Thru the Bible
with J. Vernon McGee

By J. Vernon McGee

Thru the Bible
with J. Vernon McGee

By J. Vernon McGee

VOLUME I
Genesis–Deuteronomy

Thru The Bible Radio
BOX 100
PASADENA, CALIFORNIA 91109

Published in Nashville, Tennessee, by Thomas Nelson, Inc., Publishers and distributed in Canada by Lawson Falle, Ltd., Cambridge, Ontario.

Library of Congress Cataloging in Publication Data

McGee, J. Vernon (John Vernon), 1904-
    Thru the Bible with J. Vernon McGee.

    Based on the Thru the Bible radio program.
    Includes bibliographies.
    Contents: v. 1. Genesis—Deuteronomy.
    1. Bible—Commentaries. I. Thru the Bible
(Radio program)   II. Title.
BS491.2.M37   1981   220.7'7   81-3930
ISBN 0-8407-4978-3 Royal   AACR2
ISBN 0-8407-4973-2 Nelson

Printed in the United States of America

TABLE OF CONTENTS

PREFACE

The radio broadcasts of the Thru the Bible Radio five-year program were transcribed, edited, and published first in single-volume paperbacks to accommodate the radio audience. From the beginning there was a demand that they be published in a more permanent form and in fewer volumes. This new hardback edition is an attempt to meet that need.

There has been a minimal amount of further editing for this publication. Therefore, these messages are not the word-for-word recording of the taped messages which went out over the air. The changes were necessary to accommodate a reading audience rather than a listening audience.

These are popular messages, prepared originally for a radio audience. They should not be considered a commentary on the entire Bible in any sense of that term. These messages are devoid of any attempt to present a theological or technical commentary on the Bible. Behind these messages is a great deal of research and study in order to interpret the Bible from a popular rather than from a scholarly (and too-often boring) viewpoint.

We have definitely and deliberately attempted "to put the cookies on the bottom shelf so that the kiddies could get them."

The fact that these messages have been translated into more than twenty languages for radio broadcasting and have been received with enthusiasm reveals the need for a simple teaching of the whole Bible for the masses of the world.

I am indebted to many people and to many sources for bringing this volume into existence. I should express my especial thanks to my secretary, Miss Gertrude Cutler, who supervised the editorial work; to Dr. Elliott R. Cole, my associate, who handled all the detailed work with the publishers; and finally, to my wife Ruth for tenaciously encouraging me from the beginning to put my notes and messages into printed form.

Solomon wrote, ". . . of making many books there is no end; and much study is a weariness of the flesh" (Eccl. 12:12). On a sea of books that flood the marketplace, we launch this series of THRU THE BIBLE with the hope that it might draw many to the one Book, *The Bible*.

J. VERNON McGEE

GUIDELINES FOR BIBLE STUDY

INTRODUCTION

Is the Bible Important?

The Bible is probably the most maligned Book that ever has been written. It has been attacked as no other book has ever been attacked. Yet it has ministered and does minister to literally millions of people around the globe, and it has been doing this now for several thousand years. A Book of this nature and with this tremendous impact upon the human family certainly deserves the intelligent consideration of men and women.

Sir Walter Scott, on his deathbed, asked Lockhart to read to him. Puzzled, as he scanned the shelf of books that Walter Scott had written, he asked, "What book shall I read?" And Sir Walter replied, "Why do you ask that question? There is but one book; bring the Bible." There is only one Book for any man who is dying, but it is also *the* Book for any man who is living. A great many folk do not get interested in the Bible until they get to the end of their lives or until they get into a great deal of difficulty. While it is wonderful to have a Book in which you can find comfort in a time like that, it is also a Book for you to *live*—in the full vigor of life. It is a Book to face life with today, and it's the Book which furnishes the only sure route through this world and on into the next world. It is the only Book that can enable us to meet the emergencies and cushion the shocks that come to us in life. The Bible is different from any other book.

That this Book has influenced great men who in turn have influenced the world is evident. Let me share with you some quotations.

There was an African prince who came to England and was presented to Her Majesty Queen Victoria. This prince asked a very significant question, "What is the secret of England's greatness?" The queen got a beautifully bound copy of the Bible and presented it to the prince with this statement. "This is the secret of England's greatness." I wonder if England's decline to a second-rate and then third-rate nation may be tied up in the fact that England has gotten away from the Word of God.

Prime Minister Gladstone, probably one of the greatest legal minds Britain ever produced, said, "Talk about the questions of the day! There is but one question, and that is the Gospel. That can and will correct everything. I am glad to say that about all the men at the top in Great Britain are Christians . . . I have been in public position fifty-eight years, all but eleven of them in the cabinet of the British government, and during those forty-seven years have been associated with sixty of the master minds of the century, and all but five of the sixty were Christians." I personally think that part of the problems we are having in the world today is that we have too few Christians at the top, too few who are acquainted with the Word of God.

Michael Faraday, perhaps the greatest scientist of the early 1800s, said, "But why will people go astray, when they have this blessed book of God to guide them?" Sir Isaac Newton, a scientist in the preceding century, said, "If the Bible is true, the time is coming when men shall travel at fifty miles an hour." And Voltaire, the French skeptic, commented, "Poor Isaac. He was in his dotage when he made that prophecy. It only shows what Bible study will do to an otherwise scientific mind."

It might be interesting to note what some of our early presidents had to say about the Bible. John Adams, our second president, said, "I have examined all [that is, all of Scripture] as well as my narrow sphere, my straightened means, and my busy life will allow me, and the result is that the Bible is the best book in the world. It contains more of my little philosophy than all the libraries I have seen, and such parts of it I cannot reconcile to my little philosophy I postpone for future investigation." President John Quincy Adams said, "I speak as a man of the world to men of the world; and I say to you: Search the Scriptures. The Bible is the book above all others to be read at all ages and in all conditions of human life; not to be read once or twice through then laid aside, but to be read in small portions every day." And the presidents back in those days, who made our nation great, did not get us into foreign wars and were able to solve the problems of the streets. Someone may counter, "But the problems weren't as complicated then as they are now." They were for that day, friend. Not only England but also the United States has gotten away from the Word of God. And the farther we get, the more complicated our problems become. Right now there are men in positions of authority in this land who are saying that there is no solution to our problems. That is the reason I am teaching the Word of God in its entirety—I believe it is the only solution. And, frankly, friend, we had better get back to it.

Another president, Thomas Jefferson, said, "I have always said, and always will say, that the studious perusal of the Sacred Volume will make better citizens, better husbands, and better fathers." This is something to think over today when our citizens are burning down the cities in which they live and when divorce is running rife.

Daniel Webster made this statement: "If there be anything in my style or thoughts to be commended, the credit is due to my kind parents for instilling into my mind an early love of the Scriptures." What about you today, Christian parent? Are you making a Daniel Webster in your home or a little rebel? Webster also made this statement: "I have read it [the Bible] through many times. I now make a practice of going through it once a year. It is the Book of all others for lawyers as well as divines. I pity the man who cannot find in it a rich supply of thought and rules for conduct."

Born in the East and clothed in Oriental form and imagery, the Bible walks the ways of all the world with familiar feet, and enters land after land to find its own everywhere. It has learned to speak in hundreds of languages to the heart of man. It comes into the palace to tell the monarch that he is a servant of the Most High, and into the cottage to assure the peasant that he is a son of God. Children listen to its stories with wonder and delight, and wise men ponder them as parables of life. It has a word of peace for the time of peril, a word of comfort for the time of calamity, a word of light for the hour of darkness. Its oracles are repeated in the assembly of the people, and its counsels whispered in the ear of the lonely. The wicked and the proud tremble at its warnings, but to the wounded and the penitent it has a mother's voice. The wilderness and the solitary place have been made glad by it, and the fire on the hearth has lit the reading of its well-worn pages. It has woven itself into our dearest dreams; so that love, friendship, sympathy and devotion, memory and hope put on the beautiful garments of its treasured speech, breathing of frankincense and myrrh.

—Henry van Dyke

In What Way Is the Bible Unique?

In many ways the Bible is a most unusual Book. For instance, it has a dual authorship. In other words, God is the Author of the Bible, and in another sense man is the author of the Bible. Actually, the Bible was written by about forty authors over a period of approximately fifteen hundred years. Some of these men never even heard of the others, and there was no collusion among the forty. Two or three of them could have gotten together, but the others could not have known each other. And yet they have presented a Book that has the most marvelous continuity of any book that has ever been written. Also, it is without error. Each author expressed his own feelings in his own generation. Each has his limitations, and made his mistakes—poor old Moses made mistakes, but when he was writing the Pentateuch, somehow or other no mistakes got in there. You see, it is a human Book and yet it is a God-Book.

It is a very human Book, written by men from all walks of life, prince and pauper, the highly intellectual and the very simple. For example, Dr. Luke writes almost classical Greek in a period when the Koine Greek was popular. His Greek is marvelous! But Simon Peter, the fisherman, wrote some Greek also. His is not so good, but God the Holy Spirit used both of these men. He let them express exactly their thoughts, their feelings, and yet through that method the Spirit of God was able to overrule in such a way that God said exactly what He wanted to say. That's the wonder of the Book, the Bible.

It is a God-Book. In the Bible God says twenty-five hundred times, "God said . . . the Lord has said . . . thus saith the Lord," and so on. God has made it very clear that He is speaking through this Book. It is a Book that can communicate life to you. You can even become a child of God, begotten "not by corruptible seed, but by incorruptible, by the Word of God that liveth and abideth forever." It is God's communication to man. And if God spoke out of heaven right now, He would just repeat Himself because He has said all that He wants to say to this generation. And, by the way, He didn't learn anything when He read the morning paper. When man went to the moon, he didn't discover anything that God didn't already know when He gave us the Bible. He is the same God who created this universe that we are in today.

The Bible is both divine and human. In a way it is like my Lord who walked down here and grew weary and sat down at a well. Although He was God, He was man. He talked with people down here and communicated with them. This is a Book that communicates. It speaks to mankind today. The Bible is for men as they are.

> The Bible is a corridor between two eternities down which walks the Christ of God; His invisible steps echo through the Old Testament, but we meet Him face to face in the throne room of the New; and it is through that Christ alone, crucified for me, that I have found forgiveness for sins and life eternal. The Old Testament is summed up in the word Christ; the New Testament is summed up in the word Jesus; and the summary of the whole Bible is that Jesus is the Christ.
> —Bishop Pollock

How Do You Know the Bible Is From God?

This is a good question, and it should be asked and answered.

1. Preservation—One of the objective proofs, one of the external proofs, has been the marvelous preservation of the Bible. There was a king of old—we read about him in Jeremiah—who, when the Word was sent to him, took a penknife and cut it to pieces. But it was rewritten, and we have that Word today. Down through the centuries there have been a great many Bible burnings. Today there's a great deal of antagonism toward the Bible. In our country today it is not being burned because we think that we are too civilized for such behavior. The way enemies of God's Word try to get rid of it is just to outlaw it in our schools and in many other places. (Yet we talk about our freedom of religion and freedom of speech.) In spite of all the attacks that have been made upon the Bible, it still today exists—and, of course, it's one of the best-sellers. For many years it was *the* best-seller, but it's not today. I regret to have to say that, but it is true. And that is certainly a commentary on our contemporary society. It reveals that the Bible is not really occupying the place that it once did in the history and in the life of this nation. Yet, I think the amazing preservation of the Word of God is worthy of consideration.

2. Archaeology—Another way in which we know the Bible is the Word of God is through archaeology. The spade of the archaeologist has turned up many things that have proven that this Book is the Word of God. For instance, critics for many years denied the Mosaic authorship of the Pentateuch on the basis that writing was not in existence in Moses' day. You haven't heard anybody advance that theory recently, have you? Well, of course not. For years the spade of the archaeologist has turned up again and again evidence of the validity of the Bible. The city of Jericho and the walls that fell down are one example. Now there has been some argument between Miss Kathleen Kenyon and Sir Charles Marsdon relative to specifics, but it's well established that the walls fell down, and I'll let them debate about the time and all that sort of thing. The Word of God has been substantiated there, and in many other ways archaeology has demonstrated the accuracy of the Bible. Many of the manuscripts that have been found do that also. It's quite interesting that when the Isaiah Scrolls, the Dead Sea Scrolls, were found, the liberal leaped at that because he thought he had found an argument that would discredit the Bible. However, the scrolls have not discredited the Bible, and it seems that the liberal has lost a great deal of interest in them. This is a field into which you might do some research, as I cannot go to any great length in this brief study.

3. Fulfilled Prophecy—If I were asked today whether I had just one thing to suggest as a conclusive proof that the Bible is the Word of God, do you know what I would suggest? I would suggest fulfilled prophecy. Fulfilled prophecy is the one proof that you can't escape, you can't get around. And the Bible is full of fulfilled prophecy. One-fourth of Scripture, when it was written, was prophetic; that is, it announced things that were to take place in the future. A great deal of that—in fact, a great deal more than people imagine—has already been fulfilled. We could turn to many places where prophecy has been fulfilled exactly. We find that there were many local situations that were fulfilled even in the day of the prophet. For example, Micaiah was the prophet who told Ahab that if he went out to battle as he planned, he would lose the battle and would be killed. However, Ahab's false prophets had told him he'd have a victory and would return as a victorious king. Because he didn't like what Micaiah said, Ahab ordered him locked up and fed bread and water, and said he would take care of him when he got back. But Micaiah shot back the last word, "If you come back at all, the Lord hasn't spoken by me." Well, evidently the Lord had spoken by him because Ahab didn't come back. He was killed in the battle, and his army was defeated. He had even disguised himself so that there would be no danger of his losing his life. But an enemy soldier, the Scripture says, pulled his bow at a venture; that is, when the battle was about over, he had just one arrow left in his quiver; he put it in place and shot, not really aiming at anything. But, you know, that arrow must have had Ahab's name on it, and it found him. It went right to its mark. Why? Because Micaiah had made an accurate prophecy (1 Kings 22).

On another occasion, the prophet Isaiah said that the invading Assyrian army wouldn't shoot an arrow into the city of Jerusalem (2 Kings 19:32). Well now, that's interesting. Micaiah's prophecy was fulfilled because a soldier shot an arrow by chance, pulled his bow at a venture. Wouldn't you think that among two hundred thousand soldiers—that "great host"—perhaps one might be trigger-happy and would pull his bow at a venture and let an arrow fly over the wall of Jerusalem? Well, he didn't. If the enemy had shot an arrow inside that city, they could be sure that Isaiah was not God's prophet. But he was, as was proven by this local fulfillment of his prophecy. But Isaiah also said a virgin would bring forth a child, and that was seven hundred years before it was literally fulfilled. And then, if you want a final proof, there were over three hundred prophecies concerning the first coming of Christ which were all literally fulfilled. As Jesus Christ was hanging there on the cross and dying, there was one prophecy recorded in the Old Testament that had not been fulfilled. It was, "They gave me vinegar to drink" (Ps. 69:21). Jesus said, "I thirst," and the enemy himself went and fulfilled prophecy (John 19:28–30). It's a most amazing thing. Men can't guess like that.

It has been rather amusing to watch the weatherman. During the summer season in southern California he does fine, but when we get to the change of seasons—well, your guess is as good as his. In the nation Israel, a prophet had to be accurate. If he was not accurate, he was to be put to death as a false prophet. God told His people that they would be able to distinguish a false prophet from a true prophet. A true prophet must first speak to a local situation, which Isaiah did. When that prophecy came to pass, they would know they could trust him to speak concerning the future, as Isaiah did. We can look back now and know that it was fulfilled.

There are so many other prophecies. Tyre and Sidon are over there today exactly as God's Word said twenty-five hundred years ago they would be. Egypt today is in the exact position God said it would be in. All of these are amazing, friend, and fulfilled prophecy is one of the greatest proofs that the Bible is indeed the Word of God. You see, men just can't be that accurate. Men can't guess like that—even the weatherman misses it.

Let me show you that, according to mathematical law of problematical conjecture, man could never, never prophesy. Suppose that right now I would make a prophecy. Just by way of illustration, suppose I'd say that wherever you are it's going to rain tomorrow. I'd have a 50 percent chance of being right because it'll do one of the two. But suppose that I add to that and say it would start raining tomorrow morning at nine o'clock. That would be another uncertain element. I had a fifty-fifty chance of being right at first; now I have perhaps a 25 percent chance. Every uncertain element that is added reduces by at least 50 percent the chance of my being right—the law of problematical conjecture. Now suppose that I not only say that it's going to start raining at nine o'clock, but I also say it'll stop raining at two o'clock. That has reduced my chances now another 50 percent, which brings it down to 12½ percent. Can you imagine my chance of being right now? But suppose I add three hundred uncertain elements. There's not a ghost of a chance of my being accurate. I just couldn't hit it—it would be impossible. Yet the Word of God hit it, my friend. It is accurate. The Bible has moved into that area of absolute impossibility, and that to me is absolute proof that it is the Word of God. There is nothing to compare to it at all. I have given very few examples of fulfilled prophecy, but there is in the Word of God prophecy after prophecy, and they have been fulfilled—literally fulfilled. And by the way, I would think that that indicates the method in which prophecy for the future is yet to be fulfilled.

4. Transformed Lives—I offer two final reasons as proof that the Bible is the Word of God. One is the transformed lives of believers today. I have seen what the Word of God can do in the lives of men and women. I'm thinking right now of a man in Oakland, California, who listened to my Bible-teaching program. He probably had as many problems, as many hang-ups, and he was in as much sin as any man that I know anything about. And this man began to listen to the radio program. I know of people who just hear the Gospel once and are converted. I think it's possible and that it's wonderful. But this man listened to it week after week, and he became antagonistic. He became angry. Later he said to me, "If I could have gotten to you when you were teaching the Epistle to the Romans and you told me that I was a sinner, I would have hit you in the nose," and frankly, I think he could have done it. He's much bigger and much younger than I am. I'm glad he couldn't get to me. Finally, this man turned to Christ. It has been wonderful to see what God has done in his life. Again and again and again this testimony could be multiplied. Young and old have found purpose and fulfillment in life, marriages have been saved, families reunited, individuals have been freed from alcoholism and drug addiction. Folk have had their lives transformed by coming to Christ.

When I finished seminary, I was a preacher who majored in the realm of the defense of the gospel, and I attempted to defend the Bible. In fact, I think every message I gave entered into that area. I felt if I could just get enough answers to the questions that people raise for not believing the Bible, they would believe. But I found out that the worst thing I could do was to whip a man down intellectually. The minute I did that, I made an enemy and never could win him for the Lord. So I moved out of the realm of apologetics and into another area of just giving out the Word of God as simply as I could. Only the Bible can turn a sinner into a saint.

5. Spirit of God Made it Real—Another reason that I've moved out of the realm of apologetics is because there has been a certain development in my own life. I have reached the place today where I not only believe that the Bible is the Word of God, I *know* it's the Word of God. I know it's the Word of God because the Spirit of God has made it real to my own heart and my own life. That is the thing that Paul talked to the Colossians about. He prayed that they "might be filled with the knowledge of his will in all wisdom and spiritual understanding." I also want this, because I found that the Spirit of God can confirm these things to your heart and you don't need archaeology or anything else to prove that the Bible is God's Word.

A young preacher said to me some time ago, "Dr. McGee, isn't it wonderful that they have discovered this?" He mentioned a recent discovery in particular.

And I said, "Well, I don't see anything to be excited about."

He was greatly disappointed and even chagrined that I did not respond enthusiastically. "Why, what do you mean?" he asked. "Is it possible that this hasn't impressed you?"

I answered him this way, "I already knew it was the Word of God long before the spade of the archaeologist turned that up." He asked how I knew it, and I said, "The Spirit of God has been making it real to my own heart."

I trust that the Spirit of God is going to make the Word of God not only real to you, to incorporate it into your living, but that He is also going to give you that assurance that you can say, "I *know* that it's the Word of God."

Whence but from Heaven, could men unskilled in arts,
In several ages born, in several parts,
Weave such agreeing truths, or how, or why,
Should all conspire to cheat us with a lie?
Unasked their pains, ungrateful their advice,
Starving their gain, and martyrdom their price.
                                        —Dryden

What Is Revelation? Inspiration? Illumination? Interpretation?

Revelation means that God has spoken and that God has communicated to man. *Inspiration* guarantees the revelation of God. *Illumination* has to do with the Spirit of God being the Teacher—He communicates. *Interpretation* has to do with the interpretation that you and I give to the Word of God.

Revelation

Revelation means that God has spoken. "Thus saith the Lord," and its equivalent, occurs over twenty-five hundred times. The Lord didn't want you to misunderstand that He had spoken. Notice Hebrews 1:1–2: "God, who at sundry times and in divers manners spake in time past unto the fathers by the prophets, hath in these last days spoken unto us by his Son, whom he hath appointed heir of all things, by whom also he made the worlds." Wherever you will find two persons, endowed with a reasonable degree of intelligence, who harbor the same feelings and desires, who are attracted to each other more or less, you will find communication between them. Persons of like propensities, separated from each other, delight in getting in touch with each other and rejoice in receiving communication from each other. This innate characteristic of the human heart explains the post office department, the telephone, and the telegraph. Friends communicate with friends. A husband away from home writes to his wife. A boy or girl at school will write home to dad and mom. And ever and anon there travels the scented epistle of a girl to a boy, and then the boy returns an epistle to the girl. All of this is called communication. It is the expression of the heart. I remember the thrill that came to me when I read the account of Helen Keller, shut out from the world by blindness and deafness, without means of communication; and then a way was opened up so she could communicate—probably better than many of us who can see and hear.

Now, on the basis of all this, I would like to ask you what I believe is a reasonable and certainly an intelligent question: Isn't it reasonable to conclude that God has communicated with His creatures to whom He has committed a certain degree of intelligence and whom He created in His likeness? If we did not have a revelation from God, right now I think that you and I could just wait and He would be speaking to us, because we could *expect* God to speak to us. You will notice that the writer to the Hebrews says that God in the Old Testament spoke through the prophets, and He now has spoken through Christ. Both the revelation to the prophets in the Old Testament and the revelation of Christ in the New Testament are in the Word of God, of course, and that is the only way we would know about the communication from either one. The Bible has sixty-six books, and God has spoken to us through each one of them.

This Book contains the mind of God, the state of man, the way of salvation, the doom of sinners and the happiness of believers. Its doctrines are holy, its precepts are binding, its histories are true, and its decisions are immutable. Read it to be wise, believe it to be safe and practice it to be holy. It contains light to direct you, food to support you and comfort to cheer you. It is the traveler's map, the pilgrim's staff, the pilot's compass, the soldier's sword and the Christian's character. Here paradise is restored, heaven opened and the gates of hell disclosed. Christ is its grand object, our good is its design and the glory of God its end. It should fill the memory, rule the heart, and guide the feet. Read it slowly, frequently, and prayerfully. It is given you in life and will be opened in the judgment and will be remembered forever. It involves the highest responsibility, will reward the greatest labour, and will condemn all who trifle with its sacred contents.

—Author Unknown

Inspiration

This brings us to the second great subject, which is *inspiration*. I personally believe in what is known as the plenary verbal inspiration of the Scriptures, which means that the Bible is an authoritative statement and that every word of it is the Word of God to us and for us in this day in which we live. Inspiration guarantees the revelation of God. And that is exactly what this Book says. Two men—Paul writing his last epistle to Timothy and Peter writing his last epistle—had something pretty definite to say about the Bible: "All scripture is given by inspiration of God, and is profitable for doctrine, for reproof, for correction, for instruction in righteousness, That the man of God may be perfect, thoroughly furnished unto all good works" (2 Tim. 3:16–17, New Scofield Reference Bible). Notice that *all* Scripture is given by inspiration. The word *inspiration* means "God breathed." God said through these men, as He said here through Paul, exactly what He wanted to say. He hasn't anything else to add. Peter expresses it this way: "For the prophecy came not in old time by the will of man: but holy men of God spake as they were moved by the Holy Ghost" (2 Pet. 1:21). It is very important to see that these men were moved, as it were, carried along, by the Holy Spirit of God. It was Bishop Westcott who said: "The thoughts are wedded to words as necessarily as the soul is to the body." And Dr. Keiper said, "You can as easily have music without notes, or mathematics without figures, as thoughts without words." It is not the thoughts that are inspired; it's the *words* that are inspired.

There is a little whimsical story of a girl who had taken singing lessons from a very famous teacher. He was present at her recital, and after it was over she was anxious to know his reaction. He didn't come back to congratulate her, and she asked a friend, "What did he say?"

Her loyal friend answered, "He said that you sang heavenly."

She couldn't quite believe that her teacher had said that; so she probed, "Is that *exactly* what he said?"

"Well, no, but that is what he meant."

The girl insisted, "Tell me the exact *words* that he used."

"Well, his exact words were, 'That was an unearthly noise!' "

Obviously, there is a difference between an unearthly noise and a heavenly sound. Exact words are important.

Believe me, the words of Scripture are inspired—not just the thoughts, but the words. For instance, Satan was not inspired to tell a lie, but the Bible records that he told a lie. It's the words that are inspired. And the Lord Jesus often said, "It is written," quoting the Word of God in the Old Testament—the men who wrote gave out what God had to say. In Exodus 20:1 Moses wrote: "And God spake all these words, saying . . . ." It was God who did the speaking, and Moses wrote what He said.

Over the years there have been discovered many very excellent manuscripts of the Scriptures. Speaking of the manuscripts in Britain, Sir George Kenyon, the late director and principal librarian of the British Museum, made this statement: "Thanks to these manuscripts, the ordinary reader of the Bible may feel comfortable about the soundness of the text. Apart from a few unimportant verbal alterations, natural in books transcribed by hand, the New Testament, we now feel assured, has come down intact." We can be sure today that we have that which is as close to the autographs (the original manuscripts) as anything possibly can be, and I believe in verbal plenary inspiration of the autographs.

In the second century Irenaeus, one of the church fathers, wrote: "The Scriptures indeed are perfect, forasmuch as they are spoken by the Word of God and by His Spirit." Augustine, living in the fifth century, made this statement, "Let us therefore yield ourselves and bow to the authority of the Holy Scriptures which can neither err nor deceive." And Spurgeon commented, "I can never doubt the doctrine of plenary verbal inspiration; since I so constantly see, in actual practice, how the very words that God has been pleased to use— a plural instead of a singular—are blessed to the souls of men." God speaks in this Book to our hearts and to our lives.

Illumination

Illumination means that since you and I have a Book, a God-Book and a human Book, written by men who were expressing their thoughts and at the same time writing down the Word of God, only the Spirit of God can teach it to us. Although we can get the facts of the Bible on our own, the Spirit of God will have to open our minds and hearts if we are to understand the spiritual truth that is there.

Paul, writing to the Corinthians, said, "But we speak the wisdom of God in a mystery, even the hidden wisdom, which God ordained before the world unto our glory: Which none of the princes of this world knew: for had they known it, they would not have crucified the Lord of glory. But as it is written, Eye hath not seen, nor ear heard, neither have entered into the heart of man, the things which God hath prepared for them that love him" (1 Cor. 2:7–9). Now you and I get most of what we know through the eye gate and the ear gate or by

reason. Paul tells us here that there are certain things that eye has not seen nor ear heard, certain things that you can't get into your mind at all. Then how in the world are you going to get them? "But God hath revealed them unto us by his Spirit: for the Spirit searcheth all things, yea, the deep things of God" (1 Cor. 2:10). Verse 9 sometimes goes to a funeral. The minister implies that the one who has died didn't know too much down here, but now he will know things he did not know before. While that probably is true (we will get quite an education in heaven), that is not what the verse literally says. Long before you get to the undertaker, there are a lot of things in this life that you and I can't learn through natural means. The Holy Spirit has to be our Teacher.

Remember that our Lord inquired of His disciples, "What are men saying about Me?" They said that some were saying one thing and some another. (And today you can get a different answer from almost every person you happen to ask. There are many viewpoints of Him.) Then He asked His disciples, ". . . But whom say ye that I am? And Simon Peter answered and said, Thou art the Christ, the Son of the living God. And Jesus answered and said unto him, Blessed art thou, Simon Barjona: for flesh and blood hath not revealed it unto thee, but my Father which is in heaven" (Matt. 16:15–17). God is the One who revealed the truth to Simon Peter. And today only God can open up the Word of God for us to really understand it.

On the day of the resurrection of the Lord Jesus, He walked down the Emmaus road and joined a couple of men as they walked along. Entering into their conversation, He asked them, ". . . What manner of communications are these that ye have one to another, as ye walk, and are sad? And the one of them, whose name was Cleopas, answering said unto him, Art thou only a stranger in Jerusalem, and hast not known the things which are come to pass there in these days? And he said unto them, What things? And they said unto him, Concerning Jesus of Nazareth, which was a prophet mighty in deed and word before God and all the people: And how the chief priests and our rulers delivered him to be condemned to death, and have crucified him" (Luke 24:17–20). As you will recall, Jesus had predicted that. And it is interesting to see that written prophecy had been saying it for years. Then they expressed the hope that had been theirs: "But we trusted that it had been he which should have redeemed Israel: and beside all this, to day is the third day since these things were done" (Luke 24:21). And they went on to tell about what they knew and what the women had reported: those who "were with us went to the sepulcher . . . but him they saw not" (Luke 24:24). Their hopes had dimmed, and darkness had entered their hearts. Now listen to the Lord Jesus, ". . . O fools, and slow of heart to believe all that the prophets have spoken: Ought not Christ to have suffered these things, and to enter into his glory? And beginning at Moses and all the prophets, he expounded unto them in all the scriptures the things concerning himself" (Luke 24:25–27). Wouldn't you have loved to have been there that day and heard Him go back in the Old Testament and lift out the Scriptures concerning Himself? And after He finally made Himself known to them as they sat at the evening meal, this was their comment, ". . . Did not our heart burn within us, while he talked with us by the way, and while he opened to us the scriptures?" (Luke 24:32).

You see, we are studying a Book that is different from any other book. I not only believe in the inspiration of the Bible, I believe that it is a closed Book to you unless the Spirit of God will open your heart and make it real. When Jesus returned to Jerusalem at that time, He continued teaching the disciples: "And he said unto them, These are the words which I spake unto you, while I was yet with you, that all things must be fulfilled, which were written in the law of Moses, and in the prophets, and in the psalms, concerning me" (Luke 24:44). Notice that He believed Moses wrote the Pentateuch; He believed the prophets spoke of Him and that the Psalms pointed to Him. Now here is the important verse: "Then opened he their understanding, that they might understand the scriptures" (Luke 24:45). And, friend, if He doesn't open your understanding, you're just not going to get it. That is the reason we ought to approach this Book with great humility of mind, regardless of how high our I.Q. is or the extent of our education.

Referring back to 1 Corinthians, Paul goes on to say, "Which things also we speak, not in the words which man's wisdom teacheth, but which the Holy Spirit teacheth; comparing spiritual things with spiritual. But the natural man receiveth not the things of the Spirit of God: for they are foolishness unto him: neither can he know them, because they are spiritually discerned" (1 Cor. 2:13–14, New Scofield Reference Bible). I am never disturbed when one of these unbelievers, even if he's a preacher, comes along and says he no longer believes the Bible is the Word of God; that's the way he *should* talk. After all, if he is not a believer, he cannot understand it. Mark Twain, who was no believer, said that he was not disturbed by what he did not understand in the Bible; what worried him were the things he *did* understand. There are things an unbeliever can understand, and it's those things which cause many to reject the Word of God. It was Pascal who said, "Human knowledge must be understood to be loved, but Divine knowledge must be loved to be understood."

As I leave the subject of illumination, let me add this: Only the Spirit of God can open your mind and heart to see and to accept Christ and to trust Him as your Savior. How wonderful! I have always felt as I entered the pulpit how helpless I am; believe me, Vernon McGee can't convert anyone. But I not only feel weak, I also feel mighty—not mighty in myself, but in the knowledge that the Spirit of God can take my dead words and make them real and living.

Interpretation

Interpretation has to do with the interpretation that you and I give to the Word of God. And this is the reason there are Methodists and Baptists and Presbyterians, this kind of teacher and that kind of teacher—we all have our interpretations. And where there is disagreement, somebody is evidently wrong.

There are several rules that should be followed as we attempt to interpret the Bible.

1. The overall purpose of the Bible should first be considered. And that is the reason I teach all of it—because I believe you need to have it all before you can come to any dogmatic conclusion concerning any particular verse of Scripture. It is important to take into consideration all verses that are related to that subject.

2. To whom the Scripture is addressed should next be considered. For instance, way back yonder God said to Joshua, "Arise, go over this Jordan" (Josh. 1:2). When I was over in that land, I crossed the Jordan River, but I didn't cross it to fulfill that Scripture. And I didn't say, "At last I've obeyed the Lord and have crossed over Jordan." No. When I read that verse I know the Lord is talking to Joshua—but I believe there is a tremendous lesson there for me. All Scripture is not *to* me, but all Scripture is *for* me. That is a good rule to keep in mind.

3. The immediate context before and after a Scripture should be observed. What is the passage talking about? And what other passages of Scripture deal with the same thing?

4. Discover what the original says. If you do not read Hebrew or Greek, when you read the American Standard Version you're right close to what the Lord said. Frankly, I cannot recommend the modern translations, although there are good things in them. I have found that because we are so divided doctrinally, every group that attempts to translate the Bible just naturally injects into their translation their particular viewpoint. Therefore, if the liberal is going to do the translating, you may get a taste of liberalism. If the fundamentalist is going to do the translating, you'll get his bias in certain places. However, the men who did the original English translations were men who believed that the Bible was the Word of God and handled it accordingly. When there were words they could not translate, they simply transliterated them (for instance, *Abba* and *baptizo*). The danger in modern translations is that translation is done in a dogmatic fashion. A translator must take something out of one language and put it into another language in comparable terms—identical terms if possible. Most of our modern translators are trying to get it into modern speech. And in doing so, they really miss what the original is saying. Personally, I stick by the Authorized (King James) Version. I feel that The New Scofield Reference Bible has made a tremendous step forward in making certain distinctions and corrections that needed to be made in the Authorized Version. I recommend that also, although I still use my old Scofield Reference Bible. I know my way around through the Book, and the old scout will follow the old trail. However, the important thing is to attempt to determine the exact words of the original.

5. Interpret the Bible literally. The late Dr. David Cooper has stated it well: "When the plain sense of Scripture makes common sense, seek no other sense; therefore, take every word at its primary, ordinary, usual, literal meaning unless the facts of the immediate context, studied in the light of related passages and axiomatic and fundamental truths, indicate clearly otherwise."

Guidelines

"Open thou mine eyes, that I may behold wondrous things out of thy law" [Ps. 119:18].

There are certain guidelines that each of us should follow relative to the Word of God. I guarantee that if you will follow these guidelines, blessing will come to your heart and life.

Certainly there should be these directions in the study of Scripture. Today a bottle of medicine, no matter how simple it might be, has directions for the use of it. And any little gadget that you buy in a five-and-ten-cent store has with it directions for its operation. If that is true of the things of this world, certainly the all-important Word of God should have a few directions and instructions on the study of it. I want to mention seven very simple, yet basic, preliminary steps that will be a guide for the study of the Word of God.

1. Begin with prayer.
2. Read the Bible.
3. Study the Bible.
4. Meditate on the Bible.
5. Read what others have written on the Bible.
6. Obey the Bible.
7. Pass it on to others.

You may want to add to these, but I believe these are basic and primary. Someone has put it in a very brief, cogent manner: "The Bible—know it in your head; stow it in your heart; show it in your life; sow it in the world." That is another way of saying some of the things we are going to present here.

1. Begin with Prayer.

As we saw when we dealt with the subject of illumination, the Bible differs from other books in that the Holy Spirit alone can open our minds to understand it. You can take up a book on philosophy, and if a man wrote it (and he did), then a man can understand it. The same is true of higher mathematics or any other subject. There is not a book that ever has been written by any man that another man cannot understand. But the Bible is different. The Bible cannot be understood unless the Holy Spirit is the instructor. And He *wants* to teach us. The fact of the matter is, our Lord told us, ". . . He will guide you into all truth" (John 16:13). When we open the Word of God we need to begin with the psalmist's prayer: "Open thou mine eyes, that I may behold wondrous things out of thy law" (Ps. 119:18). When the psalmist wrote these lines, he had in mind the Mosaic system, of course; but we widen that out to include the sixty-six books of the Bible and pray today, "Open thou mine eyes, that I may behold wondrous things out of thy Word."

When the apostle Paul was praying for the Ephesians, he did not pray for their health (although he may have at another time), and he did not pray that they might get wealthy (I don't know that he ever did that), but Paul's first prayer for these Ephesians is recorded in his little epistle to them: "Wherefore I also, after I heard of your faith in the Lord Jesus, and love unto all the saints, Cease not to give thanks for you, making mention of you in my prayers" (Eph. 1:15–16). Now what would Paul pray for? Here it is: "That the God of our Lord Jesus Christ, the Father of glory, may give unto you the spirit of wisdom and revelation in the knowledge of him: The eyes of your understanding being enlightened; that ye may know what is the hope of his calling, and what the riches of the glory of his inheritance in the saints" (Eph. 1:17–18). Paul's prayer, you see, is that they might have a wisdom and an understanding of the revelation of the knowledge of Him—that is, that they might know the Word of God. And that the eyes of their understanding might be enlightened, that they might know something of the hope of the calling they had in Christ. This is the prayer of the apostle Paul. And if anyone remembers me in prayer, this is exactly what I want them to pray for—that my eyes (my spiritual eyes) might be open. I believe the most important thing for you and me today is to know the will of God—and the will of God is the Word of God. We cannot know the Word of God unless the Spirit of God is our teacher. That is what Paul says over in the first epistle to the Corinthians: "Now we have received, not the spirit of the world, but the Spirit who is of God; that we might know the things that are freely given to us of God. Which things also we speak, not in the words which man's wisdom teacheth, but which the Holy Spirit teacheth, comparing spiritual things with spiritual. But the natural man receiveth not the things of the Spirit of God; for they are foolishness unto him, neither can he know them, because they are spiritually discerned" (1 Cor. 2:12–14, New Scofield Reference Bible). The reason today that so many don't get anything out of the Bible is simply because they are not letting the Spirit of God teach them. The Word of God is different from any other book, you see, because the natural man cannot receive these things. To him they are foolishness. God has given to us the Spirit that we might know the things that are freely given to us of God. He alone is our Teacher; He alone can take the Word of God and make it real and living to us.

God *wants* to communicate with us through His written Word. But it is a supernatural Book, and it will not communicate to us on the natural plane for the very simple reason that only the Spirit of God can take the things of Christ and reveal them to us. Notice this very interesting verse of Scripture: "For what man knoweth the things of a man, except the spirit of man which is in him? Even so the things of God knoweth no man, but the Spirit of God" (1 Cor. 2:11, New Scofield Reference Bible). In a very succinct and understandable manner, this gives the reason the Spirit of God must be our Teacher. You and I understand each other, but we do not understand God. I believe it is perfect nonsense to talk about a generation gap through which we cannot communicate. While it has always been true that it is difficult for an older person and a younger person to see eye to eye, we can communicate with each other because we are all human beings. We understand each other. But frankly, I don't understand God unless He is revealed to me. I used to wonder how He would feel at a funeral. Well, I find the Lord Jesus there at the funeral of Lazarus and see that He wept. I know how He feels today. I know how He feels about many things because the Spirit of God through the Word of God has revealed them to me.

When I was pastor in Nashville, Tennessee, I got up one bright morning and looked out my window. During the night about five inches of snow had fallen and covered up all the ugliness with a beautiful blanket. I sat upstairs in my study looking out over the scene when I noticed an elder of my church, who lived next door, come out on his porch with two coal scuttles filled with ashes which he was going to empty in the alley. I saw him stop and look over the landscape, and I just smiled because I knew how he felt—just like I felt, looking out on that snow that had fallen during the night. But when he started down the steps, he slipped. Not wanting to spill the ashes, he held them out and hit one of those steps with a real bump. I couldn't help but laugh. I guess if he had broken his neck I still would have laughed. But I noticed that he looked around, and when he was satisfied that nobody had seen him, he got up with great satisfaction and started out again. About half way out on the sidewalk we had a repeat performance; only this time he fell much farther because he fell all the way to the sidewalk. And it looked to me like he bounced when he hit. This time he really scanned the landscape. He didn't want anybody to see what he had done. And I knew how he felt. I would have felt the same way. He got up and looked over the landscape, went out and emptied his ashes, and when he got back to the porch, he looked over the landscape again—I don't think this time to admire the scene but to make good and sure that no one had seen him fall. I didn't say a word until Sunday morning. When I came into the church, I went right by where he sat, leaned down and said, "You sure did look funny yesterday carrying out the ashes!"

He looked at me in amazement. He said, "Did you see me?"

I said, "Yes."

"Well," he said, "I didn't think anybody saw me."

And I said, "I thought that. I knew exactly how you felt." You see, he had a human spirit and I had a human spirit—we understood each other. But who can understand God? Only the Spirit of God. And that is the reason the Holy Spirit teaches us, comparing spiritual things with spiritual.

Renan, the French skeptic, made an attack on the Word of God; yet he wrote a *Life of Jesus*. His book is divided into two sections, one is the historical section, the other is the interpretation of the life of Christ. As far as the first part is concerned, there probably has never been a more brilliant life of Christ written by any man. But his interpretation of it is positively absurd. It could have been done better by a twelve-year-old Sunday school boy. What is the explanation of that? Well, the Spirit of God does not teach you history or give you facts that you can dig out for yourself; a very clever mind can dig out those. But the interpretation is altogether different. The Spirit of God has to do the interpreting, and He alone must be the Teacher to lead us and guide us into all truth. We must have the Spirit of God to open our eyes to see.

And we are told to ask His help. In John 16 the Lord Jesus says, "I have yet many things to say unto you, but ye cannot bear them now. Howbeit when he, the Spirit of truth, is come, he will guide you into all truth: for he shall not speak of himself; but whatsoever he shall hear, that shall he speak: and he will shew you things to come. He shall glorify me: for he shall receive of mine, and shall shew it unto you. All things that the Father hath are mine; therefore said I, that he shall take of mine, and shall shew it unto you. A little while, and ye shall not see me: and again, a little while, and ye shall see me, because I go to the Father" (John 16:12–16). So the Lord Jesus is saying that we are to ask. He has many things for us, and He has sent the Holy Spirit to be the Teacher. Again in chapter 14 He says, "But the Comforter, which is the Holy Ghost, whom the Father will send in my name, he shall teach you all things, and bring all things

to your remembrance, whatsoever I have said unto you" (John 14:26). The Holy Spirit is the Teacher, and He must be the One to lead us and guide us into all truth, friend. If you ever learn anything through my Bible study program, it will not be because this poor preacher is the teacher, it will be because the Spirit of God is opening up the Word of God to you.

This, then, is the first guideline: Begin with prayer and ask the Spirit of God to be your Teacher.

2. Read the Bible.

The second guideline may seem oversimplified.

Someone asked a great Shakespearean scholar years ago, "How do you study Shakespeare?" His answer was very terse, "Read Shakespeare." And I would say to you: Read the Word of God. Do you want to know what the Bible has to say? Read the Bible. Over and above what any teacher may give you, it is all-important to read for yourself what the Bible has to say.

Dr. G. Campbell Morgan has written some very wonderful and helpful commentaries on the Bible. In fact, he has a series of books that I recommend on all sixty-six books of the Bible. I know of nothing that is any better than them, and when I started out as a student, they had a great influence on my study of the Word. It is said that he would not put pen to paper until he had read a particular book of the Bible through fifty times. So don't be weary in well doing, friend; just read the Word of God. If you don't get it the first time, read it the second time. If you don't get it the second time, read it the third time. Keep on reading it. We are to get the facts of the Word of God.

There is a very interesting incident in the Book of Nehemiah: "And all the people gathered themselves together as one man into the street that was before the water gate; and they spake unto Ezra the scribe to bring the book of the law of Moses, which the LORD had commanded to Israel. And Ezra the priest brought the law before the congregation both of men and women, and all that could hear with understanding, upon the first day of the seventh month. And he read therein before the street that was before the water gate from the morning until midday, before the men and the women, and those who could understand; and the ears of all the people were attentive unto the book of the law" (Neh. 8:1–3). This is a very remarkable passage of Scripture. You see, the Jews had been in Babylonian captivity seventy years; many of them had never heard the Word of God. It did not circulate much in that day. There were not a hundred different translations abroad nor new ones coming off the press all the time. Probably there were just one or two copies in existence, and Ezra had one of those copies. He stood and read before the water gate. "So they read in the book in the law of God distinctly, and gave the sense, and caused them to understand the reading" (Neh. 8:8). From the way the account is given, I assume that men of the tribe of Levi were stationed in certain areas among the people. After Ezra had read a certain portion, he would stop to give the people who had listened an opportunity to ask questions of the men who were stationed out there to explain the Bible to them. ". . . and the Levites, caused the people to understand the law: and the people stood in their place" (Neh. 8:7). Not only did they read the Word, but they caused the people to understand it.

We need to read the Bible.

There are so many distractions today from the study of the Word of God. And the greatest distraction we have is the church. The church is made up of committees and organizations and banquets and entertainments and promotional schemes to the extent that the Word of God is not even dealt with in many churches today. There are churches that have disbanded the preaching service altogether. Instead they have a time in which the people will be able to express themselves and say what they are thinking. I can't imagine anything more puerile or more of a waste of time than that (although it is a fine excuse to get out of preaching for a lazy preacher who will not read or study the Bible.) I find that the people who are more ignorant of the Bible than anyone else are church members. They simply do not know the Word of God. And it has been years since it has been taught in the average church. We need to read the Bible. We need to get into the Word of God—not just reading a few favorite verses, but reading the *entire* Word of God. That is the only way we are going to know it, friend. That is God's method.

WHEN YOU READ THE BIBLE THROUGH

I supposed I knew my Bible,
Reading piecemeal, hit or miss,
Now a bit of John or Matthew,
Now a snatch of Genesis,
Certain chapters of Isaiah,
Certain Psalms (the twenty-third),

Twelfth of Romans, First of Proverbs—
Yes, I thought I knew the Word!
But I found that thorough reading
Was a different thing to do,
And the way was unfamiliar
When I read the Bible through.
You who like to play at Bible,
Dip and dabble, here and there,
Just before you kneel, aweary,
And yawn through a hurried prayer;
You who treat the Crown of Writings
As you treat no other book—
Just a paragraph disjointed,
Just a crude impatient look—
Try a worthier procedure,
Try a broad and steady view;
You will kneel in very rapture
When you read the Bible through!

—Amos R. Wells

3. Study the Bible.

Someone came to Dr. G. Campbell Morgan, years ago, and said, "You speak as though you are inspired!" Dr. Morgan replied, "Inspiration is 95 percent perspiration." The Bible needs to be studied. We need to realize that the Spirit of God will not teach us something that we could get ourselves by study. I used to teach in a Bible institute, and the classes were made up of all kinds of young folks. Among them were a few very pious individuals, and I understood these young people very well after a period of time—I confess I didn't understand them at first. Their pious façade, I found, covered up a tremendous ignorance and vacuum relative to the Word of God. Some of them would not study the night before an exam. They always would give an excuse that they were busy in a prayer meeting or a service somewhere. I had the feeling that some of them believed that they could put their Bibles under their pillows at night and as they slept, the names of the kings of Israel and Judah would come up through the duck feathers! Believe me, it won't come up through the duck feathers. We have to knuckle down and study the Word of God. A fellow student in a Bible class when I was in college said, "Doctor, you have assigned us a section that is very dry." The professor, without even missing a step, said to him, "Then dampen it a little with sweat from your brow." The Bible should be studied, and it is very important we see that. There is a certain knowledge that the Spirit of God is not going to give you. I do not think He is revealing truth to lazy people. After all, you never learn logarithms or geometry or Greek by just reading a chapter

xxi   GUIDELINES

of it just before you go to sleep at night!

Now you may be shocked when I say that I do not encourage devotional reading of the Bible. But over a period of years I have learned that a great many people who are very faithful in what they call devotional reading are very ignorant of the Bible. I stayed with a family for over a week when I was holding meetings in a place in middle Tennessee. Every morning at the breakfast table we had devotions. Unfortunately, breakfast was always a little late, and Susie and Willie were rushing to get away to school. I am confident that they didn't even know what was read. Dad was wanting to get away to work, and he generally made the Bible reading very brief. Always he'd say, "Well, I'll read this familiar passage this morning because we don't have much time." And, believe me, we didn't. By the time the reading was over, Susie and Willie left the table like they were shot out of a gun, Dad got out of there almost as quickly as they did, and Mother was left with the dishes—and I wondered if she had really heard what had been read. I determined right there and then that in my home we wouldn't have devotional reading. I have always encouraged members of my family to read the Bible on their own. That is the reading that is profitable.

Someone is going to say, "But I have my devotions at night after the day is over." Now really, don't you have them right before you go to bed? You've got one foot in bed already, one eye is already closed, and you turn to a passage of Scripture to read. You cannot learn mathematics that way. You cannot learn literature that way. And you cannot learn the *Bible* that way. You have to *study* the Word of God. You ought to read it when you can give time to it. And if you can't find time, you ought to *make* time. Set apart thirty minutes or an hour. Or if you do things haphazardly like I do, read thirty minutes one day, perhaps only five minutes the next day, and two or three hours the next day, however it fits into your program. I put down no particular rule except that each person should read for himself, and boys and girls should be encouraged to read the Bible for themselves. Some folks feel that they ought to have devotional reading together. And that is fine, if the Lord leads you to do it, but I guarantee you will not be intelligent Bible students after twenty years of doing it like that. You also need to study the Word of God on your own.

It was said of John Wesley that he was a man of one Book. What made him a man of one Book? Well, he got up and read the Bible at four and five o'clock every morning—read it in five different languages. Believe me, he studied the Word of God. And you and I need to study the Word; we need to get the meaning of the Bible.

4. Meditate on the Bible.

Meditation is something that God taught His people. The Word of God was to be before the children of Israel all the time—so that they could meditate on it. "And these words, which I command thee this day, shall be in thine heart: And thou shalt teach them diligently unto thy children, and shalt talk of them when thou sittest in thine house, and when thou walkest by the way, and when thou liest down, and when thou risest up. And thou shalt bind them for a sign upon thine hand, and they shall be as frontlets between thine eyes. And thou shalt write them upon the posts of thy house, and on thy gates" (Deut. 6:6–9). Now that is an amazing statement coming from the Lord. He told them to write the Word of God upon the doorposts. In other words, wherever they turned, it was just like looking at billboards. You cannot drive up and down our streets and highways without seeing liquor signs and cigarette signs—billboards galore! Now you can understand why people today drink liquor and why they smoke cigarettes—it is before them all the time. The Lord knew human nature. He knew us. And He told His people to get the Word where they would see it. It was on their doorposts, on their gates, and they wore it on their garments. And they were to talk about it when they were walking. They were to talk about the Word when they sat down. They were to talk about it when they went to bed and until they went to sleep. God asked His people to meditate on His Word.

Now what does it really mean to meditate on the Word of God? There is a very interesting statement over in the first Psalm: "Blessed is the man that walketh not in the counsel of the ungodly, nor standeth in the way of sinners, nor sitteth in the seat of the scornful. But his delight is in the law of the LORD; and in his law doth he meditate day and night" (Ps. 1:1–2). To meditate is to ruminate, to bring to mind, and to consider over and over. Ruminating is what a cow is doing when she is chewing her cud. You know how the old cow goes out of a morning, and while the grass is fresh with dew she grazes. Then when the sun comes up and the weather is hot, the cow lies down under a tree, or stands there in the shade. You see her chewing and you wonder what in the world that cow is chewing. She will chew there for an hour or two. Well, she is meditating, friend. She is bringing the grass she ate of a morning (we are told that a cow has a complex stomach) out of one chamber and is transferring it to another. In the process she is going over it again, chewing it up good. You and I need to learn to do that in our thought processes. We are to get the Word of God, read it, have it out where we can look at it, then think about it, meditate on it.

Many times in preparing a message I'll take a verse of Scripture and spend hours doing nothing but reading it over and over, checking what others have said about it, and just keep reading it. Finally new truth will break out from that particular passage. I remember hearing Dr. Harry Ironside say that he had heard a lecture on the Song of Solomon which left him dissatisfied. He said that he read the Song of Solomon again, got down on his knees and asked God to give him an understanding of it. He did that again and again—in fact, he did it for weeks and months. Finally new light broke from that book. When I teach the Song of Solomon I generally give Dr. Ironside's interpretation for two reasons: it satisfies my own mind and heart more than does any other interpretation I have heard, and I know the man who got it had spent a great deal of time in meditation.

There are folks who write to us saying that the wife listens to our Bible study by radio at home, and the husband listens to it at work, and at the dinner table they discuss the Scripture that was covered. That is meditation; it is going back over it again. Riding along in the car alone is a good place to take a passage of Scripture and really give thought to it.

How many of you, after you have had "devotions," meditate upon that passage during the day? Most people read it and then forget it—never thinking about it again until it is called to their attention. Or, if they read it at night, they jump into bed as quickly as they can, turn out the light, and go to sleep, forgetting all about it. Meditation is almost a lost art in our contemporary society. Frankly, television in many homes absolutely blots out the possibility for meditation. It is changing the spiritual life of many families today. One of the reasons that our churches are becoming colder and more indifferent to the Word of God is simply because there is that lack of meditation upon the Word of God.

Remember the Ethiopian eunuch who was riding along reading Isaiah (Acts 8). He was actually studying Isaiah, because he was in a passage with which he was having trouble—he did not know what it meant. Here is a man who is reading and studying, and the Spirit of God is going to open the Word of God to him. That is the reason the Holy Spirit brought Philip there to explain the chapter to the Ethiopian. It opened up a new world to him, and he came to know Christ. The record says that he went on his way rejoicing. What was making him rejoice? He was meditating. He was going back over that fifty-third chapter of Isaiah.

Have you ever meditated on that Lamb who was brought as a sheep to the slaughter? Who was He? He came from heaven and identified Himself with us who like sheep have gone astray and have turned every one to our own way. And the Lord has laid on Him the iniquity of us all. Do you meditate on these things? The Ethiopian did. It always has been a matter of speculation as to what he did after that. Tradition says that he went back to his land and founded the Coptic church of Ethiopia. That could well be; we do not know. However, the interesting thing is that he went on his way rejoicing, which lets us know that he was meditating on the Word of God.

5. Read What Others Have Written on the Scriptures.

I know that this is a dangerous rule, because many folks depend on what someone else says about the Bible. Also there are many books on the market today that give wrong teaching concerning the Word of God. We need to test everything that is written by the Bible itself.

However, you and I should consult a good commentary. With each outline of the books of the Bible I list recommended books, commentaries that I have read and have found helpful. You will find it very profitable to read what others have said. Actually, you are getting all the distilled sweetness and study of the centuries when you read books written by men who have been guided in their study by the Spirit of God. You and I should profit by this. There have been some wonderful, profound works on the books of the Bible.

In addition to commentaries, a concordance is invaluable. I can recommend three: Young's concordance, Strong's concordance, and Cruden's concordance—take your pick. Also you will need a good Bible dictionary. The Davis Bible dictionary is good if you don't get the wrong edition. *Unger's Bible Dictionary* I can recommend without reservation.

Every teacher and preacher of the Gospel has a set of books that he studies. He needs them. Someone asks, "Should he present verbatim what somebody else has written?" No, he should never do that, unless he gives credit to the author. But he has a perfect right to use what others have written. I have been told that some of my feeble messages are given by others, and sometimes credit is given and sometimes no mention is made of the author at all. As far as I'm personally concerned, it makes no difference, but it does reveal the character of the individual who will use someone else's material verbatim and not give credit for it. A professor in seminary solved this problem. When someone asked him if he should quote other writers, he said, "You ought to graze on everybody's pasture, but give your own milk." And that means that you are to read what others have written, but you put it in your own thought patterns and express it your way. You have a perfect right to do that. The important thing is that we should take advantage of the study of other men in the Word of God.

6. Obey the Bible.

For the understanding and the study of the Scriptures, *obedience* is essential. Abraham is an example of this. God appeared to him when He called him out of Ur of the Chaldees and again when he was in the Promised Land. But Abraham ran off to Egypt when famine came, and during this time God had no word for him. Not until Abraham was back in the land did God appear to him again. Why? Because of lack of obedience. Until Abraham obeyed what God had already revealed to him, God was not prepared to give to him any new truth. So it is with us. When we obey, God opens up new truth for us.

Even the gospel which is given to save our souls is given for the very definite purpose of obedience. The greatest document that ever has been written on the gospel is the Epistle to the Romans. And Paul put around the gospel this matter of obedience. He begins with it: "By whom we have received grace and apostleship, for obedience to the faith among all nations, for his name" (Rom. 1:5). Again at the end of Romans, Paul comes back to this: "But now is made manifest, and by the scriptures of the prophets, according to the commandment of the everlasting God, made known to all nations for the obedience of faith" (Rom. 16:26). "Obedience of faith" is the last thing Paul says in this epistle. What is between? He sets before us what the gospel is,

that great doctrinal section; then he concludes with a section on duty—what we're to do. Paul put around the gospel this matter of obedience.

Obedience to the faith. This is where Adam and Eve went wrong. She not only listened to Satan, the enemy of God, but she also disobeyed God.

Obedience to God is very important. And we must recognize that God will not continue to reveal truth to us if we become disobedient. We must obey the Bible if we are to profit from its reading.

Also obedience is important because there are folk who measure Christianity by you and by me. Cowan has well said, "The best way to defend the Gospel is to live a life worthy of the Gospel." That is the way you prove it is the Word of God.

Four clergymen were discussing the merits of various translations of the Bible. One liked the King James Version best because of its simple, beautiful English. Another liked the American Standard Version because it is more literal and comes nearer to the Hebrew and Greek texts. Still another liked a modern translation because of its up-to-date vocabulary. The fourth minister was silent. When asked to express his opinion, he replied, "I like my mother's translation best. She translated it into life, and it was the most convincing translation I have ever seen."

You will recall that Paul wrote to the Corinthian Christians: "Ye are our epistle written in our hearts, known and read of all men: Forasmuch as ye are manifestly declared to be the epistle of Christ ministered by us, written not with ink, but with the Spirit of the living God; not in tables of stone, but in fleshy tables of the heart" (2 Cor. 3:2–3).

The Gospel is written a chapter a day
  By deeds that you do and words that you say.
Men read what you say whether faithless or true.
  Say, what is the Gospel according to you?
          —Author Unknown

That little jingle is true. Oh, how important it is to obey the Bible! I believe that today Christianity is being hurt more by those who are church members than by any other group. That is one of the reasons that we have all of this rebellion on the outside—rebellion against the establishment, which includes the church. A placard carried by one in a protest march had four words on it: "Church, no;

Jesus, yes." Candidly, the lives of a great many in the church are turning people away from the church. A barrister in England years ago was asked why he did not become a Christian. This was his answer: "I, too, might have become a Christian if I had not met so many who said they were Christians." How unfortunate that is! We need to examine our own lives in this connection. How important it is to *obey* the Word of God!

7. Pass It on to Others.

Not only read the Bible, not only study the Bible, not only meditate on the Bible, and not only read what others have written about it, but pass it on to others. That is what we all should do. You will reach a saturation point in the study of the Word unless you do share it with others. God won't let you withdraw yourself from mankind and become some sort of a walking Bible encyclopedia, knowing everything, while the rest of us remain ignorant. I think that is the reason He said: "Not forsaking the assembling of ourselves together, as the manner of some is; but exhorting one another: and so much the more, as ye see the day approaching" (Heb. 10:25).

God has told us to be witnesses. He said, "Ye shall be witnesses" (Acts 1:8). He did not say that we should be scholars, walking encyclopedias, or memory books. He did not say we should bury God's truth in a notebook. Someone has said that education is a process by which information in the professor's notebook is transferred to the student's notebook, without passing through the mind of either. Well, there is a great deal of Bible truth like that. It is not practiced, not shared. We are called to be witnesses today, therefore we ought to pass it on to others.

I learned this lesson when I was in seminary. I pastored a little church, as did five other fellows, and we found that when we were graduated, we were at least a year ahead of the other members of the class. Why? Because we were smarter than the others? No. Because we were passing it on. God was able to funnel into us a great deal more than He might have otherwise.

My friend, pass it on.

These, then, are the seven basic guidelines to follow as you take in your hands the Word of God:

1. Begin with prayer.
2. Read the Bible.
3. Study the Bible.
4. Meditate upon the Bible.
5. Read what others have written on the Bible.
6. Obey the Bible.
7. Pass it on to others.

The Book of
GENESIS
INTRODUCTION

The Book of Genesis is one of the two important key books of the Bible. The book that opens the Old Testament (Genesis) and the book that opens the New Testament (Matthew) are the two books which I feel are the key to the understanding of the Scriptures.

Before beginning this study, I would like to suggest that you read the Book of Genesis through. It would be preferable to read it at one sitting. I recognize that this may be impossible for you to do, and if you want to know the truth, I have not been able to do it in one sitting. It has taken me several sittings because of interruptions. However, if you find it possible to read through Genesis at one sitting, you will find it very profitable.

Let me give you a bird's-eye view of Genesis, a view that will cover the total spectrum of the book. There are certain things that you should note because the Book of Genesis is, actually, germane to the entire Scripture. The fact of the matter is that Genesis is a book that states many things for the first time: creation, man, woman, sin, sabbath, marriage, family, labor, civilization, culture, murder, sacrifice, races, languages, redemption, and cities.

You will also find certain phrases that occur very frequently. For instance, "these are the generations of" is an important expression used frequently because the Book of Genesis gives the families of early history. That is important to us because we are members of the human family that begins here.

A number of very interesting characters are portrayed for us. Someone has called this "the book of biographies." There are Abraham, Isaac, Jacob, Joseph, Pharaoh, and the eleven sons of Jacob besides Joseph. You will find that God is continually blessing Abraham, Isaac, Jacob, and Joseph. In addition, those who are associated with them—Lot, Abimelech, Potiphar, the butler, and Pharaoh—are also blessed of God.

In this book you will find mention of the covenant. There are frequent appearances of the Lord to the patriarchs, especially to Abraham. The altar is prominent in this book. Jealousy in the home is found here. Egypt comes before us in this book as it does nowhere else. The judgments upon sin are mentioned here, and there are evident leadings of Providence.

As we study, we need to keep in mind something that Browning wrote years ago in a grammarian's funeral essay: "Image the whole, then execute the parts. Fancy the fabric, quiet, e'er you build, e'er steel strike fire from quartz, e'er mortar dab brick." In other words, get the total picture of this book. I tell students that there are two ways of studying the Bible; one is with the telescope and the other way is with the microscope. At first, you need to get the telescopic view. After that, study it with a microscope.

A great preacher of the past, Robinson of England, has written something which I would like to write indelibly on the minds and hearts of God's people today:

We live in the age of books. They pour out for us from the press in an ever increasing multitude. And we are always reading manuals, textbooks, articles, books of devotion, books of criticism, books about the Bible, books about the Gospels, all are devoured with avidity. But what amount of time and labor do we give to the consideration of the Gospels themselves? We're constantly tempted to imagine that we get good more quickly by reading some modern statement of truth which we find comparatively easy to appropriate because it is presented to us in a shape, and from a standpoint, with which our education, or it may be partly association, has made us familiar. But the good we acquire readily is not that which enters most deeply into our being and becomes an abiding possession. It would be well if we could realize quite simply that nothing worth the having is to be gained without the winning. The great truths of nature are not offered to us in such a form as to make it easy to grasp them. The treasures of grace must be sought with all the skill and energy which are characteristic of the man who is searching for goodly pearls. (Robinson, *The Personal Life of the Clergy*.)

I love that statement because I believe that the Bible itself will speak to our hearts in a way that no other book can do. Therefore we have included the text of Scripture in this

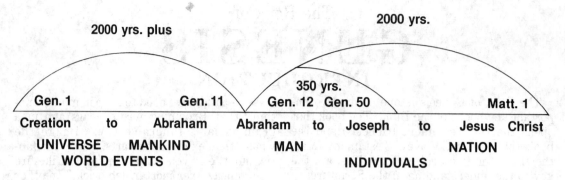

study. New translations are appearing in our day; in fact, they are coming from the presses as fast and prolifically as rabbits multiply. However, I will continue to use the Authorized or King James Version. I refuse to substitute the pungency of genius with the bland, colorless, and tasteless mediocrity of the present day.

MAJOR DIVISIONS OF THE BOOK

Where would you divide the Book of Genesis if you divided it into two parts? Notice that the first eleven chapters constitute a whole and that, beginning with chapter 12 through the remainder of the book, we find an altogether different section. The two parts differ in several ways: The first section extends from creation to Abraham. The second section extends from Abraham through Joseph. The first section deals with major *subjects*, subjects which still engage the minds of thoughtful men in our day: the Creation, the Fall, the Flood, the Tower of Babel. The second section has to do with personalities: Abraham, the man of faith; Isaac, the beloved son; Jacob, the chosen and chastened son; and Joseph, his suffering and glory.

Although that is a major division, there is another division even more significant. It has to do with *time*. The first eleven chapters cover a minimum time span of two thousand years—actually, two thousand years *plus*. I feel that it is safe to say that they may cover several hundred thousand years. I believe this first section of Genesis can cover any time in the past that you may need to fit into your particular theory, and the chances are that you would come short of it even then. At least we know the book covers a minimum of two thousand years in the first eleven chapters, but the second section of thirty-nine chapters covers only three hundred and fifty years. In fact, beginning with Genesis 12 and running all the way through the Old Testament and the New Testament, a total time span of only two thousand years is covered. Therefore, as

far as *time* is concerned, you are halfway through the Bible when you cover the first eleven chapters of Genesis.

This should suggest to your mind and heart that God had some definite purpose in giving this first section to us. Do you think that God is putting the emphasis on this first section or on the rest of the Bible? Isn't it evident that He is putting the emphasis on the last part? The first section has to do with the universe and with creation, but the last part deals with man, with nations, and with the person of Jesus Christ. God was more interested in Abraham than He was in the entire created universe. And, my friend, God is more interested in *you* and attaches more value to *you* than He does to the entire physical universe.

Let me further illustrate this. Of the eighty-nine chapters in the four Gospel records, only four chapters cover the first thirty years of the life of the Lord Jesus while eighty-five chapters cover the last three years of His life, and twenty-seven chapters cover the final eight *days* of His life. Where does that indicate that the Spirit of God is placing the emphasis? I am sure you will agree that the emphasis is on the last part, the last eight days covered by the twenty-seven chapters. And what is that all about? It's about the death, burial, and resurrection of the Lord Jesus Christ. That is the important part of the Gospel record. In other words, God has given the Gospels that you might believe that Christ died for our sins and that He was raised for our justification. That is essential. That is the all-important truth.

May I say that the first eleven chapters of Genesis are merely the introduction to the Bible, and we need to look at them in this fashion. This does not mean that we are going to pass over the first eleven chapters. Actually, we will spend quite a bit of time with them.

Genesis is the "seed plot" of the Bible, and here we find the beginning, the source, the birth of everything. The Book of Genesis is just like the bud of a beautiful rose, and it opens out into the rest of the Bible. The truth here is in germ form.

One of the best divisions which can be made of the Book of Genesis is according to the genealogies—i.e., according to the families.

Gen. 1–2:6	Book of Generations of Heavens and Earth
Gen. 2:7–6:8	Book of Generations of Adam
Gen. 6:9–9:29	Generations of Noah
Gen. 10:1–11:9	Generations of Sons of Noah
Gen. 11:10–26	Generations of Sons of Shem
Gen. 11:27–25:11	Generations of Terah
Gen. 25:12–18	Generations of Ishmael
Gen. 25:19–35:29	Generations of Isaac
Gen. 36:1–37:1	Generations of Esau
Gen. 37:2–50:26	Generations of Jacob

All of these are given to us in the Book of Genesis. It is a book of families. Genesis is an amazing book, and it will help us to look at it from this viewpoint.

OUTLINE

   6. God Makes Covenant with Abraham (Abram Becomes Abraham)—
      Confirms Promise to Abraham About a Son, Chapter 17
   7. God Reveals Coming Destruction of Sodom to Abraham—
      Abraham Intercedes on Behalf of Inhabitants, Chapter 18
   8. Angels Warn Lot—Lot Leaves Sodom
      God Destroys Cities of the Plain, Chapter 19
   9. Abraham Repeats Sin at Gerar About
      Relationship of Sarah, Chapter 20
  10. Birth of Isaac—Hagar and Ishmael Cast Out—
      Abraham at Beer-sheba, Chapter 21
  11. God Commands Abraham to Offer Isaac—
      Restrains Him—
      Reconfirms Covenant with Abraham, Chapter 22
  12. Death of Sarah—
      Abraham Purchases Machpelah Cave for Burial
      Place, Chapter 23

B. Isaac (the Beloved Son), Chapters 24–26
Choosing of a bride compares with Christ and the Church.
  1. Abraham Sends Servant for Bride for Isaac—
      Rebekah Returns with Him—
      Becomes Isaac's Bride, Chapter 24
  2. Death of Abraham—
      Birth of Esau and Jacob (twins) to Isaac and Rebekah—
      Esau Sells Birthright to Jacob, Chapter 25
  3. God Confirms Covenant to Isaac—
      Isaac Misrepresents Relationship with Rebekah—
      Isaac Digs Well in Gerar, Chapter 26

C. Jacob, Chapters 27–36
"Whom the Lord loveth He chasteneth"
  1. Jacob and Rebekah Connive
      to Get Blessing Intended for Esau, Chapter 27
  2. Jacob Leaves Home—
      At Bethel God Appears to Him—
      Confirms Abrahamic Covenant, Chapter 28
  3. Jacob Arrives in Haran—
      Meets Rachel and Uncle Laban—
      Serves for Rachel—
      Deceived into Marrying Leah, Chapter 29
  4. Birth of Sons to Jacob—
      Jacob Prepares to Leave Laban—
      Jacob's Bargain Pays Off, Chapter 30
  5. Jacob Flees from Haran—Laban Overtakes Him—
      Jacob and Laban Make Mizpah Covenant, Chapter 31
  6. Crisis in Life of Jacob: At Peniel a Man Wrestles with Him—
      Jacob's Name Changed to Israel, Chapter 32
  7. Jacob Meets Esau—
      Jacob Journeys to Shalem, Chapter 33
  8. Scandal in Jacob's Family: Dinah Defiled—
      Brothers Avenge by Slaying Men of Hamor, Chapter 34
  9. Jacob Returns to Bethel—
      Rachel Dies at Bethlehem—
      Isaac Dies at Hebron, Chapter 35
 10. Family of Esau Which Becomes Nation of Edom, Chapter 36

D. Joseph (suffering and glory), Chapters 37–50
  1. Jacob Dwells in Canaan—
      Joseph Sold into Slavery, Chapter 37

CHAPTER 1

CREATION OF THE UNIVERSE

In the beginning God created the heaven and the earth [Gen. 1:1].

This is one of the most profound statements that has ever been made, and yet we find that it is a statement that is certainly challenged in this hour in which we are living. I think that this verse is all we have of the actual creation—with the exception, as we shall see, of the creation of man and animals later on in the Book of Genesis. But this is the creation story, and I'll admit that it is a very brief story, indeed.

An incident was told by Paul Bellamy, the late city editor of the *Cleveland Plain Dealer*, that while he was making the rounds of the reporters' desks one night, he noticed one of his men grinding out a "tapeworm" on what Bellamy regarded as a relatively unimportant event. "Cut it down!" he said, "After all, the story of the creation was told in Genesis in 282 words." The reporter shot back, "Yes, and I've always thought we could have been saved a lot of arguments later if someone had just written another couple hundred."

It is interesting to note that God certainly has given us an abridged edition. The question arises: What did He have in mind when He gave us this particular section? What was the Author's purpose here? Was it His purpose to teach geology? There is a great deal of argument and disagreement at this particular juncture. Sometime ago here in California, the state board of education voted to include the biblical so-called *theory* of creation in science books. Now frankly, I'm not so sure that I'm happy about that. Someone will say that I ought to be because it is a step in the right direction. My friends, I'll tell you why I'm not happy. My concern is relative to the *character* of the teachers who teach it. We don't have enough teachers with a Christian background and with a Bible background to be able to teach it properly. Very few of the public school teachers are prepared, really, to teach the story of creation.

Dr. Ralph Girard, professor of biology and dean of the graduate division at the University of California at Davis is reported by the press to have made the comment that the "theory of creation" makes about as much sense as teaching about the stork. He asked if a scientific course on reproduction should also mention the stork theory. The very interesting thing is that the stork theory is not mentioned in the Bible at all, but the creation story is mentioned. His comparison is not quite warranted, because the Bible deals literally with this matter of procreation, and if you read your Bible carefully, you never could have the viewpoint of the stork theory! So what this man says is certainly beside the point but reveals a very antagonistic attitude toward the Bible. I'm of the opinion that this man probably knows a great deal about his particular subject, which seems to be biology, but he knows very little about the Word of God. This is quite obvious from the type of statement he has made.

This problem of origin provokes more violent controversy, wild theories, and wide disagreement than any other. Always there is the inclusion of men's hypotheses, and as a result there is a babble of voices that has drowned out the clear voice of God. Actually, there are two extreme groups who have blurred the issue, and they have muddied the waters of understanding by their dogmatic assumptions and assertions. One group is comprised of the arrogant scientists who assume that biological and philosophical evolution are the gospel truth. Their assumed axiom is "the assured finding of science," and we'll look into that in a moment. The other group is comprised of the young and proud theologians who arrogate to themselves the super-knowledge that they have discovered how God did it. They write and speak learnedly about some clever theory that reconciles science and the Bible. They look with disdain upon the great giants of biblical expositors of the past as being Bible dwarfs compared to them.

I would say that both of these groups would do well to consider a statement that was made to Job when the Lord finally appeared to him. God asked him the question: "Where wast thou when I laid the foundations of the earth? Declare, if thou hast understanding" (Job 38:4). In other words, God is saying to man, "You talk about the origin of the universe, but you don't even know where *you* were when I laid the foundation of the earth!"

There are a great many theories as to how the world began, but all of them can be boiled down to fit into a twofold classification: one is creation, and the other is speculation. All theories fall into one of these two divisions.

The theory of evolution is comprised of many different theories in our day, and some of the most reputable scientists of the past, as well as of the present, reject evolution. So we can't put down the theory of evolution as being a scientific statement like 2 + 2 = 4. Then there is the creation account in Genesis 1, which must be accepted by faith. It is very interesting that God has made it that way—by *faith* is the only way in the world by which you can accept it. Notice what the writer to the Hebrews said: "Now faith is the substance of things hoped for, the evidence of things not seen. For by it the elders obtained a good report. Through faith we understand that the worlds were framed by the word of God, so that things which are seen were not made of things which do appear" (Heb. 11:1–3). So today the great problem still remains. How did it get from nothing to something? The only way that you can ever arrive at an answer is by faith or by speculation—and speculation is very unscientific.

Now let us look at some of the theories of origin. There are those who tell us that we should accept the scientific answer. I would like to ask, what is the scientific answer? What science are we talking about? In the year 1806 Professor Lyell said that the French Institute enumerated not less than eighty geological theories which were hostile to the Scriptures, but not one of these theories is held in our day.

Moses is the human agent whom God used to write the book of Genesis, and I think he would smile at all the disturbance today regarding the creation story because he did not write it with the intention of giving a scientific account. Paul tells us the purpose of all Scripture: "All scripture *is* given by inspiration of God, and *is* profitable for doctrine, for reproof, for correction, for instruction in righteousness: That the man of God may be perfect, throughly furnished unto all good works" (2 Tim. 3:16–17). The purpose of the Scripture is for instruction in righteousness. It was not written to teach you geology or biology. It was written to show man's relationship to God and God's requirements for man and what man must do to be saved. You can write this over the first part of the book of Genesis: "What must I do to be saved?"

May I ask you, if God had given a scientific statement of creation, how many people of Moses' day could have understood it? How many people even in our day could grasp it? You must remember that the Bible was not written for only learned professors but also for simple folk of every age and in every land. If it had been written in the scientific language of Moses' time, it certainly would have been rejected.

Therefore, men have proposed several solutions relative to the origin of the universe. One is that it is an illusion. Well, that is certainly contrary to fact, is it not? And yet there are people who hold that theory. There are others who believe that it spontaneously arose out of nothing. (In a way, this is what the Bible states, although it goes further and says that God spoke it into existence; He created it.) Another view is that it had no origin but has existed eternally. A fourth view is that it was created, and this breaks down into many different theories which men hold in an attempt to explain the origin of the universe.

I have before me some of these theories which men have advanced down through the history of the world. Here is a statement by Dr. Harlow Shapely, the former director of the Harvard Observatory, who commented that we are still imbedded in abysmal ignorance of the world in which we live. He observed that "we have advanced very little, relative to the total surmisable extent of knowledge, beyond the level of wisdom acquired by animals of long racial experience. We are, to be sure, no longer afraid of strange squeaks in the dark, nor completely superstitious about the dead. On many occasions we are valiantly rational. Nevertheless, we know how much the unknown transcends what we know." In other words, we are still absolutely in the dark relative to the origin of this earth on which we live.

Dr. Loren C. Eiseley, Office of the Provost, University of Pennsylvania, was asked about this; he answered that "we do not know any more about matter and how it is produced than we know about spiritual things. Therefore, I think it is unwise to say in our present state of knowledge that the one precludes the other. The universe seems to exist as a series of emergent levels, none of which is like the level below. That man and all the rest of life have evolved and changed is undeniable, but what lies beneath these exterior manifestations, we do not know. I wish I could answer your question, but to clothe my ignorance in big words would benefit neither yourself nor me."

One article says that man is on the verge of discovering the mystery of the origin of the world. That happened to be written back in 1961. We haven't had anything new on that since then, by the way.

The biologist Edwin Conklin, speaking of evolution, stated that the probability of life originating by accident is "comparable to the probability of the unabridged dictionary originating from an explosion in a print shop." That sounds very unscientific, coming from a scientist, but it's true.

There seem to be at least three theories of the origin of the universe which even astronomists have suggested, and it is interesting to note them. One is known as the "steady state" theory, one is the "big bang" theory, and another is the "oscillating" theory.

A Caltech scientist, Dr. William A. Baum, speaking at UCLA, told the National Academy of Science that new findings tend to rule out the "steady state" theory that the universe has always existed and that new matter is continually being created. Several years ago that was the accepted theory; now they have a new theory for the origin of the universe. Dr. Baum apparently held the "big bang" theory, which is that a great explosion took place billions of years ago and that we are in for another one in probably another ten billion years. I don't think we need to worry about that a great deal, but it is an interesting theory and one that was fathered in Great Britain.

Several years ago Dr. Louis Leakey, an anthropologist (the son of a missionary, by the way) discovered in Africa what he called a missing link. He dug up pieces of a skull with well-developed teeth, called it the "nutcracker man" and claimed it belonged to a teenage youth about six hundred thousand years ago. Well, we have had theories like that before, and since we've heard no more of this one since 1961, I guess the scientific world didn't fall for it.

There are other ways for explaining the origin of man. Dr. Lawrence S. Dillon, associate professor of biology at Texas A and M College, says that man is not an animal but a plant which evolved from brown seaweed. Now maybe you have been looking in the wrong place for your grandpa and grandma. Some folks have been looking up a tree. Now we are told that we should be down at the beach pulling out seaweed because that is

grandpa and grandma! Some of this speculation really becomes ridiculous.

A long time ago I read in a leading secular magazine that: "After centuries of bitter arguments over how life on earth began, an awe-inspiring answer is emerging out of the shrewd and patient detective work in laboratories all over the world." You would think that by now we would be getting some straight answers or at least a little encouragement, but none has been forthcoming.

It was the practice, according to J.V.N. Talmage, that the dogma which scientists followed was this: "The archeological finds of prehistoric cultural objects must be so arranged that the cruder industries must always be dated earlier than those of a 'more advanced' type, regardless of where they are found." It has been a little disconcerting to find some of the advanced civilizations *underneath* those which seem to be of prehistoric time.

So many other theories are offered today about how the earth began. Dr. Klaus Mampell from Germany reportedly said that he didn't see any more reason for seeing us (the human race) connected with apes than with canary birds or kangaroos.

The evolutionary theory is divided up into many different phases and viewpoints. It has never been demonstrated as being true. It is unfortunate that when you get down to the level of the pseudo-scientists, and I'm thinking of the teachers today in our public schools who teach science, they really are not in a position to give a fair view because they were given only one viewpoint in college.

There is no unanimous acceptance of evolution even by scientists. Here is a quotation from Dr. G. A. Kerkut, of the Department of Physiology and Biochemistry at the University of South Hampton in England. Though he himself is an evolutionist, in his book, *The Implications of Evolution*, he writes: "There is a theory which states that many living animals can be observed over the course of time to undergo changes so that new species are formed. This can be called the "Special Theory of Evolution" and can be demonstrated in certain cases by experiments. On the other hand there is the theory that all of the living forms in the world have arisen from a single source which itself came from an inorganic form. This theory can be called the "General Theory of Evolution" and the evidence that supports it is not sufficiently strong to allow us to consider it as anything more than a working hypothesis." Now listen to the statement of the

Swedish botanist, Dr. Heribert Nilsson, who is also an evolutionist: "My attempts to demonstrate evolution by experiment carried on for more than forty years, have completely failed. . . . At least I should hardly be accused of having started from a preconceived anti-evolutionary standpoint. . . . It may be firmly maintained that it is not even possible to make a caricature out of paleobiological facts. The fossil material is now so complete that it has been possible to construct new classes, and the lack of transitional series cannot be explained as due to the scarcity of material. Deficiencies are real. They will never be filled. . . . The idea of an evolution rests on pure belief."

May I say to you, he is moving into the realm of religion! My friend, to be an evolutionist you have to take it by *faith*. Evolution is speculation and always has been that. But, unfortunately, a great many folk have accepted it as fact.

In our day a group of theologians (young theologians for the most part) who, not wanting to be called intellectual obscurantists, have adopted what is known as "theistic evolution." If you would like to know what one scientist says about it, Kirtly Mather, in *Science Ponders Religion*, says: "When a theologian accepts evolution as the process used by the creator, he must be willing to go all the way with it. Not only is it an orderly process, it is a continuing one. The golden age for man—if any—is in the future, not in the past. . . . Moreover, the creative process of evolution is not to be interrupted by any supernatural intervention. The evolution of the first living cells from previously existing non-living materials may represent a quantum-jump rather than an infinitesimal step along the path of progress, but it is an entirely natural development." Theistic evolution is probably the most unrealistic of all theories. It is almost an unreasonable tenet and an illogical position. There are those today who are trying to run with the hare and with the hounds. They would like to move up with the unbelievers, but they also like to carry a Scofield Bible under their arm. My friend, it is difficult to do both. It is like that old Greek race in which a contestant rode with one foot on one horse and the other foot on another horse. It was marvelous when the two horses kept on the same route. But, believe me, when one of the horses decided to go in another direction, the rider had to determine which one he was going with. That is the condition of the theistic evolutionist. He ordinari-

ly ends up riding the wrong horse, by the way.

In our day there is so much misinformation in the minds of intelligent human beings. For example, before me is a clipping from a secular magazine from several years ago. It posed a question, then answered it. First, the question: "What, according to biblical records, is the date of the creation of the world?" Now listen to the answer that was given: "4,004 B.C." How utterly ridiculous can one be?

An article in *Life* magazine concerning the origin of life said that at some indeterminate point—some say two billion years ago, some a billion and a half—life miraculously appeared on the surface of the deep. What form it took, science cannot specify. All that can be said, according to this article, is that "through some agency certain giant molecules acquired the ability to duplicate themselves." My friend, are you willing to go along with the theory that giant molecules acquired the ability to duplicate themselves?

Other ridiculous theories have been advanced. One is that man began on this earth from garbage that some prehistoric intelligence left on this earth in the dim and distant past. That statement comes from a *scientist!* While some scientists send us out to look for our ancestors in the trees, another sends us out to look at the seaweed, and now some send us to the garbage can! This is getting worse and worse, is it not? I don't know about you, but I feel that God's statement of creation still stands in this modern age.

A famous definition of evolution which Herbert Spencer gave stated that: "An integration of matter and concomitant dissipation of motion during which the matter passes from an indefinite, incoherent, homogeneity to a definite, coherent heterogeneity, and during which the retained motion undergoes a parallel transformation." You ponder that one for awhile, friend!

It still makes more sense to me to read: "In the beginning God created the heaven and the earth." Who created the universe? God did. He created it out of nothing. When? I don't know, and nobody else knows. Some men say one billion years ago, some say two billion, and now some say five billion. I personally suspect that they all are pikers. I think it was created long before that. My friend, we need to keep in mind that God has eternity behind Him. What do you think He has been doing during all the billions of years of the past? Waiting for you and me to come on the scene? No, He has been busy. He has had this creation a long time to work with. You see, He really has not told us very much, has He? It is rather presumptuous of little man down here on this earth to claim to know more than he really does know.

You cannot shape one single forest leaf,
Nor fling a mountain up, nor sink an ocean,
Presumptuous pigmy, large with unbelief!

You cannot bring one dawn of regal splendor,
Nor bid the day to shadowy twilight fall,
Nor send the pale moon forth with radiance tender;
And dare you doubt the One who has done it all?
Sherman A. Nagel, Sr.

It behooves us to just accept that majestic statement which opens the Word of God: "In the beginning God created the heaven and the earth." And with the psalmist let us consider *His* heavens, the work of *His* fingers, the moon and the stars, which *He* hast ordained (Ps. 8:3) and realize that "the heavens declare the glory of God; and the firmament sheweth his handiwork (Ps. 19:1).

The Apostle Paul wrote this to the Romans: "For the invisible things of him from the creation of the world are clearly seen, being understood by the things that are made, even his eternal power and Godhead; so that they are without excuse" (Rom. 1:20). And the writer to the Hebrews says: "Through faith we understand that the worlds were framed by the word of God, so that things which are seen were not made of things which do appear" (Heb. 11:3). We must accept creation by faith. Even science cannot tell us how something can be made out of nothing. God apparently did it just that way. And man today cannot tell when this was created.

When we compare the Genesis record with other creation accounts, the contrasts are striking indeed. Most nations have a legend of creation, and probably all of them are corruptions of the Genesis account. For example, we find one of the best accounts of a secular nation in the Babylonian tablets of creation. Notice some of the contrasts: The Babylonian tablets begin with chaos. The Bible account begins with cosmos, with perfection. "In the beginning God created the heaven and the earth." According to the Babylonian account, the heavenly bodies are gods, but they are

nothing in the world but matter according to the Bible. There is a polytheistic theology in the Babylonian account but a monotheistic truth in the Bible account. The Babylonian account says the universe is just the work of a craftsman, but the Bible says that God spoke and it came into existence. The Babylonian account is characterized by its puerility and grotesqueness, whereas the Bible presents grand and solemn realities of the Creator God who is holy and who is a Savior. The Babylonian account is definitely out of harmony with known science, but the Bible is in accord with true science.

I reject evolution because it rejects God and it rejects revelation. It denies the fall of man and the fact of sin, and it opposes the virgin birth of Christ. Therefore, I reject it with all my being. I do not believe that it is the answer to the origin of this universe.

There are three essential areas into which evolution cannot move and which evolution cannot solve. It cannot bridge the gap from nothing to something. It cannot bridge the gap from something to life. It cannot bridge the gap between life and humanity—that is, self-conscious human life with a free will.

The press, of course, is always looking for something sensational and comes up with interesting findings. One of the things which has been put in my hands is a clipping from a fellow Texan. They have found near Glenrose, Texas, down near a place where I used to live, the tracks of dinosaurs. Now, I've known about that for years. You might expect that in Texas they would find the biggest of everything, and apparently the dinosaurs were there. But now they have found something that is quite disturbing: they have found some giant human tracks in the same place. You know, that's really upsetting because it is very difficult to start out with a little amoeba or a little scum on top of the water and then find that walking back there with the dinosaurs were human beings who were much bigger than any of us today. Evolution is going to have a lot of problems in the next few years. May I predict (and I am merely echoing a prediction of a scientist) that by the end of this century the theory of evolution will be as dead as a dodo bird.

While there is a great deal more that could be said on these issues, there is a third question that arises. Not only are folk asking *who* created and *when* did He create but also *why* did He create. Believe me, this gets right down to the nitty-gritty. This is very important.

The Word of God tells us that this universe was created for His own pleasure. He saw fit to create it; He delighted in it. In the final book of the Bible we find these words: "Thou art worthy, O Lord, to receive glory and honor and power: for thou hast created all things, and for thy pleasure they are and were created" (Rev. 4:11). He created this universe because He wanted to create it. He did it for His pleasure. You may not like the universe, but He does. He never asked me about where I wanted this little world on which I live to be located in His universe. In fact, He didn't even ask me whether I wanted to be born in Texas or not. Of course, if He had given me the opportunity, I would have chosen Texas. But He didn't give me that choice. May I say to you that this universe was created for His pleasure. He saw fit to create and He delighted in the act.

The second reason that He created this universe was for His own glory. The original creation, you remember, sang that wonderful Creator's praise ". . . When the morning stars sang together, and all the sons of God shouted for joy" (Job 38:7). It was created for His glory. And in the prophecy of Isaiah are these words: ". . . I have created him for my glory, I have formed him; yea, I have made him" (Isa. 43:7). God created this universe for His own glory.

The Word of God also tells us that God created man in this universe for fellowship. He wanted to have fellowship with mankind, and so He created him a free moral agent. God could have made a bunch of robots. God could have made mechanical men and pushed a button to make them bow down to Him. But God didn't want that kind of a man. God wanted a man to be free to choose Him and to love Him and to serve Him.

My friend, in the midst of all the unbelief, the blasphemy, and the hostility toward God which is around us today, the greatest thing you can do as a human being is to publicly choose the Lord Jesus Christ. To believe in God the Father Almighty, the Maker of heaven and earth and to receive His Son, Jesus Christ, is the most glorious privilege that you and I have. We hear a lot of talk about freedom of speech and freedom of every sort, but this poor crowd around us who talks so loudly of freedom, doesn't seem to know what freedom really is. We have real freedom when we choose Jesus Christ as our Savior.

Now let's return to the first verse of Genesis: "In the beginning God created the heaven and the earth." This is a majestic verse. It is a tremendous verse. I am of the opinion that it is the doorway through which you will have to walk into the Bible. You have to believe that God is the Creator, for he that cometh to God must believe that He *is*. "In the beginning God created the heaven and the earth."

"In the beginning"—that is a beginning which you cannot date. You can estimate it as billions of years, and I think you would be accurate, but who knows how many? Certainly *man* does not know.

"God created." The word "create" is from the Hebrew word *bara*, which means to create out of nothing. This word is used only three times in the first chapter of Genesis, because it records only three acts of creation. (1) The creation of something from nothing: "In the beginning God created the heaven and the earth." (2) The creation of life: "And God created great whales, and every living creature that moveth . . ." (v. 21). That's animal life of all kinds. (3) The creation of man: "So God created man in his own image . . ." (v. 27). Theistic evolution is not the answer. It attempts to follow creation until the time of man, then considers Adam and Eve to be products of some evolutionary process. The theistic evolutionist considers the days in Genesis as periods of time, long periods of time. I do not believe that is true. God's marking off the creative days with the words, "And the evening and the morning were the first day," etc., makes it clear that He was not referring to long periods of time but to actual twenty-four hour days.

"God created the heaven and the earth." The earth is separated from the rest of creation. Why? Well, the earth is the hometown of mankind; that's where he is to be placed. We are very much interested in him because we belong to this creature. We need to realize, my friend, that you and I are creatures, creatures of God, and as creatures of God, we owe Him something.

It was years ago that Herbert Spencer said, "The most general forms into which the manifestation of the Unknowable are re-divisible are *time, space, matter, force, motion*." Those were his categories of division. A very fine personal worker, George Dewey Blomgren, was talking to an army sergeant who was a law graduate. Mr. Blomgren was attempting to witness to him. The sergeant mentioned Herbert Spencer so Mr. Blomgren replied, "Did you know that both the Bible and Spencer teach the great principle of creation?" The sergeant's eyes widened and he asked, "How's that?" The reply was, "Spencer talked about time, space, matter, force, motion. In the first two verses of Genesis we find: 'In the beginning [time] God created the heaven [space] and the earth [matter]. And the earth was without form and void; and darkness was upon the face of the deep. And the Spirit of God [force] moved [motion] upon the face of the waters.' It took Spencer fifty years to uncover this law, but here it is in fifty seconds." The sergeant had no grounds for argument and soon trusted Christ as his Savior.

It is very interesting that God has put down these great principles in the first two verses of Genesis. How important it is for us to see that.

And the earth was without form, and void; and darkness was upon the face of the deep. And the spirit of God moved upon the face of the waters [Gen. 1:2].

Although this view has been discredited by many in the past few years, I believe that a great catastrophe took place between verses 1 and 2. As far as I can see, there is an abundance of evidence for it. To begin with, look out upon this vast creation—something has happened to it! Man's trip to the moon reveals nothing in the world but a wasteland up there. How did it get that way? May I say that there came a catastrophe in God's universe.

This is specifically mentioned in regard to the earth because this is to be the place where man lives, and so the earth is described as being "without form and void."

"Darkness was upon the face of the deep" indicates the absence of God, of course.

"Without form, and void" is a very interesting expression. "Without form" is the Hebrew word *tohu,* meaning a ruin, vacancy; "void" is the Hebrew word *bohu,* meaning emptiness. Notice this statement in the prophecy of Isaiah: "For thus saith the LORD that created the heavens; God himself that formed the earth and made it; he hath established it, he created it not in vain, he formed it to be inhabited: I am the LORD; and there is none else" (Isa. 45:18). Here God says that He did not create the earth "in vain," and the Hebrew word is *tohu,* which is the same word we found in Genesis 1:2. God did not create the earth without form and void. God created this universe a cosmos, not a chaos. This is the thing which Isaiah is attempting to make clear. He created it not *tohu va bohu,* but the earth became *tohu va bohu.* God formed the earth to be inhabited, and it was God who came to this wreck and made it a habitable place for mankind.

Our current study and exploration of space has revealed, so far, that you and I live in a universe in which only the earth is habitable for human beings. I believe that Genesis is telling us that this earth *became* without form and void, that it was just as uninhabitable as the moon when the Spirit of God moved upon the face of the waters.

I believe that the entire universe came under this great catastrophe. What was the catastrophe? We can only suggest that there was some pre-Adamic creature that was on this earth. And it seems that all of this is connected with the fall of Lucifer, son of the morning, who became Satan, the devil, as we know him today. I think all of this is involved here, but God has not given us details. The fact of the matter is that He has given us very, very few details in the first chapter of Genesis.

"And the spirit of God moved." The word for "moved" means brooded, like a mother hen broods over her little chicks. He brooded upon the face of the waters. The Holy Spirit began a ministry here which we will find Him doing again and again. It is re-creation! He comes into this scene and He recreates. This is precisely what He does for us.

You will remember that the Lord Jesus said, ". . . Except a man be born of water and of the Spirit, he cannot enter into the kingdom of God" (John 3:5). The water is the Word of God. Now, if you want to make baptism the symbol for it, that's fine. But the water means the Word of God. And the Holy Spirit is the Author of it. This is very important for us to see.

CONSTRUCTION OF THE EARTH

We have seen the construction of the universe in verse 1, the convulsion of the earth in verse 2, and now we come to the construction of the earth in six days (vv. 3–31). I believe what we have here is this development.

There are several things here that I would like to call to your attention. In Exodus 20:11, it reads "For in six days the LORD made heaven and earth, the sea, and all that in them is. . . ." There is nothing in that verse about creating. It says "made"; God is taking that which is already formed and in these six days He is not "creating" but He is recreating. He is working with matter which already exists, out of the matter which He had called into existence probably billions of years before.

God created life and put it on the earth, and for the earth He created man. That is the creature we are interested in because you and I happen to be one of those creatures. This makes the Genesis record intensely important for us today.

DAY ONE—LIGHT

And God said, Let there be light: and there was light.

And God saw the light, that it was good: and God divided the light from the darkness.

And God called the light Day, and the darkness he called Night. And the evening and the morning were the first day [Gen. 1:3–5].

That must have been a twenty-four hour day—I don't see how you could get anything else out of it. Notice that God said, "Let there be light." Ten times in this chapter we will find "let there be"—let there be a firmament, let there be lights, let the waters be gathered together, etc. Someone has called these the ten commandments of creation. This is the divine decalogue that we find here.

"God said, Let there be light." This is the first time we are told that God spoke. These are His first words recorded in Scripture.

DAY TWO—AIR SPACES

And God said, Let there be a firmament in the midst of the waters, and let it divide the waters from the waters [Gen. 1:6].

"God said, Let there be a firmament"—the Hebrew word for firmament is *raqia*, meaning air spaces.

"Let it divide the waters from the waters." What does that mean? Well, God first divided the waters perpendicularly. There is water above us and water beneath us.

And God made the firmament, and divided the waters which were under the firmament from the waters which were above the firmament: and it was so [Gen. 1:7].

Out in the Hawaiian Islands, when we were there one year, five inches of rain fell in Honolulu in just a very short time—I started to say in a few minutes and I think I'm accurate in that. We were in a place where over two hundred inches of rain fall in a year. My friend, there is a whole lot of water up there if two hundred inches of it can fall! Well, that's what God did. He divided the waters above from the waters which are beneath.

And God called the firmament Heaven. And the evening and the morning were the second day [Gen. 1:8].

"God called the firmament Heaven." This is not heaven as you and I think of it. Actually, there are three heavens that are mentioned in Scripture. The Lord Jesus spoke of the birds of heaven, and I think that is the heaven mentioned in this verse. Then there are the stars of heaven, meaning the second heaven, and there is the third heaven where God dwells. So the first layer up there, the first deck, is the deck where the clouds are and where the birds fly.

DAY THREE—DRY LAND AND PLANT LIFE

And God said, Let the waters under the heaven be gathered together unto one place, and let the dry land appear: and it was so.

And God called the dry land Earth; and the gathering together of the waters called he Seas: and God saw that it was good [Gen. 1:9–10].

Now there is a horizontal division made of the waters. First the waters above were separated from the waters beneath. Now the water is separated from the land, from the earth. May I say to you, there is nothing unscientific about this. They tell us that every spot on topside of this earth on which we live today was covered with water at one time. That was evidently a judgment that had come upon the earth way back sometime in the distant eternity of the past, and we know practically nothing about it. Anything we say is speculation. God has really told us very little here. But He has told us enough so that we can believe Him, that's all.

"God called the dry land Earth." What is He getting ready to do? Well, it looks like He is getting ready to make a place where He can put man, a place that is habitable. Man is not a water creature, even though there are evolutionists who think we came from the sea and from seaweed, as we mentioned, and others who think we came out of a slop bucket! How absurd can they possibly be?

And God said, Let the earth bring forth grass, the herb yielding seed, and the fruit tree yielding fruit after his kind, whose seed is in itself, upon the earth: and it was so [Gen. 1:11].

Now God is putting plant life here because

man, until the flood, was a vegetarian. Man will eat nothing but fruit and nuts. The forming of the plant life completed the third day.

And the earth brought forth grass, and herb yielding seed after his kind, and the tree yielding fruit, whose seed was in itself, after his kind: and God saw that it was good.

And the evening and the morning were the third day [Gen. 1:12–13].

DAY FOUR—SUN, MOON, STARS APPEAR

And God said, Let there be lights in the firmament of the heaven to divide the day from the night; and let them be for signs, and for seasons, and for days, and years [Gen. 1:14].

God didn't create the sun and the moon at this time. They were already up there. God just brought them around into position.

And let them be for lights in the firmament of the heaven to give light upon the earth: and it was so.

And God made two great lights; the greater light to rule the day, and the lesser light to rule the night: he made the stars also [Gen. 1:15–16].

One of them was to take charge of the day, and the sun does that pretty well. Also the moon does a good job by night. I don't know about you, but I proposed to my wife by moonlight. That moon has a lot of influence over the night, I can assure you.

Then there is just a little clause, "He made the stars also." That was a pretty big job, by the way, but not for God. It was John Wesley who said, "God created the heavens and the earth and didn't even half try." God "made the stars also."

And God set them in the firmament of the heaven to give light upon the earth,

And to rule over the day and over the night, and to divide the light from the darkness: and God saw that it was good [Gen. 1:17–18].

You will notice that it is God who does the dividing here, "to divide the light from the darkness."

You know, He still does that! There are those today who ask, "What's the difference between right and wrong?" God has drawn all the lines. How can we know what is right?

God says what is right. God has put down certain principles. God divides the light from the darkness and there is just that much distinction between right and wrong. He is the One who makes the difference, and He still does it.

And the evening and the morning were the fourth day [Gen. 1:19].

DAY FIVE—ANIMAL LIFE

And God said, Let the waters bring forth abundantly the moving creature that hath life, and fowl that may fly above the earth in the open firmament of heaven [Gen. 1:20].

We do have a certain amount of development. This does not mean that everything came from one little cell but that God made one of each creature and there has been development from each one. God said, "Let the waters bring forth abundantly," and the next verse adds "after their kind." The word "kind" does not mean species, as even Darwin said, but it means more than that. The word is phylum. I have been reading that one scientist said he had been looking around for another word. Well, I had a professor in seminary, a very brilliant man, who gave phylum as a synonym for "kind." If you will look up that word in the dictionary, you will see that it means a direct line of descent within a group. For instance, it would include not just one horse but every animal in the horse family. God created one like that, and there has been development from each one, tremendous development. Also there has been devolution— that is, there has been development, then later there has been degeneration.

And God created great whales, and every living creature that moveth, which the waters brought forth abundantly, after their kind, and every winged fowl after his kind: and God saw that it was good [Gen. 1:21].

"And God saw that it was good." Notice that. When God does it, it's *good*.

And God blessed them, saying, Be fruitful, and multiply, and fill the waters in the seas, and let fowl multiply in the earth [Gen. 1:22].

By the way, one scientist I quoted previously said that if our schools teach the creation story, they might as well teach the stork story. Believe me, the Bible certainly gets rid of the stork story. If you read it carefully, you will notice that these animals had to "bring forth." This will be true of mankind also. You won't find little Willie under a stump, and the stork won't bring little Susie, either.

And the evening and the morning were the fifth day [Gen. 1:23].

DAY SIX—FERTILITY OF ANIMAL LIFE

And God said, Let the earth bring forth the living creature after his kind, cattle, and creeping thing, and beast of the earth after his kind: and it was so.

And God made the beast of the earth after his kind, and cattle after their kind, and every thing that creepeth upon the earth after his kind: and God saw that it was good [Gen. 1:24–25].

Notice again the expression "after his kind"—after his biological phylum. Now we will see that God separates plant life and animal life from mankind, and He says, "Let us make man in our image." This creature is of great interest to you because he happens to be your great-great, etc., grandfather, and he is mine, also. This means that you and I are cousins, although maybe not kissing cousins. But the whole human family is related.

CREATION OF MAN

And God said, Let us make man in our image, after our likeness: and let them have dominion over the fish of the sea, and over the fowl of the air, and over the cattle, and over all the earth, and over every creeping thing that creepeth upon the earth [Gen. 1:26].

The first question that arises is : *How* was man created? The next chapter will tell us that. "And let them have dominion." God gave him dominion over the earth, and I do not think this means that God made him a sort of glorified gardener for the Garden of Eden. Adam had tremendous authority given to him. We will find out a little later that God says to him that he is to do certain things relative to this creation that God has given to him.

So God created man in his own image, in the image of God created he him; male and female created he them [Gen. 1:27].

We have here just the simple fact of the creation of man. This is the third time we find the word *bara,* which means to create out of nothing. So we see that man is created; he is something new. *Bara* is the same word that occurred in the first verse of Genesis: "In the beginning God *created* the heaven and the earth." He created the physical universe. Then He created life: "And God *created* great whales, and every living creature that moveth . . ." (1:21). Now we see that God created man: "So God *created* man in his own image." God will give us the details of His creation of man in the next chapter, and we can see from this that God has left out a great deal about the creation of the universe. "In the beginning God created the heaven and the earth" is all the information He has given to us, and it's about all we can know about it. He could have filled in details, but He didn't. He will go into more detail about only one act of His creation, and that is His creation of man. Do you know why? It is because this record was written for man; God wants him to know about his origin. It is as if God were saying, "I would like very much for you to pay attention to your *own* creation and not be speculating about the creation of the universe." This verse tells us something tremendous.

"So God created man in his own image." I want to submit to you that this is one of the great statements of the Word of God. I cannot conceive of anything quite as wonderful as this. What does it mean? Well, man is like God, I think, as a trinity. Immediately someone is going to say, "Oh, I know what you mean. You mean that man is physically and mentally and spiritually a being." Yes, I believe that is true. Paul, in 1 Thessalonians 5:23, says that very thing: ". . . And I pray God your whole spirit and soul and body be preserved blameless unto the coming of our Lord Jesus Christ." Although this is true, we will see when we get into the next chapter that it actually means more than that. I think that it refers to the fact that man is a personality, and as a personality he is self-conscious, and he is one who makes his own decisions. He is a free moral agent. Apparently that is the thing which is unique about mankind. I believe this is what is meant by God creating man in His own image.

"Male and female created he them." These verses do not give to us the details of how man was created and how woman was created. We won't find that until we come to the second chapter. That is the reason that I say that God did not *intend* to give us the details concerning the creation of this great universe that we are in or He would have given us another chapter relative to that. But He offers no explanation other than He is the Creator. This puts us right back to the all-important truth which we find in the eleventh chapter of Hebrews: "Through faith we understand that the worlds were framed by the word of God, so that things which are seen were not made of things which do appear" (Heb. 11:3). Things we see today were made out of things which did not even *exist* before. The creation was made *ex nihilo*, out of nothing. Somebody says, "Explain that." My friend, I can't explain it. And evolution doesn't explain it either. Evolution has never answered the question of how nothing becomes something. It always starts with a little amoeba, or with a garbage can, or with a little piece of seaweed, or with an animal up in a tree. Our minds must have something to start with, but the Bible starts with nothing. God created! This is the tremendous revelation of this chapter.

And God blessed them, and God said unto them, Be fruitful, and multiply, and replenish the earth, and subdue it: and have dominion over the fish of the sea, and over the fowl of the air, and over every living thing that moveth upon the earth [Gen. 1:28].

We see here that God has given to this creature something unusual. First He says to man, "Be fruitful, and multiply, and replenish the earth." We will hear Him repeat that when He creates woman. God seems to be the One who introduced the subject of sex. It is quite interesting that our generation thinks that they have made a new discovery, that they are the Columbus that discovered sex. God mentions it here at the very beginning. In fact, there are four methods that God has used to get mankind into this universe. One was by *direct* creation, which produced Adam. A second way was by *indirect* creation, which produced Eve. The third was by the *virgin birth*, and this was how Jesus Christ came into the human family. The fourth way is by *natural generation*, and that is pretty well known in our day.

We have certainly dragged natural generation down to a level that God never intended for it. God created man to reproduce. This is a wonderful, glorious truth, and it is not to be made into a dirty, filthy, slimy thing as man is doing now. People are writing dirty, filthy books and calling it literature; they are producing dirty, filthy things and calling it art. Some of the critics are beginning to speak out against this, and we thank the Lord for that.

They are saying what I have long contended, that much of what is called art is revolting and repulsive and that it is not art at all. It is nothing in the world but obscene, and it is done simply for the almighty *dollar*. God never intended for sex to be abused in this way.

God created this man in His image. God is the essentially personal Being, and in giving the man an immortal soul, He gave him also a true personality. Man has a self-consciousness, he has the power of free choice, and he has a distinct moral responsibility. He is in the image of God.

"Be fruitful, and multiply, and replenish the earth." God tells man to fill the earth by reproduction. And notice that He uses the word "replenish." That is an interesting word and seems to indicate that this earth had been inhabited before by other creatures. Whatever the creatures were, they had disappeared before man was created.

God also tells man to "subdue" the earth. This, I think, is the basis of learning and of scientific exploration in our day. One of the Proverbs says this: "It is the glory of God to conceal a thing: but the honour of kings is to search out a matter" (Prov. 25:2).

God hides diamonds way down in the earth and God also puts the treasures down where man has to dig for them, and I believe that today the same thing is true about knowledge. I think it is true about the study of the Word of God. God wants us to go into the laboratory to use the test tube and the microscope, but unfortunately man comes out with an atom bomb, and he is trying to destroy the human family in our day.

"And have dominion" is God's instruction to man. Adam was not just a gardener to cut the grass. Man was created to rule this earth. I think that Adam could control the weather just as we control the air-conditioning in our homes. He *ruled* this earth. This is what we see in the Lord Jesus. When He was here on this earth, He had control over nature. He could say to a storm, "Be still." He could feed a multitude with five loaves and two fishes. It is my opinion that Adam could have done all of that until his fall. At the fall he lost the dominion that God had given him.

And God said, Behold, I have given you every herb bearing seed, which is upon the face of all the earth, and every tree, in the which is the fruit of a tree yielding seed; to you it shall be for meat [Gen. 1:29].

From this statement I assume that man was a vegetarian at first, and not until after the flood did man become a meat eater.

And to every beast of the earth, and to every fowl of the air, and to every thing that creepeth upon the earth, wherein there is life, I have given every green herb for meat: and it was so.

And God saw every thing that he had made, and, behold, it was very good. And the evening and the morning were the sixth day [Gen. 1:30–31].

This brings us to the end of chapter one, and it might be well to make a resumé at this point. What are some of the things we should note here? Well, one of these things is the fact that God is mentioned here thirty-two times. The Bible makes no attempt to prove that there is a God. Why not? Because He says, "The fool hath said in his heart, There is no God . . ." (Ps. 14:1).

The Bible is a Book written to reveal the spiritual, the religious, the redemptive truth, and that comes to us only by *faith*. So we have here the fact that God is the One who created.

In this first chapter we see the unity and power and personality of God. This is exactly what Paul wrote in Romans 1:20: "For the invisible things of him from the creation of the world are clearly seen." How are they clearly seen? "Being understood by the things that are made, even his eternal power and Godhead; so that they are without excuse." I say to you very candidly that God has shut you up to *faith* in Himself.

We will notice some other truths in this chapter. It denies polytheism: *One* God creates. Secondly, it denies the eternity of matter. The first words are: "In the beginning"— and it all had a beginning, my friend. This is true in spite of the fact that there was a time when science taught the eternity of matter. Thirdly, this chapter denies pantheism. God is before all things and He is apart from them. Fourthly, it denies fatalism—God acts in the freedom of His will.

Finally, let me enumerate the striking features in chapter 1:

(1) Order
(2) Progress
(3) Promptness
(4) Perfection

CHAPTER 2

THEME: *The Sabbath day; summary of the first five days of the restoration; man's creation; condition placed on man; woman's creation*

A great principle of revelation occurs for the first time in this chapter, but it will be found again and again in the Word of God. It is one of the fingerprints of inspiration. It is the law of recurrence or the law of recapitulation. In other words, the Spirit of God, in giving the Word of God, has a practice of stating briefly a series of great facts and truths; then He will come back and take out of the series that which is all-important, and He will elucidate and enlarge upon that particular thing. He is going to do this now in chapter 2 with the six days of creation which were given in chapter 1. This same principle is seen in the Book of Deuteronomy. Deuteronomy is the interpretation of the Law after forty years of experience with it in the wilderness. Deuteronomy is not just a repetition of the Law, but rather an interpretation of it. Likewise, we

are given not only one but *four* Gospels. Again and again, this procedure is followed throughout the Word of God.

THE SABBATH DAY

In chapter 2 that which is lifted out of the six days of creation is that which pertains to man, and we begin with the Sabbath day.

Thus the heavens and the earth were finished, and all the host of them.

And on the seventh day God ended his work which he had made; and he rested on the seventh day from all his work which he had made.

And God blessed the seventh day, and sanctified it: because that in it he had rested from all his work which God created and made [Gen. 2:1–3].

Do not miss the importance of the Sabbath day. What does it mean when it says that God rested from His work? Does it mean that God got tired, sat down to rest on the seventh day, and said that He had had a big week—that He had worked more than forty hours, and that He wanted to rest? If you look at it like that, it is perfect nonsense. God rested *from* His work. When God finished His six days of work, He looked upon it and it was very good, and there was nothing else to do. Every time I leave my office for the day, I still have work all over my desk. I have never been able to sit down and say, "I'm through. I've finished it." But *God* did. At the end of six days, He rested the seventh day because His work was complete. This is one of the greatest spiritual truths there is. The book of Hebrews tells us that as believers we enter into "rest"—that is, we enter into His *sabbath;* we enter into His perfect redemption. He died on the cross nineteen hundred years ago for you and me, and He offers us a redemption that we can enter into. Thus Paul can write: "Therefore being justified by faith, we have peace with God through our Lord Jesus Christ" (Rom. 5:1). I do not even have to lift my little finger in order to be saved—Jesus did it all.

> Jesus paid it all,
> All to Him I owe;
> Sin had left a crimson stain,
> He washed it white as snow.
> —Mrs. H. M. Hall

SUMMARY OF THE FIRST FIVE DAYS OF RESTORATION

Apparently, this vast universe we live in had been here for billions of years, but something happened to the earth and to a great deal of the creation. As a result, God moved in, the Spirit of God moved upon the face of the deep, and there was brought cosmos out of chaos.

These are the generations of the heavens and of the earth when they were created, in the day that the Lord God made the earth and the heavens [Gen. 2:4].

Actually, the word "generations" means *families.* The book of Genesis is not only the book of beginnings but also the book of the families. "These are the families of the heavens and of the earth when they were created, in the day that the Lord God made the earth and the heavens."

And every plant of the field before it was in the earth, and every herb of the field before it grew: for the Lord God had not caused it to rain upon the earth, and there was not a man to till the ground.

But there went up a mist from the earth, and watered the whole face of the ground [Gen. 2:5–6].

All this was here long before man was here upon the earth, and we can now begin to discover the purpose of God in chapter 1. In chapter 1 God was preparing a home for the man whom He would make. God is now getting ready to move this man into a place that He has prepared for him.

MAN'S CREATION

In the first chapter we saw that there was nothing, and then the inorganic came into existence: "In the beginning God created the heaven and the earth." The next step in creation was the organic, that is, the creation of life. We saw that in verse 21 where it says that God created great whales and then all animal life. He created animal life, but apparently the plant life had not been destroyed, and at the time of the re-creation, the seed was already in the earth. I would not want to be dogmatic, but this would seem to be the implication here. God has told us very little in this regard. Then man is the next step in the creation. There is actually no natural transition, and evolution cannot bridge the gap that brings us to the appearance of Homo sapiens upon the earth. The earth, therefore, was prepared for the coming of man.

And the Lord God formed man of the dust of the ground, and breathed into his nostrils the breath of life; and man became a living soul [Gen. 2:7].

This is the method of the creation of man, and again we are limited in what God has told us. Physically, man was taken out of the ground. It is quite interesting that our bodies are made up of about fifteen or sixteen chemical elements. Those same chemical elements are in the ground. The physical part of man was taken out of the dust of the ground. If we were to be boiled down into the separate chemical elements of which we are made, we would be worth very little in terms of money. I used to say $2.98, but inflation has increased that figure a little. That is the extent of our bodily worth because we were made out of the dust of the ground.

But man is more than dust. Physically, dust he is and to the dust he will return, but his spirit is going to God. Why? Because God "breathed into his nostrils the breath of life; and man became a living soul." God breathed into him "the breath of life." God gave man life which is physical or psychological, and then He gave him life which is spiritual. In other words, man now is brought into a marvelous relationship with his Creator. He has in his being a capacity for God. This is what separates man from all other creatures that are found in God's universe, as far as we know. Of course, there are the angels, but we know very little about them.

The theistic evolutionists say that mankind evolved up to this point, and then God began to work with this product of evolution. However, no form of evolutionary theory can account for human speech, it cannot account for human conscience, and it cannot account for human individuality. These are three things with which evolution has a little difficulty. It is mighty easy to take the bones of a man and compare them to the bones of some anthropoid, probably an ape, or to a horse. There is a striking similarity, I am sure, and yet there is a wide divergence also. I would expect that there would be a certain similarity because these creatures are to move in the same environment in which we move as human beings—naturally, the chassis would have to be the same. For example, there is a very striking similarity between the chassis of a Ford automobile and that of a Chevrolet automobile, but you had better not say that to the Ford Motor Company or to General Motors! They will tell you that there is a *wide* difference between the two. But there is a very striking similarity when you see the chassis. You must begin with something fixed on which you can put four wheels, one on each corner, and it must be rectangular to a certain extent. Why? Because the Ford and the Chevrolet are both going to get stuck on the freeway at five o'clock in the afternoon. A car must be able to balance, and it must have a motor to move it. So you would have a similarity, but that does not mean they came out of the same factory. I feel that such an exaggeration has been made of the similarity between man and these other creatures. Man is a different creature. God breathed into his breathing places the breath of life, and man became a living soul. Man is fearfully and wonderfully made, and that is something which we need to keep in mind.

And the LORD God planted a garden eastward in Eden; and there he put the man whom he had formed [Gen. 2:8].

I cannot tell you where the Garden of Eden is. I am sure it is somewhere in the Tigris-Euphrates valley; in fact it may be the entire valley. Originally, that valley was a very fertile place, and it still is, for that matter. It is part of "the fertile crescent." At one time, the peoples inhabiting that region did not even plant grain there; they simply harvested it, for it grew by itself. It is probable that this area will someday become the very center of the earth again.

And out of the ground made the LORD God to grow every tree that is pleasant to the sight, and good for food; the tree of life also in the midst of the garden, and the tree of knowledge of good and evil [Gen. 2:9].

These are unusual trees that are mentioned specifically, the "tree of life" and the "tree of knowledge of good and evil." I cannot tell you much about them because they are not around today; they have been removed from the scene.

The Lord God made "to grow every tree," and the trees, you will notice, were pleasant to look at and were also good for food. There was the beauty of them and the practical side of them; both were combined in them. Perhaps it can be compared to going into a furniture store and having the salesman say, "This article of furniture is very beautiful, but it's also very functional." That was the important thing in the Garden of Eden—they had some beautiful trees, but they were also functional. In fact, they were very practical—they were good for food. On this earth on which we live, we still see something of its beauty. In spite of the curse of the fall of man which is upon the earth—the fact that it brings forth the thorn and the thistle—there is still a beauty here. I remember the first time I visited the place called Hana on the island of Maui in the Hawaiian Islands. It is difficult to get there, but as we drove down that road, I had never been in such fabulous, fantastic, and wonderful foliage in my life. It is beyond description. We made a certain turn and came upon a very scenic spot. We could look down that coast and see a little peninsula protruding. There were the coconut trees, the papaya trees, the hibiscus, the bananas, the bamboo; and among the coconut trees a little church stood which the missionaries had started. We just could not help but be startled by its beauty. In fact, so much so that as we stood there, I asked the tour group with me to pause and bow their heads in prayer, and a member of our party led us in prayer. We were just privileged to see that spot. My, the Garden of Eden must have been a beautiful place!

And a river went out of Eden to water the garden; and from thence it was parted, and became into four heads.

The name of the first is Pison: that is it which compasseth the whole land of Havilah, where there is gold;

And the gold of that land is good: there is bdellium and the onyx stone.

And the name of the second river is Gihon: the same is it that compasseth the whole land of Ethiopia.

And the name of the third river is Hiddekel: that is it which goeth toward the east of Assyria. And the fourth river is Euphrates [Gen. 2:10–14].

The river in Ethiopia would be the Nile, and the Hiddekel would be the Tigris.

And the LORD God took the man, and put him into the garden of Eden to dress it and to keep it [Gen. 2:15].

This man had dominion, and the forces of nature responded at his beck and call.

CONDITION PLACED ON MAN

And the LORD God commanded the man, saying, Of every tree of the garden thou mayest freely eat:

But of the tree of the knowledge of good and evil, thou shalt not eat of it: for in the day that thou eatest thereof thou shalt surely die [Gen. 2:16–17].

It was not God's original intention for man to die, but man is now put on probation. You see, man has a free will, and privilege always creates responsibility. This is an axiomatic statement that is true. This man who is given a free will must be given a test to determine whether he will obey God or not.

Some expositors suggest that the fruit of the tree of the knowledge of good and evil was poison. On the contrary, I think it was the best fruit in the garden.

"For in the day that thou eatest thereof thou shalt surely die." Remember that man is a trinity, and he would have to die in a threefold way. Adam did not die physically until over nine hundred years after this, but God said, *"In the day* you eat, you shall die."

Death means separation, and Adam was separated from God spiritually the very day he ate, you may be sure of that.

And the LORD God said, It is not good that the man should be alone; I will make him an help meet for him [Gen. 2:18].

There was a purpose in God's putting man in the garden alone for a period of time. It was to show him that he had a need, that he needed someone to be with him.

And out of the ground the LORD God formed every beast of the field, and every fowl of the air; and brought them unto Adam to see what he would call them: and whatsoever Adam called every living creature, that was the name thereof [Gen. 2:19].

Believe me, that man had to be a smart man to name all the animals. Some wag has said that when God brought an elephant to Adam and said, "What shall we call this one?" Adam said, "Well, he looks more like an elephant than anything else." And I guess he did!

And Adam gave names to all cattle, and to the fowl of the air, and to every beast of the field; but for Adam there was not found an help meet for him [Gen. 2:20].

"An help for him"—(the word *meet* should not be here)—that is, one agreeing and answering to him, a helper as his counterpart, the other half of him. A man is but half a man until he is married, and that is very important to see. I am not here to promote marriage, and yet I would say that it is God's intention for both man and woman. The woman is to answer to the man.

WOMAN'S CREATION

And the LORD God caused a deep sleep to fall upon Adam, and he slept: and he took one of his ribs, and closed up the flesh instead thereof;

And the rib, which the LORD God had taken from man, made he a woman, and brought her unto the man [Gen. 2:21–22].

The woman is taken from Adam, from the side of Adam. Dr. Matthew Henry said that God didn't take her from the head to be his superior, or from his foot to be his inferior, but He took her from his side to be equal with him, to be along with him. That is exactly the purpose: she is to be the other half of man.

This is exactly what God meant when He said, "Wives, submit to your husbands." He means that she is to *respond*, to *answer* to him. A wife is the other part of him, the other half of him. He is only half a man without her.

Believe me, Eve was beautiful. Any woman today who is beautiful inherited it originally from mother Eve. There is no beauty that she did not have. She was a doll, let me tell you! And she was the other half of Adam.

And Adam said, This is now bone of my bones, and flesh of my flesh: she shall be called Woman, because she was taken out of Man [Gen. 2:23].

The word for "Woman" in the Hebrew language is very similar to the word for "Man." The word for man is *ish,* and the word for woman is *ishshah.* She is the other part of man and is to answer to him. God intended man to take the lead—He created him first— and He created woman to follow. The man is the aggressor—God made him that way even physically—and woman is the responder.

Do not tell me that a wife has to love her husband. God does not say that. God says that she is to respond to him. If he says to her, "I love you," then she is going to say right back to him, "I love you." When a man tells me, "My wife is very cold," that is a dead giveaway that he is not really the kind of husband he should be. If he is the right kind of husband, she will respond, because he is the one to take the lead.

Therefore shall a man leave his father and his mother, and shall cleave unto his wife: and they shall be one flesh [Gen. 2:24].

In other words, the man is now subject to his wife in the sense that he is responsible for her, and he is no longer under the control of his father and mother.

And they were both naked, the man and his wife, and were not ashamed [Gen. 2:25].

Although the Scriptures do not say so, I believe they were clothed with some sort of glory light. May I say, I think that this is the loveliest and the most precious account of the creation of woman and man. Here is a couple

whom God really joined together. There are certain things which God has given to His people that they should obey, and God has given to the human race marriage. Marriage is one of the bands which modern men are trying to throw off: "Let us break their bands asunder, and cast away their cords from us" (Ps. 2:3). What is man trying to do? He is trying to get rid of God, because God is the One who established marriage.

The creation of woman was indirect creation, for God took her out of man to reveal the fact that she is part of man. Someone has put it like this: "For woman is not undeveloped man, but diverse, not like to like, but like in difference. Yet in the long years, 'liker' must they grow, till at the last she set herself to man like perfect music unto noble words, distinct in individualities, but like each other even as those who love." The story of the creation of woman for man is one of the most beautiful stories.

The subjects of this chapter are quite wonderful: the creation of man, where he is placed, his occupation, the condition upon which he is there with a responsibility, his need for a companion, and then God's creation of woman. There is to be an identity between the husband and the wife, and God says, "Husbands, love your wives." This is the creation story.

The man who was the chaplain at Nuremberg Prison and dealt with men who had been Nazi chiefs, has written of his experiences. Speaking of his last interview with Herman Goering, one of the very few who refused to accept Christ, Chaplain Gerecke says: "That evening, around 8:30 I had a long session with Goering—during which he made sport of the story of creation, ridiculed divine inspiration of the Scriptures and made outright denial of certain Christian fundamentals." *Less than two hours later he committed suicide.* My friend, one of the ways to get rid of the alarming suicide rate is to let men and women know they are creatures of God who are responsible to their Creator. How important this is!

We have seen in chapter 2 man's kinship with God, man's worship of God, man's fellowship with God, man's service to God, man's loyalty to God, man's authority from God, and man's social life from and for God. This is the great message of this chapter.

CHAPTER 3

THEME: *The serpent denies the Word of God; the man and woman disobey the Word of God; the design of God for the future; the doctrine of redemption introduced*

We come now to what some consider to be the most important chapter of the Bible. It is conceded, I believe, by all conservative expositors to be just that. Dr. Griffith Thomas called chapter 3 the pivot of the Bible. If you doubt that, read chapters 1 and 2 of Genesis, omit chapter 3, and then read chapters 4–11. You will find that there is a tremendous vacuum that needs to be filled, that something has happened. For instance, in Genesis 1 and 2, we find man in innocence; everything is perfection, and there is fellowship between God and man. But the minute you begin with chapter 4 of Genesis and read just as far as chapter 11, you find jealousy, anger, murder, lying, wickedness, corruption, rebellion, and judgment. The question is: Where did it all come from? Where did it begin? Where did the sin originate? Actually, I do not think it originated in chapter 3 of Genesis, but as far as man is concerned, here is where it began.

Let me quote for you the statement of another concerning chapter 3: "Here we trace back to their source many of the rivers of divine truth. Here commences the great drama which is being enacted on the stage of human history and which well nigh 6,000 years has not yet completed. Here we find the divine explanation of the present fallen and ruined condition of our race. Here we learn of the subtle devices of our enemy, the devil. Here we behold the utter powerlessness of man to walk in the path of righteousness when divine grace is withheld from him. Here we discover the spiritual effects of sin, man seeking to flee from God. Here we discern the attitude of God toward the guilty sinner. Here we mark the universal tendency of human nature to cover its own moral shame by a device of man's own handiwork. Here we are taught of the gracious provision which God has made to meet our great need. Here begins that marvelous stream of prophecy which runs all through the Holy Scriptures. Here we learn that man cannot approach God except through a mediator."

THE SERPENT CASTS A SHADOW OF DOUBT ON THE WORD OF GOD

In this first section we have the setting for the temptation of man.

Now the serpent was more subtil than any beast of the field which the LORD God had made. And he said unto the woman, Yea, hath God said, Ye shall not eat of every tree of the garden? [Gen. 3:1].

The question arises: Why the temptation? If we go back to chapters 1 and 2, we find that man was created innocent, but man was not created righteous. What is righteousness? Righteousness is innocence that has been maintained in the presence of temptation. You see, temptation will either develop you or destroy you; it will do one of the two. The Garden of Eden was not a hothouse, and man was not a hothouse plant. Character must be developed, and it can only be developed in the presence of temptation. Man was created a responsible being, and he was responsible to glorify, to obey, to serve, and to be subject to divine government.

Man did not create himself—I do not think anyone claims that—but God created him. And God was not arbitrary in the condition which He laid down. He said to man, "But of the tree of the knowledge of good and evil, thou shalt not eat of it: for in the day that thou eatest thereof thou shalt surely die" (Gen. 2:17). That tree was not the only tree in the garden to eat of. It would have been very arbitrary if man would have starved to death if he had not been able to eat of the tree and if he had also been told he would die if he did eat of it. There was an abundance of trees in the garden which bore fruit; so that man did not need to eat of this tree at all. Therefore, we find that man appears on the scene a responsible creature.

In this first verse we are introduced to the serpent. Immediately the question can reasonably be asked, "Where in the world did he come from? How did he get into the Garden of Eden?" As far as I can tell from the Word of God, the serpent was not there as a slithering creature. Actually, we are not told how he came there; we are just told he was there. The Word of God leaves a great deal out. The serpent was a creature that could be used of Satan, and Satan used him. Isn't that exactly the method that Satan uses today? Paul wrote to the Corinthians: "And no marvel; for Satan himself is transformed into an angel of light" (2 Cor. 11:14). The book of Revelation says more about Satan than anywhere else in

Scripture. "And the great dragon was cast out, that old serpent, called the Devil, and Satan, which deceiveth the whole world: he was cast out into the earth, and his angels were cast out with him" (Rev. 12:9). This creature was not a slithering snake as we think of it today. That is not the picture that the Word of God gives of him at all. "And he laid hold on the dragon, that old serpent, which is the Devil, and Satan, and bound him a thousand years" (Rev. 20:2).

This is a creature with tremendous ability. There is no record of his origin here in Genesis at all. I believe that Isaiah 14 and Ezekiel 28 give us the origin of this creature and also how he became the creature that he was.

And the woman said unto the serpent, We may eat of the fruit of the trees of the garden:

But of the fruit of the tree which is in the midst of the garden, God hath said, Ye shall not eat of it, neither shall ye touch it, lest ye die [Gen. 3:2–3].

Why in the world did the serpent approach the woman? Why didn't he approach the man? When God created Adam, He had told him that he could eat of every tree of the garden, but of this one he was not to eat. Woman was created last, and she had gotten her information secondhand; she had gotten it from man. And so the serpent approached woman first. Frankly, I think that woman was created finer than man; that is, she had more compassion and sympathy in her makeup. She was probably more open to suggestion than the man. Actually, I think a woman has a nature that is more inquisitive than a man's. She is the one today who goes into the cults and isms more than anyone else and leads men into them. In fact, many of the founders of cults and isms have been women.

Satan knew what he was doing. Notice what he did. He had a very subtle method as he came. He asked her this question, which cast doubt on the Word of God, "Yea, hath God said, Ye shall not eat of every tree of the garden?" He raises a doubt in her mind and excites her curiosity. She answers, "We can eat of all the trees, but this tree God has told us, 'Ye shall not eat of it [that's all God had said, but she added something], neither shall ye touch it, lest ye die.' " I do not find where He ever said, "You are not to touch it."

THE SERPENT DENIES
THE WORD OF GOD

And the serpent said unto the woman,

Ye shall not surely die:

For God doth know that in the day ye eat thereof, then your eyes shall be opened, and ye shall be as gods, knowing good and evil [Gen. 3:4–5].

Instead of saying, "Ye shall not surely die," what he said in effect was, "Ye *certainly* shall not die. Why, that is just absolutely impossible!" He questions the love of God and the goodness of God: "If God is good, why did He put this restriction down?" The serpent implies that God is not righteous when he says, "You will not die." And he questions the holiness of God by saying, "You're going to be gods yourselves, for God doth know that in the day ye eat thereof, then your eyes shall be opened, and ye shall be as gods, knowing good and evil."

The thing that Eve did was to add to the Word of God. The liberal and the atheist take *from* the Word of God, and God has warned against that. The cults (and some fundamentalists, by the way) *add* to the Word of God, and God warns against that. There are those who say that today we are saved by law. They argue, "Yes, it is by faith, but it is faith plus something else"—and they are apt to come up with anything. The Word of God says: "Jesus answered and said unto them, This is the work of God, that ye believe on him whom he hath sent" (John 6:29). How important this is!

The serpent very subtly contradicts God, and he substitutes his word for God's word. The Book of Romans teaches the fact of the obedience of faith. Faith leads to obedience, and unbelief leads to disobedience. Doubt leads to disobedience—always.

THE MAN AND WOMAN DISOBEY
THE WORD OF GOD

And when the woman saw that the tree was good for food, and that it was pleasant to the eyes, and a tree to be desired to make one wise, she took of the fruit thereof, and did eat, and gave also unto her husband with her; and he did eat [Gen. 3:6].

Notice that the appeal the serpent made is quite an interesting one. It was an appeal to the flesh—"the tree was good for food"—but that is not all; that is not the thing that is really important. "It was pleasant to the eyes"—it was an appeal to the flesh but also an appeal to the psychological part of man, to his mind. "And a tree to be desired to make one wise"—this is an appeal to the religious side of man.

You will find that this is the exact temptation that Satan brought to the Lord Jesus in the wilderness (see Matt. 4, Mark 1, and Luke 4). First of all, he said to our Lord, "Make these stones into bread"—this was the appeal to the flesh, as the tree was good for food. Then Satan showed the Lord the kingdoms of the world and offered them to Him—that was an appeal to the mind, as the tree was pleasant to the eyes. Then finally he said, "Cast Yourself down from the temple"—this was an appeal to the religious side of man, as the tree was to be desired to make one wise. I do not think that the devil has changed his tactics today. He uses the same tactics with you and me, and the reason that he still uses them is that they work. He hasn't needed to change his tactics, for we all seem to fall for the same line.

John wrote: "For all that is in the world, the lust of the flesh, and the lust of the eyes, and the pride of life, is not of the Father, but is of the world" (1 John 2:16). "The lust of the flesh"—that is, the tree was good to eat. "The lust of the eyes"—the tree was good to look at. "The pride of life"—the tree was to be desired to make one wise. These things are not of the Father, but of the world. Jesus said that these sins of the flesh come out of the heart of man, way down deep. This is where Satan is making his appeal. This is the method that he is using in order that he might reach in and lead mankind astray. And he succeeded. They were told that they would know good and evil—and what happened? We now have the results of the fall of man.

And the eyes of them both were opened, and they knew that they were naked; and they sewed fig leaves together, and made themselves aprons [Gen. 3:7].

"And the eyes of them both were opened"—this refers to their conscience. Before the fall, man did not have a conscience; he was innocent. Innocence is ignorance of evil. Man did not make conscience. It is an accuser that each one of us has living on the inside of us. A leading psychologist in a university in Southern California, who is a Christian, said to me that the guilt complex is as much a part of man as his right arm is. Man *cannot* get rid of that guilt complex in a psychological way.

"And they knew that they were naked; and they sewed fig leaves together, and made themselves aprons." Have you ever noticed that the fig tree is the only tree that is specifi-

cally mentioned? (The tree of the knowledge of good and evil is not an apple tree. I do not know what it was, but I am almost sure it was not an apple tree.) These fig leaves concealed but did not really cover. Adam and Eve did not confess; they just attempted to cover up their sin. They were not ready to admit their lost condition.

This is the same condition of man today in religion. He goes through exercises and rituals, he joins churches, and he becomes very religious. Have you ever noticed that Christ cursed the fig tree? That is quite interesting. And He denounced religion right after that, by the way; He denounced it with all His being because religion merely covers over sin.

In this temptation Satan wanted to come between man's soul and God. In other words, he wanted to wean man from God, to win man over to himself, and to become the god of man. The temptations of the flesh would not have appealed to man in that day, anyway. He was not tempted to steal or lie or covet. He was just tempted to doubt God. What was the trouble with the rich young ruler? He did not believe God. In the parable of the tares, the tares are those who would not believe God. Notice Satan's method. First, Eve saw that the tree was good for food; second, it was pleasant to the eye; and third, it was to be desired to make one wise. Satan works from the outside to the inside, from without to within.

On the other hand, God begins with man's heart. Religion is something that you rub on the outside, but God does not begin with religion. May I make a distinction here: Christianity is not a religion; Christianity is Christ. There are a lot of religions, but the Lord Jesus went right to the fountainhead when He said, "Ye must be *born* again."

He said to the Pharisees who were very religious on the outside, "Make the inside of the platter clean. You are just like a mausoleum, beautiful on the outside with marble and flowers, but inside full of dead men's bones." What a picture! And Adam and Eve instead of confessing their sin, sewed fig leaves together as a covering. May I say to you, there is really no new style in fig leaves. Men are still going to church and going through religious exercises and good works instead of confessing the sin of their hearts.

And they heard the voice of the Lord God walking in the garden in the cool of the day: and Adam and his wife hid

themselves from the presence of the LORD God amongst the trees of the garden.

And the LORD God called unto Adam, and said unto him, Where art thou? [Gen. 3:8-9].

Religion will *separate* you from God—and Adam is lost. Adam is lost, and it is God seeking him and not man seeking God.

And he said, I heard thy voice in the garden, and I was afraid, because I was naked; and I hid myself.

And he said, Who told thee that thou wast naked? Hast thou eaten of the tree, whereof I commanded thee that thou shouldest not eat?

And the man said, The woman whom thou gavest to be with me, she gave me of the tree, and I did eat [Gen. 3:10-12].

Notice that there is no confession on Adam's part. The important thing is not so much that he blamed the woman or, as we would say in the common colloquialism of the day, "he passed the buck," but that there is no confession of sin on his part.

And the LORD God said unto the woman, What is this that thou hast done? And the woman said, The serpent beguiled me, and I did eat [Gen. 3:13].

Here is some more of that so-called "buck passing."

THE DESIGN OF GOD
FOR THE FUTURE

This man, this creature that God has made, has now turned aside from God, and God must deal with him and must judge him.

And the LORD God said unto the serpent, Because thou hast done this, thou art cursed above all cattle, and above every beast of the field; upon thy belly shalt thou go, and dust shalt thou eat all the days of thy life [Gen. 3:14].

The serpent is certainly not the slithering creature that we think of today. He was different at the beginning, and there has now been pronounced upon him this judgment from God. God pronounces a judgment upon Satan which has a tremendous effect upon man. I would urge you to memorize the following verse, for this is one that you certainly ought to know. This verse is the first prophecy of the coming of the Messiah, the Savior, into the world:

And I will put enmity between thee and the woman, and between thy seed and her seed; it shall bruise thy head, and thou shalt bruise his heel [Gen. 3:15].

"And I will put enmity between thee [that is, Satan] and the woman, and between thy seed and her seed; it [that is, Christ] shall bruise thy head, and thou shalt bruise his heel." This is a tremendous statement that is given to us here. The most prominent thought is not the ultimate victory that would come, but the long-continued struggle. This verse reveals the fact that now there is to be a long struggle between good and evil. This is exactly what you will find in the rest of the Scriptures. The Lord Jesus made this statement in His day concerning this struggle: "Ye are of your father the devil, and the lusts of your father ye will do. He was a murderer from the beginning, and abode not in the truth, because there is no truth in him. When he speaketh a lie, he speaketh of his own: for he is a liar, and the father of it" (John 8:44). "The devil" is Satan. The Lord Jesus Christ made the distinction between children of God and children of Satan. John again mentions this conflict in 1 John 3:10: "In this the children of God are manifest, and the children of the devil: whosoever doeth not righteousness is not of God, neither he that loveth not his brother." Thus we have brought before us the fact that here is a conflict, here is a struggle, and here are two seeds in the world. There will be the final victory—but the long-continued struggle is important to note. Every man must face temptation and must win his battle. Before Christ came, the victory was through obedience in faith. After Christ came, we are to identify ourselves with Christ through faith. What does it mean to be saved? It means to be *in Christ*.

Man was one of three orders of creation: angels, man, and animals. Animals were given no choice, but man and angels were given a choice. Here you have, if you please, man's choice. He has made a decision, and he is held responsible for the decision that he has made.

Notice that it says *"her* seed." It does not say the man's seed. Here is at least the suggestion of the virgin birth of Christ. When God went into that garden looking for man, He said, "Where art thou?" Any anthology of religion tells the story of man's search for God. My friend, that is not the way God tells it. Let's tell it like it is: Salvation is *God's* search for man. Man ran away from Him, and God called to him, "Where art thou?" Dr. W. H. Griffith Thomas in his book, *Genesis, A*

Devotional Commentary, makes the comment that "it is the call of Divine justice, which cannot overlook sin. It is the call of Divine sorrow, which grieves over the sinner. It is the call of Divine love, which offers redemption for sin." We have all of that in the verse before us—the promise of the coming of the Savior.

God's search for man is pictured all the way through Scripture. Paul wrote, ". . . there is none that seeketh after God" (Rom. 3:11). The Lord Jesus said, "Ye have not chosen me, but I have chosen you . . ." (John 15:16). And we can say with John, "We love him, because he first loved us" (1 John 4:19). God seeks out man, and He offers man salvation, but there is going to be a long struggle that will take place.

Unto the woman he said, I will greatly multiply thy sorrow and thy conception; in sorrow thou shalt bring forth children; and thy desire shall be to thy husband, and he shall rule over thee [Gen. 3:16].

This is the judgment upon woman. She cannot bring a child into the world without sorrow. Isn't it interesting that that should be true? The very thing that brings joy into the life and continues the human family has to come through sorrow.

And unto Adam he said, Because thou hast hearkened unto the voice of thy wife, and hast eaten of the tree, of which I commanded thee, saying, Thou shalt not eat of it: cursed is the ground for thy sake; in sorrow shalt thou eat of it all the days of thy life;

Thorns also and thistles shall it bring forth to thee; and thou shalt eat the herb of the field:

In the sweat of thy face shalt thou eat bread, till thou return unto the ground; for out of it wast thou taken: for dust thou art, and unto dust shalt thou return [Gen. 3:17–19].

This is the judgment upon man. Death now comes to man. What is death? Physical death is a separation of the person, the spirit, the soul, from the body. Ecclesiastes says: "Then shall the dust return to the earth as it was: and the spirit shall return unto God who gave it" (Eccl. 12:7). Man ultimately must answer to God. Whether he is saved or lost, he is going to have to answer to God. But Adam did not die physically the day that he ate. He did not die until more than nine hundred years later. The whole point is simply this: he died *spiritually* the moment he disobeyed; he was separated from God. Death is separation. When Paul wrote to the Ephesians that they were "dead in trespasses and sins," he did not mean that they were dead physically but that they were dead spiritually, separated from God. In that wonderful parable of the prodigal son, our Lord told about this boy who ran away from his father. When he returned, the father said to the elder son, "For this my son was dead, and is alive again; he was lost, and is found . . ." (Luke 15:24). Dead? Yes, he was dead, not physically, but he was separated from the father. To be separated from the Father means simply that—it means death. The Lord Jesus said to Martha, ". . . I am the resurrection, and the life: he that believeth in me, though he were dead, yet shall he live" (John 11:25). Again, "dead" means death spiritually, that is, separation from God. Man died spiritually the moment he ate. That is the reason he ran away from God. That is the reason he sewed fig leaves for a covering.

THE DOCTRINE OF REDEMPTION INTRODUCED

And Adam called his wife's name Eve; because she was the mother of all living [Gen. 3:20].

This does not mean that Cain and Abel were born in the Garden of Eden, but it is definite that they were born *after* the fall of Adam and Eve.

Unto Adam also and to his wife did the LORD God make coats of skins, and clothed them [Gen. 3:21].

In order to have the skins of animals, the animals have to be slain. I believe that this is the origin of sacrifice and that God made it clear to man. God rejected their fig leaves but made them clothing of skins, and when Adam and Eve left the Garden of Eden, they looked back upon a bloody sacrifice. When they looked back, they saw exactly what God had Moses put on the mercy seat in the Holy of Holies: two cherubim looking down upon the blood that was there—and that was the way to God.

There are four great lessons that we see from the fig leaves and the fact that God clothed them with skins. (1) Man must have adequate covering to approach God. You cannot come to God on the basis of your good works. You must come just as you are—a sinner. (2) Fig leaves are unacceptable; they are homemade. God does not take a homemade garment. (3) God must provide the covering. (4) The covering is only obtained through the death of the Lord Jesus.

Man must have a substitute between himself and God's wrath. That is important even in these days for man to consider. The hardest thing in the world is for man to take his rightful position before God. This anonymous poem on prayer reveals the necessity of this even in our own hearts:

> He prayed for strength that he might achieve;
> He was made weak that he might obey.
> He prayed for health that he might do greater things;
> He was given infirmity that he might do better things,
> He prayed for riches that he might be happy;
> He was given poverty that he might be wise.
> He prayed for power that he might have the praise of men;
> He was given infirmity that he might feel the need of God.
> He prayed for all things that he might enjoy life;
> He was given life that he might enjoy all things.
> He had received nothing that he asked for—all that he hoped for;

His prayer was answered—he was most blessed.

Salvation comes when you and I take our proper place as sinners before God.

And the LORD God said, Behold, the man is become as one of us, to know good and evil: and now, lest he put forth his hand, and take also of the tree of life, and eat, and live for ever:

Therefore the LORD God sent him forth from the garden of Eden, to till the ground from whence he was taken [Gen. 3:22-23].

All I can say to this is, thank God that He did not let man live eternally in sin and that God is not going to let us do that. That is really a belssing!

So he drove out the man; and he placed at the east of the garden of Eden Cherubims, and a flaming sword which turned every way, to keep the way of the tree of life [Gen. 3:24].

This does not mean that God put up a roadblock. It means that the way of life was kept open for man to come to God. But now that way is not through the tree of life. Salvation must come through a sacrifice, and when man looked back, the blood of the sacrifice is what he saw.

CHAPTER 4

THEME: The birth of Cain and Abel; God gives Cain a second chance; Cain murders Abel; the children of Cain and a godless civilization; the birth of Seth

In Genesis 3 we have the *root* of sin and in Genesis 4 the *fruit* of sin. How bad is sin? Well, in this chapter, we find that man was not just suffering from ptomaine poisoning because of having eaten the fruit of the tree of knowledge of good and evil. Chapter 4 reveals how much had really happened to the man. By his disbelief and his disobedience, he had turned away from God and had sinned in such a way that he brought upon himself and his race His judgment, because you and I are given this same kind of nature. We have the same nature

that our father had, and Adam has given all of us a pretty bad nature. All this is revealed in the story of the two sons of Adam and Eve. They had more children than this, but we are given the record of only these two at this time.

THE BIRTH OF CAIN AND ABEL

And Adam knew Eve his wife; and she conceived, and bare Cain, and said, I have gotten a man from the LORD [Gen. 4:1].

This reveals the fact that Adam and Eve certainly did not anticipate that the struggle was going to be long. When Cain was born, Eve must have said, "I have gotten the man from the Lord. God said that the seed of the woman would bruise the head of the serpent— and here he is!" But Cain was not the one. He was a murderer, he was no savior at all. It will be a long time before the Savior comes. For a minimum of six thousand years—and I think it has been longer than that—the struggle has been going on between the seed of the woman and the seed of the serpent.

And she again bare his brother Abel. And Abel was a keeper of sheep, but Cain was a tiller of the ground [Gen. 4:2].

These are the two boys that we are looking at.

And in process of time it came to pass, that Cain brought of the fruit of the ground an offering unto the LORD [Gen. 4:3].

"In process of time" actually means "at the end of days," which would mean on the Sabbath day, on the day that God had rested.

"Cain brought"—the idea of "brought" means to an appointed place. They are bringing an offering to God to an appointed place to worship. All this would indicate that they are doing it by revelation. I *know* that they are, for when we turn to Hebrews 11:4, we read: "By faith Abel offered unto God a more excellent sacrifice than Cain, by which he obtained witness that he was righteous, God testifying of his gifts: and by it he being dead yet speaketh." How could Abel offer it "by faith"? "So then faith cometh by hearing, and hearing by the word of God (Rom. 10:17). God had to have given His Word about this, or this boy Abel could never have come by faith, and that is the way he came. The other boy did not come that way. "Cain brought of the fruit of the ground." There is nothing wrong with the fruit. Don't think that he brought the leftovers—his attitude is not that of giving old clothes to the mission. I think that the fruit he brought would have won the blue ribbon in any county or state fair in the country. He brought the best of his beautiful, delicious fruit, and he brought it as an offering to the Lord.

And Abel, he also brought of the firstlings of his flock and of the fat thereof. And the LORD had respect unto Abel and to his offering:

But unto Cain and to his offering he had not respect. And Cain was very wroth, and his countenance fell [Gen. 4:4–5].

Someone may say, "I don't see anything *wrong* in the thing Cain did." In the eleventh verse of his epistle, speaking of apostates in the last days, Jude says, ". . . They have gone in the way of Cain . . ." What is the way of Cain? When Cain brought an offering to God, he did not come by faith—he came on his own. And the offering that he brought denied that human nature is evil. God said, "Bring that little blood sacrifice which will point to the Redeemer who is coming into the world. Come on that basis, and don't come by bringing the works of your own hands."

Cain's offering also denied that man was separated from God. He acted like everything was all right. This is what liberalism does today in talking about the universal fatherhood of God and the universal brotherhood of man. My friend, things are *not* all right with us today. We are *not* born children of God. We have to be born *again* to be children of God. Man is separated from God. Cain refused to recognize that, and multitudes today refuse to do so.

The third thing that Cain's offering denied was that man cannot offer works to God—Cain felt he could. Scripture says: "Not by works of righteousness which we have done, but according to his mercy he saved us, by the washing of regeneration, and renewing of the Holy Ghost" (Titus 3:5). The difference between Cain and Abel was not a character difference at all, but the difference was in the offerings which they brought. These two boys had the same background. They had the same heredity. They had the same environment. There was not that difference between them. Don't tell me that Cain got his bad disposition from an alcoholic grandfather on his father's side—he didn't have a grandfather. And don't say that Abel got his good disposition from a very fine grandmother on his mother's side. They just didn't have grandparents. They had the same heredity and the same environment. The difference was in the offerings.

That offering makes a difference in men today. No Christian takes the position that he is better than anyone else. The thing that makes him a Christian is that he recognizes that he is a sinner like everyone else and that he needs an offering, he needs a sacrifice, and he needs Someone to take his place and to die for him. Paul says of Christ: "Whom God hath set forth to be a propitiation through faith in his blood . . ." (Rom. 3:25). Therefore Paul could further write: "For they being ignorant of God's righteousness, and going about to establish their own righteousness, have not submitted themselves unto the righteousness of God" (Rom. 10:3). That is the picture of multitudes of people today. They are attempting through religion, through joining a church and doing something, to make themselves acceptable to God. God's righteousness can only come to you—because it must be a *perfect* righteousness—through Christ's providing it for you. "Who was delivered for our offences, and was raised again for our justification" (Rom. 4:25). That is, He was raised for our righteousness. He was the One who took our place. "For he hath made him to be sin for us, who knew no sin; that we might be made the righteousness of God in him" (2 Cor. 5:21). Paul says in Philippians 3:8–9, ". . . That I may win Christ, And be found in him, not having mine own righteousness, which is of the law, but that which is through the faith of Christ. . . ." The righteousness of Cain was his own righteousness. The righteousness of Abel was faith in a sacrifice that looked forward to Christ's sacrifice.

We have seen that Cain and Abel had come together to worship God. These two boys were identical. Some expositors actually believe they were twins—I think that was the position of the late Dr. Harry Rimmer. But I believe they were even closer than twins because of the fact they had no blood stream which reached way back on both sides that might cause a difference. They were the sons of Adam and Eve. However, there is a great divergence between Cain and Abel which is not necessarily a character divergence. One was accepted because of the sacrifice which he brought by faith; the other, Cain, brought his offering without any recognition from God at all.

GOD GIVES CAIN A SECOND CHANCE

And the LORD said unto Cain, Why art thou wroth? and why is thy countenance fallen?

If thou doest well, shalt thou not be accepted? and if thou doest not well, sin lieth at the door. And unto thee shall be his desire, and thou shalt rule over him [Gen. 4:6–7].

Why is Cain angry? He is angry enough that he is going to slay his brother. Back of premeditated murder there always is anger. Our Lord said that, if you are angry with your brother without a cause, you are guilty of murder. Back of anger is jealousy, and back of

jealousy is pride. There is no sense of sin whatsoever in spiritual pride. James put it in language like this: "Then when lust hath conceived, it bringeth forth sin: and sin, when it is finished, bringeth forth death" (James 1:15). Cain's anger led to murder, but back of that was his jealousy and also his pride.

And that is how God deals with him. He says to Cain, "If thou doest well, shalt thou not be accepted?" Actually, the meaning is better translated as, "Shalt thou not have excellency?" The eldest son always occupied a place of preeminence, and this boy thinks that now he will lose that. God tells him there is no reason for him to lose it if he does well. To do well would be to bring that which God had accepted from Abel, a sacrifice and the acknowledgment that he was a sinner. But not this boy—he's just angry.

"Sin lieth at the door." There are those who have interpreted this as meaning that a sin offering lies at the door; that is, that there is the little lamb lying at the door. That makes sense because that was true, but I do not think it means the sin offering here. Up to this time and beyond this time, in fact, up until Moses, as far as I can tell from the Word of God, there was no sin offering. You find the instructions given for the sin offering in the book of Leviticus. In the first part of that book, five offerings are given, and one is the sin offering. The sin offering did not come into existence until the law was given. That is the thing that Paul is saying in Romans 3:20: ". . . For by the law is the knowledge of sin." The offerings that were brought up to that time were burnt offerings. Job in his day, which obviously was before Moses, brought a burnt offering. It was not in any way a sin offering. I think if you will examine the Scriptures, you will find that that is true.

It is obvious that Cain did not realize how vulnerable to sin he was. When God said to him that "sin lieth at the door," I believe He was saying that sin like a wild beast was crouching at the door waiting to pounce on him the moment he stepped out. For that reason Cain needed a sacrifice that would be acceptable to God for sin, a sacrifice that pointed to Christ. "Not as Cain, who was of that wicked one, and slew his brother. And wherefore slew he him? Because his own works were evil, and his brother's righteous" (1 John 3:12). "If thou doest not well, sin lieth at the door." To do well would have been to bring the kind of offering that Abel had brought, a burnt offering. You find that Abraham also offered a burnt offering, for there could be no transgression until the law was given; that is, sin would not become a trespass against law until then. Therefore, you find that God actually protected this man Cain.

CAIN MURDERS ABEL

And Cain talked with Abel his brother: and it came to pass, when they were in the field, that Cain rose up against Abel his brother, and slew him.

And the LORD said unto Cain, Where is Abel thy brother? And he said, I know not: Am I my brother's keeper? [Gen. 4:8–9].

This is practically an impudent answer. He frankly had little regard for either his brother or for his God. He is trying to cover his action, but the Scriptures say, ". . . there is nothing covered, that shall not be revealed; and hid, that shall not be known" (Matt. 10:26). That is something to think over if you have any secret sins. You had better deal with them down here because they are all going to come out in God's presence someday anyway. He already knows about them—you might just as well tell Him about them. This fellow Cain tries to say that he is not guilty. "Am I my brother's keeper?"—what an impudent answer!

And he said, What hast thou done? the voice of thy brother's blood crieth unto me from the ground [Gen. 4:10].

The writer to the Hebrews uses this in Hebrews 12:24: "And to Jesus the mediator of the new covenant, and to the blood of sprinkling, that speaketh better things than that of Abel." Abel's blood spoke of murder committed. The blood of Christ speaks of redemption; it speaks of salvation.

And now art thou cursed from the earth, which hath opened her mouth to receive thy brother's blood from thy hand;

When thou tillest the ground, it shall not henceforth yield unto thee her strength; a fugitive and a vagabond shalt thou be in the earth [Gen. 4:11–12].

Yet in our day there is a curse upon the earth because of man's sin which causes it to lose its fertility. In some of the most lush sections of our earth multitudes of folk are starving. It takes great effort and ingenuity for man to make this earth produce in abundance. Certainly the blood of Abel cries out from the very earth itself—blood that was spilled in murder by a brother.

And Cain said unto the LORD, My punishment is greater than I can bear [Gen. 4:13].

If Cain's punishment was greater than he could bear, why didn't he just turn to God and confess his sin and cast himself upon God's mercy? It *was* too great for him to bear, but God was providing a Savior for him if he would only turn to Him.

Behold, thou hast driven me out this day from the face of the earth; and from thy face shall I be hid; and I shall be a fugitive and a vagabond in the earth; and it shall come to pass, that every one that findeth me shall slay me [Gen. 4:14].

Cain says now that he is to be hidden from the face of God, and of course, that is exactly what happened.

But notice now that God protects him. This is strange: God is actually harboring a murderer, a criminal.

And the LORD said unto him, Therefore whosoever slayeth Cain, vengeance shall be taken on him sevenfold. And the LORD set a mark upon Cain, lest any finding him should kill him [Gen. 4:15].

I do not know what the mark was. There has been a lot of speculation, and I do not know why I should add my speculation to all of it. But God protects Cain. There has been no law given at this time. Cain is a sinner, but he is not a transgressor because there has been no law given about murder. His great sin is that he did not bring the offering that was acceptable to God. His deeds were evil in what he brought to God, and he manifested that evil nature in slaying his brother.

THE CHILDREN OF CAIN
AND A GODLESS CIVILIZATION

We find that Cain moves out from God, and he establishes a civilization that is apart from God altogether. The children of Cain establish a godless civilization.

And Cain went out from the presence of the LORD, and dwelt in the land of Nod, on the east of Eden [Gen. 4:16].

I know a lot of folk who dwell in "the land of nod" when they are in church, but frankly, I do not know where the land of Nod really is. I have often wondered just where it is, and again, there is speculation about this. But we are told that Cain went out and dwelt in that area.

And Cain knew his wife; and she conceived, and bare Enoch: and he builded a city, and called the name of the city, after the name of his son, Enoch [Gen. 4:17].

Men have been doing this ever since. They like to call streets and cities by their own names or by names of loved ones. Even in Christian work you have schools named for individuals. Men love to do that, whether they are Christian or whether they are after the order of Cain.

But here is where urban life, city life, began: "and he builded a city, and called the name of the city, after the name of his son, Enoch." Cities have become one of the biggest problems that man has today. The cities, they say, are dying, and yet people all over the world are flocking to the cities.

And unto Enoch was born Irad: and Irad begat Mehujael: and Mehujael begat Methusael: and Methusael begat Lamech.

And Lamech took unto him two wives: the name of the one was Adah, and the name of the other Zillah [Gen. 4:18–19].

Here is the beginning of polygamy—having more than one wife. Lamech now does that which is contrary to what God intends, contrary to what God has for man. You will never find anywhere in the Scriptures that God approves of polygamy. If you read the accounts accurately, you will find that He condemns it. He gives the record of it because He is giving an *historical* record, and that is the basis on which it is given to us here.

"Adah" means *pleasure* or *adornment*. She was the first one to make it to the beauty parlor, I guess. "Zillah" means *to hide;* I suppose that means she was a coquette. My, what two girls he had for wives! No wonder he had problems. Later on we will see what happened.

Here now is the beginning of civilization, the Cainitic civilization.

And Adah bare Jabal: he was the father of such as dwell in tents, and of such as have cattle [Gen. 4:20].

"He was the father of such as dwell in tents." The apostle Paul was a tentmaker later on, but here is the first housing contractor. "And of such as have cattle"—here was the first rancher.

And his brother's name was Jubal: he was the father of all such as handle the harp and organ [Gen. 4:21].

Here is the beginning of the musicians. When we hear some of the modern music today, I am sure there are many who would agree that it must have begun with Cain's civilization!

And Zillah, she also bare Tubal-cain, an instructor of every artificer in brass and iron: and the sister of Tubal-cain was Naamah [Gen. 4:22].

Here we see the ones who are craftsmen.

And Lamech said unto his wives, Adah and Zillah, Hear my voice; ye wives of Lamech, hearken unto my speech: for I have slain a man to my wounding, and a young man to my hurt.

If Cain shall be avenged sevenfold, truly Lamech seventy and sevenfold [Gen. 4:23–24].

Lamech says, "If Cain got by with it, I can get by with it. After all, Cain did not slay in self-defense, but I have." I do not know whether he did or not, but he says that he slew in self-defense. And I do not know whether or not his two wives entered into this, or whether or not he was defending one of them. We are not told how it happened. Lamech feels that he will be *avenged* seventy and sevenfold, but our Lord told Simon Peter that he ought to *forgive* his enemy that many times.

THE BIRTH OF SETH

And Adam knew his wife again; and she bare a son, and called his name Seth: For God, said she, hath appointed me another seed instead of Abel, whom Cain slew.

And to Seth, to him also there was born a son; and he called his name Enos: then began men to call upon the name of the LORD [Gen. 4:25–26].

Apparently this was the beginning of men calling upon the name of the Lord.

CHAPTER 5

THEME: Final chapter of Adam's biography; the thrilling story of Enoch; the genealogy of Enoch to Noah

In the first section of the book of Genesis (chapters 1–11), we have world events—first the creation, then the fall, and now the Flood in chapters 5–9. In chapter 5 we have the book of the generations of Adam through Seth. Cain's line has been given to us and is now dropped. It will be mentioned again only as it crosses the godly line. This is a pattern that will be set in the book of Genesis.

In one sense, chapter 5 is one of the most discouraging and despondent chapters in the Bible. The reason is simply that it is like walking through a cemetery. God said to Adam, ". . . For in the day that thou eatest thereof thou shalt surely die" (Gen. 2:17), and they all died who were the sons of Adam. Paul says, "For as in Adam all die . . ." (1 Cor. 15:22).

FINAL CHAPTER
OF ADAM'S BIOGRAPHY

This is the book of the generations of Adam. In the day that God created man, in the likeness of God made he him;

Male and female created he them; and blessed them, and called their name Adam, in the day when they were created [Gen. 5:1–2].

"And blessed them, and called their name Adam"—not the Adamses, but Adam. He called *their* name Adam—Eve is the other half of him.

"The book of the generations of Adam." This strange expression occurs again only in the beginning of the New Testament, and there it is "the book of the generation of Jesus Christ." There are these two books, as we are already seeing that there are two lines, two seeds, and they are against each other. The struggle is going to be long between the line of Satan and the line of Christ, the accepted line. The line which we are following now is the line through Seth, and it is through this line that Christ will ultimately come.

And Adam lived an hundred and thirty years, and begat a son in his own likeness, after his image; and called his name Seth [Gen. 5:3].

When Adam was 130 years old, how old was he? In other words, when God created Adam, did He create him thirty years old or fourteen or forty-five? I do not know—anything would

be speculation. And if He created him that old, *was* he that old? And of course God could create him any age. May I say, this answers a lot of questions about the age of the earth. When someone says that certain rocks are billions of years old, they just do not know. Maybe when God created them, He created them two or three billion years old. The important thing here is that when Adam had been here 130 years, he begat a son in *his* own likeness. Adam was made in the likeness of God, but his son was born in his likeness.

And the days of Adam after he had begotten Seth were eight hundred years: and he begat sons and daughters:

And all the days that Adam lived were nine hundred and thirty years: and he died [Gen. 5:4–5].

Now we start through the graveyard. Adam begat sons and daughters, "and all the days that Adam lived were nine hundred and thirty years"—and what happened? "And he died."

In verse 8 we read what happened to Seth. He died. He had a son by the name of Enos, and what happened to him? In verse 11 we are told that he died. But he had a son, and Cainan was his son. And what happened to old Cainan? In verse 14 we find that he died too. He had a son, Mahalaleel, and what happened to him? In verse 17 it says he died. But he had a son, and his name was Jared, and, well, he died too (v. 20).

THE THRILLING STORY OF ENOCH

But before he died, Jared had a son by the name of Enoch.

And Enoch lived sixty and five years, and begat Methuselah [Gen. 5:21].

And then did Enoch die? No! He did not die. This is a dark chapter, but here is the bright spot in it.

And Enoch walked with God after he begat Methuselah three hundred years, and begat sons and daughters:

And all the days of Enoch were three hundred sixty and five years:

And Enoch walked with God: and he was not; for God took him [Gen. 5:22–24].

This is one of the most remarkable things, that in the midst of death one man is removed from this earth. It is said of Enoch that he "walked with God." This is quite remarkable, by the way. Only two men are said to have walked with God. In the next chapter, we find that Noah also walked with God. These were two antediluvians, and they walked with God. There are actually only two men in the Old Testament who did not die. One of them is Enoch, and the other, of course, is Elijah.

Enoch is one of the few before the Flood of whom we have any record at all. We are told that he did not die but that God took him—he was translated. What do we mean by *translation?* Translation is the taking of a word from one language and putting it into another language without changing its meaning. Enoch was removed from this earth; he was translated. He had to get rid of the old body which he had. He had to be a different individual—yet he had to be the same individual, just as the translated word has to be the same. Enoch was taken to heaven.

We read that Enoch lived sixty-five years, and begat Methuselah, and after that he walked with God. I do not know what the first sixty-five years of his life were. I assume that he was like the rest of the crowd—this was a very careless period, moving now into the orbit of the days of Noah. But when that little boy Methuselah was born, Enoch's walk was changed. That baby turned him to God. My friend, sometimes God puts a baby in a family just for that purpose, and if that baby will not bring you to God, nothing else will. For three hundred years after that he walked with God, and he begat other children, sons and daughters. "And all the days of Enoch were three hundred sixty and five years"—that is how long he was on this earth, but he did not die. It does not say, "And then Enoch died," but it says, "And Enoch walked with God: and he *was* not; for God took him."

The only way I know to describe this is the way a little girl described it to her mother when she came home from Sunday school. She said, "Teacher told us about Enoch and how he walked with God." Her mother said, "Well, what about Enoch?" And the little girl put it something like this: "It seems that every day God would come by and say to Enoch, 'Enoch, would you like to walk with Me?' And Enoch would come out of his house and down to the gate, and he'd go walking with God. He got to the place that he enjoyed it so much that he'd be waiting at the gate of his house every day. And God would come along and say, 'Enoch, let's take a walk.' Then one day God came by and said, 'Enoch, let's take a long walk. I have so much to tell you.' So they were walking and walking, and finally Enoch said, 'My, it's getting late in the afternoon. I'd better get back home!' And God said to him, 'Enoch, you're closer to My home than you are to your home; so you come on home with Me.' And so Enoch went home with God." I do not know how you can put it any better than that, my friend. That is exactly the story that is here.

I think that all the great truths are here in Genesis in germane. In my judgment, this is the picture of what is to come; here is the Rapture of the church. Before the judgment of the Flood, God removes Enoch.

THE GENEALOGY OF ENOCH TO NOAH

And all the days of Methuselah were nine hundred sixty and nine years: and he died [Gen. 5:27].

Methuselah lived longer than Adam. These two men, Adam and Methuselah, pretty well bridged the gap between creation and the Flood. According to our genealogy, this man Methuselah could have told Noah everything from the creation of the world. I personally feel that we have a gap in the genealogy given here. We know that in the opening of the New Testament the genealogy that is given of the Lord Jesus leaves out quite a few, and purposely so, because there is an attempt to give it in three equal segments. Certain ones are left out, but you will notice that it follows through accurately. I am sure that this genealogy is accurate, but the important thing is that we may have a gap here that would account for the fact that man has been on this earth a great deal longer than we have supposed. This is something I do not care to go into because it is quite an involved subject. Scripture is not clear right here. Why isn't it? Because God is not anxious to insist upon that. What He is trying to get over to us is the religious, the redemptive, history of mankind on this earth.

The name of Methuselah means "sending forth." Others believe that *Methuselah* meant: "When he is dead, it shall be sent." What will be sent? The Flood. As long as Methuselah lived, the Flood could not come. The very interesting thing is that according to a chronology of the genealogy of the patriarchs (shown at the end of this chapter) the year that Methuselah died is the year that the Flood came. "When he is dead, it shall be sent"—that is the meaning of his name.

GENEALOGY OF THE PATRIARCHS

These Columns Show Which of the Patriarchs Were Contemporary With Each Other

AGED

Name		Adam	Seth	Enos	Cainan	Mahalaleel	Jared	Enoch	Methuselah	Lamech	Noah	Shem	Arphaxad	Selah	Eber	Peleg	Reu	Serug	Nahor	Terah	Abram	Isaac	Jacob
Adam	Cr																						
Seth	B	130																					
Enos	B	235	105																				
Cainan	B	325	195	90																			
Mahalaleel	B	395	265	160	70																		
Jared	B	460	330	225	135	65																	
Enoch	B	622	492	387	297	227	162																
Methuselah	B	687	557	452	362	292	227	65															
Lamech	B	874	744	639	549	479	414	252	187														
Adam	D	930	800	695	605	535	470	308	243	56													
Enoch	Tr		857	752	662	592	527	365	300	113													
Seth	D		912	807	717	647	582		355	168													
Noah	B			821	731	661	596		369	182													
Enos	D			905	815	745	680		453	266	84												
Cainan	D				910	840	775		548	361	179												
Mahalaleel	D					895	830		603	416	234												
Jared	D						962		735	548	366												
Shem	B								869	682	502												
Lamech	D								964	777	595	93											
Methuselah	D								969		600	98											
The Deluge											600	98											
Arphaxad	B										602	100											
Selah	B										637	135	35										
Eber	B										667	165	65	30									
Peleg	B										701	199	99	64	34								
Reu	B										731	229	129	94	64	30							
Serug	B										763	261	161	126	96	62	32						
Nahor	B										793	291	191	156	126	92	62	30					
Terah	B										822	320	220	185	155	121	91	59	29				
Peleg	D										940	438	338	303	273	239	209	177	147	118			
Nahor	D										941	439	339	304	274		210	178	148	119			
Noah	D										950	448	348	313	283		219	187		128			
Abram	B											450	350	315	285		221	189		130			
Reu	D											468	368	333	303		239	207		148	18		
Serug	D											491	391	356	326			230		171	41		
Terah	D											525	425	390	360					205	75		
Arphaxad	D											538	438	403	373						88		
Isaac	B											550		415	385						100		
Selah	D											568		433	403						118	18	
Shem	D											600			435						150	50	
Jacob	B														445						160	60	
Abraham	D														460						175	75	15
Eber	D														464							79	19
Isaac	D																					180	120
Jacob	D																						147

Key: Cr—Creation, B—Born, D-Died, Tr—Translated.

EXAMPLE: Noah (vertical list) was born when Methuselah (horizontal list) was 369 years old.

Why did Methuselah live longer than any other person? God kept him here just to let mankind know that He is patient and merciful. God will also wait for you, my friend—all of your life. Peter speaks of the long-suffering of our God: "Which sometime were disobedient, when once the long-suffering of God waited in the days of Noah, while the ark was a-preparing, wherein few, that is, eight souls were saved by water" (1 Pet. 3:20).

As we continue down through the rest of this chapter, each man is mentioned and then his death.

And all the days of Lamech were seven hundred seventy and seven years: and he died.

And Noah was five hundred years old: and Noah begat Shem, Ham, and Japheth [Gen. 5:31–32].

It is the popular theory in the world, blindly accepted by men, and the conclusion, I think, of all philosophy, that human nature is inherently and innately good and that it can be improved. The whole program that is abroad today is that, if we will just try to improve the environment of man and his heredity, he can really be improved. Communism and socialism seek to improve man. Arminianism means that man can assist in his salvation. Modernism says that man can save himself. In other words, salvation is sort of a do-it-yourself kit that God gives to you. Some of the cults tell us that human nature is totally good and that there is no such thing as sin.

What does God say concerning man? God says that man is totally evil, totally bad. That is the condition of all of us. "There is none righteous, no, not one" (Rom. 3:10). That is the estimate of the Word of God. If you will accept God's Word for it, it will give you a truer conception of life today than is given to us by others.

Here is mankind, and we are following a godly line now. Where is it going to lead? Is it going to lead to a millennium here upon this earth? Are they going to come to Elysian fields and establish an Utopia? No. The very next chapter tells us that a Flood, a judgment from God, came upon the earth.

CHAPTER 6

THEME: *Cause of the Flood; God's deliverance from the judgment of the Flood; instructions to Noah for building the ark; passengers in the ark*

CAUSE OF THE FLOOD

In chapter 6 we see not only the Flood, but also the reason for the judgment of the Flood.

And it came to pass, when men began to multiply on the face of the earth, and daughters were born unto them,

That the sons of God saw the daughters of men that they were fair; and they took them wives of all which they chose [Gen. 6:1–2].

This matter of "the sons of God" and "the daughters of men" is something that has caused no end of discussion. There are a great many good men who take the position that "the sons of God" were angels. I personally cannot accept that at all. Most of my teachers taught that the sons of God were angels, and I recognize that a great many of the present-day expositors take that position. However, I cannot accept that view, because, if these were good angels, they would not commit this sin, and evil angels could never be designated as "sons of God." Also, the offspring here were men; they were not monstrosities. I do not know why it is assumed by so many that the offspring were giants. We will look at this more closely when we come to verse 4.

And the LORD said, My spirit shall not always strive with man, for that he also is flesh: yet his days shall be an hundred and twenty years [Gen. 6:3].

We believe that Noah preached for 120 years, and during that time the Spirit of God was striving with men. Peter makes it very clear that it was back in the days of Noah that the Spirit of God was striving with men in order that He might bring them to God—but they would not turn. "For Christ also hath once suffered for sins, the just for the unjust, that he might bring us to God, being put to death in the flesh, but quickened by the Spirit: By which also he went and preached unto the spirits in prison" (1 Pet. 3:18–19). These spirits were in prison when Peter wrote, but they were preached to in the days of Noah. How do we know that? Verse 20 reads: "Which sometime were disobedient, when once the long-suffering of God waited in the days of Noah, while the ark was a-preparing, wherein few, that is, eight souls were saved by water." When were they disobedient? During the long-suffering of God in the days of Noah—during those 120 years.

There were giants in the earth in those days; and also after that, when the sons of God came in unto the daughters of men, and they bare children to them, the same became mighty men which were of old, men of renown [Gen. 6:4].

It says, "There were giants in the earth in those days," but it does not say they are the offspring of the sons of God and the daughters of men. It does say this about the offspring: "the same became mighty men which were of old, men of renown." These were not monstrosities; they were men. The record here makes it very clear that the giants were in the earth *before* this took place, and it simply means that these offspring were outstanding individuals.

Humanity has a tremendous capacity. Man is fearfully and wonderfully made—that is a great truth we have lost sight of. This idea that man has come up from some protoplasm out of a garbage can or seaweed is utterly preposterous. It is the belief of some scientists that evolution will be repudiated, and some folk are going to look ridiculous at that time.

Evolution is nothing in the world but a theory as far as science is concerned. Nothing has been conclusive about it. It is a philosophy like any other philosophy, and it can be accepted or rejected. When it is accepted, it certainly leads to some very crazy solutions to the problems of the world, and it has gotten my country into trouble throughout the world. Anyone would think that we are the white knight riding through the world straightening out wrongs. We are wrong on the inside ourselves! I do not know why in this country today we have an intelligentsia in our colleges, our government, our news media, and our military who think they are super, that somehow or another they have arrived. It is the delusion of the hour that men think that they are greater than they really are. Man is suffering from a fall, an awful fall. He is totally depraved today, and until that is taken into consideration, we are in trouble all the way along.

Then what *do* we have here in verse 4? As I see it, Genesis is a book of genealogies—it is a book of the families. The sons of God are the godly line who have come down from Adam through Seth, and the daughters of men belong to the line of Cain. What you have here now is an intermingling and intermarriage of these two lines, until finally the entire line is totally corrupted (well, not totally; there is one exception). That is the picture that is presented to us here.

I recognize, and I want to insist upon it, that many fine expositors take the opposite view that the sons of God are actually angels. If you accept that view, you will be in good company, but I am sure that most of you want to be right and will want to go along with me. Regardless of which view you take, I hope all of us will be friends, because this is merely a matter of interpretation. It does not have anything to do with whether or not you believe the Bible but concerns only the interpretation of the facts of Scripture.

What was the condition on the earth before the Flood? What caused God to bring the judgment of the Flood?

And God saw that the wickedness of man was great in the earth, and that every imagination of the thoughts of his heart was only evil continually [Gen. 6:5].

There are four words here that ought to be emphasized and which I have marked in my Bible. "The wickedness of man was *great*." "*Every* imagination of the thoughts of his heart was *only* evil." Only evil—that is all it was—and that "*continually*." These four words reveal the condition of the human family that was upon the earth.

And it repented the LORD that he had made man on the earth, and it grieved him at his heart [Gen. 6:6].

"And it repented the LORD." What repented the Lord? The corruption of man repented the Lord. It looks as if God has changed His mind, and intends to remove man from the earth. He probably did just that with a former creation on the earth. Although it grieved God because of man's sin, thank God, He did not destroy him.

And the Lord said, I will destroy man whom I have created from the face of the earth; both man, and beast, and the creeping thing, and the fowls of the air; for it repenteth me that I have made them [Gen. 6:7].

It does not mention fish because they are in the water, and He is simply going to send more water.

GOD'S DELIVERANCE FROM THE JUDGMENT OF THE FLOOD

But Noah found grace in the eyes of the Lord [Gen. 6:8].

And why did Noah find grace?

These are the generations of Noah: Noah was a just man and perfect in his generations, and Noah walked with God [Gen. 6:9].

Why did God save Noah? Because he walked with God? Yes, but we are also told: "By faith Noah, being warned of God of things not seen as yet, moved with fear, prepared an ark to the saving of his house; by the which he condemned the world, and became heir of the righteousness which is by faith" (Heb. 11:7). It took faith to prepare an ark on dry land when it had not even drizzled! In this same chapter in Hebrews, we are told that it was by faith that Enoch was translated. You see, when the church is taken out of this world, every believer is going because the rapture is for *believers*, and the weakest saint is going out. They are going out because God extends mercy, and we are told that the mercy of God will be demonstrated at that time.

Why the Flood? Why is God going to send the Flood?

The earth also was corrupt before God, and the earth was filled with violence.

And God looked upon the earth, and, behold, it was corrupt; for all flesh had corrupted his way upon the earth [Gen. 6:11–12].

That is, man had corrupted God's way and was going his own way. He had turned from the purpose for which God had created him.

And God said unto Noah, The end of all flesh is come before me; for the earth is filled with violence through them; and, behold, I will destroy them with the earth [Gen. 6:13].

God is going to send the Flood, and I would like to mention here several reasons why.

Man had a promise of a Redeemer, and he was told that there was coming a Savior on the earth. That is the thing man should have been looking for; instead of that, he turned from God.

God had provided a sacrifice for Adam and Eve, and we find that a great, eternal principle was put down with Cain and Abel. These two boys, Cain and Abel, stand as the representatives of two great systems, two classes of people: the lost and the saved, the self-righteous and the broken-spirited, the formal professor and the genuine believer. That is what was present in the human race at this time.

And then we find that the patriarchs were living so long that the lives of Adam and Methuselah bridged the entire gap from the creation to the Flood. They certainly could have given a revelation to all mankind, which they did. Then we are told in Jude 14 and 15 that Enoch preached, he prophesied, during that period. We are also told that Noah preached during that period as he was building the ark. When Enoch disappeared, that should have alerted the people to the intervention of God in human affairs. They also knew about this man Methuselah and the meaning of his name; and when he died, they should have known the Flood was coming. Finally, there was also the ministry of the Holy Spirit. God said that His Spirit would not always strive with man. The Spirit of God *was* striving with him, but, when man totally rejected God, the Flood came in judgment upon the earth.

The entire human family has turned from God. ". . . There is none righteous, no, not one" (Rom. 3:10). There are just a few, though, who do believe Him—Noah and his family. Here is one man who walked with God; he believed God. Here is a man who still trusted God—"by faith Noah." Here is a man who was willing to risk building a boat on dry land. If the rains did not come, he certainly would be the laughingstock of the community. I think he was just that for 120 years, but Noah believed God.

There is a striking comparison in the fact that the days of Noah are to be duplicated before the Lord comes again to the earth, not for the Rapture, but to establish His kingdom. But there are some remarkable parallels that have already taken place. For instance, this chapter opened: "And it came to pass, when men began to multiply on the face of the earth, and daughters were born unto them. . . ." There was this tremendous population increase, and by that time man had spread pretty much over the earth. He was in North America, in Asia, in Europe, and in Africa. He had spread in every direction. Today we have a tremendous population explosion, and men again have increased upon the face of the earth.

Also, there is the fact that during the great tribulation period, the Holy Spirit will no longer restrain evil. He will be there to convert men, but we are told very definitely that He will not be restraining evil on the earth. God's overtures to men will be despised and rejected, and certainly they are even today. Isn't it amazing that the only ones who are listened to by the world today are the liberal Protestant and Roman Catholic ministers? You hear nothing from conservative men. They have attempted to make some sort of inroad, and they are trying their best to get back in the mainstream, but we have come to the day when, if you are going to stand for God, you will find that you will not be able to talk before a television camera very often. Instead, you must learn to protest, to march, and to deny Christ before you can expect a television interview!

Finally, the world in that day will be faced with the great problem of the Rapture—there will have been a great number of people who have mysteriously left the earth. Also there were judgments in Noah's day, and yet they did not heed them.

INSTRUCTIONS TO NOAH FOR BUILDING THE ARK

In the preparation for the Flood, God is giving the people ample opportunity.

Make thee an ark of gopher wood; rooms shalt thou make in the ark, and shalt pitch it within and without with pitch [Gen. 6:14].

"Make thee an ark of gopher wood." Gopher wood is an almost indestructible wood very much like our redwood here in California.

"Rooms shalt thou make in the ark." The word for "rooms" has the idea of *nest*. The elephant would need a room, but the mole would not need quite that much space. He could be given just a little dirt in a corner, and that is all he would need.

"And shalt pitch it within and without with pitch." The ark was to be made waterproof.

And this is the fashion which thou shalt make it of: The length of the ark shall be three hundred cubits, the breadth of it fifty cubits, and the height of it thirty cubits [Gen. 6:15].

The impression that most people have of the ark is the impression they were given by the little Sunday School pictures which made it look like a houseboat. It was, to me, a very ridiculous sort of a travesty. It was a caricature of the ark instead of a picture of it like it actually was.

To begin with, the instructions for the building of the ark reveal that it was quite sizable. "The length of the ark shall be three hundred cubits." If a cubit is eighteen inches, that ought to give you some conception of how long this ark was.

The question arises as to how they could make it substantial in that day. My friend, we are not dealing with cavemen. We are dealing with a very intelligent man. You see, the intelligence that the race has today came right through Noah, and he happened to be a very intelligent man.

Noah is not making an oceangoing ship to withstand fifty-foot waves. All he is building is a place for life, animal life and man, to stay over quite a period of time—not to go through a storm, but just to wait out the Flood. For that reason, the ark might lack a great deal that you would find on an oceangoing ship, and that would give it a great deal more room.

If a cubit is 18 inches, 300 cubits would mean that the ark was 450 feet long. That is a pretty long boat, but the relative measurements is the thing that interests me. For instance, I noted that the *New Mexico*, one of our battleships of the World War II era, was built 624 feet long, 106¼ feet wide, and with a mean draught of 29½ feet. By comparison the ark had practically the same ratio; so that you did not have a ridiculous looking boat at all, but one which would compare favorably with the way they build ships today.

A window shalt thou make to the ark, and in a cubit shalt thou finish it above; and the door of the ark shalt thou set in the side thereof; with lower, second, and third stories shalt thou make it [Gen. 6:16].

"A window shalt thou make to the ark." The window was not a little slit made in the side of the ark. Have you ever stopped to think about the stench that there might be with all those animals in there over that period of time? The window was a cubit high and went all the way around the top of the ark. The roof must have overlapped the window quite a bit. That is the way they ventilate a gymnasium today. I also noticed that at the state fair in Dallas, Texas, the buildings in which the animals were housed had that window which goes all the way around at the top. With all the animals they had there, it was not an unpleasant place to be. People were sitting in there eating their meals and also sleeping. It was very comfortable, and the odor was not bad. I have heard it said that poor Noah had to stick his head out this little window in order to live. That's ridiculous. That is man's imagination and not what the record says here at all.

"And the door of the ark shalt thou set in the side thereof." The ark had only one door, and that is important. Christ said, "I am the way" and "I am the door to the sheepfold," and He is the door to the ark.

"With lower, second, and third stories shalt thou make it." The ark had three decks, you see, and then, I take it, one either on top or on the bottom which would make four decks. Was there a door for each deck? I am rather of the opinion there was only one door and not one for each floor, but frankly, that is beside the point.

PASSENGERS IN THE ARK

And, behold, I, even I, do bring a flood of waters upon the earth, to destroy all flesh, wherein is the breath of life, from under heaven; and every thing that is in the earth shall die [Gen. 6:17].

God is bringing the judgment upon the earth—upon animal and bird and man.

But with thee will I establish my covenant; and thou shalt come into the ark, thou, and thy sons, and thy wife, and thy sons' wives with thee.

And of every living thing of all flesh, two of every sort shalt thou bring into the ark, to keep them alive with thee; they shall be male and female.

Of fowls after their kind, and of cattle after their kind, of every creeping thing of the earth after his kind, two of every sort shall come unto thee, to keep them alive [Gen. 6:18–20].

"Two of every sort shall come unto thee, to keep them alive." Noah was not a Frank Buck who

went out "to bring 'em back alive." He was not a big game hunter. He did not have to go after these animals—they came to him.

Animals in danger will do that. I remember the first time that we went into Yosemite Valley when our daughter was just a little thing. She had never seen snow before, and when we put her down in the snow, she began to whimper. But she quit when she looked over and saw a little deer. I believe we could have gone over and petted that little deer, but realizing the possible danger, of course we did not approach him any closer. When I mentioned the deer to the ranger, he laughed and said, "Yes, there's snow up in the High Sierra right now, and when there is snow up there and there's danger, they come down here and are as tame as any animal could possibly be. But the minute the snows melt in spring, they leave this area, and you couldn't get within a country mile of any of them." Why? Because when an animal is in danger, he will come to man. At the time of the Flood, I do not think Noah had any problem at all, for the animals all came to him.

And take thou unto thee of all food that is eaten, and thou shalt gather it to thee; and it shall be for food for thee, and for them.

Thus did Noah; according to all that God commanded him, so did he [Gen. 6:21–22].

Noah is now to do something very practical. It took a lot of hay in the ark to feed these animals. Some people are going to say, "But some of those animals ate meat. They would eat each other!" I do not think so. Up to the time of the Flood, apparently both men and animals were not flesh-eating. They just did not eat flesh; there were no carnivorous animals. We are told of a day in the millennium when the lion and the lamb will lie down together, and the lion will eat straw like an ox (see Isa. 11:6–7). That could certainly come to pass, for that probably was the original state of the animal.

CHAPTER 7

THEME: Noah, his family, and the animals enter the ark; destruction of all flesh and the salvation of those in the ark

NOAH, HIS FAMILY, AND THE ANIMALS ENTER THE ARK

And the Lord said unto Noah, Come thou and all thy house into the ark; for thee have I seen righteous before me in this generation [Gen. 7:1].

Why was Noah righteous? It was by faith, just as later on Abraham was counted righteous because of his faith: "And he believed in the Lord; and he counted it to him for righteousness" (Gen. 15:6). Noah believed God, and it was counted to him for righteousness. "By faith Noah . . . prepared an ark . . ." the writer to the Hebrews said (Heb. 11:7). That is the reason God saved him.

Have you ever noticed how gracious God is to this man in all of this time of judgment? Here in verse 1 He says, "Come thou. . . ." This is the same invitation that the Lord Jesus gives today to all mankind: "Come unto me, all ye that labor and are heavy laden, and I will rest you" (Matt. 11:28). Then in verse 16 of this chapter, we read, "And the Lord shut him in." Isn't that lovely? And finally, chapter 8 opens, "And God remembered Noah." How wonderful! God could very easily have forgotten all about Noah. Years later He could have said, "Oh my, I forgot all about that fellow down there. I put him in an ark and forgot about him!" That would have been too bad, wouldn't it? But God did not forget. God remembered Noah. God never forgets. He remembers you. The only thing that He does not remember is your sin if you have come to Him for salvation. Your sins He remembers no more. What a beautiful thing this is!

Now Noah and his family enter into the ark. Did you know that this story of Noah, just like the story of creation, has wandered over the face of the earth? I wish that I could give you the Babylonian account. All you have to do is to compare them to see the differences. The other accounts are utterly preposterous and ridiculous. The very fact that most nations and peoples have an account of both creation and the Flood should tell you something, my friend. It ought to tell you that there is a basis of truth for them. All of these peoples would not come up with such a record if they had been making up stories. And if you want to know which one is accurate, just make a comparison. The Babylonian account, for example, is a perfectly ridiculous story of a sort of war going on among the gods, one against the other, and that is what brought the Flood. In contrast, the Bible tells us that the Flood was a judgment of God upon man for his sin—that makes sense, by the way.

Of every clean beast thou shalt take to thee by sevens, the male and his female: and of beasts that are not clean by two, the male and his female.

Of fowls also of the air by sevens, the male and the female; to keep seed alive upon the face of all the earth [Gen. 7:2–3].

This was the basis of a lawsuit years ago against Dr. Harry Rimmer who had offered a thousand dollars to anyone who could show a contradiction in the Bible. There were several liberal theologians who testified in a court of law that this was a contradiction. Why would it first say two of each kind and now seven of each kind? Of course Dr. Rimmer won the lawsuit. All you have to do is to turn over to see that when Noah got out of the ark, he offered clean beasts as sacrifices. Where would he have gotten the clean beasts if he had not taken more than two? It was only of the clean beasts that he took seven, and now we know why. Those that were not clean went in by twos, a male and a female.

"Of fowls also of the air by sevens, the male and the female"—that is for those that are clean.

For yet seven days, and I will cause it to rain upon the earth forty days and forty nights; and every living substance that I have made will I destroy from off the face of the earth [Gen. 7:4].

For seven days the world could have knocked at the door of the ark, and frankly, they could have come in—God would have saved them. All they had to do was to believe God.

And Noah was six hundred years old when the flood of waters was upon the earth.

And Noah went in, and his sons, and his wife, and his sons' wives with him, into the ark, because of the waters of the flood.

Of clean beasts, and of beasts that are not clean, and of fowls, and of every thing that creepeth upon the earth,

There went in two and two unto Noah into the ark, the male and the female, as God had commanded Noah [Gen. 7:6–9].

Nowhere does Scripture say that Noah went out and drove the animals in. It was not necessary—they came to him.

DESTRUCTION OF ALL FLESH AND THE SALVATION OF THOSE IN THE ARK

In the six hundredth year of Noah's life, in the second month, the seventeenth day of the month, the same day were all the fountains of the great deep broken up, and the windows of heaven were opened.

And the rain was upon the earth forty days and forty nights.

And they that went in, went in male and female of all flesh, as God had commanded him: and the LORD shut him in.

And the flood was forty days upon the earth; and the waters increased, and bare up the ark, and it was lift up above the earth [Gen. 7:11–12, 16–17].

What is the scientific, historical evidence for the Flood? I am not going to enter into this subject other than to mention one of the finest books on this subject which I can highly recommend. It is *The Genesis Flood* by Henry M. Morris and John C. Whitcomb (Presbyterian and Reformed, 1960). Both of these men are thoroughly qualified to write on this subject. John Whitcomb, Th.D., professor of Old Testament at Grace Theological Seminary, and Henry M. Morris, Ph.D. from the University of Minnesota, professor of hydraulic engineering and chairman of the Department of Civil Engineering in the Virginia Polytechnic Institute, joined together and have written a book on the Genesis Flood. They show that the Flood was universal, it was a great catastrophe, and there is historical evidence for it. They also answer the uniformitarian argument (that existing processes acting in the same manner as at present are sufficient to account for all geological changes). This is one of the many different theories that have been advanced to discount the geological evidences of the universal Flood. I assume that there is an abundance of historical evidence for the Flood, and it is not necessary for me to go into it, as it has been answered in this very scholarly book.

And every living substance was destroyed which was upon the face of the ground, both man, and cattle, and the creeping things, and the fowl of the heaven; and they were destroyed from the earth: and Noah only remained alive, and they that were with him in the ark [Gen. 7:23].

On the other hand, there have recently come from the press several books by men whom I consider to be pseudointellectuals and pseudotheologians. They take the position that the Flood was local; that is, that it was confined to the Tigris-Euphrates Valley. In other words, it was sort of a big swimming pool and that is about all. *The Genesis Flood* absolutely demolishes that thought altogether, and I am sure that you realize that the Scriptures make it very clear that the Flood covered the whole earth. God said that the entire earth was going to be destroyed by the Flood. "And God said unto Noah, The end of all flesh is come before me; for the earth is filled with violence through them; and, behold, I will destroy them with the earth" (Gen. 6:13).

The human family had already gotten to North America, and the animals were certainly there—nobody would argue that point for a moment. But if you say that the Flood was not universal, then you have someone besides Noah starting the human family over again—and that is just not the way the Word of God tells it. You are on the horns of a dilemma, as I see it: you either have to accept the Word of God, or you have to reject what it says. To my judgment, to attempt to make a case for a local flood is actually, in the long run, to reject the Word of God. The Bible makes it very clear that it was a universal flood. "And every living substance was destroyed . . . and Noah only remained alive, and they that were with him in the ark."

And the waters prevailed upon the earth an hundred and fifty days [Gen. 7:24].

In other words, for a period of approximately half a year, for five months, the waters prevailed on the earth.

The Genesis Flood not only answers the question of its being a universal rather than a local flood, but it also answers this question of uniformitarianism. There are those who take the position that there was no such thing as a great convulsion or catastrophe like the Flood. I am not going into detail, except to point out that Peter makes it very clear that we should expect such scoffers. "Knowing this first, that there shall come in the last days scoffers, walking after their own lusts, And saying, Where is the promise of his coming? for since the fathers fell asleep, all things continue as they were from the beginning of the creation" (2 Peter 3:3–4). The scoffer has always been a uniformitarian, but you could not very well hold that position and accept the integrity of the Word of God at this particular point. This is very important to see.

CHAPTER 8

THEME: The rains cease; earth dries—Noah leaves the ark; Noah builds an altar and offers sacrifice

THE RAINS CEASE

And God remembered Noah, and every living thing, and all the cattle that was with him in the ark: and God made a wind to pass over the earth, and the waters assuaged;

The fountains also of the deep and the windows of heaven were stopped, and the rain from heaven was restrained;

And the waters returned from off the earth continually: and after the end of the hundred and fifty days the waters were abated.

And the ark rested in the seventh month, on the seventeenth day of the month, upon the mountains of Ararat [Gen. 8:1–4].

We are given the record not only of the building up of the Flood but also of the prevailing and now the assuaging of the Flood. We are told that "God remembered Noah"— how lovely—and that "God made a wind to pass over the earth, and the waters assuaged." It did not happen just overnight. The buildup of the waters took over 150 days, and then there were 261 days in the assuaging. That looks to me like it is something more than just a local flood.

And the waters decreased continually until the tenth month: in the tenth month, on the first day of the month, were the tops of the mountains seen.

And it came to pass at the end of forty days, that Noah opened the window of the ark which he had made [Gen. 8:5–6].

We could say that this is the beginning of the end of the Flood. Notice what Noah does:

And he sent forth a raven, which went forth to and fro, until the waters were dried up from off the earth.

Also he sent forth a dove from him, to see if the waters were abated from off the face of the ground [Gen. 8:7–8].

Frankly, Noah becomes a bird-watcher. He sends out these two birds, the raven and the dove.

But the dove found no rest for the sole of her foot, and she returned unto him into the ark, for the waters were on the face of the whole earth: then he put forth his hand, and took her, and pulled her in unto him into the ark.

And he stayed yet other seven days; and again he sent forth the dove out of the ark;

And the dove came in to him in the evening; and, lo, in her mouth was an olive leaf plucked off: so Noah knew that the waters were abated from off the earth.

And he stayed yet other seven days; and sent forth the dove; which returned not again unto him any more [Gen. 8:9–12].

I want you to see a great spiritual truth that we have here in the eighth chapter in this account of the raven and the dove. After Noah had spent over a year in the ark, he sent forth a raven, and the raven never came back. But the dove kept coming back and even brought in its beak a little bit of greenery, an olive leaf. I do not know why the dove and olive leaf have always been symbolic of peace, but they are. I cannot quite see that that is exactly the message of the dove's second return. But when the dove did not return at all, that was the sign that the judgment was over and that peace had returned to the earth. But, of course, man going out of the ark is the same type of man that all the sons of Adam were who had provoked the Flood as a judgment from God in the first place. You are going to see that there is not too much improvement in man after the Flood; in fact, there is none whatsoever.

There is a great spiritual lesson here which I

would not have you miss for anything in the world. Noah is engaged here in "bird-watching." He sends out the raven, and the raven does not come back. Why didn't that raven come back? You must recognize what that raven eats—it feeds on carrion. There was a whole lot of flesh of dead animals floating around after the Flood, and that was the kind of thing this old crow ate. He did not return to the ark because he was really going to a feast, and he was having a very wonderful time. The raven was classified as an unclean bird, by the way.

The dove is a clean bird and is so listed later on in Scripture. Remember that Noah took into the ark both the clean and the unclean animals. The dove brought back information: it was a regular homing pigeon. With the dove's second trip, Noah was now a confirmed bird-watcher—and the dove brought back evidence that the dry land was appearing. The third time, the dove did not return, and Noah knew that the waters of judgment were gone.

I have said before that all great truths of the Bible are germane in Genesis. The Bible teaches that the believer has two natures, an old and a new nature: "Therefore if any man be in Christ, he is a new creature: old things are passed away; behold, all things are become new" (2 Cor. 5:17).

The clean and the unclean are together. You and I as believers have these two natures. Our Lord said: "That which is born of the flesh is flesh; and that which is born of the Spirit is spirit" (John 3:6). And Paul writes: "For I know that in me (that is, in my flesh,) dwelleth no good thing: for to will is present with me; but how to perform that which is good I find not" (Rom. 7:18).

Paul spoke of a struggle between the two natures. And there is a struggle today between the old nature and the new nature of a believer.

The raven went out into a judged world, but he found a feast in the dead carcass because that is the thing he lived on. The bloated carcass of an elephant would have made him a banquet; I tell you, it would have been for him a bacchanalian orgy. Back and forth, he restlessly went up and down. May I say to you, that is the picture of the old nature; the old nature is like that raven. The old nature loves the things of the world and feasts on them. That is the reason so many people watch television on Sunday night and do not go to church. Don't tell me that you have some good excuse for that. You do have an old nature, but that is no excuse because you ought not to be living in the old nature.

The dove went out into a judged world, but she found no rest, no satisfaction, and she returned to the ark. The dove represents the believer in the world. The old raven went out into the world and loved it. When he found that old carcass, he probably thought the millennium had arrived! You see, it is a matter of viewpoint. A professor said to me, "This matter of what's right and wrong is relative." He's right; it is. It is what God says is right, and it is what the professor says is wrong—and he does not find very much that is wrong, by the way. What God says is wrong *is* wrong. The believer is told, "Love not the world, neither the things that are in the world . . ." (1 John 2:15). You and I are living in a judged world today. We are in the world, but not of it. We are to use it, but not to abuse it. We are not to fall in love with it, but we are to attempt to win the lost in this world and get out the Word of God. Our Lord told us, ". . . Go ye into all the world, and preach the gospel to every creature" (Mark 16:15). Let's take care of our job down here and get out the Word of God—that is the important thing. The dove recognized what kind of a world she was in, and she found no rest. She found rest only in the ark, and that ark sets forth Christ, if you please.

Let me ask you this very personal question: What kind of bird are you? Are you a raven or a dove? If you are a child of God, you have both natures—but which one are you living in today? Do you love the things of God, or don't you?

EARTH DRIES—
NOAH LEAVES THE ARK

And it came to pass in the six hundredth and first year, in the first month, the first day of the month, the waters were dried up from off the earth: and Noah removed the covering of the ark, and looked, and, behold, the face of the ground was dry [Gen. 8:13].

This brings us to 261 days, so that the total time of the Flood was 371 days, extending over a year. That also conforms to the statement of Scripture that the Flood was universal; it was not just the filling of a swimming pool—it certainly was more than that!

There have been other discoveries that have revealed something concerning the Flood, and I would like to pass on to you the words of Dr. J. E. Shelley who takes the position that the Flood was universal, that it covered the entire earth: "The most striking example of this is found in the case of the mammoths. These elephants are found buried in the frozen silt of the Tundra, Siberia, all over the length of the

Continent of Asia, and in the North of Alaska and Canada. They are found in herds on the higher ground not bogged in marshes, hundreds of thousands in number." He goes on to say that these elephants have been examined and found to have drowned. If they had just gotten bogged down, they would have died of starvation. "The farther north one goes, the more there are, till the soil of the islands of the White Sea inside the Arctic circle consists largely of their bones mingled with those of sabre-tooth tiger, giant elk, cave bear, musk ox, and with trunks of trees and trees rooted in the soil. There are now no trees in those regions, the nearest being hundreds almost thousands of miles away. The mammoth could not eat the stunted vegetation which now grows in this region for but three months in the year, a hundred square miles of which would not keep one of them alive for a month. The food in their stomachs is pine, hawthorn branches, etc. These mammoths were buried alive in the silt when that silt was soft. They and the silt were then suddenly frozen and have never been unfrozen. For they show no signs of decomposition. Mammoth ivory has been sold on the London docks for more than a thousand years. The Natural History Museum purchased a mammoth's head and tusks from the ivory store of the London Docks. This head was absolutely fresh and was covered with its original fur."

If you doubt the universality of the Flood, here is more than enough evidence to convince you.

And Noah went forth, and his sons, and his wife, and his sons' wives with him:

Every beast, every creeping thing, and every fowl, and whatsoever creepeth upon the earth, after their kinds, went forth out of the ark [Gen. 8:18–19].

NOAH BUILDS AN ALTAR AND OFFERS SACRIFICE

God is now going to make a covenant with Noah. We will see this new beginning as we get into the next chapter. This covenant is a very important one. When God made it with Noah, He made it with the human family that is on the earth today.

And Noah builded an altar unto the LORD; and took of every clean beast, and of every clean fowl, and offered burnt offerings on the altar [Gen. 8:20].

Now do you see why Noah took seven of the clean beasts and only two of the unclean? He is now offering the clean beasts as sacrifices.

The first thing that Noah did when he came out of the ark was to build an altar to the Lord and offer a sacrifice, a burnt offering, to Him. That burnt offering speaks of the person of Jesus Christ. It was offered on the basis of acceptance before God and of praise to God in recognition of Him. Without doubt, this was one of the things that caused God to be pleased with Noah at this particular time.

And the LORD smelled a sweet savor; and the LORD said in his heart, I will not again curse the ground any more for man's sake; for the imagination of man's heart is evil from his youth; neither will I again smite any more every thing living, as I have done [Gen. 8:21].

You can just write it down that that is true. What about *your* youth? Was your imagination evil or not? In our contemporary society we can see the rebellion of youth, and isn't it interesting to note the direction they have gone? They have gone in the same direction. Every imagination of man's heart is evil from his youth—and it does not improve. I was visiting in a hospital the other night. The curtain was pulled between the beds, but you could hear the next patient talking with her husband. It seemed to be a contest between those two to see who could outcuss the other one! I have never heard such profanity on the part of two human beings. May I say to you, the imagination of man's heart is evil from his youth. That just happens to be an accurate statement that was made a long time ago.

While the earth remaineth, seedtime and harvest, and cold and heat, and summer and winter, and day and night shall not cease [Gen. 8:22].

It has been suggested that the Flood was so extensive that it tilted the earth. As you know, the earth is not straight on its axis. We are off center, if you please. The magnetic center is different from the center on which we are revolving. Something happened somewhere along the line, and it is the belief of many that this is when it took place. Because the earth revolves like that, that gives us our seasons. It is sort of going around like a wobbly top. You remember that when you were young and would spin a top, the top would run down and get wobbly. That is the way the earth revolves today, and as a result we have the seasons.

Prior to the Flood, man learned the three R's: (1) *Rebellion* against God was *realized*—it came right out in the open. (2) *Revelation* from God was *rejected* by man. Noah's witness did not reach them. (3) *Repentance* was absolutely *repudiated;* there was no return to God at all. Men refused the refuge that God provided, and for 120 years Noah had no converts. These are the three R's. Men led in rebellion, they rejected the revelation, and there was no repentance on their part.

Now as this man Noah comes forth from the ark, he stands in a most unique position. He stands in the position of being the head of the human race again—the same position Adam had. It is said that we are all related to Adam, but we are closer kin than that: we are all related in Noah. In one sense, Noah is the father of all of us today.

CHAPTER 9

THEME: New instructions and arrangements; the sin of Noah and his sons

Now we come to a new beginning. It is difficult for us to realize what a revolutionary beginning it is. The dispensation of human conscience is over, and God is putting man under government—he is to govern himself. We will see something of this in the covenant which God made with Noah. And let's keep in mind that, when God made the covenant with Noah, He made it with you and me, for He made it with all mankind.

NEW INSTRUCTIONS AND ARRANGEMENTS

And God blessed Noah and his sons, and said unto them, Be fruitful, and multiply, and replenish the earth [Gen. 9:1].

The word *replenish* is meaningful here because we know that there was a civilization before the Flood, and now there is to be a civilization after the Flood. (When Adam was told to replenish the earth, we assume that there had been living creatures—I don't know what to call them—before Adam. They apparently were living creatures of God's creation; anything I could say beyond that would be pure speculation.)

Notice that the first thing God tells Noah to do is to "be fruitful, and multiply, and replenish the earth." There is to be the propagation of the race. Remember that God gave this command under special circumstances. Today we are in a time of population explosion, and there is overpopulation that is quite dangerous. However, Noah stood in an unique position. He and his family were the only folks around. Can you imagine driving down the freeway, going to work in the morning, and there are cars in front of you, cars to the right of you, cars to the left of you, cars behind you, cars honking—you're in a traffic snarl. Then about a year later you go out on the freeway and there is not another car there. Yours is the only one. You might as well take down all the traffic lights. You won't need them because you are the only one driving through. This would be quite an unusual experience for us, would it not? Well, this was the experience of Noah in his day.

And the fear of you and the dread of you shall be upon every beast of the earth, and upon every fowl of the air, upon all that moveth upon the earth, and upon all the fishes of the sea; into your hand are they delivered [Gen. 9:2].

Another part of the covenant is man's protection and rulership over the animal world. I take it that before this time the relationship was different. Apparently man had not been a meat eater before. All the animals were tame, and one is not inclined to eat an animal that is a pet. Remember that the animals *came* to Noah when the Flood was impending; they seemed to have no fear of him at all.

Now the animals will fear and dread man. However, man is responsible for the animal world. Man's treatment of the animal world is a brutal story. Man has attempted to exterminate many of the animals. Man would have slaughtered all the whales around the Hawaiian Islands for the money they could get unless the government had intervened. At one time the buffalo were in great herds in the West, but they were killed by man. Today we must have places of refuge to protect animals and bird life. It is well that we do that. The animals of Africa are being exterminated. Man is a mighty brutal creature. We need a government to protect the animals from man.

Every moving thing that liveth shall be meat for you; even as the green herb have I given you all things [Gen. 9:3].

Now God gives to man a new provision for food. Before the Flood God gave to man the green earth, the plant life, to eat. Now He tells Noah that he is able to eat animal life. There are diet faddists, and often this type of thing becomes a part of a person's religion. I once met a lady who was a vegetarian as a part of her religion, and she was quite excited when I told her that these antediluvians were all vegetarians. She thought this reinforced her argument that we should all be vegetarians, and she had her assistant take it down in her notes. However, I think she must have erased it later because I told her this: "I wouldn't make too much of it if I were you because you must remember that it was a bunch of vegetarians who were destroyed in the Flood. If diet had in any way improved them at that time, they would not have been destroyed." We see here that God now permits man to eat flesh.

However, God prohibits the eating of blood.

But flesh with the life thereof, which is the blood thereof, shall ye not eat [Gen. 9:4].

The blood should be drained out. The blood speaks of life; draining it indicates that the animal should be killed in a merciful way rather than prolonging its suffering and that it must be really dead. Although I enjoy the sport of hunting, I don't like to shoot quail, for instance, because sometimes I just wound the little fellow and it crawls away so that I can't find it. I don't like to do that. God says that when you are going to eat animals, you are to make sure that you don't eat them with their blood. It should be drained out, insuring that the animal is killed in a merciful manner.

And surely your blood of your lives will I require; at the hand of every beast will I require it, and at the hand of man; at the hand of every man's brother will I require the life of man [Gen. 9:5].

This is an interesting statement, but not so meaningful to those of us who do not live on a frontier. However, there are certain animals even we encounter—such as skunks and opossums which may be rabid or disease-carrying rodents—that pose a real danger to man.

Now the fifth and the last statement in the new covenant is the most amazing—

Whoso sheddeth man's blood, by man shall his blood be shed: for in the image of God made he man [Gen. 9:6].

Here God lays down the principle for government and protection of man. He gives the government the right of capital punishment. We have seen that in this new covenant which God has given, man is to propagate the race, he is to have the protectorate and the rulership over animals, he is given a new provision for food and a prohibition against the eating of blood. Now we see that he is given the principle of government, which is the basis of capital punishment.

May I say to you that it is amazing how the attitude of the present generation has gotten away from the Bible. You see, we do not have a Bible-oriented population anymore. It is almost totally ignorant of the Word of God. As a result, we find the judges, the lawyers, and the politicians all wanting to get rid of capital punishment. They have succeeded in many cases, and I think that finally it will be eliminated totally from American culture. At the same time we have an increase in crime and the most horrible crimes taking place. I have dealt with this subject more in detail in a booklet which I entitled, *Is Capital Punishment Christian?* I believe that capital punishment is scriptural and that it is the basis of government. The government has the right to take a life when that individual has taken someone else's life. Why? Well, I think it is quite obvious that God has ruled it so in order to protect human life.

Our lives are no longer safe on the streets and often not in our homes, either. Although I know that many officials would deny this, one reason is our attitude toward capital punishment. When a criminal knows that if he takes a life, his life is going to be sacrificed, then may I say to you, he'll think twice before he takes a life. Also, there is an idea today about getting a gun-control law. May I say that the problem is not with the gun in the hand, it is with the heart inside the man.

"Whoso sheddeth man's blood, by man shall his blood be shed" is a law that we had better get back on our statute books and get rid of this sob-sister stuff. Human government is the area into which all mankind has moved (Gentiles included). "Whoso sheddeth man's blood, by man shall his blood be shed: for in the image of God made he man" is the basis for human government. It has not been changed as far as the governments of the world are concerned.

And you, be ye fruitful, and multiply; bring forth abundantly in the earth, and multiply therein [Gen. 9:7].

This is a repetition of God's instructions in verse 1.

And God spake unto Noah, and to his sons with him, saying,

And I, behold, I establish my covenant with you, and with your seed after you [Gen. 9:8–9].

"With your seed after you" includes all the human race.

And with every living creature that is with you, of the fowl, of the cattle, and of every beast of the earth with you; from all that go out of the ark, to every beast of the earth [Gen. 9:10].

All of God's creatures are included in this covenant. Isaiah predicts that someday the lion and the lamb will lie down together and that they will not hurt or destroy. In Paul's epistle to the Romans he mentions that the whole creation is groaning and travailing in pain in this present age. May I say to you that God has made this covenant with Noah and with all of His creatures until the time His kingdom comes on earth. It is for all of Noah's descendants and "every living creature that is with you."

And I will establish my covenant with you; neither shall all flesh be cut off any more by the waters of a flood; neither shall there any more be a flood to destroy the earth [Gen. 9:11].

This is God's promise. His purpose is that He will not again destroy the earth with a flood. The next time His judgment of the earth will be by fire. We find that stated in 2 Peter 3.

In the next few verses we see the picture of the covenant, and in my opinion, really a spiritual meaning of the covenant. It is sort of a sacrament, if you please. The thing which makes it that is a visible sign to which are annexed promises.

And God said, This is the token of the covenant which I make between me and you and every living creature that is with you, for perpetual generations:

I do set my bow in the cloud, and it shall be for a token of a covenant between me and the earth [Gen. 9:12–13].

The rainbow is more or less of a sacrament, that is, a token of a covenant.

And it shall come to pass, when I bring a cloud over the earth, that the bow shall be seen in the cloud:

And I will remember my covenant, which is between me and you and every living creature of all flesh; and the waters shall no more become a flood to destroy all flesh.

And the bow shall be in the cloud; and I will look upon it, that I may remember the everlasting covenant between God and every living creature of all flesh that is upon the earth [Gen. 9:14–16].

Notice that God says, "I will look upon it" and "I will remember." God didn't say that *you* would see it; He said that *He* would see it. He said He would look upon it and it would be an "everlasting covenant between God and every living creature of all flesh that is upon the earth." That ought to be the encouragement whenever you look at a rainbow.

And God said unto Noah, This is the token of the covenant, which I have established between me and all flesh that is upon the earth [Gen. 9:17].

This is God's covenant, not merely with Noah but with all flesh that is upon the earth.

Let me say again that the rainbow could be called a sacrament because a sacrament is a visible sign to which are annexed certain promises. The Passover feast, the brazen serpent, Gideon's fleece, and in our day baptism and the Lord's Supper are such signs.

Dr. John Peter Lange once made the statement, "God's eye of grace and our eye of faith meet in the sacraments." That is what happens when man looks at the rainbow. Faith lays hold of the promise attached to the sign. You see, the merit is in what the sign speaks of. There is no faith in a promise and there is no assurance in a sign—the word and the sign go together, you see. God makes a promise and attaches a sign to it. Now the rainbow is God's answer to Noah's altar. It is as if God says, "I'll remember, and I'll look upon it." A friend of mine told me about a time he was traveling by plane across the country and going over a storm. The plane was up where the sun was shining, and all of a sudden he saw a rainbow that went all the way around, a complete circle. I guess that is the way God always sees it.

THE SIN OF NOAH AND HIS SONS

We will find something that is very disappointing in the remainder of this chapter. The question arises: When man came out of the ark after the Flood and all the sinners were dead, does that mean that there was no more sin on the earth? Well, let's look and see.

And the sons of Noah, that went forth of the ark, were Shem, and Ham, and Japheth: and Ham is the father of Canaan [Gen. 9:18].

Why is Ham's son Canaan mentioned here? For two reasons. One reason we'll see in a moment. Another reason is that when Moses wrote this record, the people of Israel were traveling to the land of Canaan, and it was encouraging for them to have this information regarding God's judgment upon the people of Canaan.

These are the three sons of Noah: and of them was the whole earth overspread.

And Noah began to be an husbandman, and he planted a vineyard:

And he drank of the wine, and was drunken; and he was uncovered within his tent [Gen. 9:19–21].

Here is the record of Noah's sin. The hard fact of the matter is that Noah got drunk, and this is sin. There is no satisfactory excuse, although many expositors have attempted to find excuses for him. One excuse is that he was ignorant of the effect of wine since no one had been drunk before. You will notice that before the Flood, drunkenness is not mentioned as one of the sins. Then there are those who hold the canopy theory about the Flood. (There are many things I have not had time to mention.) The canopy theory is that before the Flood there was an ice covering which the sunlight filtered through so that grapes did not ferment before the time of the Flood and that this was something new to Noah. Well, all I can say is that this is a new beginning in a new world, but it is old sin that is still there. This incident reveals this, and it was given to answer a big question, as we shall see.

And Ham, the father of Canaan, saw the nakedness of his father, and told his two brethren without.

And Shem and Japheth took a garment, and laid it upon both their shoulders, and went backward, and covered the nakedness of their father; and their faces were backward, and they saw not their father's nakedness.

And Noah awoke from his wine, and knew what his younger son had done unto him [Gen. 9:22–24].

Now notice what God said—

And he said, Cursed be Canaan; a servant of servants shall he be unto his brethren [Gen. 9:25].

I would have you note that God said, "Cursed be *Canaan*"—He does not put a curse on *Ham*.

A question that keeps arising is this: Is the curse of Ham upon the dark races? It certainly is not. To think otherwise is absolutely absurd. The Scripture does not teach it. The coloration of the skin, the pigment that is in the epidermis of the human family, is there because of sunlight from the outside not because of sin from within. There is no curse placed upon Ham; the curse was upon Canaan his son. We do not know in what way Canaan was involved in this incident. We are given only the bare record here, but we recognize that Canaan is mentioned for a very definite purpose. Let me repeat that it hasn't anything to do with color—it is not a curse of color put on a part of the human race. That teaching has been one of the sad things said about the black man. It is not fair to the black man and it is not fair to God—because He didn't say it. After all, the first two great civilizations were Hamitic—both the Babylonian and Egyptian civilizations were Hamitic.

Another question arises: Why did God give us a record of the sin of Noah? Well, if man had written the Book of Genesis, he would have done one of two things. He either would have covered up the sin of Noah by not mentioning it at all to make Noah a hero; or else he would have made Noah's sin a great deal more sordid than it was. But God recorded it for His own purposes.

First of all, as I have indicated, it was to encourage the children of Israel in entering the land of Canaan during the time of Moses. It let them know that God had pronounced a curse upon Canaan. He had pronounced His judgment upon the race. All you have to do is read the rest of the Old Testament and secular history to discover the fulfillment of this judgment. The Canaanites have pretty much disappeared.

God had a further reason for recording the incident of Noah's sin. In Romans 15:4 we read these words: "For whatsoever things were written aforetime were written for our learning, that we through patience and comfort of the scriptures might have hope." It was recorded to let you and me know something of the weakness of the flesh. The Lord Jesus said that the spirit is willing but the flesh is weak. And in Galatians 2:16 it is made very clear that no flesh would be justified by keeping the law: ". . . for by the works of the law shall no flesh be justified." So God has given us here the story of a man who fell, revealing the weakness of the flesh.

There is no use trying to make excuses for Noah. The bare fact is that Noah got drunk. Now, maybe you as a Christian do not get drunk. But, may I say, you and I may be living in the flesh to the extent we're just as displeasing to God as Noah was. We have, I think, a wrong conception of life in this universe that we are in. For instance, our nation has spent billions of dollars to put men on the moon, and it looks like it's not a good place to live anyway. But we spend relatively little on how to live on this earth. But God is concerned about training you and me how to live on this earth.

Let us not make some of the mistakes that are made in the consideration of this incident. We need to make it very clear that Noah did not lose his salvation. I trust that you understand that. It was an awful thing that he did—there is no excuse for it. It was his weakness of the flesh, but he was still a saved man.

And he said, Blessed be the LORD God of Shem; and Canaan shall be his servant.

God shall enlarge Japheth, and he shall dwell in the tents of Shem; and Canaan shall be his servant [Gen. 9:26–27].

As I have mentioned before, when Moses was given this revelation from God, he was leading the people of Israel to the land of Canaan. The Israelites were descendants of Shem.

And Noah lived after the flood three hundred and fifty years.

And all the days of Noah were nine hundred and fifty years: and he died [Gen. 9:28–29].

CHAPTER 10

THEME: *Sons of Japheth; sons of Ham; sons of Shem*

This is a chapter of genealogies, of families, which are the origin of the nations of the world. This chapter is far more important than the space I'm giving to it would indicate. If you are interested in ethnology and anthropology and the story of mankind on the earth, you may want a far deeper study than you will find here. H. S. Miller, who has his master's degree in ethnology, has charted the origin of the nations, using Genesis 10 as a basis for the threefold division of the human family, which is revealed in these three sons of Noah: Ham, Shem, and Japheth. Ethnology makes it evident, by the way, that neither the sons of Japheth nor the sons of Ham ever comprised what some folk call the lost ten tribes of Israel.

Here in chapter 10 we have the genealogies of all three sons of Noah.

Now these are the generations of the sons of Noah, Shem, Ham, and Japheth: and unto them were sons born after the flood [Gen. 10:1].

First we see the genealogy of Japheth (vv. 2–5), then the genealogy of Ham (vv. 6–20)—this was the outstanding people at the very beginning—and finally the genealogy of Shem (vv. 21–32). Notice that throughout the Bible God follows this same pattern of giving the rejected line first and saying a word about it, then He drops that subject entirely and does

not bring it up again. Finally, He gives the accepted line, the line which is leading to the Lord Jesus Christ.

SONS OF JAPHETH

The sons of Japheth; Gomer, and Magog, and Madai, and Javan, and Tubal, and Meshech, and Tiras [Gen. 10:2].

According to H. S. Miller's chart, the Scythians, the Slavs, Russians, Bulgarians, Bohemians, Poles, Slovaks, Croatians came from Magog. The Indians and the Iranic races—Medes, Persians, Afghans, Kurds—all came from Madai. From Javan we have the Greeks, Romans, and the Romance nationalities such as French, Spanish, Portuguese, Italian, etc. Coming from Tiras are the Thracians, the Teutons, the Germans, and then from that we have the east Germanic and the European races, the north Germanic or the Scandinavians and the west Germanic from which come the High German and the Low German, and then the Angles and the Saxons and the Jutes, the Anglo-Saxon race, the English people.

Well, I simply can't go into the whole chart, but it is an interesting study. You can see that the majority of us in America descended from these lines.

SONS OF HAM

And the sons of Ham; Cush, and Mizraim, and Phut, and Canaan [Gen. 10:6].

As you can see, Ham had other sons, but the curse was only upon Canaan. Why it was not upon the others, I am not prepared to say. From Canaan came the Phoenicians, the Hittites, the Jebusites, the Amorites, the Girgashites, the Hivites, etc.

From Ham's son Cush came the Africans—the Ethiopians, the Egyptians, the Libyans, etc. All of these races are Hamitic, you see. Now we have some detail regarding a son of Cush—

And Cush begat Nimrod: he began to be a mighty one in the earth.

He was a mighty hunter before the LORD: wherefore it is said, Even as Nimrod the mighty hunter before the LORD [Gen. 10:8–9].

"He began to be a mighty one in the earth." He wanted to become the ruler of a great world empire, and he attempted to do it.

"He was a mighty hunter before the LORD." This doesn't mean that he was a wild game hunter. Sometimes a little boy is given an air gun, and when he goes out and shoots a sparrow, his folks say, "My, look at that! He's a little Nimrod. He hit a sparrow!" But Nimrod wasn't shooting sparrows or hunting wild game in Africa. He was a hunter of men's souls—that is the thought in this passage.

And the beginning of his kindgom was Babel, and Erech, and Accad, and Calneh, in the land of Shinar [Gen. 10:10].

He was the founder of those great cities in the land of Shinar.

Nimrod has quite a story which you can get from secular history. Alexander Hislop, in his book, *The Two Babylons*, gives the background which I am not going to repeat here, but it is a fascinating story of how Nimrod was responsible for the Tower of Babel. It was he who attempted to bring together the human race after the Flood in an effort to get them united into a nation of which he could become the great world ruler. He was the rebel, the founder of Babel, the hunter of the souls of men. He was the lawless one, and he is a shadow or a type of the last world ruler, the Antichrist who is yet to appear.

The first great civilization, therefore, came out from the sons of Ham. We need to recognize that. It is so easy today to fall into the old patterns that we were taught in school a few years ago. Now the black man is wanting more study of his race. I don't blame him. He hasn't been given an opportunity in the past several hundred years. The story of the beginning of the black man is that he headed up the first two great civilizations that appeared on this earth. They were from the sons of Ham. Nimrod was a son of Ham.

I'm not going to attempt to develop that line any further. You see, we are following the pattern set by the Holy Spirit in which He gives the rejected line first and then drops it. We are going to turn now to the line that will lead to Abram and then to the nation Israel and finally to the coming of Christ into this world. It is this line which we will follow through the Old Testament. God is bidding good-bye to the rest of humanity for the time being, but He will be coming back to them later on.

Let me give you a quotation from Saphir's book, *The Divine Unity of Scripture:*

The tenth chapter of Genesis is a very remarkable chapter. Before God leaves, as it were, the nations to themselves and begins to deal with Israel, His chosen people from Abraham downward, He takes a loving farewell of all the nations of the earth, as much as to say, "I am going to leave you for a while, but I love you. I have created you: I have ordered all your future; and their different genealogies are traced."

In chapter 10 seventy nations are listed. Fourteen of them are from Japheth. Thirty of them come from Ham. Don't forget that. It will give you a different conception of the black man at his beginning. And twenty-six nations come from Shem, making a total of seventy nations listed in this genealogy.

It seems to me that God is showing us what He has done with the nations of the world. Why has the white man in our day been so prominent? Well, I'll tell you why. Because at the beginning it was the black man, the colored races, that were prominent. Then the sons of Shem made a tremendous impact upon this world during the time of David and Solomon. And you will notice that from Shem there came others, such as the Syrians, the Lydians, and the Armenians, also the Arabians from Joktan. These great nations appeared next. Apparently we are currently in the period in which the white man has come to the front. It seems to me that all three are demonstrating that, regardless of whether they are a son of Ham or a son of Shem or a son of Japheth, they are incapable of ruling this world. I believe that God is demonstrating this to us, and to see this is a tremendous thing.

SONS OF SHEM

Unto Shem also, the father of all the children of Eber, the brother of Japheth the elder, even to him were children born [Gen. 10:21].

And unto Eber were born two sons: the name of one was Peleg; for in his days was the earth divided; and his brother's name was Joktan [Gen. 10:25].

When I went over this verse in a previous Bible study, I received all sorts of weird interpretations of what was meant by "the earth was divided"—that it refers to a physical division here in the earth, that the earth had undergone some tremendous physical catastrophe. Well, my friend, all that Moses is simply doing is anticipating the next chapter in which he will give us the account of the Tower of Babel. At *that* time the earth was divided. May I say that the simple interpretation seems to be the one that a great many folk miss, and we should not miss it.

Now let's just pick up the final verse of this chapter—

These are the families of the sons of Noah, after their generations, in their nations: and by these were the nations divided in the earth after the flood [Gen. 10:32].

I want to submit to you that this is one of the great chapters of the Bible although we have given very little space to it. You can see what a rich study this would make for anyone who really wanted a fair appraisal of the human family. A great many have used this remarkable chapter for that purpose.

CHAPTER 11

THEME: The building of the Tower of Babel; from Shem to Abraham

THE BUILDING
OF THE TOWER OF BABEL

And the whole earth was of one language, and of one speech [Gen. 11:1].

I do not know what language the people spoke at that time. A friend of mine who was a fellow Texan, a preacher in Texas, facetiously said to me, "You and I are probably the only two who really know what they spoke before the Tower of Babel because it was Texan." Well, I'll be honest with you, I've come to the conclusion that it could have been something else. What the language was, we simply do not know. I believe whatever that language was will be the language that will be spoken in heaven, and it will be a much better language than we have today, with more specific nouns and verbs, adverbs, and adjectives.

And it came to pass, as they journeyed from the east, that they found a plain in the land of Shinar; and they dwelt there [Gen. 11:2].

"As they journeyed from the east"—notice it was *from* the east. Mankind was apparently moving toward the West. "They found a plain in the land of Shinar," which is in the Tigris-Euphrates Valley.

And they said one to another, Go to, let us make brick, and burn them throughly. And they had brick for stone, and slime had they for mortar [Gen. 11:3].

Down in that area there is no stone, and so they made bricks. That in itself reveals something about the substantial character of their buildings. Even today brick is a popular type of building material. Yet the brick was used there because of its practicality; it was a necessity.

And they said, Go to, let us build us a city and a tower, whose top may reach unto heaven; and let us make us a name, lest we be scattered abroad upon the face of the whole earth [Gen. 11:4].

Notice that they said, "Let *us* build *us* a city . . . and let *us* make *us* a name, lest *we* be scattered abroad." They had a bad case of perpendicular I-*itis*—let *us* make *us* a name! In my opinion, the sole purpose of this tower was for a rallying place for man.

The Tower of Babel was a ziggurat. There

are many ruins of ziggurats in the Tigris-Euphrates Valley. I have a picture of the ruins of one in Ur of the Chaldees where Abraham lived. It was made of brick, solidly constructed, and around it was a runway which went to the top. Apparently, on top of it was an altar on which, in certain instances, human sacrifices were offered. Later on children were offered, put in a red-hot idol. All of this was connected with the ziggurat in later history.

But at the time of its construction, the Tower of Babel represented the rebellion of mankind against Almighty God. Apparently it was Nimrod who led in this movement. He was the builder of the city of Babel and evidently of the Tower of Babel also. It was to be a place for him to rear a world empire that was in opposition to God.

In order to realize his ambition and to make his dreams come true, two features and factors were essential: First, he needed a center of unity, a sort of headquarters, as it were. He needed a capital, a place to assemble, a place to look to. This was why he built the city of Babel. It fulfilled one of his requirements to carry out his dream of world empire. Secondly, he needed a rallying point, not just geographical but psychological, that which gives motive—a spark, an inspiration, a song, a battle cry, sort of like a "rally-around-the-flag-boys." There had to be some impelling and compelling motivation. There had to be a monument. Lenin's tomb is where Communism meets, and in Nimrod's day it was the Tower of Babel. "Let us make us" is defiance and rebellion against God. "Let us make us a *name*" reveals an overweening ambition.

Now let's see what the Tower of Babel was *not*. It was not built as a place of refuge in time of high water. He wasn't building above the flood stage, as some expositors suggest. In fact, I consider that a very puerile interpretation. After all, Lenin's tomb is not a place of refuge when the Volga River overflows! No, this tower revealed the arrogant, defiant, rebellious attitude of man against God. God had said to man that he should scatter over the earth and replenish the earth. But man in essence answered, "Nothing doing. We're not going to scatter; we are going to get together. We are through with You." The Tower of Babel was against God.

Also, the Tower of Babel was a religious symbol. It was a ziggurat. All through that valley, as I have indicated, there are ruins of ziggurats. They were places where people worshiped the creature rather than the Creator. Some ziggurats were round, others were square, but all of them had runways leading to the top, and on the top the people carried on the worship of the sun, moon, and stars. After all, when they could see the sun, moon, and stars, they knew they were not going to have a flood, and they felt that God had been pretty mean to have sent the Flood.

Now notice God's reaction to the Tower of Babel—

And the LORD came down to see the city and the tower, which the children of men builded.

And the LORD said, Behold, the people is one, and they have all one language; and this they begin to do: and now nothing will be restrained from them, which they have imagined to do [Gen. 11:5–6].

This is a tremendous statement! Since all the people spoke one language, they didn't have the great language barrier. They could get together and pool their knowledge and resources—"and now nothing will be restrained from them, which they have imagined to do." We find here that man has a fallen nature in spite of the Flood and that he is totally depraved. God cannot ignore this rebellion, for it is a rebellion against Him. God is going to put up a protective wall. He is going to throw up a barrier. This was necessary because man is such a very capable creature. He can go to the moon and he can fly in a jet plane. I still am amazed that I can sit in a jet plane, flying five miles high in the air and be served a delicious dinner. I just can't get over it, I'll be honest with you. It seems unbelievable. *Man* has done that, friend. Man is a very competent creature.

You can see what mankind would do with one language if they all came together against God.

So notice what God did—

Go to, let us go down, and there confound their language, that they may not understand one another's speech.

So the LORD scattered them abroad from thence upon the face of all the earth: and they left off to build the city.

Therefore is the name of it called Babel; because the LORD did there confound the language of all the earth: and from thence did the LORD scatter them abroad upon the face of all the earth [Gen. 11:7–9].

Now man is scattered over the face of the earth. They were together in their rebellion, but now they can't understand one another. You know, a language barrier is a wall that is higher than the Wall of China. It is higher than the Berlin Wall and more effective. It is that which separates people, and it is stronger than any national border and any ocean.

There are a great many who say that languages developed gradually. But God said He confounded their language so that right then, while they were building, they suddenly couldn't understand each other. The building project came to a sudden halt, and folk moved away from Babel—they went in every direction.

This is a tremendous thing that took place. Here is a "speaking in tongues" when they couldn't understand each other. It is a miracle, a miracle of speaking and a miracle of hearing. They *spoke* different languages, and those who *heard* could not understand them.

Let me ask you a question: Was this a blessing in disguise, or was it a curse upon mankind? Well, for God's purposes it was a blessing. For man's development away from God, it was definitely a judgment. Down through the centuries mankind has been kept separate, and it has been a great hindrance to him. One thing that is happening today through the medium of radio and television and jet travel is that these walls are being broken down. They are tumbling down like the walls of Jericho. This is one reason that I believe God is coming down in judgment again.

Now let's put over against this tongues movement those events of the Day of Pentecost. That was another great tongues movement, and that time we find that the gospel was preached in all the languages that were understood by the people there. This was not speaking in an *unknown* tongue—that never was involved in the tongues movement to begin with. On the Day of Pentecost, God is giving His answer to the Tower of Babel. God is saying to mankind, "I have a gospel and a message for you, and I'm coming to you with the gospel in your own language."

This is the thing that God has done, and today the Bible has gone out in more languages than any other book. It is still being translated into tongues and dialects and is being brought to literally hundreds of tribes throughout the world. The gospel is for *all* mankind, and the reason and the purpose for the talking in tongues was to let the human race know that God had answered the Tower of Babel. He had a redemption for man now. The mission has been accomplished. It is no longer necessary for man to *try* to work out his salvation. He can

listen to God's message and turn to Him. The gospel is for *you*, whoever you are and whatever tongue you speak. It's for you. It's for all the nations of the world. We are told in the final book of the Bible that there will be gathered into His presence ". . . a great multitude, which no man could number, of all nations, and kindreds, and people, and tongues . . ." (Rev. 7:9).

FROM SHEM TO ABRAHAM

Now we will take up the line of Shem since it is the line which will be followed throughout the Old Testament.

These are the generations of Shem: Shem was an hundred years old, and begat Arphaxad two years after the flood [Gen. 11:10].

Shem's genealogy is given in the following verses, then we read:

And Nahor lived nine and twenty years, and begat Terah:

And Nahor lived after he begat Terah an hundred and nineteen years, and begat sons and daughters [Gen. 11:24–25].

You see that we are following the line of Terah. Why Terah? Notice the next verse:

And Terah lived seventy years, and begat Abram, Nahor, and Haran [Gen. 11:26].

Now we are going to follow the line of Abram, whom we know as Abraham.

We're following the line of Shem, and we are actually going right through the Bible following this line. The Word of God will follow this line directly to the cross of Christ. God has recorded all of this as preliminary. God now has demonstrated to man that he is in sin. In the incident of Cain and Abel, we find that Cain would not acknowledge that he was a sinner. In him we see a demonstration of the *pride* of life. At the Flood we see the sin of the *flesh* because the people then were given over to the sins of the flesh. They were indulging in violence and their every thought and imagination was evil. They were blind to their need of God. They were deaf to His claim, dead to God, dead in trespasses and sins. God gave them an invitation through Noah. They spurned the invitation and remained in the sins of the flesh. Then, here at the Tower of Babel, we see the sin of the *will*, rebellion against God. That was the Tower of Babel.

Do you have your own little Tower of Babel

which you have built? Are you in rebellion against God? Well, it is natural for human nature to be in rebellion against God.

Little Willie was being very cantankerous one evening. He was really cutting up, and his mother was having a great deal of trouble with him. Finally, she had to get him and put him in a corner—sat him down with his face to the wall and told him to sit there. She left him and went back to the living room with the rest of the family. After awhile she heard a noise in there, and she called to him, "Willie, are you standing up?" He said, "No, Mom, I'm sitting down, but I am standing up on the inside of me!"

Well, believe me, there are a lot of men and women in our day who are standing up on the inside of them, standing against God. They have built their own little Tower of Babel.

Now as we follow the line which is going to lead to Christ, here are the generations or the families of Terah—

Now these are the generations of Terah: Terah begat Abram, Nahor, and Haran; and Haran begat Lot.

And Haran died before his father Terah in the land of his nativity, in Ur of the Chaldees.

And Abram and Nahor took them wives: the name of Abram's wife was Sarai; and the name of Nahor's wife, Milcah, the daughter of Haran, the father of Milcah, and the father of Iscah.

But Sarai was barren; she had no child.

And Terah took Abram his son, and Lot the son of Haran his son's son, and Sarai his daughter in law, his son Abram's wife; and they went forth with them from Ur of the Chaldees, to go into the land of Canaan; and they came unto Haran, and dwelt there [Gen. 11:27–31].

The name *Haran* means delay.

And the days of Terah were two hundred and five years: and Terah died in Haran [Gen. 11:32].

This bit of history is given to let us know that we are going to follow Abraham, and his story will begin in the next chapter.

It is at this point that the book of Genesis—and, for that matter, the Bible as a whole—takes a turn. There is a great Grand Canyon which goes right down through the Book of Genesis. The first eleven chapters are on one side, and the last thirty-nine chapters are on the other side. In the first eleven chapters we cover over 2,000 years, as long a period as the rest of the Bible put together. Contrast that 2,000 years with the 350 years from Genesis 12 through 50. In these first eleven chapters of Genesis we have seen the Creation, the fall of man, the Flood, and the Tower of Babel. These are four great events which covered that long span of years.

CHAPTER 12

THEME: God's call and promise to Abraham; Abraham's response; Abraham's lapse of faith

The chapter before us brings us to the other side of the Grand Canyon which runs through Genesis. The atmosphere is altogether different here, and we are going to slow down to a walk. The emphasis turns from events, stupendous events, to personalities—not all of them were great but all of them were important personalities. In Genesis there are four, and others will follow in subsequent books of the Bible.

In the first eleven chapters we have seen four great events: the Creation, the fall of man,

the Flood, and the Tower of Babel. In all of these tremendous events God has been dealing with the human race as a whole. Other than Adam and Abraham, God did not appear to anyone else. God was dealing with the entire race of mankind. There is a radical change at chapter 12. Now there will be brought before us four individuals. God will no longer be dealing with events, but with a man, and from that man He will make a nation. In the first section we will see Abraham the man of faith (Gen. 12–23). Then there will be Isaac the beloved son (Gen. 24–26). Next there will be Jacob the chosen and chastened son (Gen. 27–36), and then there will be Joseph's suffering and glory (Gen. 37–50). These four patriarchs are extremely important to the understanding of the Word of God. We will be taking up their stories in the rest of the book of Genesis.

You see, God has demonstrated that He can no longer deal with the race. After the fall of man, we see the great sin of Cain. What was his great sin? *Pride.* He was angry because of the fact that deep down in his heart he was *proud* of the offering he had brought to God. And when his offering was rejected while his brother's was accepted, it caused him to *hate* his brother. His hatred led to murder, and the root of all of it was pride. Let me remind you that pride was also Satan's sin. Pride is the sin of the mind.

Then at the time of the Flood, the sin was the lust of the flesh. We saw that the actions and even the imaginations of man were to satisfy the flesh.

God had to bring the Flood to judge man at the time He did, because there was only one believer left—Noah. If God had waited even another generation, He would have lost the entire human race. God had certainly been patient with the world. He had waited 969 years, the entire life span of Methuselah. I am confident that you would say that 969 years is long enough to give anybody an opportunity to change his mind. But instead of turning to God, the people were in open rebellion, asserting a will that was against God. Following the Flood, the Tower of Babel reveals that "none seeketh after God."

After the Tower of Babel, God turns from the race of mankind to one individual. From that individual He is going to bring a nation, and to that nation He will give His revelation, and out of that nation He will bring the Redeemer. Apparently, this is the only way that God could do it. Or let me put it like this: If there were other ways, this was the *best* way. We can trust God to do the thing which is the best.

When God chose Abraham, He chose a man of faith. Abraham, by any person's measuring rod, is a great man. He is one of the greatest men who ever lived on this earth. How do you measure great men even today? Well, to begin with, the man has to be famous, and certainly Abraham measures up to that. He is probably the world's most famous man. Even in this day of radio and television, probably more people have heard of Abraham than of anyone else. More have heard of Abraham than have heard of the President of the United States, or of any head of state, or of any movie star, or of any athlete. The three great religions of the world go back to Abraham: Judaism, Islam, and Christianity. There are literally millions of people in Asia and Africa today who have heard of Abraham but have never heard of the ones who make the headlines in our country. One of the marks of a great man is fame; Abraham was a great man.

Another mark of a great man is that he must be noble of character, a generous man. Can you imagine anyone more generous than Abraham? I doubt whether there is a man alive who would do what he did. When he and his nephew came back into the land of Palestine, he told Lot to choose any portion that he wanted, and Abraham said he would take what was left. Do you think any man would do that in a business deal today? They don't even do that in a church, friend, much less in a hard-boiled business world. But Abraham was a generous man. Have you ever noticed how generous he was with the kings of Sodom and Gomorrah? He told them he wouldn't take the booty, not even so much as a shoestring, because God was the One to whom he was looking.

Thirdly, a great man must live in a momentous time. He must be, as Napoleon said, a man of destiny. The man and the right time must meet at the crossroads of life. That was certainly true of Abraham.

I believe the world would agree with me on the first three points we have mentioned. They might not agree with this one: The fourth essential of a great man is that he must be a man of faith. You will notice that all great men, even when they are not Christian, have something in which they believe. God said that Abraham was a man of faith. In the Bible record the greatest thing that is said about Abraham is that he believed God: ". . . Abraham believed God, and it was counted unto him for righteousness" (Rom. 4:3). As we go through these chapters in Genesis, we will find that God appeared to this man seven times, each time to develop faith in his life. This does not mean that he was perfect. The fact of the matter is that he failed many times. God gave him four tests, and he fell flat on his face on all four of them. But, like Simon Peter, he got up, brushed himself off and started again. May I say to you, if God has touched your heart and life, you also may fall, but you are surely going to get up and start over again. We will see this happen in Abraham's life as we go through the chapter before us.

GOD'S CALL
AND PROMISE TO ABRAHAM

The first three verses give us the threefold promise of God to Abraham (Abram), and actually this is the hub of the Bible. The rest of Scripture is an unfolding of this threefold promise.

Now the LORD had said unto Abram, Get thee out of thy country, and from thy kindred, and from thy father's house, unto a land that I will shew thee:

And I will make of thee a great nation, and I will bless thee, and make thy name great; and thou shalt be a blessing:

And I will bless them that bless thee, and curse him that curseth thee: and in thee shall all families of the earth be blessed [Gen. 12:1–3].

The first of the threefold promise is the *land.* God says, "I am going to show you a land, and I am going to give it to you." The second part of the promise is the *nation*—"I will make of thee a great nation, and I will bless thee, and make thy name great." He also promises him, "And I will bless them that bless thee, and curse him that curseth thee." The third part of the promise is that He would make him a *blessing:* "In thee shall all families of the earth be blessed." This is God's threefold promise.

Now the question arises: Has God made good on His promises to Abraham? God has certainly brought from him a great nation, and it has probably the longest tenure as a nation of any people on this earth. No one can quite match them.

How about the second promise—has Abraham been a blessing to all mankind? Yes, through the Lord Jesus Christ he has been a blessing to the whole world. Also the entire Word of God has come to us through Abraham.

God has fulfilled all His promises to Abraham—except the first one. God had said, "Abraham, I'm going to give you that land." And look at what is happening over there in our day. They are holding on to the land by their toenails, but they don't *have* it. Somebody says, "God didn't make that good." Well, let's not put it that way, my friend. Let's give God a chance. Two-thirds of the promise has been made good right to the very letter. But God said that He would not let them be in the land if they were disobedient and if they were away from Him. And they *are* away from Him today. As a result they are having trouble over there. Don't say that *God* is not making good

His promise. The fact of the matter is that God is doing exactly what He said He would do. The day will come when God will put the people of Israel back in the land, and when He does it, they won't have only a toehold. They will have the land all the way east to the Euphrates River and all the way north as far as the Hittite nation was and all the way south to the river of Egypt, which is a little river in the Arabian desert. They have never really occupied the land God gave to them. At the zenith of their power, they occupied 30,000 square miles, but that is not all that God gave them. Actually, He gave them 300,000 square miles. They have a long way to go, but they will have to get it on God's terms and in God's appointed time. The United Nations can't do anything about it, and neither can the United States or Russia settle their problem.

My friend, it is very comfortable today where I sit. I have come to the position that God is running things. It is nice to sit here without being frightened by the headlines in the newspaper and without being disturbed by what is going on in the world. God is in control, and He is going to work things out His way.

Now in the light of God's three promises to Abraham, what did he do?

ABRAHAM'S RESPONSE

In verse 1 we read: "Now the LORD *had* said unto Abram." We know from other Scriptures that God had called Abram when he lived in Ur of the Chaldees: "The God of glory appeared unto our father Abraham, when he was in Mesopotamia, before he dwelt in Charran, and said unto him, Get thee out of thy country, and from thy kindred, and come into the land which I shall shew thee. Then came he out of the land of the Chaldeans, and dwelt in Charran: and from thence, when his father was dead, he removed him into this land, wherein ye now dwell" (Acts 7:2–4). Abraham obeyed God by leaving his home, his business, and the high civilization of Ur, "not knowing whither he went." Yet it was not complete obedience because we read that he took with him some of his family. He took with him his father, Terah, and God had told Abraham not to take him. Why was it that God wanted to get him out of the land and away from his relatives? We learn the answer in the book of Joshua. ". . . Your fathers dwelt on the other side of the flood in old time, even Terah, the father of Abraham, and the father of Nachor: and they served other gods" (Josh. 24:2). They served other gods—Abraham was an idolater. The world was pretty far gone at that time. God had to move like this if He was going to save humanity. The other alternative for Him was to blot them all out and start over again. I'm glad He didn't do that. If He had, I wouldn't have been here, because I arrived here a *sinner*. The fact of the matter is, all sinners would have been blotted out. Thank God, He is a God of mercy and grace, and He saves sinners.

We'll follow the Scripture text now and call him Abram until chapter 17 where God changes his name to Abraham.

So Abram departed, as the LORD had spoken unto him; and Lot went with him: and Abram was seventy and five years old when he departed out of Haran [Gen. 12:4].

"So Abram departed, as the LORD had spoken unto him." Now he will follow God's leading to the land of Canaan.

"And Lot went with him"—oh, oh! It is still incomplete obedience; he is taking his nephew Lot with him.

And Abram took Sarai his wife, and Lot his brother's son, and all their substance that they had gathered, and the souls that they had gotten in Haran; and they went forth to go into the land of Canaan; and into the land of Canaan they came [Gen. 12:5].

Abram took Sarai, his wife, and that was all right, of course.

"And Lot his brother's son, and all their substance that they had gathered, and the souls that they had gotten in Haran." The time Abram had spent in Haran was a period of just marking time and of delaying the blessing of God. God never appeared to him again until he had moved into the land of Palestine, until he had separated at least from his closer relatives and brought only Lot with him.

"And into the land of Canaan they came"— now verse 6:

And Abram passed through the land unto the place of Sichem, unto the plain of Moreh. And the Canaanite was then in the land [Gen. 12:6].

Here is the record of the fact that the Canaanites were the descendants of Ham's son Canaan. I want to add something very important right at this point. A great many people think that Abram left a terrible place in Ur of the Chaldees and came to a land of corn and wine, a land of milk and honey, where everything was lovely. They think that Abram really bettered his lot by coming to this land. Don't

you believe it. That is not what the Bible says. And through archaeology we know that Ur of the Chaldees had a very high civilization during this time. In fact, Abram and Sarai might well have had a bathtub in their home! Ur was a great and prosperous city. Abram left all of that and came into the land of Canaan, "and the Canaanite was then in the land." The Canaanite was not civilized; he was a barbarian and a heathen, if there ever was one. Abram's purpose in coming to Canaan was certainly not to better his lot. He came in obedience to God's command.

Now he has obeyed, and notice what happens—

And the LORD, appeared unto Abram, and said, Unto thy seed will I give this land: and there builded he an altar unto the LORD, who appeared unto him [Gen. 12:7].

Abram builds an altar unto the Lord when He appears to Him this second time. While he was in Haran, the place of delay, God had not appeared to him.

You see, one of the reasons that you and I are not always blessed in the reading of the Bible is because the Bible condemns—we are not living up to the light which God has already given to us. If we would obey God, then more blessing would come. We see in Abram's experience that God did not appear again to him until after he had moved out and had begun to obey God on the light that he had. Now God appears to him again. Then Abram builds an altar, and we will see that he is a real altar-builder.

And he removed from thence unto a mountain on the east of Beth-el, and pitched his tent, having Beth-el on the west, and Hai, on the east: and there he builded an altar unto the LORD, and called upon the name of the LORD [Gen. 12:8].

Abram does two things when he gets into the land. He pitches his tent—that is like buying a home in a new subdivision and moving in. He "pitched his tent"—that's where he lived. Then "he builded an altar." That was his testimony to God, and everywhere Abram went, he left a testimony to God.

My friend, what kind of a testimony do you have? To have a testimony, you don't need to leave tracts in front of your house and you don't have to have a "Jesus Saves" bumper sticker on your car (then drive like a maniac down the freeway, as some folk do). That is no testimony at all. May I say to you that Abram quietly worshiped God, and the Canaanites soon learned that he was a man who worshiped the Lord God.

And Abram journeyed, going on still toward the south [Gen. 12:9].

South is the right direction to go for warmer weather; so this man is moving south. He has itchy feet. He's a nomad.

Now we come to the blot in his life, actually the second one.

ABRAHAM'S LAPSE OF FAITH

And there was a famine in the land: and Abram went down into Egypt to sojourn there; for the famine was grievous in the land [Gen. 12:10].

Abram was in the land, and this was the place of blessing. God never told him to leave. But a famine was in the land, and I think one morning Abram pushed back the flap of his tent, looked out, and said, "Sarai, it looks like everybody's going to Egypt. There's a famine, you know, and it's getting worse. Maybe we ought to think about going down." And I suppose Sarai said, "Anything you want to do, Abram. I'm your wife and I'll go with you." After a few days had gone by and Abram had talked to some of these travelers (probably coming from north of where he was living and bringing the news that the famine was getting worse and was moving south) I imagine that he said to Sarai one evening, "I think we had better pack up and go to Egypt." So Abram and Sarai start down to Egypt.

Notice that *God* had not told him to do that. When God had appeared to him the last time, He had said, "This is *it*, Abram, this is the land I am going to give you. You will be a blessing, and I am going to bless you here." But, you see, Abram didn't believe God. He went down into the land of Egypt. In the Bible, Egypt is a picture of the world. You will find that all the way through. I think it is still a picture of the world—this was my opinion of it when I was there. But Abram went down to Egypt.

It's amazing how the world draws Christians today. So many of them rationalize. They'll say, "You know, brother McGee, we're not able to come to church on Sunday night because we have to get up and go to work Monday morning." Well, almost everybody has to do that. And it's amazing that those same people can go to a banquet on a week night and sit through a long-winded program with lots of music and lots of talk and not worry about

getting up for work the next morning. It's amazing how the world draws Christians today and how they can rationalize.

I think that if you had met Abram going down to Egypt and had said, "Wait a minute, Abram, you're going the wrong direction—you should be staying in the land," that Abram could have given you a very good reason. He might have said, "Look, my sheep are getting pretty thin and there's not any pasture for them. Since there's plenty of grazing land for them down in Egypt, we're going down there." And that's where they went.

However, immediately there is a problem, and it concerns Sarai because she is a beautiful woman.

And it came to pass, when he was come near to enter into Egypt, that he said unto Sarai his wife, Behold now, I know that thou art a fair woman to look upon:

Therefore it shall come to pass, when the Egyptians shall see thee, that they shall say, This is his wife: and they will kill me, but they will save thee alive [Gen. 12:11–12].

As you probably know, over along the northwest shore of the Dead Sea, ancient scrolls were found in the caves there, and they are known as the Dead Sea Scrolls. At first the unbelieving scholars thought that they had found something that would disprove the Bible. But have you noticed how silent the higher critics have become? They just don't seem to have found anything that contradicts the Bible.

Among the scrolls was a set which couldn't be unrolled because they were so fragile—they had been wrapped so long that they would just shatter and come to pieces. One name could be seen, the name Lamech, so they were called part of the book of Lamech and said to be one of the apocryphal books of the Bible. Boy, how incorrect that was! The nation Israel bought them, and in the museum the experts began to moisten and soften them until they were unrolled. The scholars found that they contained Genesis 12, 13, 14, and 15, not in the Bible text but rather an interpretation of it. In the part that deals with chapter 12, it tells about the beauty of Sarai, actually describing her features and telling how beautiful she was. It confirms what we read of her in the Word of God.

The same scroll gives a description of Abram's exploration after God told him to "walk through the land in the length of it and in the breadth of it" (Gen. 13:17). The scroll gives a first person account by Abram of his journey. It confirms what the Bible has said about the land's beauty and fertility. The eyewitness (whether or not it was really Abram, we do not know) certainly confirmed the Bible record. A great many people who visit that land today can't understand how it could be called a land of milk and honey. Well, in the Book of Deuteronomy we learn what caused the desolation that is seen there today. But it was a glorious land in Abram's day.

However, there were periods of famine, and Abram left the land and went down to Egypt during such a time.

As Abram neared Egypt, he recognized that he would get into difficulty because of the beauty of his wife. So he said to Sarai,

Say, I pray thee, thou art my sister: that it may be well with me for thy sake; and my soul shall live because of thee [Gen. 12:13].

"Say, I pray thee, thou art my sister." That was half a lie, as we shall see. Half a lie is sometimes worse than a whole lie, and it certainly was intended to deceive. Abram's fears were well founded because Pharaoh did take Sarai. We know from the Book of Esther that in those days there was a period of preparation for a woman to become a wife of a ruler. And during that period of preparation, God "plagued Pharaoh and his house with great plagues," and let him know that he was not to take Sarai as his wife.

And Pharaoh called Abram, and said, What is this that thou hast done unto me? why didst thou not tell me that she was thy wife?

Why saidst thou, She is my sister? so I might have taken her to me to wife: now therefore behold thy wife, take her, and go thy way.

And Pharaoh commanded his men concerning him: and they sent him away, and his wife, and all that he had [Gen. 12:18–20].

God, you see, was overruling in the lives of Abram and Sarai, but God did not *appear* to him while he was in the land of Egypt.

CHAPTER 13

***THEME:** Abraham separates from Lot; Lot goes to Sodom; God appears to Abraham and reaffirms His promise*

In chapter 13 we see the return of Abram from the land of Egypt. Abram and Lot leave Egypt and return to the land of promise. Lot separates from Abram and goes to Sodom, and then God appears to Abram for the third time. As long as Abram is in the land of Egypt and as long as he is still holding on to Lot, God does not appear to him. The minute that he comes back to the land and there is the separation from Lot, God appears to him.

ABRAHAM SEPARATES FROM LOT

And Abram went up out of Egypt, he, and his wife, and all that he had, and Lot with him, into the south.

And Abram was very rich in cattle, in silver, and in gold [Gen. 13:1–2].

Abram was the John D. Rockefeller of that day. He was a very wealthy man at this time.

And he went on his journeys from the south even to Beth-el, unto the place where his tent had been at the beginning, between Beth-el and Hai [Gen. 13:3].

Abram went far north of Jerusalem. He had come to the south, around Hebron, and now he goes north of Jerusalem to Bethel.

Unto the place of the altar, which he had made there at the first: and there Abram called on the name of the LORD [Gen. 13:4].

Although he may stumble and fall, this man comes back to God. There is always a way back to the altar for Abram, the Prodigal Son, and any man or woman who wants to come back to God. The arms of the Father are open to receive them.

And Lot also, which went with Abram,

had flocks, and herds, and tents [Gen. 13:5].

Lot did pretty well down in the land of Egypt also.

And the land was not able to bear them, that they might dwell together: for their substance was great, so that they could not dwell together.

And there was a strife between the herdmen of Abram's cattle and the herdmen of Lot's cattle: and the Canaanite and the Perizzite dwelled then in the land [Gen. 13:6–7].

The Word of God is a marvelous Word if you just let it speak to you. Will you notice this: Abram got two things in the land of Egypt which caused him untold grief. One was riches, and the second was a little Egyptian maid by the name of Hagar. We will see more about her later. But now he has riches, and it causes him and Lot to have to separate—there is strife between them.

Did you notice this statement: "And the Canaanite and the Perizzite dwelled then in the land." Abram's herdsmen and Lot's herdsmen are fighting, and then Abram and Lot disagree. The very interesting thing is that then the Canaanite probably whispered over to the Perizzite, "Look at them! Fightin' again! When they came into this land and built an altar to the living and true God, how we looked up to Abram! When he first came here, we thought he was such a wonderful man. We knew he was honest, we knew he was truthful, but look at him now. Look at the strife they're having!" I do not think the Perizzite and the Canaanite were very well impressed by Abram and Lot at this time.

Let me say this to you, although it may step on your toes. I do not know your town, I do not know where you live, but if yours is like other towns and like the town I came from, the Methodists and the Baptists and the Presbyterians don't get along, and there is fighting. And when there are these internal fights in a church today, the unsaved man on the outside knows about it. May I say to you, he then says, "If that's Christianity, I don't want any part of it. I can get a fight outside. I don't need to join the church to get a fight." The Lord Jesus said to His own, and He says to the church today, "By this shall all men know that you are My disciples if you're fundamental and you organize a church." Oh, no! He said, "By this shall all men know that ye are my disciples, if ye have love one to another" (John 13:35). The

"Perizzite" and the "Canaanite"—those old rascals—know when your church is fighting on the inside, my friend.

I had an uncle who never came to know the Lord. My aunt used to weep and say, "Oh, he won't listen!" Do you know why? With her lived a sister, another aunt, and I used to go there sometimes on Sundays for dinner. Do you know what we had for dinner? Roast preacher! One of my aunts went to the Methodist church, the other went to the Presbyterian church, and oh, boy, did they try to outdo each other, talking about the preacher and the fights that were going on. I used to watch my uncle. He would just sit there and eat. Then he'd get up to leave and go down to his club for the afternoon. When he would come home in the evening, he wasn't drunk, but he sure had had several drinks. They never won him to Christ. There are a lot of people not being won today, my friend, because of the strife that is inside the church. This is an interesting thing: "the Canaanite and the Perizzite dwelled then in the land." And they still dwell in the land. They are right near *your* church, by the way.

And Abram said unto Lot, Let there be no strife, I pray thee, between me and thee, and between my herdmen and thy herdmen; for we be brethren.

Is not the whole land before thee? separate thyself, I pray thee, from me: if thou wilt take the left hand, then I will go to the right; or if thou depart to the right hand, then I will go to the left [Gen. 13:8–9].

It is Abram who makes the division. It took a big man to tell Lot this. In other words, Abram is saying that Lot could choose what he wanted and Abram would take what was left.

LOT GOES TO SODOM

And Lot lifted up his eyes, and beheld all the plain of Jordan, that it was well watered every where, before the LORD destroyed Sodom and Gomorrah, even as the garden of the LORD, like the land of Egypt, as thou comest unto Zoar [Gen. 13:10].

T hat was a beautiful spot in those days.

Then Lot chose him all the plain of Jordan; and Lot journeyed east: and they separated themselves the one from the other.

Abram dwelled in the land of Canaan,

plain, and pitched his tent toward Sodom [Gen. 13:11–12].

This is interesting. Probably during all the time Lot spent in that land with Abram, at night he would push back the flap of his tent and look out and say to Mrs. Lot, "Isn't that a beautiful spot down there?" In the morning he would get up and say, "My, it looks so attractive down there!" The grass is always greener in the other pasture. When the day came that Lot could make a decision and go, you know the direction he went. No man falls suddenly. It always takes place over a period of time. You lift the flap of your tent, and you pitch your tent toward Sodom—and that's the beginning. Lot lifted up his eyes, he saw the plain, and he headed in that direction. That is the biggest mistake he ever made in his life.

Lot did not know this:

But the men of Sodom were wicked and sinners before the LORD exceedingly [Gen. 13:13].

We will see later what happened to Lot and Mrs. Lot and the family down in Sodom.

GOD APPEARS TO ABRAHAM AND REAFFIRMS HIS PROMISE

And the LORD said unto Abram, after that Lot was separated from him, Lift up now thine eyes, and look from the place where thou art northward, and southward, and eastward, and westward [Gen. 13:14].

"And the LORD said unto Abram, after that Lot was separated from him"— here is the third appearance of God to this man. "Lift up now thine eyes, and look from the place where thou art northward, and southward, and eastward, and westward." This is the land God is going to give him. As God continued to appear to Abram and later on to the other patriarchs, God put sideboards around that land. In other words, He put a border to it and told them exactly what the land was. He was very specific about it.

May I just interject this thought? This ought to get rid of that song, "Beautiful Isle of Somewhere." If there ever was a song that needed *not* to be sung at a funeral, that is the one. Can you imagine Abram looking northward, eastward, southward, and westward and singing "Beautiful Isle of Somewhere" when he was standing right in the middle of it? Heaven is a real place as truly as the Promised Land is a

real place—*not* a beautiful isle of somewhere. It is a very definite place about which the Word of God is quite specific. In the Book of Revelation God makes it so specific; He puts the boundary right around it, and we can know something about it. God does not deal with that which is theoretical, but with that which is actual and real.

For all the land which thou seest, to thee will I give it, and to thy seed for ever.

And I will make thy seed as the dust of the earth: so that if a man can number the dust of the earth, then shall thy seed also be numbered [Gen. 13:15–16].

Notice what God does for this man. He labels the land and tells Abram that he is in it. He also again confirms the fact that Abram is going to have a tremendous offspring—which he has had.

Arise, walk through the land in the length of it and in the breadth of it; for I will give it unto thee [Gen. 13:17].

It is very interesting that one of the Dead Sea Scrolls describes this particular section of Genesis, and it gives a first-person account by Abraham of the land. It was a wonderful land in that day.

Then Abram removed his tent, and came and dwelt in the plain of Mamre, which is in Hebron, and built there an altar unto the LORD [Gen. 13:18].

Abram was quite an altar builder. You could always tell where Abram had been because he left a testimony. Man has left a footprint on the moon. They've left a flag up there and a little motto saying, "We have come in peace"—but they did not leave the Bible, the Word of God. That reveals the difference between the thinking of Abram and the thinking of the age and period in which we live today. The important thing to Abram was an altar to the Lord, and that is exactly what he built.

One of the meanings of *Mamre* is "richness," and *Hebron* means "communion." That is a marvelous place to dwell. In our day we can be fairly certain that we have located the tree where Abram was, and the well that is there— I have been there. It is quite an interesting spot between Hebron and Mamre, and that is where Abram dwelt. It is a good place to be: in the place of richness and of communion with God. This seems to have been Abram's home, and this is where he is buried.

CHAPTER 14

THEME: *Kings of the east capture Sodom and Gomorrah; Abraham delivers Lot; Abraham refuses booty*

In chapter 14 we find the first recorded war, one in which Abram delivers Lot; and we find the appearance of the first priest, at which time Abram is blessed by Melchizedek. These are the two great truths that are here. In one sense, this is a most remarkable chapter. It does not seem to fit in with the story at all. It seems that it could be left out, that there is a continuity without it. But it is one of the most important chapters in the Book of Genesis.

KINGS OF THE EAST CAPTURE SODOM AND GOMORRAH

And it came to pass in the days of Amraphel king of Shinar, Arioch king of Ellasar, Chedorlaomer king of Elam, and Tidal king of nations;

That these made war with Bera king of Sodom, and with Birsha king of Gomorrah, Shinab king of Admah, and Shemeber king of Zeboiim, and the king of Bela, which is Zoar [Gen. 14:1–2].

First of all, let me say that this is an historical document. In the first eleven verses, it is recorded that the kings of the east defeat the kings of Sodom and Gomorrah. For quite a few years, the critical, radical scholars rejected this, saying that these men's names do not appear in secular history at all and that this is a rather ridiculous story. But did you know that the names of these kings have been found on monuments and tablets, showing that they did exist? In fact, Amraphel is now known to be the Hammurabi of other secular history. The record that we have here is tremendously significant.

There was war, and this is the first war that is mentioned in Scripture. Mankind began early in making war. Although this is the first war recorded, I do not know that it is the first war that ever took place—I do not think that the writer intends to give that impression. The reason it is recorded is because Lot, the nephew of Abram, is involved.

All these were joined together in the vale of Siddim, which is the salt sea.

Twelve years they served Chedorlaomer, and in the thirteenth year they rebelled [Gen. 14:3–4].

The rebellion is what brought the kings of the east against Sodom and Gomorrah. These kings evidently had fought before, because the kings of the east had subjugated these cities of the plain, but the cities had reached the place of rebellion. In verses 5–11 we read the account of how the kings of the east overcame the kings who had joined together around the lower part of the Dead Sea.

And they took Lot, Abram's brother's son, who dwelt in Sodom, and his goods, and departed [Gen. 14:12].

Lot lived in Sodom and was taken captive. The reason this war is significant to the record here is that it reveals what Abram is going to do in connection with his nephew.

ABRAHAM DELIVERS LOT

And there came one that had escaped, and told Abram the Hebrew; for he dwelt in the plain of Mamre the Amorite, brother of Eshcol, and brother of Aner: and these were confederate with Abram [Gen. 14:13].

When the kings of the east left the area of Sodom and Gomorrah with their captives, they moved north along the west bank of the Dead Sea, which was not too far from Hebron and Mamre where Abram was dwelling. You can stand where Abram stood in that day and see any movement that takes place down toward the Dead Sea. So that when word was brought to Abram, he immediately began to pursue the enemy as he moved north.

"And these were confederate with Abram." Notice that Abram has a group of men that are with him. They had to stand together in that day because of the pursuit or the approach of an enemy. They either had to hang together or hang separately.

And when Abram heard that his brother was taken captive, he armed his trained servants, born in his own house, three hundred and eighteen, and pursued them unto Dan [Gen. 14:14].

This is startling, and it reveals something of the extent of Abram's possessions. This gives you some conception of the number of servants Abram had. In his own household, he could arm 318. How many did he have that he could not arm? For instance, there would also be women and children and the old folk—but he could arm 318. To have that many hired hands indicates that Abram was carrying on quite a business of raising cattle and sheep.

"And pursued them unto Dan"—Dan is up in the north.

And he divided himself against them, he and his servants, by night, and smote them, and pursued them unto Hobah, which is on the left hand of Damascus [Gen. 14:15].

Abram pursued these men all the way north to Damascus—that is quite a stretch. Apparently, what Abram did was to divide his servants. One group made an attack, probably from the rear as they were pursuing them. The other group went around, and when the enemy turned to fight the first group, the second group came down upon them. As a result, Abram was able to get a victory. At least he was able to scatter them so that they fled across the desert, leaving the people and the booty they had captured.

And he brought back all the goods, and also brought again his brother Lot, and his goods, and the women also, and the people [Gen. 14:16].

You see that they were taking the women and the other people as slaves. Abram has done a tremendous thing, and he has done it because of his nephew Lot. That is the reason all of this is mentioned here. This is very definitely not an extraneous chapter. It is a part of the life of Abram, and it is very important.

And the king of Sodom went out to meet him after his return from the slaughter of Chedorlaomer, and of the kings that were with him, at the valley of Shaveh, which is the king's dale [Gen. 14:17].

The king of Sodom went out to meet Abram. But now someone else is going to come out and meet Abram, and it is a good thing that he did, because the king of Sodom is going to put a grave temptation before Abram.

And Melchizedek king of Salem brought forth bread and wine: and he was the priest of the most high God.

And he blessed him, and said, Blessed be Abram of the most high God, possessor of heaven and earth [Gen. 14:18–19].

I have several questions here, and I am sure that you do. To begin with, where in the world did this man Melchizedek come from? He just

walks out on the page of Scripture with bread and wine, he blesses Abram, and then he walks off the page of Scripture—that's it. I wonder where he came from, I wonder where he is going, and I wonder what his business is.

I find out that he is king of Salem, but he is also priest of the most high God. But now I have another question: How did he find out about "the most high God"? He found out somewhere. *El Elohim* is the most high God, the Creator of heaven and earth; in other words, the living God, the God of Genesis 1, the God of Noah, and the God of Enoch. This is the One—He is *not* a local deity. H. C. Leupold in his book on Genesis says that this is "strictly a monotheistic conception." Dr. Samuel M. Zwemer, in his *Origin of Religion,* says that this reveals that there was monotheism before polytheism. In other words, all men had a knowledge of the living and true God. "Because that, when they knew God, they glorified him not as God, neither were thankful; but became vain in their imaginations, and their foolish heart was darkened" (Rom. 1:21). Paul goes on to say that men continued to go down to the point where they began to worship the creature more than the Creator.

Yet back in Abram's day here is a man who is high priest for the world of that day. He has a knowledge of the living and true God. He is a priest of the living and true God. He comes out, bringing bread and wine to Abram—those are the elements of the Lord's Supper! I wonder what he had in mind? How much did Melchizedek know?

Melchizedek is mentioned three times in Scripture. In addition to this passage in Genesis, he is also mentioned in Psalm 110:4, which is prophetic of Christ: ". . . Thou art a priest for ever after the order of Melchizedek." Finally, he is mentioned several times in Hebrews. After reading Hebrews, I know why nothing is said about his origin in Genesis. Nothing is said about his parents, and that is strange because the Book of Genesis is the book of families. It tells about the beginnings of these families. Every time we see mentioned a man who is important in the genealogical line (as this man Melchizedek is), his parents are mentioned. "He is the son of So-and-so," or "these are the generations of So-and-so." But we do not have the generations of Melchizedek. The writer to the Hebrews makes it very clear that the reason there is no record of Melchizedek's father or mother or beginning or ending of days is because the priesthood of Christ, in its inception, is after the order of Melchizedek. In *service*—in what our Lord did in the sacrifice of Himself and in His entering the Holy of Holies, which is heaven today—Christ's priesthood follows the order of Aaron. But in His *person*, our Lord had no beginning or ending of days, and His priesthood follows the order of Melchizedek. As King, Christ is son of Abraham, He is son of David—the Gospel of Matthew tells us that. But in the Gospel of John we read: "In the beginning was the Word, and the Word was with God, and the Word was God. . . . And the Word was made flesh, and dwelt among us, (and we beheld his glory, the glory as of the only begotten of the Father,) full of grace and truth" (John 1:1, 14). He had no beginning or ending of days as far as creation is concerned—He is the eternal God. He came out of heaven's glory, the Word was made flesh, and we beheld His glory. We have in Melchizedek a marvelous picture of the Lord Jesus Christ.

"Brought forth bread and wine." I know now why Melchizedek does this. It is because the Scriptures say, "For as often as ye eat this bread, and drink this cup, ye do shew the Lord's death till he come" (1 Cor. 11:26). Melchizedek is anticipating the death of Christ here!

On that basis he blesses Abram: "Blessed be Abram of the most high God, possessor of heaven and earth"—*El Elohim*, the Creator. This man was the high priest of the world in that day. The Lord Jesus is the great High Priest for the world today. The Lord Jesus is after the order of Melchizedek—not Aaron—as set forth here. Aaron was just for Israel and just for a tabernacle. In His person, Christ is after the order of Melchizedek.

And blessed be the most high God, which hath delivered thine enemies into thy hand. And he gave him tithes of all [Gen. 14:20].

Abram paid tithes to Melchizedek here at the very beginning. How did he know about paying tithes? Obviously, he had a revelation from God concerning this—as well as concerning other matters.

ABRAHAM REFUSES BOOTY

And the king of Sodom said unto Abram, Give me the persons, and take the goods to thyself [Gen. 14:21].

This is the temptation. According to the Code of Hammurabi of that day, this man

Abram had a perfect right to the booty and even to the persons. But the king of Sodom is clever; he says, "Give us the persons, and you take the booty—it's yours." That was a temptation to Abram. Forever after, when anybody would say, "That man Abram is certainly a wealthy man. God has blessed him," I think that the king of Sodom would have said, "Blessed him, my foot! God didn't bless him. *I* gave it to him; *I'm* the one who made him rich!" Abram knew that. Listen to him now:

And Abram said to the king of Sodom, I have lift up mine hand unto the LORD, the most high God, the possessor of heaven and earth [Gen. 14:22].

Abram is still under the influence and the blessing of Melchizedek, and it is a good thing he met Melchizedek. God always prepares us for any temptation that comes to us. He says that He will never let any temptation come to us that we are not able to bear (see 1 Cor. 10:13). God had prepared Abram for this one.

That I will not take from a thread even to a shoelatchet, and that I will not take any thing that is thine, lest thou shouldest say, I have made Abram rich [Gen. 14:23].

When Abram started out, he made a covenant with God, probably saying, "Oh, God, I am not entering this war in order to get booty. I'm not after possessions. I want to restore and recover my nephew Lot." And God permitted him to do that. Now Abram tells this to the king of Sodom as a witness to him. Abram could have said, "I worship the living and the true God. I have taken an oath that I would not take anything. You can't make me rich. I won't let you give me a shoestring or a piece of thread because, if you did even that, you would run around and say that you made me rich. If I get rich, God will have to do it."

Save only that which the young men have eaten, and the portion of the men which went with me, Aner, Eshcol, and Mamre; let them take their portion [Gen. 14:24].

But Abram says, "These other men have a right to the booty, and they can have it; but I am not taking anything. What the young men who are with me have eaten is their pay for serving you and delivering you. But as for me—you cannot give me a thing."

THEME: God's revelation of Himself as shield and reward; Abraham's faith; God's covenant with Abraham

GOD'S REVELATION OF HIMSELF AS SHIELD AND REWARD

We come to one of the high points of the Bible here in chapter 15.

After these things the word of the LORD came unto Abram in a vision, saying, Fear not, Abram: I am thy shield, and thy exceeding great reward [Gen. 15:1].

This now is the fourth time that God has appeared to Abram. God is developing this man and bringing him farther along. God does well to appear to him now because Abram has taken a tremendous step of faith in going out and rescuing Lot and in turning down the booty which the king of Sodom offered him.

"Fear not, Abram: I am thy shield." My friend, this is lovely; this is wonderful. The record does not tell us this, but let me suggest to you that perhaps during the battle, Abram got in real danger and wondered whether he would come out of it alive. God simply reminds him, "I'm your shield, Abram. I'm your shield."

"And thy exceeding great reward." In other words, God says, "You did well to turn down the booty. I am your reward; I intend to reward you." Oh, what God can do with a man today when he is willing just to believe God and look to Him!

If you think Abram is one of these pious boys who gets his halo shined every morning, you are wrong. Abram is very practical, and he is going to get right down to the nitty-gritty now. I think that God likes us to do that. I wish that we could get rid of this false piosity and the hypocritical attitude that so many fundamentalists assume today. Notice what this man Abram says—it is quite wonderful:

And Abram said, LORD God, what wilt thou give me, seeing I go childless, and the steward of my house is this Eliezer of Damascus?

And Abram said, Behold, to me thou hast given no seed: and, lo, one born in my house is mine heir [Gen. 15:2–3].

What Abram is saying to God is this: "I don't want more riches; I don't need that. The thing that's on my heart is that I'm childless and I want a son. You have promised to make me a father of nations and that my offspring will be as numberless as the sand on the seashore. But I don't have even one child!" According to the law of that day, the Code of Hammurabi, Eliezer, his steward, his head servant, who had an offspring, would in time inherit if Abram did not have a child.

And, behold, the word of the LORD came unto him, saying, This shall not be thine heir; but he that shall come forth out of thine own bowels shall be thine heir [Gen. 15:4].

God is very practical when a man will be practical with Him. He says, "I am going to give *you* a son, Abram. I am going to give you a son."

Now God took Abram by the hand and brought him forth into the night.

And he brought him forth abroad, and said, Look now toward heaven, and tell the stars, if thou be able to number them: and he said unto him, So shall thy seed be [Gen. 15:5].

This is remarkable. First God said to him that his offspring would be as numberless as the sand on the seashore, and now He says they will be as numberless as the stars in heaven. Abram could not number the stars. He could see approximately four thousand, but there were probably over fifty thousand in that area where he was looking. Abram couldn't number his offspring, and you couldn't do it today.

This man Abraham actually has two seeds. He has a physical seed, the nation Israel, and he has a spiritual seed, the church. How does the church become Abraham's spiritual seed? By faith. Paul told the Galatians that they were the sons of Abraham by faith in Jesus Christ—not in a natural line, but a spiritual seed (see Gal. 3:29).

I had the privilege of speaking to a group of very fine young Jewish men many years ago in Nashville, Tennessee. I had known some of them before I was saved and had been a very close friend of theirs. I spoke on the glories of the Mosaic law and told them that the fulfillment of it was in Christ. I began by telling them I was glad to speak to them because I knew that they were sons of Abraham. But when I told them I was a son of Abraham also, they looked in amazement one to another. And then I told them how I was a son of Abraham.

Included in God's promise were these two seeds of Abraham, and this is a very wonderful truth.

ABRAHAM'S FAITH

And he believed in the LORD; and he counted it to him for righteousness [Gen. 15:6].

This is one of the greatest statements in the Scriptures: "And he believed in the LORD." What this means is that Abram said amen to God. God has said, "I will do this for you," and Abram says to God, "I believe You. Amen. I believe it." And that was counted to him for righteousness.

Paul speaks of this in his epistle to the Romans: "What shall we say then that Abraham our father, as pertaining to the flesh, hath found? For if Abraham were justified by works, he hath whereof to glory; but not before God. For what saith the scripture? Abraham believed God, and it was counted unto him for righteousness. Now to him that worketh is the reward not reckoned of grace, but of debt. But to him that worketh not, but believeth on him that justifieth the ungodly, his faith is counted for righteousness" (Rom. 4:1–5). "What shall we say then that Abraham our father, as pertaining to the flesh, hath found"—or, that Abraham has found as pertaining to the flesh. I think that rewording brings out the meaning better.

"For what saith the scripture? Abraham believed God, and it (that is, his faith) was counted unto him for righteousness"—for that is what it was *not*, but that is what God counted it.

"Now to him that worketh is the reward not reckoned of grace, but of debt." If you can *work* for your salvation, then God *owes* it to you. But, my friend, God never saves by any other means except grace. He has never had any other method of saving, and if you ever get saved, it will be because you believe God, you accept Christ as your Savior, and you believe that God has provided salvation for you.

"But to him that worketh not [no works at all], but believeth on him that justifieth the ungodly [What kind of folk? Ungodly folk.], his faith is counted for righteousness." His faith is counted for what it is not, that is, for righteousness.

Abraham just believed God. He just accepted what God said, and he believed God. That is the way you get saved: to believe that God has done something for you, that Christ died for you and rose again. God will declare you righteous by simply accepting Christ.

In the third chapter of Galatians, we have this same great truth: "Even as Abraham believed God, and it was accounted to him for righteousness. Know ye therefore that they which are of faith, the same are the children of Abraham. And the scripture, foreseeing that God would justify the heathen through faith, preached before the gospel unto Abraham, saying, In thee shall all nations be blessed. So then they which be of faith are blessed with faithful Abraham" (Gal. 3:6–9). The faith which Abraham had made him faithful to God, but he was not saved by being faithful. He was saved by believing God. This is all-important for us to see.

GOD'S COVENANT WITH ABRAHAM

And he said unto him, I am the LORD that brought thee out of Ur of the Chaldees, to give thee this land to inherit it.

And he said, LORD God, whereby shall I know that I shall inherit it? [Gen. 15:7–8].

Again, Abram is a very practical man. He believes in dealing with reality, and I think we need to do that. We need reality today in our Christian lives. If reality is not in your life, there is nothing there. A great many people just play church today. Abram is very practical. He wants to know something, and he would like to have something in writing.

Do you know what God is probably going to tell him? God is going to say, "Abram, I'm glad you asked Me, because I am going to meet you down at the courthouse; I will go before a notary public, and I will make real this contract which I am making with you. You are going to have a son. Meet Me down there, and I will sign on the dotted line." Now, before you write me a letter and protest, let me say that you are right, that the Bible says nothing about God meeting Abram at the courthouse, and it says nothing about going to a notary public, but in the terms of the law of our day, that is exactly what God said to Abram.

Here is what God told Abram to do:

And he said unto him, Take me an heifer of three years old, and a she goat of three years old, and a ram of three years old, and a turtledove, and a young pigeon.

And he took unto him all these, and divided them in the midst, and laid each

piece one against another: but the birds divided he not [Gen. 15:9–10].

God told Abram to prepare a sacrifice. He was to get a heifer, a she goat, and a ram and divide or split them down the middle and put one half on one side and one half on the other. The turtledove and the pigeon he did not divide, but put one over here and one over there.

When men made a contract in that day, this is the way they made it. Suppose one man agreed to buy sheep from another one. They would prepare a sacrifice in this manner. The party of the first part joined hands with the party of the second part, they stated their contract, and they they walked through the sacrifice. In that day this corresponded to going down to the courthouse and signing before a notary public in our day. So we see that God is using with Abram the legal procedure of his day.

In Jeremiah 34:18 we have a reference to this custom that was prevalent in that land, not just among these people, but among all peoples in that day: "And I will give the men that have transgressed my covenant, which have not performed the words of the covenant which they had made before me, when they cut the calf in twain, and passed between the parts thereof." The method in that day was to take the sacrifice and divide it, and the men would then make the contract.

Notice that Abram got everything ready according to God's instructions.

And when the fowls came down upon the carcases, Abram drove them away [Gen. 15:11].

This is a very human scene. Abram gets everything ready, and while he is waiting for the Lord, the fowls of the air come down—the buzzard and the crow come down upon the carrion. Abram is there shooing them away, for they are ready to swoop down upon the sacrifice. If you had been there and had seen all this display of the sacrifices, knowing the custom of the day, you might have said, "Well, brother Abram, apparently the one you're making a contract with hasn't shown up. I guess he's late!" Abram would have said, "No, I don't think He's late. He just told me to get things ready and that He would be here to make the contract."

And when the sun was going down, a deep sleep fell upon Abram; and, lo, an horror of great darkness fell upon him [Gen. 15:12].

Abram is paralyzed in sleep and put aside. It seems very strange that God would paralyze him in sleep when he is supposed to be making a contract, but this is an unusual contract. God is going to go through the sacrifices because God is promising something, but Abram is not going to go through because Abram is not promising to do a thing. Abram just believed God—that's all.

That is exactly what took place over nineteen hundred years ago when God sent His Son. God the Father so loved the world that He gave His only begotten Son. And the Son agreed to come to the earth and die for the sins of the world—your sin and mine—that whosoever would believe in Him (simply accept His gift) might not perish but have everlasting life (see John 3:16). I wasn't even there nineteen hundred years ago to make a contract, but God the Father and God the Son were there, and the Son went to the cross, and He died for my sins. I was paralyzed by sin. I could not promise anything, and you couldn't either.

Abram did not promise anything either. Suppose that God had said to Abram, "Abram if you will just promise to say your prayers every night, I am going to do this for you." And suppose Abram forgot to pray one night. The contract is shot—it's broken—and therefore God does not need to make His part good. But God said that He would do His part, and He is asking man to do just one thing: to say amen to Him—that is, to believe Him. You are to believe God and believe what He has done. My friend, to believe God is salvation.

Years ago there was a dear little Scottish mother whose son had gone away to college in Glasgow and had come back an unbeliever. She talked with the boy and told about how wonderful God was and that she was sure of her salvation. The son had become skeptical, and he was a little provoked. Finally he said, "How do you know you're saved? Your little soul doesn't amount to anything." He began to compare her to the vastness of the universe and said that God could forget all about her and she couldn't be sure of her salvation. She didn't say anything, but just kept serving the boy's breakfast. Finally, when she had finished, she sat down with him and said, "You know, son, I've been thinking about it. Maybe you're right. Maybe my little soul doesn't amount to much. Maybe in the vastness of God's universe, He wouldn't miss me at all. But if He doesn't save me, He's going to lose more than I'm going to lose. I would lose only my insignificant little soul, but He would lose His reputation because He *promised* to save my soul. He agreed to do it: 'that whosoever believeth in him should not perish, but have everlasting life.' " God is the One who went through; God made the contract.

And he said unto Abram, Know of a surety that thy seed shall be a stranger in a land that is not theirs, and shall serve them; and they shall afflict them four hundred years [Gen. 15:13].

In the Scriptures it is predicted that the Hebrew people would be put out of the land three times. This is the first time. It is also predicted that they would return back to the land, and they did this time. Later on it was the Babylonian captivity. They were carried into captivity, and they returned. In A.D. 70 Jerusalem was destroyed, and for the third time they were scattered. They have never returned from that. Their current presence in the land is by no means a fulfillment of Scripture. But according to the Word of God, they will come back someday exactly as it predicts.

And also that nation, whom they shall serve, will I judge: and afterward shall they come out with great substance.

And thou shalt go to thy fathers in peace; thou shalt be buried in a good old age [Gen. 15:14–15].

They did come out of Egypt with great substance, but Abram would not live to see it, of course.

But in the fourth generation they shall come hither again; for the iniquity of the Amorites is not yet full [Gen. 15:16].

God is saying to Abram, "I cannot put you in this land now because I love Amorites also, and I want to give them a chance to turn to Me." And God gave the Amorites four hundred years—that is a long time, is it not?—to see if they would turn to Him. The only one in that land who turned to Him was that Canaanite woman, Rahab the harlot. She turned to God; she believed Him. All God asks *you* to do is to believe Him. God gave the Amorites this great period of opportunity.

And it came to pass, that, when the sun went down, and it was dark, behold a smoking furnace, and a burning lamp that passed between those pieces [Gen. 15:17].

Both of these speak of Christ. The furnace, of course, speaks of judgment. The lamp speaks of Him as the light of the world.

In the same day the LORD made a covenant with Abram, saying, Unto thy seed have I given this land, from the river of Egypt unto the great river, the river Euphrates:

The Kenites, and the Kenizzites, and the Kadmonites,

And the Hittites, and the Perizzites, and the Rephaims,

And the Amorites, and the Canaanites, and the Girgashites, and the Jebusites [Gen. 15:18–21].

God now marks out the land that He is promising to Abram. By the way, what did Abram promise to do? Nothing. He believed God. And God will save *you*—save you by grace—if you will believe what He has done for you.

CHAPTER 16

THEME: Sarai's suggestion; Hagar flees; the tests of Abraham

As we come to this chapter, I must confess that I almost wish it were not in the Bible. After Abram rose to the heights in chapter 15, you would say that he certainly is treading on high places—but he is not perfect. In chapter 16 we see the lapse of this man's faith relative to Sarai and Hagar, the Egyptian maid. We have here the unbelief of both Sarai and Abram, and the birth of Ishmael. This is certainly a letdown after the wonder of the previous chapter.

SARAI'S SUGGESTION

Now Sarai Abram's wife bare him no children: and she had an handmaid, an Egyptian, whose name was Hagar [Gen. 16:1].

Abram got two things down in the land of Egypt which really caused him trouble: one was wealth, and the other was this little Egyptian maid.

And Sarai said unto Abram, Behold now, the LORD hath restrained me from bearing: I pray thee, go in unto my maid; it may be that I may obtain children by her. And Abram hearkened to the voice of Sarai [Gen. 16:2].

The thing that Sarai suggested was the common practice of that day. When a wife could not bear a child, there was the concubine. Now don't say that God approved it. God did not approve of this at all. This was Sarai's idea, and Abram listened to her. It looks like he is surrendering his position as head of the home here, and he followed her suggestion.

And Sarai Abram's wife took Hagar her maid the Egyptian, after Abram had dwelt ten years in the land of Canaan, and gave her to her husband Abram to be his wife [Gen. 16:3].

This little Egyptian maid becomes a concubine, and this is not according to God's will. God is not going to accept the offspring at all—He didn't; He wouldn't. Why? Because it was *wrong*. Don't say that God approved this. All you can say is that this is in the record because it is an historical fact.

And he went in unto Hagar, and she conceived: and when she saw that she had conceived, her mistress was despised in her eyes [Gen. 16:4].

Hagar said, "I've mothered a child of Abram, and Sarai couldn't do it." She looked down on Sarai, you see.

And Sarai said unto Abram, My wrong be upon thee: I have given my maid into thy bosom; and when she saw that she had conceived, I was despised in her eyes: the LORD judge between me and thee [Gen. 16:5].

Don't pass this verse by. Don't assume that God approved of this. God says that it is wrong, and now Sarai sees that she has done wrong. "My wrong be upon thee"—she is *wrong*, my friend. God will not accept this, and it is going to be a real heartbreak to old Abram. But, you see, Abram and Sarai are not really trusting God as they should. After all, Abram at this time is nearly ninety years old and Sarai eighty. I think they have come to the conclusion that they are not going to have a child. Sarai could probably rationalize and say, "I think maybe this is the way God wants us to do it, for this is the custom of the day." It *was* the custom of that day, but it was contrary to God's way of doing things. We get the wrong impression if we think that just because something is recorded in the Bible God approves of it. The Bible is inspired in that it is an accurate record, but there are many things God does not approve of that are recorded in His Word.

The moral implications that you and I read into this are not quite here in the historical record. Abram and Sarai were brought up in Ur of the Chaldees where this was a common practice, and the moral angle is not the thing that for them was so wrong. The terrible thing was that they just did not believe God. The wrong that they committed by Abram taking Sarai's maid Hagar was a sin, and God treated it as such. But today we reverse the emphasis and say that taking a concubine is a sin, but we do not pay too much attention to the unbelief. Yet the unbelief was the major sin here; that is, it was lots blacker than the other.

HAGAR FLEES

But Abram said unto Sarai, Behold, thy maid is in thy hand; do to her as it pleaseth thee. And when Sarai dealt hardly with her, she fled from her face [Gen. 16:6].

Hagar took off—she ran away—and this would probably have meant death to her and certainly to the child she was carrying.

And the angel of the LORD found her by a fountain of water in the wilderness, by the fountain in the way to Shur [Gen. 16:7].

I am inclined to believe that the Angel of the Lord is none other than the preincarnate Christ. This is characteristic of Him: He is always out looking for the lost. Hagar had traveled quite a distance from home.

And he said, Hagar, Sarai's maid, whence camest thou? and whither wilt thou go? And she said, I flee from the face of my mistress Sarai.

And the angel of the LORD said unto her, Return to thy mistress, and submit thyself under her hands.

And the angel of the LORD said unto her, I will multiply thy seed exceedingly, that it shall not be numbered for multitude [Gen. 16:8–10].

In the fourth chapter of the Epistle to the Galatians, Paul uses this as an allegory. He speaks there of Hagar and her offspring as being Mount Sinai where the Mosaic law was given, and he speaks of the legality and the bondage of that law. Then he speaks of Sarai as being the one who is free. The point is that the one who belonged to Abram was Sarai—she was his wife. Many people today want to take on something different; they want to get under the law. But, my friend, as believers we have been joined to Christ. The church has been espoused to Christ, Paul says, as a chaste virgin and will someday be the bride of Christ. Therefore may I say to you, you do not want to take on the law. The law is another one that you and I just don't need; it is like Hagar, and that is the point that Paul is making in Galatians.

This is going to be a great sorrow, not only to Sarai (it already has been to her), but it is going to be an even greater sorrow to Abram later on. Hagar now comes back to give birth to a boy, that boy who happens to be Abram's son.

And the angel of the LORD said unto her, Behold, thou art with child, and shalt bear a son, and shalt call his name Ishmael; because the LORD hath heard thy affliction.

And he will be a wild man; his hand will be against every man, and every man's hand against him; and he shall dwell in the presence of all his brethren [Gen. 16:11–12].

Have you looked at this verse in light of about four thousand years of history in the Middle East? What is going on out there today? The descendants of Ishmael are wild men—that has been the story of those Bedouin tribes of the desert down through the centuries, and it is a fulfillment of the prophecy that God gave. They will tell you that they are sons of Abraham, but they are also sons of Ishmael. They are related to Abraham through Ishmael.

And she called the name of the LORD that spake unto her, Thou God seest me: for she said, Have I also here looked after him that seeth me?

Wherefore the well was called Beerlahairoi; behold, it is between Kadesh and Bered [Gen. 16:13–14].

How gracious God is to Hagar! It is not her sin, so God very graciously deals with her. Let me repeat that I believe the Angel of the Lord here is none other than the preincarnate Christ gone out to seek the lost again. He's that kind of Shepherd, and He brings to her this good word.

"And she called the name of the LORD that spake unto her, Thou God seest me." This is something new to her that she did not realize before. The Egyptians did have a very primitive idea and conception of God. "For she said, Have I also here looked after him that seeth me?" She is overwhelmed by the fact that she is seen of God. That doesn't seem to be very impressive to us today because we have a higher view of God than that. But wait just a minute! We probably come just as far short of really knowing about God as Hagar did. It is difficult for a little, finite man to conceive of the infinite God, and all of us come short of understanding and of knowing Him. I think that a theme which will engage us throughout the endless ages of eternity is just coming to know God. That is worthy of any man's study. To come to know God is something that will dignify a man's position throughout eternity.

And Hagar bare Abram a son: and Abram called his son's name, which Hagar bare, Ishmael.

And Abram was fourscore and six years old, when Hagar bare Ishmael to Abram [Gen. 16:15–16].

Remember that Ishmael was Abram's son. Abram was now eighty-six years old.

THE TESTS OF ABRAHAM

Before we go farther, I would like to make a recapitulation of the seven appearances of God to Abram, five of which we have already seen. There were certain failures in the life of Abram, but also there were successes. Actually, there were seven tests which God gave to him:

(1) God called Abram out of Ur of the Chaldees, his home, and Abram responded partially. His faith was weak and imperfect, but at least he moved out. Abram finally arrived safely in the land of Canaan, and God blessed him.

(2) Then there was a famine in the land of Canaan, and Abram fled from the land of Canaan to Egypt. There he acquired riches and Hagar—and both were stumbling blocks.

(3) Abram was given riches which are a real test. They have been a stumbling block to many a man, by the way. Frankly, I have always wished that the Lord would have let me have that kind of test rather than some of the others I've had! But nevertheless, I'm of the opinion that He could not have trusted me with

riches. Abram did not forget God, and he was certainly generous and magnanimous toward his nephew Lot. Riches resulted in his separation from Lot, and God appeared to him again.

(4) Abram was given power through his defeat of the kings of the east. That was a real test, for he happened to be the conqueror. This man Melchizedek met him, which I think strengthened Abram for the test, and so he refused the spoils of war. Afterwards, God appeared to Abram and encouraged him.

(5) God delayed giving Abram a son by his wife Sarai. Abram became impatient, and through the prompting of Sarai, he took matters into his own hands and moved outside the will of God. As a result, there was the birth of Ishmael. The Arabs of the desert today still plague the nation Israel, and they will keep right on doing that, I think, until the millennium.

Abraham's two final tests occur (6) at the destruction of Sodom and Gomorrah in chapter 18 and (7) at the offering of his son Isaac in chapter 22.

CHAPTER 17

THEME: *God gives Abraham a new name; God's covenant; Ishmael's inheritance*

Agreat many people feel that the seventeenth chapter is the most outstanding chapter of the Book of Genesis. Here God makes a covenant with Abram and confirms His promise to him about a son. He lets Abram know that Ishmael is not the one He promised to him. In one sense this chapter is the key to the Book of Genesis, and it may be a key to the entire Bible. God's covenant with Abram concerns two important items: a seed and a land. He reveals Himself to Abram by a new name—*El Shaddai*, the Almighty God—and He also gives Abram a new name. Up to this point his name was Abram; now it is changed to Abraham. *Abram* means "high father," and *Abraham* means "father of a multitude." That Ishmael was not the son God promised to Abraham is the thing this chapter makes very clear.

GOD GIVES ABRAHAM A NEW NAME

And when Abram was ninety years old and nine, the LORD appeared to Abram,

and said unto him, I am the Almighty God; walk before me, and be thou perfect [Gen. 17:1].

Think of that! Abram was eighty-six years old when Ishmael was born, and it was not until fourteen years later that Isaac was born.

"The Lord appeared to Abram, and said unto him, I am the Almighty God; walk before me, and be thou perfect." God says, "I am *El Shaddai*, the Almighty God"—this is a new name.

And I will make my covenant between me and thee, and will multiply thee exceedingly [Gen. 17:2].

Thirteen times in this chapter we find the word *covenant*. For it to appear thirteen times in twenty-seven verses obviously means that God is talking about the covenant. This is God's fifth appearance to Abram. He comes now not only to make the covenant, but also to reaffirm the promise of a son that He has made, which absolutely rules out this boy Ishmael, of course.

Paul, writing in the fourth chapter of Romans, says this: "And being not weak in faith, he considered not his own body now dead, when he was about an hundred years old, neither yet the deadness of Sarah's womb" (Rom. 4:19).

Sarah's womb actually was a tomb—it was the place of death. And out of death came life: Isaac was born. Paul concludes that fourth chapter by saying this about the Lord Jesus: "Who was delivered for our offences, and was raised again for our justification" (Rom. 4:25). Life out of death—that is the promise God is now making to this man. Abram is 99 years old, and that means that Sarai is 89 years old. When Isaac was born, Abraham was 100 years old and Sarah 90.

And Abram fell on his face: and God talked with him, saying,

As for me, behold, my covenant is with thee, and thou shalt be a father of many nations [Gen. 17:3–4].

God says to Abram that he will be a father of many nations. I suppose it could be said that this man has probably had more children than any other man that has ever lived on the earth, as far as we know. Just think of it: for four thousand years, there have been two great lines—the line of Ishmael and the line of Isaac—and there have been millions in each line. What a family! What a homecoming! Added to that, there is a spiritual seed, for we Christians are called the children of Abraham by faith in Christ. In Romans 4:16, speaking of Abraham, Paul says, ". . . who is the father of us all"—that is, of believers, of the nation Israel, and also of the Arabs, by the way. Just think of the millions of people! God says here, "I am going to make you a father of many nations," and He has made that promise good.

Neither shall thy name any more be called Abram, but thy name shall be Abraham; for a father of many nations have I made thee [Gen. 17:5].

Abram means "high father" or "father of the height" or "exalted father." *Abraham* means "father of a multitude."

I am going to inject a little story here to illustrate to you something of the faith of this man Abram. Suppose that one morning Abram and Sarai get up, and as they are working around the tent there suddenly appears a group of traders at their little oasis created by the spring at Hebron. Abram goes out to meet

them, and they want to know if they can water their camels.

There were many hospitable people in that day, and that is quite interesting. We speak of the caveman way back yonder and how terrible he was. May I say to you, in that day a stranger could not go through the country without somebody opening his home and entertaining him. But if you came into Los Angeles as a stranger, I don't know anybody who would take you in, although there are a lot of Christians in this area. Our culture is altogether different today, and we certainly lack the hospitality they had in that day.

Abram goes out to meet them, and the conversation probably sounded like this: "Sure, help yourselves, and I'll feed your stock. Would you like to stay for awhile?" They say, "No, we're on a business trip and are in a hurry to get down to Egypt."

One of the men then says, "My name is Allah," and the other says, "My name is Ali Baba. What's your name?" When Abram replies, "My name is High Father," the men exclaim, "My! Boy or girl?" Abram says, "I don't have any children." The men just laugh and say, "You mean to tell us that you don't have any children and your name is Abram? How in the world can you be a father and not have children?" And they ride off across the desert, laughing.

Six months later, they come by again. When he goes out to greet them again, they all begin to laugh, "Hello there, High Father!" But he says, "My name is not High Father anymore. It is now Father of a Multitude." The traders say, "My, must have been twins!" And then they really laugh when Abraham says, "No, I still don't have any children." They say, "How ridiculous can that be?"

Here was a man who was a father before he had any children. Abraham was Abraham, father of a multitude, by faith at that time. But four thousand years later, where you and I sit, we can say that God sure made this good. The name stuck, if you please, and he is still Abraham, the father of a multitude.

GOD'S COVENANT

And I will make thee exceeding fruitful, and I will make nations of thee, and kings shall come out of thee [Gen. 17:6].

And I will establish my covenant between me and thee and thy seed after thee in their generations for an everlasting covenant, to be a God unto thee, and to thy seed after thee [Gen. 17:6–7].

What kind of covenant did God make with Abraham? An *everlasting* covenant. If it is everlasting, is it good today? It certainly is. God promised you and me everlasting life if we will trust Christ—that is a covenant God has made. My friend, if God is not going to make good this covenant that He made with Abraham, you had better look into yours again. But I have news for you: He is going to make your covenant good, and He is also going to make Abraham's good.

And I will give unto thee, and to thy seed after thee, the land wherein thou art a stranger, all the land of Canaan, for an everlasting possession; and I will be their God [Gen. 17:8].

God tells Abraham what *He* will do. God says, "*I will.*" "I will make thee exceeding fruitful, and I will make nations of thee. . . . And I will establish my covenant between me and thee and thy seed . . . . And I will give unto thee, and to thy seed after thee . . . all the land of Canaan, for an everlasting possession."

God has made a covenant with these people that is an everlasting covenant. Since it is, it is not one that will be easily broken, and it is not one that is going to run out. God did not give them a ninety-nine-year lease on the land. God gave them an *everlasting* possession.

The Hebrew people have been in that land on three occasions, and it is theirs, but the important thing is that they occupy it only under certain conditions. First of all, God sent them down into the land of Egypt, and they were dispersed there. They went down a family of about seventy and came out a nation of at least one and one-half million. They were put out of their land again at the Babylonian captivity because they went into idolatry and were not witnessing for God. We find that they again went out of the land in A.D. 70 after they had rejected their Messiah. Actually, they have never been back. God predicted that three times they would be put out of the land and three times they would be returned. They have been returned twice. (I do not consider the present return to the land a fulfillment.) When they return the next time, I take it that it means they will never go out of the land again. The millennium will take place when God gathers and brings them back into the land.

And God said unto Abraham, Thou shalt keep my covenant therefore, thou, and thy seed after thee in their generations.

This is my covenant, which ye shall keep, between me and you and thy seed after thee; Every man child among you shall be circumcised.

And ye shall circumcise the flesh of your foreskin; and it shall be a token of the covenant betwixt me and you [Gen. 17:9–11].

Circumcision is the *badge* of the covenant. The Israelites did not circumcise themselves in order to become members of the covenant. They did this because they *had* the covenant from God. Circumcision occupied the same place that good works occupy for the believer today. You do not perform good works in order to be saved; you perform good works because you *have been* saved. That makes all the difference in the world.

When I went away from home as a boy, although I did get into a lot of trouble, the one thing that kept me from becoming an absolute renegade was the thought of my dad. I said to myself, "Because I'm a son of my father, I won't do this or enter into that." I refrained from things because of my dad. Now, I did not become his son because I did not do certain things. I already was his son. But because I was his son, I didn't do them. The badge of the covenant was circumcision. The thing that put them under the covenant wasn't circumcision, but circumcision was the badge of it, the evidence of it.

And he that is eight days old shall be circumcised among you, every man child in your generations, he that is born in the house, or bought with money of any stranger, which is not of thy seed [Gen. 17:12].

Have you noticed how meticulous the record concerning the birth of Christ is? All the law was fulfilled in connection with the birth of this little baby. It is recorded that He was the son of Abraham, the son of David; He was in the line, and on the eighth day He was circumcised. He was "born under the law," Paul says in Galatians 4:4.

He that is born in thy house, and he that is bought with thy money, must needs be circumcised: and my covenant shall be in your flesh for an everlasting covenant [Gen. 17:13].

Again, circumcision is the badge of the covenant. They did not have to do this in order to get the covenant; God had already made the covenant with them. I trust that you see this because it is so important. The same thing is true today. A great many people think that, if they join the church or are baptized, they will be saved. No, my friend, you don't do those things to get saved. If you are saved, I think you will do both of them—you'll join a church, and you'll be baptized—but you don't do that to *get* saved. We need to keep the cart where it belongs, following the horse, and not get the cart before the horse. For in fact, in the thinking of many relative to salvation, the horse is *in* the cart today.

And the uncircumcised man child whose flesh of his foreskin is not circumcised, that soul shall be cut off from his people; he hath broken my covenant [Gen. 17:14].

The fact that there were those who disobeyed (practically the entire nation disobeyed when they came out of the land of Egypt) did not militate against the covenant. That disobedience simply meant that the individual would be put out. However, as far as the nation is concerned, no individual or group could destroy this covenant which God had made with Abraham and his seed after him. It is an everlasting covenant. The man who had broken the covenant was put out, but the covenant stood. That is how marvelous it is.

And God said unto Abraham, As for Sarai thy wife, thou shalt not call her name Sarai, but Sarah shall her name be [Gen. 17:15].

Her name was Sarai before; now it is changed to Sarah.

And I will bless her, and give thee a son also of her: yea, I will bless her, and she shall be a mother of nations; kings of people shall be of her [Gen. 17:16].

If old Abraham is going to be a father of nations, then Sarah is going to be a mother of nations.

Then Abraham fell upon his face, and laughed, and said in his heart, Shall a child be born unto him that is an hundred years old? and shall Sarah, that is ninety years old, bear? [Gen. 17:17].

Old Abraham just laughed. This is not the laughter of unbelief. I think it is the laughter of just sheer joy that this could happen. I am sure that you have had this experience. Every now and then in our lives, God does something for us that is so wonderful that we just feel like laughing. You don't know anything else to do

but to laugh about it. This was something unheard of. There was "the deadness of Sarah's womb," and Abraham was "dead"—have you ever noticed how Paul described this? "(As it is written, I have made thee a father of many nations,) before him whom he believed, *even* God, who quickeneth the dead, and calleth those things which be not as though they were. Who against hope believed in hope, that he might become the father of many nations, according to that which was spoken, So shall thy seed be. And being not weak in faith, he considered not his own body now dead, when he was about an hundred years old, neither yet the deadness of Sarah's womb: He staggered not at the promise of God through unbelief; but was strong in faith, giving glory to God; And being fully persuaded that, what he had promised, he was able also to perform. And therefore it was imputed to him for righteousness" (Rom. 4:17–22). Abraham believed in God, and he is absolutely overwhelmed by the wonder and the goodness of God.

But then, all of a sudden, a thought comes to Abraham like an arrow to his heart. He thinks of a little boy who is his, a boy by the name of Ishmael.

And Abraham said unto God, O that Ishmael might live before thee! [Gen. 17:18].

Abraham is saying, "Oh, Lord, this little fellow who has been growing up in my home . . . !" Abraham is attached to Ishmael. He was fourteen years old when Abraham sent him out a little later on. I do not think that Abraham ever saw him again. My friend, I don't care what you might think of Ishmael; he was Abraham's *son*, and Abraham loved his son. It was a heartbreak for him to have to give him up.

I am of the opinion that Abraham thought many, many times, "I made a great big mistake in taking Hagar." You see, that was a sin that not only plagued him, but there has also been trouble in that land from the beginning because Abraham sinned. Don't tell me that sin is a little thing or that sin is something you get by with. "Be not deceived; God is not mocked: for whatsoever a man soweth, that shall he also reap" (Gal. 6:7). A man does not reap something similar; he reaps just that which he sowed. And this man Abraham is certainly reaping: "O that Ishmael might live before thee!"

And God said, Sarah thy wife shall bear thee a son indeed; and thou shalt call his name Isaac: and I will establish my

covenant with him for an everlasting covenant, and with his seed after him [Gen. 17:19].

In other words, God says, "No, I won't accept him. That was wrong." Don't say that God approved polygamy just because it is recorded in the Bible. I cannot see that He is approving it at all.

ISHMAEL'S INHERITANCE

And as for Ishmael, I have heard thee: Behold, I have blessed him, and will make him fruitful, and will multiply him exceedingly; twelve princes shall he beget, and I will make him a great nation.

But my covenant will I establish with Isaac, which Sarah shall bear unto thee at this set time in the next year [Gen. 17:20–21].

God holds to the promise that He has made. God is not to be deterred or deferred from this at all. He is going to do the exact thing that He said He would do. He speaks as if Isaac were already born and in their midst. He speaks of things that are not as if they are— and it *is* going to be next year.

And he left off talking with him, and God went up from Abraham [Gen. 17:22].

In other words, Abraham, you might just as well keep quiet. God has already decided this. My friend, there are things which you and I might as well stop petitioning the Lord for. There are times when you've said enough and you don't need to say any more. Sometimes folk just pester the Lord in a prayer when they already have the answer—which, of course, is *No!* God says to Abraham, "Let this alone, now. This is enough; you need not mention this anymore. I have not accepted it, and I do not intend to." God is going to hear and answer other prayers of Abraham. We will find that God listens to Abraham. However, in the case of His covenant, He is making it with Isaac not with Ishmael. That is settled, and Abraham might just as well stop trying to change God's mind. A great many people today pray about things that God maybe does not intend to hear or answer at all. I try to be very careful about asking people to pray about certain things. I want at least to feel like there is a reasonable chance of God's hearing it and answering.

And Abraham took Ishmael his son, and all that were born in his house, and all that were bought with his money, every male among the men of Abraham's house; and circumcised the flesh of their foreskin in the selfsame day, as God had said unto him.

And Abraham was ninety years old and nine, when he was circumcised in the flesh of his foreskin.

And Ishmael his son was thirteen years old, when he was circumcised in the flesh of his foreskin.

In the selfsame day was Abraham circumcised, and Ishmael his son.

And all the men of his house, born in the house, and bought with money of the stranger, were circumcised with him [Gen. 17:23–27].

Circumcision is the badge of the covenant which God has made with Abraham. Someone will ask, "Why was Ishmael included?" Hasn't God promised that Ishmael is going to be a great nation also? He is included in it in that sense, but he is not the one whom God had promised to Abraham at the beginning. He is not to be the father of the nation that God will use and the nation through which the Messiah will come.

CHAPTER 18

THEME: *God reaffirms His promise; God announces the coming destruction of Sodom and Gomorrah*

Until you get to the New Testament, you may wonder why the eighteenth and nineteenth chapters of Genesis are included in the Bible. They seem rather detached from the story of Abraham. They deal with the destruction of Sodom and Gomorrah.

Chapter 18 is a rather lengthy chapter in which God tells Abraham about the judgment of Sodom and Gomorrah and Abraham intercedes on behalf of the cities of the plain. This is an illustration, I think, of the *blessed* Christian life, of life in fellowship with God. But in chapter 19, down in Sodom and Gomorrah with Lot, we will see what I would call the *blasted* life—all because of a decision that was made.

Unfortunately, we have both kinds among Christians today—those living a blessed life and those living a blasted life. There are those who have really made shipwreck of their lives; they have gotten entirely out of the will of God. I would not suggest even for a moment that they have lost their salvation, but they sure have lost everything else. As Paul says, they are saved, ". . . yet so as by fire" (1 Cor. 3:15).

GOD REAFFIRMS HIS PROMISE

And the Lord appeared unto him in the plains of Mamre: and he sat in the tent door in the heat of the day [Gen. 18:1].

Abraham is living down there in Mamre, and he's an old man, by the way.

And he lift up his eyes and looked, and, lo, three men stood by him: and when he saw them, he ran to meet them from the tent door, and bowed himself toward the ground [Gen. 18:2].

Notice the hospitality that Abraham extends. The little story that I told in the previous chapter has a basis of fact, at least, although I don't think it ever took place. The point is that this man Abraham is a very gracious, hospitable man.

And said, My Lord, if now I have found favour in thy sight, pass not away, I pray thee, from thy servant:

Let a little water, I pray you, be fetched, and wash your feet, and rest yourselves under the tree [Gen. 18:3–4].

It seems very strange to us to tell a visiting stranger to wash his feet and come in. We wouldn't quite say that today, but this is probably the oldest custom that is known. Remember that in the Upper Room our Lord washed the disciples feet—and there is a tremendous spiritual message there. Here Abraham says, "Wash your feet." It was a token of real hospitality when someone came into a home to have him take off his shoes and wash his feet. In that day they did not take off their hat, but they did take off their shoes. Today we have reversed it. When you come to visit somebody, you leave your shoes on and take off your hat. I'm not sure which is right. I like the idea, myself, of taking off my shoes. I like to go barefooted in the summertime. I wish it were possible more often. When I am out in the Hawaiian Islands, I put my shoes away and wear thongs or go barefooted as much as possible. I don't put my shoes back on the whole time I am there. I love to go barefooted. I think this was a great custom. It sure would make you feel at home to take off your shoes, wash your feet, and rest yourself under the shade of a tree. Abraham is really entertaining these men royally.

And I will fetch a morsel of bread, and comfort ye your hearts; after that ye shall pass on: for therefore are ye come to your servant. And they said, So do, as thou hast said.

And Abraham hastened into the tent unto Sarah, and said, Make ready quickly three measures of fine meal, knead it, and make cakes upon the hearth.

And Abraham ran unto the herd, and fetched a calf tender and good, and gave it unto a young man; and he hasted to dress it.

And he took butter, and milk, and the calf which he had dressed, and set it before them; and he stood by them under the tree, and they did eat [Gen. 18:5–8].

Isn't this a marvelous way of entertaining? Abraham has prepared a sumptuous meal. He took a little calf, a servant killed and prepared it, and the chef probably barbecued it. They had veal steaks or veal roast, I imagine, and all the trimmings that went with it. "And he took butter, and milk"—my, it was a real feast! Abraham entertains these three guests.

Then we find that these guests are royal guests. In the New Testament it is suggested to us that ". . . some have entertained angels unawares" (Heb. 13:2). That was Abraham—he didn't know whom he was really entertaining.

And they said unto him, Where is Sarah thy wife? And he said, Behold, in the tent [Gen. 18:9].

It was not proper in that day—and even in the East today—for the wife to come out and be the one to entertain, especially since there were three male guests there. But now they ask and make inquiry about Sarah.

And he said, I will certainly return unto thee according to the time of life; and, lo, Sarah thy wife shall have a son. And Sarah heard it in the tent door, which was behind him [Gen. 18:10].

I think Sarah had her ear to the keyhole and had been listening in. Both Abraham and Sarah now discover that they are entertaining angels unaware.

Now Abraham and Sarah were old and well stricken in age; and it ceased to be with Sarah after the manner of women.

Therefore Sarah laughed within herself, saying, After I am waxed old shall I have pleasure, my lord being old also? [Gen. 18:11–12].

That is, Sarah asks, "Is it possible that I will have a son?"—and she laughs. Now what kind of laughter is this? I think this is the laughter which says that it is just too good to be true—that's all. Again, I'm sure that most of us have had experiences like this. God has been so good to us on a certain occasion that we just laughed. Something happened that was just too good to be true, and that was the way Sarah laughed. She is saying, "This is something just too good to be true. It just *can't* happen to me!"

And the Lord said unto Abraham, Wherefore did Sarah laugh, saying, Shall I of a surety bear a child, which am old?

Is any thing too hard for the Lord? At the time appointed I will return unto thee, according to the time of life, and Sarah shall have a son.

Then Sarah denied, saying, I laughed not; for she was afraid. And he said, Nay; but thou didst laugh [Gen. 18:13–15].

Sarah is frightened by the Lord's question and is certainly rather evasive, but she cannot avoid the truth.

And the men rose up from thence, and looked toward Sodom: and Abraham went with them to bring them on the way [Gen. 18:16].

Abraham didn't have a front gate, so he walked out with them a little farther than the front gate to bid them goodbye. And as they walked out from where Abraham lived, they could look down to Sodom and Gomorrah. When I was in that land, it was amazing to me how far you could see on a clear day. I could see from Jerusalem to Bethlehem. And from the ruins of old Samaria, I could see Jerusalem, the Mediterranean Sea, and the Sea of Galilee. I could see Mt. Hermon from most anyplace—it's tremendous. Abraham walked out a ways with these guests, and down below there, they saw Sodom and Gomorrah. They were the great resorts of that day, and they must have been very delightful and beautiful places to be.

GOD ANNOUNCES THE COMING DESTRUCTION OF SODOM AND GOMORRAH

And the Lord said, Shall I hide from Abraham that thing which I do [Gen. 18:17].

Up to this point, the Lord has not revealed to Abraham what He is going to do with Sodom and Gomorrah: He is going to destroy them. "Shall I hide from Abraham that thing which I do?"

Notice now the reason that God is *not* going to hide it from Abraham.

Seeing that Abraham shall surely become a great and mighty nation, and all the nations of the earth shall be blessed in him? [Gen. 18:18].

Abraham is going to have a tremendous influence. He is going to influence multitudes of people, including the succeeding generations. That is true right now today. As I write and as you read this book, Abraham is influencing us—we cannot avoid it.

For I know him, that he will command his children and his household after him, and they shall keep the way of the Lord, to do justice and judgment; that the Lord may bring upon Abraham that which he hath spoken of him [Gen. 18:19].

God says, "I'd better not hide it from Abraham because he will get a wrong impression of Me." Notice, by the way, that this man Abraham had discipline in his household.

And the LORD said, Because the cry of Sodom and Gomorrah is great, and because their sin is very grievous;

I will go down now, and see whether they have done altogether according to the cry of it, which is come unto me; and if not, I will know [Gen. 18:20–21].

In other words, God is saying to Abraham, "I know the situation there, but I'm going down to investigate." God never does anything hurriedly or hastily. It is a good thing that God told Abraham He was going to destroy these cities, because otherwise Abraham would have gotten a wrong impression of God. He would have thought that God was rather dictatorial and vindictive and that He was One who apparently showed no mercy for or consideration of those who were His. Abraham would really have had a distorted and warped view of God, and so God lets him know what He is going to do. Abraham now has time to turn this over in his mind. It is also a good thing that God told him because he did have a wrong idea of God and of Sodom and Gomorrah—he was wrong about many things. This is one of the reasons that God is telling us as much as He is. There are a lot of things that He does not tell us, but He has told us enough so that though a man be a fool and a wayfaring man, he needn't err therein.

And the men turned their faces from thence, and went toward Sodom: but Abraham stood yet before the LORD [Gen. 18:22].

Abraham is now waiting before the Lord.

And Abraham drew near, and said, Wilt thou also destroy the righteous with the wicked? [Gen. 18:23].

What is the first thing that enters Abraham's mind? The first thing that enters his mind, of course, is Lot. He had rescued Lot once, and now Lot is again in danger down there. I think that Abraham had wondered many times about Lot and his relationship to God, but at least he believes that Lot is a saved man. He is asking God, "What about the righteous?" I believe that Abraham would have told you that he thought there were many people in the city of Sodom who were saved. He could not understand why God would destroy the righteous with the wicked. What a picture we have here!

Peradventure there be fifty righteous within the city: wilt thou also destroy and not spare the place for the fifty righteous that are therein? [Gen. 18:24].

Abraham begins with fifty. He says to the Lord, "Lord, suppose there are fifty righteous down there in Sodom. Would You destroy the city if there were fifty righteous?"

That be far from thee to do after this manner, to slay the righteous with the wicked: and that the righteous should be as the wicked, that be far from thee: Shall not the Judge of all the earth do right? [Gen. 18:25].

That is still a question that many people ask: "Shall not the Judge of all the earth do right?" And there is an answer to it. The rest of the Bible testifies to the fact that the Judge of all the earth *always* does right. Whatever God does is right, and if you don't think He is right, the trouble is not with God, but the trouble is with you and your thinking. You are thinking wrong; you do not have all the facts; you do not know all of the details. If you did, you would know that the Judge of all the earth does right. We are wrong; He is right.

And the LORD said, If I find in Sodom fifty righteous within the city, then I will spare all the place for their sakes [Gen. 18:26].

And Abraham thinks this over.

And Abraham answered and said, Behold now, I have taken upon me to speak unto the Lord, which am but dust and ashes:

Peradventure there shall lack five of the fifty righteous: wilt thou destroy all the city for lack of five? And he said, If I find there forty and five, I will not destroy it [Gen. 18:27–28].

In other words, Abraham says, "If there are forty-five righteous left, would You destroy the city for forty-five?" And God tells him, "If I find there forty and five, I will not destroy it." This makes the man a little bit bolder, and he says to the Lord, "Suppose there are forty?" The very interesting thing is that God says, "I will not destroy it for forty." And Abraham keeps on bringing the number down. He says, "How about thirty?" God says, "If there are thirty there, I still won't do it." Abraham says, "Suppose there are twenty there?" God says, "I'll not destroy it." Abraham is overwhelmed now, and he takes another plunge: "Suppose there are ten righteous there. Would You destroy it if there are ten?" And God says, "If there are ten righteous in the city, I will not destroy it."

And the LORD went his way, as soon as he had left communing with Abraham: and Abraham returned unto his place [Gen. 18:33].

Now the question arises: Why didn't Abraham come on down below ten? I'll tell you why: At this point he is afraid that Lot is lost, and this disturbs him a great deal; so he is not going to come down any further. But he could have come down to one. He could have said, "Lord, if there is one in that city who is righteous, would You destroy the city?" Do you know what God would have said? He would have said, "If there is one who is righteous in that city, I am going to get him out of that city, because I would not destroy a righteous man with the city." How do I know that is the way it

would have been? Because that is the way it worked out. There was one righteous man there—Abraham didn't believe it, but God knew him—and that one was Lot. God said to Lot, "Get out of the city. I cannot destroy it until you are out."

Do you know that the great tribulation period cannot come as long as the church is in the world? It just cannot come, my friend, because Christ bore our judgment, and the great tribulation is part of the judgment that is coming. This is the reason that the church cannot go through it. This is a glorious picture of that truth. We are going to see that Sodom and Gomorrah are a picture of the world—and what a picture! What a condition the world is in today—it is very much like Sodom and Gomorrah. That does not mean that the Lord is going to come tomorrow. I do not know—and no one else knows—when He will come. But He could come tomorrow, and it certainly would be in keeping with the carrying out of the picture which is before us here in Genesis.

CHAPTER 19

THEME: *The angels visit Lot; destruction of the Cities of the Plain*

The preceding chapter was a picture of blessed Christian fellowship with God. But now the picture changes: We leave Hebron on the plains of Mamre where Abraham dwells and we go to the city of Sodom where Lot dwells. In this chapter Lot leaves Sodom with his wife and two daughters, and Sodom and Gomorrah are destroyed. Lot's wife turns to a pillar of salt, and then we have Lot's awful sin with his two daughters.

In chapter 19 we have a picture of that which is "the blasted life." Don't forget that this man Lot happens to be a righteous man. It is hard to believe that; if I had only this record in Genesis, I wouldn't believe it. But Simon Peter, in his epistle, says of Lot, ". . . that righteous man . . . vexed his righteous soul from day to day with their unlawful deeds" (2 Pet. 2:8). Lot lived in Sodom, but he never was happy there. It was a tragic day for him when he moved to Sodom, because he lost his family— he lost all of them if you look at the total picture. It is tragic.

There is many a man today who may be a

saved man, but due to his life style or where he lives, he loses his family, his influence, and his testimony. I have been a pastor for quite a few years, and I know Christians like Lot. Not too long ago, the son of a leader in a church which I served said to me that all he was doing was waiting for his dad to die in order to repudiate the Christian life. He thought the whole thing was phony; all he could see was hypocrisy. Of course, all he was doing was telling about his home. What a phony his dad must be! That man has lost his son, and he has lost his influence in other places, I can assure you. But I would not question his salvation. I think the man trusts Christ, but you would never know it by his life. Poor Lot! How tragic this is! This is one of two very sordid chapters in the Book of Genesis.

THE ANGELS VISIT LOT

And there came two angels to Sodom at even; and Lot sat in the gate of Sodom: and Lot seeing them rose up to meet

them; and he bowed himself with his face toward the ground [Gen. 19:1].

These two angels visit Lot in Sodom to announce judgment. Notice that Lot was sitting in the gate of Sodom. I cannot let that go by without calling attention to the fact that the ones who sat in the gate of a city were the judges. This man Lot not only moved to Sodom, but he also got into politics down there. Here he is, a petty judge sitting in the gate.

And he said, Behold now, my lords, turn in, I pray you, into your servant's house, and tarry all night, and wash your feet, and ye shall rise up early, and go on your ways. And they said, Nay; but we will abide in the street all night [Gen. 19:2].

These two men must have had dirty feet. Of course, if you had walked from the plains of Mamre down into Sodom wearing nothing but sandals, your feet would need washing, also. Again, I call your attention to this custom of that day which was practiced by those who extended hospitality to strangers.

Lot was a hospitable man. When these strangers came, he invited them to his home, and they came in. At first, however, they were reluctant. "And they said, Nay; but we will abide in the street all night." In other words, they said, "We'll just stay outside. We don't want to inconvenience you." And they said this for a purpose, of course.

And he pressed upon them greatly; and they turned in unto him, and entered into his house; and he made them a feast, and did bake unleavened bread, and they did eat [Gen. 19:3].

Now these men have another feast. They had a feast with Abraham; they now have a feast with Lot.

They had brought out something when they said, "We'll stay on the street and just sleep in the park," and Lot says to them, "You don't do that in Sodom. It's dangerous! Your life wouldn't be worth a thing if you did that." May I say that maybe Los Angeles ought to change its name to Sodom. It would not be safe for you to sleep on the streets of Los Angeles; in fact, it is not safe at all to be on the streets of Los Angeles at night. Many women who live alone will not come out to church at night. One dear saint of God told me, "I just lock my door at dark, Brother McGee, and I do not open that door until the next morning at daylight. It's not safe in my neighborhood to even walk on the street." The days of Sodom and Gomorrah

are here again, and practically for the same reason. Lot says, "No, men, do not stay on the street. It wouldn't be safe for you." When he "pressed upon them," they came in.

But before they lay down, the men of the city, even the men of Sodom, compassed the house round, both old and young, all the people from every quarter:

And they called unto Lot, and said unto him, Where are the men which came in to thee this night? bring them out unto us, that we may know them [Gen. 19:4–5].

This is a sickening scene which reveals the degradation of this city—the city of Sodom. The name that has been put on this sin from that day to this is *sodomy*. Apparently there was no attempt made in the city of Sodom to have a church for this crowd and to tell them that they were all right in spite of the fact that they practiced this thing. May I say to you that the Word of God is specific on this, and you cannot tone it down. Sodomy is an awful sin.

When this man Lot had gone down into the city of Sodom, he did not realize what kind of city it was—I'm sure of that. He got down there and found out that perversion was the order of the day, and he brought up his children, his sons and his daughters, in that atmosphere. When he earlier had pitched his tent toward Sodom, he had looked down there and had seen the lovely streets and boulevards and parks and public buildings. And he had seen the folk as they were on the outside, but he had not seen what they really were. The sin of this city is so great that God is now going to judge it. God is going to destroy the city.

Let's draw a sharp line here. There is a new attitude toward sin today. There is a gray area where sin is not really as black as we once thought it was. The church has compromised until it is pitiful. In Southern California we have a church made up of those who are homosexuals, and, lo and behold, they all admit that the pastor of the church is one also! May I say to you, the lesson of Sodom and Gomorrah is a lesson for this generation. God is *not* accepting this kind of church.

The idea today seems to be that you can become a child of God and continue on in sin. God says that is impossible—you cannot do that, and this city of Sodom is an example of that fact. Paul asks the question: "Shall we continue in sin, that grace may abound?" And the answer is "God forbid," or, Let it not be (see Rom. 6:1–2). The idea that you can be a

Christian and go on in sin is a tremendous mistake, especially to make light of it, as I judge is being done in this particular case.

This is what they were doing in Sodom and Gomorrah—and God destroyed these cities. Don't say that we have a primitive view of God in Genesis but that we have a better one today. Don't argue that, after all, Jesus received sinners. He sure did, but when He got through with them, He had changed them. The harlot who came to Him was no longer in that business. When she came to God, she changed. That is the thing that happened to other sinners. A publican came to Him, and he left the seat of customs. He gave up that which was crooked when he came to the Lord. If you have come to Christ, *you* will be changed. Many people write and try to explain to me that we are living in a new day and I need to wake up. My friend, we are living in a new day, but it just happens to be Sodom and Gomorrah all over again.

And Lot went out at the door unto them, and shut the door after him,

And said, I pray you, brethren, do not so wickedly [Gen. 19:6–7].

The men of Sodom were outside the door, asking that these guests in the home of Lot be turned over to them. Lot said, "I pray you, brethren, do not so wickedly." That is the way Lot looked at it, and he had been down there in Sodom a long time. It wasn't new morality to him; it was just old sin.

Behold now, I have two daughters which have not known man; let me, I pray you, bring them out unto you, and do ye to them as is good in your eyes: only unto these men do nothing; for therefore came they under the shadow of my roof [Gen. 19:8].

When a man entertained a guest in that day, he was responsible for him. Lot was willing to make this kind of sacrifice to protect his guests!

And they said, Stand back. And they said again, This one fellow came in to sojourn, and he will needs be a judge: now will we deal worse with thee, than with them. And they pressed sore upon the man, even Lot, and came near to break the door [Gen. 19:9].

"And they said again, This one fellow came in to sojourn, and he will needs be a judge . . . ." You see, Lot was advancing in the political area there.

But the men put forth their hand, and pulled Lot into the house to them, and shut to the door.

And they smote the men that were at the door of the house with blindness, both small and great: so that they wearied themselves to find the door [Gen. 19:10–11].

If Lot's guests had not done this, both they and Lot would have been destroyed, because that was the intention of the men of Sodom.

And the men said unto Lot, Hast thou here any besides? son in law, and thy sons, and thy daughters, and whatsoever thou hast in the city, bring them out of this place:

For we will destroy this place, because the cry of them is waxen great before the face of the LORD; and the LORD hath sent us to destroy it.

And Lot went out, and spake unto his sons in law, which married his daughters, and said, Up, get you out of this place; for the LORD will destroy this city. But he seemed as one that mocked unto his sons in law [Gen. 19:12–14].

Lot is in a very bad situation. He had spent years down in the city of Sodom. He had learned to tolerate this sort of thing, although he calls it wickedness. He had seen his sons and daughters grow up, and they apparently had married among people with those ethical standards. When the time came that Lot got this word from the Lord to leave the city, he went to his sons-in-law and said, "Let's get out of here. God is going to destroy this city." They laughed at him. They ridiculed him. I suppose they knew that the week before Lot had invested a little money in real estate there. He had lived so long as one of them, without any real difference, that they took his warning as a big joke. This man was out of the will of God in this place, and he had no witness for God. He did not win anybody for the Lord in this city. The same principle is true today: when you go down to their level, my friend, you do not win them. I think that that is being clearly demonstrated in this hour.

Frankly, I would agree with Abraham that this man Lot wasn't saved, but remember what Peter said: "And turning the cities of Sodom and Gomorrha into ashes condemned them with an overthrow, making them an ensample unto those that after should live ungodly; And delivered just Lot, vexed with the filthy conversation of the wicked: (For that righteous man dwelling among them, in seeing and hearing, vexed his righteous soul from day to day with their unlawful deeds)" (2 Pet. 2:6–8). I tell you, Lot never enjoyed it down there in Sodom. Now that he is going to leave the city, he cannot get anyone to leave with him except his wife and two single daughters.

And when the morning arose, then the angels hastened Lot, saying, Arise, take thy wife, and thy two daughters, which are here; lest thou be consumed in the iniquity of the city.

And while he lingered, the men laid hold upon his hand, and upon the hand of his wife, and upon the hand of his two daughters; the LORD being merciful unto him: and they brought him forth, and set him without the city [Gen. 19:15–16].

Here is a man who was God's man in spite of everything. If I only had the Book of Genesis, I am not sure I would believe that Lot was saved, but since Peter calls him a righteous man, we know that he was. Lot had become righteous because he had followed Abraham— he believed God, and he had offered the sacrifices. God extends mercy unto Lot, and he now believes God and gets out of the city.

And it came to pass, when they had brought them forth abroad, that he said, Escape for thy life; look not behind thee, neither stay thou in all the plain; escape to the mountain, lest thou be consumed.

And Lot said unto them, Oh, not so, my Lord:

Behold now, thy servant hath found grace in thy sight, and thou hast magnified thy mercy, which thou hast shewed unto me in saving my life; and I cannot escape to the mountain, lest some evil take me, and I die [Gen. 19:17–19].

Even Lot didn't want to leave. He would get out of the city, but he couldn't make it to the mountain.

Behold now, this city is near to flee unto, and it is a little one: Oh, let me escape thither, (is it not a little one?) and my soul shall live [Gen. 19:20].

This city was a little place called Zoar, and that is where Lot went. You see, this man came out of Sodom, but he did not come clean even out of

there. And, of course, he got into a great deal of trouble at that particular time.

DESTRUCTION OF THE CITIES OF THE PLAIN

God destroyed the cities of Sodom and Gomorrah, and we are told two things, one concerning his wife and the other concerning his daughters. Concerning his wife we read:

But his wife looked back from behind him, and she became a pillar of salt [Gen. 19:26].

I think this verse has been greatly misunderstood. Why in the world did Mrs. Lot turn and look back? I think that the reason is twofold. First of all, she turned and looked back because she did not want to leave Sodom. She loved Sodom. She loved Lot, too, but it was a *lot* of Sodom that she loved. And she didn't want to leave it. She was probably a member of the country club, the sewing club, and the Shakespeare club. In fact, there wasn't a club in town that she was not a member of. She just loved these little get-togethers in the afternoon. I'm not sure but what they met and studied religion in a nice little religious club also. She was right in the thick of it all, my friend, and she didn't want to leave. Her heart was in Sodom. Her body walked out, but she surely left her heart there.

This is a tremendous lesson for us today. I hear a great many Christians talking about how they want to see the Lord come, but they are not living as if they mean it. On Sunday morning, it is difficult to get them to leave their lovely home. And on Sunday night, they are *not* going to leave their lovely home because they love television, too. They have a color television, and they are going to look at the programs on Sunday night because there are some good ones then. But when the Lord comes, my friend, you are going to leave the television; you are going to leave that lovely home; you are going to leave everything. I have just one question to ask you: Will it break your heart to leave all of this down here?

I have asked myself that question many times. To be honest with you, I am not anxious to leave. I would love to stay. I have my friends and loved ones whom I want to be with. And I have the radio ministry that I want to continue. I'll be frank with you, I hope the Lord will just let me stay here awhile longer. But I also want to be able to say that when He does call, I will not have a thing down here which will break my heart to leave—not a thing. I love my home too, but I would just as soon go off and leave it. How do *you* feel about that today? Mrs. Lot turned and looked back, and this is one of the explanations.

The other reason that she looked back is simply that she did not believe God. God had said, "Leave the city, and don't look back." Lot didn't look back; he believed God. But Mrs. Lot did not believe God. She was not a believer, and so she didn't really make it out of the city. She was turned to a pillar of salt.

I am not going to go into the story of Lot's two daughters in verses 31–38. It is as sordid as it can be. Frankly, Lot did not do well in moving down to the city of Sodom. He lost everything except his own soul. His life is a picture of a great many people who will not judge the sins of their lives. They are saved, "yet so as by fire." The Lord has said in a very definite way to these folk who have put all their eggs in a basket like this that if they will not judge their sin down here, He *will* judge it. Apparently, that was the case in Lot's story.

I want to conclude this chapter by looking at Abraham. What did Abraham think of all this?

And Abraham gat up early in the morning to the place where he stood before the Lord:

And he looked toward Sodom and Gomorrah, and toward all the land of the plain, and beheld, and, lo, the smoke of the country went up as the smoke of a furnace [Gen. 19:27–28].

When Abraham looked down toward Sodom, I think his heart was sad. I am not sure whether or not he knew that Lot had escaped. He probably learned about it later on. When he looked down there, he probably was sad for Lot's

sake, but Abraham had not invested a dime down there. When judgment came, it did not disturb him one whit because he wasn't in love with the things of Sodom and the things of the world.

Remember that we are told, "Love not the world, neither the things that are in the world . . ." (1 John 2:15). I sometimes preach a sermon which I have entitled "Sightseeing in Sodom." First, I look at Sodom through the eyes of Lot himself: he sure had a wrong view of it. And then of Mrs. Lot: she fell in love with it. You can also sightsee in Sodom with Abraham: he lost nothing down there. Finally, you can go through Sodom with the Lord and see it as He sees it. It is too bad that the church today is not looking at the sin of sodomy as God looks at it. I do not think it is any more prevalent today than it has been in the past, but there is a tremendous percentage of our population who are homosexuals engaging in perversion. We speak of it in a more candid manner than we ever have, and it is something that is right in our midst.

What is to be the attitude of the Christian toward homosexuality? Even Lot in his day said, "You are doing wickedly." And God judged it. Isn't it enough for the child of God to know that he cannot compromise with this type of thing. This is a *sin!* The world indulges in it and then calls it a sickness. The same thing is said about the alcoholic. Sure, he's sick. Of course, he's sick. But what made him take that first drink and continue to drink until he became sick? *Sin* did it, my friend. Sin is the problem, and homosexuality is a sin. It is so labeled in the first chapter of Romans where God says He gave them up (see Rom. 1:18–32). Genesis 19 is a very important chapter for this present generation in which we are living today.

CHAPTER 20

THEME: Abraham misrepresents Sarah

Chapter 20 seems about as necessary as a fifth leg on a cow. It is a chapter that you feel as if you would like to leave out, because in it Abraham repeats the same sin which he committed when he went down into the land of Egypt and lied concerning Sarah, saying, "She is my sister." It is the same sordid story, but this chapter is put here for a very important reason. Abraham and Sarah are going to have to deal with this sin before they can have Isaac, before they can have the blessing. May I say to you, until you and I are willing to deal with the sin in our lives, there is no blessing for us.

ABRAHAM MISREPRESENTS SARAH

I am going to hit just the high points of chapter 20.

And Abraham journeyed from thence toward the south country, and dwelled between Kadesh and Shur, and sojourned in Gerar.

And Abraham said of Sarah his wife, She is my sister: and Abimelech king of Gerar sent, and took Sarah [Gen. 20:1–2].

This is quite interesting. Do you think that Sarah was beautiful? Well, at this time she is almost ninety years old, and she's beautiful. Not many senior citizens can qualify in this particular department.

Notice also that Abraham is getting quite far south in the land. He has gone beyond Kadesh-Barnea where the children of Israel later came up from Egypt and refused to enter the land. Abraham has gone down to Gerar, which I do not think he should have done, but be that as it may, he lies about Sarah again.

I want you to notice Abraham's confession because this is the thing which makes this chapter important and reveals the fact that Abraham and Sarah cannot have Isaac until they deal with this sin that is in their lives— and it goes way back.

And Abraham said, Because I thought, Surely the fear of God is not in this place; and they will slay me for my wife's sake [Gen. 20:11].

Abraham is now talking to Abimelech who is greatly disturbed that Abraham would do a thing like lying about his wife. Again, Abraham was not trusting God. He felt that he was

moving down into a godless place, but he finds out that Abimelech has a high sense of what is right and wrong. Abimelech puts a tremendous value upon character and apparently is a man who knows God. Poor Abraham doesn't look good by the side of Abimelech here.

And yet indeed she is my sister; she is the daughter of my father, but not the daughter of my mother; and she became my wife [Gen. 20:12].

Abraham lets it all out now. He says, "To tell the truth, it's half a lie. Sarah is my half sister, and she is my wife."

And it came to pass, when God caused me to wander from my father's house, that I said unto her, This is thy kindness which thou shalt shew unto me; at every place whither we shall come, say of me, He is my brother [Gen. 20:13].

Abraham did not have complete confidence and trust in God, and so when they started out, he and Sarah made a pact that anywhere they went where it looked as if Abraham might be killed because of his wife, Sarah would say that Abraham was her brother. Abraham and Sarah thought that that would keep Abraham from being killed. They made that little agreement, and they had used it down in Egypt, and here they have used it again. This sin must be dealt with before God is going to hear and answer Abraham's prayer in sending a son. Isaac will not be born until this is dealt with.

How many Christians are there who will not judge sin in their lives, and as a result, there is no blessing in their lives? If those who are in places of leadership in our fundamental churches would confess their sins and deal with the sins that are in their lives, I frankly believe that we could have revival. I do not believe there will be any blessing until sin is dealt with. Listen to Paul in 1 Corinthians: "But let a man examine himself, and so let him eat of that bread, and drink of that cup. For he that eateth and drinketh unworthily, eateth and drinketh damnation to himself, not discerning the Lord's body. For this cause many are weak and sickly among you, and many sleep. For if we would judge ourselves, we should not be judged. But when we are judged, we are chastened of the Lord, that we should not be condemned with the world" (1 Cor. 11:28–32). Blessing is being withheld from the church and from the lives of many believers because we will not deal with the sin in our lives. This is a tremendous spiritual lesson here in the twentieth chapter of the Book of Genesis.

CHAPTER 21

THEME: *The birth of Isaac; Hagar and Ishmael cast out; Abraham and Abimelech at Beer-sheba*

In the preceding chapter, we saw the sin that must be dealt with, confessed, and put away before Isaac could be born to Abraham and Sarah. Now in chapter 21 we have the birth of Isaac.

THE BIRTH OF ISAAC

And the Lord visited Sarah as he had said, and the Lord did unto Sarah as he had spoken.

For Sarah conceived, and bare Abraham a son in his old age, at the set time of which God had spoken to him [Gen. 21:1–2].

You will notice that there is a very striking similarity between the birth of Isaac and the birth of Christ. I believe that the birth of Isaac was given to us to set before mankind this great truth before Christ came. Isaac was born at the set time God had promised, and Paul says, "But when the fulness of the time was come, God sent forth his Son, made of a woman, made under the law" (Gal. 4:4).

And Abraham called the name of his son that was born unto him, whom Sarah bare to him, Isaac.

And Abraham circumcised his son Isaac being eight days old, as God had commanded him.

And Abraham was an hundred years old, when his son Isaac was born unto him.

And Sarah said, God hath made me to laugh, so that all that hear will laugh with me.

And she said, Who would have said unto Abraham, that Sarah should have given children suck? for I have born him a son in his old age [Gen. 21:3–7].

There are some very remarkable truths here that we need to lay hold of. First of all, the birth of Isaac was a miraculous birth. It was contrary to nature. In the fourth chapter of Romans, Paul writes that Abraham ". . . considered not his own body now dead . . . neither yet the deadness of Sarah's womb" (Rom. 4:19). Out of death God brings forth life: this is a miraculous birth. We need to call attention to the fact that God did not flash the supernatural birth of Christ on the world as being something new. He began to prepare men for it, and therefore way back here at the birth of Isaac we have a miraculous birth.

We also find here that God had to deal with both Sarah and Abraham. They had to recognize that they could do nothing, that it would be impossible for them to have a child. Abraham is 100 years old; Sarah is 90 years old. In other words, the birth of Isaac must be a birth that they really have nothing to do with.

And the child grew, and was weaned: and Abraham made a great feast the same day that Isaac was weaned [Gen. 21:8].

This little fellow first lived by feeding on his mother's milk, but there came a day when he had to be weaned. Even this has a lesson for us. When mamma is getting the bottle ready for the little baby in the crib, everything in his entire body is working. He's got his feet up in the air, he's got his hands up in the air, and he's yelling at the top of his voice—he wants his bottle! "As newborn babes, desire the sincere milk of the word, that ye may grow thereby" (1 Peter 2:2). It is wonderful to be a new Christian with an appetite like that for the milk of the Word. But the day comes when you are ready to start growing up as a believer. Instead of just reading Psalm 23 and John 14—wonderful as they are—try reading through the entire Bible. Grow up. Don't be a babe all of the time. Notice God's admonishment in Hebrews 5:13–14: "For every one that useth milk is unskilful in the word of righteousness: for he is a babe. But strong meat belongeth to them that are of full age. . . ." Grow up, friend.

HAGAR AND ISHMAEL CAST OUT

And Sarah saw the son of Hagar the Egyptian, which she had born unto Abraham, mocking.

Wherefore she said unto Abraham, Cast out this bondwoman and her son: for the son of this bondwoman shall not be heir with my son, even with Isaac [Gen. 21:9–10].

The coming of this little boy Isaac into the home sure did produce a great deal of difficulty. We find that the boy who was the son of Hagar, Ishmael, was mocking. We begin now to see the nature and the character of Ishmael. Up to this point, he seems to be a pretty nice boy, but now, with the appearance of this other son in the family, Ishmael really shows his true colors.

This is an illustration, by the way, of the fact that a believer has two natures. Until you are converted, you have an old nature, and that old nature controls you. You do what you want to do. As the old secular song put it, you are "doing what comes naturally." What you do that comes naturally is not always the nicest sort of thing. But when you are born again, you receive a new nature. And when you receive a new nature, that is where the trouble always begins. Paul writes in the seventh chapter of Romans of the battle going on between the old nature and the new nature: "For the good that I would I do not: but the evil which I would not, that I do" (Rom. 7:19). That is, the new nature doesn't want to, but the old nature wants to do it, and the old nature is in control. The time comes when you have to make a decision as to which nature you are going to live by. You must make a determination in this matter of yielding to the Lord. You either have to permit the Holy Spirit to move in your life, or else you have to go through life controlled by the flesh. There is no third alternative for the child of God. The son of the bondwoman must be put out. That is exactly what we have here in Genesis: the son of the bondwoman Hagar had to be put out.

And the thing was very grievous in Abraham's sight because of his son [Gen. 21:11].

After all, as far as the flesh is concerned, Ishmael is Abraham's son just as much as Isaac is. Isaac has just been born, and a little bitty baby doesn't know too much about him yet. But this boy Ishmael has been in the home for a good many years—he's a teen-ager now,

and Abraham is attached to him. The thing is very grievous if Abraham is going to have to send him away. Again, I go back to that which we said before: God did not approve of the thing which Sarah and Abraham did, and God cannot accept Ishmael. This is *sin*. God just did not approve of it, and He doesn't intend to approve of it at all. It was a heartbreak to Abraham, but in order to relieve the embarrassment, he had to send that boy away. Poor Sarah just couldn't take it with this older boy around mocking her.

As a believer you cannot live in harmony with both natures. You are going to have to make a decision. James says, "A double-minded man is unstable in all his ways" (James 1:8). This explains the instability and the insecurity among many Christians today. They want to go with the world, and yet they want to go with the Lord. They are spiritual schizophrenics, trying to do both—and you cannot do that. The Greeks had a race in which they put two horses together, and the rider would put one foot on one horse and the other foot on the other horse, and the race would start. Well, it was a great race as long as the horses were together. You and I have two natures—one is a black horse, and the other is a white horse. It would be great if they would go together, but they just will not work together. The white horse goes one way and the black horse another way. When they do this, you and I have to make up our minds which one we are going with—whether we are going to live by the old nature or the new nature. This is why we are told to yield ourselves: "yield yourselves unto God . . . and your members as instruments of righteousness unto God" (Rom. 6:13). Paul goes on to say that what the law could not do through the weakness of the flesh, the Spirit of God can now accomplish (see Rom. 8:3–4). The law tried to control man's old nature and failed. Now the Spirit of God, empowering the new nature, can accomplish what the law could never do.

The character of Ishmael, the son of Hagar, begins to be revealed. This is the nature that we find manifested later on in that nation, a nation that is antagonistic and whose hand is against his brother. This has been the picture of him down through the centuries.

In the birth of Isaac, as I have already suggested, we have a foreshadowing of the birth of the Lord Jesus Christ. God did not suddenly spring the virgin birth on mankind. He had prepared us by several miraculous births before this, including the birth of John the Baptist, the birth even of Samson, and here the birth of Isaac. I would like to call your attention to the remarkable comparison between the births of Isaac and of the Lord Jesus Christ.

(1) The birth of Isaac and the birth of Christ had both been promised. When God called Abraham out of Ur of the Chaldees twenty-five years earlier, God had said to him, "I am going to give a son to you and Sarah." Now twenty-five years have gone by, and God has made good His promise. God also said to the nation Israel, "A virgin shall conceive and bring forth a son." When the day came that Jesus was born in Bethlehem, it was a fulfillment of prophecy. Both births had been promised.

(2) With both births there was a long interval between the promise and the fulfillment. Actually, there were about twenty-five years from the time God promised it until the birth of Isaac. With the birth of Christ, you could go back many generations. For example, God had promised that there would come One in David's line—and that was a thousand years before Christ was born. This is quite a remarkable parallel here.

(3) The announcements of the births seemed incredulous and impossible to Sarah and to Mary. You will recall that the servants of the Lord visited Abraham as they were on the way to Sodom, and they announced the birth of Isaac. It just seemed impossible. Sarah laughed and said, "This thing just can't be. It is beyond belief." And, after all, who was the first one to raise a question about the virgin birth? It was Mary herself. When the angel made the announcement, she said, ". . . How shall this be, seeing I know not a man?" (Luke 1:34).

(4) Both Isaac and Jesus were named before their births. Abraham and Sarah were told that they were going to have a son and that they were going to name him Isaac. And with the birth of the Lord Jesus, we find that He was also named beforehand. The angel said to Joseph, ". . . thou shalt call his name JESUS: for he shall save his people from their sins" (Matt. 1:21).

(5) Both births occurred at God's appointed time. Verse 2 of this chapter says that at the set time which God had spoken to them of, Sarah brought forth Isaac. And regarding the birth of Jesus, we note that Paul says, "But when the fulness of the time was come, God sent forth his Son, made of a woman, made under the law" (Gal. 4:4).

(6) Both births were miraculous. The birth of Isaac was a miraculous birth, and, certainly, the birth of the Lord Jesus was—no man had any part in that.

(7) Both sons were a particular joy of their fathers. We read that "Abraham called the name of his son that was born unto him, whom Sarah bare to him, Isaac," meaning laughter. This was the name he gave his son because back at the time when God made the announcement, he laughed because of his sheer joy in it all. Referring to the Lord Jesus, we read that the Father spoke out of heaven and said, ". . . This is my beloved Son, in whom I am well pleased" (Matt. 3:17). Both sons were a joy.

(8) Both sons were obedient to their fathers, even unto death. In chapter 22 we are going to see that this boy Isaac was offered up by his father. He was not a small boy of eight or nine years. Isaac just happened to be about thirty-three years old when this took place, and he was obedient to his father even unto death. That was true of Isaac, and that was certainly true of the Lord Jesus Christ. There is a marvelous picture of the birth and life of Christ in the birth and life of Isaac.

(9) Finally, the miraculous birth of Isaac is a picture of the resurrection of Christ. We have already noted Paul's words that Abraham "considered not his own body now *dead* . . . neither yet the *deadness* of Sarah's womb" (Rom. 4:19). Out of death came life—that's resurrection, you see. After Paul emphasizes this, he goes on to say of the Lord Jesus, "Who was delivered for our offenses, and was raised again for our justification" (Rom. 4:25). We have in Isaac quite a remarkable picture of the Lord Jesus Christ.

Now we find how God graciously deals with Abraham and also with Hagar and her son Ishmael.

And God said unto Abraham, Let it not be grievous in thy sight because of the lad, and because of thy bondwoman; in all that Sarah hath said unto thee, hearken unto her voice; for in Isaac shall thy seed be called [Gen. 21:12].

God makes it clear to Abraham that He is not going to accept Ishmael as the son He had promised.

And also of the son of the bondwoman will I make a nation, because he is thy seed [Gen. 21:13].

God had said, "Of thy seed, I will make nations to come from you," and therefore He now says that a great nation will come from this boy Ishmael also.

And Abraham rose up early in the morn-

ing, and took bread, and a bottle of water, and gave it unto Hagar, putting it on her shoulder, and the child, and sent her away: and she departed, and wandered in the wilderness of Beer-sheba.

And the water was spent in the bottle, and she cast the child under one of the shrubs.

And she went, and sat her down over against him a good way off, as it were a bowshot: for she said, Let me not see the death of the child. And she sat over against him, and lift up her voice, and wept.

And God heard the voice of the lad; and the angel of God called to Hagar out of heaven, and said unto her, What aileth thee, Hagar? fear not; for God hath heard the voice of the lad where he is.

Arise, lift up the lad, and hold him in thine hand; for I will make him a great nation.

And God opened her eyes, and she saw a well of water; and she went, and filled the bottle with water, and gave the lad drink.

And God was with the lad; and he grew, and dwelt in the wilderness, and became an archer.

And he dwelt in the wilderness of Paran: and his mother took him a wife out of the land of Egypt [Gen. 21:14–21].

The Scriptures are going to drop the line of Ishmael and follow it no longer, but his descendants, the Arabs, are out there in the desert even today.

ABRAHAM AND ABIMELECH AT BEER-SHEBA

And it came to pass at that time, that Abimelech and Phichol the chief captain of his host spake unto Abraham, saying, God is with thee in all that thou doest:

Now therefore swear unto me here by God that thou wilt not deal falsely with me, nor with my son, nor with my son's son: but according to the kindness that I have done unto thee, thou shalt do unto me, and to the land wherein thou hast sojourned [Gen. 21:22–23].

In other words, Abimelech wants to make a contract or a treaty with this man Abraham—and they become good friends because of this.

Thus they made a covenant at Beer-sheba: then Abimelech rose up, and Phichol the chief captain of his host, and they returned into the land of the Philistines.

And Abraham planted a grove in Beer-sheba, and called there on the name of the LORD, the everlasting God [Gen. 21:32–33].

Abraham is calling upon God's name everywhere he goes.

And Abraham sojourned in the Philistines' land many days [Gen. 21:34].

We are told later that Abraham was always a stranger and a pilgrim in this land that God had promised to him, and this is an evidence of it.

CHAPTER 22

THEME: God commands Abraham to offer Isaac; God restrains Abraham; God reaffirms His promises; Abraham returns to Beer-sheba

In this chapter we come to another great high point of the Bible. We are walking on mountain peaks in the Book of Genesis. Chapter 22 is the account of Abraham's offering of his own son. God commanded him to offer Isaac on the altar and then restrained him at the last minute when He saw that Abraham was willing to go through with it. This chapter brings us to the seventh and last appearance of God to Abraham. After this, there is nothing more that God could ask Abraham to do. This is the supreme test that He brought to this man.

If you were to designate the ten greatest chapters of the Bible, you would almost have to include Genesis 22. One of the reasons for that is that this is the first time human sacrifice is even suggested. It is in the plan and purpose of God to make it clear to man that human sacrifice is wrong. This incident reveals that. It also reveals that God requires a life to be given up in order that He might save sinners. There is no one among the children of men worthy to take that place. God's Son was the only One. It is interesting that Paul said, "God spared not His own Son," but you might add that He *did* spare the son of Abraham and did not let him go through with the sacrifice of Isaac.

This chapter compares with Psalm 22 and Isaiah 53. The first time that I saw in this chapter these great truths which depict the cross of Christ, it was breathtaking. Not only in the birth of Isaac, but now also in the sacrifice of Isaac, there is a strange similarity to the life of our Lord.

The very interesting thing is that James makes a statement concerning this incident which may seem contradictory to other parts of the Bible: "Was not Abraham our father justified by works, when he had offered Isaac his son upon the altar?" (James 2:21). For Paul makes this statement in Romans 4: "What shall we say then that Abraham our father, as pertaining to the flesh, hath found? For if Abraham were justified by works, he hath whereof to glory; but not before God. For what saith the scripture? Abraham believed God, and it was counted unto him for righteousness" (Rom. 4:1–3). Who is right? James or Paul? My answer is that both of them are right. First of all, we need to note that both of them are talking about the same thing—faith. James is talking about the works of *faith*, not the works

of law. Paul is talking about justification before God, quoting the fifteenth chapter of Genesis, way back when Abraham was just getting under way in a walk of faith. At that time only God knew his heart, and God saw that Abraham believed Him: "And he (Abraham) believed in the Lord; and he counted it to him for righteousness" (Gen. 15:6). We can see that Abraham failed many times, and I am of the opinion that his neighbors might have said, "We don't see that he is righteous." But when the day came that he took his son to be offered on the altar, even the hardhearted Philistine had to admit that Abraham demonstrated his faith by his actions. James says that Abraham was justified by works. When was he justified? When he offered Isaac. But the question is going to arise: Did Abraham really offer Isaac upon the altar? Of course, the answer is that he didn't—but he was willing to. That very act of being willing is the act that James is talking about which reveals that Abraham had the works of faith. James is emphasizing the works of faith seen in this twenty-second chapter of Genesis, and Paul is talking about faith in his heart which Abraham had way back in the fifteenth chapter.

GOD COMMANDS ABRAHAM TO OFFER ISAAC

And it came to pass after these things, that God did tempt Abraham, and said unto him, Abraham: and he said, Behold, here I am [Gen. 22:1].

The word *tempt* is a little bit too strong; actually, the word means "test." James makes it very clear in his epistle that God never tempts anyone with evil. God tempts folks in the sense that He tests their faith. God did test Abraham, and He asked him to do something very strange.

And he said, Take now thy son, thine only son Isaac, whom thou lovest, and get thee into the land of Moriah; and offer him there for a burnt offering upon one of the mountains which I will tell thee of [Gen. 22:2].

Right after this chapter, we are told that Sarah was 127 years old when she died (see Gen. 23:1). When you put that down with this chapter, you find that this boy Isaac was not just a little lad. Sarah was 90 years old when Isaac was born and 127 when she died. That means that 37 years elapsed here. Since he is called a "lad" in this chapter, you would not gather that he actually was in his thirties—probably around 30 or 33 years of age. ·

"Take now thy son [notice how this plays upon the heartstrings of Abraham and of God Himself], thine *only* son Isaac, whom thou *lovest*." "Take now thy son"—the Lord Jesus has taken the position of the Son in the Trinity. "Thy son, thine only son"—the Lord Jesus is said to be the only begotten Son. "Thine only son Isaac, whom thou lovest"—the Lord Jesus said, "The Father loves Me."

"And get thee into the land of Moriah." It is the belief of a great many that Moriah—that is, this particular part—is the place where the temple was built centuries later and also the place that the Lord Jesus was sacrificed—right outside the city walls. When I was in Jerusalem, I had the feeling that Golgotha and the temple area were not very far apart. They belong to the same ridge. A street has been cut through there, and the ridge has been breeched, but it is the same ridge, and it is called Moriah. Let's not say that the Lord Jesus died in the exact spot—we don't know—but certainly He died on the same ridge, the same mountain, on which Abraham offered Isaac.

"And offer him there for a burnt offering upon one of the mountains which I will tell thee of." The burnt offering was the offering up until the time of Mosaic law; then a sin offering and a trespass offering were given. Here the burnt offering speaks of the person of Christ, who He is. This is an offer of a human sacrifice, and, frankly, it raises this moral question: Isn't human sacrifice wrong? Yes, it is morally wrong. Had you met Abraham on that day when he was on his way with Isaac, you might have asked him, "Where are you going, Abraham?" He would have replied, "To offer Isaac as a sacrifice." And you would have then asked, "Don't you know that that is wrong?" Abraham would have said, "Yes, I've been taught that it was wrong. I know that the heathen nations around here offer human sacrifice—the Philistines offer to Molech—but I have been taught otherwise." You would then question him further, "Then why are you doing it?" and he would explain, "All I know is that God has commanded it. I don't understand it. But I've been walking with Him now for over fifty years. He has never failed me, nor has He asked me to do anything that did not prove to

be the best thing. I don't understand this, but I believe that if I go all the way with Him that God will raise Isaac from the dead. I believe that He will do that."

This is a tremendous picture as Abraham takes Isaac with him:

And Abraham rose up early in the morning, and saddled his ass, and took two of his young men with him, and Isaac his son, and clave the wood for the burnt offering, and rose up, and went unto the place of which God had told him [Gen. 22:3].

Abraham takes Isaac with him, and he takes the wood for the burnt offering.

Then on the third day Abraham lifted up his eyes, and saw the place afar off [Gen. 22:4].

It took Abraham three days to get there, but remember that it was on the third day that Abraham received Isaac alive, back from the dead, as it were. That is the way that Abraham looked at it: Isaac was raised up to him the third day. What a picture we have here.

And Abraham said unto his young men, Abide ye here with the ass; and I and the lad will go yonder and worship, and come again to you [Gen. 22:5].

The transaction that is going to take place is between the father and the son, between Abraham and Isaac. And actually, God shut man out at the cross. At the time of the darkness at high noon, man was shut out. The night had come when no man could work, and during those last three hours, that cross became an altar on which the Lamb of God who taketh away the sin of the world was offered. The transaction was between the Father and the Son on that cross. Man was outside and was not participating at all. The picture is the same here: it is Abraham and Isaac alone.

And Abraham took the wood of the burnt offering, and laid it upon Isaac his son; and he took the fire in his hand, and a knife; and they went both of them together [Gen. 22:6].

"Abraham took the wood . . . and laid it upon Isaac his son." Remember that Christ carried His own cross. The fire here speaks of judgment, and the knife speaks of the execution of judgment and of sacrifice.

And Isaac spake unto Abraham his father, and said, My father: and he said,

Here am I, my son. And he said, Behold the fire and the wood: but where is the lamb for a burnt offering?

And Abraham said, My son, God will provide himself a lamb for a burnt offering: so they went both of them together [Gen. 22:7–8].

Verse 13 tells us that shortly after this there was a ram that was caught in the thicket by his horns, and Abraham got that ram and offered it. Abraham says here that God will provide Himself a *lamb*. But there was no *lamb* there; it was a *ram*, and there is a distinction. The Lamb was not provided until centuries later when John the Baptist marked Him out and identified Him, saying, ". . . Behold the Lamb of God, which taketh away the sin of the world" (John 1:29). "God will provide himself a lamb for a burnt offering"—it is very important to see that Abraham was speaking prophetically.

Abraham is now ready to offer this boy on the altar although he does not quite understand.

And they came to the place which God had told him of; and Abraham built an altar there, and laid the wood in order, and bound Isaac his son, and laid him on the altar upon the wood [Gen. 22:9].

Isaac is not just a little boy whom Abraham had to tie up. He is a grown man, and I believe that Isaac could have overcome Abraham if it had come to a physical encounter. But Isaac is doing this in obedience. The Lord Jesus went to the cross having said, "Not My will, but Thine be done." He went to the cross to fulfill the will of God. What a picture we have here!

And Abraham stretched forth his hand, and took the knife to slay his son [Gen. 22:10].

At this point you and I might have said, "Abraham, are you going through with it? It looks now like God is going to permit you to." He would have said, "I sure am. I've been taught that it is wrong, and I don't understand, but I've also learned to obey God."

This is a real crisis in Abraham's life. God has brought this man through four very definite crises, each of which was a real exercise of his soul, a real strain upon his heart. First of all, he was called to leave all of his relatives in Ur of the Chaldees. He was just to leave the whole group. That was a real test for Abraham. He didn't do it very well at the beginning, but, nevertheless, the break finally came. Then there was the test that came with Lot, his nephew. Abraham loved Lot—he wouldn't have been carrying Lot around with him if he hadn't. But the time came when they had to separate, and Lot went down to Sodom. Then there was the test with this boy of his, the son of Hagar, Ishmael. Abraham just cried out to God, "Oh, that Ishmael might live before Thee!" He loved that boy; he hated to be separated from him. Now Abraham comes to this supreme test, the fourth great crisis in his life: he is asked to give up Isaac. Abraham does not quite understand all the details for the very simple reason that God has told him, "In Isaac your seed shall be called." Abraham believed God would raise Isaac from the dead (see Heb. 11:19), but as far as Abraham is concerned, he is willing to go through with the sacrifice.

GOD RESTRAINS ABRAHAM

James wrote that Abraham was justified by works when he offered up his son. But wait just a minute. Did Abraham offer his son? Does your Bible say that Abraham plunged the knife into his son? No, and mine doesn't read that way either.

And the angel of the LORD called unto him out of heaven, and said, Abraham, Abraham: and he said, Here am I.

And he said, Lay not thine hand upon the lad, neither do thou any thing unto him: for now I know that thou fearest God, seeing thou hast not withheld thy son, thine only son from me [Gen. 22:11–12].

Now God knows that Abraham fears Him. How does He know? By his actions, by his works; previously it was by his faith. God sees your heart—He knows whether you are genuine or not—but your neighbors and your friends do not know. They can only know by your works. That is the reason James could say that "faith without works is dead." Faith has to produce something.

God tested Abraham. I believe that any person whom God calls, any person whom God saves, any person whom God uses is going to be tested. God tested Abraham, and God tests those who are His own today. He tests you and me, and the tests are given to us to strengthen our faith, to establish us, and to make us serviceable for Him. This man Abraham is now given the supreme test, and God will not have to ask anything of him after this.

And Abraham lifted up his eyes, and looked, and behold behind him a ram caught in a thicket by his horns: and Abraham went and took the ram, and

offered him up for a burnt offering in the stead of his son [Gen. 22:13].

All the way from the Garden of Eden down to the cross of Christ, the substitution was this little animal that pointed to His coming—and God would not permit human sacrifice. But when His Son came into the world, His Son went to the cross and died: "He that spared not his own Son, but delivered him up for us all, how shall he not with him also freely give us all things?" (Rom. 8:32). That cross became an altar on which the Lamb of God that taketh away the sin of the world was offered. It is very important to see that.

And Abraham called the name of that place Jehovah-jireh: as it is said to this day, In the mount of the LORD it shall be seen [Gen. 22:14].

Abraham now names this place which a great many people believe is where Solomon's temple was built. Golgotha, the place of a skull, is right there on that same ridge where the temple stood. There Abraham offered his son, and it was there that the Lord Jesus Christ was crucified. This is a glorious, wonderful thing to see. Abraham calls the name of this place *Jehovah-jireh*, meaning Jehovah will provide. Here is where God intervened in his behalf.

GOD REAFFIRMS HIS PROMISES

And the angel of the LORD called unto Abraham out of heaven the second time,

And said, By myself have I sworn, saith the LORD, for because thou hast done this thing, and hast not withheld thy son, thine only son [Gen. 22:15–16].

I have a question to ask: *Did* Abraham do it? No, he did not offer his son, but God says to him, "Because you have done this thing. . . ." You see, Abraham believed God, and he went far enough to let you and me know—God already knew—and to let the created universe know that he was willing to give his son. And so God counted it to him that he had done it. Abraham is justified by faith, but he is also justified before men by his works. He *demonstrated* that he had that faith.

"And hast not withheld thy son, *thine only son*." Notice how God plays upon that—because He gave His only Son.

Through this incident, God is making it clear that there will have to be a Man to stand in the gap, there will have to be a Man capable of becoming the Savior of the race if anyone is to be saved. That is a great lesson given to us

in this chapter. Abraham said that God would provide Himself a Lamb, and they found a ram and offered it. But God did provide a Lamb nineteen hundred years later in Christ. God stayed Abraham's hand and did not let him go through with the sacrifice of Isaac because it would have been wrong. God spared Abraham's son, but God did not spare His own Son but gave Him up freely for us all.

That in blessing I will bless thee, and in multiplying I will multiply thy seed as the stars of the heaven, and as the sand which is upon the sea shore; and thy seed shall possess the gate of his enemies;

And in thy seed shall all the nations of the earth be blessed; because thou hast obeyed my voice [Gen. 22:17–18].

"And in *thy seed* shall all the nations of the earth be blessed." What "seed" is God talking about here? If you go to Galatians 3:16, you will find that Paul interprets what the "seed" means: "Now to Abraham and his seed were the promises made. He saith not, And to seeds, as of many; but as of one, And to thy seed, which is Christ." Thus we have the Bible's own interpretation of the "seed."

Going back to the eighth verse, we find that Paul says this: "And the scripture, foreseeing that God would justify the heathen through faith, preached before the gospel unto Abraham, saying, In thee shall all nations be blessed" (Gal. 3:8). When did God preach the gospel to Abraham? God preached the gospel to him when He called upon him to offer his son Isaac upon the altar. God says here, "In thy seed shall all the nations of the earth be blessed," and that seed is Christ. This is the gospel as it was given to Abraham, if you please.

I would like to make a comment here concerning something that is customarily overlooked. We assume that Abraham, Isaac, Jacob, and all the Old Testament worthies were great men but that they were not as smart as we are, that they did not know as much as we know. However, I am of the opinion that Abraham knew a great deal more about the coming of Christ and the gospel than you and I give him credit for. In fact, the Lord Jesus said, "Your father Abraham rejoiced to see my day: and he saw it, and was glad" (John 8:56). So he must have known a great deal more than we realize. God had revealed much to Abraham, but the Savior was not yet come. We know today that He would not come for nineteen hundred years, but there on the top of Mount Moriah where Abraham offered Isaac was a picture of the offering and even of the resurrection of Christ! After God called Abraham to offer Isaac, it was three days before he even got to Moriah. God gave Isaac back to Abraham alive on the third day; so that this is a picture of both the death and resurrection of Christ. Paul says that God preached the gospel to Abraham, and certainly it was done here.

"And in thy seed shall *all* the nations of the earth be blessed." Today the gospel of Christ has gone out pretty much to all the world. There are many who have not heard—that is true even in our own midst—but nevertheless, the blessing has come to all nations. And the only blessing the nations have is through Christ.

"Because thou hast obeyed my voice." That obedience rested upon Abraham's faith, and faith always will lead to action. "Faith without works is dead."

ABRAHAM RETURNS TO BEER-SHEBA

So Abraham returned unto his young men, and they rose up and went together to Beer-sheba; and Abraham dwelt at Beer-sheba.

And it came to pass after these things, that it was told Abraham, saying, Behold, Milcah, she hath also born children unto thy brother Nahor [Gen. 22:19–20].

The remainder of this chapter gives us a little sidelight on the family of Abraham. Abraham had left his brother Nahor way back yonder in the land of Haran. His line will not be followed in the Scriptures, but it will cross the line of Abraham a little later on. We will go into that when we come to it. If you read the rest of this chapter, you will have quite an exercise in the pronunciation of names.

CHAPTER 23

THEME: Death and burial of Sarah

In chapter 23 we see the death of Sarah and Abraham's purchase of a cave in which to bury her, the cave of Machpelah.

And Sarah was an hundred and seven and twenty years old: these were the years of the life of Sarah.

And Sarah died in Kirjath-arba; the same is Hebron in the land of Canaan: and Abraham came to mourn for Sarah, and to weep for her [Gen. 23:1–2].

Notice that Sarah's age is given as 127 years old. She was 90 when Isaac was born, which means that at the time of her death (which took place after the offering of Isaac by several years, I suppose), Isaac was 37 years old.

We are told that Sarah died in Kirjath-arba, which is Hebron. Abraham even had to buy a cave in which to bury his dead in the very land that God had given to him. Why didn't he take Sarah somewhere else to bury her? It is because the hope they have of the future is in that land. As we move on down in this chapter, we will see that although there are the arrangements for a funeral, which is not very exciting or interesting and is perhaps even a little mor-

bid to some, it is very important to see a great truth here.

And Abraham stood up from before his dead, and spake unto the sons of Heth, saying,

I am a stranger and a sojourner with you: give me a possession of a burying-place with you, that I may bury my dead out of my sight [Gen. 23:3–4].

Abraham calls himself a stranger and a sojourner even in the Promised Land which God had promised to give to him.

And the children of Heth answered Abraham, saying unto him,

Hear us, my lord: thou art a mighty prince among us: in the choice of our sepulchres bury thy dead; none of us shall withhold from thee his sepulchre, but that thou mayest bury thy dead [Gen. 23:5–6].

This is a very generous offer made by the children of Heth who live in this land. They probably said to Abraham, "Just pick your burying spot in any of our sepulchers—that's it. We'd be delighted to have you." Abraham had made a tremendous impression. They call him "a mighty prince." This man's influence counted for something.

And Abraham stood up, and bowed himself to the people of the land, even to the children of Heth.

And he communed with them, saying, If it be your mind that I should bury my dead out of my sight; hear me, and entreat for me to Ephron the son of Zohar,

That he may give me the cave of Machpelah, which he hath, which is in the end of his field; for as much money as it is worth he shall give it me for a possession of a buryingplace amongst you [Gen. 23:7–9].

The cave of Machpelah was the place Abraham chose, but he wanted to buy it; he wanted nothing given to him. In other words, until God gives him that land, he will buy what he needs and wants. So now he actually buys a burying place.

Again I ask the question: Why didn't Abraham take Sarah somewhere else to bury her? He buried her here because it is the promised land and the hope of the future is here. As you go through the Bible, you will find that there are two great hopes and two great purposes which God has. He has an *earthly* purpose, and He has a *heavenly* purpose. He has an earthly purpose; that is, this earth on which you and I live is going into eternity. It is going to be traded in on a new model. There will be a new heaven and a new earth. But there *will* be an earth, and it will be inhabited throughout eternity. This is the promise that God gave to Abraham and to those after him. God is not going to put this earth on which you and I live in the garbage can after He gets through with the program which He is carrying out today; nor is it going to be disposed of in a wrecking yard for old and battered cars. God is not going to get rid of it. He intends to trade it in on a new model. The new earth will go into eternity, and there will be people to inhabit it. This was the hope of Abraham. Abraham wanted to be buried in that land so that, when the resurrection came, he and Sarah would be raised in that land. He never knew how many were coming after him, but there are going to be literally millions raised from the dead. This is their hope. It is an earthly hope, and it will be realized.

In the Upper Room, our Lord said this to His disciples who were schooled in the Old Testament and who had the Old Testament hope: "Let not your heart be troubled: ye believe in God, believe also in me. In my Father's house are many mansions: if it were not so, I would have told you. I go to prepare a place for you. And if I go and prepare a place for you, I will come again, and receive you unto myself; that where I am, there ye may be also" (John 14:1–3). He is speaking of the New Jerusalem which He is preparing today and which is the place to which the church will go. The New Jerusalem will be the eternal abode of the church. This teaching was brand-new to the disciples, and I am afraid that it is brand-new to a great many Christians. God never told Abraham that He would take him away from this earth to heaven. Rather, He kept telling him, "I am going to give you this land." Abraham believed God, and that was the reason that he wanted Sarah buried in that land. It became the place for him to bury his dead. He intended to be buried there, and he *is* buried there.

The exact location of Abraham's burying place is at Hebron, about twenty miles south of Jerusalem. When we made a trip there, we visited the Moslem mosque which is built over that spot. Frankly, on our entire trip through that land, I never felt uncomfortable or even a little afraid, except at Hebron. We had been warned to be very careful in Hebron, that there was a great deal of antagonism toward tourists and, actually, toward everyone who did not belong there. Of course, they allowed us to visit the mosque because it meant tourist dollars. After we went in, we looked through a little hole in the floor and down into the cave where Abraham and Sarah, Isaac and Rebekah, Jacob and Leah are all supposed to be buried. (Rachel is buried at Beth-lehem.) These folk are all buried in Israel because of their hope of being raised from the dead in that land. It is an earthly hope. Our hope as New Testament believers is a heavenly hope. I trust that that is clear to you so that you can understand why this burial was so important to Abraham at this particular time.

Abraham now makes a deal to buy the cave. Notice the transaction:

And Ephron dwelt among the children of Heth: and Ephron the Hittite answered Abraham in the audience of the children of Heth, even of all that went in at the gate of his city, saying,

Nay, my lord, hear me: the field give I thee, and the cave that is therein, I give

it thee; in the presence of the sons of my people give I it thee: bury thy dead.

And Abraham bowed down himself before the people of the land [Gen. 23:10–12].

Notice Abraham and the generosity of these people and of this man Ephron in particular. They certainly were polite in that day. We have the impression that these were cavemen who carried clubs around ready to club each other. If Abraham, Isaac, Jacob, and the other Old Testament saints—even the men who are mentioned in this chapter—were in Los Angeles today and could go back and report to their folk, I think they would say, "Do you know that our offspring are a bunch of cavemen? They're highly uncivilized! They are rude and crude and a disgrace." I think they would say that of us, but *we* have the advantage that we can talk about them. It is interesting to note how polite they are. "And Abraham bowed down himself before the people of the land."

And he spake unto Ephron in the audience of the people of the land, saying, But if thou wilt give it, I pray thee, hear me: I will give thee money for the field; take it of me, and I will bury my dead there.

And Ephron answered Abraham, saying unto him,

My lord, hearken unto me: the land is worth four hundred shekels of silver; what is that betwixt me and thee? bury therefore thy dead.

And Abraham hearkened unto Ephron;

and Abraham weighed to Ephron the silver, which he had named in the audience of the sons of Heth, four hundred shekels of silver, current money with the merchant [Gen. 23:13–16].

That is, Abraham paid for the field and cave in the legal tender of that day.

And the field of Ephron, which was in Machpelah, which was before Mamre, the field, and the cave which was therein, and all the trees that were in the field, that were in all the borders round about, were made sure.

Unto Abraham for a possession in the presence of the children of Heth, before all that went in at the gate of his city.

And after this, Abraham buried Sarah his wife in the cave of the field of Machpelah before Mamre: the same is Hebron in the land of Canaan.

And the field, and the cave that is therein, were made sure unto Abraham for a possession of a buryingplace by the sons of Heth [Gen. 23:17–20].

Apparently, this place is where the mosque is built at Hebron today. It is considered either the second or third most important mosque in the world of Islam. They have many mosques in Cairo and other places, and the ones I have seen are absolutely beautiful. The most important one, of course, would be at Mecca. I am not sure whether the one at Hebron or the one at Jerusalem would be number two, but the other would then be number three. You can see how important this is, because the Arabs all trace their lineage back to Abraham.

CHAPTER 24

THEME: A bride for Isaac

We have come in chapter 24 to a major break in this second division of Genesis. The first division (chapters 1–11) deals with *four great events*. The second and final division, chapters 12–50, deals with *four outstanding individuals*. Specifically, in Genesis 12–23 we have Abraham, the man of faith. Now in chapters 24–26 we have Isaac, the beloved son. There are three great events in the life of Isaac, and we have already seen two of them. The first was his birth, and the second was his being offered by Abraham. The third is the obtaining of his bride. They say there are three great events in a man's life—his birth, his marriage, and his death—and that he has no choice except with the second one, marriage. Sometimes a man doesn't seen to have much choice in that connection either, but, nevertheless, these are the three great events in a man's life.

We come now to the story of how Isaac secured his bride. Abraham sends his trusted servant back to the land of Haran in Mesopotamia to get a bride for Isaac—and we will see the success of the servant in securing Rebekah. This is a very wonderful love story. It reveals that God is interested in the man whom you marry, young lady, and He is interested in the young lady whom you marry, young man.

There are two institutions that God has given to the human family: one is marriage, and the other is human government (God permits man to rule himself today). These are two universal and very important institutions. When these are broken, a society will fall apart. The home is the backbone of any society—God knew that—and He established marriage, intending that it give strength and stability to society. The same thing is true relative to human government—a government must have the power to take human life in order to protect human life—that is the purpose of it. Because human life is sacred, God gave such laws.

The point here is that God is interested in your love story, and it is wonderful when you bring God into it. The first miracle that our Lord performed was at a wedding in Cana of Galilee. I do not know how many weddings He went to, but He went to that one.

The twenty-fourth chapter of Genesis is one of the richest sections of the Word of God because it tells a love story that goes way back to the very beginning. A very dramatic account is given here of the way that a bride was secured for Isaac, and again, a fantastic spiritual picture is also presented to us. There are two things that I want you to notice as we go through this chapter. One is the leading of the Lord in all the details of the lives of those involved. It is a remarkable statement that is made, time and time again, of how God led. Even in this early day, there were those in that social climate who were looking to God and following His leading. Some would have us believe that this took place in the Stone Age, when man was a caveman and pretty much uncivilized. Don't believe a word of it! Here is a record that shows that man did not start out as that kind of man at all—and we find here the leading of God. If God could lead in the lives of these folk, He can lead in your life and my life. The second thing to notice in this chapter is the straightforward manner in which Rebekah made her decision to go with the servant and become the bride of Isaac. This is a tremendous thing which we will notice as we go through.

And Abraham was old, and well stricken in age: and the LORD had blessed Abraham in all things [Gen. 24:1].

Abraham is old, well stricken in age, and the Lord has blessed him in all things. Abraham now wants to get a bride for his son Isaac, but he does not want to get a bride among the Canaanites where the people are given to idolatry and paganism, and so he will send his servant to his people, back in the land of Haran, to get a bride for Isaac.

And Abraham said unto his eldest servant of his house, that ruled over all that he had, Put, I pray thee, thy hand under my thigh [Gen. 24:2].

This is the way men took an oath in that day. They did not raise their right hands and put their left hands on a Bible. They didn't have a Bible to begin with, and frankly, I do not think it is necessary for anyone to put his hand on a Bible to swear that he is telling the truth. If he intends to lie, he will lie even if his hand is resting on a Bible. The method in that day was for a man to put his hand under the thigh of the man to whom he was going to make an oath. I think this servant was Eliezer. He was the head servant in the home of Abraham, and he had a son—remember that Abraham had called God's attention to that earlier (see Gen. 15:2–3).

And I will make thee swear by the LORD, the God of heaven, and the God of the earth, that thou shalt not take a wife unto my son of the daughters of the Canaanites, among whom I dwell [Gen. 24:3].

My Christian friend, if you have a boy or girl in your home who is marriageable, you ought to pray that he will not marry one of the "Canaanites." They are still in the land, and there is always a danger of our young people marrying one of them. If they do, as someone has put it, they are going to have the devil for their father-in-law, and they are always going to have trouble with him.

But thou shalt go unto my country, and to my kindred, and take a wife unto my son Isaac.

And the servant said unto him, Peradventure the woman will not be willing to follow me unto this land: must I needs bring thy son again unto the land from whence thou camest?

And Abraham said unto him, Beware thou that thou bring not my son thither again [Gen. 24:4–6].

In other words the servant says to Abraham, "Suppose I cannot find a girl who will come with me. Shall I come back and get Isaac to take him to that land?" And Abraham says, "Never take Isaac back! This is the place where God wants us. Do not return him to that land under any circumstances." This is very important for us to see.

The LORD God of heaven, which took me from my father's house, and from the land of my kindred, and which spake unto me, and that sware unto me, saying, Unto thy seed will I give this land; he shall send his angel before thee, and thou shalt take a wife unto my son from thence [Gen. 24:7].

Abraham is really a man of faith. He demonstrates it again and again, and here he is magnificent. He says to this servant, "You can count on God to lead you. God has promised me this." Abraham is not taking a leap in the dark—*faith* is not a leap in the dark. It *must* rest upon the Word of God. Many people say, "I believe God, and it will come to pass." That's fine. It is wonderful for you to believe God, but do you have something in writing from Him? Abraham always asked for it in writing, and he had it in writing from God. God had made a

contract with him. Abraham is really saying, "God has promised me that through my seed Isaac He is going to bring a blessing to the world. You can be sure of one thing: God has a bride back there for Isaac." You see, Abraham rests upon what God has said. We need to not be foolish today. Faith is not foolishness. It is resting upon something. It is always reasonable. It is never a leap in the dark. It is not betting your life that this or that will come to pass. It is not a gamble; it is a sure thing. Faith is the real sure thing. Abraham is sure.

And if the woman will not be willing to follow thee, then thou shalt be clear from this my oath: only bring not my son thither again [Gen. 24:8].

Abraham says, "Don't ever take my son back there, but if the woman won't come, then you are discharged." What does that mean? I think it means simply that Abraham would have told you, "God has another way of working this out. I don't know what it will be, but I am very sure that God does not want my son to marry a godless girl."

My friend, that is what faith is. Faith is acting upon *the Word of God*. Faith rests upon something. God wants us to believe *His Word* and not *just* believe. It is pious nonsense to think that you can force God to do something, that God has to do it because you believe it. I have made it through a number of years now with cancer in my body, and no one wants to be healed more than I do. Don't tell me that I don't believe in faith healing—I do. However, I have been told that I can force God, that God *will* heal me if I demand it. I do not know what His will is, but whatever His will is, that is what I want done. God wants us to bring our needs to Him, but He has to be the One to determine how He will answer our prayers. Abraham has something to rest upon. He is not demanding anything of God. He says, "If this doesn't work out, then God has another way to work it out."

And the servant put his hand under the thigh of Abraham his master, and sware to him concerning that matter [Gen. 24:9].

Now watch the servant as he goes out to get a bride for Isaac.

And the servant took ten camels of the camels of his master, and departed; for all the goods of his master were in his hand: and he arose, and went to Mesopotamia, unto the city of Nahor [Gen. 24:10].

The servant who is going to Mesopotamia to get a bride for Isaac takes ten camels along, and that means somebody had to ride them. He took along quite a retine of servants.

"For all the goods of his master were in his hand." In other words, he had charge of all the chattels and all the possessions of Abraham.

And he made his camels to kneel down without the city by a well of water at the time of the evening, even the time that women go out to draw water [Gen. 24:11].

It may seem strange to you that the women came out to draw water, but they were the ones who did the watering of the camels in that day. Very frankly, women did lots more work in those days than they do today—I mean by that, *hard* physical labor. The women were the ones who watered and took care of the stock. The men were supposed to be out trading and doing other work—they were not always loafing, by any means. But it is interesting to note that it was the custom of that day for women to go out to draw water. This servant was waiting because it was not the proper thing for him, as a stranger, to water his camels before the others who lived in that community.

This servant is depending upon God. Abraham had put all of this in the hands of the Lord, and now the servant does also:

And he said, O Lord God of my master Abraham, I pray thee, send me good speed this day, and shew kindness unto my master Abraham.

Behold, I stand here by the well of water; and the daughters of the men of the city come out to draw water:

And let it come to pass, that the damsel to whom I shall say, Let down thy pitcher, I pray thee, that I may drink; and she shall say, Drink, and I will give thy camels drink also: let the same be she that thou hast appointed for thy servant Isaac; and thereby shall I know that thou hast shewed kindness unto my master [Gen. 24:12–14].

The servant's prayer is something like this: "The daughters of the men of the city will be coming out. I do not know which one to choose, and it is just left up to me to pick one of them. I pray that the one that I pick might be the one that You pick." In other words, he calls upon the Lord to lead him in making the right choice.

Who do you think he is going to pick? Well, he is a man, and he is going to pick the best looking woman who comes out. And you can be sure of one thing—Rebekah was a good looking woman. The Puritans had the idea that beauty was of the devil. The devil *is* beautiful—he's an angel of light, by the way—but he does not have it all. After all, God is the Creator, and you have never seen a sunset or looked at a beautiful flower that He did not make. He makes women beautiful, and there is nothing wrong with that. I am sure this man is going to pick the best looking one who comes out—he'd be a pretty poor servant if he didn't.

And it came to pass, before he had done speaking, that, behold, Rebekah came out, who was born to Bethuel, son of Milcah, the wife of Nahor, Abraham's brother, with her pitcher upon her shoulder.

And the damsel was very fair to look upon, a virgin, neither had any man known her: and she went down to the well, and filled her pitcher, and came up [Gen. 24:15–16].

I told you Rebekah was good looking—I knew it was coming, of course. She was good looking—the Word of God says it, my friend, and there is nothing wrong with that. I resent it today that Hollywood, the theater, and the devil get beauty. I think that the Lord ought to have some of it. He made it to begin with, and there is nothing wrong with His using a lovely and beautiful person. I pray always that God will call fine looking men and women into His service today.

"And the damsel was *very* fair to look upon." She was not just an ordinary girl. She would have won a beauty contest. She was "a virgin, neither had any man known her."

And the servant ran to meet her, and said, Let me, I pray thee, drink a little water of thy pitcher.

And she said, Drink, my lord: and she hasted, and let down her pitcher upon her hand, and gave him drink.

And when she had done giving him drink, she said, I will draw water for thy camels also, until they have done drinking [Gen. 24:17–19].

The important thing to note is that Rebekah is a very polite and courteous girl also. She is beautiful, not dumb, and very polite.

And she hasted, and emptied her pitcher into the trough, and ran again unto the

well to draw water, and drew for all his camels [Gen. 24:20].

Remember that there were ten camels, and I do not know how long it had been since they had last filled their tanks. It was just like filling the radiator of a car to fill up those camels.

And the man wondering at her held his peace, to wit whether the LORD had made his journey prosperous or not [Gen. 24:21].

The servant just stands there in amazement. He is wondering whether this is it, whether God is leading or not—he believes He is.

And it came to pass, as the camels had done drinking, that the man took a golden earring of half a shekel weight, and two bracelets for her hands of ten shekels weight of gold;

And said, Whose daughter art thou? tell me, I pray thee: is there room in thy father's house for us to lodge in?

And she said unto him, I am the daughter of Bethuel the son of Milcah, which she bare unto Nahor [Gen. 24:22–24].

Nahor is a brother of Abraham.

She said moreover unto him, We have both straw and provender enough, and room to lodge in.

And the man bowed down his head, and worshipped the LORD [Gen. 24:25–26].

The servant sees the hand of God in this. It is wonderful to have God leading and guiding, is it not?

And he said, Blessed be the LORD God of my master Abraham, who hath not left destitute my master of his mercy and his truth: I being in the way, the LORD led me to the house of my master's brethren [Gen. 24:27].

This is a great statement here: "I being in the way, the LORD led me. . . ." The Lord leads those who are in the way—that is, those who are in *His* way, who are wanting to be led, who will be led of Him, and who will do what He wants done. God can lead a willing heart anytime.

And the damsel ran, and told them of her mother's house these things.

And Rebekah had a brother, and his name was Laban: and Laban ran out

unto the man, unto the well [Gen. 24:28–29].

Right here, let me warn you to keep your eye on Uncle Laban. He will bear watching at this point and from here on. He was greatly impressed by material things. Notice what happens:

And it came to pass, when he saw the earring and bracelets upon his sister's hands, and when he heard the words of Rebekah his sister, saying, Thus spake the man unto me; that he came unto the man; and, behold, he stood by the camels at the well [Gen. 24:30].

The servant just waited out there at the well to see whether anyone would come out to lead him into the home of Rebekah, whether he really had a welcome or not. Believe me, when old Laban saw those rings, he knew it was a very wealthy guest. Uncle Laban is not one to miss a deal. (If you doubt that, ask Jacob later on. Jacob found out that Uncle Laban was a real trader; in fact, he was a better trader than Jacob was.) So Laban went out to welcome the servant.

And he said, Come in, thou blessed of the LORD; wherefore standest thou without? for I have prepared the house, and room for the camels [Gen. 24:31].

Even old Laban recognized the fact that there was the living God, the Creator, the one God.

And the man came into the house: and he ungirded his camels, and gave straw and provender for the camels, and water to wash his feet, and the men's feet that were with him [Gen. 24:32].

Again, we have this footwashing ceremony. Note that there are quite a few men who have come with this servant. The servant is entertained royally in this home—Uncle Laban sees to that.

We have here a marvelous picture of the relationship of Christ and the church. One of the figures of speech that is used in the New Testament is that the church is someday to become the bride of Christ. This is the way the church is being won today, through the Holy Spirit whom the Father and the Son have sent into the world. The Spirit of God, like the servant of Abraham, has come to talk about Another, to take the things of Christ and show them unto us. As this servant has gone to get a bride for Isaac, so the Spirit of God is in the world to call out a bride for Christ. Notice the marvelous dramatic effect that we have here. This is an exciting story and a wonderful record of that day.

And there was set meat before him to eat: but he said, I will not eat, until I have told mine errand. And he said, Speak on [Gen. 24:33].

Abraham's servant says, "Before I can eat, I want to tell you my mission." This is also characteristic of the Holy Spirit who has come into the world to tell about Another. That is primary business as far as God is concerned. I know that there are other businesses that are very important: the business of our government, the great business of the news media, and the great corporations, the automobile and the airplane companies. All this is important, great business. But God is not continuing to deal with this world because of General Motors or the government in Washington, D.C. (whether Republican or Democrat). The stock market on Wall Street is of no great concern in heaven. The thing that is primary as far as God is concerned is to get the gospel out to the peoples of the world. The Spirit of God is here to put this first. The servant of Abraham will not eat before he has spoken, and so they tell him to speak on.

And he said, I am Abraham's servant [Gen. 24:34].

Notice that his name is not given. Likewise, the Lord Jesus said that when the Holy Spirit comes, He will not speak of Himself, but He will take the things of Mine and show them unto you (see John 16:13–15). By the way, what is the name of the Holy Spirit? He has no name. He does not come to speak of Himself; He has come to speak of Another, of Christ. Similarly, this servant is not named, but is simply called a servant of Abraham.

And the LORD hath blessed my master greatly; and he is become great: and he hath given him flocks, and herds, and silver, and gold, and menservants, and maidservants, and camels, and asses [Gen. 24:35].

The servant tells about the father's house. And that is something that the Spirit of God would have *us* know about. He convicts the world of sin, righteousness, and judgment—those are the three things that He talks about to the lost world. He would have us know that the judgment is upon a sinful earth and upon mankind. Men are lost today because they are sinners. I

hear it said that men are lost because they reject Christ. They are *not* lost because they reject Christ; they are lost because they are sinners. Whether they have heard about Him or not, they are lost sinners. That is the condition of man today. The Holy Spirit has come to let us know that there is a Savior who has borne our judgment and who has been made over to us righteousness and that we can have a standing in heaven. The Holy Spirit has come to speak of Another.

"And the LORD hath blessed my master greatly." And, my friend, our Heavenly Father is rich today in cattle and in goods. The cattle on a thousand hills are His. How great *our* Father is!

And Sarah my master's wife bare a son to my master when she was old: and unto him hath he given all that he hath [Gen. 24:36].

In an infinitely greater way, the Lord Jesus is the Inheritor, and we are joint heirs with Him today. The servant of Abraham has come to tell this family that he is after a bride for his master's son who is going to inherit all things.

And my master made me swear, saying, Thou shalt not take a wife to my son of the daughters of the Canaanites, in whose land I dwell [Gen. 24:37].

The Holy Spirit is calling out sinners, but they are sinners who are ". . . born again, not of corruptible seed, but of incorruptible, by the word of God, which liveth and abideth for ever" (1 Pet. 1:23). These are the ones He is calling out—yes, sinners—but they have been made children of God. ". . . If any man be in Christ, he is a *new* creature . . ." (2 Cor. 5:17). God is not taking "Canaanites"; His children must be transformed.

But thou shalt go unto my father's house, and to my kindred, and take a wife unto my son.

And I said unto my master, Peradventure the woman will not follow me.

And he said unto me, The LORD, before whom I walk, will send his angel with thee, and prosper thy way; and thou shalt take a wife for my son of my kindred, and of my father's house:

Then shalt thou be clear from this my oath, when thou comest to my kindred; and if they give not thee one, thou shalt be clear from my oath.

And I came this day unto the well, and said, O Lord God of my master Abraham, if now thou do prosper my way which I go:

Behold, I stand by the well of water; and it shall come to pass, that when the virgin cometh forth to draw water, and I say to her, Give me, I pray thee, a little water of thy pitcher to drink;

And she say to me, Both drink thou, and I will also draw for thy camels: let the same be the woman whom the Lord hath appointed out for my master's son.

And before I had done speaking in mine heart, behold, Rebekah came forth with her pitcher on her shoulder; and she went down unto the well, and drew water: and I said unto her, Let me drink, I pray thee.

And she made haste, and let down her pitcher from her shoulder, and said, Drink, and I will give thy camels drink also: so I drank, and she made the camels drink also.

And I asked her, and said, Whose daughter art thou? And she said, The daughter of Bethuel, Nahor's son, whom Milcah bare unto him: and I put the earring upon her face, and the bracelets upon her hands.

And I bowed down my head, and worshipped the Lord, and blessed the Lord God of my master Abraham, which had led me in the right way to take my master's brother's daughter unto his son.

And now if ye will deal kindly and truly with my master, tell me: and if not, tell me; that I may turn to the right hand, or to the left [Gen. 24:38–49].

Laban is the spokesman for this family. Listen to him:

Then Laban and Bethuel answered and said, The thing proceedeth from the Lord: we cannot speak unto thee bad or good.

Behold, Rebekah is before thee, take her and go, and let her be thy master's son's wife, as the Lord hath spoken [Gen. 24:50–51].

They say, "As far as we are concerned, this is of the Lord. You go ahead and take Rebekah."

And it came to pass, that, when Abraham's servant heard their words, he worshipped the Lord, bowing himself to the earth.

And the servant brought forth jewels of silver, and jewels of gold, and raiment, and gave them to Rebekah: he gave also to her brother and to her mother precious things [Gen. 24:52–53].

This is the way the Spirit gives to the children of God. We have the earnest, the guarantee, of the Spirit when we come to Christ. Being justified by faith, we have peace with God, we have access, we have joy, we have a hope, and we have the Holy Spirit (see Rom. 5:1–5). These are the wonderful things that have been made over to the believer today.

And they did eat and drink, he and the men that were with him, and tarried all night; and they rose up in the morning, and he said, Send me away unto my master.

And her brother and her mother said, Let the damsel abide with us a few days, at the least ten; after that she shall go [Gen. 24:54–55].

The very next morning this servant says, "I want to be on my way." I'll tell you, this is big business for him! And the brother says, "What's your hurry? Give us at least ten days to tell her good-bye. After all, we had better talk this over with her."

And he said unto them, Hinder me not, seeing the Lord hath prospered my way; send me away that I may go to my master.

And they said, We will call the damsel, and inquire at her mouth [Gen. 24:56–57].

We have come to this very important part that I think is quite wonderful. Don't miss this.

And they called Rebekah, and said unto her, Wilt thou go with this man? And she said, I will go [Gen. 24:58].

Let's take another look at this picture. It is an oriental scene, couched way back yonder in the beginning of time, at the dawn of humanity, in a way. Although I am confident that man had been on this earth thousands of years at this time, as far as we are concerned, this was approximately four thousand years ago. This family is entertaining a guest, a stranger, and they are entertaining him royally. They have fed his camels and taken care of the servants. They have set meat before him, a real feast, but he wanted to state his business.

And so he tells his strange business. He has come to get a bride for his master's son, Isaac. I can see this servant as he brings out the gifts to give to this family—gold and silver trinkets. Abraham, you must remember, was a very rich man. Then the servant begins to tell about the master. As he speaks, I see that family circle around the fire, and in the background, standing just beyond the others, I see a very beautiful girl with deep brown eyes. She is listening intently. She hears the servant tell about Abraham and about how Isaac was born. The servant tells about Isaac's miraculous birth and about his life. Then he tells about the day that his father took him yonder to the top of Mount Moriah to offer him as a sacrifice and how God spared him and would not take his life but gave him back to the father alive. And finally he tells how the father has sent him, a servant, to get a bride for Isaac. They do not want to get a bride for him from among the Canaanites. They must get one who is of like mind, one who has the same capacity for the living God, one who is born again of the Word of God. He is looking for a bride.

Rebekah has been listening all this time, and now they turn to her. No one has paid much attention to her up to this point, but now all eyes turn to her, and they say, "Rebekah, what about it? Will you go with this man?" She does not hedge or fudge or beat around the bush or hesitate. She says, "I will go."

Have you ever noticed that the men whom the Lord Jesus called as His disciples made the same instant decision? They left their nets and followed Him. Oh, I know that they went back a couple of times, but there came a day when they broke loose from those nets, and they never went back to them. They followed Him; they went with Him. The Holy Spirit is still calling today. He is the One who has taken the servant's place. You see, the Father and the Spirit sent the Son into the world to die for the world. And when the Son went back to heaven, He said He would send the Holy Spirit, the Comforter. The Spirit has now come into the world, and He is calling out a bride. He is saying, "Will you go? Here is the One who died for you. He will save you. You have to be redeemed first. You have to come as a sinner to Him, take your rightful position, and accept Him as Savior. When you do, you will be born again; you will become a child of God and be put into the church that is going to be presented to Him someday as a bride." The question is: Will

you go? Will you accept the invitation? Will you trust Christ as your Savior? This is not something about which you can beat around the bush—you either do it or you don't.

I never shall forget the time that I was speaking in a certain place in Texas. I presented Christ, and then I asked, "Will you accept Him?" I really wasn't through preaching, but I never shall forget a young man who sat there, and I could tell he was interested. He got up right there and then and walked down. It had a tremendous effect upon the audience. He was not wishywashy; there wasn't anything uncertain about him. My, I love a clean-cut decision like that! That is the way He wants you, my friend. That is the way He will accept you, and it is the only way He will accept you.

This does not end the story. They start out now, and they are going back to the promised land.

And they sent away Rebekah their sister, and her nurse, and Abraham's servant, and his men.

And they blessed Rebekah, and said unto her, Thou art our sister, be thou the mother of thousands of millions, and let thy seed possess the gate of those which hate them [Gen. 24:59–60].

This prophecy has already been fulfilled. We are not talking here about unfulfilled, but fulfilled, prophecy.

And Rebekah arose, and her damsels, and they rode upon the camels, and followed the man: and the servant took Rebekah, and went his way [Gen. 24:61].

They had a long trip back. We are not told anything about this trip, but I know that it is not easy riding a camel. I rode one from the little village outside of Cairo down to the pyramids—and that's as far as I want to ride on a camel! They call them "the ships of the desert." Well, it was as rough as any trip I have ever had on a boat. It was *rough!* They are not easy to ride, but imagine riding on those camels across the desert. I can see them after a hard day on that hot desert. At evening they stop at an oasis, the campfire is built, and they have their evening meal. As they are sitting there before going to bed to get their sleep, I hear Rebekah say to this servant, "Tell me about Isaac again." The servant says, "What do you want me to tell you?" She says, "Tell me about the way he was born. Tell me about the way his father offered him on the altar." It was like our song, "Tell me the old, old story of Jesus and His love!" And the servant says, "I told you that last night." Rebekah says, "I know, but tell it again. Tell it again." And so the servant tells it again. It never grows old. That night Rebekah has that sweet sleep, dreaming of the time when she will meet this one. The next day they start out on the journey again, and the desert isn't quite as hot, and the camel isn't quite as rough. But it is a long ways, and so they continue until they finally come in sight of the land of promise. They enter it and come down to Lahai-roi.

And Isaac came from the way of the well Lahai-roi; for he dwelt in the south country [Gen. 24:62].

This is way down in the pleasant country of Hebron and Beer-sheba.

And Isaac went out to meditate in the field at the eventide: and he lifted up his eyes, and saw, and, behold, the camels were coming [Gen. 24:63].

In this human episode, we are given a view of the coming of Christ for His bride. Many people are saying, "Won't it be wonderful when the Lord comes and we will be caught up with Him?" There is another view, and that is of those who will be with Him when He comes. Most of the church has already gone through the doorway of death, and they will be coming with Him when He comes. Their bodies will be raised and their spirits and bodies joined together. Those who are alive are to be caught up with the dead to meet the Lord in the air. Those who have gone before in death are going to see Him when He arises from the right hand of the Father and starts out to call His church to meet Him in the air. This is the picture, and what a glorious picture it is!

And Rebekah lifted up her eyes, and when she saw Isaac, she lighted off the camel.

For she had said unto the servant, What man is this that walketh in the field to meet us? And the servant had said, It is my master: therefore she took a veil, and covered herself [Gen. 24:64–65].

We as the bride of Christ will have to be clothed with the Righteousness of Christ, but *He* has been made over to us righteousness. He was delivered for our offenses, and He was raised for our justification in order that we might have a righteousness which will enable us to stand before God.

Rebekah, seeing a man walking toward them, asks who he is. Throughout the long journey she has come to know *about* him, but now she is to see him face to face. This is similar to our position even now. As Peter expressed it, "Whom having not seen, ye love . . ." (1 Peter 1:8). I wonder: When He does come, are we going to know Him? In a song there are these words: "I shall know Him, I shall know Him by the prints of the nails in His hands." I think this is the way that we are going to know Him when He comes. What a glorious, wonderful, beautiful picture we have before us!

And the servant told Isaac all things that he had done [Gen. 24:66].

The Holy Spirit has sealed us and will deliver us to Christ at the day of redemption. Believe me, it was certain that this servant of Abraham's was going to get the bride to Isaac.

Now this is the union of Isaac and Rebekah—

And Isaac brought her into his mother Sarah's tent, and took Rebekah, and she became his wife; and he loved her: and Isaac was comforted after his mother's death [Gen. 24:67].

"And he loved her"—Christ loved the church and gave Himself for her. "And Isaac was comforted after his mother's death." This reveals to us that Christ gains a great deal in our salvation. He wants us; He longs for us. Oh, that you and I might be faithful to Him, my beloved!

CHAPTER 25

THEME: Abraham marries Keturah; Abraham dies; Esau and Jacob

This is another great chapter of the Bible. It records the death of Abraham and the birth of the twins, Esau and Jacob, to Isaac and Rebekah. It gives the generations of Ishmael and also the generations of Isaac. Then there is the incident relative to the birthright. So this is a remarkable chapter, and it covers a great deal of ground.

This chapter concludes the account of Abraham's life, but, frankly, his story ended back in chapter 23 when he sent the servant out to get a bride for Isaac.

ABRAHAM MARRIES KETURAH

Then again Abraham took a wife, and her name was Keturah.

And she bare him Zimran, and Jokshan, and Medan, and Midian, and Ishbak, and Shuah [Gen. 25:1–2].

Now he has quite a family. He had his biggest family after the death of Sarah. Somebody will raise the question, "I thought that at the time of the birth of Isaac Abraham was dead as far as his capability of bringing a child into the world." Granted, he was. But when God does something, He really does it. This is the reason I believe that anything God does bears His signature. Right here we see that this man Abraham was not only able to bring Isaac into the world, but he now brings in this great family of children.

The interesting thing that we have before us here is the mention of Medan and Midian. The other boys will have nations come from them also, but I can't identify them. I'm not interested in them because they do not cross our pathway in Scripture, but Midian does. We will find later that Moses will go down into the land of Midian and take a wife from there. Remember that the Midianites are in the line of Abraham and so are the Medanites. So we find here the fact that there are other sons of Abraham, but the Lord has said it is through Isaac that Abraham's seed is called—not through any of these other sons. It is not through Ishmael, nor through Midian, nor Medan. All of these were nomads of the desert.

ABRAHAM DIES

And Abraham gave all that he had unto Isaac.

But unto the sons of the concubines, which Abraham had, Abraham gave gifts, and sent them away from Isaac his son, while he yet lived, eastward, unto the east country.

And these are the days of the years of Abraham's life which he lived, an hundred threescore and fifteen years.

Then Abraham gave up the ghost, and died in a good old age, an old man, and full of years; and was gathered to his people.

And his sons Isaac and Ishmael buried him in the cave of Machpelah, in the field of Ephron the son of Zohar the Hittite, which is before Mamre;

The field which Abraham purchased of the sons of Heth: there was Abraham buried, and Sarah his wife [Gen. 25:5–10].

Ishmael comes for the funeral because, after all, Abraham is his father. So Isaac and Ishmael together bury Abraham. Then Isaac goes down to live at the place where he first met Rebekah.

And it came to pass after the death of Abraham, that God blessed his son Isaac; and Isaac dwelt by the well Lahai-roi [Gen. 25:11].

In verses 12 to 18 we have the generations of Ishmael, Abraham's son, whom Hagar the Egyptian, Sarah's handmaid, bare unto Abraham. The list of them is given here. I call to your attention again the fact that the Holy Spirit uses this method in the Book of Genesis. The rejected line is given first and then set aside and not mentioned anymore. Then the line that is leading to Christ is given and followed. So it is after the line of Ishmael is given that we come to the line of Isaac.

ESAU AND JACOB

And these are the generations of Isaac, Abraham's son: Abraham begat Isaac [Gen. 25:19].

This is the line we are going to follow. "Abraham begat Isaac; and Isaac begat Jacob" is the way the first chapter of Matthew begins. Each of these men had other sons, as we have seen. Abraham had quite a few sons, but the genealogy of those men is not followed. It is the genealogy of Isaac that is followed. You can forget Ishmael and Midian and Medan and all the rest. They will cross paths with the descendants of Isaac time and again, but we will not follow their lines.

And Isaac was forty years old when he took Rebekah to wife, the daughter of Bethuel the Syrian of Padan-aram, the sister to Laban the Syrian.

And Isaac entreated the LORD for his wife, because she was barren: and the LORD was entreated of him, and Rebekah his wife conceived [Gen. 25: 20–21].

It is interesting that Rebekah, like Sarah, was barren. But Isaac pled with God on her behalf, and now she is pregnant with twins.

And the children struggled together within her; and she said, If it be so, why am I thus? And she went to inquire of the LORD [Gen. 25:22].

The struggle of these two boys, which began before their birth, represents *the* struggle which still goes on in the world today. There is a struggle between light and darkness, between good and evil, between the Spirit and the flesh. Every child of God knows something of this struggle which Paul sets before us in the seventh chapter of Romans.

Rebekah didn't understand the struggle which was going on within her, and she went to the Lord with the question, "Why am I thus?"

And the LORD said unto her, Two nations are in thy womb, and two manner of people shall be separated from thy bowels; and the one people shall be stronger than the other people; and the elder shall serve the younger [Gen. 25:23].

God makes the statement to her that the elder shall serve the younger. She should have believed it, and her younger son should have believed it.

And when her days to be delivered were fulfilled, behold, there were twins in her womb.

And the first came out red, all over like an hairy garment; and they called his name Esau [Gen. 25:24–25].

The name *Esau* means "red" or "earth-colored." Because he is born first, he is considered the elder. But the elder is to serve the younger.

And after that came his brother out, and his hand took hold on Esau's heel; and his name was called Jacob: and Isaac was threescore years old when she bare them [Gen. 25:26].

Isaac and Rebekah had been married for about twenty years before the children were born. The older one was Esau, and they called him "Red," if you please. Jacob took hold on Esau's heel; so they called him Jacob, meaning the usurper, because he was trying to become the elder or to take his place—but God had already promised that to him.

And the boys grew: and Esau was a cunning hunter, a man of the field; and Jacob was a plain man, dwelling in tents [Gen. 25:27].

Now we will look at these two boys as they grow up in this home. Here they are, twins, but no two boys were ever more different than these two. They not only struggled in the womb, but they are against each other from here on out. They have absolutely different viewpoints, different philosophies of life. Their thinking is different, and their attitudes are different. At the beginning, I must confess, Esau is more attractive than Jacob. But we learn that one can't always judge by the outward sign. We must judge by what takes place on the inside. We learn that in this particular case.

"The boys grew." This fellow Esau was a cunning hunter, the outdoor boy, the athletic type. He is the one we would call the all-American boy today. He went in for sports. He went in for everything that was physical, but he had no understanding or capacity or desire for spiritual things. He was only interested in that which was physical. He represents the flesh.

Jacob was a plain man. I think that you can make of that anything you want to. He lived indoors. He was mama's boy and was tied to her apron strings. You will notice that he did what she told him to do. Jacob is really a mama's boy.

And this boy Esau is papa's boy—

And Isaac loved Esau, because he did eat of his venison: but Rebekah loved Jacob [Gen. 25:28].

Here is the problem in the home. You feel that under these circumstances they are going to have trouble, and they are. When one parent is partial to one child and the other parent is partial to the other child, you have trouble. That is exactly what took place here.

Isaac loved him because he ate of his venison. Esau went out hunting, and he always got something when he went hunting. He brought home the venison. Isaac liked that, and he liked this outdoor type of boy. Rebekah loved Jacob because he was a mama's boy.

As I have said before, at this juncture the boy Esau is much more attractive than Jacob. He seems to be a more wholesome boy. The boy Jacob is cunning; he tries to be clever. The fact of the matter is that he doesn't mind stooping to do things that are absolutely wrong (And God will deal with him for this.) The interesting thing is that although Esau was very attractive on the outside, down underneath he really had no capacity for God whatever. If ever there was a man of the world, he is that man. He is just a physical man and that is all. That is all that he lived for.

Down underneath in Jacob there was a desire for the things that are spiritual. It took God a long time to rub off all the debris that was on top and to remove all the coverings in order to get down to where the spiritual desire was, but He finally did it. Before we are through with our study of Jacob (and his story goes almost all the way through the Book of Genesis), we will see that he was God's man all along, although he didn't demonstrate it until late in life.

Now we are told of an incident which took place in the home. You can well understand that the partiality shown by both father and mother would cause difficulty and conflict. It could not be called a happy home.

And Jacob sod pottage: and Esau came from the field, and he was faint:

And Esau said to Jacob, Feed me, I pray thee, with that same red pottage; for I am faint: therefore was his name called Edom.

And Jacob said, Sell me this day thy birthright.

And Esau said, Behold, I am at the point to die: and what profit shall this birthright do to me? [Gen. 25:29–32].

This incident reveals the nature of both of these men. Esau came from the field. He had been outdoors, and he was tired. He was not starving to death as some would imply. No one who had been brought up in the home of Abraham would starve to death. There would al-

ways be something for him to eat. The thing was that there was nothing prepared right at that moment but this pottage, this stew, which Jacob had made. Jacob was the indoor boy. Evidently he was a good chef.

"Feed me, I pray thee, with that same red (notice in your King James Version that the word *pottage* is in italics, meaning that the word has been supplied by the translators); for I am faint: therefore was his name called Edom." *Edom* means red or earthy just as *Esau* does. This man asks for some of the stew, and Jacob saw his chance. He is a trickster and a traitor, and he wanted the birthright. He said, "Sell me this day thy birthright."

Let's stop and look for a minute at the value of the birthright and what it means. It means that the one who had it was the head of the house. It also means that the one who had it was the priest of the family. In this particular family, it means that the one who had it would be the one who would be in the line that would lead to Christ. Do you think that Esau had valued it at all? Jacob knew that he didn't. He attached no importance to it, and he didn't want to be the priest of the family. In fact, that's the last thing that he wanted to be.

In our day, sometimes when a Christian is asked to do something for the cause of Christ, he replies, "Oh, I'm not a preacher; I can't do that!" There are too many folk today who do not *want* to do that which is spiritual. They don't even want to give the impression that they are interested in spiritual things.

That was Esau. He didn't want to give that impression. If anyone would have called him "deacon" or "preacher," it would have insulted him. He didn't want the birthright. He didn't care about being in the line that led to Christ. No one could have cared less about being in that line.

Jacob sees this, and he says to him, "I'll tell you what I'll do, if you'll give me your birthright, I'll give you a bowl of stew." Esau was very happy with the bargain. He said, "I'll be very happy to do it; what profit is the birthright to me? What do I care about the birthright? I'd rather have a bowl of stew." That is the value which he attached to spiritual things.

Let us remember that Jacob also was wrong in what he did. God had promised, "The elder shall serve the younger." The birthright is coming to Jacob in God's own time. Jacob can't wait; so he reaches out to take that which God has promised him. He takes it in a clever, tricky fashion. He should have waited for God to give it to him.

This man operated on the principle that he would do what he could for himself. He thought that as long as he could help himself there was no reason to look to God to perform it. He felt thoroughly capable of taking care of his business. At the beginning he really did rather well as far as the world would measure him. But there came a day when God sent this man off to college, and Uncle Laban was the president of the college. It was known as the college of hard knocks, and Jacob was going to learn a few things in the college of hard knocks. But here he is still operating on the principle that he is clever enough to get what is coming to him.

And Jacob said, Swear to me this day; and he sware unto him: and he sold his birthright unto Jacob.

Then Jacob gave Esau bread and pottage of lentiles; and he did eat and drink, and rose up, and went his way: **thus Esau despised his birthright [Gen. 25:33–34].**

"Esau *despised* his birthright" is the important thing to see at this juncture. So Esau sat down and ate his stew. He had surrendered his birthright because it meant nothing to him. Nothing that was spiritual meant anything to him. Unfortunately, I'm afraid we have church members like that. They have no spiritual capacity and no understanding of spiritual truths. I believe that the mark of a true Christian is one whom the Spirit of God can teach and guide. It is as if a man today had a very valuable heirloom, let's say an old family Bible which had belonged to his grandfather. Another grandson wants it and offers to give him a quarter for it. So the owner says, "Give me the twenty-five cents because I was going to throw the old thing away anyway." That is exactly what Esau would have done.

But Jacob is wrong also, and we'll see more of his cleverness and trickery in chapter 27.

CHAPTER 26

THEME: God reaffirms His covenant to Isaac; Isaac misrepresents Rebekah; Isaac in Gerar; Isaac goes to Beer-sheba

When I was a much younger preacher, this chapter did not seem to be very exciting. It is quite colorless and uninteresting, which is especially noticeable after we have studied a man like Abraham and an exciting man like Jacob who is to follow. This chapter is about Isaac. In fact, it is the only chapter that is really about Isaac, and it just isn't very thrilling. All he does is dig wells. However, in later years I've come to examine these chapters and have found that God has a message for us in this also. In fact, it is a very important message, and Paul stated it quite accurately: "For whatsoever things were written aforetime were written for our learning, that we through patience and comfort of the scriptures might have hope" (Rom. 15:4). This is a chapter that teaches patience, and some of us need that—certainly I am in that category. Yet, we would not have you get the impression that patience is all that God wants of us. The Lord also had men like Abraham, like Jacob, and like David, men who were real go-getters and who were aggressive. God can use that also. But the life of Isaac has a great message for many of us. "All scripture is given by inspiration of God, and is profitable for doctrine, for reproof, for correction, for instruction in righteousness: That the man of God may be perfect, throughly furnished unto all good works" (2 Tim. 3:16–17). With that in mind, let us come to this chapter.

Isaac, the beloved son, has the covenant confirmed to him. Then we find him dropping into the same sin of unbelief as his father Abraham had done. Finally, we see him digging wells in the land of Gerar. This doesn't seem to be very exciting but there is a message here for us; so let us not miss it.

GOD REAFFIRMS
HIS COVENANT TO ISAAC

And there was a famine in the land, beside the first famine that was in the days of Abraham. And Isaac went unto Abimelech king of the Philistines unto Gerar [Gen. 26:1].

This is now the second famine that is mentioned. You remember the famine in the days of Abraham when Abraham and Lot took off for Egypt.

And the LORD appeared unto him, and said, Go not down into Egypt; dwell in the land which I shall tell thee of [Gen. 26:2].

Why did God say that to Isaac? Well, he had an example before him of his father who had run off down to the land of Egypt. This reveals the fact that "like father, like son," sins are carried from father to son. You can talk about the generation gap all you want, but there is no generation gap of sin. It just flows right from one generation to the other. Generally, the son makes very much the same mistakes that the father did, unless something intervenes.

So God gives definite instructions to Isaac at the time of famine. And He confirms the covenant which He had made with Abraham.

Sojourn in this land, and I will be with thee, and will bless thee; for unto thee, and unto thy seed, I will give all these countries, and I will perform the oath which I sware unto Abraham thy father;

And I will make thy seed to multiply as the stars of heaven, and will give unto thy seed all these countries; and in thy seed shall all the nations of the earth be blessed [Gen. 26:3–4].

God says to Isaac, "Don't leave this land, don't go down to Egypt. I want to confirm with *you* the covenant which I made with Abraham." And He repeats the threefold promise: (1) the *land*—"I will give unto thy seed all these countries"; (2) the *nation*—"I will make thy seed to multiply as the stars of heaven"; (3) the *blessing*—"and in thy seed shall all the nations of the earth be blessed."

Because that Abraham obeyed my voice, and kept my charge, my commandments, my statutes, and my laws [Gen. 26:5].

At this point God had not yet given the Mosaic law; Abraham was not under the Mosaic system. However, the important thing is that, when God told Abraham something, he *believed* God and *acted* upon it. He demonstrated his faith by action.

We have too many folk today who complain of a lack of reality in their Christian lives. A lady came in to talk to me some time ago who said that she believed but that she just couldn't

be sure and that she didn't feel anything. Such uncertainty! I didn't have to talk to her long to find out that there was no action in her life. She was just sitting in the corner, twiddling her thumbs, saying, "I believe," and then expecting some great something to take place. That just doesn't happen. When you believe God, you act upon His promises. If you would call me right now to tell me that there is a certain amount of money in a bank in downtown Los Angeles and that you have put it in there for me and I should go down to get it, do you think I would just sit right here the rest of the day? My friend, if you know me, you would know that by the time you hung up the telephone I would have my hat on my head and I'd be going down there. Faith is what you act on. Faith is something that you step out on. Abraham believed God, and God counted it to him for righteousness. God is now telling Isaac that He wants him to be that same kind of a man.

ISAAC MISREPRESENTS REBEKAH

And Isaac dwelt in Gerar [Gen. 26:6].

Gerar is to the south. Abraham and Isaac both lived in the southern part of that land. Actually, Abraham had come into the land up north to Shechem, but he ended up living down in the southern part at Hebron, the "place of communion."

And the men of the place asked him of his wife; and he said, She is my sister: for he feared to say, She is my wife; lest, said he, the men of the place should kill me for Rebekah; because she was fair to look upon [Gen. 26:7].

Isaac is repeating the sin of his father. God had warned him not to go to Egypt; so he didn't go there but went to Gerar instead. In Gerar he must have seen the men casting glances toward Rebekah; so he says to her, "You tell them that you're my sister, not my wife." The difference between Abraham and Isaac is that Abraham told half a lie and Isaac told a whole lie. The one he is telling was cut out of the whole cloth.

And it came to pass, when he had been there a long time, that Abimelech king of the Philistines looked out at a window, and saw, and, behold, Isaac was sporting with Rebekah his wife [Gen. 26:8].

I guess they were laughing and playing together.

And Abimelech called Isaac, and said,

Behold, of a surety she is thy wife: and
how saidst thou, She is my sister? And
Isaac said unto him, Because I said,
Lest I die for her.

And Abimelech said, What is this thou
hast done unto us? one of the people
might lightly have lien with thy wife,
and thou shouldest have brought guilti-
ness upon us [Gen. 26:9–10].

Isaac had put these people in danger of committing a sin. Then Abimelech went on to
say—

And Abimelech charged all his people,
saying, He that toucheth this man or his
wife shall surely be put to death [Gen.
26:11].

Abimelech became a very good friend of
Isaac's. Isaac had the respect of the community just as Abraham had had. Both of them
were outstanding men. I mention that here
because from the rest of the chapter we might
not get the impression that Isaac is an outstanding man.

ISAAC IN GERAR

Then Isaac sowed in that land, and received in the same year an hundredfold:
and the LORD blessed him [Gen. 26:12].

God is with him, you see. That is the blessing that God promised to these people
from the day He called Abraham. It was an
earthly blessing. Later on when God put them
into that land, He told them He would bless
them in their basket; that is, it would be filled
with foodstuff. God made that promise good
when they were walking in fellowship with
Him.

We must remember that He is not promising
us that blessing. He has promised *spiritual*
blessings to us. We are told that we are blessed
with all spiritual blessings, and that is our portion today. But that blessing is on the same
terms. It depends on our walk with God. If you
will permit Him, He wants to bless you abundantly in your spiritual life. We find here that
Isaac is greatly blessed—

And the man waxed great, and went forward, and grew until he became very
great [Gen. 26:13].

Don't miss the fact that Isaac is greatly
blessed. His field brings forth an *hundredfold!*
The impression some of us have is that Abraham was outstanding, and Jacob was also, but

not Isaac. Let me say that Isaac is also outstanding.

It is significant that the life of Isaac is tied in
with that of Abraham. Isaac's birth and his life
are interwoven with Abraham's experiences.
Although Isaac was important when he was
offered there upon the altar, again it was Abraham and Isaac together. Why should it be so
presented? Well, we have already seen that all
these things happened unto them for examples
to us. It presents a wonderful picture of the
intimacy between the Lord Jesus Christ and
the Father. Jesus said, ". . . he that hath seen
me hath seen the Father . . ." (John 14:9). And
in the high priestly prayer of Jesus, He said,
". . . I have finished the work which thou
gavest me to do" (John 17:4). Also, He said,
". . . My Father worketh hitherto, and I work"
(John 5:17). Therefore, it is very proper that
the story of Isaac and the story of Abraham be
identified together.

Now here in the chapter before us we see
Isaac standing on his own two feet, and he
doesn't look too attractive. He exhibits a weakness and repeats the sin of Abraham. However, the Word of God makes it clear that Isaac
was a very great man in that land—

For he had possession of flocks, and possession of herds, and great store of servants: and the Philistines envied him
[Gen. 26:14].

The Philistines couldn't stand to see all this
prosperity—

For all the wells which his father's servants had digged in the days of Abraham
his father, the Philistines had stopped
them, and filled them with earth [Gen.
26:15].

Abraham had been digging wells in that land,
and now his son comes along and the wells
become his. But he would go out in the morning
and find that the wells were all filled up. This
was done by the Philistines and, by the way,
this is the first mention of the enmity of the
Philistines. This led to continual warfare later
on in the days of David.

And Abimelech said unto Isaac, Go from
us; for thou art much mightier than we
[Gen. 26:16].

Notice the importance of Isaac at this time.

And Isaac departed thence, and pitched
his tent in the valley of Gerar, and dwelt
there [Gen. 26:17].

This man Abimelech said, "You are causing a

great deal of difficulty now, and it would be better if you left." He had great respect for Isaac, as you can see.

Now this is a part of Isaac's life that looks like weakness, but it is not. Notice that he returns back to the land where his father Abraham had been—

And Isaac digged again the wells of water, which they had digged in the days of Abraham his father; for the Philistines had stopped them after the death of Abraham: and he called their names after the names by which his father had called them.

And Isaac's servants digged in the valley, and found there a well of springing water.

And the herdmen of Gerar did strive with Isaac's herdmen, saying, The water is ours: and he called the name of the well Esek; because they strove with him [Gen. 26:18–20].

This reveals the struggle that was carried on.

I feel that the water is a picture of the Word of God. We are to drink deeply of it. It is called the "water of the Word" and is for drinking purposes to slake our thirst, and it is also for washing. Jesus said that we are cleansed through the Word which He has spoken.

Water is a very necessary item in life. You can't have life without water. You can fly over the deserts of Arizona, New Mexico, and California and see plenty of arid land. Then all of a sudden you see an area of lush green and wonder what has happened down there. Water is the only explanation.

And, my friend, water is the explanation of the differences between God's children in any church—the water of the Word of God. There is a great difference in the lives of believers who *study* God's Word. And there will be a struggle. I think that you will always have to pay a price if you are really going to study the Word of God. The devil will permit you to do anything except get into the Word of God.

And they digged another well, and strove for that also: and he called the name of it Sitnah.

And he removed from thence, and digged another well; and for that they strove not: and he called the name of it Rehoboth; and he said, For now the LORD hath made room for us, and we shall be fruitful in the land [Gen. 26:21–22].

Then he calls the well Rehoboth. It means "there is room for us." Before that he would dig a well and they would take it away from him. He'd move up, dig another one, and they would take that away from him. He would just keep moving up. This certainly reveals that Isaac is a man of peace and a man of patience. David wouldn't have done this, I can tell you that. Simon Peter wouldn't have done that. And if you want to know the truth, Vernon McGee wouldn't have done that. It is a real lesson for us here. This is especially applicable when we apply it to the study of the Word of God.

ISAAC GOES TO BEER-SHEBA

And he went up from thence to Beer-sheba.

And the LORD appeared unto him the same night, and said, I am the God of Abraham thy father: fear not, for I am with thee, and will bless thee, and multiply thy seed for my servant Abraham's sake [Gen. 26:23–24].

God appears to him to comfort him. God appeared to all the patriarchs with the exception of Joseph. He appeared to Abraham, Isaac, and Jacob.

And he builded an altar there, and called upon the name of the LORD, and pitched his tent there: and there Isaac's servants digged a well [Gen. 26:25].

He goes on again, digging wells. You can always put a well down next to Isaac. You can put an altar down next to Abraham, and you can put a tent down next to Jacob, as we shall see later on.

Then Abimelech went to him from Gerar, and Ahuzzath one of his friends, and Phichol the chief captain of his army.

And Isaac said unto them, Wherefore come ye to me, seeing ye hate me, and have sent me away from you?

And they said, We saw certainly that the LORD was with thee: and we said, Let there be now an oath betwixt us, even betwixt us and thee, and let us make a covenant with thee;

That thou wilt do us no hurt, as we have not touched thee, and as we have done unto thee nothing but good, and have sent thee away in peace: thou art now the blessed of the LORD [Gen. 26:26–29].

Although Isaac almost seems weak in his dealing with the men of Gerar, the king of Gerar was so impressed that he followed Isaac to Beer-sheba in order to establish good relations. The influence of Isaac in that land was not that of a weak man.

And Esau was forty years old when he took to wife Judith the daughter of Beeri the Hittite, and Bashemath the daughter of Elon the Hittite:

Which were a grief of mind unto Isaac and to Rebekah [Gen. 26:34–35].

In the next chapter we will see Jacob in his true colors. Thereby hangs a tale.

CHAPTER 27

THEME: *Jacob takes Esau's birthright; Jacob flees to Laban*

This chapter has as its theme Jacob and Rebekah conniving to get the blessing of Isaac for Jacob. It is the blessing which Isaac intended for Esau. You see, Jacob wanted the blessing of his father. He knew God had promised his mother that the elder would serve the younger; so the blessing was his already. However, he did not believe God. Rebekah, his mother, did not believe God. Evidently Isaac, the father, didn't believe God or he would never have attempted to bypass Jacob and give the blessing to Esau. He followed his own feelings and appetite in contradiction to the distinct Word of God.

The method Jacob used in obtaining the birthright cannot be supported on any grounds whatsoever. He used fraud and deceit. His conduct was despicable. God did not condone this any more than He condoned the conduct of Sarah and Abraham in the matter of Hagar and Ishmael. God could not use the trickery and cleverness of Jacob. As we shall see, God deals with this man in a very definite way. Jacob had to pay for his sin in the same coin in which he sinned. You will note that as we get into this chapter.

Chapter 26 concluded with Esau, who was about forty years old, marrying two Hittite women. This was a grief to Isaac and to Rebekah. Now they recognize that, if Jacob is not to marry a Hittite or a Philistine, he must be sent away to Haran where Isaac got his bride from the family of Abraham.

JACOB TAKES ESAU'S BIRTHRIGHT

And it came to pass, that when Isaac was old, and his eyes were dim, so that he could not see, he called Esau his eldest son, and said unto him, My son: and he said unto him, Behold, here am I.

And he said, Behold now, I am old, I know not the day of my death:

Now therefore take, I pray thee, thy weapons, thy quiver and thy bow, and go out to the field, and take me some venison;

And make me savoury meat, such as I love, and bring it to me, that I may eat; that my soul may bless thee before I die [Gen. 27:1–4].

We have seen that Isaac was an outstanding man, a great man. Abimelech and the Philistines came to make a treaty with him since they feared him. He was patient and peace loving but also prominent and powerful. Here, however, he reveals that weakness of the flesh. All during his life, Esau had been his favorite while Jacob had been the favorite of Rebekah. Esau was the outdoor boy who would go out and bring in a deer or some other animal. He would barbecue it, and the old man would enjoy it. Now he is very old and he wants to bless his favorite son. He knows very well that God has said the elder will serve the younger, but he bypasses that because he wants to bless Esau. So he tells Esau to go out and bring in some meat and he will bless him because of it. What a revelation this is of this family.

Have you noticed the family strife since we have come to this last major section of Genesis? There was strife in the family of Abraham because of Hagar. Now there is strife in this family over these twins.

And Rebekah heard when Isaac spake to Esau his son. And Esau went to the field to hunt for venison, and to bring it.

And Rebekah spake unto Jacob her son,

saying, Behold, I heard thy father speak unto Esau thy brother, saying,

Bring me venison, and make me savoury meat, that I may eat, and bless thee before the LORD before my death.

Now therefore, my son, obey my voice according to that which I command thee [Gen. 27:5–8].

Rebekah overheard what Isaac said. Jacob is her favorite; so she conceives this deceitful plan. It is absolute trickery, and it cannot be condoned on any basis whatever. God is recording it as history, but He condemns it. We will see that. Remember the things that are being done here, and later you will see the chickens come home to roost for Jacob. Now Rebekah goes on to say to him:

Go now to the flock, and fetch me from thence two good kids of the goats; and I will make them savoury meat for thy father, such as he loveth:

And thou shalt bring it to thy father, that he may eat, and that he may bless thee before his death.

And Jacob said to Rebekah his mother, Behold, Esau my brother is a hairy man, and I am a smooth man [Gen. 27:9–11].

Esau was not only an outdoor man and a red man, but he was also a hairy man.

My father peradventure will feel me, and I shall seem to him as a deceiver; and I shall bring a curse upon me, and not a blessing [Gen. 27:12].

Not only will he *seem* to be a deceiver; he is a deceiver.

And his mother said unto him, Upon me be thy curse, my son; only obey my voice, and go fetch me them.

And he went, and fetched, and brought them to his mother: and his mother made savoury meat, such as his father loved.

And Rebekah took goodly raiment of her eldest son Esau, which were with her in the house, and put them upon Jacob her younger son:

And she put the skins of the kids of the goats upon his hands, and upon the smooth of his neck:

And she gave the savoury meat and the bread, which she had prepared, into the hand of her son Jacob [Gen. 27:13–17].

My friend, I can't help but comment on this. She put that skin of the kid of the goat on the back of his neck and on the back of his hands so that when his father would feel him, he'd think it was Esau. She also dressed him in Esau's clothes so he would smell like him! Apparently the deodorant that Esau was using was not very potent. The fact of the matter is, I think he was like the whimsical story I heard about two men who were working in a very tight place. One of them finally said to the other one, "Wow! I think the deodorant of one of us has quit working." The other fellow answered, "It must be yours because I don't use any!" Well, I don't think that Esau used any either, and I'm not sure he had a shower very often. Even if you couldn't see him, you could smell him.

And he came unto his father, and said, My father: and he said, Here am I; who art thou, my son?

And Jacob said unto his father, I am Esau thy firstborn; I have done according as thou badest me: arise, I pray thee, sit and eat of my venison, that thy soul may bless me.

And Isaac said unto his son, How is it that thou hast found it so quickly, my son? And he said, Because the LORD thy God brought it to me [Gen. 27:18–20].

Believe me, this boy at this particular point is typical of pious frauds. You find many such frauds even in fundamental circles today. They talk about the Lord leading them. My, sometimes the Lord "leads" them to do some very unusual things! I find out sometimes that Christian men think they can do things that the Mafia would be arrested for. But these men can very piously pray about it and *say* that it is the Lord's will. Believe me, Jacob at this point is a pious fraud. The Lord had nothing to do with this deception.

And Isaac said unto Jacob, Come near, I pray thee, that I may feel thee, my son, whether thou be my very son Esau or not.

And Jacob went near unto Isaac his father; and he felt him, and said, The voice is Jacob's voice, but the hands are the hands of Esau.

And he discerned him not, because his hands were hairy, as his brother Esau's hands: so he blessed him.

And he said, Art thou my very son Esau? And he said, I am.

And he said, Bring it near to me, and I will eat of my son's venison, that my soul may bless thee. And he brought it near to him, and he did eat: and he brought him wine, and he drank.

And his father Isaac said unto him, Come near now, and kiss me, my son.

And he came near, and kissed him: and he smelled the smell of his raiment, and blessed him, and said, See, the smell of my son is as the smell of a field which the LORD hath blessed [Gen. 27:21–27].

You can tell that Isaac suspected something was wrong, but Rebekah knew Isaac very well and she had worked out every detail.

Therefore God give thee of the dew of heaven, and the fatness of the earth, and plenty of corn and wine:

Let people serve thee, and nations bow down to thee: be lord over thy brethren, and let thy mother's sons bow down to thee: cursed be every one that curseth thee, and blessed be he that blesseth thee [Gen. 27:28–29].

Isaac is giving the blessing which *he* had received—he is passing it on. The interesting thing is that it already belonged to Jacob. God had said that it did. God had already blessed Jacob. God is not accepting this deception at all.

And it came to pass, as soon as Isaac had made an end of blessing Jacob, and Jacob was yet scarce gone out from the presence of Isaac his father, that Esau his brother came in from his hunting.

And he also had made savoury meat, and brought it unto his father, and said unto his father, Let my father arise, and eat of his son's venison, that thy soul may bless me.

And Isaac his father said unto him, Who art thou? And he said, I am thy son, thy firstborn Esau.

And Isaac trembled very exceedingly, and said, Who? where is he that hath taken venison, and brought it me, and I have eaten of all before thou camest, and have blessed him? yea, and he shall be blessed [Gen. 27:30–33].

Somebody may ask whether venison tastes like lamb or goat. It surely does. I remember several years ago when I was pastor in Pasadena that I went deer hunting in Utah with one of the officers of the church. We got a deer, and so we invited the congregation for a dinner just to have a time of good, wholesome fellowship and a lot of fun. We didn't have quite enough meat for all the people; so we bought two lamb legs and cooked that along with the rest of the meat. Nobody could tell the difference, and everyone said the venison was good. Both meats tasted very much alike.

Now Isaac really sees how he has been taken in by this plot.

And when Esau heard the words of his father, he cried with a great and exceeding bitter cry, and said unto his father, Bless me, even me also, O my father.

And he said, Thy brother came with subtilty, and hath taken away thy blessing.

And he said, Is not he rightly named Jacob? for he hath supplanted me these two times: he took away my birthright; and, behold, now he hath taken away my blessing. And he said, Hast thou not reserved a blessing for me?

And Isaac answered and said unto Esau, Behold, I have made him thy lord, and all his brethren have I given to him for servants; and with corn and wine have I sustained him: and what shall I do now unto thee, my son?

And Esau said unto his father, Hast thou but one blessing, my father? bless me, even me also, O my father. And Esau lifted up his voice, and wept.

And Isaac his father answered and said unto him, Behold, thy dwelling shall be the fatness of the earth, and of the dew of heaven from above;

And by thy sword shalt thou live, and shalt serve thy brother: and it shall come to pass when thou shalt have the dominion, that thou shalt break his yoke from off thy neck [Gen. 27:34–40].

JACOB FLEES TO LABAN

And Esau hated Jacob because of the blessing wherewith his father blessed him: and Esau said in his heart, The days of mourning for my father are at hand; then will I slay my brother Jacob [Gen. 27:41].

Esau is thinking. *My father is old and won't live much longer. Just as soon as my father dies, I'll kill Jacob. I'll get rid of him!* This is the thought of his heart, and he evidently talked about it to others.

And these words of Esau her elder son were told to Rebekah: and she sent and called Jacob her younger son, and said unto him, Behold, thy brother Esau, as touching thee, doth comfort himself, purposing to kill thee.

Now therefore, my son, obey my voice; and arise, flee thou to Laban my brother to Haran [Gen. 27:42–43].

Here again we see Rebekah taking things into her own hands. She tells Jacob, "You are going to have to leave home." Little did she know that she would pay for her part in this, her sin. She never saw this boy again. She said she would send him over there for a little while, but it was a long while and she died before he got back.

We must remember that Jacob is her favorite. She wants Jacob to go to her brother, Laban, and that is where she will send him. This is where Jacob is going to learn his lesson. This is where the chickens will come home to roost. Old Uncle Laban is going to put him through school and teach him a few things. Jacob thought he was clever, but Uncle Laban is an expert at cleverness. Poor Jacob will find he is just an amateur, and he is going to cry out to God in desperation before it is all over.

And tarry with him a few days, until thy brother's fury turn away:

Until thy brother's anger turn away from thee, and he forget that which

thou hast done to him: then I will send, and fetch thee from thence: why should I be deprived also of you both in one day? [Gen. 27:44–45].

Notice that she says she will send him away for a few days. A few days lengthened to twenty years, and during that interval she died. She never saw her boy, her pet, her favorite, again.

We can picture the life of Rebekah during those years when we consider that Esau probably did not think much of his mother after that little episode.

And Rebekah said to Isaac, I am weary of my life because of the daughters of Heth: if Jacob take a wife of the daughters of Heth, such as these which are of the daughters of the land, what good shall my life do me? [Gen. 27:46].

Remember that Esau had married these heathen, godless women. Already that was bringing sorrow into the home, and even Rebekah was overwhelmed by it. Now she tells Isaac that if Jacob stays there he will probably do the same thing. She could use this as an excellent excuse to get Jacob away from home to protect him from Esau. She has this little conference with Isaac to convince him that the thing to do is to send Jacob back to her family, to her brother Laban. Remember how Abraham's servant had gone there to get her. So now the point is to get Jacob back there to find a wife, but also to get him out of danger. Very frankly, I think that if he had stayed at home, Esau would have tried to kill him. However, the way it turned out, Rebekah was the first to die, and Jacob got back for his father's funeral. But he never again saw his mother.

CHAPTER 28

THEME: *God appears to Jacob at Bethel; Jacob makes a vow*

In the previous chapter we saw Jacob doing one of the most despicable things any man could do. He did it at the behest of his mother. You know, sometimes people excuse themselves for being mean by saying it is because their mother didn't love them when they were little. Believe me, Jacob couldn't say that. Jacob was loved and spoiled. When he was asked to do something that was not the honorable thing to do, he did it. He stole the birthright from his brother.

The birthright was already his. The formality of his father giving a blessing wasn't necessary at all. Abraham hadn't given the blessing to Isaac—*God* had! And it is God who gave it to Jacob. His trickery was not only unnecessary, but God will deal with him because of it, you can be sure of that.

The plan that Rebekah has now thought of is plausible and logical. It probably was the right thing to do in this case. She didn't mention to Isaac that she wanted to send Jacob to her brother so that he'd get away from the wrath of his brother Esau, but she did mention the fact that he could choose a wife back there from among her family.

In this chapter we will find Jacob leaving home. He comes to Beth-el where God appears to him and confirms to him the covenant made to Abraham.

And Isaac called Jacob, and blessed him, and charged him, and said unto him, Thou shalt not take a wife of the daughters of Canaan [Gen. 28:1].

All the way through the Old Testament we find that God does not want the godly to marry the ungodly. That, again, is my reason for believing that in the sixth chapter of Genesis, where it says the sons of God looked upon the daughters of men, it is saying that the godly line married with the godless line of Cain. This finally resulted in the judgment of the Flood with only one godly man left.

Intermarriage always leads to godlessness. I say this as a caution. I recognize that we are living in a day when young people are not very apt to take advice from an old preacher. They wonder what he knows about it all. Frankly, if you want to know the truth, I know a whole lot about this particular matter. I've done years of counseling and have had many, many couples come to me and have been able to watch them through the years. The story is pretty much

the same. A young lady or a young man will say they have met the right person, the one they wish to marry. That person is not a Christian. However, they want to marry that person and win him or her for the Lord. May I say this, young lady, if you cannot win him for the Lord before you get married, you will not win him after you are married. May I say this, young man, if you cannot win her for the Lord before you get married, you will not win her after you are married. God forbids the godly to marry the godless. It always entails sorrow. I have seen literally hundreds of cases, and I have never yet seen a case where it has worked. Never yet! You can't beat God! God has put it down indelibly all the way through the Word that the godly are not to marry the godless. "Be ye not unequally yoked together with unbelievers: for what fellowship hath righteousness with unrighteousness? and what communion hath light with darkness?" (2 Cor. 6:14). The New Testament strictly tells Christians that they are not to be unequally yoked. You don't get unequally yoked by sitting on a platform with an unbeliever, as some critics have accused me of doing! You do it by intermarrying. That's the way you join up with them. And God strictly forbids it.

Arise, go to Padan-aram, to the house of Bethuel thy mother's father; and take thee a wife from thence of the daughters of Laban thy mother's brother.

And God Almighty bless thee, and make thee fruitful, and multiply thee, that thou mayest be a multitude of people;

And give thee the blessing of Abraham, to thee, and to thy seed with thee; that thou mayest inherit the land wherein thou art a stranger, which God gave unto Abraham [Gen. 28:2–4].

It is obvious now that Isaac understands that God had given the blessing to Abraham, that God had transferred it to him, and that this blessing is to be passed on to his son, Jacob.

And Isaac sent away Jacob: and he went to Padan-aram unto Laban, son of Bethuel the Syrian, the brother of Rebekah, Jacob's and Esau's mother [Gen. 28:5].

If you were to give the nationality of this family, you would have to say they were Syrians because that is what they are called in the Scriptures. Sometimes the question is asked, "Was Abraham a Jew? Was he an Israelite?" No, actually he was not. There were no Israelites until the time of Jacob whose name was changed to Israel. His twelve sons were Israelites. The line came from Abraham, he is the father of the race, but you're not going to call Abraham a Midianite, I hope, and yet he is the father of the Midianites, also.

When Esau saw that Isaac had blessed Jacob, and sent him away to Padan-aram, to take him a wife from thence; and that as he blessed him he gave him a charge, saying, Thou shalt not take a wife of the daughters of Canaan;

And that Jacob obeyed his father and his mother, and was gone to Padan-aram;

And Esau seeing that the daughters of Canaan pleased not Isaac his father;

Then went Esau unto Ishmael, and took unto the wives which he had Mahalath the daughter of Ishmael Abraham's son, the sister of Nebajoth, to be his wife [Gen. 28:6–9].

Now lest someone misunderstand what I meant when I said we were through with the line of Ishmael, let me say that the Bible will not follow his line. However, his line will be mentioned as it crosses the line leading to Christ. So here, Esau goes out and marries the daughter of Ishmael. He thinks it will please his father. You see what a lack of spiritual perception he has. The Ishmaelites were as much rejected as the Canaanites or the Philistines.

GOD APPEARS TO JACOB AT BETHEL

And Jacob went out from Beer-sheba, and went toward Haran. And he lighted upon a certain place, and tarried there all night, because the sun was set; and he took of the stones of that place, and put them for his pillows, and lay down in that place to sleep [Gen. 28:10–11].

The place he has come to, as we shall see in a moment, is Beth-el, literally, "the House of God." Beth-el is twelve miles north of Jerusalem, and the home which Jacob left was probably twenty-five or thirty miles south of Jerusalem. This means that Jacob covered at least forty miles that first day. You can see that he is really hotfooting it away from Esau. He wants to get as far from him as he can, but the farther he gets away from Esau, the farther he gets away from home.

What do you think he was feeling that night? Well, he was very lonely, that is for sure. He was probably homesick. As far as the record is concerned, this was his first night away from home.

My friend, do you remember the first night that *you* were away from home? I certainly remember the first night I went away from home. We lived in the country in a little place called Springer, Oklahoma. They tell me it hasn't done any springing since then. It's still a small place, just a wide place in the road. We had some very wonderful friends who lived down the road. I suppose it couldn't have been over a mile, but at that time I thought it was five or more miles. I've been back there, and I was amazed to find out how close together things are. When I was little, I thought it was all pretty well spread out. Well, these people invited me to come down and spend the night. They had a boy about my age—we were nine or ten, I guess. He had come up to get me, and we went down to his house together. I shall never forget that experience. We had a delicious dinner, a good country dinner, and I enjoyed it that evening with these folks. Then we played hide-and-seek until it got dark which kept me occupied, but every now and then I looked into the darkness and began to get just a little homesick. Then someone said it was time to go to bed. They put a pallet down in the front room, and I put on the little nightshirt that I had brought under my arm, and I lay down on that pallet. Friend, I have never been so lonely in all my life. Homesick! Oh, how I wanted to go home! I rolled and tossed there for a long time. I finally dozed off and I slept for a while, but I awoke very early in the morning. Do you know what I did? I took off my nightshirt and put on my clothes, put my nightshirt under my arm and started running home. I didn't stop until I got there. Nobody was up, but I was sure glad to be home. First night away from home. After that, I went a long way from home, but I never was more homesick than I was that first night.

I have often wondered about Jacob. He's actually a man now, a pretty big boy, but I think he is homesick. This is the first time he is away from Rebekah. He's been tied to his mama's apron strings all of his life, and now he is untied. He is out on his own, and this is his first night away from home.

Notice what happens. He lies down and puts stones for pillows. Beth-el is a dreary place. It has been described as a bleak moorland with large, bare rocks exposed. It is twelve hundred feet above sea level, in the hills. There are many places out in the desert of California that would correspond to it.

When traveling around in the proximity of Beth-el, I was with a bus tour. Others wanted to go other places which to me weren't nearly as important as Beth-el. We drove within about a half mile of it and I wanted to walk to it, but the bus driver said we didn't have time. I could see it in the distance, and the topography looked bleak and forbidding. Yet this was the high point in the spiritual life of Jacob, not only at this time but also later in his life. So this is the place he came to, and here he lay down to sleep.

> **And he dreamed, and behold a ladder set up on the earth, and the top of it reached to heaven: and behold the angels of God ascending and descending on it. And, behold, the LORD stood above it, and said, I am the LORD God of Abraham thy father, and the God of Isaac: the land whereon thou liest, to thee will I give it, and to thy seed [Gen. 28:12–13].**

It was right in that area, by the way, where God first appeared to Abraham after he had reached the land of Palestine.

> **And thy seed shall be as the dust of the earth, and thou shalt spread abroad to the west, and to the east, and to the north, and to the south: and in thee and in thy seed shall all the families of the earth be blessed [Gen. 28:14].**

Now God is giving to Jacob exactly what He had given first to Abraham; He had repeated it to Isaac, and now He confirms it, and He reaffirms to Jacob that He will do this.

> **And, behold, I am with thee, and will keep thee in all places whither thou goest, and will bring thee again into this land; for I will not leave thee, until I have done that which I have spoken to thee of [Gen. 28:15].**

You can see that this would be comforting and helpful to a lonesome, homesick boy who really had to leave home in a hurry. He is on his way to a far country, and this first night God says to him, "I'm going to be with you, Jacob, and I'm going to bring you back to this land."

The vision that God gave to him in the dream was of a ladder that reached up to heaven. What does that ladder mean? Well, the Lord Jesus interpreted it when He called Nathanael, as recorded in John 1:45–51. By the way,

Nathanael was a wiseacre, and when he heard of Jesus, he said, "Can any good thing come out of Nazareth?" Our Lord dealt with this fellow. Nathanael asked, "How in the world do you know me like that?" And Jesus said, "Before Philip called you, when you were under the fig tree, I saw you." Nathanael's response was, "Rabbi, thou art the Son of God; thou art the King of Israel." He was pretty easy to convince, although he was a skeptic at the beginning. Let me give you the exact quote: "Jesus answered and said unto him, Because I said unto thee, I saw thee under the fig tree, believest thou? thou shalt see greater things than these. And he saith unto him, Verily, verily, I say unto you, Hereafter ye shall see heaven open, and the angels of God ascending and descending upon the Son of man" (John 1:50–51).

What is that ladder? That ladder is Christ. The angels were ascending and descending upon the Son of man. The angels ministered to Him; they were subject to His command. Nathanael will hear from the top of that ladder the voice of God, "This is my beloved Son in whom I am well pleased." My friend, God is speaking to mankind through Christ in our day. We cannot come to the Father directly. Every now and then I hear someone say in a testimony, "When I was converted, I came directly to God. I have access to God." We do *not*, my friend. We come through *Christ;* we have access to the Father through Christ. That is the only way we can get into God's presence. The Lord Jesus said, ". . . I am the way, the truth, and the life: no man cometh unto the Father, but by me" (John 14:6). The Lord Jesus Christ Himself is the ladder—not one that we can climb but one that we can trust.

This truth was given first to Jacob, the usurper. To Nathanael our Lord said, "You are an Israelite in whom there is no guile"—that is, no *Jacob*. Nathanael was a wiseacre, a humorist, but he was not a trickster like Jacob. But this man, Jacob—God is going to have to deal with him. God has given him this wonderful, glorious promise, but, oh, Jacob has so much to learn!

Isn't that true of all of us today? No wonder God has to school us. No wonder God has to discipline us. He scourges every son whom He receives. He disciplines. He did it to Abraham and He did it to Isaac. He is going to do it to Jacob. Up to this point, everything has been going Jacob's way. I received a letter from a couple who had lost their two-year-old boy suddenly one night. Up to that time everything had been going their way. They were church members, but they were hypocrites. So many people are just members of the church, yet they don't know the Lord personally. The Lord has to shake us. He allows trials to come to us to discipline us. They put iron in our backbone; they put courage in our lives and enable us to stand for God.

Jacob has a long way to go. Notice what he does—

And Jacob awaked out of his sleep, and he said, Surely the LORD is in this place; and I knew it not.

And he was afraid, and said, How dreadful is this place! this is none other but the house of God, and this is the gate of heaven [Gen. 28:16–17].

This is the passage of Scripture that I use many times in dedicating a new church. "How dreadful is this place!" I think I shock some people, especially when the congregation has come in to dedicate a lovely new facility. I get up and look around and say, "How dreadful is this place." During the rest of the time I try to win them back to being friends of mine by telling them that the place is dreadful only for a fellow like Jacob, a sinner, trying to run away from God. Every house of God, every church, ought to be a dreadful place to any sinner running away from God. It is the place where the sinner ought to be able to meet God, come face to face with God, through the Ladder who has been sent down from heaven, even Christ.

When Jacob ran away from home, he had a limited view of God. He thought that when he ran away from home, he was running away from God, also. But he found that he had not left God back home. He exclaimed, "Surely the LORD is in this place; and I knew it not!"

JACOB MAKES A VOW

And Jacob rose up early in the morning, and took the stone that he had put for his pillows, and set it up for a pillar, and poured oil upon the top of it.

And he called the name of that place Beth-el: but the name of that city was called Luz at the first [Gen. 28:18–19].

Now listen to Jacob. He has a lot to learn, and this is an evidence of it.

And Jacob vowed a vow, saying, If God will be with me, and will keep me in this way that I go, and will give me bread to eat, and raiment to put on,

So that I come again to my father's house in peace; then shall the LORD be my God [Gen. 28:20–21].

What is he doing? He wants to trade with God. He says, "Now, God, *if* You will do this for me. . . ." But God has already *told* him that He is going to do every one of these things for him—"I am going to keep you; I am going to bring you back to this land; I am going to give you this land; and I'm going to give you offspring." Then Jacob turns around and bargains with Him, "*If* You will do it, then I'll serve You."

God doesn't do business with us that way. He didn't do business that way with Jacob either. If He had, Jacob would never have made it back to that land. God brought him back into that land by His grace and mercy. When Jacob did finally come back to Bethel, he came back a wiser man. Do you know what he came back to do? To worship and praise God for His mercy. God had been merciful to him.

Many people even today say they will serve the Lord *if* He will do such and such. You won't do anything of the kind, my friend. He doesn't do business that way. He will extend mercy to you, and He will be gracious to you without asking anything in return. But He does say that if you love Him, you will really want to serve Him. That will be the bondage of love. It is the same kind of love a mother has for the little child. She becomes its slave. That's the way that He wants you and me.

And this stone, which I have set for a pillar, shall be God's house: and of all that thou shalt give me I will surely give the tenth unto thee [Gen. 28:22].

So Jacob erects this stone. He is trying to make a deal with God! And a great many of us are trying to make a deal with God. Oh, my friend, He just wants to become your *Father* through faith in Christ.

CHAPTER 29

THEME: *Jacob meets Rachel; Jacob serves for Rachel; Jacob is deceived*

Over this chapter I would like to write: "Be not deceived; God is not mocked: for whatsoever a man soweth, that shall he also reap. For he that soweth to his flesh shall of the flesh reap corruption; but he that soweth to the Spirit shall of the Spirit reap life everlasting" (Gal. 6:7–8). Probably the title that we ought to put over this chapter is "Chickens Come Home to Roost." In the beginning of this chapter we will see that Jacob begins to reap the harvest of his evil doing. The passage in Galatians is written primarily for Christians, but it expresses a universal law of God in every age. It is true in any area of life. You sow corn: you reap corn. You sow cotton; you reap cotton. You sow wheat; you reap wheat. You sow tares; you reap tares.

Examples of this principle run all the way through the Scriptures. For instance, Pharaoh slew the male children of the Hebrews, and in time his son was slain by the death angel. Ahab, through false accusations, had Naboth slain and the dogs licked his blood. God sent His prophet Elijah to Ahab with the message that, as the dogs had licked the blood of Naboth, they would lick the blood of Ahab. And that was literally fulfilled. You remember that David found this to be an inexorable law which was applicable to his own life. He committed the terrible sins of adultery and murder. God forgave him for his sin. Yet, the chickens come home to roost. He reaped what he had sown. His own daughter was raped and his son slain. Even Paul the apostle felt the weight of this law. He had given his consent at the stoning of Stephen. Later, Paul was taken outside the city of Lystra and was stoned and left for dead.

Jacob is the classic illustration of this inflexible law. Jacob had lived by his wits. He was rather cocky and clever. He had practiced deceit. He would stoop to use shady methods to accomplish his purpose. And he was proud of his cleverness. But he will reap what he has sown.

As we come to this chapter, Jacob leaves Beth-el and resumes his journey. After a period of time (I do not know how long), he arrives in Haran.

Then Jacob went on his journey, and came into the land of the people of the east.

And he looked, and behold a well in the field, and, lo, there were three flocks of sheep lying by it; for out of that well they watered the flocks: and a great stone was upon the well's mouth.

And thither were all the flocks gathered: and they rolled the stone from the well's mouth, and watered the sheep, and put the stone again upon the well's mouth in his place [Gen. 29:1–3].

We see here the importance of water in that country. It still is a very important item because there is a shortage of it in many places. It must be husbanded and protected; that is why at a certain time during the day the stone was removed from the top of the well, and then everybody watered their sheep—*everybody* got the water he needed. Then the stone was put back on to close the well.

Now Jacob arrives on the scene before they take the stone away from the well. Believe me, he is as cocky as ever.

And Jacob said unto them, My brethren, whence be ye? And they said, Of Haran are we.

And he said unto them, Know ye Laban the son of Nahor? And they said, We know him [Gen. 29:4–5].

Oh yes, they knew him. But Jacob didn't know him—yet. But, oh my, Jacob is going to get acquainted with him.

And he said unto them, Is he well? And they said, He is well: and, behold, Rachel his daughter cometh with the sheep.

And he said, Lo, it is yet high day, neither is it time that the cattle should be gathered together: water ye the sheep, and go and feed them [Gen. 29:6–7].

Here Jacob has just arrived in the land and he is telling them how to water their sheep and what they should do! This is typical of him, by the way.

And they said, We cannot, until all the flocks be gathered together, and till they roll the stone from the well's mouth; then we water the sheep [Gen. 29:8].

JACOB MEETS RACHEL

And while he yet spake with them, Rachel came with her father's sheep: for she kept them [Gen. 29:9].

R achel is a shepherdess who takes care of the sheep. This was woman's work in that day.

And it came to pass, when Jacob saw Rachel the daughter of Laban his mother's brother, and the sheep of Laban his mother's brother, that Jacob went near, and rolled the stone from the well's mouth, and watered the flock of Laban his mother's brother [Gen. 29:10].

I don't know who told him to water the flock of Laban, but he did it. Jacob is not following anyone's law but his own. He made the rules for the game as he went through life—that is, the first part of his life. He has a tremendous lesson to learn, and Uncle Laban is the one to teach him.

And Jacob kissed Rachel, and lifted up his voice, and wept [Gen. 29:11].

This verse has always been strange to me. Frankly, kissing *that* girl and then weeping is hard for me to understand! However, I am of the opinion that this boy had had a lonely trip from the moment he had left home. We need to remember that from Beth-el he had to go up by the Sea of Galilee, then up into Syria. He had to cross that desert. I suppose he had many experiences along the way. When he arrived, he was very cocky and greeted the men there in a matter-of-fact way as though he had known them all of their lives. He asks them questions, then probably in an officious way takes the stone from the mouth of the well. I suppose when he greeted this girl who was a member of his mother's family he welled up with emotion and wept. That is the only way I can explain it. But I am sure that the next time he kissed her he didn't weep!

And Jacob told Rachel that he was her father's brother, and that he was Rebekah's son: and she ran and told her father [Gen. 29:12].

You will notice that he calls himself her father's brother. The Hebrew does not make a lot of the distinctions we make today. We've got it reduced down to whether a person is a *kissing* cousin or not, but in that day if you were related, you were a brother. That is the way it is translated here and quite properly so.

But in English we would say that Jacob was her father's nephew and that he was a son of Rebekah, her father's sister.

And it came to pass, when Laban heard the tidings of Jacob his sister's son, that he ran to meet him, and embraced him, and kissed him, and brought him to his house. And he told Laban all these things [Gen. 29:13].

I imagine that Jacob had quite a bit to talk about. I wouldn't be surprised to find that he entertained them at dinner with his story of how he tricked his brother to get his birthright, and how he used trickery to get the blessing, and how clever he was. Probably he told about that night at Beth-el, too. "He told Laban all these things."

And Laban said to him, Surely thou art my bone and my flesh. And he abode with him the space of a month [Gen. 29:14].

Laban was convinced now that this was his nephew, and he says, "You're my relative, so come in and make yourself at home."

Now a month goes by, and notice what happens. Jacob is not working. He's a nephew from a far country, and he's come over to visit his uncle. I suppose he felt that he ought to have free room and board there. During that time he's courting this girl, Rachel. At least, he certainly has been casting his eyes in that direction. And I think she was casting her eyes in his direction, too.

Now, I can imagine that it was one morning at breakfast when the next incident took place.

And Laban said unto Jacob, Because thou art my brother, shouldest thou therefore serve me for nought? tell me, what shall thy wages be? [Gen. 29:15].

This Uncle Laban is clever. Who had said anything about going to work? Jacob hasn't. So Uncle Laban is very tactful and says that he doesn't want Jacob to work for him for nothing. He says that he will pay Jacob. Frankly, you don't live with Laban a month without making some sort of an arrangement to pay your board. Uncle Laban is a clever one also, and now he is going to deal with his nephew.

And Laban had two daughters: the name of the elder was Leah, and the name of the younger was Rachel [Gen. 29:16].

Here we are introduced to another daughter, Leah. Uncle Laban has been watching this boy, and he has noted that his nephew has become very much interested in his daughter Rachel, the younger of the two. The next verse tells us why—

Leah was tender eyed; but Rachel was beautiful and well favoured [Gen. 29:17].

Rachel was a very beautiful girl. Leah was "tender eyed" which is a way of saying that she was not beautiful at all.

In college when we were reading Greek and studying some of the plays of Euripides, when a fellow wanted to say something very nice about his girl, we found in the play that he would call her "cow-eyed." I always laughed about that and thought that I would turn that over in my mind before I ever considered that a compliment. Well now, the next time you meet a cow, take a look at the eyes, and you will see they are beautiful. Ever since I read that play, I have never seen a cow with ugly eyes.

But Leah was not cow-eyed, she was "tender eyed" which meant that she was sort of an ugly duckling.

So Laban has these two daughters, and it is obvious that Jacob is in love with Rachel.

JACOB SERVES FOR RACHEL

And Jacob loved Rachel; and said, I will serve thee seven years for Rachel thy younger daughter [Gen. 29:18].

We find Jacob was quite moon-eyed. So that morning at breakfast, when Uncle Laban suggested he go to work, he had something in mind himself. He knew that the boy was in love with the girl; so I don't think he was at all surprised at Jacob's answer when he asked what his wages should be. Jacob was willing to work for seven years for Rachel. This man, Laban, was driving a hard bargain.

And Laban said, It is better that I give her to thee, than that I should give her to another man: abide with me [Gen. 29:19].

Laban accepts that bargain.

Now this next verse tells us one of the loveliest things that is said about Jacob. Frankly, in the early years of Jacob's life, the only appearance of anything beautiful or fine or noble is his love for Rachel.

And Jacob served seven years for Rachel; and they seemed unto him but a few days, for the love he had to her [Gen. 29:20].

You can just see this man working. I tell you, Uncle Laban had him working hard. He worked out in the cold, out in the rain and in all sorts of weather, but he always thought of that girl Rachel. There she was to meet him after a hard day. He was desperately in love with her.

And Jacob said unto Laban, Give me my wife, for my days are fulfilled, that I may go in unto her.

And Laban gathered together all the men of the place, and made a feast [Gen. 29:21–22].

JACOB IS DECEIVED

Now notice what Uncle Laban is doing—

And it came to pass in the evening, that he took Leah his daughter, and brought her to him; and he went in unto her.

And Laban gave unto his daughter Leah Zilpah his maid for an handmaid.

And it came to pass, that in the morning, behold, it was Leah: and he said to Laban, What is this thou hast done unto me? did not I serve with thee for Rachel? wherefore then hast thou beguiled me?

And Laban said, It must not be so done in our country, to give the younger before the firstborn [Gen. 29:23–26].

At the marriage ceremony in those days, the woman was veiled, heavily veiled, so that she couldn't be seen. Poor Jacob didn't see the girl he was getting until the next morning. Lo and behold, it wasn't Rachel—it was Leah! At the moment he saw he had been tricked. I wonder if he didn't recall something of his own father when he, Jacob, had pretended to be the elder. He deceived his father, and that was the reason he had to leave home. You see, God does not approve of that type of conduct. The chickens are now coming home to roost. Jacob pretended to be the elder when he was the younger. Now he thinks he's getting the younger and he gets the elder. The tables are turned now, and it has become an awful thing for Jacob. To Jacob it is a criminal act that Laban has done, but notice how Uncle Laban passes it off. He is an expert at this type of thing. He tells Jacob that there was a little matter in the contract, a clause in the fine print, that he had forgotten to mention to Jacob. It was a custom in their country that the elder daughter must marry first, and the younger daughter could not marry until the elder daughter was married. But Uncle Laban is willing to be very generous in his dealings; so he has an offer to make.

Fulfill her week, and we will give thee this also for the service which thou shalt serve with me yet seven other years [Gen. 29:27].

This week, you see, is another seven years. Uncle Laban is getting his money's worth, isn't he? And poor Jacob is really going to school. But he is taking two wives which he shouldn't have done. He will be in trouble before it is over.

And Jacob did so, and fulfilled her week; and he gave him Rachel his daughter to wife also [Gen. 29:28].

Uncle Laban made Jacob serve twice as long as he originally agreed to. Seven years was long enough, but, believe me, *fourteen* years is a long time! This arrangement gave Jacob two wives.

You may be thinking, *Well, since this is in the Bible, God must approve of polygamy.* No, God does not approve of everything that is in the Bible—that may startle you. For instance, God didn't approve of the devil's lie. God didn't approve of David's sin, and He judged him for it. But the *record* of both events is inspired—literally, God-breathed. In other words, God said through the writer, Moses, exactly what He wanted to say. The thing that is inspired is the record of the words God gave to Moses to write down in this Book we call the Bible. In

Genesis 29 God gave an accurate record: Jacob did have two wives, and it tells us the way it came about. That is where inspiration comes in. It does not mean that God approved of everything that is recorded in the Bible. Certainly God disapproved of Jacob's having more than one wife.

May I say to you, this man Jacob had plenty of trouble in his family from here on, and it all can be traced back to his own methods which he had used. The chickens are coming home to roost.

And when the LORD saw that Leah was hated, he opened her womb; but Rachel was barren.

And Leah conceived, and bare a son, and she called his name Reuben: for she said, Surely the LORD hath looked upon my affliction; now therefore my husband will love me [Gen. 29:31–32].

Leah is a sad person because she knows her husband loves Rachel rather than her. When she becomes the mother of Reuben, it brings joy to her heart, and she feels that Jacob will love her now.

Reuben is Jacob's firstborn, but he is not the one who will begin the line leading to Christ. Rather, it will be Leah's last son, Judah. Judah was the kingly line. David was in this line, and later on, the Lord Jesus Himself, according to the flesh, came from the line of Judah. Reuben lost his position as the firstborn because of his sin. Levi was the priestly tribe. Leah was the mother of some of the outstanding sons of Jacob.

CHAPTER 30

THEME: *Birth of Jacob's sons; birth of Joseph to Rachel; Jacob prepares to leave Laban*

When we come to this chapter, we see that God is moving in spite of Jacob's sin. God is not moving because of it, but in spite of it. The theme of the chapter is the family of Jacob and the birth of his sons. Jacob longs to leave Laban, and Jacob makes a shrewd bargain with him.

BIRTH OF JACOB'S SONS

And when Rachel saw that she bare Jacob no children, Rachel envied her sister; and said unto Jacob, Give me children, or else I die [Gen. 30:1].

You see, a woman in that day was disgraced unless she had an offspring, and the more children she had, the better was her position.

And Jacob's anger was kindled against Rachel: and he said, Am I in God's stead, who hath withheld from thee the fruit of the womb?

And she said, Behold my maid Bilhah,

go in unto her; and she shall bear upon my knees, that I may also have children by her [Gen. 30:2–3].

We find here Jacob and Rachel reverting to the practice of that day. Remember that Abraham and Sarah had done the same thing. God did not approve of it then, and He is not going to approve of it now. The Bible gives us an accurate record, but that does not mean that God approved of all that was done. In fact, it is quite obvious that He disapproved of this. My, the strife that we have already called to your attention in Abraham's family. It was also in the family of Isaac. Now it is in Jacob's family already—and he is in for a great deal more trouble.

The next verses of this chapter tell of the birth of two sons of Jacob by Bilhah, Rachel's handmaid; two sons by Zilpah, Leah's handmaid; and then the birth of two more sons by Leah.

And God remembered Rachel, and God hearkened to her, and opened her womb.

And she conceived, and bare a son; and said, God hath taken away my reproach:

And she called his name Joseph; and said, The LORD shall add to me another son [Gen. 30:22–24].

This is the boy who will go down into the land of Egypt. We will follow him later in the book, as he is quite a remarkable person.

Later on Benjamin will be born to Rachel. We will conclude this chapter by listing the twelve sons of Jacob because they are important. The twelve tribes of Israel will come from them and finally the nation of Israel.

JACOB PREPARES TO LEAVE LABAN

And it came to pass, when Rachel had born Joseph, that Jacob said unto Laban, Send me away, that I may go unto mine own place, and to my country.

Give me my wives and my children, for whom I have served thee, and let me go: for thou knowest my service which I have done thee [Gen. 30:25–26].

Now listen to Uncle Laban—he's not through yet, you may be sure of that!

And Laban said unto him, I pray thee, if I have found favour in thine eyes, tarry: for I have learned by experience that the

LORD hath blessed me for thy sake [Gen. 30:27].

This is quite interesting. You may recall that Abimelech, king of Gerar, found that he was blessed when Isaac was in his midst. Now Uncle Laban has discovered that God is with Jacob and has blessed him for Jacob's sake. So Uncle Laban says, "My boy, don't rush off; don't leave me. I've been blessed, and I want to raise your wages."

And he said, Appoint me thy wages, and I will give it [Gen. 30:28].

Jacob knows by now that, any time Uncle Laban makes a deal, he is the one who will come off the winner. Jacob has learned this lesson, and he wants to leave.

And he said unto him, Thou knowest how I have served thee, and how thy cattle was with me.

For it was little which thou hadst before I came, and it is now increased unto a multitude; and the LORD hath blessed thee since my coming: and now when shall I provide for mine own house also? [Gen. 30:29–30].

Listen to Jacob complaining. He is singing the blues! He is saying, "All I've got out of all this service for you are two wives with their two maids and a house full of boys." In fact, he has eleven boys at this point. What in the world is he going to do? How is he going to feed them? He says, "God has blessed *you* and He has prospered *you*, and *I* don't have anything?"

And he said, What shall I give thee? And Jacob said, Thou shalt not give me any thing: if thou wilt do this thing for me, I will again feed and keep thy flock:

I will pass through all thy flock to-day, removing from thence all the speckled and spotted cattle, and all the brown cattle among the sheep, and the spotted and speckled among the goats: and of such shall be my hire [Gen. 30:31–32].

In other words, the pure breeds will be Laban's, but the offbreeds, those that are not blue-ribbon cattle, will be Jacob's. Jacob said, "You just let me have these, and that will be my wages." That sounds like a pretty good proposition for Laban.

So shall my righteousness answer for me in time to come, when it shall come for my hire before thy face: every one that is not speckled and spotted among the goats, and brown among the sheep, that shall be counted stolen with me.

And Laban said, Behold, I would it might be according to thy word.

And he removed that day the he goats that were ringstraked and spotted, and all the she goats that were speckled and spotted, and every one that had some white in it, and all the brown among the sheep, and gave them into the hand of his sons [Gen. 30:33–35].

They would not be able to breed with the others. Jacob would take the off-breeds so that only the full breeds would mate and bear offspring, and those would belong to Uncle Laban. The others would be his. Jacob is making a very interesting deal.

And he set three days' journey betwixt himself and Jacob: and Jacob fed the rest of Laban's flocks.

And Jacob took him rods of green popular, and of the hazel and chestnut tree; and pilled white strakes in them, and made the white appear which was in the rods.

And he set the rods which he had pilled before the flocks in the gutters in the watering troughs when the flocks came to drink, that they should conceive when they came to drink.

And the flocks conceived before the rods, and brought forth cattle ringstraked, speckled and spotted [Gen. 30:36–39].

There have been various explanations of this. There are those who say this is nothing in the world but pure superstition. Others say it is an old wives' tale and is certainly something which ought not to be in the Bible record. It is my judgment that it is important that this rec-

ord appears in the Word of God. Of course, there were genetic factors involved, but I don't feel that we should rule out this as being a superstition. The point is that both Laban and Jacob *believed* that the white streaks in the rods caused the offspring to be ringstraked. That is the important part of the story. Maybe you are too smart to believe it, but these two boys believed it. Regardless of whether or not there was value in it, Jacob is using trickery. He had been quite a trickster, but he has met an uncle who is a better trickster than he is, and now Jacob is trying to make a comeback.

This is all I will say about it at this point, and we will see that the next chapter will throw new light on this entire incident.

Now here is the list of Jacob's twelve sons who will eventually comprise the twelve tribes of the nation Israel.

Born to Leah: 1. Reuben
2. Simeon
3. Levi
4. Judah
5. Issachar
6. Zebulun
7. Dinah, daughter
Born to Bilhah, Rachel's maid:
1. Dan
2. Naphtali
Born to Zilpah, Leah's maid:
1. Gad
2. Asher
Born to Rachel: 1. Joseph
2. Benjamin

Believe me, Jacob had his hands full with these twelve boys! Also, we find that there was a girl, and her name was Dinah.

We will see in the next chapter that God has called Jacob to leave Haran and return to the land which He has promised to Abraham, to Isaac, and to Jacob. I am sure that God is thinking of Jacob's children—He doesn't want them to grow up in the environment of Laban's household.

CHAPTER 31

THEME: *Jacob flees from Haran; the Mizpah covenant*

In this chapter we find that Jacob leaves Laban without giving notice. They don't even have a farewell party for him. Laban takes out after him and overtakes him. Finally, Jacob and Laban make another contract, this time not to defraud or hurt each other. They they separate in an outwardly friendly manner.

We will see that God wants to get Jacob out of that land. He recognizes that the influence of Laban's household is not good for Jacob and his growing family. The boys are going to be heads of the twelve tribes of Israel, and God is anxious to get them out from that environment and back into Abraham's country, the country which He had promised to Abraham.

We are in a section of the Word of God which God has given to minister to our needs. It deals with a man who is a very sinful man in many ways and a man whom God would not give up. You and I can take courage from this. The Lord will never give us up as long as we keep coming back to Him. He will always receive us. If He will take a fellow like Jacob and a fellow like I am, He will take you, my friend.

You will recall that Jacob has had a pretty sad ordeal of twenty years with Uncle Laban. Uncle Laban has really given him a course in the college of hard knocks, and poor Jacob is beginning to wince because of all the pressure he has been under. However, since the new deal which he had made with Laban regarding cattle breeding, Jacob is now getting more than Uncle Laban is getting. Uncle Laban doesn't like it, nor do his sons like it.

And he heard the words of Laban's sons, saying, Jacob hath taken away all that was our father's; and of that which was our father's hath he gotten all this glory.

And Jacob beheld the countenance of Laban, and, behold, it was not toward him as before [Gen. 31:1–2].

Now Jacob has a call from God.

And the LORD said unto Jacob, Return unto the land of thy fathers, and to thy kindred; and I will be with thee.

And Jacob sent and called Rachel and Leah to the field unto his flock [Gen. 31:3–4].

God called Jacob to leave, and so he is now preparing to do that. He calls Rachel and Leah to meet him in the field because he is afraid to talk this over at home for fear some servant or possibly even Laban or Laban's sons might overhear him. He doesn't want them to see him plotting with Rachel and Leah.

And said unto them, I see your father's countenance, that it is not toward me as before; but the God of my father hath been with me.

And ye know that with all my power I have served your father [Gen. 31:5–6].

That is one thing upon which we can agree with Jacob and say to his credit. He had worked hard, but I'm of the opinion that we ought to give Laban credit for that. I believe that Laban got his money's worth out of anyone who worked for him.

And your father hath deceived me, and changed my wages ten times; but God suffered him not to hurt me [Gen. 31:7].

Notice that ten times in those twenty years old Laban had changed his wages! Poor Jacob. But when he was perplexed and frustrated, not knowing where to turn, God intervened.

If he said thus, The speckled shall be thy wages; then all the cattle bare speckled: and if he said thus, The ringstraked shall be thy hire; then bare all the cattle ringstraked.

Thus God hath taken away the cattle of your father, and given them to me [Gen. 31:8–9].

Jacob is explaining to Rachel and Leah that it is God who has blessed him, to the extent that Laban and his sons have become very jealous of him; in fact, they hate him.

Now Jacob tells the actual reason why he wants to leave—

And the angel of God spake unto me in a dream, saying, Jacob: And I said, Here am I.

And he said, Lift up now thine eyes, and see, all the rams which leap upon the cattle are ringstraked, speckled, and grisled: for I have seen all that Laban doeth unto thee [Gen. 31:11–12].

You probably thought that in the previous chapter I was not giving a satisfactory answer for what had taken place in the breeding of cattle. I was waiting until we came to this portion of Scripture, because God says, "I did it!" We don't need to look for natural explanations, although I am confident that God used one of them. However, since God didn't tell us which one it is, we simply do not know. There are several explanations, and you may take the one you want, but I like this one: God says, "I saw what Laban was doing to you, and *I* blessed you."

I am the God of Beth-el, where thou anointedst the pillar, and where thou vowedst a vow unto me: now arise, get thee out from this land, and return unto the land of thy kindred [Gen. 31:13].

"I am the God of Beth-el." God goes back to the time He appeared to this boy when he was running away, that first night away from home which he spent at Beth-el.

"Now arise, get thee out from this land, and return unto the land of thy kindred." God wants him to leave Haran because he has at this time eleven boys who are growing up, and they are already beginning to learn some things which they should not be learning. God wants to get Jacob and these boys away from the place of idolatry just as He got Abraham out of a home of idolatry.

And Rachel and Leah answered and said unto him, Is there yet any portion or inheritance for us in our father's house?

Are we not counted of him strangers? for he hath sold us, and hath quite devoured also our money [Gen. 31:14–15].

They are saying that certainly, as the daughters of their father, they should receive some inheritance, and that ought to keep Laban from being so antagonistic. But, friend, old Laban cannot be trusted.

Unfortunately, there are many Christians today who demonstrate in the way they handle their own money and the money of others that they cannot be trusted either. This is, I feel, a real test of an individual. I could tell you some stories that would make your hair stand on end. Christians, and Christian leaders, do things with money that ought not to be done.

For all the riches which God hath taken from our father, that is our's, and our children's: now then, whatsoever God hath said unto thee, do [Gen. 31:16].

I admire these two women. They tell Jacob to do whatever he wants to do. They stand with him, and apparently they feel that their father has robbed them.

JACOB FLEES FROM HARAN

Then Jacob rose up, and set his sons and his wives upon camels;

And he carried away all his cattle, and all his goods which he had gotten, the cattle of his getting, which he had gotten in Padan-aram, for to go to Isaac his father in the land of Canaan.

And Laban went to shear his sheep: and Rachel had stolen the images that were her father's [Gen. 31:17–19].

Here is a revelation of something that is quite interesting. Jacob rises up and leaves posthaste again. You remember that this is the same way he left home when he was escaping from his brother. Now he is leaving his uncle—but it is not all his fault this time. It is obvious that he is prepared for this. He has all the cattle and the servants ready to march.

"Rachel had stolen the images that were her father's." I told you that they were in a home of idolatry. God didn't want Jacob's boys to be brought up there. But, you see, Rachel had been brought up in a home of idolatry, and she wanted to take her gods with her. What a primitive notion she had! Even Jacob had thought that he could run away from God when he left his home as a boy. But at Beth-el God appeared to him. He found that he couldn't run away from God. In fact many years later David wrote: "Whither shall I go from thy spirit? or whither shall I flee from thy presence? If I ascend up into heaven, thou art there: if I make my bed in hell [sheol], behold, thou art there" (Ps. 139:7–8). That is, death won't separate you. "If I take the wings of the morning, and dwell in the uttermost parts of the sea; Even there shall thy hand lead me, and thy right hand shall hold me" (Ps. 139:9–10). You won't get away from God by even going to the moon. You simply cannot get away from Him.

"And Laban went to shear his sheep." Jacob waited until Laban went out to shear sheep. Probably Laban went quite a few miles away from home because the sheep grazed over a very large area in that day. They still do, for that matter, because it takes a large area to feed them. While Laban is away from home, Jacob just "forgets" to tell him that he is leaving.

And Jacob stole away unawares to Laban the Syrian, in that he told him not that he fled.

So he fled with all that he had; and he rose up, and passed over the river, and set his face toward the mount Gilead [Gen. 31:20–21].

They have come within sight of Mt. Gilead, which is just east of the Jordan River. They have covered a lot of ground.

And it was told Laban on the third day that Jacob was fled.

And he took his brethren with him, and pursued after him seven days' journey; and they overtook him in the mount Gilead [Gen. 31:22–23].

Laban really had been traveling fast to overtake him. You may be sure that Laban doesn't mean any good as far as Jacob is concerned. I am of the opinion that he is angry enough to kill him. But God intervened—

And God came to Laban the Syrian in a dream by night, and said unto him, Take heed that thou speak not to Jacob either good or bad [Gen. 31:24].

In other words, "You be very careful what you say and do."

Then Laban overtook Jacob. Now Jacob had pitched his tent in the mount: and Laban with his brethren pitched in the mount of Gilead [Gen. 21:25].

Listen to Uncle Laban. He's a clever rascal, by the way. He's been coming, breathing out fire and brimstone, and wanting to recover all the possessions which Jacob had taken. He probably wanted to kill Jacob and take back the two daughters and their children.

And Laban said to Jacob, What hast thou done, that thou hast stolen away unawares to me, and carried away my daughters, as captives taken with the sword?

Wherefore didst thou flee away secretly, and steal away from me; and didst not tell me, that I might have sent thee away with mirth, and with songs, with tabret, and with harp? [Gen. 31:26–27].

How clever Uncle Laban is, how diplomatic! He tries to make Jacob feel guilty for depriving his family of wonderful send-off party. He would have had a great celebration and a fond farewell. That's what he *says*, but I don't think that is what he would have done. Then he goes on to appeal to sentiment.

And hast not suffered me to kiss my sons and my daughters? thou hast now done foolishly in so doing [Gen. 31:28].

These "sons" would be his grandsons. They are destined to be very prominent as far as the history of this world is concerned.

It is in the power of my hand to do you hurt: but the God of your father spake unto me yesternight, saying, Take thou heed that thou speak not to Jacob either good or bad [Gen. 31:29].

Laban lets him know that he didn't mean good by him but that God had prevented him from doing bad.

And now, though thou wouldest needs be gone, because thou sore longedst after thy father's house, yet wherefore hast thou stolen my gods? [Gen. 31:30].

Now he asks about the stolen gods. Actually, Jacob didn't know that Rachel had stolen the gods. When he answers Laban, he is answering about his running away without letting him know.

And Jacob answered and said to Laban, Because I was afraid: for I said, Peradventure thou wouldest take by force thy daughters from me [Gen. 31:31].

Jacob knew that Laban wouldn't have let him take his wives and his family and that which belonged to him.

Now he replies to the charge of the stolen gods—

With whomsoever thou findest thy gods, let him not live: before our brethren discern thou what is thine with me, and take it to thee. For Jacob knew not that Rachel had stolen them [Gen. 31:32].

He is sure no one would have stolen them from Laban. You see, Jacob didn't believe Laban. But if you think that Laban believed Jacob, you're wrong. They had absolutely no confidence in each other. It's been a nice, pleasant twenty years together, hasn't it?

And Laban went into Jacob's tent, and into Leah's tent, and into the two maidservants' tents; but he found them not. Then went he out of Leah's tent, and entered into Rachel's tent.

Now Rachel had taken the images, and put them in the camel's furniture, and sat upon them. And Laban searched all the tent, but found them not.

And she said to her father, Let it not displease my lord that I cannot rise up before thee; for the custom of women is upon me. And he searched, but found not the images [Gen. 31:33–35].

He really expected one of his daughters to have them. Rachel is quite a clever girl herself, isn't she? She is the daughter of her father! She had taken them and put them in the camel's furniture, which is the box that went on the camel's back. Then she sat down on them and excused herself to her father. She said she couldn't get up because she didn't feel well that day. All the while, she is sitting on them. What a realistic picture we get of this family!

Rachel's taking the teraphim from her father was probably much more serious than we had imagined. The possession of those household gods implied leadership of the family, which meant that Jacob was going to inherit everything old Laban had! That is the reason Laban was so wrought up over it. He surely did not want Jacob to get his estate—he felt he had gotten too much already.

Jacob gets a little confidence now. They can't locate the images, and Jacob is sure that they aren't anywhere around. He wants to rebuke his father-in-law who has come after him.

And Jacob was wroth, and chode with Laban: and Jacob answered and said to Laban, What is my trespass? what is my sin, that thou hast so hotly pursued after me? [Gen. 31:36].

Now Jacob voices his complaint. He has passed the course in the college of hard knocks, and now he is getting his degree.

This twenty years have I been with thee; thy ewes and thy she goats have not cast their young, and the rams of thy flock have I not eaten [Gen. 31:38].

He didn't even get his meals. He had to pay for those.

That which was torn of beasts I brought not unto thee; I bare the loss of it; of my hand didst thou require it, whether stolen by day, or stolen by night [Gen. 31:39].

He couldn't even get any insurance. When a lamb was stolen or killed by a wild animal, Jacob had to pay for it. Believe me, this Laban is a hard taskmaster!

Thus I was; in the day the drought consumed me, and the frost by night; and my sleep departed from mine eyes [Gen. 31:40].

He didn't get a vacation in the summer. When the weather grew cold, he still had to stay out with the sheep and with the animals. Many nights he had to watch to protect the flock.

Thus have I been twenty years in thy house; I served thee fourteen years for thy two daughters, and six years for thy cattle: and thou hast changed my wages ten times [Gen. 31:41].

This is what has happened to Jacob. Here is the man who is clever, who thought that he could get by with sin, but God didn't let him get by with it because God has made it very clear that whatsoever a man sows, that shall he also reap. Jacob refused submission to God at home; so he had to submit to his uncle. Jacob came to receive a wife in dignity, but he was made a servant because God respects the rights of the firstborn. Jacob had deceived his father; so he was deceived by his father-in-law. Jacob, the younger, became as the older. Then he found out that he was given the older when he thought he was getting the younger. He revealed a mercenary spirit that displayed itself in the way he got the birthright, allowing his mother to cover his hands with the skins of kids of goats. Later on, we will see that his own sons will deceive him in very much the same way. They killed a kid and in its blood they dipped Joseph's coat of many colors. He deceived his father about being the favorite son, and he will be deceived about his favorite son, Joseph. Whatsoever a man sows, that shall he also reap.

Except the God of my father, the God of Abraham, and the fear of Isaac, had been with me, surely thou hadst sent me away now empty. God hath seen mine affliction and the labour of my hands, and rebuked thee yesternight [Gen. 31:42].

Jacob has had his day in court. He has vented his grievances. Now he is going to leave Laban. They bid each other good-bye and make a contract.

THE MIZPAH COVENANT

And Laban answered and said unto Jacob, These daughters are my daughters, and these children are my children, and these cattle are my cattle, and all that thou seest is mine: and what can I do this day unto these my daughters, or unto their children which they have born?

Now therefore come thou, let us make a covenant, I and thou; and let it be for a witness between me and thee [Gen. 31:43–44].

Jacob set up a stone for a pillar, a heap of stones was gathered, and a contract was made.

And Laban said, This heap is a witness between me and thee this day. Therefore was the name of it called Galeed;

And Mizpah; for he said, The LORD watch between me and thee, when we are absent one from another [Gen. 31:48–49].

The words of this contract have been used by young people's groups and other groups as a benediction. I don't think it ought to be used that way because it was a contract made between two rascals who are going to quit stealing from each other and work on somebody else! "The Lord watch between me and thee" is really saying, "May the Lord keep His eye on you so you won't steal from me any more." That is exactly what these men are saying. And after this, they separate. The pile of stones remained at Mizpah as a boundary line between Laban and Jacob. Each promised not to cross over on the other's side.

CHAPTER 32

THEME: Crisis in the life of Jacob; wrestling at Peniel; Jacob's name changed to Israel

Chapter 32 is the high point in the life of Jacob and can be called the turning point in his life. However, this is not Jacob's conversion, by any means. In spite of the fact that he was living in the flesh, this man was still God's man. This is the reason that we are told to be very careful about judging folk as to whether they are Christians or not. There are a lot of people who do not look like they are Christians, but I am almost sure that they are. Whether they are or not is in the hands of the Lord. They just don't act like Christians— that's all; they give no evidence that they are. And this man Jacob gave no such evidence, except in very faint instances when God appeared to him and he did respond in a way.

Jacob, who is God's representative and witness in the world, has been a bad witness, but he cannot continue that way, and so God is going to deal with him. To tell the truth, God will cripple him in order to get him. The Lord also disciplines us: "For whom the Lord loveth he chasteneth . . ." (Heb. 12:6). That is His method. He disciplines in that way. Lot also did not look like he was a child of God—but he was, for Peter says that Lot "vexed his righteous soul" (see 2 Pet. 2:7–8). But I tell you, Lot certainly was put through the fire. He escaped the fire of Sodom and Gomorrah, but the Lord put him through the fires of testing. This is Jacob's experience also. He got his college degree at the college of hard knocks. Un-

cle Laban was president and dean of the school. At graduation, this boy Jacob gave a pitiful valedictorian address. It took him twenty years to get his degree, and he certainly worked for it. Old Laban changed the requirements ten times. Every two years, Jacob had a new contract with Uncle Laban, and it was always to Jacob's disadvantage. This was the experience of this man.

We come now to this test in which God is going to have to deal with Jacob because he is going to represent God. God will deal with him and will move in on him in this thirty-second chapter. At the beginning, I would like to write this verse of Scripture over this chapter: "He giveth power to the faint; and to them that have no might he increaseth strength" (Isa. 40:29). This is the experience of Jacob.

CRISIS IN THE LIFE OF JACOB

And Jacob went on his way, and the angels of God met him.

And when Jacob saw them, he said, This is God's host: and he called the name of that place Mahanaim [Gen. 32:1–2].

God is beginning to deal with Jacob directly in order to bring him into the place of fruit bearing and of real, vital service and witness for Him.

And Jacob sent messengers before him

to Esau his brother unto the land of Seir, the country of Edom.

And he commanded them, saying, Thus shall ye speak unto my lord Esau; Thy servant Jacob saith thus, I have sojourned with Laban, and stayed there until now:

And I have oxen, and asses, flocks, and menservants, and womenservants: and I have sent to tell my lord, that I may find grace in thy sight [Gen. 32:3–5].

This fellow Jacob is still clever, isn't he? He just cannot let go, even after his experience with Laban. He is returning back to the land, and he remembers the last time he saw Esau twenty years ago, when Esau was breathing out threatenings against him. Notice that Jacob sends servants and instructs them, saying, "When you get to Esau my brother, say to him, 'My lord Esau.' " Of all things! And then he has them refer to himself as "Thy servant Jacob." That's not the way Jacob had spoken before. He had manipulated for the birthright and had stolen the blessing. He had been a rascal, but *now* his talk is different. I guess he had learned a few things from Uncle Laban. "My lord Esau . . . thy servant Jacob."

And the messengers returned to Jacob, saying, We came to thy brother Esau, and also he cometh to meet thee, and four hundred men with him [Gen. 32:6].

This message absolutely frightened poor Jacob because he didn't know what all that meant. Esau did not indicate his intentions to the servants at all. I suppose that Jacob quizzed them rather thoroughly and said, "Did you detect any note of animosity or bitterness or hatred toward me?" And I suppose that one of the servants said, "No, he seemed to be glad to get the information that you were coming to meet him, and now he's coming to meet you." But the fact that Esau appeared glad was no comfort to Jacob. It could mean that Esau would be glad for the opportunity of getting revenge. Anyway, poor Jacob is upset.

Then Jacob was greatly afraid and distressed: and he divided the people that was with him, and the flocks, and herds, and the camels, into two bands;

And said, If Esau come to the one company, and smite it, then the other company which is left shall escape [Gen. 32:7–8].

Jacob is in a bad way, he thinks. With this brother of his coming to him, he divides up his group. He is being clever. He reasons that if his brother strikes one group, then the other one can escape.

Notice what Jacob does now. He appeals to God in his distress:

And Jacob said, O God of my father Abraham, and God of my father Isaac, the LORD which saidst unto me, Return unto thy country, and to thy kindred, and I will deal well with thee:

I am not worthy of the least of all the mercies, and of all the truth, which thou hast shewed unto thy servant; for with my staff I passed over this Jordan; and now I am become two bands [Gen. 32:9–10].

This man now appeals to God and cries out to Him on the basis that He is the God of his father Abraham and the God of his father Isaac. I begin now to detect a little change in Jacob's life. This is the first time I have ever heard him say, "I am not worthy of the least of thy mercies." For the first time, he is acknowledging that he might be a sinner in God's sight. Do you know that there are a great many "Christians" who do not acknowledge that they are sinners? For years I knew a man who was incensed that I would indicate that he was a sinner. He told me all that he had done and that he had been saved and now was not a sinner. My friend, he is a sinner. We are all sinners, *saved by grace.* As long as we are in this life, we have that old nature that isn't even fit to go to heaven. And do you know that God is not going to let it go to heaven? Vernon McGee cannot go there. That is the reason God had to give me a new nature; the old one wasn't even fit to repair. This fellow Jacob is beginning now to say that he is not worthy. When any man begins to move toward God on that basis, he will find that God will communicate with him.

Jacob makes this very interesting statement: "for with my staff I passed over this Jordan; and now I am become two bands." He went over the Jordan with just his walking stick, his staff—that's all he had. Now he is coming back, and he has become two companies. This is Jacob for you.

Deliver me, I pray thee, from the hand of my brother, from the hand of Esau: for I fear him, lest he will come and smite me, and the mother with the children.

And thou saidst, I will surely do thee good, and make thy seed as the sand of the sea, which cannot be numbered for multitude [Gen. 32:11–12].

Jacob really cried out to God. That night was a very difficult night for him, and he didn't have any aspirins he could take.

And he lodged there that same night; and took of that which came to his hand a present for Esau his brother;

Two hundred she goats, and twenty he goats, two hundred ewes, and twenty rams,

Thirty milch camels with their colts, forty kine, and ten bulls, twenty she asses, and ten foals [Gen. 32:13–15].

Jacob is pretty generous with his stock now.

And he delivered them into the hand of his servants, every drove by themselves; and said unto his servants, Pass over before me, and put a space betwixt drove and drove [Gen. 32:16].

This is Jacob's tactic. He will send out a drove, a very rich gift, for his brother, and when that first drove arrives, Esau will say, "What is this?" The servants will reply, "We are bringing you a gift from your brother Jacob." Esau will receive that gift and then ride on a little farther to meet another drove of the same size. He will ask the servants, "Where are you going?" They will say, "We're going to meet Esau with a gift from his brother Jacob." And he will say, "I am Esau." Believe me, by the time Esau gets down where Jacob and the family are, he will be softened.

Jacob has prayed to God and has reminded the Lord, "You told me to return to my country. You said You would protect me." But does he believe God? No. He goes right ahead and makes these arrangements, which reveals that he isn't trusting God at all. I am afraid that we are often in the same position. Many of us take our burdens to the Lord in prayer. We just spread them out before Him—I do that. Then when we get through praying, we get right up and put each little burden right back on our back and start out again with them. We don't really believe Him, do we? We don't really trust Him as we should.

And he commanded the foremost, saying, When Esau my brother meeteth thee, and asketh thee, saying, Whose art thou? and whither goest thou? and whose are these before thee?

Then thou shalt say, They be thy servant Jacob's; it is a present sent unto my lord Esau: and, behold, also he is behind us.

And so commanded he the second, and the third, and all that followed the droves, saying, On this manner shall ye speak unto Esau, when ye find him.

And say ye moreover, Behold, thy servant Jacob is behind us. For he said, I will appease him with the present that goeth before me, and afterward I will see his face; peradventure he will accept of me [Gen. 32:17–20].

Esau will be met by one drove after another like that. This is the plan that Jacob is working on.

So went the present over before him: and himself lodged that night in the company.

And he rose up that night, and took his two wives, and his two womenservants, and his eleven sons, and passed over the ford Jabbok.

And he took them, and sent them over the brook, and sent over that he had [Gen. 32:21–23].

This is the night of the great experience in Jacob's life. The land where he crossed the Brook Jabbok is very desolate. When I was there, I purposely got away from my group and took a walk across the bridge that is there today. The United States built a very lovely road through that area for the Hashimite Kingdom of Jordan. There are several things in that area which you would not be able to see if there wasn't that good road, because it is quite a wilderness area. I took pictures of sheep that were drinking down at the brook Jabbok. The crossing there is a very bleak place, right down between two hills, in that very mountainous and very rugged country. Here is where Jacob came that night. He is not a happy man, and he is filled with fear and doubts. You see, chickens are coming home to roost. He had mistreated Esau. God had never told him to get the birthright or the blessing in the way he did it. God would have gotten it for him. That night Jacob sends all that he has across the brook Jabbok, but he stays on the other side so that, if his brother Esau comes, he might kill Jacob but spare the family. And so Jacob is left alone.

WRESTLING AT PENIEL

And Jacob was left alone; and there

wrestled a man with him until the breaking of the day [Gen. 32:24].

There are several things I would like to get straight as we come to this wrestling match. I have heard it said that Jacob did the wrestling. Actually, Jacob didn't want to wrestle anybody. He has Uncle Laban in back of him who doesn't mean good at all, and he has his brother Esau ahead of him. Jacob is no match for either one. He is caught now between a rock and a hard place, and he doesn't know which way to turn. Do you think he wanted to take on a third opponent that night? I don't think so.

Years ago *Time* magazine, reporting in the sports section concerning the votes for the greatest wrestler, said that not a vote went to the most famous athlete in history, wrestling Jacob. Lo and behold, the magazine received a letter from someone who wrote asking them to tell something about this wrestler Jacob. The writer of the letter had never heard of him before! And evidently he had never read his Bible at all. Jacob is no wrestler—let's make that very clear here at the beginning. That night he was alone because he wanted to be alone, and he wasn't looking for a fight.

This is the question: Who is this one who wrestled with Jacob that night? There has been a great deal of speculation about who it is, but I think He is none other than the preincarnate Christ. There is some evidence for this in the prophecy of Hosea: "Ephraim feedeth on wind, and followeth after the east wind: he daily increaseth lies and desolation; and they do make a covenant with the Assyrians, and oil is carried into Egypt. The LORD hath also a controversy with Judah, and will punish Jacob according to his ways; according to his doings will he recompense him. He took his brother by the heel in the womb, and by his strength he had power with God: Yea, he had power over the angel, and prevailed: he wept, and made supplication unto him: he found him in Beth-el, and there he spake with us; Even the LORD God of hosts; the LORD is his memorial" (Hos. 12:1–5). "The LORD is his memorial"—or, "the Lord is His name." It was none other than Jehovah, the preincarnate Christ, who wrestled with Jacob that night.

And when he saw that he prevailed not against him, he touched the hollow of his thigh; and the hollow of Jacob's thigh was out of joint, as he wrestled with him [Gen. 32:25].

Old Jacob is not going to give up easily; he is not that kind of man—and he struggled against

Him. Finally, this One who wrestled with him crippled him.

And he said, Let me go, for the day breaketh. And he said, I will not let thee go, except thou bless me [Gen. 32:26].

What happens now? Jacob is just holding on; he's not wrestling. He is just holding on to this One. He found out that you do not get anywhere with God by struggling and resisting. The only way that you get anywhere with Him is by yielding and just holding on to Him. Abraham had learned that, and that is why he said amen to God. He believed God, and He counted it to him for righteousness. Abraham reached the end of his rope and put his arms around God. My friend, when you get in that condition, then you trust God. When you are willing to hold on, He is there ready to help you.

JACOB'S NAME CHANGED TO ISRAEL

And he said unto him, What is thy name? And he said, Jacob.

And he said, Thy name shall be called no more Jacob, but Israel: for as a prince hast thou power with God and with men, and hast prevailed [Gen. 32:27–28].

He is not Jacob anymore—the one who is the usurper, the trickster—but Israel, "for as a prince hast thou power with God and with men, and hast prevailed." Now the new nature of Israel will be manifested in the life of this man.

And Jacob asked him, and said, Tell me, I pray thee, thy name. And he said, Wherefore is it that thou dost ask after my name? And he blessed him there.

And Jacob called the name of the place Peniel: for I have seen God face to face, and my life is preserved [Gen. 32:29–30].

Jacob had seen the Angel of the Lord, the preincarnate Christ.

And as he passed over Penuel the sun rose upon him, and he halted upon his thigh.

Therefore the children of Israel eat not of the sinew which shrank, which is upon the hollow of the thigh, unto this day: because he touched the hollow of Jacob's thigh in the sinew that shrank [Gen. 32:31–32].

God had to cripple Jacob in order to get him, but He got him. This man Jacob refused to give in at first—that was typical of him. He knew a few holds, and he thought that after awhile he would be able to overcome. Finally, he found out he couldn't overcome, but he would not surrender. And so what did God do? Certainly, with His superior strength, in a moment God could have pinned down Jacob's shoulders—but He wouldn't have pinned down his *will*. Jacob was like the little boy whose mama made him sit in a corner in his room. After awhile she heard a noise in there, and she called to him, "Willie, are you sitting down?" He said, "Yes, I'm sitting down, but I'm standing up on the inside of me!" That is precisely what would have happened to Jacob. He would have been standing up on the inside of himself—he wasn't ready to yield.

Notice how God deals with him. He touches the hollow of Jacob's thigh. Just a touch of the finger of God, and this man becomes helpless. But you see, God is not pinning down his shoulders. Now Jacob holds on to Him. The Man says, "Let Me go," and Jacob says, "No, I want Your blessing." He's clinging to God now. The struggling and striving are over, and from here on Jacob is going to manifest a spiritual nature, dependence upon God. You will not find the change happening in a moment's notice. Psychologists tell us that certain synaptic connections are set up in our nervous systems so that we do things by habit. We are creatures of habit. This man will lapse back into his old ways many times, but we begin to see something different in him now. Before we are through with him, we will find that he is a real man of God.

First, we saw him at his home and then in the land of Haran where he was a man of the flesh. Here at Peniel, at the brook Jabbok, we find him fighting. After this, and all the way through down into Egypt, we see him as a man of faith. First a man of the flesh, then a man who is fighting and struggling, and finally a man of the faith.

In the New Testament another young man,

a son of Jacob by the name of Saul of Tarsus, tells us his struggle in chapter 7 of Romans. There were three periods in his life. When he was converted, he thought he could live the Christian life. That's where I made my mistake also. When I became a Christian, I frankly thought I could live the Christian life. After all, Vernon McGee didn't need any help. I thought it was easy, but I didn't *do* it, and that was the hard part. That is where Paul had his problem: "For the good that I would I do not: but the evil which I would not, that I do" (Rom. 7:19).

Paul found out that not only was there no good in the old nature, but there also was no strength or power in the new nature. Finally we hear him crying out, "O wretched man that I am! who shall deliver me from the body of this death?" (Rom. 7:24). Then something happened, and in verse 25 he says, "I thank God through Jesus Christ our Lord. . . ." It is through Him that you will have to do all your thanking, because that is where your help is going to come—through Him. ". . . So then with the mind I myself serve the law of God; but with the flesh the law of sin" (Rom. 7:25). That is the way that it is with all of us. We have that old nature, and it cannot do anything that will please God. In fact, Paul went on to say that it was against God.

"Because the carnal mind is enmity against God: for it is not subject to the law of God, neither indeed can be. So then they that are in the flesh cannot please God" (Rom. 8:7–8). We cannot please God in the flesh. Finally, Paul found victory by yielding to the Spirit of God. What the law could not do, the Spirit now is able to do in our lives. How does one do it? It is not until you and I yield to Him that we can please Him. *Yield* means that it is an act of the will of a regenerated person submitting himself to the will of God. And that is exactly what Jacob did. Jacob won, but he got the victory, not by fighting and struggling, but by *yielding*. What a picture we have here in him, and we are told that all these things happened unto them as examples to us (see 1 Cor. 10:11).

CHAPTER 33

In the previous chapter we saw the high point in the life of Jacob, which was his encounter with God. On that night "a man" wrestled with him, and the "man," not Jacob, did the wrestling. Jacob was not looking for another fight. He has Uncle Laban in back of him and Brother Esau ahead of him, and the last time he saw both of them they were breathing out threatenings against him. This man Jacob is not in a position to take on someone else. Therefore, the "man" took the initiative; He was the aggressor. He was, as we have seen, the preincarnate Christ. Jacob resisted Him until the touch of God crippled him. Then, recognizing at last who He was, Jacob clung to Him until He blessed him. From this point on we will begin to see a change in Jacob. As we follow his life in the chapter before us, we will think that we have met a new man. To tell the truth, he *is* a new man.

JACOB MEETS ESAU

And Jacob lifted up his eyes, and looked, and, behold, Esau came, and with him four hundred men. And he divided the children unto Leah, and unto Rachel, and unto the two handmaids [Gen. 33:1].

Jacob wants to spare his family; so he separates them from the others.

And he put the handmaids and their children foremost, and Leah and her children after, and Rachel and Joseph hindermost.

And he passed over before them, and bowed himself to the ground seven times, until he came near to his brother [Gen. 33:2–3].

I would love to have a picture of Jacob meeting his brother Esau! I suppose that while he was a mile away from him, he started bowing. He is coming with his hat in his hand because Esau has four hundred men with him, and Jacob doesn't know if he is coming as friend or foe.

And Esau ran to meet him, and embraced him, and fell on his neck, and kissed him: and they wept [Gen. 33:4].

Well, they are twins, they are brothers. Let bygones be bygones. It looks as if God has certainly touched Esau's heart because he had sworn vengeance that he would kill Jacob.

And he lifted up his eyes, and saw the women and the children; and said, Who are those with thee? And he said, The children which God hath graciously given thy servant.

Then the handmaidens came near, they and their children, and they bowed themselves.

And Leah also with her children came near, and bowed themselves: and after came Joseph near and Rachel, and they bowed themselves [Gen. 33:5–7].

Jacob introduces his family to his brother.

And he said, What meanest thou by all this drove which I met? And he said, These are to find grace in the sight of my lord [Gen. 33:8].

Apparently Jacob believes for a moment that his strategy of approaching his brother has worked. But it wasn't necessary. Listen to Esau—what a change!

And Esau said, I have enough, my brother; keep that thou hast unto thyself [Gen. 33:9].

Esau is saying, "You didn't need to send that to me. I have plenty already."

And Jacob said, Nay, I pray thee, if now I have found grace in thy sight, then receive my present at my hand: for therefore I have seen thy face, as though I had seen the face of God, and thou wast pleased with me.

Take, I pray thee, my blessing that is brought to thee; because God hath dealt graciously with me, and because I have enough. And he urged him, and he took it [Gen. 33:10–11].

This is almost a humorous scene. Up to this time, each was trying to get something from the other. This was especially true of Jacob. Now we find Jacob in a new role altogether. Here he is insisting that his brother take a gift. Esau says, "You don't have to give it to me. I have plenty." But Jacob *insists* that he accept it. Believe me, something has happened to Jacob!

He reminds me of Zacchaeus in the New Testament. When our Lord called him down and went with him into his house, something happened to Zacchaeus. He wasn't the same man that climbed up into the tree. He said he would no longer be the tax collector who had been stealing from people and had been dishonest. He wanted to return, not only anything that he had taken in a wrong way, but he wanted to restore it fourfold. What a change had taken place! You could certainly tell which house Jesus had visited.

Certainly there is a change that has taken place in Jacob. Before he had traded a bowl of stew to get a birthright; now he is willing to give flocks and herds to his brother for nothing! In fact, Jacob *insists* that he take them. Esau finally accepted the gift. In that day and in that land if one refused to take a gift which was urged upon him, it was considered an insult. Therefore, Esau takes the gift.

And he said, Let us take our journey, and let us go, and I will go before thee [Gen. 33:12].

Esau is saying, "Now as you return to the land, let me go before you, show you the way, and be a protection for you."

And he said unto him. My lord knoweth that the children are tender, and the flocks and herds with young are with me: and if men should overdrive them one day, all the flock will die [Gen. 33:13].

Jacob says, "I'm moving my family, and we have little ones, also we have young among the flocks and herds. We can't go very fast. You, of course, with that army of four hundred will probably want to move much faster; so you go ahead."

Let my lord, I pray thee, pass over before his servant: and I will lead on softly, according as the cattle that goeth before me and the children be able to endure, until I come unto my lord unto Seir [Gen. 33:14].

Jacob says, "I can't keep up with you, Brother Esau. I'll just have to set my own pace. You go on ahead."

And Esau said, Let me now leave with thee some of the folk that are with me. And he said, What needeth it? let me find grace in the sight of my lord.

So Esau returned that day on his way unto Seir [Gen. 33:15–16].

Esau lived in Southern Canaan in Seir, the "land of Edom," at this time. After their father's death, he moved to Mount Seir, which God subsequently gave to Esau for a possession (Deut. 2:5).

JACOB JOURNEYS TO SHALEM

And Jacob journeyed to Succoth, and built him an house, and made booths for his cattle: therefore the name of the place is called Succoth [Gen. 33:17].

Now let us not pass by so quickly and easily here that we do not pay attention to what has happened. A great change has come over this man Jacob. You see, all of Jacob's clever scheming to present a gift to his brother Esau has just come to naught. God had prepared the heart of Laban not to harm Jacob, and God had prepared the heart of Esau to receive Jacob. Now he has peace on both fronts. Esau did not want the gift of Jacob because Esau himself had an abundance. When Jacob insisted, he took the gift out of courtesy. Both these brothers seem to be generous and genuine in their reconciliation. We have no reason to doubt it. Since Esau is now prosperous, and since he attached no particular value to his birthright anyway, there is no reason why he should not be reconciled to his twin brother.

Now the sunshine is beginning to fall on Jacob's life. Laban is appeased and Esau is reconciled. God had arranged all of this for him. Had Jacob been left to his own cupidity and his own cleverness, he would have come to his death in a violent manner. Before too long Jacob is going to look back over his life, and when he does, he is going to see the hand of God in his life, and he is going to give God the glory. However, the evil that he has sown is yet to bring forth a full harvest. Trouble is in the offing for this man. It is there waiting for him.

Esau rides off to Seir, and we bid good-bye to him for the time being. He will be back, however, for the funeral of his father Isaac, as we will see in chapter 35.

And Jacob came to Shalem, a city of Shechem, which is in the land of Canaan, when he came from Padan-aram; and pitched his tent before the city.

And he bought a parcel of a field, where he had spread his tent, at the hand of the children of Hamor, Shechem's father, for an hundred pieces of money [Gen. 33:18–19].

Jacob is sometimes criticized because he stopped here at Succoth and at Shalem and did not proceed on to Beth-el. Actually, we ought not to expect too much of Jacob at this time. He's been crippled, and he is just learning to walk with his spiritual legs.

And he erected there an altar, and called it El-elohe-Israel [Gen. 33:20].

Jacob builds an altar here, just as his grandfather Abraham was accustomed to building altars wherever he went. The fine feature is that Jacob identifies his new name with the name of God. He calls it El-elohe-Israel which means, "God, the God of Israel." This indicates real growth in a man who is just learning to walk. Let's put it like this. This man is on the way to Beth-el, but he hasn't arrived there yet. First he journeys to Succoth.

CHAPTER 34

THEME: Dinah defiled by Shechem; Simeon and Levi slay the men of Hamor

Frankly, Jacob made a mistake by stopping in Shalem, for there is going to be a scandal at this point in the family of this man. Dinah, the daughter of Jacob by Leah, is defiled by Shechem, son of Hamor the Hivite. Then Simeon and Levi, Dinah's full brothers, avenge this act by slaying all the inhabitants of the city of Hamor. This cannot be justified, and it is a dark blot on the family of Jacob. It reveals the fact that Jacob did not get away too soon when he left his uncle Laban down in the land of Haran. We need to see that God was right in getting him away from that environment.

There are two things that God spends a great deal of time with in Genesis. First of all, there is the heredity. God is very much concerned that a believer marry a believer and that a believer not marry an unbeliever. That is important for the sake of heredity. The second thing of concern is the environment of the individual. We see this especially in the life of Jacob. He has a big family. Not only were there twelve sons, but there were also daughters. We are given the record of only this one daughter because she features in this very sad chapter.

There is something else for us to note that is important to the understanding of Genesis, and that is that there is trouble in the families. Have you noticed that? There was strife and trouble in the family of Abraham. There was strife and trouble in the family of Isaac. Esau was Isaac's favorite, and Rebekah's favorite was her son Jacob—and that caused a great deal of trouble in the family. Now we will see that there was a great deal of trouble in the family of Jacob.

Jacob stops and stays in Shalem for awhile,

and it is going to cause a great deal of sorrow to him. Very frankly, chapter 34 is a sad, sordid chapter, and this must have been a heartbreak to old Jacob at this time. Jacob (or Israel, as we should call him) has built an altar, and he is now giving a testimony to the living and true God. There is a change in his life, but it is a slow growth, a development. This should be a lesson to us today: Don't expect that, as a Christian, you are going to become full grown overnight. God adopts us as full-grown sons into the family where we are able to understand divine truth because the Holy Spirit is our Teacher. But our spiritual growth and our progress are very slow. We may learn truths in the Bible, but we will find that in our lives we are very much like Simon Peter, stumbling here and falling down there. Thank God that Simon Peter kept getting up and brushing himself off, and there came a day when he had a very close walk with the Lord. In fact, he walked to a cross even as our Lord did. You and I need to recognize that in our own lives the growth is slow, and therefore the growth in others will also be slow. Sometimes parents of converted children expect too much of them. Let's not expect too much of other folk, but let's also expect a great deal of ourselves.

There are three chapters in the Book of Genesis that are not pretty at all, and they all concern the children of Leah, the elder daughter of Laban who was given to Jacob. I believe that this gives evidence of the fact that God does not approve plurality of marriages. The very fact that it was forced on Jacob to a certain extent did not make it right, by any means—Jacob at least went along with it. We find in this section that the children of Leah are all involved in sin. She had four boys. In this chapter it is Simeon and Levi. In chapter 35 we come to another of the sons, Reuben, the first-born. In chapter 38 it will be Judah. Every one of Leah's sons turned out rather badly, and there was flagrant sin in their lives.

We have already noted that there was a great deal of strife in all of these families, but now another element has entered in. There is sordidness and a shoddiness that has seeped into the family of Jacob that was not in the family of Abraham or of Isaac. They had a great deal of difficulty and many problems, but nothing like we see in Jacob's family. Again, God wanted to get this man Jacob and his family out from the home of Laban, out from that atmosphere, because the very atmosphere gave the background for these awful sins that are mentioned here.

DINAH DEFILED BY SHECHEM

Jacob has stopped here at Shalem and has bought himself a nice little place out in the suburban area of town. He is attempting, as it were, to orient himself to the culture of that day. Well, it wasn't a good place, and God wants to separate this man from this area also. And believe me, after you read this chapter, you will come to the conclusion that God had *better* separate him from it!

And Dinah the daughter of Leah, which she bare unto Jacob, went out to see the daughters of the land [Gen. 34:1].

Dinah went visiting in this town of Shalem.

And when Shechem the son of Hamor the Hivite, prince of the country, saw her, he took her, and lay with her, and defiled her [Gen. 34:2].

Let me put it in the language of the news media today: He raped her. If they can say it in print and on radio and television, certainly this poor preacher can say it. Sin needs to be spelled out. There was a time when sin was sin, but now they've taken the "s" off of it, and you're in the "in" group if you're a sinner. But that's not the way God spells sin. He still spells it S-I-N. And you will notice that "I" is right in the middle of the word—that's where all of us are.

And his soul clave unto Dinah the daughter of Jacob, and he loved the damsel, and spake kindly unto the damsel.

And Shechem spake unto his father Hamor, saying, Get me this damsel to wife [Gen. 34:3–4].

The very interesting thing is that the boy Shechem was apparently in love with the girl and really wanted to marry her.

And Jacob heard that he had defiled Dinah his daughter: now his sons were with his cattle in the field: and Jacob held his peace until they were come.

And Hamor the father of Shechem went out unto Jacob to commune with him.

And the sons of Jacob came out of the field when they heard it: and the men were grieved, and they were very wroth, because he had wrought folly in Israel in lying with Jacob's daughter; which thing ought not to be done [Gen. 34:5–7].

We certainly agree that it should not have been done, but it had been, and now the fellow wants to marry her. When Jacob heard it, he waited for his boys to come in, and they had a war counsel. I am of the opinion that Jacob probably should not have made as much of it as he did. When Hamor, the father of Shechem, came out to him, it is obvious that he wanted to get the girl for his son's wife. Jacob probably should have yielded to that, because that was, shall I say, the best way out at the time. Certainly, the way it was handled was not the best by any means, and God did not approve of it.

And Hamor communed with them, saying, The soul of my son Shechem longeth for your daughter: I pray you give her him to wife

And make ye marriages with us, and give your daughters unto us, and take our daughters unto you [Gen. 34:8–9].

Although intermarriage would have been wrong, it seems that Dinah should have been given to Shechem because that would have prevented a worse sin. This, of course, is hindsight, and "Monday morning quarterbacks" are not always right.

And ye shall dwell with us: and the land shall be before you; dwell and trade ye therein, and get you possessions therein.

And Shechem said unto her father and unto her brethren, Let me find grace in your eyes, and what ye shall say unto me I will give.

Ask me never so much dowry and gift, and I will give according as ye shall say unto me: but give me the damsel to wife [Gen. 34:10–12].

All of this reveals that Jacob is going to have to move on. This is no place for him, mixing with these people in this land.

And the sons of Jacob answered Shechem and Hamor his father deceitfully, and said, because he had defiled Dinah their sister [Gen. 34:13].

I feel that Jacob should certainly have taken the leadership in his family. First of all, he should have prevented his sons from deceiving Shechem and Hamor.

And they said unto them, We cannot do this thing, to give our sister to one that is uncircumcised; for that were a reproach unto us [Gen. 34:14].

The thing that disturbs me about this incident is that the real reproach—the sin of rape—is ignored, and they make the reproach on the basis of the rule which God had given them regarding intermarriage with the uncircumcised.

But in this will we consent unto you: If ye will be as we be, that every male of you be circumcised;

Then will we give our daughters unto you, and we will take your daughters to us, and we will dwell with you, and we will become one people.

But if ye will not hearken unto us, to be circumcised; then will we take our daughter, and we will be gone [Gen. 34:15–17].

The thing that Jacob's sons ask them to do is to go through the ritual of circumcision.

This ought to be a warning today to a great many people. I recall one couple who came to me for counseling and asked me to perform their marriage ceremony. I would not unite them in marriage because he was not a Christian, and she claimed that she would not marry him unless he became a Christian. I talked with him, and he said he would accept Christ. We had prayer, and then I asked him, "What have you really done?" I have never heard such hemming and hawing and beating around the bush as this boy did. Very frankly, I said right in front of him, "Young lady, I'll not perform the ceremony. I don't think the young man is converted." They felt that I was being very harsh, and they went down the street and got another preacher to perform the ceremony. After they were married, she tried to get him to go to church. Of course, he had a good reason for not coming to hear me preach because I'd

been so cruel to him, but then she agreed to go to another church, and they went two or three times. Finally, he just said to her point-blank, "Really, I'm not a Christian." Just to go through the ceremony of joining the church and even of saying you trust Christ doesn't mean you have. I find that faith doesn't seem to mean very much to a great many people today. They think it is enough just to nod your head. It is a tremendous experience, my friend, to trust Christ as your Savior. There's nothing quite like it, nothing to compare to it in this world. When you trust Christ as Savior, it does something for you. It didn't do anything for that boy.

Mark Twain had the same experience. He was not a Christian, and he was in love with a very beautiful, wonderful Christian girl. She would not marry him until he became a Christian. He professed to have accepted Christ as his Savior, and they started out their marriage that way. Well, Mark Twain became very famous, and he was entertained by many famous people in the world. One day when he came back to his home in Missouri and she wanted to go to church, he said, "Look, I can't keep up the front any longer. You go on to church. I know now that I'm not a Christian." May I say that made a very unhappy home, and it absolutely spoiled the life of this lovely Christian girl.

Here the sons of Jacob are saying, "If you'll go through the rite of circumcision, it will make everything all right." A great many people think that if you join the church, nod your head, and are able to use the right vocabulary and quote the right verse, that means you are a Christian. My friend, that does not mean you are a Christian. If you have trusted in Christ, something has happened, and you are a different person.

And their words pleased Hamor, and Shechem Hamor's son.

And the young man deferred not to do the thing, because he had delight in Jacob's daughter: and he was more honourable than all the house of his father [Gen. 34:18–19].

I agree that this boy is doing the honorable thing at this point.

And Hamor and Shechem his son came unto the gate of their city, and communed with the men of their city, saying,

These men are peaceable with us; therefore let them dwell in the land, and trade

therein; for the land, behold, it is large enough for them; let us take their daughters to us for wives, and let us give them our daughters.

Only herein will the men consent unto us for to dwell with us, to be one people, if every male among us be circumcised, as they are circumcised.

Shall not their cattle and their substance and every beast of theirs be ours? only let us consent unto them, and they will dwell with us [Gen. 34:20–23].

In other words, through intermarriage these men expected to eventually own everything that Jacob had.

And unto Hamor and unto Shechem his son hearkened all that went out of the gate of his city; and every male was circumcised, all that went out of the gate of his city [Gen. 34:24].

Performing the rite of circumcision on unbelievers was as phony as it could be. It is like joining a church when you are unconverted.

SIMEON AND LEVI SLAY THE MEN OF HAMOR

And it came to pass on the third day, when they were sore, that two of the sons of Jacob, Simeon and Levi, Dinah's brethren, took each man his sword, and came upon the city boldly, and slew all the males [Gen. 34:25].

This was real trickery. Simeon and Levi were Dinah's full brothers, and they wanted to get revenge. In their revenge, they go too far. Neither the rape nor the fact that Hamor intended to dispossess Jacob and his sons of the great wealth which Jacob had accumulated in Haran can in any way justify the brutal act of Simeon and Levi, but it does reveal the impossible situation of dealing with the inhabitants of that land. The thing they have done is a very terrible thing.

And they slew Hamor and Shechem his son with the edge of the sword, and took Dinah out of Shechem's house, and went out.

The sons of Jacob came upon the slain, and spoiled the city, because they had defiled their sister [Gen. 34:26–27].

The other sons joined in on this. This reveals greed in the family of Jacob that is not right and which they had learned in the home of Laban.

They took their sheep, and their oxen, and their asses, and that which was in the city, and that which was in the field,

And all their wealth, and all their little ones, and their wives took they captive, and spoiled even all that was in the house.

And Jacob said to Simeon and Levi, Ye have troubled me to make me to stink among the inhabitants of the land, among the Canaanites and the Perizzites: and I being few in number, they shall gather themselves together against me, and slay me; and I shall be destroyed, I and my house [Gen. 34:28–30].

Notice something that is obviously wrong here in the life of Jacob. Jacob rebukes Simeon and Levi for giving him a bad name, but he doesn't rebuke them for the sin that they have committed. We sometimes get a wrong perspective of sin and of our actions. We think only of the *effect* that it is going to have. There are many men and women in our churches who will not take a stand on certain issues. Why? Well, the little crowd they run with may not accept them. They are with a little clique, and they don't dare stand for anything that the little clique wouldn't stand for. It is never a question of whether it is right or wrong; it's a question of whether it ingratiates them to the crowd. God have mercy on Christians who shape their lives by those who are around them and who are constantly looking for the effect their conduct is going to have on others. They do not look on whether this is the right thing or the Christian thing or whether as a child of God this is something they should or should not do. This is the reason our churches are filled with those who compromise, and it is little wonder that we have so many frustrated, unhappy Christians today. It is a wonderful thing to stand for the truth, and when you stand for it, then you don't have to compromise. How wonderful it is when we will do that. Poor old Jacob is growing, but he hasn't grown that far.

Then these boys, of course, attempt to defend themselves:

And they said, Should he deal with our sister as with an harlot? [Gen. 34:31].

That's a good question. I would say that if they wanted to take the judgment into their own hands, they first of all should have heard this boy out and let him marry their sister. It would have been the best thing to do under the circumstances, but it is not the right thing, by any means. Certainly that would have been better than to go to the extreme of murdering the inhabitants of that land. There is no excuse that can be offered, and I have no defense to offer for them at all. They should not have done the thing that they did, but we must understand that they were not living in the light of Romans 12:19–21 which says: "Dearly beloved, avenge not yourselves, but rather give place unto wrath: for it is written, Vengeance is mine; I will repay, saith the Lord. Therefore if thine enemy hunger, feed him; if he thirst, give him drink: for in so doing thou shalt heap coals of fire on his head. Be not overcome of evil, but overcome evil with good." For a Christian today Romans 12 is the policy that he should follow. The very minute we attempt to take revenge or get vengeance, it means that we are no longer walking by faith. We are saying that we cannot trust God to work it out. However, I am not sure that you could bring Jacob—and certainly not his sons—up to such a spiritual level at that particular time. But you cannot justify this terrible deed which they have committed. You can well understand that they acted because of their feeling for their sister and the shame which had been brought upon the family. Jacob was beginning to see that a whole lot of chickens—not just a few—were coming home to roost.

CHAPTER 35

THEME: *Jacob returns to Beth-el; God renews the covenant; Rachel dies at the birth of Benjamin; death of Isaac*

After the study in chapter 34, you may have come to the conclusion that I made a blunder when I said that Jacob's life changed at Peniel. Actually, we did not see too much change in what took place in the thirty-fourth chapter. That is quite true, but there was a change that took place. I hesitate to call Jacob's experience at Peniel a crisis experience because I am afraid that this matter of a crisis experience has been overdrawn by a great many. There are some folk who feel that, if you don't have a second experience, you just haven't had anything. The fact of the matter is that that's not true. Some have a wonderful crisis experience, and I'm sure that many of us can turn back to that in our lives. But there are those who cannot or do not and have never mentioned it as being something very important in their lives. But when Jacob came to Peniel, a tremendous thing happened to him. All the way from the beginning of the life of Jacob until Peniel, his life was characterized by the rise of self, the assertion of the flesh—that's Jacob and nothing but that. What really happened at Peniel was the fall of self. He went down like a deflated tire. He had been pumped up like a balloon, and he went down to practically nothing. But actually, chapter 34 evidences that he was not yet walking by faith.

As soon as Esau had turned his back and started home, Jacob took his family down to Shalem. It is a tragic move. Jacob was still depending upon his own cleverness. Dinah was raped, and Simeon and Levi, her full brothers, went into the city of Shalem to the prince who was responsible. Although he wanted to marry her, they murdered him, and the sons of Jacob conducted a slaughter that would make a gang shooting in Chicago look pretty tame. When they came home, Jacob said, "You have made my name to smell among the people of my land."

Many expositors say that it was a tragic thing for Jacob to stop in Shalem, and I must say that I have to go along with that partially. But I have one question to ask: Was Jacob ready for Beth-el? Was he ready for the experiences that God was going to give him? No, I think that the tragic things that took place in chapter 34 were the result of a man who had been walking in the energy of the flesh. There had been a deflation of self, but there was no discernible faith in God. Because he did not have faith to go on to Beth-el, he stopped at Shalem. These tragic things which took place in his life reveal that this man was not a leader in his own family. He was not taking the proper place that he should have. He was no spiritual giant, by any means. And to have those eleven boys to herd was really a job for which this man Jacob was not prepared. After this tragic event, Jacob now is beginning to see the hand of God in his life, and now he makes the decision that he probably should have made beforehand.

JACOB RETURNS TO BETH-EL

And God said unto Jacob, Arise, go up to Beth-el, and dwell there: and make there an altar unto God, that appeared unto thee when thou fleddest from the face of Esau thy brother [Gen. 35:1].

Now God is calling this man back to Beth-el. After this sad experience, he is prepared to go. You see, he didn't have faith to move out before, but Jacob now begins to take the spiritual leadership in his home.

Then Jacob said unto his household, and to all that were with him, Put away the strange gods that are among you, and be clean, and change your garments [Gen. 35:2].

There are several things that Jacob tells his household to do. First of all, they are to "put away the strange gods that are among you." We are almost shocked at this. You will recall that when Jacob fled with Rachel and Leah, Rachel slipped out with the family gods. Apparently, she had sat on them while riding the camel—she just crawled on top of the luggage that was on the camel's back and sat down because these little images were underneath. Jacob did not know at the time that she had taken them. He was very honest when he told Laban that the little images were not in his entourage at all. That may have been one of the few times he was truthful with Laban. He really had not known they were there.

When they were discovered, I think that we would all assume that Jacob would get rid of them because he knew of the living and true God. In fact, he had had a personal encounter with Him. But he didn't get rid of the images, and now we find that his entire family is worshiping these strange gods. For the first time, Jacob is the one to take the spiritual leadership, and he says, "Let's get rid of these false gods, these strange gods." The first thing they have to do is to put away that which is wrong.

There are too many folk who six days a week are serving some other god, and on Sunday they try to serve the Lord. Many Christians, even fundamental believers, have their strange gods, and then they wonder why their service in the church on Sunday is not a thrilling experience. My friend, you are going to have to put away your strange gods. I don't know what yours might be. It could be covetousness. There is many a good fundamental businessman who is out after every dollar he can get. He gives more devotion to getting the dollar than he does to serving the Lord on Sunday. And then he wonders what is wrong with his spiritual life. If you are going to come back to Beth-el where you met God at the beginning, then, my friend, you must put away those things that are wrong.

Then Jacob says, "Be clean." For the believer, that means confession of sins. You have to deal with sin in your life. You cannot come to church on Sunday and dismiss the way you have lived during the week that has just passed. After all, you take a physical bath and use a deodorant before you come to church, and yet there is spiritual body odor in our churches because there is no confession of the sin, no cleansing. "If we confess our sins, he is faithful and just to forgive us our sins, and to cleanse us from all unrighteousness" (1 John 1:9). There must be the confession. He will forgive, but we must confess.

"And change your garments." In other words, get rid of the old garments. In Scripture "garments" speak of habits. We speak of an equestrian wearing a riding habit or of a football player wearing a uniform—which is his habit. In like manner, the child of God should dress in a way to mirror who he is and to whom he belongs. Do you wear the habits of the Lord? Can you be detected in business or in school or in the neighborhood as being a little different in your life? You *are* wearing a habit. The day that Jacob went back to Beth-el, he started living for God. Up to then, I don't think he was. Now he says, "Let's go back to Beth-el"—that's the thing that we must do.

And let us arise, and go up to Beth-el; and I will make there an altar unto God, who answered me in the day of my distress, and was with me in the way which I went [Gen. 35:3].

Abraham and Isaac had made altars, and now Jacob will make an altar—thank God for that. He will now have a witness for God.

"Who answered me in the day of my distress, and was with me in the way which I went." The thing that Jacob remembered is that when he was running away from home as a young man, homesick and lonesome, he had come to Beth-el, and God had been faithful to him. God had said, "I will be faithful to you." The years had gone by, and God certainly had been faithful to him. Now God says, "You've got to go back to Beth-el. You have to go back to where you started. You have to begin there."

We need to recognize that the years we spend in living a shoddy, shabby Christian life are a waste of time, absolutely a waste of time. God called the children of Israel to get out of Egypt and into the land of promise. God appeared to them and told them to go into the land, but they didn't go in. Forty years they wandered around, and then God appeared to Joshua and said, "Go into the land." He picked up right where He had left off. They had wasted forty years. How many people are wasting their lives as Christians? My, the tremendous spiritual lessons that are here for us! I don't know about you, but some of us are just like Jacob, and that's the reason this is so applicable to us today. Thank God that He says He is the God of Jacob. I love that! If He'll be the God of Jacob, He'll be the God of J. Vernon McGee also—that's wonderful! This chapter is a great encouragement to us.

Notice that Jacob is assuming authority in his home.

And they gave unto Jacob all the strange gods which were in their hand, and all their earrings which were in their ears; and Jacob hid them under the oak which was by Shechem [Gen. 35:4].

Let me pause to say that earrings were associated with worship in that day—there is a great deal said in Scripture about that. The earrings identified them as idolaters, and so they are going to get rid of them.

"Jacob hid them under the oak which was by Shechem." Jacob got rid of them. They're not stored away—they're buried. They must be put away because it is now going to be a new life.

And they journeyed: and the terror of God was upon the cities that were round about them, and they did not pursue after the sons of Jacob.

So Jacob came to Luz, which is in the land of Canaan, that is, Beth-el, he and all the people that were with him [Gen. 35:5–6].

This place was called Luz before Jacob changed the name to Beth-el, and the people in that day knew it as Luz, not as Beth-el. We know it today as Beth-el.

And he built there an altar, and called the place El-beth-el: because there God appeared unto him, when he fled from the face of his brother [Gen. 35:7].

Beth-el, meaning "the house of God," was the name that Jacob had given to it before. Now he calls it *El-Beth-el*, which means *"God* of the house of God." This reveals spiritual growth in Jacob's life.

Now here is a very interesting sidelight:

But Deborah Rebekah's nurse died, and she was buried beneath Beth-el under an oak: and the name of it was called Allon-bachuth [Gen. 35:8].

Since Deborah was with Jacob at this time, we assume that Rebekah had already died, and Scripture does not tell us when her death took place. Poor Jacob never saw his mother again. That part is not as tragic as the fact that she never saw him again—she had just sent him away for a little while, you know. The nurse apparently had brought a message of Rebekah's death and had come to stay with Jacob—and now she dies.

GOD RENEWS THE COVENANT

And God appeared unto Jacob again, when he came out of Padan-aram, and blessed him [Gen. 35:9].

All those years God had been trying to deal with Jacob. Now he picks up right where He had met him when he came to Beth-el as a young man. Those years he spent down there with Uncle Laban, in many ways, were wasted years.

And God said unto him, Thy name is Jacob: thy name shall not be called any more Jacob, but Israel shall be thy name: and he called his name Israel.

And God said unto him, I am God Almighty: be fruitful and multiply; a nation and a company of nations shall be of thee, and kings shall come out of thy loins [Gen. 35:10–11].

"I am God Almighty." Remember that that is what He had told Abraham.

And the land which I gave Abraham and Isaac, to thee I will give it, and to thy seed after thee will I give the land [Gen. 35:12].

The Lord considers that pretty important property, by the way. This now is the third time He has promised them the land—first to Abraham, then to Isaac, and now to Jacob. The Lord had to tell each one of these men about it two or three times; in fact, He told Abraham many times.

And God went up from him in the place where he talked with him.

And Jacob set up a pillar in the place where he talked with him, even a pillar of stone: and he poured a drink offering thereon, and he poured oil thereon.

And Jacob called the name of the place where God spake with him, Beth-el [Gen. 35:13–15].

Here is the first mention of a drink offering. In the Book of Leviticus, five offerings are given, but not a drink offering. In fact, no instruction is given about it at all, but it is mentioned. Evidently this is one of the oldest offerings, and it has a very wonderful meaning to the believer today. The drink offering was just poured on the other offerings, and it went up in steam. Paul told the Philippians that that is the way he wanted his life to be—just poured out like a drink offering.

RACHEL DIES
AT THE BIRTH OF BENJAMIN

And they journeyed from Beth-el; and there was but a little way to come to Ephrath: and Rachel travailed, and she had hard labour [Gen. 35:16].

Rachel had one son Joseph, but now she has a second son.

And it came to pass, when she was in hard labour, that the midwife said unto her, Fear not; thou shalt have this son also.

And it came to pass, as her soul was in departing, (for she died) that she called his name Ben-oni: but his father called him Benjamin [Gen. 35:17–18].

What a wonderful thing this is—not the death of Rachel, but the way this took place. She says, "Call him 'son of my sorrow,' " but Jacob looked down at him and said, "I've lost my lovely Rachel, and this little fellow looks like her, so I'll just call him Benjamin, 'son of my right hand.' " Jacob was partial to the sons of Rachel.

Jacob's love for Rachel was perhaps the only fine thing in his life during those years in Pandan-aram when there was so much evidence of the flesh and of self-seeking. He loved Rachel—there is no question about that. He was totally devoted to her. He was willing to do almost anything for her, such as permitting her to keep the images she had taken from her father. I don't think that Leah would have gotten by with it—or anyone else for that matter. But he was indulgent with Rachel. She had

given Jacob his son Joseph, and now she gives birth to Benjamin. And it was at the birth of her second son that she died. His life meant her death. It was a great heartbreak to Jacob.

The other ten boys were no joy to him at all. God reminded him, I think, every day for twenty-four hours of the day that it was sinful to have more than one wife. He didn't need all of them. However, God will overrule, of course. (And He overrules in your life and mine. We can thank Him for that!) But the facts reveal that God did not approve of this plural marriage. This is especially obvious in the treatment which Joseph received from his half brothers.

Jacob loved Joseph and Benjamin and, very frankly, the other boys were jealous of that. He should not have shown such partiality to Joseph because he had experienced the results of partiality in his own home—he had been the one whom his father had more or less pushed aside. He knew the trouble it had caused. Although I don't try to defend Jacob, we can sympathize with him. He had lost his lovely Rachel, but he had Benjamin. While it was true that the boy was the son of Rachel's sorrow, Jacob could not call him Benoni. He was not the son of *his* sorrow; he was the son of his right hand, his walking stick, his staff, the one he would lean on in his old age. It is important to recognize this because it will help us understand the great sorrow Jacob will go through later on. All of it will have its roots in Jacob's sin. God does not approve of the wrong in our lives, my friend. We think we can get by with it, but we will not get by with it—anymore than Jacob got by with it.

And Rachel died, and was buried in the way to Ephrath, which is Bethlehem [Gen. 35:19].

She is buried there today. I have several pictures that I have taken of her tomb that is there.

And Jacob set a pillar upon her grave: that is the pillar of Rachel's grave unto this day [Gen. 35:20].

That is, it was there until the time Moses wrote this, but it is also there to this very day.

And Israel journeyed, and spread his tent beyond the tower of Edar [Gen. 35:21].

In verses 22–26 we have a listing of the sons of Jacob by his different wives. Actually, Joseph and Benjamin were the two boys that were outstanding. The others just didn't turn out well. Again, this proves the fact that God does not bless a plurality of wives. The family of Jacob ought to illustrate that fact to us. Although Uncle Laban was responsible, of course, Jacob went along with it.

DEATH OF ISAAC

And Isaac gave up the ghost, and died, and was gathered unto his people, being old and full of days: and his sons Esau and Jacob buried him [Gen. 35:29].

I suspect that the death of their father Isaac was the only occasion which brought these two boys together in the years following Jacob's return to the land.

Have you noticed that this chapter is made prominent by death? First there is the death of Deborah, the maid of Rebekah. In this there is the suggestion of the death of Rebekah herself. Then there is the death of lovely Rachel. Finally, the chapter closes with the death of Isaac.

CHAPTER 36

THEME: Esau moves from Canaan to Mount Seir

This chapter deals entirely with the family of Esau which became the nation of Edom. Although it may not be too interesting for the average reader, it is a marvelous study for one who wants to follow through on these names and the peoples who came from them. You will find that some of the names mentioned here are names that one hears out on that great Arabian desert today. Omar, the tentmaker, belongs out there, as do Teman and Zepho and Kenaz and Korah. Well, here is the family of Esau, and they are still located out in that area.

The family of Esau settled in Edom, which is right south and east of the Dead Sea. It is a mountainous area, and the capital of Edom, the rock-hewn city of Petra, stands there today. Prophecy in the books of Isaiah, Jeremiah, Ezekiel, and Obadiah concerning Edom has been remarkably fulfilled.

The nation of Edom came from Esau. Three times in this chapter it is made very clear that Esau is the father of Edom—in fact, the names are synonymous (notice verse 8, for example). Then what is the difference between Esau and Edom? Well, when we first met Esau, we saw him as a boy in the family of Isaac. He was the outdoor, rugged type, a fine-looking athletic boy, by the way. Outwardly he looked attractive, but if there ever was a man of the flesh, Esau was that man.

Years ago a Christian girl talked to me about a fine-looking young man whom she had met. To tell the truth, they were both fine-looking young people. She had been born in China. Her father was in the oil business and had been made very wealthy. She met this young man who was a bank clerk, a very poor boy. I had been a bank clerk when I was a young fellow, and I knew that a lot of bank clerks look around for a good marriage. They notice the daughters of customers who have money in the bank. So this boy had met the girl. He was a handsome brute, fine-looking, the rugged type. To me he looked like Esau. She was a lovely Christian girl who had been led to the Lord by a missionary while in China. She insisted on marrying this young man, hoping that he would come to the Lord. I had talked with him and knew he had no notion of coming to the Lord, but he wanted to marry that girl. She was beautiful and she had money—and he was a man of the flesh. I told them I could not perform the ceremony. She was quite provoked with me, but later on she came back to tell me that she was divorced. She told me she had never known a person so given over to the things that were secular and carnal and of the flesh. She said she never dreamed there could be a person who would never in his entire life have a high, noble, spiritual, wonderful thought. She said he was as crude as one could possibly be. On the surface he gave a good impression, and he had been well mannered and chivalrous when they were courting, but underneath the facade he was crude and rude. Well, that is Esau, also. If you had been an attractive young lady in Esau's day and had seen him there in his family, the chances are that you would have been glad to date him. He was an attractive young man, but he was a man of the flesh.

Perhaps someone will want to argue with God about His choice of Jacob over Esau. Esau looked so good on the outside. Could God have made a mistake? Well, over in the little prophecy of Obadiah we see Esau unveiled. One little Esau has become about one hundred thousand Edomites. Each one of them is a little Esau. Now take a look at the nation and you will see what came from Esau. It is like putting Esau under a microscope; he is greatly enlarged. What do we see? We see a nation filled with pride. God said to Edom: "The pride of thine heart hath deceived thee, thou that dwellest in the clefts of the rock, whose habitation is high; that saith in his heart, Who shall bring me down to the ground? Though thou exalt thyself as the eagle, and though thou set thy nest among the stars, thence will I bring thee down, saith the LORD" (Obad. 1:3–4). The pride of their heart was a declaration of independence, a soul that says it can live without God and does not have a need for God. That is Esau.

In the last book of the Old Testament God says, "Jacob have I loved and Esau have I hated." God never said that until over one thousand years after these men lived, but God knew the heart of Esau at the beginning. After they worked their way out in history, it is obvious to us all that God was accurate.

Now these are the generations of Esau, who is Edom [Gen. 36:1].

Again we are told that Esau is Edom.

Esau took his wives of the daughters of Canaan; Adah the daugher of Elon the Hittite, and Aholibamah the daughter of Anah the daugher of Zibeon the Hivite;

And Bashemath Ishmael's daughter, sister of Nebajoth [Gen. 36:2–3].

Esau, you recall, had married two Canaanite women and also an Ishmaelite woman.

And Esau took his wives, and his sons, and his daughters, and all the persons of his house, and his cattle, and all his beasts, and all his substance, which he had got in the land of Canaan; and went into the country from the face of his brother Jacob.

For their riches were more than that they might dwell together; and the land wherein they were strangers could not bear them because of their cattle [Gen. 36:6–7].

Remember that Abraham and Lot had had that same problem. There was not enough grazing land for them. Each one had too many cattle. They had separated and now Esau leaves the Promised Land, leaves it on his own, due to economic circumstances.

Thus dwelt Esau in mount Seir: Esau is Edom [Gen. 36:8].

Now Esau moves from "the land of Seir" in Canaan, where he lived when Jacob returned from Padan-aram (Gen. 32:3), to Mount Seir, which I have already described.

And Timna was concubine to Eliphaz Esau's son; and she bare to Eliphaz Amalek: these were the sons of Adah Esau's wife [Gen. 36:12].

This is the beginning of the Amalekites. Down through the centuries those tribes which were there in the desert pushed out in many directions. Many of them pushed across North Africa. All the Arab tribes came from Abraham—through Hagar, the Egyptian, and through Keturah, whom he married after the death of Sarah. And there has been intermarriage between the tribes. They belong to the same family that Israelites belong to.

In the Mideast I met an Arab who expressed hostility to a statement I had made about the nation Israel in a message I had given to our tour group. Although he was a Christian Arab, he told me how he hated the nation Israel. I said to him, "But he is your *brother*." Believe me, that did antagonize him! He said, "I have no relationship with him at all." I insisted that he did. I said, "You are both Semitic people. You are a Semite as much as they are." Well, he had to admit that was true.

So this chapter is important as it shows these relationships. The Spirit of God uses a great deal of printer's ink to tell us about this.

We find some humor in this chapter, too.

These were dukes of the sons of Esau: the sons of Eliphaz the firstborn son of Esau; duke Teman, duke Omar, duke Zepho, duke Kenaz [Gen. 36:15].

Where in the world did they get these dukes? Well, here is the beginning of nobility—they just assumed these titles. Each one of them became a duke. It is not just a nickname—they mean business by it. The beginning of nobility is in the family of Esau.

These are the sons of Esau, who is Edom, and these are their dukes [Gen. 36:19].

They have dukes in the family now. A great many people in my country can trace their ancestry back to royalty. It makes me wonder if anybody who came from Europe were folk who worked in vineyards, made pottery, and ran shoe shops. Everybody seems to have come from royalty. Well, Esau turned out quite a few of them. In fact, he went further than producing dukes—

And these are the kings that reigned in the land of Edom, before there reigned any king over the children of Israel [Gen. 36:31].

This business of having kings was not God's plan for His people. But this was the lifestyle of Edom. They had dukes and kings over them. If you had belonged to the family of Esau, you would have needed a title, because that is the type of folk they were. It is interesting to note that the people of Esau had kings long before the people of Israel had kings. In fact, later on the people of Israel will say to Samuel, ". . .make us a king to judge us like all the nations" (1 Sam. 8:5). They could have said, "Our brothers down south, the Edomites, have kings. We would like to have kings like they do."

And these are the names of the dukes that came of Esau, according to their families, after their places, by their names; duke Timnah, duke Alvah, duke Jetheth,

Duke Aholibamah, duke Elah, duke Pinon,

Duke Kenaz, duke Teman, duke Mibzar,

Duke Magdiel, duke Iram: these be the dukes of Edom, according to their habitations in the land of their possession: he is Esau the father of the Edomites [Gen. 36:40–43].

This is the family history of the rejected line. When the chapter gives the final resumé, it lists again the dukes that came from the line of Esau. There must have been a lot of bowing and scraping to each other when they got together. "I want you to meet my brother here. He is Duke Alvah" and "I want you to meet my friend. He is Duke Timnah." And the kings—I doubt if you could even get in to see them!

This is a very interesting chapter for anyone who is interested in the study of anthropology or ethnology. A chapter like this gives a family history which probably extends farther back than any other source could go.

So the chapter closes with a list of the dukes and mentions again that their habitation is in the land of their possession which is Edom. "He is Esau the father of the Edomites." We see the working out of this in the prophecies of Obadiah and in Malachi. This is quite remarkable, friend, and something we cannot just pass by.

CHAPTER 37

THEME: Cause of strife in Jacob's family; the dreams of Joseph; Jacob sends Joseph to his brethren; Joseph sold into slavery

As we resume the story of the line of Abraham, Isaac, and Jacob, we come to the fourth outstanding figure in this last section of Genesis. From here, all the way through the Book of Genesis, the central figure is Joseph, although we are still dealing with the family of Jacob. More chapters are devoted to Joseph than to Abraham or Isaac or to anyone else. More chapters are devoted to Joseph than to the first whole period from Genesis 1–11. This should cause the thoughtful student to pause and ask why Joseph should be given such prominence in Scripture.

There are probably several reasons. One is that the life of Joseph is a good and honorable life. He is the living example of the verse: "Finally, brethren, whatsoever things are true, whatsoever things are honest, whatsoever things are just, whatsoever things are pure, whatsoever things are lovely, whatsoever things are of good report; if there be any virtue, and if there be any praise, think on these things" (Phil. 4:8). God wants us to have whatever is good, virtuous, and great before us, and Joseph's life is just that.

There is a second reason, and it is a great one. There is no one in Scripture who is more like Christ in his person and experiences than Joseph. Yet nowhere in the New Testament is Joseph given to us as a type of Christ. However, the parallel cannot be accidental. As we go on into his story, we shall mention many of these parallels. There are at least thirty which I shall list later.

So now we resume the story of the line of Jacob which is that line leading to the Messiah, the Christ. Jacob is living in Canaan as the story of Joseph begins.

CAUSE OF STRIFE IN JACOB'S FAMILY

And Jacob dwelt in the land wherein his father was a stranger, in the land of Canaan [Gen. 37:1].

Jacob has moved down, apparently, south of Bethlehem and has come to Hebron. This is the place where Abraham had made his home. This is the place of fellowship, of communion with God.

These are the generations of Jacob. Joseph, being seventeen years old, was feeding the flock with his brethren; and the lad was with the sons of Bilhah, and with the sons of Zilpah, his father's wives: and Joseph brought unto his father their evil report [Gen. 37:2].

We can see that the bunch of boys Jacob had were real problem children (with the exception of Joseph and Benjamin). It took these men a long time to learn the lessons God would teach them.

Notice now that the emphasis shifts from Jacob to Joseph. Joseph was only seventeen, just a teenager, when this incident took place. He was the youngest of the boys out there with the flocks. Benjamin was still too young, you see, and was still at home. Joseph brought to his father a bad report about the other boys. Of course, they didn't like that. I'm sure they called him a tattletale.

Now Israel loved Joseph more than all his children, because he was the son of his old age: and he made him a coat of many colours [Gen. 37:3].

Jacob should have learned a lesson in his own home. He knew that to play favorites would cause trouble in a family. His own father had favored the elder brother, and Jacob knew what it was to be discriminated against. But here he practices the very same thing. We can understand his feelings, knowing that Rachel was the wife whom he really loved—she was the one fine thing in his life—and Joseph is really a fine boy, and Jacob loves him dearly. While all this is true, it still is not an excuse. He should not have made him that coat of many colors.

Another possible translation of "coat of many colours" would be the "coat with sleeves," a long-sleeved robe. You see, the ordinary robe in those days consisted of one piece of cloth about ten feet long. They would put a hole in the middle of it and stick the head through this hole. Half of the cloth would drop down the front of the body and half the cloth down the back of the body. They would tie it together around the waist or seam up the sides, and that would be their coat. They didn't have sleeves. So to put sleeves in the coat of any person would set him off from the others. And certainly a coat of many colors would set him apart, also.

And when his brethren saw that their father loved him more than all his brethren, they hated him, and could not speak peaceably unto him [Gen. 37:4].

Naturally, the brothers hated him for being the favorite of his father. They couldn't even speak peaceably to him. So here we see strife in this family also. I tell you, I don't care whose family it is, sin will ruin it. Sin ruins lives, and sin ruins families; sin ruins communities, and it ruins nations. This is the problem with our families and cities and nations today. There is just one cause: God calls it *sin*.

So here we find that this boy Joseph is the object of discrimination. His father discriminates in his love for him. The brothers discriminate in their hatred against him.

THE DREAMS OF JOSEPH

And Joseph dreamed a dream, and he told it his brethren: and they hated him yet the more.

And he said unto them, Hear, I pray you, this dream which I have dreamed [Gen. 37:5–6].

How can we explain his conduct here? Why would he go to his father and tattle on his brothers in the first place when he knew it would incur their hatred? Well, I think he just didn't know how bad this world can be. He had no idea how bad his brothers were. I'm of the opinion that he was a rather gullible boy at this time. It took him a long time to find out about the ways of the world, but he certainly did learn. Eventually he probably knew as much about the world and the wickedness of man to man as anyone. But that was later on, not now.

You can just imagine how Joseph has been protected. His father centered all of his affection on Rachel. He had fallen in love with her at first sight and had worked fourteen years for her. Then many years went by before she bore him a child. Finally Joseph was born. What a delight that must have been for Jacob. But now Rachel is gone; so he centers his affection on this boy. He shouldn't have done that—he has other sons to raise—but that is what he has done. Joseph has been loved and protected.

For, behold, we were binding sheaves in the field, and, lo, my sheaf arose, and also stood upright; and, behold, your sheaves stood round about, and made obeisance to my sheaf.

And his brethren said to him, Shalt thou indeed reign over us? or shalt thou indeed have dominion over us? And they hated him yet the more for his dreams, and for his words [Gen. 37:7–8].

Can't you imagine how they sneered? I'm sure they were cynical. They didn't really believe that he would rule over them. Yet, they hated him because he had this dream. This doesn't end the dreams, though. He had another one.

And he dreamed yet another dream, and told it his brethren, and said, Behold, I have dreamed a dream more; and, behold, the sun and the moon and the eleven stars made obeisance to me.

And he told it to his father, and to his brethren: and his father rebuked him, and said unto him, What is this dream that thou hast dreamed? Shall I and thy mother and thy brethren indeed come to bow down ourselves to thee to the earth?

And his brethren envied him; but his father observed the saying [Gen. 37: 9–11].

He told them this dream and they understood what he was talking about. This same image appears in Revelation 12:1 where a woman is described clothed with the sun, and the moon is under her feet, and she had a crown of twelve stars upon her head. That means the nation of Israel. These brethren understood that Joseph was telling them about themselves, the sons of Israel.

We are seeing the nation of Israel at its beginning here. Genesis is like a bud, and the flower opens up as we go through the Scripture. Here is a bud that is not going to open up until we get into the Book of Revelation. It is a late bloomer, by the way, but it is going to open up there. We need to understand what is being said rather than try to make guesses. We don't need to be guessing when it is made this clear.

Old Jacob understood it exactly, and he chided, "Does this mean that your father, your mother, and your brothers are going to bow down to you!" All Joseph could answer was, "That was the dream." He didn't try to interpret it because it was evident. His brothers just dismissed it, paid no attention to it. They thought it wasn't even in the realm of possibility, as far as they were concerned. They knew that not one of them would ever bow down to Joseph! But Jacob observed the saying.

JACOB SENDS JOSEPH TO HIS BRETHREN

And his brethren went to feed their father's flock in Shechem [Gen. 37:12].

At this time, Jacob and his family were living around Hebron, which was twenty or more miles south of Jerusalem. And Shechem is that far north of Jerusalem, so that these boys are grazing the sheep a long ways from home. We can see that they grazed their sheep over that entire area.

And Israel said unto Joseph, Do not thy brethren feed the flock in Shechem? come, and I will send thee unto them. And he said to him, Here am I [Gen. 37:13].

Joseph said, "All right, I'll go." He was very obedient to his father, you will notice.

And he said to him, Go, I pray thee, see whether it be well with thy brethren, and well with the flocks; and bring me word again. So he sent him out of the vale of Hebron, and he came to Shechem [Gen. 37:14].

Joseph had traveled all the way from Hebron to Shechem. When he reached Shechem, he began to look around for them. That is rugged terrain up there, and this boy couldn't locate them.

And a certain man found him, and, behold, he was wandering in the field: and the man asked him, saying, What seekest thou? [Gen. 37:15].

I can imagine that this man had seen Joseph pass his tent several times; so he asks him who he is looking for.

And he said, I seek my brethren: tell me, I pray thee, where they feed their flocks.

And the man said, They are departed hence; for I heard them say, Let us go to Dothan. And Joseph went after his

brethren, and found them in Dothan [Gen. 37:16–17].

Dothan is a long way north of Shechem. It is near the Valley of Esdraelon, and this is where the brothers have moved the sheep. And at last Joseph found them—there they were.

And when they saw him afar off, even before he came near unto them, they conspired against him to slay him.

And they said one to another, Behold, this dreamer cometh.

Come now therefore, and let us slay him, and cast him into some pit, and we will say, Some evil beast hath devoured him: and we shall see what will become of his dreams [Gen. 37:18–20].

How they hated Joseph! Here they are probably almost one hundred miles from home, and they say to each other, "Let's get rid of him now, and we'll see what will become of his dreams!"

Before we go on with the story, I want to call to your attention the comparison of Joseph to the Lord Jesus. You just should not miss the analogy.

1. The *birth* of Joseph was miraculous in that it was by the intervention of God as an answer to prayer. The Lord Jesus is virgin born. His birth was certainly miraculous!
2. Joseph was *loved* by his father. The Lord Jesus was *loved* by His Father, who declared, "This is My beloved Son."
3. Joseph had the coat of many colors which set him apart. Christ was set apart in that He was "separate from sinners."
4. Joseph announced that he was to *rule* over his brethren. The Lord Jesus presented Himself as the Messiah. Just as they ridiculed Joseph's message, so they also ridiculed Jesus. In fact, nailed to His cross were the words: THIS IS JESUS THE KING OF THE JEWS.
5. Joseph was *sent* by his father to his brethren. Jesus was *sent* to His brethren—He came first to the lost sheep of the house of Israel.
6. Joseph was *hated* by his brethren without a cause, and the Lord Jesus was *hated* by His brethren without a cause.

As we return to the story now, remember that Joseph is approaching his brothers, and they are plotting against him. He is wearing that coat of many colors or with the sleeves, which was a mark of position. We must remem-

ber that Joseph was younger than his brothers yet was in a position above them. So there is all this hatred and jealousy—to the point of murder!

Reuben has already lost his position as the firstborn. However, he stands in a good light here. He has more mature judgment than the others.

And Reuben heard it, and he delivered him out of their hands; and said, Let us not kill him [Gen. 37:21].

They would have killed him right then and there if Reuben had not intervened.

And Reuben said unto them, Shed no blood, but cast him into this pit that is in the wilderness, and lay no hand upon him; that he might rid him out of their hands, to deliver him to his father again [Gen. 37:22].

It was Reuben's avowed purpose, after Joseph had been put into the pit, to slip back again and take him out of the pit and take him home to his father.

And it came to pass, when Joseph was come unto his brethren, that they stripped Joseph out of his coat, his coat of many colours that was on him [Gen. 37:23].

That coat Joseph wore was like waving a red flag in front of a bull. They hated it because it set him apart from them. According to the law of primogeniture, the older brothers had a prior claim; so they stripped off from Joseph the hated coat.

And they took him, and cast him into a pit: and the pit was empty, there was no water in it.

And they sat down to eat bread: and they lifted up their eyes and looked, and, behold, a company of Ishmeelites came from Gilead with their camels bearing spicery and balm and myrrh, going to carry it down to Egypt [Gen. 37:24–25].

This was a caravan of traders that was going by.

And Judah said unto his brethren, What profit is it if we slay our brother, and conceal his blood?

Come, and let us sell him to the Ishmeelites, and let not our hand be upon him; for he is our brother and our flesh. And his brethren were content [Gen. 37:26–27].

Now Judah intervenes when he sees some traders going by. It is a very mercenary plan that he has, but at least he doesn't want murder to take place. He doesn't want the blood of Joseph to be on their hands. The brothers were satisfied with the suggestion because what they wanted was to get rid of him—they didn't care how it was accomplished. They realized the Ishmeelites would take him down to Egypt and would sell him there as a slave. At least they would be rid of him. Slavery in most places was a living death, and they knew they would certainly never hear from him again.

Then there passed by Midianites merchantmen; and they drew and lifted up Joseph out of the pit, and sold Joseph to the Ishmeelites for twenty pieces of silver: and they brought Joseph into Egypt [Gen. 37:28].

At this point you are probably thinking that Moses (who wrote the Genesis record) should make up his mind. First he calls them Ishmeelites, then Midianites, and then he calls them Ishmeelites again. So who are they? Is this an error in the Bible? Sometime ago a student brought to me a little booklet, which had been handed to him, listing a thousand or two thousand so-called errors in the Bible. After looking it over, the only errors I found were in that little book—not in the Bible. One of the so-called errors was this matter of calling the men of this caravan Ishmeelites, then Midianites, then Ishmeelites again.

This is an interesting point, and it deserves a closer look. First of all, it reveals how the critic and those who hate the Bible can interpret as an error something that actually shows the accuracy of the biblical record.

Who are the Ishmeelites? They are the descendants of Ishmael, the son of Abraham. Who are the Midianites? They are the descendants of Midian, a son of Abraham. Ishmael was the son of Abraham by Hagar, and Midian was the son of Abraham by Keturah whom he married after the death of Sarah. They are all brethren—they are actually kin to this group of boys who are selling their brother! At this time, who was an Israelite? Well, there were only twelve of them. How many Ishmeelites do you think there might be by this time? Ishmael was older than Isaac, so maybe there were one hundred or more. How many Midianites would there be? Well, Midian was born after Isaac; so there couldn't be too many—maybe a dozen or more. These were little groups, and in that day travel was dangerous. They were going across the desert to Egypt. They joined together for

protection, and they joined together for a common interest. They were going on a business trip to Egypt, and, since they were related, they understood each other and joined together.

May I say that the Word of God makes good sense if you just let it make good sense. We are the folk that don't make the good sense. Ignorance adds a great deal to what people consider contradictions in the Bible. You can see that Moses understood what the situation was, and he wrote precisely.

JOSEPH SOLD INTO SLAVERY

So the brothers sell Joseph to the Ishmaelites who take him down to Egypt.

And Reuben returned unto the pit; and, behold, Joseph was not in the pit; and he rent his clothes.

And he returned unto his brethren, and said, The child is not; and I, whither shall I go?

And they took Joseph's coat, and killed a kid of the goats, and dipped the coat in the blood [Gen. 37:29–31].

Scripture does not tell us whether they told Reuben what they actually had done, but I'm of the opinion they did. And they probably said it was no use chasing after the merchants because they were a long way off by now; so he might as well help them think up a good story to tell Jacob.

And they sent the coat of many colours, and they brought it to their father; and said, This have we found: know now whether it be thy son's coat or no [Gen. 37:32].

Pretty clever, isn't it? They act as if they had never seen Joseph. They pretend they just found this coat. Believe me, they knew that hated coat! But they pretend they don't recognize it and ask their father whether he recognizes it. Jacob knew whose coat it was. He comes to a natural conclusion and, of course, the conclusion to which the brothers intended for him to come.

And he knew it, and said, It is my son's coat; an evil beast hath devoured him; Joseph is without doubt rent in pieces [Gen. 37:33].

Let's pause and take another look at this. They killed a kid of the goats and used that blood on the coat. Does this matter of deceiving a father with a goat remind us of something we've heard before? Remember that when Rebekah and Jacob were conniving, they used a kid for the savory meat dish, and they took the skin of the goat and put it on the hands and arms of Jacob to deceive his father. Now the brothers of Joseph are using the blood of a goat to deceive their father, who is none other than Jacob himself. They hand the coat to him and say, "Do you recognize it? We just found it up there in the mountains. It looks like a wild beast must have got to him." Old Jacob came to the conclusion that his son Joseph had been killed.

Notice this very carefully. Jacob is deceived in exactly the same way that he had deceived. "Be not deceived; God is not mocked: for whatsoever a man soweth, that shall he also reap" (Gal. 6:7)—not something else, not something similar, but the *same thing*. This man Jacob did some bad sowing. He used deception, and now that he is a father, he is deceived in the identical way that he had deceived his own father years before.

When we sow corn, we reap corn. When we sow tares, we reap tares. We get exactly what we sow. This is true in any realm you wish to move in today. It is true in the physical realm, in the moral, and in the spiritual realm. That is true also for the believer. If you think you can get by with sin because you are a child of God, you have another thought coming. In fact, you'd better take that other thought and not commit the sin because God is no respecter of persons. He said this is the way it is going to be, and you are not an exception. I talked to a minister who had gotten involved with another man's wife. As I talked with him, he tried to justify himself on the basis that he was someone special to the Lord. He felt that because he was who he was, he could operate on a little different plane and by a different rule book than anyone else. But he found that God is no respecter of persons.

Now notice the grief of Jacob—

And Jacob rent his clothes, and put sackcloth upon his loins, and mourned for his son many days.

And all his sons and all his daughters rose up to comfort him; but he refused to be comforted: and he said, For I will go down into the grave unto my son mourning. Thus his father wept for him [Gen. 37:34–35].

Perhaps some will think his grief is a demonstration of how much Jacob loved his son Joseph. I'll admit that he certainly loved this boy. But it reveals that Jacob had not learned to walk by faith yet, friend. You recall the experience he had at Peniel. It was the deflation of the old ego. The flesh collapsed there, but now he must learn to walk by faith. He hasn't learned that yet. In fact, the faith of Jacob is mentioned in the eleventh chapter of Hebrews, but nothing in his life is mentioned there as an example of his faith until the time of his death. Then faith is exhibited.

Compare his grief here to the grief of a man like David (2 Sam. 12:15–23). David wept over the baby boy of his who died. He loved that little one just as much as Jacob loved Joseph, but David was a man of faith. He knew the little one couldn't come back to him, and he also knew that he was going to the little fellow some day. What faith! You see, Jacob is not walking by faith, friend. This is abnormal grief.

Christian friend, perhaps you have lost a loved one. Perhaps you just can't get over it. I want to say to you kindly, not brutally, but kindly: learn to walk by faith. You manifest faith when you recognize that you can't bring that one back by grieving. It does no good at all. If you are a child of God and you are grieving over one who is a child of God, then walk by faith. You will see that one again and never be separated. The world has no faith—they grieve as those without hope. Christian friend, *you* can walk by faith.

Now the final verse of this chapter follows Joseph to Egypt—

And the Midianites sold him into Egypt unto Potiphar, an officer of Pharaoh's, and captain of the guard [Gen. 37:36].

We will leave Joseph right there and pick up his story in chapter 39.

CHAPTER 38

THEME: *The sin and shame of Judah*

This is another chapter that seems to be about as necessary as a fifth leg on a cow. After you have read the story, you may wish that it had been left out of the Bible. Many people have asked me why this chapter is in the Word of God. I agree that it is one of the worst chapters in the Bible, but it gives us some background on the tribe of Judah, out of which the Lord Jesus Christ came. This fact makes it important that it be included in the biblical record. In this chapter you will read names like Judah and Tamar and Pharez and Zerah. If you think they sound familiar, it is because you have read them in the first chapter of Matthew. They are in the genealogy of the Lord Jesus Christ. My friend, that is an amazing thing! Our Lord came into a sinful line. He was made in all points like as we are, yet He Himself was without sin. He came into that human line where all have sinned and come short of the glory of God.

This chapter deals with the sin and the shame of Judah. This leads me to say that the sons of Jacob were certainly not very much of a comfort to him. It looks as if all the sons were problem children, with the exception of Joseph and Benjamin. And Joseph was no comfort because his father was heartbroken about his disappearance. All of this reveals to us that Jacob spent too much time in Padan-aram accumulating a fortune rather than teaching his children. How different he was from Abraham. You remember that God had said of Abraham: "For I know him, that he will command his children and his household after him, and they shall keep the way of the LORD, to do justice and judgment; that the LORD may bring upon Abraham that which he hath spoken of him" (Gen. 18:19).

Well, Jacob didn't do that. He was so busy down there contending with Uncle Laban that he didn't have much time for his boys. That was tragic, because each one of them seemed to have gotten involved in something that was very sinful.

There is, I believe, a further reason for including this chapter in the Word of God at this juncture. Beginning with the next chapter, we go down to the land of Egypt with Joseph. God is sending Joseph ahead, as he very clearly detected from the fortuitous concurrence of circumstances in his life, to prepare the way for the coming down of the children of Israel into Egypt. It would preserve their lives during the famine in Canaan, but more than that, it would get them out of the land of Canaan from the abominable Canaanites into the seclusion of the land of Goshen in Egypt. Had Jacob and his family continued on in Canaan, they would have dropped down to the level of the Canaanites. The chapter before us reveals the necessity of getting the family of Jacob away from the degrading influence of the Canaanites.

This is the story of Judah, whose line will be the kingly line among the tribes of Israel.

And it came to pass at that time, that Judah went down from his brethren, and turned in to a certain Adullamite, whose name was Hirah.

And Judah saw there a daughter of a certain Canaanite, whose name was Shuah; and he took her, and went in unto her [Gen. 38:1–2].

He went down to do business with a certain Adullamite, and when he got down there he saw this Canaanite woman, and he had an affair with her.

And she conceived, and bare a son; and he called his name Er [Gen. 38:3].

Judah called his name Er—and Judah certainly had *erred;* he had sinned—

And she conceived again, and bare a son; and she called his name Onan.

And she yet again conceived, and bare a son; and called his name Shelah: and he was at Chezib, when she bare him.

And Judah took a wife for Er his first-born, whose name was Tamar [Gen. 38:4–6].

This is the first appearance of Tamar. She gets into the genealogy of Christ this way! Now, look at this family. It is just loaded with sin.

And Er, Judah's firstborn, was wicked in the sight of the LORD; and the LORD slew him.

And Judah said unto Onan, Go in unto thy brother's wife, and marry her, and raise up seed to thy brother.

And Onan knew that the seed should not be his; and it came to pass, when he went in unto his brother's wife, that he spilled

it on the ground, lest that he should give seed to his brother.

And the thing which he did displeased the Lord: wherefore he slew him also [Gen. 38:7–10].

This reminds us of the present hour when there is so much emphasis on sex.

Then said Judah to Tamar his daughter in law, Remain a widow at thy father's house, till Shelah my son be grown: for he said, Lest peradventure he die also, as his brethren did. And Tamar went and dwelt in her father's house [Gen. 38:11].

It was the custom of that day that when a man died, his brother was to marry his widow. Onan refused to do it, and he was smitten with death.

Now Judah has another son who is growing up, and he tells his daughter-in-law to follow the custom of returning to her father's house until the younger son is ready for marriage.

And in process of time the daughter of Shuah Judah's wife died; and Judah was comforted, and went up unto his sheep-shearers to Timnath, he and his friend Hirah the Adullamite.

And it was told Tamar, saying, Behold thy father in law goeth up to Timnath to shear his sheep [Gen. 38:12–13].

Apparently this deal that Judah had, which concerned seeing this Adullamite by the name of Hirah, was in connection with sheep. They were raising sheep and must have had a tremendous flock together. Judah goes up there to shear them. In the meantime, Tamar has been waiting all this while at home. She comes to the conclusion that Judah is not going to give Shelah to her as her husband.

And she put her widow's garments off from her, and covered her with a veil, and wrapped herself, and sat in an open place, which is by the way to Timnath; for she saw that Shelah was grown, and she was not given unto him to wife [Gen. 38:14].

Shelah was, of course, the third son of Judah. Tamar sees that Judah doesn't intend to give her to him as his wife; so she takes action. She takes off her widow's clothes and sits by the wayside with her face covered as was the custom of harlots.

And he turned unto her by the way, and

said, Go to, I pray thee, let me come in unto thee; (for he knew not that she was his daughter in law.) And she said, What wilt thou give me, that thou mayest come in unto me? [Gen. 38:16].**

We get a picture of Judah. He had propositioned the Canaanite woman, Shuah's daughter. Now he does the same thing with Tamar. This is a very black picture and an ugly story that we have here. Judah thought she was a harlot. She saw the opportunity of taking advantage of him, and she did it.

And he said, I will send thee a kid from the flock. And she said, Wilt thou give me a pledge, till thou send it?

And he said, What pledge shall I give thee? And she said, Thy signet, and thy bracelets, and thy staff that is in thine hand. And he gave it her, and came in unto her, and she conceived by him.

And she arose, and went away, and laid by her veil from her, and put on the garments of her widowhood.

And Judah sent the kid by the hand of his friend the Adullamite, to receive his pledge from the woman's hand; but he found her not [Gen. 38:17–20].

Judah sent his friend into town who said, "I'm looking for the harlot that is here."

Then he asked the men of that place, saying, Where is the harlot, that was openly by the way side? And they said, There was no harlot in this place.

And he returned to Judah, and said, I cannot find her; and also the men of the place said, that there was no harlot in this place.

And Judah said, Let her take it to her, lest we be shamed: behold, I sent this kid, and thou hast not found her.

And it came to pass about three months after, that it was told Judah, saying, Tamar thy daughter in law hath played the harlot; and also, behold, she is with child by whoredom. And Judah said, Bring her forth, and let her be burnt [Gen. 38:21–24].

That's Judah. Here is the old double standard. God doesn't approve of these things, friend. It is here in His Word, but that doesn't mean that He approves of it. His people are acting just like the Canaanites, which is the reason He is going to get them out of this land and take them down into the land of Egypt. There He is going to separate them and isolate them in the land of Goshen to get them away from this terrible influence. This episode reveals the necessity for God to do this.

Judah is acting in a way that is unspeakable it is so bad. The fact of the matter is, he is quick to see the sin in somebody else, but he can't see it in himself. It reminds us of the time Nathan went in to David and told him the story about the fellow who had one little ewe lamb. When Nathan said the rich man came and took it away, David was quick to condemn the rich man. David reacted just like Judah does here. David said he wanted that rich man stoned to death. Then Nathan declared that David himself was the man. It is interesting that we can all see sin so clearly in other people, but we can't see it within our own being.

The charge against Judah is really a double one. His sin is terrible in itself, but it was with his own daughter-in-law! This is the way the Canaanites lived. We think that we are in a sex revolution today and there is a *new* sexual freedom. My friend, for centuries the heathen have had sexual freedom. That's part of heathendom, and it is the reason they lived as low as they did. It is the reason they were judged and removed from the scene. The Canaanites are gone. They have disappeared. God has judged them. That ought to be a message to any person. Yet a great many people don't seem to get the message—even Christians! You wonder why this chapter is in the Bible. It is in the Bible as a warning to us. It is in the Bible to let us know that God did not approve of sin, and it explains why God took Israel out of the land of Palestine and down into the land of Egypt.

Tamar is then brought into the presence of her father-in-law.

When she was brought forth, she sent to her father in law, saying, By the man, whose these are, am I with child: and she said, Discern, I pray thee, whose are these, the signet, and bracelets, and staff [Gen. 38:25].

Judah was going to have her burnt. But she said, "Well, I would like you to know who the father of the child is; he is the one who owns these articles that I'm showing you." Judah looked at them and had to admit they were his own.

And Judah acknowledged them, and said, She hath been more righteous than I; because that I gave her not to Shelah my son. And he knew her again no more [Gen. 38:26].

This was repulsive even to Judah, but we can see how he had adopted some of the customs of the Canaanites.

May I pause for a moment to make an application? Remember, all these things are written for our learning. They are examples unto us. Today we hear that if we are going to witness to this generation and if we are going to communicate to them, we've got to get down to their level. I disagree with that. God has never used that method to witness. God has always, under all circumstances, asked His people to live on a high and lofty plane.

I can well imagine one of our present-day theologians going up to Noah and saying, "Brother Noah, you're spending all your time working on this boat, and it is silly for you to be doing that. We're having a big party over in Babylon tonight. They just got in a new shipment of marijuana and we are really going to blow our minds. We're going to pass around the grass and we're going to have a high time and take a little trip. You don't need to build that boat for a trip; we'll give you a trip. Come on over." Noah, of course, would refuse. So the theologian would ask Noah, "How do you expect to reach all the hippies of Babylon? How are you going to reach the Babylonian beeboppers unless you are willing to come down and communicate with them?" The fact of the matter is, God never asked Noah to come down to "communicate." God asked him to give *His* message.

And this is what God asks us to do in our day. I am firmly convinced that if God's people would give out His Word and live lives that would commend the gospel, He would make their witness effective. There are many pastors in our day who are so afraid they will lose the crowd that they do anything to attract people to their church—and some of them are having their problems. But God has never asked us to compromise. God does ask us to give out the Word of God—regardless of the size of our congregation.

This reminds me of the story about Dr. Scofield who was invited to speak over in North Carolina. The first service was on a rainy night, and very few people came to hear him speak. The pastor felt that he must apologize to Dr. Scofield; so he reached over and told him that he was sorry so few people had come to hear a man of his caliber. Dr. Scofield replied to the pastor, "My Lord had only twelve men to speak to, and since He had only twelve men and never complained, who is C. I. Scofield that he should complain about a small crowd?" Friend, this is a lesson for our generation to learn. We so often think that there must be crowds or else God is not in it. Maybe God has called us to witness to a few. But I have news for you: If you give out the Word of God, it will have its effect. My friend, the Word of God is powerful, and God is looking for clean vessels through whom he can give it out.

Well, Judah had certainly lowered himself to the level of the Canaanites, and look at the results.

And it came to pass in the time of her travail, that, behold, twins were in her womb.

And it came to pass, when she travailed, that the one put out his hand: and the midwife took and bound upon his hand a scarlet thread, saying, This came out first.

And it came to pass, as he drew back his hand, that, behold, his brother came out: and she said, How hast thou broken forth? this breach be upon thee: therefore his name was called Pharez.

And afterward came out his brother, that had the scarlet thread upon his hand: and his name was called Zerah [Gen. 38:27–30].

Now if we turn over to the New Testament, we will find the genealogy of the Lord Jesus in Matthew, chapter 1. There we read: "Abraham begat Isaac; and Isaac begat Jacob; and Jacob begat Judas and his brethren; and Judas begat Phares and Zara of Thamar; and Phares begat Esrom; and Esrom began Aram (Matt. 1:2–3). Then as we follow through the genealogy, we come to this verse: "And Jacob begat Joseph the husband of Mary, of whom was born Jesus, who is called Christ (Matt. 1:16). It is an amazing thing that the Lord Jesus Christ, according to the flesh, should come through the line of Judah and Tamar! When He came into the human family, He came in a sinful line. He was made sin for us, He who knew no sin, that we might be made the righteousness of God in Him (see 2 Cor. 5:21).

CHAPTER 39

THEME: *Overseer in the house of Potiphar; tempted, then framed by Potiphar's wife; Joseph imprisoned*

We return to the story of Joseph after the interlude of chapter 38, which we classified as one of the worst chapters in the Bible because it certainly tells a sordid story of the man Judah.

We will discover that Joseph is altogether different from Judah. I have always felt that Joseph and Benjamin got a great deal of teaching, instruction, and personal attention that the other ten boys did not receive. These seemed to be the only two boys in whom Jacob was interested.

Because of the hatred and animosity of Joseph's brothers, he was sold into slavery and taken to the land of Egypt.

To be in a foreign land and sold into slavery is a very dreary prospect for a seventeen-year-old boy. There is certainly nothing in the outward aspect of things to bring any encouragement to his heart. Joseph seems to be more or less a hardluck boy. Even in the land of Egypt, just as things would begin to move smoothly for him, something else would happen. Of course, it always happened for a purpose, even though that was difficult for Joseph to see.

There is no person in the Old Testament in whose life the purpose of God is more clearly seen than Joseph. The providence of God is manifest in every detail of his life. The hand of God is upon him and the leading of the Lord evident, but Joseph is the one patriarch to whom God did not appear directly, according to the text of Scripture. God appeared to Abraham, Isaac, and Jacob, but not to Joseph. Yet the direction of God in his life is more clearly seen than in any other. He is the Old Testament example of Romans 8:28: "And we know that all things work together for good to them that love God, to them who are the called according to his purpose." Joseph himself expressed it in rather vivid language. At the death of their father, Joseph's brothers felt that Joseph might turn on them, and they came to him asking for mercy. He told them that he held no grudge against them at all and said, "But as for you, ye thought evil against me; but God meant it unto good, to bring to pass, as it is this day, to save much people alive" (Gen. 50:20). Although everything seemed to go wrong for him and the outward aspect was dark—it looked *terrible*—each event was a step bringing to fruition God's purpose in this man's life.

My friend, in our own lives we need to reckon on the fact that ". . . whom the Lord loveth he chasteneth, and scourgeth every son whom he receiveth" (Heb. 12:6). If we are the children of God, in the will of God, we can have the assurance of God that nothing comes to us without His permission. God works all things together for good to them who love Him. Even our misfortunes, heartbreaks, and sufferings are for our good and His glory.

There is a hedge about every child of God, and nothing gets through it without the permission of God. You remember that, when Satan wanted to test Job, he said to God: "Hast not thou made an hedge about him, and about his house, and about all that he hath on every side? thou hast blessed the work of his hands, and his substance is increased in the land" (Job 1:10). Satan asked God to let the hedge down. Even if Satan gets God's permission to test us, still all things will work for our good.

Dr. Torrey used to say that Romans 8:28 is the soft pillow for a tired heart. And someone else has put it like this: "God nothing does, nor suffers to be done, but what we would ourselves, if we but could see through all events of things as well as He."

There is another aspect of the life of Joseph which should be an encouragement to every child of God. None of God's children today have ever had a direct revelation from God. Some modern false prophets claim to the contrary, but God has not appeared directly to any person today. It is for our encouragement that God did not appear to Joseph directly because we can still know that He is leading and directing us.

Now let's follow this young man Joseph and see what is going to happen to him.

OVERSEER
IN THE HOUSE OF POTIPHAR

And Joseph was brought down to Egypt; and Potiphar, an officer of Pharaoh, captain of the guard, an Egyptian, bought him of the hands of the Ishmeelites, which had brought him down thither [Gen. 39:1].

This fine-looking young man, seventeen years old, would be a prize as a slave in the market. He was bought by Potiphar who was a captain of the guard. Potiphar was in the military, he had his office in the Pentagon of that day, and he was part of the brass, a prominent official.

And the LORD was with Joseph, and he was a prosperous man; and he was in the house of his master the Egyptian [Gen. 39:2].

Immediately, when he gets into the home of Potiphar who is an officer of Pharaoh, it is obvious that the Lord is with Joseph. Blessing came to that home when Joseph came.

And his master saw that the LORD was with him, and that the LORD made all that he did to prosper in his hand [Gen. 39:3].

Life is great up to this point. You'd like to add that they all lived happily ever after, but they didn't. This is not a story; it is reality. The child of God is going to encounter temptation, trouble, and problems in this world. This is what is going to happen to Joseph.

And Joseph found grace in his sight, and he served him: and he made him overseer over his house, and all that he had he put into his hand [Gen. 39:4].

Just think of this! Because of the way Joseph serves, he is elevated to the position of handling all the material substance—the chattels and probably even the real estate—of Potiphar. The man trusted him with everything.

And it came to pass from the time that he had made him overseer in his house, and over all that he had, that the LORD blessed the Egyptian's house for Joseph's sake; and the blessing of the LORD was upon all that he had in the house, and in the field.

And he left all that he had in Joseph's hand; and he knew not aught he had, save the bread which he did eat. And Joseph was a goodly person, and well favoured [Gen. 39:5–6].

Potiphar trusted Joseph so much that he never even demanded an accounting—he didn't have to hire a C.P.A. to go over the books. He believed in the integrity of this young man.

The only thing that Potiphar worried about, as an officer of Pharaoh, was that he should please Pharaoh and do a good job there. He let Joseph handle his personal affairs. When he sat down at the table, the food was put before him. That's all that he was interested in because he trusted this young man.

TEMPTED, THEN FRAMED BY POTIPHAR'S WIFE

Now notice what happens—

And it came to pass after these things, that his master's wife cast her eyes upon Joseph; and she said, Lie with me [Gen. 39:7].

Potiphar had given him the full run of his home, and Joseph had charge of everything. While Joseph was busy, Potiphar's wife was also busy. She was busy scheming. Joseph was a handsome young man. It may be that Potiphar was an old man because it was generally the custom in that day for an older man to have a young wife. She sees Joseph, and she attempts to entice him.

But he refused, and said unto his master's wife, Behold, my master wotteth not what is with me in the house, and he hath committed all that he hath to my hand;

There is none greater in this house than I; neither hath he kept back any thing from me but thee, because thou art his wife: how then can I do this great wickedness, and sin against God? [Gen. 39: 8–9].

Now do you notice that this young man is serving *God* in all of this? When he went down to Egypt, it was a land filled with idolatry just as much as Babylon was. In that land of idolatry, Joseph maintained a testimony for the living and true God and a high moral standard. When this woman enticed him, he said, "My master has turned over everything to me but you— you are his *wife*." Notice what a high viewpoint Joseph had on marriage.

You see, God has given marriage to all mankind. When a person begins to despise the marriage vows, he is beginning to despise God, my friend. A man who will break his marriage vows will generally break any vow he has made to God. It has been interesting for me to note in my ministry that a divorced person, that is, one who gets divorced because he or she has been unfaithful, generally will get as far from

God as any person possibly can. I've seen that happen again and again.

Joseph here is attempting to be true to God. What a high viewpoint he has! Yet, look at what is going to come to pass because he attempts to serve the living and true God.

And it came to pass, as she spake to Joseph day by day, that he hearkened not unto her, to lie by her, or to be with her [Gen. 39:10].

This man, Potiphar, as an officer of Pharaoh, would be away from home a great deal. Maybe he was away from home too much. This woman didn't tempt Joseph only one time, but again and again and again. It was a constant temptation to him, yet this young man did not yield. You can imagine that there begins to well up in her a boiling resentment against Joseph. The old bromide has it, "Hell hath no fury like that of a woman scorned." Believe me, she is going to take revenge on Joseph.

And it came to pass about this time, that Joseph went into the house to do his business; and there was none of the men of the house there within.

And she caught him by his garment, saying, Lie with me: and he left his garment in her hand, and fled, and got him out.

And it came to pass, when she saw that he had left his garment in her hand, and was fled forth,

That she called unto the men of her house, and spake unto them, saying, See, he hath brought in an Hebrew unto us to mock us; he came in unto me to lie with me, and I cried with a loud voice [Gen. 39:11–14].

Things weren't so well between Potiphar and his wife. Notice how she speaks of him in such a mean, degrading way. She says that *he* brought in a Hebrew to mock them. In other words, the wife probably had been guilty of this before. The man whom I feel most sorry for is Potiphar. He is the sap if there ever was one. Possibly he suspected something all along.

She is beginning now to cover up her tracks—

And it came to pass, when he heard that I lifted up my voice and cried, that he left his garment with me, and fled, and got him out.

And she laid up his garment by her, until his lord came home [Gen. 39:15–16].

So here is the boy Joseph in his teens, down there alone in Egypt, and he is being framed in the most dastardly manner. She brings this charge against Joseph to the other men. Her husband was away from home; so she has all this story built up to tell him when he arrives.

And she spake unto him, according to these words, saying, The Hebrew servant, which thou hast brought unto us, came in unto me to mock me:

And it came to pass, as I lifted up my voice and cried, that he left his garment with me, and fled out.

And it came to pass, when his master heard the words of his wife, which she spake unto him, saying, After this manner did thy servant to me; that his wrath was kindled [Gen. 39:17–19].

On the surface it seems that Potiphar believes her story, at least it made him angry at the moment. He was an officer in the army of Pharaoh and must have been a pretty sharp man to be among the brass. But he certainly was a stupid husband. It is my personal feeling that he recognized the kind of wife he had and thought the expedient thing was to throw Joseph into prison and forget the whole matter. I feel sorry for him, married to this woman. I'm of the opinion that she had been unfaithful many times before and that Joseph was just another one in her series of conquests—only it just didn't work with Joseph, so she framed him.

JOSEPH IMPRISONED

And Joseph's master took him, and put him into the prison, a place where the king's prisoners were bound: and he was there in the prison [Gen. 39:20].

This boy is certainly having bad luck, is he not? There at home he was the favorite of his father, wearing a coat of many colors. The next thing he knew, his brothers had taken off the coat and put him down in a pit. He hears them dickering with some tradesmen, and then he is sold down to Egypt. He was only seventeen years old, and I am of the opinion that on the way down, and after he got there, he spent many nights wetting the pillow with his tears. He certainly was homesick.

Now he's getting along in this new position, just elevated to a high position because he is a capable and fine-looking young man. Then the wife of Potiphar attempts to lure him to commit sin. His high moral standard prevents him from yielding. As a result of that, she frames him. This poor boy just doesn't stand a chance.

We need to remember that, although Joseph had been elevated in his position, he is still a slave. Potiphar's wife would be like Caesar's wife—one just wouldn't dare say anything about her. Obviously her word would be accepted. Poor Joseph! He doesn't need to even open his mouth. He is declared guilty before he can make any kind of a defense at all. He immediately finds himself put into prison, the prison where the prisoners of Pharaoh were placed.

But the LORD was with Joseph, and shewed him mercy, and gave him favour in the sight of the keeper of the prison.

And the keeper of the prison committed to Joseph's hand all the prisoners that were in the prison; and whatsoever they did there, he was the doer of it.

The keeper of the prison looked not to any thing that was under his hand; because the LORD was with him, and that which he did, the LORD made it to prosper [Gen. 39:21–23].

The hand of God is obvious in this young man's life, but over against it are the terrible things that happen to him. Now he finds himself in prison. How discouraging that would have been to the average person. But the interesting thing is that the Lord is with Joseph. Although He does not appear to him, as He had to the other patriarchs, He shows him mercy. First He causes the keeper of the prison to like him and to trust him. Although Joseph is naturally a very attractive young man and has tremendous ability, yet the important thing to note is that all of this would have come to naught had not God been with him. God is with him and is leading him. All of these experiences are moving toward the accomplishment of a purpose in this young man's life.

Joseph recognized this, and it gave him a buoyancy, an attitude of optimism. The circumstances did not get him down. He lived on top of his circumstances. I have a preacher friend who tells me my problem is that the circumstances are all on top of me! I think many of us live that way. But Joseph was one who was living on top of his circumstances. The

Lord was with him. He recognized the hand of God in his life, and so he was not discouraged. Discouragement is one of the finest weapons Satan has—discouragement and disappointment. This young man seems to have surmounted all of his circumstances. He reminds us of the passage in Hebrews: "Now no chastening for the present seemeth to be joyous, but grievous: nevertheless afterward it yieldeth the peaceable fruit of righteousness unto them which are exercised thereby" (Heb. 12:11).

Certainly the chastening of the Lord is going to yield the peaceable fruit of righteousness in the life of this young man.

The story of Joseph reveals that not every man has his price. Satan says that he does, but there have been several men whom Satan could not buy. Joseph was one of these. Job was another, and the apostle Paul was still another. Satan despises mankind, but these and many more are men whom Satan found he could not buy.

Is it the will of God that Joseph be in prison? Well, my friend, it is almost essential that he be there. We'll see that in the next chapter.

CHAPTER 40

THEME: *Joseph interprets dreams for the butler and baker; fulfillment of the dreams*

This chapter, rather than advancing the story of Joseph, seems to slow it down to absolutely no movement at all. We see Joseph in prison, and he is delayed and circumscribed by the ingratitude of the chief butler of Pharaoh. We may ask what all this means. May I say to you that all of this is accomplishing God's plan and purpose in Joseph's life. We will see this as we get into the chapter.

In chapter 37 we started a comparison between Joseph and the Lord Jesus. Now that we are farther along in the story, let us stop to make some more comparisons:

1. Joseph was sent to his brethren. The Lord Jesus Christ was sent to His brethren, the lost sheep of the house of Israel.

2. Joseph was hated by his brethren without a cause, and this is what the Lord Jesus says about Himself, "They hated me without a cause."

3. Joseph was sold by his own brothers, and the Lord Jesus was sold by one of His own brethren.

4. Joseph was sold for twenty pieces of silver. The Lord Jesus was sold for thirty pieces of silver.

5. The brothers plotted to kill Joseph. The brethren plotted to kill the Lord Jesus— "He came unto His own, and His own received Him not."

6. Joseph was put into the pit which was meant to be a place of death for him. The Lord Jesus was crucified.

7. Joseph was raised up out of that pit. The Lord Jesus was raised from the dead on the third day.

8. Joseph obeyed his father. The Lord Jesus obeyed His Father so that He could say that He always did the things which pleased His Father.

9. Joseph's father had sent him to seek his brethren. We are told that the Lord Jesus Christ came to do the will of His Father when He came here to seek His brethren.

10. Joseph was mocked by his brethren. When they saw him coming, they said, "Behold, this dreamer cometh." The Lord Jesus was mocked by His brethren. When He was on the cross, they said, "If He be the Christ, let Him come down now from the cross."

11. The brothers refused to receive Joseph, and the brethren of the Lord Jesus, the Jews, refused to receive Him.

12. They took counsel to kill Joseph, and we are told they took counsel to plot the death of the Lord Jesus.

13. Joseph's coat dripping with blood was returned to his father. They took the coat of the Lord Jesus and gambled for it.

14. After Joseph was sold into Egypt, he was lost sight of for many years. Christ ascended up into heaven. He told His disciples that they should see Him no more until His return.

15. Joseph was tempted by the world, the flesh, and the devil, and he resisted. The Lord Jesus was tempted by the world, the flesh, and the devil, and He won the victory.

16. Joseph became the savior of the world during this period, in the physical sense—he

saved them from starvation. The Lord Jesus Christ in every sense is the Savior of the whole world.

17. Joseph was hated by his brothers, and they delivered him to the Gentiles. He couldn't defend himself, and he was unjustly accused. The Lord Jesus was also delivered by His own to the religious rulers who in turn delivered Him to the Gentiles. He was innocent.

18. Pilate did not believe the accusation which was brought against the Lord Jesus. He found Him innocent, yet he scourged Him. And Joseph had to suffer although Potiphar probably knew that he was innocent. Potiphar had to keep up a front before Pharaoh as Pilate had to keep up a front before Caesar.

19. Joseph found favor in the sight of the jailer. And in the case of Jesus, the Roman centurion said of Him, "Truly, this was the Son of God."

20. Joseph was numbered with the transgressors. He was a blessing to the butler, and he was judgment for the baker. The Lord Jesus was crucified between two thieves. One was judged and the other was blessed.

In the chapter before us we will begin to see why it was the will of God that Joseph be in prison at this time.

JOSEPH INTERPRETS DREAMS FOR THE BUTLER AND BAKER

And it came to pass after these things, that the butler of the king of Egypt and his baker had offended their lord the king of Egypt.

And Pharaoh was wroth against two of his officers, against the chief of the butlers, and against the chief of the bakers.

And he put them in ward in the house of the captain of the guard, into the prison, the place where Joseph was bound [Gen. 40:1–3].

That was no accident!

What does this reveal? It certainly reveals to us the arbitrary and dictatorial position and policy that the pharaohs of Egypt had. I don't know what the baker did—maybe he burned the biscuits for breakfast. For some whim, Pharaoh put him into prison. What did the butler do? Maybe he was bringing up a glass of wine to Pharaoh and stubbed his toe and spilled it on the Persian rug that was there. I don't know. It isn't told us why both the baker

and the butler of Pharaoh were in the prison, but the important thing is that they are put where Joseph is. Joseph occupies a good position, even here in the prison. Everywhere he went, his ability was certainly recognized. "A man's gift maketh room for him, and bringeth him before great men" (Prov. 18:16). Certainly this was true for Joseph. And God is moving in his life with a very definite purpose.

And the captain of the guard charged Joseph with them, and he served them: and they continued a season in ward [Gen. 40:4].

Joseph got acquainted with them because he had charge of them. It was his business to take care of them while they were in prison.

And they dreamed a dream both of them, each man his dream in one night, each man according to the interpretation of his dream, the butler and the baker of the king of Egypt, which were bound in the prison.

And Joseph came in unto them in the morning, and looked upon them, and, behold, they were sad [Gen. 40:5–6].

Joseph was an optimistic type of individual, always bright and sharp, and he finds these two fellows, who occupy positions with Pharaoh, sitting dolefully with very dark looks upon their faces.

And he asked Pharaoh's officers that were with him in the ward of his lord's house, saying, Wherefore look ye so sadly today?

And they said unto him, We have dreamed a dream, and there is no interpreter of it. And Joseph said unto them, Do not interpretations belong to God? tell me them, I pray you [Gen. 40:7–8].

Joseph gives God all the glory in this. Later on we will find another young Hebrew in a foreign court who will do the same thing—Daniel also gave God the glory. I wish Christians today would do this. Anything you or I do for the Lord should be done to the praise of God. Make sure that God gets the glory for it. I believe that one of the reasons many of us are not blessed as much as the Lord would like to bless us is because when we do receive something wonderful, we take it for granted and we do not give God the glory for it. We need to give God the glory. Joseph should give God the glory, and he does! He says, "Do not interpretations belong to God?"

And the chief butler told his dream to Joseph, and said to him, In my dream, behold, a vine was before me;

And in the vine were three branches: and it was as though it budded, and her blossoms shot forth; and the clusters thereof brought forth ripe grapes:

And Pharaoh's cup was in my hand: and I took the grapes, and pressed them into Pharaoh's cup, and I gave the cup into Pharaoh's hand.

And Joseph said unto him, This is the interpretation of it: The three branches are three days:

Yet within three days shall Pharaoh lift up thine head, and restore thee unto thy place: and thou shalt deliver Pharaoh's cup into his hand, after the former manner when thou wast his butler [Gen. 40:9-13].

It is interesting to see that God used dreams in the Old Testament. We don't find God moving that way in the New Testament, because then the canon of Scripture was complete. We don't need dreams today, but in that day, God did speak in dreams, and He used symbols that were meaningful to them. A butler would understand about serving wine—that was what he did for Pharaoh. Later on we will find King Nebuchadnezzar has a dream of an image. Now he was certainly acquainted with images and with idols—that would be something that he could understand very well.

Joseph was able to interpret the dream and promised the butler that he would be restored in three days.

But think on me when it shall be well with thee, and show kindness, I pray thee, unto me, and make mention of me unto Pharaoh, and bring me out of this house [Gen. 40:14].

He says, "Now you will be out of here in three days, but I'll be here until I rot unless somebody moves in my behalf. I've interpreted your dream—please don't forget me!"

Now he gives him something of his background—

For indeed I was stolen away out of the land of the Hebrews: and here also have I done nothing that they should put me into the dungeon [Gen. 40:15].

Although the record doesn't tell us, the butler probably promised that he would speak to Pharaoh in Joseph's behalf.

When the chief baker saw that the interpretation was good, he said unto Joseph, I also was in my dream, and, behold, I had three white baskets on my head:

And in the uppermost basket there was of all manner of bakemeats for Pharaoh; and the birds did eat them out of the basket upon my head [Gen. 40:16-17].

The dream of the baker is in a symbol meaningful to him. He can understand a basket filled with little cookies, sweetmeats.

And Joseph answered and said, This is the interpretation thereof: The three baskets are three days:

Yet within three days shall Pharaoh lift up thy head from off thee, and shall hang thee on a tree; and the birds shall eat thy flesh from off thee [Gen. 40:18-19].

Joseph interprets his dream for him but warns that it is not going to be good for him. In three days he is to be taken out and hanged, and the birds will eat his flesh.

FULFILLMENT OF THE DREAMS

And it came to pass the third day, which was Pharaoh's birthday, that he made a feast unto all his servants: and he lifted up the head of the chief butler and of the chief baker among his servants.

And he restored the chief butler unto his butlership again; and he gave the cup into Pharaoh's hand:

But he hanged the chief baker: as Joseph had interpreted to them.

Yet did not the chief butler remember Joseph, but forgat him [Gen. 40:20-23].

Poor Joseph! This seems like a hopeless predicament now. Here he is, not only a slave, but one who has been falsely accused. Believe me, the prison bars are just as real as if he were guilty of some crime. The poor boy is here, and it is the purpose of Potiphar to forget him. That is his way of covering up the scandal that was in his own home. Joseph has to pay for Potiphar's cover-up. Joseph's one glimmer of light had been that the butler would remember him to Pharaoh. This seemed to be such a marvelous way of getting the ear of Pharaoh. But the butler is so elated with going back to his job and being in favor with Pharaoh again that he forgets all about poor Joseph. God wants to leave him there for a purpose. Suppose the butler had said to Pharaoh, "There is a prisoner down there who is innocent. He should not be there—he has been falsely accused. And he interpreted my dream for me. I sure would appreciate it, Pharaoh, if you would let him out." Suppose Pharaoh had let him out, don't you see what would have happened? He would have been at home in the land of Canaan at the time that Pharaoh needed him to interpret his dream. God wants to keep him nearby, and prison is a convenient place to keep him—there will be no difficulty in Pharaoh's finding him when he needs him.

In spite of the discouragement, Joseph believed that God was moving in his life, and there were fruits of faith which were apparent. He was faithful in every relationship of his life. He was faithful to Potiphar. In prison he was faithful to the keeper of the prison. He was faithful to God, always giving Him the glory. We will see later on that he will be faithful to Pharaoh, and he will be faithful to his own brothers. You see, Joseph's faith made him faithful. My friend, I believe that if you are truly a believer, you will be faithful.

We are living in a day when one of the tragic things happening is that there are so few Christians one can depend upon. I have a friend who is the head of a large Christian organization. We had a chance to sit together alone in a foreign city, just he and I. He was telling me some of the problems he had. He is in a tremendous organization, and yet he was telling me how few men he could really trust in his organization. Remember, this is a *Christian* organization. We see so few men in true faithfulness to their positions. We thank God for those who are. I have always thanked the Lord that He has put around me, everywhere I have ever been, a few faithful ones. I tell you, they are dear ones who are a great encouragement.

Joseph was that kind of a man. His faith made him faithful. It also gave him his optimistic outlook on life, even under all his trials and temptations. And it was faith that gave him his sympathetic and kindly attitude toward everyone. Notice how kind he was to the butler and the baker. And later on we will see his kindness to his brothers. Another thing that his faith did for him was to make him a very humble man. He gave *God* the glory for all his achievements. What a wonderful person he was! And what was responsible? Well, he *believed* God. He believed God as his father Abraham had believed Him, and this was the fruit that faith produced in his life.

Here is Joseph—forgotten in the prison. But Someone has not forgotten him; God has not forgotten him, and He is at work in his life.

Friend, this has a message for you and me. I don't know what your circumstances are right now, but I do know, judging from the letters that I get, that many folk are in a hard place. One man wrote to me, "I am between a rock and a hard place. Things look very dark." You don't see the way out, and you wonder if God cares. That is the reason God has given this story of Joseph. He wants you to know that He cares and that He is moving in your life. If you are His child, He is permitting things to happen to you for your own good. His chastisements are always for our good. Friend, we can't miss! How wonderful our God is!

CHAPTER 41

THEME: The dreams of Pharaoh; Joseph is made overseer of Egypt; Joseph's two sons—Manasseh and Ephraim

What a difference this chapter is from the previous one where we left Joseph down in jail, forgotten, forlorn, and forsaken. Yet all of this was happening to him for God's purposes in his life. If we could recognize God's hand in our lives today, it would give us a different outlook on life! In the chapter before us we will see that Joseph is released from prison when he interprets the dreams of Pharaoh. He is made overseer over the entire land of Egypt, and he marries Asenath, the daughter of the Priest of On, who bears him Manasseh and Ephraim.

This is a story of rags to riches. I know of no fictitious story more thrilling than this episode in the life of Joseph. In this chapter we can certainly see the hand of God in his life. And Joseph was conscious of God's care even during the days of adversity. This developed in him many virtues which are the fruit of the Spirit. One of them was patience. The truth expressed in Romans 5:3 that tribulation (or trouble) worketh patience is definitely illustrated in the life of Joseph.

We find here that this boy is brought into the presence of Pharaoh, the Gentile king, just as later on Daniel will be brought in before Nebuchadnezzar. Both of them are to interpret dreams.

Then we will consider the famine at the end of the chapter. What purpose of God is to be accomplished by this? God will use it to get the family of Jacob out of Canaan, away from the sins of the Canaanites and to bring them to Egypt to settle in the secluded spot of Goshen. That is one of His objectives. God had, I am sure, many other reasons, but this one is obvious.

As we go along, I hope you are still taking note of the ways in which Joseph is like the Lord Jesus Christ. We will make more of these comparisons later on. It is something important for us to be noting.

THE DREAMS OF PHARAOH

Remember that in the previous chapter Pharaoh's butler and baker were put in the same prison where Joseph was incarcerated. Joseph interpreted their dreams correctly—the baker was hanged, and the butler was restored to his position. Joseph had begged the butler to remember his plight and speak of it to Pharaoh, but he had not done so. Now God gives Pharaoh a dream—

And it came to pass at the end of two full years, that Pharaoh dreamed: and, behold, he stood by the river [Gen. 41:1].

Notice that it has been two full years since the close of the previous chapter. Joseph has spent two more years in jail, waiting for something to happen.

Here is Pharaoh's dream—

And, behold, there came up out of the river seven well favoured kine and fatfleshed; and they fed in a meadow.

And, behold, seven other kine came up after them out of the river, ill favoured and leanfleshed; and stood by the other kine upon the brink of the river [Gen. 41:2–3].

"Kine" are cows. We are talking about cattle here. He saw seven cows that were well-fed, fine looking, fat cattle. Then he saw seven really skinny cows.

And the ill favoured and leanfleshed kine did eat up the seven well favoured and fat kine. So Pharaoh awoke [Gen. 41:4].

Pharaoh woke up and wondered what the dream meant. He didn't have the interpretation, but there was nobody to help him that day.

And he slept and dreamed the second time: and, behold, seven ears of corn came up upon one stalk, rank and good.

And, behold, seven thin ears and blasted with the east wind sprung up after them.

And the seven thin ears devoured the seven rank and full ears. And Pharaoh awoke, and, behold, it was a dream.

And it came to pass in the morning that his spirit was troubled; and he sent and called for all the magicians of Egypt, and all the wise men thereof: and Pharaoh told them his dream; but there was none that could interpret them unto Pharaoh [Gen. 41:5–8].

While all of these magicians and wise men were called in and Pharaoh was telling them his dream, the chief butler was there listening. After all, his position was to stand before Pharaoh and get him anything that he wanted. When none of the wise men could give Pharaoh an interpretation, the butler spoke up—

Then spake the chief butler unto Pharaoh, saying, I do remember my faults this day [Gen. 41:9].

I would call it a little more than a "fault!" It was a *sin*, in my opinion. But, you see, all of this was in the providence of God. We would call them the fortuitous concurrence of circumstances. The difficult experiences of Joseph could not be understood at the time, but God was letting them happen for a purpose. Now the chief butler says, "Oh, I just remembered that I promised a young fellow down there in prison that I would speak to you about him. And, by the way, Pharaoh, *he* can interpret dreams." Now he tells Pharaoh his own experience—

Pharaoh was wroth with his servants, and put me in ward in the captain of the guard's house, both me and the chief baker:

And we dreamed a dream in one night, I and he; we dreamed each man according to the interpretation of his dream.

And there was there with us a young man, an Hebrew, servant to the captain of the guard; and we told him, and he interpreted to us our dreams; to each man according to his dream he did interpret.

And it came to pass, as he interpreted to us, so it was; me he restored unto mine office, and him he hanged [Gen. 41:10–13].

Pharaoh said, "Well, we've tried everybody else around here, and since that young man interpreted your dream and that of the baker, let's have him come because I have the feeling that my dreams are very significant."

Then Pharaoh sent and called Joseph, and they brought him hastily out of the dungeon: and he shaved himself, and changed his raiment, and came in unto Pharaoh [Gen. 41:14].

Note that Joseph shaved himself. You must remember that the Hebrews were not shaving in that day. But have you noticed that the statues and paintings of the Egyptians show a cleanshaven people? Many of the rulers sported a little goatee to add dignity to their position—if they couldn't grow their own, they wore a false one—but generally the Egyptians were without hair on their faces.

There is a tremendous message in this. This man is lifted up out of the prison now. He shaves, and changes his prison garb for proper court clothing. This is a new life that is before him. It is like a resurrection; he is raised up. Now he goes to the Gentiles. What a tremendous picture of Christ this gives to us here.

And Pharaoh said unto Joseph, I have dreamed a dream, and there is none that can interpret it: and I have heard say of thee, that thou canst understand a dream to interpret it [Gen. 41:15].

Notice how Joseph gives God the glory—

And Joseph answered Pharaoh, saying, It is not in me: God shall give Pharaoh an answer of peace [Gen. 41:16].

From Joseph's viewpoint, God must receive the glory. Again let me say that the child of God should be very careful that God gets the glory for all of his accomplishments. If what we do is a blessing, it is because God is doing it through us. Joseph is aware of this, and he says, "It is not in *me*—I can't interpret it—but *God* shall give Pharaoh an answer of peace."

Pharaoh repeats the dreams to Joseph. Actually, it is one dream of two parts, and it is treated as a single dream.

And Joseph said unto Pharaoh, The dream of Pharaoh is one: God hath shewed Pharaoh what he is about to do [Gen. 41:25].

Joseph says that the dream is one—both speak of the same thing. And the fact that it was repeated, given to Pharaoh twice, adds to its importance. The reason for the dream is that God is letting Pharaoh know what He is about to do. Here is the interpretation—

The seven good kine are seven years; and the seven good ears are seven years: the dream is one.

And the seven thin and ill favoured kine that came up after them are seven years; and the seven empty ears blasted with the east wind shall be seven years of famine.

This is the thing which I have spoken unto Pharaoh: What God is about to do he sheweth unto Pharaoh.

Behold, there come seven years of great plenty throughout all the land of Egypt:

And there shall arise after them seven years of famine; and all the plenty shall be forgotten in the land of Egypt; and the famine shall consume the land;

And the plenty shall not be known in the land by reason of that famine following; for it shall be very grievous [Gen. 41:26–31].

This, you see, is a prediction. There are to be seven years of plenty and then seven years of famine.

And for that the dream was doubled unto Pharaoh twice; it is because the thing is established by God, and God will shortly bring it to pass [Gen. 41:32].

The famine had been determined by God, and He wants Pharaoh to know about it. Now here is the advice of Joseph to Pharaoh—

Now therefore let Pharaoh look out a man discreet and wise, and set him over the land of Egypt.

Let Pharaoh do this, and let him appoint officers over the land, and take up the fifth part of the land of Egypt in the seven plenteous years.

And let them gather all the food of those good years that come, and lay up corn under the hand of Pharaoh, and let them keep food in the cities.

And that food shall be for store to the land against the seven years of famine, which shall be in the land of Egypt; that the land perish not through the famine.

And the thing was good in the eyes of Pharaoh, and in the eyes of all his servants [Gen. 41:33–37].

Joseph advises Pharaoh to collect all the surplus during the seven years of plenty and keep it in store for the lean years.

JOSEPH IS MADE OVERSEER OF EGYPT

And Pharaoh said unto his servants, Can we find such a one as this is, a man in whom the spirit of God is?

And Pharaoh said unto Joseph, Forasmuch as God hath shewed thee all this, there is none so discreet and wise as thou art:

Thou shalt be over my house, and according unto thy word shall all my people be ruled: only in the throne will I be greater than thou.

And Pharaoh said unto Joseph, See, I have set thee over all the land of Egypt [Gen. 41:38–41].

Notice the significance of this. At the beginning this boy had been in the back of the prison, forgotten, forsaken, and forlorn. Now he is brought out at the right psychological moment because nobody else can interpret the dream of Pharaoh. Not only does he interpret it, but in his enthusiasm and because he is a man of ability, he suggests what Pharaoh should do. God is leading him in all of this, of course.

There is to be a worldwide famine, a famine so severe that even Egypt will be affected. Because Egypt is an irrigated land, it is not dependent upon rainfall. The Upper Nile, the Blue Nile, comes down from central Africa and furnishes the water upon which Egypt depends. Egypt gets about an inch of rainfall in a good year; so it is famine all the time as far as rainfall is concerned. But the Nile overflows the land every year, bringing not only water, but sediment which fertilizes the soil. However, God has warned that there will be seven years of famine which will affect Egypt, also.

As Pharaoh listens to Joseph, what he says makes sense. It is too bad that in my own nation there have not been men in our government who have had some sense of the future. Our foreign policy since the years before World War II, even from the days of Hitler's rise to power, has been more or less a first-aid program, something rushed in as an emergency measure. Someone once asked Gladstone what is the measure of a great statesman. He said it is the man who knows the direction God is going for the next fifty years. Well, here in Genesis, Pharaoh is told what is going to happen for the next fourteen years. Our nation could use a man like this, also.

Now, who could take over better than Joseph? Pharaoh recognized that he was a man of ability. Now don't you see how God had been training him in the home of Potiphar? We may wonder why in the world God ever let him go into that home in the first place. Now we realize that he had received quite a bit of training in the home of Potiphar where he had charge of everything the man owned. Now he is going to have charge of everything in the land of Egypt. This is a tremendous transition in his life. He went all the way from the back of the jail to the throne next to that of Pharaoh.

And Pharaoh took off his ring from his hand, and put it upon Joseph's hand, and arrayed him in vestures of fine linen, and put a gold chain about his neck [Gen. 41:42].

By the way, that ring had a signet on it. When that was put down in wax, it was just the same as Pharaoh's signature. Pharaoh is making Joseph his agent. He has the right to use the king's signature.

And he made him to ride in the second chariot which he had; and they cried before him, Bow the knee: and he made him ruler over all the land of Egypt.

And Pharaoh said unto Joseph, I am Pharaoh, and without thee shall no man lift up his hand or foot in all the land of Egypt.

And Pharaoh called Joseph's name Zaphnath-paaneah; and he gave him to wife Asenath the daughter of Poti-pherah priest of On. And Joseph went out over all the land of Egypt [Gen. 41:43–45].

I like the name Joe better than I like *Zaphnath-paaneah*, but that was the name that Pharaoh gave to him. It is a Coptic name, and it means "the revealer of secret things."

And Joseph was thirty years old when he stood before Pharaoh king of Egypt. And Joseph went out from the presence of Pharaoh, and went throughout all the land of Egypt [Gen. 41:46].

We are told Joseph's age here, and we see that he has been in the land of Egypt for thirteen years. We know that two of those years were spent in prison after the episode with the butler and the baker. He probably had been in the prison a year or so before that. So he may have been in the house of Potiphar close to ten years. This gives us some idea of how his life was divided into time periods while he was in the land of Egypt.

After these thirteen years in Egypt, Joseph finds himself in a position which would correspond, I believe, to prime minister. He was second only to Pharaoh in the land of Egypt. Have you ever wondered why Pharaoh was so willing to accept him? Primarily, of course, the answer is that God was with him. All the way along we have been seeing that. The hand of God, by His providence, was leading this man. Joseph says himself that the brothers meant it for evil but that God meant it for good. It is wonderful to know that.

There may be another very practical reason for Pharaoh's accepting Joseph so readily. Many scholars hold that the Pharaoh at this particular time in history was one of the Hyksos kings. The Hyksos were not native Egyptians but were Bedouins from the Arabian Desert. They were a nomadic group, and for a period they came in and took over the throne of Egypt. If this is true (and I think it is), Pharaoh was actually closer in nationality to Joseph than to the Egyptians, and this gave him confidence in Joseph. Actually, these Hyksos kings found it a little difficult to find someone in Egypt who would be loyal and faithful to them. Faithfulness was certainly characteristic of Joseph. His confidence that God was moving in his life produced in him a faithfulness to whomever he was attached. He was faithful to his task because he knew that God was in it. A racial bond with Pharaoh may well be a reason that Joseph found such a ready reception with him at this time, and he certainly proved to be faithful to him, as we shall see.

By the way, the Hyksos kings were later expelled from Egypt, which I believe to be the reason that in Exodus 1:8 we read: "Now there arose up a new king over Egypt, which knew not Joseph." The Pharaoh of the oppression certainly had no fellow-feeling with the Hebrews!

Note that Pharaoh placed a chain about Joseph's neck, which gave him the same authority that Pharaoh had. Also, Pharaoh gave him for a bride the daughter of the priest of On. Her name, *Asenath*, means "dedicated to Neith (the Egyptian Minerva)." Evidently, she came right out of heathenism.

This event in Joseph's life furnishes another parallel with the life of the Lord Jesus. Joseph had a Gentile bride, and the Lord Jesus Christ is presently calling out of this world a Gentile bride, which we call the church.

And in this same verse there is still another parallel; Joseph stood before Pharaoh when he was thirty years old, and the Lord Jesus began His ministry when He was thirty years of age. So at thirty, Joseph takes up his work in Egypt. During these seven years of plenty, he is gathering into storehouses the abundant produce of the land.

And in the seven plenteous years the earth brought forth by handfuls.

And he gathered up all the food of the seven years, which were in the land of Egypt, and laid up the food in the cities: the food of the field, which was round

about every city, laid he up in the same [Gen. 41:47–48].

Notice that he "laid up the food in the cities." He was planning ahead for easy distribution. I remember that during the depression of the 1930s men stood in the lines of the soup kitchens of Chicago and New York, and the lines were blocks long. Although at that time there was an abundance of food, there was a problem of distribution. But Joseph is doing a very practical thing. He is laying up the food in the cities. He is gathering up the surplus, and he is putting it in the cities, ready for distribution.

And Joseph gathered corn as the sand of the sea, very much, until he left numbering; for it was without number [Gen. 41:49].

Egypt was the breadbasket of the world. Under Joseph's management, I tell you, it seemed like two or three breadbaskets!

JOSEPH'S TWO SONS— MANASSEH AND EPHRAIM

Now we pause for a little family note—

And unto Joseph were born two sons before the years of famine came, which Asenath the daughter of Poti-pherah priest of On bare unto him.

And Joseph called the name of the firstborn Manasseh: For God, said he, hath made me forget all my toil, and all my father's house.

And the name of the second called he Ephraim: For God hath caused me to be fruitful in the land of my affliction [Gen. 41:50–52].

These boys were born before the famine. He called his first son *Manasseh*. I'd say a good name for him would be "Amnesia" because it means that God had made Joseph "forget." He was so much involved that he forgot about his father's house. He'd been a homesick boy at first, but he's not anymore.

In the first part of this chapter we saw that Joseph, when he was released from prison, changed his clothes and shaved himself before appearing before Pharaoh. It may seem to you that shaving may not be very important, that only the Gillette Company would be interested

in that fact. But to us it has a symbolic interest. The Hebrews wore beards, and when Joseph shaved himself and changed his clothing, it speaks to me of resurrection because he laid aside the old life and began the new life. From that point on, he dresses like an Egyptian; he talks like an Egyptian; he lives like an Egyptian. He says "God made me forget." So he names his son Manasseh—and you may call him Amnesia if you want to!

The next boy he names *Ephraim* because that means "fruitful." So you can call this next boy "Ambrosia" if you like. Someone may object that this is free translating. Maybe it is, but if you put those two boys' names into their English counterparts, that is exactly what they are. His boys were Amnesia and Ambrosia. Joseph gave them these names because God had made him forget his father's house and had made him fruitful in the land of Egypt.

And the seven years of plenteousness, that was in the land of Egypt, were ended [Gen. 41:53].

The seven years of bountiful crops are over now, and the famine will begin. At this time Joseph is thirty-seven years old. Keep that in mind for the next chapter.

And the seven years of dearth began to come, according as Joseph had said: and the dearth was in all lands; but in all the land of Egypt there was bread.

And when all the land of Egypt was famished, the people cried to Pharaoh for bread: and Pharaoh said unto all the Egyptians, Go unto Joseph; what he saith to you, do [Gen. 41:54–55].

May I call your attention to the fact that Joseph is the one who had the bread. There is another parallel here. Jesus Christ said, "I am the bread of life."

And the famine was over all the face of the earth: and Joseph opened all the storehouses, and sold unto the Egyptians; and the famine waxed sore in the land of Egypt.

And all countries came into Egypt to Joseph for to buy corn; because that the famine was so sore in all lands [Gen. 41:56–57].

Notice that the famine is worldwide.

CHAPTER 42

THEME: Jacob sends ten sons to Egypt; Simeon left as hostage; nine brothers return home

The dramatic incidents in the life of Joseph are beginning to unfold. The pattern of God in using Joseph to preserve the race during the famine and the removal of Jacob and his sons to Egypt begins to emerge in clear detail. When Joseph was back in that dungeon, he couldn't see all of this. But he believed God. He is a man, who, because of his faith, was always enthusiastic and optimistic. Frankly, I wish my faith would get down far enough into shoe leather so that regardless of what happened, and regardless of what the circumstances are, I could be optimistic. I tell you, it doesn't take much rain or many dark clouds to make me less optimistic than I should be. I'm sure that is true of many of us today.

Joseph is in a unique position. I think you could almost guess what is going to happen. The famine is over all the earth, and all the earth is coming to Egypt to get grain. Guess who's coming for dinner!

The famine forces Jacob to send his ten sons to Egypt to buy food. Why only ten? Why didn't he send Benjamin? He didn't want to lose Benjamin. It would have killed him to have lost Benjamin.

Joseph recognized his brothers, but they did not recognize Joseph. Why not? Well, there are several reasons. First of all, they thought he was dead; so they were not looking for him at all. They never expected to see him again, but he did expect to see them.

Then, we must remember that many years had gone by. He was seventeen when they sold him, and now he is thirty-seven years old, plus however many years the famine has been going on. Let's say it was one year; so they hadn't seen him in twenty-one years. He's almost forty and he is dressed like an Egyptian, speaks and acts like an Egyptian.

But we are getting ahead of our story—

JACOB SENDS TEN SONS TO EGYPT

Now when Jacob saw that there was corn in Egypt, Jacob said unto his sons, Why do ye look one upon another? [Gen. 42:1].

They were looking at each other in a doleful way, not knowing where to turn or what to do.

And he said, Behold, I have heard that there is corn in Egypt: get you down thither, and buy for us from thence; that we may live, and not die [Gen. 42:2].

This illustrates faith. A great many people say that faith is so mysterious to them and that they don't know *how* to believe. I talked to a man who did not want to believe, but his argument was, "Well, how can I believe?" Notice here how Jacob believed. He heard something: "I have *heard* that there is corn in Egypt." He believed it, believed that it would bring life to them. So he acted upon his belief: "Get you down thither, and buy for us from thence; that we may live, and not die." My friend, that is what saving faith is. Some folk ask, "How can I believe in Jesus?" Can you imagine Jacob standing there before his ten sons and saying, "I've heard that there is corn down in Egypt, but how am I going to believe it?" Well, the way to believe it is to act upon it. The Bible says, ". . . *Believe* on the Lord Jesus Christ, and thou shalt be saved . . ." (Acts 16:31). You hear something and you believe it. That is what old Jacob did. That is the way he got corn which brought life to his family. And the way you and I get eternal life is through faith in Christ.

And Joseph's ten brethren went down to buy corn in Egypt.

But Benjamin, Joseph's brother, Jacob sent not with his brethren; for he said, Lest peradventure mischief befall him [Gen. 42:3–4].

Suppose mischief befalls the other ten boys, then what? Well, for one thing they are older. But if you want to know the truth, it wouldn't hurt Jacob as much as to lose Benjamin. Benjamin and Joseph were Rachel's boys, and Rachel was the wife he had deeply loved. And now he sends out all ten and keeps only Benjamin with him.

And the sons of Israel came to buy corn among those that came: for the famine was in the land of Canaan [Gen. 42:5].

Now we come to this dramatic moment—

And Joseph was the governor over the land, and he it was that sold to all the people of the land: and Joseph's brethren came, and bowed down themselves before him with their faces to the earth [Gen. 42:6].

Joseph has been watching for them. He knew they would have to come. There had been delegations there from all over the inhabited earth of that day. The famine was worldwide. So he watches, and lo and behold, here come the ten men. They all bow down before him. They got right down on their faces before Joseph. You wonder how he felt. By the way, what do you think of? Here is the literal fulfillment of the dreams of Joseph. Do you remember how he had dreamed as a boy that all the sheaves bowed down to his sheaf? Here it is taking place—all his older brothers are down on their faces before him.

And Joseph saw his brethren, and he knew them, but made himself strange unto them, and spake roughly unto them; and he said unto them, Whence come ye? And they said, From the land of Canaan to buy food.

And Joseph knew his brethren, but they knew not him [Gen. 42:7–8].

Do you know why he treated them roughly? He is testing them. We will find that he is going to test them all the way through. He is going to ask them some penetrating questions.

And Joseph remembered the dreams which he dreamed of them, and said unto them, Ye are spies; to see the nakedness of the land ye are come.

And they said unto him, Nay, my lord, but to buy food are thy servants come.

We are all one man's sons; we are true men, thy servants are no spies [Gen. 42:9–11].

Believe me, Joseph is pouring it on—

And he said unto them, Nay, but to see the nakedness of the land ye are come.

And they said, Thy servants are twelve brethren, the sons of one man in the land of Canaan; and, behold, the youngest is this day with our father, and one is not [Gen. 42:12–13].

He is trying to get as much information as he can about his family without letting them know who he is. He accuses them of being spies.

There are only ten men there before him. They confess that they are really twelve and that one is home with their father. The other "is not" is what they think. In other words, they consider Joseph dead, but there he is standing before them!

Now for the third time Joseph accuses them of being spies.

And Joseph said unto them, That is it that I spake unto you, saying, Ye are spies:

Hereby ye shall be proved: By the life of Pharaoh ye shall not go forth hence, except your youngest brother come hither.

Send one of you, and let him fetch your brother, and ye shall be kept in prison, that your words may be proved, whether there be any truth in you: or else by the life of Pharaoh surely ye are spies [Gen. 42:14–16].

Joseph is attempting to make contact with his youngest brother. These men are really half brothers of his, but Benjamin is his full brother, and he wants to see him. This is the way he attempts to accomplish this.

And he put them all together into ward three days [Gen. 42:17].

He locks them up in the town bastille.

Things look bad for them now, and they wonder what is going to happen.

And Joseph said unto them the third day, This do, and live; for I fear God [Gen. 42:18].

If there was anything that should have given the brothers an inkling of an idea who Joseph was, this statement was it. He says, "I fear God." Apparently in that day there were people other than just Jacob and his family who knew God. They knew that the way to God was by sacrifice. However, this sort of thing probably would not have excited the interest of these brethren. Maybe it even made them a little suspicious of this man. At least he gave a testimony for God. I want you to note that Joseph never misses an opportunity to give a testimony for God. Certainly he is giving one here. He always gives God the glory as the One who is directing his life. At least the statement that he fears God should have encouraged the brothers to believe that they would be treated justly at his hand.

If ye be true men, let one of your brethren be bound in the house of your prison: go ye, carry corn for the famine of your houses:

But bring your youngest brother unto me; so shall your words be verified, and ye shall not die. And they did so [Gen. 42:19–20].

These brothers are men, some of them being over fifty years old, and now they find themselves in a real predicament. They are being dealt with by one who fears God, but they are afraid because they don't know what he is going to do. Joseph makes the pretext of testing them to see whether they are true men, but what he really wants is for his younger brother to come the next time.

And they said one to another, We are verily guilty concerning our brother, in that we saw the anguish of his soul, when he besought us, and we would not hear; therefore is this distress come upon us [Gen. 42:21].

What is taking place here is quite interesting. They are speaking in Hebrew, and Joseph can understand them. Joseph has been speaking to them through an interpreter. He didn't need to, but he did because he is posing as an Egyptian. They are making a real confession of their guilt.

And Reuben answered them, saying, Spake I not unto you, saying, Do not sin against the child; and ye would not hear? therefore, behold, also his blood is required [Gen. 42:22].

They feel that what is happening to them is the vengeance of God upon them for the way they treated Joseph.

SIMEON LEFT AS HOSTAGE

And they knew not that Joseph understood them; for he spake unto them by an interpreter.

And he turned himself about from them, and wept; and returned to them again, and communed with them, and took from them Simeon, and bound him before their eyes [Gen. 42:23–24].

They say that this evil thing is coming upon them because of the evil they had done to Joseph. They are really repentant now. Joseph hears every bit of it, and he is moved toward them. He would love to walk up to them, throw his arms around each one of them, and call them "brother." But he dares not do it because he would never get Benjamin here.

He gives them a real test now. They must leave one of the brothers, and it is Simeon who is to stay. Joseph was so moved, so emotionally charged by all this that he had to weep. But he goes aside and washes his face; then comes in again as if nothing has happened.

I don't have any idea why they chose Simeon. I take it that while Joseph was gone out of the room, his brothers made the choice for Simeon to stay, and Joseph accepted that choice.

Then Joseph commanded to fill their sacks with corn, and to restore every man's money into his sack, and to give them provision for the way: and thus did he unto them [Gen. 42:25].

He just couldn't take their money. So he not only gave them back their payment for the grain, but he gave them food for the trip home.

And they laded their asses with the corn, and departed thence.

And as one of them opened his sack to give his ass provender in the inn, he espied his money; for, behold, it was in his sack's mouth.

And he said unto his brethren, My money is restored; and, lo, it is even in my sack: and their heart failed them, and they were afraid, saying one to another, What is this that God hath done unto us? [Gen. 42:26–28].

They feel that this is the judgment of God upon them. Ordinarily it would have been good news and a wonderful thing to have your money returned to you! Let me ask you this: Wouldn't you like to go down to your favorite supermarket to do your weekend grocery shopping, load up several of those great big carts and buy for your whole family; then wouldn't you like to open up your grocery sack at home and find that they had given you back all of the money you had paid for the groceries? Do you think that would be bad news to you? Especially, would it worry you if you learned that the grocer was giving this to you as a gift from him? Don't we all agree that under ordinary circumstances that would be good news? We would actually take it as an encouragement.

Well, it wasn't that for these men. They already feel that they are in hot water with this hard-boiled ruler down there in Egypt who has made it so difficult for them. This only adds to their concern.

We may wonder why they didn't go back to Egypt immediately. What would you have done under the circumstances? I think they feared they would really be in hot water had they gone back. Then this man would accuse them of stealing the money. They are not taking any chances. They are going on home, intending to bring the money back when they return.

And they came unto Jacob their father unto the land of Canaan, and told him all that befell unto them; saying,

The man, who is the lord of the land, spake roughly to us, and took us for spies of the country.

And we said unto him, We are true men; we are no spies:

We be twelve brethren, sons of our father; one is not, and the youngest is this day with our father in the land of Canaan.

And the man, the lord of the country, said unto us, Hereby shall I know that ye are true men; leave one of your brethren here with me, and take food for the famine of your households, and be gone:

And bring your youngest brother unto me: then shall I know that ye are no spies, but that ye are true men: so will I deliver you your brother, and ye shall traffick in the land [Gen. 42:29–34].

Remember that they have left Simeon down there in Egypt.

And it came to pass as they emptied their sacks, that, behold, every man's bundle of money was in his sack: and when both they and their father saw the bundles of money, they were afraid [Gen. 42:35].

They thought it was a trick, of course.

And Jacob their father said unto them, Me have ye bereaved of my children: Joseph is not, and Simeon is not, and ye will take Benjamin away: all these things are against me [Gen. 42:36].

Poor old Jacob! He's not the cocky individual we once knew, nor is he quite the man of faith that we shall see a little later. But he is growing. He is not bragging now but is very pessimistic. He says, "All these things are against me." His son, Joseph, would not have said such a thing, but Jacob is saying it. Joseph would have said the same thing that Paul wrote so many years later: "And we know that all things work together for good to them that love God, to them who are the called according to his purpose" (Rom. 8:28). "Being confident of this very thing, that he which hath begun a good work in you will perform it until the day of Jesus Christ" (Phil. 1:6).

And Reuben spake unto his father, saying, Slay my two sons, if I bring him not to thee: deliver him into my hand, and I will bring him to thee again.

And he said, My son shall not go down with you; for his brother is dead, and he is left alone: if mischief befall him by the way in the which ye go, then shall ye bring down my gray hairs with sorrow to the grave [Gen. 42:37–38].

Jacob's life was wrapped up in the life of this boy Benjamin. You see, Joseph was his favorite because he was the firstborn of his lovely Rachel. Now Joseph is gone, which is a heartbreak to him. Now he faces the chance that he may lose this other son of Rachel, and he says that if this takes place he will die. Very candidly, he would have. His life was absolutely tied up in the life of Benjamin. He is the son of his right hand. He is the walking stick for Jacob. Jacob leans on him. That is what he has been doing these past years; so Jacob says that he will not let him go down to Egypt. In the meantime, poor Simeon is down there cooling his heels in jail!

CHAPTER 43

THEME: *Jacob sends his sons to Egypt; the brothers are enter-tained in Joseph's home*

Due to the seriousness of the famine, the sons of Jacob are forced to return to Egypt with Benjamin where they again have an audience with Joseph and present Benjamin. Joseph does not make himself known unto them at this time.

This is doubtless the most dramatic chapter in the Book of Genesis. I know of nothing that is quite as moving as the appearance of Benjamin before Joseph. The thing that brings them down to the land again is the seriousness of the famine. If the famine had lifted, I think Simeon would have spent the rest of his life in jail down in the land of Egypt, at least until Joseph released him.

JACOB SENDS HIS SONS TO EGYPT

And the famine was sore in the land.

And it came to pass, when they had eaten up the corn which they had brought out of Egypt, their father said unto them, Go again, buy us a little food [Gen. 43:1–2].

Jacob realized they would starve to death if they didn't go down to Egypt again.

And Judah spake unto him, saying, The man did solemnly protest unto us, saying, Ye shall not see my face, except your brother be with you.

If thou wilt send our brother with us, we will go down and buy thee food:

But if thou wilt not send him, we will not go down: for the man said unto us, Ye shall not see my face, except your brother be with you [Gen. 43:3–5].

"The man" is their brother Joseph, but they do not know it. He had presented to them a cut-and-dried proposition, and they knew he meant it. Judah tells his father very definitely, "If we go down there, we *must* have Benjamin with us. You wouldn't send him before, but there is no use going if he is not with us this time because the man won't see us."

And Israel said, Wherefore dealt ye so ill with me, as to tell the man whether ye had yet a brother?

And they said, The man asked us straitly of our state, and of our kindred, saying, Is your father yet alive? have ye another brother? and we told him according to the tenor of these words: could we certainly know that he would say, Bring your brother down? [Gen. 43:6–7].

Poor old Jacob is really frustrated. He says, "Why in the world did you tell the man in the first place that you even had another brother?" He doesn't realize that Joseph knew it anyway. But Jacob wishes his sons had kept their mouths shut.

And Judah said unto Israel his father, Send the lad with me, and we will arise and go; that we may live, and not die, both we, and thou, and also our little ones.

I will be surety for him; of my hand shalt thou require him: if I bring him not unto thee, and set him before thee, then let me bear the blame for ever [Gen. 43:8–9].

The brothers were really quite reasonable in their answer to their father. They told him that they hadn't intended to tell "the man" everything but that he kept probing them. He was going to get his information and wouldn't stop until he did—we know that. Then Judah comes forward as a surety for Benjamin.

Friend, you and I have a Surety today, and He came from the tribe of Judah. The Lord Jesus took that place and became my Shepherd, took my place and took my penalty. I was not able to meet His standard. I was not able to come up to His level. But the Lord Jesus stepped in and became my Surety and gave His life for me. What a picture of Christ we have here!

For except we had lingered, surely now we had returned this second time [Gen. 43:10].

Judah says, "If you had let Benjamin go, we would have been there and back home by this time."

And their father Israel said unto them, If it must be so now, do this; take of the best fruits in the land in your vessels, and carry down the man a present, a little balm, and a little honey, spices, and myrrh, nuts, and almonds [Gen. 43:11].

You will notice here that the thing they lacked

was grain. They lacked bread, the staff of life. Apparently they had honey, nuts, and spices. So Jacob says they should send the man a gift. "Let's get on the sweet side of him" is actually what he is saying with the gift.

And take double money in your hand; and the money that was brought again in the mouth of your sacks, carry it again in your hand; peradventure it was an oversight:

Take also your brother, and arise, go again unto the man:

And God Almighty give you mercy before the man, that he may send away your other brother, and Benjamin. If I be bereaved of my children, I am bereaved [Gen. 43:12–14].

So old Jacob relinquishes Benjamin and lets him go along with his older brothers.

Now the dramatic moment comes when they stand again before Joseph.

And the men took that present, and they took double money in their hand, and Benjamin; and rose up, and went down to Egypt, and stood before Joseph [Gen. 43:15].

You can well imagine Joseph's emotion as his eye singled out Benjamin!

THE BROTHERS ARE ENTERTAINED IN JOSEPH'S HOME

And when Joseph saw Benjamin with them, he said to the ruler of his house, Bring these men home, and slay, and make ready; for these men shall dine with me at noon.

And the man did as Joseph bade; and the man brought the men into Joseph's house [Gen. 43:16–17].

The reason for Joseph's inviting them to his home is obvious. He wants to talk with them in the privacy of his own home.

And the men were afraid, because they were brought into Joseph's house; and they said, Because of the money that was returned in our sacks at the first time are we brought in; that he may seek occasion against us, and fall upon us, and take us for bondmen, and our asses [Gen. 43:18].

These men are really panicky now. They can't imagine him inviting them to his home for any

good purpose. He had dealt with them so harshly before, and now he is inviting them to lunch!

Again, here is something that under ordinary circumstances would be something to brag about. Wouldn't you brag if the President of the United States had invited you to the Blue Room, or, better yet, the dining room for dinner? You would think it was a wonderful privilege. Yet, for these men, such a privilege brings no joy whatsoever. You see, they have a guilt complex. They feel guilty about everything that happens because they are the ones who sold their brother. Guilt changes joy into misery. In their fears, they wonder and begin to speculate. Could this man be plotting to take them as slaves because of the money in the sacks? Well, *they* had not hesitated to make a slave of Joseph when they sold him to the Ishmeelites for slavery in Egypt.

And they came near to the steward of Joseph's house, and they communed with him at the door of the house.

And said, O sir, we came indeed down at the first time to buy food:

And it came to pass, when we came to the inn, that we opened our sacks, and, behold, every man's money was in the mouth of his sack, our money in full weight: and we have brought it again in our hand.

And other money have we brought down in our hands to buy food: we cannot tell who put our money in our sacks [Gen. 43:19–22].

They are beginning to apologize, explain, and plead. They even appeal to this man who is conducting them to Joseph's home—who evidently was an official.

And he said, Peace be to you, fear not: your God, and the God of your father, hath given you treasure in your sacks: I had your money. And he brought Simeon out unto them [Gen. 43:23].

Apparently, this man, through the testimony of Joseph, had come to a knowledge of the living and true God. I think that Joseph had at least partially let him in on what was taking place. When he said, "I had your money," I imagine that frightened the brothers all the more.

And the man brought the men into Joseph's house, and gave them water,

and they washed their feet; and he gave their asses provender [Gen. 43:24].

Here we see the custom of foot washing again. We saw it in the life of Abraham and then again down in the city of Sodom. It was the custom of that day.

And they made ready the present against Joseph came at noon: for they heard that they should eat bread there.

And when Joseph came home, they brought him the present which was in their hand into the house, and bowed themselves to him to the earth [Gen. 43:25–26].

Remember that old Jacob had told his sons to take a present to "the man." Notice that they "bowed themselves to him to the earth." Again the boyhood dreams of Joseph are being fulfilled.

And he asked them of their welfare, and said, Is your father well, the old man of whom ye spake? Is he yet alive? [Gen. 43:27].

This is a dramatic moment! Joseph is probably seated, not necessarily on a throne, but on an elevation of prominence, as his brothers bow before him. When they stand to their feet, Joseph looks them right in the eye, and they look at him. Joseph asks, "Is your father well, the old man of whom ye spake? Is he still alive?" You see, Joseph is acutely interested because he is *his* father, also.

And they answered, Thy servant our father is in good health, he is yet alive. And they bowed down their heads, and made obeisance [Gen. 43:28].

Here they go down on their faces again. I would love to have a picture of this, wouldn't you? Benjamin is with them, and he goes down on his face, too.

And he lifted up his eyes, and saw his brother Benjamin, his mother's son, and said, Is this your younger brother, of whom ye spake unto me? And he said, God be gracious unto thee, my son [Gen. 43:29].

Joseph looks at his brother Benjamin, "his mother's son." The others are his half brothers, but this boy is his full brother, his mother's son. He asks, "Is this your younger brother, of whom ye spake unto me?" I suppose the brothers nodded. Joseph said to Ben-

jamin, "God be gracious unto thee, my son." What a dramatic moment! And Joseph can't contain his emotion—

And Joseph made haste; for his bowels did yearn upon his brother: and he sought where to weep; and he entered into his chamber, and wept there [Gen. 43:30].

"His bowels did yearn upon his brother"—that is, he was deeply moved, and his heart went out to him. I suppose he said to his brothers, "Excuse me for a moment—someone wants me on the telephone," and he got out of the room as quickly as he could. He went into his own private quarters and he wept. After all these years, he sees his own brother Benjamin. It has been about twenty-two years. Joseph is almost forty now, and Benjamin is a young man.

And he washed his face, and went out, and refrained himself, and said, Set on bread [Gen. 43:31].

This is a marvelous, wonderful picture of something that is yet to be fulfilled. I hope that you will see this. The prophet Zechariah tells us that Jesus Christ is going to make Himself known unto His brethren someday. They are going to ask Him about the piercing of His side and the nail prints in His hands. He is going to say to them in that day, "These I received in the house of My friends." Then they will recognize Him, and they will weep. He is the One who has provided salvation for them. He is the One who gave His life for their redemption. This is going to take place when the Lord Jesus comes back to the earth. He will be revealed to His brethren, the nation Israel. There will be a remnant there who will know Him. Many of His brethren did not believe on Him when He came the first time, but at that time they are going to know Him.

Likewise, the brothers of Joseph are the ones who delivered him into slavery. They sold him, got rid of him. But now he is going to make himself known to his brethren. Someday our Lord Jesus Christ is going to do just that.

My Christian friend, beware of anti-Semitism. Regardless of how blind the nation of Israel is or what they engage in today, and regardless if they are not all lovely people, it is still true that they are the brethren of our Lord. There is coming the day when He is going to make Himself known to them. It is a family affair. We had better let His family alone. No real Christian can engage in anti-Semitism.

After Joseph had gone to his private quarters to weep, he regained control of his emotions, washed his face and returned to his brothers. He said, "Let's eat."

And they set on for him by himself, and for them by themselves, and for the Egyptians, which did eat with him, by themselves: because the Egyptians might not eat bread with the Hebrews: for that is an abomination unto the Egyptians [Gen. 43:32].

There are several things about this meal that the brothers would have noticed had they not been so frightened. The first thing is that Joseph did not eat with the Egyptians. The Egyptians ate alone. Joseph was separate from them. The brothers may have thought this was simply because he was the brass, the head man in this particular place.

Now here is something else—

And they sat before him, the firstborn according to his birthright, and the youngest according to his youth: and the men marvelled one at another [Gen. 43:33].

Joseph arranged the place cards, and he put Reuben in his proper place, he put Benjamin in his proper place, and all the brothers were in their right order, according to their ages. They looked at each other in amazement and wondered how he knew all that.

And he took and sent messes unto them from before him: but Benjamin's mess was five times so much as any of theirs. And they drank, and were merry with him [Gen. 43:34].

Also notice that he served their plates. I wish our Authorized Version had used another word here instead of "messes" because that sounds messy, but of course it means portions. And again, he just could not refrain from showing his affection for his own brother Benjamin, so that he gave him five times as much. Now that young man had been through a famine, and this was his first real meal for a long time.

"And they drank, and were merry with him." It was a glorious affair. And what a wonderful day it will be when Joseph finally reveals himself to his brethren.

CHAPTER 44

THEME: *Joseph sends his brothers home; Judah volunteers to take Benjamin's place*

Again, we have a wonderful and dramatic chapter before us. Joseph has something else up his sleeve when he sends his brothers away with the grain. He tests his brothers relative to their relationship and their affection to Benjamin and their father. Remember, they had sold *him* into slavery. Have they changed? Will they be willing to let Benjamin go into slavery to save themselves? He needs to satisfy his mind in this regard before he makes himself known to them. The test he uses here would give him absolute proof that his brothers would not repeat the episode that he had experienced at their hands.

Judah acts as the spokesman for the group, and he is brought into a wonderful picture here. He is willing to take the place of Benjamin, and his eloquent defense of Benjamin is one of the most moving passages in the Bible.

JOSEPH SENDS BROTHERS HOME

And he commanded the steward of his house, saying, Fill the men's sacks with food, as much as they can carry, and put every man's money in his sack's mouth.

And put my cup, the silver cup, in the sack's mouth of the youngest, and his corn money. And he did according to the word that Joseph had spoken.

As soon as the morning was light, the men were sent away, they and their asses.

And when they were gone out of the city, and not yet far off, Joseph said unto his steward, Up, follow after the men; and when thou dost overtake them, say unto them, Wherefore have ye rewarded evil for good?

Is not this it in which my lord drinketh, and whereby indeed he divineth? ye have done evil in so doing [Gen. 44:1–5].

Joseph sends them away, and the brothers start out, thinking everything is all right. They have no idea of the cup in the sack of Benjamin. But the steward of Joseph's house comes after them with specific instructions. When the brothers get out a little way, they are overtaken. Here comes a whole troop after them, and they are accused of taking the cup belonging to Joseph.

And he overtook them, and he spake unto them these same words.

And they said unto him, Wherefore saith my lord these words? God forbid that thy servants should do according to this thing [Gen. 44:6–7].

Note that the steward says that Joseph uses this cup for "divining." Remember that Joseph was a prophet, and he was able to foretell the future. We know that is so because he interpreted the dreams of the baker, the butler, and of Pharaoh. He may have used this cup, or maybe that was part of the ruse that he used. We must understand that his gift of prophecy was a gift that God had given him, and this was before there was any written revelation. We are not to get a cup and look at tea leaves, nor are we to watch the horoscope—that is all absolute nonsense. It reveals the sad spiritual condition of people today when they turn to that sort of thing. Joseph had a gift. It was not in the cup. His gift was from God.

Behold, the money, which we found in our sacks' mouths, we brought again unto thee out of the land of Canaan: how then should we steal out of thy lord's house silver or gold?

With whomsoever of thy servants it be found, both let him die, and we also will be my lord's bondmen [Gen. 44:8–9].

They were so sure that none of them had the cup.

And he said, Now also let it be according unto your words: he with whom it is found shall be my servant; and ye shall be blameless.

Then they speedily took down every man his sack to the ground, and opened every man his sack.

And he searched, and began at the eldest, and left at the youngest: and the cup was found in Benjamin's sack [Gen. 44:10–12].

Of course, Joseph had instructed his steward to put the cup in Benjamin's sack.

Then they rent their clothes, and laded every man his ass, and returned to the city [Gen. 44:13].

They "rent" or tore their clothes as a gesture of extreme distress. They all turned around to go back. They are not going home without Benjamin, you may be sure of that. Here they fall on the ground before Joseph again. This time it is in dismay and in agony—

And Judah and his brethren came to Joseph's house; for he was yet there: and they fell before him on the ground.

And Joseph said unto them, What deed is this that ye have done? wot ye not that such a man as I can certainly divine? [Gen. 44:14–15].

JUDAH VOLUNTEERS
TO TAKE BENJAMIN'S PLACE

Judah comes to the front, and the nobility of this man really stands out now. Remember it is from the tribe of Judah that the Saviour is to come. This man makes one of the finest speeches ever recorded. He makes a full confession that it is because of their sin that this has come upon them.

And Judah said, What shall we say unto my lord? what shall we speak? or how shall we clear ourselves? God hath found out the iniquity of thy servants: behold, we are my lord's servants, both we, and he also with whom the cup is found.

And he said, God forbid that I should do so: but the man in whose hand the cup is found, he shall be my servant; and as for you, get you up in peace unto your father [Gen. 44:16–17].

Joseph wants to test them now in regard to their love for their brother. He says that Benjamin is the guilty one; so it is Benjamin who must stay. They had sold *him* into slavery; now he says, "Just leave Benjamin here, and he can be my slave. He is the guilty one. The rest of you can go home." Now listen to Judah—

Then Judah came near unto him, and said, Oh my lord, let thy servant, I pray thee, speak a word in my lord's ears, and let not thine anger burn against thy servant: for thou art even as Pharaoh [Gen. 44:18].

You can see the position which Joseph occupies in Egypt.

My lord asked his servants, saying, Have ye a father, or a brother?

And we said unto my lord, We have a father, an old man, and a child of his old age, a little one; and his brother is dead, and he alone is left of his mother, and his father loveth him.

And thou saidst unto thy servants, Bring him down unto me, that I may set mine eyes upon him.

And we said unto my lord, The lad cannot leave his father: for if he should leave his father, his father would die.

And thou saidst unto thy servants, Except your youngest brother come down with you, ye shall see my face no more.

And it came to pass when we came up unto thy servant my father, we told him the words of my lord.

And our father said, Go again, and buy us a little food.

And we said, We cannot go down: if our youngest brother be with us, then will we go down: for we may not see the man's face, except our youngest brother be with us.

And thy servant my father said unto us, Ye know that my wife bare me two sons:

And the one went out from me, and I said, Surely he is torn in pieces; and I saw him not since:

And if ye take this also from me, and mischief befall him, ye shall bring down my gray hairs with sorrow to the grave [Gen. 44:19–29].

Judah here in this statement is recounting what has happened and the feelings of their father. Actually, the father had been deceived, and Joseph can see that now. He now knows exactly what the brothers told their father had happened to him so long ago. I believe that this is the first time any one of them has said that much. They had said previously that he "was not," meaning that he was dead.

We can see something else. Jacob is growing in grace, but he hasn't arrived. Instead of trusting the Lord, he is leaning on this boy Benjamin. If anything had happened to Benjamin, it would have killed him—he would have gone down into his grave, sorrowing.

There are Christians today who reveal a very wonderful faith in God at the time when death comes to a loved one. Others actually collapse when this happens. I don't care how much you love a member of your family, friend, if you both are children of God, you know you are going to see each other again someday. The one walking by faith is not going to collapse at a time like that. Therefore, we can recognize that Jacob has not yet arrived. Although he is growing in grace, he still does not have a complete trust in God.

Now therefore when I come to thy servant my father, and the lad be not with us; seeing that his life is bound up in the lad's life;

It shall come to pass, when he seeth that the lad is not with us, that he will die; and thy servants shall bring down the gray hairs of thy servant our father with sorrow to the grave [Gen. 44:30–31].

You notice the concern that Judah has here for old Jacob. Judah is the spokesman for the group. I think any one of the other brothers would have made this same statement.

For thy servant became surety for the lad unto my father, saying, If I bring him not unto thee, then I shall bear the blame to my father for ever.

Now therefore, I pray thee, let thy servant abide instead of the lad a bondman to my lord; and let the lad go up with his brethren.

For how shall I go up to my father, and the lad be not with me? lest peradventure I see the evil that shall come on my father [Gen. 44:32–34].

Again, Judah is the spokesman for the group, and any one of them would have offered himself. Joseph tests his brothers, and they all pass the test. Rather than to see Benjamin go into slavery, they are willing to take his place.

My friend, later on in history there came One in the line of Judah, the Lion of the tribe of Judah, who bore the penalty for the guilty. ". . . God commendeth his love toward us, in that, while we were yet sinners, Christ died for us" (Rom. 5:8). Christ took the place of the guilty.

CHAPTER 45

THEME: *Joseph reveals his identity; Joseph invites his family to Egypt*

The story from the previous chapters continues right on in the chapter before us. Joseph reveals himself to his brethren and identifies himself with them.

JOSEPH REVEALS HIS IDENTITY

Then Joseph could not refrain himself before all them that stood by him; and he cried, Cause every man to go out from me. And there stood no man with him, while Joseph made himself known unto his brethren [Gen. 45:1].

Joseph clears the room.

And he wept aloud: and the Egyptians and the house of Pharaoh heard [Gen. 45:2].

This time Joseph could not get out of the room. He just breaks down and begins to weep. No one knows why except Joseph. His own brethren at this time do not know, and the servants who are there do not know. Now there is no further reason for Joseph to conceal his identity from them, as he has fully tested his brethren.

Let me repeat that the day is coming when the Lord Jesus Christ is going to make Himself known unto His brethren, the Jews. When He came the first time, "he came unto his own, and his own received him not" (John 1:11). In fact, they delivered Him up to be crucified. But when He comes the second time, He will make Himself known to His own people. "And one shall say unto him, What are these wounds in thine hands? Then he shall answer, Those with which I was wounded in the house of my friends" (Zech. 13:6). Christ will make Himself known to His brethren. And "in that day there shall be a fountain opened to the house of David and to the inhabitants of Jerusalem for sin and for uncleanness" (Zech. 13:1). It will be a family affair between the Lord Jesus and His brethren. The episode of Joseph revealing himself to his brothers gives us a little inkling of how wonderful that day of Christ's revelation will be.

Joseph is so charged with emotion that he can't contain himself. In the house of Pharaoh they can hear the weeping. They can't understand what is happening over at Joseph's house.

And Joseph said unto his brethren, I am Joseph: doth my father yet live? And his brethren could not answer him; for they were troubled at his presence [Gen. 45:3].

"Troubled" in our translation is really not strong enough. The brothers were *terrified* at his presence. I tell you, if you think they were afraid before, they were really terrified now. It had been close to twenty-five years since they had seen him when they sold him to the Ishmaelites, and they are sure that now he will want to get his revenge. They are too shocked and frightened to speak.

And Joseph said unto his brethren, Come near to me, I pray you. And they came near. And he said, I am Joseph your brother, whom ye sold into Egypt [Gen. 45:4].

"I'm your brother." Here is a dramatic moment! Can you imagine how they feel? Notice the reaction of Joseph here. He is not angry, and he does not seek revenge. That would be the normal, human reaction. Then why doesn't he seek revenge?

Now therefore be not grieved, nor angry with yourselves, that ye sold me hither: for God did send me before you to preserve life [Gen. 45:5].

You see, the thing that Joseph could see in all of this was that God had permitted it for a purpose. God was moving in his life.

For these two years hath the famine been in the land: and yet there are five years, in the which there shall neither be earing nor harvest.

And God sent me before you to preserve you a posterity in the earth, and to save your lives by a great deliverance.

So now it was not you that sent me hither, but God: and he hath made me a father to Pharaoh, and lord of all his house, and a ruler throughout all the land of Egypt [Gen. 45:6–8].

If you and I could see the hand of God in our lives, would we become angry and seek revenge? I don't think we would. Again this man gives the glory to God.

Joseph was seventeen when he was brought

into Egypt. He was thirty when he stood before Pharaoh. There had been seven years of plenty and now there have passed two years of famine. So Joseph is thirty-nine years old and had been living in the land of Egypt for twenty-two years. He sees the hand of God in all of this.

JOSEPH INVITES HIS FAMILY TO EGYPT

Haste ye, and go up to my father, and say unto him, Thus saith thy son Joseph, God hath made me lord of all Egypt: come down unto me, tarry not:

And thou shalt dwell in the land of Goshen, and thou shalt be near unto me, thou, and thy children, and thy children's children, and thy flocks, and thy herds, and all that thou hast:

And there will I nourish thee; for yet there are five years of famine; lest thou, and thy household, and all that thou hast, come to poverty [Gen. 45:9–11].

Jacob and his family could not have survived had they stayed in the land of Palestine at this particular time. They would have perished. Joseph wants to bring them down to the land of Goshen which is actually the best part of Egypt. It is in that land that God is going to make them a nation, sheltered from the rest of the world. The lives of the brothers revealed that they needed to get out of the land of Canaan.

And, behold, your eyes see, and the eyes of my brother Benjamin, that it is my mouth that speaketh unto you [Gen. 45:12].

I think that they stood there absolutely spellbound and were down on their faces and then up again and that they had absolutely nothing to say as they listened to Joseph speaking words that seemed unbelievable—they would have been unbelievable but Joseph was right there before them.

And ye shall tell my father of all my glory in Egypt, and of all that ye have seen; and ye shall haste and bring down my father hither.

And he fell upon his brother Benjamin's neck, and wept; and Benjamin wept upon his neck [Gen. 45:13–14].

This is a tender scene between these two full brothers. Joseph and Benjamin are both marvelous men.

Moreover he kissed all his brethren, and wept upon them: and after that his brethren talked with him [Gen. 45:15].

The other brothers were stunned, but now they begin to recover their senses, and they have quite a talk.

And then the news begins to be spread abroad.

And the fame thereof was heard in Pharaoh's house, saying, Joseph's brethren are come: and it pleased Pharaoh well, and his servants [Gen. 45:16].

There was all this noise in the house of Joseph, and the people could hear it. Pharaoh wanted to know what was going on, and I suppose he asked one of the servants from Joseph's house what it all meant. The servant probably said, "Well, you know those eleven men who came down from Canaan—they're Joseph's *brothers!*" It delighted Pharaoh. Why would it delight him? Remember that Pharaoh was probably a Hyksos king and of the same racial strain as Joseph and his family. He hadn't been able to trust the Egyptians too much and was pleased with Joseph's faithfulness; so he was delighted that there were going to be more like him.

And Pharaoh said unto Joseph, Say unto thy brethren, This do ye; lade your beasts, and go, get you unto the land of Canaan;

And take your father and your households, and come unto me: and I will give you the good of the land of Egypt, and ye shall eat the fat of the land.

Now thou art commanded, this do ye; take you wagons out of the land of Egypt for your little ones, and for your wives, and bring your father, and come [Gen. 45:17–19].

Notice that Pharaoh orders wagons to be sent. The wheel was quite an invention, and these men from Canaan were not using wagons yet, but the Egyptians were more advanced.

Also regard not your stuff; for the good of all the land of Egypt is yours [Gen. 45:20].

"You won't need to bring anything extra; we'll furnish everything you need."

And the children of Israel did so: and Joseph gave them wagons, according to the commandment of Pharaoh, and gave them provision for the way.

To all of them he gave each man changes of raiment; but to Benjamin he gave three hundred pieces of silver, and five changes of raiment.

And to his father he sent after this manner; ten asses laden with the good things of Egypt, and ten she asses laden with corn and bread and meat for his father by the way.

So he sent his brethren away, and they departed: and he said unto them, See that ye fall not out by the way.

And they went up out of Egypt, and came into the land of Canaan unto Jacob their father.

And told him, saying, Joseph is yet alive, and he is governor over all the land of Egypt. And Jacob's heart fainted, for he believed them not [Gen. 45:21–26].

He just could not believe it was true.

And they told him all the words of Joseph, which he had said unto them: and when he saw the wagons which Joseph had sent to carry him, the spirit of Jacob their father revived [Gen. 45:27].

Finally old Jacob was convinced, and he began to exhibit some enthusiasm.

And Israel said, It is enough; Joseph my son is yet alive: I will go and see him before I die [Gen. 45:28].

What thrilling developments we are seeing here! The prospect of seeing Joseph certainly influenced Jacob to make the decision to go down to Egypt. Do you think that he intended to remain in Egypt? I don't think so. I think he intended to pay a brief visit to his son and then return back home as soon as the famine was over. But he never returned to Canaan except for a burial, his own. He died in the land of Egypt. Although his whole family lived there, he was buried in the land of Canaan.

CHAPTER 46

THEME: Jacob and family move to Egypt; Jacob and Joseph reunited

Jacob probably thought he was going to Egypt for only a few years, and even then it was with some reluctance and hesitation that he consented going there. God had instructed Abraham to stay out of Egypt, and Abraham had been in trouble down there. God had said the same thing to Isaac. So now the question is, should Jacob go down into the land of Egypt? He needs a little more encouragement than the invitation from his son Joseph or even from Pharaoh. He needs to have a green light from God.

JACOB AND FAMILY MOVE TO EGYPT

And Israel took his journey with all that he had, and came to Beer-sheba, and offered sacrifices unto the God of his father Isaac [Gen. 46:1].

Here is the amazing thing: he offered sacrifices to the God of his father Isaac. The first time he left that land going to the land of Haran, he had come to Beth-el. Was he looking for God? No, he thought he had run away from Him. He wasn't seeking the mind of God at all, nor was he asking for His leading. What a contrast there is between young Jacob and the servant of Abraham. The servant of Abraham never took a step without looking to God, but Jacob didn't think that he needed God in his life at all. It took a long time for him to learn that was not the proper way to go through life.

How many Christians today go through the entire week and leave God pretty much out of their program. They make their own decisions and do what they want to do. Then they come to church on Sunday, are very religious and are willing to do God's will—they think God's will for them is merely to go to church and maybe teach a Sunday school class. Then they tell God good-bye on Sunday night. The rest of the week God is not in the picture for them.

This man Jacob, for most of his life, had not been looking to God, but now, as he comes to Beer-sheba, he offers sacrifices unto the God of his father Isaac.

Now God is going to be gracious and appear to him—

And God spake unto Israel in the visions of the night, and said, Jacob, Jacob. And he said, Here am I.

And he said, I am God, the God of thy father: fear not to go down into Egypt; for I will there make of thee a great nation [Gen. 46:2–3].

Now God is promising that He will make of Jacob a great nation down in the land of Egypt. You may be wondering if God did that. We find the answer in the next book of the Bible: "And the children of Israel were fruitful, and increased abundantly, and multiplied, and waxed exceeding mighty; and the land was filled with them" (Exod. 1:7). There was a real population explosion of Israelites in the land of Egypt. What is the explanation of that? God is making good His promise to Jacob. "I am God, the God of thy Father; fear not to go down into Egypt: for I will there make of thee a great nation." God made good that which He promised to him.

I will go down with thee into Egypt; and I will also surely bring thee up again: and Joseph shall put his hand upon thine eyes.

And Jacob rose up from Beer-sheba: and the sons of Israel carried Jacob their father, and their little ones, and their wives, in the wagons which Pharaoh had sent to carry him [Gen. 46:4–5].

Pharaoh, you recall, had sent these wagons from Egypt. They put Jacob in one of the wagons, and here they go.

The life of Jacob can be divided into three geographical locations: the land of Haran, the land of Canaan, and the land of Egypt. These are not only geographical areas, but they denote three spiritual levels. Jacob left the land with just a staff. When he came into Haran, he was God's man living in the flesh. He came out of Haran, running. He was running away from his father-in-law and was afraid to meet his own brother Esau. Then in the land of Canaan Jacob had his wrestling match, but he is God's man who is fighting in his own strength. Now he is going to Egypt. He is not walking in his own strength, and he is not running away anymore. He is now walking by faith.

Although Joseph is prominent in this section of Genesis, be sure to mark the evidences of the spiritual man of faith in the life of Jacob. Jacob has become the man that God wanted him to be, and only God can make this kind of man.

Let me state this again. Jacob's life in Haran typifies the man of God who is living in the flesh. Jacob's life in the land of Canaan typifies the man of God who is fighting in his own strength. Jacob's life in Egypt typifies the man of God who is walking by faith.

This, I believe, is true also for a great many of us today. There was that time in our lives when we came in contact with the gospel, the Word of God, and we turned to Him. Then there was that period of struggle when we thought we could live our lives in our own strength. Perhaps that lasted for years. Then there came the time when we did grow in grace and in the knowledge of our Lord Jesus Christ and began to walk by faith.

And they took their cattle, and their goods, which they had gotten in the land of Canaan, and came into Egypt, Jacob, and all his seed with him:

His sons, and his son's sons with him, his daughters, and his son's daughters, and all his seed brought he with him into Egypt [Gen. 46:6–7].

Because of the famine, Jacob had to take everyone—children and grandchildren. And all of their livestock had to go with them since it could not have survived the famine.

The following verses give the genealogy of Jacob. It is very important because it is the genealogy which will lead to Jesus Christ and will be followed through the rest of the Bible. After listing all of Jacob's descendants, we read this:

All the souls that came with Jacob into Egypt, which came out of his loins, besides Jacob's sons' wives, all the souls were threescore and six [Gen. 46:26].

From Jacob there were sixty-six people who came with him from Canaan into Egypt. Of course, Joseph and his family were already in Egypt—

And the sons of Joseph, which were born him in Egypt, were two souls: all the souls of the house of Jacob, which came into Egypt, were threescore and ten [Gen. 46:27].

This brought the total household of Jacob to seventy souls.

Notice that each son of Jacob and his offspring are listed by name. Why are these lists of names given to us in the Scriptures?

Doesn't God have more important information to give to us? My friend, there is nothing more important than our Lord Jesus Christ, and this is the genealogy that leads to Him. We will find some of these names in the genealogy in the first chapter of Matthew, at the beginning of the New Testament. Again, we will find some of these names in the genealogy given to us in Luke, chapter 3. These lists of names are important for that reason.

There is another reason, and it is very personal. Have you heard of the Lamb's Book of Life? The question is: Is *your* name written there? Just as you got into the line of Adam (and we all are in that line), you get into the line of Christ—that is, by birth. But in the case of the Lamb's Book of Life, you get there by the *new* birth which comes about by receiving Christ as your personal Savior. When you do that, you become a child of God.

How important are you? Well, I don't know you—probably have never heard of you—but God knows *you*. In fact, He has numbered the very hairs of your head! He knows you better than anyone else knows you. He knows you and loves you more than your mother ever did—I don't imagine that she ever counted the hairs of your head! God did. God knows you *personally*.

In Jacob's genealogy there are names that mean nothing to me. In watching the news on television, I saw the crowd of young folk at a rock festival, a mob of about two hundred thousand dirty, filthy folk. They may have needed a bath to begin with, but it had just rained, and they were covered with mud. As I looked at them, I thought, *God knows each one of them, and God loves each one. They are not thinking of Him, but each one is precious in God's sight, and Christ died for each one.* My friend, here you are in the midst of a great population explosion with literally millions of people around you, yet *you* are an individual to God. And the names listed in Jacob's genealogy are people whom I don't know. Candidly, I'm not interested in them. But God is. He delighted in putting their names down because they were His. This again causes me to ask you the question: Is your name written in the Lamb's Book of Life?

Now here comes Jacob with all of his family to the land of Egypt.

And he sent Judah before him unto Joseph, to direct his face unto Goshen; and they came into the land of Goshen [Gen. 36:28].

JACOB AND JOSEPH REUNITED

What a picture we have here—

And Joseph made ready his chariot, and went up to meet Israel his father, to Goshen, and presented himself unto him; and he fell on his neck, and wept on his neck a good while [Gen. 46:29].

Joseph fell on the neck of his father and embraced him, and he wept there. The Word of God says it was a good while. I don't know how long a "good while" is, but it does mean that it wasn't just a brisk handshake that had no meaning. The emotion was quite real. Oh, what a marvelous meeting this was!

And Israel said unto Joseph, Now let me die, since I have seen thy face, because thou art yet alive [Gen. 46:30].

What a joy this was to old Jacob! Frankly, friend, I think that Jacob was an old man about ready to die. I believe he barely made this trip, but God sustained him. We will find that he is permitted to live for a few years in the land of Egypt. Israel and Joseph have these last years together. Notice that Jacob is now "the child of God who lives by faith." Therefore, he is called by his name *Israel*.

And Joseph said unto his brethren, and unto his father's house, I will go up, and shew Pharaoh, and say unto him, My brethren, and my father's house, which were in the land of Canaan, are come unto me;

And the men are shepherds, for their trade hath been to feed cattle; and they have brought their flocks, and their herds, and all that they have.

And it shall come to pass, when Pharaoh shall call you, and shall say, What is your occupation?

That ye shall say, Thy servants' trade hath been about cattle from our youth even until now, both we, and also our fathers: that ye may dwell in the land of Goshen; for every shepherd is an abomination unto the Egyptians [Gen. 46:31–34].

They had the same problem in Egypt in that day as we had in the western part of the United States. I remember when I was a boy in West Texas that, if a man tried to raise sheep in that area, he was in trouble. He found he didn't have any friends at all, and I mean he was in *real* trouble. Just so, the Egyptians didn't care for shepherds.

It is interesting that the Word of God has had so much to say about shepherds. These people were shepherds who raised their own sheep, and they still do in the land of Israel. "Shepherd" is the figure of speech which is used to describe our Lord. He is the Good Shepherd who gives His life for the sheep. He is the Great Shepherd of His sheep who watches over them today. He is the Chief Shepherd who is yet to appear. He calls Himself the Shepherd.

And, my friend, He is an abomination to the world. He is not received today. I am speaking of the real Jesus Christ. Liberalism has concocted a Jesus which the world will accept. They have made an idol that doesn't even look like the Lord Jesus of the Bible. The one they talk about is not virgin born; he never performed miracles; he did not die for the sins of the world; and he was not raised bodily from the dead. The Jesus of the liberal never lived. There is no record of a Jesus like that. The only One we have records of was virgin born, performed miracles, died for the sins of the world, and arose bodily from the grave. That is the Shepherd whom the world doesn't like. He is still an abomination to the world.

Shepherds were an abomination to the Egyptians. Joseph tells his brothers to tell Pharaoh that they are shepherds and that they raise cattle. Actually, they had both cattle and sheep. We will find later that Pharaoh will give them the land of Goshen and will ask them to take care of his sheep so that the children of Israel became the shepherds in the land of Egypt.

It is really quite wonderful to see that now the family of Jacob is living in the land of Goshen. This is to be their home for a long time. After the death of Joseph, they will become slaves in the land of Egypt, but God will be with them through all that time. They will become a great nation down there, and then God will lead them out under Moses.

There is no record that God ever appeared to Joseph, yet we certainly see the providence of God in the life of Joseph. It is obvious to us now that he had to come ahead to prepare the way so that the entire family of Jacob could survive in the land of Egypt.

CHAPTER 47

THEME: *Joseph presents father and brothers to Pharaoh; Joseph promises Jacob burial in Canaan*

We have seen how Jacob and all his family have arrived in the land of Egypt. Joseph, as a move of strategy, brought them into the land of Goshen. This actually was the richest land in that day, but right now they are in the midst of a famine and no land is very valuable to the owner at this particular time.

We are going to find that this is the best chapter in the life of Jacob so far. Jacob doesn't appear in a good light when we first meet him in Scripture. In fact, not until he makes his trip to Egypt do we begin to see that he has become a man of faith. This chapter, more than any other, reveals that.

The famine becomes more intense as it draws to an end. Although the people of the world are involved in this, Canaan and Egypt are the lands which are mentioned because they are the particular areas in the development of the story which is told to us here.

JOSEPH PRESENTS FATHER AND BROTHERS TO PHARAOH

Then Joseph came and told Pharaoh, and said, My Father and my brethren, and their flocks, and their herds, and all that they have, are come out of the land of Canaan; and, behold, they are in the land of Goshen [Gen. 47:1].

Joseph is going to present his father and his brothers to the Pharaoh of Egypt. He put them in the land of Goshen before he asked for a place for them. You can see the strategy in that. If they were already there, Pharaoh would be more apt to give them that land. After all, they would already be moved in and have unpacked their goods.

And he took some of his brethren, even five men, and presented them unto Pharaoh.

And Pharaoh said unto his brethren, What is your occupation? And they said unto Pharaoh, Thy servants are shepherds, both we, and also our fathers [Gen. 47:2–3].

We saw that shepherds and cattlemen didn't get along in those days. Egyptians just didn't care for shepherds, neither did they care for shepherding. So that opened up an opportunity for the children of Israel to do something that the Egyptians would not want to do.

They said moreover unto Pharaoh, For to sojourn in the land are we come; for thy servants have no pasture for their flocks; for the famine is sore in the land of Canaan: now therefore, we pray thee, let thy servants dwell in the land of Goshen.

And Pharaoh spake unto Joseph, saying, Thy father and thy brethren are come unto thee:

The land of Egypt is before thee; in the best of the land make thy father and brethren to dwell; in the land of Goshen let them dwell: and if thou knowest any men of activity among them, then make them rulers over my cattle [Gen. 47: 4–6].

Since shepherding was not popular for the Egyptians, Pharaoh needed someone to care for his cattle.

Now Joseph presents his own father to Pharaoh, and this is really quite remarkable. I want you to notice that Jacob now stands in the best light in which we've ever seen him during our study of him.

And Joseph brought in Jacob his father, and set him before Pharaoh: and Jacob blessed Pharaoh [Gen. 47:7].

Notice that it is Jacob who is blessing Pharaoh. He is beginning to live up to his name. He is a witness for God now. The lesser is always blessed of the greater, and Jacob blesses Pharaoh as a witness for God.

And Pharaoh said unto Jacob, How old art thou? [Gen. 47:8].

At this point, if Jacob were living by that old nature which controlled him at the beginning, he would have said, "Well, Pharaoh, I am 130 years old, and I want to tell you what I have accomplished in my lifetime. I would like to tell you how I outsmarted my brother when I was a young fellow and how I became rich by out-

smarting my father-in-law." And he could have bragged about his family—"I've got twelve sons. . . ." He could have gone on and on. But Jacob is a different man now. Listen to him—

And Jacob said unto Pharaoh, The days of the years of my pilgrimage are an hundred and thirty years: few and evil have the days of the years of my life been, and have not attained unto the days of the years of the life of my fathers in the days of their pilgrimage [Gen. 47:9].

First of all, notice that he was 130 years old when he came down to the land of Egypt, and he will be 147 years old when he dies. Therefore, he will spend 17 years in the land of Egypt. I imagine that he was right on the verge of death—one foot in the grave and the other foot on a banana peel—when he came down to Egypt. But the joy of finding Joseph alive and of being with him in Egypt prolonged his life 17 years.

Again, this audience with Pharaoh is an opportunity for the old man to boast, but notice how changed this man Jacob is. He says that he is 130 years old and his life is really nothing to brag about. "Few and evil have the days of the years of my life been." He doesn't brag about pulling a trick on his old father. Instead, he says he doesn't measure up to his fathers. I "have not attained unto the days of the years of the life of my fathers in the days of their pilgrimage." Isn't this a changed man? It doesn't sound like the old Jacob, does it? He's giving glory to God for his life, and he is making no boast that he has accomplished a great deal.

And Jacob blessed Pharaoh, and went out from before Pharaoh [Gen. 47:10].

Frankly, my feeling is that Jacob has arrived. What an opportunity he has to boast, but he doesn't take advantage of it. Someone else might have thought, *Pharaoh is a great ruler, but I want him to know that I was a pretty big man up yonder in the land of Canaan!* But Jacob doesn't brag—he is just a sinner, saved by the grace of God.

In our day we hear so much boasting on the part of many Christians. Sometimes in our own circles, we attempt to applaud certain men for what they have done. We talk about how great they are. Well, if we all told the truth, we would say that we are just a bunch of sinners and we haven't anything to brag about except a wonderful Savior who has been gracious and patient with us down through the years. He is all any of us have to boast about.

Neither can we say that we are superior to our fathers. A friend of mind, who is now a seminary professor, told me how ashamed he had been of his dad. When he first went off to college, his dad was coming to that college to speak because he was a preacher and a Bible teacher. My friend said he was so ashamed of his dad that he wouldn't even go to the meeting where he spoke. He pretended to be sick so he would not have to go. He said, "I was so ashamed of him that I didn't want to be known as his son!" He spent four years in college and then went into the business world for a couple of years. He said, "I had a rough time, and I changed my thinking about my dad. I had thought he was pretty stupid, but I realized that he had supported his family and had been an excellent Bible teacher. After I had experienced some rough times in the business world, I came home, and my, how my dad had improved! No one has ever learned as much as my dad had learned during those brief years I had been away from home!" He came to the conclusion his dad was a lot smarter than he had thought him to be. Isn't that same kind of story true of many of us? But it is not true of Jacob here. He takes a humble place because he is a changed man now.

And Joseph placed his father and his brethren, and gave them a possession in the land of Egypt, in the best of the land, in the land of Rameses, as Pharaoh had commanded [Gen. 47:11].

The land of Rameses is the land of Goshen.

And Joseph nourished his father, and his brethren, and all his father's household, with bread, according to their families.

And there was no bread in all the land; for the famine was very sore, so that the land of Egypt and all the land of Canaan fainted by reason of the famine [Gen. 47:12–13].

The reason that only Egypt and Canaan are mentioned is because they are the two geographical locations which are involved in our story. If Jacob had remained in Canaan with his family, they would have perished. Grain had been stored in the land of Egypt, but the land is not producing grain anymore. Evidently the famine has spread all over Africa, because the Nile River is not overflowing, which is so necessary for Egypt's crop production.

And Joseph gathered up all the money that was found in the land of Egypt, and in the land of Canaan, for the corn which they bought: and Joseph brought the money into Pharaoh's house [Gen. 47:14].

We are coming now to something for which Joseph has been criticized. People say he took advantage of poverty and he bought up the land. In other words, he closed in on the mortgages and bought the land. I feel that this is an unfair criticism of Joseph. To begin with, he is the agent of Pharaoh. None of this is for himself; he is making no effort to enrich himself. He was not crooked in any sense of the word. He did not gain personally because of the famine.

An illustration of this is the scarcity of and demand for uranium during wartime in my own country. When some men found that they had uranium in their properties—especially in Arizona—they were paid handsome sums for their land. Were they taking advantage of their government? I don't think so. The law of supply and demand was in operation.

It seems to me that this same principle was in operation in the land of Egypt. Joseph bought the land for Pharaoh, and he is enabling the people to live by furnishing them food. I think that Joseph stayed within the confines of the law of supply and demand.

And when money failed in the land of Egypt, and in the land of Canaan, all the Egyptians came unto Joseph, and said, Give us bread: for why should we die in thy presence? for the money faileth. And Joseph said, Give your cattle; and I will give you for your cattle, if money fail.

And they brought their cattle unto Joseph: and Joseph gave them bread in exchange for horses, and for the flocks, and for the cattle of the herds, and for the asses: and he fed them with bread for all their cattle for that year.

When that year was ended, they came unto him the second year, and said unto him, We will not hide it from my lord, how that our money is spent; my lord also hath our herds of cattle; there is not aught left in the sight of my lord, but our bodies, and our lands:

Wherefore shall we die before thine eyes, both we and our land? buy us and our land for bread, and we and our land will be servants unto Pharaoh: and give

us seed, that we may live, and not die, that the land be not desolate.

And Joseph bought all the land of Egypt for Pharaoh; for the Egyptians sold every man his field, because the famine prevailed over them: so the land became Pharaoh's [Gen. 47:15–20].

There is no doubt that the famine was a very terrible thing.

And as for the people, he removed them to cities from one end of the borders of Egypt even to the other end thereof [Gen. 47:21].

There was a great migration into the urban areas so that they would be near the center of supply where the grain was stored. You remember that Joseph had chosen these centers throughout Egypt at the very beginning. He now brings the people where they will be close to the supply of food.

Then Joseph said unto the people, Behold, I have bought you this day and your land for Pharaoh: lo, here is seed for you, and ye shall sow the land.

And it shall come to pass in the increase, that ye shall give the fifth part unto Pharaoh, and four parts shall be your own, for seed of the field, and for your food, and for them of your households, and for food for your little ones [Gen. 47:23–24].

Joseph knows that the famine will be ended the next year; so he tells the people to sow their grain.

And they said, Thou hast saved our lives; let us find grace in the sight of my lord, and we will be Pharaoh's servants.

And Joseph made it a law over the land of Egypt unto this day, that Pharaoh should have the fifth part; except the land of the priests only, which became not Pharaoh's [Gen. 47:25–26].

JOSEPH PROMISES JACOB BURIAL IN CANAAN

And Israel dwelt in the land of Egypt, in the country of Goshen; and they had possessions therein, and grew, and multiplied exceedingly.

And Jacob lived in the land of Egypt seventeen years; so the whole age of Jacob was an hundred forty and seven years.

And the time drew nigh that Israel must die: and he called his son Joseph, and said unto him, If now I have found grace in thy sight, put, I pray thee, thy hand under my thigh, and deal kindly and truly with me; bury me not, I pray thee, in Egypt:

But I will lie with my fathers, and thou shalt carry me out of Egypt, and bury me in their buryingplace. And he said, I will do as thou hast said.

And he said, Swear unto me. And he sware unto him. And Israel bowed himself upon the bed's head [Gen. 47:27–31].

I think there are several factors which entered into Jacob's request to be buried back in the land of Canaan. First of all, he is now 147 years old, and he becomes alarmed that he will die in the land of Egypt. I think that is clear to him now. Then, the success of Joseph in acquiring all the land for Pharaoh makes him believe that his family might become comfortable in Egypt and never want to return to Canaan. His age certainly told him that he would die shortly.

We need to recognize this request as an evidence of the faith of Jacob in the covenant which God had made with his fathers. We need to note this because it will come up several times as we go through the Bible. The hope of the Old Testament is an *earthly* hope. Abraham believed that he would be raised from the dead in that land, so he wanted to be buried there. Isaac believed the same. Now Jacob is expressing that same faith. You see, the hope in the Old Testament is not to be caught up to meet the Lord in the air and enter the city of the New Jerusalem, which is the eternal and permanent abode of the *church*.

The hope of the Old Testament is in Christ's kingdom which will be set up on this earth. When that happens, Israel's great hope will be fulfilled, and these people will be raised for that kingdom. The first thousand years of it will be a time of testing, and after that the eternal kingdom will continue on and on. This is why Jacob does not want to be buried in Egypt. If he had no faith or hope in God's promise to him, what difference would it make where he was buried?

For the believer today it makes no difference where we are buried. At the time of the Rapture, wherever we are, we shall be raised, and our bodies will join our spirits; that is, if we have died before the Rapture takes place. If we are still living, then we shall be changed and caught up to meet the Lord in the air. So it won't make any difference if we are buried in Egypt or in Canaan or in Los Angeles, or in Timbuctoo. The living "in Christ" and the dead "in Christ" in all of these places will be caught up. It won't make any difference where we are. We don't need to go to a launching pad in Florida and take off from there. No, our hope is a heavenly hope!

The hope of the Old Testament is an earthly hope, and the fact that Jacob wants to be buried back in the land is an evidence of his faith in the resurrection. He hopes to be raised from the dead in the Promised Land. Jacob is now becoming a man of faith.

CHAPTER 48

THEME: *Joseph visits Jacob during his last illness; Jacob blesses Ephraim and Manasseh*

This tells us of Jacob's last sickness and his blessing of the two sons of Joseph. We are told in Hebrews 11:21 that "by faith Jacob, when he was a dying, blessed both the sons of Joseph; and worshipped, leaning upon the top of his staff."

This chapter gives us another occasion to see further evidences of the spiritual growth of Jacob. He has come a long, long way since his early days. We may feel that it is unfortunate that these traits which appear in the last days of Jacob were not present in his early life. But isn't it wonderful to be able to observe in this that spiritual life is a growth and a development! It is not some sensational experience which takes place in a moment of time, but it is described scripturally as a walk in the Spirit. There was too much of the old nature in Jacob when he was a young man, and the new nature is not discerned until he is an old man.

A fine-looking young couple in Memphis, Tennessee, had come forward after a service. I asked them what they came forward for. They said they wanted all that God had for them. I found out they came forward every Sunday. They thought they would have some sensational, momentous experience that would all of a sudden make them fully grown Christians. Scripture tells us we are to ". . . *grow* in grace, and in the knowledge of our Lord and Saviour Jesus Christ" (2 Pet. 3:18). We see in Jacob that we must wait for the fruit of the Spirit to develop. But thank God for the possibility of growth in our lives and for the patience of God which permits it. Also, we can thank Him that He doesn't move in, as we would, and try to force growth. God very patiently dealt with Jacob, and He will deal very patiently with you and me.

JOSEPH VISITS JACOB DURING HIS LAST ILLNESS

And it came to pass after these things, that one told Joseph, Behold, thy father is sick: and he took with him his two sons, Manasseh and Ephraim.

And one told Jacob, and said, Behold, thy son Joseph cometh unto thee: and Israel strengthened himself, and sat upon the bed.

And Jacob said unto Joseph, God Almighty appeared unto me at Luz in the land of Canaan, and blessed me [Gen. 48:1–3].

Can you imagine the thrill that fills the heart of this old man? Here comes Joseph, his favorite son, with his two young boys. Jacob never dreamed he would see Joseph again because he thought he had been killed. Yet he sees Joseph elevated to this important position in Egypt, and he can trace the way God had worked out the affairs of his life. Jacob had been in Egypt for seventeen years now. He is an old man and is dying, but he musters his strength to sit at the edge of his bed. Notice that his thinking goes back to the time God appeared to him at Luz, and he says to Joseph, "God Almighty appeared unto me at Luz in the land of Canaan, and blessed me." Jacob has come a long way. We see now the *faith* of Jacob. He is now trusting God. He is not bragging about himself. As a young man he was clever and could get what he wanted—or so he thought—and he would use any kind of method to get it. But now, as he looks back over his life, he remembers when God appeared to him at Bethel, both when he was leaving the land of

Canaan and when he was returning. He says, "God appeared to me there, and God blessed me."

Now we see the faith of Jacob—

And said unto me, Behold, I will make thee fruitful, and multiply thee, and I will make of thee a multitude of people; and will give this land to thy seed after thee for an everlasting possession [Gen. 48:4].

Let's pay especial attention to God's promise that Jacob mentions, which runs through the Old and New Testaments. He made the promise to the line of the patriarchs: Abraham, Isaac, and Jacob. There are three specific points to the covenant: (1) the *nation*, (2) the *land*, and (3) the *blessing*. But the two important things for Jacob right here are these: (1) "I will make thee fruitful, and multiply thee, and I will make of thee a multitude of people"; (2) "and will give this land to thy seed after thee for an everlasting possession."

The third part of the covenant is important for you and me. "In thee shall all the families of the earth be blessed."

The reason that you and I are sitting down with the Bible right now is because God has made good two-thirds of this promise which He covenanted thousands of years ago. The one-third is still not fulfilled. The Jews do not have the land of Israel yet. Oh, they have a little border of it, but it is certainly a bone of contention. When they get the land from the hand of God, they will live there in peace. Every man will be under his vine and his fig tree. They will own property and pay no taxes. That sounds like the millennium, doesn't it? Well, that is what it will be.

JACOB BLESSES
EPHRAIM AND MANASSEH

And now thy two sons, Ephraim and Manasseh, which were born unto thee in the land of Egypt before I came unto thee into Egypt, are mine; as Reuben and Simeon, they shall be mine.

And thy issue, which thou begettest after them, shall be thine, and shall be called after the name of their brethren in their inheritance [Gen. 48:5–6].

These two grandsons, the two sons of Joseph, will each become a tribe. One would conclude that there are thirteen tribes of Israel, since there are twelve sons, and now the two sons of Joseph are each to become a tribe. There was no tribe of Joseph, but there

were the tribes of Ephraim and Manasseh, and that makes thirteen in any man's mathematics. Yet the Bible counts twelve tribes. You see, the tribe of Levi was not counted as a tribe. They became the high priestly tribe and were not given any land or territory but were scattered as priests throughout the other tribes. So they were not counted as a tribe. You may consider that to be a rather devious way of counting, but I didn't do it; the Word of God counts it that way. That is the way God wanted it to be, and so that is the way God made it.

Ephraim and Manasseh are over seventeen-years-old because they were born before Jacob came to Egypt. They each become a tribe.

Notice now that Jacob's mind goes back to Rachel, his beloved, the mother of Joseph.

And as for me, when I came from Padan, Rachel died by me in the land of Canaan in the way, when yet there was but a little way to come unto Ephrath: and I buried her there in the way of Ephrath; the same is Beth-lehem [Gen. 48:7].

My friend, when you and I sing "O Little Town of Bethlehem," we think of the birth of Jesus, but if Jacob could hear us, he would think primarily of the death of his beloved and beautiful Rachel. Here he is on his deathbed, and his thoughts go back to the place where he buried her. That was his heartbreak.

And Israel beheld Joseph's sons, and said, Who are these?

And Joseph said unto his father, They are my sons, whom God hath given me in this place. And he said, Bring them, I pray thee, unto me, and I will bless them [Gen. 48:8–9]

Have you noticed that both Isaac and Jacob had trouble seeing when they got old? The brightness of the sun may have something to do with it. Even today there is a lot of eye disease in the Mideast countries. When I was in the Arab countries, I noticed a great many old people who seemed to have difficulty getting around. They weren't entirely blind, but they certainly couldn't see very well. So we notice here that Jacob didn't recognize the boys.

Now the eyes of Israel were dim for age, so that he could not see. And he brought them near unto him; and he kissed them, and embraced them [Gen. 48:10].

Perhaps the fellows are a little embarrassed by their grandfather's show of affection for them.

And Israel said unto Joseph, I had not thought to see thy face: and, lo, God hath shewed me also thy seed.

And Joseph brought them out from between his knees, and he bowed himself with his face to the earth [Gen. 48:11–12].

It seems that the two boys tried to get away from their grandfather when he lavished his affection upon them.

And Joseph took them both, Ephraim in his right hand toward Israel's left hand, and Manasseh in his left hand toward Israel's right hand, and brought them near unto him [Gen. 48:13].

Joseph is bringing the boys to their grandfather that he might bless them. The one who would stand before Israel at his right hand would be the one with priority.

And Israel stretched out his right hand, and laid it upon Ephraim's head, who was the younger, and his left hand upon Manasseh's head, guiding his hands wittingly; for Manasseh was the firstborn [Gen. 48:14].

Ephraim is to become the leader above Manasseh. Later on we will see that the tribe of Manasseh marched under the banner of the tribe of Ephraim in the wilderness march, as described in Numbers. Joshua came out of the tribe of Ephraim, by the way, and there were many great men from that tribe. It became the tribe with priority—there is no question about that.

Do you see what happened here? Even though Jacob couldn't see too well, he could tell what Joseph was doing. Joseph was pushing the older son to the position of Jacob's right hand and the younger son toward the left hand. So what did old Jacob do? Well, he just switched hands. He crossed his hands and put his right hand on the younger son.

Why did he do this? There is no doubt that he had tender affection for both boys. They were the sons of his favorite son Joseph. He knowingly gives the blessing to the younger, and I think one reason may have been that he was the younger and he had received the blessing. So he passes the blessing on to the younger son here.

This is an interesting principle that runs all the way through the Scriptures. For instance, in the choice of David, David was the youngest of the sons of Jesse. Why did God choose him? God is illustrating for you and me a great spiritual truth. God does not accept primogeniture—that is, natural birth. Never will He accept it. There must be the new birth. Therefore, God does not pay attention to our customs. We say that the oldest boy has the responsibility in a family. Well, the oldest boy is not the one whom God always chooses. That is, God does not choose the natural man—He chooses no man because of his natural ability. How we need to learn this truth in our day! Now don't misunderstand me. God can use talent, but it must be dedicated to Him! If it took talent alone to bring about revival, we would have had revival in California years ago. We have Christian talent all around, but we don't have revival. Why not? Because the talent is not dedicated to God. I tell you, my friend, it must be *yielded* to Him to be used of Him.

And old Jacob crossed his hands as he laid them on the heads of his grandsons so that he gave the younger boy the priority.

And he blessed Joseph, and said, God, before whom my fathers Abraham and Isaac did walk, the God which fed me all my life long unto this day [Gen. 48:15].

"The *God* which *fed* me *all my life long* unto this day." He reaches spiritual heights here, my friend.

The Angel which redeemed me from all evil, bless the lads; and let my name be named on them, and the name of my fathers Abraham and Isaac; and let them grow into a multitude in the midst of the earth [Gen. 48:16].

"The Angel which redeemed me from all evil, bless the lads." He has nothing to boast about except a wonderful Redeemer. And they did "grow into a multitude in the midst of the earth" just as he said.

And when Joseph saw that his father laid his right hand upon the head of Ephraim, it displeased him; and he held up his father's hand, to remove it from Ephraim's head unto Manasseh's head. And Joseph said unto his father, Not so, my father: for this is the firstborn; put thy right hand upon his head [Gen. 48:17–18].

Watch old Jacob's reaction—

And his father refused, and said, I know it, my son, I know it; he also shall become a people, and he also shall be great: but truly his younger brother

shall be greater than he, and his seed shall become a multitude of nations [Gen. 48:19].

"His seed shall become a multitude of nations"—that's important to see.

Joseph had better accept this because he is not the oldest, either. He happens to be one of the youngest, and yet the blessing is given to *his* sons.

And he blessed them that day, saying, In thee shall Israel bless, saying, God make thee as Ephraim and as Manasseh: and he set Ephraim before Manasseh.

And Israel said unto Joseph, Behold, I die: but God shall be with you, and bring you again unto the land of your fathers [Gen. 48:20–21].

Notice Jacob's *faith* in God.

Moreover I have given to thee one portion above thy brethren, which I took out of the hand of the Amorite with my sword and with my bow [Gen. 48:22].

That is, Joseph, through his *two* sons, would have a greater inheritance than the other brothers would have.

This apparently was a personal gift made by Jacob to Joseph (see John 4:5). It was a ridge near Sychar where Joseph was buried. It compensated for the fact that two tribes came from Joseph and they needed more territory. It was a parcel of land which Jacob first bought from the Amorite, then later they retook it by force. Jacob returned the compliment, and by force he reclaimed it. It has been an area of controversy up to the present time. It is here that modern Israel wants to build on the west bank.

CHAPTER 49

THEME: *Jacob's deathbed blessing and prophecy; final words and death of Jacob*

This is another remarkable chapter, as it is the deathbed scene of old Jacob. In fact, in the previous chapter we saw him on that deathbed as he strengthened himself, sat upon the bed, and blessed the sons of Joseph.

After that interview, the rest of Jacob's sons came in, so that around him now are all twelve of his sons. He has a farewell message for each of them. He begins with the eldest and goes right down the list. Anything that a man says on his deathbed is important because generally, if he ever tells the truth, he tells it on his deathbed. This deathbed message is dramatic because it is prophetic. It tells what will happen to the twelve sons of Jacob when they become tribes. What was prophetic then has now become largely historical.

This is our final opportunity to see another evidence of faith in the life of Jacob. He spoke to his boys who were to become the twelve tribes in the nation of Israel and would be dwelling in the land of Canaan. What faith! Remember that the Canaanite was then in the land and that Jacob's family was favorably situated in Egypt.

JACOB'S DEATHBED BLESSING AND PROPHECY

And Jacob called unto his sons, and said, Gather yourselves together, that I may tell you that which shall befall you in the last days [Gen. 49:1].

We come here to an important expression. We will find that there are certain expressions which the Bible uses over and over again. One of those expressions is right here: "in the last days." The last days of the nation Israel will be different from the last days of the church. There is a very sharp dispensational distinction which needs to be made. Now he is talking about the last days of the nation Israel and what is going to happen then to the twelve tribes which will develop from his sons and will form the nation.

A friend of mine in seminary (a very intelligent young man who did a great deal of studying) wrote his thesis on the prophecies concerning the twelve sons of Jacob and the tribes that came from them. I enjoyed talking with him because he always had something new to offer. I came to appreciate at that time the marvelous fulfillment there has been of these prophecies to the tribes, especially those given by Moses in Deuteronomy 33.

Many folk talk about the fact that certain prophecies concerning the nation Israel have been fulfilled, and that is true. But we can narrow it down further by dividing Israel into twelve parts and recognizing that God has had something to say concerning each of the twelve. Not only have His prophecies concerning the nation been fulfilled, but prophecies concerning each tribe have been fulfilled. My friend, that makes it remarkable indeed. In the chapter before us we will see the prophecies of what will befall each tribe in the "last days." While some of them have been fulfilled already, most of them wait final fulfillment. I will be hitting only the highlights, but if you want a more comprehensive study, I recommend two sources listed in the bibliography at the end of this book: *Paradise to Prison: Studies in Genesis* by Davis, and *The Genesis Record* by Morris.

Gather yourselves together, and hear, ye sons of Jacob; and hearken unto Israel your father [Gen. 49:2].

Here now is the old man sitting up in bed. I've seen pictures of him stretched out in bed looking like he wouldn't be able to raise his head. But that is not true! He was leaning on his staff, as we learn in Hebrews 11:21. Frankly, old Jacob had been on the go all of his life, and he wanted to keep going. Death is really an embarrassment. It comes at a most inconvenient time, a time when we want to keep going down here. (I have made appointments two years ahead, and I don't know whether I'll fulfill them or not. I accept them with one stipulation: "provided I'm alive.") Jacob found that he couldn't keep going. He was leaning on his staff. He wanted to keep going, but he couldn't. What a remarkable man he was in many ways.

Reuben, thou art my firstborn, my might, and the beginning of my strength, the excellency of dignity, and the excellency of power:

Unstable as water, thou shalt not excel; because thou wentest up to thy father's bed; then defiledst thou it: he went up to my couch [Gen. 49:3–4].

These patriarchs recognized the great subject of heredity that is of so much concern today. Like father, like son. Jacob recognizes that and

sees that this boy Reuben is a great deal like himself. "Unstable as water" could have described Jacob in his early years. It was true of his oldest son, also. "Thou shalt not excel." Reuben never did. He never did win a blue ribbon. He won a couple of red ribbons and some white ribbons, but he was never in first place.

There are a lot of folk like that today. They are satisfied and do not wish to excel. I have a preacher friend who is a wonderful man. He could have been an outstanding writer, but he didn't want to be. I think he wrote two little pamphlets. He could have been a great Bible teacher, but he didn't want to be. He just did what he wanted to do. He was satisfied with the red ribbon and never won a blue ribbon.

The story about Reuben which Jacob mentions here is a sordid story. I didn't dwell on it when we went through Genesis because I see no reason to dwell on that. Contemporary literature, plays, movies, and television give us enough of the sordid to make us sick of it. God does not intend for us to dwell on man's sins. In fact, He gives us these instructions: "Finally, brethren, whatsoever things are true, whatsoever things are honest, whatsoever things are just, whatsoever things are pure, whatsoever things are lovely, whatsoever things are of good report; if there be any virtue, and if there be any praise, think on these things" (Phil. 4:8). But God records human sins to that we may have an accurate picture of the human family.

The next two boys are classed together. They were full brothers, sons of Leah.

Simeon and Levi are brethren; instruments of cruelty are in their habitations [Gen. 49:5].

You remember how they went to Shalem, a city of Shechem, and killed all the inhabitants of the city because one man was guilty of raping their own sister. They took their revenge on the whole town! They should not have done that, of course, and Jacob reminds them of this.

O my soul, come not thou into their secret; unto their assembly, mine honour, be not thou united; for in their anger they slew a man, and in their selfwill they digged down a wall.

Cursed be their anger, for it was fierce; and their wrath, for it was cruel: I will divide them in Jacob, and scatter them in Israel [Gen. 49:6–7].

In Levi, we see an exhibition of the marvelous grace of God. It is true that they were scattered in Israel, but this was because they were made the priestly tribe. It was the grace of God that could take a cruel person like Levi and make him the head of the priestly tribe.

It is the grace of God that has transformed us sinners into a kingdom of priests, my friend. All believers are priests today. Among them are converted drunkards, converted harlots, converted murderers. I have had several of them in the churches where I have served. How did they become priests in the kingdom of God? Just as we all did—by the marvelous grace of God. "Forasmuch as ye know that ye were not redeemed with corruptible things, as silver and gold, from your vain conversation received by tradition from your fathers; But with the precious blood of Christ, as of a lamb without blemish and without spot" (1 Pet. 1:18–19). Then he goes on in 1 Peter 2:5 to say, "Ye also, as living stones, are built up a spiritual house, an holy priesthood, to offer up spiritual sacrifices, acceptable to God by Jesus Christ." Who is he talking about? Those who have been redeemed by the precious blood of Christ!

Reuben lost first place, and Simeon and Levi have also lost first place. The king will not come from any of these tribes. There is another boy who was also a sinner. We will see what the grace of God did for him:

Judah, thou art he whom thy brethren shall praise: thy hand shall be in the neck of thine enemies; thy father's children shall bow down before thee [Gen. 49:8].

"Thy father's children shall bow down before thee." Why? Because the Lord Jesus Christ came from the line of Judah, and it is before Him that all will bow.

Judah is a lion's whelp: from the prey, my son, thou art gone up: he stooped down, he couched as a lion, and as an old lion; who shall rouse him up? [Gen. 49:9].

Here is one of the most remarkable prophecies of Scripture—

The sceptre shall not depart from Judah, nor a lawgiver from between his feet, until Shiloh come; and unto him shall the gathering of the people be [Gen. 49:10].

"Until Shiloh come"—Shiloh is the ruler.

This is one of the more remarkable prophecies in all the Word of God. Already we have

been told that there will be a seed of the woman. That was the first prophecy of Christ: "And I will put enmity between thee and the woman, and between thy seed and her seed; it shall bruise thy head, and thou shalt bruise his heel" (Gen. 3:15). The "seed" of the woman is the One who will do the bruising of the serpent's head. He will be the One to get the victory. This first prophecy was in Genesis; then that Seed was confirmed to Abraham, to Isaac, and to Jacob. Now it is confirmed to Judah—out of Judah's line He is coming. Also, the word *shiloh* means "rest and tranquility." Christ is the One who will bring rest. Remember that when the Lord Jesus walked here on earth, He turned from those who had rejected Him, and He said to the populace, "Come unto me, all ye that labor and are heavy laden, and I will rest you" (Matt. 11:28). That is Shiloh—Shiloh had come.

Not only is Christ Shiloh, but also He is the One who will hold the sceptre. The sceptre of this universe will be held in nail-pierced hands. In the last part of verse 24 of this chapter we read that from God will come the *Shepherd*, the *Stone* of Israel. So this Shiloh is also a shepherd and a stone. When we get to Numbers 24:17 we will find that a Star is prophesied. Think of all that the coming of Christ means. He is the *Seed* promised to the woman and to the patriarchs. He is the *Shiloh* who brings rest. He is the *King* who holds the sceptre. He is the *Shepherd* who gave His life, and He is the chief *Shepherd* who is coming someday. He is the *Stone* that the builders disallowed but who is now become the headstone of the corner. He is the *Star*, the bright and morning Star for His church. This is the line that went from Adam to Seth (after Abel was murdered). From Seth it went through Noah to Shem and to Abraham, Isaac, and Jacob, and now to Judah. Friend, don't miss this wonderful fact that God is moving according to a pattern and a program here. This is very important for us to see.

Binding his foal unto the vine, and his ass's colt unto the choice vine; he washed his garments in wine, and his clothes in the blood of grapes:

His eyes shall be red with wine, and his teeth white with milk [Gen. 49:11–12].

Who is this talking about? It is Christ who came riding into Jerusalem on a little donkey, offering Himself as the Messiah, the King, and the Savior. "He washed his garments in wine"—what kind of wine? Blood, His own blood. But when Christ comes the next time, His garments will be red. The question is asked, "Wherefore art thou red in thine apparel, and thy garments like him that treadeth in the winevat?" (Isa. 63:2). At this time it will not be His own blood but the blood of His enemies. This predicts Christ's second coming when He returns in judgment.

The prophecy given to Judah is one of the most remarkable prophecies in the Scriptures.

Zebulun shall dwell at the haven of the sea; and he shall be for an haven of ships; and his border shall be unto Zidon [Gen. 49:13].

Zebulun was the tribe which lived along the coast up in the northern part of the land.

Issachar is a strong ass couching down between two burdens:

And he saw that rest was good, and the land that it was pleasant; and bowed his shoulder to bear, and became a servant unto tribute [Gen. 49:14–15].

Issachar was also finally located way up in the northern part of the land. They were the ones who did a great deal of the work that constituted the backbone of the nation. They were the workers, and that is the thought here. We hear a great deal about the silent majority today, that is, the average person like you and me. We don't get on television. It is the unusual, often the peculiar, people whom we see on television and whom people consider to be great. People try to convince us that these are the kind of folk who are the important people. But, my friend, they are not the backbone of this nation, or of any nation. The little tribes, like Zebulun and Issachar, which we tend to pass over were really the backbone of the nation Israel when they got settled in the Promised Land.

Dan shall judge his people, as one of the tribes of Israel.

Dan shall be a serpent by the way, an adder in the path, that biteth the horse heels, so that his rider shall fall backward.

I have waited for thy salvation, O LORD [Gen. 49:16–18].

Dan is going to need the salvation of the Lord because Dan will be one of the tribes which actually will lead in rebellion. We will see that when we get on in our study through Scripture.

Gad, a troop shall overcome him: but he shall overcome at the last [Gen. 49:19].

This was another tribe that settled up in the northern part of the country. Actually, Dan was the most northern so that when the extent of the land of Israel is described, it is expressed as "from Dan to Beer-sheba."

Out of Asher his bread shall be fat, and he shall yield royal dainties.

Naphtali is a hind let loose: he giveth goodly words [Gen. 49:20–21].

As I mentioned earlier, a fellow student in seminary wrote his thesis on the fulfillment of each of these prophecies concerning the twelve sons of Jacob. I have not made a personal study of this, but if you are a student, you would find such a research very rewarding. Throughout the remainder of the Bible, every person with whom it deals personally comes from one of the tribes of Israel.

Joseph is a fruitful bough, even a fruitful bough by a well; whose branches run over the wall [Gen. 49:22].

Joseph had left the land of Canaan and had gone down into Egypt, but he was still a witness for God there. Later, his sons, Ephraim and Manasseh, would be put in the territory which was Samaria later in history. That was called Gentile territory in Christ's day. It was a great place to witness, and the gospel did go into that area. Our Lord Himself ministered there. In John 4 we have the record of His witness to the Samaritan people, beginning with a woman at a well.

The archers have sorely grieved him, and shot at him, and hated him:

But his bow abode in strength, and the arms of his hands were made strong by the hands of the mighty God of Jacob; (from thence is the shepherd, the stone of Israel:)

Even by the God of thy father, who shall help thee; and by the Almighty, who shall bless thee with blessings of heaven above, blessings of the deep that lieth under, blessings of the breasts, and of the womb [Gen. 49:23–25].

The two tribes that came from Joseph, Ephraim, and Manasseh, became very prominent and important tribes—so much so that out of them came the *division* of the kingdom. They were that powerful.

The blessings of thy father have pre-vailed above the blessings of my pro-genitors unto the utmost bound of the everlasting hills: they shall be on the head of Joseph, and on the crown of the head of him that was separate from his brethren [Gen. 49:26].

Note that Jacob is trying to tie Joseph, and the two tribes which will come from him, back to the God of Israel, the Creator, the Redeemer. Why? Well, these tribes, especially Ephraim, led Israel into idolatry. Jeroboam, who led in the rebellion and placed the two golden calves at Israel's borders, came from the tribe of Ephraim. So here on his deathbed, Jacob calls them back, back to the God of his fathers.

Benjamin shall ravin as a wolf: in the morning he shall devour the prey, and at night he shall divide the spoil [Gen. 49:27].

This is a strange prophecy concerning Ben-jamin. Benjamin was closely identified with Judah, so much so that Benjamin went with the tribe of Judah at the division of the king-dom. The tribe of Benjamin was the only one that stayed with the house of David.

FINAL WORDS AND DEATH OF JACOB

And he charged them, and said unto them, I am to be gathered unto my peo-ple: bury me with my fathers in the cave that is in the field of Ephron the Hittite [Gen. 49:29].

We see that death to Jacob was not the end of it all. He was going to be with his people. He wanted his body to be buried in the cave that Abraham had bought and paid for. He wanted to make sure that he stayed in that land until the day when he would be raised from the dead to live in that land.

In the cave that is in the field of Mach-pelah, which is before Mamre, in the land of Canaan, which Abraham bought with the field of Ephron the Hittite for a possession of a buryingplace [Gen. 49:30].

We can see how much this man knew of his own family history. I don't imagine that he was carrying with him a written record at this time, yet he carried this information in his mind.

There they buried Abraham and Sarah his wife; there they buried Isaac and Rebekah his wife; and there I buried Leah [Gen. 49:31].

It is not so much that he was interested in being buried by Leah (after all, Rachel was buried up in Beth-lehem), but he wants to be buried where he will be raised from the dead at the resurrection so he will be right there when God fulfills His promises to the nation Israel.

The purchase of the field and of the cave that is therein was from the children of Heth.

And when Jacob had made an end of commanding his sons, he gathered up his feet into the bed, and yielded up the ghost, and was gathered unto his people [Gen. 49:32–33].

It is interesting to see that up to the very last Jacob kept his feet on the floor. He started out in life as a man of the flesh. He took hold of his brother's heel at birth which was why he was called *Jacob*, "the supplanter." He lived up to that name which was certainly characteristic of him. He held on to everything that he could find, and he was always trying to be first. He started out on all fours, and he took what he wanted by any method. As a young man he walked on his own two feet in his own strength and ability. He depended on his own clever-ness and ingenuity. He thought he could take care of himself and did not need God. He was self-sufficient, self-opinionated, self-assertive, aggressive, contemptible, and despicable.

At Peniel God crippled him. God had to "break" him to get him, and I think God was prepared to break his neck! After that, he went through life limping. He had to go on three legs, using a staff or walking stick, be-cause he could no longer walk by himself. Here, before his death, he is sitting on the bed, leaning on his staff. Now the time has come. He pulls his feet up into the bed, puts down the staff, and lies down to die. This is Jacob. He has walked a long way through life. He ends in a final act of faith, looking forward to the day when he would be raised from the dead in the land, according to the promise of God.

"These all died in faith, not having received the promises, but having seen them afar off, and were persuaded of them, and embraced them, and confessed that they were strangers and pilgrims on the earth" (Heb. 11:13).

CHAPTER 50

THEME: Burial of Jacob in Canaan; Joseph allays the fears of his brethren; death and burial of Joseph in Egypt

This chapter tells of the burial of Jacob in Canaan and the death and burial of Joseph in Egypt. There is, therefore, a touch of sadness about this last chapter of Genesis. We have already called attention to the emphasis put upon death in the Book of Genesis. God had told Adam, ". . . For in the day that thou eatest thereof thou shalt surely die" (Gen. 2:17). Paul wrote later, ". . . so death passed upon all men, for that all have sinned" (Rom. 5:12). The Book of Genesis is a full example of the fact of sin and the reality of death. It opens with God and man in the Garden of Eden and ends in a coffin in Egypt. This book recounts the entrance of sin into the human family but also relates the faithfulness of God in providing a way of life for man.

BURIAL OF JACOB IN CANAAN

And Joseph fell upon his father's face, and wept upon him, and kissed him [Gen. 50:1].

Naturally, he sorrowed. He loved his father.

And Joseph commanded his servants the physicians to embalm his father: and the physicians embalmed Israel [Gen. 50:2].

We know that the Egyptians were quite expert at this sort of thing. We hear of the mummies of Egypt. They had a method of preserving bodies that we have not learned yet today. So Joseph called in the physicians to embalm his father. We don't laugh at a funeral, but I can't help but smile when I think of their making old Jacob up into a mummy, and I am of the opinion that his mummy is in Hebron today.

Remember, it had been his request to be taken and buried in the cave of Machpelah because his hope is an earthly hope. When he is raised from the dead, he will be there in the land with the nation Israel. The hope of the believer today, the member of the church of our Lord Jesus Christ, is to be caught up with the Lord in the air and to go to a place called the New Jerusalem out in space. There are two different hopes, and they are both glorious.

And forty days were fulfilled for him; for so are fulfilled the days of those which are embalmed: and the Egyptians mourned for him threescore and ten days [Gen. 50:3].

It took them forty days to embalm. Evidently there were several processes involved. And we note that the Egyptians mourned for him. I don't think this was professional mourning. I think he had become a real saint in the land of Egypt and was probably respected as the father of Joseph. Joseph was the deliverer, but I believe that his father Jacob was at this time a real saint of God.

And when the days of his mourning were past, Joseph spake unto the house of Pharaoh, saying, If now I have found grace in your eyes, speak, I pray you, in the ears of Pharaoh, saying,

My father made me swear, saying, Lo, I die: in my grave which I have digged for me in the land of Canaan, there shalt thou bury me. Now therefore let me go up, I pray thee, and bury my father, and I will come again.

And Pharaoh said, Go up, and bury thy father, according as he made thee swear.

And Joseph went up to bury his father: and with him went up all the servants of Pharaoh, the elders of his house, and all the elders of the land of Egypt [Gen. 50:4–7].

You can see how this man was greatly respected, loved, and honored in the land of Egypt. This is probably the longest funeral procession that the world has ever seen. It went all the way from Egypt to Hebron in Canaan.

And all the house of Joseph, and his brethren, and his father's house: only their little ones, and their flocks, and their herds, they left in the land of Goshen [Gen. 50:8].

One wonders whether Pharaoh required that they leave their little ones and their flocks so that he could be sure they would come back. Pharaoh didn't want to lose Joseph because he still needed him.

And there went up with him both chariots and horsemen: and it was a very great company.

And they came to the threshingfloor of Atad, which is beyond Jordan, and there they mourned with a great and very sore lamentation: and he made a mourning for his father seven days.

And when the inhabitants of the land, the Canaanites, saw the mourning in the floor of Atad, they said, This is a grievous mourning to the Egyptians: wherefore the name of it was called Abel-mizraim, which is beyond Jordan.

And his sons did unto him according as he commanded them:

For his sons carried him into the land of Canaan, and buried him in the cave of the field of Machpelah, which Abraham bought with the field for a possession of a buryingplace of Ephron the Hittite, before Mamre [Gen. 50:9–13].

You may wonder why Jacob wasn't buried with Rachel in Beth-lehem, which was probably not more than twenty miles farther north. I think the reason is stated here. Abraham had bought this cave, and Jacob wanted to be buried with his fathers in a place that was bought and paid for to make sure that he would stay in the land. So he was buried with the other patriarchs. They all had the same hope of resurrection.

JOSEPH ALLAYS THE FEARS OF HIS BRETHREN

And Joseph returned into Egypt, he, and his brethren, and all that went up with him to bury his father, after he had buried his father.

And when Joseph's brethren saw that their father was dead, they said, Joseph will peradventure hate us, and will certainly requite us all the evil which we did unto him.

And they sent a messenger unto Joseph, saying, Thy father did command before he died, saying,

So shall ye say unto Joseph, Forgive, I pray thee now, the trespass of thy brethren, and their sin; for they did unto thee evil: and now, we pray thee, forgive the trespass of the servants of the God of thy father. And Joseph wept when they spake unto him [Gen. 50:14–17].

E vidently the brothers had gone to Jacob before he died and had expressed their fears regarding what would happen to them after he was gone. They were afraid that Joseph would turn on them and be against them once the father was gone. So Jacob had given them a message to tell to Joseph, and he was sure that Joseph would not persecute them or attempt to get even with them. When the brothers do come to Joseph with this confession, Joseph breaks into weeping because of it. Now they are repenting because of their sin.

And his brethren also went and fell down before his face; and they said, Behold, we be thy servants [Gen. 50:18].

You see, the prophecy of their falling down before him has repeatedly come true.

And Joseph said unto them, Fear not: for am I in the place of God? [Gen. 50:19].

Joseph gives God the glory in every case.

Now here is a remarkable verse of Scripture—

But as for you, ye thought evil against me; but God meant it unto good, to bring to pass, as it is this day, to save much people alive [Gen. 50:20].

Friend, God has a far-off purpose that you and I do not see. I must confess how human *I* am about this because I can't see any further than my nose when trouble comes to me, and I ask, "Why does God permit this to happen?" We need to remember that He has a good purpose in view. He is not going to let anything happen to you unless it will accomplish a good purpose in your life.

Now listen to Joseph—

Now therefore fear ye not: I will nourish you, and your little ones. And he comforted them, and spake kindly unto them.

And Joseph dwelt in Egypt, he, and his father's house: and Joseph lived an hundred and ten years.

And Joseph saw Ephraim's children of the third generation: the children also of Machir the son of Manasseh were brought up upon Joseph's knees [Gen. 50:21–23].

I take this to mean that Joseph was a great-great-grandfather.

DEATH AND BURIAL OF JOSEPH IN EGYPT

And Joseph said unto his brethren, I die: and God will surely visit you, and bring you out of this land unto the land which he sware to Abraham, to Isaac, and to Jacob.

And Joseph took an oath of the children of Israel, saying, God will surely visit you, and ye shall carry up my bones from hence.

So Joseph died, being an hundred and ten years old: and they embalmed him, and he was put in a coffin in Egypt [Gen. 50:24–26].

This is the way the Book of Genesis ends. It began with God creating the heaven and the earth, and it ends with a coffin in Egypt. What had happened to the human family? Sin had intruded into the creation of God.

Why was not Joseph taken up to Canaan and buried there at this time? I think it is obvious that Joseph was a hero in the land of Egypt and his family would not have been permitted to remove his body from Egypt at that time. I think he was one of the outstanding patriots whom the Egyptians reverenced. Probably they had a monument raised at his grave.

But Joseph says to his own people, "When you go back to Canaan, don't leave my bones down here!" In Joseph we see the same hope that we saw in Jacob; that is, a confidence that God would give them the land of Canaan as an eternal possession. And they wanted to be raised from the dead in their own land. Joseph believed that God would raise up His earthly people to inherit the land of promise.

The Book of Hebrews mentions this as the crowning act of faith in the life of Joseph. "By faith Joseph, when he died, made mention of the departing of the children of Israel; and gave commandment concerning his bones" (Heb. 11:22).

In Exodus 13 we will see how wonderfully God honored Joseph and answered his request. Moses and the children of Israel took the bones of Joseph with them when they left Egypt.

BIBLIOGRAPHY

Barnhouse, Donald Grey. *Genesis: A Devotional Exposition*. Grand Rapids, Michigan: Zondervan Publishing House, 1973.

Borland, James A. *Christ in the Old Testament*. Chicago, Illinois: Moody Press, 1978.

Davis, John J. *Paradise to Prison: Studies in Genesis*. Grand Rapids, Michigan: Baker Book House, 1975.

De Haan, M. R. *Genesis and Evolution*. Grand Rapids, Michigan: Zondervan Publishing House, 1962.

De Haan, M. R. *The Days of Noah*. Grand Rapids, Michigan: Zondervan Publishing House, 1962.

Jensen, Irving L. *Genesis—A Self-Study Guide*. Chicago, Illinois: Moody Press, 1967.

Mackintosh, C. H. *Genesis to Deuteronomy*. Neptune, New Jersey: Loizeaux Brothers, 1972.

Meyer, F. B. *Abraham: The Obedience of Faith*. Fort Washington, Pennsylvania: Christian Literature Crusade, n.d.

Meyer, F. B. *Israel: A Prince With God*. Fort Washington, Pennsylvania: Christian Literature Crusade, n.d.

Meyer, F. B. *Joseph: Beloved—Hated—Exalted*. Fort Washington, Pennsylvania: Christian Literature Crusade, n.d.

Morgan, G. Campbell. *The Unfolding Message of the Bible*. Old Tappan, New Jersey: Fleming H. Revell Company, n.d.

Morris, Henry M. *The Genesis Record: A Scientific and Devotional Commentary*. Grand Rapids, Michigan: Baker Book House, 1976.

Morris, Henry M. and Whitcomb, John C., Jr. *The Genesis Flood*. Grand Rapids, Michigan: Baker Book House, 1961.

Pink, Arthur W. *Gleanings in Genesis*. Chicago, Illinois: Moody Press, 1922.

Stigers, Harold. *A Commentary on Genesis*. Grand Rapids, Michigan: Zondervan Publishing House, 1975.

Thomas, W. H. Griffith. *Genesis: A Devotional Commentary*. Grand Rapids, Michigan: Eerdmans Publishing Company, 1946.

Unger, Merrill F. *Unger's Bible Commentary*, Vol. I. Chicago, Illinois: Moody Press, 1980.

Vos, Howard F. *Beginnings in the Old Testament*. Chicago, Illinois: Moody Press, 1975.

Wood, Leon J. *Genesis: A Study Guide Commentary*. Grand Rapids, Michigan: Zondervan Publishing House, 1975.

For additional material on creation, the Flood, and science, write to:

The Institute for Creation Research
2100 Greenfield
El Cahon, California 92021
Dr. Henry M. Morris, Director

The Book of
EXODUS
INTRODUCTION

Exodus continues the account which was begun in Genesis, although there was a lapse of at least 3½ centuries. Genesis 15:13 says that the seed of Abraham would spend 400 years in Egypt. Exodus 12:40 says that it was 430 years, and Galatians 3:16–17 confirms it. It was 430 years from the call of Abraham, and 400 years from the time that God told Abraham.

Exodus means "the way out" and tells the story of redemption by blood and by power. The message of Exodus is stated in Hebrews 11:23-29, which says: "By faith Moses, when he was born, was hid three months of his parents, because they saw he was a proper child; and they were not afraid of the king's commandment. By faith Moses, when he was come to years, refused to be called the son of Pharaoh's daughter; choosing rather to suffer affliction with the people of God, than to enjoy the pleasures of sin for a season; esteeming the reproach of Christ greater riches than the treasures in Egypt: for he had respect unto the recompense of the reward. By faith he forsook Egypt, not fearing the wrath of the king: for he endured, as seeing him who is invisible. Through faith he kept the passover, and the sprinkling of blood, lest he that destroyed the firstborn should touch them. By faith they passed through the Red sea as by dry land: which the Egyptians assaying to do were drowned."

The word which opens Exodus is a conjunction that is better translated *and* rather than *now*. Exodus has been called the sequel to Genesis. Dr. G. Campbell Morgan wrote, "In the Book of Exodus nothing is commenced, nothing is finished."

Genesis 46:27 tells us that seventy souls of Jacob entered Egypt. It is conservatively estimated that 2,100,000 left Egypt at the time of the Exodus. Although it is impossible to be certain about dates in this early period, it would seem that Joseph entered Egypt under the Hyksos or shepherd kings who were Semitic conquerors, and were related to Abraham, Isaac, and Jacob. Actually the Israelites may have been their only friends, as they were hated by Egyptians. Finally they were driven out by a native Egyptian dynasty which was understandably hostile to foreigners. In this line was the Pharaoh of the oppression and the one "who knew not Joseph."

Moses figures prominently in the book of Exodus. He is the author of the Pentateuch which includes the first five books of the Old Testament—Genesis, Exodus, Leviticus, Numbers, and Deuteronomy. In the Book of Exodus, Moses' life is divided into three forty-year periods:

1. Forty years in Pharaoh's palace in Egypt,
2. Forty years in the desert in Midian,
3. Forty years in the wilderness as leader of Israel.

Moses' training in Egypt, evidently in the Temple of the Sun, did not prepare him to follow God in leading Israel out of Egypt. God trained him in the desert for forty years to reveal to him that he could *not* deliver Israel alone. God gave Moses a B.D. (Backside of the Desert) degree.

It should be noted that after God prepared Moses to deliver his people, He sent him back to Egypt after forty years. Moses is to assemble elders of Israel and go to Pharaoh. Pharaoh will refuse to let Israel go. His refusal will open the contest between God and the gods of Egypt. Egypt was dominated by idolatry—"gods many and lords many." There were thousands of temples and millions of idols. Behind idolatry was Satan. There was *power* in the religion of Egypt—"Now as Jannes and Jambres withstood Moses, so do these also resist the truth: men of corrupt minds, reprobate concerning the faith" (2 Tim. 3:8). Pharaoh asked, ". . . Who is the LORD, that I should obey his voice to let Israel go? I know not the LORD, neither will I let Israel go" (Exod. 5:2). God introduced Himself. Pharaoh got acquainted with God and acknowledged Him as God. "And Pharaoh sent, and called for Moses and Aaron, and said unto them, I have sinned this time: the LORD is righteous, and I and my people are wicked" (Exod. 9:27). "Then Pharaoh called for Moses and Aaron in haste; and he said, I have sinned against the LORD your God, and against you" (Exod. 10:16).

A question arises from this episode: Why the plagues? They were God's battle with the gods of Egypt. Each plague was directed against a particular god in Egypt. "For I will pass through the land of Egypt this night, and will smite all the firstborn in the land of Egypt, both man and beast; and against all the gods of Egypt I will execute judgment: I am the LORD" (Exod. 12:12). God wanted to reveal to His own people that He, the LORD, was far greater than any god of Egypt and that He had power to deliver them.

OUTLINE

I. A Deliverer, Chapters 1–11
A. Slavery of Israel in Egypt, Chapter 1
B. Birth of Moses—First Forty Years in Pharaoh's Palace, Chapter 2
C. Call of Moses—Second Forty Years in Midian, Chapter 3
   (Incident of burning bush)
D. Return of Moses to Egypt—Announcement of Deliverance to Israel, Chapter 4
E. Contest with Pharaoh, Chapters 5–11
   (9 plagues against idolatry of Egypt, battle of the gods)

II. Deliverance (by Blood and Power), Chapters 12–14
A. Institution of Passover—Tenth Plague, Death of Firstborn (Blood), Chapter 12
B. Crossing Red Sea—Destruction of Army of Egypt (Power), Chapters 13–14

III. Marching to Mount Sinai (Spiritual Education), Chapters 15–18
   (7 experiences correspond to Christian experience)
A. Song of Redeemed—Wilderness of Shur, Chapter 15:1–22
   (No bed of roses after redemption)
B. Marah, Bitter Water Sweetened by Tree, Chapter 15:23–26
   (Cross sweetens bitter experiences of life)
C. Elim (Fruitful Christian Experience), Chapter 15:27
D. Wilderness of Sin—Manna and Quail, Chapter 16
   (Christ is the Bread of life.)
E. Smitten Rock ("That Rock was Christ"), Chapter 17:1–7
F. Amalek (the Flesh), 17:8–16
   (Victory on the hill top, Deut. 25:17–18)
G. Jethro, Priest of Midian, Chapter 18
   (Worldly wisdom in contrast to revelation)

IV. The Law (Condemnation), Chapters 19–24
A. Arrival at Mount Sinai—Agreement to Accept the Law, Chapter 19
B. Ten Commandments—Order for the Altar, Chapter 20
C. Social Legislation, Chapters 21–24

V. Blueprint and Construction of Tabernacle, Chapters 25–40
   (A pattern and picture of Christ)
A. Blueprint for Tabernacle—Pattern of Garments for High Priest, Chapters 25–30
B. Workmen for Tabernacle—Sabbath a Sign to Israel, Chapter 31
C. Golden Calf—Broken Law—Moses' Intercession Second Tables of the Law, Chapters 32–35
D. Construction of Tabernacle, Chapters 36–39
E. Tabernacle Erected—Filled with Glory of the Lord, Chapter 40
   (Exodus begins in gloom and ends in glory)

CHAPTER 1

THEME: Israel in Egypt; the heroism of two women

The first few verses of Exodus connect it with the account of Genesis. Those who came down into Egypt are listed first and the years between are quickly covered. Exodus 1:7 continues the Genesis account.

The *key verse* in this book is Exodus 20:2, which says, "I am the LORD thy God, which have brought thee out of the land of Egypt, out of the house of bondage."

ISRAEL IN EGYPT

Now these are the names of the children of Israel, which came into Egypt; every man and his household came with Jacob.

Reuben, Simeon, Levi, and Judah,

Issachar, Zebulun, and Benjamin,

Dan, and Naphtali, Gad, and Asher.

And all the souls that came out of the loins of Jacob were seventy souls: for Joseph was in Egypt already.

And Joseph died, and all his brethren, and all that generation [Exod. 1:1–6].

Exodus is the sequel to Genesis. The death of Joseph concludes Genesis. Exodus 1:6 tells us that Joseph, all of his brethren, and all that generation had died. Three and one-half centuries have passed.

In Genesis chapter 46 God said that Israel would increase and multiply and become a great nation in the land of Egypt. As we come to verse seven, this prophecy has actually taken place.

And the children of Israel were fruitful, and increased abundantly, and multiplied, and waxed exceeding mighty; and the land was filled with them [Exod. 1:7].

Verse eight indicates that a great change has taken place.

Now there arose up a new king over Egypt, which knew not Joseph [Exod. 1:8].

A new Pharaoh has come to the throne of Egypt who has never heard of Joseph. Perhaps the Hyksos, or shepherd kings, who were Semites, had been deposed and the former dynasty of Egyptian kings sat on the throne again. The new king never knew Joseph and felt no indebtedness to him or his descendants.

There is a tremendous lesson to be learned in verse eight. I have often wondered why movements today which specialize in reaching children have not used this verse. It should be used. There is a continual responsibility of teaching the Word of God to each generation. If we neglect to teach the Bible, the time will come when it will be forgotten.

A Coca-Cola executive in Texas once told me that a certain percentage of each bottle is spent for advertising. I kidded him about having to advertise such a well-known product. I mentioned to this man that I had once seen thirteen Coca-Cola advertisements in a small town in Texas and thought that was overdoing it. He said, "Not so!" Then he asked me, "When was the last time you saw a can of Arbuckle coffee?" I told him that it had been a popular brand when I was a boy, but I had not seen any lately. "They thought," he replied, "that they did not need to advertise."

Now there arose in Egypt a Pharaoh that did not know Joseph. And there is always a new generation that has never heard about the Lord Jesus Christ. I was shocked not long ago when I realized my own daughter and son-in-law had no knowledge of the depression. They are of a new generation that did not live through the depression. They did not understand what some of us older folk went through in the way of hardship and suffering. Therefore it is always necessary to teach the next generation what happened in previous generations. And so there arose a generation who never heard of Joseph. At one time Joseph was so well known that he was a hero and his body could not even be taken from the land.

The new Pharaoh who came to power was not as kindly disposed toward the Israelites as had been his predecessors.

And he said unto his people, Behold, the people of the children of Israel are more and mightier than we:

Come on, let us deal wisely with them; lest they multiply, and it come to pass, that, when there falleth out any war, they join also unto our enemies, and fight against us, and so get them up out of the land [Exod. 1:9–10].

It was a real possibility that Israel might have joined forces with the enemy against Egypt. Although Pharaoh wanted slaves, the simple way to solve the problem would have been to let Israel go. Instead of releasing Israel, Pharaoh decided to use worldly wisdom to take care of the difficulty.

Therefore they did set over them taskmasters to afflict them with their burdens. And they built for Pharaoh treasure cities, Pithom and Raamses [Exod. 1:11].

The children of Israel were forced to do hard labor. They did not build the pyramids because they had already been in existence many, many years. They were, however, forced to build treasure cities. They built the treasure cities of Pithom and Raamses. They constructed the cities with bricks which they as slaves were forced to make. At the beginning of their slavery the Israelites were provided with straw to make their bricks. As Pharaoh's persecution of them increased, they were compelled to hunt for their own straw and at the same time produce the exact number of bricks they had made before. Dr. Kyle, one of my professors, brought a brick to class one day that had been taken out of the city of Raamses. The brick was made without straw. The Biblical record of Israel's bondage in Egypt needs no defense; the brick only confirms that the record is accurate.

There is no doubt that the Israelites were in a difficult position in Egypt. The Egyptians made life harder and harder for Israel.

But the more they afflicted them, the more they multiplied and grew. And they were grieved because of the children of Israel [Exod. 1:12].

God told Abraham that Israel would have times of hardship in Egypt. Genesis 15:13 says, "And he said unto Abram, Know of a surety that thy seed shall be a stranger in a land that is not theirs, and shall serve them; and they shall afflict them four hundred years." Three things are predicted in this verse. The Israelites were to be strangers in a strange land; they were to be servants, that is, slaves; they were to be afflicted. All of these predictions had come true in just the first few verses of Exodus 1.

The more the Egyptians afflicted the Israelites, the more they multiplied and grew.

And the Egyptians made the children of Israel to serve with rigour:

And they made their lives bitter with hard bondage, in mortar, and in brick, and in all manner of service in the field:

all their service, wherein they made them serve, was with rigour.

And the king of Egypt spake to the Hebrew midwives, of which the name of the one was Shiphrah, and the name of the other Puah [Exod. 1:13–15].

The Egyptians not only made slaves of the Israelites, they mistreated them also. In spite of the persecution, God's blessing rested upon them and their numbers increased greatly. The king noticed the rapid growth of his slave nation and spoke to the Hebrew midwives in an attempt to solve the problem.

It is interesting to note the meaning of the names of these two women. Shiphrah means "beauty." Puah means "splendor." Have you ever noticed the silhouette pictures of Egyptian women? Beauty and splendor characterized the women in the land of Egypt. These women apparently occupied high official positions in Egypt and were in charge of the nurses who were responsible for delivering babies.

And he said, When ye do the office of a midwife to the Hebrew women, and see them upon the stools; if it be a son, then ye shall kill him: but if it be a daughter, then she shall live [Exod. 1:16].

This is another attempt of Satan to destroy the line leading to the Lord Jesus Christ. Satanic attempts to cut off the line leading to Christ run all the way through the Bible from the Old Testament to the New Testament. Many attempts have been made to destroy the Jews, and it is quite interesting to note the way anti-Semitism has spread throughout the world. It is satanic in its origin, and therefore no child of God should have any part in it. It is generally people with no knowledge of God who persecute the Jews.

Someone is undoubtedly thinking, "Yes, but during the Dark Ages, the Church engaged in anti-Semitism." This is true. But it was the Dark Ages and the Church was far from the Word of God, involved in external religious affairs. In my opinion no person can study the Word of God and become anti-Semitic.

THE HEROISM OF TWO WOMEN

As Satan attempted to get rid of the children of Israel, God intervened.

But the midwives feared God, and did not as the king of Egypt commanded them, but saved the men children alive.

And the king of Egypt called for the midwives, and said unto them, Why

have ye done this thing, and have saved the men children alive?

And the midwives said unto Pharaoh, Because the Hebrew women are not as the Egyptian women; for they are lively, and are delivered ere the midwives come in unto them.

Therefore God dealt well with the midwives: and the people multiplied, and waxed very mighty [Exod. 1:17–20].

This attempt to destroy all the male Hebrew children was a political maneuver that did not work out.

And it came to pass, because the midwives feared God, that he made them houses [Exod. 1:21].

These women had to choose whether to obey Pharaoh or God. They had learned to fear God and their obedience was seen and rewarded by God. He gave Shiphrah and Puah both a name and a place in Israel, and they were greatly respected in the land.

And Pharaoh charged all his people, saying, Every son that is born ye shall cast into the river, and every daughter ye shall save alive [Exod. 1:22].

If this order had been carried out, Israel would soon have been exterminated. Pharaoh's orders were not obeyed, and the succeeding chapters in Exodus clearly show it. God raises up Moses to deliver the children of Israel out of Egyptian bondage. Exodus is the great book on redemption. It reveals, in picture form, how God delivers us today—from sin, the world, the flesh, and the devil—and saves us for heaven.

CHAPTER 2

THEME: The birth of Moses; Moses' first attempt to help his people; Moses in Midian takes a Gentile bride

In this chapter we have before us Moses the deliverer. He is prominent as the deliverer of Israel in the first eleven chapters of Exodus.

Exodus is the great book of redemption. Nothing is begun or ended in this book. It is simply a continuation of the story that started in Genesis and continues on into the Books of Leviticus and Numbers.

THE BIRTH OF MOSES

And there went a man of the house of Levi, and took to wife a daughter of Levi.

And the woman conceived, and bare a son: and when she saw him that he was a goodly child, she hid him three months [Exod. 2:1–2].

This is the age-old story of the man who sees a woman, falls in love with her, and marries her. She loves him in return, and they have a child. This is what human life is all about, and that is the story we have here.

Moses is writing this account of his parents and of his own birth, and it is a modest record. This is why we must turn to other portions of the Bible to give us more information about the events in Exodus. If given the opportunity, most of us would want to tell about our parents in detail, but Moses did not even mention his parents by name. They were ordinary people. They were in slavery. They were members of the tribe of Levi. That is all Moses says at this point. Later on we are given their names as Amram and Jochebed.

Verse two tells us only that Moses was a good, healthy child. Moses also seems quite reticent about giving his own record in any detail.

And when she could not longer hide him, she took for him an ark of bulrushes, and daubed it with slime and with pitch, and put the child therein; and she laid it in the flags by the river's brink [Exod. 2:3].

Moses was not only a healthy child, but he also had a good set of lungs. His parents could hide him at first, but the day came when Moses could really scream at the top of his voice. What a contrast this is to several years later when the Lord asks him to be His spokesman to Pharaoh and Moses says that he cannot speak. Many of us are good at crying like babies, but as adults we do not do so well for the Lord.

Jochebed had a serious problem. She could no longer hide her child. A lot of pious people would have acted differently from this mother by saying, "Well, we're just going to trust the Lord." That is a wonderful statement to make, but do you really trust the Lord when you are playing the fool? Jochebed would have been foolish to keep her child in the house when a guard passing by might have heard his cry. It would have meant instant death for Moses.

I can hear someone saying, "You know the child would not cry when the guard passed by." How do you know? Faith is *not* a leap in the dark, as I heard a liberal say some years ago. God asks us to believe that which is good and solid. God never asks us to do foolish things. Jochebed did a sensible thing. She made a little ark and put Moses in it.

And his sister stood afar off, to wit what would be done to him [Exod. 2:4].

In addition to fashioning the ark, Jochebed also sent Moses' sister to watch it and find out what would happen to her brother. Her sensible actions indicated that she was trusting God.

And the daughter of Pharaoh came down to wash herself at the river; and her maidens walked along by the river's side; and when she saw the ark among the flags, she sent her maid to fetch it [Exod. 2:5].

Now the hand of the Lord is revealed. The Lord is going to intervene in this situation. This is what the Lord does when you use common sense, and Jochebed had demonstrated sensibleness. Pharaoh's daughter came to the Nile River to wash. It was undoubtedly a secluded spot. And there was an ark. She had one of her attendants bring the ark to her.

And when she had opened it, she saw the child: and, behold, the babe wept. And she had compassion on him, and said, This is one of the Hebrews' children [Exod. 2:6].

At that very moment was the right time for the child to cry. In fact, the Lord pinched little Moses and he let out a yelp. And God brought together two things that He has made—a baby's cry and a woman's heart. Pharaoh's daughter just could not pass this little baby by.

Then said his sister to Pharaoh's daughter. Shall I go and call to thee a nurse of

the Hebrew women, that she may nurse the child for thee? [Exod. 2:7].

Miriam, Moses' sister, made a very helpful suggestion to the princess. And later on she is not going to let her young brother forget it. This is a very human story we are reading, friends. God has something to tell us on every page of His Book.

And Pharaoh's daughter said to her, Go. And the maid went and called the child's mother [Exod. 2:8].

This is a real turn of events, and it shows how God really moves when we act sensibly and move by faith sensibly. The very mother of the child was called to nurse him and be *paid* for it! You cannot beat that, friends. You cannot beat God when He is moving in our hearts and lives.

And Pharaoh's daughter said unto her, Take this child away, and nurse it for me, and I will give thee thy wages. And the woman took the child, and nursed it.

And the child grew, and she brought him unto Pharaoh's daughter, and he became her son. And she called his name Moses: and she said, Because I drew him out of the water [Exod. 2:9–10].

The name *Moses* means "drawer out" and Pharaoh's daughter named him this because she had drawn him out of the water. Although the identification of the Pharaoh of the oppression is a controversial subject and a matter of speculation, Pharaoh's daughter may have been the oldest daughter of Rameses II, or she may have been his sister. According to the Egyptian customs of the day, her firstborn son had the right to the throne. Moses would have been the next Pharaoh had Rameses II and his queen remained childless.

MOSES' FIRST ATTEMPT TO HELP HIS PEOPLE

The first forty years of Moses' life were spent in the courts of Pharaoh. He was raised and trained like an Egyptian. He looked like an Egyptian, talked like an Egyptian, and acted like an Egyptian. He was recognized as an Egyptian when he went to Midian, as we shall see later in the Book of Exodus.

Moses was educated in the great Temple of the Sun which was the outstanding university of the day. We underrate what the Egyptians knew and accomplished. Their knowledge of astronomy was phenomenal. They knew the exact distance to the sun. They worked on the theory that the earth was round and not flat.

They knew a great deal about chemistry which is evidenced by the way they were able to embalm the dead. We have no process to equal it today. Their workmanship and ability with colors were fantastic. Their colors are brighter than any we have today. I am confident that our paint companies would give anything if they knew the formulas used for color by the Egyptians. They are bright, beautiful, and startling after four thousand years. (I have to paint my house about every four years!)

In addition to all of their other accomplishments, the Egyptians also had a tremendous library. And Moses, we are told, was learned in all the wisdom of the Egyptians. The one great lack in Moses' education was that he was not taught how to serve God. But do not underestimate Moses; he was an outstanding man. Stephen, in the Book of Acts, gives us some insight into this period of Moses' life: "In which time Moses was born, and was exceeding fair, and nourished up in his father's house three months: And when he was cast out, Pharaoh's daughter took him up, and nourished him for her own son. And Moses was learned in all the wisdom of the Egyptians, and was mighty in words and in deeds. And when he was full forty years old, it came into his heart to visit his brethren the children of Israel. And seeing one of them suffer wrong, he defended him, and avenged him that was oppressed, and smote the Egyptian: For he supposed his brethren would have understood how that God by his hand would deliver them: but they understood not. And the next day he shewed himself unto them as they strove, and would have set them at one again, saying, Sirs, ye are brethren; why do ye wrong one to another? But he that did his neighbour wrong thrust him away, saying, Who made thee a ruler and a judge over us? Wilt thou kill me, as thou diddest the Egyptian yesterday? Then fled Moses at this saying . . ." (Acts 7:20–29).

In other words, all of his training in Egypt did not prepare Moses to deliver the children of Israel. One day when he was out he saw one of his brethren being persecuted and beaten by one of the slave drivers, and Moses killed the guard. Moses looked around him to see if his deed had been seen—but, he did not look up. He should have looked up to God who would have forbidden him to do a thing like this because Moses is forty years ahead of God in delivering the children of Israel. Therefore God is going to put him out on the back side of the desert.

Now when Pharaoh heard this thing, he sought to slay Moses. But Moses fled from the face of Pharaoh, and dwelt in the land of Midian: and he sat down by a well [Exod. 2:15].

MOSES IN MIDIAN TAKES A GENTILE BRIDE

Moses had spent forty years in Egypt but it did not prepare him for what was to come.

Now the priest of Midian had seven daughters: and they came and drew water, and filled the troughs to water their father's flock.

And the shepherds came and drove them away: but Moses stood up and helped them, and watered their flock.

And when they came to Reuel their father, he said, How is it that ye are come so soon today?

And they said, An Egyptian delivered us out of the hand of the shepherds, and also drew water enough for us, and watered the flock.

And he said unto his daughters, And where is he? why is it that ye have left the man? call him, that he may eat bread.

And Moses was content to dwell with the man: and he gave Moses Zipporah his daughter [Exod. 2:16–21].

Zipporah is given to Moses, and he takes a bride. It is interesting that many of the men in the Old Testament are figures of Christ. Although not all details of their lives typify Christ—they couldn't—they certainly picture Christ in some way. Moses was a murderer in sharp contrast to Christ our Savior. However, Moses was a type of Christ in that he was God's chosen deliverer; he was rejected by Israel and turned to the Gentiles, taking a Gentile bride; afterward he again appears as Israel's deliverer and is accepted.

And so we find Moses in the land of Midian. For the next forty years it will be his home. Two sons are born to him. In the desert he will begin his preparation to be the deliverer of Israel from their Egyptian bondage. There has always been a question relative to Moses' marital state. I am sure he must have loved his wife, but the record we have does not reveal a wonderful relationship. This part of his life is one of the things that Moses more or less passes over. The name Zipporah means "sparrow" which may indicate a small, nervous person.

And she bare him a son, and he called his name Gershom: for he said, I have been a stranger in a strange land.

And it came to pass in process of time, that the king of Egypt died: and the children of Israel sighed by reason of the bondage, and they cried, and their cry came up unto God by reason of the bondage.

And God heard their groaning, and God remembered his covenant with Abraham, with Isaac, and with Jacob.

And God looked upon the children of Israel, and God had respect unto them [Exod. 2:22–25].

God is getting ready to deliver the children of Israel. Moses has been trained to be that deliverer. God did not choose to deliver the Israelites because they were superior to the Egyptians, or because they had been true and faithful to Him, or because they had not gone into idolatry. These people had been most unfaithful to God. They served idols rather than Him. You will recall that, after they had been delivered from Egypt and Moses had led them into the wilderness, the Israelites could not wait to make a golden calf to worship. God's desire was to deliver them because they were in a helpless, hopeless position in slavery. Unless someone intervened in their behalf, they would have perished.

God gives two reasons for delivering Israel:
1. He heard their groanings.
2. He remembered His covenant with Abraham, Isaac, and Jacob.

The desperate, hopeless condition of Israel appealed to the heart of God. And His promise to bring Abraham's offspring back into the land after 400 years caused God to devise a plan to deliver them.

Why do you think God has redeemed *you* (that is, if you are redeemed)? God saved us for the same reason He saved Israel. He found nothing in us that called for His salvation. He makes it quite clear that we are not saved because of any merit we possess. Paul explains it in Romans 3:23–24, "For all have sinned, and come short of the glory of God; Being justified freely by his grace through the redemption that is in Christ Jesus." The word *freely* means "without a cause." We have been saved from our sins without a cause. It is the same word our Lord used when He said that He was hated without a cause (John 15:25). God did not look at me and say, "My, you are white and Protes-

tant, honest and hardworking, and I'm going to redeem you." The fact of the matter is that God saw us in the blackness and darkness of sin and ignorance. He saw that we were hopelessly lost and not able to save ourselves.

God's love provided a Savior. God so loved us that He gave His only begotten Son, John 3:16 tells us. However, it was not His love that saved us; it was His *grace*. We are saved without out a cause by His grace through the redemption that is in Christ Jesus.

Many people believe God saw something in them worthy of salvation. They believe God saved them as sinners, but it was because He saw what lovely people they would become. May I say that this idea is entirely erroneous. We will never become lovely. Each of us has the old nature in which no good dwells. In Romans 7:18 Paul says, "For I know that in me (that is, in my flesh,) dwelleth no good thing . . . ." It is a shoe that really pinches to be told that there is no good in man at all. There never has been and never will be anything good in us. This is why we cannot produce anything good. This is why God gives us a new nature when we are saved, and why the old nature eventually must be destroyed.

God saw no good in Israel. But He heard Israel's cry in bondage and redeemed them. God saw our desperate condition and saved us. God had a plan, but He did not ask the human race what they thought about it. God did not say, "This is my plan for your salvation. If it pleases you, I will go through with it." No sir! God the Father so loved the world that He sent His Son to die for the sins of the world. The Son agreed to come, and the Father agreed to save anyone who trusted Jesus Christ for salvation. God says to us, "This is the salvation I offer you. Take it or leave it." He wants us to take it but leaves the choice up to each individual.

There was a little Scotch lady who worked hard taking in washing in order to send her son to the university. When he came home for vacation, his mind was filled with doubts about God from the liberal teaching he had received. He did not want his mother to know about the change in his thinking. She kept telling him how wonderful it was of God to save her and how she knew she was saved. Finally he could not listen to more of her talk and said, "Mother, you do not seem to realize how small you are in this universe. If you lost your soul, God would not miss it at all. It would not amount to anything." She did not reply right away but kept putting dinner on the table. Finally she said, "I've been thinking about what you said. You are right. My little soul does not amount to much; I would not lose much and God would not lose much. But if He does not save me, He will lose more than I will. He promised that if I would trust Jesus He would save me. If He breaks His word, He will lose His reputation and mar His character."

This is what God is saying to mankind. There was nothing attractive about the children of Israel but He heard their cry. There is nothing lovely about us either that would cause Him to save us. God made a covenant with Abraham, Isaac, and Jacob that promised the redemption of Israel. He also agreed to save anyone that trusts Jesus Christ as Savior. Grace is love in action. He saves us by His grace, and His great love has provided redemption.

CHAPTER 3

THEME: The call of Moses; the commissioning of Moses

Moses' forty years in Midian have come to an end. All of his schooling in Egypt was not enough to prepare him for his great work of delivering Israel from bondage. God equipped him for this task by forty years of preparation in the desert area of Midian.

THE CALL OF MOSES

Now Moses kept the flock of Jethro his father in law, the priest of Midian: and he led the flock to the backside of the desert, and came to the mountain of God, even to Horeb.

And the angel of the LORD appeared unto him in a flame of fire out of the midst of a bush: and he looked, and, behold, the bush burned with fire, and the bush was not consumed [Exod. 3:1–2].

Moses turned aside to see why the bush was burning but was not consumed. One of the greatest proofs of the accuracy of Scripture is the existence of the nation Israel. Years ago an emperor of Germany asked his chaplain the question, "What is the greatest proof that the Bible is the Word of God? That proof is somewhere in my kingdom." Without hesitation the chaplain said, "The Jew, sir. He is the proof." He is the burning bush that ought to cause the unbeliever to turn aside and take a look today. It is amazing that he has existed down through the centuries. From the days of Moses to the present hour he has been in existence. Other nations have come and gone, and he has attended the funeral of all of them. He is still around. Israel has been in the fire of persecution from the bondage in Egypt through the centuries to the present hour. But like the burning bush Israel has not been consumed.

By the way, when is the last time you saw a Midianite? Have you seen the flag of Midian? Do you know anything about the government of Midian? You do not and I do not because Midian is gone. It has disappeared.

The angel of the Lord who appeared to Moses is none other than the pre-incarnate Christ. Some people would debate this conclusion, but this is my conviction after years of studying the Word of God.

And Moses said, I will now turn aside, and see this great sight, why the bush is not burnt.

And when the LORD saw that he turned aside to see, God called unto him out of the midst of the bush, and said, Moses, Moses. And he said, Here am I.

And he said, Draw not nigh hither: put off thy shoes from off thy feet, for the place whereon thou standest is holy ground [Exod. 3:3–5].

God had to correct Moses' manners. Although Moses had been brought up in the court of Pharaoh, he didn't know enough to take off his shoes in the presence of a holy God. And I'm afraid many folk today get familiar with God. God is teaching him a great lesson about the holiness of God. We need to learn this lesson too.

Moreover he said, I am the God of thy father, the God of Abraham, the God of Isaac, and the God of Jacob. And Moses hid his face; for he was afraid to look upon God [Exod. 3:6].

Moses did *not* look upon God. If he had, he would have looked upon the revelation of God, the Lord Jesus Christ veiled in human form. It can still be said, "No man hath seen God at any time; the only begotten Son, which is in the bosom of the Father, he hath declared him" (John 1:18). The only way you can know God is through the Lord Jesus Christ.

And the LORD said, I have surely seen the affliction of my people which are in Egypt, and have heard their cry by reason of their taskmasters; for I know their sorrows;

And I am come down to deliver them out of the hand of the Egyptians, and to bring them up out of that land unto a good land and a large, unto a land flowing with milk and honey; unto the place of the Canaanites, and the Hittites, and the Amorites, and the Perizzites, and the Hivites, and the Jebusites [Exod. 3:7–8].

When God redeems, He not only redeems *from* something, He always redeems *unto* something. We have been saved from sin unto holiness and heaven. Paul explains this concept in Ephesians 2:5–6: "Even when we were dead in sins, [God] hath quickened us together with Christ, (by grace ye are saved;) And hath raised us up together, and made us sit together in heavenly places in Christ Jesus." God has raised us up and given us a position in Christ. If you are saved today, you are completely saved. You will be just as saved a million years from now as you are today because you are in Christ. You have been brought out of Adam and put in Christ. You have been brought out of death and put into life. You have been brought out of darkness and put into light. You have been brought out of hell, if you please, and put into heaven. That is *redemption:* it is *out of* and *into.*

God said, "I am going to take the children of Israel out of bondage and into a good land." That is the salvation of God. That is redemption.

Now therefore, behold, the cry of the children of Israel is come unto me: and I have also seen the oppression wherewith the Egyptians oppress them.

Come now therefore, and I will send thee unto Pharaoh, that thou mayest bring forth my people the children of Israel out of Egypt.

And Moses said unto God, Who am I, that I should go unto Pharaoh, and that I should bring forth the children of Israel out of Egypt? [Exod. 3:9–11].

Do you notice what has happened to Moses?

Forty years before this moment, he was ready to deliver Israel. He was cocky and almost arrogant. He slew an Egyptian and delivered one of his brethren from persecution because he thought his act would be understood. He thought he could deliver Israel by himself. He found out that he could not, and God took him to the back side of the desert for special training that would fit him for the job. He learned how really weak he was. He learned he could not deliver Israel by himself.

Now Moses is saying to God, "Who am *I*? I cannot do what you are asking me to do." My friends, *now* God can use him. This is God's way of training all of His men. God had to take the boy David who could slay a giant and put him out into the caves and dens of the earth where he was hunted like a partridge. He found out how weak he was. Then God could make him a king.

Elijah the prophet was brave enough to walk right into the court of Ahab and Jezebel and tell them that ". . . there shall not be dew nor rain these years, but according to my word" (1 Kings 17:1). Elijah was not as brave as he seemed. God put him out in the desert where He trains His men. Elijah drank from a brook. There was a drought that caused the brook to dry up. He watched the brook grow smaller and smaller and said, "My life is no more than a dried up brook." He was right. Then Elijah spent some more time eating out of an empty flour barrel. He found out he was nothing and God was everything. When Elijah realized this, God used him to face the prophets of Baal and bring down fire from heaven.

Paul puts it this way, "Therefore I take pleasure in infirmities, in reproaches, in necessities, in persecutions, in distresses for Christ's sake: for when I am weak, then am I strong" (2 Cor. 12:10). This certainly is a paradox. It is, however, what God was teaching Moses. When Moses learned that he could not deliver Israel, but that God could do it through him, God was ready to use him.

One of the reasons many of us are not used of God today is we are too strong. Have you ever stopped to think about that? God cannot use us when we are too strong. It is out of weakness that we are made strong. The apostle Paul said, "But God hath chosen the foolish things of the world to confound the wise; and God hath chosen the weak things of the world to confound the things which are mighty" (1 Cor. 1:27). Moses and Paul recognized that God could move through them when they were weak. It is amazing what God can do through a weak vessel.

And he said, Certainly I will be with thee; and this shall be a token unto thee, that I have sent thee: When thou hast brought forth the people out of Egypt, ye shall serve God upon this mountain.

And Moses said unto God, Behold, when I come unto the children of Israel, and shall say unto them, The God of your fathers hath sent me unto you; and they shall say to me, What is his name? what shall I say unto them? [Exod. 3:12–13].

This question Moses asked is a natural one. I am sure all of us would have asked the same question. Moses was afraid that the children of Israel would not accept him. He did not know how to explain God to them. He did not know how he was ever going to get the Israelites to this mountain of God. These were the problems Moses faced. Notice how God answered him.

And God said unto Moses, I AM THAT I AM: and he said, Thus shalt thou say unto the children of Israel, I AM hath sent me unto you [Exod. 3:14].

There is undoubtedly more included in the name "I AM" than has ever been brought out, but there are several things of primary importance that should be considered. The name "I AM" is a tetragram, or a word of four letters. We translate it JEHOVAH. It has also been translated as *YAHWEH*. How do you pronounce it? It became a sacred name, a holy name, to the children of Israel to such an extent they actually forgot how to pronounce it. To avoid profaning His name, they did not use it. Which name, then, is correct? Is it Jehovah or Yahweh? No one knows. But "I AM" is God's name.

In Genesis God is Creator. He is Elohim, the mighty God, the self-existing One; I AM WHO I AM. This is the God who is sending Moses to deliver the children of Israel.

Psalm 135:13 says, "Thy name, O LORD, endureth for ever; and thy memorial, O LORD, throughout all generations." The name "LORD" in this verse can be translated "I AM WHO I AM." It is important to see that this name speaks of the fact that *GOD IS*.

THE COMMISSIONING OF MOSES

The time had come for the fulfillment of Joseph's promise as stated in Genesis 50:25: ". . . God will surely visit you . . . ."

And God said moreover unto Moses, Thus shalt thou say unto the children of Israel, The LORD God of your fathers, the God of Abraham, the God of Isaac, and the God of Jacob, hath sent me unto you: this is my name for ever, and this is my memorial unto all generations [Exod. 3:15].

God had appeared to Abraham, Isaac, and Jacob. This same God was sending Moses to the children of Israel, and the procedure he was to employ is given in the next few verses.

Go, and gather the elders of Israel together, and say unto them, The LORD God of your fathers, the God of Abraham, of Isaac, and of Jacob, appeared unto me, saying, I have surely visited you, and seen that which is done to you in Egypt:

And I have said, I will bring you up out of the affliction of Egypt unto the land of the Canaanites, and the Hittites, and the Amorites, and the Perizzites, and the Hivites, and the Jebusites, unto a land flowing with milk and honey.

And they shall hearken to thy voice: and thou shalt come, thou and the elders of Israel, unto the king of Egypt, and ye shall say unto him, The LORD God of the Hebrews hath met with us: and now let us go, we beseech thee, three days' journey into the wilderness, that we may sacrifice to the LORD our God.

And I am sure that the king of Egypt will not let you go, no, not by a mighty hand.

And I will stretch out my hand, and smite Egypt with all my wonders which I will do in the midst thereof: and after that he will let you go [Exod. 3:16–20].

God has given Moses the agenda and course to follow. He is to tell the elders of Israel about God's plan of deliverance. Then he and the elders are to go to Pharaoh and ask to be allowed to journey three days into the wilderness to sacrifice to their God as a nation. The intention was to break gently Israel's plan to Pharaoh rather than bluntly stating, "We are leaving and going back to the land of Canaan for good."

God tells Moses that Pharaoh will refuse to let Israel go. Pharaoh's refusal in this matter will open up God's campaign against the gods of Egypt. After that campaign, even though God will show His mighty wonders, Pharaoh will still steadfastly refuse to let Israel go. God will then bring plagues that will cause Pharaoh to change his mind and send Israel on its way from Egypt. God has a plan to deliver Israel, and deliver them He will.

And I will give this people favour in the sight of the Egyptians: and it shall come to pass, that, when ye go, ye shall not go empty:

But every woman shall borrow of her neighbour, and of her that sojourneth in her house, jewels of silver, and jewels of gold, and raiment: and ye shall put them upon your sons, and upon your daughters; and ye shall spoil the Egyptians [Exod. 3:21–22].

The word *borrow* in this passage does not mean to steal but to collect back wages. The Israelites had been slaves without pay. God tells them to collect their back wages for several hundred years' work. They would leave Egypt recompensed for years of toil. God was caring for His people.

CHAPTER 4

THEME: Moses' objections to being Israel's deliverer; Aaron becomes Moses' spokesman; Moses returns to Egypt

This chapter tells us of the return of Moses to Egypt and the marvelous way in which God deals with his misgivings. Moses has many questions in his mind and many hurdles to surmount but God has an answer for every objection of Moses.

MOSES' OBJECTIONS TO BEING ISRAEL'S DELIVERER

Moses had several reasons why he felt he was the wrong man for the job God wanted him to do.

And Moses answered and said, But, behold, they will not believe me, nor hearken unto my voice: for they will say, The Lord hath not appeared unto thee.

And the Lord said unto him, What is that in thine hand? And he said, A rod [Exod. 4:1–2].

In the days to come Moses would use the rod in many different ways. It would become his badge of authority. It would be a testimony to Israel and Egypt of God's presence with Moses. It would also serve as a source of strength to him.

And he said, Cast it on the ground. And he cast it on the ground, and it became a serpent; and Moses fled from before it [Exod. 4:3].

When Moses cast the rod to the ground, it became a vicious monster. Note that there is no power in the rod. It is simply an instrument and can be used by Satan as well as by God. For example, liken a dollar bill to the rod. The dollar can be used to help pay for a murder or for prostitution, gambling, liquor, etc. In other words that dollar can become a serpent. Only when that dollar, or the rod, is put in the hand of a man of God who is moved by the power of God can it be used for God. This is an important lesson God is teaching in this passage.

And the Lord said unto Moses, Put forth thine hand, and take it by the tail. And he put forth his hand, and caught it, and it became a rod in his hand [Exod. 4:4].

Many people consider the automobile, radio, and television to be of the devil. The devil can use all of these instruments, but they can also be used for God. Grab that serpent by the tail, friends! Use your automobile to take some dear saint to church or some of your unsaved friends to hear the Word of God preached. Support Christian programs on television and radio. Do your part to make the media an instrument of God rather than an instrument of the devil. *You* make them a rod in the hand of God.

God called Moses to deliver the children of Israel from the bondage of Egypt. He trained him for forty years in the desert and commissioned him at the burning bush. This man, who at one time was so eager that he ran ahead of God, is now reluctant to accept his God-given office of deliverer. He began to give God his objections and God put a rod in his hand. He learns that when the rod is used according to the will of God in the hand of a man yielded to God, it becomes his badge of authority. In addition to the rod, however, God gives Moses another token of assurance and teaches him an important lesson as he is about to assume the great responsibility of leading Israel out of Egypt.

And the LORD said furthermore unto him, Put now thine hand into thy bosom. And he put his hand into his bosom: and when he took it out, behold, his hand was leprous as snow.

And he said, Put thine hand into thy bosom again. And he put his hand into his bosom again; and plucked it out of his bosom, and, behold, it was turned again as his other flesh.

And it shall come to pass, if they will not believe thee, neither hearken to the voice of the first sign, that they will believe the voice of the latter sign [Exod. 4:6–8].

The great message here is for Moses in particular. His bosom speaks of his inner life. Proverbs 4:23 says, "Keep thy heart with all diligence; for out of it are the issues of life." In other words, the hand will do the bidding of the heart. God wanted to put the rod in the hand of a man yielded to Him. Now he wants Moses' hand to be in accord with his heart. The Lord made this statement in Matthew 7:17: "Even so every good tree bringeth forth good fruit; but a corrupt tree bringeth forth evil fruit." Then in Luke 6:45 the Lord says, "A good man out of the good treasure of his heart bringeth forth that which is good; and an evil man out of the evil treasure of his heart bringeth forth that which is evil: for of the abundance of the heart his mouth speaketh." God is saying to Moses that He wants his *hand* and his *heart*. God is saying the same thing to us today. God does not want our money and our abilities. God wants you and He wants me. If He gets us, then He will get the rest, too.

Moses put his hand in his bosom and it came out leprous. He put his hand into his bosom again and it came out clean. Out of your heart will ultimately come what you are. God wanted that rod in the hand of a man yielded to Him. He wanted that man's hand to move in the same direction as his yielded heart. This is the great lesson God had for Moses, the children of Israel, and for us today.

And Moses said unto the LORD, O my Lord, I am not eloquent, neither hereto-

fore, nor since thou hast spoken unto thy servant: but I am slow of speech, and of a slow tongue [Exod. 4:10].

Moses now offers another objection. He says, "Lord, you need an eloquent speaker for the job and I cannot speak well." Moses is quite able to speak when it is time, but he is giving an excuse. He feels inadequate.

And the LORD said unto him, Who hath made man's mouth? or who maketh the dumb, or deaf, or the seeing, or the blind? have not I the LORD?

Now therefore go, and I will be with thy mouth, and teach thee what thou shalt say [Exod. 4:11-12].

God is telling Moses that He not only wants his hand but He wants his mouth also. He promises to be with Moses' mouth and teach him what to say. Out of the heart proceed the issues of life and "what is in the well of the heart will come up through the bucket of the mouth." God wanted the heart of Moses.

And he said, O my Lord, send, I pray thee, by the hand of him whom thou wilt send [Exod. 4:13].

Moses is trying to find a substitute.

AARON BECOMES MOSES' SPOKESMAN

And the anger of the LORD was kindled against Moses, and he said, Is not Aaron the Levite thy brother? I know that he can speak well. And also, behold, he cometh forth to meet thee: and when he seeth thee, he will be glad in his heart.

And thou shalt speak unto him, and put words in his mouth: and I will be with thy mouth, and with his mouth, and will teach you what ye shall do.

And he shall be thy spokesman unto the people: and he shall be, even he shall be to thee instead of a mouth, and thou shalt be to him instead of God [Exod. 4:14–16].

Moses made a great mistake in asking God for a spokesman. God allowed it, but He did not want a divided command. You will find out that it caused problems as the children of Israel journeyed through the wilderness. In the Book of Numbers we will discover that Aaron was involved in making a golden calf for Israel to worship while Moses was on Mount Sinai! This was a terrible blunder on the part of

Aaron, and it came as the result of a divided command. Other problems crop up in the Book of Numbers. God did not need Aaron for the job of delivering the children of Israel; all He needed was Moses. Moses was reluctant to trust God all the way, and God had to send another man with him. We need to recognize our weakness, but when God calls us to do a job we should respond with trust. God will enable us to do the job He calls us to do.

And thou shalt take this rod in thine hand, wherewith thou shalt do signs.

And Moses went and returned to Jethro his father in law, and said unto him, Let me go, I pray thee, and return unto my brethren which are in Egypt, and see whether they be yet alive. And Jethro said to Moses, Go in peace [Exod. 4:17–18].

MOSES RETURNS TO EGYPT

And the LORD said unto Moses in Midian, Go, return into Egypt: for all the men are dead which sought thy life [Exod. 4:19].

There is a new Pharaoh in Egypt. The Pharaoh who had ordered Moses' death is now dead and Moses can safely return to Egypt.

And Moses took his wife and his sons, and set them upon an ass, and he returned to the land of Egypt: and Moses took the rod of God in his hand.

And the LORD said unto Moses, When thou goest to return into Egypt, see that thou do all those wonders before Pharaoh, which I have put in thine hand: but I will harden his heart, that he shall not let the people go [Exod. 4:20–21].

The fact that God says He will harden Pharaoh's heart has always presented a problem. This problem comes up again when we consider the plagues, and we will study it then in more detail and arrive at a satisfactory solution.

And thou shalt say unto Pharaoh, Thus saith the LORD, Israel is my son, even my firstborn [Exod. 4:22].

God did not call the individual Israelite a son of God, but He did say of the nation, "Israel is my son, even my firstborn."

And I say unto thee, Let my son go, that he may serve me: and if thou refuse to let him go, behold, I will slay thy son, even thy firstborn [Exod. 4:23].

God was very lenient in dealing with Pharaoh and the Egyptians. He told Pharaoh at the beginning of the contest, "Either let my son Israel go or I will slay your son." God sent many plagues before He touched the firstborn of Egypt, giving him ample time to acknowledge the true God and let Israel go, but Pharaoh did not avail himself of the opportunity.

And it came to pass by the way in the inn, that the LORD met him, and sought to kill him [Exod. 4:24].

This is a strange verse, but it reveals the third real objection of Moses. He had neglected to circumcise his sons. Circumcision was the evidence or seal of the covenant of God made with Abraham. If Moses would proclaim God's will to others, he too had to be obedient to God's will. God had to forcibly remind Moses of his disobedience.

Then Zipporah took a sharp stone, and cut off the foreskin of her son, and cast it at his feet, and said, Surely a bloody husband art thou to me.

So he let him go: then she said, A bloody husband thou art, because of the circumcision [Exod. 4:25–26].

This incident is difficult to understand, and we must retrace our steps somewhat to examine the problem. When Moses fled as a fugitive from Egypt, he went to the land of Midian. The Midianites were the offspring of Abraham and Keturah. These people were monotheistic. They were not idolaters but worshiped one God. Moses felt at home with these people. He became close friends with the Priest of Midian who had seven daughters. Moses married his daughter Zipporah—a name that sounds like a modern gadget to take the place of buttons. Actually, as we have said before, her name means "sparrow" or "little bird." The wife of Moses was the first "Lady Bird."

God blessed Moses' home in the beginning. His first son Gershom, meaning "stranger" was born in Midian. Moses had been a stranger in his land, but he had made it his home.

In Moses' married life, unfortunately, there was a problem. God called Moses at the burning bush and commissioned him to go to Egypt. Pharaoh was dead and it was safe for Moses to return. As Moses started his journey to Egypt, God attempted to kill him. Why? Moses had neglected the rite of circumcising his son. Circumcision was the badge and seal of God's covenant with Abraham that was designed to teach the Israelites to have no confidence in the flesh. The flesh was to be cut away, and each Israelite was to place his trust in God.

Genesis 15:6, Psalm 106:31, Romans 4:3, and Galatians 3:6 tell us that Abraham believed God and it was counted unto him as righteousness. Isaac and Jacob followed the example of Abraham. They were Israelites by birth, but circumcision was the badge of it. It was an act of faith for them to perform that rite. Circumcision was the evidence that a man was the son of Abraham. It was an evidence of their faith.

Apparently Zipporah had resisted the ordinance of circumcision, and Moses had not insisted upon it. Perhaps Moses did not feel this act was so important, and obviously his wife felt it was a foolish and bloody thing to do. At any rate, Moses did not want to precipitate a marital rift. Moses' wife was not atheistic; she was monotheistic. She was simply resisting the ordinance of God, and Moses did not want to make an issue of it. Moses could stand up against Pharaoh, but he could not stand up against his wife. Moses could tell Israel when they were wrong, but he did not oppose his wife when she was wrong.

Moses obviously thought he could get away with this area of disobedience. He just let it slide like many Christian workers do who neglect their own families while trying to fix up other people's families. God intervened in Moses' life. He waylaid him on the way to Egypt and revealed to him the seriousness of the situation. There is a real danger when husband and wife do not agree completely in spiritual matters. That is the reason Scripture warns against believers and non-believers getting married.

It was Zipporah who performed the rite of circumcision upon their son to save the life of Moses. Therefore what she did was an act of faith on her part. She claimed the promise of the covenant with Abraham—the redemption of blood with no confidence in the flesh. After the circumcision of their son, perhaps when they reached Egypt, Moses saw the problem, and sent her back home to be with her father. Later on the wilderness march we shall see that Jethro, Moses' father-in-law, brought Zipporah to him and they were reconciled.

And the LORD said to Aaron, Go into the wilderness to meet Moses. And he went, and met him in the mount of God, and kissed him.

And Moses told Aaron all the words of the LORD who had sent him, and all the signs which he had commanded him.

And Moses and Aaron went and gathered together all the elders of the children of Israel:

And Aaron spake all the words which the LORD had spoken unto Moses, and did the signs in the sight of the people.

And the people believed: and when they heard that the LORD had visited the children of Israel, and that he had looked upon their affliction, then they bowed their heads and worshipped [Exod. 4:27–31].

This is a great worship scene that we have here. These people come now to faith in God. And it will be on this basis that God will lead them out of the land of Egypt.

CHAPTER 5

THEME: *Moses' appeal for Israel's deliverance; the increase of Israel's burden; Moses' prayer*

Chapter 5 begins the contest with Pharaoh. The plagues are leveled against the idolatry of Egypt. It is actually a battle of God with the gods of Egypt. Moses returned to Egypt after an absence of forty years. The deliverer is prepared now to deliver his people. He was to assemble the elders of Israel, and they were to go to Pharaoh and present their request. Pharaoh refused to let Israel go, and this opened the struggle between God and the gods of Egypt.

The plagues were not haphazard. God did not send a plague of frogs and then say, "I wonder what calamity I should send next?" Probably nothing was ever quite so organized and meaningful as these plagues. They were directed very definitely toward the idolatry of Egypt.

Pharaoh asked the question, "Who is the Lord? I do not know Him, and I do not intend to let Israel go." So God introduced Himself and did it by bringing plagues on the land of Egypt. In Exodus 7:5 the Lord makes it very clear what He has in mind: "And the Egyptians shall know that I am the LORD, when I stretch forth mine hand upon Egypt, and bring out the children of Israel from among them." God used the plagues to deliver His people and to let the Egyptians know who He was.

Each plague was leveled at a different god of Egypt. There were thousands of temples, millions of idols, and about three thousand gods in Egypt. That will outdo anything we have in this country today. There was power in the religion of Egypt. The Egyptians were not fools. We have transistor radios, color television, and have been to the moon, but that does not mean we are superior. All of our knowledge is based on that which has been handed down from the past. We have been building upon the knowledge that has come to us through the centuries. Paul makes it clear that there was power in the Egyptian religions in 2 Timothy 3:8 when he says, "Now as Jannes and Jambres withstood Moses, so do these also resist the truth: men of corrupt minds, reprobate concerning the faith." The power in Egyptian religion was satanic and Satan grants power to those who worship him. The oracle at Delphi in the Greek period is an example of it.

God directed His plagues against the idolatry in Egypt, against Pharaoh, and against Satan. It was a battle of the gods. Exodus 12:12 confirms it: "For I will pass through the land of Egypt this night, and will smite all the firstborn in the land of Egypt, both man and beast; and against all the gods of Egypt I will execute judgment: I am the LORD." God exposed the gods of Egypt as false, and He revealed to Israel His ability to deliver them. These Israelites had been born in the brickyards in the midst of idolatry, and God had to show them that He was superior.

A brief outline of each plague might be helpful at this point in order to see that there was some sense to them. When Moses first stood before Pharaoh, he changed his rod into a serpent. The wise men of Egypt performed the same miracle. This reveals that Satan has definite powers. After this demonstration came the ten plagues.

1. *Water turned to blood* (Exod. 7:19–25): The fertility of the land of Egypt depended upon the overflow of the Nile River to bring it both fertilizer and water. Therefore this river was sacred to the god Osiris—whose all-seeing eye is found in many Egyptian paintings. Pagan rites were held every spring when the river brought life out of death. When the water was turned to blood, it brought death instead of life. The wise men of Egypt also imitated this plague with their sorcery.

2. *The plague of frogs* (Exod. 8:1–15): One of the most beautiful temples in Memphis was the temple to Heka, the ugly frog-headed goddess. It was an offense to kill the sacred frog, but if you found them in your house, bed, food, and underfoot everywhere, as the Egyptians did, you might feel like killing them. But they were sacred. The wise men also duplicated this plague which might indicate that their success up to this point was accomplished by sleight-of-hand tricks or some similar magical device.

3. *The plague of lice* (Exod. 8:16–20): The Egyptians worshiped the earth-god Geb. But "the dust of the land became lice throughout all the land of Egypt." This which was sacred to Geb they now despise. Pharaoh did not ask that this plague be taken away, and the Egyptian sorcerers could not reproduce this pestilence. They seem to have acknowledged that the One who brought this plague was supreme over the gods of Egypt.

4. *The plague of flies* (Exod. 8:20–32): It is thought by some that the swarms of flies were actually masses of the sacred beetle. And Khepara was the beetle-god. The beetle, or scarab, is found in the Egyptian tombs and speaks of

eternal life. These beetles were sacred to Ra the sun-god.

5. *The plague of murrain* (Exod. 9:1–7): Murrain was a disease that affected cattle. The second largest temple that Egypt ever built was located in Memphis and was for the worship of the black bull Apis. You could say that this plague caused the Egyptians to worship a sick cow!

6. *The plague of boils* (Exod. 9:8–17): The priests of all the religions of Egypt had to be spotless—with no mark or blemish on their bodies—in order to serve in the temples. Well, they had a moratorium on worship in Egypt during this period because of the boils that were on all the priests. None of them could serve anywhere. It was actually a judgment on the entire religion of Egypt.

7. *The plague of hail* (Exod. 9:18–35): God demonstrates His power with the plague of hail over the sky-goddess who is powerless in her own domain.

8. *The plague of locusts* (Exod. 10:1–20): The judgment of the locusts was against the insect gods. The plague of locusts meant the crops were cursed. This was an evidence of the judgment of God as found in the books of Joel and Revelation also.

9. *The plague of darkness* (Exod. 10:21–29): God moved in with darkness against the chief god that was worshiped—the sun-god Ra. The sun disc is the most familiar symbol found in Egyptian ruins. The plague of darkness shows the utter helplessness of Ra.

10. *Death of the firstborn* (Exod. 11–12:36): According to the religion of Egypt, the first-born belonged to the gods of Egypt. In other words, God took what was set aside for the gods of Egypt. God was teaching the Egyptians who He was. He was convincing Pharaoh that he was *God.* Also He was bringing His own people to the place where they were willing to acknowledge Him as their God. This was the final act of judgment that would free Israel from Egyptian bondage.

It is important to understand that there was purpose in the plagues of Egypt. God challenged the gods of Egypt to a contest and defeated them.

You can imagine the idolatry that was in the land of Egypt. Yet God through Isaiah predicted that the time would come when every idol would disappear from Egypt. And today Egypt is a Moslem country that does not permit idols at all. Every idol has disappeared, as God said they would.

MOSES' APPEAL
FOR ISRAEL'S DELIVERANCE

In chapter 5 the contest begins with Pharaoh and the battle begins with the Egyptian gods.

And afterward Moses and Aaron went in, and told Pharaoh, Thus saith the Lord God of Israel, Let my people go, that they may hold a feast unto me in the wilderness [Exod. 5:1].

Sacrificing to God in the wilderness was the first step toward Israel's freedom. Moses and Aaron did not rush into the presence of Pharaoh and say, "Let my people go. We are leaving Egypt and going to the promised land." They simply requested that Israel be allowed to go out into the wilderness and worship. They were preparing Pharaoh and softening him up for what would ultimately come. Now notice the reaction of Pharaoh.

And Pharaoh said, Who is the Lord, that I should obey his voice to let Israel go? I know not the Lord, neither will I let Israel go [Exod. 5:2].

The expression "Let my people go" has been made famous in a picture. I wish we could make the question "Who is the Lord?" famous. It is the best question of all today because you have to know Him before there can be any deliverance for you. Pharaoh made two definite statements: (1) I do not know the Lord, and, (2) I do not intend to let Israel go. In a short time Pharaoh would become acquainted with the God of Israel in a terrible way, and he would let the Israelites go.

And they said, The God of the Hebrews hath met with us: let us go, we pray thee, three days' journey into the desert, and sacrifice unto the Lord our God; lest he fall upon us with pestilence, or with the sword [Exod. 5:3].

God wants us to worship Him. He will judge us if we do not take this step now.

And the king of Egypt said unto them, Wherefore do ye, Moses and Aaron, let the people from their works? get you unto your burdens.

And Pharaoh said, Behold, the people of the land now are many, and ye make them rest from their burdens [Exod. 5:4–5].

Moses had been having mass meetings with his people. They were restless and wanted to leave Egypt. Pharaoh saw the problem this presented, and his answer was to send them back to the brickyards. This is exactly what he did and increased their difficulties at the same time.

THE INCREASE OF ISRAEL'S BURDEN

And Pharaoh commanded the same day the taskmasters of the people, and their officers, saying,

Ye shall no more give the people straw to make brick, as heretofore: let them go and gather straw for themselves.

And the tale of the bricks, which they did make heretofore, ye shall lay upon them; ye shall not diminish aught thereof: for they be idle; therefore they cry, saying, Let us go and sacrifice to our God [Exod. 5:6–8].

Pharaoh thought Israel was asking for a holiday. He reasoned that if they wanted some time off, they must not be working hard enough. Straw was withheld from them, and they were forced to produce the same number of bricks and gather the straw, too. Their daily tasks increased so that they served with rigor.

Then the officers of the children of Israel came and cried unto Pharaoh, saying, Wherefore dealest thou thus with thy servants?

There is no straw given unto thy servants, and they say to us, Make brick: and, behold, thy servants are beaten; but the fault is in thine own people.

But he said, Ye are idle, ye are idle: therefore ye say, Let us go and do sacrifice to the LORD.

Go therefore now, and work; for there shall no straw be given you, yet shall ye deliver the tale of bricks.

And the officers of the children of Israel did see that they were in evil case, after it was said, Ye shall not minish aught from your bricks of your daily task.

And they met Moses and Aaron, who stood in the way, as they came forth from Pharaoh:

And they said unto them, The LORD look upon you, and judge; because ye have made our savour to be abhorred in the eyes of Pharaoh, and in the eyes of his servants, to put a sword in their hand to slay us [Exod. 5:15–21].

The children of Israel blamed Moses and Aaron for their increased burden. They accused these two men of hindering rather than helping them and of giving Pharaoh an excuse to make life more unbearable for them.

MOSES' PRAYER

And Moses returned unto the LORD, and said, Lord, wherefore hast thou so evil entreated this people? why is it that thou hast sent me?

For since I came to Pharaoh to speak in thy name, he hath done evil to this people; neither hast thou delivered thy people at all [Exod. 5:22–23].

Moses is impatient. He is complaining to God. "I've come down here to deliver them at Your instructions. But instead of letting them go, Pharaoh has only made life more difficult for the children of Israel." Moses could not see the entire picture, but God was moving slowly and patiently to work out His plan. In chapter 6 God encourages Moses and the children of Israel and renews His promise to deliver them. God has much to teach Moses, the Israelites, the Egyptians, and Pharaoh.

CHAPTER 6

*THEME: Jehovah's answer to Moses' prayer; a partial
genealogy of Israel; renewal of Moses' commission*

Chapter 6 is a continuation of the last part of chapter 5. The time for the plagues to descend upon Egypt is at hand. The battle of the gods is about to begin. What has led up to this moment? In retrospect we find that the first thing Moses, Aaron, and the elders of Israel did was ask Pharaoh for permission to go out into the wilderness and sacrifice unto the Lord for three days. Pharaoh's answer was no because he "did not know the Lord." He then increased the burden of the Israelites. The children of Israel complained to Moses who in turn complained to the Lord.

God wanted to assure Moses of who He was and what He was going to do. The God of Abraham, Isaac, and Jacob had heard the groanings of Israel and was going to deliver them. God wanted Moses to look at the past history of Israel and see how He had kept them. God had demonstrated time and time again His love for Israel and His desire to help them. God had intervened many times in their behalf.

God also intervenes in our behalf today. I am certain he has for me—maybe you are not sure of God's working in your life. Philippians 1:6 says: "Being confident of this very thing, that he which hath begun a good work in you will perform it until the day of Jesus Christ." God knows our needs today. He knows our desperate condition. He can and *wants* to help us just as He helped Israel in Egypt.

JEHOVAH'S ANSWER
TO MOSES' PRAYER

Jehovah, the self-existing One, speaks to Moses to give him encouragement, hope, and confidence.

Then the LORD said unto Moses, Now shalt thou see what I will do to Pharaoh: for with a strong hand shall he let them go, and with a strong hand shall he drive them out of his land [Exod. 6:1].

Jehovah is telling Moses that He is THE LORD. He does not have to make preparations for the future. He is self-existing and needs no reserve. God is not dependent upon anything in creation. He does not lean upon anything; rather, all of creation leans upon Him for support. God wanted Moses to lean upon Him too.

And God spake unto Moses, and said unto him, I am the LORD:

And I appeared unto Abraham, unto Isaac, and unto Jacob, by the name of God Almighty, but by my name JEHOVAH was I not known to them.

And I have also established my covenant with them, to give them the land of Canaan, the land of their pilgrimage, wherein they were strangers.

And I have also heard the groaning of the children of Israel, whom the Egyptians keep in bondage; and I have remembered my covenant [Exod. 6:2–5].

God is telling Moses that He had appeared to Abraham, Isaac, and Jacob—but not as Jehovah. God, as Jehovah, was going to redeem His people, adopt them as His own, deliver them from bondage, and lead them to the Promised Land. By all of this they would know God as Jehovah, a part of His character that He had not revealed to Abraham, Isaac, and Jacob.

In verses 6 to 8 God reveals the seven "I wills" of redemption. These verses paint a marvelous portrait picture for us today and were a great encouragement to Moses in that day. God announces who He is and what He is going to do. We have a Savior today who tells us who He is and what He is going to do. He is able to save to the uttermost all who come to Him.

Wherefore say unto the children of Israel, I am the LORD, and I will bring you out from under the burdens of the Egyptians, and I will rid you out of their bondage, and I will redeem you with a stretched out arm, and with great judgments:

And I will take you to me for a people, and I will be to you a God: and ye shall know that I am the LORD your God, which bringeth you out from under the burdens of the Egyptians.

And I will bring you in unto the land, concerning the which I did swear to give it to Abraham, to Isaac, and to Jacob; and I will give it you for an heritage: I am the LORD [Exod. 6:6–8].

The seven "I wills" of redemption are:
1. I will bring you out from under the burdens of the Egyptians.
2. I will rid you out of their bondage.

3. I will redeem you with an outstretched arm.
4. I will take you to me for a people.
5. I will be to you a God.
6. I will bring you into the land.
7. I will give it to you for an heritage.

I will bring you out from under your burdens: The corollary and parallel to our redemption in Christ is found in this statement. We carry a burden of sin today. The things of the world are an oppression to the heart. We are told not to love the world. God can deliver us from the burden of sin through faith in Jesus Christ.

I will rid you out of bondage: God will deliver you from the *slavery* of sin. I received a remarkable letter from a man that bears out the fact that God is able to deliver from the bondage of sin. This man is brilliant but he lived in sin. He has had at least six illegitimate children as the result of affairs with that many women. And the work by which he made a living was not altogether honest. This fellow had as checkered a career as anyone I have ever heard about. Then he began listening to our *Thru The Bible* radio broadcast day after day, and the Word of God reached into his life. As he drank in the truths of the Bible, the darkness began to roll away, and the light broke through into his heart and life. He realized he was not trusting the Lord Jesus Christ as his Savior. God redeemed this man. Redemption is His business.

The Israelites were in the land of Egypt living a life of bondage. God said, "I am going to take you out of this place. I am going to rid you of your bondage."

I will redeem you with an outstretched arm: This is the mighty bared arm spoken of by Isaiah the prophet: "Who hath believed our report? and to whom is the arm of the LORD revealed?" (Isa. 53:1) Well, I don't know to whom it is being revealed. God is doing a work of redemption in the hearts and lives of men and women today. Each of us needs a Savior from sin because we are corrupt in His sight. He loved us enough to die for us in order that we might be saved. If He was willing to do that, we must be willing to come as sinners to the Lord. If we place our faith in the work of Jesus Christ for us, we will be saved. God has a great plan of salvation but man must come to Him for it. He will redeem you with an outstretched arm.

I will take you to me for a people: Just think—God has lifted us out of the muck and mire of sin and made us His sons by faith in Christ Jesus! Now He tells us, "I will be to you

a God." God does not save us and then run off and leave us. He wants to be our God. If you are really saved, you will not go on living as if God does not exist. If you have trusted Jesus Christ as Savior, it will transform your life. He will become your God and you will bow down to Him and acknowledge who He is. God wants to redeem you. He wants you to know Christ as Savior and Lord. He wants you to know you are saved. He wants to be your God. He wants us for His people.

I will be to you a God: God chose believers in Christ before the foundation of the world which places it before all time—in eternity past. The reason for the choice was not found in the believers, but in the all-wise purpose of God. He does not struggle to love His own in spite of their failures. God loves His own because it is His nature to love. He wants to be our God.

I will bring you into the land: The land is Canaan. It was promised by God to Abraham, Isaac, and Jacob. Canaan is *not* a picture of heaven. It is a picture of the Christian life as believers should be living it. Canaan typifies the heavenlies where we are blessed with all spiritual blessing—the believer has to walk worthy of his high calling for perfect enjoyment of spiritual blessing. This is done through the filling of the Spirit (Eph. 4:1–5:18). There is also warfare and battles to win. Believers sometimes live as if they are bankrupt in the wilderness of the world and never enter into the riches of His grace and mercy. Are you living today in the life, light, and love of a living Savior?

I will give you the land for an heritage: Paul, in the fifth chapter of Romans, makes it clear that we have been justified by faith and have peace with God through the Lord Jesus Christ. We have access to Him. We have joy in the midst of trouble. We have been given the Holy Spirit of God to indwell us, and the love of God has been made real to us. We have been delivered from the wrath to come and are saved from the Great Tribulation period. What kind of salvation do you have, friend, that you talk about but has not transformed your life or redeemed you from something? These verses tell of our heritage and picture our salvation.

And Moses spake so unto the children of Israel: but they hearkened not unto Moses for anguish of spirit, and for cruel bondage [Exod. 6:9].

Your heart must go out to the children of Israel at a time like this. They found it impossible to believe Moses because he had not helped their cause but had only been responsible for their increased burden.

And the LORD spake unto Moses, saying,

Go in, speak unto Pharaoh king of Egypt, that he let the children of Israel go out of his land.

And Moses spake before the LORD, saying, Behold, the children of Israel have not hearkened unto me; how then shall Pharaoh hear me, who am of uncircumcised lips?

And the LORD spake unto Moses and unto Aaron, and gave them a charge unto the children of Israel, and unto Pharaoh king of Egypt, to bring the children of Israel out of the land of Egypt [Exod. 6:10–13].

Moses was not accepted by the children of Israel; he was not accepted by Pharaoh. God told him to speak to Pharaoh again and Moses is reluctant to go. His eyes are on the circumstances rather than on God.

A PARTIAL GENEALOGY OF ISRAEL

In the midst of all these difficulties and circumstances we come to a very strange occurrence. God is careful to list the families of Israel again—an important item as far as the Old Testament is concerned. Frankly, reading all these names is boring to me and puts me to sleep, but they are important and thrilling to God. He is insistent that the genealogies be recorded. God wants us to know whom we are reading about and who His children are. God feels the same way about you and me. He wants us to be the sons of God through faith in Christ.

These be the heads of their fathers' houses: The sons of Reuben the firstborn of Israel. . . . And the sons of Simeon. . . . And these are the names of the sons of Levi according to their generations; Gershon, and Kohath, and Merari; and the years of the life of Levi were an hundred thirty and seven years [Exod. 6:14–16].

Gershon, Kohath, and Merari are the three sons of Levi. They are the men who will take the tabernacle through the wilderness. The name Cohen comes from the name Kohath, but the average Jew today could not tell you what tribe he belongs to.

And the sons of Kohath; Amram, and Izhar, and Hebron, and Uzziel. . . .

And Amram took him Jochebed his father's sister to wife; and she bare him Aaron and Moses: and the years of the life of Amram were an hundred and thirty and seven years [Exod. 6:18–20].

In this passage the parents of Aaron and Moses are named—Amram and his wife Jochebed. The question has been asked, "Why wasn't the life of Aaron in as much jeopardy as the life of Moses when the command to kill the Hebrew babies was given by Pharaoh?" The answer is simply that Aaron was older than Moses, and the decree had not been made yet. It was not until Pharaoh saw how quickly the Israelites were increasing in number that he issued his orders.

The next few verses continue to deal with the genealogy and I want to pick up my train of thought with verse 26.

These are that Aaron and Moses, to whom the LORD said, Bring out the children of Israel from the land of Egypt according to their armies.

These are they which spake to Pharaoh king of Egypt, to bring out the children of Israel from Egypt: these are that Moses and Aaron [Exod. 6:26–27].

We saw in verse 12 that Moses was discouraged. Neither the circumcised nor the uncircumcised will accept him. At this juncture God steps in and gives the background of who Moses is. He has to live up to his claims before he can deliver the children of Israel.

There are those today who say that it is not essential to believe the virgin birth of Christ. I say that it is absolutely essential to believe it. It is part of the credentials of Christ. You do not have to trust in His virgin birth to be saved—when I came to Christ I never *heard* of the virgin birth. You must trust in His death and resurrection to be saved. But when you are saved, you will come to know Him. And when you know Him, you'll find out He's virgin born. If He was not virgin born, then you have made a mistake in trusting Him because He is not who He claims to be. No one who is truly saved will deny the virgin birth of Jesus Christ.

It is also essential that Moses and Aaron are who they claim to be. It has been forty years since Moses left Egypt. In the meantime he has married the daughter of the priest of Midian. Now here he is back in Egypt. Who is he anyway? This genealogy tells who he is. He belongs to the tribe of Levi, and his father and mother are Amram and Jochebed. The genealogy provides the necessary credentials for Moses to accomplish the work he is sent to do in the land of Egypt.

RENEWAL OF MOSES' COMMISSION

On the basis of the credentials, God renews His call to Moses and Aaron.

And it came to pass on the day when the LORD spake unto Moses in the land of Egypt,

That the LORD spake unto Moses, saying, I am the LORD: speak thou unto Pharaoh king of Egypt all that I say unto thee.

And Moses said before the LORD, Behold, I am of uncircumcised lips, and how shall Pharaoh hearken unto me? [Exod. 6:28–30].

Moses is making excuses again. It is not a very pleasant task he has to perform. He has been rejected all along the way. Even after he shows his credentials of being in the tribe of Levi, he is rejected. Now Levi was the son of Jacob, Jacob was the son of Isaac, and Isaac was the son of Abraham. God made the promises concerning the children of Israel to Abraham. "I'm in the right line," says Moses, "but I hesitate to go." Moses does not have much faith.

CHAPTER 7

***THEME:** The renewal of Moses' commission—continued; the Egyptian magicians; the first plague—water turned to blood*

The battle between the Lord God of Israel and the Egyptian gods has not yet been joined, but we are coming to it now. God has been preparing the children of Israel, Moses and Aaron, and even old Pharaoh for the engagement.

Moses is going to stand before Pharaoh, but Aaron will do the speaking. Was Moses tongue-tied, did he stutter, or did he have some other speech impediment? My personal feeling is that Moses' problem was psychological. After forty years in the wilderness he may have felt inadequate and fearful.

God wanted to make it very clear, however, that He, and not Moses, was going to deliver the children of Israel. By the way, that is one reason it is so difficult for God to move today in our individual lives or in the church. There is always some person or some organization who is taking the credit. When we are always getting in the way to take the credit, the mighty bared arm of God is not revealed. God had to put the human element out of the way because He cannot use the flesh. God, speaking through the apostle Paul, tells us this in Romans 7:18, "For I know that in me (that is, in my flesh,) dwelleth no good thing: for to will is present with me; but how to perform that which is good I find not." It is difficult for some people to believe that there is no good in man because they rather count on it, especially in a time of emergency. But God does not want our

flesh. He cannot use it; He will not use it. God has set the flesh aside, and Aaron will speak for Moses.

THE RENEWAL OF MOSES' COMMISSION—CONTINUED

And the LORD said unto Moses, See, I have made thee a god to Pharaoh: and Aaron thy brother shall be thy prophet [Exod. 7:1].

This is one of the finest definitions you will find of a prophet. Moses was going to be a god to Pharaoh. Aaron was going to be the spokesman for Moses. Aaron would be a prophet. A prophet is one who speaks for God, one who has a message from God to the people. A prophet is the opposite of a priest. He comes out from God and goes to the people, but a priest represents the people before God. A priest is not to speak for God and a prophet is not to represent the people. He is to represent God. Aaron is to represent Moses before the people, and Moses is to represent God before both the people and Pharaoh.

Thou shalt speak all that I command thee: and Aaron thy brother shall speak unto Pharaoh, that he send the children of Israel out of his land.

And I will harden Pharaoh's heart, and multiply my signs and my wonders in the land of Egypt [Exod. 7:2–3].

What does it mean to harden Pharaoh's heart? Did God harden Pharaoh's heart? Yes, but in this way: If Pharaoh were a tenderhearted, sweet fellow who desired to turn to God and was happy to have Moses deliver the children of Israel because Pharaoh wanted to do something for them, then it was mean of God to harden the heart of this wonderful Pharaoh. If that is the way you read it, friends, you are not reading it right. The hardening is a figurative word, which can mean twisting, as with a rope. It means God twisted the heart of Pharaoh. He was going to squeeze out what was in it. God forced him to do the thing he really wanted to do.

Pharaoh was like the politicians of today who will not say what they actually mean. They feel one way and speak another way. Pharaoh did not want to let the children of Israel go, and yet he wanted to appear as a benevolent ruler. He wanted everyone to think he was a generous man, but in this matter of Israel he was hard. Well, God is going to bring Pharaoh into court and make him admit how he really feels.

There are certain men who have to be taken into court before they will do what they have already agreed to do. A Los Angeles contractor told me that he had to take a man to court before the man would honor a contract. He would not fulfill his obligations until the law got after him. That is what God is doing to Pharaoh. God is bringing Pharaoh into court and saying, "You are going to reveal the thing that is actually in your heart. You cannot say one thing and do something else." God is going to force the king's hand in this particular matter. By the way, this is exactly what God is going to do with every individual that will someday come into His presence. You will be seen as you really are. There will be no more camouflage. This is a rather frightening thing for some of us, is it not?

But Pharaoh shall not hearken unto you, that I may lay my hand upon Egypt, and bring forth mine armies, and my people the children of Israel, out of the land of Egypt by great judgments.

And the Egyptians shall know that I am the LORD, when I stretch forth mine hand upon Egypt, and bring out the children of Israel from among them [Exod. 7:4–5].

In other words, Pharaoh will stand revealed for what he is, and the Lord God of Israel will be revealed for who He is. The Egyptians will know, and the Israelites will have it confirmed, and Moses and Aaron will be justified.

And Moses and Aaron did as the LORD commanded them, so did they.

And Moses was fourscore years old, and Aaron fourscore and three years old, when they spake unto Pharaoh [Exod. 7:6–7].

Aaron was three years older than Moses.

And the LORD spake unto Moses and unto Aaron, saying.

When Pharaoh shall speak unto you, saying, Shew a miracle for you: then thou shalt say unto Aaron, Take thy rod, and cast it before Pharaoh, and it shall become a serpent [Exod. 7:8–9].

Pharaoh is probably going to ask Moses and Aaron. "Where are your credentials? You have come before me and made this excessive demand upon me; now show me your authority." Aaron's rod was to be the badge of authority.

THE EGYPTIAN MAGICIANS

And Moses and Aaron went in unto Pharaoh, and they did so as the LORD had commanded: and Aaron cast down his rod before Pharaoh, and before his servants, and it became a serpent [Exod. 7:10].

There is some question about the word *serpent* in this passage because there is very little history concerning the snake in Egypt. Actually the word used here is *crocodile*. During the days of Moses there were many of these creatures living in the Nile river and ponds throughout the land. The rod changed into a crocodile.

You will find as we study the plagues that God was dealing with the whole realm of zoology. That is, the gods of Egypt were either animal or bird or insect. Paul wrote about it when he said, "Professing themselves to be wise, they became fools, And changed the glory of the uncorruptible God into an image made like to corruptible man, and to birds, and fourfooted beasts, and creeping things" (Rom. 1:22–23).

The Egyptians symbolized everything. They took an abstract idea and put it into the concrete form of an image. They had deities which represented every phase and function of life. They did not miss a thing. They changed monotheism into polytheism. As Sir Wallis Budge has stated it, "They believed in the existence of one great God, self-produced, self-existent, almighty, and eternal." Unfortunately, they felt "that this Being was too great and mighty to concern Himself with the affairs and destinies of human beings." Therefore He "permitted the management of this world . . . to fall into the hands of hordes of 'gods' and demons, and good and bad spirits." This is what the Egyptians believed.

This is the very thing Paul found when he went to Athens. He found a monument to the "unknown God." "For as I passed by, and beheld your devotions, I found an altar with this inscription, TO THE UNKNOWN GOD. Whom therefore ye ignorantly worship, him declare I unto you" (Acts 17:23). If a man worships all of these different gods, he cannot know the living and true God. So the Lord God of Israel attacks the gods of Egypt to show who He is.

The Hebrew word *tannin* translated "serpent" in this chapter is not translated "serpent" anywhere else in the Bible. In the books of Isaiah and Ezekiel it is rendered "dragon." The word is actually satanic in its meaning, and that is probably why the translators used the word *serpent*. Regardless of the reason, the fact remains that the Egyptians worshiped the crocodile. It occupied a large place in the worship and religion of Egypt. Sebak was a deity of evil with a crocodile head. Apepi, the perpetual arch enemy of all the solar gods, appeared in the form of a crocodile. The Egyptians engaged in a magical ritual which was performed in the temple of Amen-Ra in the city of Thebes. Apepi lived in the nethermost part of the heaven and endeavored every day to prevent the rising of the sun god Ra. He stirred up lightning, thunder, tempests, storms, hurricanes, rain, and tried to obscure the light of the sun by filling the sky with clouds, mists, fog and blackness. The Egyptian ritual was an attempt to destroy Apepi. It was a prominent worship of Egypt and the first thing against which God delivers a blow. Aaron's rod is changed into a crocodile!

Then Pharaoh also called the wise men and the sorcerers: now the magicians of Egypt, they also did in like manner with their enchantments [Exod. 7:11].

The magicians of Egypt duplicated the miracle of Aaron's rod. Perhaps it would be better to say they imitated the miracle. Whatever and however they did it, they made a pretty good show of it. Paul, however, has a word to say about it in 2 Timothy 3:8, "Now as Jannes and Jambres withstood Moses, so do these also

resist the truth: men of corrupt minds, reprobate concerning the faith." These magicians resisted the living and true God.

For they cast down every man his rod, and they became serpents: but Aaron's rod swallowed up their rods.

And he hardened Pharaoh's heart, that he hearkened not unto them: as the Lord had said [Exod. 7:12–13].

It is interesting that the Egyptians worship the crocodile and it is Aaron's rod that swallows up their crocodiles. This should have impressed Pharaoh, but it did not. Pharaoh hardened his heart and persisted in his set ways.

THE FIRST PLAGUE—WATER TURNED TO BLOOD

And the Lord said unto Moses, Pharaoh's heart is hardened, he refuseth to let the people go.

Get thee unto Pharaoh in the morning; lo, he goeth out unto the water; and thou shalt stand by the river's brink against he come; and the rod which was turned to a serpent shalt thou take in thine hand.

And thou shalt say unto him. The Lord God of the Hebrews hath sent me unto thee, saying, Let my people go, that they may serve me in the wilderness: and, behold, hitherto thou wouldest not hear.

Thus saith the Lord, In this thou shalt know that I am the Lord: behold, I will smite with the rod that is in mine hand upon the waters which are in the river, and they shall be turned to blood.

And the fish that is in the river shall die, and the river shall stink; and the Egyptians shall loathe to drink of the water of the river.

And the Lord spake unto Moses, Say unto Aaron, Take thy rod, and stretch out thine hand upon the waters of Egypt, upon their streams, upon their rivers, and upon their ponds, and upon all their pools of water, that they may become blood; and that there may be blood throughout all the land of Egypt, both in vessels of wood, and in vessels of stone [Exod. 7:14–19].

This is another blow at the worship in Egypt. The sacred Nile River is turned to blood. The Egyptians depicted the Nile as Hapi, a fat man with the breasts of a woman which indicated the powers of fertility and nourishment. There was a hymn they sang in the temple to this god which went something like this:

> Thou waterest the fields which Ra created . . .
> Thou art the bringer of food . . . creator of all good things.
> Thou fillest the storehouses . . .
> Thou hast care for the poor and needy.

The Nile River was the life-blood of Egypt. But it had to be water to be their "life-blood." Now that river is blood and becomes death to them. What had been a blessing in Egypt is now a curse. This is God's judgment.

And the magicians of Egypt did so with their enchantments: and Pharaoh's heart was hardened, neither did he hearken unto them; as the Lord had said.

And Pharaoh turned and went into his house, neither did he set his heart to this also.

And all the Egyptians digged round about the river for water to drink; for they could not drink of the water of the river.

And seven days were fulfilled, after that the Lord had smitten the river [Exod. 7:22–25].

This plague lasted for seven days. Pharaoh was not convinced this was the hand of God because his magicians were able to duplicate the plague. This is an amazing thing! It was a manifestation of the power of Satan, of course, but they were powerless to change the blood back into pure water.

CHAPTER 8

THEME: *The second plague—frogs; the third plague—lice; the fourth plague—flies*

The plagues continue upon the land of Egypt. God is directing His attack against a people immersed in idolatry.

THE SECOND PLAGUE—FROGS

Frogs were represented by Heka, a frog-headed goddess. Also Hapi was depicted as holding a frog out of whose mouth flowed a stream of nourishment. This indicates the close relationship between the god of the Nile and the frog goddess, one of the oldest and mother of goddesses. She was the goddess of fertility and rebirth, the patroness of midwives. One Egyptian picture shows Heka reciting spells to effect the resurrection of Osiris. Also a carving shows her kneeling before the queen and superintending at the birth of Hatshepset.

And the Lord spake unto Moses, Go unto Pharaoh, and say unto him, Thus saith the Lord, Let my people go, that they may serve me.

And if thou refuse to let them go, behold, I will smite all thy borders with frogs:

And the river shall bring forth frogs abundantly, which shall go up and come into thine house, and into thy bedchamber, and upon thy bed, and into the house of thy servants, and upon thy people, and into thine ovens, and into thy kneadingtroughs:

And the frogs shall come up both on thee, and upon thy people, and upon all thy servants.

And the Lord spake unto Moses, Say unto Aaron, Stretch forth thine hand with thy rod over the streams, over the rivers, and over the ponds, and cause frogs to come up upon the land of Egypt [Exod. 8:1–5].

Frogs were everywhere—in Egyptian bedrooms, in kitchens, in every room in the house, in kneadingtroughs and in ovens. When they walked, they walked on frogs; when they sat, they sat on frogs. It was a terrible situation. One frog could not do very much, but many frogs caused great consternation. Of course they were sacred and should not be killed.

And Aaron stretched out his hand over the waters of Egypt; and the frogs came up, and covered the land of Egypt.

And the magicians did so with their enchantments, and brought up frogs upon the land of Egypt [Exod. 8:6–7].

Once again the Egyptian magicians duplicated the plague of frogs. This reveals the power of Satan.

Then Pharaoh called for Moses and Aaron, and said, Entreat the Lord, that he may take away the frogs from me, and from my people; and I will let the people go, that they may do sacrifice unto the Lord.

And Moses said unto Pharaoh, Glory over me: when shall I entreat for thee, and for thy servants, and for thy people, to destroy the frogs from thee and thy houses, that they may remain in the river only?

And he said, To-morrow. And he said, Be it according to thy word: that thou mayest know that there is none like unto the Lord our God.

And the frogs shall depart from thee, and from thy houses, and from thy servants, and from thy people; they shall remain in the river only [Exod. 8:8–11].

It is interesting to note that although the magicians could multiply the frogs, they could not remove them. Pharaoh was so upset by this plague that he was ready to promise anything. God was beginning to force this king to acknowledge who He is.

And Moses and Aaron went out from Pharaoh: and Moses cried unto the Lord because of the frogs which he had brought against Pharaoh.

And the Lord did according to the word of Moses; and the frogs died out of the houses, out of the villages, and out of the fields.

And they gathered them together upon heaps: and the land stank.

But when Pharaoh saw that there was respite, he hardened his heart, and hearkened not unto them; as the Lord had said [Exod. 8:12–15].

This passage gives us a more comprehensive picture of the hardening of Pharaoh's heart. We are told that he hardened his own heart.

God's part in this was to bring to the surface that which was already there.

THE THIRD PLAGUE—LICE

And the Lord said unto Moses, Say unto Aaron, Stretch out thy rod, and smite the dust of the land, that it may become lice throughout all the land of Egypt.

And they did so; for Aaron stretched out his hand with his rod, and smote the dust of the earth, and it became lice in man, and in beast; all the dust of the land became lice throughout all the land of Egypt.

And the magicians did so with their enchantments to bring forth lice, but they could not: so there were lice upon man, and upon beast.

Then the magicians said unto Pharaoh, This is the finger of God: and Pharaoh's heart was hardened, and he hearkened not unto them; as the Lord had said [Exod. 8:16–19].

Up to this point the magicians were able to duplicate every miracle wrought by the hand of God. For some reason they were powerless to reproduce this plague. If it was by trickery that they duplicated the miracles, at least during this plague they finally acknowledged the finger of God in the plagues. Gradually God was convincing the Egyptians that He alone was God.

The worship of these gods entered into the very life of the Egyptians and into their daily routines. This judgment brought loathing upon Geb, the earth god. Geb was closely related to the earth in all of its states. Geb was the one who made his report to Osiris on the state of the harvest.

The word *lice* could mean gnats or mosquitoes. Its root means to "cover" or "nip" or "pinch." It is interesting that the nipping, pinching, or covering could not be fulfilled by a gnat or a mosquito. It is, however, a good description of lice. A leading zoologist has said that the mites form an enormous order whose leading function, to a large extent, is to play the scavenger. You can well imagine with the land stinking with frogs that there were crowds of lice. The lice could eventually rid the land of the frogs and could therefore become a blessing as well as a curse.

Regardless of the apparent help the lice might have been, one man tells about his experience with them in Egypt: "I noticed that the sand appeared to be in motion. Close . . .

inspection revealed . . . that the surface of the ground was a moving mass of minute ticks, thousands of which were crawling up my legs . . . I beat a hasty retreat, pondering the words of the Scriptures, 'the dust of the land became lice throughout all the land of Egypt.' "

The plague of lice could not be duplicated by the Egyptian magicians. God is beginning to level His judgment against life itself in the land of Egypt.

THE FOURTH PLAGUE—FLIES

And the LORD said unto Moses, Rise up early in the morning, and stand before Pharaoh; lo, he cometh forth to the water; and say unto him, Thus saith the LORD, Let my people go, that they may serve me.

Else, if thou wilt not let my people go, behold, I will send swarms of flies upon thee, and upon thy servants, and upon thy people, and into thy houses: and the houses of the Egyptians shall be full of swarms of flies, and also the ground whereon they are.

And I will sever in that day the land of Goshen, in which my people dwell, that no swarms of flies shall be there; to the end thou mayest know that I am the LORD in the midst of the earth.

And I will put a division between my people and thy people: to-morrow shall this sign be [Exod. 8:20–23].

Up until this time the plagues had touched both the lands of Egypt and Goshen where the children of Israel lived. Many people were probably telling Pharaoh that since Goshen was also affected by the plagues, the phenomena of the plagues had a natural explanation. Maybe they attributed the vexation to one of the Egyptian gods. Everything becomes crystal clear at this juncture, however, when God declares that from now on there was to be distinction and none of the following plagues would touch the land of Goshen, the home of Israel. From now on, judgment would fall only upon the land of Egypt.

The fourth judgment is the plague of flies. These "flies" were most likely the sacred beetle or scarab as they were known in Egypt. These scarabs, many of gold, are found in the tombs in Egypt. They were sacred to the sun god Ra. The severity of this plague is reflected in the fact that Pharaoh was willing to reach some sort of compromise with Moses at this time. Notice the proposal that Pharaoh made as the sacred beetle invaded the land.

And the LORD did so; and there came a grievous swarm of flies into the house of Pharaoh, and into his servants' houses, and into all the land of Egypt: the land was corrupted by reason of the swarm of flies.

And Pharaoh called for Moses and for Aaron, and said, Go ye, sacrifice to your God in the land,

And Moses said, It is not meet so to do; for we shall sacrifice the abomination of the Egyptians to the LORD our God: lo, shall we sacrifice the abomination of the Egyptians before their eyes, and will they not stone us?

We will go three days' journey into the wilderness, and sacrifice to the LORD our God, as he shall command us [Exod. 8:24–27].

The Egyptian scarab spoke of eternal life. Imagine this most sacred thing becoming a curse to the people and a plague upon the land. Pharaoh wanted to work out a compromise; he made four compromises in all before the plagues came to an end. Moses and Aaron wanted the children of Israel to go three days' journey into the wilderness and sacrifice. Pharaoh said, "All right, you may sacrifice, but *stay in the land.*" This is the same kind of compromise that many Christians make. It is always satanic. This compromise says we can be Christians but not narrow ones. Be a broad-minded Christian and don't change your life. If your life doesn't change, you are not a Christian. Now don't accuse me of saying you have to perform good works to be a Christian. I didn't say it that way. We are saved by faith in Christ and nothing else—works are excluded. But when you put your faith in Christ to save you, it will change your life. That is where Christian conduct comes in. The inner man must be changed first. My point is that the contemporary church has made many compromises and for the most part is still in the land of Egypt. You cannot tell the difference today between the average Christian and the average man of the world.

The facts tell us that over fifty percent of the citizens of the United States are members of some religious body. Whenever I am on a plane and they are serving cocktails, I play a game to pass the time. At first I counted the people having cocktails but that became too big an undertaking; so now I just count the people who do not have drinks. The other day I was on a plane where only four people did not take cocktails. Now friends, there must have been some church members on that airplane. They were sacrificing in the land of Egypt. They were broad-minded and did not want to be "square." They wanted to live like the world.

We are in a race today with two horses. One horse is black and one is white. If you decide to ride them and put one foot on one horse and one foot on the other, you will soon make a strange discovery. These horses will run in opposite directions. You must make up your mind which horse you want to ride. Moses will not accept Pharaoh's compromise. Moses insists on Israel's going three days' journey into the wilderness to sacrifice to the Lord God.

Next Pharaoh decides on a second compromise.

And Pharaoh said, I will let you go, that ye may sacrifice to the Lord your God in the wilderness; only ye shall not go very far away: entreat for me [Exod. 8:28].

Pharaoh's concession this time is just a shade different from his other one. He says, "Do not go very far away and also entreat for me." This, again, is the same kind of compromise that we find many churches (even fundamental ones) adopting—the program of the world.

They run their entire program on the basis of banquets, promotion, contests, and so forth. Many churches are so much like the world that it is difficult to tell them from the Rotary Club, or any knife-and-fork club whose membership is made up largely of those who do not know Christ.

And Moses said, Behold, I go out from thee, and I will entreat the Lord that the swarms of flies may depart from Pharaoh, from his servants, and from his people, to-morrow: but let not Pharaoh deal deceitfully any more in not letting the people go to sacrifice to the Lord.

And Moses went out from Pharaoh, and entreated the Lord.

And the Lord did according to the word of Moses; and he removed the swarms of flies from Pharaoh, from his servants, and from his people; there remained not one.

And Pharaoh hardened his heart at this time also, neither would he let the people go [Exod. 8:29–32].

Pharaoh is hardening his heart and God is making him reveal what is already in his heart.

CHAPTER 9

THEME: *The fifth plague—murrain; the sixth plague—boils; the seventh plague—hail*

God continues to deal with the stubborn heart of Pharaoh and with his people. So long as Pharaoh resists the Lord God, anguish and disaster will be poured out upon the land of Egypt and its inhabitants. Up to this chapter we are told that Pharaoh hardened his own heart, and now we are told that God hardened Pharaoh's heart. Pharaoh's continual refusal to acknowledge the Lord God and obey His wishes has brought about God's power in destruction. God wants to shower blessings upon us and wants to save us, but our refusal can turn blessing to cursing. So is the case with Pharaoh.

THE FIFTH PLAGUE—MURRAIN

Then the Lord said unto Moses, Go in

unto Pharaoh, and tell him, Thus saith the Lord God of the Hebrews, Let my people go, that they may serve me.

For if thou refuse to let them go, and wilt hold them still,

Behold, the hand of the Lord is upon thy cattle which is in the field, upon the horses, upon the asses, upon the camels, upon the oxen, and upon the sheep: there shall be a very grievous murrain.

And the Lord shall sever between the cattle of Israel and the cattle of Egypt: and there shall nothing die of all that is the children's of Israel.

And the Lord appointed a set time,

saying, To-morrow the LORD shall do this thing in the land.

And the LORD did that thing on the morrow, and all the cattle of Egypt died: but of the cattle of the children of Israel died not one.

And Pharaoh sent, and, behold, there was not one of the cattle of the Israelites dead. And the heart of Pharaoh was hardened, and he did not let the people go [Exod. 9:1–7].

A person would think that by this time Pharaoh would be impressed and let the children of Israel go. The fact is obvious that God is involved in this plague and that He is dealing with this king and his people.

With a tour group I made a trip out to the pyramids. When we got back, one of the men who knew the area said, "Did you see the mummies of the bulls?" We said, "No." "Well," he said, "you missed the most important thing." So several in our group went back out there to get pictures of them. I was not interested in going twelve miles in all that heat to see mummies of bulls! But they are there—literally hundreds of them, reverently entombed in sarcophagi. Archaeologists have just begun unearthing them. Apis, the black bull, was worshiped in Egypt. The second largest temple that Egypt built was located in Memphis and was for the worship of the black bull Apis. Apis was supposed to be an embodiment of Ptah of Memphis. Apis, thought to be engendered by a moonbeam was distinguished by several characteristics. A new Apis was always believed to be born upon the death of the old. The dead bull was embalmed and buried in Memphis. His soul then passed to the world beyond as Osiris-Apis.

You might say that what they had here is the worship of a sick cow. God must have smiled at this. God is leveling His judgments against this awful, frightful institution of idolatry that had such a hold upon the Egyptian people as well as on the Israelites. We shall see later that Israel, too, had gone into idolatry.

THE SIXTH PLAGUE—BOILS

And the LORD said unto Moses and unto Aaron, Take to you handfuls of ashes of the furnace, and let Moses sprinkle it toward the heaven in the sight of Pharaoh.

And it shall become small dust in all the land of Egypt, and shall be a boil breaking forth with blains upon man, and upon beast, throughout all the land of Egypt.

And they took ashes of the furnace, and stood before Pharaoh; and Moses sprinkled it up toward heaven; and it became a boil breaking forth with blains upon man, and upon beast [Exod. 9:8–10].

It is only an assumption, but this plague probably began right in the presence of Pharaoh, and he may have been the first one to get boils.

And the magicians could not stand before Moses because of the boils; for the boil was upon the magicians, and upon all the Egyptians [Exod. 9:11].

Pharaoh had with him at all times his magicians or wise men who counselled him. They were able to duplicate the first three plagues and miracles. The rest they were unable to duplicate, and now in this judgment they have boils too! I can imagine they left in a hurry.

For the first time God is touching man as well as beast with judgment. He is afflicting man's physical body. The priests who served in the Egyptian temples had to be clean, without any type of breaking out or sickness. Suddenly this plague of boils comes upon them and they are unclean, unfit to serve in the temples. This brings to a halt all of the false worship in Egypt.

I walked over part of the ruins of the city of Memphis. The ruins are practically all gone now, but archaeologists know something of the extent of that great city. Up one thoroughfare and down the other was temple after temple. There were over one thousand temples in Memphis, and priests served in all of them. You can imagine what this plague of boils did to the services in these temples. Everything slowed to a standstill. All the bright lights went off!

About the time I was in this city I remember reading about a strike in Las Vegas. There on "glitter gulch" are probably more neon lights than any place in the world. I have been told that if you fly in an airplane over Las Vegas at night, it is so bright that you think the sun is coming up. Well, they had a strike and the lights went out. Motels closed and the people left. It was such a startling event that the strike was settled immediately.

Conditions were similar in the land of Egypt to those in Las Vegas during the strike. False religion was out of business. Everyone had boils. The priests could not serve in the temples. There were probably signs on the temples, which said, CLOSED BECAUSE OF SICKNESS.

And the LORD hardened the heart of Pharaoh, and he hearkened not unto them; as the LORD had spoken unto Moses.

And the LORD said unto Moses, Rise up early in the morning, and stand before Pharaoh, and say unto him, Thus saith the LORD God of the Hebrews, Let my people go, that they may serve me [Exod. 9:12–13].

Even though Pharaoh himself is afflicted with boils, God continues to ask for the release of His people through His servant Moses. How many times have we read, "Let my people go that they may serve me"? How many times have we read God's request, "Let my people go"? Still Pharaoh refuses to let Israel leave the land. His heart is hard.

For I will at this time send all my plagues upon thine heart, and upon thy servants, and upon thy people; that thou mayest know that there is none like me in all the earth.

For now I will stretch out my hand, that I may smite thee and thy people with pestilence; and thou shalt be cut off from the earth.

And in very deed for this cause have I raised thee up, for to shew in thee my power; and that my name may be declared throughout all the earth.

As yet exaltest thou thyself against my people, that thou wilt not let them go [Exod. 9:14–17].

God is going to use Pharaoh to demonstrate His power throughout all of the earth. Here is a case of God using the wrath of man to praise Him. Psalm 76:10 says, "Surely the wrath of man shall praise thee . . . ."

THE SEVENTH PLAGUE—HAIL

Behold, tomorrow about this time I will cause it to rain a very grievous hail, such as hath not been in Egypt since the foundation thereof even until now [Exod. 9:18].

Egypt is essentially a land of little rain. The average is less than an inch in one year. God tells them that they are going to have rain—but a kind they can do without.

Send therefore now, and gather thy cattle, and all that thou hast in the field; for upon every man and beast which shall be found in the field, and shall not be brought home, the hail shall come down upon them, and they shall die.

He that feared the word of the LORD among the servants of Pharaoh made his servants and his cattle flee into the houses [Exod. 9:19–20].

This is a question of whether or not they believed God. God said, "Get yourselves and your cattle inside." Many people did not believe the words of God, and they suffered from the judgment. God gave them a chance, but it was their choice whether or not they believed what He said. The same holds true today.

And he that regarded not the word of the LORD left his servants and his cattle in the field [Exod. 9:21].

This plague was directed against Isis (sometimes represented as cow-headed), goddess of fertility and considered the goddess of the air. She is the mythical daughter of Set and Nut, the sister and wife of Osiris, and the mother of Horus. It is said that the tears of Isis falling into the Nile River caused it to overflow its banks and bring nourishment to the land. Isis was a prominent goddess in Egypt, and the plague of hail was directed against her.

It is important to note that this plague touches mankind, as well as the animals.

And the LORD said unto Moses, Stretch forth thine hand toward heaven, that there may be hail in all the land of Egypt, upon man, and upon beast, and upon every herb of the field, throughout the land of Egypt.

And Moses stretched forth his rod toward heaven: and the LORD sent thunder and hail, and the fire ran along upon the ground; and the LORD rained hail upon the land of Egypt.

So there was hail, and fire mingled with the hail, very grievous, such as there was none like it in all the land of Egypt since it became a nation.

And the hail smote throughout all the land of Egypt all that was in the field, both man and beast; and the hail smote every herb of the field, and brake every tree of the field [Exod. 9:22–25].

Those who did not believe God made no provision for protection. The message God gave to the Egyptians is the same one He gives to the world today. Judgment is coming. Man is not wise to go on as if nothing is going to happen. It was that way in the days of Noah, and it will be that way when Christ comes again in judgment. Many people in Egypt did not believe God, and they paid the price for their unbelief. All God asks is that you believe Him.

Only in the land of Goshen, where the children of Israel were, was there no hail [Exod. 9:26].

From this point on, the land of Goshen is spared from the plagues coming upon the land of Egypt.

And Pharaoh sent, and called for Moses and Aaron, and said unto them, I have sinned this time: the Lord is righteous, and I and my people are wicked [Exod. 9:27].

This is the first time that Pharaoh has made any admission of sin.

And the flax and the barley was smitten: for the barley was in the ear, and the flax was bolled [Exod. 9:31].

The wheat and rye were not smitten in the same way, verse 32 tells us, because they were not yet grown up. It was all beaten down. This was a judgment against the Egyptian food and clothing.

And the heart of Pharaoh was hardened, neither would he let the children of Israel go; as the Lord had spoken by Moses [Exod. 9:35].

God is striking at the Egyptians in an attempt to wake them up and shake them out of their false worship. Pharaoh, leader of the people, continues to harden his heart.

CHAPTER 10

THEME: *Pharaoh is threatened with a plague of locusts; the eighth plague—locusts; the ninth plague—darkness; the Lord's claim on Israel*

PHARAOH IS THREATENED WITH A PLAGUE OF LOCUSTS

A person begins to wonder what it is going to take to cause Pharaoh to let Israel go.

And the Lord said unto Moses, Go in unto Pharaoh: for I have hardened his heart, and the heart of his servants, that I might shew these my signs before him:

And that thou mayest tell in the ears of thy son, and of thy son's son, what things I have wrought in Egypt, and my signs which I have done among them; that ye may know how that I am the Lord [Exod. 10:1-2].

God has many reasons for doing what He does. One reason for the plagues was to make Pharaoh reveal that he was a godless man. God could have taken the children of Israel out of the land immediately without making any contact with Pharaoh. If He had, the critic would say that God certainly was not fair to Pharaoh. He should have given him an opportunity to let Israel go, and He should have given him an opportunity for salvation. Well, friend, that is

exactly what God has done. God also wanted to demonstrate to His people what He was able to do before He took them into the wilderness. He wanted them to know that He was well able to bring them into the land promised to Abraham, Isaac, and Jacob. That story has been told through the observance of the Passover for nearly four thousand years.

And Moses and Aaron came in unto Pharaoh, and said unto him, Thus saith the Lord God of the Hebrews. How long wilt thou refuse to humble thyself before me? let my people go, that they may serve me.

Else, if thou refuse to let my people go, behold, tomorrow will I bring the locusts into thy coast:

And they shall cover the face of the earth, that one cannot be able to see the earth: and they shall eat the residue of that which is escaped, which remaineth unto you from the hail, and shall eat every tree which groweth for you out of the field:

And they shall fill thy houses, and the houses of all thy servants, and the houses of all the Egyptians; which neither thy fathers, nor thy fathers' fathers have seen, since the day that they were upon the earth unto this day. And he turned himself, and went out from Pharaoh.

And Pharaoh's servants said unto him. How long shall this man be a snare unto us? let the men go, that they may serve the LORD their God: knowest thou not yet that Egypt is destroyed? [Exod. 10:3–7].

Pharaoh's servants try to reason with him, "Don't you realize that Egypt is destroyed? How much longer are you going to permit it? Let them go!" So, once again, Moses and Aaron are brought into the presence of Pharaoh.

THE EIGHTH PLAGUE—LOCUSTS

And Moses and Aaron were brought again unto Pharaoh: and he said unto them, Go, serve the LORD your God: but who are they that shall go?

And Moses said, We will go with our young and with our old, with our sons and with our daughters, with our flocks and with our herds will we go; for we must hold a feast unto the LORD.

And he said unto them, Let the LORD be so with you, as I will let you go, and your little ones: look to it: for evil is before you [Exod. 10:8–10].

Pharaoh is very angry that they would not accept his compromise.

Not so: go now ye that are men, and serve the LORD: for that ye did desire. And they were driven out from Pharaoh's presence [Exod. 10:11].

Pharaoh told Moses that the adults could go into the wilderness and sacrifice but they were to go without the children. Pharaoh suspected, undoubtedly, that if Israel would go three days' journey into the wilderness they would keep going. He wants to stop them, and he knows that if he keeps the children, the adults will come back.

Just as Pharaoh tempted and tested Moses with compromise, so the child of God today is tempted with compromise. Children all across the country are being brought up in an educational system that is absolutely contrary to the teachings of Christianity. The child of God is told that he must learn to get along in the world, make all the money he can, and get involved in the world. I have been a pastor for over thirty years, and again and again I have seen Christian parents want the best for their children. They want them to have the best education. They want them to succeed and be rich. One after another has fallen and departed from the Lord. Many members of churches I have served have lost their children to the world. Wanting the "best" of the world for their children is the most subtle temptation that can come to Christian parents.

What do you expect, my friends, when you send your children to these worldly institutions and they come home thoroughly brainwashed? Why do you say, "My, how could he do that when he was brought up in a Christian home?" The problem is that he was not actually raised in a Christian home. The parents of many young people may be lovely Christian people but they did not really train their children in Christian precepts and values. They were so anxious and ambitious for them to get on in the world that they lost them.

Moses and Aaron would *not* accept Pharaoh's compromise, and this made him angry. His anger did not accomplish a thing, however, because another plague was about to begin.

And the LORD said unto Moses, Stretch out thine hand over the land of Egypt for the locusts, that they may come up upon the land of Egypt, and eat every herb of the land, even all that the hail hath left.

And Moses stretched forth his rod over the land of Egypt, and the LORD brought an east wind upon the land all that day, and all that night; and when it was morning, the east wind brought the locusts.

And the locusts went up over all the land of Egypt, and rested in all the coasts of Egypt: very grievous were they; before them there were no such locusts as they, neither after them shall be such.

For they covered the face of the whole earth, so that the land was darkened; and they did eat every herb of the land, and all the fruit of the trees which the hail had left: and there remained not any green thing in the trees, or in the herbs of the field, through all the land of Egypt [Exod. 10:12–15].

There are several interesting things revealed in this judgment of locusts. Notice that they did not appear miraculously, as did some of the other plagues. An east wind brought them from another place, possibly from somewhere in Asia. Locusts were prominent in the Asian area and this wind had brought them over a broad expanse of desert, and they were pretty hungry when they arrived in the green Nile Valley. They absolutely stripped the land of vegetation.

The locust is used in Scripture as a picture of judgment. A plague of locusts is probably one of the worst things man has to face. The prophet Joel described a plague of locusts in the past, which is a matter of history, then predicted a judgment that is yet future for mankind. The Book of Revelation also mentions a great plague of locusts that will come upon the earth. These insects probably had a greater effect upon the land of Egypt than any of the previous plagues that had come upon the land.

Then Pharaoh called for Moses and Aaron in haste; and he said, I have sinned against the LORD your God, and against you [Exod. 10:16].

This is another time Pharaoh has made an admission of sin.

Now therefore forgive, I pray thee, my sin only this once, and entreat the LORD your God, that he may take away from me this death only.

And he went out from Pharaoh, and entreated the LORD.

And the LORD turned a mighty strong west wind, which took away the locusts, and cast them into the Red sea; there remained not one locust in all the coasts of Egypt.

But the LORD hardened Pharaoh's heart, so that he would not let the children of Israel go [Exod. 10:17–20].

There is a method in the way God is dealing with the Egyptians and a systematic and orderly way in which He is sending the plagues. The first plagues were directed against the different gods, goddesses, and idols that infested the land. Now God is beginning to direct the plagues in a manner that works a tremendous hardship upon the people and their struggle to stay alive. The plague of locusts certainly has its effect, and the people try to convince Pharaoh that things are bad.

This causes Pharaoh to temporarily repent. The minute the plague is removed, however, Pharaoh changes his mind and goes back to his original position. God is going to force him to let the children of Israel go.

THE NINTH PLAGUE—DARKNESS

And the LORD said unto Moses, Stretch out thine hand toward heaven, that there may be darkness over the land of Egypt, even darkness which may be felt.

And Moses stretched forth his hand toward heaven; and there was a thick darkness in all the land of Egypt three days:

They saw not one another, neither rose any from his place for three days: but all the children of Israel had light in their dwellings [Exod. 10:21–23].

Have you ever been in a place where you could feel the darkness? The only time I have actually felt darkness was down in Carlsbad Caverns. Years ago on a tour of the cave they turned out the lights and the group sang "Rock of Ages." It was very effective. I am told they no longer sing this song because of criticism from some unbelievers, but the blackness of the darkness in that cave could be felt. I have never been in darkness like that before or since, and it was this kind of darkness that was over the land of Egypt. The judgment was upon the sun-god Ra. Darkness came over the land of Egypt in the daytime. God moved in with darkness against the chief god that they worshiped. The sun disc is the most familiar symbol the Egyptians used; it is in all of their art. The plague of darkness showed the utter helplessness of Ra. This darkness was a miracle of God, and it caused Pharaoh to propose a fourth compromise. This was the last compromise he made before he allowed the children of Israel to leave the land of Egypt.

THE LORD'S CLAIM ON ISRAEL

And Pharaoh called unto Moses, and said, Go ye, serve the LORD; only let your flocks and your herds be stayed: let your little ones also go with you [Exod. 10:24].

You would think that just leaving their flocks and herds behind would be a compromise that Moses might make for the Israelites. Pharaoh has come a long way in making concessions to Moses, and you would think this one would be agreeable. Once again there is a lesson here for the modern-day Christian. God called Israel to leave Egypt "lock, stock, and barrel." The children were not to be left in Egypt to be raised in their educational system. If we expect to bring our children up in the wisdom of the world and expect them to pour all of their energies into becoming successful, we should also be prepared to lose them to the world. I listened to a mother tell about how she had sent her son to a godless school, and how he was being advanced. She didn't mention to me that he had lost his faith, although he had. He had graduated from this school, was given a high position. I see his name in print many times. Then she came with tears in her eyes to tell me how her son had turned his back upon everything she held sacred. Well, that's the way she started him out. The world is subtle.

There are also many Christians today who leave their "flocks and herds in the land of Egypt." Egypt, by the way, is a picture of the world. Many Christians are faithful in the church, support their pastor, give to the Lord's work and all the rest, but they do business in the land of Egypt. They put their flocks and herds in Egypt above everything else. If they had to make a choice to serve God or make a trip to Egypt for their flocks and herds, you know which direction they would go.

It is interesting that many Christians say, "I serve the Lord on Sunday, but during the week I am out in the cold-hearted business world." Many of these so-called Christians live so much like folk of the world that it is difficult to tell them apart. They live like everyone else in the land of Egypt. I am of the opinion that the Rapture of the church will break the hearts of a great many Christians because it will separate them from their investments in the world. They will have to leave their safe-deposit boxes, savings accounts, their stocks and bonds, and real estate. This is what they have given their time and hearts to, and it will cause them great grief to leave them behind.

Notice what Moses says to this compromise. Moses tells Pharaoh that there will be *no* compromise.

And Moses said, Thou must give us also sacrifices and burnt offerings, that we may sacrifice unto the Lord our God.

Our cattle also shall go with us: there shall not an hoof be left behind: for thereof must we take to serve the Lord our God; and we know not with what we must serve the Lord, until we come thither.

But the Lord hardened Pharaoh's heart, and he would not let them go.

And Pharaoh said unto him, Get thee from me, take heed to thyself, see my face no more; for in that day thou seest my face thou shalt die.

And Moses said, Thou hast spoken well, I will see thy face again no more [Exod. 10:25–29].

There would be no compromise.

CHAPTER 11

***THEME:** The Israelites ask Egyptians for jewels; the firstborn of Egypt are threatened with death*

This is the final chapter in this section of the contest with Pharaoh. The death of the firstborn is the final act of judgment upon Egypt before Israel is freed from the yoke of bondage. Pharaoh should have learned by this time that it is futile to enter into conflict with God. God has been longsuffering and forgiving, but He must make Pharaoh understand that it is time for Israel to leave Egypt. All of Egypt was inclined to take Pharaoh's side in this contest with God and He must deliver one final blow upon Egypt in His attempt to teach them the lessons they need to learn.

THE ISRAELITES ASK
FOR EGYPTIAN JEWELS

And the Lord said unto Moses, Yet will I bring one plague more upon Pharaoh, and upon Egypt: afterwards he will let you go hence: when he shall let you go, he shall surely thrust you out hence altogether.

Speak now in the ears of the people, and let every man borrow of his neighbour, and every woman of her neighbour, jewels of silver, and jewels of gold.

And the LORD gave the people favour in the sight of the Egyptians. Moreover the man Moses was very great in the land of Egypt, in the sight of Pharaoh's servants, and in the sight of the people [Exod. 11:1–3].

The word "borrow" in this passage simply means to collect back wages. The Israelites had served for years as slaves and had never received any payment for their labors. Now they were going to get their money. They were literally to go to their neighbors and ask for their back wages. The Lord gave the Israelites favor in the eyes of the Egyptians, and they were glad to pay the children of Israel their just payment.

THE FIRSTBORN OF EGYPT ARE THREATENED WITH DEATH

And Moses said, Thus saith the LORD, About midnight will I go out into the midst of Egypt.

And all the firstborn in the land of Egypt shall die, from the firstborn of Pharaoh that sitteth upon his throne, even unto the firstborn of the maidservant that is behind the mill; and all the firstborn of beasts.

And there shall be a great cry throughout all the land of Egypt, such as there was none like it, nor shall be like it any more.

But against any of the children of Israel shall not a dog move his tongue, against man or beast: that ye may know how that the LORD doth put a difference between the Egyptians and Israel.

And all these thy servants shall come down unto me, and bow down themselves unto me, saying, Get thee out, and all the people that follow thee: and after that I will go out. And he went out from Pharaoh in a great anger.

And the LORD said unto Moses, Pharaoh shall not hearken unto you; that my wonders may be multiplied in the land of Egypt.

And Moses and Aaron did all these wonders before Pharaoh; and the LORD hardened Pharaoh's heart, so that he would not let the children of Israel go out of his land [Exod. 11:4–10].

Now the firstborn of both man and beast belonged to the gods of Egypt. The Lord God will claim the firstfruits of the Egyptian gods. He is going to show that there is a difference between the children of Israel and the Egyptians. The difference did not lie in the death angel which passed over both the lands of Egypt and Goshen. It did not lie in the fact that one race was Jew and one was Gentile. The difference lay in the blood of the lamb put upon the doorpost. Each home protected by the blood would not be touched by the death angel. This was the beginning of the oldest religious holiday of the Jews, the Passover Feast. The Passover is one of the most eloquent portraits of the Lord Jesus Christ found in the Old Testament.

CHAPTER 12

THEME: The beginning of Israel's religious year; institution of the Feast of the Passover; the tenth plague—death of the firstborn; the Israelites are driven out of Egypt

The Feast of the Passover was instituted as a memorial to Israel's deliverance from Egypt and their adoption as Jehovah's nation. The Passover is a festival that laid the foundation of the nation Israel's birth into a new relationship with God.

THE BEGINNING OF ISRAEL'S RELIGIOUS YEAR

Chapter 12 is a high point in the Book of Exodus. Here we find the institution of the Feast of the Passover. It is a picture of that which Paul speaks of in 1 Corinthians 5:7, "... For even Christ our passover is sacrificed for us." Christ is in this chapter.

And the Lord spake unto Moses and Aaron in the land of Egypt, saying,

This month shall be unto you the beginning of months: it shall be the first month of the year to you [Exod. 12:1–2].

This chapter brings us to a new division in the Book of Exodus. The first division (chapters 1–11) deals with Moses, the deliverer. Chapters 12–14 deal with the deliverance of Israel. The first was a deliverer, now it's the deliverance. The deliverance is actually not by Moses. The deliverance is first by blood. That's the Passover Feast, the death of the firstborn. Then in chapters 13 and 14, crossing the Red Sea and the destruction of the army of Egypt are by power. God delivered them by blood and by power. And our redemption today is by blood and by power. The blood that the Lord Jesus Christ shed on the cross paid the penalty for our sins. The power of the Holy Spirit makes it real and effectual in our sinful hearts. Zechariah 4:6 says, "... Not by might, nor by power, but by my spirit, saith the Lord of hosts." Redemption is the work of the Lord Jesus on the cross for us and the work of the Holy Spirit in us.

Verses 1 and 2 of this chapter tell of the birthday of a nation. When Israel entered Egypt, it was as a family. When they made their exit from Egypt, it was as a nation. The interesting point is that God puts the emphasis on the family here because the family comprises the building blocks out of which the nation was made. You remember how Pharaoh forced the Israelites to make bricks without straw. All the time that Israel was in bondage,

God made them the bricks of the family for the building of a nation out of the straws of individuals. An old cliché says, "No nation is stronger than the families of that nation."

The zero hour has come for Israel. The countdown begins in this chapter for the exodus of the children of Israel out of Egypt.

INSTITUTION OF THE FEAST OF THE PASSOVER

Speak ye unto all the congregation of Israel, saying, In the tenth day of this month they shall take to them every man a lamb, according to the house of their fathers, a lamb for an house [Exod. 12:3].

There are two prominent points of emphasis in this verse: (1) the blood, and (2) the family. The Israelites have become a nation and God is going to deliver them, but He will do it by families and by the individuals in the family. There was to be a lamb in every house. The lamb, of course, speaks of the blood that will be put on the doorpost.

And if the household be too little for the lamb, let him and his neighbour next unto his house take it according to the number of the souls; every man according to his eating shall make your count for the lamb [Exod. 12:4].

This verse does not say anything about the lamb being too little for the household. This would not happen; the lamb is sufficient. It is possible, however, that the household might be too little for the lamb. God is interested in each individual member of the family. Each family was to have a lamb, but what if a man and his wife were childless or had married children who lived apart from them? This couple is then supposed to join with a neighbor who is in the same position and divide the lamb. Each individual in each family is to receive a part of the lamb. The celebration of the Feast of the Passover is to be a personal, private matter. It is redemption for the nation, yes, but it centers in the family. It must be received and accepted by each individual member in the family. The Passover is a family affair.

God is presenting the modus operandi by which He is going to save individuals. No one is saved because he is the member of a nation or a family. Take, for example, the account of the Philippian jailor and the salvation of his household as told in the Book of Acts, chapter 17. His family was not saved because the jailor believed, but because each member of his family made a transaction with *the Lamb;* each had to partake of the Lamb. That was true here. Every member had to exhibit his faith in this way. ". . .Believe on the Lord Jesus Christ, and thou shalt be saved, and thy house" (Acts 16:31) does not mean that if you believe, your family will be saved. No! Your family will have to believe on the Lord Jesus Christ, and then they will be saved. Each one will have to participate and partake of it in order to come in under the protection and the redemption of the blood that is out on the doorpost of the house.

We have come to a fateful night in the land of Egypt. The final plague is about to descend upon the people. The Israelites in the land of Goshen were spared during the last three plagues, and God's people were delivered from judgment, but they were not redeemed. Now they have to be redeemed and exhibit faith in the blood.

Your lamb shall be without blemish, a male of the first year: ye shall take it out from the sheep, or from the goats:

And ye shall keep it up until the fourteenth day of the same month: and the whole assembly of the congregation of Israel shall kill it in the evening [Exod. 12:5–6].

This portion of Scripture is quite interesting. Note that each family had a lamb. Thousands of lambs must have been slain that evening, but the sixth verse reads, "Israel shall kill *it* in the evening." These many lambs were speaking of another Lamb. God looked at all of these lambs as that one Lamb, the Lord Jesus Christ, who was the Passover offered for us. This feast was pointing to the coming of the Lord Jesus Christ into the world.

And they shall take of the blood, and strike it on the two side posts and on the upper door post of the houses, wherein they shall eat it [Exod. 12:7].

The children of Israel were to put the blood of the lamb outside on the door. Upon seeing the blood, the death angel would pass over the house. I believe there is a picture given here that will answer a question that is asked many times: What will happen to the little children of believers at the time of the Rapture? If small children are in the house when the Lord comes for His own, will He take the Mom and Dad and leave the little ones behind? This chapter shows us that God will not leave the young ones behind.

Inside the home the family is eating the lamb, and by faith they are partaking of Christ. The young children do not know what is taking place. Will they be left behind in Egypt when Israel goes out from the land? If a little one has not yet reached the age of accountability, will he be slain? Oh no, friend, the blood covers everyone in the family. God will not leave small children behind at the time of the Rapture any more than He left them behind when the Israelites were redeemed and left the land of Egypt.

And they shall eat the flesh in that night, roast with fire, and unleavened bread; and with bitter herbs they shall eat it [Exod. 12:8].

Each instruction connected with this feast had a specific meaning and message. This verse speaks of the fellowship of the family. The family entered into the celebration of the Passover *together.* I want to make a statement now that will cause some heated reactions. Today, in our very highly organized church programs, we put the juniors in one place, the junior high group in another place, and the senior high group in still another place. Can't you just hear Moses telling the Israelites to take their babies over to the nursery in Pharaoh's palace because that is where he was raised! Then he might tell them to take the juniors over to the volleyball court, and so forth. May I say to you that a lot of the children would have missed out on the Exodus that night. The observance of the Passover was a family affair, and I am afraid that our churches today are guilty of dividing families. Families should be together in church.

When I was a young preacher in Tennessee, I held meetings in many country churches and had the best time of my life. I would start preaching in the evening to families who might have a baby with them. The mother would cradle a restless child in her arms, and I learned to out-talk them. If I can't out-talk a six-month-old child, there is something radically wrong! So I learned to preach above them. Then the baby would go to sleep, and the mother would take it to the back of the church and put the child on a pallet. She would come back and sit with her husband and maybe two or three other children. Mothers would pop up like popcorn all over the assembly and put their children on the pallets and return to sit with their families. This went on night after night.

One member told me about a preacher who had held meetings in the church about a year ago. He told the congregation that he was a greater preacher than the apostle Paul. He paused for a moment after making that statement because he knew the people would question it. "I am a greater preacher than Paul because he preached until midnight and put only one person to sleep. I have not preached for thirty minutes, and I have put a dozen to sleep." On that basis, friends, I too, am a great preacher!

These small country churches were not very well organized, but they produced some wonderful saints of God. I do not have any confidence in the revolutionary crowd storming our campuses today. We have done it wrong, friends. God's pattern was family centered and we have departed from this pattern.

We are also told in this verse that they were to eat the flesh of the lamb roast with fire. Fire speaks of judgment. There must be judgment of sin. They were to eat the lamb with unleavened bread. Leaven speaks of sin, and unleavened bread speaks of Christ as the One we are to feed upon. They were also to partake of this meal with bitter herbs. Although there are different meanings attached to these herbs, in this context I believe it means that our experience will not always be sweet after we have received Jesus Christ as Savior. The bitter herbs go with redemption.

Eat not of it raw, nor sodden at all with water, but roast with fire; his head with his legs, and with the purtenance thereof [Exod. 12:9].

This sacrifice could not be eaten raw because it spoke of the judgment of sin in human lives, and this requires sacrifice and the fire of judgment. When a person comes to Christ, he comes as a sinner. The sacrifice was not to be soaked with water. This simply means that we must trust Christ and Him alone. Unfortunately there are many today who are trusting in water for their salvation. Everything was to be roasted. It was the judgment of fire.

And thus shall ye eat it; with your loins girded, your shoes on your feet, and your staff in your hand; and ye shall eat it in haste: it is the LORD's passover.

For I will pass through the land of Egypt this night, and will smite all the firstborn in the land of Egypt, both man and beast; and against all the gods of Egypt I will execute judgment: I am the LORD [Exod. 12:11–12].

Friend, when you come to Christ, you should have your loins girded and be ready to get out of the world and no longer be involved in it. I do not believe that you can be converted and continue living a sinful life. This does not mean that you will not sin occasionally, but it does mean that you will not make a habit of living in a pattern of sin.

We had a remarkable instance of a woman in Los Angeles who ran a liquor store and was converted to Christ. She called me by phone and said she was getting out of the liquor business. She said, "If you tell me to take a hammer and break every bottle in the store, I will do it." But it was all she had. I told her to sell the business. She sold it and is a wonderful Christian today.

You will get out of "Egypt" if the blood has been put on the doorposts. You are to eat the sacrificial lamb with your loins girt about, ready to go.

God had directed His plagues, one at a time, against the principal gods of Egypt. All of the gods demanded the offering of the firstborn. Now God is turning His guns against all the Egyptian idols.

And the blood shall be to you for a token upon the houses where ye are: and when I see the blood, I will pass over you, and the plague shall not be upon you to destroy you, when I smite the land of Egypt [Exod. 12:13].

The Israelites were not saved because they were the seed of Abraham. If the Egyptians had obeyed God's command, they, too, would have been saved. God said, "When I see the *blood*, I will pass over you." No one was saved because he was doing the best he could, or because he was honest, or because he was a good person. God said, "When I see the *blood*, I will pass over you." They were not to run out of the house during the night and look at the blood; they were to have confidence and faith in it. They were not saved because they went through the ceremony of circumcision, or because they belonged to some church. God said, "When I see the *blood*, I will pass over you." The death angel was not making a survey of the neighborhood. They were not to open a window and tell the death angel how good they were and how much charity work they had done. Any man who put his neck out of a window that night would have died. God said, "When I see the blood, I will pass over you." Nothing needed to be added. Who was saved that night? Those who believed God. Those who had sprinkled the blood upon their doorposts and trusted in it. Although I do not understand it completely, I believe what God says. He tells me that the shed blood of Christ will save me and nothing else will.

God said that when he saw the blood, he would pass over that home. The blood was not some mystic or superstitious sign. A great principle runs all the way through the Word of God that without shedding of blood, there is no remission of sins. In other words, God cannot arbitrarily or big-heartedly shut His eyes to sin and do nothing about it, any more than can a judge today when the guilty are brought before him. The judge should apply the law to the guilty, and the penalty should be paid. Part of our problem in America today is the laxity in law enforcement. But God's law is inexorable in the universe—"The soul that sinneth, it shall die." The death sentence is upon all of us. But God is gracious, and an innocent life may be substituted for the guilty. Up until Christ came, it was a lamb. Then Jesus was ". . . the Lamb of God, which taketh away the sin of the world" (John 1:29). If we receive Christ, we are saved from the judgment that we deserve as sinners.

Now on that night in Egypt, there was the death of the firstborn in every home that was not protected by the blood. The application of the blood on the doorposts and the lintels of the home was an indication of faith, you see. That answers to the appropriation of a personal faith in Christ.

There followed the Passover Feast. In the Book of Leviticus there are instructions given for the Passover and then the Feast of Unleavened Bread, which actually was part of it, but took place after the Passover Feast.

And this day shall be unto you for a memorial; and ye shall keep it a feast to the LORD throughout your generations; ye shall keep it a feast by an ordinance for ever.

Seven days shall ye eat unleavened bread; even the first day ye shall put away leaven out of your houses: for whosoever eateth leavened bread from the first day until the seventh day, that soul shall be cut off from Israel.

And in the first day there shall be an holy convocation, and in the seventh day there shall be an holy convocation to you; no manner of work shall be done in them, save that which every man

must eat, that only may be done of you [Exod. 12:14–16].

Actually, this has nothing to do with the death angel passing over. It has nothing to do with their salvation. This is a feast of fellowship for those within the home. It is a duty, of course—God commanded it—and it is also a privilege. They are to have fellowship with God.

And ye shall observe the feast of unleavened bread; for in this selfsame day have I brought your armies out of the land of Egypt: therefore shall ye observe this day in your generations by an ordinance for ever [Exod. 12:17].

They ate the unleavened bread on the wilderness march because on the night of the Passover they were expelled from Egypt. And they ate the bread for seven days.

Notice that it is unleavened bread. If they ate leavened bread they were cut off—that is, cut off from fellowship.

Leaven is mentioned eight times between verses 14 and 20.

Seven days shall there be no leaven found in your houses: for whosoever eateth that which is leavened, even that soul shall be cut off from the congregation of Israel, whether he be a stranger, or born in the land.

Ye shall eat nothing leavened; in all your habitations shall ye eat unleavened bread [Exod. 12:19–20].

Leaven is a principle of evil. It represents that which is evil and offensive. In the thirteenth chapter of Matthew there is a parable about a woman hiding leaven in three measures of meal. That leaven is not the gospel because leaven is a principle of evil. The three measures of meal represents the Word of God, and leaven (evil) has been put into it. It is amazing to see the amount of error being taught today, and how many gullible folk believe it. "Leaven" is being mixed into the teaching of the Word. All of the cults and "isms" use the Bible, but mix false doctrine with it. This is what the children of Israel were told to avoid.

Our Lord made this matter of "leaven" clear in the Gospel of Matthew. Matthew 16:6 says, "Then Jesus said unto them, Take heed and beware of the leaven of the Pharisees and of the Sadducees." Then Matthew 16:11 continues, "How is it that ye do not understand that I spake it not to you concerning bread, that ye should beware of the leaven of the Pharisees and of the Sadducees?" The Lord's disciples, at this time, thought He was speaking about physical bread. Later they understood that the Lord was speaking about the *doctrine* of the Pharisees, which was evil.

Unleavened bread is not palatable. There are a great many people who do not like the study of the Bible, the pure, unleavened Word of God. Many people love to come to church for the social time, or the music, or the beauty of the place, but not for the Word of God. They do not want the Word of God because it is not palatable to them.

I have been in Israel during the Feast of Unleavened Bread and never got so tired of unleavened bread in my life because I was brought up in the South where we had hot biscuits that puff right up. What a wonderful night it was when this feast came to an end and they brought out the real bread. It tasted good to the natural man. Unleavened bread is not as tasty as the leavened bread is, but the Word of God is the food that is good for the child of God.

And ye shall take a bunch of hyssop, and dip it in the blood that is in the basin, and strike the lintel and the two side posts with the blood that is in the basin; and none of you shall go out at the door of his house until the morning.

For the LORD will pass through to smite the Egyptians; and when he seeth the blood upon the lintel, and on the two side posts, the LORD will pass over the door, and will not suffer the destroyer to come in unto your houses to smite you [Exod. 12:22–23].

Have you wondered how they put the blood on the door posts? Hyssop is a fluffy little plant that grows around rocks. It was used to apply the blood to the house. Hyssop, to me, represents faith. That is the way the blood of Christ is applied to your heart and life. You trust what Christ has done when He died for you.

THE TENTH PLAGUE—
DEATH OF THE FIRSTBORN

This is the last judgment and the last plague to come upon the land of Egypt. God had prepared His people for it. The land of Goshen had escaped the last three plagues but could not escape this one unless there was blood on the doorposts. Any Egyptian could follow the example of the Israelites—put blood on his doorpost and believe God—and the death angel would have spared the firstborn in his house. It is going to surprise many people someday when they discover that the Lord

Jesus is not going to ask which church they belonged to. If you have trusted Christ as your Savior, the Holy Spirit of God has baptized you into the body of believers, and you are a member of the true church.

And it came to pass, that at midnight the LORD smote all the firstborn in the land of Egypt, from the firstborn of Pharaoh that sat on his throne unto the firstborn of the captive that was in the dungeon; and all the firstborn of cattle.

And Pharaoh rose up in the night, he, and all his servants, and all the Egyptians; and there was a great cry in Egypt; for there was not a house where there was not one dead [Exod. 12:29–30].

This final judgment claimed the life of the firstborn in each house. Up to this point God had not touched human life. Now he does, but do not say that God is a murderer. "The Lord gives and the Lord takes away; blessed be the name of the Lord." He who creates life has the authority to take it away.

THE ISRAELITES ARE DRIVEN
OUT OF EGYPT

That night Pharaoh got up:

And he called for Moses and Aaron by night, and said, Rise up, and get you forth from among my people, both ye and the children of Israel; and go, serve the LORD, as ye have said.

Also take your flocks and your herds, as ye have said, and be gone; and bless me also [Exod. 12:31–32].

Pharaoh finally has had to give up. Until now he has been reluctant to give in to Moses' demands but this plague reached in and touched his own son. God did not begin by touching the lives of the firstborn; He began the contest with Pharaoh by changing Aaron's rod into a crocodile. If Pharaoh had believed God, the children of Israel could have left the land and he would have spared his people the judgments. The blame, therefore, should not belong to God.

And the Egyptians were urgent upon the people, that they might send them out of the land in haste; for they said, We be all dead men [Exod. 12:33].

The Egyptians did not know where the judgment of God would end. God had taken their firstborn; what would He do next? Perhaps He would bring death to all the Egyptians, and so Pharaoh and the people told the Israelites to get out of the land because they feared for their own lives.

And the people took their dough before it was leavened, their kneadingtroughs being bound up in their clothes upon their shoulders.

And the children of Israel did according to the word of Moses; and they borrowed of the Egyptians jewels of silver, and jewels of gold, and raiment [Exod. 12:34–35].

The word "borrow" is the Hebrew *shaal*, meaning "to ask." God gave them favor in the sight of the Egyptians so that when they asked, the Egyptians *gave* (not lent) them whatever they wanted. It was God's way of simply collecting back wages for their years of slave labor in Egypt. The Egyptians owed the Israelites so much in back wages that the children of Israel spoiled them; that is, Israel left with much of Egypt's wealth.

And the children of Israel journeyed from Rameses to Succoth, about six hundred thousand on foot that were men, beside children [Exod. 12:37].

It would seem that there came out of the land of Egypt well over one million people. There were six hundred thousand men on foot besides all the women and children.

Then our attention is called to another interesting fact:

And a mixed multitude went up also with them; and flocks, and herds, even very much cattle [Exod. 12:38].

In addition to the Israelites that left Egypt, a mixed multitude left with them. They will be the cause of much trouble in the camp of Israel. We learn more about them in the Book of Numbers; the mixed multitude are troublemakers. Factually, they are half-breeds. An Egyptian married a Jewish maiden or a Hebrew married an Egyptian maiden. The offspring of a union like this had to make a decision—shall he go out of the land of Egypt with the Israelites or stay with the Egyptians? Many of the mixed multitude left the land and many stayed. Those who left, often wondered if they had made a mistake, and when trouble and hardship came they were the first to complain. They were not Israelites in the true sense of the word.

One of the big problems in Israel today is the mixed multitude, those who have a Gentile parent. Are they Israelites? Also we have a problem in the church with those who join the church but are not saved. I have been a pastor for a long time, and I have never believed that a troublemaker in a church is really a child of God. (But let's understand what we mean by troublemakers. We deal with that in Num. 11.)

And they baked unleavened cakes of the dough which they brought forth out of Egypt, for it was not leavened; because they were thrust out of Egypt, and could not tarry, neither had they prepared for themselves any victual.

Now the sojourning of the children of Israel, who dwelt in Egypt, was four hundred and thirty years.

And it came to pass at the end of the four hundred and thirty years, even the selfsame day it came to pass, that all the hosts of the LORD went out from the land of Egypt.

It is a night to be much observed unto the LORD for bringing them out from the land of Egypt: this is that night of the LORD to be observed of all the children of Israel in their generations [Exod. 12:39–42].

The celebration of the Passover goes back to the exodus of Israel out of the land of Egypt. They were never to forget what the Lord God did for them until the King comes again and the Millennium is established. And then they will forget it. We will see that later.

All the congregation of Israel shall keep it.

And when a stranger shall sojourn with thee, and will keep the passover to the LORD, let all his males be circumcised, and then let him come near and keep it; and he shall be as one that is born in the land: for no uncircumcised person shall eat thereof [Exod. 12:47–48].

Only those who identified themselves by faith with the people of God could take part in this observance. If a Gentile wanted to identify himself in belief with Israel, he was welcome.

One law shall be to him that is homeborn, and unto the stranger that sojourneth among you.

Thus did all the children of Israel; as the LORD commanded Moses and Aaron, so did they.

And it came to pass the selfsame day, that the LORD did bring the children of Israel out of the land of Egypt by their armies [Exod. 12:49–51].

As we follow the children of Israel out of Egypt, to the Red Sea and into the wilderness, we will learn lessons that correspond to experiences in the Christian life today.

CHAPTER 13

THEME: Israel's firstborn sanctified to God; journey to Etham by divine guidance

ISRAEL'S FIRSTBORN SANCTIFIED TO GOD

The children of Israel are leaving the land of Egypt and moving toward the Red Sea.

And the LORD spake unto Moses, saying,

Sanctify unto me all the firstborn, whatsoever openeth the womb among the children of Israel, both of man and of beast: it is mine.

And Moses said unto the people, Remember this day, in which ye came out from Egypt, out of the house of bondage; for by strength of hand the LORD brought you out from this place: there shall no leavened bread be eaten [Exod. 13:1–3].

The firstborn in Egypt had died. The gods of Egypt had always claimed the firstborn as their own, and now God claims the firstborn of Israel as His own. He wants the first from believers today, also. Many Christians do not give Him the first place. God claims our best, our very best; God claims the first in everything. Even though He wants first place in our lives, many believers put Him last, and that creates a problem. If we have time, we work for the Lord, but most of our time is spent on personal interests and amusements. We usually give the Lord what is left over.

I remember hearing Billy Sunday tell a story years ago. He was riding across the country with William Wrigley, the chewing gum man. Mr. Wrigley was a Christian, and as they rode on the train he told Billy Sunday that he had made it a practice in his life to give the Lord one tenth of everything that he made, and he added that it was not the last tenth he made that he gave to the Lord. William Wrigley gave the Lord the *first* tenth of his earnings. It is quite interesting how the Lord blessed him and prospered him. Now God doesn't guaran-

tee material prosperity to anyone, but it is interesting how He has blessed men and women who put Him first. And to put Him first means no half truth in *saying* we put Him first—no compromising.

The children of Israel have just come out of Egypt where they served for years as slaves. Then God immediately requires of them their firstborn. Many of them probably said, "Look, Lord, you have just delivered us out of slavery and now you are claiming our firstborn for your own!" The Lord Jesus Christ does the same thing for you and me. He saves us out of the bondage of sin, delivers us, and sets us free. God says, "If the Son therefore shall make you free, ye shall be free indeed" (John 8:36). The Lord is also saying that He wants us to give ourselves to Him. You say, "I'm free!" Are you really free? You have been bought with a price—the precious blood of Jesus Christ. The blessing comes when you give yourself to Him voluntarily and put Him first.

And it shall be when the LORD shall bring thee into the land of the Canaanites, and the Hittites, and the Amorites, and the Hivites, and the Jebusites, which he sware unto thy fathers to give thee, a land flowing with milk and honey, that thou shalt keep this service in this month [Exod. 13:5].

In other words, the Israelites were to observe the Passover Feast and the Feast of Unleavened Bread.

Seven days thou shalt eat unleavened bread, and in the seventh day shall be a feast to the LORD.

Unleavened bread shall be eaten seven days; and there shall no leavened bread be seen with thee, neither shall there be leaven seen with thee in all thy quarters [Exod. 13:6–7].

When the Israelites left Egypt, they took on their journey their kneading-troughs and the dough that was in them. This was leavened dough and God says, "I want you to get rid of that. Unleavened bread shall be eaten seven days, and there shall no leavened bread be seen with thee nor in thy house."

And thou shalt shew thy son in that day, saying, This is done because of that which the LORD did unto me when I came forth out of Egypt [Exod. 13:8].

This observance was to be passed from one generation to the other so that the people would always remember that God delivered them out of the land of Egypt.

And it shall be for a sign unto thee upon thine hand, and for a memorial between thine eyes, that the LORD's law may be in thy mouth: for with a strong hand hath the LORD brought thee out of Egypt.

Thou shalt therefore keep this ordinance in his season from year to year.

And it shall be when the LORD shall bring thee into the land of the Canaanites, as he sware unto thee and to thy fathers, and shall give it thee,

That thou shalt set apart unto the LORD all that openeth the matrix, and every firstling that cometh of a beast which thou hast; the males shall be the LORD's [Exod. 13:9–12].

The firstborn of all the stock that belonged to the children of Israel belonged to the Lord.

And every firstling of an ass thou shalt redeem with a lamb; and if thou wilt not redeem it, then thou shalt break his neck: and all the firstborn of man among thy children shalt thou redeem [Exod. 13:13].

Every firstling of an ass was to be redeemed with a lamb. God did not want one of these long-eared animals as an offering. The offering had to be a lamb. The firstborn of man among their children were to be redeemed, as we shall see later on, by silver. Silver was the redemption money.

And it shall be when thy son asketh thee in time to come, saying, What is this? that thou shalt say unto him, By strength of hand the LORD brought us out from Egypt, from the house of bondage:

And it came to pass, when Pharaoh would hardly let us go, that the LORD slew all the firstborn in the land of Egypt, both the firstborn of man, and the firstborn of beast: therefore I sacrifice to the LORD all that openeth the matrix, being males; but all the firstborn of my children I redeem [Exod. 13:14–15].

This observance was to remind the Israelites that God delivered them out of the land of Egypt. The firstborn of their sons had to be redeemed by silver. We are told in 1 Peter 1:18–19 that, "Forasmuch as ye know that ye were not redeemed with corruptible things, as silver and gold, from your vain conversation received by tradition from your fathers; but with the precious blood of Christ, as of a lamb without blemish and without spot."

And it came to pass, when Pharaoh had let the people go, that God led them not through the way of the land of the Philistines, although that was near; for God said, Lest peradventure the people repent when they see war, and they return to Egypt [Exod. 13:17].

The Israelites had just come out of slavery, and they were not prepared for warfare. The shortest way for them to go to the land which God had given them was up the sea coast. During the 1967 Six-Day war in the land of Palestine, the Israelites moved right down the sea coast and moved the Egyptians right out. Of course, the Israelites had tanks and planes to do it. They were prepared. The Israelites coming out of Egyptian slavery had no weapons to fight with; so God graciously took them through the wilderness. It was a longer route to the land, but it would spare any warfare. They would not have to face an enemy until they entered the land. It took them forty years to get through the wilderness and into the Promised Land. By then they would have an army and be equipped, as we shall see.

Someone might say, "But God could have delivered them by some miracle." This is true, but this kind of an attitude makes me sick. Some Christians think that God should perform a miracle for them every minute. They feel that they have the right to command the Lord to intervene for them if they are sick or in trouble. It is not a question of His ability; He certainly can do it. Rather, it is a question of the *way* God wants to do it. He is following a plan. And when it is necessary, God will perform a miracle for us—but only to accomplish His will and way in our lives.

God could have brought the Israelites through the land of the Philistines by a miracle. Had they been attacked, God could have delivered them. When it is necessary, God is prepared to perform miracles but only to accomplish His will.

But God led the people about, through the way of the wilderness of the Red sea: and the children of Israel went up harnessed out of the land of Egypt [Exod. 13:18].

The word "harnessed" is an interesting word. It means that the children of Israel left Egypt in an orderly manner. They did not come out of the land like a mob but in an organized way. They did not have an army but they lined up five in a row. If you had seen them going through the wilderness, you would have observed a most orderly group.

And Moses took the bones of Joseph with him: for he had straitly sworn the children of Israel, saying, God will surely visit you; and ye shall carry up my bones away hence with you [Exod. 13:19].

When the Israelites left Egypt, Moses took the bones of Joseph. There is an interesting passage in Genesis 50:24 which says, "And Joseph said unto his brethren, I die: and God will surely visit you, and bring you out of this land unto the land which he sware to Abraham, to Isaac, and to Jacob." Genesis 50:25 continues by saying. "And Joseph took an oath of the children of Israel, saying, God will surely visit you, and ye shall carry up my bones from hence." At least two hundred years had elapsed since Joseph had spoken these words, but now the time had come. When he died, he was a national hero and would have to be buried in Egypt. But eventually a Pharaoh arose who did not know Joseph. Since Joseph was no longer a national hero, his bones could be removed from Egypt without protest.

Joseph wanted to be buried in the Promised Land. But why remove his body and bury it in the land? If Joseph knew he would be raised from the dead someday and taken up to heaven, what difference would it make if his launching pad was in Egypt or in the land of Israel? Well, the fact of the matter is that he was not expecting to go to heaven. He expected to be raised in the resurrection of his people *in* that land for the Millennium—and then for eternity. This will be heaven for them. This was the hope of Joseph, and it is also the hope of Moses. By faith Moses takes the bones of Joseph to the Promised Land.

JOURNEY TO ETHAM
BY DIVINE GUIDANCE

And they took their journey from Succoth, and encamped in Etham, in the edge of the wilderness.

And the LORD went before them by day in a pillar of a cloud, to lead them the way; and by night in a pillar of fire, to give them light; to go by day and night:

He took not away the pillar of the cloud by day, nor the pillar of fire by night, from before the people [Exod. 13:20–22].

The children of Israel are moving toward the hot, burning desert that even Moses called a great and terrible wilderness. They went through it and did not even get sunburned because they had a pillar of cloud over them by day. This nation had something that no other nation has ever had: the Glory, the visible presence of God. When Paul was defining his kinsman, he said, "Who are Israelites; to whom pertaineth the adoption, and the glory. . . ." (Rom. 9:4). These people had the glory, the visible presence of God.

Not even the church has the visible presence of God with it. Nothing visible has been given to the church. Ephesians 1:3 tells us that God ". . .hath blessed us with all *spiritual* blessings in heavenly places in Christ." They were looking forward to the coming of Christ, and *we* look back to an historical event. We do not need the visible presence of God in order to walk by faith. They needed the "glory" because the redemption had not yet been worked out in history as it has now.

God made every preparation for every eventuality in order to bring His people safely through the wilderness.

CHAPTER 14

THEME: Pharaoh and his army pursue Israel; God's victory over Egypt

PHARAOH AND HIS ARMY PURSUE ISRAEL

And the LORD spake unto Moses, saying,

Speak unto the children of Israel, that they turn and encamp before Pi-hahiroth, between Migdol and the sea, over against Baal-zephon: before it shall ye encamp by the sea [Exod. 14: 1–2].

It is impossible to locate these places definitely, but they were somewhere between the Nile River and the Red Sea.

For Pharaoh will say of the children of Israel, They are entangled in the land, the wilderness hath shut them in [Exod. 14:3].

Pharaoh has spies watching the children of Israel. The movement of two and one half million people would be difficult to conceal anyway. Pharaoh expects the Israelites to move up the coastal route and through the land of the Philistines. When they head toward the wilderness, he thinks they are lost and do not know where they are going. God says that when he thinks they are trapped, he will pursue them. It is obvious that Pharaoh let the Israelites go reluctantly. God is not through with this man Pharaoh yet.

And I will harden Pharaoh's heart, that he shall follow after them; and I will be honoured upon Pharaoh, and upon all his host; that the Egyptians may know that I am the LORD. And they did so [Exod. 14:4].

You would think that the Egyptians had experienced enough disaster, but something even more profound is going to take place that will convince them.

And it was told the king of Egypt that the people fled: and the heart of Pharaoh and of his servants was turned against the people, and they said, Why have we done this, that we have let Israel go from serving us?

And he made ready his chariot, and took his people with him:

And he took six hundred chosen chariots, and all the chariots of Egypt, and captains over every one of them [Exod. 14:5–7].

The host of Egypt moves against the children of Israel with six hundred chariots. You can imagine what that number of chariots could do to a poor, helpless, defenseless people—especially women, children and cattle. They would make havoc and hash of them!

And the LORD hardened the heart of Pharaoh king of Egypt, and he pursued after the children of Israel: and the children of Israel went out with an high hand.

But the Egyptians pursued after them, all the horses and chariots of Pharaoh, and his horsemen, and his army, and overtook them encamping by the sea, beside Pi-hahiroth, before Baal-zephon.

And when Pharaoh drew nigh, the children of Israel lifted up their eyes, and, behold, the Egyptians marched after them; and they were sore afraid: and the children of Israel cried out unto the LORD [Exod. 14:8–10].

The Red Sea is ahead of the Israelites, and the hosts of Egypt are behind them. These poor defenseless people are caught between the devil and the deep blue sea. From a natural viewpoint, the Israelites are in a bad spot.

And they said unto Moses, Because there were no graves in Egypt, hast thou taken us away to die in the wilderness? wherefore hast thou dealt thus with us, to carry us forth out of Egypt? [Exod. 14:11].

This is a rather ironic statement, and I am sure it was even more so in that day. The great pyramids stood as monuments to the burial places of kings. Mummies were all over the place in Egypt; it was a great burying ground. The children of Israel were saying, "Did you bring us all the way out into the wilderness to die because there was not room to bury us in the land of Egypt?" The Israelites are sure they are going to be slaughtered out in the wilderness.

Is not this the word that we did tell thee in Egypt, saying, Let us alone, that we may serve the Egyptians? For it had been better for us to serve the Egyptians, than that we should die in the wilderness [Exod. 14:12].

The Israelites, when they were in the land of Egypt, cried out for deliverance. God provided the opportunity for them to leave; but the minute they were in danger, they wanted to return to Egypt.

Now notice what God is going to do for His people. They are helpless and hopeless without the aid of God. If they are to be redeemed, God will have to do it. I wish we could get that objective viewpoint of ourselves today because we are just like the Israelites. If we could go with the astronauts to the moon and look down on this little earth of ours, we would see people lost in sin. Actually our world is a pretty hopeless place; a great burying ground. In Romans 5:12 Paul tells us, "Wherefore, as by one man sin entered into the world, and death by sin; and so death passed upon all men, for that all have sinned." Man has been on the march for over five thousand years. Where is he marching to? Man is marching to the grave. It isn't pretty, but it is true. Man is the most colossal failure in God's universe.

GOD'S VICTORY OVER EGYPT

Look at these children of Israel. Unless God moves on their behalf, they are doomed. And you and I could never be redeemed unless God did it, friends. Redemption is the work of the Lord. Jonah said, ". . . Salvation is of the LORD" (Jonah 2:9); King David made the same statement, and that is the message of the New Testament.

> And Moses said unto the people, Fear ye not, stand still, and see the salvation of the LORD, which he will shew to you to-day: for the Egyptians whom ye have seen to-day, ye shall see them again no more for ever [Exod. 14:13].

The Lord will work in behalf of His people; all they have to do is accept and receive His salvation. They are to stand still and God will do the work. Remember, you cannot lift a little finger to work out your salvation. All you have to do is accept what God has done for you.

> The LORD shall fight for you, and ye shall hold your peace [Exod. 14:14].

God will bring salvation to His people and will bring the peace that comes from having sins forgiven.

> And the LORD said unto Moses, Wherefore criest thou unto me? speak unto the children of Israel, that they go forward:

> But lift thou up thy rod, and stretch out thine hand over the sea, and divide it:

> and the children of Israel shall go on dry ground through the midst of the sea [Exod. 14:15–16].

The Israelites are to stand still and see the salvation of the Lord. But when it is wrought they are to lay hold of His instructions by faith. Their faith will be evidenced in whether or not they will go forward.

Many natural explanations are offered as to how the children of Israel crossed the sea. First, I believe it is well established by reputable, conservative historians and theologians that the exodus of Israel is an historical fact. The problem for most people comes in trying to figure out *how* they crossed the Red Sea. Some say that the wind blew the water back. But there was a wall of water on both sides of the path. Others say that some sort of a natural phenomenon rolled back the sea. Still others claim that an earthquake took place at the exact moment they were ready to cross the sea. The thing that must be faced here is that a miracle took place. You either accept it or you do not. God, by a miracle, opened the sea and the Israelites walked through it on dry ground.

When the Israelites crossed the sea, they crossed to the other side dry-shod. There was not even enough water for them to get their feet damp. It would be difficult to explain this apart from a direct miracle.

> And I, behold, I will harden the hearts of the Egyptians, and they shall follow them: and I will get me honour upon Pharaoh, and upon all his host, upon his chariots, and upon his horsemen [Exod. 14:17].

Had you been at the water's edge when Pharaoh started to follow the children of Israel across the Red Sea, you would have said to him, "I suppose that you recognize that you are doing this because your heart and the hearts of your people are hardened by God, and you really don't want to do it." I think Pharaoh and his army would have laughed at you and replied, "We are chasing the Israelites because we want to." The fact is that God is forcing the Egyptians to do the thing that is in their hearts.

> And the Egyptians shall know that I am the LORD, when I have gotten me honour upon Pharaoh, upon his chariots, and upon his horsemen.

> And the angel of God, which went before the camp of Israel, removed and went behind them; and the pillar of the cloud

went from before their face, and stood behind them:

And it came between the camp of the Egyptians and the camp of Israel; and it was a cloud and darkness to them, but it gave light by night to these: so that the one came not near the other all the night.

And Moses stretched out his hand over the sea; and the LORD caused the sea to go back by a strong east wind all that night, and made the sea dry land, and the waters were divided [Exod. 14: 18–21].

There are several things to take note of in this passage. First of all, the Egyptians mentioned in verse 18 are the people who are left back in the land of Egypt. Israel will cross safely to the other side of the Red Sea, and Pharaoh and his army will perish in the waters of that sea, and the Egyptians left in the land will know that the God of the Israelites is the *Lord*. In verse 19 the "angel of God" is mentioned. I believe the Angel of God was none other than the pre-incarnate Christ. It was God Himself who stood between the Egyptians and the Israelites. When a strong east wind came, it caused the sea to go back. A natural wind could never have made a wall of water on both sides.

And the children of Israel went into the midst of the sea upon the dry ground: and the waters were a wall unto them on their right hand, and on their left.

And the Egyptians pursued, and went in after them to the midst of the sea, even all Pharaoh's horses, his chariots, and his horsemen.

And it came to pass, that in the morning watch the LORD looked unto the host of the Egyptians through the pillar of fire and of the cloud, and troubled the host of the Egyptians,

And took off their chariot wheels, that they drove them heavily: so that the Egyptians said, Let us flee from the face of Israel; for the LORD fighteth for them against the Egyptians [Exod. 14:22–25].

As God works out His plan to deliver His people, once again we see that He worked through the pillar of fire and the cloud, which I believe represent the Holy Spirit. They were led, as the child of God should be led today, by the Spirit of God.

It becomes clear to the Egyptians that what is happening to them is certainly supernatural. They want to retreat and escape the forces which are against them.

And the LORD said unto Moses, Stretch out thine hand over the sea, that the waters may come again upon the Egyptians, upon their chariots, and upon their horsemen.

And Moses stretched forth his hand over the sea, and the sea returned to his strength when the morning appeared; and the Egyptians fled against it; and the LORD overthrew the Egyptians in the midst of the sea.

And the waters returned, and covered the chariots, and the horsemen, and all the host of Pharaoh that came into the sea after them; there remained not so much as one of them [Exod. 14:26–28].

This account needs close observation because it is a *miracle*. There is no natural way to explain what happened. Many conservative men, although they believe in the Word of God and are saved by faith alone in Christ, try to explain the crossing of the Red Sea in some natural way. When you read this record, it is impossible to explain it naturally. God says it is a miracle and you either take it or leave it.

But the children of Israel walked upon dry land in the midst of the sea; and the waters were a wall unto them on their right hand, and on their left [Exod. 14:29].

This is a miracle. Twice, now, this has been made clear to us. They walked on dry land through the midst of the sea. The waters were a wall to them on the left side and on the right side. You cannot explain it on a natural basis.

Thus the LORD saved Israel that day out of the hand of the Egyptians; and Israel saw the Egyptians dead upon the sea shore.

And Israel saw that great work which the LORD did upon the Egyptians: and the people feared the LORD, and believed the LORD, and his servant Moses [Exod. 14:30–31].

These two verses state the purpose for God's deliverance of Israel. At the beginning of their wilderness march they saw the power of God when He delivered them by blood out of Egypt. Now at the Red Sea He demonstrates

His power again by taking them safely across the sea and by destroying the Egyptians pursuing them. God delivers His children by power.

CHAPTER 15

THEME: Israel's song of redemption; Israel murmurs because they lack water

ISRAEL'S SONG OF REDEMPTION

Immediately upon their safe journey across the Red Sea, the children of Israel join in singing a song.

Then sang Moses and the children of Israel this song unto the LORD, and spake, saying, I will sing unto the LORD, for he hath triumphed gloriously: the horse and his rider hath he thrown into the sea.

The LORD is my strength and song, and he is become my salvation: he is my God, and I will prepare him an habitation; my father's God, and I will exalt him.

The LORD is a man of war: the LORD is his name [Exod. 15:1–3].

They are singing lustily now. This is the same crowd, friends, that only a few hours before on the other side of the Red Sea were moaning, crying out that they wanted to go back to Egypt and saying, "Because there were no graves in Egypt, hast thou taken us away to die in the wilderness?" We are told in 1 Corinthians 10:11 that, ". . . all these things happened unto them for ensamples: and they are written for our admonition, upon whom the ends of the world are come."

God uses this experience to teach us a very important truth. "Moreover, brethren, I would not that ye should be ignorant, how that all our fathers were under the cloud, and all passed through the sea; and were all baptized unto Moses in the cloud and in the sea" (1 Cor. 10:1–2). How were the children of Israel baptized unto Moses? It could not have been by water because they crossed the sea dry-shod. Not a drop of water fell upon them. If you want to talk about water, take a good look at the Egyptians; they were the ones who got wet. Then what does it mean that the Israelites were baptized unto Moses in the cloud and in the sea? It means that they were identified. The primary meaning of *baptism* is identifica-

tion. The ritual of baptism is the baptism of water, and I believe it is important. It sets forth the real baptism which is of the Holy Spirit and identifies us with Christ and puts us in Christ. Now how were the Israelites baptized unto Moses? They complained on one side of the sea, and when they crossed to the other side, they sang the song of Moses. They were identified with Moses. They were delivered through him.

"By faith they passed through the Red sea as by dry land: which the Egyptians assaying to do were drowned" (Heb. 11:29). It was "by faith" that the Israelites crossed the sea. Whose faith was it? It was not the faith of the children of Israel because they did not have any until they crossed over the sea. They were identified with Moses. It was Moses' faith. It was Moses who smote the Red Sea. It was Moses who led them across. When they reached the other side of the sea, it was Moses who lifted the song of deliverance. Now they have seen the salvation of God. They are identified with Moses. They have been baptized unto Moses.

Friends, this is what happens when you trust the Lord Jesus Christ as Savior. He is the One who takes us out of the Egyptian bondage and the Egyptian darkness of this world. He leads us across the Red Sea. It is His deliverance and His salvation and His redemption. He brings us to the place where we can lift a song of redemption unto Him. Then we are joined to Him. We are baptized into Christ. First Corinthians 12:13 says, "For by one Spirit are we all baptized into one body, whether we be Jews or Gentiles, whether we be bond or free; and have been all made to drink into one Spirit." The Holy Spirit is the one who joins us to Christ and causes us to become one with Him. It is a wonderful thing to be joined to Him!

A dear little lady talking about the assurance of her salvation once said, "Nobody can take you out of His hand." Someone replied, "Well, you might slip through His fingers."

And she replied, "Oh my no, I couldn't slip through His fingers; I am one of His fingers." That is true, friends. We are members of the body of Christ. The Holy Spirit of God joins us to Him. What a wonderful redemption we have in Christ! What happened to Israel is an example for us. It is a picture of our redemption and what the Spirit of God does when we trust the Lord Jesus Christ as Savior.

Before the Israelites joined in with Moses to sing to their God the song of redemption, they were singing the blues, the Desert Blues. Before they crossed the sea, they sang the blues loud and long, and they will be returning to the Desert Blues again because it will be their theme song as they travel through the desert. For a time, however, they lustily sang the song of redemption.

This song can be compared with the song of Deborah and Barak in the Book of Judges. There are many songs in the Bible. David composed and sang many songs found in the Psalms. You will find that his songs are great songs. Even Jeremiah had a song, even though it was often with a wail. Other prophets had songs throughout the Old Testament.

The New Testament opens with songs. Dr. Luke records several of them. There is the song of Elizabeth when word was brought to her that she was to have a child. Mary sang a song when she learned she was to be the mother of the Lord Jesus Christ. Other great songs were connected with the birth of Christ. Finally in the Book of Revelation we get a glimpse into heaven as we see a great company gathered around the throne of God singing a new song. Probably that is going to be the first time I will be able to sing. Up to the present time I don't do very well, but by that time— with a new body and a new voice—I am sure I will be able to sing a new song.

With all the talk about peace today it might be well for everyone to read this song of Moses. It tells us that Jehovah is a man of war. In the nineteenth chapter of Revelation we see Him coming to earth and putting down all unrighteousness. Until He does that, the earth will never have peace. In Matthew 10:34 the Lord said, "Think not that I am come to send peace on earth: I came not to send peace, but a sword." These words were spoken about His first coming to the earth. The second time He comes to earth He will bring peace with the sword. That is the only way to rid the earth of unrighteousness.

This song of Moses and the Israelites recounts the wonderful experience they had in crossing the Red Sea. Their song told the story of what they had seen God do and of what God had done for them. It was something they were not apt to forget, but this song certainly kept the experience before them.

> **Pharaoh's chariots and his host hath he cast into the sea: his chosen captains also are drowned in the Red sea.**

> **The depths have covered them: they sank into the bottom as a stone.**

> **Thy right hand, O LORD, is become glorious in power: thy right hand, O LORD, hath dashed in pieces the enemy [Exod. 15:4–6].**

The Israelites are celebrating their deliverance. Egypt and the Egyptians represent to them the world, slavery, their hopelessness, and helplessness. Now they have been redeemed. That is the sum and substance of their song.

Remember that they have come out of a land of idolatry. Each plague had been leveled at one of the Egyptian gods. Now what is the conclusion they have come to?

> **Who is like unto thee, O LORD, among the gods? who is like thee, glorious in holiness, fearful in praises, doing wonders? [Exod. 15:11].**

God is teaching them great lessons concerning Himself.

> **Thou stretchedst out thy right hand, the earth swallowed them.**

> **Thou in thy mercy hast led forth the people which thou hast redeemed: thou hast guided them in thy strength unto thy holy habitation [Exod. 15:12–13].**

Israel was a redeemed people. The redemption of the people had to come first. That is the important thing today. God is not asking you to do one thing for Him until you have been redeemed and have accepted His salvation accomplished by Jesus Christ upon the cross. He is not asking you for anything. He is not demanding that the world do anything. God is not saying, "If you will prove yourself, come up to a higher standard, wash your face, rake your yard, and put up a good front, I am willing to be your good neighbor." God does not want anything from the world. He is saying to a lost world, "What will you do with My Son who died for you?" Listen once again to verse 13: "Thou in thy mercy hast led forth the people which thou hast redeemed: thou hast guided them in thy strength unto thy holy habitation."

It sounds as if they are already in the Promised Land. As far as God is concerned, they are in the land because He is going to take them there.

The LORD shall reign for ever and ever.

For the horse of Pharaoh went in with his chariots and with his horsemen into the sea, and the LORD brought again the waters of the sea upon them; but the children of Israel went on dry land in the midst of the sea [Exod. 15:18–19].

Now we are introduced to a girl we have not heard about since the birth of Moses—Miriam, the sister of Moses and Aaron.

And Miriam the prophetess, the sister of Aaron, took a timbrel in her hand; and all the women went out after her with timbrels and with dances.

And Miriam answered them, Sing ye to the LORD, for he hath triumphed gloriously; the horse and his rider hath he thrown into the sea [Exod. 15:20–21].

This is the conclusion of this song of praise and thanksgiving to God for His deliverance.

ISRAEL MURMURS BECAUSE THEY LACK WATER

Israel is across the sea now. They have had a wonderful time of praise, singing the song of Moses. They are a redeemed people. You would think that from now on life would be a bed of roses and that they would be delivered from all of their difficulties. There should not have been a cloud in the sky, a thorn along the path, nor a sigh from any of the congregation. They went three days' journey into the wilderness and what happened to them? They thirsted!

So Moses brought Israel from the Red sea, and they went out into the wilderness of Shur; and they went three days in the wilderness, and found no water [Exod. 15:22].

Egypt had been a land of plenty and with water in abundance. Quite suddenly the children of Israel crossed the Red Sea and found themselves in different circumstances. Water was not available anymore. The cisterns of Egypt were gone and they had not found the fountains of living water. I believe this is the experience of every born-again child of God. After salvation, the believer finds that the cisterns of Egypt do not satisfy at all. There is a period of soul-thirst. This is the period of time

Paul speaks of in Philippians 3:7 when he says, "But what things were gain to me, those I counted loss for Christ." Then the apostle Paul reveals a great thirst, a tremendous yearning, when he says in Philippians 3:10, "That I may know him, and the power of his resurrection, and the fellowship of his sufferings, being made conformable unto his death." This is the experience of the child of God after he is redeemed.

I would like to share a personal experience with you. I remember the time God definitely put His hand upon me for the ministry. I came to know the peace of God through trust in Christ. I wanted to study for the ministry, but for the moment I was working in a bank and traveling with a pretty fast crowd. I thought I was having a great time. I was actually the chairman of a dance committee. In those days you always had to have bootleg liquor to dance. I had committed my life to the Lord, but I decided not to break off with the old life all of a sudden. I'd make a gradual break. I decided to go to the dance that night, but I would not dance—just stand in the stag line and visit around a little bit. I was offered a drink at least a dozen times, and each time turned it down. Finally I met a fellow who worked at the bank with me and had a grudge. I was promoted into a position ahead of him, and he had never forgiven me for it. It was not my fault, because I was not in charge of the bank and did not hand out promotions, but he had never forgiven me. He took advantage of every opportunity to get at me some way, and this evening he said, "This is a pretty place for a preacher to be!" He used some strong language to drive the point home to me, too. I came to the conclusion that what he said was right and, like a little whipped dog, I went down the stairs and out onto the street. I could hear the orchestra playing in the distance, and I almost turned around and went back. I wanted to go back and say to the fellow, "Look, I think I will stay here with the gang." Thank God I did not!

There is always that trip into the wilderness after you are saved. You get a little thirsty, but the cisterns of Egypt just will not satisfy you anymore. You look for living water and actually do not know where to find it. At that time I knew very little about the Bible and couldn't find my way around in it at all. But I soon found John 7:37: "In the last day, that great day of the feast, Jesus stood and cried, saying, If any man thirst, let him come unto me, and drink." What a wonderful thing it was to come to Him!

Thirsting and not finding water was their

first experience. Now they have a second experience that was not much better.

And when they came to Marah, they could not drink of the waters of Marah, for they were bitter: therefore the name of it was called Marah.

And the people murmured against Moses, saying, What shall we drink?

And he cried unto the LORD: and the LORD shewed him a tree, which when he had cast into the waters, the waters were made sweet: there he made for them a statute and an ordinance, and there he proved them.

And said, If thou wilt diligently hearken to the voice of the LORD thy God, and wilt do that which is right in his sight, and wilt give ear to his commandments, and keep all his statutes, I will put none of these diseases upon thee, which I have brought upon the Egyptians: for I am the LORD that healeth thee [Exod. 15:23–26].

Their second experience on the other side of the sea is the bitter water of Marah. They have gone three days' journey into the wilderness and are thirsty. When they finally come to water, it is bitter and unfit to drink. And remember that the children of Israel are now redeemed people. Marah was on the path where God led them. He had marked it out for them.

You may not realize it, but the oasis of Marah is a normal Christian experience. When a bitter experience comes to a Christian, it is a puzzling and perplexing thing. Some people say, "Why does God let this happen to me?" I cannot tell you why certain things befall Christians, but I do know that God is not punishing them. He is educating them and preparing them for something. The Lord said, "In the world ye shall have tribulation." Right on your pathway there is a Marah. In the pathway of every believer there is a Marah. God has arranged it all. Someone has said, "Disappointments are God's appointments." I have found this to be true.

Once a young person said to me, "I wanted to go to school. I wanted to prepare for the mission field, but my father died and I had to help support my mother; so I could not go to school." When I was a pastor in Nashville, the superintendent of our junior department was a beautiful, sweet, uncomplaining, young woman. She was prematurely gray, and one day I inquired why. I was told that at one time she was engaged to one of the finest young men in the church. They were to be married, but he was called away to war and was killed. It caused her hair to turn gray. That was the "Marah" in her life.

Friend, there are many frustrations, disappointments, and sorrows in life. Your plans can be torn up like a jigsaw puzzle. You may have a little grave on a hillside somewhere. I have. May I say that we all have our Marahs. You will not bypass them. You cannot detour around them, skip over them, or tunnel under them.

God uses a branding iron. I remember West Texas, in the spring of the year when the calves were branded. As a boy I would see the branding iron put down on a little fellow. Oh, how he bellowed! It made me feel sort of sad to hear him cry. But from then on everyone knew to whom he belonged. After a calf was branded, it would not get lost. God does that for us today.

What was it that made the bitter water of Marah sweet? We are told that a tree cast into the water made it sweet. Deuteronomy 21:23 says, "he that is hanged is accursed of God . . ." and in Galatians 3:13 it says, ". . . Cursed is every one that hangeth on a tree." Jesus Christ died on a tree, and it is that cross that makes the experiences of life sweet. He tasted death for every man, and took the sting out of death. "O death, where is thy sting? O grave, where is thy victory?" says 1 Corinthians 15:55. It is the cross of Christ that makes sweet the Marah experiences of life.

And they came to Elim, where were twelve wells of water, and threescore and ten palm trees: and they encamped there by the waters [Exod. 15:27].

Elim was a place of abundant blessing and fruitfulness. There were seventy palm trees and twelve wells. After the bitterness of Marah, God brought His people to Elim. "Weeping may endure for a night, but joy cometh in the morning." Simon Peter may be locked in the inner prison, but the angel is going to open the door. Paul and Silas may be beaten at midnight, but an earthquake will free them. There is a Marah along the pilgrim pathway today; but, friend, there is also an Elim. God's plan for usefulness always leads to Marah and to Elim. Joseph, you remember, had that experience. Moses did, Elijah did, David did, Adoniram Judson did, John G. Paton did. And I am sure you and I will have that also. Beyond every Marah there is an

Elim. Beyond every shadow, there is an Elim. Beyond every cloud, there is the sun. Beyond every shadow, there is the light. Beyond every trial, there is a triumph, and beyond every storm, there is a rainbow. George Matheson wrote, "I trace the rainbow through the rain." This is the way God leads us. All of these things happened to Israel for examples to us.

CHAPTER 16

THEME: Israel murmurs because they lack food; manna and quail are provided by God; manna described and collected; the Sabbath given to Israel

We have been studying the experiences of the nation Israel. After they left the land of Egypt and crossed the Red Sea and came to Mount Sinai, there are *seven* recorded experiences which correspond to the Christian experience. So far they have sung the song of Moses, gone three days without water, arrived at Marah where the water was bitter, and then journeyed to Elim where there was water and trees in abundance. Elim is a picture of the fruitful Christian experience, and God promises to bring us to this place. Now we come to the Wilderness of Sin, the manna and the quail. And we find that Christ is the Bread of life.

ISRAEL MURMURS
BECAUSE THEY LACK FOOD

And they took their journey from Elim, and all the congregation of the children of Israel came unto the wilderness of Sin, which is between Elim and Sinai, on the fifteenth day of the second month after their departing out of the land of Egypt.

And the whole congregation of the children of Israel murmured against Moses and Aaron in the wilderness:

And the children of Israel said unto them, Would to God we had died by the hand of the LORD in the land of Egypt, when we sat by the flesh pots, and when we did eat bread to the full; for ye have brought us forth into this wilderness, to kill this whole assembly with hunger [Exod. 16:1-3].

It has been only about two and one half months since the Israelites left Egypt. They started murmuring when they came to the Red Sea. When they crossed the sea, they sang the song of Moses, the song of redemption. But it was not long before they began to murmur again and to sing the Desert Blues. We would call them a bunch of gripers. They wanted to be delivered from the slavery of Egypt, but after they journeyed into the wilderness, they ran short of water and food and began to complain. They remembered the fleshpots of Egypt and longed for them. There are many people who have been saved out of sin, then wanted to go back to the old life. Many of us have had that temptation.

A man told me in Nashville that he was saved out of a life of bootlegging and heavy drinking. When he was converted, he knew every bootlegging joint in Nashville, and for the first few months after he was saved he did not dare go by one of those places because he knew he would go in. He said, "I looked back at those old fleshpots but, thank God, today I hate them."

MANNA AND QUAIL
ARE PROVIDED BY GOD

God had no intention of letting His people starve. His plan was to lead them through the wilderness, and He had promised to take care of them.

Then said the LORD unto Moses, Behold, I will rain bread from heaven for you; and the people shall go out and gather a certain rate every day, that I may prove them, whether they will walk in my law, or no.

And it shall come to pass, that on the sixth day they shall prepare that which they bring in; and it shall be twice as much as they gather daily.

And Moses and Aaron said unto all the children of Israel, At even, then ye shall know that the LORD hath brought you out from the land of Egypt:

And in the morning, then ye shall see the glory of the LORD; for that he heareth your murmurings against the LORD: and what are we, that ye murmur against us? [Exod. 16:4–7].

Moses and Aaron asked the congregation, "Why are you murmuring against us? We are only human. We cannot do anything. We cannot provide for you. God has heard your murmurings and you will see the glory of God." Every time Israel murmured, the glory of God appeared. This tells us that God does not like griping, complaining, fault-finding Christians. The church is filled with complaining Christians. If you are in a church where you have to murmur, complain, and gripe, get out and go somewhere else.

And Moses said, This shall be, when the LORD shall give you in the evening flesh to eat, and in the morning bread to the full; for that the LORD heareth your murmurings which ye murmur against him: and what are we? your murmurings are not against us, but against the LORD [Exod. 16:8].

You should be very careful when you begin to gripe about things at church. Are you griping about the preacher because he is not as friendly as you think he ought to be, or because he did not shake hands with you last Sunday, or because he has not been around to visit you lately? Are you murmuring against him? Aren't you really against him because he teaches the Word of God and represents God in your church? Sometimes we preachers murmur, too, and we all should be careful that we are not murmuring against God. This is one thing that God does not like.

And Moses spake unto Aaron, Say unto all the congregation of the children of Israel, Come near before the LORD: for he hath heard your murmurings.

And it came to pass, as Aaron spake unto the whole congregation of the children of Israel, that they looked toward the wilderness, and, behold, the glory of the LORD appeared in the cloud.

And the LORD spake unto Moses, saying,

I have heard the murmurings of the children of Israel: speak unto them, saying, At even ye shall eat flesh, and in the morning ye shall be filled with bread; and ye shall know that I am the LORD your God.

And it came to pass, that at even the quails came up, and covered the camp: and in the morning the dew lay round about the host [Exod. 16:9–13].

God not only gave the Israelites manna but He sent quail also. They had quail on toast, or on manna, and it was mighty good eating.

MANNA DESCRIBED AND COLLECTED

Manna was Israel's sustenance as they journeyed through the wilderness.

And when the dew that lay was gone up, behold, upon the face of the wilderness there lay a small round thing, as small as the hoar frost on the ground.

And when the children of Israel saw it, they said one to another, It is manna: for they wist not what it was. And Moses said unto them, This is the bread which the LORD hath given you to eat.

This is the thing which the LORD hath commanded, Gather of it every man according to his eating, an omer for every man, according to the number of your persons; take ye every man for them which are in his tents [Exod. 16:14–16].

The Israelites were to gather only enough manna for the day.

And the children of Israel did so, and gathered, some more, some less.

And when they did mete it with an omer, he that gathered much had nothing over, and he that gathered little had no lack; they gathered every man according to his eating [Exod. 16:17–18].

The glutton did not get more than his share.

And Moses said, Let no man leave of it till the morning.

Notwithstanding they hearkened not unto Moses; but some of them left of it until the morning, and it bred worms, and stank: and Moses was wroth with them.

And they gathered it every morning, every man according to his eating: and when the sun waxed hot, it melted [Exod. 16:19–21].

The manna was to be gathered every morning. Each man was to gather it. This was to be a personal experience. The manna speaks of the Lord Jesus Christ as the Bread of Life. The

Gospel of John, chapter 6, confirms this: "Then Jesus said unto them, Verily, verily, I say unto you, Moses gave you not that bread from heaven; but my Father giveth you the true bread from heaven. For the bread of God is he which cometh down from heaven, and giveth life unto the world. Then said they unto him, Lord, evermore give us this bread. And Jesus said unto them, I am the bread of life: he that cometh to me shall never hunger; and he that believeth on me shall never thirst" (John 6:32–35).

And it came to pass, that on the sixth day they gathered twice as much bread, two omers for one man: and all the rulers of the congregation came and told Moses.

And he said unto them, This is that which the LORD hath said, To-morrow is the rest of the holy sabbath unto the LORD: bake that which ye will bake to-day, and seethe that ye will seethe; and that which remaineth over lay up for you to be kept until the morning.

And they laid it up till the morning, as Moses bade: and it did not stink, neither was there any worm therein [Exod. 16:22–24].

God would supply day by day, but before the Sabbath day they were to get enough for two days.

Manna is that which represents Christ as the Bread of Life who came down from heaven to give His life for the world. Jesus Christ is the true Bread. He is the one who gives us life and sustenance.

In Deuteronomy 8:4 we find that during the forty years that the Israelites wandered in the wilderness their feet did not swell. I have been told by a medical missionary that one of the causes of foot-swelling in the Orient is an improper diet. It is interesting that the manna had all the vitamins they needed to keep their feet from swelling as they journeyed through the wilderness. The manna was adequate to meet their needs.

THE SABBATH GIVEN TO ISRAEL

And Moses said, Eat that to-day; for to-day is a sabbath unto the LORD: to-day ye shall not find it in the field.

Six days ye shall gather it; but on the seventh day, which is the sabbath, in it there shall be none [Exod. 16:25–26].

The Sabbath day was given to Israel *before* the formal giving of law.

And the house of Israel called the name thereof Manna: and it was like coriander seed, white; and the taste of it was like wafers made with honey [Exod. 16:31].

How would you describe manna? It is difficult to explain. It was a wonderful food that contained all the nourishment Israel needed. It tasted, I think, about like anything they wanted it to taste like. It was a very exciting food, but it started the mixed multitude complaining. Numbers 11:4–5 records an incident which helps us to properly understand manna. "And the mixed multitude that was among them fell a-lusting: and the children of Israel also wept again, and said, Who shall give us flesh to eat? We remember the fish, which we did eat in Egypt freely; the cucumbers, and the melons, and the leeks, and the onions, and the garlick." This is what the mixed multitude missed in the wilderness, away from the land of Egypt.

The list of foods that they missed included those which grew on or under the ground. They were condiments without real nourishment like the cucumbers, the melons, the leeks, the onions, and garlic. When you eat some of those things, friends, you are not very attractive. Someone has said, "An apple a day keeps the doctor away." Well, an onion a day keeps everybody away. These are the things that the people of the world eat. They do not satisfy because they are nothing but condiments. The mixed multitude remembered what they had in Egypt and hungered for it.

In Numbers 11:6 it says, "But now our soul is dried away: there is nothing at all, beside this manna, before our eyes." They complained that there was nothing to eat but manna. Numbers 11:7 continues, "And the manna was as coriander seed, and the colour thereof as the colour of bdellium." It is as if God is saying, "These people despise my food which is like fried chicken, ice cream, and angel food cake all rolled into one." Manna was not a monotonous food, but the mixed multitude did not want it.

Numbers 11:8 goes on to say, "And the people went about, and gathered it, and ground it in mills, or beat it in a mortar, and baked it in pans, and made cakes of it: and the taste of it was as the taste of fresh oil." Manna could be fixed in many ways. They could grind it, beat it, bake it in pans, or make a casserole. They probably published *Mother Moses' Cookbook* with 1001 recipes. The children of Israel, however, despised God's heavenly food and complained about eating it. They grew tired of eating manna. They longed for the fleshpots of Egypt. They wanted to go back to that from which they had been delivered.

That is the story, I am afraid, of some people who have been converted, and have been delivered out of "Egypt." Every now and then they take a side trip back to get the leeks, the onions, and the garlic. There are Christians today who need to make a complete break with the old life. Friend, you can't go on living like the world, living on the things of Egypt, and be serviceable to God and have the peace of God in your heart. There must be a break with Egypt. We must live on the true Manna that comes from heaven, even the Lord Jesus Christ.

And Moses said, This is the thing which the LORD commandeth, Fill an omer of it to be kept for your generations; that they may see the bread wherewith I have fed you in the wilderness, when I brought you forth from the land of Egypt.

And Moses said unto Aaron, Take a pot, and put an omer full of manna therein, and lay it up before the LORD, to be kept for your generations [Exod. 16:32–33].

A pot of manna was put in the ark, which is described in greater detail in the final part of Exodus. In the ark were placed three things: (1) Aaron's rod that budded, (2) the pot of manna, and (3) the Ten Commandments. The Law speaks of the fact that Christ alone kept the Law. He fulfilled it for you and me. The manna also speaks of Christ's death for us. He is provided as spiritual food for us. Aaron's rod that budded speaks of His resurrection. Then placed over the ark, serving as the lid, was the mercy seat where the blood was sprinkled.

Christ alone was able to meet the demands of God. He alone is able to save, and He can save us because He shed His own blood. Because of that, God can extend mercy to man, the sinner.

And the children of Israel did eat manna forty years, until they came to a land inhabited; they did eat manna, until they came unto the borders of the land of Canaan.

Now an omer is the tenth part of an ephah [Exod. 16:35–36].

These two verses tell us that the children of Israel ate manna for forty years, and we are told what their daily ration was. When they finally came into the Promised Land, the manna ceased, and they ate the old corn of the land again. Then they also complained about the old corn. They discoverd that the manna was an exciting food after all. It was, in fact, exotic, compared to the old corn.

The interesting thing about this is that many people live on experience after they have been saved. They have been to the cross, which speaks of the death of the Lord Jesus Christ, but they go right on talking about their experience. When they give a testimony, they speak only of experience. They do not like Bible study because it is old corn. It is the Word of God that our Lord wants us to feed upon. If you haven't had that taste of manna yet, I suggest that you come to Christ and taste of it. Psalm 34:8 says, "O taste and see that the LORD is good: blessed is the man that trusteth in him." In addition to this, John 6:51 quotes Jesus as saying, "I am the living bread which came down from heaven: if any man eat of this bread, he shall live for ever: and the bread that I will give is my flesh, which I will give for the life of the world."

CHAPTER 17

THEME: Water flows from the smitten rock; contention with Amalek

The children of Israel have left the land of Egypt and are on a wilderness march. They are on their way to Mount Sinai. Along the way Israel has had seven experiences that are pictures of the Christian life. Remember, ". . . all these things happened unto them for ensamples: and they are written for our admonition, upon whom the ends of the world are come" (1 Cor. 10:11). All Christians will do well to read and heed these lessons. These lessons are given to us in picture form and their meaning is clear.

WATER FLOWS
FROM THE SMITTEN ROCK

As they journey through the desert, the children of Israel thirst and once again they murmur.

And all the congregation of the children of Israel journeyed from the wilderness of Sin, after their journeys, according to the commandment of the LORD, and pitched in Rephidim: and there was no water for the people to drink.

Wherefore the people did chide with Moses, and said, Give us water that we may drink. And Moses said unto them, Why chide ye with me? wherefore do ye tempt the LORD?

And the people thirsted there for water; and the people murmured against Moses, and said, Wherefore is this that thou hast brought us up out of Egypt, to kill us and our children and our cattle with thirst? [Exod. 17:1–3].

The children of Israel were everlastingly complaining. They have a need and start to complain. God graciously meets their need. Then something else comes up and they begin to cry out, complain, and find fault. Many churches are in this same spiritual condition yet they think they are in excellent condition.

And Moses cried unto the LORD, saying, What shall I do unto this people? they be almost ready to stone me [Exod. 17:4].

About this time Moses was probably ready to turn his job over to somebody else. Notice God's provision for Israel.

And the LORD said unto Moses, Go on before the people, and take with thee of the elders of Israel; and thy rod, wherewith thou smotest the river, take in thine hand, and go [Exod. 17:5].

This is the rod given to Moses when he went back to Egypt. It was to be a badge and seal of the authority and power of Moses.

Behold, I will stand before thee there upon the rock in Horeb; and thou shalt smite the rock, and there shall come water out of it, that the people may drink. And Moses did so in the sight of the elders of Israel.

And he called the name of the place Massah, and Meribah, because of the chiding of the children of Israel, and because they tempted the LORD, saying, Is the LORD among us, or not? [Exod. 17: 6–7].

This is the first mention of the "rock" and the "water" that came out of that rock. What does the rock represent? We are not left to guesswork or our own speculation or our own wisdom. The Holy Spirit of God explains it in 1 Corinthians 10:1–4 which tells us, "Moreover, brethren, I would not that ye should be ignorant, how that all our fathers were under the cloud, and all passed through the sea; And were all baptized unto Moses in the cloud and in the sea; And did all eat the same spiritual meat; And did all drink the same spiritual drink: for they drank of that spiritual Rock that followed them: and that Rock was Christ."

The bread that Israel ate was manna, which was a picture of Christ, the Bread of Life. Christ is also the Water of Life, and the rock is a picture of Him. It contrasts the unbelief of the people (you see, they doubted God here) with the solid rock. Israel was leaning on cobwebs and broken reeds. The small cloud of doubt was hiding the face of God from them.

The rock is a beautiful portrait of the Lord Jesus Christ. Psalm 61:2 says, "From the end of the earth will I cry unto thee, when my heart is overwhelmed: lead me to the rock that is higher than I." That is Christ. Again the Psalmist says, "And they remembered that God was their rock, and the high God their redeemer" (Psalm 78:35). Then Peter tells us, "Wherefore also it is contained in the scripture, Behold, I lay in Sion a chief corner stone, elect, precious: and he that believeth on him shall not be confounded. Unto you therefore which believe he is precious: but unto them which be disobedient, the stone which the builders disallowed, the same is made the head of the corner, And a stone of stumbling, and a rock of offence, even to them which stumble at the word, being disobedient: whereunto also they were appointed" (1 Pet. 2:6–8). Finally, the apostle Paul gives us this advice in 1 Corinthians 3:11, "For other foundation can no man lay than that is laid, which is Jesus Christ."

The Lord Jesus, as one hymn says, is "a Rock in a weary land." Although this is a marvelous picture of Him as the foundation—the one upon whom we rest and the one upon whom the church is built—a rock is the last place we go for a drink of water. I do not mean to be facetious, but you could not even get hard water from a rock. That would be like getting blood from a turnip or orange juice from a doorknob. You can admire a rock's sterling qualities and durability. There are great lessons to be learned from it. You can test it and analyze it, but you cannot drink it. Jesus is a Rock, but His beautiful life and durability will not save you. His teachings will not redeem your soul. His life and teachings are like polished marble which are engraved and, though you apply them to your life with Carborundum or optician's rouge, they still won't save you. The application of the principles taught by the Lord Jesus may polish you a little, but He is still that Rock against which you can dash your foot.

You can fall on the Rock Christ Jesus for salvation, but no human effort is able to get water from this Rock. Only when the rock was smitten did it bring forth life-giving waters. Jesus was crucified, and nothing short of believing that He died in your place and bore your sins on that cross will save you. The smitten rock is a picture of the death of Jesus Christ.

In Numbers we are told a second time that the children of Israel complained that they had no water. The first time Israel murmured about being thirsty God told Moses to strike the rock and water gushed forth. In Numbers, however, God gives Moses different instructions. God tells Moses: "Take the rod, and gather thou the assembly together, thou, and Aaron thy brother, and *speak ye unto the rock* before their eyes; and it shall give forth his water, and thou shalt bring forth to them water out of the rock: so thou shalt give the congregation and their beasts drink" (Num. 20:8). Moses was to *speak* to the rock because the rock had already been *smitten*. Christ was crucified nineteen hundred years ago, and when

He said on the cross, ". . . It is finished . . ." (John 19:30), it was indeed finished. Christ does not have to be crucified again. God is satisfied with what Jesus did for you. The question is, "Are you satisfied with the work Christ did for you on the cross?" He died to save you. All that God is asking is that you believe in His Son.

From the Rock, Christ Jesus, come spiritual blessings today. The waters of blessing gush forth to relieve parched lips. Ephesians 1:3 informs us that, "Blessed be the God and Father of our Lord Jesus Christ, who hath blessed us with all spiritual blessings in heavenly places in Christ." The Rock was smitten *once* and from it flows an abundance of water. The fountain is brimfull. The stream is bank full. The world is not able to contain it. But in spite of that, there are many men's souls that are shriveled up and tongues that are parched. Millions of people are dying for want of spiritual drink. The channel is blocked, logjammed by doubts, corroded by sin, and insulated by indifference. The channel is also dammed by those who profess to know Jesus Christ but who in reality do not know Him.

Friends, I am disturbed and distressed as I look about. The world is thirsty. I ask you personally and particularly, Have you been to that smitten Rock for a drink of living water? God says if you drink of that water you will never thirst again.

CONTENTION WITH AMALEK

During their wilderness march the Israelites ran into the Amalekites, who represent the flesh in Scripture. This experience is yet another lesson we would do well to learn.

Then came Amalek, and fought with Israel in Rephidim [Exod. 17:8].

Amalek was a descendant of Esau, and the Amalekites had become enemies of Israel. They never ceased to be Israel's enemies. For the *first* time the children of Israel engage in warfare.

And Moses said unto Joshua, Choose us out men, and go out, fight with Amalek: to-morrow I will stand on the top of the hill with the rod of God in mine hand.

So Joshua did as Moses had said to him, and fought with Amalek: and Moses, Aaron, and Hur went up to the top of the hill [Exod. 17:9–10].

Esau was a picture of the flesh. As Israel could not overcome Amalek by their own efforts, neither can you nor I overcome the flesh by our own efforts. The flesh wars against the spirit and the spirit against the flesh. Paul explains it in Galatians 5:17, "For the flesh lusteth against the Spirit, and the Spirit against the flesh: and these are contrary the one to the other: so that ye cannot do the things that ye would." This is the picture we have in the wilderness as Israel and Amalek war against each other.

And it came to pass, when Moses held up his hand, that Israel prevailed: and when he let down his hand, Amalek prevailed.

But Moses' hands were heavy; and they took a stone, and put it under him, and he sat thereon; and Aaron and Hur stayed up his hands, the one on the one side, and the other on the other side; and his hands were steady until the going down of the sun [Exod. 17:11–12].

Careful observation reveals that the battle was actually fought on top of the mountain. It was fought by prayer. This battle was not won by Israel's fighting ability because they were not experienced soldiers nor adept at warfare yet. This battle was fought and won by Moses. The moment Moses was no longer able to hold his hands up, the children of Israel began to lose the fight. If it had not been for Moses, Israel would have lost the battle. The important thing to remember is that the Holy Spirit is the only One who can give us victory over the flesh. Victory comes as the believer walks in the Spirit. When you and I act independently of the Spirit, Amalek, or the flesh, wins an easy victory. When Moses' hands were held up, the Israelites won. You and I never will be able to overcome the flesh. It is only the Spirit of God who can do that.

And Joshua discomfited Amalek and his people with the edge of the sword.

And the LORD said unto Moses, Write this for a memorial in a book, and rehearse it in the ears of Joshua: for I will

utterly put out the remembrance of Amalek from under heaven [Exod. 17:13–14].

It is time to stop and consider this man Joshua. He is the one who is going to succeed Moses. We can see that he is already being prepared for this position. He is an ordinary man but God is preparing him for the task that is ahead of him. God instructs Moses to rehearse in the ears of Joshua that Amalek is to be destroyed.

Now God is going to get rid of the flesh. Thank God for that. When the Lord takes the church to heaven, He will change it. 1 Corinthians 15:52 confirms this: "In a moment, in the twinkling of an eye, at the last trump: for the trumpet shall sound, and the dead shall be raised incorruptible, and we shall be changed." If the Lord took the church to heaven as it is now, without changing it, heaven would be just like this old earth because we would wreck the place with our old natures. I have been dragging my old nature around like a corpse for years. I would like to get rid of it, and I have tried to get rid of it, but it keeps asserting itself again and again. Thank God that He has promised to get rid of Vernon McGee's old nature one day. Those who belong to Christ will some day be changed and made fit for heaven.

And Moses built an altar, and called the name of it Jehovah-nissi:

For he said, Because the LORD hath sworn that the LORD will have war with Amalek from generation to generation [Exod. 17:15–16].

There are three important things to remember. First, God is going to get rid of Amalek. In other words, God is going to get rid of the old nature. Secondly, the Lord will never compromise with the old nature. He will have war with Amalek from generation to generation. The third important item is that this constant conflict will go on as long as we live in this life. The flesh and the spirit will always war against each other. Only the Holy Spirit of God can give us victory. We need to recognize this fact.

CHAPTER 18

THEME: The visit of Jethro, Moses' father-in-law; Jethro's advice to appoint judges accepted by Moses

In chapter 18 we come to the last of the seven experiences the children of Israel had between Egypt and Mount Sinai. God has been leading Moses directly by revelation but now Moses turns to worldly wisdom for help rather than to God for revelation.

THE VISIT OF JETHRO, MOSES' FATHER-IN-LAW

Jethro, the priest of Midian, visits Moses. He brought Moses' wife and children with him. While with Moses, they have a nice visit; you might call it a family reunion.

When Jethro, the priest of Midian, Moses' father-in-law, heard of all that God had done for Moses, and for Israel his people, and that the LORD had brought Israel out of Egypt;

Then Jethro, Moses' father-in-law, took Zipporah, Moses' wife, after he had sent her back,

And her two sons; of which the name of the one was Gershom; for he said, I have been an alien in a strange land:

And the name of the other was Eliezer; for the God of my father, said he, was mine help, and delivered me from the sword of Pharaoh [Exod. 18:1–4].

Moses has come now into the land of Midian with this great company of Israelites. Here the father-in-law of Moses brings his wife and sons to him. Apparently, when they went down to Egypt, after that experience when she called him a bloody husband, he sent her back home—then or shortly after that. There is no record of her being in Egypt when the exodus took place. But now Jethro brings her and her two sons to Moses. So this is a family reunion.

And Jethro, Moses' father-in-law, came with his sons and his wife unto Moses into the wilderness, where he encamped at the mount of God:

And he said unto Moses, I thy father-in-law Jethro am come unto thee, and thy wife, and her two sons with her.

And Moses went out to meet his father-in-law, and did obeisance, and kissed him; and they asked each other of their welfare; and they came into the tent [Exod. 18:5–7].

It is an interesting thing to note the marvelous relationship between Moses and his father-in-law. They seem to be very close, buddies in fact. Moses tells him all that God has done in leading the children of Israel out of Egypt. Jethro shows great interest in everything that Moses relates to him. In fact, when Moses went out to greet his family, we are told that he kissed his father-in-law but nothing is said about him kissing his wife. This passage says nothing about Moses being glad to see his sons either. All of this seems to confirm our previous conclusion that Moses' family relationship was not as it should have been.

And Moses told his father-in-law all that the LORD had done unto Pharaoh and to the Egyptians for Israel's sake, and all the travail that had come upon them by the way, and how the LORD delivered them.

And Jethro rejoiced for all the goodness which the LORD had done to Israel, whom he had delivered out of the hand of the Egyptians.

And Jethro said, Blessed be the LORD, who hath delivered you out of the hand of the Egyptians, and out of the hand of Pharaoh, who hath delivered the people from under the hand of the Egyptians.

Now I know that the LORD is greater than all gods: for in the thing wherein they dealt proudly he was above them.

And Jethro, Moses' father-in-law, took a burnt offering and sacrifices for God: and Aaron came, and all the elders of Israel, to eat bread with Moses' father-in-law before God [Exod. 18:8–12].

Jethro was probably skeptical when Moses, while still in Midian, announced that he was going to deliver the children of Israel from their yoke of bondage in Egypt. Probably he told his neighbors, "I don't know what has come over my son-in-law. He has big ideas. He thinks God has called him to deliver the Israelites out of Egypt. I just don't believe that the God he serves can do that." Well, God did do it, and this apparently brought Jethro to a saving knowledge of God. This is evidenced by the fact that he offered burnt offerings to God.

JETHRO'S ADVICE TO APPOINT
JUDGES ACCEPTED BY MOSES

And it came to pass on the morrow, that Moses sat to judge the people: and the people stood by Moses from the morning unto the evening.

And when Moses' father-in-law saw all that he did to the people, he said, What is this thing that thou doest to the people? why sittest thou thyself alone, and all the people stand by thee from morning unto even?

And Moses said unto his father-in-law, Because the people come unto me to inquire of God:

When they have a matter, they come unto me; and I judge between one and another, and I do make them know the statutes of God, and his laws.

And Moses' father-in-law said unto him, The thing that thou doest is not good.

Thou wilt surely wear away, both thou, and this people that is with thee: for this thing is too heavy for thee; thou art not able to perform it thyself alone [Exod. 18:13–18].

Moses' father-in-law obviously loved him, had great respect for him, and was enthusiastic about him. As he has brought Moses' family to be with him, he stays on for a few days and sees how busy Moses is, judging the people. So he comes up with a suggestion to lighten the load of Moses.

Hearken now unto my voice, I will give thee counsel, and God shall be with thee: Be thou for the people to Godward, that thou mayest bring the causes unto God:

And thou shalt teach them ordinances and laws, and shalt shew them the way wherein they must walk, and the work that they must do.

Moreover thou shalt provide out of all the people able men, such as fear God, men of truth, hating covetousness; and place such over them, to be rulers of thousands, and rulers of hundreds, rulers of fifties, and rulers of tens:

And let them judge the people at all seasons: and it shall be, that every great matter they shall bring unto thee, but every small matter they shall judge: so

shall it be easier for thyself, and they shall bear the burden with thee.

If thou shalt do this thing, and God command thee so, then thou shalt be able to endure, and all this people shall also go to their place in peace.

So Moses hearkened to the voice of his father-in-law, and did all that he had said.

And Moses chose able men out of all Israel, and made them heads over the people, rulers of thousands, rulers of hundreds, rulers of fifties, and rulers of tens.

And they judged the people at all seasons: the hard causes they brought unto Moses, but every small matter they judged themselves.

And Moses let his father-in-law depart; and he went his way into his own land [Exod. 18:19–27].

Jethro suggested that judges be appointed to help Moses take care of the problems of the people. Someone is apt to say, "What is wrong with his suggestion?" Well, on the surface, everything looks fine.

One thing must be remembered—there are two kinds of wisdom in this world, the wisdom of God and the wisdom of this world. Jethro's proposal was based on the wisdom of the world. When you follow the pattern of the world, you do not look to God. One of the reasons the church is in such trouble today is because men have been brought into the church and put on a board or given a place of prominence because they have been successful in business. They attempt to run the church by the methods of the world, and they have no spiritual discernment whatsoever. The program of the world does not work in the church.

The recommendations that Jethro made were good. They would take the load off Moses and expedite matters. They would provide an orderly system and conserve time. Jethro's proposition looked like a very attractive package. His suggestion was sincere, and he meant well. He was concerned about Moses' health, and you cannot help but love him for this. The thing, however, that we need to note is that it was not the will of God. God permitted it all right, but He did not suggest it.

A careful examination of this passage will reveal the subtle and sinister character of this man's advice. First of all, God had given no such instructions to Moses concerning this matter. Jethro's suggestion actually questioned the wisdom, judgment, and the love of God. Jethro was actually saying that God was not doing the best that He could for Moses. If God really loved Moses and cared for him, He would have made this suggestion a long time ago. Friends, I hear in back of Jethro's statement the hiss of the serpent made known so long ago in the Garden of Eden. The serpent had suggested to Eve, "Oh, if you could only eat of that tree, you would be wise and God has not permitted you to do that. God is not doing the best that He could do for you." Jethro's suggestion implies the same thing. But if this were the best method, God would have made this arrangement before.

The second thing to note is that God had been dealing directly with Moses. He was equipping him for the great task of delivering Israel. God did not want a third party brought in. He did not want others included who would dissipate or insulate the power of God in coming directly to Moses. Remember that God spoke face-to-face with Moses. There are many people who do not like to do business directly with God. They would rather deal with other people. They would rather go through a man, a church, a ceremony, a book, or even go to a musical concert. All of these have their place. But, friend, we need to go directly to God. God didn't want this crowd brought into it.

The third thing to notice, as we look at this passage, is that Jethro's suggestion created an organization out of which came the seventy, the Sanhedrin, which one night about 1500 years after this met together and plotted the death of the Son of God! Moses didn't need this organization. God gave Moses power for the task and these arduous duties. These seventy men were no more efficient for God than one man. After all, it is the Spirit that quickeneth and gives man power.

There are people who feel that what the church needs for success is the right method. Right now there are many preachers who are acting rather foolishly by trying to identify themselves with the "new generation." They say that they want to communicate with the new generation. There is a seminary in Southern California that majors in identifying and communicating with people. I have never heard of them really reaching down and touching lives in Southern California. They just cannot do it. God does not need a method, an organization, numbers, a system, a ritual, or good works. God sweeps aside all the wisdom of the world so that there is nothing between your soul and Him. The wisdom of the world and the wisdom of God are contradictory—so much so that one is wisdom and the other is foolishness. In 1 Corinthians 3:18–19 God says, "Let no man deceive himself. If any man among you seemeth to be wise in this world, let him become a fool, that he may be wise. For the wisdom of this world is foolishness with God. For it is written, He taketh the wise in their own craftiness."

The apostle Paul tells us in 1 Corinthians 2:4, ". . . my speech and my preaching was not with enticing words of man's wisdom, but in demonstration of the Spirit and of power." We do not need to be clever and use the intellectual approach to win men to Christ. What we do need is the wisdom of God to guide us. We need the power of God and not new methods. My friend, do you rely on the wisdom of the world or do you look to God to guide you with that wisdom that is from above?

CHAPTER 19

THEME: Moses delivers God's message; Israel prepares for a visitation from God

Chapters 19 through 24 deal with the Law. The children of Israel have arrived at Mount Sinai, and here they agree to accept the Law. In fact, what they do is exchange grace for law.

> **In the third month, when the children of Israel were gone forth out of the land of Egypt, the same day came they into the wilderness of Sinai.**

> **For they were departed from Rephidim, and were come to the desert of Sinai, and had pitched in the wilderness; and there Israel camped before the mount [Exod. 19:1–2].**

The children of Israel have arrived at Mount Sinai, the place where the Law is going to be given. God is going to deal graciously with His people. He is going to give them the opportunity of deciding whether they want to go on with God leading them—the way He has for the period of time since they left Egypt until they arrived at the mount—or whether they would rather accept and receive the Law.

MOSES DELIVERS GOD'S MESSAGE

> **And Moses went up unto God, and the LORD called unto him out of the mountain, saying, Thus shalt thou say to the house of Jacob, and tell the children of Israel; Ye have seen what I did unto the Egyptians, and how I bare you on eagles' wings, and brought you unto myself [Exod. 19:3–4].**

That's traveling by grace!

> **Now therefore, if ye will obey my voice indeed, and keep my covenant, then ye shall be a peculiar treasure unto me above all people: for all the earth is mine [Exod. 19:5].**

The children of Israel travelled from Egypt to Mount Sinai by the grace of God. Then God asks them if they want to receive the Law and commandments, and they foolishly agree to accept it instead of saying that they enjoyed the trip on eagles' wings from Egypt to Mount Sinai.

God reminded them of what He had done to the Egyptians and how He had borne the children of Israel on eagles' wings. Perhaps a few words should be said about the eagle. The eagle is a bird of prey, which Job 9:26 corroborates by saying, "They are passed away as the swift ships: as the eagle that hasteth to the prey." The Lord Jesus Christ Himself said, "For wheresoever the carcase is, there will the eagles be gathered together" (Matt. 24:28). Yet the eagle is used as a symbol of God and deity in Scripture. In the Book of Ezekiel deity is represented by the face of an eagle. In the fourth chapter of the Book of Revelation deity is pictured by a flying eagle. The eagle is admired for its wings and its ability to soar to the heights. In other words, the eagle is the jet plane of the bird family, and the wings of the eagle are definitely a symbol of deity. God said to Israel in Exodus 19:4, "Ye have seen what I did unto the Egyptians, and how I bare you on eagles' wings, and brought you unto myself." That, friends, is God's marvelous, infinite, wonderful grace. By grace God brought Israel out of Egypt and to Mount Sinai. God had found them helpless and hopeless in the slavery of Egypt, and He delivered them. He redeemed them by blood. The same night the death angel passed over, the children of Israel marched out of Egypt. They came to the Red Sea where Pharaoh could have slaughtered them like animals, but God intervened. And God brought them across the Red Sea by power. You see, He is bearing them on eagles' wings.

On the way from Egypt to Mount Sinai, Israel had seven experiences which correspond to our Christian experiences. God gave Israel manna when they were hungry and water when they were thirsty. God sweetened the bitter waters of Marah. God delivered them from Amalek. All the way God bore Israel on eagles' wings, and that is the way He bears us today. He leads us by His grace, and we walk by faith.

Now at Mount Sinai God reminds Israel how He has led and cared for them. Then He gives them a choice—grace or law. God asks them if they will keep the commandments if He gives them to Israel. They are going to exchange grace for law. A great many people do that today. This is unfortunate because we live in a day when God saves by grace. God does not save by law. What a contrast there is between law and grace.

Law demands—grace gives.

Law says "do"—grace says "believe."

Law exacts—grace bestows.

Law says "work"—grace says "rest."

Law threatens, pronouncing a curse,—grace entreats, pronouncing a blessing. Law says "Do, and thou shalt live"—grace says, "Live, and thou shalt do." Law condemns the best man—grace saves the worst man.

The Law reveals the character of God—it also reveals the weakness of man. In Romans 3:19 Paul says, "Now we know that what things soever the law saith, it saith to them who are under the law: that every mouth may be stopped, and all the world may become guilty before God."

God never gave the Law as a means of salvation. No one was ever saved by keeping the Law. You can't mention a single one. Moses was a murderer; he also lost his temper and disobeyed God. Why then was the Law given? There was a definite reason which is stated in Galatians 3:19—"Wherefore then serveth the law? It was added because of transgressions, till the seed should come to whom the promise was made . . . ." The law was given to reveal that we are sinners. It was given temporarily until the Seed would come. The seed spoken of in this verse is the Lord Jesus Christ. Paul goes on to say in Galatians 3:24 that, ". . . the law was our schoolmaster to bring us unto Christ, that we might be justified by faith."

The "schoolmaster" is not a school teacher, but a slave in the home of a Roman patrician that took care of the child. He clothed, washed, dressed him, blew his nose when needed, and paddled him when necessary. When the child was old enough to attend school, the schoolmaster took him. The word for schoolmaster is *paidagōgos*, meaning a "child conductor," one who takes a little child by the hand and leads him to the school. The Law is our schoolmaster, our *paidagōgos*. It takes us by the hand, like a little child, and leads us to the cross and says, "My little one, you need a Savior. You are a sinner and you need to be saved."

And ye shall be unto me a kingdom of priests, and an holy nation. These are the words which thou shalt speak unto the children of Israel [Exod. 19:6].

God originally intended for Israel to be a kingdom of priests. All of the tribes were to be priests. Because of their failure to enter the land at Kadesh-Barnea and because they made and worshiped a golden calf while Moses was on the mountain receiving God's law, only one tribe was chosen to be a priestly tribe. God's ultimate goal in the Millennium, however, is to make the entire nation a kingdom of priests. This will happen long after the church is removed from this earth and is in heaven with the Lord Jesus Christ in the New Jerusalem.

And Moses came and called for the elders of the people, and laid before their faces all these words which the Lord commanded him [Exod. 19:7].

Listen to these people—what confidence they had!

And all the people answered together, and said, All that the Lord hath spoken we will do. And Moses returned the words of the people unto the Lord [Exod. 19:8].

The giving of the Law to the nation Israel at Mount Sinai was the beginning of the dispensation of Law. This dispensation extends from Mount Sinai to the cross of Calvary, from the Exodus to the Cross. It is the revelation to a people, living under ideal conditions, that they cannot keep the Law. Israel said, "All that the Lord hath spoken *we will do*." They said, "Bring it on; we'll keep it" before they even knew what it was! Then they demonstrated for fifteen hundred years that they could not keep the Law. This is the attitude of a great many people today—they think the natural man can please God. The natural man cannot keep the Law and he fails terribly in the attempt. The Law was given to control the old nature but it cannot, because the old nature is a revolutionary which cannot be controlled. Paul sums it up in Romans 8:6–7 like this, "For to be carnally minded is death; but to be spiritually minded is life and peace. Because the carnal mind is enmity against God: for it is not subject to the law of God, neither indeed can be."

You and I have an old nature. It is at enmity with God. It can never be obedient to God and can never please Him. Have you made that discovery in your own life? Have you found that you are a failure at meeting God's standards? Thank God that He has made another arrangement!

There is nothing that makes a greater hypocrite out of a person than for him to say, "I keep the Law!" No one can measure up to God's standards. Look at Israel. God is going to give them the Law and they say, "Bring it on, we are ready to keep it." What a display of self-confidence and arrogance. Yet there are multitudes of men and women today that claim they keep the Law even after God clearly demonstrated that no one can be saved by the Law—because no one can keep the Law. It was tried out under ideal conditions by the nation Israel.

ISRAEL PREPARES FOR
A VISITATION BY GOD

And the LORD said unto Moses, Lo, I come unto thee in a thick cloud, that the people may hear when I speak with thee, and believe thee for ever. And Moses told the words of the people unto the LORD [Exod. 19:9].

There are some people who think that the giving of the Law was a beautiful event. Years ago a very cultured and refined southern lady said to me, "Mr. McGee, don't you think the giving of the Law was a beautiful, lovely thing?" I think I shocked her when I replied, "I do not see anything beautiful in it. It was a frightful and terrifying thing!"

And the LORD said unto Moses, Go unto the people, and sanctify them to-day and to-morrow, and let them wash their clothes.

And be ready against the third day: for the third day the LORD will come down in the sight of all the people upon mount Sinai [Exod. 19:10–11].

What a tremendous scene, but listen to what followed:

And thou shalt set bounds unto the people round about, saying, Take heed to yourselves, that ye go not up into the mount, or touch the border of it: whosoever toucheth the mount shall be surely put to death [Exod. 19:12].

Does this sound like a beautiful scene? The children of Israel were told not to get near the mount and not to touch it or they would die. That, friends, is not beautiful; it is dreadful!

There shall not an hand touch it, but he shall surely be stoned, or shot through; whether it be beast or man, it shall not live: when the trumpet soundeth long, they shall come up to the mount.

And Moses went down from the mount unto the people, and sanctified the people; and they washed their clothes.

And he said unto the people, Be ready against the third day: come not at your wives.

And it came to pass on the third day in the morning, that there were thunders and lightnings, and a thick cloud upon the mount, and the voice of the trumpet exceeding loud; so that all the people that was in the camp trembled [Exod. 19:13–16].

This is not a circus parade going by, but this is the giving of God's law. It was a terrifying experience and the people trembled because it was frightening.

And Moses brought forth the people out of the camp to meet with God; and they stood at the nether part of the mount.

And mount Sinai was altogether on a smoke, because the LORD descended upon it in fire: and the smoke thereof ascended as the smoke of a furnace, and the whole mount quaked greatly.

And when the voice of the trumpet sounded long, and waxed louder and louder, Moses spake, and God answered him by a voice.

And the LORD came down upon mount Sinai, on the top of the mount: and the LORD called Moses up to the top of the mount; and Moses went up.

And the LORD said unto Moses, Go down, charge the people, lest they break through unto the LORD to gaze, and many of them perish [Exod. 19:17–21].

Some of the Israelites think they might see something spectacular, but they will not see anything. They will only hear a voice and it is still true to this day that "No man hath seen God at any time; the only begotten Son, which is in the bosom of the Father, he hath declared him" (John 1:18).

And let the priests also, which come near to the LORD, sanctify themselves, lest the LORD break forth upon them.

And Moses said unto the LORD, The people cannot come up to mount Sinai: for thou chargedst us, saying, Set bounds about the mount, and sanctify it.

And the LORD said unto him, Away, get thee down, and thou shalt come up, thou, and Aaron with thee: but let not the priests and the people break through to come up unto the LORD, lest he break forth upon them.

So Moses went down unto the people, and spake unto them [Exod. 19:22–25].

Israel's pledge to keep the Law was a mistake they never would have made had they known more about themselves and how weak they were. There is a great contrast between that dispensation of law and our dispensation of grace.

THEME: The giving of the Ten Commandments; the effect of God's visit; instructions concerning the altar

In chapter 20 of Exodus we have the giving of the Law. The Ten Commandments are given first but they are only part of the Law. Instructions pertaining to the altar are also given; the Law and the altar go together. The Law revealed that man is a sinner and needs a Savior. There must be an altar upon which to offer the sacrifice; there must be the shedding of blood for sin. You have a mirror in your bathroom, which is a picture of the Law, and there is a basin underneath the mirror. You do not wash yourself with the mirror; it only reveals the dirt. Just so, the Law is the mirror that reveals our sin. And beneath that mirror there is a wash basin.

There is a fountain filled with blood
    Drawn from Immanuel's veins,
And sinners plunged beneath *that* flood,
    Lose all their guilty stains.

THE GIVING
OF THE TEN COMMANDMENTS

The first part of the Law given to Israel was the Ten Commandments which was a moral code.

And God spake all these words, saying,

I am the LORD thy God, which have brought thee out of the land of Egypt, out of the house of bondage [Exod. 20:1–2].

God says, "I brought you out of Egypt and the house of bondage, and upon that basis I want to give you My law." Israel asked for the Law and God obliged them and He gave them the Ten Commandments first.

Several things need to be mentioned as we look at the Ten Commandments. The first one is the "new morality." The new morality goes back before the giving of the Law. In fact, it came right out of the Garden of Eden when man first disobeyed God. The new morality existed before the Flood and after the Flood. Today it is far from new. We love to think that we are sophisticated and refined sinners. We are not—we are just crude sinners in the raw—natural sinners. The Ten Commandments put before us God's standards. No man can play fast and loose with the Ten Commandments and get by with it.

On Blackwell's Island there was a graveyard for criminals. On one grave was a marker which read, "Here lies the fragments of John Smith who contradicted His Maker, played football with the Ten Commandments, and departed this life at the age of thirty-five. His mother and wife weep for him. Nobody else does. May he rest in peace." That grave marker revealed a man who tried to defy the law of God. No person can play football with the Ten Commandments and escape the punishment of God.

Often times the charge is made against those of us who preach the grace of God that we do not have a proper appreciation for the Law. We are charged with despising it, rejecting it, and actually teaching that because we are not saved by the Law, it can be violated at will and broken with impunity. This is not true at all. On the contrary, every preacher who teaches the grace of God and has a true perspective of the nature of salvation by faith, realizes the lofty character of the Law. Paul answers the problem in Romans 6:1–2 which says, "What shall we say then? Shall we continue in sin, that grace may abound? God forbid. How shall we, that are dead to sin, live any longer therein?"

If you think you can continue to live in sin and break the Ten Commandments at will, then, my friend, you are not saved by the grace of God. When you are really saved, you want to please God and want to do His will which is revealed in the Ten Commandments. Therefore I think every preacher of the grace of God has a respect and reverence for God's law. We say with the psalmist, "O how love I thy law! it is my meditation all the day."

What is the Law? Someone has defined it as the transcript of the mind of God. That is a defective definition. The Law is the expression of the mind of God relative to what man ought to be. There is no grace or mercy in the Law at all. The Law is an expression of the holy will of God. The psalmist in Psalm 19:7 says, "The law of the LORD is perfect, converting the soul: the testimony of the LORD is sure, making wise the simple." The Law requires perfection on your part. I have never met anyone who has measured up to God's standard. The Law is not some vague notion, and it does not have anything to do with good intentions. It requires perfect obedience, for the Law of the Lord is perfect.

The Law of the Lord is right. Our notions of

right and wrong are colored by our environment and by the fact that we have a fallen nature. The Law is a revelation of God. God has drawn the line between right and wrong. How do you know what is right? God tells us what is right. This present generation who wants freedom so badly is questioning what is right. "Why is it wrong to steal?" they ask. They do not mind stealing. But they like the commandment "Thou shalt not kill" because they say it is wrong for the government to commit murder by executing criminals. How inconsistent this crowd is! How ignorant they are of the law. Why is it wrong to lie or to steal? Because God says it is wrong. You may say, "It is for the good of mankind." Of course it is. The Law would be a wonderful thing if man could keep it. Man cannot keep the Law, however, and the jails, the locks on the doors, and the fact that you have to sign ten pieces of paper to borrow money from a bank because they do not trust you, are all testimony to this fact. There was a day when a man's word was his bond, but that is no longer true today. The law is a norm for human conduct. Stealing, lying, and adultery are wrong because God says they are wrong.

The Law never enforces itself. The Lawgiver must have power. God enforces His laws with a tremendous impact. Take the law of gravitation, for example. You can go up as high as you want to but you had better not turn loose. The law of gravitation is in operation and you cannot reverse it. You may think you can, but in the long run you will be the loser.

Many people think they can break the Ten Commandments right and left and get by with it. That reminds me of the whimsical story of the man who jumped off the Empire State Building in New York City. As he went sailing by the fiftieth floor, a man looked out the window and said to him, "Well, how is it?" The falling man replied, "So far, so good." That is not where the law of gravitation enforces itself. Fifty more floors down and the man will find out, "So far, *not* so good." The interesting thing is that a law must be enforced to be a law and therefore God says in Ezekiel 18:4, ". . . the soul that sinneth, it shall die." The Law must be enforced and the breaker of the Law must pay the penalty.

There is another viewpoint that needs to be corrected and that is the confounding of law and grace and putting them into one system. Putting law and grace into the same system is to rob the Law of its majesty and meaning. There is no love in the Law. There is no grace in the law. Grace is robbed of its goodness and

glory when it is mixed with the Law. Grace is stripped of its wonder, attractiveness and desire. The sinner's needs are not met when law and grace are bound together. The Law sets forth what man ought to be. Grace sets forth what God is. The majesty of the Law is something that we do need to recognize.

The Law reveals who God is and the vast yawning chasm between God and man. Paul asked the question in Galatians 4:21, "Tell me, ye that desire to be under the law, do ye not hear the law?" You had better listen to what the Law says because man has been weighed in the balances by the Ten Commandments and has been found wanting. You do not measure yourself by others. It is very easy for the man on Mt. Whitney to look down at the man on the ant hill and say, "I am higher than you are." The man on Mt. Whitney, however, did not make it to the moon, or to heaven either. You just do not measure up to God's standard.

The Law also reveals who man is and his inability to bridge the gap between himself and God. Romans 3:19 tells us, "Now we know that what things soever the law saith, it saith to them who are under the law: that every mouth may be stopped, and all the world may become guilty before God." Paul says in Romans 8:3, "For what the law could not do, in that it was weak through the flesh, God sending his own Son in the likeness of sinful flesh, and for sin, condemned sin in the flesh." The fault does not lie in the Law but in us.

The Law is a mirror, as we have already seen, that reveals man in his sinful condition. Many people look in the mirror and think they are all right. This reminds me of the fairy story in which a queen looked in her mirror and said, "Mirror, mirror, on the wall, who is fairest of them all?" She wanted the mirror to say that she was, but the mirror told the truth and said she wasn't—someone else was fairer. And the interesting thing today is that a great many folk look at the mirror (the Ten Commandments in the Word of God) and they say the same thing, "Mirror, mirror on the wall, who is fairest of them all?" The difference is that they answer their own question and say, "*I* am." They think they are keeping the Law. My friend, you need to look in the mirror more closely and let the mirror do the answering.

The Law never made a man a sinner; it revealed the fact that man was a sinner. The Law was given to bring a man to Christ, as we have seen. It was our schoolmaster to take us by the hand, lead us to the cross, and tell us, "Little man, you need a Savior because you are a sinner."

THE TEN COMMANDMENTS

Now let's look at the Ten Commandments. They are divided into two different major divisions. One part deals with man's relationship to God, and the other part deals with man's relationship to man.

Thou shalt have no other gods before me [Exod. 20:3].

God is condemning polytheism, which is the belief in more than one god. There is no commandment against atheism—there was none in those days because they were too close to the creation and the original revelation of God. The atheists begin to appear during the time of King David, and they were called fools. Psalm 53:1 says, "The fool hath said in his heart, There is no God. . . ." Today the atheist can be a college professor and considered to be a brain and an intellectual, but God says he is a fool. There are many atheists today because we are so far from our origin, and men are not willing to accept the revelation of God in His Word.

God told Israel, "Thou shalt have no other gods before me." God instructed the nation in this manner because in that day it was mighty hard for man to keep balanced. In that day it was popular to worship many gods. Today it is popular not to worship any god. My, how the pendulum of the clock has moved! The important thing to note in this verse is the fact that God is condemning polytheism. Paul elaborates upon this subject in Romans 1:21–25 which states, "Because that, when they knew God, they glorified him not as God, neither were thankful; but became vain in their imaginations, and their foolish heart was darkened. Professing themselves to be wise, they became fools, And changed the glory of the uncorruptible God into an image made like to corruptible man, and to birds, and fourfooted beasts, and creeping things. Wherefore God also gave them up to uncleanness through the lusts of their own hearts, to dishonour their own bodies between themselves: Who changed the truth of God into a lie, and worshipped and served the creature more than the Creator, who is blessed for ever. Amen."

Thou shalt not make unto thee any graven image, or any likeness of any thing that is in heaven above, or that is in the earth beneath, or that is in the water under the earth:

Thou shalt not bow down thyself to them, nor serve them: for I the Lord thy God am a jealous God, visiting the iniquity of the fathers upon the children unto the third and fourth generation of them that hate me [Exod. 20:4–5].

Some people may feel that this passage does not apply to us today. Colossians 3:5 tells us that ". . . covetousness . . . is idolatry." Anything that you give yourself to, especially in abandonment, becomes your "god." Many people do not worship Bacchus, the cloven-footed Greek and Roman god of wine and revelry of long ago, but they worship the bottle just the same. There are millions of alcoholics in our country right now. The liquor interests like to tell us about how much of the tax burden they carry, when actually they do not pay a fraction of the bill for the casualties they cause by their product. A lot of propaganda is being fed to this generation and large groups of people are being brainwashed. Whether or not folk recognize it, they worship the god Bacchus.

Other people worship Aphrodite, that is, the goddess of sex. Some people worship money. Anything to which you give your time, heart, and soul, becomes your God. God says that we are not to have any gods before Him.

Thou shalt not take the name of the Lord thy God in vain; for the Lord will not hold him guiltless that taketh his name in vain [Exod. 20:7].

Using the Lord's name in "vain" means in the way of blasphemy. This is very prevalent in our day and age. But His commandment still stands. It is wrong to use God's name in vain because He is God and He is holy! It also reveals a lack of vocabulary. Many people cannot express themselves without using profanity. A man who was wonderfully converted several years ago in Texas once told me, "When I was converted, I lost over half of my vocabulary!" And this is what he meant.

Now the fourth commandment:

Remember the sabbath day, to keep it holy.

Six days shalt thou labour, and do all thy work:

But the seventh day is the sabbath of the Lord thy God: in it thou shalt not do any work, thou, nor thy son, nor thy daughter, thy manservant, nor thy maidservant, nor thy cattle, nor thy stranger that is within thy gates:

For in six days the Lord made heaven and earth, the sea, and all that in them is, and rested the seventh day: wherefore the Lord blessed the sabbath day, and hallowed it [Exod. 20:8–11].

The Sabbath day was given to the nation Israel in a very unusual way. It was a covenant, a token between God and the children of Israel. We shall see that in Exodus 31:13–17. The exact day, in my opinion, is not important. After all, the calendar changes that have been made make it impossible for us to know whether our seventh day is our Saturday or not. I do not think it is. But that is beside the point because, as far as we are concerned, it makes no difference what day we observe. We keep what we believe is the first day of the week. It may or may not be. But we recognize the first day of our week because our Lord came back from the dead on that day. All of this will be dealt with later on in the Book of Exodus.

Next we come to the section of the commandments which deal with man's relationship with man. It begins in the home.

Honor thy father and thy mother: that thy days may be long upon the land which the Lord thy God giveth thee [Exod. 20:12].

A father and a mother should be worthy of the honor of their children. We will speak more of this commandment later.

The sixth commandment says:

Thou shalt not kill [Exod. 20:13].

This verse is used by many people who are opposed to a particular war. Many young men have talked to me about it. They say, "You should not kill; therefore, you should not be a soldier." The commandment "Thou shalt not kill" was *not* given to a nation; it was given to the individual. One man should not kill another. No one should go to any country on his own, and kill. "Thou shalt not kill" has nothing to do with soldier service or with the execution of a criminal. A nation is given an authority to protect human life by taking human life. "Thou shalt not kill" is a commandment to the individual and it is speaking of murder, which our Lord said comes from anger—and we are not even to be angry with our brother.

The seventh commandment says:

Thou shalt not commit adultery [Exod. 20:14].

We are living today in the middle of a sex revolution. Sex is certainly not new, but it is still adultery when it is committed outside of wedlock. God makes this very clear. Man may think he has changed this commandment but he has not. This commandment still stands.

The eighth commandment says:

Thou shalt not steal [Exod. 20:15].

The point I would like to make here is that if you are permitted to commit adultery, then you should be permitted to steal and so forth. This whole package goes together. If one is all right to indulge in, then all should be right; if one is wrong, then all are wrong.

The ninth commandment says:

Thou shalt not bear false witness against thy neighbour [Exod. 20:16].

Bearing false witness against your neighbor is lying.

The tenth commandment says:

Thou shalt not covet thy neighbour's house, thou shalt not covet thy neighbour's wife, nor his manservant, nor his maidservant, nor his ox, nor his ass, nor any thing that is thy neighbour's [Exod. 20:17].

Covetousness, according to the apostle Paul in Colossians 3:5, is idolatry. This is one of the great sins of the present hour. God condemns killing, adultery, stealing, bearing false witness, and covetousness. We will have an occasion to look at the Ten Commandments in a different way later on.

THE EFFECT OF GOD'S VISIT

God has given the children of Israel the moral code which is the Ten Commandments. However, there is more to the Law than the moral code. God will also give them that part of the Law which deals with social legislation. He will also give them instructions concerning an altar and the building of the tabernacle. The Book of Leviticus gives in detail the service of the tabernacle. It is all part of the Law. It all goes in one package.

And all the people saw the thunderings, and the lightnings, and the noise of the trumpet, and the mountain smoking: and when the people saw it, they removed, and stood afar off.

And they said unto Moses, Speak thou with us, and we will hear: but let not God speak with us, lest we die [Exod. 20:18–19].

When the Israelites saw the thunder and lightning, they were afraid and backed away from the mount.

And Moses said unto the people, Fear not: for God is come to prove you, and that his fear may be before your faces, that ye sin not [Exod. 20:20].

The Law presented a very high standard. The Law of the Lord is perfect. It demands perfection. If you are trying to be saved by keeping the Law, you will have to be *perfect*. If you are not perfect, you cannot be saved by the Law. I thank God that under grace He can take a poor sinner like me and save me. Grace reveals something of the goodness and wonder of our God.

And the people stood afar off, and Moses drew near unto the thick darkness where God was.

And the Lord said unto Moses, Thus thou shalt say unto the children of Israel, Ye have seen that I have talked with you from heaven.

Ye shall not make with me gods of silver, neither shall ye make unto you gods of gold [Exod. 20:21–23].

It is important to see why God appears in just this way to the children of Israel. I think it is evident that God wants to impress upon them that He is the living God. Remember that they were reared in Egypt with idols all around them—and they were and are idolatrous, as we shall see. They are worshiping the creature rather than the Creator. God is moving closer to these people than He ever has before.

INSTRUCTIONS
CONCERNING THE ALTAR

God has given Israel the Ten Commandments. Now along with the commandments God gives instructions for an altar. An altar is used for sacrifice. The altar speaks of the cross of Christ and the blood that He shed. This altar is the one they built before the tabernacle was made. Apparently everywhere they journeyed they made one like this.

An altar of earth thou shalt make unto me, and shalt sacrifice thereon thy burnt offerings, and thy peace offerings, thy sheep, and thine oxen: in all places where I record my name I will come unto thee, and I will bless thee [Exod. 20:24].

There is no mention of presenting a sin offering on this altar. The peace offering reveals that man needs a sacrifice that will reconcile him to God, and that Christ did make peace by the blood of His cross. The burnt offering speaks of who Christ is; it speaks of His worthiness and ability to save.

This altar was to be made of earth and was the place upon which the Israelites were to sacrifice burnt offerings and peace offerings. The sin and trespass offerings were given to Israel later.

And if thou wilt make me an altar of stone, thou shalt not build it of hewn stone: for if thou lift up thy tool upon it, thou hast polluted it [Exod. 20:25].

There is an important lesson in this verse. God wanted them to build a plain altar of stone with no engraving. Perhaps an engraver would want to make the altar appealing, attractive looking, and very beautiful. The moment a tool is put to the stones, it is polluted. God rejects it. Today we have gone way past "engraving" in our churches. We have come to the place where we feel that everything connected with worship should be beautiful. We want soft music, dim lights, and beautiful colors. We want the sermon to be given in very low tones and in a dignified manner, as flowery as possible. Well, we've been through such a period. And we have found that liberalism has emptied our churches. There is nothing wrong with an attractive place to worship. I am for soft lights, beautiful music, and flowery speaking. But when any of these things obscure the message of the Cross and take attention away from the Lord Jesus Christ who died on that cross, then God is offended. God does not want this to happen.

When Paul went to the city of Corinth, you will recall, he found the Corinthians to be quite philosophical. Many of the heathen priests connected with the heathen religions tried to identify with all the sins of Corinth. When Paul arrived, these secondhand philosophers wanted to argue, discuss, and appear intellectual. These Corinthians were going in every direction. Paul had a similar experience in Athens. He tells these Corinthians, "For I determined not to know any thing among you, save Jesus Christ, and him crucified" (1 Cor. 2:2). Friends, if "Jesus Christ and him crucified" is left out of the message, I do not care how high the steeple is, how loud the church bell is, how beautiful the sanctuary is, how soft the music is, or how educated the preacher is—it is not a church and, as far as God is concerned, it is polluted.

Neither shalt thou go up by steps unto mine altar, that thy nakedness be not discovered thereon [Exod. 20:26].

Many people would like to build nice lovely steps up to the altar. That would be very convenient. In that day a man wore a kind of a skirt and to climb steps he would have to lift that skirt and his nakedness would be revealed. God says, "I do not want to see your nakedness." That which speaks of the flesh God cannot use.

Let me make this very personal. Anything that Vernon McGee does that is of the flesh, God hates and will not use. God does not want a display of the flesh in anything that has to do with His work. We need to guard against this type of thing. It disturbs me when people see only the preacher and do not see the One he is trying to present. I personally do not like anyone to tell me that I preached a beautiful sermon. The last thing I want to do is preach a beautiful sermon. I want to preach about a beautiful Savior and when people hear me preach, I want them to say, "Isn't Jesus wonderful!"

I have had very few real compliments since I have been a minister, but one I remember well. When I was a pastor as a student in Georgia, I used to preach in a church on the side of a red clay hill. One morning after the message everyone left but a country boy. He wore high yellow shoes that buttoned all the way, and he waited around, as timid as could be. Finally he came up to me with tears in his eyes. He took hold of my hand and said, "My, I did not know Jesus was so wonderful." He wanted to say something else but he was too choked with emotion; so he turned and walked out of the little church. That church today is in the middle of a city, but in those days it was in the middle of a cotton patch. I watched that country boy walk across the cotton patch, and said to myself, "Oh God, let me so preach that people will know that Jesus is wonderful." That was a compliment and I have not had many like it.

We do not need the display of the flesh in the ministry, in the pulpit, or in church work. We need to preach Jesus Christ and Him crucified.

CHAPTER 21

THEME: *The law concerning master and servant relationships; the law concerning personal injuries*

THE LAW CONCERNING MASTER AND SERVANT RELATIONSHIPS

In Exodus 21 we come to social legislation. This part of the Law is an important issue at this time because the Israelites had been slaves in Egypt.

Now these are the judgments which thou shalt set before them.

If thou buy an Hebrew servant, six years he shall serve: and in the seventh he shall go out free for nothing [Exod. 21:1–2].

These two verses clearly state that the Israelites could never permanently make one of their own brethren a slave.

If he came in by himself, he shall go out by himself: if he were married, then his wife shall go out with him.

If his master have given him a wife, and she have born him sons or daughters; the wife and her children shall be her master's, and he shall go out by himself.

And if the servant shall plainly say, I love my master, my wife, and my children; I will not go out free:

Then his master shall bring him unto the judges; he shall also bring him to the door, or unto the door post; and his master shall bore his ear through with an awl; and he shall serve him for ever [Exod. 21:3–6].

This remarkable law states that if a man is a slave, after seven years he can go free. If he was married when he became a slave, he can take his wife with him. If he married while a slave, that is, if he married a woman who was already a slave of his master, at the end of seven years he could go free, but his wife would still belong to the master. He would be free but his wife would not. He could, however, if he loved his wife and master, decide to stay of his own free will. If he decides to stay, his master is to bore his ear lobe through with an awl signifying that he will serve his master forever.

This is a beautiful picture of the Lord Jesus Christ. He came to this earth and took upon

Himself our humanity. And we were all slaves of sin. He could have gone out free. He could have returned to heaven, to His position in the Godhead, without going through the doorway of death. He did not have to die upon the cross. But He willingly came down to earth and took upon Himself our humanity. "And being found in fashion as a man, he humbled himself, and became obedient unto death, even the death of the cross" (Phil. 2:8).

Psalm 40:6–8 goes on to say, "Sacrifice and offering thou didst not desire; mine ears hast thou opened: burnt offering and sin offering hast thou not required. Then said I, Lo, I come: in the volume of the book it is written of me, I delight to do thy will, O my God: yea, thy law is within my heart." This passage refers to Christ, because Hebrews 10:5–9 tells us that it does. It was fulfilled when our Lord came to this earth. "Wherefore when he cometh into the world [speaking of Christ], he saith, Sacrifice and offering thou wouldest not, but a body hast thou prepared me [it was not only his ear that was "digged," or bored through with an awl, but God gave Him a body which He will have throughout eternity]: in burnt offerings and sacrifices for sin thou hast had no pleasure. Then said I, Lo, I come (in the volume of the book it is written of me) to do thy will, O God. Above when he said, Sacrifice and offering and burnt offerings and offering for sin thou wouldest not, neither hadst pleasure therein; which are offered by the law; Then said he, Lo, I come to do thy will, O God. He taketh away the first, that he may establish the second." Christ was "made like unto His brethren." He chose not to go out free without us. He could have left this earth without dying, but He said, "I love My Bride. I love the sinner." So He became obedient unto death, even the death of the cross so that He could redeem us from the slavery of sin. What a picture this is of Christ—placed right here after the giving of the Ten Commandments.

THE LAW
CONCERNING PERSONAL INJURIES

He that smiteth a man, so that he die, shall be surely put to death [Exod. 21:12].

This verse is the basis for capital punishment. Some people believe that "Thou shalt not kill" means that the government has no right to exact a death penalty. However, God commanded the nation Israel to put to death any murderer.

And if a man lie not in wait, but God deliver him into his hand; then I will appoint thee a place whither he shall flee [Exod. 21:13].

There were six cities of refuge placed throughout the land of Palestine. These were set up in convenient locations so that one charged with manslaughter could avail himself of the shelter they afforded until the matter in which he was involved could be settled. We will speak more of the cities of refuge later.

But if a man come presumptuously upon his neighbour, to slay him with guile; thou shalt take him from mine altar, that he may die [Exod. 21:14].

If a man commits a premeditated murder, that man is to be executed. If a man kills someone in self-defense while trying to defend himself, without premeditation, that man would not merit execution.

And he that smiteth his father, or his mother, shall be surely put to death [Exod. 21:15].

This is God's protection for the home.

And he that stealeth a man, and selleth him, or if he be found in his hand, he shall surely be put to death [Exod. 21:16].

God did not approve of slavery at all and, in fact, He condemned it. It was a great system in that day, but God dealt with it.

And he that curseth his father, or his mother, shall surely be put to death.

And if men strive together, and one smite another with a stone, or with his fist, and he die not, but keepeth his bed:

If he rise again, and walk abroad upon his staff, then shall he that smote him be quit: only he shall pay for the loss of his time, and shall cause him to be thoroughly healed [Exod. 21:17–19].

In other words, the one who was responsible for the injury was to reimburse the injured—both for his time and medical expenses.

The above laws and the other laws presented in the rest of this chapter are the basis of the laws of our land. They form the basic platform of law and order that is necessary for a civilized nation to build upon.

Verses 24 and 25 sum it all up by saying:

Eye for eye, tooth for tooth, hand for hand, foot for foot.

Burning for burning, wound for wound, stripe for stripe [Exod. 21:24–25].

In other words, these two verses state the law of reciprocity. Law must be enforced if there is to be law and order and protection for human life and property.

Thank God, we do not have to depend on keeping the Law for our salvation. There is One who is prepared to extend grace to us that we may be saved, even the Lord Jesus Christ.

CHAPTER 22

THEME: *The law concerning property rights; the law concerning crimes against humanity*

THE LAW CONCERNING PROPERTY RIGHTS

There are those who raise the question today, "What is right and what is wrong?" Some say that what is right and wrong is relative. A college professor, who claims to be an atheist, was discussing this with me. He maintained that right and wrong are relative, that what he would think is right and what I would think is right could be poles apart. Then he asked me, "On what do you base your dogmatic conclusions?" I said, "I base them on the Word of God." I went on to tell him that my nature was just like his nature, and that I would like to give in in certain places, and I would like to let the bars down here and there, but God has given me a standard to follow. The interesting thing is that God's standard has produced a society in which there has been a measure of law and justice.

The laws presented in chapters 21 to 24 deal with everyday nitty-gritty living. In some ways it is boring reading and similar to reading a lawbook. However, most of our laws are based upon these precepts. I am glad that the Word of God says, "Thou shalt not kill." It protects me and my family. I am happy the Bible says, "Thou shalt not steal." It protects what little property I have. These and the other laws are basic to having order in a society.

If a man shall steal an ox, or a sheep, and kill it, or sell it; he shall restore five oxen for an ox, and four sheep for a sheep [Exod. 22:1].

I cannot tell you why *five* oxen should be restored for an ox or *four* sheep for one sheep. In the New Testament, however, Zacchaeus referred to this principle: "And Zacchaeus stood, and said unto the Lord; Behold, Lord, the half of my goods I give to the poor; and if I have taken any thing from any man by false accusation, I restore him *fourfold*" (Luke 19:8). Why did he say fourfold? He was referring to the Mosaic Law.

Our law today says that if you destroy another man's property, you must pay the damages. All that our society demands when you damage or destroy some other person's property is to replace the item or pay what it is worth. God's law of restoring fourfold is much better with human nature the way it is. If we had to restore fourfold anything that we destroyed or damaged, we would be more careful. Human nature is always the same, and God is always the same. God deals with man on the basis that is best for him.

If a thief be found breaking up, and be smitten that he die, there shall no blood be shed for him [Exod. 22:2].

This law gives you the right to self-protection. Not long ago a thief broke into a man's place and the homeowner shot him. He sued the homeowner for several thousand dollars in damages. The case went to court and the thief won the judgment on the grounds that the homeowner had no right to shoot him, according to the decision of some asinine judge! In order to pay the damages the homeowner had to sell his property. And there was no judgment against the thief at all! In our day there is a great emphasis on protecting the rights of the *guilty* at the expense of the rights of the *innocent*.

God's law protects a man's property and his home. Under this principle a man is justified in protecting his property, his home, and his loved ones.

God's laws are basic principles which give society law and order. If mankind had followed God's social legislation as given in the Book of Exodus, we would not have the social problems we are having in the cities of the United States. Our entire legal system, which was founded on the Word of God, is riddled with men who do not know the Bible because they are so far from it themselves. Their entire background is such that they are not properly able to interpret the Law.

The Constitution of the United States was written by men, not all of whom were Christian (in fact, most of them were Deists), but they had a certain respect for the Word of God. I recently heard a man say that Thomas Jefferson ridiculed the Bible. He did not. Quotations from Thomas Jefferson show that he had great respect for the Word of God even though he did not believe in the miraculous and actually did not follow it in his personal life. But we have men who administer law today with no background in the Bible whatever. Because of this we are in trouble, deep trouble.

If the sun be risen upon him, there shall be blood shed for him; for he should make full restitution; if he have nothing, then he shall be sold for his theft [Exod. 22:3].

If a man steals, he has to make restitution for that which he has stolen, even to the point of selling himself into slavery to help make the payment.

If a man shall cause a field or vineyard to be eaten, and shall put in his beast, and shall feed in another man's field; of the best of his own field, and of the best of his own vineyard, shall he make restitution [Exod. 22:5].

If a man's cow or sheep breaks through into another man's field and they cause damage, he is to make restitution.

If fire break out, and catch in thorns, so that the stacks of corn, or the standing corn, or the field, be consumed therewith; he that kindled the fire shall surely make restitution [Exod. 22:6].

This is a practical verse that shows us the right way to do things. It is another basic principle for the welfare of mankind on earth. God gave the Mosaic system to Israel so that they would be an example to the nations of the world.

THE LAW CONCERNING CRIMES AGAINST HUMANITY

And if a man entice a maid that is not betrothed, and lie with her, he shall surely endow her to be his wife [Exod. 22:16].

In other words, if a man rapes a girl, he will be forced to marry her. Things are certainly different in our day and age.

If her father utterly refuse to give her unto him, he shall pay money according to the dowry of virgins [Exod. 22:17].

If her father does not agree to the marriage, the rapist must pay a penalty for what he has done.

Thou shalt not suffer a witch to live [Exod. 22:18].

Today we are seeing a resurgence of Satan worship and of the supernatural. This trend is potent and it is real. We shall be dealing with this further in the Book of Deuteronomy.

Whosoever lieth with a beast shall surely be put to death [Exod. 22:19].

Having sexual intercourse with a beast shows just how low man can go. Why did God make a law like this? Well, because this was being done. And we are seeing a recurrence of this unspeakably degrading practice in our "enlightened" society.

He that sacrificeth unto any god, save unto the LORD only, he shall be utterly destroyed [Exod. 22:20].

This, of course, was the most severe penalty. Had it been followed to the letter, we would have a much better society today. Utterly destroying anyone who sacrifices to any other god but the LORD is harsh but, after all, when you have a cancer, you want to rid yourself of it. This is what God is talking about.

Thou shalt neither vex a stranger, nor oppress him: for ye were strangers in the land of Egypt [Exod. 22:21].

This is God's "Good Neighbor" policy.

Ye shall not afflict any widow, or fatherless child [Exod. 22:22].

Child labor laws were established after the Wesleyan Revival, friends. The Word of God has been basic to all of the great movements that have brought blessing to mankind. What about the fatherless child? Did the orphans' home begin in atheistic countries or under Christian auspices?

If thou afflict them in any wise, and they cry at all unto me, I will surely hear their cry:

And my wrath shall wax hot, and I will kill you with the sword; and your wives shall be widows, and your children fatherless [Exod. 22:23–24].

I believe that God protects the helpless. Great judgment is coming for those individuals who have mistreated folk in need.

If thou lend money to any of my people that is poor by thee, thou shalt not be to him as an usurer, neither shalt thou lay upon him usury [Exod. 22:25].

If one person lends money to another, he is not to charge excessive interest. God says it is wrong to take advantage of others.

These are some of God's laws, and more are given in Exodus 23.

CHAPTER 23

THEME: *The law concerning property rights—continued; the law concerning the land and the Sabbath; the law concerning national feasts*

THE LAW CONCERNING PROPERTY RIGHTS—CONTINUED

Thou shalt not raise a false report: put not thine hand with the wicked to be an unrighteous witness [Exod. 23:1].

Be careful what you say; this is God's rule of conduct. A gossiper is as bad as a murderer, a thief, or an adulterer in your midst, yet in our society a gossiper gets by easily.

Thou shalt not follow a multitude to do evil; neither shalt thou speak in a cause to decline after many to wrest judgment [Exod. 23:2].

If we were to follow God's precept, "Thou shalt not follow a multitude to do evil," it would put us out of the marching, protesting and rioting business. Also it would rid our society of the growing menace of gangs. I talked with a very attractive young fellow in this category. He said he dressed as he did because he wanted liberty and freedom. I noticed there were several thousand dressed just like him. So I asked him, "Would you dare dress differently? Would they accept you?" He said, "No." Then I said, "When they protest, you have to get in line and protest, don't you?" He said, "Yes, I do." "Well," I replied, "then you really do not have much freedom, do you? You have to do certain things. When they protest, you have to protest. When they dress a certain way, you have to dress a certain way. This is not freedom." My friend, freedom is not following a multitude to do evil!

Neither shalt thou countenance a poor man in his cause [Exod. 23:3].

Judgment should not be swayed toward the rich or toward the poor. Judgment and justice should be exercised fairly. The Romans depicted justice as a woman, tender but also blindfolded. She was no respecter of persons and held a sword in one hand and scales in the other. The sword meant that when the judgment was handed down, there would be the execution of the penalty. The scales meant that justice would be fair. Judgment should be exercised without respect of persons.

THE LAW CONCERNING THE LAND AND THE SABBATH

Once again God gives Israel this law concerning the Sabbath day and the sabbatic year.

And six years thou shalt sow thy land, and shalt gather in the fruits thereof:

But the seventh year thou shalt let it rest and lie still; that the poor of thy people may eat: and what they leave the beasts of the field shall eat. In like manner thou shalt deal with thy vineyard, and with thy oliveyard [Exod. 23:10–11].

God will review this law with Israel when they go into the land. The subjects of the Sabbath day, the sabbatic year and the year of Jubilee are dealt with in the Book of Leviticus. Briefly, the Sabbath day was the seventh day of the week and was a day of strict rest. The Sabbatic year was the septennial rest for the land from all cultivation. The year of Jubilee is also called the year of liberty. Every fiftieth year the Hebrews who had been forced to sell themselves into slavery became free. Lands that had been sold reverted to their original owners.

It is interesting to note that folk today who claim to be Sabbath keepers, are attempting to keep only the Sabbath *day*. They ignore the Sabbath year (especially if they are farmers) and disregard completely the year of Jubilee.

THE LAW
CONCERNING NATIONAL FEASTS

Three times thou shalt keep a feast unto me in the year.

Thou shalt keep the feast of unleavened bread: (thou shalt eat unleavened bread seven days, as I commanded thee, in the time appointed of the month Abib: for in it thou camest out from Egypt: and none shall appear before me empty:)

And the feast of harvest, the firstfruits of thy labours, which thou has sown in the field: and the feast of ingathering, which is in the end of the year, when thou hast gathered in thy labours out of the field.

Three times in the year all thy males shall appear before the Lord GOD [Exod. 23:14–17].

Three times a year all the Hebrew males were to appear before the Lord God in Jerusalem. There were three feasts that were to be celebrated: (1) the Feast of the Passover; (2) the Feast of Pentecost; (3) the Feast of Tabernacles. The Feast of the Passover, you will recall, was instituted in memory of Israel's preservation from the last plague brought against the land of Egypt and her deliverance from that land of bondage. Before the people of Israel enter the Promised Land, these will be discussed in detail.

Behold, I send an Angel before thee, to keep thee in the way, and to bring thee into the place which I have prepared.

Beware of him, and obey his voice, provoke him not; for he will not pardon your transgressions: for my name is in him [Exod. 23:20–21].

Who is this Angel? Other Scriptures shed light on the answer. First Corinthians 10:4 says, "And did all drink the same spiritual drink: for they drank of that spiritual Rock that followed them: and that Rock was Christ." First Corinthians 10:9–10 continues, "Neither let us tempt Christ, as some of them also tempted, and were destroyed of serpents. Neither murmur ye, as some of them also murmured, and were destroyed of the destroyer." It is the Lord Jesus that they were to obey. He is definitely the one in view here.

For mine Angel shall go before thee, and bring thee in unto the Amorites, and the Hittites, and the Perizzites, and the Canaanites, the Hivites, and the Jebusites: and I will cut them off [Exod. 23:23].

God told Israel that He intended to put the enemy out of the land because of their sin. Now the Lord says to them:

I will send my fear before thee, and will destroy all the people to whom thou shalt come, and I will make all thine enemies turn their backs unto thee [Exod. 23:27].

God is telling Israel that it is His intention to put them in the land of Israel and make it their land. Then God tells them:

Thou shalt make no covenant with them, nor with their gods.

They shall not dwell in thy land, lest they make thee sin against me: for if thou serve their gods, it will surely be a snare unto thee [Exod. 23:32–33].

The children of Israel were not to make any covenants with the inhabitants of the land nor with their gods. Joshua made the mistake of making a covenant with the Gibeonites. He did not do enough investigating. Of course the reason the nation of Israel finally went into Babylonian captivity was because they went into idolatry and served other gods. In other words, they did not heed God's warning.

CHAPTER 24

THEME: *Order of worship before the existence of the tabernacle;*
the children of Israel acknowledge the covenant; Moses ascends
Mount Sinai alone

Exodus 24 concludes the section on social legislation begun in Exodus 21. We have found that the law of Moses is much more than the brief Ten Commandments and that the area of social legislation covers a great deal of ground.

ORDER OF WORSHIP BEFORE
THE EXISTENCE OF
THE TABERNACLE

And he said unto Moses, Come up unto the Lord, thou, and Aaron, Nadab, and Abihu, and seventy of the elders of Israel; and worship ye afar off [Exod. 24:1].

God told these men to come up into the mountain, but even these men who were in a very unique position at that time were told to *worship afar off.* How different things were under law than they are under grace. How different their situation was from when God was bringing them along the path from Egypt on eagle's wings of grace. Under law man must worship afar off but today Ephesians 2:13 tells us, "But now in Christ Jesus ye who sometimes were far off are made nigh by the blood of Christ." God saves us and leads us along life's pathway today by His grace.

And Moses alone shall come near the Lord: but they shall not come nigh; neither shall the people go up with him.

And Moses came and told the people all the words of the Lord, and all the judgments: and all the people answered with one voice, and said, All the words which the Lord hath said will we do [Exod. 24:2–3].

This is the second time that the children of Israel have given an affirmative answer when God asked them if they wanted His commandments and Law. They are very self-confident, self-sufficient, and almost arrogant when they tell God, "Yes, we want your Law." They promise to do all of the words of the Lord even before they have them all. They have been given the Ten Commandments and believe they can keep them.

One wonders how Israel could be so deceived. But I am even more puzzled by the many people who still believe they are living by the Law. Those who believe they are meeting God's standard are deceived, and it is a terrible thing. First John 1:8 tells us: "If we say that we have no sin, we deceive ourselves, and the truth is not in us." You won't be deceiving your neighbors, you will not deceive your wife nor husband nor loved ones, but you certainly can deceive yourself. If you say that you do not sin, you deceive yourself. You would think that a man who says he has no sin ought to have also a little truth in him. But John says there is no truth in him at all. In case you missed it, John repeats it in 1 John 1:10, which says, "If we say that we have not sinned, we make him a liar, and his word is not in us." He said that if you say that you have not sinned, you have made God a liar. Friends, God is no liar. I wouldn't call Him that if I were you. The best thing to do is not boast of your goodness. My, the arrogance of the children of Israel in saying, "All the words which the Lord hath said we will do!" You will notice, however, that they did not keep all His words.

THE CHILDREN OF ISRAEL
ACKNOWLEDGE THE COVENANT

And Moses wrote all the words of the Lord, and rose up early in the morning, and builded an altar under the hill, and twelve pillars, according to the twelve tribes of Israel.

And he sent young men of the children of Israel, which offered burnt offerings, and sacrificed peace offerings of oxen unto the Lord.

And Moses took half of the blood, and put it in basins; and half of the blood he sprinkled on the altar.

And he took the book of the covenant, and read in the audience of the people: and they said, All that the Lord hath said will we do, and be obedient [Exod. 24:4–7].

These Israelites were certainly confident. In fact, they were filled with self-confidence. They really thought they could keep God's law, and that is the worst kind of self-deception. They promised to obey God, but they did not. The natural man believes he can please God, but he cannot. You and I cannot please God because no man can meet God's standard. We forget that we are actually members of a totally depraved race as far as God is concerned. If you doubt it, just look around the world and note the lawlessness. Look at the sin, the confusion, the atheism, and the godlessness on every hand. God is absolutely right when He says in Romans 3:10, ". . .There is none righteous, no, not one." We live in a day when sin is called good and bad is called good. The prophets said that such a day would come. Well, we certainly have arrived.

And Moses took the blood, and sprinkled it on the people, and said, Behold the blood of the covenant which the LORD hath made with you concerning all these words [Exod. 24:8].

Even before God gives the law to them, the Israelites are sprinkled with blood to let them know that there must be a sacrifice. Hebrews 9:22 says, "And almost all things are by the law purged with blood; and without shedding of blood is no remission." God will repeat this many times. Life must be given up, and a penalty must be paid before any of us can go to heaven.

MOSES ASCENDS
MOUNT SINAI ALONE

Then went up Moses, and Aaron, Nadab, and Abihu, and seventy of the elders of Israel:

And they saw the God of Israel: and there was under his feet as it were a paved work of a sapphire stone, and as it were the body of heaven in his clearness [Exod. 24:9–10].

"They *saw* the God of Israel" needs to be understood in the light of other Scriptures. Actually no one has seen God because He is a Spirit. John 1:18 tells us that, "No man hath seen God at any time; the only begotten Son, which is in the bosom of the Father, he hath declared him." What they saw was a representation of God. I sincerely doubt that we shall see God the Father throughout eternity. Jesus Christ is probably the closest view we will have of the Father. But He will be enough to satisfy our hearts. All that we know today about the Father is through the Son. I do not know how God the Father looks, or feels, or thinks, because God has told us in Isaiah 55:8–9, "For my thoughts are not your thoughts, neither are your ways my ways, saith the LORD. For as the heavens are higher than the earth, so are my ways higher than

your ways, and my thoughts than your thoughts." But Jesus has revealed Him to us. Moses, Aaron, Nadab, Abihu, and the seventy elders of Israel did not see God the Father but they saw a representation of God.

And upon the nobles of the children of Israel he laid not his hand: also they saw God, and did eat and drink [Exod. 24:11].

In this verse, as in the previous one, they saw a representation of God. Later on Moses asks to see God because all he had seen was a representation. Moses wanted to *see* God. Also to see God was Philip's plea in the upper room. "Philip saith unto him, Lord, shew us the Father, and it sufficeth us. Jesus saith unto him, Have I been so long time with you, and yet hast thou not known me, Philip? he that hath seen me hath seen the Father; and how sayest thou then, Shew us the Father?" (John 14:8–9). If you want to see God, friends, you will have to go through Jesus Christ.

I have heard earnest laymen give testimony to the fact that they can come directly into the presence of God since their salvation. The truth is that we do not come directly into God's presence; we have a mediator. "For there is one God, and one mediator between God and men, the man Christ Jesus" (1 Tim. 2:5). You come to God through Christ Jesus the mediator. Christ is the *daysman* Job longed for. Christ puts one hand in the Father's hand and one in your hand and brings you and God together. We do not reach God the Father on our own, and we must recognize that.

And Moses rose up, and his minister Joshua: and Moses went up into the mount of God [Exod. 24:13].

Now Joshua is beginning to appear in the picture more. God is preparing him to succeed Moses. He is a young man, and God has many things to teach him before he is prepared to lead Israel.

And he said unto the elders, Tarry ye here for us, until we come again unto you: and, behold, Aaron and Hur are with you: if any man have any matters to do, let him come unto them.

And Moses went up into the mount, and a cloud covered the mount.

And the glory of the LORD abode upon mount Sinai, and the cloud covered it six days: and the seventh day he called unto Moses out of the midst of the cloud.

And the sight of the glory of the LORD was like devouring fire on the top of the mount in the eyes of the children of Israel.

And Moses went into the midst of the cloud, and gat him up into the mount:

and Moses was in the mount forty days and forty nights [Exod. 24:14–18].

It was during this time on Mount Sinai that Moses received the instructions presented in the rest of this book.

CHAPTER 25

THEME: *Materials to be used for the tabernacle; instructions for constructing the ark of the covenant; the table of showbread; the golden lampstand*

In chapters 25 through 30 of Exodus, God gives Israel the blueprint for the tabernacle and the pattern for the garments for the high priest. Next we have the construction and erection of the tabernacle and the fact that it was filled with the glory of the Lord. The tabernacle was to be the center of Israel's life because it was there where man would approach God.

MATERIALS TO BE USED FOR THE TABERNACLE

And the LORD spake unto Moses, saying,

Speak unto the children of Israel, that they bring me an offering: of every man that giveth it willingly with his heart ye shall take my offering [Exod. 25:1–2].

Israel had been out of slavery for only a few months, yet the Lord asks them to make a contribution to help build the tabernacle. The amazing thing is that the children of Israel gave so much they were told to stop giving! Friends, a thing like this does not happen very often. I was a pastor for a long time, and I never had to restrain folk from giving to the church. But Moses did!

Following are the items they were to bring:

And this is the offering which ye shall take of them; gold, and silver, and brass,

And blue, and purple, and scarlet, and fine linen, and goats' hair,

And rams' skins dyed red, and badgers' skins, and shittim wood,

Oil for the light, spices for anointing oil, and for sweet incense,

Onyx stones, and stones to be set in the ephod, and in the breastplate [Exod. 25:3–7].

Our first reaction is, "Where did they obtain these items?" Remember that Israel had just been delivered out of slavery and this was part of the four hundred years back wages that they collected on their way out of the land of Egypt. Exodus 12:36 reminds us that ". . . the LORD gave the people favour in the sight of the Egyptians, so that they lent unto them such things as they required. And they spoiled the Egyptians." When Israel left Egypt, they took out tremendous wealth. It has been estimated that at least five million dollars worth of material went into the construction of the tabernacle alone. The tabernacle was small in size because it had to be carried on the wilderness march, but it was very ornate, rich and beautiful.

And let them make me a sanctuary; that I may dwell among them [Exod. 25:8].

God never said that He was going to *live* in the tabernacle in the sense that He was restricted to a geographical spot. He did say, however, that He would *dwell* between the cherubim. 1 Samuel 4:4, 2 Samuel 6:2, 2 Kings 19:15 and Isaiah 37:16 all give testimony to this fact. Israel was a theocracy and Jehovah was the King. Israel was to be ruled by God. His throne was between the cherubim, and this is where man met God. The idea which exists today that God dwells in a building made by hands is not true. That is a pagan notion. Some people call a church building "God's house." It is not God's house because He does not dwell in a building and never did. Solomon expressed it accurately, "But will God indeed dwell on the earth?

behold, the heaven and heaven of heavens cannot contain thee; how much less this house I have builded?" (1 Kings 8:27). The tabernacle was to be the place where man meets with God. "The LORD reigneth; let the people tremble: he sitteth between the cherubims; let the earth be moved" (Ps. 99:1). The ark was God's throne and it was the first article of furniture that they were to build.

According to all that I shew thee, after the pattern of the tabernacle, and the pattern of all the instruments thereof, even so shall ye make it [Exod. 25:9].

The Book of Hebrews tells us that this earthly tabernacle was patterned after the tabernacle in heaven. The question arises, "Is there a literal tabernacle in heaven?" I take the position that there is because God says there is. I take this literally and feel that if God had meant something else, He would have made that clear also. Hebrews 8:5 says, "Who serve unto the example and shadow of heavenly things, as Moses was admonished of God when he was about to make the tabernacle: for, See, saith he, that thou make all things according to the pattern shewed to thee in the mount." Hebrews 9:23–24 goes on to say, "It was therefore necessary that the patterns of things in the heavens should be purified with these; but the heavenly things themselves with better sacrifices than these. For Christ is not entered into the holy places made with hands, which are the figures of the true; but into heaven itself, now to appear in the presence of God for us."

INSTRUCTIONS FOR CONSTRUCTING THE ARK OF THE COVENANT

The outer court was an enclosed place around the tabernacle proper, 100 cubits long by 50 cubits wide. The cubit was a unit of measure based on the length of the forearm from the tip of the middle finger to the elbow. If you measure yours, you will find it is about eighteen inches—if you are a small person it will be shorter than that; if you are tall, it will be longer. So the length of a cubit varied, but was about eighteen inches. If you will consult the floor plan of the tabernacle, you will see that in the outer court were the brazen altar and the laver (Exod. 30:28). The tabernacle proper was divided into two compartments, the Holy Place and the Holy of Holies. The tabernacle itself was thirty cubits long and ten cubits wide and ten cubits high. The Holy Place was twenty by ten cubits. The Holy of Holies was ten cubits long, ten cubits wide,

and ten cubits high, thus making it a perfect cube.

The furniture in the Holy Place consisted of the table of showbread, the golden lampstand, and the altar of incense. In the Holy of Holies were the ark of the covenant and the mercy seat. In the outer court were two articles of furniture: the brazen altar and the layer. Enclosing it was a fence of white linen.

And they shall make an ark of shittim wood: two cubits and a half shall be the length thereof, and a cubit and a half the breadth thereof, and a cubit and a half the height thereof.

And thou shalt overlay it with pure gold, within and without shalt thou overlay it, and shalt make upon it a crown of gold round about.

And thou shalt cast four rings of gold for it, and put them in the four corners thereof; and two rings shall be in the one side of it, and two rings in the other side of it.

And thou shalt make staves of shittim wood, and overlay them with gold [Exod. 25:10–13].

The ark and the mercy seat above it was the place where God would meet with the children of Israel. It was the place for them to approach their God. It was the sanctum sanctorum of the tabernacle. Notice that the first article of furniture is the ark. We are approaching it from God's viewpoint, from the inside looking out. The ark was in the Holy of Holies where God's presence dwelt. If we were approaching it from man's viewpoint, we would come first to the gate of the tabernacle, then the brazen altar and the laver.

The tabernacle was fashioned in such a way that it could be carried as the Israelites marched through the wilderness. It was put together when they made camp and taken down when they moved to another place. Each piece of furniture in the tabernacle was equipped with rings and staves so that it could be easily carried through the wilderness.

The mercy seat, which formed a top for the ark, was considered a separate piece of furniture.

And thou shalt make a mercy seat of pure gold: two cubits and a half shall be the length thereof, and a cubit and a half the breadth thereof.

And thou shalt make two cherubims of

gold, of beaten work shalt thou make them, in the two ends of the mercy seat.

And make one cherub on the one end, and the other cherub on the other end: even of the mercy seat shall ye make the cherubims on the two ends thereof [Exod. 25:17–19].

Notice what God now says:

And the cherubims shall stretch forth their wings on high, covering the mercy seat with their wings, and their faces shall look one to another; toward the mercy seat shall the faces of the cherubims be [Exod. 25:20].

The cherubim looked down upon the mercy seat.

And thou shalt put the mercy seat above upon the ark; and in the ark thou shalt put the testimony that I shall give thee.

And there I will meet with thee, and I will commune with thee from above the mercy seat, from between the two cherubims which are upon the ark of the testimony, of all things which I will give thee in commandment unto the children of Israel [Exod. 25:21–22].

The ark was a chest covered inside and outside with gold. It was made of shittim wood which was more or less indestructible and much like the redwood of California. It was a perfect symbol of the Lord Jesus Christ in His deity and humanity. Jesus Christ was the God-man; His deity was represented by the gold and His humanity was represented by the wood.

The ark could not be spoken of as merely a wooden chest because it also was a gold chest. It could not be called a golden chest because it was also a chest of wood. It required both gold and wood to maintain the symbolism pointing to Christ as the God-man. There is no mingling of the two. To overlook this duality is to entertain a monstrous notion of His person. There is no doctrine in Scripture so filled with infinite mystery and so removed from the realm of explanation as the hypostatical union of Christ, the God-man. Yet there is no symbol so simple as the ark that describes this union of God and man in one body. A mere box made of wood and gold speaks of things unfathomable. Truly God chooses the simple things to confound the wise. That simple box tells the whole story, as far as man can take it in, of the unsearchable mystery of the blessed person of the Lord Jesus Christ.

The ark was covered with gold both inside and outside. Colossians 2:9 tells us, "For in him dwelleth all the fulness of the Godhead bodily." Jesus Christ was not merely a thaumaturgist, that is, a wonder-worker. Nor was He a man with an overdeveloped God consciousness. He *was* God! He spoke as God. He put Himself on the same plane as God. In John 14:1, 9, our Savior says, "Let not your heart be troubled: ye believe in God, believe also in me. . . . Have I been so long time with you, and yet hast thou not known me, Philip? he that hath seen me hath seen the Father. . . ." Yes, He was God.

He was also perfectly man. He grew tired. He sat down to rest at a well in Samaria in the heat of the day. He slept, He ate, He drank, He laughed, He wept, and beyond all that, He suffered and died. All of these are human characteristics. The gold and the wood in the ark were both required, yet neither was mingled with the other. Nor was the identity of one lost in the other. Christ was both God and man, but the two natures were never fused or merged. He never functioned at the same time as both God and man. What He did was either perfectly human or perfectly divine.

The ark was not an empty box. It contained three items which are enumerated in Hebrews 9:4; "Which had the golden censer, and the ark of the covenant overlaid round about with gold, wherein was the golden pot that had manna, and Aaron's rod that budded, and the tables of the covenant." The contents of the ark were also symbolic. Aaron's rod that budded speaks of the Lord's resurrection. The manna speaks of the fact that Christ is the Bread of Life. The Ten Commandments speak of the life He lived on earth fulfilling the Law in all points and fulfilling the prophecies spoken of Him.

The tables of the covenant speak of the Kingship of Christ. He was born a King. He lived a King. He died a King, and He rose from the dead a King. He is coming again to earth as King. God's program is moving today and has been moving from eternity past to the time when Christ shall rule over this earth. Earth needs a ruler. Man needs a King. Someday He is coming as King of Kings and Lord of Lords.

The pot of manna speaks of Christ as a prophet. He spoke for God as John 6:32 clearly shows, ". . . Verily, verily, I say unto you, Moses gave you not that bread from heaven; but my Father giveth you the true bread from heaven." Jesus Christ was also God's message to man. He was the *Logos*, the Word of God, the very alphabet of God, the Alpha and Omega. He is God's final message to man. Since Christ came to earth as God-man, heaven has been silent because God has no addenda to place after Christ. He has no post-script to the letter because Christ is the embodiment of that letter. God told out His heart in Christ.

Aaron's rod that budded speaks of the work of Christ as priest. The prophet spoke for God before man; the priest spoke for man before God. As priest Christ offered Himself. As a priest He passed into heaven. Even now He sits at God's right hand in heaven. Jesus Christ the God-man was raised from the dead and He is the unique example of resurrection up to the present hour. Easter lilies and eggs do not speak of the resurrection, but Aaron's rod that budded does. It was an old dead stick that came alive. The ark speaks of Christ as prophet, priest, and king. "And the Word was made flesh, and dwelt among us, (and we beheld his glory, the glory as of the only begotten of the Father,) full of grace and truth" (John 1:14).

The mercy seat rested on top of the ark. It served as the top for the chest, the ark, but it was a separate piece of furniture. It was made of pure gold with cherubim on each end with their wings spread, overshadowing it, and looking down upon the top where the blood was placed. It was here the high priest sprinkled the blood of the sacrifice. It was the blood that made it the *mercy* seat. This too was symbolic of the work of Christ. Christ literally presented His blood in heaven after His death on the cross. A critic recommended my book, *The Tabernacle, God's Portrait of Christ*, but warned people that I took everything literally and must be watched carefully because I held the position that Christ offered His blood in heaven. The critic felt this was crude. I do not believe this is crude because the blood of Christ is not crude; it is precious. Peter calls his Savior's blood "precious" in 1 Peter 1:18–19, "Forasmuch as ye know that ye were not redeemed with corruptible things, as silver and gold, from your vain conversation received by tradition from your fathers; But with the precious blood of Christ, as of a lamb without blemish and without spot." Christ's blood is more precious than silver or gold. The most valuable thing in heaven is the blood He shed for man on earth. He presented His blood as He entered heaven and that is what makes God's throne a mercy seat for us today. We are bidden to come to God today on the basis of the fact that Jesus Christ, our great High Priest, has offered His own blood for our sins. Hebrews 4:14–16 reminds us that, "Seeing then that we have a great high priest, that is passed into the heavens, Jesus the Son of God, let us hold fast our profession. For we have not an high priest which cannot be touched with the feeling of our infirmities; but was in all points tempted like as we are, yet without sin. Let us therefore come boldly unto the throne of grace, that we may obtain mercy, and find grace to help in time of need."

You and I approach God through our great High Priest in heaven. He is the living Christ at God's right hand. Through Him we find mercy and help. Many believers are trying to fight the battle down here alone. They are trying to meet the issues of life alone. Friends, you and I are not able to do it. We are not strong enough. We need help. And we are not availing ourselves of the help Christ offers. Paul prayed for the Ephesians that the mighty power that worked in Christ, bringing Him from the dead, might work in them (Eph. 1:19–20). We see very little of that power working in believers today. We need to lay hold of it by faith because we have a High Priest who is at God's right hand.

The high priest who served in this tabernacle rushed into the Holy Place, sprinkled the blood on the mercy seat, and rushed out again. Christ, our High Priest, when He made His offering, sat down at God's right hand and is still there for us today. He died down here to save us. He lives in heaven to keep us saved. And we should keep in contact with Him. Have you had a talk with Him today?

We have looked now at the articles of furniture in the Holy of Holies: the ark and the mercy seat. Now we will consider the furniture in the second compartment, the Holy Place.

THE TABLE OF SHOWBREAD

There are three articles of furniture in the Holy Place: (1) the golden lampstand, (2) the table of showbread, and (3) the altar of incense. Inside the Holy Place is the place of worship. The golden lampstand is one of the most perfect figures of Christ that we have. The table of showbread speaks of Him as being the Bread of Life. The altar of incense speaks of prayer—that the Lord is our great intercessor today, and we pray to the Father through Him.

The table of showbread has twelve loaves of bread on it. There are many explanations of how these loaves were arranged but the important thing to remember is that each loaf represents a tribe of Israel. In other words, God was providing equality for all.

Thou shalt also make a table of shittim wood: two cubits shall be the length

thereof, and a cubit the breadth thereof, and a cubit and a half the height thereof [Exod. 25:23].

You will notice that the table of showbread is two cubits long, and a cubit wide—twice as long as it is wide. It is a cubit and one half high. The table of showbread is the same height as the ark of the covenant.

And thou shalt overlay it with pure gold, and make thereto a crown of gold round about [Exod. 25:24].

The "crown of gold" is a border around the table to keep the bread from falling off.

And thou shalt make unto it a border of an hand breadth round about, and thou shalt make a golden crown to the border thereof round about.

And thou shalt make for it four rings of gold, and put the rings in the four corners that are on the four feet thereof [Exod. 25:25–26].

Once again we are told that staves were to be put through these rings in order that the table might be carried through the wilderness as the children of Israel journeyed. It was carried on the shoulders of the priests.

And thou shalt make the dishes thereof, and spoons thereof, and covers thereof, and bowls thereof, to cover withal: of pure gold shalt thou make them.

And thou shalt set upon the table shewbread before me alway [Exod. 25:29–30].

The bread is a type of Christ. Therefore the table is a type of Christ. It pictures Him. The table of showbread suggests many things: it speaks of sustenance, provision, and supply. It is the table of salvation. Our Lord gave a parable in Matthew 22:1–14 which tells about the marriage of the king's son. The invited guests refused to come, and this provoked the king to deal with the rejectors. Having done so, the king extended the invitation to include those in the highways and byways. They were bidden to come and eat. Thus the invitation has gone out today to the world to come and partake of the salvation as it is in the Lord Jesus Christ.

It is also a table of provision. God, as Creator, provides all food for man and beast. Whether you like it or not, friend, you eat every day at God's table in the physical realm. Yet how few recognize this truth and give thanks to Him for His bounty. God is the one who provides for us.

This table also speaks of the Lord's Supper, as instituted by the Lord Himself just prior to His death upon the cross. It is a table for believers. The table of showbread is a prefiguration of Christ as the sustainer of spiritual life for the believer.

The table was two cubits long, one cubit wide, and one and one half cubits high. It was made of shittim wood and overlaid with gold. The almost incorruptible shittim (acacia) wood speaks of His humanity. This wood was a product of the earth but was not subject to the action of it in a chemical way. In the same way our Lord had a body made of earth elements and conceived in the womb of a virgin. The gold speaks of His deity but the gold is not produced by the earth; it is separate from it and has an inherent value. Christ was not of the earth in His deity. He was God. He came from glory.

On the table were placed twelve loaves of bread. The table and the bread are spoken of as one. We do the same thing today when we say, "The Lord's table." We do not eat the table, but we associate the table with the food. This metonymy is common in Scripture.

The bread was changed each Sabbath. The bread which was removed was eaten with wine by the priestly family in the Holy Place. This table doesn't prefigure Christ in the same way that manna does. Although both speak of Christ, it is not in the same connection. The manna speaks of Christ as the *life-giver*. He interpreted this Himself in John 6:32 when He said, ". . . Verily, verily, I say unto you, Moses gave you not that bread from heaven; but my Father giveth you the true bread from heaven." A short time later, in John 6:35, Jesus said, ". . . I am the bread of life: he that cometh to me shall never hunger; and he that believeth on me shall never thirst."

Now the showbread also speaks of Christ as the *life-sustainer*. Eternal life is a gift and is the manna which came down from heaven. The person who receives manna receives eternal life. However, eternal life requires a special food to sustain it and help it grow and find strength. The showbread pictures Christ as that special food for those who have partaken of the manna of life.

The Lord Jesus Christ is seen in another illustration that He also used. The showbread was made of grain which was ground and unleavened, made into bread and baked. Leviticus 24:5 says, "And thou shalt take fine flour, and bake twelve cakes thereof: two tenth deals shall be in one cake." Then we find that the Lord Jesus said, "Verily, verily, I say unto you, Except a corn of wheat fall into the ground and die, it abideth alone: but if it die, it bringeth forth much fruit" (John 12:24). The Lord Jesus Christ was ground in the mill of suffering. In His anguish Christ said in John 12:27, "Now is my soul troubled; and what shall I say? Father, save me from this hour: but for this cause came I unto this hour." John 12:31–32 tells us that He was brought into the fire of suffering and judgment. "Now is the judgment of this world: now shall the prince of this world be cast out. And I, if I be lifted up from the earth, will draw all men unto me." Jesus Christ came forth from the tomb in newness of life because His soul did not see corruption. Now He lives a resurrection life. He is the showbread now for believers to feed upon to sustain eternal life and promote growth. The Christian is to feed upon the living Christ. He is to appropriate Christ as He is today, living at God's right hand. Jesus Christ said, ". . . I am the bread of life . . ." (John 6:35).

There is an ancient proverb which contains the thought that a thing grows by what it feeds upon. And a book on the subject of dieting is entitled, *You Are What You Eat*. The difficulty today is that we have too many Christians who are not feeding upon Christ. You have to feed on Him in order to grow. In 2 Corinthians 5:16 Paul tells us, "Wherefore henceforth know we no man after the flesh: yea, though we have known Christ after the flesh, yet now henceforth know we him no more." We no longer know Christ after the flesh. We must feed upon Him as He is today. He is the living Christ and we are to grow by looking to Him.

THE GOLDEN LAMPSTAND

The next article of furniture is the lampstand, in most translations called the candlestick, but it was really a lampstand.

And thou shalt make a candlestick of pure gold: of beaten work shall the candlestick be made: his shaft, and his branches, his bowls, his knops, and his flowers, shall be of the same.

And six branches shall come out of the sides of it; three branches of the candlestick out of the one side, and three branches of the candlestick out of the other side:

Three bowls made like unto almonds, with a knop and a flower in one branch; and three bowls made like almonds in the other branch, with a knop and a flower: so in the six branches that come out of the candlestick [Exod. 25:31–33].

As the description continues from verses 34–39, the reading becomes rather tedious. Verse 40 says:

And look that thou make them after their pattern, which was shewed thee in the mount [Exod. 25:40].

The lampstand is probably the most perfect picture of Christ found in the tabernacle furniture. It sets Him forth as pure gold and speaks of His deity. It sets Him forth as He is—*God*. Worship has to do with walking in the light. This is a very important fact to see.

We have studied the table of showbread and have seen that it spoke of the fact that when we worship God we must feed on the Lord Jesus Christ. If you go to church and you are only entertained, or given a book review, or listen to some social issue being debated, or hear how you can improve your city, you are not having a worship service. You are just having a meeting. You only worship God when you feed upon Him who is the table of showbread.

Now in order to worship God, you must also walk in the light. Christ is the light, as symbolized by the lampstand in the Holy Place. If you wanted natural light, you had to go outside the tabernacle. If you wanted to walk in the light of the lampstand, you had to go inside the tabernacle. John 1:9 tells us that Jesus Christ is the ". . . true Light, which lighteth every man that cometh into the world." You will find that there are people who counsel others by "words." We are told that through philosophy and vain deceit we can be deceived. Listen to the words of Paul in Colossians 2:8, "Beware lest any man spoil you through philosophy and vain deceit, after the tradition of men, after the rudiments of the world, and not after Christ." Christ is not just another philosopher who "darkened counsel by words without knowledge." He is the Son of God, and in Him there is no darkness at all.

The lampstand was actually made of one piece of gold. It was beaten work, highly ornamented. It had a central shaft, but extending from that shaft were three branches on each side, making a total of seven branches in all. Each branch was like the limb of an almond tree with fruit and blossom. At the top was an open almond blossom, and it was here that the lamps filled with oil were placed.

The almond blossoms looked like wood but they were gold. They remind us of Aaron's rod that budded. When Aaron's priestly prerogative was in question, the budding of his almond rod established his right to the priesthood. The almond rod, a dead branch, was made to live and bear fruit. Christ was established as the Son of God by His resurrection from the dead. The resurrection did not make Christ the Son of God because He was already that from the eternal counsels of God; the resurrection only confirmed it. Aaron was the God-appointed high priest and this position was confirmed by the resurrection of the dead almond rod. The resurrection of Christ likewise established His priesthood. Christ is our great High Priest. He became a man and partook of our nature, "tempted in all points as we are, yet without sin." But the primary basis of His priesthood is His deity. The priest represented man before God. And Christ, as God who became man, is now the God-man who represents man. There is Someone in heaven who knows and understands me! He is able to help me. The resurrection which declared Him to be the Son of God likewise declared His right to the priesthood.

It is interesting to note that no measurements are given for the lampstand. Why? Because you can't put a yardstick down on Deity, friend. You cannot measure Him as the Son of God. You can't understand Him. He is beyond the computation of man. Yet He also was perfectly human. His deity and humanity are never fused. Along with the fact that Jesus wept was the fact that He commanded Lazarus to come forth.

The lampstand gave light in the Holy Place. It was the place of worship. Notice that the lampstand held up the lighted lamps. In turn, the lamps revealed the beauty of the lampstand. The oil in the lamps represents the Holy Spirit. Christ said of the Holy Spirit in John 14:26, "But the Comforter, which is the Holy Ghost, whom the Father will send in my name, he shall teach you all things, and bring all things to your remembrance, whatsoever I have said unto you." When you and I study the Word together, we meet around the person of Christ, and it is the Holy Spirit who takes the things of Christ and shows them unto us—just as those lamps reveal the beauty of the lampstand. The Holy Spirit reveals Christ as the Son of God, the One who came to earth on our behalf and who lives in heaven to intercede for us.

CHAPTER 26

THEME: *The curtains of the tabernacle; the boards and sockets of the tabernacle; the veils*

THE CURTAINS OF THE TABERNACLE

Over the tabernacle proper were four coverings. The first covering was linen and it covered that part of the tabernacle that was 30 cubits long, 10 cubits wide and 10 cubits high. This linen covering came down the sides of the tabernacle but was not permitted to touch the ground.

Moreover thou shalt make the tabernacle with ten curtains of fine twined linen, and blue, and purple, and scarlet: with cherubims of cunning work shalt thou make them [Exod. 26:1].

The linen covering was beautiful and the result of fine work.

And thou shalt make curtains of goats' hair to be a covering upon the tabernacle: eleven curtains shalt thou make [Exod. 26:7].

These curtains had to be sewn together.

The length of one curtain shall be thirty cubits, and the breadth of one curtain four cubits: and the eleven curtains shall be all of one measure [Exod. 26:8].

The length of one curtain was to be 30 cubits which means it would exactly cover the top and sides of the tabernacle. They were held together with loops and rings.

And thou shalt make a covering for the tent of rams' skins dyed red, and a covering above of badgers' skins [Exod. 26:14].

The third covering was made of rams' skins dyed red and the fourth covering was badgers' skins, or more correctly, sealskins. The women used to wear sealskin coats and this tabernacle was probably the first one that ever wore a sealskin coat!

Now each of these coverings had symbolic meaning. The first covering was fine-twined,

Egyptian linen with cherubim woven in the material. It did not touch the ground, and its beauty could only be seen on the inside of the tabernacle. This covering could not be seen from the outside at all and, frankly, the beauty of the Lord Jesus Christ can not be seen by the world. He can only satisfy His own people. It is important for believers to worship Him because we not only need to feed on Him, but we need to behold Him in His beauty. In Psalm 17:8, David said, "Keep me as the apple of the eye; hide me under the shadow of thy wings." The wings of the cherubim were woven in the linen cloth *over* the tabernacle. But *under* His wings is a good place for us to be hidden, and we should worship Him who is worthy of our worship.

The second curtain was made of goats' hair and it touched the ground. This curtain speaks of Christ's worth for sinners. It is symbolic of the death of Christ, and this is the message that is to be given to the world. We read in Hebrews 9:26, "For then must he often have suffered since the foundation of the world: but now once in the end of the world hath he appeared to put away sin by the sacrifice of himself." The word *world* in this verse is better translated "age." He has appeared, and this is the message that should go forth. This is the story which the goats' hair curtain tells.

The third covering was made of rams' skin dyed red. This curtain speaks of the strength and vigor of Christ and His offering on the cross. This curtain shows the outward aspect of His offering as our substitute.

The fourth curtain was made of badgers' skins (sealskins). After forty years in the wilderness this curtain was marred by time and weather, but it always protected that which was within. This covering speaks of Christ's walk before men. Just as the linen covering was inside to show His beauty to the believer, so the sealskin covering had no beauty to reveal. Isaiah 53:2 tells us this about Christ: ". . . he hath no form nor comeliness; and when we shall see him, there is no beauty that we should desire him." There is no beauty on the outside that we should desire Him; we have to go inside to behold His beauty. The world does not see in Him what we see in Him.

THE BOARDS AND SOCKETS OF THE TABERNACLE

And thou shalt make boards for the tabernacle of shittim wood standing up.

Ten cubits shall be the length of a board, and a cubit and a half shall be the breadth of one board.

Two tenons shall there be in one board, set in order one against another: thus shalt thou make for all the boards of the tabernacle.

And thou shalt make the boards for the tabernacle, twenty boards on the south side southward.

And thou shalt make forty sockets of silver under the twenty boards; two sockets under one board for his two tenons, and two sockets under another board for his two tenons [Exod. 26:15–19].

These boards were made of shittim wood which was a very durable wood like redwood. It was practically indestructible. These boards were covered with gold. There were twenty boards on each side and ten in the rear of the tabernacle. There was a certain amount of overlapping, of course, but this actually constituted the tabernacle proper. Rings were placed in the boards and bars ran through the rings, thus holding the tabernacle together.

Everything in the tabernacle speaks of either the person or work of Christ. Every covering, every thread, and every article of furniture reveals some facet of the Savior. As the bars held the tabernacle together, so the Holy Spirit of God holds true believers together today. Believers should be held together by the Spirit. In fact, believers are told "to keep the unity of the Spirit in the bond of peace."

The curtains covering the tabernacle each bore a different color and each had its own significance. There was blue, a heavenly color. There was scarlet, which speaks of Christ's blood. There was a blending of the blue and scarlet which produced a purple color that speaks of royalty. The blue and scarlet speak of heaven touching earth, or the humanity of Christ. The purple speaks of Him as King of the Jews. The boards, bars, and rings were overlaid with gold which speaks of the deity of the Lord Jesus Christ.

THE VEILS

And thou shalt make a veil of blue, and purple, and scarlet, and fine twined linen of cunning work: with cherubims shall it be made:

And thou shalt hang it upon four pillars of shittim wood overlaid with gold: their hooks shall be of gold, upon the four sockets of silver [Exod. 26:31–32].

The veil was hung upon four pillars and speaks of the humanity of Jesus Christ. The pillars were made of shittim wood covered with gold, with silver sockets attached. These speak of deity taking hold of earth through redemption. There was no capital on top of these pillars, which made them different from the other pillars in the tabernacle; they were just cut off. Isaiah 53:8 tells us, "He was taken from prison and from judgment: and who shall declare his generation? for he was cut off out of the land of the living: for the transgression of my people was he stricken." Jesus Christ was cut off out of the land of the living—He lived to be only thirty-three years old.

Now the veil was made of fine-twined linen and was the only entrance to the Holy of Holies. The veil speaks of the humanity of Christ. When Christ was on the cross, He dismissed His spirit. At the moment of His death the veil was torn in two, representing the fracture of His spirit and His body. When the veil in the temple was rent in two, the way into God's presence was open. The only way to get to God today is through the Lord Jesus Christ. There is only one entrance to the Holy of Holies and only one way to God. In John 14:6 Jesus Himself said, ". . . I am the way, the truth, and the life: no man cometh unto the Father, but by me."

Some people believe that you can come to God if you are sincere and belong to some church. Do not believe it. You will not find this type of thinking in the Word of God.

What a wonderful picture the veil is. It shows us the humanity of Christ. Friends, it is the death of Jesus Christ that saves us. His spotless life condemns us. When I stand before the veil, I am condemned. I see myself as not able to pass into the presence of God. We read in Matthew 27:50–51 that, "Jesus, when he had cried again with a loud voice, yielded up the ghost. And, behold, the veil of the temple was rent in twain from the top to the bottom; and the earth did quake, and the rocks rent." The death of Jesus Christ provides access to God, and the rent veil pictures it.

Then there is another hanging:

And thou shalt make an hanging for the door of the tent, of blue, and purple, and scarlet, and fine twined linen, wrought with needlework.

And thou shalt make for the hanging five pillars of shittim wood, and overlay them with gold, and their hooks shall be of gold: and thou shalt cast five sockets of brass for them [Exod. 26:36–37].

This veil, or hanging, led to the Holy Place, the place of worship where the golden lampstand, table of showbread, and altar of incense were located. Now, friend, we cannot worship God any old way. We have to come through the Lord Jesus Christ. We have to come in spirit and in truth. Jesus said, ". . . I am the way, the truth, and the life: no man cometh unto the Father, but by me" (John 14:6).

Both veils prefigure our Lord Jesus Christ.

CHAPTER 27

THEME: *The brazen altar; the court of the tabernacle; oil for the lamp*

Notice now as we move outside the tabernacle proper to the court that the articles of furniture are made of brass: the brazen altar and the brazen laver. Inside, you recall, the articles of furniture were of gold. As you get closer to God, the emphasis is on the person of Christ. As you move farther out, the emphasis is on the work of Christ.

THE BRAZEN ALTAR

And thou shalt make an altar of shittim wood, five cubits long, and five cubits broad; the altar shall be foursquare: and the height thereof shall be three cubits.

And thou shalt make the horns of it upon the four corners thereof: his horns shall be of the same: and thou shalt overlay it with brass.

And thou shalt make his pans to receive his ashes, and his shovels, and his basins, and his fleshhooks, and his firepans: all the vessels thereof thou shalt make of brass [Exod. 27:1–3].

The furniture in the outer court is made of brass which represents judgment of sin. The sin question must be settled in the court before entrance can be made into the Holy Place. The furniture in the Holy Place was all of gold and pictures communion with God and worship of God. There is no sin in the Holy Place. The sin question is dealt with in the outer court.

Man is standing on the outside. How is he going to approach God? The first thing he must have is a substitute to die for him. Man might avoid meeting God, but if he wants to meet God and not die, he must have a substitute. Someone will have to die on that brazen altar for him. Sometimes this altar is called the table of the Lord, and it is called the altar of burnt offering. This is where God deals with the sinner. It speaks of the cross of Christ, and of the fact that He is actually the One who died in man's stead. It is as Paul said in Ephesians 5:2, "And walk in love, as Christ also hath loved us, and hath given himself for us an offering and a sacrifice to God for a sweet-smelling savour." Christ is our burnt offering. The altar was made by man but the pattern is in heaven. The cross was God's chosen altar of sacrifice. The Lord Jesus Christ was delivered by the determinate counsel and foreknowledge of God to die on the cross. Christ, therefore, is more than just a good man. He is that and also He is the Lamb slain from the foundation of the world. There is no approach to God except by the brazen altar. There a victim must be sacrificed and must be claimed as the substitute. John 1:29 tells us, "The next day John seeth Jesus coming unto him, and saith, Behold the Lamb of God, which taketh away the sin of the world." The apostle John spoke of Christ as that substitute upon the brazen altar. That is what the cross became in those last three hours when darkness descended and Christ paid for the sins of the world.

We are told in John 1:12 that ". . . as many as received him, to them gave he power to become the sons of God, even to them that believe on his name." Man could not worship, pray, or serve God until he came to the brazen altar. Every priest, every Levite, had to come to this altar. Friends, "the way of the cross leads home." If Jesus Christ had not gone by the brazen altar, we would have no access to God.

Jesus Christ is not only the Lamb that died for us, He is also the *risen* Lamb. The Apostle John tells us in Revelation 5:6 that he saw a ". . . Lamb as it had been slain . . ." The brazen altar stood at the entrance of the tabernacle. The cross of Christ stands before heaven—it was raised on this earth but there is no entrance to heaven except by this cross.

The brass which covered the altar speaks of judgment. The shittim wood covered with brass speaks of His strength for sacrifice. What a picture this is of the cross of Christ!

THE COURT OF THE TABERNACLE

And thou shalt make the court of the tabernacle: for the south side southward there shall be hangings for the court of fine twined linen of an hundred cubits long for one side:

And for the gate of the court shall be an hanging of twenty cubits, of blue, and purple, and scarlet, and fine twined linen, wrought with needlework: and their pillars shall be four, and their sockets four [Exod. 27:9, 16].

Once again the colors of the hangings tell a story. Blue was a heavenly color and spoke of the fact that Christ came from heaven. Scarlet spoke of Christ's humanity and the blood that He shed for mankind. The purple was a blending of the blue and scarlet, the color of royalty, speaking of Christ's kingship. This was the hanging for the gate of the court through which the priests and Levites entered. This entrance was only five cubits high and the fence that went around the outside of the tabernacle was one hundred cubits by fifty cubits, and was covered with white linen all the way around. It separated those on the inside from those on the outside.

OIL FOR THE LAMP

The conclusion of this chapter is quite interesting. It deals with the oil for the lamp, and it is unusual that this subject should be brought up at this particular place.

And thou shalt command the children of Israel, that they bring thee pure oil olive beaten for the light, to cause the lamp to burn always [Exod. 27:20].

Oil, as has already been pointed out, speaks of the Holy Spirit of God—Zechariah's interpretation of the lampstand: ". . . Not by might, nor by power, but by my *spirit* saith the LORD of hosts" (Zech. 4:6). The *light* is that which the Holy Spirit gives. The Holy Spirit will not speak of Himself, but He takes the things of Christ and shows them unto us.

In the tabernacle of the congregation without the veil, which is before the

testimony, Aaron and his sons shall order it from evening to morning before the LORD: it shall be a statute for ever unto their generations on the behalf of the children of Israel [Exod. 27:21].

The burning light speaks of Christ. Now all that has changed—the Lord Jesus Christ has gone back to heaven. Matthew 5:14 tells us: "Ye are the light of the world. . . ." You and I do not make much light. It is only the Spirit of God that can use us. The first picture we have of Christ in the Book of Revelation shows Him walking in the midst of the lampstands. He is trying to keep the church's light of witness alive and burning on earth. Christ is dealing with those who are His own.

A word or two should be said about two articles of furniture not yet mentioned. One piece of furniture is the altar of incense which is mentioned over in Exodus chapter 30. If you were going to worship God, you had to come by this altar.

The other article of furniture not yet mentioned is the brazen laver. The laver made one clean to worship God. At the brazen altar you received Jesus Christ as Savior, and at the brazen laver you are washed and cleansed by the Holy Spirit of God. Then you are permitted to go and worship God.

CHAPTER 28

THEME: Aaron and his sons set apart for the priesthood; the ephod; the breastplate; the Urim and Thummim; the robe of the ephod

AARON AND HIS SONS SET APART FOR THE PRIESTHOOD

We have seen that every thread, color, and chord in the tabernacle suggest the person and work of Christ. Now we come to the ones who are going to serve in the tabernacle. The Levites were to care for the tabernacle, and Aaron and his sons were to be the priests. Aaron was to be the high priest.

And take thou unto thee Aaron thy brother, and his sons with him, from among the children of Israel, that he may minister unto me in the priest's office, even Aaron, Nadab and Abihu, Eleazar and Ithamar, Aaron's sons.

And thou shalt make holy garments for Aaron thy brother for glory and for beauty [Exod. 28:1–2].

In order for Aaron to serve as high priest he had to have certain garments. And these garments speak of Christ. It is true that most of the instructions given in Exodus do not make very thrilling reading, nor do they read like a detective or a mystery story, but they do reveal Christ. Do you wonder why God gave us all of these instructions? Little children learn by pictures. The Bible is a picture book and God wants us to learn the truths He has for us by looking at the "pictures" He has given us.

These garments were not holy in the sense that you and I think of holy today. The Hebrew word for *holy* means "set apart." These garments were set apart for the service of God. Anything that is set apart for God is holy.

Suppose you have ten dollars in your pocketbook and you want to give one dollar to the Lord's work. You may have received that ten dollars from a store, and the store may have received it from a gambler, who in turn may have received it from a prostitute, who may have gotten it from a thief and so on. But the minute you set that money aside for God, it is holy. Anything set aside for God is holy.

These are holy garments and are to be used in the service of God. I do not wear a robe like the Levites used to wear but when I was a pastor I had a mohair suit which I wore exclusively in the pulpit. I had a great deal of fun kidding my intimate friends about my "holy suit." When I preach, I have on my holy clothes and, in one sense, I am accurate because anything set aside for the service of God is holy.

Notice that these garments are for the glory of God and they are beautiful. I love that. Things do not have to be ugly, friends, just because they are used in the service of God. I personally resent that the world, the flesh, and the devil seem to get everything that is beautiful. Why can't we give God some of the beauty? He is the one who made beauty. If you do not think He splashes color around, watch a sunset, or look at the leaves in the fall. Look at the heavens during a clear sunny day and then watch them during a storm. God majors in colors and beauty, and these garments for the priests were to be beautiful and for the glory of God.

And thou shalt speak unto all that are wise-hearted, whom I have filled with the spirit of wisdom, that they may make Aaron's garments to consecrate him, that he may minister unto me in the priest's office [Exod. 28:3].

Aaron is to be set aside for the ministry of the great high priest. These are to be his garments:

And these are the garments which they shall make; a breastplate, and an ephod, and a robe, and a broidered coat, a mitre, and a girdle: and they shall make holy garments for Aaron thy brother, and his sons, that he may minister unto me in the priest's office [Exod. 28:4].

Here are six garments that are to be used in the service of God. They are to be worn by Aaron and then, of course, passed on to those who shall succeed him in the office.

And they shall take gold, and blue, and purple, and scarlet, and fine linen [Exod. 28:5].

These garments are to be made out of the very best material. I feel like God ought to have the very best, but I must confess that we must be very careful about this subject. Never in my ministry have I driven an automobile that is considered expensive, like a Cadillac or a Lincoln. One time a man offered to buy me an expensive car and I refused. I happen to drive a Chevrolet but, quite frankly, I feel I have as much right to drive a Cadillac. Now this is where I must be careful. Right now I know a certain minister who is coming under great criticism because several people went out to his headquarters one day and found nothing but Cadillacs parked around the place. The type of ministry in which he is engaged begs and urges people to give money to his work and there are those who feel the money received is not being spent wisely.

May I say that money sent into a ministry should not be spent needlessly. We ought to be very careful what we do with contributions. I have attempted to follow a pattern of being very careful with money because I ask people to give to my radio ministry. For this reason I

drive a Chevrolet. So if anyone is thinking about giving me a Cadillac, forget it. Seriously, we need to be careful. On the other hand, we should recognize that God's work should have the very best, and that does not necessarily mean a Cadillac.

When we moved into our new headquarters, we needed to settle the question of what kind of equipment we should have. Should the machine used to make the radio tapes be a cheap model? No! The tapes are very important and so we got the best machine we could find. We feel that good equipment for God's work is essential; God's work ought to have it. I trust that you understand what I am saying because I believe that God is being cheated and robbed. Malachi asked this question, "Will a man rob God? Yet ye have robbed me. But ye say, Wherein have we robbed thee? In tithes and offerings" (Mal. 3:8). God knows that a man will rob Him. Man was that way in Moses' day and man is still the same today.

THE EPHOD

And they shall make the ephod of gold, of blue, and of purple, of scarlet, and fine twined linen, with cunning work.

It shall have the two shoulderpieces thereof joined at the two edges thereof; and so it shall be joined together.

And the curious girdle of the ephod, which is upon it, shall be of the same, according to the work thereof; even of gold, of blue, and purple, and scarlet, and fine twined linen.

And thou shalt take two onyx stones, and grave on them the names of the children of Israel [Exod. 28:6–9].

The ephod is difficult to describe. It was worn over the linen garment. Two long pieces of cloth were brought together and fastened by a stone on one shoulder and a stone on the other shoulder. The material was gathered in the middle with a girdle. Six of the names of the children of Israel were engraved on one onyx stone and six names were engraved on the other. When the high priest went into the presence of God, he carried the children of Israel on his shoulders. That speaks of the strength and power of the high priest. Hebrews 7:25 tells us about Jesus Christ our High Priest: "Wherefore he is able also to save them to the uttermost that come unto God by him, seeing he ever liveth to make intercession for them." Christ is able to save us, you see. He has strength and power.

Do you remember the parable He gave about the little lost sheep? The shepherd went out and found him and put him on his shoulders (Luke 15:1–7). Jesus Christ carries me on His shoulders and that is where He carries you, friend. From time to time I get off His shoulders but He is right there to lift me back to that place of safety and continue to carry me. What a lovely picture the ephod gives us of Christ.

THE BREASTPLATE

And thou shalt make the breastplate of judgment with cunning work; after the work of the ephod thou shalt make it; of gold, of blue, and of purple, and of scarlet, and of fine twined linen, shalt thou make it.

Foursquare it shall be being doubled; a span shall be the length thereof, and a span shall be the breadth thereof [Exod. 28:15–16].

The best way to describe the breastplate is to call it a vest—but a very beautiful one—that went over the garment. It was a breastplate of judgment. Why? Well, friends, it pictures the fact that sin has been judged. We need the breastplate of righteousness today as believers. You see, the breastplate covers the vile heart within us. That is the only way we could stand in the presence of God. It means that our sins are judged. The righteousness of Christ has been made over to us. So this is called the breastplate of judgment.

The breastplate was, in a way, part of the ephod. The ephod and the breastplate went together and was a thing of beauty.

And thou shalt set in it settings of stones, even four rows of stones: the first row shall be a sardius, a topaz, and a carbuncle: this shall be the first row.

And the second row shall be an emerald, a sapphire, and a diamond.

And the third row a ligure, an agate, and an amethyst.

And the fourth row a beryl, and an onyx, and a jasper: they shall be set in gold in their inclosings [Exod. 28:17–20].

On the breastplate of the great high priest were these twelve precious stones which were arranged three in a row, and there were four rows.

And the stones shall be with the names of the children of Israel, twelve, according to their names, like the engravings of a signet; every one with his name shall they be according to the twelve tribes [Exod. 28:21].

These stones are also found in the Book of Revelation where we are told that they form the foundation of the New Jerusalem. Each stone was a different color and together they formed a flashing and beautiful display. I am of the opinion that God's universe is filled with color, and when sin is finally removed we will see it flash with color.

These twelve stones are quite interesting. When the high priest went into God's presence wearing the breastplate, he pictured the Lord Jesus Christ who is at the right hand of God interceding for us. The Lord not only carries us on His shoulders, the place of power and ability, but He carries us on His breast. We are engraven on His heart. He loves us! What a picture this is of His love for us.

THE URIM AND THUMMIM

And thou shalt put in the breastplate of judgment the Urim and the Thummim; and they shall be upon Aaron's heart, when he goeth in before the LORD: and Aaron shall bear the judgment of the children of Israel upon his heart before the LORD continually [Exod. 28:30].

I am going to tell you a secret and I do not want you to tell anyone. I do not know what the Urim and the Thummim were. I have read books by about twenty-five different authors and have discovered that they do not know either. The interesting thing is that they had something to do with determining the will of God. Just how, I do not know. Some people think the Urim and Thummim were dice, but I do not believe it. Whatever they were, they determined the will of God. God has kept the details obscure for a very good reason—some nut would try to produce a Urim and Thummim today and would claim that it would give us all the answers. We have a lot of people around today trying to give us the answers without the Urim and Thummim! God wants us to go to Him for the answers.

THE ROBE OF THE EPHOD

And beneath upon the hem of it thou shalt make pomegranates of blue, and of purple, and of scarlet, round about the hem thereof; and bells of gold between them round about:

A golden bell and a pomegranate, a golden bell and a pomegranate, upon

the hem of the robe round about [Exod. 28:33–34].

The first sermon I preached in California was on the golden bells and pomegranates. I told the congregation I did not know exactly what a pomegranate was. Well, I found that they are grown in Southern California. By nine o'clock that evening I had at least twenty bushels of pomegranates on my back porch! I know what they are now.

The pomegranates speak of fruit, and the bells speak of witness. We should have both of these in our lives. We ought to be a witness for Christ, and there ought to be the fruit of the Holy Spirit (Gal. 5:22–23) in our lives. You should not be handing out tracts, friends, unless you are making the right kind of "tracks" in this world. Too many people want to witness but do not have a life to back it up. There are also some folk who have a life to back up a witness, but who do not witness. We ought to have a bell and a pomegranate, a bell and a pomegranate.

And it shall be upon Aaron to minister: and his sound shall be heard when he goeth in unto the holy place before the LORD, and when he cometh out, that he die not [Exod. 28:35].

These symbols of life and witness would give a sound as the high priest went in and out of the sanctuary. "That he die not" alerts them to the fact that if he should default in the ritual he would be stricken dead.

And thou shalt make a plate of pure gold, and grave upon it, like the engravings of a signet, HOLINESS TO THE LORD.

And thou shalt put it on a blue lace, that it may be upon the mitre; upon the forefront of the mitre it shall be.

And it shall be upon Aaron's forehead, that Aaron may bear the iniquity of the holy things, which the children of Israel shall hallow in all their holy gifts; and it shall be always upon his forehead, that they may be accepted before the LORD [Exod. 28:36–38].

These garments distinguished the high priest from the other priests, and they set forth the glories and beauties of our High Priest who is "holy, harmless, undefiled, separate from sinners." He died down here to save us. He lives at God's right hand to keep us saved.

And thou shalt embroider the coat of fine linen, and thou shalt make the mitre of fine linen, and thou shalt make the girdle of needlework.

And for Aaron's sons thou shalt make coats, and thou shalt make for them girdles, and bonnets shalt thou make for them, for glory and for beauty.

And thou shalt put them upon Aaron thy brother, and his sons with him; and shalt anoint them, and consecrate them, and sanctify them, that they may minister unto me in the priest's office.

And thou shalt make them linen breeches to cover their nakedness; from the loins even unto the thighs they shall reach:

And they shall be upon Aaron, and upon his sons, when they come in unto the tabernacle of the congregation, or when they come near unto the altar to minister in the holy place; that they bear not iniquity, and die: it shall be a statute for ever unto him and his seed after him [Exod. 28:39–43].

God wanted no nudity in the service for Him (and we should keep this in mind for today). God wanted no display of the flesh. These garments were a covering over any work of the flesh.

CHAPTER 29

THEME: The consecration of the priests; the sacrifices of the consecration; the food of the priests; the continual burnt offering

THE CONSECRATION OF THE PRIESTS

Chapter 29 is a long chapter, and not all of it is as interesting and thrilling reading as it might be. I am confident, however, that the Spirit of God wants to use it to minister to us. This is God's *A-B-C Book* for us and it contains great spiritual lessons.

And this is the thing that thou shalt do unto them to hallow them, to minister unto me in the priest's office: Take one young bullock, and two rams without blemish [Exod. 29:1].

Consecration for a believer is nothing that *he* does for himself. It is something that God does for him. It rests upon the finished work of Christ. It *has* to rest there.

And unleavened bread, and cakes unleavened tempered with oil, and wafers unleavened anointed with oil: of wheaten flour shalt thou make them.

And thou shalt put them into one basket, and bring them in the basket, with the bullock and the two rams.

And Aaron and his sons thou shalt bring unto the door of the tabernacle of the congregation, and shalt wash them with water [Exod. 29:2–4].

The washing is typical of regeneration. Titus 3:5 tells us it is: "Not by works of righteousness which we have done, but according to his mercy he saved us, by the washing of regeneration, and renewing of the Holy Ghost." The washing mentioned in this passage has to do with regeneration. The laver deals with a different type of washing altogether.

Now Moses is going to put the garments upon Aaron.

And thou shalt take the garments, and put upon Aaron the coat, and the robe of the ephod, and the ephod, and the breastplate, and gird him with the curious girdle of the ephod:

And thou shalt put the mitre upon his head, and put the holy crown upon the mitre.

Then shalt thou take the anointing oil, and pour it upon his head, and anoint him.

And thou shalt bring his sons, and put coats upon them.

And thou shalt gird them with girdles, Aaron and his sons, and put the bonnets on them: and the priest's office shall be theirs for a perpetual statute: and thou shalt consecrate Aaron and his sons [Exod. 29:5–9].

Consecration is what God does rather than what we do. I hear so much today about "consecration services" where people promise to do something. I have promised God big things in the past and have never quite made good. I do not like to think of that as being consecration. It is not what I promise Him. Rather, consecration is coming to God with empty hands, confessing our weakness and our inability to do anything, then letting God do the rest.

If you read the prayers of Moses, Elijah, David, and Samuel in the Old Testament, and Paul in the New Testament, you will find that these men never came to God on the basis of what they were, who they were, or what they promised God that they would do. I have attended fagot services for years. I have watched people put a little chip or limb on the fire and then give a testimony about the things they were going to do for God. I have heard enough promises at those fagot services to turn the world upside down for God. Unfortunately, many of those promises are never kept because we really do not have much to offer God, do we? Maybe you have something to offer Him, but I do not. The thing is that we need to come to Him with empty hands and allow Him to fill them.

THE SACRIFICES OF THE CONSECRATION

And thou shalt cause a bullock to be brought before the tabernacle of the congregation: and Aaron and his sons shall put their hands upon the head of the bullock [Exod. 29:10].

The high priest and his family put their hands upon the bullock. There are many people who believe that the laying on of hands transmits something magical or spiritual. It does not. That is not the purpose of the laying on of hands. The only thing you can transfer to another man by the laying on of hands is disease germs. This is all that is passed on. The laying on of hands on an animal speaks of identification. When a sinner came up to the altar and put his hands on the head of the animal he had brought, it meant that the animal was taking his place.

In the church I served for many years we had over one hundred missionaries. When a missionary went to his or her field of service, we held a consecration service to set that missionary aside for service. We put our hands on them. So far I have never transferred anything to a missionary yet. The purpose for the service was identification. The missionaries were identified with us and they represented us on the field. I consider that when I put hands on a missionary, he is identified with me in the ministry, and I have a certain responsibility to pray for him and support him. The laying on of hands means identification.

The bullock took Aaron's place. It will die for him because he is a sinner. This is the burnt offering. In Leviticus we shall go over these offerings in detail. Even in the Garden of Eden there was a burnt offering. The altar that we have identified as the brazen altar is sometimes called the altar of burnt offering because it was here that the main sacrifice was offered. The main sacrifice, which was the burnt offering and the first one, sets forth the person of Christ—who He is. The altar speaks of what He has done for us.

THE FOOD OF THE PRIESTS

And thou shalt take the breast of the ram of Aaron's consecration, and wave it for a wave offering before the LORD: and it shall be thy part.

And thou shalt sanctify the breast of the wave offering, and the shoulder of the heave offering, which is waved, and which is heaved up, of the ram of the consecration, even of that which is for Aaron, and of that which is for his sons [Exod. 29:26–27].

Once again in Leviticus you will find that a part of an offering went to Aaron and the priest as their part. You see, the Levites were apportioned no land for farming in the nation, and this is the way God provided for their support. The Levites were to serve in the tabernacle and later in the temple, and they would receive a part of the offering.

THE CONTINUAL BURNT OFFERING

The continual burnt offering was to be continually offered.

Now this is that which thou shalt offer upon the altar; two lambs of the first year day by day continually.

The one lamb thou shalt offer in the morning; and the other lamb thou shalt offer at even:

And with the one lamb a tenth deal of flour mingled with the fourth part of an hin of beaten oil; and the fourth part of an hin of wine for a drink offering [Exod. 29:38–40].

Once again the Book of Leviticus gives us the details of the continual burnt offering. This offering was a daily sacrifice; a lamb was offered in the morning and a lamb was offered in the evening. It speaks of the fact that the people needed a continual reminder that someone was needed to take their place and that their sin merited death. There must be the shedding of blood for sin.

The Book of Hebrews brings out this truth: "For then must he often have suffered since the foundation of the world: but now once in the end of the world hath he appeared to put away sin by the sacrifice of himself" (Heb. 9:26). This verse, of course, is speaking about the sacrifice of the Lord Jesus Christ. The blood of bulls, goats, and lambs could not take away sin, but the blood of Jesus Christ could. His sacrifice is adequate. The Lord has dealt adequately with sin. He died only once. Once in the end of the age He appeared to put away sin by the sacrifice of Himself.

CHAPTER 30

THEME: The altar of incense; the ransomed may worship; the cleansed may worship; the anointed may worship; the incense

THE ALTAR OF INCENSE

This is the great worship chapter. In looking at the first compartment of the tabernacle proper, the Holy Place, we see three articles of furniture. All speak of worship. We have already considered the lampstand and the table of showbread, but there is also an altar here. It is the altar of incense. The table of showbread and the golden lampstand typify God's people meeting and fellowshiping together. (This is *not* where you meet together and gossip, but where you feed on the person of Jesus Christ. It is a banquet.) The altar of incense is the place of prayer.

And thou shalt make an altar to burn incense upon: of shittim wood shalt thou make it.

A cubit shall be the length thereof, and a cubit the breadth thereof; foursquare shall it be: and two cubits shall be the height thereof: the horns thereof shall be of the same [Exod. 30:1–2].

The instructions tell us that this was a small altar.

And thou shalt overlay it with pure gold, the top thereof, and the sides thereof round about, and the horns thereof; and thou shalt make unto it a crown of gold round about.

And two golden rings shalt thou make to it under the crown of it, by the two corners thereof, upon the two sides of it shalt thou make it; and they shall be for places for the staves to bear it withal [Exod. 30:3–4].

Even this small piece of furniture had rings so that staves could be put through them and it could be carried upon the shoulders of the priests. In the Book of Numbers we are told that on the wilderness march the Levites carried the articles of furniture.

And thou shalt put it before the veil that is by the ark of the testimony, before the mercy seat that is over the testimony, where I will meet with thee [Exod. 30:6].

This altar was placed right by the veil, and the ark and mercy seat were on the other side of the veil. It stood in the Holy Place, the place of worship.

And Aaron shall burn thereon sweet incense every morning: when he dresseth the lamps, he shall burn incense upon it.

And when Aaron lighteth the lamps at even, he shall burn incense upon it, a perpetual incense before the LORD throughout your generations [Exod. 30:7–8].

This was not an altar of sacrifice.

Ye shall offer no strange incense thereon, nor burnt sacrifice, nor meat offering; neither shall ye pour drink offering thereon [Exod. 30:9].

Only incense, and only a certain kind of incense, was to be placed upon this altar. The priests would go in and burn incense every time they would light the lamps of the lampstand. This altar speaks of prayer, and we know this because the Bible uses incense as a symbol of prayer and praise in many places. David, for example, in Psalm 141:2 says, "Let my prayer be set forth before thee as incense . . . ." The Book of Revelation gives us this picture of incense: "And another angel came and stood at the altar, having a golden censer; and there was given unto him much incense, that he should offer it with the prayers of all saints upon the golden altar which was before the throne" (Rev. 8:3). Luke 1:9 tells us that "According to the custom of the priest's office, his [Zacharias'] lot was to burn incense when he went into the temple of the Lord." Zacharias was a member of the tribe of Levi and he served in the temple. He was serving at the altar of incense, according to this verse, and it was at the time of prayer. Dr. Luke opens the New Testament—chronologically—with Zacharias at the altar of incense. In other words, God broke His silence of four hundred years at the altar of incense by giving a message to Zacharias there.

Incense, therefore, is a figure of the Lord Jesus Christ, our Intercessor. Aaron ministered in the place of worship and Aaron is a figure of Christ in this particular sense, although Christ is actually a priest after the order of Melchizedek (Heb. 7). In Hebrews 9 we find a strange thing—the altar of incense is placed in the Holy of Holies. It looks as if the writer of Hebrews didn't know where it belonged! Why did he locate it in the Holy of

Holies rather than in the Holy Place as it is in Exodus? Because when he wrote, the veil had been rent in two. Christ had offered Himself down here. His flesh had been rent, and He had died upon the cross. But He ascended back to heaven, and the altar of incense is in heaven today. We come to God through Jesus Christ. He is our great Intercessor. Christ is in heaven, and the altar speaks of the place where He stands. When we come to God in prayer, we have to come through the Lord Jesus Christ.

I have heard lots of people say, "Now that I am saved, I can go directly to God." No, you cannot! You go to God through Christ. He is the One who brings us into the presence of God. Christ is in heaven praying for us. It was wonderful for the children of Israel to know that their high priest was in the tabernacle, at the altar of incense, praying for them. It is wonderful for us to know that Jesus Christ, our great High Priest, is praying for us.

Christ does not pray for the world. Did you know that? In His high priestly prayer He says, "I pray for them: I pray not for the world, but for them which thou hast given me; for they are thine" (John 17:9). You say, "Why doesn't He pray for the world?" Jesus Christ *died* for the world. And the Holy Spirit is down here to make the offer of Christ real to those who will receive Him. Christ could do no more than die for the sins of the world. He is in heaven praying for those who have received Him as Savior. I am glad that He is doing this because if He were not, we could not accomplish very much on earth. What a precious thing it is to have a great High Priest who prays for us. God hears our prayers because of who Christ is and what He did for us on the cross.

Ephesians 1:6 says, "To the praise of the glory of his grace, wherein he hath made us accepted in the beloved." Because of Jesus Christ, God the Father accepts us in the Beloved. In Matthew 17:5, Mark 9:7 and Luke 9:35 God the Father said, "This is my beloved Son, hear him." We are not only to hear Him, we are to pray through Him. Jesus Christ told us in John 14:14: "If ye shall ask any thing in my name, I will do it." This is what it means to pray in the Spirit.

You will notice that this altar is separated from the other articles of furniture. Only the priests could worship here. Even King Uzziah was smitten with leprosy when he tried to intrude here (2 Chron. 26:16–21). Only priests can pray today—and every true believer in Christ is a priest. There is a great deal of sentimental rubbish told around today that a person can lead any sort of sinful life he pleases, reject Christ, and then in time of trouble, perhaps when his mother is in the hospital, this reprobate can get on his knees before God and expect an answer. Motion pictures have shown scenes like this, and some sentimental preachers talk about such things happening, but God says He will not answer prayers like this. Let us be very careful about this, friends. The altar of incense is where priests go. The *only* prayer a sinner can pray is "God be merciful to me, a sinner." God will hear and answer that prayer when it is offered to Him.

Verse 8 tells us that there is to be "a perpetual incense before the LORD throughout your generations." There is to be continual praise to God. In 1 Thessalonians we are told to "pray without ceasing." The incense was to be upon the altar in the morning and the evening.

When the high priest went inside and offered incense on the altar, he spent some time in the tabernacle. That incense stayed upon his garments and when he came outside, the people could smell him. You might say that he was wearing the right kind of fragrance. When the great high priest walked by, people caught the fragrance. They said, "My, doesn't he smell good!" The trouble with most saints today is that they are not wearing the right kind of cologne. The right cologne is *prayer*. Let your prayers ascend before God as sweet incense, and it will permeate your garments— if you spend time in prayer.

THE RANSOMED MAY WORSHIP

When thou takest the sum of the children of Israel after their number, then shall they give every man a ransom for his soul unto the LORD, when thou numberest them; that there be no plague among them, when thou numberest them.

This they shall give, every one that passeth among them that are numbered, half a shekel after the shekel of the sanctuary: (a shekel is twenty gerahs:) an half shekel shall be the offering of the LORD [Exod. 30:12–13].

This is the second requirement of worship. There will be no plague among them because they are going to be redeemed. They were to be ransomed with silver. Silver is the metal of redemption and a type of redemption. Everyone that worshiped had to be redeemed. We hear a great deal today about public worship. Actually there is no such thing. Only the redeemed can worship, but the way is open to "whosoever will" for redemption.

THE CLEANSED MAY WORSHIP

Not only must worshipers be redeemed, they must also be cleansed. That brings us to the laver. The laver is located in the outer court and is made of brass, along with the brazen altar. This is where God settles the sin question and where He deals with our sin. The brazen laver is where God deals with our sins as saints. Saints sometimes sin. This idea that saints are heavenly is just not true. As one anonymous poet has said:

> To dwell above
> With saints of love
> O that will be glory!
> But to stay below
> With saints *I* know
> That is another story!

And the Lord spake unto Moses saying,

Thou shalt also make a laver of brass, and his foot also of brass, to wash withal: and thou shalt put it between the tabernacle of the congregation and the altar, and thou shalt put water therein.

For Aaron and his sons shall wash their hands and their feet thereat:

When they go into the tabernacle of the congregation, they shall wash with water, that they die not; or when they come near to the altar to minister, to burn offering made by fire unto the Lord [Exod. 30:17–20].

The priest could not come into the tabernacle to serve unless he had first washed. The priest got contaminated when he was on the outside. When you go to church and do not enjoy the service, maybe it is not just because the preacher is dull. Maybe you are a dirty saint. When you have the combination of a dull preacher and a dirty saint, you do not have a very exciting service.

We get dirty in this world, and we cannot worship until we are cleansed. That is why the Lord washed the disciples' feet. He is still doing that today. We need to go to the laver, friends. That is the first thing the priest did. If they were going to the brazen altar, they washed before and after. If they were going into the Holy Place, they washed before they came in and washed when they came out. I am of the opinion that the matter of washing was very important. It was so important, in fact, that I can imagine one priest saying to another

priest at the laver, "How many times have you been here today?" The other priest might reply, "Nearly a dozen times." And the first priest would say, "Well, I've been up here over a dozen times. And look at my hands—I have dishpan hands because I have washed so much. I wonder why God wants us to do this so often?" And Aaron, standing in the background, might have said, "The Lord wants you to wash and wash and wash so that you will *know* that you have to be holy. You cannot worship Him, serve Him, or be of use to Him unless you have been cleaned up."

The idea that a dirty saint can serve God acceptably simply is not true. Every now and then you hear of some man getting involved with a woman, and folk say, "My, I do not understand how a thing like that can happen to one who is doing a great work for God." The man might have been a preacher or a fine Christian worker, but if you check his work, you will find out that it is wood, hay, and stubble. In 1 Corinthians 3:12–15 we learn that, ". . . if any man build upon this foundation gold, silver, precious stones, wood, hay, stubble; Every man's work shall be made manifest: for the day shall declare it, because it shall be revealed by fire; and the fire shall try every man's work of what sort it is. If any man's work abide which he hath built thereupon, he shall receive a reward. If any man's work shall be burned, he shall suffer loss: but he himself shall be saved; yet so as by fire." His "great work" amounts to nothing in God's sight. God wants us to be clean.

The *priests* were to wash in the brazen laver. *We* are to come to Him in confession. First John 1:9 tells us that "If we confess our sins, he is faithful and just to forgive us our sins, and to cleanse us from all unrighteousness." This laver of brass pictures our sanctification. We must wash if we are going to serve God. We must wash if we are going to be used by God. We must be clean. Not only should our garments smell like sweet incense, but our bodies should be washed with pure water. The pure water is the Word of God.

The laver was made out of brass. The women brought their highly polished brass mirrors to make the laver. They did not have glass mirrors then. The mirrors revealed dirt and that was the purpose of the laver. The laver cleansed the priest, and the laver pictures the Word of God. The Bible is a mirror and when we look into it, our sin is revealed. We then need to confess that sin and be cleansed.

Now you are not to confess your sin publicly; you go to Jesus Christ in private. That laver is in heaven. I think that every Sunday, before we ever go inside the church, we should confess our sins for the week. Do not tell me that you don't get dirty. Your eyes get dirty. Your mind gets dirty. Your hands get dirty. Your feet get dirty. You get dirty all right. One of the big troubles in our churches today is that there is too much spiritual B.O. We need to confess our sins to Him and wash before we go in to worship. God does not accept worship until it comes from a cleansed heart nor will He accept service except from a cleansed heart.

THE ANOINTED MAY WORSHIP

And thou shalt make it an oil of holy ointment, an ointment compound after the art of the apothecary: it shall be an holy anointing oil.

And thou shalt anoint the tabernacle of the congregation therewith, and the ark of the testimony,

And the table and all his vessels . . . [Exod. 30:25–27a].

What is the anointing for us today? It is the anointing of the Holy Spirit. We have an anointing that enables us to understand the Word of God. That is the reason the Bible is being made real to so many today. It is not the teacher nor the preacher; it is the Spirit of God using the Word of God. Only the Spirit can anoint you. You do not have to go to some man and have him pour oil on you. You can go to God right now and say, "God, open my heart and mind and life to understand your Word." First John 2:20 says, "But ye have an unction from the Holy One, and ye know all things." The word "unction" means *anointing* and it is ours.

First John 2:27 goes on to say, "But the anointing which ye have received of him abideth in you, and ye need not that any man teach you: but as the same anointing teacheth you of all things, and is truth, and is no lie, and even as it hath taught you, ye shall abide in him." The Holy Spirit is the one who can open your mind and heart when you go to work with God to understand His Word. What a blessing He will bring to your heart! There are so many people today who are asking the questions, "What is life all about? What shall I do today? How shall I communicate my needs?" Oh my dear friends, ask God to let the Holy Spirit of God make real His Word to your hearts, and true joy will be yours.

THE INCENSE

And the LORD said unto Moses, Take unto thee sweet spices, stacte, and onycha, and galbanum; these sweet spices with pure frankincense: of each shall there be a like weight:

And thou shalt make it a perfume, a confection after the art of the apothecary, tempered together, pure and holy:

And thou shalt beat some of it very small, and put of it before the testimony in the tabernacle of the congregation . . . [Exod. 30:34–36a].

Now the incense, as we are told in verse 34, was made of sweet spices, stacte, and onycha, and galbanum, along with pure frankincense. Stacte was a resinous gum that oozed from trees on Mount Gilead. It was called the balm of Gilead. The onycha came from a species of shell fish that resembled a crab. The galbanum was taken from the leaves of a Syrian plant. These were blended with pure frankincense. It was a secret formula, long since lost. The mixture of these spices gave off a sweet incense, and it was not to be duplicated nor replaced.

And as for the perfume which thou shalt make, ye shall not make to yourselves according to the composition thereof: it shall be unto thee holy for the LORD.

Whosoever shall make like unto that, to smell thereto, shall even be cut off from his people [Exod. 30:37–38].

No one was to use this formula for himself. Neither would God accept any counterfeit.

The altar speaks to us of prayer and worship. It is a place where we are to offer our praise, thanksgiving, and our requests. It is not to be duplicated. This formula was not to be used in an attempt to try and make the incense or worship pleasing to the natural man. You cannot make worship pleasing to the natural man. We are to worship God in spirit and in truth. All sorts of things are used to try and trap people into going to church. Nothing but the Word of God should be used to accomplish this. Make sure that the Word of God is foremost, and that everything centers around the Word of God.

In closing, I want to mention again that there were two altars. The burnt altar is where God deals with a sinner. It speaks of the earth and the sin of man. The altar of incense speaks of heaven and holiness. The burnt altar speaks of what Christ did for us on earth. The incense altar speaks of what Christ is doing for us in heaven today. It also speaks of our prayers and our part in worship. It speaks of Christ who prays for us. He is the one who truly praises God and prays for us. He is the one who genuinely worships God for us. He is our intercessor.

How are we to learn to worship? Well, not at the bloody altar where you go as a sinner and take Christ as your Savior. You enter the Holy Place and come to the golden altar. There is no sacrifice there because the sin question was settled outside. When you worship God, the sin question has to be settled. The very basis rests upon the fact that this altar once a year was consecrated with blood. As believers, we are accepted in the Beloved before God. God hears our prayers because of what Christ has done.

CHAPTER 31

THEME: The call of Spirit-filled craftsmen; the Sabbath day becomes a sign

THE CALL
OF SPIRIT-FILLED CRAFTSMEN

This chapter seems to be a departure from the study of the tabernacle, but actually it is not. What we have here is an interval between the giving of the Law and the instructions of the tabernacle. Moses spent a great deal of time on Mt. Sinai, receiving all the instructions. The children of Israel became somewhat impatient while they were waiting for him to return. This chapter tells us about the workmen who made the tabernacle and about one in particular who was given a special gift for making the articles of furniture, especially the more difficult pieces.

And the LORD spake unto Moses, saying,

See, I have called by name Bezaleel the son of Uri, the son of Hur, of the tribe of Judah:

And I have filled him with the spirit of God, in wisdom, and in understanding, and in knowledge, and in all manner of workmanship,

To devise cunning works, to work in gold, and in silver, and in brass,

And in cutting of stones, to set them, and in carving of timber, to work in all manner of workmanship.

And I, behold, I have given with him Aholiab, the son of Ahisamach, of the tribe of Dan: and in the hearts of all that are wise hearted I have put wisdom, that they may make all that I have commanded thee [Exod. 31:1–6].

These men and their helpers were given special gifts for craftsmanship. They made the tabernacle furniture and also the garments. The Spirit of God equipped them for their work. The question might arise as to the trade of Bezaleel before God called him to do this work. I believe craftsmanship was his trade, and that he worked with gold and silver and other delicate things. But he was given a special gift from God to do His work.

My feeling is that whatever a man is equipped to do, that is the thing he should do unless God makes it clear that he should do otherwise. I find today that there are those who cannot speak well before an audience and yet want to. I know several laymen who are determined that they are going to be speakers, but they are not equipped for it. They have no trace of the gift of speaking, but they stubbornly continue to speak when other useful gifts they have go to waste. I know a man in radio work who is a technical expert but all he wants to do is speak. He has a special gift, and I think he should confine himself to the gift God has given him.

When I was a pastor in Nashville, one of the deacons of my church came to me the first day I arrived and asked me never to call on him for public prayer. "It scares me to death; I have stage fright and I cannot seem to overcome my fear. It must be abnormal, but I make a fool of myself when I try to speak in public," he said. This man was the superintendent of a street car company and held an executive position, but he confessed to me that he could not do any public speaking that made sense. He did tell me, however, that if there was anything that needed to be done around the church, to let him know. He turned out to be a wonderful helper and he was right there whenever I called on him. Before I left that church, I was thanking

God that this man did not have the gift of public speaking because it made him faithful to the gift that God had given him.

Bezaleel could have been very much like some laymen today. He could have said, "Look here, Lord, I want to wear these high priestly garments like Aaron. I want to serve You like that." But God said, "That is not the way I want you to serve me." In one sense this man's gift is more important than Aaron's gift. His gift was essential for the building of the tabernacle. God will give you a gift, friend, that will develop the talents that you have. God gives us talents, but He wants us to dedicate them to Him. Let's allow the Holy Spirit to take us and use us.

We do not all have the same talents and gifts. There is a wrong impression circulating in the church today that if you cannot sing in the choir, teach a Sunday school class, speak publicly, or be an usher, you are pretty much out of the picture. I think there are literally hundreds of gifts that God gives to men to serve Him. It is up to the individual to determine what is his gift. Whatever gift God has given you, He would like the Spirit of God to take it and use it for His service.

THE SABBATH DAY BECOMES A SIGN

There is something else in this chapter that is of profound interest and is important to see. It has to do with the Sabbath day. It is something that many people pass over. The Sabbath day was given to man right after creation, and it was observed universally. When we come to the Mosaic system, we find that God made it one of the Ten Commandments for the children of Israel. At this time God makes it quite clear that the Sabbath is *only* for the children of Israel.

And the Lord spake unto Moses, saying,

Speak thou also unto the children of Israel, saying, Verily my sabbaths ye shall keep: for it is a sign between me and you throughout your generations; that ye may know that I am the Lord that doth sanctify you [Exod. 31:12–13].

The Sabbath was given specifically to Israel. I do not believe it was ever given to the church.

When someone asks me, "When was the Sabbath day changed?" I always reply that it never was changed. It was done away with, as far as the church is concerned. We are not under the Sabbath day which is Saturday. We do not observe Saturday—Jesus was dead that day and we are not serving a dead Christ. On the first day of the week Jesus Christ rose from the dead. The church from the very beginning met on the first day of the week. That is when the church was born; the day of Pentecost was on the day *after* the Sabbath. The Sabbath was first given to the entire human race but man turned away from God, and God gave the Sabbath exclusively to Israel.

Ye shall keep the sabbath therefore; for it is holy unto you: every one that defileth it shall surely be put to death: for whosoever doeth any work therein, that soul shall be cut off from among his people [Exod. 31:14].

I would like to ask the people who claim to keep the Sabbath if they keep it all the time. And are those of their number who do not keep the Sabbath all the time put to death as the law requires?

Six days may work be done; but in the seventh is the sabbath of rest, holy to the Lord: whosoever doeth any work in the sabbath day, he shall surely be put to death [Exod. 31:15].

If a man was found gathering sticks on the Sabbath day, he was stoned to death in Israel.

Wherefore the children of Israel shall keep the sabbath, to observe the sabbath throughout their generations, for a perpetual covenant.

It is a sign between me and the children of Israel for ever: for in six days the Lord made heaven and earth, and on the seventh day he rested, and was refreshed [Exod. 31:16–17].

This passage expressly says that the children of Israel, not the church, were to keep the Sabbath. The Israelites are an earthly people belonging to the first creation. The church is a new creation and it was given a new day to observe which is the first day of the week.

CHAPTER 32

THE GOLDEN CALF

This chapter presents tragedy as far as the children of Israel are concerned, and yet it is here we see one of the greatest teachings and revelations concerning our God. Also, this is one of the greatest lessons on prayer found in the Bible.

And when the people saw that Moses delayed to come down out of the mount, the people gathered themselves together unto Aaron, and said unto him, Up, make us gods, which shall go before us; for as for this Moses, the man that brought us up out of the land of Egypt, we wot not what is become of him [Exod. 32:1].

The word *wot* simply means we "know" not. The people thought Moses was gone, probably had been killed. Since he was gone, they wanted to make idols (gods) to lead them on the wilderness march. Right away they lapsed into idolatry. You would think Aaron, who was the high priest, would try to stop them, but he did not. Aaron went along with the liberalism of the people wanting to return to idolatry.

And Aaron said unto them, Break off the golden earrings, which are in the ears of your wives, of your sons, and of your daughters, and bring them unto me [Exod. 32:2].

During that time earrings were a sign of idolatry (see Genesis 35:4). It was a sign that these people were serving the gods of Egypt. Now they were to bring these earrings to Aaron.

And all the people brake off the golden earrings which were in their ears, and brought them unto Aaron.

And he received them at their hand, and fashioned it with a graving tool, after he had made it a molten calf: and they said, These be thy gods, O Israel, which brought thee up out of the land of Egypt [Exod. 32:3–4].

Can you imagine these people lapsing into idolatry this quickly? It would be inconceivable to me if it were not for the fact that I have watched the church lapse into apostasy that I never dreamed I would live to see.

And they rose up early on the morrow, and offered burnt offerings, and brought peace offerings; and the people sat down to eat and to drink, and rose up to play [Exod. 32:6].

Gross immorality was involved here. They have already departed from God after they had told Him that they would keep all of His commandments. As you can see, they are not keeping any of them.

All this time Moses is on the mountain receiving the Law, the instructions, and the blueprint for the tabernacle.

CONDEMNATION OF ISRAEL'S APOSTASY

And the LORD said unto Moses, Go, get thee down; for thy people, which thou broughtest out of the land of Egypt, have corrupted themselves:

They have turned aside quickly out of the way which I commanded them: they have made them a molten calf, and have worshipped it, and have sacrificed thereunto, and said, These be thy gods, O Israel, which have brought thee up out of the land of Egypt [Exod. 32:7–8].

God did not redeem Israel because they were superior, greater, or better than any other nation. They were none of these things. God said, "I knew you were a stiffnecked people."

And the LORD said unto Moses, I have seen this people, and, behold, it is a stiffnecked people:

Now therefore let me alone, that my wrath may wax hot against them, and that I may consume them: and I will make of thee a great nation [Exod. 32:9–10].

This was a real temptation to Moses. God is saying, "Moses, I will use you like I used Abraham, and I will make of you a great nation and I will still be able to make good my covenant with Abraham." Now notice what Moses does. He is an example of one of the greatest prayers in all of Scripture.

And Moses besought the LORD his God, and said, LORD, why doth thy wrath wax

hot against thy people, which thou hast brought forth out of the land of Egypt with great power, and with a mighty hand? [Exod. 32:11].

God asks Moses to "remember." God says, "Moses, get thee down, for *thy* people that *thou* hast brought forth out of the land of Egypt have corrupted themselves." Now Moses really talks back to God. (There is none of this pious piffle that you hear today in so many prayers. We have so much hypocrisy in some of our prayers that it is no wonder prayer meetings are dead. If we would talk honestly and frankly to God, prayer meeting would be the most exciting meeting in the church.) Listen to what Moses said, "Lord, I think You made a mistake. I do not recall bringing any people out of Egypt. And they are not *my* people; they are *Your* people. You brought them out of Egypt and You did it with a mighty hand. I could not bring them out. You have made a mistake, Lord." Can you imagine talking to God like that? Moses did!

Wherefore should the Egyptians speak, and say, For mischief did he bring them out, to slay them in the mountains, and to consume them from the face of the earth? Turn from thy fierce wrath, and repent of this evil against thy people [Exod. 32:12].

Then Moses tells the Lord, "You brought Your people out of the land of Egypt, but suppose that You do not take them into the land. The Egyptians would say that You were able to lead them out of Egypt but not able to take them into the land. They are Your people, Lord. You promised to bring them into the land."

Next, Moses gives God a third reason for turning aside from His wrath against the Israelites.

Remember Abraham, Isaac, and Israel, thy servants, to whom thou swarest by thine own self, and saidst unto them, I will multiply your seed as the stars of heaven, and all this land that I have spoken of will I give unto your seed, and they shall inherit it for ever [Exod. 32:13].

Moses continues, "Lord, remember Abraham, Isaac, and Israel; You made a promise to them. You promised to multiply their seed and give them a land."

And the LORD repented of the evil which he thought to do unto his people [Exod. 32:14].

When Moses prayed like that, it moved the arm of God. If we were more honest in praying, we would see more answers—that is, more visible answers to our prayers. We always receive an answer to our prayers, but I think the Lord tells most of us no because we do not really pray honestly to Him.

JUDGMENT

And Moses turned, and went down from the mount, and the two tables of the testimony were in his hand: the tables were written on both their sides: on the one side and on the other were they written.

And the tables were the work of God, and the writing was the writing of God, graven upon the tables.

And when Joshua heard the noise of the people as they shouted, he said unto Moses. There is a noise of war in the camp.

And he said, It is not the voice of them that shout for mastery, neither is it the voice of them that cry for being overcome: but the noise of them that sing do I hear [Exod. 32:15–18].

The children of Israel were having a high old time, friends. They were worshiping their golden calf and living in sin.

And it came to pass, as soon as he came nigh unto the camp, that he saw the calf, and the dancing: and Moses' anger waxed hot, and he cast the tables out of his hands, and brake them beneath the mount.

And he took the calf which they had made, and burnt it in the fire, and ground it to powder, and strawed it upon the water, and made the children of Israel drink of it.

And Moses said unto Aaron, What did this people unto thee, that thou hast brought so great a sin upon them? [Exod. 32:19–21].

Now listen to Aaron try to crawfish out of it all. This would really be humorous, if it were not so serious a matter.

And Aaron said, Let not the anger of my lord wax hot: thou knowest the people, that they are set on mischief.

For they said unto me, Make us gods, which shall go before us: for as for this

Moses, the man that brought us up out of the land of Egypt, we wot not what is become of him [Exod. 32:22–23].

In other words, Moses is getting the blame for what happened. The children of Israel thought that Moses had deserted them, and so they turned to the golden calf. Aaron continues:

And I said unto them. Whosoever hath any gold, let them break it off. So they gave it me: then I cast it into the fire, and there came out this calf [Exod. 32:24].

You cannot help but laugh at Aaron's statement. I think Moses must have laughed with incredulity. "You mean, Aaron, that you poured gold into the fire and the calf walked out?" A few verses back we were told, you remember, that Aaron fashioned the calf with tools. What Aaron did was lie.

And when Moses saw that the people were naked; (for Aaron had made them naked unto their shame among their enemies) [Exod. 32:25].

This matter of nudism, sex, and dope is not new. I think you can look at the Israelites in this instance and see the whole bit. Moses will see this thing through. He is really angry. At the same time, however, notice what an intercessor he is for these people. He lays hold of the heart of God and moves the hand of God.

It is time for Moses to move in with extreme surgery. When you have cancer, and I know this from personal experience, you want to try to get rid of it. If it means cutting away half of your body, you want to get rid of it. Sin is an awful cancer, and God uses extreme surgery in this case by slaying those who were guilty.

Then Moses stood in the gate of the camp, and said, Who is on the LORD's side? let him come unto me. And all the sons of Levi gathered themselves together unto him.

And he said unto them. Thus saith the LORD God of Israel, Put every man his sword by his side, and go in and out from gate to gate throughout the camp, and slay every man his brother, and every man his companion, and every man his neighbour [Exod. 32:26–27].

This judgment is serious and extreme. It had to be that because there had been terrible sin. Liberalism has crept into our churches and we have allowed it to stay there unchecked. I can remember when I came before a church court to be examined for the ministry. A young fellow from a liberal seminary was also there to be examined. I have never seen anyone who knew as little theology and Bible as this boy, and what he did know he had all mixed up. It was clear that he had little knowledge and no faith. He could never even explain the great doctrines of the faith. In fact, one man very patiently said to him, "Well, if you don't believe it, at least you ought to know what you don't believe!" But he didn't. Then one old man who knew this boy's father, said, "This boy's father was a great preacher in the past. He was sound in the faith and I know that one day this boy will come around and will get straightened out." It was not unanimous but the council accepted him. It made me sick at heart to be brought in at the same time with a fellow who did not believe anything at all.

The way this council handled the situation is not the way Moses would have handled it! He would not have drawn a sword and slain the fellow, but he would not have accepted him as a preacher. He would have given that boy a Bible and told him to go to Bible school, learn a little Bible, and then come back and he could be examined again and see if he was fit for the ministry. Because of similar actions by other councils, liberalism has come into the organized church and has taken over. You cannot compromise with sin. Someone has said, "Compromise is immoral," and it is especially immoral in the church. Moses did not do a very good job of compromising. He used extreme surgery.

And the children of Levi did according to the word of Moses: and there fell of the people that day about three thousand men [Exod. 32:28].

Those that were guilty were slain, and that cleaned up the camp pretty well. Many people are apt to say that this was brutal. Look at it this way. Was it better to cut out the cancer now and save the nation or let the cancer grow and destroy the nation? Think of the men, women, and children in the camp who were not guilty. If the men who had led Israel into idolatry had been allowed to live, the nation would never have entered the Promised Land. That, of course, is what is happening in the church in many places. I see church after church lose its importance and its influence and become useless because it allowed liberalism to creep in. We are soft and sentimental and silly. Sometimes we are even stupid in the way we handle evil.

THE INTERCESSION OF MOSES

And it came to pass on the morrow, that Moses said unto the people, Ye have sinned a great sin: and now I will go up unto the LORD; peradventure I shall make an atonement for your sin [Exod. 32:30].

An atonement *covered* up sin. That is the way sin was handled before Jesus Christ came to earth and died on the cross. After the cross, sin is removed. Now Moses gives his fourth reason for taking the children of Israel into the Promised Land.

And Moses returned unto the LORD, and said, Oh, this people have sinned a great sin, and have made them gods of gold [Exod. 32:31].

What is this? Confession. If you want to get along with God, you will have to agree with Him about sin. Sin is sin and it must be confessed. It does not matter who you are, either. These are God's chosen people, the children of Israel, and Moses says, "We have sinned!" Israel had sinned a great sin and made gods of gold. Moses spelled out the sin before God. And, friends, when we confess our sin to God, we should spell it out. Tell God exactly what it is.

Yet now, if thou wilt forgive their sin—; and if not, blot me, I pray thee, out of thy book which thou hast written [Exod. 32:32].

Moses said, "I take my place with the people. I identify myself with them, and if You intend to blot them out, blot me out also." Remember that God had told Moses that He could still make good His covenant to Abraham, Isaac, and Jacob by simply making a nation from Moses. But Moses said, "No, I identify myself with the people. If You do not intend to bring them into the land, then blot me out with them." Notice that what moves the heart of God moves the hand of God.

And the LORD said unto Moses, Whosoever hath sinned against me, him will I blot out of my book [Exod. 32:33].

God deals individually and personally with sin.

Therefore now go, lead the people unto the place of which I have spoken unto thee: behold, mine Angel shall go before thee: nevertheless in the day when I visit I will visit their sin upon them.

And the LORD plagued the people, because they made the calf, which Aaron made [Exod. 32:34–35].

God will deal with sin personally. He will, however, take the people into the land. Those that had not sinned in the idolatry of the calf would be led by the Angel of God. Now the Angel of the Lord in the Old Testament is the visible presence of Christ—the pre-incarnate Christ. Because of Moses' intercession, God has not given up His people. This should impress upon us the extreme importance of prayer.

CHAPTER 33

THEME: Israel's journey continues; the tabernacle is placed outside the camp; Moses' prayer and the Lord's answer

ISRAEL'S JOURNEY CONTINUES

And the LORD said unto Moses, Depart, and go up hence, thou and the people which thou hast brought up out of the land of Egypt, unto the land which I sware unto Abraham, to Isaac, and to Jacob, saying, Unto thy seed will I give it:

And I will send an angel before thee; and I will drive out the Canaanite, the Amo-

rite, and the Hittite, and the Perizzite, the Hivite, and the Jebusite [Exod. 33:1–2].

God is preparing Israel to enter the land. We will see them resume their wilderness march in the Book of Numbers. (The Book of Leviticus is the continuation of the instructions for the service of the tabernacle which they are just setting up in the Book of Exodus.)

Unto a land flowing with milk and

honey: for I will not go up in the midst of thee: for thou art a stiffnecked people: lest I consume thee in the way.

And when the people heard these evil tidings, they mourned: and no man did put on him his ornaments [Exod. 33:3–4].

These ornaments, as we have already seen, were heathen. Their earrings, for example, demonstrated the fact that they were still worshiping the gods of Egypt. The earrings were a sign of it. This is very much like the wearing of a cross, although it is meaningless today as an identification of a Christian.

For the LORD had said unto Moses, Say unto the children of Israel, Ye are a stiffnecked people: I will come up into the midst of thee in a moment, and consume thee: therefore now put off thy ornaments from thee, that I may know what to do unto thee [Exod. 33:5].

This is the *third* time God has called Israel a stiff-necked people. God is making it clear to them that He had not come to redeem His people because they were superior.

God asks them to remove the signs that show they are heathen and pagan and take a stand for God. I personally believe that is the reason that baptism (water baptism) was so important in the early church. It was an evidence that a person had left the old and was taking a stand for the new. This should give that type of testimony today. And so:

And the children of Israel stripped themselves of their ornaments by the mount Horeb [Exod. 33:6].

THE TABERNACLE IS PLACED OUTSIDE THE CAMP

And Moses took the tabernacle, and pitched it without the camp, afar off from the camp, and called it the Tabernacle of the congregation. And it came to pass, that every one which sought the LORD went out unto the tabernacle of the congregation, which was without the camp [Exod. 33:7].

As the tabernacle is being constructed, Moses has it set up without the camp, or outside the camp. The tabernacle at this point is only a tent of meeting. It was probably just a tent or maybe the outer fence that later enclosed the tabernacle.

And it came to pass, when Moses went out unto the tabernacle, that all the people rose up, and stood every man at his tent door, and looked after Moses, until he was gone into the tabernacle.

And it came to pass, as Moses entered into the tabernacle, the cloudy pillar descended, and stood at the door of the tabernacle, and the LORD talked with Moses [Exod. 33:8–9].

Tabernacle Floor Plan

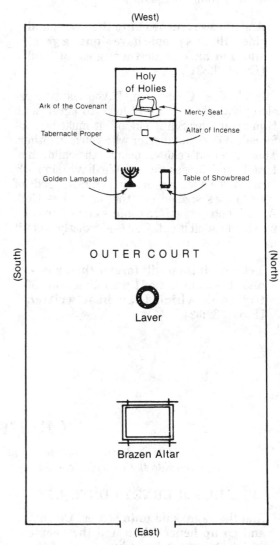

(West)

Holy of Holies

Ark of the Covenant

Mercy Seat

Tabernacle Proper

Altar of Incense

Golden Lampstand

Table of Showbread

(South)

(North)

OUTER COURT

Laver

Brazen Altar

(East)

The question arises, "Has anyone seen God?" John 1:18 tells us that no man has seen God at any time. John 14:9 reveals that those who have seen Jesus Christ have seen the Father. The Lord Jesus Christ is the revelation of God veiled in human flesh. In the Old Testament one of His names was "Angel of the Lord." It was the Angel of the Lord that talked with Moses.

And the LORD spake unto Moses face to face, as a man speaketh unto his friend [Exod. 33:11a].

Just as friends speak to each other face to face, God and Moses talked. Yet Moses did not see God.

And he turned again into the camp: but his servant Joshua, the son of Nun, a young man, departed not out of the tabernacle [Exod. 33:11b].

Once again Joshua is mentioned. He is the man God is preparing to succeed Moses. I do not think that anyone suspected it at the time, but when we get to the Book of Joshua, we will see that he was probably the most unlikely person of all to succeed Moses.

MOSES' PRAYER
AND THE LORD'S ANSWER

And Moses said unto the LORD, See, thou sayest unto me. Bring up this people: and thou hast not let me know whom thou wilt send with me. Yet thou hast said, I know thee by name, and thou hast also found grace in my sight.

Now therefore, I pray thee, if I have found grace in thy sight, shew me now thy way, that I may know thee, that I may find grace in thy sight: and consider that this nation is thy people [Exod. 33:12–13).

Moses was asking for the same thing that Paul did in Philippians 3:10, "That I may know him. . . ." It is the same thing that Philip meant when in John 14:8 he said, ". . . Shew us the Father, and it sufficeth us." I believe every sincere child of God has a desire to know God.

And he said, My presence shall go with thee, and I will give thee rest.

And he said unto him, If thy presence go not with me, carry us not up hence [Exod. 33:14–15].

Moses knew that he needed the presence of God with him. He knew that he could not make it on his own.

For wherein shall it be known here that I and thy people have found grace in thy sight? is it not in that thou goest with us? so shall we be separated, I and thy people, from all the people that are upon the face of the earth [Exod. 33:16].

It is important to notice that God made the Israelites a peculiar people for a very definite reason. The church is also to be a peculiar people today. This means we are to be a people for God; it does not mean that we are to be oddballs.

And the LORD said unto Moses, I will do this thing also that thou hast spoken: for thou hast found grace in my sight, and I know thee by name [Exod. 33:17].

Moses is becoming very intimate with God.

And he said, I beseech thee, shew me thy glory [Exod. 33:18].

Moses could not actually *see* God face to face.

And he said, I will make all my goodness pass before thee, and I will proclaim the name of the LORD before thee: and will be gracious to whom I will be gracious, and will shew mercy on whom I will shew mercy [Exod. 33:19].

Paul uses this verse in Romans 9:15 when he says, "For he saith to Moses, I will have mercy on whom I will have mercy, and I will have compassion on whom I will have compassion."

And he said, Thou canst not see my face: for there shall no man see me, and live [Exod. 33:20].

It is a fact, friend, you are *not* going to see God face to face.

And the LORD said, Behold, there is a place by me, and thou shalt stand upon a rock:

And it shall come to pass, while my glory passeth by, that I will put thee in a clift of the rock, and will cover thee with my hand while I pass by:

And I will take away mine hand, and thou shalt see my back parts: but my face shall not be seen [Exod. 33:21–23].

This passage is speaking about the glory being a representation of God. The Lord Jesus said that when He comes the second time, there would be the sign of the Son of man in heaven. Matthew 24:30 states: "And then shall appear the sign of the Son of man in heaven: and then shall all the tribes of the earth mourn, and they shall see the Son of man coming in the clouds of heaven with power and great glory." I think that sign is the shekinah glory spoken of in Exodus 33:21–23. When Christ took upon Himself human flesh, the glory was not there. He took a humble place and put aside His glory, but He was still God. That is why He could say, "He that hath seen me hath seen the Father."

We are not going to see God. We will see the Lord Jesus Christ and He will be in human form because that is the form He took here on earth. Today He is in a glorified body, and someday we shall be like Him we are told in 1 John 3:2 which says, "Beloved, now are we the sons of God, and it doth not yet appear what we shall be: but we know that, when he shall appear, we shall be like him; for we shall see him as he is." This is the anticipation and hope of believers who are walking by faith. That is the way Moses is going to walk. He knew that God's presence had to go with him or failure would be the result.

We need His presence today also to face the problems of everyday life.

CHAPTER 34

THEME: The tables of the Law renewed; Moses' commission is renewed; Moses' face shines

THE TABLES OF THE LAW RENEWED

And the LORD said unto Moses, Hew thee two tables of stone like unto the first: and I will write upon these tables the words that were in the first tables, which thou brakest.

And be ready in the morning, and come up in the morning unto mount Sinai, and present thyself there to me in the top of the mount.

And no man shall come up with thee, neither let any man be seen throughout all the mount; neither let the flocks nor the herds feed before that mount.

And he hewed two tables of stone like unto the first; and Moses rose up early in the morning, and went up unto mount Sinai, as the LORD had commanded him, and took in his hand the two tables of stone [Exod. 34:1–4].

These are the second tables of the Law. The first tables were broken by Moses when he descended Mt. Sinai and found that the children of Israel had made a golden calf and were worshiping it. He now comes back to the mount with blank tables of stone.

And the LORD descended in the cloud, and stood with him there, and proclaimed the name of the LORD [Exod. 34:5].

The Lord is now proclaiming His name. This is a tremendous advance for both Moses and the children of Israel. A name has meaning. When you hear the name Caesar, what do you think of? When you hear the name Abraham Lincoln, what do you think of? You conjure up certain images in your mind. God is now proclaiming His name and He wants the Israelites to remember their experiences with Him since they left the land of Egypt.

And the LORD passed by before him, and proclaimed, The LORD, The LORD God, merciful and gracious, longsuffering, and abundant in goodness and truth,

Keeping mercy for thousands, forgiving iniquity and transgression and sin, and that will by no means clear the guilty . . . [Exod. 34:6–7a].

God does not extend mercy by shutting His eyes to the guilty or by saying, "I will just forget that sin." Sin must be punished and a penalty must be paid. God by no means clears the guilty. What happens then? How does He keep His mercy and take care of iniquity at the same time? A sacrifice has been provided. The sacrifices Israel made in that day did not *take away* sin but they pointed to that "Perfect Sacrifice," the Lord Jesus Christ, who, when He did come, put away sin by His death on the cross.

. . . visiting the iniquity of the fathers upon the children, and upon the children's children, unto the third and to the fourth generation [Exod. 34:7b].

It is a good thing to remember that today you can commit a sin that will affect your children, your grandchildren, your great-grandchildren, and your great-great-grandchildren.

I took a certain course in abnormal psychology in college—psychology was my second major. I almost accepted a scholarship to go on with my studies in this field. One day we went on a tour of a mental hospital in Oliver, Tennessee. We were shown different forms of abnormality. All of the patients were suffering from one mental disease or another. After we had seen one particular group, a member of our class asked the doctor what caused these diseases. The doctor simply replied, "It was either the sins of the father or the grandfather, or it could have been the sins of the great-grandfather."

A doctor in Nashville took me to the hospital one morning where he was going to operate on some blind children, although it would give them only partial sight. "What made them blind?" I asked. He replied, "It was the sins of their fathers." Believe me, friend, you cannot break His laws with impunity. God is always the same. His laws do not change. But thank God "He keeps mercy for thousands, forgiving iniquity." If we only turn to Him, we will find mercy.

And Moses made haste, and bowed his head toward the earth, and worshipped.

And he said, If now I have found grace in thy sight, O Lord, let my Lord, I pray thee, go among us; for it is a stiffnecked people; and pardon our iniquity and our sin, and take us for thine inheritance [Exod. 34:8–9].

This is about the fourth time these people have been called stiff-necked. I hope by this time that you realize God never saved the nation Israel because they were superior, or because they were doing so well, or because they promised to do good. They are a stiff-necked people.

MOSES' COMMISSION IS RENEWED

And he said, Behold, I make a covenant: before all thy people I will do marvels, such as have not been done in all the earth, nor in any nation: and all the people among which thou art shall see the work of the Lord: for it is a terrible thing that I will do with thee [Exod. 34:10].

The word *terrible* means "to incite terror." This word does not have the same meaning as we give to *terrible*. It was part of the shield of God that He was putting around His people. They would have been devoured by the enemy if He had not done this.

Observe thou that which I command thee this day: behold, I drive out before thee the Amorite, and the Canaanite, and the Hittite, and the Perizzite, and the Hivite, and the Jebusite [Exod. 34:11].

God says that He will drive out all of their enemies and this is the third time He has mentioned this.

Take heed to thyself, lest thou make a covenant with the inhabitants of the land whither thou goest, lest it be for a snare in the midst of thee [Exod. 34:12].

God warned them not to make a covenant with any of the people of the land. When the Gibeonites came to Joshua (in the Book of Joshua), they tricked the Israelites. They pretended that they had come from afar and had old stale bread to prove it—to Joshua, at least. Why didn't God want Israel to make covenants with the people in the land of Canaan? If they made any covenants with these people, it would become a snare to them and lead them back into idolatry.

But ye shall destroy their altars, break their images, and cut down their groves:

For thou shalt worship no other god: for the Lord, whose name is Jealous, is a jealous God [Exod. 34:13–14].

He is a jealous God and does not want to share His honor and glory with false gods. There is no reason to apologize for God's being jealous either. I once heard a wife say, "My husband is not jealous of me." She was boasting of that fact. But I could have told her that if her husband was not jealous, he did not love her. Anything or any person you love, you are jealous of, and do not like to share with others. You can be jealous in an evil way, but this is not what we are talking about. When you love a person, you have a concern and you care for them.

Lest thou make a covenant with the inhabitants of the land, and they go a-whoring after their gods, and do sacrifice unto their gods, and one call thee, and thou eat of his sacrifice;

And thou take of their daughters unto thy sons, and their daughters go a-whoring after their gods, and make thy sons go a-whoring after their gods.

Thou shalt make thee no molten gods [Exod. 34:15–17].

The land of Canaan was covered with idolatry just like a dog is covered with fleas. The land was filled with gross immorality, and God is warning Israel to keep herself separate from people engaged in these activities and make no covenant with them at all. Israel was to either destroy them or drive them out of the land. The critics down through the years have decried this. Apparently they have not investigated the reason for this extreme measure. Of course the obvious reason is that God was protecting his own from the horror of idolatry. But there is another reason. It is known today that venereal disease was in epidemic proportions among the inhabitants of Canaan. God was attempting to protect His people from the ravages of disease. Israel disobeyed God and did not completely clear the land of these people and suffered the sad consequences. Finally God sent Israel, disobedient and corrupt, into Babylonian captivity.

> The feast of unleavened bread shalt thou keep. Seven days thou shalt eat unleavened bread, as I commanded thee, in the time of the month Abib: for in the month Abib thou camest out from Egypt [Exod. 34:18].

God is preparing Israel to enter the land by reestablishing the feasts and sabbaths.

> Thrice in the year shall all your menchildren appear before the Lord GOD, the God of Israel [Exod. 34:23].

God then goes on and gives many details concerning different things that the children of Israel were to do and were not to do.

> Thou shalt not offer the blood of my sacrifice with leaven; neither shall the sacrifice of the feast of the passover be left unto the morning.

> The first of the first fruits of thy land thou shalt bring unto the house of the LORD thy God. Thou shalt not seethe a kid in his mother's milk [Exod. 34: 25–26].

The Israelites were to put God *first!* To "seethe a kid" means, of course, to boil it. It is not to be boiled in its mother's milk. That is, they were to avoid doing the unnatural thing.

MOSES' FACE SHINES

> And it came to pass, when Moses came down from mount Sinai with the two tables of testimony in Moses' hand, when he came down from the mount, that Moses wist not that the skin of his face shone while he talked with him.

> And when Aaron and all the children of Israel saw Moses, behold, the skin of his face shone; and they were afraid to come nigh him.

> And Moses called unto them; and Aaron and all the rulers of the congregation returned unto him: and Moses talked with them.

> And afterward all the children of Israel came nigh: and he gave them in commandment all that the LORD had spoken with him in mount Sinai.

> And till Moses had done speaking with them, he put a veil on his face.

> But when Moses went in before the LORD to speak with him, he took the veil off, until he came out. And he came out, and spake unto the children of Israel that which he was commanded.

> And the children of Israel saw the face of Moses, that the skin of Moses' face shone: and Moses put the veil upon his face again, until he went in to speak with him [Exod. 34:29–35].

CHAPTER 35

THEME: The Sabbath reemphasized; free gifts for the tabernacle; Bezaleel and Aholiab called to the work

THE SABBATH REEMPHASIZED

In this chapter the Lord returns to talk to Israel about the Sabbath day. This is the third time.

And Moses gathered all the congregation of the children of Israel together, and said unto them, These are the words which the Lord hath commanded, that ye should do them.

Six days shall work be done, but on the seventh day there shall be to you an holy day, a sabbath of rest to the Lord: whosoever doeth work therein shall be put to death.

Ye shall kindle no fire throughout your habitations upon the sabbath day [Exod. 35:1–3].

The Lord insists that the first reason for the Sabbath is that it belongs to the first creation. God rested on the Sabbath day. As mankind left the creative hand of God, he began to wander away from God. There came the day when mankind as a whole no longer recognized God but began to worship the creature. And man gave up keeping the Sabbath day. Now God said that the Sabbath was a peculiar sign between Himself and the children of Israel. God began to lay down rules that actually apply more to Israel in the Promised Land than to any other place. If anyone did work on the Sabbath day, he was stoned to death. It would be very hard to carry on our society without someone working on the Sabbath day, which is Saturday. Suppose no fire was kindled on the Sabbath. This would cause great problems in the frozen North. God's laws were made to suit the land in which Israel lived.

FREE GIFTS FOR THE TABERNACLE

And Moses spake unto all the congregation of the children of Israel, saying, This is the thing which the Lord commanded, saying,

Take ye from among you an offering unto the Lord: whosoever is of a willing heart, let him bring it, an offering of the Lord; gold, and silver, and brass [Exod. 35:4–5].

These gifts for the making of the tabernacle were to be voluntary. The people were not required to bring anything. There was no demand put upon them at all. This is not the tithe. This is a voluntary gift. They were to bring other things besides the gold, silver, and brass, as we shall see.

And blue, and purple, and scarlet, and fine linen, and goats' hair.

And rams' skins dyed red, and badgers' skins, and shittim wood,

And oil for the light, and spices for anointing oil, and for the sweet incense,

And onyx stones, and stones to be set for the ephod, and for the breastplate [Exod. 35:6–9].

These are the different things that the children of Israel could give to the building of the tabernacle. In that day there was no such thing as legal tender. The method of barter was the exchange of goods; so the Israelites were giving things rather than money to the Lord's work.

This is still a way people can serve the Lord. Several years ago in San Diego a man donated two ampex recorders to our radio ministry. These recorders were very valuable and came to us at the time when we were really in need of them. Many people think that you have to always write out a check—do not misunderstand, we need money too—but the Lord can also be served when you donate things to His service.

The question is repeatedly asked, "Where did the children of Israel get the different articles they gave to the tabernacle when they had been *slaves* in Egypt?" Remember that God said that they would come out of Egypt with great wealth (Gen. 15:14). He made sure they collected their back wages. The Egyptians were so glad to rid the land of the Israelites that they gave them whatever they asked. So Israel left with a great deal of the wealth of Egypt.

BEZALEEL AND AHOLIAB CALLED TO THE WORK

And Moses said unto the children of Israel, See, the Lord hath called by name Bezaleel the son of Uri, the son of Hur, of the tribe of Judah;

And he hath filled him with the spirit of

God, in wisdom, in understanding, and in knowledge, and in all manner of workmanship [Exod. 35:30–31].

Bezaleel is the man God equipped to make the articles of furniture that are so important in the tabernacle.

And he hath put in his heart that he may teach, both he, and Aholiab, the son of Ahisamach, of the tribe of Dan [Exod. 35:34].

God gave Bezaleel the ability to pass on his gift to others.

Them hath he filled with wisdom of heart, to work all manner of work, of the engraver, and of the cunning workman, and of the embroiderer, in blue, and in purple, in scarlet, and in fine linen, and of the weaver, even of them that do any work, and of those that devise cunning work [Exod. 35:35].

The tabernacle was a beautiful object. It was a jewel in the desert. It was not large, not a great warehouse, only a small building. It has been estimated that about five million dollars went into the construction of the tabernacle according to the value of the metals of a few years ago. The value in inflationary times would even be greater. The tabernacle was God's precious jewel; a picture of His Son, Jesus Christ.

The tabernacle erected, and the tents of Israel around it.

CHAPTER 36

THEME: Construction of the tabernacle

This chapter returns us to the tabernacle. We have already seen the instructions regarding how to build it. Now we see they are building it according to instructions. Following the blueprint is very important because the tabernacle is God's portrait of Christ. It reveals Him.

Then wrought Bezaleel and Aholiab, and every wise-hearted man, in whom the LORD put wisdom and understanding to know how to work all manner of work for the service of the sanctuary, according to all that the LORD had commanded [Exod. 36:1].

Every member of the crew, which was probably a large number of folk, was engaged in the building of the tabernacle with the wisdom and understanding God has given him. The man in charge was Bezaleel.

And Moses called Bezaleel and Aholiab, and every wise-hearted man, in whose heart the LORD had put wisdom, even every one whose heart stirred him up to come unto the work to do it [Exod. 36:2].

Now notice something here that is very important and essential in the work of the Lord. If you are serving the Lord grudgingly, do not do it. God cannot use this kind of an attitude. Building the tabernacle are men who are carving out beautiful articles of furniture that are to be used in the worship of the Lord. This is not a "job" to them. They are not watching the clock. They do not belong to a union. They do not just work a certain number of hours a week and quit. They are not building the tabernacle because it is their duty. They are not working because they have to work. They have been slaves in the past and here they are slaving again, but this time because they want to. Their hearts are in their work. That is the way you are to do God's work.

A young preacher once told me, "I like the ministry but I do not like preaching." I suggested he get out of the ministry. The ministry is no place for a man who does not *love* to study and preach the Word of God. If a preacher cannot do his job with enthusiasm and preach with enthusiasm, he should not be in the ministry.

I once listened to a former student of mine preach. What a hassle, what an effort, what a lack of enthusiasm! My friend, if you cannot preach or serve the Lord with verve, vigor, and vitality, don't do it at all. God doesn't want people in His service who would rather be doing something else.

Notice Bezaleel rushing at top speed. Is he going to a football game, a baseball game, or some social? No! Bezaleel is going to work—work for the Lord. You know, if people came to church next Sunday filled with enthusiasm, the whole town would soon be coming out to see what in the world was happening in the church. It would be a revival. God's work is to be done with joy and happiness. We are to serve Him with gladness. In Romans 14:5 the apostle Paul said, ". . . Let every man be fully persuaded in his own mind." This is how we are to serve the Lord. We are to be fully persuaded that we are serving Him because we want to and because we are eager to please Him. Again, in 1 Corinthians 9:16 Paul tells us, ". . . Woe is unto me, if I preach not the gospel!" Paul *wanted* to preach the Gospel.

Those three hundred men of Gideon that went down to the water did not lean over the edge and lap it up. They dipped their hands in the water and brought it up to their mouths, watching for the enemy. They said, "Where are those Midianites? We want to get them." This account is found in Judges 7:5–7. This is the kind of enthusiasm we need in the church today. We are bogged down with too many dead saints, and I mean they are dead before they are buried.

And they received of Moses all the offering, which the children of Israel had brought for the work of the service of the sanctuary, to make it withal. And they brought yet unto him free offerings every morning.

And all the wise men, that wrought all the work of the sanctuary, came every man from his work which they made:

And they spake unto Moses, saying, The people bring much more than enough for the service of the work, which the LORD commanded to make [Exod. 36: 3–5].

This is the only place on record, that I know of, where the people had to be asked to stop giving. They brought a great deal more than was needed to build and furnish the tabernacle. I have never seen an offering like this in my ministry! Nor have I ever heard of an offering like this before or after.

And Moses gave commandment, and they caused it to be proclaimed throughout the camp, saying, Let neither man nor woman make any more work for the offering of the sanctuary. So the people were restrained from bringing [Exod. 36:6].

The people are urged not to give, and they have to be restrained and told that they have brought enough. This is really amazing in the light of the fact that these people were fresh out of slavery. They had never owned anything before and now that they had riches you would think they would not be so willing to give it away. But they give liberally, joyfully, and enthusiastically to their God. Whatever you do for God, this is the way you should do it. That is the way God wants it done.

God wants us to give joyfully. There was a motto years ago that said, "Give 'til it hurts." God says, "If it hurts, don't give." Our worship of God should be with joy, and so should our giving.

It seems in this chapter that we are going over the different articles and part of the tabernacle again. It sounds like repetition, but before we were given the blueprint for the tabernacle, and now we come to the execution of the job. We not only need a blueprint and materials, but we need to go to work. The people of Israel are beginning the work in this chapter.

And every wise-hearted man among them that wrought the work of the tabernacle made ten curtains of fine twined linen, and blue, and purple, and scarlet: with cherubims of cunning work made he them [Exod. 36:8].

This was the covering of all the tabernacle. It was the covering that went on first the articles of furniture when they went out on the wilderness march. It was the fence outside. This fine twined Egyptian linen speaks of the righteousness of Christ. It speaks of His character and His work. It speaks of the righteousness that He provides for us so that we might be clothed to stand in God's presence. The important thing to notice is that Christ is adequate to meet our needs. He is able to save us. He is able to deliver us. He is able to keep us.

The curtains of goats' hair, the covering of rams' skins and the boards and sockets also speak of the person of Christ in one way or another. Now the tabernacle was thirty cubits long by ten cubits wide by ten cubits high. It was made of acacia wood, and the boards were overlaid with gold all the way around. The boards were one and one-half cubits wide. On the wilderness march they were very heavy to carry and were carried in wagons. (However all of the articles of furniture were carried on the shoulders of the priests of the tribe of Levi.) The golden boards were to be placed upright but each one had certain sockets that fitted down into sockets of silver, and the entire tabernacle rested upon silver—silver typifies redemption. The tabernacle was held together by bars. Certain rings were put in each board, and when it was set up, these bars slipped through the rings and bound the tabernacle together. It was a very compact building.

The tabernacle had an inner veil that separated the main tabernacle into two compartments; the smaller compartment was called the Holy of Holies and the larger compartment was called the Holy Place. Everything in the tabernacle pictured some part of the person or work of the Lord Jesus Christ.

CHAPTER 37

THEME: *The plan of the tabernacle*

Everything mentioned in this chapter has been dealt with in previous chapters in the Book of Exodus. Rather than repeating the Scriptures which have been quoted in previous chapters, I will recap some of the highlights and the things which I feel are of primary importance.

The two articles of furniture in the outer court were the brazen altar and the laver. When you stepped inside the Holy Place, there were three articles of furniture: the golden lampstand, the table of showbread, and the altar of incense. In the Holy of Holies was the ark of the covenant and the mercy seat.

There were three compartments to the tabernacle. And there were three entrances to the tabernacle. (1) There was a gate through the linen fence that surrounded the tabernacle. (2) There was an entrance which led into the Holy Place. (3) The third entrance led into the

Holy of Holies, where only the high priest went once a year on the great Day of Atonement (as we shall see in Leviticus) and sprinkled blood on the mercy seat—which is what made it a *mercy* seat.

There were seven articles of furniture arranged in such a way as to give us a wonderful picture. The brazen altar speaks of the cross of Christ where we receive forgiveness of sin. The laver speaks of the fact that Christ washes or cleanses those who are His own. The laver is where we confess our sins, and receive his forgiveness and cleansing.

The Holy Place is the place of worship. In it is the golden lampstand typifying Christ, the Light of the World. The table of showbread pictures Christ as the Bread of Life upon which we feed. The altar of incense is the place of prayer. It speaks of the fact that Christ is our Intercessor. In the Epistle to the Hebrews the

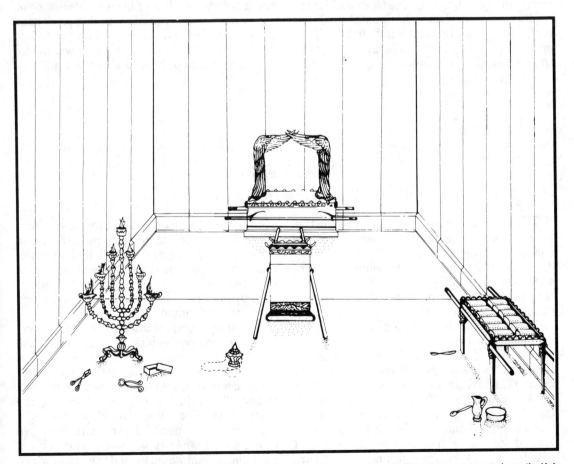

The artist, George Howell, has sketched the tabernacle interior without the separating veil. The rear compartment shows the Holy of Holies which housed the ark of the covenant. The front compartment pictures the Holy Place in which were the lampstand, the altar of incense, and the table of showbread.

altar of incense is placed in the Holy of Holies (rather than in the Holy Place) because our Intercessor is now in heaven. But the altar of incense is outside in the Holy Place also where you and I can come today. When believers want to worship God, they come into the Holy Place. Confession, praise, thanksgiving, intercession, making requests—these are the things that have to do with worship. And all of this is in the Holy Place. If you want the light which the world gives, you go outside, but if you want light from the lampstand, you must come inside. In order to serve Christ you cannot walk by the wisdom of the world but by the light of the Word of God.

The Holy of Holies pictures Jesus Christ in the presence of God. In the Book of Hebrews we are told to come to the throne of grace. The mercy seat pictures this, and this is where we find grace to help and mercy in time of need. There is a mercy seat for believers in heaven.

When Christ came to earth, He not only fulfilled the picture of the tabernacle, He did something quite unusual. The tabernacle in the wilderness was always horizontal with the earth. It was set up on the flat surface of the ground, with its pillars and boards fitting into the sockets they put down. But when Christ came to pay the price for our sins, He made the tabernacle perpendicular. The cross was the brazen altar where the Lamb of God was offered for our sins. He died down here to save us. But He returned to heaven where He lives today to keep us saved. The Holy of Holies is in heaven today. We do not go horizontally to God by going to a building or to a man, but we look to heaven and go directly to Him—through Jesus Christ. "For there is one God, and one mediator between God and men, the man Christ Jesus" (1 Tim. 2:5).

Where are you today, friend, in relation to the tabernacle? Do you need to stand at the brazen altar and be saved? There are many folk—even church members—who need to go there. Are you a soiled Christian who needs to confess your sins at the laver and be cleansed? Or are you walking in darkness today? Step inside the Holy Place and walk by the light of the golden lampstand. Maybe your spiritual life is a little anemic, and you need to feed on the Bread of Life to gain nourishment. Maybe your prayer life is beggarly and you need to stand before the altar of incense. Perhaps you are in trouble and you need mercy, grace, and help. Well, there is a mercy seat for you today. Go there and accept the help that is waiting for you. God wants to bless and guide you.

CHAPTER 38

THEME: The plan of the tabernacle—continued

We are still looking at the tabernacle in this chapter. Beginning at chapter 25, the blueprint for the tabernacle was given in every detail. Now Bezaleel and his helpers are constructing the building. In fact, by chapter 38 the tabernacle has been constructed, as I understand it, but has not yet been set in order. This chapter pays particular attention to the outer court.

As we shall see in the Book of Numbers, Israel traveled when the pillar of cloud started moving. The ark on the shoulders of the priests led the procession. When the cloud rested, Israel set up camp. The ark was put down on the desert sand and the tabernacle was set up around it. The siding of the gold-covered boards was put in place around it, the bars were slipped through the rings of the boards, and that bound the tabernacle together. Then over the boards were placed four coverings; the linen, goats' skins dyed red, the rams' skins, and the badger or sealskins for protection. The beauty of the tabernacle had to be seen from within. Everything in it spoke of worship, praise, adoration to God, and blessing to the individual.

The outer court, enclosed by the linen fence, was one hundred cubits by fifty cubits and contained the brazen altar and laver. This is where the sin question was settled. The sinner would come to the gate and stand there as a sinner. The priest would lead him into the outer court. The sinner would put his right hand upon the head of the animal he had brought—whether it be lamb, goat, or ox. Then the animal was slain and the priest would offer it on the altar. That was as far as the individual went; from then on he went in the person of his priest. The priest had to stop at the laver and wash so that he could enter the Holy Place. In the Holy Place were three articles of furniture: the golden lampstand, the table of showbread, and the altar of incense, all of which spoke of worship. Next came the veil which separated the Holy Place from the Holy of Holies, and the priest did not dare go beyond that. He did not go into the Holy of Holies, where were the ark of the covenant and the mercy seat, because only the high priest entered this room and only once a year in behalf of the nation.

And he made the altar of burnt offering of shittim wood: five cubits was the length thereof, and five cubits the breadth thereof; it was foursquare; and three cubits the height thereof [Exod. 38:1].

On the brazen altar the victim was offered and sin was judged. It was here the individual or the nation came to take care of the sin problem. When this altar was constructed, no other altar could be made. This was *the* approach to God and any other altar built anywhere else would have been blasphemy. It was in the place of prominence because the sin question was settled here. There could be no such thing as worship or blessing until one had come to the brazen altar.

The horns on the altar speak of strength— the ability of Jesus Christ to save. There are many instructions and details about the approach and care of this altar. There had to be certain pots, pans, staves and rings, etc. The important thing to remember, however, is its function of settling the sin problem.

And he made the laver of brass, and the foot of it of brass, of the looking glasses of the women assembling, which assembled at the door of the tabernacle of the congregation [Exod. 38:8].

The mirrors spoken of here were made of brass which was highly polished. Women have not changed; they carried mirrors in that day, too. The laver was made from these mirrors. The mirror represents the Word of God. It is the Bible that shows the believer his need for cleansing. The laver was there for cleansing. We have the same thing in our bathrooms today. We have a mirror, and beneath the mirror is a wash basin. The mirror does not wash the dirt off, and neither can the Law save you. You can rub up against it all you want to but the dirt remains. However, "there is a fountain filled with blood, drawn from Immanuel's veins, and

sinners plunged beneath that flood lose all their guilty stains."

And he made the court: on the south side southward the hangings of the court were of fine twined linen, an hundred cubits:

Their pillars were twenty, and their brasen sockets twenty; the hooks of the pillars and their fillets were of silver.

And for the north side the hangings were an hundred cubits, their pillars were twenty, and their sockets of brass twenty; the hooks of the pillars and their fillets of silver [Exod. 38:9–11].

The fine twined linen speaks of the humanity of Christ, and it actually separated man from God.

I was greatly disturbed at this Easter season when someone handed me an article concerning a message that a so-called conservative president of a seminary gave at one of these "knife and fork" clubs. I had spoken at this club years ago. It was reported that this preacher said that all we had to do was follow the teachings of Jesus and peace would come to the world—even if you denied the deity of Christ. Well, that just is not true. There can be no peace for man apart from the shed blood of Christ. That linen fence, which pictured the humanity of Christ, shut man out from God. The *life* of Christ does not save us; it condemns us! It is the death of Christ that saves us. When we have preachers that pretend to be conservative giving a message like that, no wonder there is so much confusion in the world today! The Word of God, and especially the tabernacle, is like a picture book. If you just look at the picture you can understand that the life and teachings of Christ cannot save you. To begin with, you could not measure up to His life or His teachings. Nonsense to the contrary has been ground out by liberalism for years and has gotten us into the difficulty we are in today. It is time that someone puts it right on the line and tells the truth. The teachings of Christ cannot save you, friends. The death of Christ on the cross saves you. That is the reason the brazen altar was there. The white linen fence shut out man from God, and God from man. Although the sockets for the tabernacle proper were silver, the sockets for the fence were brass. Brass, as we have already seen, is the metal of judgment. The picture of Christ in Revelation 1:15 speaks of his feet like "fine brass." I tell you, friend, that sin has to be judged. Man must recognize that he is a sinner. He cannot come into God's presence until the sin question is settled.

The hooks of the pillars and the fillets were of silver, however, and silver is the metal of redemption. The fence of the outer court kept man out, but God made a way for him to enter. He found a way to judge sin and provided a redemption for man that he might be clothed in the righteousness of Christ. What a picture! You can look at the tabernacle and get the gospel. God has given it to us in picture form.

There was an entrance to the court. Man did not climb over the fence. He had to come in through the gate.

And the hanging for the gate of the court was needle work, of blue, and purple, and scarlet, and fine twined linen: and twenty cubits was the length, and the height in the breadth was five cubits, answerable to the hangings of the court [Exod. 38:18].

All of the material and color speaks of the person of Christ. We have been through this before, but it will not hurt to repeat. Blue speaks of the fact that He came from heaven as deity. The scarlet speaks of His humanity and the blood He shed for mankind. The blue and scarlet combined make purple which speaks of His royalty. He was born King of the Jews.

The gate was as high as the fence was on the outside. It was about seven and one-half feet and that would be pretty hard even for a basketball player to look over. There was no way to get into the court except through this entrance. It was a wide entrance, wide enough for any sinner to enter, but it was the *only* way one could enter. Christ has said that He is the *way*, the *truth*, and the *life*. I like to think of the gate into the court as being the *way*.

The next of the three entrances that would bring one into the very presence of God, is the entrance into the Holy Place. I like to think of that as being "the truth." Christ also said that if you are going to worship God, you will have to worship Him in spirit and in *truth*. I do not mean to be harsh, but "worship" in a church that denies who Christ is and what He has done is not true worship. You have to worship Him in truth. You cannot deny the deity of Christ and the fact that He died for you and still worship Him. It would be best for a lot of people if they did not go to church (that is, to certain churches) at all. Their own condition is not good, and the church they are attending is insulting the Lord Jesus Christ by denying His deity.

Then the final entrance which brought one

into the very Holy of Holies was the entrance through the veil which speaks of the life Christ gave up on the cross. When He died, that veil was torn in two from the top to the bottom, signifying that the way to God was now open. That is *life*. Christ is the *way*, the *truth*, and the *life*. No one comes into the presence of the Father but by Him (John 14:6).

Next I want to call your attention to the question of the individual Israelite. The nation Israel is called a "son." God never called the individual Israelite, son. The question was, and is today, "Who is a Jew?" Is a Jew one who has been born a Jew or does his religion make him a Jew? In the Old Testament you had to be born a Jew to be one. And God made a provision that everyone had to be redeemed, which means that each individual had to be a born again one. Israel was a chosen nation, but each individual had to be redeemed.

And the silver of them that were numbered of the congregation was an hundred talents, and a thousand seven hundred and threescore and fifteen shekels, after the shekel of the sanctuary:

A bekah for every man, that is, half a shekel, after the shekel of the sanctuary, for every one that went to be numbered, from twenty years old and upward, for six hundred thousand and three thousand and five hundred and fifty men [Exod. 38:25–26].

The Jews brought silver because it was the metal of redemption. Every Israelite had to be redeemed to be acceptable. We have been redeemed by the precious blood of Christ which is more precious than silver or gold. Now, every individual Israelite was not saved. Only a remnant of the nation was saved, just as not all church members are saved.

A very small percentage of church members today are saved. A wealthy man in Tulsa, Oklahoma, told me that for a long time he and his wife "played" church. "We sat down with the rest of the hypocrites. None of us were born again; we just put up a front. Before the sun went down we were all drunk." Being a church member doesn't mean very much in these days in which we live. You have to be redeemed. And the children of Israel had to be redeemed.

And of the hundred talents of silver were cast the sockets of the sanctuary, and the sockets of the veil; an hundred sock-

ets of the hundred talents, a talent for a socket [Exod. 38:27].

The sockets were made out of the redemption money. This is where the tabernacle proper was placed. It rested upon silver. It rested upon redemption. Every individual will have to personally accept the redemption that is in Christ Jesus. You have to pay the redemption price. What is it? Well, it is not silver or gold. The only condition is that you must be thirsty. Would you like to have a drink of the water of life? It is free. Salvation is free, but it is not cheap. It cost God everything. He gave His Son to die on the cross and to pay the price of our redemption. We are redeemed by His blood.

In the wilderness, redemption was forced upon the nation of Israel. But when they got into the land, if they wanted to be numbered with the redeemed, they had to pay the price of redemption. Thank God it has already been paid for *us*. It does not cost any money. It does not have any price—but you must be thirsty for it. Do you want to be saved? Do you recognize that you have a need, that you are a sinner? Then come. The price has been paid. Christ has shed His precious blood for you. It enables you to come to God and to be accepted by Him through Christ.

CHAPTER 39

THEME: *The holy garments of the high priest*

A aron was the high priest, and the garments he wore all spoke of the person of Christ. We have already been given the pattern for these garments.

And of the blue, and purple, and scarlet, they made cloths of service, to do service in the holy place, and made the holy garments for Aaron; as the LORD commanded Moses.

And he made the ephod of gold, blue, and purple, and scarlet, and fine twined linen [Exod. 39:1–2].

These garments are called "holy" because they are set apart for the service of God.

And the curious girdle of his ephod, that was upon it, was of the same, according to the work thereof; of gold, blue, and purple, and scarlet, and fine twined linen; as the LORD commanded Moses [Exod. 39:5].

It was "curious" in the sense that it was woven in an unusual way. There were eight articles of clothing worn by the high priest. Four were the same or similar to those worn by all the priests. Four were peculiar to him and separated him from the other priests; they were "garments for glory and for beauty." This is a picture of our great High Priest, the Lord Jesus Christ, in all His extraordinary graces and glory. Each article of clothing was symbolic.

On the great Day of Atonement when Aaron took the blood into the Holy of Holies, he laid aside all of his garments of beauty and glory and wore only the simple linen garments that the other priests wore. He must be unadorned but pure.

The white linen that the priests wore speaks of righteousness. Isaiah 52:11 says, "Depart ye, depart ye, go ye out from thence, touch no unclean thing; go ye out of the midst of her; be ye clean, that bear the vessels of the LORD." God still says this. I do not believe that God uses a sinful preacher, teacher, or layman, no matter how prominent or talented he may be. They are doing nothing for God because He will not accept their work. They are building with wood, hay, and stubble. We must be clothed with the righteousness of Christ and then live a life to back it up. This is one lesson taught in these basic garments.

It is interesting to note that when Aaron went into the Holy of Holies to offer the sacrifice for the sin of the people, he laid aside his garments of glory and beauty. When the Lord Jesus came to earth, He did not lay aside His deity, but He did lay aside the garments of glory and beauty—that is, He laid aside His prerogatives as God. He laid aside the shekinah glory and came to earth as a human being; He was born a baby. Man was looking for a king, not a baby. Then He offered Himself as a sacrifice for sin. He died in His humanity.

To say that *God* died on the cross is not quite

accurate. I wonder what they mean by "death." When Jesus Christ died on the cross, He was separated from God, that is true. There was a rift in the Godhead, to be sure, when Christ was made sin for us who knew no sin (2 Cor. 5:21). But even at that moment, God was in Christ, reconciling the world unto Himself (2 Cor. 5:19). This is a mystery, friends, that I cannot penetrate. I have read the works of many theologians and have found that they have not penetrated it either.

These garments of beauty and glory were really lovely. The high priest was richly attired and colorful. He wore the ephod which had two stones, one on each shoulder, with six of the names of the tribes engraved on one stone and six on the other, which speaks of the strength and ability of our Lord, that great Shepherd of the sheep. When one sheep gets lost, our Great Savior finds it, puts it on His shoulders and brings it back. Thank God that we have a Shepherd who can put us on His shoulders and bring us safely back to the fold. He is able to save to the uttermost all who come unto God through Him (Heb. 7:25).

The high priest also wore a breastplate which was somewhat like a vest. It had twelve stones on it, and it was a thing of great beauty. Possibly it had some sort of pocket where the Urim and Thummim were placed. The Urim and Thummim had something to do with prediction. We are not told how it worked. The beautiful stones on the breastplate speak of the fact that Christ carries us on His heart today. He loves us. "For God so loved the world, that He gave his only begotten Son, that whosoever believeth in him should not perish, but have everlasting life" (John 3:16). These stones depict His great love for us.

Now on the robe of the ephod were the golden bells and pomegranates so that when the high priest was serving, those bells could be heard ringing as he went into the Holy Place. The pomegranates speak of the fruitful life of the believer. The bells speak of the testimony of that life. When the priest was in the Holy Place, the Israelites could say, "Well, he is in there, in the place of worship, serving for us. We know he is there because we can hear the bells." That is what worship should mean to us, friend. Our high priest is representing us in God's presence. It ought to draw us to the person of Christ.

I used to have an elder in one of my churches when I was a young man who was a great encouragement to me. He was a wonderful man of God and he would come to me on Sunday morning and say, "Well, you rang the bell today." If you want to know the truth, I really did not. I preached some lousy sermons in those days but his point was, because he was a student of the Bible, that he was able to come into the presence of Christ through the preaching of the Word of God.

To hear the bells of the high priest was a wonderful experience. What a picture the garments of the priest give! The mitre on his head said, "HOLINESS UNTO THE LORD." This speaks of holiness and has to do with the inner life, but the important thing is that it means the high priest is wholly given to the work of the ministry. *Holy* means anything that is set aside for the use of God.

There is something I would like to say to preachers today. I have been a preacher for a long time now and I know there are a great many people who want a preacher to do everything under the sun. They want him to socialize, backslap, hold hands, be nursemaid, as well as preach. No wonder many preachers have nervous breakdowns. Many preachers are nothing more than wet nurses for a lot of little babies in Christ. They go around burping them all the time. The preacher who stands in the pulpit today ought to be able to wear the mitre "HOLINESS UNTO THE LORD." That is, he should have time to prepare a message. He should have time to spend before God in prayer. I am amazed at the number of people who invite the preacher out on a Saturday night. That should be his day for meditation and preparation. I once had an elder say to me, "Vernon, I appreciate your coming to see me, but I will tell you what I would like you to do. I would like you to spend time preparing a message instead of visiting me. Business is difficult today, and I get weary and discouraged. When I come to church on Sunday, I want to hear something that comes from God. I need help and I hope you will spend Saturday preparing so that I will be able to hear from heaven on Sunday morning and evening."

I think he had a right to say that. My friend, we need to recognize the fact that preachers ought to wear the mitre. Without it, our ministry for the Lord will not be effective.

CHAPTER 40

THEME: *The tabernacle erected and filled with the shekinah glory*

In this chapter the tabernacle is set up. I want to deal with only one thing because we have already dealt with every article of furniture and the garments of the priest. When Moses had the tabernacle set up in the camp of Israel, an amazing thing happened.

Then a cloud covered the tent of the congregation, and the glory of the LORD filled the tabernacle.

And Moses was not able to enter into the tent of the congregation, because the cloud abode thereon, and the glory of the LORD filled the tabernacle.

And when the cloud was taken up from over the tabernacle, the children of Israel went onward in all their journeys:

But if the cloud were not taken up, then they journeyed not till the day that it was taken up.

For the cloud of the LORD was upon the tabernacle by day, and fire was on it by night, in the sight of all the house of Israel, throughout all their journeys [Exod. 40:34–38].

When the apostle Paul attempts to identify the Israelites in the Book of Romans, he enumerates several things that set them apart from other peoples. One was the *shekinah* glory (Rom. 9:4). The Israelites were the only people to ever have the glory of God, the visible presence of God. That is what led them through the great and terrible wilderness. The cloud would lift in the morning if they were to journey that day. If it did not lift, the children of Israel stayed in the camp. They did not attempt to move that day. They never moved by their own wisdom or judgment. They did not vote on whether or not they should move, and Moses did not make the decision—the cloud did!

We sometimes say in our churches that Christ is the Head of the church. How about your church? Is He the Head of *your* church? Are we following the cloud today or do we put a man on the church board because he is a successful businessman? You hear people say today, "I want to talk to my preacher about this problem. I want him to tell me what to do." We who are pastors are not experts at telling people what they should do. We cannot solve everyone's marital problems. But there is a pillar of cloud today although most people do not see it. It is the Holy Spirit of God. He ought to be the One to lead us and guide us. Oh, how He is neglected! We are always appealing to someone human or something outside of God for help. But we need preachers, teachers, and laymen who are filled with the *Spirit* of God. Our churches need leaders who pay attention to the Word of God, and who want to do the will of God. There is no visible cloud over the church today, but the Holy Spirit of God wants to lead and guide us.

This concludes our studies in the Book of Exodus. It opened in the gloom of the brickyards of Egypt, and it closed in the glorious presence of the Lord in the tabernacle. It was His presence that led them through the wilderness. God wants to deliver you from the gloom of the slavery of sin and to bring you into the glory of His presence and into the very center of His will where He can lead and guide you. What a wonderful book is Exodus!

BIBLIOGRAPHY

Borland, James A. *Christ in the Old Testament*. Chicago, Illinois: Moody Press, 1978.

Davis, John J. *Moses and the Gods of Egypt*. Grand Rapids, Michigan: Baker Book House, 1971.

Epp, Theodore H. *Moses*, Lincoln, Nebraska: Back to the Bible Broadcast, 1975.

Gaebelein, Arno C. *Annotated Bible*. Vol. I. Neptune, New Jersey: Loizeaux Brothers, 1917.

Grant, F. W. *Numerical Bible*. Neptune, New Jersey: Loizeaux Brothers, 1891.

Gray, James M. *Synthetic Bible Studies*. Westwood, New Jersey: Fleming H. Revell Company, 1906.

Jensen, Irving L. *Exodus*. Chicago, Illinois: Moody Press, 1967.

Mackintosh, C. H. (C.H.M.). *Notes on the Pentateuch*. Neptune, New Jersey: Loizeaux Brothers, 1880.

McGee, J. Vernon. *The Tabernacle, God's Portrait of Christ*. Pasadena, California: Thru the Bible Books.

Meyer, F. B. *Exodus*. Grand Rapids, Michigan: Kregel Publications, 1952.

Meyer, F. B. *Moses: The Servant of God*. Fort Washington, Pennsylvania: Christian Literature Crusade, n.d.,

Morgan, G. Campbell. *The Unfolding Message of the Bible*. Old Tappan, New Jersey: Fleming H. Revell Company.

Pink, Arthur W. *Gleanings in Exodus*. Chicago, Illinois: Moody Press, 1922.

Ridout, Samuel. *Lectures on the Tabernacle*. Neptune, New Jersey: Loizeaux Brothers, 1914.

Thomas, W. H. Griffith. *Through the Pentateuch Chapter by Chapter*. Grand Rapids, Michigan: William B. Eerdmans Company, 1957.

Unger, Merrill F. *Unger's Bible Handbook*. Chicago, Illinois: Moody Press, 1966.

Vos, Howard F. *Beginnings in the Old Testament*. Chicago, Illinois: Moody Press, 1975.

The Book of
LEVITICUS
INTRODUCTION

Many years ago, I read a statement by Dr. S. H. Kellogg saying that he considered the Book of Leviticus the most important book in the Bible. I felt that he must have had his tongue in cheek to make a statement like that. Then I heard a great preacher in Memphis, Tennessee, Dr. Albert C. Dudley, say that he considered the Book of Leviticus the greatest book in the Bible.

Several years ago I made an experiment on our radio program, and actually I didn't know what would happen as I began teaching this book. I wanted to study it and I wanted to see if it was such a great book, and I must confess that I had misgivings as to the value of Leviticus for a popular exposition on the Bible. However, I discovered that it is a thrilling book, and not only that, but I can now honestly say that I consider the Book of Leviticus one of the most important books of the Bible. If it were possible for me to get the message of this book into the hearts of all people who are trying to be religious, all cults and "isms" would end. A knowledge of the Book of Leviticus would accomplish that.

The Book of Leviticus was written by Moses. It is a part of the Pentateuch, the first five books of the Bible.

In the Book of Leviticus, the children of Israel were marking time at Mount Sinai. The book opens and closes at the same geographical spot, Mount Sinai, where God gave the Law. You will remember that Exodus concluded with the construction of the tabernacle according to God's instructions and then the filling of the tabernacle with the glory of the Lord. Leviticus continues by giving the order and rules of worship in the tabernacle. Leviticus is the great book on worship.

The book opens with the Hebrew word *Va-yick-rah*, which means "and He called." God has now moved to the tabernacle and speaks from there; He no longer speaks from Mount Sinai. He calls the people to meet with Him at the tabernacle. He tells them how they are to come and how they are to walk before Him. The exact meaning of the church, the *ekklesia*, is the "called out ones." We are also those who have been called out. In that day, God spoke from the tabernacle and asked them to come to Him. Today, the Lord Jesus calls us to Him-self. He says, "My sheep hear my voice" (John 10:27). So this book has a wonderful message for us today.

Leviticus is the book of worship. Sacrifice, ceremony, ritual, liturgy, instructions, washings, convocations, holy days, observances, conditions, and warnings crowd this book. All these physical exercises were given to teach spiritual truths. Paul wrote: "Now all these things happened unto them for ensamples: and they are written for our admonition, upon whom the ends of the world are come" (1 Cor. 10:11). In 1 Corinthians 10:6 he says, "Now these things were our examples . . .". "For whatsoever things were written aforetime were written for our learning, that we through patience and comfort of the scriptures might have hope" (Rom. 15:4).

Peter tells us that the Old Testament holds spiritual truths for us. "Of which salvation the prophets have inquired and searched diligently, who prophesied of the grace that should come unto you: Searching what, or what manner of time the Spirit of Christ which was in them did signify, when it testified beforehand the sufferings of Christ, and the glory that should follow. Unto whom it was revealed, that not unto themselves, but unto us they did minister the things, which are now reported unto you . . ." (1 Pet. 1:10–12). Hebrews 11:13 says, "These all died in faith, not having received the promises, but having seen them afar off, and were persuaded of them, and embraced them, and confessed that they were strangers and pilgrims on the earth."

Leviticus has some wonderful instruction for us today for it reveals Christ in a most remarkable manner. Tyndale, in his *Prologue into the Third Book of Moses*, said, "Though sacrifices and ceremonies can be no ground or foundation to build upon—that is, though we can prove nought with them—yet when we have once found Christ and his mysteries, then we may borrow figures, that is to say, allegories, similitudes, and examples, to open Christ, and the secrets of God hid in Christ, even unto the quick: and can declare them more lively and sensibly with them than with all the words of the world."

Worship for us today is no longer by ritual or in a specific place. You remember that the people of Israel had been going through ceremonies and they had their rituals, but Jesus said to the woman at the well in Samaria, ". . . Woman, believe me, the hour cometh, when ye shall neither in this mountain, nor yet at Jerusalem, worship the Father. Ye worship ye know not what: we know what we worship: for salvation is of the Jews. But the hour cometh, and now is, when the true worshippers shall worship the Father in spirit and in truth: for the Father seeketh such to worship him. God is a Spirit: and they that worship him must worship him in spirit and in truth" (John 4:21–24).

The keynote to the book is holiness unto Jehovah. The message of the book is twofold:

1. Leviticus teaches that the way to God is by sacrifice. The word *atonement* occurs 45 times in this book. Atonement means to "cover up." The blood of bulls and goats did not actually take away sin. It covered over sin until Christ came to take away all sins. This is what Paul is referring to in Romans 3:25: "Whom God hath set forth to be a propitiation through faith in his blood, to declare his righteousness for the remission of sins that are past, through the forbearance of God."

The sins that are past are the sins back in the Old Testament. You see, God never accepted the blood of bulls and goats as the final payment for sin, but He required that blood be shed. It was an atonement to *cover over* the sins until Christ came. In other words, God saved "on credit" in the Old Testament. When Christ came, as the hymn accurately states it, "Jesus paid it all." This is true as far as the past is concerned, and as far as the present is concerned, and as far as the future is concerned.

One of the key verses in Leviticus, dealing with atonement, is found in Leviticus 17:11, "For the life of the flesh is in the blood: and I have given it to you upon the altar to make an atonement for your souls: for it is the blood that maketh an atonement for the soul." The way to God is by sacrifice and without the shedding of blood, there is no remission of sins.

2. Leviticus teaches that the walk with God is by sanctification. The word *holiness* occurs 87 times in this book. "And ye shall be holy unto me: for I the LORD am holy, and have severed you from other people, that ye should be mine" (Lev. 20:26).

God gave strict laws governing the diet, social life, and daily details involving every physical aspect of the lives of His people. These laws have a greater spiritual application to His people today. That is the reason I think we ought to study Leviticus. You see, access to

God is secured for the sinner today through the shed blood of Christ. The writer to the Hebrews stated it this way: "Nor yet that he should offer himself often, as the high priest entereth into the holy place every year with blood of others; For then must he often have suffered since the foundation of the world: but now once in the end of the world [literally, end of the age] hath he appeared to put away sin by the sacrifice of himself" (Heb. 9:25–26).

Those who are redeemed by the blood of Christ must live a holy life if they are to enjoy and worship God. "Now the God of peace, that brought again from the dead our Lord Jesus, that great shepherd of the sheep, through the blood of the everlasting covenant, Make you perfect in every good work to do his will, working in you that which is well-pleasing in his sight, through Jesus Christ; to whom be glory for ever and ever. Amen" (Heb. 13:20–21).

Leviticus is a remarkable book, as the contents are considered in the light of the New Testament. This book is about as dull as anything possible could be to the average Christian and you won't find very many classes or individuals reading and studying the Book of Leviticus. Yet, it is a remarkable book.

1. The five offerings which open this book are clear, crystal-cut cameos of Christ. They depict His hypostatical person in depth and His death in detail (chapters 1–7).

2. The consecration of the priests reveals how shallow and inadequate is our thinking of Christian consecration (chapters 8–10).

3. The diet God provided for His people was sanitary and therapeutic, and contains much spiritual food for our souls (chapter 11).

4. Attention is given to motherhood and is a further example of God's thinking concerning womanhood (chapter 12).

5. The prominence given to leprosy and its treatment, in the heart of this book on worship, demands our attention. Why is there this extended section on leprosy? Those who have been given gracious insights into Scripture have found here a type of sin and its defiling effect on man in his relation to God. The cleansing of the leper finds its fulfillment in the death and resurrection of Christ as typified in a most unusual sacrifice of two birds (chapters 13–15). My friend if you and I would escape the defilement of sin in this world, we need to know a great deal about the death and resurrection of Christ and the application of it to our lives.

6. The great Day of Atonement is a full-length portrait of the sacrifice of Christ (chapter 16).

7. The importance of the burnt altar in the tabernacle, highlights the essential characteristic of the cross of Christ (chapter 17).

8. The emphasis in this book of instructions concerning seemingly minute details in the daily lives of God's people reveals how God intends the human family to be involved with Him (chapters 18–22). God wants to get involved in your business, in your family life, in your social life. My friend, let us beware lest we shut Him out of our lives.

9. The list of feasts furnishes a prophetic program of God's agenda for all time (chapter 23).

10. The laws governing the land of Palestine furnish an interpretation of its checkered history and an insight into its future prominence. There are a lot of prophecies in this book. The nation Israel and the Promised Land are intertwined and interwoven from here to eternity (chapters 24–27).

There is a relationship in the first three books of the Bible:

In Genesis we see man ruined.

In Exodus we see man redeemed.

In Leviticus we see man worshiping God.

We can also make a comparison and contrast between Exodus and Leviticus. In the Book of Exodus we see the offer of pardon; Leviticus offers purity. In Exodus we have God's approach to man; in Leviticus it is man's approach to God. In Exodus, Christ is the Savior; in Leviticus, He is the Sanctifier. In Exodus man's guilt is prominent; in Leviticus man's defilement is prominent. In Exodus, God speaks out of the mount; in Leviticus, He speaks out of the tabernacle. In Exodus man is made nigh to God; in Leviticus man is kept nigh to God.

OUTLINE

CHAPTER 1

THEME: *The burnt offering; regulations, ritual, and reason for the burnt sacrifice; the law of the burnt sacrifice*

This is the oldest offering known to man. It was the offering of Abel, Noah, and Abraham. All the offerings were made on the brazen altar but because the burnt offering was made there, the brazen altar is also called the burnt altar. It received its name from this sacrifice. This offering is recorded first of the five offerings because of its prominence and priority. This offering is a picture of Christ in depth as well as in death. A man cannot probe the full meaning of this offering because it sets before us what God sees in Christ. We can't see as much as He does. Here is a profound mystery that only the Holy Spirit can reveal.

The burnt offering shows the person of Christ. He is our substitute. Paul reveals this in Ephesians 5:2, "And walk in love, as Christ also hath loved us, and hath given himself for us an offering and a sacrifice to God for a sweet-smelling savour."

REGULATIONS
FOR THE BURNT SACRIFICE

And the LORD called unto Moses, and spake unto him out of the tabernacle of the congregation, saying [Lev. 1:1].

God called unto Moses out of the tabernacle. No longer is He speaking from the top of Mount Sinai in thunder and lightning, as when He gave the commandments. Here He calls to Moses from the tabernacle in reconciliation.

"And the LORD called"—His call is for those who will hear His voice. That is important to see. God is calling to men today to be reconciled to Him. The church is a called-out body, and they are the elect because they are called. "For the Jews require a sign, and the Greeks seek after wisdom: But we preach Christ crucified, unto the Jews a stumblingblock, and unto the Greeks foolishness; But unto them which are called, both Jews and Greeks, Christ the power of God, and the wisdom of God" (1 Cor. 1:22–24).

"Called" doesn't mean those who only hear; it means those who have heard and responded. I would like to ask you this question: Have you heard Him and have you responded to Him?

Speak unto the children of Israel, and say unto them, If any man of you bring an offering unto the LORD, ye shall bring your offering of the cattle, even of the herd, and of the flock [Lev. 1:2].

"If any man" means "whosoever will may come."

If his offering be a burnt sacrifice of the herd, let him offer a male without blemish: he shall offer it of his own voluntary will at the door of the tabernacle of the congregation before the LORD [Lev. 1:3].

"He shall offer it of his own voluntary will." May I say, this is free will with a vengeance. The Lord Jesus said, "If any man thirst, let him come . . . ." This is an all-inclusive invitation to the human family. None are excluded except those who exclude themselves. The Lord Jesus gives only one condition, "If any man thirst." You may say, "I don't thirst." Well, then maybe this isn't for you. But if you do thirst, He asks you to come to Him. He can satisfy you. Isaiah included this in his invitation, "Ho, every one that thirsteth, come ye to the waters . . ." (Isa. 55:1). Anyone can come to Christ if he chooses to come. There must be a need and a desire. If you have that, come!

Two types of animals were used for the burnt offering. Animals of the herd are cattle and of the flock are sheep. Wild animals that were animals of prey were excluded. Carnivorous animals were forbidden in all sacrifices. Animals that live by slaying other animals could never reveal Christ, who came to give His life a ransom for many.

A further restriction was that the animal must be a clean animal and it must be domesticated. It could not be taken in the hunt. Only that which was valuable and dear to the owner could be offered because it prefigures Christ. God spared not His own Son. Christ suffered on the cross, but the Father suffered in heaven. The final restriction reveals that the animal was one that was obedient to man. My, what a picture this is! Christ was the obedient servant. He came to minister and He was obedient unto death.

The burnt offering is the offering that is mentioned up to the time of Leviticus and it was the only offering that was made by those who wanted an approach to God. The burnt sacrifice is called *olah* in the Hebrew. It means "that which ascends." It is not irreverent to say that the burnt sacrifice went up in smoke. It was wholly consumed on the altar; nothing remained but the ashes. This reveals that the burnt offering is what God sees in Christ. Paul said in Ephesians 5:2 that Christ gave Himself ". . . an offering and a sacrifice to God for a sweet-smelling savour." Here in Leviticus 1 we find in verses 9, 13, and 17 that the sacrifice is "a sweet savour unto the LORD." This is what God sees in Christ. It may not be what you see in Him or what I see in Him. It is what God sees in Him, and that is the thing that is all-important. God is saying that He is satisfied with what Jesus did for your sins and for my sins. God is satisfied that Jesus has paid it all for you and that He can save you to the uttermost if you will put your trust in Him. The question is, "Are you satisfied with that?"

You will notice that it says the sacrifice is to be a male, and that speaks of strength. It speaks of the fact that the Lord Jesus is mighty to save, and that He is able to save to the uttermost (Heb. 7:25). Then, the sacrifice was to be without blemish which means the animal was to be ideally perfect. This speaks of the perfections of Christ. ". . . In him is no sin" (1 John 3:5). "Who did no sin . . ." (1 Pet. 2:22). ". . . Who knew no sin. . ." (2 Cor. 5:21). "Who is holy, harmless, undefiled, separate from sinners . . ." (Heb. 7:26). He is the beloved Son of whom the Father could say, ". . . I am well pleased" (Matt. 3:17).

He shall offer it of his own "voluntary will" is translated "that he may be accepted before Jehovah" in the American Standard Version of 1901. Because of the atoning death of the little animal, the sinner was received by God. The animal had to be offered, not in life, but in death. This was absolutely imperative. It is *not* the spotless life of Christ and our approval of Him that saves us. Only His death can save the sinner.

In the Gospels we find that when He died, the veil of the temple was torn in two. It was His death which opened the way to God; it was His death which saves the sinner. You see, the veil represents His flesh (Heb. 10:20). His perfect life shuts us out from God. What God demands is a life that is perfect like the life of Christ, and you and I can't reproduce it. His life is the standard. The Father could say concerning Jesus, ". . . This is my beloved Son, in whom I am well pleased" (Matt. 3:17). You and I just can't measure up to that. The life of Christ therefore cannot save us. It shuts us out from God, just as the veil shut man out from God in the tabernacle. We must have another basis on which we can come to God. That way is through the death of Christ. That is what tore the veil. The minute you and I come through the death of Christ, the way to God is open. It is the death of Christ that saves the sinner.

The offering was to be brought of his own voluntary will. You don't have to come to Christ. But if you want to be saved, then you will have to come to Christ. God has no other way. The Lord Jesus said, ". . . no man cometh unto the Father, but by me" (John 14:6). You may think that is dogmatic and narrow. I'll tell you something—it is! But the interesting thing is that it will bring you to God. Now, you don't have to come; that is where your free will enters in. You do not have to come, *but*, if you want to come to God, then you must come this one way because God has elected that this is the only way! You cannot come to God on the basis of your own "righteousness." He cannot accept your righteousness; He won't have any of it. "Not by works of righteousness which we have done, but according to his mercy he saved us . . ." (Titus 3:5).

"At the door of the tabernacle" is another imperative. They couldn't offer the sacrifice anywhere else. This was to keep Israel from idolatry. They were prone to lapse into idolatry again and again, and finally their idolatry was the reason for the Babylonian captivity. And this, by the way, has a message for us. It is to keep us from presuming that we can come to God *our* way, on *our* terms. We do not make the terms by which we come to God. God makes the terms, my friend. "But we are all as an unclean thing, and all our righteousnesses are as filthy rags . . ." (Isa. 64:6). God won't accept our righteousness. A great many people think that the righteousness of God is just a projection, on a little higher level, of the righteousness of man. Nothing of the kind! It is altogether holy! The *only* righteousness which God can accept is the righteousness of God which is through faith in Christ. You can't work for it. You can't buy it. God cannot accept our poor righteousness—it will simply go down the drain. The offering must be at the door of the tabernacle. Friends, there is no other way to come to God but His way. The Lord Jesus said, "No man cometh unto the Father, but by me."

And he shall put his hand upon the head of the burnt offering; and it shall be accepted for him to make atonement for him [Lev. 1:4].

"He shall put his hand upon the head of the burnt offering." Dr. Kellogg calls this "an act of designation." This is revealed in Leviticus 24:14 where the witnesses were to lay their hands on the blasphemer before he was stoned to death. Moses laid his hands on Joshua, designating him as his successor. Dr. Kellogg wrote a very fine book on Leviticus, which may be out of print now, but I would suggest you buy one if you can find it in a secondhand bookstore. Here is a quotation from it. He is speaking of the laying on of the hand upon the head of the animal, and he says, "It symbolized a transfer, according to God's merciful provision, of an obligation to suffer for sin, from the offerer to the innocent victim. Henceforth, the victim stood in the offerer's place, and was dealt with accordingly."

In other words, when the man went in and put his hand on the head of the little animal that was to be slain, he was designating this little animal to take his place. The man was confessing that he deserved to die. Friends, when you take Christ as your Savior, you are saying that you are a sinner and that you can't save yourself. You want to turn from your sins and you want to turn to the Savior and you want to live for Him. The little animal was dying a substitutionary death in the place of the offerer. That is what Christ did for us. When you accept Christ, you put your hand on Him; that is, you designate Him as your Savior.

People today seem to have the idea that there is some merit in the act of laying on of hands. They think there is some transfer of power. The only thing that can be transferred by laying on of hands is disease germs. But it does designate someone who is taking your place. When we as church leaders place our hands on a missionary, as the church in Antioch did to Paul and Barnabas, we are designating that one to go out in our place and as our representative.

Christ took our place. This is what it means when it says, ". . . He hath made him to be sin for us . . ." (2 Cor. 5:21) and "Who was delivered for our offences . . ." (Rom. 4:25).

The Hebrew here means to lay the hand so as to lean heavily upon another. "Thy wrath lieth hard upon me . . ." (Ps. 88:7). This part of the ceremony speaks of atonement and acceptance through the death of the victim— "it shall be accepted for him to make atonement for him."

We have said before that atonement means to cover, not to remove. "For it is not possible that the blood of bulls and of goats should take away sins" (Heb. 10:4). Only the Lamb of God can remove sin.

This offering was done publicly. He went down to the tabernacle, he walked to the side of the altar, and there he slew the little animal. It was a public act. A sinner needs to confess Christ publicly. By faith, we place our hand on Christ, but the public needs to know that we do it. I think this is primarily the meaning of baptism today. Baptism means "to be identified with." This is a public confession of being identified with Christ in His death and in His resurrection. This is the reason water baptism was so important in the early church.

THE RITUAL
FOR THE BURNT SACRIFICE

And he shall kill the bullock before the LORD: and the priests, Aaron's sons, shall bring the blood, and sprinkle the blood round about upon the altar that is by the door of the tabernacle of the congregation [Lev. 1:5].

Now we come to the ritual for the burnt offering. A proper offering having been chosen—that is, the right kind of animal—the sinner brings the victim to the entrance of the tabernacle where he is met by a priest. The sinner himself slays the victim. (There is an exception in verses 14, 15.) "For the wages of sin is death . . ." (Rom. 6:23). Here the innocent dies for the guilty. Just so, "Christ also hath once suffered for sins, the just for the unjust . . ." (1 Pet. 3:18).

Our sins put Jesus Christ to death. If you want it made very personal, *my* sin is responsible for the death of Christ; *your* sin is responsible for the death of Christ. I get a little weary of hearing people argue about who is responsible for the death of Christ. They indict the religious rulers, the nation Israel, or the Roman nation. My friend, people can argue all they wish; the fact is that if I hadn't been a sinner and if you hadn't been a sinner, nobody would have put Him to death. It was our sin that put Him to death!

Every sacrifice had to be slain. Either the sinner, or the priest acting for the nation, slew the victim. There was no forgiveness apart from the shed blood of the victim. So today, only the blood of Christ can cleanse us from all sin. After the slaying of the victim, the priest took over by sprinkling the blood about the altar. The blood represented life and the sprinkling presented it to God.

And he shall flay the burnt offering, and cut it into his pieces.

And the sons of Aaron the priest shall put fire upon the altar, and lay the wood in order upon the fire:

And the priests, Aaron's sons, shall lay the parts, the head, and the fat, in order

upon the wood that is on the fire which is upon the altar:

But his inwards and his legs shall he wash in water: and the priest shall burn all on the altar, to be a burnt sacrifice, an offering made by fire, of a sweet savour unto the LORD [Lev. 1:6–9].

Everything had to be done decently and in order. God is not the author of confusion. The offering was to be cut into pieces so that it might be exposed and so it could be more easily consumed by the fire. The inner life of the Lord Jesus has been open for inspection for over 1900 years. He has been examined more than any other person. There is more disagreement concerning Him than anyone else. This was true at the time He lived and it is still true today. He still asks the question, "Whom do men say that I the Son of man am?" There are all kinds of opinions today and some of them are blasphemous. Yet it is still true that He is "holy, harmless, undefiled, separate from sinners." Jesus Christ, who has been under examination all these years, is still the One who is altogether lovely.

And if his offering be of the flocks, namely, of the sheep, or of the goats, for a burnt sacrifice; he shall bring it a male without blemish.

And he shall kill it on the side of the altar northward before the LORD: and the priests, Aaron's sons, shall sprinkle his blood round about upon the altar.

And he shall cut it into his pieces, with his head and his fat: and the priest shall lay them in order on the wood that is on the fire which is upon the altar:

But he shall wash the inwards and the legs with water: and the priest shall bring it all, and burn it upon the altar: it is a burnt sacrifice, an offering made by fire, of a sweet savour unto the LORD [Lev. 1:10–13].

Notice again, the offering is cut in pieces and totally exposed.

Fire was to be used on the altar. The fire does not necessarily represent hell, vengeance, or wrath. I disagree with those who magnify that so much. Fire did not represent that at the burning bush. Fire oftentimes represents the purifying energy and the resistless power of God. "And he shall sit as a refiner and purifier of silver: and he shall purify the sons of

Levi, and purge them as gold and silver . . ." (Mal. 3:3). Fire is that resistless energy of God which sometimes destroys and sometimes cleanses and sometimes consumes. The *nature of the object* determines the process it will take.

Here in the burnt offering, it speaks of the total commitment of Christ to God. It is absolute consecration. In our experience this is essential also, if we are to worship God in spirit and in truth. "For the LORD thy God is a consuming fire, even a jealous God" (Deut. 4:24).

My friend, you cannot just play around and get very far with God. That is the reason there is so much that is phony in Christian service today. I want to say it kindly but emphatically—you are not serving God unless you are letting Him cleanse and purify your life. We have forgotten this matter of holiness today. How we need it in our churches and in our own lives!

And if the burnt sacrifice for his offering to the LORD be of fowls, then he shall bring his offering of turtledoves, or of young pigeons.

And the priest shall bring it unto the altar, and wring off his head, and burn it on the altar; and the blood thereof shall be wrung out at the side of the altar:

And he shall pluck away his crop with his feathers, and cast it beside the altar on the east part, by the place of the ashes [Lev. 1:14–16].

Poverty was no excuse for not bringing an offering to God. A bird could be substituted for an animal. Anyone could have a bird and offer it. Did you notice that when our Lord was born, His parents offered turtledoves? His parents were poor and He was born in poverty.

THE REASON
FOR THE BURNT SACRIFICE

And he shall cleave it with the wings thereof, but shall not divide it asunder: and the priest shall burn it upon the altar, upon the wood that is upon the fire: it is a burnt sacrifice, an offering made by fire, of a sweet savour unto the LORD [Lev. 1:17].

This is the third time it is mentioned that it is a sweet savor to the Lord. This makes it clear that this was the reason for the sacrifice. It is what God sees in Jesus Christ.

THE LAW
OF THE BURNT SACRIFICE

The law of the burnt offering is found in Leviticus 6:8–13. The morning and the evening offerings were burnt sacrifices offered by Aaron and the priests for the nation to God (Exod. 29:38–46). It was called the *continual* burnt offering. Christ in consecration *ever* lives to make intercession for us. This is most beautifully expressed in an ancient "Order for the Visitation of the Sick," attributed to Anselm of Canterbury:

"The minister shall say to the sick man: Dost thou believe that thou canst not be saved but by the death of Christ? The sick man answereth, Yes. Then let it be said unto him: Go to, then, and whilst thy soul abideth in thee, put all thy confidence in this death alone; place thy trust in no other thing; commit thyself wholly to this death; cover thyself wholly with this alone . . . And if God would judge thee, say: Lord! I place the death of our Lord Jesus Christ between me and Thy judgment; otherwise I will not contend or enter into judgment with Thee.

"And if He shall say unto thee that thou art a sinner, say: I place the death of our Lord Jesus Christ between me and my sins. If He shall say unto thee, that thou hast deserved damnation, say: Lord! I put the death of our Lord Jesus Christ between Thee and all my sins; and I offer His merits for my own, which I should have, and have not.

"And whosoever of us can thus speak, to him the promise speaks from out the shadows of the tent of meeting: 'This Christ, the Lamb of God, the true burnt offering, shall be accepted for thee, to make atonement for thee!' "

This is the law of the burnt offering. God is satisfied with Jesus and He sees us in Christ. He is satisfied, then, with us. "But now the righteousness of God without the law is manifested, being witnessed by the law and the prophets; Even the righteousness of God which is by faith of Jesus Christ unto all and upon all them that believe: for there is no difference: For all have sinned, and come short of the glory of God; Being justified freely by his grace through the redemption that is in Christ Jesus" (Rom. 3:21–24).

My friend, do you have the sacrifice of Christ between you and your sins? Has His blood been shed that *you* might live? Have you trusted Him today? God sees Christ as the only One who can satisfy Him for your sins. Have you seen Him like that? Are you still trying to bring your little puny self and your little goodness to offer to God? God won't take that. He only accepts what Christ has done for you and He counts the righteousness of Christ as your righteousness. Trust Him today and live!

CHAPTER 2

THEME: *Offerings mixed but unbaked; offerings mixed and baked; offering of firstfruits; the law of the meal offering*

The offerings speak of the person of Christ and of the work of Christ. The burnt offering was a picture of Christ in depth as well as in death. The meal offering reveals the humanity of Jesus in all its perfection and loveliness.

As you read this, you will see it is like a recipe for bread. That is exactly what it is. It is really the *meal* offering. The Authorized Version calls it a meat offering, which is a misleading term for us today, as no meat was connected with it at all. There is no shedding of blood; so this offering was different from the others. However, it was generally offered with some offering in which there was the shedding of blood. This meal offering could be offered either baked or unbaked. Aaron and his sons received a portion of this offering for themselves. It was to be eaten by all the males in the family of Aaron.

The meal or food offering sets forth the humanity of Jesus in all His perfections. His deity is not in view here. He was perfectly human, and He was the perfect human. God's goal for man is fulfilled in Jesus. He is the second man, but the last Adam. There will be no more Adams, but there will be some more men who are made just like Him. He is the last Adam, the Head of a new people. "Beloved, now are we the sons of God, and it doth not yet appear what we shall be: but we know that, when he shall appear, we shall be like him; for we shall see him as he is" (1 John 3:2).

Friends, man as he is in the world today is the most colossal failure in God's universe. Have you ever stopped to think about that? The Scriptures are outspoken and specific at this point. "They are all gone out of the way, [the original here suggests that they are a wreck] they are together become unprofitable . . ." and ". . . all have sinned, and come short of the glory of God" (Rom. 3:12 and 23).

God cannot save us on the basis of our keeping His Law for the very simple reason that God sees our imperfections. We cannot fulfill or keep the Law. We cannot render perfection to Him. God can't save us in our imperfections because He is a holy God and demands absolute righteousness and perfection. Imperfection is the very best that we can do. Therefore, mankind is a failure.

"The way of peace they have not known" is confirmed in every morning newspaper. Why is this? Because war and violence are in the very heart of man. It is almost amusing to hear about the peace demonstrations that end up in a *brawl*! With feverish energy man is presently trying to perfect fiendish instruments of frightful destruction. Surely this is not the goal of man!

God has another purpose in view for man and if you want to see what He has in mind, look at Jesus. Here is the Man who pleased God. There was a glory in His manhood. The loveliness of Jesus was truly a sweet perfume. His coming was a doxology; His stay was a blessing; His departure was a benediction. His winsomeness has filled the world with a new hope and ideal concerning man.

There are two important aspects of this offering: the ingredients which are included and the ingredients which are excluded.

OFFERINGS MIXED BUT UNBAKED

And when any will offer a meat offering unto the LORD, his offering shall be of fine flour; and he shall pour oil upon it, and put frankincense thereon [Lev. 2:1].

The offering was to be made of fine flour and fine flour in that day was a little unusual. They didn't have the great mills as we have today in Minneapolis. Actually, they ground it by hand in a kind of rock bowl. They used a pestle, with which they just beat the grain down. It was often very coarse and uneven if the grinder was careless or in a hurry. If the flour was to be very fine, it meant they must spend a great deal of time with it. This offering

had to be made of very fine flour which means that it was well beaten.

This sets before us the Lord Jesus in His personality. Today I am sure we would use the expression that He had a well-integrated personality. He was a normal person. Actually, I think He was the only normal person who has ever been on this earth. Sin has made all of the human race lumpy, one-sided, abnormal. One part of our personalities has overdeveloped at the expense of some other area of our personality.

In college I studied abnormal psychology. In my last year of college I went to see the professor of the department and said that I needed to talk to him. I told him that when we looked at the etiology of the disease of every form of abnormality that we had been studying, I found that I had symptoms of all these forms of abnormality. He broke out in laughter and said to me, "I was wondering when you would come. All the rest of the class has been here. They all have it, and I have it, too." You see, all of us do. Recently a leading psychologist made the statement that all of mankind today is a little "off." We are all just a little off-center. Jesus was the only normal person.

Notice how uneven were the characters of men in the Bible. Samson was enabled to perform great physical feats, but he seems to have been weak both in will and mind. In fact, he was a sissy. Paul was a mental giant, but he appeared to be weak in body. Simon Peter was moved by his emotions, even declaring that he would die for Jesus, yet he denied Him, which reveals a definite weakness in the area of the volition. King Saul was self-willed and stubborn, unable to bow the knee in obedience to God. This led to his dismissal and then to his death. All of these men were lumpy. They had over and underdeveloped personalities.

In contrast to them and all of us, Jesus was well balanced. He had equal poise in all areas of His personality. He could drive the money changers from the temple, and He could take the little children into His arms. When He was twelve years old, the religious rulers marvelled at His wisdom. When He began to teach, the people were amazed, saying, ". . . How knoweth this man letters, having never learned?" (John 7:15). Nevertheless, the Lord Jesus never appealed to His intellect as the basis for any judgment. Have you ever noticed that this was never the criterion for His conduct? He came to do the Father's will, and that was the motive for His actions.

Jesus could weep at the tomb of Lazarus or over the indifferent city of Jerusalem. At the same time, He would raise Lazarus from the dead, and He would pronounce a severe judgment on Jerusalem (which was literally fulfilled). He wasn't swayed or guided by His emotions. He was never self-willed, yet nothing could hinder Him from going to Jerusalem to die. At all times He could say, "Not as I will, but as thou wilt." "For I came down from heaven, not to do mine own will, but the will of him that sent me" (John 6:38). His own volitional nature was not the guideline for His action. He was even; all of us are lumpy.

"He shall pour oil upon it"—olive oil speaks of the Holy Spirit. You will notice that here it is "oil upon it." In verses 4 and 5 it is "mingled with oil"; in verse 6 it is "pour oil thereon"; in verse 7 it is "with oil." The offering was drenched with oil. The oil was a very important part of the offering and was applied in many different ways.

The prominence of the Holy Spirit in the human life of Jesus is very noticeable. He was born of the Spirit—"mingled with oil" (Luke 1:35). He was baptized of the Spirit—"oil upon it" (Matt. 3:16–17). He was led of the Spirit—"pour oil thereon" (Mark 1:12). He taught, performed miracles, and offered Himself in the power of the Holy Spirit—"with oil" (John 3:34; Matt. 12:28).

If the Lord Jesus in His perfect humanity needed the Holy Spirit, surely you and I need Him to an even greater extent. We can do nothing of ourselves.

Frankincense was made from a secret formula. It evidently was a form of incense with which it was mixed (Exod. 30:34), but was distinguished from it. It was made from some part of a plant or tree, perhaps the bark or leaves, and it exuded its fragrance only when crushed, beaten, burned, or put under pressure. This speaks of the life of the Lord Jesus as He manifested the fragrance of His life under the fires of tension, pressures, and persecution. This is what the Father saw in Him as the One in whom He delighted. There was a special fragrance about His life, and there should be a fragrance in our lives also, since we belong to Him.

And he shall bring it to Aaron's sons the priests: and he shall take thereout his handful of the flour thereof, and of the oil thereof, with all the frankincense thereof; and the priest shall burn the memorial of it upon the altar, to be an offering made by fire, of a sweet savour unto the LORD [Lev. 2:2].

The priests received a portion of the meal offering. They were to take out a percentage of each item. Apparently the remainder was mixed and then burnt upon the altar.

And the remnant of the meat offerings shall be Aaron's and his sons': it is a thing most holy of the offerings of the LORD made by fire [Lev. 2:3].

Emphasis is laid upon the fact that this offering was burnt upon the altar although no blood was shed in connection with it. Great emphasis is placed upon the fire (verses 2, 9, 16 and chapter 6:15, 17–18).

OFFERINGS MIXED AND BAKED

And if thou bring an oblation of a meat offering baken in the oven, it shall be unleavened cakes of fine flour mingled with oil, or unleavened wafers anointed with oil.

And if thy oblation be a meat offering baken in a pan, it shall be of fine flour unleavened, mingled with oil.

Thou shalt part it in pieces, and pour oil thereon: it is a meat offering.

And if thy oblation be a meat offering baken in the fryingpan, it shall be made of fine flour with oil.

And thou shalt bring the meat offering that is made of these things unto the LORD: and when it is presented unto the priest, he shall bring it unto the altar.

And the priest shall take from the meat offering a memorial thereof, and shall burn it upon the altar: it is an offering made by fire, of a sweet savour unto the LORD.

And that which is left of the meat offering shall be Aaron's and his sons': it is a thing most holy of the offerings of the LORD made by fire [Lev. 2:4–10].

These are detailed instructions for the ritual of the meal offering and it sounds, very frankly, like a recipe for making bread. The emphasis upon the fine flour and the oil is repeated again and again. Also, the fire is mentioned over and over. I want to say with great emphasis that the fire here does not symbolize hell under any circumstance. It is God's purifying energy and power which brought out the sweetness in the life of Christ.

In verse 9 it is specifically declared to be a "sweet savour unto the Lord." The final and full meaning of this offering is what God sees in

Christ. His sweetness came out under pressure. In your experience and mine sweetness doesn't always come out from us when we are under pressure. I've heard some Christians say some very ugly things when they were under tension. But as more tension was placed on Him, the sweeter He was. The Lord Jesus could say, "And he that sent me is with me: the Father hath not left me alone; for I do always those things that please him" (John 8:29).

What was left of the meal offering was to be Aaron's and his sons'. Believers have the high privilege of sharing Christ with God the Father. What do you see in Him? Is there sweetness about Him? Have you smelled the sweetness and fragrance of His life?

"Then Jesus said unto them, Verily, verily, I say unto you, Except ye eat the flesh of the Son of man, and drink his blood, ye have no life in you. Whoso eateth my flesh, and drinketh my blood, hath eternal life; and I will raise him up at the last day. For my flesh is meat indeed, and my blood is drink indeed. He that eateth my flesh, and drinketh my blood, dwelleth in me, and I in him. As the living Father hath sent me, and I live by the Father: so he that eateth me, even he shall live by me. This is that bread which came down from heaven: not as your fathers did eat manna, and are dead: he that eateth of this bread shall live for ever" (John 6:53–58). If you want any sweetness in your life, and if I want any, we must partake of Christ. Not literally, of course. We are not cannibals. We partake of Him by faith and we appropriate Him into our lives. As we partake of Him, the sweetness of His life should come into our lives.

No meat offering, which ye shall bring unto the Lord, shall be made with leaven: for ye shall burn no leaven, nor any honey, in any offering of the Lord made by fire [Lev. 2:11].

The ingredients excluded in this offering are as prominent as the ingredients included. The two mentioned here by name are leaven and honey.

Leaven will be mentioned in the Scriptures again and again. Leaven in Scripture is everywhere presented as a principle of evil. The Lord Jesus Christ warned His disciples of the leaven of the Pharisees. He was talking about the doctrine of the Pharisees, their teaching. That is the leaven. Evil teaching is the leaven. Leaven is the principle of evil. Leaven is to be excluded from the offering. This speaks of the fact that there is no evil in Christ. There is no sin in the life of Christ.

Honey was also excluded. It represents natural sweetness. It will sour, just as leaven is a souring thing. There are Christians who assume a pious pose in public. They wear a Sunday smile. They call everyone "brother" and "my dear so-and-so." Their halo is polished with the latest miracle cleanser. Yet these same folk can and do engage in vicious slander and malicious gossip. They are more dangerous than a killer with a gun. May I say to you that there are a lot of folk who have honey in their lives.

The Lord Jesus told it like it is, friends. There was no corrupting principle in the life of Jesus. He did not exhibit honey sweetness, nor was there any leaven in His speech that made it acceptable to the natural man.

As for the oblation of the firstfruits, ye shall offer them unto the Lord: but they shall not be burnt on the altar for a sweet savour [Lev. 2:12].

This offering was a sweet savor sacrifice, but it was not to derive its sweetness from the palatable ingredient of leaven nor the natural sweetness of honey.

And every oblation of thy meat offering shalt thou season with salt; neither shalt thou suffer the salt of the covenant of thy God to be lacking from thy meat offering: with all thine offerings thou shalt offer salt [Lev. 2:13].

Salt is the final ingredient which was included in the meal offering. Salt is a preservative and is the opposite of leaven. Leaven produces decay; salt preserves from corruption. "The salt of the covenant" is still eaten among Arabs as a seal to bind one in faithful obedience to a covenant.

Salt was the token of faithfulness between the offerer and God. Christ is faithful. This is one of His many-faceted names. He is Faithful and True (Rev. 19:11). He is the Lord Jesus.

Christ offered Himself to God. We can offer ourselves to God because of His mercy. We ought to be found faithful. Christians are to be the salt in the world. We do this by offering ourselves as a living sacrifice to God (Rom. 12:1–2).

OFFERING OF FIRSTFRUITS

And if thou offer a meat offering of thy firstfruits unto the Lord, thou shalt offer for the meat offering of thy first-

fruits green ears of corn dried by the fire, even corn beaten out of full ears.

And thou shalt put oil upon it, and lay frankincense thereon: it is a meat offering.

And the priest shall burn the memorial of it, part of the beaten corn thereof, and part of the oil thereof, with all the frankincense thereof: it is an offering made by fire unto the LORD [Lev. 2: 14–16].

The Feast of Firstfruits, as given in Leviticus 23:9–14, was a meal offering as well as the Feast of Pentecost.

THE LAW OF THE MEAL OFFERING

The law of the meal offering is given in Leviticus 6:14–23. It reveals that with every burnt sacrifice in the morning and in the evening, a meal offering was also made. (See Exod. 29:39–40.)

The meal offering sets forth Christ in His consecration. It also represents the consecration of believers in Christ. It pictures the perfect humanity of Christ.

CHAPTER 3

THEME: A sacrifice from the herd; a sacrifice from the flock; a sacrifice from the goats; the law of the peace offering

This offering speaks of the communion and fellowship of believers with God the Father through our Lord Jesus Christ. The only way you and I can come to God is through Jesus Christ. He is the Way!

No single offering can set forth the manifold wonders of the person of Christ and the many facets of His glory. Just as we need four Gospels in the New Testament to set forth His earthly life, so also we need the five offerings of Leviticus to set forth His person and work.

We will notice that there are striking similarities between the peace offering and the burnt offering but we will also note sharp contrast. So the peace offering is also a unique offering.

The peace offering does not speak of the peace that Christ made through His blood on the cross, as that has to do with sin and comes properly under the non-sweet savor offerings. It is concerning Christ being made our Peace as regards sin that Paul writes in Colossians 1:20–22: "And, having made peace through the blood of his cross, by him to reconcile all things unto himself; by him, I say, whether they be things in earth, or things in heaven. And you, that were sometime alienated and enemies in your mind by wicked works, yet now hath he reconciled In the body of his flesh through death, to present you holy and unblameable and unreproveable in his sight." That is not the peace offering.

Rather, the peace offering speaks more spe-

cifically of the peace to which Paul referred in Ephesians, the peace which brings all believers into communion with the Father by the Holy Spirit, through the Lord Jesus Christ. "But now in Christ Jesus ye who sometimes were far off are made nigh by the blood of Christ. For he is our peace, who hath made both one, and hath broken down the middle wall of partition between us; Having abolished in his flesh the enmity, even the law of commandments contained in ordinances; for to make in himself of twain one new man, so making peace; And that he might reconcile both unto God in one body by the cross, having slain the enmity thereby: And came and preached peace to you which were afar off, and to them that were nigh. For through him we both have access by one Spirit unto the Father. Now therefore ye are no more strangers and foreigners, but fellow-citizens with the saints, and of the household of God; And are built upon the foundation of the apostles and prophets, Jesus Christ himself being the chief corner stone; In whom all the building fitly framed together groweth unto an holy temple in the Lord: In whom ye also are builded together for an habitation of God through the Spirit" (Eph. 2:13–22).

In the peace offering, the emphasis is not upon the peace that He made by the blood of the cross, but upon the peace He *is* because of the blood of the cross. He is the meeting place of all believers together and of each believer with God the Father. Christ is the only one who can break down the walls that separate individuals, families, religions, races, and nations. All are made one in Christ. Then they become a habitation of God in the Spirit and have access to the Father. You see, only believers can join together in partaking of the wonders, the beauties, and the glories of Christ. They can have communion with the Father and fellowship one with another as they share the things of Christ.

This is what the apostle John is saying. "That which we have seen and heard declare we unto you, that ye also may have fellowship with us: and truly our fellowship is with the Father, and with his Son Jesus Christ" (1 John 1:3). The peace offering brings us together. It is only as we meet around the person of Christ that we can be drawn together. Friends, don't tell me to have fellowship with every Tom, Dick, and Harry! I cannot. But there is *nothing* that keeps me from fellowshipping with any person, I don't care who he is, *if* he can meet with me around the person of Christ. We are all made one there. We are all on the same level there. We can all enjoy the person of Christ.

A SACRIFICE FROM THE HERD

And if his oblation be a sacrifice of peace offering, if he offer it of the herd; whether it be a male or female, he shall offer it without blemish before the LORD [Lev. 3:1].

The peace offering is in one sense all comprehensive. The sinner can come to God because Christ made peace by the blood of His cross. There is also communion with God and fellowship with Him on the basis of peace by the blood of His cross. Christ and His work of redemption is the complete satisfaction for peace. The emphasis of the peace offering, however, is chiefly on the communion.

What is the Gospel appeal to the sinner? Well, it is like this. God says to you and me as sinners, "You are lost. You are alienated from Me, so I will have to consign you to the darkness of eternity." If God did that, He would be just and holy and all the angels in heaven would sing praises to His name. But, my friend, God is satisfied with what Jesus did for you and now you can come to God. The Gospel message is this: "God is reconciled!" The question is, "Will you be reconciled?" God is satisfied with what Jesus did. That is the message. That is the good news. God has already turned to you. Will you turn to Him? He will accept you because of what Christ has done. Will you be satisfied with Christ and what He has done, and will you come to God and have fellowship? That is the peace that you can know.

The peace offering is different from the burnt offering in several respects. In the burnt offering only a male could be offered: but here it can be either a male or female—but without blemish. The offerer will never find as much in Christ as God finds in Him. In the burnt offering it speaks of what God sees in Christ. In the peace offering it is the offerer who finds something in Christ. The female offering was permitted because here the capacity of the offerer to enjoy Christ is in view. The offerer will never find as much in Christ as God finds in Him.

And he shall lay his hand upon the head of his offering, and kill it at the door of the tabernacle of the congregation: and Aaron's sons the priests shall sprinkle the blood upon the altar round about [Lev. 3:2].

Up to this point, it duplicates the burnt offering.

And he shall offer of the sacrifice of the peace offering an offering made by fire unto the LORD; the fat that covereth the inwards, and all the fat that is upon the inwards.

And the two kidneys, and the fat that is on them, which is by the flanks, and the caul above the liver, with the kidneys, it shall he take away [Lev. 3:3–4].

Here the contrast with the burnt sacrifice is noted. *All* of the burnt offering was placed on that altar. In the peace offering, only a portion was offered. The portion was specified. It was to be the choice portion which included the fat and the inward parts. These speak of the hidden riches, the precious qualities, the priceless value of the character of Christ that God alone knows.

Sometimes a loved one knows the real worth of a great man who has been bitterly assailed in public. Early in my ministry, I became acquainted with a great preacher, and he and his family became my friends. An attack was made upon him, and harsh things were said about him. His family knew and I knew that they were lies. Just so, there are a lot of things said about Christ that are not true. A great many people say, "I don't understand this and I don't understand that about Christ." There is a lot I don't understand about Him either. But God knows Him! God sees more in Him than you and I can see. God sees the inward parts. We just don't know Him. That is why Paul cried out, "That I may know him, and the power of his resurrection, and the fellowship of his sufferings . . ." (Phil. 3:10).

And Aaron's sons shall burn it on the altar upon the burnt sacrifice, which is upon the wood that is on the fire: it is an offering made by fire, of a sweet savour unto the LORD [Lev. 3:5].

The offering was consumed by fire and this speaks of the total dedication of Christ and His human testing and sufferings. It is specifically labeled, "a sweet savour unto the LORD." The emphasis is still upon the person of Christ and not upon His work. It is His perfect life that is in view, not His death for sin. His sufferings in life were not for the sins of the world. Even in the first three hours on the cross, His suffering was at the hands of men. It was during the last three hours on the cross that it became an altar on which the Son of God was offered. Darkness veiled from the eye of man those last three hours when it pleased the Lord to bruise Him, when He put Him to grief, when He made His soul an offering for sin (Isa. 53:10).

Notice that the peace offering was put together with the burnt offering. They belong together in order to get the full view of the inward values and glories of Christ.

A SACRIFICE FROM THE FLOCK

And if his offering for a sacrifice of peace offering unto the LORD be of the flock; male or female, he shall offer it without blemish.

If he offer a lamb for his offering, then shall he offer it before the LORD [Lev. 3:6–7].

The lamb sets forth in a peculiar way the character of Christ and is, therefore, unusually appropriate as a sacrifice in the peace offering.

By contrast the bullock, or the heifer from the herd, sets forth the servant side of our Lord's ministry. The bullock was a domesticated animal, used to bear burdens and to plow fields, and so represented transportation and commerce in that day. The bullock was a servant and a friend of man. The bullock represents Christ as a servant. This is the aspect of Christ's ministry which is set forth in the Gospel of Mark. We need to emphasize that Christ as a servant was not a bellboy or a shoeshiner

for man. He did not run at man's bidding. The Gospel of Mark sets Him forth as *God's* Servant. He came to do the will of God.

However, the *lamb* sets forth Christ in His complete identification with man in life and in death. Have you ever noticed that? At the beginning of His ministry, John the Baptist pointed Him out as ". . . the Lamb of God, which taketh away the sin of the world" (John 1:29). That referred to His work. Later, he said, ". . . Behold the Lamb of God!" (John 1:36)—referring to His Person.

From the beginning, the lamb has set forth His quality and ability to take the place of man in bearing the sin of the world. The very first offering made by Abel was the sacrifice of a lamb. I think that God clothed Adam and Eve with lambs' skins. I can't prove that but I believe it in view of the fact that Abel brought a lamb.

Isaiah 53 makes it very clear that Jesus Christ was our substitute, carrying our sins and iniquities. ". . . He is brought as a lamb to the slaughter, and as a sheep before her shearers is dumb, so he openeth not his mouth" (Isa. 53:7). He is pictured as a lamb. The Lamb becomes our substitute.

He is also called a lamb in His resurrection. "And I beheld, and, lo, in the midst of the throne and of the four beasts, and in the midst of the elders, stood a Lamb as it had been slain, having seven horns and seven eyes, which are the seven Spirits of God sent forth into all the earth" (Rev. 5:6). Again, He is a Lamb in His return in glory. "And said to the mountains and rocks, Fall on us, and hide us from the face of him that sitteth on the throne, and from the wrath of the Lamb: For the great day of his wrath is come; and who shall be able to stand?" (Rev. 6:16–17).

The lamb is probably the most complete representation of Christ of all the sacrifices.

And he shall lay his hand upon the head of his offering, and kill it before the tabernacle of the congregation: and Aaron's sons shall sprinkle the blood thereof round about upon the altar.

And he shall offer of the sacrifice of the peace offering an offering made by fire unto the LORD; the fat thereof, and the whole rump, it shall he take off hard by the backbone; and the fat that covereth the inwards, and all the fat that is upon the inwards,

And the two kidneys, and the fat that is upon them, which is by the flanks, and

the caul above the liver, with the kidneys, it shall he take away [Lev. 3:8–10].

The ritual is similar to that given concerning one of the herd. The fat was God's portion. It was considered the better part of the animal. A fat animal was the best type, and the best was offered to God.

There are many passages to illustrate that fat was considered the best: ". . . Go your way, eat the fat, and drink the sweet . . ." (Neh. 8:10). "And in this mountain shall the LORD of hosts make unto all people a feast of fat things, a feast of wines on the lees, of fat things full of marrow, of wines on the lees well refined" (Isa. 25:6). "And bring hither the fatted calf, and kill it; and let us eat, and be merry" (Luke 15:23). Today, those of us who need to reduce our weight try not to eat the fat, but it is obvious that the fat was considered the choice part. God precisely declared, "all the fat that is upon the inwards and the two kidneys and the fat that is upon them" was to be for Him. God demanded the best.

We see here the deep and full meaning of the peace offering. Fellowship with God rests upon the blood of Christ, it is true, but there is another aspect of this fellowship. To make it complete and final there must be the presentation of the life of the believer in total dedication. Both of these aspects are included by Jesus Christ in His wonderful, inclusive invitation: "Come unto me, all ye that labour and are heavy laden, and I will give you rest" (Matt. 11:28). There is a rest that He gives, which is typified by the shed blood. This is the rest of redemption. "Take my yoke upon you, and learn of me; for I am meek and lowly in heart: and ye shall find rest unto your souls. For my yoke is easy, and my burden is light" (Matt. 11:29–30)—this is a rest that we find, which is represented by the fat. We must come to Him and offer ourselves to Him. This is the rest of dedication.

The expression "the whole rump" is translated in the American Standard Version of 1901 as "the fat tail entire." This has reference to a special breed of sheep peculiar to that geographical area. The tail of this breed weighs as much as 15 pounds, and is very fatty.

And the priest shall burn it upon the altar: it is the food of the offering made by fire unto the LORD [Lev. 3:11].

This is a strange clause and some have tried to associate it with pagan offerings. We know from an Assyrian inscription of Esarhaddon that offerers sacrificed victims to the gods and then feasted with the gods. However in the peace offering, the very opposite is true. God feasts the offerer. God makes this very clear in Deuteronomy 12:6–7: "And thither ye shall bring your burnt offerings, and your sacrifices, and your tithes, and heave offerings of your hand, and your vows, and your freewill offerings, and the firstlings of your herds and of your flocks: And there ye shall eat before the LORD your God, and ye shall rejoice in all that ye put your hand unto, ye and your households, wherein the LORD thy God hath blessed thee." The fat was totally consumed, but the priest received the breast and the shoulder. The offerer ate the remainder, and he did it in God's house. God was the host and the offerer, the sinner, was the guest.

Heathenism has it backwards and that was the basis of Isaiah's charge against Israel when they went into idolatry. "But ye are they that forsake the LORD, that forget my holy mountain, that prepare a table for that troop, and that furnish the drink offering unto that number" (Isa. 65:11). The American Standard Version says, "that prepare a table for Fortune, and that fill up mingled wine unto Destiny."

God provides the table in the peace offering! This throws light upon many verses of Scripture: "Thou preparest a table before me in the presence of mine enemies . . ." (Ps. 23:5). "They shall be abundantly satisfied with the fatness of thy house . . ." (Ps. 36:8). "I am the living bread which came down from heaven: if any man eat of this bread, he shall live for ever . . . . so he that eateth me, even he shall live by me" (John 6:51, 57). ". . . Take, eat; this is my body" (Matt. 26:26).

The Lord prepares the table of salvation and fellowship. This is emphasized in the peace offering. This helps us to understand the parable of the prodigal son. It is the Father who kills the fatted calf when the son is restored to fellowship. In the parable of the great supper, it is the Lord who invites, ". . . Come; for all things are now ready" (Luke 14:17). This is the table of salvation which God has provided. And then read 1 John chapter 1 again and again. Fellowship with God rests upon the redemption of Christ through His blood and upon our knowing Christ and confessing our sins. First we accept God's salvation by accepting Jesus Christ as our Savior; then we come to the table of fellowship.

Modern man thinks he can provide a table of salvation of his own works and invite God to come and eat. My friend, that is a purely pagan notion. God provides the table of salvation; God provides the table of fellowship.

A SACRIFICE FROM THE GOATS

And if his offering be a goat, then he shall offer it before the LORD [Lev. 3:12].

This is the third and final type of sacrifice for the peace offering. All three types of sacrifice are essential to portray the different aspects of Christ in the peace offering. The goat represents the complete identification of Christ as adequate to take away the sin of man. He was made sin for us. That is not just a nice statement but an actual fact. He is the propitiation for our sins, which means that He adequately and totally paid the penalty for our sins. You hear the expression, "I don't want anyone to make a goat of me." Well, friends, Christ was willing to be made a goat for you. He took the full penalty of your sin and my sin. His offering for sin is clearly set forth in Hebrews 10:6–14.

The ritual of it follows the pattern of the offering of the herd and of the flock.

And he shall lay his hand upon the head of it, and kill it before the tabernacle of the congregation: and the sons of Aaron shall sprinkle the blood thereof upon the altar round about.

And he shall offer thereof his offering, even an offering made by fire unto the LORD; the fat that covereth the inwards, and all the fat that is upon the inwards,

And the two kidneys, and the fat that is upon them, which is by the flanks, and the caul above the liver, with the kidneys, it shall he take away.

And the priest shall burn them upon the altar: it is the food of the offering made by fire for a sweet savour: all the fat is the LORD's.

It shall be a perpetual statute for your generations throughout all your dwellings, that ye eat neither fat nor blood [Lev. 3:13–17].

There are two statements here that should detain us for a moment: "all the fat is the Lord's" and "that ye eat neither fat nor blood." These two prohibitions are indeed striking. They are amplified in the law of the peace offerings in chapter 7.

The reason for the prohibition of eating blood is stated in Leviticus 17:10–14, and we will go into that later in our study.

The reason for the prohibition of eating the fat is given here. The fat is the Lord's. Man was reminded that he was redeemed by blood. That is the basis and ground of our acceptance before God. That brings us to the table of communion and fellowship with God. But the fat is the Lord's. He demands the best. If we are to enjoy to the fullest our fellowship with Him, it is imperative that we give Him our best. There must be total dedication to Him. Loving sacrifice of our lives must follow our redemption in order to enter into His sweet peace of communion. This is the message of Romans 12, John 15:14, and Philippians 3:10–14. Salvation is by the blood. Sanctification and service are by the fat.

THE LAW
OF THE PEACE OFFERING

The law of the peace offering is given in Lev. 7:11–38. It is the most extensive of all the instructions of the five offerings and it is the last. The value of the other offerings must be entered into before we can enjoy the peace of God.

We will go into more detail in chapter 7. Suffice it to say here that Aaron and his sons, the priests, received as their portion of the peace offering the breast and the shoulder. The breast speaks of the love of Christ for us and the shoulder speaks of the power and strength of Christ. He is able to save to the uttermost. This is our portion in Christ.

Do you hear Him, Christian friend, do you hear Him in His peace offering?

CHAPTER 4

THEME: *Sins of ignorance; sins of the priest; sins of the congregation; sins of the ruler; sins of the common people; the law of the sin offering*

This is the first of the non-sweet savor offerings. The three sweet savor offerings set forth the *person* of Christ in all of His glorious character. The two non-sweet savor offerings set forth the *work* of Christ on the cross for sin. The sin offering speaks of sin as a nature. The trespass offering speaks of sin as an act. You see, man is a sinner by nature, and he is a sinner because of what he does. He does what he does because he is a sinner by nature.

Several striking features of the sin offering set it apart from the other offerings and distinguish its importance:

1. It is the longest account of any offering since it is twice as long as any of the other four. The burnt offering was 17 verses; the meal offering, 16 verses; the peace offering, 17 verses; the trespass offering, 19 verses; the sin offering, 35 verses. Evidently the Spirit of God thought this was very important.

2. The sin offering was an entirely new offering. Up to this time, there is no record anywhere of a sin offering. There is no previous record of it occurring in Scripture. No heathen nation had anything that was even similar to it.

3. From the time of the giving of the Law, it became the most important and significant offering. You see, man was a sinner before the giving of the Law, but actually it was the Law which revealed to him that he was a sinner. The sin offering was offered during all of the feasts—Passover, Pentecost, Trumpets, and Tabernacles. It was offered on the great Day of Atonement (Yom Kippur). It brought the High Priest into the Holy of Holies.

4. It is in contrast to the burnt sacrifice, although it was made in the same place. "Speak unto Aaron and to his sons, saying, This is the law of the sin offering: In the place where the burnt offering is killed shall the sin offering be killed before the LORD: it is most holy" (Lev. 6:25).

Where the burnt offering leaves off, the sin offering begins. The burnt offering tells *who* Christ *is*; the sin offering tells *what* Christ *did*. In the burnt offering Christ meets the demands of God's high and holy standard; in the sin offering Christ meets the deep and desperate needs of man. In the burnt offering we see the preciousness of Christ; in the sin offering we see the hatefulness of sin.

The burnt offering was a voluntary offering; the sin offering was commanded. The burnt offering ascended; the sin offering was poured out. The one went up and the other went down.

SINS OF IGNORANCE

And the LORD spake unto Moses, saying,

Speak unto the children of Israel, saying, If a soul shall sin through ignorance against any of the commandments of the LORD concerning things which ought not to be done, and shall do against any of them [Lev. 4:1–2].

The emphasis here is upon a sin committed in ignorance. If a man sinned wilfully and deliberately, this offering did not avail. "He that despised Moses' law died without mercy under two or three witnesses" (Heb. 10:28). This speaks of the fact that there is no salvation for a person who wilfully rejects Jesus Christ. "For if we sin wilfully after that we have received the knowledge of the truth, there remaineth no more sacrifice for sins, But a certain fearful looking for of judgment and fiery indignation, which shall devour the adversaries" (Heb. 10:26–27).

Sins of ignorance reveal the underlying truth that man is a sinner by nature. My friend, I must say this to you: You are a sinner whether you know it or not. You are a sinner by nature, and so am I. That is the reason we commit sins. Regardless of the estimation of any given time or custom, man is a sinner. God's attitude toward sin does not change. We do those things which are contrary to God because it is impossible for the natural man to do anything that will please God. Natural man does not have that capacity. He is a sinner by nature. These sins must be called to man's attention. It is sin regardless of who commits it.

The sin offering gave a profound conviction of sin. This conviction stands out in the literature of the race. The deep guilt complex of man must be diagnosed before an adequate remedy can be prescribed.

Listen to the Psalmist, "Search me, O God, and know my heart: try me, and know my thoughts: And see if there be any wicked way in me, and lead me in the way everlasting" (Ps. 139:23–24). "Against thee, thee only, have I sinned, and done this evil in thy sight: that thou mightest be justified when thou speakest, and be clear when thou judgest" (Ps. 51:4).

This is what I call getting on the Lord Jesus Christ's couch instead of going to the psychiatrist's couch. A great many people with a guilt complex go to the psychiatrists today. One would get the impression that the psychiatrist or psychologist has a skill that the Word of God does not reveal. I think that is a wrong impression. The Word of God contains the remedy for man today. If you have a problem and you are bothered with a guilt complex, a personality problem, why don't you go to the Lord's couch and cry out, "Search me, O God, and know my heart. Try me. See if there be any wicked way in me." My friend, our problem is not that our mothers didn't give us all the love we should have had when we were little brats; our problem is that we are sinners by nature. So let's get on God's couch and tell Him that.

The sins of ignorance were acts committed by a person who at the time did not know they were sin. "Who can understand his errors? cleanse thou me from secret faults" (Ps. 19:12). How we need to confess to God that we are sinful human beings! If you can't think of anything special to confess, then just confess who you are, a sinner.

A group of men gathered regularly for prayer and one man would always pray, "Lord, if we have committed any sin, forgive us." The men got tired of this little formula and one of them said to him, "Why don't you tell Him what the sin is?" The man answered, "Well, I don't know what it is." The leader said, "Why don't you take a guess at it?" And do you know, the man's first guess was right! We need to confess our sins to God!

If a man sinned through ignorance, rashness, or accident, God made provision for his deliverance. He established the cities of refuge (Num. 35:11). God has a refuge for you too, my friend; He has a remedy for you. "My little children, these things write I unto you, that ye sin not. And if any man sin, we have an advocate with the Father, Jesus Christ the righteous" (1 John 2:1).

Paul explains the reason he was the chief of sinners and why he obtained mercy. He was a blasphemer and a persecutor and injurious, but he obtained mercy because he did it ignorantly in unbelief. He goes on to say, "And the grace of our Lord was exceeding abundant with faith and love which is in Christ Jesus. This is a faithful saying, and worthy of all acceptation, that Christ Jesus came into the world to save sinners; of whom I am chief" (1 Tim. 1:14–15).

My Dad died when I was fourteen, and soon I was obliged to go into the business world. There I teamed up with the wrong crowd. I was out doing things that a man twenty-five years old was doing, and I was just sixteen years old. I'm not offering an excuse, but I really didn't know then how bad it was. Then there came that day when I received Christ, and from that day to this, I look back and hate myself for what I did. Thank God, friend, there is a sin offering. Christ died for me; so I can go and tell Him all about it. I don't need to crawl up on anybody's couch and tell him about it. It's none of his business. But it sure is God's business and I must tell Him about it. He forgives me because He took care of all my sin at the cross.

The sin offering teaches us that we must see ourselves as God sees us. It brings before us the consciousness of sin and our own unworthiness, but also God's provision. "I acknowledged my sin unto thee, and mine iniquity have I not hid. I said, I will confess my transgressions unto the LORD; and thou forgavest the iniquity of my sin" (Ps. 32:5). It lifts the guilt complex.

The sin offering taught its own inadequacy. "Sacrifice and offering thou didst not desire; mine ears hast thou opened: burnt offering and sin offering hast thou not required" (Ps. 40:6). It pointed the way to God's perfect satisfaction for sin and His forgiveness. "Having therefore, brethren, boldness to enter into the holiest by the blood of Jesus, By a new and living way, which he hath consecrated for us, through the veil, that is to say, his flesh; And having an high priest over the house of God; Let us draw near with a true heart in full assurance of faith, having our hearts sprinkled from an evil conscience, and our bodies washed with pure water" (Heb. 10:19–22). Now you and I, sinners, can come into His presence with boldness. Why? Because Jesus is our sin offering, even for these sins of ignorance.

Sin through ignorance brings to our attention another side of God's justice and His absolute fairness in dealing with man. God will deal with man in equity. There will be degrees of punishment as there will be degrees of rewards. The degree of responsibility is also recognized in the sin offering as we shall see in the different classes of people who are considered here.

SINS OF THE PRIEST

If the priest that is anointed do sin

according to the sin of the people; then let him bring for his sin, which he hath sinned, a young bullock without blemish unto the LORD for a sin offering [Lev. 4:3].

The sin of the priest is considered first, for he stood in the place of leadership. If he was wrong, the people were wrong. His sin was their sin. Like priest, like people. He was to bring a young bullock, the most valuable animal of all, as his offering. You see that the position of the one who sinned determined the type of animal for the sin sacrifice. His sin was no different, but his responsibility was greater.

It is still the same today. "Therefore to him that knoweth to do good, and doeth it not, to him it is sin" (James 4:17). "My brethren, be not many masters, knowing that we shall receive the greater condemnation" (James 3:1). Do you want to be a preacher? It makes you more responsible. Do you want to sing a solo? It makes you responsible. Do you want to be a deacon or an officer in the church, or a teacher of a Sunday School class? Then you are more responsible than anyone else. Privilege carries with it a responsibility, and God Himself will hold you to that responsibility.

That is what is clearly shown here. "According to the sins of the people" could be more properly translated "so as to cause the people to sin." This points out the responsibility of the priest. He was a mere human being and he was subject to the same temptations as the remainder of the race. "For the law maketh men high priests which have infirmity . . ." (Heb. 7:28). It is in this point that there is a radical difference between Christ, our great High Priest, and the priests of the order of Aaron. "For we have not an high priest which cannot be touched with the feeling of our infirmities; but was in all points tempted like as we are, yet without sin" (Heb. 4:15).

And he shall bring the bullock unto the door of the tabernacle of the congregation before the LORD; and shall lay his hand upon the bullock's head, and kill the bullock before the LORD [Lev. 4:4].

This is the ritual for the sin offering. In this part of the ritual there is a similarity to the burnt offering.

And the priest that is anointed shall take of the bullock's blood, and bring it to the tabernacle of the congregation:

And the priest shall dip his finger in the blood, and sprinkle of the blood seven times before the LORD, before the veil of the sanctuary.

And the priest shall put some of the blood upon the horns of the altar of sweet incense before the LORD, which is in the tabernacle of the congregation; and shall pour all the blood of the bullock at the bottom of the altar of the burnt offering, which is at the door of the tabernacle of the congregation [Lev. 4:5-7].

To sprinkle the blood seven times before the veil secured God's relationship with the offender. To put some of the blood on the horns of the altar of incense, the place of prayer, was to restore the privilege of worship to the offender. Our acceptance by God and our worship of Him are dependent upon the blood of Jesus Christ. "If we confess our sins, he is faithful and just to forgive us our sins, and to cleanse us from all unrighteousness" (1 John 1:9). "And almost all things are by the law purged with blood; and without shedding of blood is no remission" (Heb. 9:22).

The remainder of the blood was poured out at the bottom of the brazen altar. This satisfied the conscience of the sinner and removed the guilt complex. This was the remedy for the conviction of sin and the only remedy that could satisfy the mind and heart.

My friend, the important thing for you to understand is that when Christ forgives you your sin, He also forgives *you*. There is nothing more to be said about it. He has put it in the bottom of the sea. He has removed it as far as the east is from the west. He has removed it so that He will not even remember it. He settles the sin question. That rids us of our guilt complexes. You need never wonder whether He has really forgiven you. He took away all your sin and guilt. *All* of it. When you come to Christ and see Him, you will find Him adequate.

And he shall take off from it all the fat of the bullock for the sin offering; the fat that covereth the inwards, and all the fat that is upon the inwards,

And the two kidneys, and the fat that is upon them, which is by the flanks, and the caul above the liver, with the kidneys, it shall he take away,

As it was taken off from the bullock of the sacrifice of peace offerings: and the priest shall burn them upon the altar of the burnt offering [Lev. 4:8-10].

Here the ritual of the sin sacrifice follows that of the peace offering. The sin has been forgiven. Fellowship is restored and service is again restored. The fat is offered to be burned on the altar. Remember that the fat represents the very best.

And the skin of the bullock, and all his flesh, with his head, and with his legs, and his inwards, and his dung,

Even the whole bullock shall he carry forth without the camp unto a clean place, where the ashes are poured out, and burn him on the wood with fire: where the ashes are poured out shall he be burnt [Lev. 4:11–12].

At this point there is a radical departure from the other offerings. The remainder of the bullock was taken without the camp and burned there. We believe that this is simply an emphasis upon the exceeding sinfulness of sin. This animal was the sin offering—there is no thought of consecration or signifying the person of Christ. Rather, this is Christ, the sin-bearer, the One who was made sin for us. This deeper meaning is given to us in Hebrews. "We have an altar, whereof they have no right to eat which serve the tabernacle. For the bodies of those beasts, whose blood is brought into the sanctuary by the high priest for sin, are burned without the camp. Wherefore Jesus also, that he might sanctify the people with his own blood, suffered without the gate. Let us go forth therefore unto him without the camp, bearing his reproach. For here have we no continuing city, but we seek one to come" (Heb. 13:10–14). Let us ponder this Scripture well. Religion can never satisfy the heart or meet the requirements of a God who is holy. Only the death of Christ on the cross can give us forgiveness of sins. We are sinners by nature and we are not fit for heaven. If God would consign this entire world into a lost eternity, the angels in heaven would still sing, "Holy, holy, holy!" But thank God, He didn't do that. He loved us so much that He sent Jesus Christ to be made sin for us. Don't try to solve the problem of your sin in any other way than to turn and trust Christ. He is adequate. He meets the deep need in your heart and soul. He alone can offer you forgiveness for sin. The death of Christ on the cross as our sin-bearer is the only solution there is to sin. That is the meaning of that part of the animal which had to be burned outside the camp.

SINS OF THE CONGREGATION

And if the whole congregation of Israel

sin through ignorance, and the thing be hid from the eyes of the assembly, and they have done somewhat against any of the commandments of the LORD concerning things which should not be done, and are guilty;

When the sin, which they have sinned against it, is known, then the congregation shall offer a young bullock for the sin, and bring him before the tabernacle of the congregation [Lev. 4:13–14].

The victim for the entire congregation was the same as for the priest. A young bullock was the most valuable animal for offering. You see, the high priest represented the entire congregation before the Lord, so the requirement would be the same.

I think there is another lesson here. There is not only an individual responsibility before God but there is also a corporate responsibility. God judges nations, and many people who didn't participate in the sin of the nation are judged along with it.

When Jerusalem was destroyed in A.D. 70, the whole nation went into captivity. When the Roman Empire disintegrated, everyone went down with it. Friends, you and I are responsible since we are a part of the nation.

God also judges churches and local congregations. I hear people say that they are going to stay in a liberal church and try to witness to it. Where do they get that idea? It's not in the Word of God. If you identify yourself with a church which does not teach the truth from the Word of God, God will judge you right along with that church. Your responsibility is an individual responsibility, but when you join yourself with something, you are placed under corporate responsibility also. When the Lord sent His messages to the seven churches of Asia in the Book of Revelation, the message was to the churches and to every member of each church.

And the elders of the congregation shall lay their hands upon the head of the bullock before the LORD: and the bullock shall be killed before the LORD [Lev. 4:15].

The elders represented the nation. Similarly, the elders in the Book of Revelation represent the church.

Now the ritual here is identical with the offering of the priest. I'll not go over that again. It is explained in verses 16–21.

SINS OF THE RULER

When a ruler hath sinned, and done somewhat through ignorance against any of the commandments of the LORD his God concerning things which should not be done, and is guilty;

Or, if his sin, wherein he hath sinned, come to his knowledge; he shall bring his offering, a kid of the goats, a male without blemish [Lev. 4:22–23].

You will notice that all these different groups are to bring an offering because they are sinners. Their responsibility is different in each case, but they are all guilty. This has reference to a civil ruler. People who are rulers are often charged inaccurately and there is gossip about them. This must be real guilt. His sin must come to his knowledge and then he shall bring his offering. Again, the ruler is in a place of responsibility. His offering was of less worth than that of the priest or the entire congregation, but it was of more value than that of a private person.

This teaches us the lesson that rulers are ordained of God and thereby are responsible to God. Unfortunately, our politicians today do not seek to please God. I have listened to many of their speeches and I have yet to hear one of them, Democrat or Republican, say that he feels that he has a responsibility to God. They are always trying to please the people. You hear them talk of their constituents. God says that they are responsible to Him!

The ruler was to bring an offering of a kid of the goats, a male without blemish. The offering was not as valuable as the bullock. The ritual and the procedure for the offering for the ruler follow the same steps as that for the priest and for the people. You see, the sin of the man is the same as if he were a private citizen. The value of the animal he must sacrifice indicates the degree of his responsibility.

SINS OF THE COMMON PEOPLE

And if any one of the common people sin through ignorance, while he doeth somewhat against any of the commandments of the LORD concerning things which ought not to be done, and be guilty [Lev. 4:27].

This is now talking about the common person, the private citizen. The offering is for a sin through ignorance but a sin against a commandment of God. It was against something specifically stated as being forbidden.

His guilt cannot be just hearsay, but the guilt must be established.

Again, this offering was to lift the guilt complex and satisfy the conscience. Only the death of Christ can lift the crushing guilt complex from modern man. Psychological procedures have not been able to accomplish this. A person's conscience may be seared with a hot iron and the guilt may be transferred from one area to another, but deep in the human heart the strange guilt complex lingers. It is removed only when it is brought to Christ for His forgiveness.

Or if his sin, which he hath sinned, come to his knowledge: then he shall bring his offering, a kid of the goats, a female without blemish, for his sin which he hath sinned [Lev. 4:28].

If a sin comes to his knowledge later, then it is no longer a sin through ignorance, but it requires the same sacrifice. What does the believer do today? He has come to Christ as a lost sinner and accepted Him as his Savior. Then, when he finds that he has sinned, he confesses it to God. "If we confess our sins, he is faithful and just to forgive us our sins, and to cleanse us from all unrighteousness" (1 John 1:9).

A female kid of the goats was an offering of less value than any previous offering. Yet, an offering was required. All of these offerings point to the death of Christ.

Again, the ritual is the same for all classifications of humanity. A female lamb was also acceptable according to verse 32, and again the ritual of the lamb was the same.

The important clause to notice is, "it shall be forgiven him" in verse 31 and verse 35. The important truth is that complete forgiveness was secured for the sinner. Total absolution was accomplished. This is exactly what was accomplished for us when Christ died. "In whom we have redemption through his blood, the forgiveness of sins, according to the riches of his grace" (Eph. 1:7).

THE LAW OF THE SIN OFFERING

And the LORD spake unto Moses, saying,

Speak unto Aaron and to his sons, saying, This is the law of the sin offering: In the place where the burnt offering is killed shall the sin offering be killed before the LORD: it is most holy [Lev. 6:24–25].

The place for the sin offering was the same as the place for the burnt offering. Both refer to Christ. The sin offering was holy.

The priest that offereth it for sin shall eat it: in the holy place shall it be eaten, in the court of the tabernacle of the congregation.

Whatsoever shall touch the flesh thereof shall be holy: and when there is sprinkled of the blood thereof upon any garment, thou shalt wash that whereon it was sprinkled in the holy place [Lev. 6:26–27].

The sin offering was holy. You remember that Christ on the cross cried out to God with words from Psalm 22. "My God, my God, why hast thou forsaken me? why art thou so far from helping me, and from the words of my roaring? O my God, I cry in the daytime, but thou hearest not; and in the night season, and am not silent. But thou art holy, O thou that inhabitest the praises of Israel (Ps. 22:1–3).

Christ became sin for us on the cross and yet He was holy. God withdrew from Him and yet God was in Christ reconciling the world to Himself. I don't understand it; this is a great mystery. He was holy and is still holy yet our sin was put on Him. We will never know or understand what He suffered on the cross; because He is holy and since we are not, we do not know what suffering really is.

But the earthen vessel wherein it is sodden shall be broken: and if it be sodden

in a brasen pot, it shall be both scoured, and rinsed in water.

All the males among the priests shall eat thereof: it is most holy.

And no sin offering, whereof any of the blood is brought into the tabernacle of the congregation to reconcile withal in the holy place, shall be eaten: it shall be burnt in the fire [Lev. 6:28–30].

The law is meticulous even concerning the vessels. You see, the offering was for sin, and sin is the opposite of holiness. God is giving the final reminder of this.

"Let the wicked forsake his way, and the unrighteous man his thoughts: and let him return unto the LORD, and he will have mercy upon him; and to our God, for he will abundantly pardon. For my thoughts are not your thoughts, neither are your ways my ways, saith the LORD. For as the heavens are higher than the earth, so are my ways higher than your ways, and my thoughts than your thoughts" (Isa. 55:7–9). We need to be reminded of the fact that He saved us *from* sin, not *to* sin. That is very important for us to note. Paul writes, "What shall we say then? Shall we continue in sin, that grace may abound? God forbid. How shall we, that are dead to sin, live any longer therein?" (Rom. 6:1–2).

CHAPTER 5

***THEME:** The trespass offering: specific acts of sin committed in ignorance; non-specific acts of sin committed in ignorance*

Some expositors treat the first 13 verses of this chapter as part of the sin offering. There is ample justification for this, as the word *trespass* in verses 6 and 7 can be translated "guilt" and should be "for his guilt." In verses 6, 7, 9, and 11, the sin offering is required for the trespass because the act of sin is caused by the nature of sin. All sin comes from the same source: the sin nature. You and I inherited it from Adam. The ax must be laid at the root as well as at the fruit.

In our discussion here, we shall treat the entire chapter as the trespass offering. The word *trespass* has very much the same meaning in the King James translation as it does in present-day use of the word. We all under-

stand a "No Trespassing" sign. It means we are not to invade the rights of others. Liberty is a word which is much misused and abused today. Many folk go around parading, burning things, destroying things, and talking about liberty. Friend, you are free to swing your fist in any direction that you please, but your liberty ends where my nose begins. A trespass is the invasion of the rights of either God or man.

For example, withholding tithes from God was counted a trespass in Israel. We have the example of Achan who took the accursed thing and this was considered a trespass (Josh. 7:1).

We must always remember that our trespasses arise out of our sin nature. Man is totally depraved and actually has no capacity for

God whatsoever. God makes it very clear that He cannot and will not accept the works of unsaved men to accomplish their salvation. Their righteousness is as filthy rags. He does not save by works of righteousness, but He saves us by His grace. It is impossible for an unsaved man to please God "Because the carnal mind is enmity against God: for it is not subject to the law of God, neither indeed can be" (Rom. 8:7). When Jesus was on this earth, religious folk came to Him with this question, "Then said they unto him, What shall we do, that we might work the works of God? Jesus answered and said unto them, This is the work of God, that ye believe on him whom he hath sent" (John 6:28–29). The apostles had the same answer, ". . . Believe on the Lord Jesus Christ, and thou shalt be saved . . ." (Acts 16:31).

SPECIFIC ACTS OF SIN COMMITTED IN IGNORANCE

The list of sins enumerated here is obviously not an exhaustive list but gives us examples of a limitless number which could be named. These are sins of individuals, not of the entire congregation. Most of the section deals with the remedy and not the disease. So we find the emphasis is upon the type of offering and not on the character of the offerer, as it was in the sin offering.

And if a soul sin, and hear the voice of swearing, and is a witness, whether he hath seen or known of it; if he do not utter it, then he shall bear his iniquity [Lev. 5:1].

Let me say again that the four specific sins listed here are merely examples. I think one could fill up the rest of the Book of Leviticus with specific sins if one named them all. I understand some preacher made up a list of 800 specific sins that he had thought of. He was swamped with letters from people who wanted the list of sins. They thought maybe there was something they were missing since they couldn't think of 800 sins. Well, here we are given a few examples.

"And if a soul sin, and hear the voice of swearing" could be better translated, "if a person sin in this respect that he hears the voice of adjuration." It has to do with the hearing of an oath and being a witness. If a witness has seen or knows something, but he withholds the truth to the detriment of some individual, then that is a sin of omission.

There are sins of omission today. Some folk come into church today thinking their hands are clean because they haven't murdered or stolen. Listen to James: "Therefore to him that knoweth to do good, and doeth it not, to him it is sin" (James 4:17).

Solomon prayed to God concerning this very issue of not telling the truth when a witness ought to tell the truth. "If any man trespass against his neighbour, and an oath be laid upon him to cause him to swear, and the oath come before thine altar in this house: Then hear thou in heaven, and do, and judge thy servants, condemning the wicked, to bring his way upon his head; and justifying the righteous, to give him according to his righteousness" (1 Kings 8:31–32).

Let me give you an example of this. The town gossip is crossing the square of the town and she sees the president of the bank crossing the street. His secretary is also leaving the bank to go to lunch and a car hits her as she is crossing the street. The bank president rushes over and picks her up in his arms and takes her into a doctor's office. The gossip runs to the telephone to call the wife of the bank president and says, "Do you know, Madge, I saw your husband with another woman in his arms!" Now although that was a fact, it wasn't the whole truth! She is withholding important information. That is a sin of omission.

I was in a meeting of Christian men who were talking about the pastor and they gave certain information that was accurate. But it wasn't the whole truth. They told only a part of it; they didn't tell the whole situation. They were willing to let that group of men believe that they had heard the whole story. That is a trespass. It is one of the most vicious sins that can be committed. Notice here that it is Number One on God's Sin Parade! Over in the Book of Proverbs we find a list of things which God hates and in that list of seven we find "a lying tongue" (Prov. 6:17).

You remember that Jesus was quiet during most of His trial. We are told that He held His peace. But when He was put under oath, He broke His silence. Then He was no longer dumb like a sheep before her shearers is dumb. ". . . And the high priest answered and said unto him, I adjure thee by the living God, that thou tell us whether thou be the Christ, the Son of God. Jesus saith unto him, Thou hast said: nevertheless I say unto you, Hereafter shall ye see the Son of man sitting on the right hand of power, and coming in the clouds of heaven" (Matt. 26:63–64). You see, under oath He did not hold His peace, but spoke out in witness. He told the whole truth.

Or if a soul touch any unclean thing, whether it be a carcase of an unclean beast, or a carcase of unclean cattle, or the carcase of unclean creeping things, and if it be hidden from him; he also shall be unclean, and guilty [Lev. 5:2].

This is the law concerning uncleanness. A man might become polluted by contact with a dead animal without being aware of it while others witnessed it. A dead carcase caused uncleanness by contact. Why? Probably for health reasons.

This also speaks to Christians today. We can't be out in the world without becoming unclean by seeing things and hearing things and thinking things. We are unclean. We may not even realize that we have come into contact with the unclean. It may be hidden from us so we are not even aware of it. But we are not to rush into God's presence until we are cleansed. This is why the Psalmist says, "Who can understand his errors? cleanse thou me from secret faults" (Ps. 19:12).

We should not only pray for forgiveness in general, we are to name our specific failures to God and ask Him for forgiveness. But more than that, we should pray for forgiveness of sins that we may be unaware of. Sometimes we are unclean and do not realize it.

Or if he touch the uncleanness of man, whatsoever uncleanness it be that a man shall be defiled withal, and it be hid from him; when he knoweth of it, then he shall be guilty [Lev. 5:3].

This is similar to the case of the unclean animal, yet God makes a distinction between man and beast. The penalty for this is more severe than for touching the beast (Lev. 11:24 and Num. 19:11–16). Apparently there were other distinctions of uncleanness concerning man other than death.

Or if a soul swear, pronouncing with his lips to do evil, or to do good, whatsoever it be that a man shall pronounce with an oath, and it be hid from him; when he knoweth of it, then he shall be guilty in one of these [Lev. 5:4].

Careless speech is involved in this instance. Sometimes we promise to do something, and then we don't do it. We promise that we will serve the Lord. Jephthah is an example of a man promising to do something very rash—to offer his daughter. Simon Peter boldly declared that he would not deny Christ, but would die defending Him.

Today I hear people making some very rash promises. In fact, I think some of our songs are dynamite, to tell the truth. In our songs we promise to give all to Him, to follow Him, to die for Him. We sing them so glibly that we don't even know what we are singing.

Also I think it is careless speech and presumptuous when we try to demand of God an answer to our prayers. We need always to remember that our prayers are to be in accordance with His will. If we ask anything according to His will, He heareth us. Where did we get the idea that we could demand anything of God?

"Then he shall be guilty in one of these" refers to the four things which have been listed. Many more could have been included.

And it shall be, when he shall be guilty in one of these things, that he shall confess that he hath sinned in that thing:

And he shall bring his trespass offering unto the LORD for his sin which he hath sinned, a female from the flock, a lamb or a kid of the goats, for a sin offering: and the priest shall make an atonement for him concerning his sin [Lev. 5:5–6].

Confession is commanded for the first time. The other offerings were an open admission of guilt. This one has to do with secret sins. They were hidden sins even though they be against God and man.

You remember in Joshua 7, when Achan took the wedge of gold and the Babylonish garment, that trespass had to be dealt with publicly because it was that kind of a sin. The laying on of hands in the other offerings was evidently an admission of sin. Here confession must come first, then the offering. In the sweet savor offerings, the offerings preceded any thought of confession. The opposite is true here.

I think this is what our Lord had in mind in the Sermon on the Mount. "Therefore if thou bring thy gift to the altar, and there rememberest that thy brother hath aught against thee; Leave there thy gift before the altar, and go thy way; first be reconciled to thy brother, and then come and offer thy gift" (Matt. 5:23–24). The believer today is to confess his sin to God privately but he is to make restitution to the injured party.

The trespass offering simply means the offering of guilt. It was a sin offering, since all sin stems from the sin nature. We are not sinners because we sin; we sin because we are sinners with a sin nature.

Since this offering is for an act of sin which is one of the many facets of the sin nature, the value of the offering was not as great as the value of the sin offering in chapter 4.

And if he be not able to bring a lamb, then he shall bring for his trespass, which he hath committed, two turtle doves, or two young pigeons, unto the Lord; one for a sin offering, and the other for a burnt offering [Lev. 5:7].

The emphasis in the trespass offering is not in the character or position of the offerer, but in the sacrifice itself. Two turtledoves were required, as one was for a sin offering and one was for a burnt offering. The person and the work of Christ are represented in the poorest of offerings. This was the sacrifice of the poor. Christ preached glad tidings to the poor.

Notice that it is labeled a sin offering because it arises from the sin nature.

And he shall bring them unto the priest, who shall offer that which is for the sin offering first, and wring off his head from his neck, but shall not divide it asunder:

And he shall sprinkle of the blood of the sin offering upon the side of the altar; and the rest of the blood shall be wrung out at the bottom of the altar: it is a sin offering [Lev. 5:8–9].

Blood must be shed, though the head of the bird was not removed from the body.

And he shall offer the second for a burnt offering, according to the manner: and the priest shall make an atonement for him for his sin which he hath sinned, and it shall be forgiven him [Lev. 5:10].

The sinner has complete forgiveness even with the little bird. All of this points to Christ as the one sacrifice.

But if he be not able to bring two turtle-doves, or two young pigeons, then he that sinned shall bring for his offering the tenth part of an ephah of fine flour for a sin offering; he shall put no oil upon it, neither shall he put any frank-incense thereon: for it is a sin offering [Lev. 5:11].

The poorest of the poor was not left out. If one could not bring a bird, he could bring what amounted to a piece of bread. This sacrifice was still a substitute for him.

Then shall he bring it to the priest, and the priest shall take his handful of it, even a memorial thereof, and burn it on the altar, according to the offerings made by fire unto the Lord: it is a sin offering.

And the priest shall make an atonement for him as touching his sin that he hath sinned in one of these, and it shall be forgiven him: and the remnant shall be the priest's, as a meat offering [Lev. 5:12–13].

NON-SPECIFIC ACTS OF SIN COMMITTED IN IGNORANCE

And the Lord spake unto Moses, saying,

If a soul commit a trespass, and sin through ignorance, in the holy things of the Lord; then he shall bring for his trespass unto the Lord a ram without blemish out of the flocks, with thy estimation by shekels of silver, after the shekel of the sanctuary, for a trespass offering.

And he shall make amends for the harm that he hath done in the holy thing, and shall add the fifth part thereto, and give it unto the priest: and the priest shall make an atonement for him with the ram of the trespass offering, and it shall be forgiven him [Lev. 5:14–16].

These trespass offerings emphasize the fact that there has been an invasion of the rights of both God and man. Harm to others is the feature which requires that reparation had to be performed. The principal had to be restored *plus* a fifth part. This must be what Zacchaeus had in mind when he told the Lord that he would give half his goods to the poor and restore fourfold what he had taken from any man by false accusation (Luke 19:8).

The chief wrong committed through ignorance seems to apply to robbing God in connection with tithes and offerings. We find this again in Malachi: "Will a man rob God? Yet ye have robbed me. But ye say, Wherein have we robbed thee? In tithes and offerings. Ye are cursed with a curse: for ye have robbed me, even this whole nation" (Mal. 3:8–9). The Lord promises them blessing if they will bring their tithes, such blessing that there shall not be room to receive it.

Ecclesiastes 5:5 warns, "Better is it that thou shouldest not vow, than that thou shouldest vow and not pay." For this kind of neglect, this trespass against God, the offering must be valuable. It must be a ram. This points us to Christ, who is precious. "But with the precious blood of Christ, as of a lamb without blemish and without spot" (1 Pet. 1:19). Through this offering there was forgiveness for the sinner who committed the trespass in ignorance.

And if a soul sin, and commit any of these things which are forbidden to be done by the commandments of the LORD; though he wist it not, yet is he guilty, and shall bear his iniquity.

And he shall bring a ram without blemish out of the flock, with thy estimation, for a trespass offering, unto the priest: and the priest shall make an atonement for him concerning his ignorance

wherein he erred and wist it not, and it shall be forgiven him.

It is a trespass offering: he hath certainly trespassed against the LORD [Lev. 5:17–19].

This apparently had to do with breaking any of the commandments of God in ignorance. Ignorance of the law is no excuse. This is also true in civil law. In spite of the lack of knowledge of the commandment, the offender was guilty and was held liable. Here again, the ram is given as the only animal for the trespass offering.

This offering in its ritual followed the pattern of the sin offering, except in the sprinkling of the blood, which followed the pattern of the burnt and peace offerings. We will see this in more detail in chapter 7.

CHAPTER 6

THEME: Conclusion of rules concerning the trespass offering; law concerning the burnt offering; concerning the meal offering; concerning the sin offering

Chapters 6 and 7 present the law of the offerings. Actually, the law of the offerings concerned the priests and their particular part in them and portion of them. It could be called the special rules for the priests who minister at the altar of God.

This section opens with specific directions to the priests and a command for Aaron and his sons. Since the priests served at the altar, they were involved in all of the offerings that were made on the burnt altar. All of this is a shadow of the reality in heaven where Christ, our great High Priest, serves. "For every high priest is ordained to offer gifts and sacrifices: wherefore it is of necessity that this man have somewhat also to offer. For if he were on earth, he should not be a priest, seeing that there are priests that offer gifts according to the law: Who serve unto the example and shadow of heavenly things, as Moses was admonished of God when he was about to make the tabernacle: for, See, saith he, that thou make all things according to the pattern shewed to thee in the mount" (Heb. 8:3–5).

There is another striking feature. Christ is not only the priest but He is also the sacrifice.

He offered Himself. "Wherefore when he cometh into the world, he saith, Sacrifice and offering thou wouldest not, but a body hast thou prepared me: In burnt offerings and sacrifices for sin thou hast had no pleasure. Then said I, Lo, I come (in the volume of the book it is written of me,) to do thy will, O God. Above when he said, Sacrifice and offering and burnt offerings and offering for sin thou wouldest not, neither hadst pleasure therein; which are offered by the law; Then said he, Lo, I come to do thy will, O God. He taketh away the first, that he may establish the second. By the which will we are sanctified through the offering of the body of Jesus Christ once for all. And every priest standeth daily ministering and offering often times the same sacrifices, which can never take away sins: But this man, after he had offered one sacrifice for sins for ever, sat down on the right hand of God" (Heb. 10:5–12).

We need to be so aware of this today. There are a great many religions which have elaborate rituals with marching and robes and candles and routines. I suppose in all our churches we do a lot of things that really are not worthwhile. God is a Spirit and must be worshiped in spirit and in truth. God gave us this great spiritual truth here in the book of Hebrews so that we would see that.

You and I have a High Priest in heaven and He is just as busy as can be. When it says that He sat down, it means that redemption was complete. It is similar to saying that God rested on the seventh day because creation was complete. It doesn't mean that He was tired and stopped doing anything. Just so, the Lord Jesus doesn't sit down because He is tired and doesn't want to do anything. He is busy! He died down here on this earth to save us. He lives up at the right hand of God to keep us saved. You and I ought to keep in touch with Him. This is reality! This is spiritual! The trouble today is that we are out of touch with the *living* Christ. He is no longer a reality to us.

The greatest compliment I ever heard given about a preacher was for the one whom I succeeded in Nashville, Tennessee. A butcher in the market said to me, "I understand you are following Dr. Allen. You know, there is something about that man. Every time I meet him, I feel like he just left Jesus around the corner." I want to tell you, friends, Dr. Allen meant business with Jesus. Jesus Christ was a reality in his life.

CONCLUSION OF RULES CONCERNING THE TRESPASS OFFERING

Again, the sins listed are merely examples of a longer list of trespasses which could be given. They are sins committed against one's neighbor in the daily run of affairs.

And the LORD spake unto Moses, saying,

If a soul sin, and commit a trespass against the LORD, and lie unto his neighbour in that which was delivered him to keep, or in fellowship, or in a thing taken away by violence, or hath deceived his neighbour;

Or have found that which was lost, and lieth concerning it, and sweareth falsely; in any of all these that a man doeth, sinning therein:

Then it shall be, because he hath sinned, and is guilty, that he shall restore that which he took violently away, or the thing which he hath deceitfully gotten, or that which was delivered him to keep, or the lost thing which he found.

Or all that about which he hath sworn falsely; he shall even restore it in the

principal, and shall add the fifth part more thereto, and give it unto him to whom it appertaineth, in the day of his trespass offering.

And he shall bring his trespass offering unto the LORD, a ram without blemish out of the flock, with thy estimation, for a trespass offering, unto the priest:

And the priest shall make an atonement for him before the LORD: and it shall be forgiven him for any thing of all that he hath done in trespassing therein [Lev. 6:1–7].

This would appear to be a separate revelation from God, distinct from the preceding chapter. It shows that sin against a neighbor is a sin against God. That is why Jesus said, "Therefore all things whatsoever ye would that men should do to you, do ye even so to them: for this is the law and the prophets" (Matt. 7:12).

Certain specific sins are mentioned here. Lying about borrowed articles and responsibility for articles left for safe keeping are mentioned. We find an example of this in 2 Kings 6:5 when the students of Elisha lost the borrowed ax. "Fellowship" in this passage actually refers to a business partnership. "Taking by violence" would be a forced transaction such as Ahab taking Naboth's vineyard in 1 Kings 21:2–16. "Deceiving his neighbor" would mean lying to the neighbor in not reporting having found a lost article.

May I say again, sins against one's fellowman are also sins against God. We see here again that restitution had to be made with an additional penalty of one fifth added. A fifth would be a double tithe. This was followed by the trespass offering. Again, it is the ram that is the victim. God is showing that He is no respecter of persons.

The trespass offering was vital to the spiritual life of the individual Israelite. "Fools make a mock at sin: but among the righteous there is favour" (Prov. 14:9). A sense of sin renders Jesus precious to the soul.

CONCERNING THE BURNT OFFERING

And the LORD spake unto Moses, saying,

Command Aaron and his sons, saying, This is the law of the burnt offering: It is the burnt offering because of the burning upon the altar all night unto the morning and the fire of the altar shall be burning in it [Lev. 6:8–9].

The fire on the altar was to burn continually, that is, while the tabernacle was set up and not on the wilderness march. The burnt offering was left on the altar all night and the fire was kept burning so that the whole offering would be consumed.

This speaks of the continual consecration of Christ. It was the Lord Jesus who could say, ". . . I do always those things that please him " (John 8:29). He displays this love and obedience in His high priestly prayer, "And for their sakes I sanctify myself, that they also might be sanctified through the truth" (John 17:19). Or listen to Him in John 4:31–32: "In the meanwhile his disciples prayed him, saying, Master, eat. But he said unto them, I have meat to eat that ye know not of."

This also speaks of the fact that we are to offer ourselves a living sacrifice to God (Rom. 12:1–2). I find that when I crawl upon the altar and the fire gets hot, I crawl off. I don't know about you, but I see a lot of folk doing that too. I wish I could say that I always do the things that please Him. The Lord Jesus could say it, but I can't. There is a challenge to every believer today because God delights in the continual obedience of His children. That should give us real food for thought.

Remember that this was the issue when Samuel rebuked King Saul. "And Samuel said, Hath the LORD as great delight in burnt offerings and sacrifices, as in obeying the voice of the LORD? Behold, to obey is better than sacrifice, and to hearken than the fat of rams. For rebellion is as the sin of witchcraft, and stubbornness is as iniquity and idolatry. Because thou hast rejected the word of the LORD, he hath also rejected thee from being king" (1 Sam. 15:22–23).

Today you and I need to offer our own hearts and lives to Him, if we belong to Him, that is, if we are saved. God forbid that we simply make empty professions. What is it that God wants us to do? ". . . This is the work of God, that ye believe on him whom he hath sent" (John 6:29).

And the priest shall put on his linen garment, and his linen breeches shall he put upon his flesh, and take up the ashes which the fire hath consumed with the burnt offering on the altar, and he shall put them beside the altar.

And he shall put off his garments, and put on other garments, and carry forth the ashes without the camp unto a clean place [Lev. 6:10–11].

God gave instructions even to the detail of the garment the priest was to wear. He was not only to put on the long robe, which was common to all the priests, but also the linen breeches. Why? The flesh must be covered totally. God is teaching that He *cannot* accept the works of the flesh.

"Now the works of the flesh are manifest, which are these; Adultery, fornication, uncleanness, lasciviousness, Idolatry, witchcraft, hatred, variance, emulations, wrath, strife, seditions, heresies, Envyings, murders, drunkenness, revellings, and such like: of the which I tell you before, as I have also told you in time past, that they which do such things shall not inherit the kingdom of God" (Gal. 5:19–21). God cannot accept the works of the flesh. It is only the fruit of the Holy Spirit which is acceptable to Him. The Spirit of God must produce this in our lives. "But the fruit of the Spirit is love, joy, peace, longsuffering, gentleness, goodness, faith, Meekness, temperance: against such there is no law" (Gal. 5:22–23).

The priest removed the garments he wore when he removed the ashes, and he put on a fresh suit. This was a continual reminder of the utter pollution of sin. The ashes of the altar spoke primarily of the judgment of sin and even the ashes were contaminated. They must be taken out and put in a clean place. What a picture this is of the defilement of sin!

And the fire upon the altar shall be burning in it; it shall not be put out: and the priest shall burn wood on it every morning, and lay the burnt offering in order upon it; and he shall burn thereon the fat of the peace offerings.

The fire shall ever be burning upon the altar; it shall never go out [Lev. 6: 12–13].

This is another reminder that the fire is to burn continually and is repeated again in verse 13. A fresh supply of wood was to be made in the morning and a burnt offering made for the whole camp. This was the morning sacrifice. The peace offering was then put on the burnt offering.

The continual burning on the altar should remind us that the fire of God burns continually. For those who reject Jesus Christ, this means the fire of God's wrath. "He that believeth on the Son hath everlasting life: and he that believeth not the Son shall not see life; but the wrath of God abideth on him" (John 3:36).

CONCERNING THE MEAL OFFERING

And this is the law of the meat offering:

the sons of Aaron shall offer it before the LORD, before the altar.

And he shall take of it his handful, of the flour of the meat offering, and of the oil thereof, and all the frankincense which is upon the meat offering, and shall burn it upon the altar for a sweet savour, even the memorial of it, unto the LORD [Lev. 6:14–15].

Again the instructions are directed to the priests. The offerer is a worshiper who stands before the altar rejoicing before God. The priest performs for him.

And the remainder thereof shall Aaron and his sons eat: with unleavened bread shall it be eaten in the holy place; in the court of the tabernacle of the congregation they shall eat it.

It shall not be baken with leaven. I have given it unto them for their portion of my offerings made by fire; it is most holy, as is the sin offering, and as the trespass offering [Lev. 6:16–17].

"With unleavened bread shall it be eaten" is translated in the Septuagint, "unleavened shall it be eaten." The holy place where it was eaten was evidently the outer court of the tabernacle. It was holy because God was there. God's presence makes any place holy. Remember Moses was told to take off his shoes because the ground on which he stood was *holy* ground (Exod. 3:5). And Peter says that at the Transfiguration, they were with Him in the *holy* mount (2 Pet. 1:18).

All the males among the children of Aaron shall eat of it. It shall be a statute for ever in your generations concerning the offerings of the LORD made by fire: every one that toucheth them shall be holy [Lev. 6:18].

All believers can participate in the enjoyment of the beauties and glories of the holy humanity of our Lord. My friend, you and I need to rejoice in Him more than we do.

And the LORD spake unto Moses, saying,

This is the offering of Aaron and of his sons, which they shall offer unto the LORD in the day when he is anointed; the tenth part of an ephah of fine flour for a meat offering perpetual, half of it in the morning, and half thereof at night.

In a pan it shall be made with oil; and when it is baken, thou shalt bring it in:

and the baken pieces of the meat offering shalt thou offer for a sweet savour unto the LORD.

And the priest of his sons that is anointed in his stead shall offer it: it is a statute for ever unto the LORD; it shall be wholly burnt.

For every meat offering for the priest shall be wholly burnt: it shall not be eaten [Lev. 6:19–23].

The priests were not only to eat but also they were to offer a tithe of the meal offering. The priest who received a tenth was in turn to offer a tenth. All of the tithe must be offered. The priests must give as well as receive.

Ministers today should set an example for their congregation in the matter of giving. The offering plate should be passed to the members of the church staff even if they are sitting on the platform during a service. We are all to have a part in giving.

CONCERNING THE SIN OFFERING

And the LORD spake unto Moses, saying,

Speak unto Aaron and to his sons, saying, This is the law of the sin offering: In the place where the burnt offering is killed shall the sin offering be killed before the LORD; it is most holy.

The priest that offereth it for sin shall eat it: in the holy place shall it be eaten, in the court of the tabernacle of the congregation.

Whatsoever shall touch the flesh thereof shall be holy: and when there is sprinkled of the blood thereof upon any garment, thou shalt wash that whereon it was sprinkled in the holy place.

But the earthen vessel wherein it is sodden shall be broken: and if it be sodden in a brasen pot, it shall be both scoured, and rinsed in water.

All the males among the priests shall eat thereof: it is most holy.

And no sin offering, whereof any of the blood is brought into the tabernacle of the congregation to reconcile withal in the holy place, shall be eaten: it shall be burnt in the fire [Lev. 6:24–30].

The instructions are again given to the priests. The sin offering, which speaks of the work of Christ on the cross, was to be offered where the burnt offering was sacrificed. The burnt offering speaks of the person of Christ. Christ must be holy, harmless, and free from sin to be a satisfactory offering for sin. He must be able to save. This is why the virgin birth is essential in the plan of salvation. This is the One who was conceived by the Holy Spirit in a virgin. The sin offering was holy because Christ was free from sin—though He was made sin for us. It was my sin and your sin that caused Him to die, not His sin. He didn't die simply because He was arrested by the Romans. He could have stepped off this earth at any moment. He told Peter that He could call for legions of angels, if He wished to do so. He was made sin for us and He died in our place.

CHAPTER 7

THEME: *Concerning the trespass offering; concerning the peace offering*

The instructions to the priests are continued for these two offerings. These two offerings were more personal than the others. The trespass concerned the individual Israelite, and was not a congregational matter. The peace must finally be enjoyed by the individual in the body of believers.

The emphasis is upon the service of the priest. This is a picture of what the Lord Jesus has done and is doing for us today at God's right hand. He is still girded with the towel of service. He still cleanses. "If we confess our sins, he is faithful and just to forgive us our sins, and to cleanse us from all unrighteousness" (1 John 1:9).

CONCERNING THE TRESPASS OFFERING

Likewise this is the law of the trespass offering: it is most holy.

In the place where they kill the burnt offering shall they kill the trespass offering: and the blood thereof shall he sprinkle round about upon the altar.

And he shall offer of it all the fat thereof; the rump, and the fat that covereth the inwards,

And the two kidneys, and the fat that is on them, which is by the flanks, and the caul that is above the liver, with the kidneys, it shall he take away:

And the priest shall burn them upon the altar for an offering made by fire unto the LORD: it is a trespass offering.

Every male among the priests shall eat thereof: it shall be eaten in the holy place: it is most holy.

As the sin offering is, so is the trespass offering: there is one law for them: the priest that maketh atonement therewith shall have it [Lev. 7:1–7].

The ritual of the trespass offering follows the same pattern as that of the sin offering. Although it is for acts of sin, the offerer is reminded that the sacrifice is holy. The worth and merit of Christ cannot be over emphasized. When we see our sin nature and our sinful acts in all their enormity and frightfulness, then we shall see the wonder, greatness, and holiness of Christ. My friend, you will never appreciate the Lord Jesus as your Savior until you see yourself as the terrible sinner that you are. *I'm* not calling you a low-down sinner. That is what the *Word of God* calls each one of us.

The blood is mentioned but is not emphasized as it is in the sin offering. We are told, however, that there is one law for them. There is a danger that we may tend to make the blood a commonplace thing. It should be dealt with reverently and reticently. It is precious, and we should be on guard that we do not treat that which is precious and holy as if it were commonplace.

And the priest that offereth any man's burnt offering, even the priest shall have to himself the skin of the burnt offering which he hath offered [Lev. 7:8].

Actually there was one part of the animal that was not burned. It was the skin, and that went to the priest. This speaks of being covered or clothed in the righteousness of Christ. God is satisfied with the Lord Jesus, and He sees us as being *in* Christ. "Even the righteousness of God which is by faith of Jesus Christ unto all and upon all them that believe: for there is no difference" (Rom. 3:22). Being clothed in Christ's righteousness is what Jesus referred to in His parable of the wedding feast. The man who entered without being clothed in a wedding garment was bound and cast out (Matt. 22:11-13).

> **And all the meat offering that is baken in the oven, and all that is dressed in the fryingpan, and in the pan, shall be the priest's that offereth it.**

> **And every meat offering, mingled with oil, and dry, shall all the sons of Aaron have, one as much as another [Lev. 7: 9-10].**

Everything baked in the oven or dressed in the frying pan was to be for the priests. This particular type of meal offering went to the priests in its entirety.

CONCERNING THE PEACE OFFERING

> **And this is the law of the sacrifice of peace offerings, which he shall offer unto the LORD.**

> **If he offer it for a thanksgiving, then he shall offer with the sacrifice of thanksgiving unleavened cakes mingled with oil, and unleavened wafers anointed with oil, and cakes mingled with oil, of fine flour, fried [Lev. 7:11-12].**

The emphasis here is upon the fact that it must be a freewill offering. The reason is for thanksgiving. This has a special meaning for believers. "By him therefore let us offer the sacrifice of praise to God continually, that is, the fruit of our lips giving thanks to his name" (Heb. 13:15). The fruit of our lips should be giving thanks to His name. Friend, we cannot come to church to worship unless we are prepared to offer the sacrifice of praise to God. A complaining, criticizing Christian is in no position to worship God. How important this is!

> **Besides the cakes, he shall offer for his offering leavened bread with the sacrifice of thanksgiving of his peace offerings.**

> **And of it he shall offer one out of the whole oblation for an heave offering unto the LORD, and it shall be the priest's that sprinkleth the blood of the peace offerings [Lev. 7:13-14].**

Notice this very carefully. In verse 12, the cakes and wafers were to be unleavened. In verse 13, the bread was to be leavened. This seems strange. Why should this be when leaven is a principle of evil? It is because in verse 12 it is showing Christ as our peace offering and he is without sin, without leaven. In verse 13, it is the offerer who gives thanks for his participation in the peace. His sins have been forgiven and he has peace with God but there is still evil in him; leaven is still present. Peace with God does not depend on the believer attaining sinless perfection. The leaven is still there. Oh, how important it is to realize this! "If we say that we have no sin, we deceive ourselves, and the truth is not in us" (1 John 1:8). The believer is to confess his sin for forgiveness and cleansing, then he is to walk by the new nature in the power of the Holy Spirit. "For sin shall not have dominion over you . . ." (Rom. 6:14). The leavened bread was a heave offering. It was to be elevated toward heaven. Just so, our hearts are to be opened to God for Him to search us and know us and to lead us in the way everlasting (Ps. 139:23-24).

> **And the flesh of the sacrifice of his peace offerings for thanksgiving shall be eaten the same day that it is offered; he shall not leave any of it until the morning.**

> **But if the sacrifice of his offering be a vow, or a voluntary offering, it shall be eaten the same day that he offereth his sacrifice: and on the morrow also the remainder of it shall be eaten:**

> **But the remainder of the flesh of the sacrifice on the third day shall be burnt with fire.**

> **And if any of the flesh of the sacrifice of his peace offerings be eaten at all on the third day, it shall not be accepted, neither shall it be imputed unto him that offereth it: it shall be an abomination, and the soul that eateth of it shall bear his iniquity [Lev. 7:15-18].**

The peace offering was to be eaten at once. There was to be no delay. Thus, we are to stay very close to Christ for peace of conscience and for power over temptation. My friend, stay close to Christ! He gives peace only to those who are His own, to those who have entered into this glorious, wonderful fellowship with Him. We must look to Him and rest upon Him.

When you find that Christ is adequate and wonderful, then the peace of God that passeth all understanding will enter into your heart. What a picture these sacrifices are of the Lord Jesus!

Now I am going to pick some verses out of the rest of the chapter.

And the flesh that toucheth any unclean thing shall not be eaten; it shall be burnt with fire: and as for the flesh, all that be clean shall eat thereof.

But the soul that eateth of the flesh of the sacrifice of peace offerings, that pertain unto the LORD, having his uncleanness upon him, even that soul shall be cut off from his people [Lev. 7:19–20].

An unclean person who ate of the peace offering was excommunicated. Even so today, there must be confession of sin on the part of the believer if he is to enter into fellowship with God.

And the LORD spake unto Moses, saying,

Speak unto the children of Israel, saying, Ye shall eat no manner of fat, of ox, or of sheep, or of goat.

Moreover ye shall eat no manner of blood, whether it be of fowl or of beast, in any of your dwellings.

Whatsoever soul it be that eateth any manner of blood, even that soul shall be cut off from his people [Lev. 7:22–23, 26–27].

We have already discussed the prohibition of eating blood. This is to remind us that man was redeemed by blood and that this is the basis and ground of our acceptance before God. They were also forbidden to eat the fat because the fat belonged to the Lord.

And the LORD spake unto Moses, saying,

Speak unto the children of Israel, saying, He that offereth the sacrifice of his peace offerings unto the LORD shall bring his oblation unto the LORD of the sacrifice of his peace offerings.

His own hands shall bring the offerings of the LORD made by fire, the fat with the breast, it shall he bring, that the breast may be waved for a wave offering before the LORD.

And the priest shall burn the fat upon the altar: but the breast shall be Aaron's and his sons'.

And the right shoulder shall ye give unto the priest for an heave offering of the sacrifices of your peace offerings.

He among the sons of Aaron, that offereth the blood of the peace offerings, and the fat, shall have the right shoulder for his part.

For the wave breast and the heave shoulder have I taken of the children of Israel from off the sacrifices of their peace offerings, and have given them unto Aaron the priest and unto his sons by a statute for ever from among the children of Israel [Lev. 7:28–34].

Aaron, his sons, and the priests received as their portion of the peace offering the breast and the shoulder. The breast speaks of the love of Christ for us. "But God commendeth his love toward us, in that, while we were yet sinners, Christ died for us" (Rom. 5:8). ". . . who loved me, and gave himself for me" (Gal. 2:20). ". . . having loved his own which were in the world, he loved them unto the end" (John 13:1).

The shoulder speaks of the power and strength of Christ. He is able to save to the uttermost. "My sheep hear my voice, and I know them, and they follow me: And I give unto them eternal life; and they shall never perish, neither shall any man pluck them out of my hand. My father, which gave them me, is greater than all; and no man is able to pluck them out of my Father's hand. I and my Father are one" (John 10:27–30).

He loves His own with an everlasting love and He can save to the uttermost. This is *our* portion in Christ!

All of these sacrifices in the Old Testament were not an end in themselves. The Old Testament saint was saved by faith just as we are saved by faith. "Offer the sacrifices of righteousness, and put your trust in the LORD" (Ps. 4:5). God was pleased when the sacrifices were brought in faith and in thanksgiving (Ps. 50:12–15 and 51:19). God was displeased when the sacrifices were brought as a dull routine and were polluted (Mal. 1:7–14).

All the sacrifices in the Old Testament demanded a more perfect antitype. This is found in Christ! "So Christ was once offered to bear the sins of many; and unto them that look for him shall he appear the second time without sin unto salvation" (Heb. 9:28).

This is the portion of the anointing of Aaron, and of the anointing of his sons, out of the offerings of the LORD made by fire, in the day when he presented them

to minister unto the LORD in the priest's office;

Which the LORD commanded to be given them of the children of Israel, in the day that he anointed them, by a statute for ever throughout their generations.

This is the law of the burnt offering, of the meat offering, and of the sin offering, and of the trespass offering, and of the consecrations, and of the sacrifice of the peace offerings;

Which the LORD commanded Moses in mount Sinai, in the day that he commanded the children of Israel to offer their oblations unto the LORD, in the wilderness of Sinai [Lev. 7:35–38].

God sums up here the instructions given to Aaron and the priests in the law of the offerings of chapters 6 and 7.

CHAPTER 8

THEME: Calling the congregation to witness the ritual of consecration of the priests; cleansing Aaron and his sons; clothing of the high priest; consecration of the high priest; clothing and cleansing the priests and Aaron; commandments given to Aaron and his sons

For the law maketh men high priests which have infirmity; but the word of the oath, which was since the law, maketh the Son, who is consecrated for evermore (Heb. 7:28).

We come now to an altogether new section concerning the consecration of the priests. The consecration of the priests is important because it will throw a great deal of light on what is called consecration today in our churches. May I say that much of what we call consecration today is a pretty sorry substitute for the real article.

Our attention is now directed to the priests and not the sacrifices. We leave the brazen altar now and turn to the brazen laver. It was at the brazen altar that God dealt with the sin question for the sinner once and for all. But that doesn't mean that the saved sinner was perfect. He still sinned, unfortunately; so God must take him to the brazen laver where He washed him and kept him clean.

God still washes us and keeps us clean at the brazen laver. Jesus Christ is still girded with that towel of service and He washes us in the brazen laver of His blood and that keeps on cleansing us from all sin.

Israel had a priesthood and this was written for them. In fact, the book of Leviticus really is written for the Levites. It was God's original intention to make the entire nation of Israel a kingdom of priests. "And ye shall be unto me a kingdom of priests, and an holy nation . . ." (Exod. 19:6). Their sin in the matter of the golden calf prevented this. Instead, only one tribe was taken, the tribe of Levi. Out of this tribe only one man was chosen as the high priest and that was Aaron.

The church today is a priesthood, and Christ is the great High Priest. ". . . We have such an high priest, who is set on the right hand of the throne of the Majesty in the heavens" (Heb. 8:1). "But ye are a chosen generation, a royal priesthood, an holy nation, a peculiar people; that ye should shew forth the praises of him who hath called you out of darkness into his marvelous light" (1 Pet. 2:9). "And hast made us unto our God kings and priests: and we shall reign on the earth" (Rev. 5:10). "And hath made us kings and priests unto God and his Father; to him be glory and dominion for ever and ever. Amen" (Rev. 1:6). "We have an altar, whereof they have no right to eat which serve the tabernacle" (Heb. 13:10). That altar today is in heaven. It is at the throne of grace.

In the future, after the church is gone, I believe that the nation Israel will be the priests on the earth during the Millennium.

The definition of a priest was not left to man's invention but is explained in the Scripture. "For every high priest taken from among men is ordained for men in things pertaining to God, that he may offer both gifts and sacrifices for sins" (Heb. 5:1). Priesthood in the Scriptures bears no similarity to any order of priests in any religion at the present time.

A priest is one who represents man before

God. He goes in to God on behalf of man. He is the opposite of a prophet. A prophet comes out from God, to speak for God, to man. A priest comes out from man and goes to God, to speak for man to God, and to represent man.

You can see that the Lord Jesus is both Prophet and Priest. He came out from God and spoke for God to man. He reveals God to man. Now He has gone from man back to God and is our great High Priest. He represents us there. In fact, we are in Him! My friend, if you are not in Him, then you are not up there. You and I could never get there on our own.

A knowledge of the tabernacle is essential to an understanding of the Book of Leviticus and especially of the priesthood. The typology of the tabernacle and of the priesthood is so rich in meaning and detail that there is a danger of emphasizing one facet to the exclusion of another and thereby giving a wrong inference. I do think we need to note that the outer court of the tabernacle represents the world down here. This is where Christ bled and died. The Holy Place is the unseen to which our great High Priest has gone.

Actually, this is what happened when the Lord Jesus died on the cross and then went back up to heaven. He took the tabernacle and the meaning of it which was horizontal here on the earth and He made it perpendicular. That is, the altar is down here—this is where He died on the cross. The Holy Place is up there, and He is even now in the Holy of Holies. Listen to these passages which explain this. "Seeing then that we have a great high priest, that is passed into the heavens, Jesus the Son of God, let us hold fast our profession" (Heb. 4:14). "But Christ being come an high priest of good things to come, by a greater and more perfect tabernacle, not made with hands, that is to say, not of this building" (Heb. 9:11). "Now of the things which we have spoken this is the sum: We have such an high priest, who is set on the right hand of the throne of the Majesty in the heavens; A minister of the sanctuary, and of the true tabernacle, which the Lord pitched, and not man" (Heb. 8:1–2). "It was therefore necessary that the patterns of things in the heavens should be purified with these; but the heavenly things themselves with better sacrifices than these. For Christ is not entered into the holy places made with hands, which are the figures of the true; but into heaven itself, now to appear in the presence of God for us" (Heb. 9:23–24).

He is up yonder today. I wish we could bring this reality into our faith. We attend church and go through a little ritual and often the realities of our faith are forgotten. He is up yonder, friend, right now. You are to approach God through Him. We are told to come with boldness. He appears now in the presence of God *for us*. My friend, you are not alone down here. There is availability with God through Christ. The tabernacle is now perpendicular and the Holy of Holies is in heaven.

Twelve times in this chapter it is stated that the Lord commanded Moses. The final clincher is the last verse, "So Aaron and his sons did all things which the LORD commanded by the hand of Moses" (Lev. 8:36). These are the things which God commanded. Consecration must be the way He says it is to be done!

Some people believe in a late dating of the Book of Leviticus as the invention of the priesthood. Yet it says here that this was all done as God commanded it. Do you believe in the inspired Word of God? Then you cannot accept the late dating of Leviticus, but believe the inerrancy of Scripture and that this was done at the command of God.

CALLING OF THE CONGREGATION TO WITNESS THE RITUAL

And the LORD spake unto Moses, saying,

Take Aaron and his sons with him, and the garments, and the anointing oil, and a bullock for the sin offering, and two rams, and a basket of unleavened bread;

And gather thou all the congregation together unto the door of the tabernacle of the congregation [Lev. 8:1–3].

Moses is commanded to bring Aaron and his sons, with all the articles which are to be used in the consecration of the priests, to the door of the tabernacle. This sounds somewhat like a grocery list, but every item it mentions is very important.

Then he is to gather the congregation together to witness the ritual of consecrating the priests. This is to be a very impressive service. They will see that God takes feeble men and sets them aside for His service. I feel like saying a Hallelujah to that because He will do that for you and for me. "For the law maketh men high priests which have infirmity; but the word of the oath, which was since the law, maketh the Son, who is consecrated for evermore" (Heb. 7:28). Christ was really consecrated. In a sense no one else is really consecrated. But the marvellous thing is that God will accept men with infirmities. If He demanded perfection, we would all be left out. Thank God, He takes them as they are, infirm.

And Moses did as the LORD commanded him; and the assembly was gathered together unto the door of the tabernacle of the congregation.

And Moses said unto the congregation, This is the thing which the LORD commanded to be done [Lev. 8:4–5].

Moses does what he is commanded to do. The people likewise obey and come together for this service. Moses gives a word of explanation that he is following the instructions of the Lord in all that he does.

CLEANSING OF AARON AND HIS SONS

And Moses brought Aaron and his sons, and washed them with water [Lev. 8:6].

Moses brings Aaron and his sons to the laver for washing. He gives them a bath, if you please. This signifies that they are to be holy, pure, and clean if they are to serve the Lord. They have already been to the altar for forgiveness, but they need cleansing.

A great many people today say that they are qualified for service because they are saved. Now it is true that salvation is the prime requisite, but for service one must also be cleansed. You must be cleansed to be used! Listen to these verses from Scripture: "Not by works of righteousness which we have done, but according to his mercy he saved us, by the washing of regeneration, and renewing of the Holy Ghost" (Titus 3:5). "Let us draw near with a true heart in full assurance of faith, having our hearts sprinkled from an evil conscience, and our bodies washed with pure water" (Heb. 10:22). "That he might sanctify and cleanse it with the washing of water by the word" (Eph. 5:26). "Jesus saith to him, He that is washed needeth not save to wash his feet, but is clean every whit: and ye are clean, but not all" (John 13:10). "If we confess our sins, he is faithful and just to forgive us our sins, and to cleanse us from all unrighteousness" (1 John 1:9).

The Holy Ghost renews us as we go along, but we need a washing from the Lord. With what does He wash us? What is the cleansing agent? It is the Word of God. That is what cleanses us. The Lord said that His disciples needed to be washed because their feet were dirty. They all had a bath; that is, they all had been saved (except Judas), but they still needed their feet washed so that they might have fellowship with Him. This cleansing is for service.

How do we get that washing? It is by *confession* that we are forgiven and cleansed. Do you want to be used of God? Then go confess your sins, dear Christian. That is the first step. This is God's way. This is His command. We either must do it His way or we cannot be of service. He has His way of doing things and we need to learn and obey His ways.

CLOTHING OF THE HIGH PRIEST

And he put upon him the coat, and girded him with the girdle, and clothed him with the robe, and put the ephod upon him, and he girded him with the curious girdle of the ephod, and bound it unto him therewith [Lev. 8:7].

The clothing of the high priest is a picture of our great High Priest in all His extraordinary graces and glory. Each article of clothing was symbolic. There were eight articles worn by the high priest. Four were the same or similar to those worn by all the priests. Four were peculiar to him, and separated him from the other priests. They were garments for glory and for beauty.

The four which were common to all the priests were as follows: the coat, the girdle, the turban or mitre or bonnet, and the breeches. These were all made of white linen, with the exception of the turban. The white linen speaks of righteousness. Every believer is clothed in the righteousness of Christ. It is essential for service to be thus clothed, and to be girded is necessary for active obedience. The coat and girdle mentioned in this verse were the basic garments which all the priests wore. These garments are described in detail in Exodus 28.

And he put the breastplate upon him: also he put in the breastplate the Urim and the Thummim [Lev. 8:8].

The breastplate is also described in Exodus 28. The Urim and Thummim were placed in the breastplate. *Urim* means "light" and *Thummim* means "perfections," so these were the lights and perfections. I do not know exactly how they functioned. Some think that they had to do with the Law and that possibly the Law was written on stones. In Psalm 19 there is a reference to this. "The law of the LORD is perfect, [perfections—Thummim], converting the soul: the testimony of the LORD is sure, making wise the simple " (Ps. 19:7). "The statutes of the LORD are right, rejoicing the heart: the commandment of the LORD is pure, enlightening the eyes [light—Urim]" (Ps. 19:8).

Apparently the Urim and Thummim had something to do with determining the will of God. There is a spiritual application for us. We need the Word of God today, and we need the leading of God to determine the will of God in our lives.

And he put the mitre upon his head; also upon the mitre, even upon his forefront, did he put the golden plate, the holy crown; as the LORD commanded Moses [Lev. 8:9].

The mitre of the high priest had put upon it the golden crown described in Exodus 28. Remember that graven upon it was HOLINESS TO THE LORD. These garments distinguished the high priest from the other priests. They set forth the glories and beauties of our great High Priest who died down here to save us and lives at God's right hand to keep us saved. "For if, when we were enemies, we were reconciled to God by the death of his Son, much more, being reconciled, we shall be saved by his life" (Rom. 5:10). ". . . because I live, ye shall live also" (John 14:19).

The sons of Aaron were at his side clothed in simple linen. This is a picture of our great High Priest with His many sons who are being gathered with Him and who are clothed in His righteousness. "For it became him, for whom are all things, and by whom are all things, in bringing many sons unto glory, to make the captain of their salvation perfect through sufferings" (Heb. 2:10). We come to Christ as lost sinners and He covers us with His righteousness.

The priest carried stones on each shoulder with six of the names of the twelve tribes on each shoulder. The twelve stones on the breastplate had a name of each of the tribes on each, one tribe on each stone. The great high priest carried the nation of Israel on his shoulder and upon his heart. The shoulder speaks of strength and the heart speaks of love.

CONSECRATION OF THE HIGH PRIEST

And Moses took the anointing oil, and anointed the tabernacle and all that was therein, and sanctified them [Lev. 8:10].

The tabernacle and all the vessels of the ministry had been sprinkled with blood (Heb. 9:21). Now it is anointed with oil. They were already redeemed and cleansed by the blood. Now they are anointed with the oil which symbolizes the Holy Spirit. Now the Holy Spirit is free to move and work in the worship and service of the tabernacle. "God is a Spirit: and they that worship him must worship him in spirit and in truth" (John 4:24).

And he sprinkled thereof upon the altar seven times, and anointed the altar and all his vessels, both the laver and his foot, to sanctify them.

And he poured of the anointing oil upon Aaron's head, and anointed him, to sanctify him [Lev. 8:11–12].

The act of sprinkling the oil speaks of sanctification. All was now ready for use, having been set apart for the service of God. Aaron was not sprinkled but anointed with the oil. He was just covered with oil! "It is like the precious ointment upon the head, that ran down upon the beard, even Aaron's beard: that went down to the skirts of his garments" (Ps. 133:2).

Just so the Holy Spirit (of whom oil is the symbol) was poured out upon Christ at His baptism. It is distinctly stated that ". . . God giveth not the Spirit by *measure* unto him" (John 3:34). In other words, God gives to His Son the Holy Spirit without measure.

It must be noted that the oil was poured on Aaron before the priests had the blood applied to them. Our High Priest needed no offering for sin. We do; He did not. "Thou hast loved righteousness, and hated iniquity; therefore God, even thy God, hath anointed thee with the oil of gladness above thy fellows" (Heb. 1:9).

CLOTHING OF THE PRIESTS

And Moses brought Aaron's sons, and put coats upon them, and girded them with girdles, and put bonnets upon them; as the LORD commanded Moses [Lev. 8:13].

We are told again that this was was all done according to the commandment of the Lord. This reminds us once more that we must stand clothed in the righteousness of Christ.

CLEANSING OF THE PRIESTS AND AARON

And he brought the bullock for the sin offering: and Aaron and his sons laid their hands upon the head of the bullock for the sin offering [Lev. 8:14].

The bullock was the sin offering for the high priest. The four sons of Aaron could claim it as their offering, too. Their sins are transferred to the victim. That is understood by the laying on of hands. God wrote indelibly in their souls and burned it into their hearts that they were sinners, even though they were in the service of God.

You will find as you go through the Word of God that God's men have always been conscious of the fact that they are sinners. "For innumerable evils have compassed me about: mine iniquities have taken hold upon me, so that I am not able to look up; they are more than the hairs of mine head: therefore my heart faileth me" (Ps. 40:12). Friend, do you feel that you are that kind of a sinner? God can do something for you if you are like that. After all, if you don't get sick enough to go to the doctor, you won't go to him. If you aren't sure that you are a real sinner, you are not apt to go to Christ. "For mine iniquities are gone over mine head: as an heavy burden they are too heavy for me" (Ps. 38:4).

Friends, if you have a load that is too heavy for you, get someone else to carry it for you. There is Someone who says, "Come unto me all ye that labor and are heavy laden. I will give you rest. I'll take your burdens." And don't try to fool God. He knows all about you; so you might just as well tell Him the whole story.

And he slew it; and Moses took the blood, and put it upon the horns of the altar round about with his finger, and purified the altar, and poured the blood at the bottom of the altar, and sanctified it, to make reconciliation upon it.

And he took all the fat that was upon the inwards, and the caul above the liver, and the two kidneys, and their fat, and Moses burned it upon the altar.

But the bullock, and his hide, his flesh, and his dung, he burnt with fire without the camp; as the LORD commanded Moses [Lev. 8:15–17].

This ritual is meaningless until we understand the spiritual lesson. They follow the ritual of the sin offering with the exception that the blood is put on the horns of the brazen altar rather than on the golden altar. Even the altar which is used for the bloody sacrifices must be dedicated with blood. This is to remind us that there is no merit in the wood of the cross. There are a lot of people today who feel there is some merit in the cross itself. There is no merit in the cross! *The merit is in the One who shed His blood for us there.* Though He became sin for us, He was not polluted with sin. He was not stained with sin. He was "made sin" and yet He was "separate from sinners." Again, we notice that all this was done at the commandment of God.

And he brought the ram for the burnt offering: and Aaron and his sons laid their hands upon the head of the ram.

And he killed it; and Moses sprinkled the blood upon the altar round about.

And he cut the ram into pieces; and Moses burnt the head, and the pieces, and the fat.

And he washed the inwards and the legs in water; and Moses burnt the whole ram upon the altar: it was a burnt sacrifice for a sweet savour, and an offering made by fire unto the LORD; as the LORD commanded Moses [Lev. 8:18–21].

They now go through the ritual of the burnt offering. The burnt offering followed the sin offering. It is impossible to comprehend the beauties and merits of Christ until the sin question has been dealt with in a manner satisfactory to God. The sin offering represents what Christ did for us on the cross. The burnt offering represents who He is. You can never really know Him until you come to Him first to save you and you accept Him as your substitute for sin. He paid the penalty for your sin. That is of prime importance to know.

Actually, *fellowship* in the New Testament means to share the things of Christ. Only those who are the blood-bought believers can share the things of Christ. The priests had to go inside the holy place to see the beauties of that place. The outside was not very pretty. Just so, the unbelieving world does not see the beauty of Christ and rejects Him, but the child of God is finding new beauties and glories in Him every day.

And he brought the other ram, the ram of consecration: and Aaron and his sons laid their hands upon the head of the ram.

And he slew it; and Moses took of the blood of it, and put it upon the tip of Aaron's right ear, and upon the thumb of his right hand, and upon the great toe of his right foot.

And he brought Aaron's sons and Moses put of the blood upon the tip of their right ear, and upon the thumbs of their right hands, and upon the great toes of their right feet: and Moses sprinkled the blood upon the altar round about [Lev. 8:22–24].

The ram of consecration was actually a trespass offering. No peace offerings were made. Why not? Because the priests were already in the sanctuary, the place of fellowship and communion.

The blood-tipped ear symbolizes the ear that will hear the voice of God. Without that, friend, you are not going to hear Him. The natural man does not receive the things of Christ. The blood-tipped hand was essential for service. It is impossible to serve the Lord before one is saved. The blood-tipped foot was essential for the walk before God. All of this is symbolic of the fact that the *total* personality must be presented to God.

> **And he took the fat, and the rump, and all the fat that was upon the inwards, and the caul above the liver, and the two kidneys, and their fat, and the right shoulder:**
>
> **And out of the basket of unleavened bread, that was before the LORD, he took one unleavened cake, and a cake of oiled bread, and one wafer, and put them on the fat, and upon the right shoulder:**
>
> **And he put all upon Aaron's hands, and upon his sons' hands, and waved them for a wave offering before the LORD.**
>
> **And Moses took them from off their hands, and burnt them on the altar upon the burnt offering: they were consecrations for a sweet savour: it is an offering made by fire unto the LORD.**
>
> **And Moses took the breast, and waved it for a wave offering before the LORD: for of the ram of consecration it was Moses' part; as the LORD commanded Moses [Lev. 8:25–29].**

These verses tell that they took parts from all the offerings and put them together and placed them in the hands of Aaron and his sons. They then waved them before the Lord. This was total commitment to God on the basis of the value of one offering. "So Christ was once offered to bear the sins of many; and unto them that look for him shall he appear the second time without sin unto salvation" (Heb. 9:28).

> **And Moses took of the anointing oil, and of the blood which was upon the altar, and sprinkled it upon Aaron, and upon his garments, and upon his sons, and upon his sons' garments with him; and sanctified Aaron, and his garments, and his sons, and his sons' garments with him [Lev. 8:30].**

Now the priests together with Aaron are consecrated with blood and oil. Blood is for the forgiveness of sins, the work of Christ; the oil is for the anointing of the Spirit of God. (The instructions for this were given in Exodus 29:21.) This speaks of the Lord Jesus who said, "And for their sakes I sanctify myself, that they also might be sanctified through the truth" (John 17:19).

This should also remind us that believers are to walk before the world as the blood-bought children of God. This is what Jude meant "And others save with fear, pulling them out of the fire; hating even the garment spotted by the flesh" (Jude 23). You see, we can go through consecration services and make promises of consecration, but the real question is what your neighbors think about you. What do the folk where you go to school think of you? Do the people with whom you work think that you are serving God? Do they think you are consecrated?

I heard a wonderful thing about a Christian the other day. An unsaved man said, "I don't know much about that fellow's religion, but if I ever get religion, I want his kind." I'm afraid that too often what the world sees of the Christian is not really very appealing. Our life should be so that it would attract the man out in the world to the Lord Jesus Christ.

COMMANDMENTS GIVEN TO AARON AND HIS SONS

> **And Moses said unto Aaron and to his sons, Boil the flesh at the door of the tabernacle of the congregation: and there eat it with the bread that is in the basket of consecrations, as I commanded, saying, Aaron and his sons shall eat it.**
>
> **And that which remaineth of the flesh and of the bread shall ye burn with fire [Lev. 8:31–32].**

I told you at the beginning of this section that this sounds like a grocery list, and this is how this section on consecration ends. They are to eat the food that is left. This typifies the fact that believers are now to feed upon the finished work of Christ. Peace and satisfaction are the portion of the believers only in ratio to the measure in which they feed on Christ. Nothing is to be left. All must be consumed or burnt with fire. Nothing is to be left to spoil or waste. Oh, how God's people need to feed upon Him!

> **And ye shall not go out of the door of the tabernacle of the congregation in seven days, until the days of your consecration be at an end: for seven days shall he consecrate you.**

As he hath done this day, so the LORD
hath commanded to do, to make an
atonement for you.

Therefore shall ye abide at the door of
the tabernacle of the congregation day
and night seven days, and keep the
charge of the LORD, that ye die not: for
so I am commanded.

So Aaron and his sons did all things
which the LORD commanded by the hand
of Moses [Lev. 8:33–36].

There were to be seven days of consecration
and meditation. They were to remain continually on duty at the door of the tabernacle.
So it is with our great High Priest who ever
lives to make intercession for His own. You
may wake up at 2:00 A.M., and He is right up
there for you. You may be out in a difficult and
dark place, but He is right up there for you. He
is always available!

All this was done at the commandment of
God. This is emphasized, as it is repeated in
each of the last three verses of this chapter.
The reason for this will be made clear in the
next chapter.

CHAPTER 9

*THEME: Aaron prepares to begin his service; Aaron offers the
sin offering; Aaron offers the burnt offering; Aaron offers the
meal and peace offerings; Aaron blesses the people and the glory
of the Lord appears*

This chapter is intensely interesting, as it
not only marks the initiation of Aaron and
his sons into the service of the priesthood, but
it gives in detail the daily ritual of the service of
the priests. With the exception of the great
Day of Atonement, very little detail is given in
the remainder of Scripture relative to the daily
ritual.

This marks the time when the priest for the
first time became a priest. Although one was
born in Aaron's line, he was not fully a priest
until he was consecrated. The Hebrew word
for consecration literally means "to fill the
hand." That means we come to God with empty
hands. Consecration isn't a promise to go out
as a missionary or to do something else for the
Lord. Consecration means to come to the Lord
with empty hands and ask, "Lord, what will
You have me to do?" *He* does the filling! That is
consecration.

Too many folk think they must bring something to God if they are to be consecrated. Some
folk seem to think they are giving the Lord a
whole lot if they give themselves. We're not
giving Him very much, friends. When He got
me, all He got was just so much sin. That's all.

The Septuagint adopted the Greek word
teleioo to express consecration. This expresses
the same thought. *Telos* means "end," and it
means "the purpose," meaning to accomplish
what God wants you to accomplish. It means to

fulfill the end for which you were born. We
were born for the purpose of completing the
body of Christ. And He was born for the purpose of coming down here to accomplish the
will of God in order that He might bring us
home to glory. "For it became him, for whom
are all things, and by whom are all things, in
bringing many sons unto glory, to make the
captain of their salvation perfect through sufferings" (Heb. 2:10). You see, Jesus was consecrated. He had a purpose. "For the law maketh
men high priests which have infirmity; but the
word of the oath, which was since the law,
maketh the Son, who is consecrated for evermore" (Heb. 7:28).

In this chapter it is the office of Jesus, not
His character, which is in view. It is Jesus
accomplishing the purpose, the God-given purpose, in His office.

AARON PREPARES
TO BEGIN HIS SERVICE

And it came to pass on the eighth day,
that Moses called Aaron and his sons,
and the elders of Israel;

And he said unto Aaron, Take thee a
young calf for a sin offering, and a ram
for a burnt offering, without blemish,
and offer them before the LORD [Lev.
9:1–2].

All of this was done at the commandment of God. They had carried out the details of the seven days and now, on the eighth day, Aaron was to begin his service as the high priest. The eighth day is the first day of the week! That is the day that Jesus came back from the dead. Christ entered into His office as High Priest after His death and resurrection.

Hebrews 8:4 and 9:10–12 tell us that if Christ were on earth, He would not be a priest. It was after He ascended into heaven that He became a High Priest in the tabernacle not made with hands, up in heaven. By His own blood He entered into the Holy Place.

As Aaron entered into his office as high priest on the first day of the week, his four sons were there as witnesses. Likewise, we have four Gospels which bear witness to the fact of the death and resurrection of Christ. We today have a perfect and complete Priest. "And being made perfect, he became the author of eternal salvation unto all them that obey him" (Heb. 5:9). We obey Him when we believe Him and believe on Him. We obey Him, after we are believers, when we attempt to do His will. That is consecration, friends. We come to him empty; we hold out our empty hands and ask Christ to fill us.

Aaron was not our great High Priest. He needed to make a sin offering for himself. The high priest on all great public occasions began by making an offering for himself. By this he was declaring that he was not the Christ but that there would be One who comes after him. He would be the great High Priest— "Who needeth not daily, as those high priests, to offer up sacrifice, first for his own sins, and then for the people's: for this he did once, when he offered up himself" (Heb. 7:27).

And unto the children of Israel thou shalt speak, saying, Take ye a kid of the goats for a sin offering; and a calf and a lamb, both of the first year, without blemish, for a burnt offering;

Also a bullock and a ram for peace offerings, to sacrifice before the LORD; and a meat offering mingled with oil: for to day the LORD will appear unto you [Lev. 9:3–4].

Aaron was commanded to have the people bring all the offerings to God with the exception of the trespass offering. At the very beginning there was no need for the trespass offering because they had not had time to commit a trespass. They offered the regular kid of the goats for the sin offering; a double offering of a calf and a lamb for the burnt offering; a double offering of a bullock and a ram for the peace offering; and the regular meal offering. The glory of the Lord was to appear to them that day. This was to show that through the death of Christ, on to the resurrected High Priest at God's right hand, is the way we approach God.

And they brought that which Moses commanded before the tabernacle of the congregation: and all the congregation drew near and stood before the LORD.

And Moses said, This is the thing which the LORD commanded that ye should do: and the glory of the LORD shall appear unto you.

And Moses said unto Aaron, Go unto the altar, and offer thy sin offering, and thy burnt offering, and make an atonement for thyself, and for the people: and offer the offering of the people, and make an atonement for them; as the LORD commanded [Lev. 9:5–7].

The people obey, and Moses assures them that the glory of the Lord will appear to them.

AARON OFFERS THE SIN OFFERING

Aaron therefore went unto the altar, and slew the calf of the sin offering, which was for himself.

And the sons of Aaron brought the blood unto him: and he dipped his finger in the blood, and put it upon the horns of the altar, and poured out the blood at the bottom of the altar:

But the fat, and the kidneys, and the caul above the liver of the sin offering, he burnt upon the altar; as the LORD commanded Moses.

And the flesh and the hide he burnt with fire without the camp [Lev. 9:8–11].

These verses describe how Aaron carried out the ritual of the sin offering in meticulous detail. The sin offering was made first. Why? When the offerings were first presented, the burnt offering was first and the sin offering came last. Well, you see, the offerings were first presented from God's viewpoint. But now we are approaching God from man's viewpoint. Man comes to God as a sinner. You and I, my friend, come as sinners. It is the sin question which must be settled first. "In whom we have redemption through his blood, the forgiveness of sins, according to the riches of his grace" (Eph. 1:7).

AARON OFFERS THE BURNT OFFERING

The ritual for the burnt offering was followed in meticulous detail. First Aaron offered for himself.

And he slew the burnt offering: and Aaron's sons presented unto him the blood, which he sprinkled round about upon the altar.

And they presented the burnt offering unto him, with the pieces thereof, and the head: and he burnt them upon the altar.

And he did wash the inwards and the legs, and burnt them upon the burnt offering on the altar [Lev. 9:12–14].

The sin offering and the burnt offering for the people was then presented.

And he brought the people's offering, and took the goat, which was the sin offering for the people, and slew it, and offered it for sin, as the first.

And he brought the burnt offering, and offered it according to the manner [Lev. 9:15–16].

All of this is a picture of Christ. "Yet it pleased the LORD to bruise him; he hath put him to grief: when thou shalt make his soul an offering for sin, he shall see his seed, he shall prolong his days, and the pleasure of the LORD shall prosper in his hand" (Isa. 53:10). "For he hath made him to be sin for us, who knew no sin; that we might be made the righteousness of God in him" (2 Cor. 5:21).

The sin offering is made sin. Christ had the sin of the world pressed down upon Him as one great globe, a whole world, of sin.

AARON OFFERS THE MEAL AND PEACE OFFERINGS

And he brought the meat offering, and took an handful thereof, and burnt it upon the altar, beside the burnt sacrifice of the morning.

He slew also the bullock and the ram for a sacrifice of peace offerings, which was for the people: and Aaron's sons presented unto him the blood, which he sprinkled upon the altar round about,

And the fat of the bullock and of the ram, the rump, and that which covereth the inwards, and the kidneys, and the caul above the liver:

And they put the fat upon the breasts, and he burnt the fat upon the altar:

And the breasts and the right shoulder Aaron waved for a wave offering before the LORD; as Moses commanded [Lev. 9:17–21].

The meal offering followed the regular ritual. The same is true for the peace offering. Aaron, as the representative for the nation, presents the sacrifices before the Lord through the shedding of the blood. The people are accepted. Blessing will follow.

AARON BLESSES THE PEOPLE AND THE GLORY OF THE LORD APPEARS

And Aaron lifted up his hand toward the people, and blessed them, and came down from offering of the sin offering, and the burnt offering, and peace offerings.

And Moses and Aaron went into the tabernacle of the congregation, and came out, and blessed the people: and the glory of the LORD appeared unto all the people.

And there came a fire out from before the LORD, and consumed upon the altar the burnt offering and the fat: which when all the people saw, they shouted, and fell on their faces [Lev. 9:22–24].

Blessing follows the offering of the three offerings: the sin offering, the burnt offering, and the peace offering. Then Moses and Aaron retired into the tabernacle. It is thought that at the time of the evening sacrifice they came forth to bless the people and then the glory of the Lord appeared. All is complete now. The people shout and fall on their faces in adoration and praise.

Christ is now entered into the Holy Place, which is in heaven itself, to appear there for you and me today. Oh, my friend, lay hold of this *living* Christ. Fall before Him in adoration and praise.

CHAPTER 10

THEME: *Incident concerning Nadab and Abihu, sons of Aaron;*
instructions coming out of the incident; injunctions concerning
the offerings in connection with the incident

The Book of Leviticus has very little narrative, but is filled with instructions, rituals, regulations, and laws. This chapter offers a change of pace in the reading for it is a narrative. However, the interest is almost obliterated because it is a horrible tragedy which is recorded here.

This is another blot on man's long and sordid history of sin and willfulness. It is the record of the rebellion and disobedience of the two sons of Aaron. It follows the glorious day of dedication recorded in the preceding chapter. So often we find this happening. After a flush of victory, there is defeat—as in the Book of Joshua, the victory of Jericho is followed by the ignoble defeat at Ai.

The presumption of Nadab and Abihu is frightening in the light of the clear teaching which God gave at Sinai. "And let the priests also, which come near to the LORD, sanctify themselves, lest the LORD break forth upon them" (Exod. 19:22). In Exodus 30:34–38 God gave to Moses the formula for the incense to be used in the tabernacle and said, "As for the perfume which thou shalt make, ye shall not make to yourselves according to the composition thereof: it shall be unto thee holy for the LORD. Whosoever shall make like unto that, to smell thereto, shall even be cut off from his people" (Exod. 30:37–38).

The holiness of God is set forth at the beginning of the age of Law by this incident. The holiness of God is set forth at the beginning of the age of Grace by the incident concerning Ananias and Sapphira. Death was the drastic penalty in both cases. Our God is holy, and He deals with His children on that level. "For our God is a consuming fire" (Heb. 12:29) is something we all need to learn today. "Knowing therefore the terror of the Lord, we persuade men . . ." (2 Cor. 5:11). This is something we need to recognize today.

There is a warning in Hebrews 12:25: "See that ye refuse not him that speaketh. For if they escaped not who refused him that spake on earth, much more shall not we escape, if we turn away from him that speaketh from heaven." This is one of the great sins of the hour. People are not hearing what God has to say in His Word.

INCIDENT CONCERNING NADAB AND ABIHU, SONS OF AARON

And Nadab and Abihu, the sons of Aaron, took either of them his censer, and put fire therein, and put incense thereon, and offered strange fire before the LORD, which he commanded them not.

And there went out fire from the LORD, and devoured them, and they died before the LORD [Lev. 10:1–2].

It may be argued that the penalty of death was too severe for the transgression committed. But notice particularly what God says here, "Which he commanded them not." This reveals something of the enormity of the crime, and therefore the penalty is just. This was willful and deliberate disobedience to the expressed command of God.

Precisely what did they do which brought down such severe judgment upon them? This act has been called "will-worship" and that is what it is. What did they do wrong? I'd like to make three suggestions:

1. They probably did not light the censer of incense from coals from off the altar, which was the fire which had come down from heaven. It apparently was understood that this must be done. This was the practice on the Great Day of Atonement as is clearly stated in Leviticus 16:12: "And he shall take a censer full of burning coals of fire from off the altar before the Lord, and his hands full of sweet incense beaten small, and bring it within the veil." This was the same ritual followed at the time of the rebellion of Korah (Num. 16:46). It must be assumed that this method was the only correct one. The ritual they followed was contrary to God's way.

2. Their timing was out of step with the God-given ritual. The ritual for the day had been completed. They should have consulted Aaron in this matter. Apparently, they wanted to repeat the marvelous display of the preceding chapter. Isn't this a problem today, when with our will-worship we try to duplicate what God has done? There are many who try to duplicate the experience of the day of Pente-

cost. God is sovereign! His will must be followed even as to the timing. The Spirit of God will move according to His own will. We should simply make ourselves available and obedient to Him.

3. Others have supposed that they intruded beyond the veil which was expressly forbidden. There is justification for their viewpoint as stated in Leviticus 16:1–2: "And the LORD spake unto Moses after the death of the two sons of Aaron, when they offered before the LORD, and died; And the LORD said unto Moses, Speak unto Aaron thy brother, that he come not at all times into the holy place within the veil before the mercy seat, which is upon the ark; that he die not: for I will appear in the cloud upon the mercy seat."

It would seem that this prohibition came out of the incident of Nadab and Abihu. They were wrong as to the place they should come. God had commanded them as to the manner, the time, and the place. They were wrong in all three.

Some may still think that God surely uses extreme surgery. It *does* reveal that our God is a jealous God. He is sovereign in all His dealings, and those who come to Him must come on His terms. It is still true that to obey is better than sacrifice. God will not accept worship in our own will, no matter how sincere. We need to note here, too, that the high position of these men offered them no immunity.

The sudden execution of judgment here is startling. There is no escaping the statement that the fire was from the Lord. Let us recognize that judgment is not foreign to the age of Grace. It may not always be this sudden. "For this cause many are weak and sickly among you, and many sleep" (1 Cor. 11:30). In the case of Ananias and Sapphira it was just as sudden and sure.

This does not mean that the believer in Christ can lose his salvation! Nadab and Abihu, and Ananias and Sapphira did not lose their salvation. Neither did the believers in the Corinthian congregation. This is made very clear. "For if we would judge ourselves, we should not be judged. But when we are judged, we are chastened of the Lord, that we should not be condemned with the world" (1 Cor. 11:31–32).

Physical death is oftentimes a judgment for the child of God. There is a sin unto death (1 John 5:16) but it is physical death. The child of God is not condemned with the world. These judgments in both the Old and New Testaments are examples to believers that will-worship is detestable to God. The be-

liever must come to God in God's way. The believing sinner must worship God's way.

Hebrews 10:19–22 tells us very definitely that we are to come to God with boldness, but that it must be by the blood of Jesus. We come because we have an High Priest over the house of God. We are to come ". . . with a true heart in full assurance of faith, having our hearts sprinkled from an evil conscience, and our bodies washed with pure water." God makes a difference! "And that ye may put difference between holy and unholy, and between unclean and clean" (Lev. 10:10). Don't get the idea that God can't move in with judgment today.

Let me get very personal. A friend of mine, who knows me very well, said, "McGee, since you have had cancer and you know you still have cancer in your body now, did it ever occur to you that maybe it is a judgment from God?" I told this brother, "You know, I have waked up in the stillness and darkness of the night and I've thought just that, and I have cried out to God." May I say to you, I don't exclude myself. If we don't judge ourselves, God will judge us, so that we are not condemned with the world! God does all things well! When I say these things to you, remember that I am going through it. This fellow knows what he is talking about.

What an illustration this is that sometime Jesus will come in fiery judgment upon the lost world. Enoch preached this! Enoch prophesied, ". . . Behold, the Lord cometh with ten thousands of his saints, To execute judgment upon all, and to convince all that are ungodly among them of all their ungodly deeds which they have ungodly committed, and of all their hard speeches which ungodly sinners have spoken against him" (Jude 14–15). Peter said the same thing. "And if the righteous scarcely be saved, where shall the ungodly and the sinner appear?" (1 Pet. 4:18).

Then Moses said unto Aaron, This is it that the LORD spake, saying, I will be sanctified in them that come nigh me, and before all the people I will be glorified. And Aaron held his peace.

And Moses called Mishael and Elzaphan, the sons of Uzziel the uncle of Aaron, and said unto them, Come near, carry your brethren from before the sanctuary out of the camp.

So they went near, and carried them in their coats out of the camp; as Moses had said [Lev. 10:3–5].

When the news spread throughout the hosts of Israel, the people must have gathered about the tabernacle to view the dead bodies of these young men. Moses quoted the words of the Lord to give them an explanation for the judgment. "And let the priests also, which come near to the LORD, sanctify themselves, lest the LORD break forth upon them" (Exod. 19:22).

Those who have been brought into a particular nearness to God must exercise a sharp insight into the holiness and the righteous demands of God. "You only have I known of all the families of the earth: therefore I will punish you for all your iniquities" (Amos 3:2). As God judged His people Israel, so God judges His saints today in order that the world may know He is a holy God.

Aaron's attitude and conduct are noticeable. He maintains a demeanor of silence. There is no cry of disappointment, grief, or resentment toward God. He bows in heartbroken submission to the will of God. His grief must have been deep, but he can say nothing against the sovereign will of God. You notice God says, "I will be sanctified in them that come nigh me."

Moses called upon two of the priests who were cousins of the slain men to remove the dead bodies from before the sanctuary. As the people looked on in awe, they were carried out of the camp.

INSTRUCTIONS COMING OUT OF THE INCIDENT

And Moses said unto Aaron, and unto Eleazar and unto Ithamar, his sons, Uncover not your heads, neither rend your clothes; lest ye die, and lest wrath come upon all the people: but let your brethren, the whole house of Israel, bewail the burning which the LORD hath kindled.

And ye shall not go out from the door of the tabernacle of the congregation, lest ye die: for the anointing oil of the LORD is upon you. And they did according to the word of Moses [Lev. 10:6–7].

A restriction is placed on Aaron and his two remaining sons. They were not to mourn outwardly. There is a twofold reason for this. The first is clearly stated, "the anointing oil of the LORD is upon you." They were set aside to represent the people before God, and they were God's representatives before the people. They were to continue in their office that there might be a mediator between God and man lest wrath should come upon the people and the judgment of death be upon them. In the second

place, they were not to show the outward signs of mourning which would contradict the action of God in judging their loved ones. It must be added that they must have gone about their office with sad hearts. They were serving God and there must be no evidence of rebellion against Him.

And the LORD spake unto Aaron, saying,

Do not drink wine nor strong drink, thou, nor thy sons with thee, when ye go into the tabernacle of the congregation, lest ye die: it shall be a statute for ever throughout your generations [Lev. 10:8–9].

It would appear from this instruction that Nadab and Abihu had acted under the influence of alcohol. This is one of the finest examples in Scripture against the use and abuse of alcohol or drugs. The priest is to serve the Lord with a clear, steady, and sober mind. Today we have the advocates of the use of drugs in religion. My friend, God despises such an approach to Him. This is the same thing that Paul meant when he said, "And be not drunk with wine, wherein is excess; but be filled with the Spirit" (Eph. 5:18). The believer is to draw his dynamic and his zeal from the Spirit of the Lord and not from frail and human props. What a lesson this is against drugs and alcohol for us today.

And that ye may put difference between holy and unholy, and between unclean and clean;

And that ye may teach the children of Israel all the statutes which the LORD hath spoken unto them by the hand of Moses [Lev. 10:10–11].

The use of wine dulls the senses so that a sharp distinction cannot be made between the holy and the unholy. True values are distorted and there is a breakdown in morals as a result of the use and abuse of alcohol. The priest must keep the statutes of the Lord so that he can teach them to the people. It is the filling of the Holy Spirit that is needed for the study and the teaching of the Word of God.

INJUNCTIONS CONCERNING THE OFFERINGS

And Moses spake unto Aaron, and unto Eleazar and unto Ithamar, his sons that were left, Take the meat offering that remaineth of the offerings of the LORD made by fire, and eat it without leaven beside the altar: for it is most holy:

And ye shall eat it in the holy place, because it is thy due, and thy sons' due, of the sacrifices of the LORD made by fire: for so I am commanded.

And the wave breast and heave shoulder shall ye eat in a clean place; thou, and thy sons, and thy daughters with thee: for they be thy due, and thy sons' due, which are given out of the sacrifices of peace offerings of the children of Israel.

The heave shoulder and the wave breast shall they bring with the offerings made by fire of the fat, to wave it for a wave offering before the LORD; and it shall be thine, and thy sons' with thee, by a statute for ever; as the LORD hath commanded [Lev. 10:12–15].

Moses repeats the commandments which concern both the meal offering and the peace offering. A portion of the offering was to be eaten by them in the holy place. This evidently is the outer court beside the burnt altar. It is holy because it was set aside for the service of God. The wave breast and the heave shoulder should be eaten in a clean place. Apparently they could take this to eat in their homes which would be ceremonially clean.

And Moses diligently sought the goat of the sin offering, and, behold, it was burnt: and he was angry with Eleazar and Ithamar, the sons of Aaron which were left alive, saying,

Wherefore have ye not eaten the sin offering in the holy place, seeing it is most holy, and God hath given it you to bear the iniquity of the congregation, to make atonement for them before the LORD?

Behold, the blood of it was not brought in within the holy place: ye should indeed have eaten it in the holy place, as I commanded [Lev. 10:16–18].

Now here is another tragic incident with action contrary to the will of God. We find failure on the part of the two other sons of Aaron, but here it is a sin of omission. It was not a deliberate and willful sin, as was that of the two dead sons. The sin offering was to be eaten in the holy place and that had not been done. Although the blood had been offered, the portion that belonged to the priests had not been eaten. They had omitted doing this, possibly not realizing the importance of it.

And Aaron said unto Moses, Behold, this day have they offered their sin offering and their burnt offering before the LORD; and such things have befallen me: and if I had eaten the sin offering to day, should it have been accepted in the sight of the LORD?

And when Moses heard that, he was content [Lev. 10:19–20].

Aaron assumed responsibility for his sons. Apparently the tragic incident had caused not only a loss of appetite but also a feeling of unworthiness in continuing to serve before God. Moses was satisfied with the explanation. I think at this point old Aaron felt like resigning.

There is tremendous truth for us to draw from this incident. These men came to God on their own. They were willful and this was blasphemy. God judged them. People today ask me whether it is wrong for them to belong to a church which denies the deity of Christ. Friends, do you think anyone can come to God in such a place, apart from God's will and God's terms? If God struck today as He struck Nadab and Abihu, I think half the church members would be dead. The liberals would be struck for denying the deity of Christ and the forgiveness of His sacrifice for us. Many fundamental church members would be struck down like Ananias and Sapphira for their hypocrisy, their lying to the Holy Spirit. God is dealing in mercy today, giving time for repentance and for men to come to the knowledge of the truth. Otherwise many people would be struck dead.

There is a wonderful lesson for you and for me. When we come to God, we must come on His terms. This is not an arrangement which we can make. We are not making the rules. God is the One who saves and He is the One who says how we shall be saved. Jesus Christ says that no man comes to the Father but by Him.

CHAPTER 11

THEME: The food of God's people—clean and unclean animals; contact with carcasses of unclean animals; contact with carcasses of clean animals; contamination of creeping creatures; classification of clean and unclean made by a holy God

This is a most unusual chapter. We have come now to a radical bifurcation in this book. The subject matter is changed from the priests to the people; from offerings to God to food for man; from worship before God to the walk in this world. The change is made from the sacred to the secular without any change of pace or level. There is no thought that this is anything different.

Today we make a false distinction between the sacred and the secular. We think if it is in the church it is sacred. Even gossip in the church seems to be regarded as sacred (especially if it is couched as a prayer request!). If gossip is outside the church, then it is secular. Friend, all and any of our work can be done to the glory of God. Someone has said,

I want to dig a ditch so straight and true
That God can look it through.

Friends, you cannot make a distinction between the sacred and the secular. God moves right out here from that which we would call sacred to that which we would call secular, and He makes no distinction.

This chapter is so unusual because God gives a diet, a menu, for the children of Israel to follow. They are to eat certain things and they are not to eat the things which God keeps off the menu. So here is the important question: Could the God of this vast universe be interested in what His creatures have for dinner? Could the One who orders all of creation prepare a menu for man? This chapter gives the answer: God was and is interested in the details of the lives of His people. No detail is too minute to escape His interest and His concern.

A lady asked G. Campbell Morgan whether he thought we ought to pray to God about the little things in our lives. His answer was, "Madam, can you mention anything in your life that is big to God?" You see, we tend to divide things in our lives as big problems and little problems. They are not divided that way before God. They are all little problems to Him. Yet nothing is too small for His attention and care. There are so many injunctions to us to pray about everything, to worry about nothing.

There are great spiritual lessons for us in this section, as we shall see; but there is also a very real and practical aspect which, because it pertained to Israel, we sometimes ignore. Since God forbade the eating of certain animals and permitted the eating of others, it must be assumed that there was a health factor involved. They could eat certain animals, fish, and birds but not others. It was not a superstition and it was more than a religious rite to make a distinction between clean and unclean animals. Since God prescribed certain animals for the diet of His people, and since He definitely forbade others, there must be some benefit in following that diet. History should demonstrate that God had good and sufficient grounds for making His distinctions. Now it is true that God could have acted in an arbitrary fashion in setting up these lines of separation between clean and unclean, but, ordinarily, God acted for the good of His people. Does history show this to be the case in these matters?

Well, the interesting thing we will find is that the animals which were forbidden to be eaten were largely unclean feeders. The animals rejected by the Mosaic system are more liable to disease.

Let me give a quotation from Dr. S. H. Kellogg: One of the greatest discoveries of modern science is the fact that a large number of diseases to which animals are liable are due to the presence of low forms of parasitic life. To such diseases those which are unclean in their feeding will be especially exposed, while none will perhaps be found wholly exempt. Another discovery of recent times which has a no less important bearing on the question raised by this chapter is the now ascertained fact that many of these parasitic diseases are common to both animals and men, and may be communicated from the former to the latter" (*The Book of Leviticus*, p. 314).

He goes on to list the parasite trichinae in swine, diphtheria in turkeys, and glanders in horses. Evidently Moses didn't understand about these diseases and certainly the physicians in Egypt didn't know about them. But God knew! God made these distinctions between clean and unclean. Does this work out in history? It certainly does.

Listen to the statement of Dr. Noel de Mussy, presented to the Paris Academy of Medicine in 1885: "The idea of parasitic and infectious maladies, which has conquered so great a position in modern pathology, appears to have greatly occupied the mind of Moses and to have dominated all his hygienic rules. He excluded from Hebrew dietary *animals particularly liable to parasites;* and as it is in the blood, that the germs and spores of infectious disease circulate, he orders that they must be drained of their blood before serving for food."

How did Moses know that? Well, Moses wouldn't have known it, but God told him.

I quote Dr. Kellogg again. "Even so long ago as the days when the plague was desolating Europe, the Jews so universally escaped infection that, by this their exemption, the popular suspicion was excited into fury, and they were accused of causing the fearful mortality among their Gentile neighbors by poisoning the wells and springs."

Professor Hosmer wrote: "Throughout the entire history of Israel, the wisdom of the ancient lawgivers in these respects has been remarkably shown. In times of pestilence the Jews have suffered far less than others; as regards longevity and general health, they have in every age been noteworthy, and, at the present day, in the life-insurance offices, the life of a Jew is said to be worth much more than that of men of other stock."

Dr. Behrends also states: "In Prussia, the mean duration of Jewish life averages five years more than that of the general population." Now, of course, today the Jews are breaking down their rules about diet, and the gap is closing. There were times when the life of the Jews was actually twice that of their Gentile neighbors.

There are some lessons in this for us today. We are apt to condemn Israel for placing such a great emphasis on the physical while missing the spiritual implications. At the same time, we tend to place such an emphasis on the spiritual that we ignore the physical altogether. A Christian should not ignore his body as to the food he eats, the use and abuse of the body, and the care of it. He should keep in mind that the body is the tabernacle of God today and the very temple of the Holy Spirit. Because a thing is physical does not preclude it from being spiritual.

At the same time, we are told very definitely today, that we can eat whatever we wish to eat. If you want to eat rattlesnake meat, you may eat rattlesnake meat. There is no spiritual value in eating or not eating certain foods. In fact, it is a superstition when you approach it like that. Let us look at several Scriptures concerning this:

"I know, and am persuaded by the Lord Jesus, that there is nothing unclean of itself: but to him that esteemeth any thing to be unclean, to him it is unclean" (Rom. 14:14).

"But meat commendeth us not to God: for neither, if we eat, are we the better; neither, if we eat not, are we the worse" (1 Cor. 8:8).

"Meats for the belly, and the belly for meats: but God shall destroy both it and them . . ." (1 Cor. 6:13).

"Whether therefore ye eat, or drink, or Whatsoever ye do, do all to the glory of God" (1 Cor. 10:31).

We should point out that gluttony is strictly forbidden and temperance, or self-control, is a command for a believer under grace.

CLEAN AND UNCLEAN ANIMALS (ON THE LAND)

And the LORD spake unto Moses and to Aaron, saying unto them,

Speak unto the children of Israel, saying, These are the beasts which ye shall eat among all the beasts that are on the earth [Lev. 11:1–2].

God draws a strict line of demarcation between light and darkness, night and day, black and white, right and wrong, clean and unclean. And by the way, God is the One who makes the difference between light and darkness. It is His intent to sharpen man's discriminating nature so that he is sensitive to these God-made distinctions. God wants man to love the good and to loathe the evil. This present age is witnessing the dulling of man's sensibilities to the sharp distinctions between right and wrong and good and bad. Man tries to put everything in life in the gray zone of amorality. God draws these distinctions to drive man to the altar and the shed blood of Christ for cleansing and for forgiveness.

God makes the rules. Someone asks, "How do you know what is right?" The answer is that *right* is what God says is right! This is *His* universe. Do you know any better rules than the ones He has made? He's made the rules for the physical realm. (Do you want to defy the law of gravity and jump off the earth? It's an expensive trip, and it will cost you millions of dollars to do it. It put our government in debt to do it, and it will put you in debt to do it.)

God moves into the realm of the everyday life and nothing comes closer to that than what man eats. God declares certain things to be clean and certain to be unclean. Man is to be reminded that he lives in a world where sin abounds. Man must learn to choose the good and shun the evil.

The distinction was moral, yet the clean creatures were wholesome and gave nourishment to the body. The distinction of the clean and unclean animals is older than the Mosaic economy, and we know that Noah recognized such a division.

It is noticeable that the choice of edible animals, fish, and fowl, follow generally the pattern of civilized man down through the centuries to the present day. That is no accident. God made the distinction and there are certain animals you want and some you don't want to eat. Another feature we should note is that certain animals were probably healthful in that land and in that day which might not be true elsewhere. Today we have no command concerning clean and unclean animals for food.

There are great moral issues involved in this chapter. Man lives in a world of sin, and God requires recognition of this fact. Choices must be made. Fallen man outside of Eden still has a "tree" of which God says he must not eat. I think the moral objective is primary. You remember that when Peter saw the sheet come down with all kinds of animals and birds in it, he didn't want to eat when God told him to eat. God then told him, "Don't you call unclean what God has called clean" (Acts 10:11–15). In other words, God makes the rules, and man must make his decisions according to God's rules. This is a tremendous moral lesson.

Whatsoever parteth the hoof, and is clovenfooted, and cheweth the cud, among the beasts, that shall ye eat [Lev. 11:3].

This was the rule to be followed to determine the animals to be eaten. This was repeated in Deuteronomy 14:6, and in that chapter it lists the ox, the sheep, the goat, the hart, the roebuck, the fallow deer, the wild goat, the pygarg, the wild ox, and the chamois.

In Leviticus, the principle and rule is given with a few examples of those which are unclean. In Deuteronomy, the principle and rule are not emphasized, but a more extended list of the clean animals is given. Leviticus emphasizes the negative; Deuteronomy emphasizes the positive.

In Leviticus the division of clean and unclean is sharply drawn although this is not a new commandment. The distinction does not follow any biological division, but a health factor was involved.

Some heathen nations, Persia for example, attributed the creation of certain animals to the good god while other animals were the product of a bad god. God created all the animals. Neither did the nature of the animal, as representing some sin or virtue, make the distinction. For example, the lion was unclean, but it represents the Lord Jesus Christ and is the symbol of the tribe of Judah. That is why Christ is called the Lion of the tribe of Judah.

There is not some mysterious connection between the soul and the body as one finds in some heathen cults today. The nature of the animal is not transferred to the one who eats it. That's just nonsense and superstition. Some vegetarians think people become cruel because they eat animal meat. Well, I've seen some pretty mean folk who are vegetarians. May I say, such ideas are nonsense.

For Israel, the distinction between the clean and unclean animals was part of God's plan to keep them separate from all nations. Even today *Kosher* has a particular meaning to everyone. They were constantly reminded that they lived in a world where choices had to be made.

For the Christian there are some spiritual applications. We have already shown that there is no merit in following a ritual regarding meat. But it is interesting to note that "to meditate" is a figurative expression of a cow chewing the cud. "But his delight is in the law of the LORD; and in his law doth he meditate day and night" (Ps. 1:2). Meditating is a valid application for the chewing of the cud for the spiritual benefit of believers. Likewise, the parting of the hoof speaks of the walk of the believer in separation. "I therefore, the prisoner of the LORD, beseech you that ye walk worthy of the vocation wherewith ye are called" (Eph. 4:1). "And walk in love, as Christ also hath loved us . . . . See then that ye walk circumspectly, not as fools, but as wise" (Eph. 5:2, 15). The relationship between the study of the Word of God and the walk of the believer is intimately tied together. "But continue thou in the things which thou hast learned and hast been assured of, knowing of whom thou hast learned them; And that from a child thou hast known the holy scriptures, which are able to make thee wise unto salvation through faith which is in Christ Jesus" (2 Tim. 3:14–15). "But be ye doers of the word, and not hearers only, deceiving your own selves" (James 1:22). My friend, the walk of the believer is tied up with the Word of God. If you are going through this world, you will have to chew the cud, the Word of God, and you will need to have that separated walk that only the Word can produce. The Bible-studying believer, who puts into practice the teaching of the Word of God, identifies himself as a child of God by his work and his walk.

Friend, what kind of tracks are you making? I remember the story of a man years ago when someone tried to hand him a tract. He asked what it was and was told it was a tract. He handed it back and said he couldn't read it. He said, "I'll just watch your tracks."

Nevertheless these shall ye not eat of them that chew the cud, or of them that divide the hoof: as the camel, because he cheweth the cud, but divideth not the hoof; he is unclean unto you.

And the coney, because he cheweth the cud, but divideth not the hoof, he is unclean unto you.

And the hare, because he cheweth the cud, but divideth not the hoof; he is unclean unto you.

And the swine, though he divide the hoof, and be clovenfooted, yet he cheweth not the cud; he is unclean to you.

Of their flesh shall ye not eat, and their carcase shall ye not touch; they are unclean to you [Lev. 11:4–8].

This is an extended list of animals which are unclean. Evidently, there must have been some question about these animals. Only vegetable-eating animals chew the cud. This eliminated the carnivorous animals.

God warned about eating a camel. The reaction would be, "Who would want to?" Don't you think this adds a note of humor to the words of our Lord when He accused the Pharisees of straining at a gnat and swallowing a camel? The camel wasn't only lumpy; he was unclean. A coney is something like a rabbit and lives in rocky places. This corresponds to our rabbit. It is quite interesting to me that today there are those who emphasize that one should not eat pork but I have never heard them mention that one should not eat rabbit. The swine divides the hoof but does not chew the cud. The pig seems to be constantly eating but does not chew the cud. It is interesting to note that pork is still a difficult meat to digest. Swine are an unclean animal. They are unclean in their eating habits.

The Israelite was even forbidden to have contract with the dead carcass of these unclean animals. The spiritual implications of this are unavoidable.

CLEAN AND UNCLEAN CREATURES (ON THE WATER)

These shall ye eat of all that are in the waters: whatsoever hath fins and scales in the waters, in the seas, and in the rivers, them shall ye eat.

And all that have not fins and scales in the seas, and in the rivers, of all that move in the waters, and of any living thing which is in the waters, they shall be an abomination unto you:

They shall be even an abomination unto you; ye shall not eat of their flesh, but ye shall have their carcases in abomination.

Whatsoever hath no fins nor scales in the waters, that shall be an abomination unto you [Lev. 11:9–12].

There is a sharp line drawn here as well as among animals. The clean fish must be characterized by two visible marks—fins and scales—to be clean. This rule applied to both fresh and salt water fish. Crawling creatures in the water were forbidden, which would eliminate a great segment of the creatures of the waters. No examples are given, probably because the distinction is very clear cut.

Israel depended on the supply of fish from the Mediterranean Sea, the Sea of Galilee, and the Jordan River. Fish played a prominent part in the diet of the nation. One of the gates of Jerusalem was called the fish gate. This is where the fish from the Mediterranean were brought in, and it is interesting that this was a problem in the times of Nehemiah. The fishermen would bring in their fish on the Sabbath day (Neh. 13:16–22).

The important role of fishing in the earthly ministry of the Lord Jesus Christ is well known to the student of the New Testament. The first disciples our Lord called were fishermen. They were told that they were to become fishers of men.

Jesus told the parable that the kingdom of heaven is like a net which caught good fish and bad fish (Matt. 13:47–50). What was the method of determining the good from the bad fish? It is not whether the fish were large or small but would be according to the Levitical law. A fish that has both fins and scales is clean, or good. Now how is this like the judgment of the wicked from among the just? Well, the believer is the one who is propelled by the Holy Spirit and who is clothed in the righteousness of Christ. Those are the two identifying marks. Those are the fins and the scales, if you please.

CLEAN AND UNCLEAN FLYING CREATURES (IN THE AIR)

And these are they which ye shall have in abomination among the fowls; they shall not be eaten, they are an abomination: the eagle, and the ossifrage, and the osprey,

And the vulture, and the kite after his kind;

Every raven after his kind;

And the owl, and the night hawk, and the cuckoo, and the hawk after his kind,

And the little owl, and the cormorant, and the great owl,

And the swan, and the pelican, and the gier eagle,

And the stork, the heron after her kind, and the lapwing, and the bat [Lev. 11:13–19].

On the birds there are no visible markers like there are on the fish and the animals. But they seem to have in common that they are all unclean feeders. For the most part, they feed on dead carcasses of animals, fish, and other fowl.

A list of unclean birds of Palestine are given. This is another point that reveals that the Mosaic system was intended for the nation Israel and also for the particular land of Palestine. Some of these birds sound strange to us. They fall into the family of the eagles and the hawks, the vultures and the ravens, the owls and cormorants, and the swans and pelicans. They don't even sound appetizing. They are the "dirty birdies" because of their feeding habits. Now remember, some people eat some of these birds today. I can't say I would like any of them, but whether we eat them or don't eat them makes no difference—meat will not commend us to God. The point is that it was teaching Israel to make a distinction. They had to make a decision about what was clean and unclean.

The lesson for us today is that we must make decisions about our conduct and our profession. We have to make the decision about whether to accept Christ or not, whether to study the Word of God or not, whether to walk in a way pleasing to God or not. That is the application for us today.

This section throws some light on the experience of Elijah. He was fed by the ravens—dirty birds. Elijah did not eat the ravens, but they fed him. This was an humbling experience for this man of God who obeyed God in every detail.

CLEAN AND UNCLEAN CREEPING CREATURES (ON THE GROUND)

All fowls that creep, going upon all four, shall be an abomination unto you.

Yet these may ye eat of every flying creeping thing that goeth upon all four, which have legs above their feet, to leap withal upon the earth;

Even these of them ye may eat; the locust after his kind, and the bald locust after his kind, and the beetle after his kind, and the grasshopper after his kind.

But all other flying creeping things, which have four feet, shall be an abomination unto you [Lev. 11:20–23].

Well, folks, you can leave all of these off my menu. However, we must note that some of them are clean. These were apparently four species of locusts. The locust was the regular species; the bald locust had a protuberance; the beetle was a locust with a protuberance and a tail; the grasshopper was a locust with a tail but without a protuberance. So they were permitted to eat these four kinds of locusts. But, friends, if you're having me over for dinner, let's have something else on the menu! Although they don't appeal to me, there is nothing religiously or ceremonially unclean about them. John the Baptist had a scriptural diet when he ate locusts and wild honey.

CONTACT WITH CARCASSES OF UNCLEAN ANIMALS

And for these ye shall be unclean: whosoever toucheth the carcase of them shall be unclean until the even.

And whosoever beareth aught of the carcase of them shall wash his clothes, and be unclean until the even.

The carcases of every beast which divideth the hoof, and is not clovenfooted, nor cheweth the cud, are unclean unto

you: every one that toucheth them shall be unclean.

And whatsoever goeth upon his paws, among all manner of beasts that go on all four, those are unclean unto you: whoso toucheth their carcase shall be unclean until the even.

And he that beareth the carcase of them shall wash his clothes, and be unclean until the even: they are unclean unto you [Lev. 11:24–28].

Not only was Israel forbidden to eat unclean animals, but also they were forbidden to touch the carcass of an unclean animal. Contamination by contact is the principle here. This was a great principle of life that was restated in the days of the return of Israel after the captivity. "Thus saith the LORD of hosts; Ask now the priests concerning the law, saying, If one bear holy flesh in the skirt of his garment, and with his skirt do touch bread, or pottage, or wine, or oil, or any meat, shall it be holy? And the priests answered and said, No. Then said Haggai, If one that is unclean by a dead body touch any of these, shall it be unclean? And the priests answered and said, It shall be unclean" (Hag. 2:11–13).

There is a very important principle set before us here. Cleanness or holiness is not transferred by contact. On the contrary, dirt, sin, and unholiness are transferred by contact. In other words, it is impossible to bring holiness out of the unholy. But the unclean can affect the clean. An unrighteous man cannot produce righteous works which are acceptable to God. You cannot bring righteousness out of unrighteousness.

This principle operates as a law in every realm of life and in all strata of society. A gallon of dirty water is not made clean by adding a gallon of clean water. On the other hand, one drop of dirty water will contaminate the clean water. A boy with the measles is never cured by contact with a boy who is well, but the well boy may very well catch the measles from the sick boy. A Christian cannot mingle with the world and play with sin without becoming contaminated. Where do we get the idea that a Christian can dabble with drugs and drinking and night clubs and wild parties? Some claim that the way to reach the lost is to meet them on their level. Well, do they reach the lost that way? No, they are contaminated and take part in those sins themselves. The New Testament is clear on this. "And others save with fear, pulling them out of the fire; hating even the

garment spotted by the flesh" (Jude 23). It is a terrible mistake to mix and mingle with sin. We are to beware of all contamination.

An Israelite was reminded of this great principle when he walked along the road and saw a dead dog or a dead bear. He was forbidden to carry the carcass or any part of it. He was not to take a bone or the skin for any use. If he inadvertently touched the carcass of an unclean animal, he was to wash his garments and remain unclean until the end of the day.

These are great spiritual lessons for us. The Christian is sanctified by the redemption of Christ and is clothed with His garments of righteousness. But we walk through the world where we can become contaminated. We still have the old nature. Not until we lay down this body in death will we be completely and totally sanctified and removed from the very presence of sin.

These also shall be unclean unto you among the creeping things that creep upon the earth; the weasel, and the mouse, and the tortoise after his kind,

And the ferret, and the chameleon, and the lizard, and the snail, and the mole.

These are unclean to you among all that creep: whosoever doth touch them, when they be dead, shall be unclean until the even [Lev. 11:29–31].

These are creatures that live on the ground or under the ground. They must have been rather commonplace but they were to be avoided by the Israelite. The carcass of a mole could contaminate him as much as the carcass of an elephant. So he was constantly reminded that he lived in a world of fallen creatures, and that little sins are as heinous in God's sight as big sins. The mote and the beam are alike to God. "Little sins" are also sin and must be avoided.

And upon whatsoever any of them, when they are dead, doth fall, it shall be unclean; whether it be any vessel of wood, or raiment, or skin, or sack, whatsoever vessel it be, wherein any work is done, it must be put into water, and it shall be unclean until the even; so it shall be cleansed.

And every earthen vessel, whereinto any of them falleth, whatsoever is in it shall be unclean; and ye shall break it.

Of all meat which may be eaten, that on which such water cometh shall be unclean: and all drink that may be drunk in every such vessel shall be unclean.

And every thing whereupon any part of their carcase falleth shall be unclean; whether it be oven, or ranges for pots, they shall be broken down: for they are unclean, and shall be unclean unto you.

Nevertheless a fountain or pit, wherein there is plenty of water, shall be clean: but that which toucheth their carcase shall be unclean [Lev. 11:32–36].

Now we go into the kitchen. It must have been a commonplace experience for some rodent to get into the kitchen of that day and fall into one of the vessels and die. Any earthen vessel had to be broken and the water or grain or whatever was in it had to be thrown out. A bronze vessel was to be scoured clean. You see, God taught His people cleanliness in the preparation of food. And He was teaching them a lesson in holiness. *Every* vessel was holy to God and it was all to remain clean. In the Mosaic system, cleanliness was next to godliness and this applied to even the smallest detail in domestic situations. God guarded His people against contamination and pollution.

If the dead carcass fell into a fountain or a lake, the water was not contaminated. It was too big and too fresh.

Isn't it wonderful that the Lord Jesus Christ is the fountain of living water? He is *not* contaminated by contact with the sinner or the sick, the leper or the woman with an issue of blood. Jesus said: "But whosoever drinketh of the water that I shall give him shall never thirst; but the water that I shall give him shall be in him a well of water springing up into everlasting life" (John 4:14). Also "In the last day, that great day of the feast, Jesus stood and cried, saying, If any man thirst, let him come unto me, and drink. He that believeth on me, as the scripture hath said, out of his belly shall flow rivers of living water" (John 7:37–38).

And if any part of their carcase fall upon any sowing seed which is to be sown, it shall be clean.

But if any water be put upon the seed, and any part of their carcase fall thereon, it shall be unclean unto you [Lev. 11:37–38].

Now we leave the kitchen and go out into the field and the food production. Dry seed that was to be sown could not be contaminated by contact with a carcass of the unclean. However, if the seed was wet, then its shell or armor had been penetrated and it was unclean.

This is why the child of God needs a shell or armor today. We are told, "Put on the whole armour of God, that ye may be able to stand against the wiles of the devil" (Eph. 6:11).

CONTACT WITH CARCASSES OF CLEAN ANIMALS

And if any beast, of which ye may eat, die; he that toucheth the carcase thereof shall be unclean until the even.

And he that eateth of the carcase of it shall wash his clothes, and be unclean until the even: he also that beareth the carcase of it shall wash his clothes, and be unclean until the even [Lev. 11:39–40].

Any clean animal that died of itself or of disease was unclean. In Malachi 1:8 God forbade the sacrifice of any animal that was lame or sick. God will not accept the second-best or the castoff from us either.

CONTAMINATION OF CREEPING CREATURES

And every creeping thing that creepeth upon the earth shall be an abomination; it shall not be eaten.

Whatsoever goeth upon the belly, and whatsoever goeth upon all four, or whatsoever hath more feet among all creeping things that creep upon the earth, them ye shall not eat; for they are an abomination.

Ye shall not make yourselves abominable with any creeping thing that creepeth, neither shall ye make yourselves unclean with them, that ye should be defiled thereby [Lev. 11:41–43].

Everything that crept on the earth or that went on its belly was unclean. God gives the reason they should not become unclean with them:

For I am the LORD your God: ye shall therefore sanctify yourselves, and ye shall be holy; for I am holy: neither shall ye defile yourselves with any manner of creeping thing that creepeth upon the earth.

For I am the LORD that bringeth you up out of the land of Egypt, to be your God: ye shall therefore be holy, for I am holy [Lev. 11:44–45].

All creeping things were unclean as representatives of the fall of man when the serpent was cursed and made to crawl on its belly.

CLASSIFICATION OF CLEAN AND UNCLEAN MADE BY A HOLY GOD

This is the law of the beasts, and of the fowl, and of every living creature that moveth in the waters, and of every creature that creepeth upon the earth:

To make a difference between the unclean and the clean, and between the beast that may be eaten and the beast that may not be eaten [Lev. 11:46–47].

It is God who makes the sharp distinction between the clean and the unclean. Holiness in little things is essential. This is the real test for God's man. The acid test of any life of any of God's people is this. God says, "I am your Lord. I am holy. Be ye holy."

My friend, you must make the decision as to whether you are going to walk with God and for God in this contaminated world. This is the lesson for us from his chapter of the clean and the unclean.

CHAPTER 12

THEME: *Cleansing of a mother after childbirth; a sacrifice for atonement*

In the preceding chapter we saw the contamination of sin by contact. The external character of sin was emphasized—we live in a world surrounded by sin.

This chapter places the emphasis on the internal character of sin. Not only do we become sinners by contact, but we are sinners by birth. And this chapter is the law concerning motherhood, the transmission of sin by inheritance. The very nature that we inherit is a fallen, sinful nature. David said, "Behold, I was shapen in iniquity, and in sin did my mother conceive me" (Ps. 51:5). This chapter is in the field of obstetrics, as the former chapter was in the field of dietetics and pediatrics. Our Lord is the Great Physician and He is the specialist in all fields.

Pagan peoples entertained superstitious notions about the uncleanness of women in childbirth. There is not a shred of that notion in the Levitical economy, as we hope to point out. It was also a pagan practice to place women in an inferior position to man. This law does not contain a breath of that idea, as the Mosaic economy lifted womanhood and ennobled motherhood in contrast to the base heathenism that surrounded the nation Israel.

Obviously there were certain hygienic benefits in the practice of these God-given laws—as we saw in the matter of diet. God was caring for His people physically, and at the same time was teaching them (and us) the great spiritual truth that we are born in sin.

There is a doctrine today that is almost totally rejected, and that is the total depravity of man—but man is certainly *demonstrating* it! Our news media is full of it, and man's total depravity is quite obvious. We are told: "Wherefore, as by one man sin entered into the world, and death by sin; and so death passed upon all men, for that all have sinned" (Rom. 5:12).

The world thinks of innocence, virtue, and goodness in the picture of a young mother holding a sweet, cuddly baby in her arms. But God paints a different picture, an opposite portrait, in this chapter. There's the young mother holding the precious baby, but he's not a picture of innocence and sinlessness. He is a picture of uncleanness and sin. Do you know what happened? That mother brought into the world a sinner. That's all she could bring into the world because she is a sinner—and papa's a sinner too.

S. H. Kellogg has this comment: "In the birth of a child, the special original curse against the woman is regarded by the law as reaching its fullest, most consummate and significant expression. For the extreme evil of the state of sin into which the first woman, by that first sin, brought all womanhood, is seen most of all in this, that now woman, by means of those powers given her for good and blessing, can bring into the world only a child of sin" (*The Book of Leviticus*, p. 314).

You recall that God said to the first woman: ". . . I will greatly multiply thy sorrow and thy conception; in sorrow thou shalt bring forth children; and thy desire shall be to thy husband, and he shall rule over thee" (Gen. 3:16). Not only would the woman travail in bringing a child into the world, but the chances are that child would be a heartbreak to her because that child is a sinner.

That is, I think, what Paul had in mind when he put down certain regulations concerning woman's place in public worship. He says: "But I suffer not a woman to teach, nor to usurp authority over the man, but to be in silence" (1 Tim. 2:12). He is talking about the place of doctrinal leadership in the church, and I think the reason is twofold. Adam was created first, and also in the transgression the woman was the one who was deceived. "For Adam was first formed, then Eve. And Adam was not deceived, but the woman being deceived was in the transgression" (1 Tim. 2:13–14). This is not teaching the superiority of man over woman. Rather, it is a matter of order and headship. Secondly, the woman was first in the transgression—she was the leader there.

The fact that a Christian mother travails in the birth of her child is an evidence of God's judgment, but it certainly does not mean she loses her salvation when she brings a sinner into the world. "Notwithstanding she shall be saved in childbearing, if they continue in faith and charity and holiness with sobriety" (1 Tim. 2:15). She is not saved *by* childbearing; she is saved *through* childbearing. In other words, she does not become unclean and lose her salvation by bringing a sinner into the world. The evidence of her salvation is in her faith, love, holy living, and sobriety. "Uncleanness" under the Law reminded her that she had brought a sinner into the world. "Travail" under grace reminds the mother today that a sinner has been born even though she is a believer.

When Paul the apostle said to the Philippian jailer, "Believe on the Lord Jesus Christ, and thou shalt be saved, and thy house" (Acts 16:31) he didn't mean that his family would be saved just because he believed on the Lord. Neither does it mean that your children are saved just because you are a believer. Discipline has broken down in the homes of America because too many parents think they are raising a sweet little flower when what they have is a stinkweed! That, my friend, is what you and I are, and that is what we have brought into the world. Again and again I asked my daughter, "Are you sure you trust Christ? Are you saved?" She asked me once, "Why do you keep asking me?" And I told her, "I just want to make sure." She has my nature and I happen to know that this nature of mine is a lost nature. She is not automatically saved just because I am a Christian and a preacher of the Gospel.

This raises another question. Someone said, "If my baby is born a sinner and he dies in infancy, is he lost because he is a sinner?" No. In Adam all die, and that's the reason the little one died. But the Lord Jesus said, "Take heed that ye despise not one of these little ones; for I say unto you, That in heaven their angels [spirits] do always behold the face of my Father which is in heaven" (Matt. 18:10). The word "angels" should be translated *spirits*—their spirits behold the face of the Father. In other words, when that little infant dies, his spirit goes to be with the Father. Why? Because Christ came down and died for sinners, and the little one has not reached the age of accountability. The minute he does, then he has to make a decision for Christ.

I like the quaint epitaph that Robert Robertson placed over the graves of his four children:

> Bold infidelity, turn pale and die,
> Beneath this stone four infants' ashes lie;
> Say are they lost or saved,
> If death's by sin, they sinned for they lie here;
> If Heaven's by works, in Heaven they can't appear.
> Reason—Ah, how depraved.
> Reverse the Bible's sacred page, the knot's untied,
> They died, for Adam sinned; they live, for Jesus died.

CLEANSING OF A MOTHER AT THE BIRTH OF A MALE CHILD

And the LORD spake unto Moses, saying,

Speak unto the children of Israel, saying, If a woman have conceived seed, and born a man child: then she shall be unclean seven days; according to the days of the separation for her infirmity shall she be unclean [Lev. 12:1–2].

The mother is unclean because she has brought a sinner into the world. Eve thought she had brought the Savior into the world when Cain was born, but she had brought into the world only a sinner—the first murderer. Now this Levitical ritual is to remind women that they were bringing into the world the same kind of a baby that Eve had brought into the world. They cannot do good. They can only sin.

Her uncleanness is divided into two periods. The first period was seven days. We shall see in the next verse that the male child was circumcised on the eighth day. Circumcision was the badge given to Abraham.

I realize that the idea of uncleanness of motherhood conflicts with the popular notion of motherhood and the little baby, but we need to emphasize that the babies we are bringing into the world are sinners. They are going to run undisciplined. They will be revolutionaries. They will adopt the new morality, which is just old-fashioned sin. The whole philosophy of life has been entirely wrong. We need to start raising children by the Scripture and not by Dr. Spock. This has been the cause of deep problems during my entire time in the ministry—I have seen parents after parents raise their children in this way.

And in the eighth day the flesh of his foreskin shall be circumcised.

And she shall then continue in the blood of her purifying three and thirty days; she shall touch no hallowed thing, nor come into the sanctuary, until the days of her purifying be fulfilled [Lev. 12: 3–4].

We have mentioned that the mother's period of uncleanness is divided into two periods. The first was seven days, and then the male child was circumcised on the eighth day. Being born an Israelite did not include him in the covenant until the baby was circumcised. Each Israelite was first of all a son of Adam and was born outside the covenant. This is what Paul means in Romans 9:6–7: ". . . For they are not all Israel, which are of Israel: Neither, because they are the seed of Abraham, are they all children . . ." Natural birth does not bring a man into a right relationship with God. Natural birth separates a man from God! God owes us nothing. He sent His Son out of His grace to us.

The second period of the mother's uncleanness was for thirty-three days so that the total time was forty days. This reaffirms the fact that the rite of circumcision had a meaning of cleansing. It was God's way in the Old Testament of saying, ". . . Suffer little children, and forbid them not to come unto me . . ." (Matt. 19:14). The circumcision of the male child removed some of the sin from the mother. His acceptance meant her acceptance also. She is reminded that she is still a sinner, and thirty-three more days are required for her cleansing.

It is interesting to note that Jesus was circumcised on the eighth day. Then Jesus was brought to the temple when the days of Mary's purification according to the law of Moses were accomplished (Luke 2:21–23). Mary was a sinner even though she brought the sinless Savior into the world. His birth did not save her. Only her new birth by accepting Jesus as her own Savior could save her.

Jesus was circumcised to fulfill the law of Moses. He came to fulfill, not to destroy the Law. He was made (born) under the Law. Thus he identified Himself perfectly with His people.

CLEANSING OF THE MOTHER AT THE BIRTH OF A FEMALE CHILD

But if she bear a maid child, then she shall be unclean two weeks, as in her separation: and she shall continue in the blood of her purifying threescore and six days [Lev. 12:5].

The time is doubled for the cleansing at the birth of a female child. I don't know why this was so, but obviously the circumcision of the male child had something to do with the reduction of the days and it relieved some of the curse.

Grace brings us to a new day. "For as many of you as have been baptized into Christ have put on Christ. There is neither Jew nor Greek, there is neither bond nor free, there is neither male nor female: for ye are all one in Christ Jesus. And if ye be Christ's, then are ye Abraham's seed, and heirs according to the promise" (Gal. 3:27–29).

CLEANSING OF THE MOTHER BY BRINGING A SACRIFICE FOR ATONEMENT

And when the days of her purifying are fulfilled, for a son, or for a daughter, she shall bring a lamb of the first year for a burnt offering, and a young pigeon, or a turtledove, for a sin offering, unto the door of the tabernacle of the congregation, unto the priest:

Who shall offer it before the LORD, and make an atonement for her; and she shall be cleansed from the issue of her blood. This is the law for her that hath born a male or a female.

And if she be not able to bring a lamb, then she shall bring two turtles, or two young pigeons; the one for the burnt offering, and the other for a sin offer-

ing: and the priest shall make an atonement for her, and she shall be clean
[Lev. 12:6–8].

The mother brought a burnt offering and a
sin offering to God and the priest offered it
for her. She certainly was not saved just by
bringing children into the world, as some
claim. She had to have a sacrifice. A mother
must trust the Lord Jesus Christ. With that in
mind, she is prepared to raise her child as a
sinner who needs to accept Christ. Oh, how the
home needs that today!

You remember that when the Lord Jesus
was born, his mother brought turtle-doves because the poor could bring them as an offering.

She had to have an offering because she was a
sinner; she was not sinless. She brought an
offering. But there was no offering for the
Lord Jesus. No offering was ever made for
Jesus or by Jesus. He is the sinless One. He
was *the* offering for the sin of the world. He is
the Lamb of God.

Friends, think on these things. We live in a
world that has gone crazy, has gone mad. This
world has turned its back upon the Almighty
God, and the judgment of God is beginning to
fall upon the world. We are demonstrating the
fact that only sinners are born into this world
and that all people need the saving grace of
God. All people need the shed blood of Christ
to pay the penalty for their sins.

CHAPTER 13

THEME: *Diagnosis of leprosy; disposal of lepers' garments*

This is concerned with the exceeding sinfulness of sin. "For out of the heart proceed
evil thoughts, murders, adulteries, fornications, thefts, false witness, blasphemies:
These are the things which defile a man: but to
eat with unwashen hands defileth not a man"
(Matt. 15:19–20).

We come now to another unusual section of
this book, the section on leprosy. Someone
may ask whether this is practical for today.
May I say that all of this book is practical. We
are in the section of the book which we have
entitled "Holiness in Daily Life." God is concerned with the conduct of His children. We
saw that He is concerned with their food; now
in chapters 13, 14, and 15 we find He is concerned with leprosy and the cleansing of running issues.

Leprosy and running issues of the flesh are
accurate symbols of the manifestation of sin in
the heart of man. It shows the exceeding sinfulness of sin and the effect of sin in action. The
emphasis of Leviticus is on sin.

In the heart of this book on worship of a holy
God is this extended section on leprosy and
issues in the flesh. The filthiness and repulsiveness of sin are represented in leprosy. The
hopelessness and deadliness of sin are accurately portrayed. The leper who trudged down
a hot, dusty, oriental road crying out, "Unclean! Unclean!" was a reminder to the

Israelite that he, too, was a moral leper who
needed supernatural cleansing.

Perhaps you are one of those who thinks that
you will be saved by your works and that you
don't need Christ as your Savior. May I say
that if you could go to heaven just like you are,
without Christ, you would go through heaven
crying out, "Unclean! Unclean!" No angel
would touch you with a twenty foot pole. You
couldn't come anywhere near the presence of
God.

You see, man has the idea that he has some
kind of claim on God, but we have no claim
upon Him whatsoever. He owes us nothing.
He could blot out of existence this little earth
that we live on, and it would not even make a
dent in this universe. But thank God, He loves
us. I'm so glad He loves us! That is the only
thing that could bind Him to us.

God is driving a point home to us, and it is
the same point He was driving home to Israel:
Sin is exceeding sinful. This comparison between leprosy and sin is a recurring theme in
the Scripture: "There is no soundness in my
flesh because of thine anger; neither is there
any rest in my bones because of my sin . . . .
My wounds stink and are corrupt because of
my foolishness . . . . For my loins are filled
with a loathsome disease: and there is no
soundness in my flesh. . . . For I will declare
mine iniquity; I will be sorry for my sin" (Ps.

38:3, 5, 7, 18). That is the way we look to God.

Isaiah also had leprosy in his thinking as he described the sins of his people: "From the sole of the foot even unto the head there is no soundness in it; but wounds, and bruises, and putrefying sores: they have not been closed, neither bound up, neither mollified with ointment" (Isa. 1:6). "Surely he hath borne our griefs, and carried our sorrows: yet we did esteem him stricken, smitten of God, and afflicted. But he was wounded for our transgressions, he was bruised for our iniquities: the chastisement of our peace was upon him; and with his stripes we are healed" (Isa. 53:4–5). Now, some folk say he is talking about leprosy here and that he is referring to a physical disease. No, my friend, Isaiah is talking about sin being laid on the Lord Jesus Christ. Can we be sure of that? Listen to the apostle Peter: "Who his own self bare our sins in his own body on the tree, that we, being dead to sins, should live unto righteousness: by whose stripes ye were healed" (1 Pet. 2:24).

We were dead in sin and He bare our sins in His own body on the tree. By His stripes we are healed. Now it is true that physical disease is a manifestation of sin and that behind disease germs there lies sin. If there were no sin, there would be neither death nor sickness.

There are two important considerations we should take into account as we get into this chapter.

1. The Bible does not agree with the generally accepted view that leprosy was incurable in that day. Cleansing is mentioned in Leviticus 14:2. There were supernatural cures such as Naaman's in 2 Kings 5. Some expositors think that Job had leprosy. Since there was no scientific diagnosis of the disease in those days, there has been discussion on what the leprosy was. They had medicines in that day which they used for the cure of leprosy.

This chapter and the following do not contain a cure for leprosy. This should be carefully noted. It gives instructions to the priest on how a case of leprosy is to be determined, and the measures to be taken to prevent it spreading in the camp. After it had been cleansed, there was a ritual to be followed. It is not a cure that is presented here. In chapter 14 it deals with the ceremonial cleansing of the leper after his cure and not the cure itself. The main objective was to teach great spiritual truths in connection with the cleansing of leprosy as a type of sin.

2. This is not a scientific treatise on the detection, prevention, and cure of leprosy. There is *no* attempt to give a medical diagnosis of the disease. The diagnosis was a practical one which was adjusted to the knowledge of that day. It has direct and definite spiritual lessons for *this* day. The ritual was ceremonial rather than curative.

There has been some discussion on the part of some Christian physicians as to whether leprosy as we know it is the disease that the Mosaic system is considering. There has been much written in the past, both pro and con. It would seem that the descriptions in these chapters describe leprosy as we understand this loathsome and death-dealing disease but includes also elephantiasis, skin diseases, running issues, cancer, tumors, and social diseases. This is illustrated in chapter 15, and we will amplify this aspect when we come to that chapter. After all, only the first stages of leprosy are described here. By the time the person was declared to be a leper, he was ejected from society.

This chapter deals with the cleansing of leprosy, not the cure of leprosy. The leper was cleansed after he had been cured.

DIAGNOSIS OF A NEW CASE OF LEPROSY

And the Lord spake unto Moses and Aaron, saying,

When a man shall have in the skin of his flesh a rising, a scab, or bright spot, and it be in the skin of his flesh like the plague of leprosy; then he shall be brought unto Aaron the priest, or unto one of his sons the priests [Lev. 13:1–2].

Compared to modern techniques of diagnosis, the methods of Leviticus seem very crude. The procedure was adapted to the knowledge of that day. The diagnosis was not done in order to prescribe a treatment, but rather, it was a religious ritual. This needs to be stated emphatically.

Now friends, since I have a cancer, I know how my doctor treated me. He looked at it and just by looking he came to the conclusion that it was a cancer. It was not until a biopsy had been taken in a scientific way that they decided that they should operate. So in that day, they could have known a great deal more than we realize. The priests handled literally thousands of cases, I think, and so they would know what to look for. Perhaps this isn't as crude as we today think that it was. It may have actually been a pretty good diagnostic system. Still, the emphasis here is upon the spiritual ceremony rather than the physical catharsis.

Three symptoms are identified here: a rising

or boil, a scab or small tumor, a bright spot. These are symptoms of leprosy, but the person having such a symptom need not necessarily be a leper. The first step was to bring the patient with a symptom to Aaron or one of the priests.

Just so, any manifestation of sin, either small or great, should be brought immediately to our Great High Priest, who is also the Great Physician. We are to pray about everything. That includes every manifestation of sin. That is the place to go when we are physically sick, too. I received a caustic letter not so long ago telling me not to be so proud and go to a certain healer. They said I would be healed if my pride would be overcome. Friends, I took my case to the Great Physician, the Lord Jesus. I go there when I sin, and I go there when I am sick. That is the place to go first. That doesn't mean I didn't go to a doctor when I got sick. But I went to the Lord Jesus first! "Let us therefore come boldly unto the throne of grace, that we may obtain mercy, and find grace to help in time of need . . . . Wherefore he is able also to save them to the uttermost that come unto God by him, seeing he ever liveth to make intercession for them" (Heb. 4:16; 7:25). "If we confess our sins, he is faithful and just to forgive us our sins, and to cleanse us from all unrighteousness" (1 John 1:9).

And the priest shall look on the plague in the skin of the flesh: and when the hair in the plague is turned white, and the plague in sight be deeper than the skin of his flesh, it is a plague of leprosy: and the priest shall look on him, and pronounce him unclean [Lev. 13:3].

There was no rash judgment made. The man or woman was carefully watched over a period of time. If a lesion on the skin began to disappear, the person was dismissed. If the hair turned white, it was becoming dead and showed that the disease was beneath the skin. Then the priest would pronounce the person unclean.

The Great Physician has made a thorough inspection of us and has made a diagnosis. "Their throat is an open sepulchre; with their tongues they have used deceit; the poison of asps is under their lips: Whose mouth is full of cursing and bitterness: Their feet are swift to shed blood: Destruction and misery are in their ways" (Rom. 3:13–16). God says, "All have sinned." We are unclean. You see, just like any doctor, the Great Physician asks us to open our mouth and He looks down our throat. Then He asks us to stick out our tongue and there He finds deceit and lying. We are all spiritual lep-

ers. God cannot have lepers in heaven. He must cure them before they get there.

Leprosy is a type of sin.

1. It becomes overt in loathsome ways. One night a drunken man came in off the street and sat in our warm auditorium. Suddenly he collapsed and fell out of the seat. We had to call an ambulance. By the time the ambulance got there, he was a mess. May I say to you, sin is loathsome in many ways.

2. It is a horrible disease. Dr. Kellogg wrote, "From among all diseases, leprosy has been selected by the Holy Ghost to stand . . . as the supreme type of sin, as seen by God!"

3. It begins in a small way, "a rising, a scab, a bright spot." Finally it delivers a death-dealing blow. What is at first so very small becomes a frightful and dreadful condition. Lepers in most countries today are isolated from the populace and are segregated into hospitals or colonies. Those of us who have seen pictures of lepers from missionaries in Africa or Asia realize what a dread disease it is. A century ago a missionary, William Thompson, described leprosy in Palestine in *The Land and the Book:* "As I was approaching Jerusalem, I was startled by the sudden apparition of a crowd of beggars, sans eyes, sans nose, sans hair, sans everything . . . . They held up their handless arms, unearthly sounds gurgled through throats without palates; in a word, I was horrified!" (Vol. I, pp. 530–531).

Sin seems ever so infinitesimal in a child. It may appear as a bright spot at first. The parents and relatives think little Willie is cute when he acts up, yells and kicks his feet in the air. Unless Willie is disciplined and is led to a saving knowledge of Christ, he will become lawless and even criminal. Lenin, Stalin, Hitler were all cute little babies once upon a time.

No drunkard ever became an alcoholic by taking one drink, but no man ever became an alcoholic who did not take the first drink. All sins start small.

4. Leprosy not only progresses slowly from a small beginning, but it progresses surely. From a little beginning, it advances surely and steadily to a tragic crisis. I quote Dr. Thompson again: "It comes on by degrees in different parts of the body: the hair falls from the head and eyebrows; the nails loosen, decay, and drop off; joint after joint of the fingers and toes shrink up and slowly fall away: the gums are absorbed, and the teeth disappear; the nose, the eyes, the tongue, and the palate are slowly consumed; and, finally, the wretched victim sinks into the earth and disappears."

This is the way God says sin is. "Then when

lust hath conceived, it bringeth forth sin: and sin, when it is finished, bringeth forth death" (James 1:15).

Leprosy is a living death. A leper was treated as a dead man. The wages of sin is death. "Be not deceived; God is not mocked: for whatsoever a man soweth, that shall he also reap. For he that soweth to his flesh shall of the flesh reap corruption; but he that soweth to the Spirit shall of the Spirit reap life everlasting" (Gal. 6:7–8).

Like leprosy, sin destroys the whole man. Both are corrosive in their effect, working slowly and surely, until finally they break out in an angry display that eventuates in death. No man ever went wrong overnight. Leprosy did not kill in a day—it is not like a heart attack. The leper's life was a walking death. Just so, the sinner is also dead even while he lives. Paul writes, "And you hath he quickened, who were dead in trespasses and sins; Wherein in time past ye walked according to the course of this world . . ." (Eph. 2:1–2).

The final, desperate, and inescapable end of sin and leprosy is death.

5. Leprosy does not produce sharp and unbearable pain as some other diseases. Leprosy keeps the man sad and restless. Likewise, sin produces a restlessness and sadness in man that is evident in our culture. Folks want to be amused, want to be made to laugh because they are sad. Crowds flock to places of amusement, to the night clubs, to be entertained. Take a look at the sad faces with vacant stares. Watch the cars filled with restless folk going nowhere fast. We have a generation with itchy feet. It is leprosy.

Finally sin brings a person to the point of not having any feeling, just as Paul said, "Who being past feeling have given themselves over unto lasciviousness, to work all uncleanness with greediness" (Eph. 4:19). They lapse into a state of sad contentment. They can reach the state of having a ". . . conscience seared with a hot iron" (1 Tim. 4:2).

6. Leprosy is thought to be hereditary. Whether it is or not, sin is! All that sinners can bring into the world are more sinners. I am interested in the insight of a contemporary psychologist who recognizes that while the assumption of education is that "the moral nature of man is capable of improvement," the assumption of traditional Christianity is that "the moral nature of man is corrupt, or absolutely bad." He further observes that while education assumes that an exterior "human agent" may be the means of man's "moral improvement," traditional Christianity assumes

that "the agent is God" and that rather than the moral nature of man being improved," it is exchanged for a new one."

7. Finally, leprosy and sin separate from God. It seemed cruel that the leper was not only shut out from society, but also from the sanctuary. It must be remembered that God is holy, the Author of righteousness and cleanliness. Therefore, leprosy is a fitting symbol of sin that separates from God. "But your iniquities have separated between you and your God, and your sins have hid his face from you, that he will not hear" (Isa. 59:2). In the New Jerusalem, the unforgiven and unwashed sinner is shut out from the presence of God according to Revelation 21:27 and 22:15.

So leprosy stands as a perfect type of sin. It is sin, as it were, made visible in the flesh. The priest was to look on the leper and pronounce him unclean. Just so, the Great Physician looks on the human family and pronounces it unclean. He does this so that we might come to Him for cleansing. He is ready to touch the leper and make him clean.

I have spent a long time in the beginning of this chapter because it is so important to see the analogy here and get the great spiritual message for us today. There is not much being said about sin today, yet our basic problem is sin!

If the bright spot be white in the skin of his flesh, and in sight be not deeper than the skin, and the hair thereof be not turned white; then the priest shall shut up him that hath the plague seven days [Lev. 13:4].

Now in this verse we see that there was no haste in making the judgment. Likewise, God is slow to anger in His relationship with us. God is very patient and He grants every opportunity to the sinner. ". . . The LORD, The LORD God, merciful and gracious, longsuffering, and abundant in goodness and truth, Keeping mercy for thousands, forgiving iniquity and transgression and sin, and that will by no means clear the guilty; visiting the iniquity of the fathers upon the children, and upon the children's children, unto the third and to the fourth generation" (Exod. 34:6–7). That verse is in the Old Testament. What does the New Testament say about the patience of God? "The Lord is not slack concerning his promise, as some men count slackness; but is longsuffering to us-ward, not willing that any should perish, but that all should come to repentance" (2 Pet. 3:9).

You see, the priest shut up the man for

seven days. He thought it was leprosy, but he was patient with him. Just so, God has shut up the world in quarantine for the disease of sin. "For God hath concluded them all in unbelief, that he might have mercy upon all" (Rom. 11:32). "But the scripture hath concluded all under sin, that the promise by faith of Jesus Christ might be given to them that believe" (Gal. 3:22). "Concluded" means to shut up together. God has the world shut up in quarantine, my friend, and He is not going to let man get very far out into His universe. It is rather amusing that when they brought the men back from the moon, they checked to see if they had brought any disease down to this earth. We have enough disease down here. Do you think we left any disease up there? God has us here under quarantine so that He might have mercy on us.

> And the priest shall look on him the seventh day: and, behold, if the plague in his sight be at a stay, and the plague spread not in the skin; then the priest shall shut him up seven days more [Lev. 13:5].

After seven days the priest makes another inspection and if there is still an element of uncertainty, then the patient is placed in quarantine for seven more days. There was not a rash or hasty judgment. We should learn from this that we are not to make hasty and rash judgments of others. It is a serious matter to make a false charge against another believer. Paul told Timothy, "Against an elder receive not an accusation, but before two or three witnesses" (1 Tim. 5:19). He also warned that at the end times there would be false accusers.

When I was a pastor I made a rule that no one could come to me to criticize a church officer unless the accused man was present to hear it. Do you know how many accusations I heard in the last twenty-one years? Just one. We need to be careful.

> And the priest shall look on him again the seventh day: and, behold, if the plague be somewhat dark, and the plague spread not in the skin, the priest shall pronounce him clean: it is but a scab: and we shall wash his clothes, and be clean [Lev. 13:6].

If the plague in the skin has not spread in fourteen days, but has improved, it obviously was not leprosy and the man is pronounced clean. Those were sweet words for the man, and he surely could sing a jubilee song. He did not need to be separated from his loved ones, but was clean and could go back to them.

Remember that the Lord touched the leper who came to Him and made him clean. More than that, He says to the spiritual lepers that their sins are forgiven. He healed the physical disease to demonstrate that He is the Savior who can forgive sins. Remember how the scribes and the Pharisees asked, ". . . Who can forgive sins, but God alone?" (Luke 5:21). So Jesus first told the man who was paralyzed that his sins were forgiven. Then He said, "But that ye may know that the Son of man hath power upon earth to forgive sins, I say unto thee, Arise, and take up thy couch, and go into thine house." It is important to recognize that Jesus has the authority to do both. (See Luke 5:17–26).

> But if the scab spread much abroad in the skin, after that he hath been seen of the priest for his cleansing, he shall be seen of the priest again:

> And if the priest see that, behold, the scab spreadeth in the skin, then the priest shall pronounce him unclean: it is a leprosy [Lev. 13:7–8].

This is the dark side of the picture. This would now be the third inspection. Does God give a man a second chance? My friend, God will give the sinner a thousand chances, if that is what it takes.

Finally the verdict must be rendered. The man is declared a leper. It is an awful sentence. The man is put out. Contrast this to the man who was hanging under the sentence of leprosy and was expecting to be put out but then was declared to be clean. That cleansed man did not live like a leper from that day on. He is clean and he lives clean. What a lesson that is for us!

There are some folk who make a profession of being converted. They can stand inspection for a while but finally the awful disease of sin will break out in its frightful symptoms and it is obvious they are unclean. John speaks of this in 1 John 2:19, "They went out from us, but they were not of us; for if they had been of us, they would no doubt have continued with us: but they went out, that they might be made manifest that they were not all of us." Peter describes these unclean and immoral lepers as the dog returning to his own vomit and the sow returning to the mire (2 Pet. 2:22).

DIAGNOSIS OF AN OLD CASE OF LEPROSY

> When the plague of leprosy is in a man, then he shall be brought unto the priest;

And the priest shall see him: and, behold, if the rising be white in the skin, and it have turned the hair white, and there be quick raw flesh in the rising;

It is an old leprosy in the skin of his flesh, and the priest shall pronounce him unclean, and shall not shut him up: for he is unclean [Lev. 13:9-11].

This is a case of old leprosy, or we might call it chronic leprosy. There was no need to shut this man up for observation because he was definitely a leper.

There are hardened sinners who are so obviously sinners that even their best friends tell them so. Under this class would come the spiritual Mafia, the murderer and the thief and the alcoholic and the drug addict. These people are under the slavery of their sin and only a supernatural remedy can help in cases like this.

The polished and slick church member who is unsaved does not believe that he has leprosy. He resents being told that he is a lost sinner. The hardened sinner is easier to reach than he, and is more open to the Gospel message. He *knows* he has leprosy.

And if a leprosy break out abroad in the skin, and the leprosy cover all the skin of him that hath the plague from his head even to his foot . . . Then the priest shall consider . . . he shall pronounce him clean that hath the plague: it is all turned white: he is clean.

But when raw flesh appeareth in him, he shall be unclean . . . it is a leprosy . . . .

Or if the raw flesh turn again, and be changed unto white . . . then the priest shall pronounce him clean that hath the plague: he is clean [Lev. 13:12-17].

This section shows another aspect of old leprosy. Although the entire body is covered, it does not necessarily follow that the case is hopeless. The remarkable statement here is that if the flesh has turned white, the patient is declared clean. This seems to indicate clearly that no sinner is hopeless. This may be what Isaiah meant when he wrote: "Why should ye be stricken any more? ye will revolt more and more: the whole head is sick, and the whole heart faint" (Isa. 1:5). Then follows the great invitation of the Great Physician, "Come now, and let us reason together, saith the LORD: though your sins be as scarlet, they shall be as white as snow; though they be red like crimson, they shall be as wool" (Isa. 1:18).

Notice that the true mark and symptom of leprosy is the raw flesh. The Bible has much to say about the flesh, even flesh as it is manifested in the believer: ". . . for all flesh had corrupted his way upon the earth" (Gen. 6:12). ". . . the flesh profiteth nothing . . ." (John 6:63). "For I know that in me, (that is, in my flesh,) dwelleth no good thing . . ." (Rom. 7:18). "That no flesh should glory in his presence . . . flesh and blood cannot inherit the kingdom of God . . ." (1 Cor. 1:29 and 15:50). ". . . fulfilling the desires of the flesh and of the mind; and were by nature the children of wrath, even as others" (Eph. 2:3). "For we are the circumcision, which worship God in the spirit, and rejoice in Christ Jesus, and have no confidence in the flesh" (Phil. 3:3). "And others save with fear, pulling them out of the fire; hating even the garment spotted by the flesh" (Jude 23).

It is obvious from these passages that the raw flesh is the old nature which was judged on the cross. When it manifests itself in a believer, God must judge it. The flesh can never please God. Only that which the Holy Spirit produces in the life of the believer is acceptable to God.

DIAGNOSIS OF LEPROSY FROM A BOIL OR A BURN

The flesh also, in which, even in the skin thereof, was a boil, and is healed,

And in the place of the boil there be a white rising, or a bright spot, white, and somewhat reddish, and it be shewed to the priest;

And if, when the priest seeth it, behold, it be in sight lower than the skin, and the hair thereof be turned white; the priest shall pronounce him unclean: it is a plague of leprosy broken out of the boil.

But if the priest look on it, and, behold, there be no white hairs therein, and if it be not lower than the skin, but be somewhat dark; then the priest shall shut him up seven days:

And if it spread much abroad in the skin, then the priest shall pronounce him unclean: it is a plague.

But if the bright spot stay in his place, and spread not, it is a burning boil; and the priest shall pronounce him clean [Lev. 13:18-23].

These verses give the details of the inspection of a boil. It was to be inspected by the priest because of a possibility of leprosy beginning there. It is just like a small sore which may become cancerous. They followed the same process as in the new case of leprosy. If there were white hair in the boil and it penetrated lower than the skin, these indicated deep-seated trouble. The seven days of inspection permitted the priest to determine which direction the boil would take.

There is always the danger of old sins spreading and becoming malignant. Often a new convert speaks of deliverance from some evil habit and then years later that old sore may break out again. It does happen. The person who has had such an experience may have been unsaved all along, or he may have been genuinely saved but the old flesh is reappearing. A careful inspection should be made and no cursory judgment is to be pronounced.

Several years ago, a man who was an alcoholic accepted Christ as his Savior. Then he got sick and I went to visit him. I found out he wasn't really sick of anything. The place reeked of alcohol. He began to weep and said he'd slipped back. May I say to you, one might feel like taking a fellow like that and putting him across your knee and paddling him. But that wouldn't do a bit of good. We need to make an inspection and diagnose the leprosy. But we need to tell that man that his leprosy can be cured. He has a Savior. We are not to stand there and condemn him and scold him and then leave. That would make him feel bad and make me feel bad. No one would be helped. This man needed to know that he had a Savior who would forgive him. The Savior heals the leprosy that breaks out.

Or if there be any flesh, in the skin whereof there is a hot burning, and the quick flesh that burneth have a white bright spot, somewhat reddish, or white;

Then the priest shall look upon it: and, behold, if the hair in the bright spot be turned white, and it be in sight deeper than the skin; it is a leprosy broken out of the burning: wherefore the priest shall pronounce him unclean: it is the plague of leprosy.

But if the priest look on it, and, behold, there be no white hair in the bright spot, and it be no lower than the other skin, but be somewhat dark; then the priest shall shut him up seven days:

And the priest shall look upon him the seventh day: and if it be spread much abroad in the skin, then the priest shall pronounce him unclean: it is the plague of leprosy.

And if the bright spot stay in his place, and spread not in the skin, but it be somewhat dark; it is a rising of the burning, and the priest shall pronounce him clean: for it is an inflammation of the burning [Lev. 13:24–28].

This describes a leprosy that comes from a hot burning. This hot burning is not a definite identification. It would be a burning from a hot object or it might mean the burning of an infection that has fever in it. At any rate, there was the danger of leprosy developing in it.

This seems to confirm the Scriptures that teach us that the flesh must be kept under close observation, for it can break out in the most alarming manner. "I speak after the manner of men because of the infirmity of your flesh: for as ye have yielded your members servants to uncleanness and to iniquity unto iniquity; even so now yield your members servants to righteousness unto holiness" (Rom. 6:19). "But I keep under my body, and bring it into subjection: lest that by any means, when I have preached to others, I myself should be a castaway" (1 Cor. 9:27).

All of these passages teach us to watch carefully for the presence of a pimple in the flesh. The flesh cannot please God.

DIAGNOSIS OF LEPROSY LOCATED IN THE HEAD OR THE BEARD

If a man or woman have a plague upon the head or the beard,

Then the priest shall see the plague: and, behold, if it be in sight deeper than the skin; and there be in it a yellow thin hair; then the priest shall pronounce him unclean: it is a dry scall, even a leprosy upon the head or beard [Lev. 13:29–30].

Leprosy could break out in the most unlikely spots. If it were hidden by the hair of the head or beard, it might not be discovered for some time. Special observation must be made of leprosy in these areas. The same techniques were applied here as to any other area to determine the presence of leprosy. A yellow hair indicated that the infection was beneath the epidermis and was leprosy.

You know, sin sometimes insinuates itself into the chief places in the church, into a Sunday School teachers' meeting or a board meeting or a mission meeting. It enervates and vitiates the witness of the entire body of believers when there is sin at the head. Again, one must be careful in judging these things. There must be time to make a judgment.

And if the priest look on the plague of the scall, and, behold, it be not in sight deeper than the skin, and that there is no black hair in it; then the priest shall shut up him that hath the plague of the scall seven days:

And in the seventh day the priest shall look on the plague: and, behold, if the scall spread not, and there be in it no yellow hair, and the scall be not in sight deeper than the skin;

He shall be shaven, but the scall shall he not shave; and the priest shall shut up him that hath the scall seven days more:

And in the seventh day the priest shall look on the scall: and, behold, if the scall be not spread in the skin, nor be in sight deeper than the skin; then the priest shall pronounce him clean: and he shall wash his clothes, and be clean.

But if the scall spread much in the skin after his cleansing;

Then the priest shall look on him: and, behold, if the scall be spread in the skin, the priest shall not seek for yellow hair; he is unclean.

But if the scall be in his sight at a stay, and that there is black hair grown up therein; the scall is healed, he is clean: and the priest shall pronounce him clean [Lev. 13:31–37].

So these verses go on to show that it might not be leprosy. Here again time is taken before a judgment is made and the patient is put in quarantine for seven days and then another period of seven days if that is necessary. This should teach us that accusations against the leadership in God's work should be received with a great deal of caution. Careful investigation must be made before a decision is determined.

The priest was given ample opportunity to observe the lesions. If the lesion spread later, the priest could still declare the man unclean. On the other hand, if black hair began to grow in the lesion, the priest shall pronounce the man clean.

If a man also or a woman have in the skin of their flesh bright spots, even white bright spots;

Then the priest shall look: and, behold, if the bright spots in the skin of their flesh be darkish white; it is a freckled spot that groweth in the skin; he is clean [Lev. 13:38–39].

These verses point out that a freckle is not leprosy, and then the following verses show that baldness is not leprosy, although leprosy can break out in a bald spot.

And the man whose hair is fallen off his head, he is bald; yet is he clean.

And he that hath his hair fallen off from the part of his head toward his face, he is forehead bald: yet is he clean.

And if there be in the bald head, or bald forehead, a white reddish sore; it is a leprosy sprung up in his bald head, or his bald forehead.

Then the priest shall look upon it: and, behold, if the rising of the sore be white reddish in his bald head, or in his bald forehead, as the leprosy appeareth in the skin of the flesh;

He is a leprous man, he is unclean: the priest shall pronounce him utterly unclean; his plague is in his head [Lev. 13:40–44].

DISPOSAL OF LEPERS' GARMENTS

And the leper in whom the plague is, his clothes shall be rent, and his head bare, and he shall put a covering upon his upper lip, and shall cry, Unclean, unclean [Lev. 13:45].

The garments of a leper were to be torn. He was to cover his upper lip and go about crying, "Unclean, unclean." The condition of the leper is revealed in his awful state. He was capable of transmitting the disease by contact.

The sinner spreads his sin wherever he goes! His disease is contagious and he infects others. A father has a right to live his own life as he pleases, but he has no right to take a precious son to hell with him. Many fathers are doing just that. The leper had defiled everything that was around him. That is what this teaches us. Even the garments would spread the infection. Just so, everything sin touches is defiled by it.

All the days wherein the plague shall be in him he shall be defiled; he is unclean:

he shall dwell alone; without the camp shall his habitation be [Lev. 13:46].

Many sinners comfort themselves by saying they will have plenty of company in hell. Notice that the leper was alone. He was separate.

The garment also that the plague of leprosy is in, whether it be a woollen garment, or a linen garment;

Whether it be in the warp, or woof; of linen, or of woollen; whether in a skin, or in any thing made of skin;

And if the plague be greenish or reddish in the garment, or in the skin, either in the warp, or in the woof, or in any thing of skin; it is a plague of leprosy, and shall be shewed unto the priest:

And the priest shall look upon the plague, and shut up it that hath the plague seven days:

And he shall look on the plague on the seventh day: if the plague be spread in the garment, either in the warp, or in the woof, or in a skin, or in any work that is made of skin; the plague is a fretting leprosy; it is unclean.

He shall therefore burn that garment, whether warp or woof, in woollen or in linen, or any thing of skin, wherein the plague is: for it is a fretting leprosy; it shall be burnt in the fire.

And if the priest shall look, and, behold, the plague be not spread in the garment, either in the warp, or in the woof or in any thing of skin;

Then the priest shall command that they wash the thing wherein the plague is, and he shall shut it up seven days more:

And the priest shall look on the plague, after that it is washed: and, behold, if the plague have not changed his colour, and the plague be not spread; it is unclean; thou shalt burn it in the fire; it is fret inward, whether it be bare within or without.

And if the priest look, and, behold, the plague be somewhat dark after the washing of it; then he shall rend it out of the garment, or out of the skin, or out of the warp, or out of the woof:

And if it appear still in the garment, either in the warp, or in the woof, or in any thing of skin; it is a spreading plague: thou shalt burn that wherein the plague is with fire.

And the garment, either warp, or woof, or whatsoever thing of skin it be, which thou shalt wash, if the plague be departed from them, then it shall be washed the second time, and shall be clean.

This is the law of the plague of leprosy in a garment of woollen or linen, either in the warp, or woof, or any thing of skins, to pronounce it clean, or to pronounce it unclean [Lev. 13:47–59].

This is an extended passage relative to the disposing of the garments. The quality of the garment made no difference. The best garments were just as infected as the cheap garments. There is a great lesson for us to learn through this. The righteousness of man is filthy rags in God's sight. Anything a sinner does or touches is contaminated by his sin.

Even the garments of those with lesser infections were to be washed. This passage shows an amazing insight into the spread of infection. We are all as an unclean thing and we, too, need washing. Only God has the remedy for the sinner.

CHAPTER 14

THEME: Ceremonial cleansing of the leper; ceremonial cleansing a house of leprosy; ceremonial law for cleansing leprosy and issues of the flesh

Again, I must insist that we are not being given a cure for leprosy. This is the ceremonial cleansing. In the preceding chapter we saw the details of the decisions in diagnosing the leprosy. There evidently were those lepers who were cured by the treatment of that day—whatever it was, and also there were those who were healed supernaturally. We know today there is a cure for leprosy. It is not an incurable disease, and Scripture does not present it as such. It was a terrible disease and is used to teach us tremendous spiritual lessons about sin.

This chapter casts a ray of light and hope into the darkness of the leper's plight. We note that no physician's prescription is given for the treatment and cure of leprosy. Rather, it shows the ceremonial cleansing which follows the cure. This alludes to the redemption of the sinner. The ritual is entirely symbolic, yet there is a therapeutic value in the washing and cleansing.

When man sinned in the Garden of Eden, sin separated God and man. This barrier of sin moved in a twofold direction in that it affected both God and man. It moved upward toward God and made man guilty before a holy God. It moved downward toward man, and man became polluted and contaminated with sin. Leprosy is a picture of sin in its pollution and contamination.

The remarkable feature in this chapter is the unique ceremony of cleansing and the treatment of a plague of leprosy in a house. The house is treated as a leper, obviously emphasizing the thought of contagion.

CEREMONIAL CLEANSING
OF THE LEPER WITHOUT THE CAMP

And the Lord spake unto Moses, saying,

This shall be the law of the leper in the day of his cleansing: He shall be brought unto the priest:

And the priest shall go forth out of the camp; and the priest shall look, and, behold, if the plague of leprosy be healed in the leper [Lev. 14:1–3].

We notice that the priest is not going out to heal the leper but is going out to see if he has been healed. That is important. This is

the "law of the leper in the day of his cleansing." This is a ritual which was to be followed precisely. It is a ceremonial cleansing which followed the cure of the leprosy. The man had been pronounced a leper by the priest. Now the priest must declare him cleansed. The priest must go out to the leper and meet him where he is. The leper would not dare to come into society, among the people, for he was forbidden to do that. He was shut out. Therefore, the priest must go to him. We find this mentioned in Luke 17:12, "And as he entered into a certain village, there met him ten men that were lepers, which stood afar off."

There is a wonderful parallel here to the person and work of our High Priest and Great Physician. He came forth from heaven's glory to this sin-cursed earth where man was suffering from the leprosy of sin. Friends, we can't go up into the society of heaven when we are lepers. We've done well to make it to the moon, but the men didn't get rid of their sin when they went to the moon. No, it was necessary for the Lord Jesus to come out of heaven's glory to this earth. The hymn states it very accurately, "Out of the ivory palaces into a world of woe." That is His story!

There is a great deal of emphasis placed on this. The second chapter of Hebrews tells about this: "But we see Jesus, who was made a little lower than the angels for the suffering of death, crowned with glory and honour; that he by the grace of God should taste death for every man. For it became him, for whom are all things, and by whom are all things, in bringing many sons unto glory, to make the captain of their salvation perfect through sufferings . . . . Forasmuch then as the children are partakers of flesh and blood, he also himself likewise took part of the same; that through death he might destroy him that had the power of death, that is, the devil . . . . For verily he took not on him the nature of angels; but he took on him the seed of Abraham. Wherefore in all things it behoved him to be made like unto his brethren, that he might be a merciful and faithful high priest in things pertaining to God, to make reconciliation for the sins of the people" (Heb. 2:9–10, 14, 16–17). He came out of heaven's glory, down to this earth. The Priest had to come to the leper! "But when the fulness of the time was come, God sent forth his Son, made of a woman, made under the law, To redeem them that were under the law, that we might receive the adoption of sons" (Gal. 4:4–5).

We need to emphasize that He still goes all the way to the sinner to heal his plague of sin. "Behold, I stand at the door, and knock: if any man hear my voice, and open the door, I will come in to him, and will sup with him, and he with me" (Rev. 3:20). God has declared that the heart of man is vile, and so it is God who must pronounce a man clean. He alone can cleanse. ". . . and the blood of Jesus Christ his Son cleanseth us from all sin" (1 John 1:7).

Now notice what the priest did when he came to the leper.

Then shall the priest command to take for him that is to be cleansed two birds alive and clean, and cedar wood, and scarlet, and hyssop:

And the priest shall command that one of the birds be killed in an earthen vessel over running water:

As for the living bird, he shall take it, and the cedar wood, and the scarlet, and the hyssop, and shall dip them and the living bird in the blood of the bird that was killed over the running water:

And he shall sprinkle upon him that is to be cleansed from the leprosy seven times, and shall pronounce him clean, and shall let the living bird loose into the open field [Lev. 14:4–7].

Didn't I tell you this could be an unusual ceremony? I don't think there is anything, anywhere, as unusual as this. All other sacrifices were to be made at the altar of the tabernacle and, later, of the temple at the command of God. This is the exception. The leper was shut out from the tabernacle, and so it was necessary for the priest to come to him.

The brazen altar for the sacrifices speaks of the cross of Christ. But, you see, that cross had to be down here on this earth. He had to come down here to meet us where we are. Friends, we were shut out from God. We were strangers and afar off, without hope and without God in the world. He had to come here to meet us in our need.

There were two live, clean birds used in this sacrifice. Most likely they were doves. One was killed—to represent the death of Christ. The other was living—to represent the resurrection of Christ. These are the two facets of the Gospel. Paul says, "For I delivered unto you first of all that which I also received, how that Christ died for our sins according to the scriptures; And that he was buried, and that he rose again the third day according to the scriptures" (1 Cor. 15:3–4). Two birds: death and resurrection!

Then notice that they used cedar wood. This, I think, is a symbol of the perfect humanity of Christ. The wood was incorruptible. It served a practical purpose as the handle of a brush to which the hyssop was tied with the scarlet ring. The scarlet was evidently scarlet wool.

The scarlet, I believe, is the sign of faith in the blood. It reminds us that Rahab was instructed to put out a scarlet cord as an evidence of her faith.

Hyssop is a plant that grows upon rocks in damp places. It represents the faith of the individual. "Purge me with hyssop, and I shall be clean: wash me, and I shall be whiter than snow" (Ps. 51:7). It is the appropriation and the application of the redemption in Christ. You see, one can stand at the sidelines and nod his head and say he believes that Jesus died and rose again. That is not saving faith. The question is whether or not you have appropriated it for yourself. Have you actually put your trust in Him? Also it is the application of the death of Christ and the blood of Christ to sin in the believer's life. "But if we walk in the light, as he is in the light, we have fellowship one with another, and the blood of Jesus Christ his Son cleanseth us from all sin" (1 John 1:7).

The earthen vessel speaks of the humanity of Christ. He took upon Himself our flesh, our humanity. Paul calls himself an earthen vessel in 2 Corinthians 4:7. The earthen vessel is this body which we have. The emphasis is upon the weakness and infirmity of humanity. "For we have not an high priest which cannot be touched with the feeling of our infirmities; but was in all points tempted like as we are, yet without sin" (Heb. 4:15).

Running water is living water. This water was taken from a running stream or fountain. This speaks of both the Word of God and the Spirit of God.

The ritual is both unusual and beautiful. One of the birds is slain over the earthen vessel in which there is the living water. This represents the death of Christ who offered Himself by the eternal Spirit. "How much more shall the blood of Christ, who through the eternal Spirit offered himself without spot to God, purge your conscience from dead works to serve the living God?" (Heb. 9:14).

It was essential to have the two birds to

carry out the typical meaning of resurrection. The live bird was dipped in the blood of the slain bird to identify him with the bird that was slain. Then the live bird was given its freedom, permitting it to fly away. Christ was delivered for our offenses and raised for our justification to give us the liberty to stand steadfast in Christ. "Stand fast therefore in the liberty wherewith Christ hath made us free, and be not entangled again with the yoke of bondage" (Gal. 5:1). That means not to get entangled again with religion and regulations and ritual and law. Christ took our place, died our death, paid our penalty. He was raised for us. If He died for us down here, then we died in Him (2 Cor. 5:14–15) and we were raised in Him and we are in Him up yonder at the right hand of God (Eph. 1:1–6). Friends, the believer is as free as the birds of the heavens and is delivered from religion and ritual and law. The believer is now the bond-slave of the Lord Jesus Christ. He is subject to Christ's will and way. "If ye love me, keep my commandments" (John 14:15).

"He shall sprinkle upon him that is to be cleansed from the leprosy seven times." Seven is the number of completeness and finality. This settled forever the question of whether the leper was cleansed or not. There are only two kinds of people in this world, friends—there are lepers and cleansed lepers. That is, there are lost sinners and saved sinners. That is all.

Living water and blood meet in this ceremony. John was careful to note for us that when Christ died and the soldier pierced His side, blood and water came forth (John 19:34–35). He repeats the fact that Jesus Christ came by water and the blood in his epistle (1 John 5:6).

The Gnostics in John's day taught that Jesus was not God but that God came upon Him at baptism (that is the water) and departed from Him at the cross (that is the blood). John insists that Jesus Christ was God from the very beginning when He was made flesh and that He was God on the cross when He shed His precious blood. "And there are three that bear witness in earth, the Spirit, and the water, and the blood: and these three agree in one" (1 John 5:8). The ceremony and offering concerning the leper bore this out and illustrates this great truth.

And he that is to be cleansed shall wash his clothes, and shave off all his hair, and wash himself in water, that he may be clean: and after that he shall come

into the camp, and shall tarry abroad out of his tent seven days.

But it shall be on the seventh day, that he shall shave all his hair off his head and his beard and his eyebrows, even all his hair he shall shave off: and he shall wash his clothes, also he shall wash his flesh in water, and he shall be clean [Lev. 14:8–9].

Now you'll have to admit that this is unusual also. The sacrificial ceremony has been completed denoting that the leper has been cleansed and accepted. Now, before he enters back into society, this further ritual shows that his old life has ended for him and a new life opens before him. The clothes represent the habits of life, his life style. The shaving off of all the hair of his body emphasizes the radical and revolutionary change that is taking place in his life.

Friends, when a believer comes to Christ, there is going to be a change! The putting away of the flesh is essential to a consistent walk before the world. The Lord Jesus said, "Ye shall know them by their fruits" (Matt. 7:16). That is still the test tube for His own.

Again, the seven days indicate a complete cycle of testing and inspection. He is to be tested before he returns to society. I think that sometimes we let new converts give a testimony too soon. Believers are to be put up and watched for a while. There must be a newness of life.

At the end of this time, he washed himself thoroughly. The child of God needs to be continually washed. "Now ye are clean through the word which I have spoken unto you" (John 15:3). "Sanctify them through thy truth: thy word is truth" (John 17:17). Friend, you can never be cleansed or sanctified, set apart for God's use, until you are saturated with the Word of God. How important that is!

May I say that the seven days for the believer, the time of completeness, is when God completes the earthly journey of His church. Then He will present her to Himself as a cleansed church (Eph. 5:25–27). In the meantime the believer is in the process of being sanctified. This is the practical aspect. There should be a daily growth, a development in faith and in practice. Holiness is to the spiritual life what health is to the physical body.

CEREMONIAL CLEANSING
OF THE LEPER WITHIN THE CAMP

And on the eighth day he shall take two he lambs without blemish, and one ewe

lamb of the first year without blemish, and three tenth deals of fine flour for a meat offering, mingled with oil, and one log of oil [Lev. 14:10].

The cleansed leper is now fit to enter the congregation of the Lord, but when he does, he must take his place with the other Israelites and present the offerings that every member of the congregation brought before the Lord. He brings two he lambs, one ewe lamb, fine flour, oil, and a log of oil. These are all the offerings which the average Israelite would normally make in his lifetime. It indicated the full acceptance of the cleansed leper.

And the priest that maketh him clean shall present the man that is to be made clean, and those things, before the Lord, at the door of the tabernacle of the congregation:

And the priest shall take one he lamb, and offer him for a trespass offering, and the log of oil, and wave them for a wave offering before the Lord:

And he shall slay the lamb in the place where he shall kill the sin offering and the burnt offering, in the holy place: for as the sin offering is the priest's, so is the trespass offering: it is most holy:

And the priest shall take some of the blood of the trespass offering, and the priest shall put it upon the tip of the right ear of him that is to be cleansed, and upon the thumb of his right hand, and upon the great toe of his right foot:

And the priest shall take some of the log of oil, and pour it into the palm of his own left hand:

And the priest shall dip his right finger in the oil that is in his left hand, and shall sprinkle of the oil with his finger seven times before the Lord:

And of the rest of the oil that is in his hand shall the priest put upon the tip of the right ear of him that is to be cleansed, and upon the thumb of his right hand, and upon the great toe of his right foot, upon the blood of the trespass offering:

And the remnant of the oil that is in the priest's hand he shall pour upon the head of him that is to be cleansed: and the priest shall make an atonement for him before the Lord.

And the priest shall offer the sin offering, and make an atonement for him that is to be cleansed from his uncleanness; and afterward he shall kill the burnt offering:

And the priest shall offer the burnt offering and the meat offering upon the altar: and the priest shall make an atonement for him, and he shall be clean [Lev. 14:11–20].

This extended passage in the Authorized Version is in a single sentence. The action here is one continuous ceremony which encompasses all the offerings and means that the cleansed leper now stands before the door of the tabernacle just as any other Israelite.

He brings a he lamb for a trespass offering to remind him that he is still a sinner who sins and who needs the cleansing blood of Christ applied by the Holy Spirit to his life. The other he lamb is for a sin offering, because the cleansed leper still has his sin nature. The ewe lamb is for a burnt offering to set forth the person of Christ as God sees Him. The fine flour mingled with oil speaks of the meal offering which sets forth the loveliness of the humanity of Christ. The blood put upon the tip of his right ear indicates that he can now hear the voice of the Son of God saying, "Thy faith hath made thee whole." The blood on the right thumb indicates that with clean hands he can now serve God. The blood on his right toe indicates that the cleansed leper can now walk in the way of God. The oil poured on his head indicates he is now totally dedicated to God.

All these offerings speak of Christ, through whom the cleansed leper is acceptable to God. There is nothing special about him just because he is a cleansed leper. Too often we see Christians who feel that somehow they are different and special. They withdraw from the others and think they are better than the others. My friend, we each must come just as all the rest come. Everyone must be acceptable to God through Christ. We each need to be washed. You remember that Peter protested to the Lord Jesus that He would never wash his feet. Our Lord answered, ". . . If I wash thee not, thou hast no part with me" (John 13:8). There is a great lesson in this for you and for me. Yes, the leper was brought back and yes, he had been cleansed of his leprosy, but he stood with the rest of the congregation before God. He still stood as a sinner and he needed the constant cleansing before God.

Verses 21–32 explain the offering he could bring if he were poor. It would be logical to think that a person who had been a leper would not be able to afford an elaborate ritual. Again, the provision of God for the poor is marvelous. No one is shut out because of poverty. Turtle-doves or pigeons could be substituted in the offering.

And if he be poor, and cannot get so much; then he shall take one lamb for a trespass offering to be waved, to make an atonement for him, and one tenth deal of fine flour mingled with oil for a meat offering, and a log of oil;

And two turtledoves, or two young pi-geons, such as he is able to get; and the one shall be a sin offering, and the other a burnt offering.

And he shall bring them on the eighth day for his cleansing unto the priest, unto the door of the tabernacle of the congregation, before the Lord.

And the priest shall take the lamb of the trespass offering, and the log of oil, and the priest shall wave them for a wave offering before the Lord:

And he shall kill the lamb of the trespass offering, and the priest shall take some of the blood of the trespass offering, and put it upon the tip of the right ear of him that is to be cleansed, and upon the thumb of his right hand, and upon the great toe of his right foot:

And the priest shall pour of the oil into the palm of his own left hand:

And the priest shall sprinkle with his right finger some of the oil that is in his left hand seven times before the Lord:

And the priest shall put of the oil that is in his hand upon the tip of the right ear of him that is to be cleansed, and upon the thumb of his right hand, and upon the great toe of his right foot, upon the place of the blood of the trespass offering:

And the rest of the oil that is in the priest's hand he shall put upon the head of him that is to be cleansed, to make an atonement for him before the Lord.

And he shall offer the one of the turtle-doves, or of the young pigeons, such as he can get;

Even such as he is able to get, the one for a sin offering, and the other for a burnt

offering, with the meat offering: and the priest shall make an atonement for him that is to be cleansed before the Lord.

This is the law of him in whom is the plague of leprosy, whose hand is not able to get that which pertaineth to his cleansing [Lev. 14:21–32].

CEREMONIAL CLEANSING
OF A HOUSE
WHEREIN HAS BEEN LEPROSY

And the Lord spake unto Moses and unto Aaron, saying,

When ye be come into the land of Ca-naan, which I give to you for a posses-sion, and I put the plague of leprosy in a house of the land of your possession;

And he that owneth the house shall come and tell the priest, saying, It seemeth to me there is as it were a plague in the house:

Then the priest shall command that they empty the house, before the priest go into it to see the plague, that all that is in the house be not made unclean: and afterward the priest shall go in to see the house [Lev. 14:33–36].

I must confess that a house would be an un-usual place to find leprosy. It is hard to know exactly what this meant. Perhaps it was some fungus growth or dry rot which entered into the fabric of the house. The priest would examine the house for greenish or reddish streaks and would examine it again in seven days to see if the plague were spreading.

The picture is that we live in an old house down here, which is our body. And we live in this world which is also contaminated by sin. The old house we live in is filled with leprosy.

There are three stages in the ceremonial cleansing of the house. First, the house was emptied of the furniture and occupants. The priest inspected it and then shut it up for seven days before making another inspection. If he then found a trace of leprosy, he removed the plaster from the infected part and took away the diseased stones.

And if the plague come again, and break out in the house, after that he hath taken away the stones, and after he hath scraped the house, and after it is plas-tered;

Then the priest shall come and look, and

behold, if the plague be spread in the house, it is a fretting leprosy in the house: it is unclean.

And he shall break down the house, the stones of it, and the timber thereof, and all the mortar of the house; and he shall carry them forth out of the city unto an unclean place.

Moreover, he that goeth into the house all the while that it is shut up shall be unclean until the even.

And he that lieth in the house shall wash his clothes; and he that eateth in the house shall wash his clothes [Lev. 14:43–47].

If the priest found remnants of the infection in the renovated house, then the house was to be demolished and removed.

You know, there will be a time when God will demolish this earth that is tainted with leprosy. He is going to make it clean. There will be a new heaven and a new earth and they will be free from sin.

And if the priest shall come in, and look upon it, and, behold, the plague hath not spread in the house, after the house was plastered; then the priest shall pronounce the house clean, because the plague is healed [Lev. 14:48].

The same ritual of the two birds is followed here as in the case of the ceremonial cleansing of the leper.

And he shall take to cleanse the house two birds, and cedar wood, and scarlet, and hyssop:

And he shall kill the one of the birds in an earthen vessel over running water:

And he shall take the cedar wood, and the hyssop, and the scarlet, and the living bird, and dip them in the blood of the slain bird, and in the running water, and sprinkle the house seven times:

And he shall cleanse the house with the blood of the bird, and with the running water, and with the living bird, and with the cedar wood, and with the hyssop, and with the scarlet:

But he shall let go the living bird out of the city into the open fields, and make an atonement for the house: and it shall be clean [Lev. 14:49–53].

CEREMONIAL LAW FOR CLEANSING OF LEPROSY AND ISSUES OF THE FLESH

This is the law for all manner of plague of leprosy, and scall,

And for the leprosy of a garment, and of a house,

And for a rising, and for a scab, and for a bright spot:

To teach when it is unclean, and when it is clean: this is the law of leprosy [Lev. 14:54–57].

This seems to be an emphatic enforcement of the law concerning the cleansing of the leprosy. Notice that the primary purpose of the ritual was to teach. "To teach when it is unclean, and when it is clean."

This is a great spiritual lesson and it is meant to teach us. You and I have spiritual leprosy. If either you or I went to heaven without Jesus Christ, without trusting Him, we would cry out, "Unclean, unclean," and we would be cast out. In Christ, we are accepted in the Beloved! My friend, where are you today? Are you a leper who has come to Jesus Christ for cleansing or are you still unclean?

CHAPTER 15

THEME: *Running issues of the man; running issues of the woman; repulsiveness and regulations of running issues*

We have had two chapters on this matter of leprosy, and that has been bad enough, but it is going to get worse in this chapter. We are hearing a great deal about the pollution of our ecology in these days but there is a pollution of our souls also, and of our minds—of our entire beings. These running sores are highly contagious and infectious and they reveal to us the exceeding sinfulness of sin. Human nature is an overflowing cesspool and a sewer of uncleanness. Not only is human nature defiled, but it is defiling; not only is it corrupt, but it is corrupting. This chapter holds up the mirror to human nature, and after one look, no flesh can glory in His sight.

One would think that leprosy was the worst of the diseases but actually it was not as contagious and contaminating as running issues. I would like to quote Dr. Leiker who is an authority on leprosy. "Leprosy is caused by tiny germs called leprosy bacilli, which can be seen only through a microscope. The bacilli were discovered in 1873 by the Norwegian doctor, Hansen. That is why leprosy is sometimes called Hansen's disease. The bacilli are present in large numbers in the skin of certain types of leprosy patients. They pass from these patients to the skin of healthy people, mainly by bodily contact. They then enter the skin through tiny wounds and scratches, where they may live and multiply. Only infectious patients—those who have many bacilli in their skin—are able to spread the disease. Many patients have no bacilli left in their skin and therefore they do not pass on the disease.

"Frequent bathing, washing of clothes, and keeping a clean house will help to prevent the disease, because many bacilli can be washed away with water and soap before they enter the skin. The most important thing is to avoid bodily contact with infectious cases of leprosy. The germs are not carried by air or by insects. There is no proof that leprosy is spread in other ways, but it may be that the disease is spread occasionally by means other than bodily contact.

"You may use patients' clothes, sleeping mats, tools, and so on, without risk, provided they are washed with hot water and soap and have been in the sun for at least 24 hours. There is no danger in visiting patients' homes, or even in shaking hands with them, but you should wash your hands afterwards. There is no reason to fear leprosy if these simple safeguards are taken."

Leprosy was a disease that could not be kept a secret for long. It worked slowly, but it would finally break out. In contrast, running issues could be kept secret for a lifetime. These represent the thought life of man as well as the overt act of sin. "And God saw that the wickedness of man was great in the earth, and that every imagination of the thoughts of his heart was only evil continually" (Gen. 6:5). This has to do with that part of human nature that is defiled and that affects others. "Who can bring a clean thing out of an unclean? Not one" (Job 14:4). "Who can understand his errors? Cleanse thou me from secret faults" (Ps. 19:12). "For I know that in me (that is, in my flesh,) dwelleth no good thing: for to will is present with me; but how to perform that which is good I find not" (Rom. 7:18). Here we have the nature of man that is hidden. No one else may know about it. This is what we know down deep in our hearts. Yet, this secret sin can be passed on to others.

Some famous men have commented on the secret sin of man: "I see no fault committed which I too might not have committed" (Goethe). "Every man knows that of himself which he dares not tell to his dearest friends" (Dr. Samuel Johnson). "I do not know what the heart of a villain may be—I only know that of a virtuous man, and that is frightful" (Count de Maistre). "Go to your own bosom. Knock there: and ask your heart what it doth know" (Shakespeare). "Why is there no man who *confesses* his vices? It is because he has not yet laid them aside. It is a *waking* man only who can tell his dreams" (Seneca).

The curse of sin has affected man's power in the propagation of the race. Man is only capable of producing after his kind—a sinner as he is. The very fountain of the race is polluted. Many of these running issues are connected with the generative organs of the race. For the most part, they are the social diseases. There is filthiness and defilement connected with sexual sins that is appalling. David cried out to God, "Purge me with hyssop, and I shall be clean: wash me, and I shall be whiter than snow. . . . Create in me a clean heart, O God; and renew a right spirit within me" (Ps. 51: 7, 10).

Today people talk about the new morality. It

is interesting that they turn out the same old diseases with the new morality. Today the social diseases, venereal diseases, are increasing at an alarming rate. It is of epidemic proportions both in this country and in places abroad where our soldiers are stationed. That is the way sin is. And it robs a person of the joy of his salvation.

It seems strange that God would talk so much about such a repulsive subject. However, He gives to man a comprehensive view of the exceeding sinfulness of sin. We get an unusual view of it in this chapter. We need to recall the words of Paul, "For whatsoever things were written aforetime were written for our learning, that we through patience and comfort of the scriptures might have hope" (Rom. 15:4).

RUNNING ISSUES OF THE MAN

And the Lord spake unto Moses and to Aaron, saying [Lev. 15:1].

God addressed both Moses and Aaron. In chapter 14 where the "law of the leper" was under consideration, only the law-giver Moses was addressed. Aaron, as the high priest, is a prophetic picture of our Great High Priest. Only the Lord Jesus can give comfort and understanding to the afflicted as well as the extending of mercy and grace. Our High Priest cannot be touched by our sin, but He can be touched with a feeling of our infirmities, because He was in all points tempted as we are, yet without sin (Heb. 4:14–15 and Heb. 2:17–18).

Speak unto the children of Israel, and say unto them, When any man hath a running issue out of his flesh, because of his issue he is unclean.

And this shall be his uncleanness in his issue: whether his flesh run with his issue, or his flesh be stopped from his issue, it is his uncleanness [Lev. 15:2–3].

This vivid language reveals how sickening, disgusting, abhorrent, offensive, impure, repugnant, and utterly corrupt and corrupting the human nature is. The pus of sin is flowing from the human heart. We can see it all around us and in us. The defilement is here. We cannot rub shoulders with each other without it affecting our lives because human nature is not only corrupt, it is corrupting. You and I influence one another. I live my life in you, and you live your life in me. It cannot be otherwise. You are a preacher, whether you know it or not. You are preaching by your life.

When I was a pastor in Pasadena, I knew a very godly woman whose son was a drunkard. They lived a little way from the church. One could always tell when he was on what is called a "toot" because he would use both sides of the street on the way home. His mother was distressed and ashamed, and she asked me to talk with him. One day I saw him weaving down the street and I brought him into my study to talk with him. I told him how low-down he was, called him a sinner and a disgrace. I called him everything you could possibly call such a man, and he just hung his head and took it all. Then I said, "Don't you know that you are preaching by your life?" He asked, "Are you calling me a preacher?" When I told him he was, he got up the best he could as drunk as he was and wanted to fight me. You could call him anything else in the world but a preacher!

Well, my friend, whoever you are, you are a preacher. You are preaching some message by your life. You are influencing someone.

Human nature is corrupting because it is sinful. Even the regenerated man still carries his old sinful flesh. Listen to the words of the Lord Jesus:

"But those things which proceed out of the mouth come forth from the heart; and they defile the man. For out of the heart proceed evil thoughts, murders, adulteries, fornications, thefts, false witness, blasphemies: These are the things which defile a man: but to eat with unwashen hands defileth not a man" (Matt. 15:18–20).

It is amazing today how many people are interested in religious ceremonies. Even though they go through those religious ceremonies, they have a heart that is just as filthy as it possibly can be. We all have that kind of heart, unless it has been cleansed by the blood of Christ.

James makes it very practical. "But every man is tempted, when he is drawn away of his own lust, and enticed. Then when lust hath conceived, it bringeth forth sin: and sin, when it is finished, bringeth forth death" (James 1:14–15). Paul cried out in despair, ". . . I know that in me (that is, in my flesh,) dwelleth no good thing . . ." (Rom. 7:18). The sore of sin may be visible or invisible; it may be oozing blood and pus, or it may not appear on the surface, yet it is there. The uncleanness in view here is in the thought life and the secret sins—secret to man but open before God. "Behold, thou desirest truth in the inward parts: and in the hidden part thou shalt make me to know wisdom" (Ps. 51:6). This passage should humble the proud man and show how utterly disgusting he is in the light of God's presence. Listen to David: "Against thee, thee only, have I sinned, and done this evil in thy sight: that thou mightest be justified when thou speakest, and be clear when thou judgest" (Ps. 51:4).

God has emphasized in His Word again and again that sin is exceeding sinful. Read Ezekiel 16:1–13 in which God makes it very clear to Israel that they had no virtues or attractions but were utterly disgusting to Him. They were polluted and their genealogy was bad. Or read the entire chapter of Isaiah 59, where he says, "But your iniquities have separated between you and your God, and your sins have hid his face from you, that he will not hear."

Every bed, whereon he lieth that hath the issue, is unclean: and every thing, whereon he sitteth, shall be unclean.

And whosoever toucheth his bed shall wash his clothes, and bathe himself in water, and be unclean until the even.

And he that sitteth on any thing whereon he sat that hath the issue shall wash his clothes, and bathe himself in water, and be unclean until the even.

And he that toucheth the flesh of him that hath the issue shall wash his clothes, and bathe himself in water, and be unclean until the even [Lev. 15:4–7].

Everything he sits on, everything he touches is unclean.

God is concerned with the personal life of His people. His law reaches into the minute areas of their lives. He even watches over them while they are asleep! The man with an unclean issue contaminated the bed upon which he slept, and even his dreams were impure. Many a person spends a sleepless night, not counting sheep, but recalling his sins with lustful pleasure. God is interested in what we think when we lie upon our pillows. He wants to control our thought life. "Finally, brethren, whatsoever things are true, whatsoever things are honest, whatsoever things are just, whatsoever things are pure, whatsoever things are lovely, whatsoever things are of good report; if there be any virtue, and if there be any praise, think on these things" (Phil. 4:8).

God is interested in you! He is interested in you when you lie down and when you walk about. He is interested in what you touch. When we sit upon a chair in social conversation, God is interested in our conversation. Do we spread the virus of contamination? Also

God is interested in our business and social contacts. Physical contact of the clean with the unclean always spreads the disease to the clean.

My friend we cannot be with people or even just walk down the street without becoming soiled. We hear four-letter words, we see pictures, we are lured by advertising and propaganda. We are constantly soiled. We need to be aware of this and to confess our sin and to be cleansed by God. We all have this leprosy of sin, these running sores, these hidden sins.

And if he that hath the issue spit upon him that is clean; then he shall wash his clothes, and bathe himself in water, and be unclean until the even.

And what saddle soever he rideth upon that hath the issue shall be unclean.

And whosoever toucheth any thing that was under him shall be unclean until the even: and he that beareth any of those things shall wash his clothes, and bathe himself in water, and be unclean until the even.

And whomsoever he toucheth that hath the issue, and hath not rinsed his hands in water, he shall wash his clothes, and bathe himself in water, and be unclean until the even.

And the vessel of earth, that he toucheth which hath the issue, shall be broken: and every vessel of wood shall be rinsed in water [Lev. 15:8–12].

This gets down to where a person almost feels disgusted, but it reveals the nastiness of sin by contact. The former regulations had to do with conduct in the home and now this pertains to contact on the street or in a public place. Some of this we might call accidental contact.

We find this today. A believer often finds himself in a public place or on the street and some vile, dirty-minded person opens his mouth and spews out undiluted profanity and unspeakable blasphemy. This is contaminating. A believer may feel dirty after leaving such a group, and he is dirty. He needs to wash himself. That is the reason it is so very important for us to stay in the Word of God. "Wherewithal shall a young man cleanse his way? by taking heed thereto according to thy word" (Ps. 119:9). We get dirty in this life!

Listen to these words of Jesus: ". . . If I wash thee not, thou hast no part with me" (John 13:8). This means we cannot have fellowship with the Lord Jesus if we are not washed by Him. "Now ye are clean through the word which I have spoken unto you" (John 15:3). "Sanctify them through thy truth: thy word is truth" (John 17:17).

And when he that hath an issue is cleansed of his issue; then he shall number to himself seven days for his cleansing, and wash his clothes, and bathe his flesh in running water, and shall be clean.

And on the eighth day he shall take to him two turtledoves, or two young pigeons, and come before the LORD unto the door of the tabernacle of the congregation, and give them unto the priest:

And the priest shall offer them, the one for a sin offering, and the other for a burnt offering; and the priest shall make an atonement for him before the LORD for his issue [Lev. 15:13–15].

Here, again, we have both the water and the blood introduced. The blood removes the guilt of sin and the water removes the stain of sin. The Holy Spirit must apply the sacrifice of Christ to those secret sins which are in our lives today.

Friend, do you see what this is describing? It is a sordid chapter, and yet we must confess that it is a picture of you and me. We need to confess and be cleansed of our secret sins. "I acknowledged my sin unto thee, and mine iniquity have I not hid. I said, I will confess my transgressions unto the LORD; and thou forgavest the iniquity of my sin" (Ps. 32:5). "If we confess our sins, he is faithful and just to forgive us our sins, and to cleanse us from all unrighteousness" (1 John 1:9).

And if any man's seed of copulation go out from him, then he shall wash all his flesh in water, and be unclean until the even.

And every garment, and every skin, whereon is the seed of copulation, shall be washed with water, and be unclean until the even.

The woman also with whom man shall lie with seed of copulation, they shall both bathe themselves in water, and be unclean until the even [Lev. 15:16–18].

It is obvious that this is referring to venereal diseases. Today these diseases are like an epidemic. God guards against these social diseases. God is interested in the procreation of

the race. God gave this gift to man for his good and inspiration, and so guards this system carefully. Man is always in danger of debasing himself in that which was to be the noblest experiences.

Our Lord teaches that unholy desires and lustful thoughts are to be avoided, for they are sin. "Ye have heard that it was said by them of old time, Thou shalt not commit adultery: But I say unto you, That whosoever looketh on a woman to lust after her hath committed adultery with her already in his heart" (Matt. 5:27–28).

RUNNING ISSUES OF THE WOMAN

And if a woman have an issue, and her issue in her flesh be blood, she shall be put apart seven days: and whosoever toucheth her shall be unclean until the even.

And every thing that she lieth upon in her separation shall be unclean: every thing also that she sitteth upon shall be unclean.

And whosoever toucheth her bed shall wash his clothes, and bathe himself in water, and be unclean until the even.

And whosoever toucheth any thing that she sat upon shall wash his clothes, and bathe himself in water, and be unclean until the even.

And if it be on her bed, or on any thing whereon she sitteth, when he toucheth it, he shall be unclean until the even.

And if any man lie with her at all, and her flowers be upon him, he shall be unclean seven days; and all the bed whereon he lieth shall be unclean [Lev. 15:19–24].

These verses evidently refer to the uncleanness of a woman during her normal menstrual period. She was separated from her friends and her loved ones during this period. She was treated as an outcast and a leper (Num. 5:2). This seems to be unusually severe. The only explanation we have to offer is that this is a reminder of the fall of man as recorded in Genesis. The penalty was death. Man is reminded that he had a bad beginning and has nothing in which to glory. Sinful man can produce only sin.

And if a woman have an issue of her blood many days out of the time of her separation, or if it run beyond the time

of her separation; all the days of the issue of her uncleanness shall be as the days of her separation: she shall be unclean.

Every bed whereon she lieth all the days of her issue shall be unto her as the bed of her separation: and whatsoever she sitteth upon shall be unclean, as the uncleanness of her separation.

And whosoever toucheth those things shall be unclean, and shall wash his clothes, and bathe himself in water, and be unclean until the even.

But if she be cleansed of her issue, then she shall number to herself seven days, and after that she shall be clean.

And on the eighth day she shall take unto her two turtles, or two young pigeons, and bring them unto the priest, to the door of the tabernacle of the congregation [Lev. 15:25–29].

This section deals with an abnormal issue. This gives rules for her separation and the fact that she contaminates the bed she lies on and anyone who touches the things which she contaminates. It also explains the offering she is to bring when she is cleansed of her issue.

This gives us some insight into the plight of the woman with the issue of blood who came to Christ for healing (Luke 8:43–48). The Law had shut her out from contact with others, yet she touched Jesus. The Law had shut her out from the temple and from the public worship of God. The grace of our Lord healed her and restored her, and He commended her faith. Jesus is the fountain for the cleansing of the uncleanness of our hearts.

REPULSIVENESS AND REGULATIONS OF RUNNING ISSUES

Thus shall ye separate the children of Israel from their uncleanness; that they die not in their uncleanness, when they defile my tabernacle that is among them.

This is the law of him that hath an issue, and of him whose seed goeth from him, and is defiled therewith;

And of her that is sick of her flowers, and of him that hath an issue, of the man, and of the woman, and of him that lieth with her that is unclean [Lev. 15:31–33].

Sexual sins are obviously under primary consideration in the closing verses of the chapter concerning running issues. It is referring to venereal disease, and death was the penalty for the failure to obey the commandments regulating running issues.

Hidden sin is not a trivial matter to God. Neither does He ignore the secret sins of believers. "Know ye not that ye are the temple of God, and that the Spirit of God dwelleth in you? If any man defile the temple of God, him shall God destroy; for the temple of God is holy, which temple ye are" (1 Cor. 3:16–17). We belong to God and we are the temple of the Holy Spirit. Abuse of that temple can be a sin unto death. There is a sin unto death. "If any man see his brother sin a sin which is not unto death, he shall ask, and he shall give him life for them that sin not unto death. There is a sin unto death: I do not say that he shall pray for it" (1 John 5:16). It is possible for a believer to commit a sin so that God takes him home. There is no use praying for him, because God is going to take him home. How do you know what that sin is? You don't know. But we are to remember that God deals with His own children in judgment when that is necessary. That does not mean that everyone who dies is taken home under judgment. Yet, there is a sin unto death and God calls His children home when they continue to be disobedient. The disobedience may be in this area of secret sins.

A mother may warn her little boy not to fight with the boy next door. She tells him that if they can't play without fighting, he must come into the house. She may issue this warning several times and each time she finds him fighting. Finally, she goes out and gets precious little Willie and leads him into the house. Little Willie says, "Mama, I don't want to come in," but into the house he goes! He doesn't want to come in, but neither will he obey. God is a good disciplinarian, by the way. Sometimes a child of His keeps on sinning and commits a sin unto death; so the Father just takes him on home.

"But your iniquities have separated between you and your God, and your sins have hid his face from you, that he will not hear" (Isa. 59:2). The child of God needs to recognize this and he needs to confess his sin. There can be secret sins which the believer does not confess. If, then, God strikes him down, let us not blame God for it. The blame lies with the individual.

We are living in an age that has gone mad over sex. Sexual sins are rampant and venereal disease is becoming an epidemic. What a lesson we have in this chapter. I'm glad to close the page on this chapter because it is such an ugly picture. Yet, it is the picture of the human family and we are part of that family.

We will come now to the sixteenth chapter and it is like going out of darkness into light. We have come out of a tunnel and will enter the clear noonday sun.

CHAPTER 16

THEME: The great Day of Atonement—Preparation of the priest; preparation of the place; preparation of the people

This chapter holds the greatest spiritual lesson for us. The subjects treated so far in Leviticus have been offerings, priests, and sin. None of these have dealt finally and completely with sin. We now come to that which more completely than any other deals with the subject of sin. It at least points more specifically and adequately to the work of Christ in redemption. It is a shadow of His redemptive work.

"Let no man therefore judge you in meat, or in drink, or in respect of an holyday, or of the new moon, or of the sabbath days: Which are a shadow of things to come; but the body is of Christ" (Col. 2:16–17). A shadow is a picture. Although a picture is a poor substitute for the real thing or the real person, it points to the reality. Years ago Hengstenberg commented, "The elucidation of the doctrine of types, now entirely neglected, is an important problem of future theologians." The picture, or type, of this great Day of Atonement merits our careful study.

Dr. Kellogg states the significance of the great Day of Atonement in this fashion: "[It] was perhaps the most important and characteristic in the whole Mosaic legislation." The rabbis designated the Day of Atonement with the simple word *Yoma*, "The Day." It was on this day that sin was dealt with in a more adequate way than in any other ceremony of the Mosaic system.

Notice in verse 16, ". . . and because of their transgressions in all their sins." Then in verse 22, "And the goat shall bear upon him all their iniquities . . ." and in verse 21, ". . . and confess over him all the iniquities of the children of Israel . . . ." He will make atonement for all their transgressions, all their iniquities, all their sins! This was the best that the law had to offer until Christ should come.

The instructions and restrictions of this day grew out of the historical incident of the rebellion and disobedience of Nadab and Abihu, sons of Aaron, when they intruded into the Holy of Holies of the tabernacle, and were immediately put to death by the direct judgment of God (chapter 10). Some writers treat these two chapters together.

The Day of Atonement was observed in the seventh month and on the tenth day. These numbers are significant in most of Scripture. The seventh is the sabbatic month and denotes rest and cessation from works. Surely it is not amiss that this month was chosen to set forth the rest of redemption that is in Christ. "For he that is entered into his rest, he also hath ceased from his own works, as God did from his" (Heb. 4:10).

Ten is another prominent number in Scripture, and seems to convey the idea of that which expresses God's complete will and way. There were the Ten Commandments—God could have given another, but He did not. God requested the tithe, the tenth, and the remnant of Israel is defined as a tenth (Isa. 6:13). *Ten* expresses God's mind and purpose. The tenth day expresses the truth that Christ came to do the will of God. It pleased the Lord to bruise Him, He hath put Him to grief. He came in the fullness of time, at the appointed hour.

The word for "atonement" is the Hebrew *kaphar*, which means "to cover." God did not take away sins in the Old Testament; He covered them until Christ came and removed them. There are a number of Scriptures which teach this. "And the times of this ignorance God winked at [overlooked]; but now commandeth all men everywhere to repent" (Acts 17:30). "Being justified freely by his grace through the redemption that is in Christ Jesus: Whom God hath set forth to be a propitiation [that is, a mercy seat] through faith in his blood, to declare his righteousness for the remission of sins that are past, through the forebearance of God" (Rom. 3:24–25). "And for this cause he is the mediator of the new testament, that by means of death, for the redemption of the transgressions that were under the first testament, they which are called might receive the promise of eternal inheritance" (Heb. 9:15). "The Holy Ghost this signifying, that the way into the holiest of all was not yet made manifest, while as the first tabernacle was yet standing: Which was a figure for the time then present, in which were offered both gifts and sacrifices, that could not make him that did the service perfect, as pertaining to the conscience" (Heb. 9:8–9).

The Day of Atonement pointed to Christ and His redemption as did no other sacrifice, ceremony, or ordinance of the Old Testament. It reveals Christ, as our Great High Priest, going into the Holy of Holies for us.

PREPARATION OF THE PRIEST

And the LORD spake unto Moses after the death of the two sons of Aaron, when they offered before the LORD, and died;

And the LORD said unto Moses, Speak unto Aaron thy brother, that he come not at all times into the holy place within the veil before the mercy seat, which is upon the ark; that he die not: for I will appear in the cloud upon the mercy seat [Lev. 16:1–2].

The instructions, ordinances, and rituals for the great Day of Atonement were made essential after the incident of the death of Nadab and Abihu, who intruded into the Holy Place and were slain by the direct judgment of God. The great Day of Atonement offered an explanation for the sudden death of these two men. The utter holiness of God and the utter sinfulness of man are made clear in this service.

There is a great gulf between God and man, but it is not fixed. Thank God for that! It has been bridged. Today God offers encouragement to man to come to Him but, my friend, you must come God's way. When you come God's way, you can come with boldness. "Having therefore, brethren, boldness to enter into the holiest by the blood of Jesus, By a new and living way, which he hath consecrated for us, through the veil, that is to say, his flesh; And having an high priest over the house of God; Let us draw near with a true heart in full assurance of faith, having our hearts sprinkled from an evil conscience, and our bodies washed with pure water" (Heb. 10:19–22). "For through him [Christ Jesus] we both have access by one Spirit unto the Father" (Eph. 2:18). The invitation is to *come*. That means we are to come God's way. If we do, then we can come with great assurance.

You will notice that all this was done because these two sons of Aaron had intruded into the Holy of Holies. God now says, "You can't at all times come into My place." For us today it is different. We can come any time and any place and enter into the presence of God; that is, provided we come through Christ.

I actually think it is sinful for some people to pray. A minister who rejects Christ and who prays publicly to God, but does not come to God through Jesus Christ is coming to God in some other way which God will not accept. That is the sin of Nadab and Abihu.

Thus shall Aaron come into the holy place: with a young bullock for a sin offering, and a ram for a burnt offering.

He shall put on the holy linen coat, and he shall have the linen breeches upon his flesh, and shall be girded with a linen girdle, and with the linen mitre shall he be attired: these are holy garments; therefore shall he wash his flesh in water, and so put them on [Lev. 16:3–4].

The unique and significant feature about this day was that the high priest alone performed the ritual. He had no assistance whatsoever. "And there shall be no man in the tabernacle of the congregation when he goeth in to make an atonement in the holy place . . ." (v. 17). It was all his work, from the menial tasks to the high priestly offices. All the other priests retired from the tabernacle. He alone entered, for the work of atonement was his.

This is important to see because he pictured Christ. Christ was alone with the sins of the world. "My God, my God, why hast thou forsaken me? why art thou so far from helping me, and from the words of my roaring?" (Ps. 22:1). Christ was forsaken of both God and man when He was made sin for us. Nevertheless, He and the Father were in fellowship regarding the plan of salvation. "Behold, the hour cometh, yea, is now come, that ye shall be scattered, every man to his own, and shall leave me alone: and yet I am not alone, because the Father is with me" (John 16:32). This is a great mystery. ". . . God was in Christ, reconciling the world unto himself . . ." (2 Cor. 5:19).

The high priest laid aside his garments of glory and beauty. He became attired in the same linen garb as the other priests. He washed himself and put on the linen garments only. He must be unadorned but pure.

This is a beautiful foreshadowing of Christ, our High Priest, who laid aside His glory and took upon Himself human flesh to die on the cross. "In the beginning was the Word, and the Word was with God, and the Word was God . . . . And the Word was made flesh, and dwelt among us, (and we beheld his glory, the glory as of the only begotten of the Father,) full of grace and truth . . . . No man hath seen God at any time; the only begotten Son, which is in the bosom of the Father, he hath declared him" (John 1:1, 14, 18). Our LORD did not lay aside His deity, but He put aside His glory when He came down to this earth and became a man. "Let this mind be in you, which was also in Christ Jesus: Who, being in the form of God, thought it not robbery to be equal with God: But made himself of no reputation, and took upon him the form of a servant, and was made in the likeness of men: And being found in fashion as a man, he humbled himself, and became obedient unto death, even the death of the cross" (Phil. 2:5–8).

And he shall take of the congregation of the children of Israel two kids of the goats for a sin offering, and one ram for a burnt offering.

And Aaron shall offer his bullock of the sin offering, which is for himself, and made an atonement for himself, and for his house [Lev. 16:5–6].

This gives the final personal preparation of Aaron for this all-important day. Aaron offered a sin offering for himself and his family and maybe included the entire tribe of Levi.

This phase of the great Day of Atonement finds no counterpart in the life and work of Christ. He had no sin. He was without sin. He did not die for Himself. He was made sin for us. He never made an offering for Himself. The offering of turtledoves which was brought to the temple when He was a baby was for the cleansing of Mary, His mother. It was to remind her that she was a sinner. There is no record of a sacrifice or an offering for Jesus. But Aaron had to make an offering for himself first, and then he could make an offering for the people.

PREPARATION OF THE PLACE

And he shall take the two goats, and present them before the LORD at the door of the tabernacle of the congregation.

And Aaron shall cast lots upon the two goats; one lot for the LORD, and the other lot for the scapegoat.

And Aaron shall bring the goat upon which the LORD's lot fell, and offer him for a sin offering.

But the goat, on which the lot fell to be the scapegoat, shall be presented alive before the LORD, to make an atonement with him, and to let him go for a scapegoat into the wilderness.

And Aaron shall bring the bullock of the sin offering, which is for himself, and shall make an atonement for himself, and for his house, and shall kill the bullock of the sin offering which is for himself:

And he shall take a censer full of burning coals of fire from off the altar before the LORD, and his hands full of sweet incense beaten small, and bring it within the veil:

And he shall put the incense upon the fire before the LORD, that the cloud of the incense may cover the mercy seat that is upon the testimony, that he die not:

And he shall take of the blood of the bullock, and sprinkle it with his finger upon the mercy seat eastward; and before the mercy seat shall he sprinkle of the blood with his finger seven times [Lev. 16:7–14].

It is well to note here that the two goats constituted one sin offering. Each presented a distinct aspect of the remission of sin. One was offered as a sin offering. The other was taken into the wilderness.

The goat sent into the wilderness was called the scapegoat. The Hebrew word is *lo-azazel*. There has been some confusion as to its meaning. The word applies primarily to the goat and its destination into the wilderness. The view of the Septuagint, Luther, Kellogg, and Andrew Bonar is that it means an entire and utter removal. Endersheim gives it the meaning, "wholly to go away." It is definitely a part of the sin offering. One lot fell on the goat to be sent away and one lot fell on the goat to be offered.

Before anything was done to the goats, Aaron had to enter the Holy of Holies with the blood of the bullock for himself and for his house. So it is not exactly accurate to say that the high priest went in only one time. He went in on only one day of the year, but he went in twice on that day.

The brazen altar was in the outer court. The bullock for his sin offering would be slain as in any other sin offering. Something new is added at the conclusion of the offering. On the way into the Holy of Holies, as he passed the laver, I am confident that he washed his hands and his feet. Then, in the Holy Place, he was to take a censer full of burning coals of fire from the golden altar of incense and with his hands full of sweet incense, he would place the incense upon the coals in the censer. When he passed the veil into the Holy of Holies, the cloud of smoke would fill the Holy of Holies. The ark and the mercy seat were in the Holy of Holies. He would take the blood of the bullock which he had brought in a basin with him, dip his finger into it, and sprinkle it before the mercy seat seven times. The blood made the top of the box a *mercy* seat. Seven times denotes a complete and adequate atonement.

I'm sure this was an awesome day for the high priest. He must perform accurately and meticulously in the presence of God. The slightest deviation would mean instant death. He probably rehearsed the ritual many times before the performance actually took place. As far as we know, no high priest ever died in the Holy of Holies. The only two who died were Nadab and Abihu.

Christ was made sin for us on the cross. This is the counterpart to the brazen altar in the tabernacle. Then, as our Great High Priest, He entered into heaven and offered His own blood for our sins. Now the throne of God is a mercy seat for us. All of this is clearly taught us in Hebrews 9 and 10. Whereas Aaron went with fear and trembling, we are bidden to come with boldness according to Hebrews 4:16. Where he did not dare linger and could come only one day in the year, *we* are bidden to come constantly. Christ, our High Priest, carried His own blood and the sweet incense of His own intercession into heaven, and He is there today at God's right hand.

After Aaron had gone in for himself and his house, he was to go into the Holy of Holies for the people.

Then shall he kill the goat of the sin offering, that is for the people, and bring his blood within the veil, and do with that blood as he did with the blood of the bullock, and sprinkle it upon the mercy seat, and before the mercy seat:

And he shall make an atonement for the holy place, because of the uncleanness of the child of Israel, and because of their transgressions in all their sins: and so shall he do for the tabernacle of the congregation, that remaineth among them in the midst of their uncleanness.

And there shall be no man in the tabernacle of the congregation when he goeth in to make an atonement in the holy place, until he come out, and have made an atonement for himself, and for his household, and for all the congregation of Israel.

And he shall go out unto the altar that is before the LORD, and make an atonement for it; and shall take of the blood of the bullock, and of the blood of the goat, and put it upon the horns of the altar round about.

And he shall sprinkle of the blood upon it with his finger seven times, and cleanse it, and hallow it from the uncleanness of the children of Israel [Lev. 16:15–19].

Now he is going in, not only for himself and his family, but for the children of Israel. This is done because of their transgressions and because of their uncleanness. The same ritual is followed in slaying the goat as in the slaying of the bullock for Aaron. He goes into the Holy of Holies as before, but now the atonement covers the Holy Place itself because of the contamination of Israel. Even the brazen altar itself must have the blood applied because this is where the sins of Israel were confessed and atoned; it is polluted because of the sin of the people.

All of this is to remind us of the One who died on the cross for us. It is not the cross that is important; the importance is in the One who died on the cross. "Forasmuch as ye know that ye were not redeemed with corruptible things, as silver and gold, from your vain conversation received by tradition from your fathers; But with the precious blood of Christ, as of a lamb without blemish and without spot" (1 Pet. 1:18–19).

All of this revealed the inadequacy of the ritual of the blood of bulls and goats. "It was therefore necessary that the patterns of things in the heavens should be purified with these; but the heavenly things themselves with better sacrifices than these" (Heb. 9:23). I believe that in heaven Jesus Christ literally offered His blood; that He bore it to the Holy of Holies of which the tabernacle Holy of Holies is but a pattern. Now I know some people don't like to hear of the blood, and they consider such a literal interpretation to be crude. You will notice that the apostle Peter calls it the "precious blood of Christ." I believe that the blood of Christ will be at the throne of God to remind us throughout the endless ages of eternity that our salvation was purchased at a tremendous price. Christ shed His blood on the cross and then He presented His blood for your sins and my sins. We have been redeemed by the precious blood of Christ.

PREPARATION OF THE PEOPLE

And when he hath made an end of reconciling the holy place, and the tabernacle of the congregation, and the altar, he shall bring the live goat:

And Aaron shall lay both his hands upon the head of the live goat, and confess over him all the iniquities of the children of Israel, and all their transgressions in all their sins, putting them upon the head of the goat, and shall send him away by the hand of a fit man into the wilderness:

And the goat shall bear upon him all their iniquities unto a land not inhabited: and he shall let go the goat in the wilderness [Lev. 16:20–22].

On this day the great high priest functioned alone. Aaron had sprinkled the blood of "the Lord's goat" on the mercy seat and now he places his bloody hands on the head of the live goat and confesses the sins of Israel. It must have been a sordid list of sins, but down the list he went. The laying on of hands denotes the fact that this goat is now identified as the sins of Israel.

Of Christ it is said, ". . . the LORD hath laid on him the iniquity of us all" (Isa. 53:6). "For he hath made him to be sin for us . . ." (2 Cor. 5:21) is reality. Ambrose said, "The thief knew that those wounds in the body of Christ were not the wounds of Christ, but of the thief."

Then Aaron put that goat into the hands of a man who had no personal interest in it, and Israelites were stationed at intervals to see that the job was done. The live goat finally disappeared into the wilderness, never to be seen or found again. The news that the goat was gone was relayed from station to station so that it was known a few minutes later in the temple.

Just as the news was passed from station to station, so the good news that Christ has taken away our sins has been passed from Matthew, Mark, Luke, and John to Paul the Apostle, then to the early church fathers, and finally to me and to you. Christ has put away our sins in a perfect and complete manner. The scapegoat illustrates several Scriptures in this connection: "As far as the east is from the west, so far hath he removed our transgressions from us" (Ps. 103:12). "Behold, for peace I had great bitterness: but thou hast in love to my soul delivered it from the pit of corruption: for thou hast cast all my sins behind thy back" (Isa. 38:17). "I have blotted out, as a thick cloud, thy transgressions, and, as a cloud, thy sins: return unto me; for I have redeemed thee" (Isa. 44:22). "In those days, and in that time, saith the LORD, the iniquity of Israel shall be sought for, and there shall be none; and the sins of Judah, and they shall not be found: for I will pardon them whom I reserve" (Jer. 50:20). "And they shall teach no more every man his neighbour, and every man his brother, saying, Know the LORD: for they shall all know me, from the least of them unto the greatest of them, saith the LORD: for I will forgive their iniquity, and I will remember their sin no more" (Jer. 31:34).

What does the great Day of Atonement mean to the Christian? It is a holy day for us too. When the high priest is there with his bloody hands on the head of the goat, I think of my Lord on the cross. John pointed Him out, ". . . Behold the Lamb of God, which taketh away the sin of the world" (John 1:29).

". . . If we walk in the light, as he is in the light, we have fellowship one with another, and the blood of Jesus Christ his Son cleanseth us from all sin" (1 John 1:7). Dean Law has well said, "Faith transfers our sins; Christ removes them; God forgets them."

And Aaron shall come into the tabernacle of the congregation, and shall put off the linen garments, which he put on when he went into the holy place, and shall leave them there:

And he shall wash his flesh with water in the holy place, and put on his garments, and come forth, and offer his burnt offering, and the burnt offering of the people, and make an atonement for himself, and for the people [Lev. 16:23–24].

The ritual of the great Day of Atonement has now been completed. Without being irreverent, let me say that all that was left for Aaron to do was to wash up. This finds no counterpart in Christ. When His work was finished, He sat down at the right hand of God. Aaron did not *dare* enter the holy place for another year, but our Lord sits in the presence of the Father because there is no taint of sin upon Him now— even though He bore all sins upon the tree.

Verse 25 says that the fat of the sin offering is treated as a burnt offering. This protects the person of Christ from any implication of sin, even though He was made sin for us.

And he that let go the goat for the scapegoat shall wash his clothes, and bathe his flesh in water, and afterward come into the camp.

And the bullock for the sin offering, and the goat for the sin offering, whose blood was brought in to make atonement in the holy place, shall one carry forth without the camp; and they shall burn in the fire their skins, and their flesh, and their dung.

And he that burneth them shall wash his clothes, and bathe his flesh in water, and afterward he shall come into the camp [Lev. 16:26–28].

The one who led the goat into the wilderness was contaminated by contact with the live goat and must wash his clothes and bathe himself. The carcasses of the bullock and goat were taken without the camp and burned, and the people who did that had to wash themselves. I tell you, God was impressing these people with the fact they were sinners, lost sinners. He is showing that He is holy and that sin separates from God. Friends, we were separated from God by sin, but Christ died for us. He is the One who took away our sins when He entered into the Holy Place with His own blood.

And this shall be a statute for ever unto you: that in the seventh month, on the tenth day of the month, ye shall afflict your souls, and do no work at all, whether it be one of your own country, or a stranger that sojourneth among you:

For on that day shall the priest make an atonement for you, to cleanse you, that ye may be clean from all your sins before the LORD.

It shall be a sabbath of rest unto you, and ye shall afflict your souls, by a statute for ever.

And the priest, whom he shall anoint, and whom he shall consecrate to minister in the priest's office in his father's stead, shall make the atonement, and shall put on the linen clothes, even the holy garments:

And he shall make an atonement for the holy sanctuary, and he shall make an atonement for the tabernacle of the congregation, and for the altar, and he shall make an atonement for the priests, and for all the people of the congregation.

And this shall be an everlasting statute unto you, to make an atonement for the children of Israel for all their sins once a year. And he did as the LORD commanded Moses [Lev. 16:29–34].

The Day of Atonement is the only day of mourning and fasting which God gave His people. On this day you don't say, "Happy Yom Kippur" or "Merry Yom Kippur" because that is not the way the day is celebrated. It was the day to afflict the soul because of sin. It was mourning for sin. This is the basis for fasting in the Old Testament.

This day was to be observed until the permanent and eternal sacrifice for sin came. It was fulfilled by Christ in His death.

> "Man of Sorrows!" what a name
> For the Son of God who came
> Ruined sinners to reclaim!
> Hallelujah! what a Saviour!
>
> Bearing shame and scoffing rude,
> In my place condemned He stood;
> Sealed my pardon with His blood;
> Hallelujah! what a Saviour!
>
> Guilty, vile and helpless, we;
> Spotless Lamb of God was He:
> "Full atonement!" can it be?
> Hallelujah! what a Saviour!
>
> "Lifted up" was He to die,
> "It is finished," was His cry;
> Now in heav'n exalted high;
> Hallelujah! what a Saviour!
>
> When He comes, our glorious King,
> All His ransomed home to bring,
> Then anew this song we'll sing:
> Hallelujah! what a Savior!
>
> —P. P. Bliss

CHAPTER 17

THEME: *One place of sacrifice; the offense of occult goat worship; the offering of sacrifice at the tabernacle; the obligation not to eat blood*

Leviticus is an exciting book as it is unfolding and opening up great basic and bedrock truths for the Christian today. Though these things were given to the nation Israel in a literal way, and though the reason for doing these things has passed away, yet all of this contains great spiritual lessons for us today. It answers many questions and gives new insights for the understanding and appreciation of the New Testament. I rejoice that many are coming to a personal relationship with Christ through the study of Leviticus.

Some people treat this chapter as an extension of the previous chapter. There is a sequence here, it is true, but the subject is different. Consideration is now given to the one place of sacrifice and the value of the blood.

This chapter had direct application to the wilderness march and the period that Israel was camped about the tabernacle. It has to do with ethical rather than ceremonial considerations. Clean domestic animals for food were to be slain at the tabernacle. Only verses 8 and 9 in this chapter have to do specifically with the ceremonial offering of a sacrifice to God.

After Israel was scattered throughout the land of Palestine, some of them lived a hundred or more miles from the tabernacle. It would not have been feasible or even possible for them to bring the animals they were to use for food and slay them at the tabernacle. In Deuteronomy God revised these instructions to them when they were ready to enter the land (Deut. 12:15–16 and 20–25).

Why did God give such instructions? Israel was fresh out of Egypt where they had been surrounded by idolatry. They had worshiped the idols of Egypt, and there was always the danger of lapsing back into idolatry. They had worshiped the nature gods of Egypt. In verse 7 the word translated "devils" is actually *seirim* which means "hairy one" and refers to goats. The Egyptians worshiped Mendes, the goat god, and the Greeks worshiped the goat god as Pan—familiar to us from Greek literature and art depicted with tail, horns, and cloven feet. Medieval Christianity then identified this form as the devil. We get our word *panic* from this period of time when it described the terror that the devil caused.

From this we see that Israel was forbidden to kill any animal in any place but the tabernacle in order to prevent them from making it an offering to Pan, the goat god.

Then, we learn that under no circumstance was the blood to be eaten. The reason is given specifically: it represents the life. There is a twofold reason behind this. 1. Life is sacred—even animals are not to be slain needlessly. 2. Blood speaks of the sacrifice of Christ. It was the means of expiation, the symbol of reconciliation, and the type of the one great vicarious, substitutionary sacrifice of Christ. Life is sacred and must be protected, but Christ must give His life so that the sinner can have life. Blood and life are synonymous. Man was never to eat blood. But he is to "drink the blood of Christ," which means to appropriate by faith in the shed blood of Christ the life of Christ which He gave up so that we might live. Let us love, praise, and talk about the blood. Too often, even in our churches, there is a soft-pedal placed on the topic of sin. My friend, it always follows that when there is a hesitation to mention sin, there is an equal playing down of the precious blood of Christ.

A famous preacher who came to Washington years ago was approached by a dowager who said, "Doctor, I do hope that you will not talk too much about the blood, as our former preacher did." His answer was enlightening, "Madam, I will not say too much about the blood." She interrupted, "I am so glad to hear that!" Then he added, "It is impossible to say too much about the blood!"

THE ONE PLACE OF SACRIFICE

And the Lord spake unto Moses, saying,

Speak unto Aaron, and unto his sons, and unto all the children of Israel, and say unto them; This is the thing which the Lord hath commanded, saying [Lev. 17:1–2].

These instructions were not for Moses and Aaron alone, but they were also for the sons of Aaron and for the entire nation of Israel. It is obvious that God is reaching now into the personal and private lives of the people. He not only made a difference between the clean and unclean animals in chapter 11, but now He puts down the regulations by which they were to eat the clean animals. The lives of His people are to be different from the heathen round about them. They are told that again in the next chapter, as we shall see (Lev. 18:3).

> **What man soever there be of the house of Israel, that killeth an ox, or lamb, or goat, in the camp, or that killeth it out of the camp,**
>
> **And bringeth it not unto the door of the tabernacle of the congregation, to offer an offering unto the LORD before the tabernacle of the LORD; blood shall be imputed unto that man; he hath shed blood; and that man shall be cut off from among his people:**
>
> **To the end that the children of Israel may bring their sacrifices, which they offer in the open field, even that they may bring them unto the LORD, unto the door of the tabernacle of the congregation, unto the priest, and offer them for peace offerings unto the LORD.**
>
> **And the priest shall sprinkle the blood upon the altar of the LORD at the door of the tabernacle of the congregation, and burn the fat for a sweet savour unto the LORD [Lev. 17:3–6].**

This is another of those strange laws and it does not concern the ceremonial offering of sacrifices. When you look at it carefully, you will note that these animals were for food for God's people. In other words, God is demanding that they bring Him to the dinner table! By this token, the heathen gods were shut out.

Why was God so strict about this? If they were going to have a lamb for dinner, they had to bring it to the door of the tabernacle to slay it. Maybe some of them didn't want their neighbors to know they were having company. Maybe some of them forgot to invite their mother-in-law for dinner. All this made no difference. They must slay the animal at the tabernacle. This was done because of their background. You see, among the heathen the meat was offered to an idol before it was eaten. God was putting up a roadblock to hinder His people from taking the long road to idolatry, spiritual darkness, and judgment.

When they lived down in Egypt, even though they were in slavery, they were idolaters just like the Egyptians. God did not redeem them because they were superior. God redeemed them because He had heard their cry and because He had made a promise to Abraham, Isaac, and Jacob. When God makes a covenant, He keeps it. How do I know they were idolaters in Egypt? Because Scripture says they were. "In the day that I lifted up mine hand unto them, to bring them forth of the land of Egypt into a land that I had espied for them, flowing with milk and honey, which is the glory of all lands: Then said I unto them, Cast ye away every man the abominations of his eyes, and defile not yourselves with the idols of Egypt: I am the LORD your God. But they rebelled against me, and would not hearken unto me: they did not every man cast away the abominations of their eyes, neither did they forsake the idols of Egypt: then I said, I will pour out my fury upon them, to accomplish my anger against them in the midst of the land of Egypt" (Ezek. 20:6–8). God is trying to break them from that sordid background in the land of Egypt. They had worshiped animals, and the shedding of blood and the offering of the meat was used in idolatry.

One needs to understand this background to get the significance of Paul's injunctions to the Corinthians in 1 Corinthians 8:1–13 and 10:1–33. The Corinthians were idolatrous and they brought their animal and offered it to their idols. They left their animal there; the meat was taken into the temple and sold in the meat market there. The best filet mignon of that day would have been bought at the heathen temple; it was the local supermarket. By the time of the New Testament, the godly Israelite had been so schooled that he refused to buy this meat that had been offered to idols. The converted Gentiles didn't have any qualms about eating the meat that had been offered to idols, realizing that the idol was nothing. But the Jewish Christian didn't like to eat with the Gentile Christian because of this difference over meat offered to idols. This chapter in Leviticus, you see, gives the background for the passage to the Corinthians.

It is interesting to note that when the great Council of Jerusalem handed down the decision, James spoke for the group and said, "Wherefore my sentence is, that we trouble not them, which from among the Gentiles are turned to God: But that we write unto them, that they abstain from pollutions of idols, and from fornication, and from things strangled, and from blood" (Acts 15:19–20). God was teaching the Gentile believers that life is sacred.

May I mention here that the slaughter of animals for food is still associated with heathen worship among the Hindus and in Persia.

Actually, the children of Israel had very little meat to eat in the wilderness. I think the incident concerning the quail indicated that. They complained because they didn't have any meat to eat and cried, ". . . Who shall give us flesh to eat?" (Num. 11:4). This was true of all nations of antiquity, and even today nations in the East are short on meat. Some are actually vegetarian in their diets.

A clean animal for food for the table was to be killed at the door of the tabernacle. The blood would be poured out there. The blood was placed upon the altar, and the fat was offered as a sweet savour. The sacrifice was a peace offering. The remainder of the animal was returned to the owner, and he could prepare it for his table. You can see why the Jewish believers resented the Gentiles eating meat bought at a heathen temple.

THE OFFENSE
OF OCCULT GOAT WORSHIP

And they shall no more offer their sacrifices unto devils, after whom they have gone a-whoring. This shall be a statute for ever unto them throughout their generations [Lev. 17:7].

I have already mentioned that the word *devils* in this verse is literally "hairy ones," or goats. The same word is used in 2 Chronicles 11:15: "And he ordained him priests for the high places, and for the devils [literally, goats] and for the calves which he had made." That is how Jeroboam, the son of Nebat, made Israel to sin.

This refers to nature worship, degrading and licentious, associated with the god Pan. God is saying to His people, "Don't you do that! You bring that animal to the door of the tabernacle." This is why there was the severe penalty as stated in the fourth verse. The details had to be changed when they entered into the land, but the principle that is taught here is eternal.

This is very, very important for us to see today. They lived under the danger of returning to idolatry and to gross immorality, and right now we are experiencing a return to this matter of nature worship. My friend, all this business today of going back to primitive living is a return to the same sort of thing. God wanted to protect them and wants to protect us from idolatry and immorality.

THE OFFERING OF SACRIFICE
AT THE TABERNACLE

And thou shalt say unto them, Whatsoever man there be of the house of Israel, or of the strangers which sojourn among you, that offereth a burnt offering or sacrifice,

And bringeth it not unto the door of the tabernacle of the congregation, to offer it unto the LORD; even that man shall be cut off from among his people [Lev. 17:8–9].

God is specific about bringing an animal for their own food or bringing it for an offering. God did not let them present an animal as an offering and then take it home to eat. Now, in these two verses, He is talking about bringing an animal for a burnt offering. When the animal was brought as an offering, they had to make the offering according to the law of the burnt offering. There was only one place for sacrifice. The Lord repeated this again and again in order to deter Israel from idolatry.

It was applicable to the strangers and foreigners who had established residence in Israel. There was always the danger of the influence from the presence of the heathen in their midst. The tendency was to resort to the ways of the heathen rather than to win them over to the Lord.

We are told today, "Wherefore, my dearly beloved, flee from idolatry" (1 Cor. 10:14). And again, "Be ye not unequally yoked together with unbelievers: for what fellowship hath righteousness with unrighteousness? and what communion hath light with darkness? And what concord hath Christ with Belial? . . . . Wherefore come out from among them, and be ye separate, saith the Lord, and touch not the unclean thing; and I will receive you" (2 Cor. 6:14–17).

This is a great principle which is carried over to the church. There is a danger of association with the unbeliever in religion, politics, marriage, business, or social life. God has placed a warning about this in His Word.

THE OBLIGATION NOT TO EAT BLOOD

And whatsoever man there be of the house of Israel, or of the strangers that sojourn among you, that eateth any manner of blood; I will even set my face against that soul that eateth blood, and will cut him off from among his people.

For the life of the flesh is in the blood: and I have given it to you upon the altar to make an atonement for your souls: for it is the blood that maketh an atonement for the soul [Lev. 17:10–11].

I consider verse 11 one of the key verses of this book. The life is in the blood. This is restated in verse 14. This is the basis of all sacrifice.

Therefore I said unto the children of Israel, No soul of you shall eat blood, neither shall any stranger that sojourneth among you eat blood.

And whatsoever man there be of the children of Israel, or of the strangers that sojourn among you, which hunteth and catcheth any beast or fowl that may be eaten; he shall even pour out the blood thereof, and cover it with dust.

For it is the life of all flesh; the blood of it is for the life thereof: therefore I said unto the children of Israel, Ye shall eat the blood of no manner of flesh: for the life of all flesh is the blood thereof: whosoever eateth it shall be cut off [Lev. 17:12–14].

Jesus Christ said something very interesting. "Whoso eateth my flesh, and drinketh my blood, hath eternal life; and I will raise him up at the last day. For my flesh is meat indeed, and my blood is drink indeed. He that eateth my flesh, and drinketh my blood, dwelleth in me, and I in him" (John 6:54–56). Because the life of the flesh is in the blood, Jesus is saying that we are to accept His shed blood for our sins in faith and then we receive life. Jesus shed His blood and gave His life. The life is in the blood.

This is a great, eternal truth. This explains why Abel's sacrifice was more excellent than Cain's. It is the blood that maketh an atonement for the soul. The blood of Christ is the only thing that can wash away sin. There is nothing offensive about the blood; the offense is in our sin.

> What can wash away my sin?
> Nothing but the blood of Jesus;
> What can make me whole again?
> Nothing but the blood of Jesus.
> Oh! precious is the flow
> That makes me white as snow;
> No other fount I know,
> Nothing but the blood of Jesus.

CHAPTER 18

THEME: Immorality condemned, amplification of the seventh commandment—Preamble to social prohibitions; sexual relations with relatives forbidden; sundry sexual sins prohibited; offspring forbidden to be offered to Molech; perversion of sex prohibited; nations in Palestine cast out for committing these sins

Up to this point the laws concerning ceremonial cleansing have been given. The rules regulated the ritual of religion. In chapters 18, 19, and 20, we find a special section which applies the Ten Commandments to life situations. God is now dealing with the moral aspects of the lives of His people. Friends, we are getting right down to the nitty-gritty.

This section opens with a preamble in 18:1–5 and closes with a formal postscript at the close of chapter 20. These are very important because they give the reason for the restrictions and regulations of the social life of His people.

We are living in a day when the moral foundations have been broken up and removed. "Who makes the rules, and what is right and wrong?" asks the sneering skeptic. This preamble and postscript give us a twofold explanation:

(1) Three times in the preamble, verses 2, 4, and 5, the Word says "I am the LORD." God makes the rules! Breaking the Ten Commandments is wrong because God says it is wrong. (2) The postscript gives the second reason. "And ye shall be holy unto me: for I the LORD am holy, and have severed you from other people, that ye should be mine" (Lev. 20:26). God demands that His people be holy. Purity in all life's situations is the command of God.

This chapter deals with the seventh commandment primarily. It spells out in detail what is meant by adultery. Sexual sins are the subject. These are the sins which mark a decadent society and the decline and fall of empires.

PREAMBLE TO SOCIAL PROHIBITIONS

And the LORD spake unto Moses, saying,

Speak unto the children of Israel, and say unto them, I am the LORD your God.

After the doings of the land of Egypt, wherein ye dwelt, shall ye not do: and after the doings of the land of Canaan, whither I bring you, shall ye not do; neither shall ye walk in their ordinances.

Ye shall do my judgments, and keep mine ordinances, to walk therein: I am the LORD your God.

Ye shall therefore keep my statutes, and my judgments: which if a man do, he shall live in them: I am the LORD [Lev. 18:1–5].

They have just come out of Egypt, and there they had done all these things which are forbidden. The disgusting sins which will be mentioned were a way of life for the Egyptians. God had to separate His people from the influence of that sinful environment. They were going to the land of Canaan, a land flowing with milk and honey. But that isn't all that was in Canaan—the Canaanites were there, and they also were immoral. God saw that the children of Israel were caught, as we would say, between the devil and the deep blue sea, or between a rock and a hard place. The Egyptians were behind them, the Canaanites were ahead of them, and both of them were grossly immoral.

We are living in a day when they talk about a sexual revolution. I wonder whether people have read the eighteenth chapter of Leviticus. May I say to you, there is nothing new about sexual perversion at all. It is the same old immorality that they had in Egypt and in Canaan.

God says, "I am the LORD, your God," and "I am the LORD." Who makes the rules? God makes the rules. Maybe someone says, "But I don't want to follow them." Well, that is up to you, but God still makes the rules! Breaking the Ten Commandments is wrong because God says it is wrong. That ought to be enough to satisfy the heart of the child of God. The skeptic would not be satisfied with any argument since he makes his own rules, and he is his own god.

By the way, if you can create a whole universe—and you will need a whole planetary system with a sun and a moon and a few stars—then you can make your own ten commandments. But as long as you are living in God's world, breathing His air, using His sunshine, drinking His water, walking on His earth, and not even paying rent for it, you had better obey His commands. He tells us that if we break His Commandments, we will pay for it. And, my friend, you will pay! You may not be arrested by the local police, but you will stand before Him some day.

The things that God said were immoral are still immoral today. Listen to the New Testament: "Not in the lust of concupiscence, even as the Gentiles which know not God: That no man go beyond and defraud his brother in any matter: because that the Lord is the avenger of all such, as we also have forewarned you and testified. For God hath not called us unto uncleanness, but unto holiness" (1 Thess. 4:5–7). "This I say therefore, and testify in the Lord, that ye henceforth walk not as other Gentiles walk, in the vanity of their mind, Having the understanding darkened, being alienated from the life of God through the ignorance that is in them, because of the blindness of their heart: Who being past feeling have given themselves over unto lasciviousness, to work all uncleanness with greediness" (Eph. 4:17–19). "But now I have written unto you not to keep company, if any man that is called a brother be a fornicator, or covetous, or an idolater, or a railer, or a drunkard, or an extortioner; with such an one no not to eat" (1 Cor. 5:11). "Whereby are given unto us exceeding great and precious promises: that by these ye might be partakers of the divine nature, having escaped the corruption that is in the world through lust" (2 Pet. 1:4).

These passages from the Epistles of the New Testament are speaking to you and to me. The child of God in any age is called to holy living. "Know ye not that ye are the temple of God, and that the Spirit of God dwelleth in you? If any man defile the temple of God, him shall God destroy; for the temple of God is holy, which temple ye are" (1 Cor. 3:16–17). "According as he hath chosen us in him before the foundation of the world, that we should be holy and without blame before him in love" (Eph. 1:4). "Because it is written, Be ye holy; for I am holy" (1 Pet. 1:16). God is calling us to holiness. We need to emphasize holiness. God asks us to be holy.

There is another truth that I do not want you to miss, friends. Many folk say that if you are going to reach the crowds, you've got to go down and live with them. You've got to be like they are. This has been tried, both by individuals and by groups. And do you know what? They don't reach the crowd; they become a part of the crowd. May I say to you, God has called us to holiness. Folk who have really reached men for Christ have been those whose *lives* commended the Gospel they preached.

For example, England was a pretty wicked place during the eighteenth century, and they called the followers of John Wesley, "holy people." In fact, they gave them the name "Methodists" because their methods were different from the methods of the world.

God says, "I am Jehovah." Someone may say, "Well, I'm not a Christian, and I'm just not interested." May I say to you that God is declaring His sovereignty. God created this universe and He is the One who is running it. And He says, "I am your God." He is a reconciled God. He knows our frame and yet He loves us. Friend, if you are reconciled to God, you will want to please Him. The child of God can be filled with the Holy Spirit so that he will not commit these sins of the flesh, but will produce the fruit of the Spirit.

SEXUAL RELATIONS
WITH RELATIVES FORBIDDEN

None of you shall approach to any that is near to kin to him, to uncover their nakedness: I am the Lord (Lev. 18:6).

The blanket statement is made that no person is to have sexual relations with a near relative. This entire section amplifies the seventh commandment. Here it refers to anyone who has the same blood relationship as the other person. Now it goes on. God is specific. And the reason He gives is, "I am the Lord."

The nakedness of thy father, or the nakedness of thy mother, shalt thou not uncover: she is thy mother; thou shalt not uncover her nakedness.

The nakedness of thy father's wife shalt thou not uncover: it is thy father's nakedness [Lev. 18:7–8].

This warns against disgusting incest. Yet this sin was in the Corinthian church. Paul condemned it with great feeling. "It is reported commonly that there is fornication among you, and such fornication as is not so much as named among the Gentiles, that one should have his father's wife" (1 Cor. 5:1).

These are things that are talked about today, aren't they? Well, God talks about them, too. Don't tell me things are different today. God has spelled out exactly what is sin. Nobody can make a mistake about this, friends.

The nakedness of thy sister, the daughter of thy father, or daughter of thy mother, whether she be born at home, or born abroad, even their nakedness thou shalt not uncover.

The nakedness of thy son's daughter, or of thy daughter's daughter, even their nakedness thou shalt not uncover: for theirs is thine own nakedness.

The nakedness of thy father's wife's daughter, begotten of thy father, she is thy sister, thou shalt not uncover her nakedness.

Thou shalt not uncover the nakedness of thy father's sister: she is thy father's near kinswoman.

Thou shalt not uncover the nakedness of thy mother's sister: for she is thy mother's near kinswoman.

Thou shalt not uncover the nakedness of thy father's brother, thou shalt not approach to his wife: she is thine aunt.

Thou shalt not uncover the nakedness of thy daughter-in-law: she is thy son's wife: thou shalt not uncover her nakedness [Lev. 18:9–15].

The different human relationships which are established by blood or marriage are dealt with specifically in this section. Relatives are thrown together in a domestic situation in which adultery could be practiced. God put up these barriers to prevent this.

Egypt practiced these sins, especially those mentioned in verse 9. The Pharaohs and the Ptolemies practiced intermarriage of brother and sister.

In the beginning, there was no law against this. Cain and Seth had to marry their own sisters. Abraham married his half sister. However the Law now halts this practice.

Thou shalt not uncover the nakedness of thy brother's wife: it is thy brother's nakedness [Lev. 18:16].

There is an exception to this verse and that is in the law of the kinsman-redeemer as stated in Deuteronomy 25:5–10.

SUNDRY SEXUAL SINS PROHIBITED

Thou shalt not uncover the nakedness of a woman and her daughter, neither shalt thou take her son's daughter, or her daughter's daughter, to uncover her nakedness; for they are her near kinswomen: it is wickedness.

Neither shalt thou take a wife to her sister, to vex her, to uncover her nakedness, beside the other in her life time [Lev. 18:17–18].

This relationship is not by blood, but by marriage. Because of the close relationship of the wife to a daughter or son, any marriage is forbidden. Evidently both of these verses have reference to having two wives at the same time. It is labeled incest here, instead of bigamy. Notice the Berkeley Version on these two verses: "Do not expose the nakedness of both a woman and her daughter; neither take her son's daughter or her daughter's daughter to expose her; they are blood relatives. It is incest. While your wife is still living do not take her sister for a rival to expose her nakedness" (Lev. 18:17–18).

This was the problem poor Jacob faced in having two sisters as wives—Leah and Rachel. The story of this family was certainly not a happy one. Remember, however, that Jacob lived before the Ten Commandments had been given.

Also thou shalt not approach unto a woman to uncover her nakedness, as long as she is put apart for her uncleanness [Lev. 18:19].

Lawful marital relations of a husband and wife were forbidden at certain times. The sensual mind must be made subject to the law of God.

Moreover thou shalt not lie carnally with thy neighbour's wife, to defile thyself with her [Lev. 18:20].

Believe me, God is throwing up these bulwarks to protect the home from the licentious practices of the heathen round about them. The family on earth was to mirror the family in heaven (Eph. 3:15). Purity of living was to be the badge of God's family. There was a holy place in the tabernacle for *worship;* the home was a holy place in the nation for *living.* The New Testament also has a great deal about this. It would be well to read 1 Corinthians 7 in this connection.

OFFSPRING FORBIDDEN
TO BE OFFERED TO MOLECH

And thou shalt not let any of thy seed pass through the fire to Molech, neither shalt thou profane the name of thy God: I am the LORD [Lev. 18:21].

"Thy seed" means their children. This verse may seem to be out of place in this chapter, but the pagan worship of Molech was closely related with sex. The image of old Molech was heated red-hot, and the bodies of children were placed in its arms. It is hard to imagine the horror of this. There are those who

believe that such a thing could never have happened. However, the Scriptures make other references to this same practice. ". . . and the Sepharvites burnt their children in fire to Adrammelech and Anammelech, the gods of Sepharvaim" (2 Kings 17:31). "And they have built the high places of Tophet, which is in the valley of the son of Hinnom, to burn their sons and their daughters in the fire; which I commanded them not, neither came it into my heart" (Jer. 7:31). This terrible practice profanes the holy name of God (Lev. 20:3). The unnatural brutality of this pagan rite was a deep profaning of the name of the true God. God's love of children is evident in Scripture from Genesis to Revelation. The Lord Jesus said, "Let them come to Me."

PERVERSION OF SEX PROHIBITED

Thou shalt not lie with mankind, as with womankind: it is abomination [Lev. 18:22].

It is hard to believe that right here in downtown Los Angeles, a church put on a dance for sexual perverts. I am told they had over 700 people at that dance. It was so disgusting that a hard-boiled newspaper writer went down to write it up, but walked out. Yet a "church" engaged in that. My friend, God condemns it! In the Old Testament He condemns it; in the New Testament He condemns it. "Wherefore God also gave them up to uncleanness through the lusts of their own hearts, to dishonour their own bodies between themselves: Who changed the truth of God into a lie, and worshipped and served the creature more than the Creator, who is blessed for ever. Amen. For this cause God gave them up unto vile affections: for even their women did change the natural use into that which is against nature: And likewise also the men, leaving the natural use of the woman, burned in their lust one toward another; men with men working that which is unseemly, and receiving in themselves that recompence of their error which was meet. And even as they did not like to retain God in their knowledge, God gave them over to a reprobate mind, to do those things which are not convenient" (Rom. 1: 24–28).

The depravity that is mentioned here is common today. The United States is like Sodom and Gomorrah. It makes me weep to see the way my country is going. I love this country. It's the land of my birth. I hate to see these dirty, filthy, immoral people bringing us into judgment. Believe me, friends, the judgment of God is already upon us today. We can't have peace abroad and we can't have peace at home. Why not? "There is no peace, saith the LORD, unto the wicked" (Isa. 48:22).

Neither shalt thou lie with any beast to defile thyself therewith: neither shall any woman stand before a beast to lie down thereto: it is confusion [Lev. 18:23].

This is indeed unspeakable. This was practiced in the fertility cults and nature worship. Licentiousness is always connected with idolatry in the most debased fashion. And if you think this is not being practiced today, then you should talk to the police department in a city like Los Angeles. They can tell you.

NATIONS IN PALESTINE CAST OUT FOR COMMITTING THESE SINS

Defile not ye yourselves in any of these things: for in all these the nations are defiled which I cast out before you:

And the land is defiled: therefore I do visit the iniquity thereof upon it, and the land itself vomiteth out her inhabitants [Lev. 18:24–25].

The nations in Palestine were cast out because they committed these abominable and atrocious sins. That is the reason they were put off the land. A lot of soft-hearted and soft-headed preachers today weep because God put out the Canaanites. Here is the reason God put them out. God couldn't tolerate what was taking place. The land of the Canaanites was eaten up with venereal disease. Why do you suppose God told them not to take even a wedge of gold or to touch a garment in the city of Jericho? They were guilty of the vilest sins imaginable. Don't you think that God put them out for a good reason? After all, if the tenant doesn't pay rent, he can be put out. God happened to own that land.

My friend that is the way you and I occupy this earth down here. Our "three score years and ten" is just a lease. The land is God's. It is His business and it would be well for us to make His business our business. His business is the one that will prevail.

Ye shall therefore keep my statutes and my judgments, and shall not commit any of these abominations; neither any of your own nation, nor any stranger that sojourneth among you:

(For all these abominations have the men of the land done, which were before you, and the land is defiled;)

That the land spue not you out also, when ye defile it, as it spued out the nations that were before you.

For whosoever shall commit any of these abominations, even the souls that commit them shall be cut off from among their people.

Therefore shall ye keep mine ordinance, that ye commit not any one of these abominable customs, which were committed before you, and that ye defile not yourselves therein: I am the LORD your God [Lev. 18:26–30].

God gives a double warning to His people that if they pursue a pattern similar to those who preceded them in the land, the same judgment, if not worse, would befall them. God's land must be holy. God's ultimate goal is that righteousness will cover the earth.

CHAPTER 19

THEME: *Man's relationship to God; man's relationship to the poor; man's relationship to his neighbor; man's relationships in different life situations*

We are in that section of the book where the Ten Commandments are explained in terms of the social life of the nation. I can't think of anything more practical than this particular section. God's Law is to tell us this one thing: ". . . Ye shall be holy: for I the LORD your God am holy" (Lev. 19:2). This was fundamental and basic to all facets of the life of Israel. It explained everything which God commanded or demanded. It entered into the web and woof of their daily routine. Holiness in daily life with all of its relationships was paramount in the everyday living of God's people. That is something that needs to be reemphasized today, by the way. This is not just theory. God intended it to be brought right into our lives.

The Law can not produce the holiness which it demands. It demanded, but it did not supply. It revealed the righteousness of the Law, but the high level which it demanded could not be attained by human effort. "Now we know that what things soever the law saith, it saith to them who are under the law: that every mouth may be stopped, and all the world may become guilty before God. Therefore by the deeds of the law there shall no flesh be justified in his sight: for by the law is the knowledge of sin" (Rom. 3:19–20).

How wonderful it is that God has given us His Holy Spirit to indwell us. This is the dynamic that is needed for Christian living.

The reason given in this chapter, "I am the LORD your God" or "I am the LORD" occurs sixteen times in this chapter. God draws the line between right and wrong. He alone makes the sharp distinction between the holy and unholy. No other reason needs to be given.

MAN'S RELATIONSHIP TO GOD

And the LORD spake unto Moses, saying,

Speak unto all the congregation of the children of Israel, and say unto them. Ye shall be holy: for I the LORD your God am holy [Lev. 19:1–2].

God gives these instructions to Moses the lawgiver, and they amplify a portion of the Ten Commandments. God exacts holy conduct on the basis that He is holy. It is well to note that God still enjoins the same conduct today. "Whether therefore ye eat, or drink, or whatsoever ye do, do all to the glory of God" (1 Cor. 10:31). "Therefore if any man be in Christ, he is a new creature: old things are passed away; behold, all things are become new" (2 Cor. 5:17). "Wherefore gird up the loins of your mind, be sober, and hope to the end for the grace that is to be brought unto you at the revelation of Jesus Christ; As obedient children, not fashioning yourselves according to the former lusts in your ignorance: But as he which hath called you is holy, so be ye holy in all manner of conversation; Because it is written. Be ye holy; for I am holy" (1 Pet. 1:13–16).

The major difference between the conduct required under law and under grace is that today the dynamic is supplied to the believer in the person of the Holy Spirit. We are joined to the living Christ. Old things have passed away. We are no longer joined to Adam, and we are no longer joined to a legal system. We are joined to Christ and we are to seek to please Him. You see, under the Law they tried to keep the commandments by their own effort. They were to learn that the flesh will always fail. In contrast to this, we have the Spirit of God *in* us. "For what the law could not do, in that it was weak through the flesh, God sending his own Son in the likeness of sinful flesh, and for sin, condemned sin in the flesh: That the righteousness of the law might be fulfilled in us, who walk not after the flesh, but after the Spirit" (Rom. 8:3–4). "But the fruit of the Spirit is love, joy, peace, longsuffering, gentleness, goodness, faith, Meekness, temperance: against such there is no law" (Gal. 5:22–23). The Law never went as far as this. The Son of God wants to bring us up to a high plane.

Now, in emphasizing certain of the commandments they were to keep, God will emphasize those particular areas in which they were weak. The history of Israel will show us that God understood their weak points. They were instructed about the sabbath, the avoidance of idolatry, the bringing of proper offerings to God. These are areas in which they later broke down. God is asking them to be holy in their daily life.

Ye shall fear every man his mother, and his father, and keep my sabbaths: I am the LORD your God [Lev. 19:3].

One might think it is strange that God should begin with the commandment to honor father and mother. But it is not so strange when we consider that the parent stands in the place of God for the child and that the child learns to obey God by first obeying the parent. When you are going to get down to the nitty-gritty, you must begin at home.

Then He adds, "And keep my sabbaths." God demanded one-seventh of man's time as well as one-tenth of his possessions.

These two commandments mentioned first encompass the two major divisions of the Ten Commandments. There is duty to man and duty to God. The Lord Jesus Christ summed it all up as love to God and love to man. He said this is the sum total of the law (Matt. 22:36–40).

The sabbath law does not rest upon a moral basis but was an arbitrary command of God given to Israel. Israel, in apostasy and decline, sinned at this point. They refused to observe the sabbaths. "Saying, When will the new moon be gone, that we may sell corn? and the sabbath, that we may set forth wheat, making the ephah small, and the shekel great, and falsifying the balances by deceit?" (Amos 8:5). This was God's charge and case against the nation.

Turn ye not unto idols, nor make to yourselves molten gods: I am the LORD your God [Lev. 19:4].

This covers the first two commandments. The thought here is not even to cast a glance at idolatry. Heathen worship appealed to the eye with its pomp and ceremony. It still does. Look at the pageantry and meaningless rituals that you see in religion today. It is "eye service." They were not to look on idols and they were not to make idols. God ridicules the idols because they are nothing and can do nothing.

And if ye offer a sacrifice of peace offerings unto the LORD, ye shall offer it at your own will.

It shall be eaten the same day ye offer it, and on the morrow: and if aught remain until the third day, it shall be burnt in the fire.

And if it be eaten at all on the third day, it is abominable: it shall not be accepted.

Therefore every one that eateth it shall bear his iniquity, because he hath profaned the hallowed thing of the LORD:

and that soul shall be cut off from among his people [Lev. 19:5–8].

There is nothing new added here. However, we should point out again that the peace offering was to be made voluntarily. Even though it was a voluntary offering, the offerer was not relieved from following scrupulously the rules that were prescribed. Any deviation from the prescribed order penalized the man as an example to the people.

I find today that there are those in Christian service who seem to think they can take special liberties that no one else can take. Or some people think that because they have given a large contribution to the church they should have special privileges and special attention. Notice that the peace offering was given voluntarily but the detail had to be followed through meticulously. We must all come to God on God's terms. Any deviation from the prescribed order penalized the man as an example to the people. This was a positive law, not a moral law. Because of that, there was the more danger of failure. How many people today make a pledge to the church and then feel that they don't need to go through with it if they don't wish to. God says, "If you are going to do it voluntarily, then do it right."

I had to go out to a television station to make a tape to be aired locally. They were taping a very popular program and so I stayed to watch. I was so impressed by the dedication of the people who were putting it on that I stayed a long time to watch and someone might ask me why I did that. Well, I've been among Christians so long that it did me good to get among people who were dedicated. Of course I understand why they are dedicated—they are dedicated to greed. They were being paid a handsome sum to do that show, but I'll tell you, they gave it everything they had.

Too many Christians excuse what they are doing by saying it is just volunteer work. God may say, "If you are going to do it, then do it right when you come to Me." Don't volunteer to do God's work unless you are going to give it everything you have. I'm of the opinion there will be a lot of Christians judged someday because of their laziness. Some folk glory in the fact they took a job. "Look, I taught a Sunday School class." My friend, how many times were you late? How many times did you fail to prepare the lesson? I tell you, the crowd in the television show knew their parts. But I see Sunday School teachers flipping through the quarterly, trying to find something to say. I think God is going to judge us on that someday.

He tells us not to come to Him with a voluntary offering unless we come the right way.

MAN'S RELATIONSHIP TO THE POOR

And when ye reap the harvest of your land, thou shalt not wholly reap the corners of thy field, neither shalt thou gather the gleanings of thy harvest.

And thou shalt not glean thy vineyard, neither shalt thou gather every grape of thy vineyard; thou shalt leave them for the poor and stranger: I am the LORD your God [Lev. 19:9–10].

This was God's marvelous provision for the poor. God did not put anyone on charity. He never let anyone sit down and do nothing and receive a welfare check. The poor were taken care of by being given the opportunity to work. This was a marvelous balance between heartless capitalism and godless socialism. Whatever a farmer did not reap his first time around must be left for the poor. The ancient method of harvesting by hand left 10% to 20% of the grain in the field. The same law applied to their vineyards. I was at a meeting in Turlock, California, and a man told me to go out to the vineyard and help myself to the grapes because he knew how I loved grapes. It was after the harvest and the pickers were all gone. I could have filled a truck with grapes if I had had one there. That night at the meeting I told the folks that I had been out gleaning. That is the way God took care of His people. His method of dealing with poverty enabled both rich and poor to acknowledge the good hand of God.

MAN'S RELATIONSHIP TO HIS NEIGHBOR

Ye shall not steal, neither deal falsely, neither lie one to another.

And ye shall not swear by my name falsely, neither shalt thou profane the name of thy God: I am the LORD [Lev. 19:11–12].

This restates the eighth and ninth commandments. "Thou shalt not steal. Thou shalt not bear false witness against thy neighbour" (Exod. 20:15–16). Stealing, defrauding, lying, and perjury are all included here. To deal falsely is a form of stealing according to God's definition.

The third commandment is included in verse 12. God's name is holy. In business God's man is to demonstrate the holiness of God's name by his honest and true business dealings.

Thou shalt not defraud thy neighbour, neither rob him: the wages of him that is hired shall not abide with thee all night until the morning [Lev. 19:13].

We are to pay any man working for us. May I say to you, I think God would be on the side of labor. My Dad was a working man and I remember him in overalls more than any other way. He built cotton gins in Texas and many times, I found out, he was beaten financially. Listen to James: "Go to now, ye rich men, weep and howl for your miseries that shall come upon you. Your riches are corrupted, and your garments are moth-eaten" (James 5:1–2). Verse 6 of the same chapter goes on to say, "Ye have condemned and killed the just; and he doth not resist you." Godless labor is a terrible thing and so is godless capitalism. Right now I think we are in real danger from the latter.

Thou shalt not curse the deaf, nor put a stumbling block before the blind, but shalt fear thy God: I am the LORD [Lev. 19:14].

A blind man told me how he was cheated by a salesman who came to him. May I say to you, these terrible things are still done today. God put a double emphasis on His name in consideration of the deaf and blind. It is God's concern for the weak, helpless, and infirm, and it is His rebuke against the hardheartedness of man.

Ye shall do no unrighteousness in judgment: thou shalt not respect the person of the poor, nor honour the person of the mighty: but in righteousness shalt thou judge thy neighbour [Lev. 19:15].

Here is a word for the judge sitting on the bench, and how our judges need this word today! The judge on the bench is to understand that he is to judge as God judges. I wish some of them would remember that they are in that position, not because some politician put them there, but because they represent Almighty God. And they are to judge impartially.

Shakespeare wrote in *King Henry VIII:* "Heaven is above all yet; there sits a judge that no king can corrupt." Socrates said, "Four things belong to a judge, to hear courteously, to answer wisely, to consider soberly, and to decide impartially."

Thou shalt not go up and down as a talebearer among thy people: neither shalt thou stand against the blood of thy neighbour: I am the LORD.

Thou shalt not hate thy brother in thine heart: thou shalt in any wise rebuke thy neighbour, and not suffer sin upon him.

Thou shalt not avenge, nor bear any grudge against the children of thy people, but thou shalt love thy neighbour as thyself: I am the Lord [Lev. 19:16–18].

Talebearing is slander. It is best to remain silent if to tell the truth will ruin a neighbor.

Sir Walter Scott wrote, "Low breathed talkers, minion lispers cutting honest throats by whispers." Someone else has said, "You cannot believe everything you hear, but you can repeat it." James has a great deal to say about this, and I wrote a little booklet on his epistle called *Hell on Fire*. Do you know what hell on fire is? It is the little tongue that is in your mouth. It is an awful thing. It is the most dangerous thing in the world, more dangerous than an atom bomb.

"Stand against the blood" means to murder. Hatred is not put on a par with murder, but it is forbidden. Our Lord linked them together and said that if you hate, you are a murderer (Matt. 5:21–22).

The answer to all these negative prohibitions is found in the positive, "But thou shalt love thy neighbour as thyself." Paul summed up all this for the Christian: "Brethren, if a man be overtaken in a fault, ye which are spiritual, restore such an one in the spirit of meekness; considering thyself, lest thou also be tempted" (Gal. 6:1).

MAN'S RELATIONSHIPS IN DIFFERENT LIFE SITUATIONS

Ye shall keep my statutes, Thou shalt not let thy cattle gender with a diverse kind: thou shalt not sow thy field with mingled seed: neither shall a garment mingled of linen and woollen come upon thee [Lev. 19:19].

Do you know what happens when you wash such a garment? God is teaching them great spiritual truths with symbols and ceremonies. They were not to have hybrid animals and plants. This was to teach them that there is to be no mingling of truth and error. This is brought out by our Lord's parable of the wheat and the tares (Matt. 13). Paul says, "Ye cannot drink the cup of the Lord, and the cup of devils: ye cannot be partakers of the Lord's table, and of the table of devils" (1 Cor. 10:21). Christ said, ". . . Ye cannot serve God and mammon" (Luke 16:13).

And whosoever lieth carnally with a woman, that is a bondmaid, betrothed to an husband, and not at all redeemed, nor freedom given her; she shall be scourged; they shall not be put to death, because she was not free.

And he shall bring his trespass offering unto the Lord, unto the door of the tabernacle of the congregation, even a ram for a trespass offering.

And the priest shall make an atonement for him with the ram of the trespass offering before the Lord for his sin which he hath done: and the sin which he hath done shall be forgiven him [Lev. 19:20–22].

This goes back to the seventh commandment. This protects the bond-woman. This raises the natural question, "Is God lending approval to slavery?" No. God is recognizing the sinful situation caused by the hard hearts of men, just as He did in the case of divorce (Matt. 19:8). It was recognized as a sin on the part of the man, for he had to bring a trespass offering. The woman did not bring an offering.

And when ye shall come into the land, and shall have planted all manner of trees for food, then ye shall count the fruit thereof as uncircumcised: three years shall it be as uncircumcised unto you: it shall not be eaten of.

But in the fourth year all the fruit thereof shall be holy to praise the Lord withal.

And in the fifth year shall ye eat of the fruit thereof, that it may yield unto you the increase thereof: I am the Lord your God [Lev. 19:23–25].

This law seems strange to those of us who are not dendrologists. We are told, however, that young fruit trees will grow faster and yield better fruit if the buds are nipped off (circumcised) the first few years. The Lord knew that. The spiritual lesson was that the first fruits belong to God. And it taught that "Every good gift and every perfect gift is from above, and cometh down from the Father of lights . . ." (James 1:17).

Ye shall not eat any thing with the blood: neither shall ye use enchantment, nor observe times.

Ye shall not round the corners of your heads, neither shalt thou mar the corners of thy beard.

Ye shall not make any cuttings in your flesh for the dead, nor print any marks upon you: I am the LORD [Lev. 19: 26–28].

There are six commandments here that condemn the practices and superstitions of the heathen. They were not to eat flesh with the blood in it. They were not to trim their hair and leave little tufts of it. They were not to act like the heathen when a loved one dies.

Do not prostitute thy daughter, to cause her to be a whore: lest the land fall to whoredom, and the land become full of wickedness [Lev. 19:29].

This is a condemnation of a heathen practice which prevails to this day among some people. I have read that men in this country go through college with the money their wives earn as harlots. How terrible!

Ye shall keep my sabbaths, and reverence my sanctuary: I am the LORD [Lev. 19:30].

The Sabbath was a sign of the relationship between God and the children of Israel, and it was to be observed strictly. This is brought out in detail in Exodus 31:13–17.

Regard not them that have familiar spirits, neither seek after wizards, to be defiled by them: I am the LORD your God [Lev. 19:31].

This is one of the many warnings against spiritism and demonism. The supernatural and satanic character of this practice is recognized in the Scriptures and rejected.

Thou shalt rise up before the hoary head, and honour the face of the old man, and fear thy God: I am the LORD [Lev. 19:32].

Respect is to be shown old age. This also is repeated in the Scriptures.

And if a stranger sojourn with thee in your land, ye shall not vex him.

But the stranger that dwelleth with you shall be unto you as one born among you, and thou shalt love him as thyself; for ye were strangers in the land of Egypt: I am the LORD your God [Lev. 19:33–34].

The stranger among them was to be treated kindly and was to be loved. He was a reminder to them that they were strangers in Egypt. The stranger was a neighbor.

Ye shall do no unrighteousness in judgment, in meteyard, in weight, or in measure.

Just balances, just weights, a just ephah, and a just hin, shall ye have: I am the LORD your God, which brought you out of the land of Egypt [Lev. 19: 35–36].

Business transactions were to be honest. Measures and weights were to be honest. God's children are to be different from others because they represent God even in their business dealings.

Therefore shall ye observe all my statutes, and all my judgments, and do them: I am the LORD [Lev. 19:37].

God is the Lord. That is reason enough for obedience to what He commands. Can you think of anything to add to that?

CHAPTER 20

THEME: Capital punishment for those who offer their children to Molech; capital punishment for those who practice spiritism; capital punishment for those who curse father or mother; capital punishment for those who commit adultery; certain offenses which require lesser penalty; conclusion to the law of holiness

Dr. Andrew A. Bonar, in his book on Leviticus, calls this chapter "Warnings Against the Sins of the Former Inhabitants." In other words, these were the sins of the Canaanites.

It appears that the death penalty was exacted for breaking any one of the Ten Commandments. Not all of them are listed here under the penal code for the death penalty. Only a few are given as examples. For example, murder is not listed in this chapter, but we learn elsewhere about the death penalty for it. For this reason I infer that the penalty for breaking any of the Ten Commandments was death.

God instituted capital punishment! He is just and righteous, and He applied the death penalty with unsparing severity.

Nowhere in the Word of God is punishment given for the purpose of reforming the criminal. That was not the objective. Punishment of a crime is for the moral good of the people. Punishment of a crime is a deterrent to crime. It will cut down the crime rate. One of the reasons for the spread of lawlessness like a dreadful plague throughout this land is due to the fact that we have weak judges who will not enforce the law.

We hear a great many sob sisters cry about the death penalty. God instituted capital punishment for good and sufficient reasons. There must be the satisfaction of outraged justice. Justice and righteousness demand punishment. The majesty, law, and holiness of God have been outraged, and so crime must be punished.

If you don't believe in the death penalty, let me ask you a question. Do you mean to say that you are better than God? God makes no apology for the death penalty. Listen to Him: "So ye shall not pollute the land wherein ye are: for blood it defileth the land: and the land cannot be cleansed of the blood that is shed therein, but by the blood of him that shed it" (Num. 35:33). Remember that the Books of Matthew and Luke tell us that the blood of Abel cries out from the ground.

Let me ask you another question. Suppose a sadistic criminal took your little child by the heels and dashed his head against a stone. What would you think should be done to him?

I'm talking about *yours* now, not the children of someone else in another state. It's easy to be theoretical and ideal as long as it doesn't involve you. Here in California a man raped a girl and killed the fellow she was with. A crowd was parading at the governor's mansion and parading at the penitentiary, protesting the death sentence. What about the girl? She is in a mental institution, a raving maniac. *Her* parents believe in capital punishment. I tell you, when you are talking about your own, that changes the color of the picture altogether. God says these people should be punished.

Modern man in his efforts to be soft has abolished the death penalty in the name of this enlightened age. But it still stands in the Word of God as the most humanitarian procedure for the good of all men.

CAPITAL PUNISHMENT FOR THOSE WHO OFFER THEIR CHILDREN TO MOLECH

And the Lord spake unto Moses, saying [Lev. 20:1].

God is speaking to Moses now, not to Aaron or the people. He is speaking to the lawgiver because this is about the penal code. Paul says that those in positions of authority who rule over us do not carry the sword in vain. They are to use it (Rom. 13). A judge has no right to let a sadistic criminal, a psychotic criminal, loose on society to endanger your family and mine.

Someone will say that the electric chair is a mean old chair. That's right, it is. In that day, they were executed by stoning. That's not pretty either. No one has claimed it was pretty. It is an awful thing, a horrible thing. Don't forget, the crime committed is also horrible.

Again, thou shalt say to the children of Israel, Whosoever he be of the children of Israel, or of the strangers that sojourn in Israel, that giveth any of his seed unto Molech; he shall surely be put to death: the people of the land shall stone him with stones [Lev. 20:2].

The worship of Molech was savage, satanic, cruel, and brutal. Children were offered as sacrifices to the idol of Molech which was heated red hot. According to historians, the arms of the idol were outstretched and the child was cast "into a gaping hole, full of fire." This was fiendish and demoniacal. What a contrast is Jesus who stretched out His arms to receive little children! "But Jesus said, Suffer little children, and forbid them not, to come unto me: for of such is the kingdom of heaven" (Matt. 19:14). Stoning to death was the penalty for this crime of "giving his seed to Molech," and it is difficult to see how any would oppose the sentence. Stoning is almost too good for them.

Friends, the child brutality today in our land could be curtailed if our judges would punish parents who brutally treat the little ones who can't protect themselves. The judge should protect them.

And I will set my face against that man, and will cut him off from among his people: because he hath given of his seed unto Molech, to defile my sanctuary, and to profane my holy name [Lev. 20:3].

This is the strongest language possible. "I will set my face against that man." Was this an unpardonable sin? I don't know, but every word is a terrible invective. "I will cut him off from among his people." This sin was a sin against God. It defiles His sanctuary and profanes His holy name. In Ezekiel 23:37–39, we find that the children of Israel did just this, and it was one of the reasons that God's judgment came upon them. Remember that idolatry was high treason in a nation that was a theocracy.

And if the people of the land do any ways hide their eyes from the man, when he giveth of his seed unto Molech, and kill him not:

Then I will set my face against that man, and against his family, and will cut him off, and all that go a-whoring after him, to commit whoredom with Molech, from among their people [Lev. 20:4–5].

For a man to remain silent when a neighbor worshiped Molech by offering his child was to make him a partner in crime. To be soft-hearted and soft-headed in executing the penalty made a man guilty. He was to be cut off from the people, which was tantamount to the death penalty.

CAPITAL PUNISHMENT FOR THOSE WHO PRACTICE SPIRITISM

And the soul that turneth after such as have familiar spirits, and after wizards, to go a-whoring after them, I will even set my face against that soul, and will cut him off from among his people [Lev. 20:6].

This was another practice of the Canaanites who were then in the land. This was false religion which was definitely satanic. Someone may object that it was not the real thing and lacked the supernatural. Frankly, there is supernaturalism manifested in Satan worship. The fact of the matter is that the Lord Jesus Himself warned that there would appear finally an antichrist who would be able to perform miracles, and that, if it were possible, he would deceive the very elect. Satan is a liar and the father of the lie. God says that He will set His face against the soul that turns to this kind of false worship.

A man also or woman that hath a familiar spirit, or that is a wizard, shall surely be put to death: they shall stone them with stones: their blood shall be upon them [Lev. 20:27].

I bring this verse up into this section as it too deals with satanic superstition. Demon possession is a reality and has existed in all ages. In this modern age, many cults and "isms" are promoted by those who are demon possessed. This is all the work of Satan. The death penalty was exacted for participating in or practicing these satanic rites of the occult.

Some people are surprised that worshipers of Satan have power. Sure, the devil has power! A departure from the Word of God and a departure from God always leads into error, and this gives rise to the false cults which we find today.

Why did God exact the death penalty for participating in these satanic rites of the occult?

Sanctify yourselves therefore, and be ye holy: for I am the LORD your God.

And ye shall keep my statutes, and do them: I am the LORD which sanctify you [Lev. 20:7–8].

These verses offer a good and sufficient reason for the death penalty. The people were to be holy because they belonged to God, and He was holy. Any deviation from this standard was a serious breach of conduct. To practice the abominations that have been named was to turn from God to Satan. It was spiritual adultery and treason. Today people do not seem to realize how serious that can be. This is God's universe. God is a reality, friends. God's statutes are never to be taken lightly.

CAPITAL PUNISHMENT FOR THOSE WHO CURSE FATHER OR MOTHER

For every one that curseth his father or his mother shall be surely put to death: he hath cursed his father or his mother: his blood shall be upon him [Lev. 20:9].

The fifth commandment was not to be considered of minor importance. In Leviticus 19:3 the Israelite was instructed to fear his father and mother. Now the death penalty was inflicted for cursing father and mother. In Romans 1:31 Paul spoke of those "without natural affection." And we are told that in the last days children will be disobedient to parents, and men will be without natural affection (2 Tim. 3:2–3). This characterized the heathen of the past and will characterize the last days. The punishment stated here is extreme.

We need to mention here that the Bible also offers grace in this regard. The Lord Jesus told the parable of the prodigal son who came home and was received by the father. That is grace. "If we confess our sins, he is faithful and just to forgive us our sins, and to cleanse us from all unrighteousness" (1 John 1:9).

CAPITAL PUNISHMENT FOR THOSE WHO COMMIT ADULTERY

And the man that committeth adultery with another man's wife, even he that committeth adultery with his neighbour's wife, the adulterer and the adulteress shall surely be put to death.

And the man that lieth with his father's wife hath uncovered his father's nakedness: both of them shall surely be put to death; their blood shall be upon them.

And if a man lie with his daughter-in-law, both of them shall surely be put to death: they have wrought confusion; their blood shall be upon them.

If a man also lie with mankind, as he lieth with a woman, both of them have committed an abomination: they shall surely be put to death; their blood shall be upon them.

And if a man take a wife and her mother, it is wickedness: they shall be burnt with fire, both he and they; that there be no wickedness among you.

And if a man lie with a beast, he shall surely be put to death: and ye shall slay the beast.

And if a woman approach unto any beast, and lie down thereto, thou shalt kill the woman, and the beast: they shall surely be put to death; their blood shall be upon them [Lev. 20:10–16].

This entire section contains unspeakable and even unbelievable sins. Adultery in every form and shape was punished with death. Sins of sex have caused the most powerful empires to topple. I would say that sex and liquor were the two causes of the fall of Babylon, Egypt, Rome, and France. What a warning this is for our nation!

This is a rebuke against lax morals today. These sins brought down fire and brimstone on Sodom and Gomorrah. These are the sins which cause God to give up a people (Rom. 1:24–28).

In spite of the awful immorality of these sins and the severity of the punishment, the Savior stands ready to forgive any who will come to Him. He put His sacrificial death between this sin and the woman taken in adultery. His sacrificial death atones for you, my friend, if you will come to him for forgiveness.

CERTAIN OFFENSES WHICH REQUIRE A LESSER PENALTY

And if a man shall take his sister, his father's daughter, or his mother's daughter, and see her nakedness, and she see his nakedness; it is a wicked thing: and they shall be cut off in the sight of their people: he hath uncovered his sister's nakedness; he shall bear his iniquity.

And if a man shall lie with a woman having her sickness, and shall uncover her nakedness; he hath discovered her fountain, and she hath uncovered the fountain of her blood: and both of them shall be cut off from among their people.

And thou shalt not uncover the nakedness of thy mother's sister, nor of thy father's sister: for he uncovereth his near kin: they shall bear their iniquity.

And if a man shall lie with his uncle's wife, he hath uncovered his uncle's nakedness: they shall bear their sin: they shall die childless.

And if a man shall take his brother's wife, it is an unclean thing: he hath un-

covered his brother's nakedness; they shall be childless [Lev. 20:17–21].

Incest with a full or half sister was forbidden and the penalty was to be executed publicly. God demanded cleanliness in every detail of his people's lives; especially as it had to do with sexual relations. God forbade sexual relations between those who were near of kin. He did not say that they would not bear children, but that they should die childless—the children would die before the parents who were guilty of this crime.

CONCLUSION TO THE LAW OF HOLINESS

Ye shall therefore keep all my statutes, and all my judgments, and do them: that the land, whither I bring you to dwell therein, spue you not out [Lev. 20:22].

God put the Canaanites out of the land because they committed these awful sins. He warns Israel that He will put them out of the land if they do the same things. God is no respecter of persons. Do you know that their failure to obey God brought on them the Babylonian captivity? Listen to the record: "Manasseh was twelve years old when he began to reign, and reigned fifty and five years in Jerusalem. . . . And he did that which was evil in the sight of the LORD, after the abominations of the heathen, whom the LORD cast out before the children of Israel. . . . And he made his son pass through the fire, and observed times, and used enchantments, and dealt with familiar spirits and wizards: he wrought much wickedness in the sight of the LORD, to provoke him to anger . . . . Manasseh seduced them to do more evil than did the nations whom the LORD destroyed before the children of Israel" (2 Kings 21:1–2, 6, 9).

And ye shall not walk in the manners of the nation, which I cast out before you: for they committed all these things, and therefore I abhorred them [Lev. 20:23].

This should answer the question as to the justice of God in destroying some of the nations which occupied Palestine. As a result of these sins they were eaten up with social diseases. God forbade His people to take or touch anything in the city of Jericho at the time of the conquest. Evidently venereal diseases had reached epidemic proportions.

But I have said unto you, Ye shall inherit their land, and I will give it unto you to possess it, a land that floweth with milk and honey: I am the LORD your God, which have separated you from other people [Lev. 20:24].

It was a land flowing with milk and honey. Timber covered that land. What happened to it? "Even all nations shall say, Wherefore hath the LORD done thus unto this land? what meaneth the heat of this great anger? Then men shall say, Because they have forsaken the covenant of the LORD God of their fathers, which he made with them when he brought them forth out of the land of Egypt: For they went and served other gods, and worshipped them, gods whom they knew not, and whom he had not given unto them: And the anger of the LORD was kindled against this land, to bring upon it all the curses that are written in this book: And the LORD rooted them out of their land in anger, and in wrath, and in great indignation, and cast them into another land, as it is this day" (Deut. 29:24–28). They are planting trees over there today. When I was there, I set out five trees; one for each member of my family, one for the church that I served, and one for a Jewish friend.

Ye shall therefore put difference between clean beasts and unclean, and between unclean fowls and clean: and ye shall not make your souls abominable by beast, or by fowl, or by any manner of living thing that creepeth on the ground, which I have separated from you as unclean [Lev. 20:25].

God reviews the statutes which were to make His people a different and a holy people. He began with their diet, and He concludes with it.

And ye shall be holy unto me: for I the LORD am holy, and have severed you from other people, that ye should be mine [Lev. 20:26].

They are out of the land because they did not obey God. They were to be a holy nation like unto their God who is holy. "But," you may say, "they are in the land." May I ask how they are getting along? They have had trouble every minute they have been back in the land. Do you know what the problem is? They went back to the land but they did not return to God. When they do return to God—which they will do someday—then there will be blessing in that land. God hasn't changed His mind, friends.

This should be a lesson to us and to our nation. God is high and holy, and He demands holiness. This is the key to Leviticus.

CHAPTER 21

THEME: *Defilement of priesthood prevented in human kinship and friendship; disqualifications for priestly function*

We have been studying the law as directed to the people from chapter 11 through chapter 20. Now we come to the law for the personal purity of the priests. This is found in chapters 21 and 22. We will find a certain amount of repetition here.

It had been God's original intention that the entire nation should be a kingdom of priests (Exod. 19:5–6). Their disobedience in the matter of the golden calf destroyed the possibility of the realization of a perfect and ideal society. In the Millennium, the perfect society will be attained. Then the entire nation of Israel will be the priests here on the earth for the earthly people, the Gentile nations. Through the Millennium and through eternity, there are the three groups of the human family: (1) the Church of Jesus Christ in the New Jerusalem, (2) the nation Israel here on this earth, (3) the saved Gentiles on this earth.

After Israel's failure, God chose only one tribe to be the priests, the tribe of Levi. In Israel, therefore, there were the congregation, the priesthood, and the high priest. The higher position required a higher obligation. The greater responsibility demanded a higher way of life.

The church today is called a royal priesthood. Every believer is a priest and has access to the throne of grace today. Every believer-priest is required to live a holy life which is possible only by the power of the indwelling Holy Spirit. "And above all things have fervent charity among yourselves: for charity shall cover the multitude of sins. Use hospitality one to another without grudging. As every man hath received the gift, even so minister the same one to another, as good stewards of the manifold grace of God. If any man speak, let him speak as the oracles of God; if any man minister, let him do it as of the ability which God giveth: that God in all things may be glorified through Jesus Christ, to whom be praise and dominion for ever and ever. Amen" (1 Pet. 4:8–11). He also said, "But ye are a chosen generation, a royal priesthood, an holy nation, a peculiar people; that ye should shew forth the praises of him who hath called you out of darkness into his marvellous light: Which in time past were not a people, but are now the people of God: which had not obtained mercy, but now have obtained mercy" (1 Pet. 2:9–10).

As God's people we are called to a higher way of life. "This I say therefore, and testify in the Lord, that ye henceforth walk not as other Gentiles walk, in the vanity of their mind. . . . That ye put off concerning the former conversation the old man, which is corrupt according to the deceitful lusts; And be renewed in the spirit of your mind; And that ye put on the new man, which after God is created in righteousness and true holiness" (Eph. 4:17, 22–24). The child of God is saved by grace and has been called to a high place in his life.

A believer should be careful about accepting an office in the church. If he does become an officer, he should measure up to that responsibility. I have very little patience with men who accept an office in the church and then say they are not able to come to the mid-week service or come on Sunday night. Well, my brother, you should not have accepted the office. Responsibility, you see, comes through privilege. It is a privilege to serve the Lord in an office. You have been elevated. Then live up to it.

Jesus Christ is our Great High Priest and He measured up to His office. "For such an high priest became us, who is holy, harmless, undefiled, separate from sinners, and made higher than the heavens; who needeth not daily, as those high priests, to offer up sacrifice, first for his own sins, and then for the people's: for this he did once, when he offered up himself. For the law maketh men high priests which have infirmity; but the word of the oath, which was since the law, maketh the Son, who is consecrated for evermore" (Heb. 7:26–28). The Lord Jesus Christ is both the priest and the sacrifice. He offered Himself.

The priests and the high priest now come under the purview of the law. Let us look at it.

DEFILEMENT OF PRIESTHOOD PREVENTED IN HUMAN KINSHIP AND FRIENDSHIP

And the LORD said unto Moses, Speak unto the priests the sons of Aaron, and say unto them, There shall none be defiled for the dead among his people:

But for his kin, that is near unto him, that is, for his mother, and for his father, and for his son, and for his daughter, and for his brother.

And for his sister a virgin, that is nigh unto him, which hath had no husband: for her may he be defiled [Lev. 21:1–3].

Moses is to address this section to the priests. Death is a penalty of sin, and the idea is that they are not to be contaminated with sin. Physical contact with the dead brings defilement. The priest was permitted to defile himself for close relatives. These listed here are all blood relations and by nature close to the priest. He must be permitted to express his feelings of sympathy and grief as a priest of God. He must be a type of Jesus who could weep at the grave of Lazarus and was touched with the feelings of our infirmities. He was not, however, permitted to defile himself for the dead of any others. He could mourn in his heart, but was denied physical contact.

But he shall not defile himself, being a chief man among his people, to profane himself [Lev. 21:4].

The office he occupied required of him a stricter separation than any common man among the people.

There are places that I don't go, not because they are wrong, but because I am an ordained minister and I don't want to give any occasion for offense to anyone. I believe that pastors, deacons, elders, Sunday School teachers, and all others who serve in the church, should all be extremely careful about where they go, what they do and say. God is going to hold you and me more responsible if He has placed us in a position of responsibility.

They shall not make baldness upon their head, neither shall they shave off the corner of their beard, nor make any cuttings in their flesh [Lev. 21:5].

This was something the heathen did, and they did it as an act of mourning for the dead. The priest was not to practice these superstitious, pagan practices that were all around him.

They shall be holy unto their God, and not profane the name of their God: for the offerings of the LORD made by fire, and the bread of their God, they do offer: therefore they shall be holy [Lev. 21:6].

Their mourning was to befit those who were cupbearers of the King, "the bread of their God." Their position demanded dignity and restraint as God's representatives. The same applies to God's representatives in the church today: "For a bishop must be blameless, as the steward of God; not selfwilled, not soon angry, not given to wine, no striker, not given to filthy lucre; But a lover of hospitality, a lover of good men, sober, just, holy, temperate" (Titus 1:7–8).

They shall not take a wife that is a whore, or profane; neither shall they take a woman put away from her husband: for he is holy unto his God.

Thou shalt sanctify him therefore; for he offereth the bread of thy God: he shall be holy unto thee: for I the LORD, which sanctify you, am holy [Lev. 21:7–8].

This refers to his personal and private life, and in that, too, he is to reveal the holiness of God because of his position. He shall not marry a harlot, profane woman, or a divorced person. The reason given is because he is serving God—"offereth the bread of thy God."

The priest is a type of Christ. Also the body of believers, called the *bride* of Christ, is to be cleansed before she is presented to Him without spot and wrinkle (Eph. 5:26–27).

The church leader is to be an example to others in this particular matter. May I say right here that I get many letters from both men and women who were divorced before they were saved. Some of the men want to enter the ministry and the women wish to become missionaries. I know one cannot generalize about these things, but I do want to say that I think it is almost sinful the way certain innocent people who had an unfortunate experience in their lives—many of them before they were saved—are shut out from an office because of that past experience in which they were not guilty at all. I encourage these people to go ahead and prepare for the ministry or the mission field. But I warn them to also be prepared to weather the criticism of some "saint" who thinks he is speaking for God. Also, they will find certain churches that will shut them out. Yet I encourage them to go ahead with their preparation because there will be a place for them. And there is. We need to recognize that in this day there are a great many people who are the innocent victims of divorce.

Another thing we need to recognize is that the wife of a pastor is not an assistant pastor. She is simply the wife of the pastor; that is the role she is to fill. She must be the kind of person who would be a credit to the office that the man occupies. It is not required of her that she must play the piano and the organ, sing in the choir, lead the missionary society, and on and on.

And the daughter of any priest, if she profane herself by playing the whore, she profaneth her father: she shall be burnt with fire [Lev. 21:9].

Why? Because of the position of her father. She was to receive the severest of penalties if she disgraced the office of her father.

And he that is the high priest among his brethren, upon whose head the anointing oil was poured, and that is consecrated to put on the garments, shall not uncover his head, nor rend his clothes;

Neither shall he go in to any dead body, nor defile himself for his father, or for his mother;

Neither shall he go out of the sanctuary, nor profane the sanctuary of his God: for the crown of the anointing oil of his God is upon him: I am the LORD [Lev. 21:10–12].

This is the first mention of the high priest. As God's anointed priest, he is to be separated unto the Lord. He was to wear the crown on which were inscribed the words "Holiness unto the Lord" as a continual reminder of who he is, whose he is, and whom he serves.

He is not to rend his holy garments. He was not to be a violent man. At the trial of Jesus this law was broken when the high priest emotionally tore his clothes (Matt. 26:65). Neither was the high priest to attend the funeral of either his father or mother. The anointing oil had been poured upon him, and he must be totally dedicated to God and separated from sin because of his position.

The Lord Jesus Christ had the anointing oil poured upon Him and He came to do the Father's will even unto death. He demands just such dedication on the part of His followers.

And he shall take a wife in her virginity.

A widow, or a divorced woman, or profane, or an harlot, these shall he not take: but he shall take a virgin of his own people to wife.

Neither shall he profane his seed among his people: for I the LORD do sanctify him [Lev. 21:13–15].

His wife too must measure up to the position of the holy office. He is forbidden to marry a harlot, a profane or a divorced woman.

DISQUALIFICATIONS FOR PRIESTLY FUNCTION

The following verses list disqualifications for the priestly function. It includes blindness, lameness, flat nose, dwarfism, scabs, and other deformities and blemishes.

And the LORD spake unto Moses, saying.

Speak unto Aaron, saying. Whosoever he be of thy seed in their generations that hath any blemish, let him not approach to offer the bread of his God.

For whatsoever man he be that hath a blemish, he shall not approach: a blind man, or a lame, or he that hath a flat nose, or any thing superfluous.

Or, a man that is brokenfooted, or brokenhanded.

Or crookback, or a dwarf, or that hath a blemish in his eye, or be scurvy, or scabbed, or hath his stones broken;

No man that hath a blemish of the seed of Aaron the priest shall come nigh to offer the offerings of the LORD made by fire: he hath a blemish; he shall not come nigh to offer the bread of his God [Lev. 21:16–21].

Why should this be? Just as no sacrifice was to be offered that had a blemish, by the same token no priest was to serve in the tabernacle if he had a blemish. Both the offering and the offerer represent Christ and there is no blemish in Him, either in His person or in His work. Christ is the perfect High Priest. There is no blemish in Him but rather beauty and glory and excellency.

He shall eat the bread of his God, both of the most holy, and of the holy.

Only he shall not go in unto the veil, nor come nigh unto the altar, because he hath a blemish, that he profane not my sanctuaries: for I the LORD do sanctify them [Lev. 21:22–23].

Although those with a blemish were forbidden to serve, they were not shut out from the table of the Lord. God provided for them. This is in contrast to the treatment the pagan world gave the unfit.

There is a spiritual lesson for us here. There are many believers who have some serious handicap either physically, morally, ethically, or spiritually. This would bar them from certain forms of service, yet they are genuine saints of God who have all the rights and privileges of believers in every respect.

When I was studying for the ministry, I taught a young fellow in Sunday School who was in junior high school at the time. He was a marvelous athlete, but he had a cleft palate with a speech impediment. He came to me one day and told me that he would like to be a minister. Now, how do you talk to a young fellow like that? I tried to explain to him that

he was a wonderful athlete, but that his speech was a handicap and suggested he find something in Christian work which would not require public speaking. I've followed this man through the years. He became a football coach at a college. His influence for Christ was as great or greater than any minister's. They learned to admire this man as an athlete and then, with his speech impediment, he would tell them about Jesus Christ and it made a real impact upon them.

CHAPTER 22

THEME: *Defilement of the priesthood through disease, diet, and the dead; discernment of the offerings brought by the people*

DEFILEMENT OF THE PRIESTHOOD THROUGH DISEASE, DIET, AND THE DEAD

And the LORD spake unto Moses, saying,

Speak unto Aaron and to his sons, that they separate themselves from the holy things of the children of Israel, and that they profane not my holy name in those things which they hallow unto me: I am the LORD [Lev. 22:1–2].

There was to be a separation of the sacred and the secular. Aaron was not to bring the things of the tabernacle home with him. The lesson for us is that we are not to treat the sacred and holy things of God as if they were commonplace.

Say unto them, Whosoever he be of all your seed among your generations, that goeth unto the holy things, which the children of Israel hallow unto the LORD, having his uncleanness upon him, that soul shall be cut off from my presence: I am the LORD [Lev. 22:3].

The priest is not to go about his office in a careless and slipshod manner. God requires that he should be put out of the office of the priesthood if he does that. I believe there is a spiritual application for the believer today. "For if we would judge ourselves, we should not be judged. But when we are judged, we are chastened of the Lord, that we should not be condemned with the world" (1 Cor. 11:31–32).

God proceeds to enumerate all manner of

uncleanness which would disqualify the priest from carrying out his priestly duties.

What man soever of the seed of Aaron is a leper, or hath a running issue; he shall not eat of the holy things, until he be clean. And whoso toucheth any thing that is unclean by the dead, or a man whose seed goeth from him;

Or whosoever toucheth any creeping thing, whereby he may be made unclean, or a man of whom he may take uncleanness, whatsoever uncleanness he hath;

The soul which hath touched any such shall be unclean until even, and shall not eat of the holy things, unless he wash his flesh with water.

And when the sun is down, he shall be clean, and shall afterward eat of the holy things; because it is his food.

That which dieth of itself, or is torn with beasts, he shall not eat to defile himself therewith: I am the LORD.

They shall therefore keep mine ordinance, lest they bear sin for it, and die therefore, if they profane it: I the LORD do sanctify them [Lev. 22:4–9].

The priests were to be holy in their relationships in their homes, in their social contacts, in their business contacts, in anything where they touched the world. The priests were set apart to be holy unto the Lord. They were to be an example to others. Some of the things mentioned are the same as those given for all of Israel. The priest had no special privileges. Uncleanness in the common man and uncleanness in the priest were to be ceremonially cleansed. The private life of the priest must match his public office and service.

There shall no stranger eat of the holy thing: a sojourner of the priest, or an hired servant, shall not eat of the holy thing [Lev. 22:10].

The priest must preserve the sanctity of the tabernacle by excluding the stranger. Only the sons of God can worship God.

But if the priest buy any soul with his money, he shall eat of it, and he that is born in his house: they shall eat of his meat.

If the priest's daughter also be married unto a stranger, she may not eat of an offering of the holy things.

But if the priest's daughter be a widow, or divorced, and have no child, and is returned unto her father's house, as in her youth, she shall eat of her father's meat: but there shall no stranger eat thereof [Lev. 22:11–13].

The verses go on to explain that only those who belong to the priest, who were born in his house, can eat of his meat. If a priest's daughter married a Gentile, she was excluded from access to the holy things. If she were widowed or divorced and returned to her father's house, she could eat her father's meat. The prodigal son or daughter may return home and find a welcome.

And if a man eat of the holy thing unwittingly, then he shall put the fifth part thereof unto it, and shall give it unto the priest with the holy thing.

And they shall not profane the holy things of the children of Israel, which they offer unto the LORD;

Or suffer them to bear the iniquity of trespass, when they eat their holy things: for I the LORD do sanctify them [Lev. 22:14–16].

Ignorance of the law affords no excuse. The man who eats of the holy things unwittingly is guilty. A fine is exacted of him. This placed an added responsibility upon the priests to guard the holy place.

The unbelieving world gains its impression of the church from the members of the church. Indifference and irreverence is detected immediately by the outside unbeliever, and his attitude and conduct is governed accordingly. The Lord Jesus said, "Woe unto the world because of offences! for it must needs be that offences come; but woe to that man by whom the offence cometh" (Matt. 18:7).

DISCERNMENT OF THE OFFERINGS BROUGHT BY THE PEOPLE

And the LORD spake unto Moses, saying,

Speak unto Aaron, and to his sons, and unto all the children of Israel, and say unto them, Whatsoever he be of the house of Israel, or of the strangers in Israel, that will offer his oblation for all his vows, and for all his freewill offerings, which they will offer unto the LORD for a burnt offering:

Ye shall offer at your own will a male without blemish, of the beeves, of the sheep, or of the goats.

But whatsoever hath a blemish, that shall ye not offer: for it shall not be acceptable for you [Lev. 22:17–20].

This section contains rules and regulations for the people in bringing their offerings, and these rules must be strictly enforced by the priests. The regulations apply to the people, but the enforcement applies to the priests. No offering with a blemish was to be permitted because the offerings pointed to Christ. Any departure from this was to lower the concept of the person of Christ and the holy demands of God.

And whosoever offereth a sacrifice of peace offerings unto the LORD to accomplish his vow, or a freewill offering in beeves or sheep, it shall be perfect to be accepted; there shall be no blemish therein.

Blind, or broken, or maimed, or having a wen, or scurvy, or scabbed, ye shall not offer these unto the LORD, nor make an offering by fire of them upon the altar unto the LORD.

Either a bullock or a lamb that hath any thing superfluous or lacking in his parts, that mayest thou offer for a freewill offering; but for a vow it shall not be accepted.

Ye shall not offer unto the LORD that which is bruised, or crushed, or broken,

or cut; neither shall ye make any offering thereof in your land.

Neither from a stranger's hand shall ye offer the bread of your God of any of these; because their corruption is in them, and blemishes be in them: they shall not be accepted for you.

And the LORD spake unto Moses, saying,

When a bullock, or a sheep, or a goat, is brought forth, then it shall be seven days under the dam; and from the eighth day and thenceforth it shall be accepted for an offering made by fire unto the LORD.

And whether it be cow or ewe, ye shall not kill it and her young both in one day [Lev. 22:21–28].

Natural deformity in an animal as well as bruises and cuts and broken bones comprised the blemishes. Any of these should make them reject the animal as an offering. No stranger was to make an offering. And any offering animal was to be at least over seven days old. Seven represents completion—it was to have lived a complete cycle.

It was at this point of offering animals without blemish that Israel failed miserably. They brought that which was torn and lame and sick for their offerings and God called forth from the prophets a denunciation of their offerings. We find this in Malachi 1:6–14.

And when ye will offer a sacrifice of thanksgiving unto the LORD, offer it at your own will.

On the same day it shall be eaten up; ye shall leave none of it until the morrow: I am the LORD [Lev. 22:29–30].

The offering was to be a freewill offering. This type of offering must represent the Father who gave His Son in love and the Son who came ". . . for the joy that was set before him . . ." (Heb. 12:2). The offering must be eaten the same day. No opportunity must be allowed for the slightest bit of corruption.

Therefore shall ye keep my commandments, and do them: I am the LORD.

Neither shall ye profane my holy name; but I will be hallowed among the children of Israel: I am the LORD which hallow you,

That brought you out of the land of Egypt, to be your God: I am the LORD [Lev. 22:31–33].

They were to be a witness for God. They were not to go as witnesses to the ends of the earth as you and I have been called to do today. They were called to serve God as a nation. As they did this, the whole world would come to Jerusalem. God's holy name was to be represented in every act of worship.

What was to be the motivation for their obedience? Dr. Andrew A. Bonar gives five reasons:

1. "I am the Lord"
2. "I will be hallowed among the children of Israel"
3. "I am the Lord which hallow you"
4. "I am the Lord which brought you out of Egypt"
5. "Your God."

"I am the Lord which hallow you." There is liberty for the believer today, but liberty does not grant license. The holiness and righteousness of God must be zealously maintained in all our worship.

"I am the Lord which brought you out of Egypt." God has saved you, my friend. God saves you by grace. He didn't save you with the idea of exacting commensurate work from you. Then it wouldn't be grace. I do not agree with the words of the song, "I gave My life for thee, what hast thou done for Me?" Grace does not demand payment. But let me ask you a question. Do you love Him? Do you *want* to serve Him? The wife doesn't fix a birthday dinner for her husband because it is her duty. She does it because she loves the old boy! And the true believer will serve God because he loves Him.

"I am the LORD which hallow you, that brought you out of the land of Egypt, *to be your God.*" Is He your God, my friend? If He is, then you represent Him. The world is reading you. Remember the little poem:

The Gospel is written a chapter a day
By the deeds that you do and words that
    you say.
Men read what you say whether faithless
    or true.
Say, what is the Gospel according to you?

Men are not reading the Bible today. They are reading you and me. What are they reading in you, my friend?

This is a remarkable chapter of God's solemn festivals. The holy holidays were times of joy. There was mourning on only one of them, the great Day of Atonement. The others were to be times of joy and rejoicing. God never wanted a weeping people to come before Him; He wanted a rejoicing people. These festivals provide God's calendar for all time.

John Peter Lange gives the meaning of the so-called feasts as "a fixed, appointed time." It is sometimes translated a "set time." Perhaps "holy seasons" would be the most appropriate translation.

Details for most of these feasts are given elsewhere in Scripture. Here they are given in an orderly and purposeful arrangement. There are seven feasts, excluding the Sabbath day, which is given first. The Sabbath day was not a feast day, but is included because it furnishes the yardstick for the measuring of time. The number seven is as prominent in this chapter as in the Book of Revelation. It is the dimension of time.

The Sabbath day is the seventh day. Pentecost is the feast of the seventh week; the seventh new moon with its following Day of Atonement and feast of Tabernacles is the feast of the seventh month. In the twenty-fifth chapter we will have occasion to consider the Sabbatic year and the year of Jubilee, all adjusted to the number seven. There were seven days of unleavened bread, and seven days of dwelling in tabernacles in the feast of the Tabernacles.

These days of holy convocation served a twofold purpose: a practical purpose and a prophetic purpose. On the practical plane they served both a social and commercial purpose. They brought the twelve tribes together in worship and fellowship. All males were required to go to Jerusalem to worship on three occasions: at the feasts of Passover, Pentecost, and Tabernacles (Deut. 16:16). You can see that this would have a tendency to unite the nation and knit the tribes together. The people would come from all sections of the kingdom and exchange ideas as well as merchandise. Failure to follow these instructions was one of the contributing factors in dividing the nation into northern and southern kingdoms.

Most of these feasts were geared into the agricultural life of the land, especially the harvesting of the crops. This was especially true of the feasts of Firstfruits, Pentecost, and Tabernacles. This brought the worship of Jehovah down to the grain field, the vineyard, and the fig orchard. Praise to God was united with the work of the people. The sweat of their brow became a sacred thing.

The primary purpose of these feast days was to give a prophetic picture of all future time. Each one of these feasts has found or will find a fulfillment in time. Most of them have been fulfilled. We will point this out as we go along.

We are no longer to observe days and seasons because Christ has fulfilled them. "Let no man therefore judge you in meat, or in drink, or in respect of an holyday, or of the new moon, or of the sabbath days: Which are a shadow of things to come; but the body is of Christ" (Col. 2:16–17).

I should mention that all the festivals and observances are not included in this chapter. The Sabbatic year and the year of Jubilee are found in chapter 25, and the New Moons in Numbers 28:11–15.

THE HOLY SEASONS OF THE SABBATH

And the LORD spake unto Moses, saying,

Speak unto the children of Israel, and say unto them, Concerning the feasts of the LORD, which ye shall proclaim to be holy convocations, even these are my feasts.

Six days shall work be done: but the seventh day is the sabbath of rest, an holy convocation; ye shall do no work therein: it is the sabbath of the LORD in all your dwellings [Lev. 23:1–3].

If you will notice, as we go through this book, God always directs His instructions to certain people, and it is well to note the ones to whom He is directing the instruction. He tells Moses as the lawgiver, and he in turn is to tell the people. Even though the feasts will involve the tabernacle, the priests are not specifically mentioned. The people were to come together, and the feasts were to fit into the yearly calendar of Israel.

    Passover—the crucifixion and death of Christ
    Unleavened Bread—the fellowship we have with Christ because of His death
    Firstfruits—the resurrection of Christ
    Pentecost—the beginning of the church
    Trumpets—Israel brought back into the land (future)
    Great Day of Atonement—the work of Christ upon the cross for us
    Tabernacles—the time when Israel is in the land (future)

The weekly Sabbath cannot properly be labeled one of the feast days. It is pre-Mosaic and goes back to the original creation. It was repeated to Israel, and in Deuteronomy an additional reason for its observance is given. "And remember that thou wast a servant in the land of Egypt, and that the LORD thy God brought thee out thence through a mighty hand and by a stretched out arm: therefore the LORD thy God commanded thee to keep the sabbath day" (Deut. 5:15).

When they were slaves down in Egypt, they had to work every day. The Sabbath day is tied in with their deliverance. Now that they have been delivered from Egypt, they are to set aside one day to worship God. There is to be cessation from all labor and activity.

When the early church set aside a day of the week to come together, they chose Sunday, the first day of the week, because it was the day our Lord came back from the dead. That is the day full deliverance was given to us. "Who was delivered for our offences, and was raised again for our justification" (Rom. 4:25). The Sabbath day belongs to the old creation. We belong to the new creation. ". . . if any man be in Christ, he is a new creature [creation] . . ." (2 Cor. 5:17). We honor Christ by setting aside the first day of the week.

The Sabbath was a yardstick of time for Israel. It spoke of cessation from all labor and activity and looked forward to a new week when there would be a new creation. It was also prophetic in that it looked forward to redemption. Man lost his rest in the first creation, but now rest is his through redemption. "There remaineth therefore a rest to the people of God. For he that is entered into his rest, he also hath ceased from his own works, as God did from his. Let us labour therefore to enter into that rest, lest any man fall after the same example of unbelief" (Heb. 4:9–11). Our rest comes through redemption and redemption only. There is a rest for the people of God. What is it? Our sins are forgiven. "Come unto me, all ye that labour and are heavy laden, and I will give you rest" (Matt. 11:28). Rest and redemption are the twofold aspect of the Sabbath day.

The Sabbath day was not a feast day. It is geared to the week and not to the year. It was not a feast, but a set time.

THE HOLY SEASON OF PASSOVER

These are the feasts of the LORD, even holy convocations, which ye shall proclaim in their seasons.

In the fourteenth day of the first month at even is the LORD's passover [Lev. 23:4–5].

The description of the feast was given to us back in Exodus 12, but here it is placed in the calendar of God. This verse makes it clear that the feasts begin properly with the Passover and not the Sabbath. In Exodus 12:2 God said, "This month shall be unto you the beginning of months: it shall be the first month of the year to you." This holy season represents the sacrificial death of Christ and the value of His blood. "Purge out therefore the old leaven, that ye may be a new lump, as ye are unleavened. For even Christ our passover is sacrificed for us" (1 Cor. 5:7).

The Passover originated in the historical event of the last plague in Egypt by the slaying of the firstborn. Israel was instructed to slay a lamb and put the blood of the lamb on the doorposts of their homes. They were to stay inside, roast the lamb, and eat it. The angel of death would pass over every door which was marked with the blood. When we get to Numbers 9, we will find that Israel kept the Passover when they were encamped at Mount Sinai.

The Passover was brought to its fulfillment the night of the arrest of the Lord Jesus Christ after He had observed the Passover with His disciples, and had instituted a new feast on the dying embers of the old. Then we see the Lamb slain in Revelation 5:6. I think the Passover will be observed again in the Kingdom. "For I say unto you, I will not any more eat thereof, until it be fulfilled in the kingdom of God" (Luke 22:16).

THE HOLY SEASON
OF UNLEAVENED BREAD

And on the fifteenth day of the same month is the feast of unleavened bread unto the Lord: seven days ye must eat unleavened bread.

In the first day ye shall have an holy convocation: ye shall do no servile work therein.

But ye shall offer an offering made by fire unto the Lord seven days: in the seventh day is an holy convocation: ye shall do no servile work therein [Lev. 23:6–8].

Although this is considered a separate feast, it is closely aligned with the Passover. Passover was observed one day, and the next day—the first day of the week—began the feast of Unleavened Bread. Its historical origin is in direct connection with the Passover (Exod. 12:14–28). Unleavened bread was to be eaten for seven days beginning on the day after Passover. In Matthew and Mark the Passover and Unleavened Bread are considered as one feast.

Leaven here, as elsewhere, is the symbol of evil. The unleavened bread speaks of fellowship with Christ based on His redemption and maintained by the holy walk of the believer (1 Cor. 5:7–8).

No servile work was to be done. On those days the participants were to rest from their daily occupations. There were to be offerings made by fire which refer to burnt offerings, meal offerings, and sin offerings. The first and the seventh days of the week of Unleavened Bread were the particular days of an "holy convocation."

The Passover speaks of the death of Christ for our sins. After that, we are not to maintain fellowship with Him on the basis of the fact that He died for us. We are to remain clean by confessing our sins as we go along. Our Lord said to His men, ". . . If I wash thee not, thou hast no part with me" (John 13:8). It signifies that the value of the blood of Christ continues for the believer after he is saved. "But if we walk in the light, as he is in the light, we have fellowship one with another, and the blood of Jesus Christ his Son cleanseth us from all sin" (1 John 1:7). The blood of Jesus Christ *keeps on* keeping us clean. That is the meaning of the feast of Mazzoth, Unleavened Bread.

THE HOLY SEASON OF
FIRST FRUITS

And the Lord spake unto Moses, saying,

Speak unto the children of Israel, and say unto them, When ye be come into the land which I give unto you, and shall reap the harvest thereof, then ye shall bring a sheaf of the firstfruits of your harvest unto the priest:

And he shall wave the sheaf before the Lord, to be accepted for you: on the morrow after the sabbath the priest shall wave it [Lev. 23:9–11].

This feast could not be observed until Israel got out of the wilderness and into the Promised Land. When they had sowed their grain in the land, they were to watch for the first heading of the barley. When they would see a stalk here and there, they would cut each one down and put them together to make a sheaf. This was then brought to the tabernacle, and the priest would offer it to the Lord.

The exact day that he did this is not stated. It may have been the first day of Unleavened Bread or the last day of that feast. The important item to note is that it was done on the first day of the week. This is so important because Christ is called the firstfruits. "But now is Christ risen from the dead, and become the firstfruits of them that slept" (1 Cor. 15:20). "But every man in his own order: Christ the firstfruits; afterward they that are Christ's at his coming" (1 Cor. 15:23). The time of His resurrection is clearly stated in Matthew 28:1: "In the end of the sabbath, as it began to dawn toward the first day of the week, came Mary Magdalene and the other Mary to see the sepulchre." On the first day of the week, Christ, "the firstfruits" was resurrected from the dead.

Someday the church will be included in resurrection, but so far He is the only One who has been raised in a glorified body. At the rapture of the church, we shall all rise. There will be a coming out of the graves just as Christ did. He is the firstfruits, afterwards they that are Christ's at His coming. "Verily, verily, I say unto you, Except a corn of wheat fall into the ground and die, it abideth alone: but if it die, *it bringeth forth much fruit*" (John 12:24).

You see, the offering of the firstfruits indicated that there would be a harvest to follow. Believers are that harvest.

And ye shall offer that day when ye wave the sheaf an he lamb without blemish of the first year for a burnt offering unto the Lord.

And the meat offering thereof shall be

two tenth deals of fine flour mingled with oil, an offering made by fire unto the LORD for a sweet savour: and the drink offering thereof shall be of wine, the fourth part of an hin.

And ye shall eat neither bread, nor parched corn, nor green ears, until the selfsame day that ye have brought an offering unto your God: it shall be a statute for ever throughout your generations in all your dwellings [Lev. 23:12–14].

Offerings accompanied the celebration of this day. No sin offering was included because that was included in the death of Christ—that is where He settled the sin question. These offerings are a sweet savor. "For he hath made him to be sin for us, who knew no sin; that we might be made the righteousness of God in him" (2 Cor. 5:21). ". . . because I live, ye shall live also" (John 14:19). This is a glorious truth that we have here.

The new crop of grain could not be enjoyed until this offering was waved before Jehovah. For the believer, the death and resurrection of Christ brings us into new relationships and blessings. "Therefore if any man be in Christ, he is a new creature: old things are passed away; behold, all things are become new" (2 Cor. 5:17). That doesn't mean that just a few habits change. It means we are taken out of the old Adam, and we are joined to the Lord Jesus Christ. Now we have a new purpose, a new goal, a new joy, and new life—and that would affect a few old habits, would it not? He makes all things new.

THE HOLY SEASON OF PENTECOST

Notice the orderly, chronological sequence that we have here. Passover tells us that Christ, our Passover, is sacrificed for us. Unleavened Bread is sharing the things of Christ, fellowship with Him. Then Firstfruits signifies Christ's resurrection, the firstfruits from the dead. Now we come to Pentecost.

And ye shall count unto you from the morrow after the sabbath, from the day that ye brought the sheaf of the wave offering; seven sabbaths shall be complete:

Even unto the morrow after the seventh sabbath shall ye number fifty days; and ye shall offer a new meat offering unto the LORD [Lev. 23:15–16].

There are several things we need to note about Pentecost because there is so much being made of it today that is absolutely un-

scriptural. The feast of Pentecost always fell on the first day of the week. They counted seven sabbaths, which would be seven weeks or forty-nine days, then the fiftieth day, the day after the seventh sabbath, the first day of the week, was Pentecost. This was fifty days after the offering of the wave sheaf of firstfruits.

The church was born on the first day of the week. It was on the first day of the week that our Lord arose. Doesn't that tell us something? Wouldn't it be rather odd for the church to go back and observe the old Sabbath which belonged to the old creation when the church is a new creation? When the church meets on the first day of the week, we are celebrating our Lord's resurrection and the birthday of the church. This festival is also called the feast of Weeks.

The typical meaning of Pentecost is not left to man's speculation. "And when the day of Pentecost was fully come, they were all with one accord in one place . . . . And they were all filled with the Holy Ghost, and began to speak with other tongues, as the Spirit gave them utterance" (Acts 2:1, 4). "When the day of Pentecost was fully come" doesn't mean at twelve noon or at six in the evening. "The day of Pentecost was fully come" means the fulfillment of that for which it was given in Leviticus. It denotes the coming of the Holy Spirit to baptize believers into the body of Christ and to begin the calling out of the church. Pentecost is the birthday of the church.

It was fifty days after the resurrection of Christ that the Holy Spirit came. God was running according to His calendar and on time.

They were to offer a new meal offering. That is a type of the church. The church is something new. Christ didn't say that he would give us an old garment and patch it up. He came to bring a brand new robe of righteousness. To be in Christ is to be clothed with His righteousness. That is how God sees us.

We need to note the time sequence. After the resurrection of the Lord Jesus, He showed Himself alive for forty days. Then, just before He ascended into heaven, He said to His own that they should not depart from Jerusalem, but wait for the promise of the Father. He told them they should be endued with power from on high (Luke 24:49). In Acts 1:5 it states: ". . . but ye shall be baptized with the Holy Ghost not many days hence." Ten days later, on the day of Pentecost, the Spirit of God came upon them.

Ye shall bring out of your habitations two wave loaves of two tenth deals: they shall be of fine flour; they shall be baken with leaven; they are the first-fruits unto the LORD [Lev. 23:17].

Do you notice anything startling about this verse? We have said that leaven is the principle of evil and that it was not to be in the offerings. Here is the exception. This is typifying the church, and it is a new offering in that it is a meal offering with *leaven* included. What does it mean? It means there is evil in the church. This is obvious to the most casual observer.

I was a pastor for forty years. I have served in four different states from the Atlantic to the Pacific. I have been in some wonderful churches, and I look back on those years with a real joy. I've had wonderful fellowship with the members of these churches. They have loved me and I loved them; we have been very close. However I happen to be able to testify that there is evil in the church. That is why leaven is included in this offering. This speaks of the visible church down on earth, the church as you and I see it and know it. There is evil in it. The Lord knew that long before the church even existed!

And ye shall offer with the bread seven lambs without blemish of the first year, and one young bullock, and two rams: they shall be for a burnt offering unto the LORD, with their meat offering, and their drink offerings, even an offering made by fire, of sweet savour unto the LORD.

Then ye shall sacrifice one kid of the goats for a sin offering, and two lambs of the first year for a sacrifice of peace offerings.

And the priest shall wave them with the bread of the firstfruits for a wave offering before the LORD, with the two lambs: they shall be holy to the LORD for the priest [Lev. 23:18–20].

All the offerings are to be made at this time. All that Christ is and all that He has done have been made over to the church. Believers can draw upon Him for everything. You can come to Him for salvation, first of all. You can come to Him for help and for mercy, for sympathy and for comfort. You can come to Him in all the situations of life. All the offerings were made at this time.

Isn't it interesting how the Lord, in these pictures, is giving to you and me some of the greatest truths? He uses pictures rather than cold, theological terms.

And ye shall proclaim on the selfsame day, that it may be an holy convocation unto you: ye shall do no servile work therein: it shall be a statute for ever in all your dwellings throughout your generations [Lev. 23:21].

They were to rest on that day and cease from their own works. That is what you and I are to do when we come to Christ. "Not by works of righteousness which we have done, but according to his mercy he saved us, by the washing of regeneration, and renewing of the Holy Ghost" (Titus 3:5).

And when ye reap the harvest of your land, thou shalt not make clean riddance of the corners of thy field when thou reapest, neither shall thou gather any gleaning of thy harvest: thou shalt leave them unto the poor, and to the stranger: I am the LORD your God [Lev. 23:22].

The holy day was adapted to the land. In the midst of the celebration they were to remember the poor and the stranger.

That is the practical side of the work of the church and of all believers today. We have been saved by grace, but we should attempt to get the Word of God out to folk and be helpful to them. I do not believe the church has any right to engage in any social service in which they do not present the Gospel. We are to feed people and reach out to them in their need, but along with this we must present the Gospel to them. We should remember that a man with an empty stomach is not going to be very eager to listen to the Gospel. James has some things to say about that (James 2:14–20).

This also looks forward to the great harvest at the end of the age, after the Rapture of the church, when God will remember the Gentiles. James 1:18 says, "Of his own will begat he us with the word of truth, that we should be a kind of firstfruits of his creatures." The early church was Jewish and was firstfruits, but it was to be followed by a great company of Gentiles. Our Lord tells about the end of the age: "The field is the world; the good seed are the children of the kingdom; but the tares are the children of the wicked one; The enemy that sowed them is the devil; the harvest is the end of the world; and the reapers are the angels" (Matt. 13:38–39). This is the judgment at the end of the age. Angels are not connected in any way to the Rapture. This is the judgment that is coming that is in mind here. "Behold my servant, whom I uphold; mine elect, in whom my soul delighteth; I have put my spirit upon him: he shall bring forth judgment to the Gentiles" (Isa. 42:1).

THE HOLY SEASON OF TRUMPETS

And the LORD spake unto Moses, saying,

Speak unto the children of Israel, saying, In the seventh month, in the first day of the month, shall ye have a sabbath, a memorial of blowing of trumpets, an holy convocation.

Ye shall do no servile work therein; but ye shall offer an offering made by fire unto the LORD [Lev. 23:23–25].

The date here is important. Three feasts take place in the seventh month. It is sort of a sabbatic month, just as there is a sabbatic day and a sabbatic year. This marked the beginning of the civil year as Passover marked the beginning of the religious year.

The blowing of two silver trumpets were used in moving Israel through the wilderness (Num. 10). The trumpets were blown seven times to get them on the march. There are seven trumpets in the Revelation which cover the great tribulation period and which will see Israel restored to the land for the kingdom age. "And it shall come to pass in that day, that the great trumpet shall be blown, and they shall come which were ready to perish in the land of Assyria, and the outcasts in the land of Egypt, and shall worship the LORD in the holy mount at Jerusalem" (Isa. 27:13). "And he shall send his angels with a great sound of a trumpet, and they shall gather together his elect from the four winds, from one end of heaven to the other" (Matt. 24:31).

Before the restoration of Israel the church will have left the earth already. They will hear the voice of the Lord like a trumpet. These are now the people left on earth who will hear the sound of the trumpet.

"Blessed is the people that know the joyful sound: they shall walk, O LORD, in the light of thy countenance" (Ps. 89:15).

The trumpets are connected with the coming judgment.

THE HOLY SEASON OF
THE GREAT DAY OF ATONEMENT

And the LORD spake unto Moses, saying,

Also on the tenth day of this seventh month there shall be a day of atonement: it shall be an holy convocation unto you; and ye shall afflict your souls, and offer an offering made by fire unto the LORD.

And ye shall do no work in that same day: for it is a day of atonement, to make an atonement for you before the LORD your God.

For whatsoever soul it be that shall not be afflicted in that same day, he shall be cut off from among his people.

And whatsoever soul it be that doeth any work in that same day, the same soul will I destroy from among his people.

Ye shall do no manner of work: it shall be a statute for ever throughout your generations in all your dwellings.

It shall be unto you a sabbath of rest, and ye shall afflict your souls: in the ninth day of the month at even, from even unto even, shall ye celebrate your sabbath [Lev. 23:26–32].

The great Day of Atonement was fully covered in chapter 16. Three times Scripture says, "Ye shall afflict your souls." It was a solemn day rather than a feast day, which was different from all the others.

In contrast to this, it is interesting to note that the trumpet of Jubilee was sounded every fifty years on the Day of Atonement, and that it denoted joy and rejoicing (Lev. 25:8–9). There is deliverance when the price is paid for your salvation and mine. That is the year of Jubilee. What a glorious year that must have been!

THE HOLY SEASON OF
TABERNACLES

And the LORD spake unto Moses, saying,

Speak unto the children of Israel, saying, The fifteenth day of this seventh month shall be the feast of tabernacles for seven days unto the LORD.

On the first day shall be an holy convocation: ye shall do no servile work therein.

Seven days ye shall offer an offering made by fire unto the LORD: on the

eighth day shall be an holy convocation unto you; and ye shall offer an offering made by fire unto the LORD: it is a solemn assembly; and ye shall do no servile work therein [Lev. 23:33–36].

This is the third feast in the seventh month. It was both a memorial and a prophetic holy season. It followed the great Day of Atonement by only a few days. As a memorial, it spoke of their days of wandering in the wilderness when they dwelt in booths. It points prophetically to the time when God will have fully removed their sin, and they will dwell again safely in the Promised Land. "And I will pour upon the house of David, and upon the inhabitants of Jerusalem, the spirit of grace and of supplications: and they shall look upon me whom they have pierced, and they shall mourn for him, as one mourneth for his only son, and shall be in bitterness for him, as one that is in bitterness for his firstborn" (Zech. 12:10). "In that day there shall be a fountain opened to the house of David and to the inhabitants of Jerusalem for sin and for uncleanness" (Zech. 13:1). "But they shall sit every man under his vine and under his fig tree; and none shall make them afraid: for the mouth of the LORD of hosts hath spoken it" (Mic. 4:4).

These are the feasts of the LORD, which ye shall proclaim to be holy convocations, to offer an offering made by fire unto the LORD, a burnt offering, and a meat offering, a sacrifice, and drink offerings, every thing upon his day:

Beside the sabbaths of the LORD, and beside your gifts, and beside all your vows, and beside all your freewill offerings, which ye give unto the LORD [Lev. 23:37–38].

This is a special emphasis on the feast days to reveal in what God delights for the benefit of His people.

Also in the fifteenth day of the seventh month, when ye have gathered in the fruit of the land, ye shall keep a feast unto the LORD seven days: on the first day shall be a sabbath, and on the eighth day shall be a sabbath.

And ye shall take you on the first day the boughs of goodly trees, branches of palm trees, and the boughs of thick trees, and willows of the brook; and ye shall rejoice before the LORD your God seven days.

And ye shall keep it a feast unto the LORD seven days in the year. It shall be a statute for ever in your generations: ye shall celebrate it in the seventh month.

Ye shall dwell in booths seven days: all that are Israelites born shall dwell in booths:

That your generations may know that I made the children of Israel to dwell in booths, when I brought them out of the land of Egypt: I am the LORD your God.

And Moses declared unto the children of Israel the feasts of the LORD [Lev. 23:39–44].

After the great Day of Atonement when there was made a full expiation of their sins, and the harvest and fruit of the land were gathered in, there was observed this very joyful occasion. They were to dwell in booths to remind them of the wilderness wanderings, but also to point them to the future. Hebrews 11 tells us that they all died in faith, not having received the promises, but having seen them afar off. They were persuaded of them and they embraced them. They were looking forward to that day when they would not dwell in booths as in the wilderness, but they would be in the millennial age. That is the hope for this earth.

This holy season will be observed during the millennium: "And it shall come to pass, that every one that is left of all the nations which came against Jerusalem shall even go up from year to year to worship the King, the LORD of hosts, and to keep the feast of tabernacles. And it shall be, that whoso will not come up of all the families of the earth unto Jerusalem to worship the King, the LORD of hosts, even upon them shall be no rain. And if the family of Egypt go not up, and come not, that have no rain; there shall be the plague, wherewith the LORD will smite the heathen that come not up to keep the feast of tabernacles" (Zech. 14:16–18). You will find it interesting to read that whole chapter of Zechariah 14.

This feast is not only prophetic of the millennium, but also points to eternity and the everlasting kingdom. "And I heard a great voice out of heaven saying, Behold, the tabernacle of God is with men, and he will dwell with them, and they shall be his people, and God himself shall be with them, and be their God" (Rev. 21:3). This is the fulfillment of the great feast of Tabernacles. For seven days in the seventh month they were to rejoice. This speaks of the final and full rejoicing of God's earthly people. (His heavenly people will be with Him in the New Jerusalem.) Friends, there is a great future ahead for us!

CHAPTER 24

THEME: Olive oil for the golden lampstand; fine flour for the table of showbread; death penalty for the sin of blasphemy

This chapter seems to be out of place with what has gone before. The items in this chapter seem to be disconnected. The oil for the lampstand and the bread for the table do not seem to belong between the Feast of Tabernacles and the Sabbatic year. Nevertheless, this is the method the Holy Spirit uses on another occasion. In Numbers 8:1–4 there are the instructions for lighting the lights, and a brief description is inserted between the gifts of the princes and the cleansing of the Levites. I think it teaches that all is to be done in the light and leading of the Holy Spirit. The same lesson is to be drawn here. The celebrations of the feasts and the observances of the Sabbatic and Jubilee years must be performed in the light of the Holy Spirit and in the strength and power of Christ. That is very important.

There are some practical implications which must not be overlooked. The people were to furnish the oil for the lampstand and the fine flour for the bread on the table. God made them participants in the provision and worship of the tabernacle. God, by some miracle, could have furnished the oil and the flour and the workmanship for the table and the lampstand. However, He wanted the people to participate.

That is the way I feel about getting out the Word of God. In every local congregation there are ways for you to get involved in the work of the Lord. Just keep your eyes open and you will notice something to do. I remember when I was teaching a little Bible study to a Boy Scout troop. I doubt whether any one of those boys ever did a good deed—they almost put me in the hospital! I really had to be stern with them. A couple of men from the church came in one night and saw what a problem I had with those boys. So they volunteered their help. It was wonderful to have them sit with the boys while I taught the Bible study.

All those who love the Word of God should get involved in getting the message to people.

God says, "You bring the oil; you bring the flour."

The importance of the lampstand cannot be overlooked. It was probably the most accurate and beautiful picture of Christ in all the tabernacle. It was solid gold and beautifully wrought into seven branches of almond boughs from one main stem.

Aaron had sole charge of the lights of the lampstand to keep them burning (Exod. 30:7–8). It is important to see that today the lamps are in the hands of our Great High Priest. Jesus Christ has said that He is the Light of the world. Before He left, He told His own that they were to be the light of the world. Paul uses this same idea when he says, ". . . among whom ye shine as lights in the world" (Phil. 2:15). In Revelation 1 and 2, the Lord Jesus Christ as our Great High Priest walks in the midst of the lampstands today to keep us shining. He pours in the oil which is the filling with the Holy Spirit. He trims the wicks so that the light will burn brighter. He removes the light when it refuses to burn—this is the sin unto death which John mentions in his epistle.

Therefore the insertion of the lampstand and the showbread in this section is not out of place.

The second incident in the book of Leviticus is found in this chapter. The son of an Israelitish mother and an Egyptian father blasphemed. This is another example of the problem and difficulty presented by the mixed multitude that came out of Egypt with Israel. They were problem children and troublemakers. They correspond to those in the church today who are torn between the world on one hand and serving God on the other.

OLIVE OIL
FOR THE GOLDEN LAMPSTAND

And the LORD spake unto Moses, saying.

Command the children of Israel, that they bring unto thee pure oil olive beaten for the light, to cause the lamps to burn continually [Lev. 24:1–2].

The people of Israel were to furnish the olive oil, and since the seven lamps burned continually, both day and night, this was no small item. This gave each Israelite, as well as the tribe of Levi, an interest in the service of the tabernacle. The olive oil was to be pure, free from leaves and all impurities. It was not to be pressed out, but beaten out, to produce the very finest grade. The best was to be used, for the oil speaks of the Holy Spirit.

Without the veil of the testimony, in the tabernacle of the congregation, shall Aaron order it from the evening unto the morning before the Lord continually: it shall be a statute for ever in your generations.

He shall order the lamps upon the pure candlestick before the Lord continually [Lev. 24:3–4].

The lamps were to be kept lit continually while the tabernacle was set up. (Obviously, when they marched in the wilderness, they did not hold up lighted candlesticks.) And we note that Aaron alone controlled the use and the service of the lampstand. "And Aaron shall burn thereon sweet incense every morning: when he dresseth the lamps, he shall burn incense upon it. And when Aaron lighteth the lamps at even, he shall burn incense upon it, a perpetual incense before the Lord throughout your generations" (Exod. 30:7–8).

The Lord Jesus Christ is walking in the midst of the lampstands today. He is our Great High Priest. He trims them every now and then as He moves into our hearts and lives. Sometimes He must snuff out a light that is giving off smoke instead of light.

FINE FLOUR
FOR THE TABLE OF SHOWBREAD

And thou shalt take fine bread, and bake twelve cakes thereof: two tenth deals shall be in one cake.

And thou shalt set them in two rows, six on a row, upon the pure table before the Lord.

And thou shalt put pure frankincense upon each row, that it may be on the bread for a memorial even an offering

made by fire unto the Lord [Lev. 24: 5–7].

The fine flour was to be furnished by the people, as was the olive oil. As the oil speaks of the Holy Spirit, so the bread speaks of Christ. "And Jesus said unto them, I am the bread of life: he that cometh to me shall never hunger; and he that believeth on me shall never thirst" (John 6:35).

Fine flour means it was of wheat. The frankincense was a natural gum to be a gift from the people. The bread speaks of Christ, and the frankincense speaks of the wonderful fragrance of His humanity.

Every sabbath he shall set it in order before the Lord continually, being taken from the children of Israel by an everlasting covenant.

And it shall be Aaron's and his sons'; and they shall eat it in the holy place: for it is most holy unto him of the offerings of the Lord made by fire by a perpetual statute [Lev. 24:8–9].

The bread would stay on the table for a week. It was to be changed on the Sabbath, and the old bread was to be eaten by Aaron and his sons—and always in the Holy Place. When David and his men were in desperate need, Ahimelech gave him some of the showbread to eat (1 Sam. 21:4–6). Our Lord calls attention to this when they criticized His disciples for eating grain on the Sabbath day (Matt. 12:3–4).

The bread and the light speak of Christ. "I am the living bread which came down from heaven: if any man eat of this bread, he shall live for ever: and the bread that I will give is my flesh, which I will give for the life of the world" (John 6:51). "Then spake Jesus again unto them, saying, I am the light of the world: he that followeth me shall not walk in darkness, but shall have the light of life" (John 8:12).

We must feed on Him if we are to serve Him. And anything we do for Him must be done in His light through the Holy Spirit.

DEATH PENALTY
FOR THE SIN OF BLASPHEMY

There are only two incidents or episodes recorded in the book of Leviticus. One is the incident of Nadab and Abihu back in Leviticus 10, and now we come to this incident. It seems entirely out of keeping with the instructions given here, but we need to recognize the fact that God is teaching a great lesson concerning blasphemy.

And the son of an Israelitish woman, whose father was an Egyptian, went out among the children of Israel: and this son of the Israelitish woman and a man of Israel strove together in the camp;

And the Israelitish woman's son blasphemed the name of the LORD, and cursed. And they brought him unto Moses: (and his mother's name was Shelomith, the daughter of Dibri, of the tribe of Dan:)

And they put him in ward, that the mind of the LORD might be shewed them [Lev. 24:10–12].

This boy who did the blaspheming is a half-breed whose mother was of the tribe of Dan and whose father was an Egyptian. There was a mixed multitude that went out of Egypt along with the children of Israel (Exod. 12:38). We are going to see that this group started trouble in the camp; they would murmur and cause strife. "And the mixed multitude that was among them fell a-lusting: and the children of Israel also wept again, and said, Who shall give us flesh to eat?" (Num. 11:4).

We can see why these would be problem children, troublemakers. When the day came for the children of Israel to leave the land of Egypt and go out into the Promised Land, the Egyptian father would stay in Egypt and the Israelitish mother would go. There is a separation right there.

This is one of the reasons that God told His people then (and He tells us now) that there should not be intermarriage between a believer and an unbeliever. This does not have anything to do with race. It is wrong for a believer to marry an unbeliever regardless of the color of the skin. Even though both are the same color, it is still wrong for a believer to marry an unbeliever. *God* says that. I would never have known it is wrong if God hadn't said it.

This half-breed boy has a problem. He must make a decision whether to go the way of the father or the way of the mother. The problem is that the decision is never really made. Sure, he made an initial decision, but then in his mind the question would always reappear, *I wonder if I should have done the other thing and stayed with Dad.* This mixed multitude has an eternal question mark before them. It was a hard decision to leave Egypt in the first place. Then their thoughts constantly go back to Egypt, and when the going gets rough, they are the first to complain.

Now, friends, we have those same people in the church today. There is the unsaved person in the church who wants one foot in the church but he has the other foot out in the world. They are the troublemakers. It has always made me wonder whether the troublemaker is really a saved person. I cannot understand a really born-again believer in the Lord Jesus Christ trying to block the giving out of the Word of God. The greatest opposition I have had to my radio broadcast that gives out the Word of God, has not come from those outside the church; it has been the church members who have tried to wreck this radio program. I was never so shocked in my life. One would expect them to say, "Brother, God bless you. I hope you can get the Word of God out to people." No, my friend they didn't want to have any part in it.

Now this boy got into a fight. We can easily understand how that could come about. He did not have a place in the tribe of Dan, but was a hanger-on who had access to the camp of Israel. After he got into the fight, he blasphemed the name of God. He cursed the name of the Lord, that name which was so sacred in Israel that it was not even voiced. It evidently was the Hebrew tetragrammaton YHWH. There is even a question today about how to pronounce the name of the Lord. Is it Jehovah or Jahweh? The name is so holy that the Israelites did not even pronounce it, but this blasphemer could pronounce it!

I was invited to a private club by one of the members, and we had lunch there. A man at the table next to us used the name of God more than I have ever used it in any sermon. But He didn't use it like I use it in a sermon! He was blaspheming. And God feels no differently about him than He did about this half-breed boy in Leviticus.

And the LORD spake unto Moses, saying,

Bring forth him that hath cursed without the camp; and let all that heard him lay their hands upon his head, and let all the congregation stone him.

And thou shalt speak unto the children of Israel, saying, Whosoever curseth his God shall bear his sin.

And he that blasphemeth the name of the LORD, he shall surely be put to death, and all the congregation shall certainly stone him: as well the

stranger, as he that is born in the land, when he blasphemeth the name of the Lord, shall be put to death [Lev. 24:13–16].

God handed down His verdict of guilty, and the penalty was death by stoning. The seriousness of the crime is measured by the penalty which God inflicted. All who heard the blasphemy must place their hands on his head, denoting a placing of guilt solely on the young man. The death penalty is required for blaspheming God, and it is established that the penalty shall be paid by both the Israelite and the stranger.

And he that killeth any man shall surely be put to death.

And he that killeth a beast shall make it good; beast for beast.

And if a man cause a blemish in his neighbour; as he hath done, so shall it be done to him;

Breach for breach, eye for eye, tooth for tooth: as he hath caused a blemish in a man, so shall it be done to him again.

And he that killeth a beast, he shall restore it: and he that killeth a man, he shall be put to death.

Ye shall have one manner of law, as well for the stranger, as for one of your own country: for I am the Lord your God [Lev. 24:17–22].

We have developed some soft notions. The penalty for murdering a man is stated right here. War protesters like to print "Thou shalt not kill" on their banners. I am still waiting to see a banner that says "He that killeth any man shall surely be put to death."

There was established here what is known as *lex talionis*, an eye for an eye and a tooth for a tooth. This was the penalty which was inflicted literally. One law applied to both the Israelite and the stranger.

And Moses spake to the children of Israel, that they should bring forth him that had cursed out of the camp, and stone him with stones. And the children of Israel did as the Lord commanded Moses [Lev. 24:23].

There is a great moral lesson here. The name of our God is sacred and must be protected. Blasphemy is a crime of the deepest hue. Also, human life is sacred and must be protected. God provides also for the protection of personal property.

God is righteous in all His dealings. We, too, are guilty before God— "The soul that sinneth, it shall die." But Christ has borne our sentence of death. "Surely he hath borne our griefs, and carried our sorrows: yet we did esteem him stricken, smitten of God, and afflicted. But he was wounded for our transgressions, he was bruised for our iniquities: the chastisement of our peace was upon him; and with his stripes we are healed. All we like sheep have gone astray; we have turned every one to his own way; and the Lord hath laid on him the iniquity of us all" (Isa. 53:4–6).

CHAPTER 25

THEME: The sabbatical year; the year of Jubilee; the redemption of property; the redemption of persons

Not only was the Mosaic economy directed to the people of Israel, but it also pertained particularly to the land of Palestine. This is emphasized in this chapter. The laws given here could not be enforced until Israel entered the land of Canaan. They could not possibly be adapted to the wilderness. There is a constant and almost monotonous reference to and repetition of the word *land*— "When ye come into the land," "rest unto the land," and "proclaim liberty throughout all the land." That last phrase is found ten times. Everything in this chapter is tied down to the land which God gave Israel. The Mosaic economy was directed to a peculiar people, Israel, and to a particular land, Palestine. Furthermore, it is directed to a people engaged in agriculture.

There are those who try to saddle the Old Testament Law as a way of life upon the church. These laws don't fit in California, and they won't fit other areas of our nation. "Proclaim liberty throughout all the land" is inscribed on our Liberty Bell in Philadelphia. Yet, we need always remember that these laws were given to a particular people in a particular land.

One cannot read Leviticus, nor the rest of the Bible, without noticing the recurrence of the number *seven*. It is the number used to denote completeness. It does not mean perfection in every instance, but it denotes completeness. There is a definite connection of the many occurrences of the number seven in Leviticus with the number seven in Revelation. Both books use it in a structural way. Time was divided into sevens both for the civil and ceremonial calendars. There is the seventh day, the seventh week, the seventh month, the seventh year. The calendar was geared to sabbatic times and the Levitical code was run on wheels of seven cycles. This occurs again in Revelation.

God rested on the seventh day, not because He was tired, but because He had completed creation in six days, and there was no more to do. The Sabbath was made the basic unit of measurement of time, and then from the Sabbath there were ever-expanding units of time measurement.

THE SABBATICAL YEAR

And the Lord spake unto Moses in mount Sinai, saying [Lev. 25:1].

It should be noted that this reverts back to Mt. Sinai, but it is to be put into effect when they get into the Land. Remember that God spoke out of the tabernacle in Leviticus 1:1.

Speak unto the children of Israel, and say unto them. When ye come into the land which I give you, then shall the land keep a sabbath unto the Lord [Lev. 25:2].

This is amazing. There is a sabbath for the land as well as for man. The seventh day is for man, and the seventh year is for the land.

The seventh day hearkens back to creation when God rested from His labors, for His work of creation was complete. *Sabbath* means rest, and in its ultimate meaning it refers to the rest of redemption. "There remaineth therefore a rest to the people of God. For he that is entered into his rest, he also hath ceased from his own works, as God did from his. Let us labour therefore to enter into

that rest, lest any man fall after the same example of unbelief" (Heb. 4:9–11). *Rest* in these verses means literally "keeping of a sabbath."

It is obvious in this day of scientific agriculture that letting the land lie fallow on the seventh year was good for the land. It was also a rest for those who tilled the soil, although they could discharge other necessary duties. This Sabbatical year for the land was to deliver the Israelite from covetousness. Actually, it was the breaking of this regulation concerning the Sabbatical year that sent Israel into the seventy years Babylonian captivity (2 Chron. 36:21). They failed to keep seventy sabbatic years over a period of 490 years; so they went into captivity for seventy years.

Six years thou shalt sow thy field, and six years thou shalt prune thy vineyard, and gather in the fruit thereof;

But in the seventh year shall be a sabbath of rest unto the land, a sabbath for the Lord: thou shalt neither sow thy field, nor prune thy vineyard [Lev. 25:3–4].

This makes it perfectly clear that the Sabbatical year related to the land. They were to sow their fields and prune their vineyards for six years, and then neither sow nor prune on the seventh year. There is a curse upon the earth as well as upon man, and it is by the sweat of man's brow that he extracts bread from the soil. There will be a day when the curse shall be lifted from creation (Rom. 8:20–22 and Isa. 35:1–2).

The southland where I was reared has learned, to its sorrow, that one should let the land lie fallow. A great deal of the land has been worn out by planting cotton every year, year after year. The Sabbatical year was actually a good agricultural principle which God gave to them. It is quite interesting that God knows all about farming, isn't it?

That which groweth of its own accord of thy harvest thou shalt not reap, neither gather the grapes of thy vine undressed: for it is a year of rest unto the land.

And the sabbath of the land shall be meat for you: for thee, and for thy servant, and for thy maid, and for thy hired servant, and for thy stranger that sojourneth with thee.

And for thy cattle, and for the beast that are in thy land, shall all the increase thereof be meat [Lev. 25:5–7].

This shows how the physical needs of the people were supplied during the Sabbatical year. The land was so productive that it was not necessary to plant each year. In the Euphrates Valley, in the days of Abraham, it was not necessary to plant at all. The grain grew without planting. The ground in Israel produced enough to supply the needs of the owner, his servants, and the stranger. Even the cattle could survive and probably grew fat by grazing on the untilled land. God took care of both man and beast, Israelite and stranger, rich and poor during the year of rest. They were all given enough to eat. However, they could not harvest anything to market it.

Years ago, before all the subdivisions were built, there were many fine vineyards near Pasadena. I had a very fine neighbor who had a wonderful vineyard of Concord grapes. He was a generous man and he would always bring me a basket or two during the season. He was a Seventh Day Adventist and at times he would try to goad me about the Sabbath day. He would ask me why I didn't keep the Sabbath day. I would tell him that I did keep the Sabbath day—on Saturday and on Sunday and on Monday and on Tuesday and every day of the week. I tried to explain to him that *sabbath* means rest and that we have entered into the rest of redemption. We have ceased from works and put our trust in Jesus Christ which makes every day a day of rest, a rest in Jesus Christ. Of course, he didn't like it that way. Then I would ask him a question. "Are you keeping the Mosaic Law? Are you keeping the Sabbath as they did in Israel?" He assured me that he was. Then I showed him chapter 25 of Leviticus. I told him there was not a Sabbath day only, but there was also a Sabbatical year. In that year the poor people could go into the vineyard and glean grapes. I asked him to let me know when he would observe that Sabbatical year so I could get my basket and glean some of his grapes. He answered, "You'd better not go into that vineyard without my permission!" May I say to you, he was not keeping the Mosaic Law. He was keeping only a small part of it. He did not keep the Sabbatical year nor the year of Jubilee.

God was teaching Israel several lessons. He never permitted any one of them to monopolize the land so that the poor people were not taken care of. God was protecting the land and the poor people at the same time. Also He was teaching them that the land was cursed but that the time would come when the land would produce in abundance.

Today, people worry about the population explosion and the inability of the earth to produce enough food for the people. When the curse is removed, my friend, this earth will produce in a way never seen since the fall of man. God is the supplier of all human needs. God is the owner of this earth.

THE YEAR OF JUBILEE

And thou shalt number seven sabbaths of years unto thee, seven times seven years; and the space of the seven sabbaths of years shall be unto thee forty and nine years [Lev. 25:8].

This continues in the multiples of seven. Seven Sabbatical years were numbered and this made forty-nine years. Then, the following year, the fiftieth, was set aside as the year of Jubilee. The year of Jubilee was a continuing of the number seven to the ever-ascending scale of the calendar. It was the largest unit of time—fifty years.

Today we operate by leases. People may have a fifty-year lease or a ninety-nine-year lease. God worked on that basis, also. There were two years of Jubilee in every century.

Then shalt thou cause the trumpet of the jubile to sound on the tenth day of the seventh month, in the day of atonement shall ye make the trumpet sound throughout all your land [Lev. 25:9].

This was the crowning point of the entire sabbatical structure of the nation. It was the *SHeNATH HAYOBHEL*, the year of Jubilee. In many respects it was the most anticipated and joyful period of the Mosaic economy. The *KEREN HAYOBHEL* meant the horn of a ram, and in the time the *YOBHEL* came to mean trumpet. It is translated twenty-one times as "jubilee," five times as "ram's horn," and once as "trumpet."

After Israel was settled in the land, it is difficult to see how one blast of the trumpet could be heard from Dan to Beersheba. It is reasonable to conclude that in every populated area there was a simultaneous blowing of the ram's horn to usher in the year of Jubilee. I think it would begin at the tabernacle or temple. There would be a person stationed far enough away to be able to hear it, and then the trumpet note would be passed on and on out to the very end of the land.

And ye shall hallow the fiftieth year, and proclaim liberty throughout all the land unto all the inhabitants thereof: it

shall be a jubile unto you; and ye shall return every man unto his possession, and ye shall return every man unto his family [Lev. 25:10].

In that day people could mortgage their land, but in the year of Jubilee that land would return back to the original owner. This was the way God protected the land from leaving the original owner. The land could be taken away for a period of fifty years, but in the year of Jubilee the land went back to the original owner or to his descendants.

If a man had sold himself into slavery, when that trumpet was sounded he went free. The shackles were broken.

This is how we are freed today. The Greek word for trumpet is *kerux* and the verb *kerusso* means to proclaim or to herald. The year of Jubilee is likened to this age of grace when the Gospel is preached to slaves of sin and captives of Satan. "But God be thanked, that ye were the servants of sin, but ye have obeyed from the heart that form of doctrine which was delivered you. Being then made free from sin, ye became the servants of righteousness. For the wages of sin is death; but the gift of God is eternal life through Jesus Christ our Lord" (Rom. 6:17–18, 23). The Lord Jesus Christ said, "And ye shall know the truth, and the truth shall make you free. . . . If the Son therefore shall make you free, ye shall be free indeed" (John 8:32, 36).

In the year of Jubilee everything went free. All mortgages were canceled. When you come to Jesus Christ, my friend, the sin question is settled. He paid the penalty. It is all settled, and you go free. He makes you free! "But now being made free from sin, and become servants to God, ye have your fruit unto holiness, and the end everlasting life" (Rom. 6:22). "Stand fast therefore in the liberty wherewith Christ hath made us free, and be not entangled again with the yoke of bondage" (Gal. 5:1).

In this connection it is interesting to note the words of our Lord in the synagogue at Nazareth: "And there was delivered unto him the book of the prophet Esaias. And when he had opened the book, he found the place where it was written, The Spirit of the Lord is upon me, because he hath anointed me to preach the gospel to the poor; he hath sent me to heal the brokenhearted, to preach deliverance to the captives, and recovering of sight to the blind, to set at liberty them that are bruised, To preach the acceptable year of the Lord. And he closed the book, and he gave it again to the minister, and sat down. And the eyes of all them that were in the synagogue were fastened on him. And he began to say unto them, This day is this scripture fulfilled in your ears" (Luke 4:17–21).

"To preach the gospel to the poor" is to herald it, to trumpet it. Isn't this the year of Jubilee—to heal the brokenhearted, to preach deliverance to the captives, to set at liberty them that are bruised?

Possibly the best application and final fulfillment of the year of Jubilee will be in the Millennium as it relates directly to the nation Israel. I would encourage you to read Isaiah 11, 35 and 40, Jeremiah 23, Micah 4, and Revelation 20.

A jubile, shall that fiftieth year be unto you: ye shall not sow, neither reap that which groweth of itself in it, nor gather the grapes in it of thy vine undressed.

For it is the jubile; it shall be holy unto you: ye shall eat the increase thereof out of the field [Lev. 25:11–12].

The year of Jubilee followed a Sabbatical year when the land lay fallow. God promised to provide providentially for them. They were to obey. God would provide.

In the year of this jubile ye shall return every man unto his possession.

And if thou sell aught unto thy neighbour, or buyest aught of thy neighbour's hand, ye shall not oppress one another:

According to the number of years after the jubile thou shalt buy of thy neighbour, and according unto the number of years of the fruits he shall sell unto thee:

According to the multitude of years thou shalt increase the price thereof, and according to the fewness of years thou shalt diminish the price of it: for according to the number of the years of the fruits doth he sell unto thee.

Ye shall not therefore oppress one another; but thou shalt fear thy God: for I am the LORD your God.

Wherefore ye shall do my statutes, and keep my judgments, and do them; and ye shall dwell in the land in safety.

And the land shall yield her fruit, and ye shall eat your fill, and dwell therein in safety.

And if ye shall say, What shall we eat the seventh year? behold, we shall not sow, nor gather in our increase:

Then I will command my blessing upon you in the sixth year, and it shall bring forth fruit for three years.

And ye shall sow the eighth year, and eat yet of old fruit until the ninth year; until her fruits come in ye shall eat of the old store.

The land shall not be sold for ever: for the land is mine; for ye are strangers and sojourners with me.

And in all the land of your possession ye shall grant a redemption for the land [Lev. 25:13–24].

This section explains that all property and possessions were to be returned to the original owner. This prevented any one individual or group from getting possession of most of the land while the rest became extremely poor. It preserved a balance in Israel. This was not a choice between communism and capitalism, but it was God's plan. He retained ownership of the land and Israel held it in perpetuity.

God promised His blessing upon them. He promised to bless the land in the sixth year. They would sow again on the eighth year and they would eat of the old fruit of the land until the ninth year when it would produce again. God makes it very clear to them in verse 23: "The land shall not be sold for ever: for the land is mine."

THE REDEMPTION OF PROPERTY

If thy brother be waxen poor, and hath sold away some of his possession, and if any of his kin come to redeem it, then shall he redeem that which his brother sold.

And if the man have none to redeem it, and himself be able to redeem it;

Then let him count the years of the sale thereof, and restore the overplus unto the man to whom he sold it; that he may return unto his possession [Lev. 25:25–27].

It was a long time from one year of Jubilee to the next. If a man lost his property shortly after a Jubilee, there was the possibility he would not be alive to enjoy it the next time a year of Jubilee came around. So God made another provision for the recovery of the land. If there was a rich relative, he was able to redeem the property if he was willing to do so, and then the land could be restored to the original owner. It depended on the willingness of the kinsman. This is the law of the kinsman-redeemer which we will see in operation in the Book of Ruth.

But if he be not able to restore it to him, then that which is sold shall remain in the hand of him that hath bought it until the year of jubile: and in the jubile it shall go out, and he shall return unto his possession.

And if a man sell a dwelling house in a walled city, then he may redeem it within a whole year after it is sold; within a full year may he redeem it.

And if it be not redeemed within the space of a full year, then the house that is in the walled city shall be established for ever to him that bought it throughout his generations: it shall not go out in the jubile.

But the houses of the villages which have no wall round about them shall be counted as the fields of the country: they may be redeemed, and they shall go out in the jubile.

Notwithstanding the cities of the Levites, and the houses of the cities of their possession, may the Levites redeem at any time.

And if a man purchase of the Levites, then the house that was sold, and the city of his possession, shall go out in the year of jubile: for the houses of the cities of the Levites are their possession among the children of Israel.

But the field of the suburbs of their cities may not be sold; for it is their perpetual possession [Lev. 25:28–34].

Laws were also made concerning dwellings and buildings on property. Depreciation was taken into consideration. There were different rules applying to the Levites.

THE REDEMPTION OF PERSONS

And if thy brother be waxen poor, and fallen in decay with thee; then thou shalt relieve him: yea, though he be a stranger, or a sojourner; that he may live with thee.

Take thou no usury of him, or increase: but fear thy God; that thy brother may live with thee.

Thou shalt not give him thy money upon usury, nor lend him thy victuals for increase.

God was explicit about the care of unfortunate folk. They were to be helped; they were not to be taken advantage of.

I am the LORD your God, which brought you forth out of the land of Egypt, to give you the land of Canaan, and to be your God.

And if thy brother that dwelleth by thee be waxen poor, and be sold unto thee; thou shalt not compel him to serve as a bondservant:

But as an hired servant, and as a sojourner, he shall be with thee, and shall serve thee unto the year of jubile:

And then shall he depart from thee, both he and his children with him, and shall return unto his own family, and unto the possession of his fathers shall he return.

For they are my servants, which I brought forth out of the land of Egypt: they shall not be sold as bondmen.

Thou shalt not rule over him with rigour; but shalt fear thy God.

Both thy bondmen, and thy bondmaids, which thou shalt have, shall be of the heathen that are round about you; of them shall ye buy bondmen and bondmaids.

Moreover, of the children of the strangers that do sojourn among you, of them shall ye buy, and of their families that are with you, which they begat in your land: and they shall be your possession.

And ye shall take them as an inheritance for your children after you, to inherit them for a possession; they shall be your bondmen for ever: but over your brethren the children of Israel, ye shall not rule one over another with rigour [Lev. 25:38–46].

The poor brother who probably had a low I.Q. was to be protected from becoming a slave. He was to be treated as a hired servant, not as a slave. They were permitted to have only foreigners as slaves—which was a great step forward in a world of slavery. It is the adaption of the Mosaic Law to the mores of that day.

And if a sojourner or stranger wax rich by thee, and thy brother that dwelleth by him wax poor, and sell himself unto the stranger or sojourner by thee, or to the stock of the stranger's family:

After that he is sold he may be redeemed again; one of his brethren may redeem him:

Either his uncle, or his uncle's son, may redeem him, or any that is nigh of kin unto him of his family may redeem him; or if he be able, he may redeem himself.

And he shall reckon with him that bought him from the year that he was sold to him unto the year of jubile: and the price of his sale shall be according unto the number of years, according to the time of a hired servant shall it be with him.

If there be yet many years behind, according unto them he shall give again the price of his redemption out of the money that he was bought for.

And if there remain but few years unto the year of jubile, then he shall count with him, and according unto his years shall he give him again the price of his redemption.

And as a yearly hired servant shall he be with him: and the other shall not rule with rigour over him in thy sight.

And if he be not redeemed in these years, then he shall go out in the year of jubile, both he, and his children with him.

For unto me the children of Israel are servants; they are my servants whom I brought forth out of the land of Egypt: I am the LORD your God [Lev. 25:47–55].

This is the application of the law of Jubilee to the person (see verse 10) who not only had lost his property, but had to sell his person as well. He could have the services of a kinsman-redeemer if there was one who was willing and able to deliver him before the year of Jubilee.

You and I have a Kinsman-Redeemer. He is rich. Yet, for our sakes He was willing to become poor so that He might shed His precious blood to redeem us. He has redeemed not only our persons but He has also paid the price for this cursed earth. It too will be redeemed from the curse that is on it now. The law of the kinsman-redeemer points to our Lord Jesus Christ who is our Kinsman-Redeemer.

CHAPTER 26

THEME: *Prologue to Israel's Magna Charta of the land; promise of blessing; pronouncement of judgment; prediction predicated on promise to patriarchs*

This is a marvelous chapter. It is a prophetic history that covers Israel's entire tenure of the Promised Land until the present hour and gives the conditions in the future on which they will occupy the land.

This section stands in a peculiar relationship to the remainder of the book of Leviticus. There are not great spiritual lessons and pictures here, but this is the direct word of Jehovah to the nation Israel concerning their future. This is history prewritten and reveals the basis on which Israel entered the land of Canaan and their tenancy there.

This is an "iffy" chapter. "If" occurs nine times and it has to do with the conditions on which they occupy the land. God says "I will" twenty-four times. God will act and react according to their response to the "if." God gave them the land, but their occupancy of it is determined by their answer to the "if." Obedience is the ground of blessing in the land. This chapter is not only the calendar of their history, but it serves as the barometer of their blessings. Their presence in the land, rainfall, and bountiful crops denote the favor of God. Their absence from the land, famine, and drought denote the judgment of God because of their disobedience.

You and I are blessed with all spiritual blessings in the heavenlies in Christ Jesus. However there are some "ifs" connected to that also. God loves you and wants to shower you with His blessings. But you can put up an umbrella of indifference, you can put up an umbrella of sin, you can put up an umbrella of stepping out of the will of God. When you do that, the sunshine of His love won't get through to you. You must put down your umbrella to experience His spiritual blessings.

PROLOGUE TO ISRAEL'S MAGNA CHARTA OF THE LAND

Ye shall make you no idols nor graven image, neither rear you up a standing image, neither shall ye set up any image of stone in your land, to bow down unto it: for I am the Lord your God.

Ye shall keep my sabbaths, and reverence my sanctuary: I am the Lord [Lev. 26:1–2].

These two verses sum up the first part of the Ten Commandments, man's relationship with God. These are essential for Israel to maintain residence in the land. They are to meet these injunctions if they are to occupy that land. The land is given to them, but their enjoyment of it, their occupation of it, depends upon their obedience to God.

1. They are to make no idols.

The Hebrew word for an idol *(elilim)* means a "nothing." They shall make no *nothings*. It's pretty hard to make a *nothing*, friends, and yet there are a great many folk who make a *nothing* of their relationship to God. Anything that takes the place of God is a *nothing*.

The word given for graven images means a carved wooden image. And the word for the image of stone means sculptured stone idols. The people were not to worship an image, nor even worship before an image. This is a repetition of what had already been told the people back in Leviticus 19:30.

2. Keep the Sabbaths.

3. Reverence the Sanctuary.

The Sabbath, the Sanctuary, and this matter of worshiping God, all come in one package. The character of Jehovah is the basis for obeying these injunctions. "I am the Lord."

PROMISE OF BLESSING

If ye walk in my statutes, and keep my commandments, and do them;

Then I will give you rain in due season, and the land shall yield her increase, and the trees of the field shall yield their fruit.

And your threshing shall reach unto the vintage, and the vintage shall reach unto the sowing time: and ye shall eat your bread to the full, and dwell in your land safely.

And I will give peace in the land, and ye shall lie down, and none shall make you afraid: and I will rid evil beasts out of the land, neither shall the sword go through your land [Lev. 26:3–6].

You notice this starts with an "if." *If* they walk in the prescribed manner, then God promised these things. Their occupancy of the land is contingent upon the obedience to God's revealed will to them. God recognizes their free will. *If* you will obey, then God will bless.

It seems that in that land the primary evidence of the blessing of God in response to their obedience is rainfall. We find this repeated in Deuteronomy and in the prophets. "And I will make them and the places round about my hill a blessing; and I will cause the shower to come down in his season; there shall be showers of blessing. And the tree of the field shall yield her fruit, and the earth shall yield her increase, and they shall be safe in their land, and shall know that I am the LORD . . ." (Ezek. 34:26–27).

The prophets look forward to the day when this will be accomplished in Israel. It is a day yet to come. "Behold, the days come, saith the LORD, that the plowman shall overtake the reaper, and the treader of grapes him that soweth seed; and the mountains shall drop sweet wine, and all the hills shall melt" (Amos 9:13). "Be glad then, ye children of Zion, and rejoice in the LORD your God: for he hath given you the former rain moderately, and he will cause to come down for you the rain, the former rain, and the latter rain in the first month. And the floors shall be full of wheat, and the vats shall overflow with wine and oil" (Joel 2:23–24).

God's promise to them is the occupation of that land, showers, fruitfulness, peace. It's interesting that that little nation can't have peace today. It's no use for us to point our finger at them because the rest of us can't have peace either. It's all tied up in one little word "if." God has promised to bless *if* certain things are done.

And ye shall chase your enemies, and they shall fall before you by the word.

And five of you shall chase an hundred, and an hundred of you shall put ten thousand to flight: and your enemies shall fall before you by the sword [Lev. 26:7–8].

Victory over their enemies would be a part of their blessing. Many times this was literally fulfilled, as you know. When they would return to God, God would raise up a Samuel, a David, a Deborah, a Gideon, or an Elijah. All these were raised up because God was making good His promise. They would be victorious over their enemies as part of their blessing. "One man of you shall chase a thousand: for the LORD your God, he it is that fighteth for you, as he hath promised you" (Josh. 23:10).

For I will have respect unto you, and make you fruitful, and multiply you, and establish my covenant with you.

And ye shall eat old store, and bring forth the old because of the new [Lev. 26:9–10].

A population explosion in Israel would be part of the blessing. Today the world doesn't think that is a blessing at all. The increase in the population would not present the problem of food shortage because the food would be so multiplied that they would have to remove the old to make room for the new.

And I will set my tabernacle among you: and my soul shall not abhor you [Lev. 26:11].

Don't tell me that God does not abhor sin. Of course He does. And He will not compromise with it in your life or my life. The tabernacle in their midst was an evident token of blessing. This is the great hope of the future which will be fulfilled finally for the eternal earth.

"And I heard a great voice out of heaven saying, Behold, the tabernacle of God is with men, and he will dwell with them, and they shall be his people, and God himself shall be with them, and be their God" (Rev. 21:3).

And I will walk among you, and will be your God, and ye shall be my people [Lev. 26:12].

God promises to fellowship with those who obey Him. That is also what He tells us today.

". . . if we walk in the light, as he is in the light, we have fellowship one with another, and the blood of Jesus Christ his Son cleanseth us from all sin" (1 John 1:7). God wants to have fellowship with us. "And what agreement hath the temple of God with idols? for ye are the temple of the living God; as God hath said, I will dwell in them, and walk in them; and I will be their God, and they shall be my people" (2 Cor. 6:16).

I am the Lord your God, which brought you forth out of the land of Egypt, that ye should not be their bondmen; and I have broken the bands of your yoke, and made you go upright [Lev. 26:13].

The future promise of blessing rests upon the solid history of the past when God delivered them from Egypt. He is saying to them, "I have done this for you in the past; don't you know I will do it for you in the future?" He tells us the same thing today. "Being confident of this very thing, that he which hath begun a good work in you will perform it until the day of Jesus Christ" (Phil. 1:6). You can be confident that since He has brought you up to this moment, He is going to lead you right through to the day of Jesus Christ. I'll say a *Hallelujah* to that!

PRONOUNCEMENT OF JUDGMENT

But if ye will not hearken unto me, and will not do all these commandments;

And if ye shall despise my statutes, or if your soul abhor my judgments, so that ye will not do all my commandments, but that ye break my covenant [Lev. 26:14–15].

L isten to His three "ifs" in these two verses. These are the "ifs" of a breach of the covenant: refusal to hear, refusal to do, despising and abhorring God's statutes and judgments. Breaking God's covenant would bring judgment upon the people and the land.

I also will do this unto you; I will even appoint over you terror, consumption, and the burning ague, that shall consume the eyes, and cause sorrow of heart; and ye shall sow your seed in vain, for your enemies shall eat it.

And I will set my face against you, and ye shall be slain before your enemies: they that hate you shall reign over you; and ye shall flee when none pursueth you [Lev. 26:16–17].

This is the first degree judgment—terror, consumption, burning ague, sorrow of heart, and crop failure. Their enemies will slay them, enslave them, and cause them great fear. This happened often in their sad and sordid history. We read that the anger of the Lord waxed hot against Israel, and He delivered them into the hands of spoilers who spoiled them (Judg. 2:14, 3:8, and 4:2).

What the prophets did in their messages was call their attention to the fact that they had broken the covenant which God had made with them. "And they shall eat up thine harvest, and thy bread, which thy sons and thy daughters should eat . . ." (Jer. 5:17). "Thou shalt sow, but thou shalt not reap; thou shalt tread the olives, but thou shalt not anoint thee with oil; and sweet wine, but shalt not drink wine" (Mic. 6:15).

And if ye will not yet for all this hearken unto me, then I will punish you seven times more for your sins.

And I will break the pride of your power; and I will make your heaven as iron, and your earth as brass:

And your strength shall be spent in vain: for your land shall not yield her increase, neither shall the trees of the land yield their fruits [Lev. 26:18–20].

This is the second degree of judgment. If they were obdurate and continual in their disobedience, then God would judge them seven times, which indicates a complete and absolute judgment. Their pride would be broken. There would be no rain; there would be continual crop failure.

And if ye walk contrary unto me, and will not hearken unto me; I will bring seven times more plagues upon you according to your sins.

I will also send wild beasts among you, which shall rob you of your children, and destroy your cattle, and make you few in number; and your high ways shall be desolate [Lev. 26:21–22].

This is the third degree judgment. Plagues and wild beasts will decimate the population. All of this came upon them. Read in Judges where they travelled on the byways while the highways were unoccupied. Man has lost his dominion over nature.

And if ye will not be reformed by me by these things, but will walk contrary unto me;

Then will I also walk contrary unto you, and will punish you yet seven times for your sins.

And I will bring a sword upon you, that shall avenge the quarrel of my covenant: and when ye are gathered together within your cities, I will send the pestilence among you; and ye shall be delivered into the hand of the enemy.

And when I have broken the staff of your bread, ten women shall bake your bread in one oven, and they shall deliver you your bread again by weight: and ye shall eat and not be satisfied [Lev. 26:23–26].

This is the fourth degree judgment. Notice the repetition of the number seven, which indicates completeness. The enemy will breach their defenses, and the pestilence will strike the people. Captivity would be the end result.

Ezekiel warned them that a third part would die of the pestilence and with famine, a third part would fall by the sword, and a third part would be scattered (Ezek. 5:12). Isaiah, Jeremiah and Ezekiel all warned them of famine which would overtake them. It all happened.

This will take place again at the time of the Great Tribulation, as we find it in the sixth chapter of the Book of Revelation.

And if ye will not for all this hearken unto me, but walk contrary unto me;

Then I will walk contrary unto you also in fury; and I, even I, will chastise you seven times for your sins.

And ye shall eat the flesh of your sons, and the flesh of your daughters shall ye eat [Lev. 26:27–29].

This seems terribly harsh, and one would think it could never come to pass. But it did.

And I will destroy your high places, and cut down your images, and cast your carcases upon the carcases of your idols, and my soul shall abhor you.

And I will make your cities waste, and bring your sanctuaries unto desolation, and I will not smell the savour of your sweet odours.

And I will bring the land into desolation: and your enemies which dwell therein shall be astonished at it.

And I will scatter you among the heathen, and will draw out a sword after you: and your land shall be desolate, and your cities waste [Lev. 26:30–33].

This is the fifth degree judgment, and it is extreme. It was the result of warfare in the siege of the cities. This was fulfilled in the siege of Samaria (2 Kings 6:28–29), and again in the siege of Jerusalem by the Babylonians under Nebuchadnezzar (Lam. 2:20 and 4:10), and again when Titus the Roman attacked Jerusalem in A.D. 70. Verse 33 is a picture of the land as it stood for 1900 years. God does what He says He will do.

Then shall the land enjoy her sabbaths, as long as it lieth desolate, and ye be in your enemies' land; even then shall the land rest, and enjoy her sabbaths.

As long as it lieth desolate it shall rest; because it did not rest in your sabbaths, when ye dwelt upon it [Lev. 26:34–35].

Here is the reason they went into the Babylonian captivity. During 490 years Israel failed to give the land its sabbaths. That means the land missed seventy sabbath years. The people of Israel thought they were getting by with it, but finally God said it was enough. If they wouldn't give the land its sabbaths, God would. So He put them out of the land for seventy years. How accurate God is! This is why the Babylonian captivity lasted seventy years (2 Chron. 36:21).

And upon them that are left alive of you I will send a faintness into their hearts in the lands of their enemies; and the sound of a shaken leaf shall chase them; and they shall flee, as fleeing from a sword; and they shall fall when none pursueth.

And they shall fall one upon another, as it were before a sword, when none pursueth: and ye shall have no power to stand before your enemies.

And ye shall perish among the heathen, and the land of your enemies shall eat you up.

And they that are left of you shall pine away in their iniquity in your enemies' lands; and also in the iniquities of their fathers shall they pine away with them [Lev. 26:36–39].

This is an accurate prophetic portrayal of the Jew since the days of the Babylonian captivity, as he has been scattered among the nations. Wave after wave of anti-Semitism has descended upon him to destroy him. This section is a striking picture of the Nazi anti-Semitic movement. You can see that this Book of Leviticus is up-to-date.

PREDICTION PREDICATED ON PROMISE TO PATRIARCHS

If they shall confess their iniquity, and the iniquity of their fathers, with their trespass which they trespassed against me, and that also they have walked contrary unto me;

And that I also have walked contrary unto them, and have brought them into the land of their enemies; if then their uncircumcised hearts be humbled, and they then accept of the punishment of their iniquity:

Then will I remember my covenant with Jacob, and also my covenant with Isaac, and also my covenant with Abraham will I remember; and I will remember the land [Lev. 26:40–42].

All of their past iniquity does not destroy the fact that Israel holds the title deed to that land. This is a remarkable prophecy and one that God says He will fulfill when the time has come. God will not utterly destroy them because of His covenant with Abraham and the other patriarchs. We found in the book of Exodus that when Israel was in slavery in Egypt, God heard their groaning, God remembered His covenant with Abraham, Isaac, and Jacob, and so God delivered them out of Egypt (Exod. 2:24–25).

Now God tells them they can stay in the land if they will obey Him. If not, they must leave the land. But if they will repent and turn to God when they are out of the land, then He will bring them back into the land. So we find that Daniel turned to God in prayer when he was down in Babylon. He turned his face toward Jerusalem, he confessed his sins and the sins of his people, and when he did that, God heard. God sent a messenger to him to tell him they would return to the land. And they did return back to the land!

God still has a future purpose for the nation which the judgment of the past cannot nullify.

Read Romans 11:1–25 and Jeremiah 31:31–34 in this connection.

The land also shall be left of them, and shall enjoy her sabbaths, while she lieth desolate without them: and they shall accept of the punishment of their iniquity: because, even because they despised my judgments, and because their soul abhorred my statutes.

And yet for all that, when they be in the land of their enemies, I will not cast them away, neither will I abhor them, to destroy them utterly, and to break my covenant with them: for I am the LORD their God [Lev. 26:43–44].

This is a remarkable passage of Scripture. Can you say that God is through with the nation Israel after you have read this passage? If you believe that God means what He says, then He is not through with them at all.

But I will for their sakes remember the covenant of their ancestors, whom I brought forth out of the land of Egypt in the sight of the heathen, that I might be their God: I am the LORD.

These are the statutes and judgments and laws, which the LORD made between him and the children of Israel in mount Sinai by the hand of Moses [Lev. 26:45–46].

They brought judgment upon Palestine just as Adam brought judgment upon the whole earth by his sin. Because of God's covenant with their fathers, He will return them to the land and restore all that He had promised to them.

We have come to the end of the giving of these laws here in Leviticus. God confirms the Pentateuch here as given through Moses. This verse seems to end the book, but it doesn't.

God looks down through the ages to their repeated failures and His faithfulness and final victory. Moses could not bring them eternal blessings, although he was a mediator. The world must look to Another. John gives us the answer: "For the law was given by Moses, but grace and truth came by Jesus Christ" (John 1:17).

CHAPTER 27

THEME: Commutation of vows concerning persons; commutation of vows concerning animals; commutation of vows concerning houses; commutation of vows concerning land; concerning three things which are the Lord's apart from a vow

When you begin to read this chapter, you wonder why it is here. It seems to be an addendum or a postscript to the Book of Leviticus. All the expositors note this, and some actually consider this a major problem of the book. J. A. Seiss doesn't include it with the Book of Leviticus, and Dr. Langley treats it as an appendix. Although the subject matter seems to be extraneous and unrelated to the contents of the book, I see no reason to make a mountain out of a mole hill.

I think there is a definite purpose in placing this chapter last. Dr. S. H. Kellogg notes with real spiritual perception that what has preceded this chapter is obligatory, while this is voluntary. Actually, this makes a beautiful and fitting climax to the book of worship.

In much this same way, chapter 21 of John's Gospel follows the climax of chapter 20. In chapter 20 the risen Lord has revealed Himself to His disciples and has sent them out into the world. But wait a minute—He has a message to Simon Peter in chapter 21, "If you love Me, feed My sheep." It is voluntary, and the basis for it is love. That is God's method.

A striking feature about the vows is that they are voluntary. They follow the commandments, ceremonies, and ordinances. It is going the second mile after God has required the first mile. They are the response of a grateful heart. However, it is important to note that after a promise has been made to God, it is essential that it be fulfilled.

The natural response of a saved person is to ask what he can do for the Lord since the Lord has done so much for him. We find this expressed many times in the Scripture. "What shall I render unto the LORD for all his benefits toward me?" (Ps. 116:12). The apostle Paul wrote to the believers of his day, "I beseech you therefore, brethren, by the mercies of God, that ye present your bodies a living sacrifice, holy, acceptable unto God, which is your reasonable service" (Rom. 12:1). This is not a command. He says, "I *beseech* you." In Titus 2:11 he wrote, "For the grace of God that bringeth salvation hath appeared to all men." What does it do? Does it demand something? No. "Teaching us that, denying ungodliness and worldly lusts, we should live soberly, righteously, and godly, in this pres-

ent world" (Titus 2:12). Micah evidently had this chapter in mind when he wrote, "He hath shewed thee, O man, what is good; and what does the LORD require of thee, but to do justly, and to love mercy, and to walk humbly with thy God?" (Mic. 6:8).

Every normal believer wants to do something for God. He wants to pledge something to God. The deepest problem is to find something worthy to pledge to God. Ephraim Syrus wrote, "I pronounce my life wretched, because it is unprofitable." David Brainerd cried, "O that my soul were holy as He is holy! O that it were pure as Christ is pure, and perfect as my Father in Heaven is perfect! These are the sweetest commands in God's book, comprising all others. And shall I break them? Must I break them? Am I under a necessity of it as long as I live in the world? O my soul! woe, woe is me that I am a sinner." What can a saved sinner offer to God? This chapter answers that question.

Once a vow was made, it became mandatory. "It is a snare to the man who devoureth that which is holy, and after vows to make inquiry" (Prov. 20:25). You make the inquiry first so you know what you are doing. "When thou vowest a vow unto God, defer not to pay it; for he hath no pleasure in fools: pay that which thou hast vowed. Better is it that thou shouldest not vow, than that thou shouldest vow and not pay. Suffer not thy mouth to cause thy flesh to sin; neither say thou before the angel, that it was an error: wherefore should God be angry at thy voice, and destroy the work of thine hands?" (Eccl. 5:4–6).

There were promissory vows and there were vows of renunciation. These vows figured large in the life of the nation. Then there was the Nazarite vow which is given in detail in Numbers 6. The most notable vow is the one made by Jephthah. "And Jephthah vowed a vow unto the LORD, and said, If thou shalt without fail deliver the children of Ammon into mine hands, then it shall be, that whatsoever cometh forth of the doors of my house to meet me, when I return in peace from the children of Ammon, shall surely be the LORD's, and I will offer it up for a burnt offering" (Judg. 11:30–31). We know that God strictly forbade human sacrifice. I believe the original can also be translated, ". . . when I return in peace from the children of Ammon, shall surely be the LORD's, or I will offer up a burnt offering." Remember that it was his daughter who ran out to greet him. He did not sacrifice his daughter, but he did offer her up to the Lord. This is made clear in Judges 11:39-40: "And it came to pass at the end of two months, that she returned unto her father, who did with her according to his vow which he had vowed: and she knew no man. And it was a custom in Israel, That the daughters of Israel went yearly to lament the daughter of Jephthah the Gileadite four days in a year." In other words, she did not marry. For a Hebrew woman, this was a terrible thing. She was dedicated wholly to the Lord. Jephthah offered her to the Lord, but he did not sacrifice her by killing her.

It was a rash vow that he had made, but at least he kept it. If a vow was not kept, a trespass and sin offering must be made (Lev. 5: 4-6).

I believe that God will hold you to your vow. A great many Christians today are not keeping their vows to God. If you do not intend to keep a vow, or you think lightly about your dealing with God, then you had better take a second look at it. I think that there are many Christians who have been set aside today. There are many who are being judged and many who have fallen asleep as Paul says. Remember, God is not asking you to make a vow. It is voluntary. But if you do promise God something, be sure you go through with it. "When thou shalt vow a vow unto the LORD thy God, thou shalt not be slack to pay it: for the LORD thy God will surely require it of thee; and it would be sin in thee. But if thou shalt forbear to vow, it shall be no sin in thee. That which is gone out of thy lips thou shalt keep and perform; even a freewill offering, according as thou has vowed unto the LORD thy God, which thou hast promised with thy mouth" (Deut. 23:21-23).

COMMUTATION OF VOWS CONCERNING PERSONS

And the LORD spake unto Moses, saying.

Speak unto the children of Israel, and say unto them. When a man shall make a singular vow, the persons shall be for the LORD by thy estimation [Lev. 27: 1-2].

"Making a singular vow," means to single out something of value, parti-cularly precious to the individual. Remember how David would not offer to God something which had been donated to him. ". . . Nay; but I will surely buy it of thee at a price: neither will I offer burnt offerings unto the LORD my God of that which doth cost me nothing. . ." (2 Sam. 24:24).

If you are in a church and you are attempting to give to God some offering that costs you nothing, may God have mercy on you! We are not under a tithe system today. Israel was, but we are not. God does not require a tithe of us. We are to give a freewill offering. I can promise you that if you are cheap with God, God will be cheap with you.

A successful business man was asked the secret of his success. He said, "As the Lord shovels it in, I shovel it out; the more I shovel it out, the more the Lord shovels it in." Now, that is not to say that the Lord is promising to bless us with money. He has many kinds of blessings for us. However, I do believe that some of us are poor today and some of us have such a hard time financially because of the way we deal with God.

A man came to me when the stock market crashed, and he brought in some stock which he offered with this comment, "Now that it is going down, I might just as well give it to the church." God have mercy on that kind of giving. We are to give something of value. It should cost us something.

And thy estimation shall be of the male from twenty years old even unto sixty years old, even thy estimation shall be fifty shekels of silver, after the shekel of the sanctuary.

And if it be a female, then thy estimation shall be thirty shekels [Lev. 27: 3-4].

When a person was dedicated by a vow to God, it did not mean that individual must serve in the tabernacle—that was the peculiar service of the Levites. A redemption price could be paid for the person which would relieve him of that service. This is called the commutation price of the person.

A man between the ages of twenty and sixty was of greater value because of the amount of work he could do. The labor value seemed to be the standard of evaluation. A male in the prime of life could render the most service. "By thy estimation" meant that which was the current value among the people.

The labor value of a female would be less, but the important feature is that a female could be devoted to God. I think this makes it clear that the daughter of Jephthah was not offered as a human sacrifice but remained unmarried and was vowed to God.

Hannah brought little Samuel to the temple as a thanksgiving offering to God in payment of her vow. She said, "For this child I prayed; and the LORD hath given me my petition which I asked of him: Therefore also I have lent him to the LORD; as long as he liveth he shall be lent to the LORD. . ." (1 Sam. 1:27–28). She kept her vow.

Have you ever come to God and presented yourself to Him? Have you presented your children to God? Your grandchildren? Have you presented your possessions to Him? He hasn't commanded you to do that, but He has said that you may do it. If you do it, then it is mandatory that you make good.

And if it be from five years old even unto twenty years old, then thy estimation shall be of the male twenty shekels, and for the female ten shekels.

And if it be from a month old even unto five years old, then thy estimation shall be of the male five shekels of silver, and for the female thy estimation shall be three shekels of silver.

And if it be from sixty years old and above; if it be a male, then thy estimation shall be fifteen shekels, and for the female ten shekels.

But if he be poorer than thy estimation, then he shall present himself before the priest, and the priest shall value him; according to his ability that vowed shall the priest value him [Lev. 27:5–8].

You see that the scale of values was determined by age and not by social position, riches, or prestige. The value was based on the ability to labor. Notice how wonderfully God provided for the poor so they could participate in this voluntary service. A fair and equitable price was set by the priest according to the man's ability to pay. The widow's mite is of more value in heaven than the rich gifts of the wealthy and affluent.

There is another striking feature about the vowing of persons. Ordinarily in human affairs, a man pays for the service of another. In the law of vows this is reversed and a man pays to serve God. It is a privilege to serve God.

COMMUTATION OF VOWS CONCERNING ANIMALS

And if it be a beast, whereof men bring an offering unto the LORD, all that any man giveth of such unto the LORD shall be holy.

He shall not alter it, nor change it, a good for a bad, or a bad for a good: and if he shall at all change beast for beast, then it and the exchange thereof shall be holy [Lev. 27:9–10].

When I was pastor of a little country church, a member of the church took me out to his barn lot and showed me a calf. He told me he had given it to the LORD. To tell you the truth, that calf didn't look as if it would live, and I suspect that is the reason he gave it to the Lord. Well, that calf became a blue-ribbon prize winner! Then the man told me, "You know, this is such a fine animal that I thought I'd better keep it. I have another animal over here that I'm giving to the Lord instead." He sold it and gave the money to the church, and felt very comfortable about what he had done.

God says, "Don't substitute." If you have promised to do something for God, go through with it. Remember the sin of Ananias and Sapphira. They said they were giving to the Lord the entire price of a piece of land, but they didn't go through with it. They didn't have to give all of it to God. Peter told them that while it was theirs, they were perfectly free to do with it what they wished. It was a voluntary offering, but then they tried to withhold some of it from God.

This that we are talking about is real today. God holds us to our vows. If you have promised Him something and haven't made good, it is still on His books. We are dealing with a God of reality.

And if it be any unclean beast, of which they do not offer a sacrifice unto the LORD then he shall present the beast before the priest:

And the priest shall value it, whether it be good or bad: as thou valuest it, who art the priest, so shall it be.

But if he will at all redeem it, then he shall add a fifth part thereof unto thy estimation [Lev. 27:11–13].

An unclean animal could be pledged in a vow, but it would not be offered in sacrifice. The priest would value the animal, the man would pay the price of redemption and add a fifth of the price as a sort of fine for offering an unclean animal.

COMMUTATION OF VOWS
CONCERNING HOUSES

And when a man shall sanctify his house to be holy unto the LORD, then the priest shall estimate it, whether it be good or bad: as the priest shall estimate it, so shall it stand.

And if he that sanctified it will redeem his house, then he shall add the fifth part of the money of thy estimation unto it, and it shall be his [Lev. 27:14–15].

The home of a man is his most sacred material possession. He could pledge it to the Lord. I think a Christian home, as well as the children of Christians, should be dedicated to God. The man could continue to live in his house and begin paying rent to God as the owner. If he did not continue paying his rent, he was to add a fifth when he redeemed it. Again this was a sort of fine in recognition of God's ownership.

A man asked me to come out to dedicate his house. He said he wanted it to be God's house, and I could come out there any time I wanted to. Well, I had a house of my own and didn't need to be running out to his house. If he really meant that it was God's house, then he should pay God rent for it as a recognition of God's ownership. You may ask me whether I think this is that literal. Yes, I think it is just that literal. We make vows to God of our freewill. Then we prove whether or not we are genuine in our vows. This gets right down to the nitty-gritty where you and I live.

COMMUTATION OF VOWS
CONCERNING LAND

And if a man shall sanctify unto the LORD some part of a field of his possession, then thy estimation shall be according to the seed thereof: an homer of barley seed shall be valued at fifty shekels of silver.

If he sanctify his field from the year of jubile, according to thy estimation it shall stand.

But if he sanctify his field after the jubile, then the priest shall reckon unto him the money according to the years that remain, even unto the year of the jubile, and it shall be abated from thy estimation.

And if he that sanctified the field will in any wise redeem it, then he shall add the fifth part of the money of thy estimation unto it, and it shall be assured to him.

And if he will not redeem the field, or if he have sold the field to another man, it shall not be redeemed any more.

But the field, when it goeth out in the jubile, shall be holy unto the LORD, as a field devoted; the possession thereof shall be the priest's.

And if a man sanctify unto the LORD a field which he hath bought, which is not of the fields of his possession;

Then the priest shall reckon unto him the worth of thy estimation, even unto the year of the jubile: and he shall give thine estimation in that day, as a holy thing unto the LORD.

In the year of the jubile the field shall return unto him of whom it was bought, even to him to whom the possession of the land did belong.

And all thy estimations shall be according to the shekel of the sanctuary: twenty gerahs shall be the shekel [Lev. 27:16–25].

This must have been a very complicated system. Land could be dedicated to God even though the land belonged to God. The land was evaluated on the basis of its productivity and in relation to the year of Jubilee. All land returned to the original owner at that time. This was taken into account if a man dedicated the land to the Lord just shortly before the year of Jubilee as a gesture of generosity. In fact he might be a very selfish man. A man could not dedicate a borrowed field to God. God knows the heart of man.

CONCERNING THREE THINGS
WHICH ARE THE LORD'S
APART FROM A VOW

Only the firstling of the beasts, which should be the LORD's firstling, no man shall sanctify it; whether it be ox, or sheep: it is the LORD's.

And if it be of an unclean beast, then he shall redeem it according to thine estimation, and shall add a fifth part of it thereto: or if it be not redeemed, then it shall be sold according to thy estimation [Lev. 27:26–27].

The firstborn of both man and beast were already claimed by the Lord and could not be devoted to the Lord in a vow. God insisted that His rights be observed.

Notwithstanding no devoted thing, that a man shall devote unto the LORD of all that he hath, both of man and beast, and of the field of his possession, shall be sold or redeemed: every devoted thing is most holy unto the LORD.

None devoted, which shall be devoted of men, shall be redeemed; but shall surely be put to death [Lev. 27:28–29].

The second classification of things which could not be devoted in a vow was that which was already pledged in a vow to God. In Joshua we learn that Jericho was devoted to God for destruction. Because Achan took of that which God had told them they should utterly destroy, Achan was destroyed (Josh. 6 and 7).

And all the tithe of the land, whether of the seed of the land, or of the fruit of the tree, is the LORD's: it is holy unto the LORD.

And if a man will at all redeem aught of his tithes, he shall add thereto the fifth part thereof.

And concerning the tithe of the herd, or of the flock, even of whatsoever passeth under the rod, the tenth shall be holy unto the LORD.

He shall not search whether it be good or bad, neither shall he change it: and if he change it at all, then both it and the change thereof shall be holy; it shall not be redeemed [Lev. 27:30–33].

The tithe was the third thing which already belonged to God and could not be pledged in a vow.

These are the commandments, which the LORD commanded Moses for the children of Israel in mount Sinai [Lev. 27:34].

This verse concludes the Book of Leviticus and sums it up. It also reveals that chapter 27 is not an addendum but part and parcel of the thinking of God for man under law.

The believer can be thankful for the grace of God in this day. "For the grace of God that bringeth salvation hath appeared to all men, teaching us that, denying ungodliness and worldly lusts, we should live soberly, righteously, and godly, in this present world; Looking for that blessed hope, and the glorious appearing of the great God and our Saviour Jesus Christ; Who gave himself for us, that he might redeem us from all iniquity, and purify unto himself a peculiar people, zealous of good works" (Titus 2:11–14).

BIBLIOGRAPHY

Gaebelein, Arno C. *Annotated Bible* Vol. 1. Neptune, New Jersey: Loizeaux Brothers, 1917.

Grant, F. W. *Numerical Bible*. Neptune, New Jersey: Loizeaux Brothers, 1891.

Gray, James M. *Synthetic Bible Studies*. Westwood, New Jersey: Fleming H. Revell Co., 1906.

Heslop, W. G. *Lessons from Leviticus*. Grand Rapids, Michigan: Kregel Publications, 1945.

Ironside, H. A. *Lectures on the Levitical Offerings*. Neptune, New Jersey: Loizeaux Brothers, 1929.

Jamieson, Robert; Faucett, H. R.; and Brown, D. *Commentary on the Bible*. 3 vols. Grand Rapids, Michigan: Wm. B. Eerdmans Publishing Co., 1945.

Jensen, Irving L. *Leviticus*. Chicago, Illinois: Moody Press, 1967.

Jukes, Andrew. *The Law of the Offerings*. Grand Rapids, Michigan: Kregel Publications, 1870.

Kellogg, S. H. *The Book of Leviticus*. New York, New York: George H. Doran Co., 1908.

Kelly, William. *Lectures Introductory to the Pentateuch*. Oak Park, Illinois: Bible Truth Publishers, 1870.

Mackintosh, C. H. (C.H.M.). *Notes on the Pentateuch*. Neptune, New Jersey: Loizeaux Brothers, 1880.

McGee, J. Vernon. *Learning Through Leviticus*. 2 vols. Pasadena, California: Thru the Bible Books, 1964.

Thomas, W. H. Griffith. *Through the Pentateuch Chapter by Chapter*. Grand Rapids, Michigan: Wm. B. Eerdmans Publishing Co., 1957.

Unger, Merrill F. *Unger's Bible Handbook*. Chicago, Illinois: Moody Press, 1966.

The Book of
NUMBERS

INTRODUCTION

The Book of Numbers, called *Arithmoi* (meaning "Arithmetic") in the Septuagint, gets its name from the census in chapters 1 and 26. Numbers takes up the story where Exodus left off. It is the fourth book of the Pentateuch.

You will recall that in Genesis, the first book of the Pentateuch, we have the creation and fall of man and many beginnings. We have the beginning of Israel—not a nation yet, but a growing family that migrates down to Egypt to escape extinction by famine.

In Exodus we find the family becoming a nation in Egypt. We see them in slavery by the brick kilns of Egypt; then we see God delivering them by the hand of Moses and bringing them through the wilderness as far as Mount Sinai.

In the Book of Leviticus we see the children of Israel marking time at Mount Sinai while God gives the Law and the tabernacle. God calls them to Himself and tells them how to come.

In the Book of Numbers we see the children of Israel depart from Mount Sinai and march to Kadesh-barnea. After their failure at Kadesh-barnea, they began to wander until that generation died in the wilderness. The years of wandering were a veritable saga of suffering, a trek of tragedy, and a story of straying.

"Pilgrim's Progress" is an apt theme for this book. Here we find the walking, wandering, working, warring, witnessing, and worshiping of God's pilgrims. It is a handbook for pilgrims in this world. In the words of the hymnwriter, "Chart and compass come from Thee." This is a road map for the wilderness of this world.

This book is helpful for us today. The lessons which the children of Israel had to learn are the lessons that you and I will need to learn, which is the reason God recorded this history for you and me. "For whatsoever things were written aforetime were written for our learning, that we through patience and comfort of the scriptures might have hope" (Rom. 15:4).

"Now all these things happened unto them for ensamples: and they are written for our admonition, upon whom the ends of the world are come" (1 Cor. 10:11).

"These all died in faith, not having received the promises, but having seen them afar off, and were persuaded of them, and embraced them, and confessed that they were strangers and pilgrims on the earth" (Heb. 11:13).

"Dearly beloved, I beseech you as strangers and pilgrims, abstain from fleshly lusts, which war against the soul" (1 Pet. 2:11).

"I have given them thy word; and the world hath hated them, because they are not of the world, even as I am not of the world. I pray not that thou shouldest take them out of the world, but that thou shouldest keep them from the evil" (John 17:14–15).

The first five books of the Bible, called the Pentateuch (since *pentateuch* means "five books"), were written by Moses. They are identified in Scripture as the Law. Although the Mosaic authorship has been questioned, it is affirmed by conservative scholars and confirmed by archaeology. Bible believers unanimously accept the Mosaic authorship.

It is interesting to note that the distance from Mount Sinai to Kadesh-barnea was from 150 to 200 miles—a journey, in that time, of eleven days (Deut. 1:2). The Israelites spent thirty days at Kibroth. They spent forty years on a journey that should have taken forty days because their walking was turned to wandering. Since they refused to go into the land, they did not advance an inch after Kadesh-barnea. At the end of their wanderings they came back to the same place, Kadesh-barnea. What was the reason? Unbelief.

Between the census in the first chapter and the census in the twenty-sixth chapter, we find a divine history of the wanderings of the Israelites in the wilderness for about thirty-eight years and ten months, commencing with the first movement of the camp after the tabernacle was reared.

A comparison of the two sets of census figures will show that their number was decimated. Numbers 1:46 says there were 603,550 fighting men. Numbers 26:51 states that there were 601,730 fighting men. This represents a loss of 1,820 fighting men. God's command was for them to be fruitful and multiply, but they were losing instead of gaining during the years in the wilderness.

The census helps us to ascertain the number that had come out of Egypt. I am giving to you the estimate of Dr. Melvin Grove Kyle, who was a great Egyptologist and one of the editors of the *International Standard Bible Encyclopedia* and also, at one time, editor on the staff of *The National Geographic*. He was a great man and a great archaeologist—and as dull as any lecturer can be. However, a person could get a wealth of information if he would make the effort to listen to him. I must say that I found him intensely interesting. Dr. Kyle figured that with about 600,000 fighting men there would be approximately 400,000 women. He set a figure at 200,000 senior citizens and 800,000 children. Then there was a mixed multitude that followed, which he estimated to be about 100,000. This gives a total estimate of 2,100,000 people, which does not include the tribe of Levi. Between 2,000,000 and 3,000,000 would be the number who came out of the land of Egypt!

Included in this book are three illustrations that are helpful in this study. Two of them show the tabernacle and the way the children of Israel camped around it. The other illustration shows the order by which they marched.

Don't think for a moment that this was a mob going through the wilderness helter-skelter. No group ever marched more orderly than this group. As we study this, I am sure you will be impressed by the way God insisted upon the order of this camp.

This is God's method. To the church He said, "Let all things be done decently and in order" (1 Cor. 14:40). He is a God of order. Have you ever pulled aside the petals of a rose and looked deeply into it? He put the rose together nicely, didn't He? Have you noticed the way He shaped a tree? Have you noted the orderly arrangement of every fruit and vegetable you pick up? Have you observed the orderliness of this universe? Things are not flying around, bumping into each other. There is plenty of space to maneuver because the Lord has arranged it so. We live in a remarkable universe which reveals a God of power and a God of order. The Psalmist said, "The fool hath said in his heart, There is no God . . ." (Ps. 14:1). Nobody but a fool could be an atheist. This universe shouts out the message. The order of the universe evidences it. The power of this tremendous universe reveals that there is a Person in control of it. Not only does it reveal a Person, but it reveals His genius.

OUTLINE

I. Fitting out the Nation Israel for Wilderness March, Chapters 1–8
  A. Order of the Camp, Chapters 1–4
    1. First Census, Chapter 1
    2. Standards and Positions of 12 Tribes on Wilderness March, Chapter 2
    3. Census, Position, and Service of Levites on Wilderness March, Chapter 3
    4. Service of Levites about the Tabernacle, Chapter 4
  B. Cleansing the Camp, Chapters 5–8
    1. Restitution and Jealousy Offering, Chapter 5
    2. Vow of the Nazarite, Chapter 6
    3. Gifts of the Princes, Chapter 7
    4. Light of Lampstand and Laver for Levites, Chapter 8

II. Forward March!, Chapters 9–10
  A. Passover and Covering Cloud, Chapter 9
  B. Order of March, Chapter 10

III. From Sinai to Kadesh-Barnea, Chapters 11–12
  A. Complaining and Murmuring of People Displeasing to the Lord, Chapter 11
  B. Jealousy of Miriam and Aaron; Judgment of Miriam, Chapter 12

IV. Failure at Kadesh-Barnea, Chapters 13–14
  A. Spies Chosen and Sent into Land of Canaan, Chapter 13
  B. Israel Refuses to Enter Because of Unbelief, Chapter 14

V. Faltering, Fumbling, and Fussing through the Wilderness, Chapters 15–25
  A. God's Blessing Delayed; His Purpose Not Destroyed, Chapter 15
  B. Incidents Relating to the Priesthood, Chapters 16–19
    1. Gainsaying of Korah, Chapter 16
    2. Aaron's Rod That Budded, Chapter 17
    3. Confirmation of Priesthood, Chapter 18
    4. Offering and Ashes of Red Heifer, Chapter 19
  C. Deaths of Miriam and Aaron; Water from the Rock, Chapter 20
  D. First Victory of Israel; First Song; Serpent of Brass, Chapter 21
  E. The Prophet Balaam, Chapters 22–25
    1. The Way of Balaam, Chapter 22
    2. The Error of Balaam, Chapter 23
    3. The Doctrine of Balaam, Chapters 24–25

VI. Future: New Generation Prepares to Enter Land, Chapters 26–36
  A. Census of New Generation, Chapter 26
  B. Woman's Place under Law, Chapter 27
  C. The Law of Offerings, Chapters 28–29
  D. Law of Vows, Chapter 30
  E. Judgment of Midian, Chapter 31
  F. Reuben and Gad Ask for Land on Wrong Side of Jordan, Chapter 32
  G. Log of the Journeys, Chapter 33
  H. Borders of the Promised Land, Chapter 34
  I. Cities of Refuge Given to Levites, Chapter 35
  J. Law of Land Regarding Inheritance, Chapter 36

CHAPTER 1

And the Lord spake unto Moses in the wilderness of Sinai, in the tabernacle of the congregation, on the first day of the second month, in the second year after they were come out of the land of Egypt, saying [Num. 1:1].

THE FIRST CENSUS

God spoke to Moses in the wilderness, but He spoke from the tabernacle. The tabernacle was in the wilderness. Just so, the church today is in the world. The Lord Jesus prayed, "I pray not that thou shouldest take them out of the world, but that thou shouldest keep them from the evil" (John 17:15). The church is in the world.

God spoke from the tabernacle. The building of God today is made of flesh and blood, true believers who compose what we call the church. "Now therefore ye are no more strangers and foreigners, but fellow-citizens with the saints, and of the household of God; And are built upon the foundation of the apostles and prophets, Jesus Christ himself being the chief corner stone; In whom all the building fitly framed together groweth unto an holy temple in the Lord: In whom ye also are builded together for an habitation of God through the Spirit" (Eph. 2:19–22). This church is made up of people who ". . . are his workmanship, created in Christ Jesus unto good works, which God hath before ordained that we should walk in them" (Eph. 2:10).

Take ye the sum of all the congregation of the children of Israel, after their families, by the house of their fathers, with the number of their names, every male by their polls;

From twenty years old and upward, all that are able to go forth to war in Israel: thou and Aaron shall number them by their armies [Num. 1:2–3].

The children of Israel are to be numbered, and they are to be numbered for the purpose of building up an army. An army is for warfare. As slaves in the land of Egypt, God fought for them; they were not asked to fight. Now that they have been brought out of Egypt into the wilderness, they are to fight their enemies. And their enemies are out there waiting for them.

May I say that you and I who are believers living in this world have enemies also. These enemies are quite real, by the way. Again let me refer back to the Epistle to the Ephesians where we are told about the warfare of believers in this world today. "Finally, my brethren, be strong in the Lord, and in the power of his might. Put on the whole armour of God, that ye may be able to stand against the wiles of the devil. For we wrestle not against flesh and blood, but against principalities, against powers, against the rulers of the darkness of this world, against spiritual wickedness in high places" (Eph. 6:10–12).

God has saved us by His infinite, marvelous, wonderful grace. But you and I are in a world that is wicked and rough. Like the children of Israel out in the wilderness, we are in the wilderness of this world, which is full of sin. Although God has *saved* us by His marvelous grace, we have an enemy to fight. Paul wrote this to a young preacher, "Thou therefore endure hardness, as a good soldier of Jesus Christ" (2 Tim. 2:3). Again, he tells him, "Fight the good fight of faith, lay hold on eternal life, whereunto thou art also called . . ." (1 Tim. 6:12).

Now for the first time the Israelites hear of war. In this book we will find wars and trumpets, battles and giants—all of that. You and I live in that kind of world yet today.

In our day some folk seem to think that all one must do is say, "Peace," and there will be peace. They talk about making love and not war. Yet, they cause dissension and trouble while they talk about peace! They know nothing about true peace. They don't seem to understand that we live in a big, bad world, that there are some bad folks around us, and that there will be fights and wars whether we like it or not. That is one of the terrible things about our world.

And with you there shall be a man of every tribe; every one head of the house of his fathers [Num. 1:4].

The way this book starts off here with this census doesn't sound exactly thrilling. It's not like a mystery story on television. One would think we have here 54 verses of unnecessary details which are quite boring, but we need to remember that these details were important to God. If we will see the great truths that are here, we will find it thrilling for us.

First of all, we see that God is interested in the individuals. Mass movements have their place and play their role but God is interested in redeemed individuals. He is interested in *every* individual.

Moses and Aaron were to take a census and they were to have one assistant from each tribe. The names of these assistants are given here, which are too monotonous to quote, yet they reveal that every name there was important to God and has meaning. If one understands the Hebrew meaning of the names, it will give a wonderful message.

And these are the names of the men that shall stand with you; of the tribe of Reuben; Elizur the son of Shedeur [Num. 1:5].

That doesn't sound very interesting or thrilling, but let me explain it. Reuben was the eldest son of Jacob, and he was set aside. We are told, "Reuben, thou art my firstborn, my might, and the beginning of my strength, the excellency of dignity, and the excellency of power: Unstable as water, thou shalt not excel; because thou wentest up to thy father's bed; then defiledst thou it: he went up to my couch" (Gen. 49:3–4). Reuben—unstable as water.

Now the man chosen out of this tribe was to be a different kind of man. Elizur, the son of Shedeur, was the man. *Elizur* means "My God is a rock" and *Shedeur* means "The Almighty is a fire." I like that. This man Elizur, "My God is a rock," may belong to a tribe that is unstable as water, but he knows a Rock that is stable. He reminds me of the little Scottish lady who said, "I may tremble on the Rock, but the Rock never trembles under me." Remember that they had sung in the song of Moses that God was their Rock. This fellow had learned that. He knew that God is a Rock in a weary land. He is the foundation Rock for us to rest on also. It is wonderful to know, my friend, that you may be an unstable person and come from an unstable family, but there is a Rock for you. "My God is a Rock."

And they assembled all the congregation together on the first day of the second month, and they declared their pedigrees after their families, by the house of their fathers, according to the number of the names, from twenty years old and upward, by their polls [Num. 1:18].

Why did they declare their pedigree? Why are pedigrees so important in the Word of God? They serve a threefold purpose.

1. They were interesting and beneficial to those who were concerned. It's well to know something of your ancestry, what kind of stock you came from.

2. The reason some names and genealogies are omitted in the Bible and others are recorded is because it was important to preserve the genealogy of Jesus Christ. We saw in our study of Genesis how the rejected line was given first and then dropped and forgotten. Then the genealogical line which would lead to the Lord Jesus is given, and this line is followed all the way through the Scriptures.

The New Testament opens with a genealogy, and the whole New Testament stands or falls on the accuracy of that genealogy. This genealogy was kept on record, and probably was open on display, in the temple of that day. Probably the enemy checked it many times, hoping to find that Jesus did not have the legal right to the throne of David. It is interesting that the accuracy of the genealogy of Jesus Christ was never questioned by His enemies.

3. God forbade intermarriage, and a true Israelite had to be able to declare his pedigree. They were the beneficiaries of the covenant made to Abraham. Also the genealogy was necessary to determine who was eligible for the priesthood. We find an example of this in the Book of Nehemiah. "And of the priests: the children of Habaiah, the children of Koz, the children of Barzillai, which took one of the daughters of Barzillai the Gileadite to wife, and was called after their name. These sought their register among those that were reckoned by genealogy, but it was not found: therefore were they, as polluted, put from the priesthood" (Neh. 7:63–64). Levites who could not declare their genealogy were put out of the priesthood.

There is a message in all of this for us today. Can you imagine a young man of that day being called up and asked, "Are you an Israelite?" If he answered, "Well, I hope I'm an Israelite, but I can't be sure until I die," what do you think would have happened? They would have pushed him aside! Suppose another young man stepped up and they asked, "Are you an Israelite?" What do you think they would have done to him if he answered, "Well, I try to be an Israelite, I'm working real hard at it, and I hope to become one"? Would that have been acceptable? Do you see how important it was for them to declare that they were Israelites? Each one must know that he was the son of Abraham.

Now I have a question for you—a quite personal question. Can you declare your pedigree as a Christian? If you don't know whether you can or not, may I say to you that you had better be able to declare it. Listen to this: "Beloved, now are we the sons of God, and it doth not yet appear what we shall be: but we know that, when he shall appear, we shall be like him; for we shall see him as he is" (1 John 3:2). Can *you* say that, my friend?

How can you become a son of God? "For ye are all the children of God by faith in Christ Jesus" (Gal. 3:26). There is no other way. You become a son of God by faith in Christ Jesus. "But as many as received him, [the Lord Jesus], to them gave he power to become the sons of God, even to them that believe on his name" (John 1:12). The authority to become the sons of God is given to those who do no more nor less than simply believe in His name.

And our genealogy is important! If we are a true child of God through faith in Christ, then we are heirs of God and joint heirs of Christ! "And if ye be Christ's, then are ye Abraham's seed, and heirs according to the promise" (Gal. 3:29). "For as many as are led by the Spirit of God, they are the sons of God. For ye have not received the spirit of bondage again to fear; but ye have received the Spirit of adoption, whereby we cry, Abba, Father. The Spirit itself beareth witness with our spirit, that we are the children of God: And if children, then heirs; heirs of God, and joint-heirs with Christ; if so be that we suffer with him, that we may be also glorified together" (Rom. 8:14–17).

You can *know* it. You can be born again through the blood of Christ and so be a member of the family of God. That is the only way! In this wilderness journey today, you must know who you are! You must know that you are a child of God. If you are not sure of that, you ought to make sure of it and you *can* make sure of it. How can you be sure? By taking God at His Word. It is not what you think or what you feel; He says that if you put your trust in Christ, you are His child. You can rest on the Word of God.

Here we are given the twelve tribes of Israel and the numbers in each tribe. If you were to take an adding machine and go through this chapter, you would find that it is accurate.

HOW ISRAEL ENCAMPED ON WILDERNESS MARCH

CHART OF CAMP

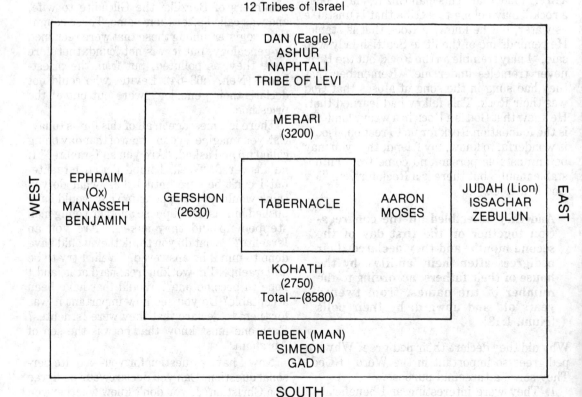

NORTH

12 Tribes of Israel

DAN (Eagle)
ASHUR
NAPHTALI
TRIBE OF LEVI

MERARI
(3200)

WEST

EPHRAIM
(Ox)
MANASSEH
BENJAMIN

GERSHON
(2630)

TABERNACLE

AARON
MOSES

JUDAH (Lion)
ISSACHAR
ZEBULUN

EAST

KOHATH
(2750)
Total--(8580)

REUBEN (MAN)
SIMEON
GAD

SOUTH

Those that were numbered of them, even of the tribe of Reuben, were forty and six thousand and five hundred.

Those that were numbered of them, even of the tribe of Simeon, were fifty and nine thousand and three hundred [Num. 1:21, 23].

So it goes down the list until verse 46.

Even all they that were numbered were six hundred thousand and three thousand and five hundred and fifty [Num. 1:46].

Now we will notice that the Levites were not numbered.

But the Levites after the tribe of their fathers were not numbered among them.

For the LORD had spoken unto Moses, saying,

Only thou shalt not number the tribe of Levi, neither take the sum of them among the children of Israel:

But thou shalt appoint the Levites over the tabernacle of testimony, and over all the vessels thereof, and over all things that belong to it: they shall bear the tabernacle, and all the vessels thereof; and they shall minister unto it, and shall encamp round about the tabernacle. [Num. 1:47–50].

The reason they were not numbered for warfare was that they had full charge of the tabernacle. They would put it up in the evening when they came into camp, and they would take it down whenever they were ready to march.

And when the tabernacle setteth forward, the Levites shall take it down: and when the tabernacle is to be pitched, the Levites shall set it up: and the stranger that cometh nigh shall be put to death.

And the children of Israel shall pitch their tents, every man by his own camp, and every man by his own standard, throughout their hosts.

But the Levites shall pitch round about the tabernacle of testimony, that there be no wrath upon the congregation of the children of Israel: and the Levites shall keep the charge of the tabernacle of testimony [Num. 1:51–53].

The children of Israel had to know who they were, hence the genealogy. It was also important that each of them should know where he belonged. He had a definite place assigned to him in the camp. The same is true for us. We need to know our pedigree, the fact that we belong to the family of God as His children. And, we need to know where we belong. We'll see more of this in the next chapter.

CHAPTER 2

THEME: *The arrangement of the camp*

In chapter 1 we learned about the census. Each Israelite had to know who he was. He also had to know where he belonged. During all these years in the wilderness, the camp positions and the order of their marching were orderly and according to God's direction.

We are told that they raised standards over their camps. These were banners that were put up over them. Just what was on these banners? Let me quote to you from two great scholars of the Old Testament, Keil and Delitzsch, in their *Commentary on the Pentateuch*, Volume III: "Neither the Mosaic law, nor the Old Testament generally gives us any intimation as to the form or character of the standard (*deqhel*). According to rabbinical tradition, the standard of Judah bore the figure of a lion, that of Reuben the likeness of a man, or of a man's head, that of Ephraim the figure of an ox, and that of Dan the figure of an eagle; so that the four living creatures united in the cherubic forms described by Ezekiel were represented upon these four standards."

I don't want to make too much of that because there is a danger in trying to read too much into it. There are people who go so far as to find in their arrangement about the camp a picture of the way the stars are arranged in heaven, the signs of the Zodiac! Also there are people who try to find the gospel written in the stars or try to find their future written in the stars. Shakespeare said, "It's not in our stars but in ourselves that we are underlings." Our problem is within ourselves, not up yonder in the stars. We won't find the gospel in the stars; we find it in the Word of God. Without the Word of God we would not suspect that the gospel was in the stars. Mankind is not without excuse because they could read the gospel in the stars but because all creation reveals God's eternal power and Godhead. Whether the standards bore a name or emblem is unimportant, and we know that tradition is not always accurate.

THE ARRANGEMENT OF THE CAMP

And the LORD spake unto Moses and unto Aaron, saying,

Every man of the children of Israel shall pitch by his own standard, with the ensign of their father's house: far off about the tabernacle of the congregation shall they pitch.

And on the east side toward the rising of the sun shall they of the standard of the camp of Judah pitch throughout their armies: and Nahshon the son of Amminadab shall be captain of the children of Judah [Num. 2:1–3].

Notice that they all camp in reference to the tabernacle. The tabernacle would be placed in the camp and then the children of Israel would camp around it. They would put up their standards to mark their place in the camp.

On the east side was Judah. The tribe of Issachar (v. 5) and the tribe of Zebulun (v. 7) camped with Judah under the same standard. If the emblem on that standard was a lion, then when these three tribes saw the standard with the lion, they knew where they belonged.

On the south side shall be the standard of the camp of Reuben according to their armies: and the captain of the children of Reuben shall be Elizur the son of Shedeur [Num. 2:10].

The tribe of Reuben was on the south side and Simeon (v. 12) and Gad (v. 14) camped with Reuben.

On the west side shall be the standard of the camp of Ephraim according to their armies: and the captain of the sons of Ephraim shall be Elishama the son of Ammihud [Num. 2:18].

On the west the tribes of Manasseh (v. 20) and Benjamin (v. 22) camped with Ephraim under his emblem.

The standard of the camp of Dan shall be on the north side by their armies: and the captain of the children of Dan shall be Ahiezer the son of Ammishaddai [Num. 2:25].

The tribes of Asher (v. 27) and Naphtali (v. 29) camped with Dan under his standard.

The children of Israel camped in an orderly way. Each family in each tribe knew where it belonged in that tribe.

But the Levites were not numbered among the children of Israel; as the LORD commanded Moses.

And the children of Israel did according to all that the LORD commanded Moses: so they pitched by their standards, and so they set forward, every one after their families, according to the house of their fathers [Num. 2:33–34].

We have learned now that they must know who they were and where they belonged. They must know their pedigree in order to know their place in the camp. They could not go to war unless they were sure of their position.

Just so, Christian warfare is not carried on in the realm of doubts and fears but in the clear light of a sure salvation. Our enemies today are the world, the flesh, and the devil. My friend, they will overcome you if you are not sure of your salvation.

Every person in the church of the Lord Jesus Christ has a God-appointed place. All service in the church is to be directed by the Holy Spirit. We are told that by one Spirit we are all baptized into one body. When you were put into the body, you were put in as a member. "For as the body is one, and hath many members, and all the members of that one body, being many, are one body: so also is Christ. For by one Spirit are we all baptized into one body, whether we be Jews or Gentiles, whether we be bond or free; and have been all made to drink into one Spirit. For the body is not one member, but many" (1 Cor. 12:12–14).

When He puts you into that body, He puts you there to serve. Every believer has a gift. *You* have a gift. The exercise of that gift is your Christian service.

There are many members of the human body and each has its function. There are over 20 bones in the foot alone. So in the body of Christ there are many gifts and each of us is to exercise his gift. You and I are to find out what our gift is. I believe that God rewards His own by the exercise of that gift. Although the Holy Spirit divides to every man severally as He wills, I do believe that 1 Corinthians 12:31 indicates we can pray and covet the best gifts. As a young man, I heard Dr. Ironside teach the Bible, and I asked God to let me teach like he taught. God heard and answered my prayer in a wonderful way. Although I can't teach like he did, God has permitted me to have a teaching ministry which I wanted and asked Him for. I think that we may covet earnestly the best gifts, but recognize this is all under the sovereign control of the Holy Spirit.

Remember Dorcas? She made clothes. You remember that when she died, they called in Simon Peter and the widows showed him the clothes Dorcas had made for them. Simon Peter probably said, "We had better raise this woman from the dead. The church needs her!" And God raised her from the dead.

Friend, you ought to find your place in the camp. Are you usurping another's place? Are you occupying a place in the church that you really can't fill and that belongs to someone else? We ought to encourage each member of our church to find his place, and that should hearten the humblest member of the church. You have a gift and God wants you to exercise it. Don't try to do someone else's job. You do what God has called you to do.

CHAPTER 3

THEME: *Aaron and Moses; tribe of Levi given to Aaron; three families of Levi; census of firstborn of all Israel*

As we come to the third chapter, we can see that God is preparing the children of Israel for the wilderness march. First of all, there must be the order of the camp. We have seen that there was a census so that the men of war might be chosen. The people needed to be certain who they were, and to have the assurance that they were sons of Abraham. Then they needed the standards for the order of the camp so they would know where they belonged.

Chapter 3 will give us a look at the tribe of Levi and what they are to do. This is the tribe that had the oversight of the tabernacle. Although they were not included in the first census, a census is taken of them separately so that they may be assigned to a definite position in the camp.

AARON AND MOSES

These also are the generations of Aaron and Moses in the day that the LORD spake with Moses in mount Sinai.

And these are the names of the sons of Aaron; Nadab the firstborn, and Abihu, Eleazar, and Ithamar.

These are the names of the sons of Aaron, the priests which were anointed, whom he consecrated to minister in the priest's office.

And Nadab and Abihu died before the LORD, when they offered strange fire before the LORD, in the wilderness of Sinai, and they had no children: and Eleazar and Ithamar ministered in the priest's office in the sight of Aaron their father [Num. 3:1–4].

First, we are given the family of Aaron and of Moses. What we have here confirms the record that was given in the Book of Leviticus. Nadab and Abihu were destroyed because they intruded into the high priest's office, which they should not have done.

TRIBE OF LEVI GIVEN TO AARON

And the LORD spake unto Moses, saying,

Bring the tribe of Levi near, and present them before Aaron the priest, that they may minister unto him.

And they shall keep his charge, and the charge of the whole congregation before the tabernacle of the congregation, to do the service of the tabernacle [Num. 3:5–7].

The tribe of Levi was given to the high priest, Aaron, to assist him. You and I, in the church as believers, are a priesthood of believers. As such, we have been given to our Great High Priest. Listen to the Lord Jesus in

His high-priestly prayer: "I have manifested thy name unto the men which thou gavest me out of the world: thine they were, and thou gavest them me; and they have kept thy word" (John 17:6). Believers, which collectively are called the church, have been given to the Lord Jesus. This entire chapter records His wonderful prayer for us. We have been given as a love gift from the Father to the Son. Some of us may feel that He didn't get very much. We need to remember that it is not what we are now, but what He is going to make out of us, that is important.

This giving of the Levites to Aaron is mentioned again.

And thou shalt give the Levites unto Aaron and to his sons: they are wholly given unto him out of the children of Israel [Num. 3:9].

Now the reason is stated:

And I, behold, I have taken the Levites from among the children of Israel instead of all the firstborn that openeth the matrix among the children of Israel: therefore the Levites shall be mine;

Because all the firstborn are mine; for on the day that I smote all the firstborn in the land of Egypt I hallowed unto me all the firstborn in Israel, both man and beast: mine shall they be: I am the LORD [Num. 3:12–13].

That was the way God put it back there. I think today He still asks every family to give Him not only our possessions but to give Him the members of our household. Have you dedicated your own to the Lord? Have you turned them over to Him? It is a wonderful thing to be able to dedicate your own to Him.

The firstborn belongs to the Lord. That doesn't mean that he must go into the ministry, but he was to be redeemed to show that he belonged to God. In Israel, instead of taking the firstborn from each tribe, God had them numbered; and He took the tribe of Levi.

THREE FAMILIES OF LEVI

And the LORD spake unto Moses in the wilderness of Sinai, saying,

Number the children of Levi after the house of their fathers, by their families: every male from a month old and upward shalt thou number them.

And Moses numbered them according to the word of the LORD, as he was commanded.

And these were the sons of Levi by their names; Gershon, and Kohath, and Merari [Num. 3:14–17].

There were three families in the tribe of Levi, families of his three sons: Gershon, Kohath, and Merari.

The family of Gershon is counted. They are told to pitch their tents behind the tabernacle westward. Their assignment was to take care of the curtains, coverings and cords of the tabernacle (vv. 21–26).

The family of Kohath is counted. They are to pitch on the side of the tabernacle southward. Their assignment is to be in charge of the articles of furniture of the tabernacle (vv. 27–32).

The family of Merari is counted. They are to pitch on the side of the tabernacle northward. Their assignment is to be in charge of the boards, bars, pillars, sockets, and vessels of the tabernacle (vv. 33–37).

We can now visualize the pattern of Israel encamped on the wilderness march. The tabernacle formed a rectangle in the center of the camp. Another rectangle was formed around the tabernacle by the camps of the Levites. Still another, larger rectangle was formed around that by the camps of the twelve tribes. The tabernacle was always set with the door to the east. Aaron and Moses with their families camped before the door of the tabernacle on the east side. Merari was on the north, Gershon on the west, Kohath on the south. These formed the rectangle surrounding the tabernacle. Then beyond this were the camps of Judah, Issachar, Zebulun on the east; Dan, Ashur, Naphthali on the north; Ephraim, Manasseh, Benjamin on the west; Reuben, Simeon, and Gad on the south.

All that were numbered of the Levites, which Moses and Aaron numbered at the commandment of the LORD, throughout their families, all the males from a month old and upward, were twenty and two thousand [Num. 3:39].

CENSUS OF FIRSTBORN
OF ALL ISRAEL

And the LORD said unto Moses, Number all the firstborn of the males of the children of Israel from a month old and upward, and take the number of their names.

And thou shalt take the Levites for me (I am the LORD) instead of all the firstborn among the children of Israel; and the cattle of the Levites instead of all the

firstlings among the cattle of the children of Israel [Num. 3:40–41].

So Moses numbered all the firstborn among the children of Israel and found there were 22,273 males from a month old and upward who were the firstborn. This meant there were 273 more firstborn males than there were Levites; so this additional number was to be redeemed with five shekels apiece, and this was to be given to Aaron and his sons.

To the critic of the Bible there appears in this chapter contradictions in the numbers given. Rather than to devote space to a study of this kind, I refer the interested reader to the very fine work done by Keil and Delitzsch in the third volume of their *Commentary on the Old Testament*.

CHAPTER 4

THEME: *Who is to serve; the order of service*

The three families of the tribe of Levi had service to perform about the tabernacle. This chapter tells us who is to serve, what was the order of their service, and how many there were in the tribe who served.

WHO IS TO SERVE

And the Lord spake unto Moses and unto Aaron, saying,

Take the sum of the sons of Kohath from among the sons of Levi, after their families, by the house of their fathers,

From thirty years old and upward even until fifty years old, all that enter into the host, to do the work in the tabernacle of the congregation [Num. 4:1–3].

The prime of life for the Levites was from thirty to fifty years. Those were the years they were to serve.

THE ORDER OF SERVICE

This shall be the service of the sons of Kohath in the tabernacle of the congregation, about the most holy things:

And when the camp setteth forward, Aaron shall come, and his sons, and they shall take down the covering veil, and cover the ark of testimony with it:

And shall put thereon the covering of badgers' skins, and shall spread over it a cloth wholly of blue, and shall put in the staves thereof.

And when Aaron and his sons have made an end of covering the sanctuary, and all the vessels of the sanctuary, as the camp is to set forward; after that, the sons of Kohath shall come to bear it: but they shall not touch any holy thing, lest they die. These things are the burden of the sons of Kohath in the tabernacle of the congregation [Num. 4:4–6, 15].

The only ones who ever saw the articles that belonged in the Holy of Holies—the ark and the mercy seat—were Aaron and his sons. Those articles were carefully covered by Aaron and his sons before the Kohathites came to carry them.

This is the service of the families of the Gershonites, to serve, and for burdens:

And they shall bear the curtains of the tabernacle, and the tabernacle of the congregation, his covering, and the covering of the badgers' skins that is above upon it, and the hanging for the door of the tabernacle of the congregation [Num. 4:24–25].

It goes on to list some of the other hangings and cords which were the responsibility of the families of Gershon.

As for the sons of Merari . . .

And this is the charge of their burden, according to all their service in the tabernacle of the congregation; the boards of the tabernacle, and the bars thereof, and the pillars thereof, and sockets thereof,

And the pillars of the court round about, and their sockets, and their pins, and their cords, with all their instruments, and with all their service: and by name ye shall reckon the instruments of the

charge of their burden [Num. 4:29, 31–32].

Merari carried the heavy articles, the pillars and the boards and the bars; the Kohathites carried the articles of furniture; Gershon, it would seem, had the easiest job carrying the curtains and coverings and cords.

I'd like for you to get a picture of what happened when they moved. When Moses and Aaron would come out of the tabernacle in the morning, they didn't need to talk things over. Moses didn't say, "Well, let's have a meeting of the board of elders or the board of deacons, and let's find out whether or not we should march today." They didn't depend on that type of thing. They watched to see if the pillar of cloud lifted from off the tabernacle. If it lifted, it meant that they were to march. If it did not lift, it meant that they were to stay in camp that day. Moses and Aaron simply had to watch and follow the leading that the Spirit of God gave them, for that pillar of cloud represented the Spirit of God.

The child of God should be led like that today. Not that we see a visible pillar of cloud, but we should be led by the same Spirit of God. "For as many as are led by the Spirit of God, they are the sons of God" (Rom. 8:14). The Spirit of God wants to lead the sons of God.

When the pillar of cloud lifted, immediately Aaron and his sons went into the Holy Place, and they went first to the veil. You will remember that on the other side of the veil, in the Holy of Holies, was the ark and the mercy seat. I believe that the ark and the mercy seat were put up against the veil, not against the back wall. This means that when the high priest went into the Holy of Holies, he turned around and faced east as he sprinkled the blood on the mercy seat. The high priest did that on one day of the year only. On this day of moving they did not go inside the veil. The veil was held up by rings and the high priest would let it down, and then drop the veil down over the mercy seat and the ark. Then they would put the linen cloth around it and its other coverings, and finally they would put around it the outside cover of the tabernacle. When that was concluded, and all the vessels were wrapped, the Kohathites were permitted to come in. There were staves that fit into the rings on all of these articles of furniture. The Kohathites would come in and pick up the furniture by these staves and carry it out. The priests who carried the ark would lead the way out to the front and would wait for the pillar of cloud to guide them.

We will see their marching order in a later chapter.

In the evening, it must have been a thrilling sight to see them set up a new camp. Every man knew what he was to do. Every man was carrying his particular part of the tabernacle and had been carrying it during the day's march. When they set up camp, the very first thing that was put down was the ark. The whole camp was arranged according to that. The Kohathites carrying the other articles of furniture would put them down in their relation to the ark, and then the boards and the curtains were set up around them. In other words, the furniture was put in first. Now that's not the way we build a house today, but remember this was designed for a march and it had to be mobile.

Each man had his assignment. I'm of the opinion that the camp went up in a hurry, and I mean in a hurry. I think that within about thirty minutes of the time they came to rest and the ark was put down, the tabernacle was ready to be used.

Let me illustrate this. In my first pastorate in Nashville, Tennessee, I was single and I spent a lot of time with the young people. When the circus would come to town, we would go out to the railroad yards to be there when the circus arrived at two o'clock in the morning. You could hear the animals cry, but there was no other sound. They would put the cars on the side track, and the minute those cars came to a standstill, a whole army of men would come out of those cars. The train would not have been stopped more than five minutes before the wagons were rolling off the flat cars; the circus was unloaded and moving out to the circus grounds.

A cook tent would be erected and many of the roustabouts would have coffee and breakfast while another crew would put up the big tent, the big top; then this crew would come in for breakfast while the other workers would go out to put in the seats and circus rings and hang the trapezes. I tell you, every man knew his job and it was interesting to watch. By ten o'clock in the morning everything was in order and ready for business. By noon the big circus parade would be on the street.

This was most interesting to me. We would spend the whole night watching the circus when it came to town. I would tell my young folk, "I'm of the opinion that this is the way it was done when the children of Israel came into camp."

When Israel came into camp, the Kohathites would put down the articles of furniture. Then

Merari would come in with the boards and the bars and put up his part. Then Gershon would put on the coverings. Finally, the high priest would remove the veil and hang that. What a thrill it must have been to watch Israel come into camp. After forty years of practice they must have been pretty good at it.

As each Levite had his assignment, just so, every Christian has a gift and a job God wants him to do. I believe God will reward you for doing what He wants you to do. We are not to do what *we* choose to do, but we are to exercise the gifts that He has given us.

Suppose there was a fellow who carried that tent pin for the northwest corner of the tabernacle, and he got weary of his job. One day as he was driving in his pin, he said, "I'm tired of this. For twenty years now I've been carrying that tent pin. I come here in the morning, and loosen it and pull it out of the ground, put it on my shoulder, and take it over on the wagon with my family. Nobody seems to recognize how hard I work. Nobody rewards me for what I do. Moses never has called me up and given me a medal. I'm tired of this job and I'm going to quit carrying this pin." One morning when they were taking down the tabernacle, his pin was hard to loosen from the ground and he got disgusted and left it there. He thought, "Nobody will pay any attention anyway. My job is not very important. All I do is

carry a tent pin; so I think I'll just leave it today."

Can you imagine the problem that next evening? They would try to set up the tabernacle but the northwest corner pin would not be there. The men would report it to Moses, and they would look up this man who was to carry that pin. Moses would ask, "Where is the tent pin?" and the man would answer, "I left it back there where we camped last night." Then Moses would ask him why he left it, and the man would answer, "I don't think that my job is really important." Moses would say, "Not important! We can't put up the tabernacle without it. You will have to sit there all night holding that cord yourself because you are responsible for that tent pin!"

My friend, who is to determine who does the most important thing in God's service today? That man had been faithful for twenty years; then all of a sudden he just went haywire, and notice what it did to the setting up of the tabernacle. How many children of God today think their service is unimportant? God is not going to reward you for the amount of work you have done, but for your faithfulness in doing that which He has called you to do. If you are carrying that tent pin from the northwest corner, don't forget to carry it today. The job the Lord has given you to do is very important to Him.

CHAPTER 5

THEME: *Defilement by disease and death; restitution; the jealousy offering*

You may have thought that this is not a very interesting book, but I hope that by now you have changed your mind. There is interesting material in it and a pertinent message for us in these days.

We have seen the orderly arrangement of the camp which was a preparation for the wilderness march. There had to be this preparation. The Christian today needs to recognize that he is a pilgrim going through the wilderness of this world. Everything and everyone must be in his place for the walk, the work, the war, and the worship of the wilderness.

We come now to instructions concerning cleansing the camp, which includes chapters 5 through 8. As we come to this section on the

cleansing of the camp, we need to recognize that the reason for cleansing is that they (and we) are serving a *holy* God.

DEFILEMENT BY DISEASE AND DEATH

And the Lord spake unto Moses, saying,

Command the children of Israel, that they put out of the camp every leper, and every one that hath an issue, and whosoever is defiled by the dead:

Both male and female shall ye put out, without the camp shall ye put them; that they defile not their camps, in the midst whereof I dwell.

And the children of Israel did so, and put them out without the camp: as the LORD spake unto Moses, so did the children of Israel [Num. 5:1–4].

They were to put the leper out of the camp. That may seem cruel to us, but there was a very definite reason for it. There was the danger of contamination and transmission of disease. And we read that the camp was not to be defiled because God dwelt in the midst of the camp.

God commanded that certain ones were to be put out of the camp. This was not done by those who thought they were superior or wanted to assert their spiritual prerogatives. It was by *God's* command. Who were to be excluded from the camp? First of all, the leper. We saw in the Book of Leviticus that leprosy was a type of sin. Any outburst from within, an issue in the body, represents the flesh, the unregenerate nature of man. Sins of the flesh must be dealt with.

We need to recognize that if we are going to walk with God, if we are going to have fellowship with Him, there must be a cleansing of our lives. Recently I heard of a preacher who died as an alcoholic, yet people talked about what a blessing he was. I discount that, because God is not a fool. He does not bless nor will He walk with us when we are living in conscious sin. "For our God is a consuming fire" (Heb. 12:29). "God is greatly to be feared in the assembly of the saints, and to be had in reverence of all them that are about him" (Ps. 89:7). Today a great deal of the problems and difficulties and sickness and heartache is caused by Christian people who will not deal with the sin in their lives. In our churches today, we shut our eyes to sin in the lives of the people.

In Israel there were certain ones who had to be put out of the camp!

When we get to the Book of Joshua, we will see that Israel could not get a victory at Ai because Achan had sinned and had covered it up. It had to be brought to light and dealt with before Israel could have a victory.

I believe that there could be revival today if more preachers, church officers, Sunday School teachers, choir directors, and singers would deal with the sins in their lives. Sins of the flesh are like a leprosy. God will not bless until that sin is dealt with.

RESTITUTION

And the LORD spake unto Moses, saying,

Speak unto the children of Israel, When a man or woman shall commit any sin that men commit, to do a trespass against the LORD, and that person be guilty;

Then they shall confess their sin which they have done: and he shall recompense his trespass with the principal thereof, and add unto it the fifth part thereof, and give it unto him against whom he hath trespassed [Num. 5:5–7].

This is what Zacchaeus was offering to do. "Behold, Lord, the half of my goods I give to the poor; and if I have taken any thing from any man by false accusation, I restore him fourfold" (Luke 19:8). He was actually going farther than the Mosaic Law required him to go.

We see here that a restitution was to be made. Repentance, therefore, is more than simply saying, "I'm sorry." A relationship between God and the individual cannot be made sweet until the relationship is made right between the individuals. "For godly sorrow worketh repentance to salvation not to be repented of: but the sorrow of the world worketh death" (2 Cor. 7:10). Many people today think that repentance means shedding a few tears and then going merrily on their way. It is much more than that. It is making things right by making restitution to the individual who has been injured. We are to confess our sins to God, that is true. But we must remember that our Lord also said this: "Therefore if thou bring thy gift to the altar, and there rememberest that thy brother hath aught against thee; Leave there thy gift before the altar, and go thy way; first be reconciled to thy brother, and then come and offer thy gift" (Matt. 5:23–24). The world has the idea one can shed a few tears and eat humble pie for a while and then everything is right again. That is what is called the "sorrow of the world" in Corinthians, and that kind of repentance is meaningless.

My Dad used to tell about a little boat on the Mississippi River. It had a little bitty boiler and a great big whistle. When that boat was going upstream and blew its whistle, it would drift back. It couldn't go upstream and blow its whistle at the same time! There are a lot of people like that today. Their repentance is like the blowing of the whistle. They shed tears in profusion, but there is no turning from sin, no turning to God, no restitution to the one they have injured. For this reason there is no progress in their Christian lives.

THE JEALOUSY OFFERING

And the LORD spake unto Moses, saying,

Speak unto the children of Israel, and say unto them, If any man's wife go aside, and commit a trespass against him,

And a man lie with her carnally, and it be hid from the eyes of her husband, and be kept close, and she be defiled, and there be no witness against her, neither she be taken with the manner;

And the spirit of jealousy come upon him, and he be jealous of his wife, and she be defiled: or if the spirit of jealousy come upon him, and he be jealous of his wife, and she be not defiled:

Then shall the man bring his wife unto the priest, and he shall bring her offering for her, the tenth part of an ephah of barley meal; he shall pour no oil upon it, nor put frankincense thereon; for it is an offering of jealousy, an offering of memorial, bringing iniquity to remembrance.

And the priest shall set the woman before the LORD, and uncover the woman's head, and put the offering of memorial in her hands, which is the jealousy offering: and the priest shall have in his hand the bitter water that causeth the curse:

And the priest shall charge her by an oath, and say unto the woman, If no man have lain with thee, and if thou hast not gone aside to uncleanness with another instead of thy husband, be thou free from this bitter water that causeth the curse [Num. 5:11–15, 18–19].

The verses following tell us that the woman was to drink the bitter water and if it caused her belly to swell and her thigh to rot, she was to be a curse among her people. If she was not defiled, but was clean, then she should be free. This test would have a tremendous psychological effect upon a person, especially if she were guilty.

Why isn't the man subjected to the same test? The Bible does not teach a double standard. In this case, the husband was suspicious of the wife. Could a husband be guilty? Of course. We saw in Leviticus, and will see again in Deuteronomy, that if a man or woman were taken in adultery, *both* of them were to be stoned to death. There is no double standard in the Bible. Then why is only the woman to be tested? Because this is a picture of Christ and the church. There can be no suspicion of Christ, but there is suspicion of the church, I can assure you. I know the church rather well, and, believe me, it is under suspicion!

But this is a jealousy offering. Can God be jealous? Yes, He says that He is a jealous God. Many times He says, "I the LORD thy God am a jealous God." It is not the low human kind of jealousy like the jealousy of a person who is goaded by an Iago, but the jealousy of love.

When I hear a wife say, "My husband is not jealous of me," I want to say to her, "Lady, don't mention it. If your husband is not jealous of you, it is because he doesn't love you. So I don't think I would mention it, if I were you." If a man really loves a woman, he is jealous of her, and the same thing would be true of a woman who loves a man. This is the way God is jealous. He loves us, and He wants our love in return. He is jealous of us! He doesn't want us to give our time and our affection to the things of this world.

Now, in this test of jealousy, if the wife was shown to be innocent, she was exonerated. Actually, this law protected her from a jealous husband. This worked in her behalf in a very wonderful way.

Certainly this reveals again that the Word of God is very clear on this matter of fidelity to the marriage vow. Today we are seeing a great letdown of that, and it is becoming the accepted thing that the marriage vow is not to be taken seriously. *God* will hold you to it—I can assure you of that. A great many of the problems of this world today begin in the home. They are being made by those who are treating lightly the marriage vow. God cannot, nor will He bless a nation where this situation prevails.

CHAPTER 6

THEME: *Nazarite vow; the triune blessing*

We come now to something that is quite remarkable: the vow of the Nazarite. This was a voluntary vow. Any man or woman of Israel who wanted to become a Nazarite could do so. He could take the vow for a certain period of time or for a lifetime. God did not command it; it was purely voluntary. But if any of His people wanted a closer walk with Him, this is what they could do.

NAZARITE VOW

And the Lord spake unto Moses, saying,

Speak unto the children of Israel, and say unto them, When either man or woman shall separate themselves to vow a vow of a Nazarite, to separate themselves unto the Lord:

He shall separate himself from wine and strong drink, and shall drink no vinegar of wine, or vinegar of strong drink, neither shall he drink any liquor of grapes, nor eat moist grapes, or dried [Num. 6:1–3].

When a person took this voluntary vow of the Nazarite, there were three things he was forbidden to do.

First, he was not to drink wine or strong drink. Anything that came from the vine was forbidden him. This has nothing to do with the question of whether it is right or wrong to drink wine. May I say this, and I want to say it carefully and I want you to hear me carefully. The Christian standard is not a standard of right or wrong. The question is this: What is your *purpose* in doing what you are doing? Are you doing it to please Christ? Do you want to be a Nazarite? Do you want to live for Him? That is the question. People will ask me whether it is right for a Christian to drink wine. My friend, I won't argue that point. I won't argue right or wrong with you. I want to know whether you really want to please Christ. Wine, in the Scriptures, is a symbol of earthly joy; it is to cheer the heart. The whole point here is that the Nazarite was to find his joy in the Lord.

There are a great many Christians today who do not find their joy in the things of God, in the Word of God, or in fellowship with Christ. They find their joy in the things of this world. I go to a great number of church banquets, and I know there are church members there who would never come to a weekday meeting unless it was a banquet. I always feel sorry for those Christians who, like the poor woman, got crumbs from God's table. Don't misunderstand me; there is nothing wrong with banquets, but when they go to Christian banquets, they get crumbs—that's all. There would be the time of eating, then a few pious things would be said; someone would take a verse of Scripture and say some sweet things about it, and everyone would leave, feeling very spiritual and very satisfied and even challenged. But they would drop right back and live just as they had always lived. I feel sorry for them.

Where do you find joy, friend? I ask you that very personally. Do you need the stimulants of this world in order to enjoy "Christian" things? Can you really get joy out of studying the Word of God? Does prayer turn you off or turn you on? My, how many of us today think we are being really Christian and really spiritual when all we have been doing is bringing the world into our activities!

Second, when a person took the Nazarite vow, he was not to shave his head.

All the days of the vow of his separation there shall no razor come upon his head: until the days be fulfilled, in the which he separateth himself unto the Lord, he shall be holy, and shall let the locks of the hair of his head grow [Num. 6:5].

Paul says in 1 Corinthians 11:14, "Doth not even nature itself teach you, that, if a man have long hair, it is a shame unto him?" I wish we could hang signs to state this in public places. I still think it is a shame for a man to have long hair. I agree with the apostle Paul; it is a shame to the man. Therefore, the Nazarite must be willing to bear shame for Christ. His long hair would indicate that he was willing to share that position with Christ who said, "But I am a worm, and no man; a reproach of men, and despised of the people" (Ps. 22:6).

Third, he who took the Nazarite vow was not to touch a dead body.

All the days that he separateth himself unto the Lord he shall come at no dead body.

He shall not make himself unclean for his father, or for his mother, for his brother, or for his sister, when they die: because the consecration of his God is upon his head [Num. 6:6–7].

We read in chapter 5 that a leper was to be taken out of the camp and also whoever was defiled by the dead. You see, the world is the place of death. I think one can say that death is the deepest mark that is on this world today. Death is the seal of a sin-cursed earth. It is the judgment which God pronounced. It was because of sin that death came into the world. In order to deal with death, sin must be dealt with, because the wages of sin is death.

The Nazarite was not to touch a dead body. He was to be separate from the world. The Lord was to be first in his life. Remember the Lord Jesus said, "He that loveth father or mother more than me is not worthy of me: and he that loveth son or daughter more than me is not worthy of me" (Matt. 10:37). He is to be put above loved ones. He has top priority. Remember that this vow is voluntary. He doesn't command the vow of the Nazarite. But if one wanted to take this vow and dedicate his life to Him, he could do so.

Do you find your joy in the Lord? Are you willing to bear shame for Him, to take an humble place for Him? Are you willing to put Him first, above everything in this life? You see, although the believer today doesn't take a Nazarite vow, there is the offer of a closer walk with the Lord. It is voluntary. You must want it. It is an act of dedication. It is incorrect to call it consecration; you cannot consecrate yourself. Only God can consecrate you. Actually, what we do is come to God with empty hands, offering nothing but ourselves to Him—our devotion, our worship, our love, our service, our time.

Sometimes when you stand for God, you will find you must stand alone. He must be first in your life. Many people today talk about being consecrated Christians, but they wouldn't dare do anything that would offend the little clique in their church. They are afraid they might find themselves outside, which would be much better for them because some of these church cliques are not of God and can be a very cruel crowd! Yet, there are folk who think they are consecrated, who do not have the strength or stamina to stand against such a clique; so they just go along with the crowd. You see, if you want to give yourself to the Lord, Christ must have top priority. You must find your satisfaction and your joy in Him.

All the days of his separation he is holy unto the Lord [Num. 6:8].

I'm of the opinion that a great many folk today are missing a great blessing. Perhaps even now you are going through a particular time of trial. Why not set yourself aside for God? If you are a Christian, give yourself to God in a very definite way. It won't remove the trial, but it will make it more bearable. The Lord Jesus said, "Come unto me, all ye that labour and are heavy laden, and I will give you rest. Take my yoke upon you, and learn of me; for I am meek and lowly in heart: and ye shall find rest unto your souls" (Matt. 11:28–29). It is wonderful to be yoked with Him.

And if any man die very suddenly by him, and he hath defiled the head of his consecration; then he shall shave his head in the day of his cleansing, on the seventh day shall he shave it.

And on the eighth day he shall bring two turtles, or two young pigeons, to the priest, to the door of the tabernacle of the congregation [Num. 6:9–10].

God is very earnest about having a vow to Him kept. If the Nazarite was defiled, he was to bring a sacrifice. God does not require a vow, but when a vow is made, He expects it to be kept, and it is a serious matter if it is broken.

I am confident that there are a great many Christians who promised God things that they never made good, and that explains their sad spiritual plight today. Through the years of my ministry, I have watched some people come to church every Sunday with their halos brightly shined. They would be so pious that you'd think any moment they would sprout wings and fly away. Yet, these people would let the Lord down, over and over again. Then, later on, something would come up in their lives that would make shipwreck of their faith.

A great many people today will not make a pledge to God because they are afraid they may not keep it. People are afraid to put it on the line with God. They are afraid to pledge something financial, for example, because they might see a new car or a new television set and buy that instead. So they don't want to commit themselves about something to God. May I say, I believe this is one reason people miss out on blessings today.

Now it is true, God goes into great detail here to reveal that He does expect us to follow through right down to the details. It is also true that we shouldn't pledge something to God and then decide to do something or to buy something else instead. But, if we make an agreement with God and stick with it, He will bless. God is very serious and very practical about these matters, and we should be also. God will always bless us if we are faithful to Him and to the promise we make to Him.

There is a great spiritual lesson here for us. This is something you should think about very seriously today.

THE TRIUNE BLESSING

And the Lord spake unto Moses, saying,

Speak unto Aaron and unto his sons, saying, On this wise ye shall bless the children of Israel, saying unto them,

The Lord bless thee, and keep thee:

The Lord make his face shine upon thee, and be gracious unto thee:

The Lord lift up his countenance upon thee, and give thee peace.

And they shall put my name upon the children of Israel; and I will bless them [Num. 6:22–27].

Here we find the Trinity in the Old Testament. God the Father is the source of all blessing. The Lord Jesus is the One who makes His face to shine upon us. The Holy Spirit lifts up His countenance upon us and gives us peace. This is the only way we can come to God and experience the peace of God. He is the One who makes these things real to our hearts.

The triune God gives them this blessing. The census has been taken, and they all know their pedigree. The standards have been raised; so they all know where they belong. They are to follow their standard, and they are to camp in their assigned place in the camp with their own tribe and their own family. The camp has been cleansed. Now the Lord blesses them. It is the only way God can bless.

Many churches today are not experiencing the blessing of God. The problem is that they are not properly prepared for the march. They are trying to start out without first setting things in order. They are like a soldier who forgot to put on his belt one morning. Believe me it is pretty hard to march and carry a gun without your belt or suspenders! And there are churches like that, my friend. They are starting out before things are set in order. Paul is writing to the church when he says, "Let all things be done decently and in order" (1 Cor. 14:40). Know your pedigree; that is, know you are a child of God; know your standard; know what your gift is and use it for Him; and keep your life clean.

What a wonderful blessing there is here. God the Father keeps us; the Son makes His face to shine upon us—He is the light of the world; God the Holy Spirit gives us peace. What a glorious chapter this is!

CHAPTER 7

THEME: *Gifts of the princes*

We come now to another rather remarkable chapter. This is next to the longest chapter in the Bible. The longest chapter in the Bible is Psalm 119, which is all about the Word of God. Here we find eighty-nine verses, and do you know what they are all about? The gifts of the princes. They enumerate each item that they brought. It's really a monotonous chapter, because it is repetition again and again. All the princes are mentioned, and we are told exactly what each one of them gave. This has a very important message for you and me.

GIFTS OF THE PRINCES

And it came to pass on the day that Moses had fully set up the tabernacle, and had anointed it, and sanctified it, and all the instruments thereof, both the altar and all the vessels thereof, and had anointed them, and sanctified them;

That the princes of Israel, heads of the house of their fathers, who were the princes of the tribes, and were over them that were numbered, offered:

And the Lord said unto Moses, They shall offer their offering, each prince on his day, for the dedicating of the altar.

And he that offered his offering the first day was Nahshon the son of Amminadab, of the tribe of Judah:

And his offering was one silver charger, the weight thereof was an hundred and thirty shekels, one silver bowl of sev-

enty shekels, after the shekel of the sanctuary; both of them were full of fine flour mingled with oil for a meat offering:

One spoon of ten shekels of gold, full of incense:

One young bullock, one ram, one lamb of the first year, for a burnt offering:

One kid of the goats for a sin offering:

And for a sacrifice of peace offerings, two oxen, five rams, five he goats, five lambs of the first year: this was the offering of Nahshon the son of Amminadab [Num. 7:1–2, 11–17].

Do you know this man, Nahshon? I don't. All I know about this man is that he offered these gifts, but God knew him and God took note of the gifts that he brought.

Do you find his offering interesting? I don't, really. It sounds sort of like a shopping list.

Now the next man came:

On the second day Nethaneel the son of Zuar, prince of Issachar, did offer [Num. 7:18].

Now do you know what he did? He did the same thing—brought the identical offering. Couldn't the Bible just have a ditto mark there for his offering? Couldn't the Spirit of God have said simply that it was the same? No, the Spirit of God recorded very carefully and in detail what each one brought. Each man is listed here by name, and, as far as I know, this is all he ever did for the Lord. This whole long chapter is about these men and what they gave to the Lord. Even a spoonful of incense was recorded!

Now, our Lord said, "But when thou doest alms, let not thy left hand know what thy right hand doeth" (Matt. 6:3), and a great many people had better not let the right hand know what the left hand is doing, because both hands are doing so little for the Lord. They should be ashamed of their hands, both right and left. But I have news for you. Little as it is, the Lord records what you do for Him.

Remember that the Gospel of Luke tells how the Lord Jesus sat over against the treasury one day. Was He nosy, do you think? Did He have any business there? He certainly did. He just happened to be the Lord of Glory and the Lord of the temple. He watched how the peo-

The tabernacle erected, and the tents of Israel around it.

ple gave. The rich gave rich gifts. They were large gifts, and He noted that. Then He watched a widow put in two little coppers. In comparison to the richness of that temple, to the ornateness and wealth of it, she didn't add anything. But Jesus didn't think of it that way. She gave all she had, and to Jesus hers was the largest gift of all. It is recorded in heaven. You may be sure of that.

Jesus knows exactly what you give to Him, and He knows how much you keep for yourself. I don't like this pious talk of some people saying what they give is just between them and the Lord. I wonder if they realize the Lord is recording it.

This is a remarkable chapter. It is eighty-nine verses long, and one of the most monotonous things I've ever read, but I think the Lord still looks it over. I think He opens the books and says, "Well, look here what this prince gave." He takes note of all the gifts.

Friend, you have never done anything for Him that is not recorded, and you will be rewarded for that. We ought to talk more freely about these things because they are important to God.

CHAPTER 8

THEME: *The light of the lampstand; Levites cleansed*

This chapter surprises us by beginning with instructions for lighting the lampstand in the Holy Place. At first it seems that the lampstand is out of place—that belongs back in Exodus where instructions were given for the tabernacle. But as we look at it more closely, we see that God has a good reason for mentioning it here.

Chapter 8 continues the section regarding the cleansing operation in preparation for the wilderness march. Those who were going to follow God and serve Him had to be clean.

THE LIGHT OF THE LAMPSTAND

And the LORD spake unto Moses, saying,

Speak unto Aaron, and say unto him, When thou lightest the lamps, the seven lamps shall give light over against the candlestick.

And Aaron did so; he lighted the lamps thereof over against the candlestick, as the LORD commanded Moses.

And this work of the candlestick was of beaten gold, unto the shaft thereof, unto the flowers thereof, was beaten work: according unto the pattern which the LORD had shewed Moses, so he made the candlestick [Num. 8:1–4].

This beautiful lampstand was one of the articles of furniture in the tabernacle. It was made of beaten gold, the work of an artisan who had shaped it into the form of branches of almonds with a great almond blossom at the top of each branch to hold the lamps. The lights on the top revealed the beauty of the lampstand.

This is the most perfect picture of Christ that we find in the tabernacle. The lighted lamps represent the Holy Spirit who reveals the beauty of Christ. The lampstand is symbolic of Christ who sent the Holy Spirit into the world. The Spirit of God takes the things of Christ and shows them to us.

Now we understand why the lampstand is mentioned here between the gifts of the princes and the cleansing of the Levites. It reminds us that everything must be done in the light of the presence of Christ.

What does that mean to you and me? It means that our gifts to Him and our service for Him must be done in the light of His presence. In other words, it must be done according to His Word. This is where the church is to get its instructions—not from a book of church order or some other place—but from the Word of God.

The lampstand is the light, and the Lord Jesus Christ calls Himself the Light of the world. He is revealed in the Word of God.

LEVITES CLEANSED

The remainder of the chapter deals with the cleansing of the Levites. They had to come to the laver for cleansing although they had already been to the brazen altar, which speaks of the cross of Christ. Now we find that God will keep His servants clean.

And the Lord spake unto Moses, saying,

Take the Levites from among the children of Israel, and cleanse them [Num. 8:5–6].

Friend, if God is going to use you, He'll have to clean you. He will have His own way of doing it. Now notice how the Levites were cleansed.

And thus shalt thou do unto them, to cleanse them: Sprinkle water of purifying upon them, and let them shave all their flesh, and let them wash their clothes, and so make themselves clean.

Then let them take a young bullock with his meat offering, even fine flour mingled with oil, and another young bullock shalt thou take for a sin offering [Num. 8:7–8].

First, they must be sprinkled with the water of purifying. This was done at the laver. Secondly, they were to shave all their flesh. Thirdly, they were to wash their clothes to make themselves clean. Fourthly, they were to offer a sin offering and a burnt offering.

Do you remember what God had said about Levi? Levi was one of the sons of Jacob, and when Jacob blessed him, this is what he said: "Simeon and Levi are brethren; instruments of cruelty are in their habitations. O my soul, come not thou into their secret; unto their assembly, mine honour, be not thou united: for in their anger they slew a man, and in their selfwill they digged down a wall. Cursed be their anger, for it was fierce; and their wrath, for it was cruel: I will divide them in Jacob, and scatter them in Israel" (Gen. 49:5–7). Obviously they needed to be cleansed.

The important thing for the child of God today is not *how* you walk, but *where* you walk. "But if we walk in the light, as he is in the light, we have fellowship one with another, and the blood of Jesus Christ his Son cleanseth us from all sin" (1 John 1:7). You see, the light and the laver are placed together here. When you walk in the light, you see that there is imperfection in your life. Then you go to the laver to remove it, which symbolizes the confession of your sins.

Notice that there are four steps that are given here for cleansing.

1. "Sprinkle the water of purifying upon them." You remember that when Christ washed the disciples' feet, Simon Peter objected. The Lord Jesus told him, "If I wash thee not, thou hast no part with me" (John 13:8). That means, you will not have fellowship with Me, you will have no part with Me. John explains this in his Epistle. "If we walk in the light, as he is in the light, we have fellowship one with another." Yes, but when I walk in the light, I see things that are wrong in my life. What am I to do then? "And the blood of Jesus Christ his Son cleanseth us from all sin." It keeps on cleansing us from all sin as we confess our sins to Him. "If we confess our sins, he is faithful and just to forgive us our sins, and to cleanse us from all unrighteousness" (1 John 1:7 and 9). This is most important, friends. This is for believers. If you are to serve God, you must confess your sins. The brazen altar is the place where the sinner comes to God for salvation; the laver is the place the believer, the saint of God, comes to be cleansed.

2. "Let them shave all their flesh." The word of God is alive, and "powerful, and sharper than any two-edged sword, piercing even to the dividing asunder of soul and spirit, and of the joints and marrow, and is a discerner of the thoughts and intents of the heart" (Heb. 4:12). The Word of God can dig down into your life and find things wrong there that you didn't know were wrong. You don't need that sharp razor, you see. You don't think there is a spot on you? Then get out the razor and start using the Word of God. It's a light and it's also a sharp razor.

3. "Let them wash their clothes." A garment speaks of the habits of life. We even call them a riding habit or a walking habit to identify the use of the garment. We need to wash our garments—we have certain habits that we need to get rid of because they are hurting our testimony for the Lord.

4. "Take for a sin offering." There was to be a bullock for a burnt offering and a meal offering and another young bullock for a sin offering. These offerings, as we have already seen, speak of Christ. The burnt offering speaks of who He is. The meal offering speaks of His sinless perfection. The peace offering speaks of the fact that He made peace by the blood of His cross. The sin offering speaks of what He has done for us. In other words, all of this cleansing, all of this that is done, is done in the light of the person and work of Christ. He did all of this for us. He did it in order that we might serve Him.

And thou shalt bring the Levites before the tabernacle of the congregation: and thou shalt gather the whole assembly of the children of Israel together:

And thou shalt bring the Levites before the Lord: and the children of Israel

shall put their hands upon the Levites:

And Aaron shall offer the Levites before the LORD for an offering of the children of Israel, that they may execute the service of the LORD [Num. 8:9–11].

Now, let us understand this very clearly. You can sing a solo, you can preach a sermon, you can teach a Sunday school class, you can be an officer in the church, but you are not effective until you walk in the light of the Word of God, until you have been to Him for cleansing. You must see yourself in the light of the Word of God. You know you come short, you confess your sins to Him, and you know He forgives you and cleanses you. You use that sharp razor that takes off that which offends. You need to watch your habits if you are to be used of God. Many a man has let a bad habit ruin his testimony. And the cleansing must all rest upon the person and work of Christ.

We see that all this was done so that the Levites might serve the Lord.

Thus shalt thou separate the Levites from among the children of Israel: and the Levites shall be mine.

And I have given the Levites as a gift to Aaron and to his sons from among the children of Israel, to do the service of the children of Israel in the tabernacle of the congregation, and to make an atonement for the children of Israel: that there be no plague among the children of Israel, when the children of Israel come nigh unto the sanctuary [Num. 8:14, 19].

Remember that we have mentioned before how our Lord, in His high priestly prayer, says of the believers, ". . . thine they were, and thou gavest them me . . ." (John 17:6). The Lord Jesus Christ paid a price and redeemed us back to God by His own blood. Now the Father has given us as a gift back to the Lord Jesus Christ. We belong to Him.

Now service to Him does not rest upon rules and regulations and law. That is not the way to serve the Lord Jesus. We serve Him because we love Him. We are in a new relationship to Him. We have been joined to Him; we are a part of Him. What a thrill it is to know it is not a matter of following little rules and regulations. Instead it is a matter of wanting to please Him. How wonderful this is.

This is it that belongeth unto the Levites: from twenty and five years old and upward they shall go in to wait upon the service of the tabernacle of the congregation:

And from the age of fifty years they shall cease waiting upon the service thereof, and shall serve no more:

But shall minister with their brethren in the tabernacle of the congregation, to keep the charge, and shall do no service. Thus shalt thou do unto the Levites touching their charge [Num. 8:24–26].

The Levites were permitted to serve in the tabernacle at the age of twenty-five years. Back in the fourth chapter we learned that they could not enter into priestly service until the age of thirty years. The priests served from age thirty to fifty. The Levites who served around in the tabernacle, putting it up, taking it down—just any kind of service— were from age twenty-five to fifty years. Back in Numbers 1:3 we saw that the census of those able to go to war included the ones who were twenty years old and upward.

This raises the question of the age of accountability. When we come to Numbers 14:29 we read, "Your carcases shall fall in this wilderness; and all that were numbered of you, according to your whole number, from twenty years old and upward, which have murmured against me." Apparently in this instance, twenty years was the age of accountability. The boy who was nineteen years old would be permitted to enter the land. The twenty-year-old boy who had murmured would die in the wilderness.

I would like to suggest that the age of accountability may be older than we tend to think it is. We think maybe a little child is responsible. I don't think so. A little child can accept the Lord. In fact there are many on record as young as four years old who have received Christ. But the age of accountability must be somewhat later than that, and I'm of the opinion it will be different for different people. We see here that God made it different for the different forms of service. A man could be a soldier at twenty years; a Levite could work in the tabernacle at twenty-five years; a priest began his priestly service at thirty years. The important thing is that we should instruct boys and girls and encourage them to come to the Lord as soon as possible. It is so important for our children to trust in the Lord Jesus.

CHAPTER 9

THEME: *Passover observed on wilderness march; pillar of cloud by day, pillar of fire by night*

PASSOVER OBSERVED ON WILDERNESS MARCH

And the LORD spake unto Moses in the wilderness of Sinai, in the first month of the second year after they were come out of the land of Egypt, saying,

Let the children of Israel also keep the passover at his appointed season [Num. 9:1–2].

Israel was to celebrate the Passover while they were in the wilderness. So they kept the Passover on this, the second year after they left Egypt. During the celebration a problem arose. There were certain men who were defiled by a dead body so that they could not keep the Passover. They came and reported it to Moses and Aaron and asked what they should do.

And Moses said unto them, Stand still, and I will hear what the LORD will command concerning you [Num. 9:8].

Moses didn't appeal to a book of church order; he didn't appeal to *Robert's Rules of Order.* He appealed to God. I repeat again what I have said so often. We are to appeal to the Word of God today. That is the authority for the child of God. Now I realize there will be different ideas on the interpretation of the Word of God. That is why we should study it and be sensible in our interpretation of it.

And the LORD spake unto Moses, saying,

Speak unto the children of Israel, saying, If any man of you or of your posterity shall be unclean by reason of a dead body, or be in a journey afar off, yet he shall keep the passover unto the LORD.

The fourteenth day of the second month at even they shall keep it, and eat it with unleavened bread and bitter herbs [Num. 9:9–11].

Those who were unable to keep the Passover at the appointed time were to have a delayed Passover and celebrate it a month later.

PILLAR OF CLOUD BY DAY, PILLAR OF FIRE BY NIGHT

And on the day that the tabernacle was reared up the cloud covered the tabernacle, namely, the tent of the testimony: and at even there was upon the tabernacle as it were the appearance of fire, until the morning.

So it was alway: the cloud covered it by day, and the appearance of fire by night [Num. 9:15–16].

The children of Israel had a covering cloud, which was the Shekinah glory. This was one of many things that made them different from any other nation. When Paul was writing to the Romans and wanted to give some of the identifying marks of the Israelites, he wrote this, "Who are Israelites; to whom pertaineth the adoption, and the glory, and the covenants, and the giving of the law, and the service of God, and the promises; Whose are the fathers, and of whom as concerning the flesh Christ came, who is over all, God blessed for ever. Amen" (Rom. 9:4–5). You see, he mentions the glory. These were the only people who ever had the visible presence of God with them.

At the commandment of the LORD the children of Israel journeyed, and at the commandment of the LORD they pitched: as long as the cloud abode upon the tabernacle they rested in their tents.

And when the cloud tarried long upon the tabernacle many days, then the children of Israel kept the charge of the LORD, and journeyed not [Num. 9:18–19].

Moses was not the one who decided whether they would march today or tomorrow, or whether they would stay in camp for several days. God decided that.

We need to recognize today that the Lord Jesus Christ is the Head of the church. He is the One who should lead. The problem is that the church is so busy going its own way that oftentimes He isn't even consulted. But Christ is still the Head of His church, and those who are His will follow Him.

You will notice that sometimes they stayed in camp for several days, even months, and they were about a year at Mount Sinai. They were out there in that wilderness for forty years.

Or whether it were two days, or a month, or a year, that the cloud tarried upon the tabernacle, remaining thereon, the children of Israel abode in their tents, and journeyed not: but when it was taken up, they journeyed.

At the commandment of the LORD they rested in the tents, and at the commandment of the LORD they journeyed: they kept the charge of the LORD, at the commandment of the LORD by the hand of Moses [Num. 9:22–23].

When the pillar of cloud lifted in the morning, they knew it was a day for them to journey. The Levites would go immediately to take down the tabernacle, and I believe they could do this in thirty minutes or so, and would put it up just as quickly in the evening when they came to rest. Then the pillar of cloud that had led them would settle down over the tabernacle. This pillar of cloud and pillar of fire was the Shekinah glory that was the visible presence of God. After their wilderness journey was over, and they were settled in the Land, Solomon erected a temple to replace the mobile tabernacle. "And it came to pass, when the priests were come out of the holy place, that the cloud filled the house of the LORD, So that the priests could not stand to minister because of the cloud: for the glory of the LORD had filled the house of the LORD" (1 Kings 8:10–11). God, you see, hallowed the temple with His presence. However, later in their history when Israel turned from her God, the Shekinah glory left the temple. Ezekiel tells of its hesitant departure, as though reluctant to leave, then of its lifting up and disappearance into the heavens.

Of the Lord Jesus, John wrote, "And we beheld his glory," but not many saw it at His first coming. It was His glory that He laid aside when He came to this earth—not his deity, but His glory.

When He comes again, there will be "the sign of the Son of man in heaven," and I believe that sign will be the Shekinah glory. Christ will return to earth in all His glory.

That sign is not for the church. We are never given a visible presence of God. Rather, we are given the *inward* presence of God, the Holy Spirit indwelling us. The Spirit of God is *in* the believer today. What wonderful truths there are here for us.

CHAPTER 10

THEME: *Silver trumpets; order of march*

The last preparation for the march is the instructions for making two silver trumpets. The wilderness march will then begin in verse 11 of this chapter.

SILVER TRUMPETS

And the LORD spake unto Moses, saying,

Make thee two trumpets of silver; of a whole piece shalt thou make them: that thou mayest use them for the calling of the assembly, and for the journeying of the camps [Num. 10:1–2].

Two is the number of witness—it is in the mouth of two witnesses that a matter is established. These two trumpets were used to move Israel on the wilderness march.

And when they shall blow with them, all the assembly shall assemble themselves

THE ORDER BY WHICH THEY MARCHED IS GIVEN IN 10:11-36.

	Section 7	Section 6	Section 5	Section 4	Section 3	Section 2	Section 1	
Mixed	Dan	Ephraim	Kohathites	Reuben	Gershon Merari	Judah "Praise"	Moses Aaron Ark	
Multitude	bearing standard (vs. 25)	bearing standard (vs. 22)	bearing sanctuary (vs. 21)	bearing standard (vs. 18)	bearing tabernacle (vs. 17)	bearing standard (vs. 14)	(vs. 33)	FORWARD MARCH!
	Asher Naphtali	Manasseh Benjamin	Sons of Levi	Simeon Gad	Sons of Levi	Issachar Zebulun		

to thee at the door of the tabernacle of the congregation.

And if they blow but with one trumpet, then the princes, which are heads of the thousands of Israel, shall gather themselves unto thee [Num. 10:3–4].

The blowing of one trumpet brought the princes together. This reminds us that there is to be a last trump for the church. That last trump, I believe, is the voice of Christ which will be His last call. He has sent out invitation after invitation. His final invitation to the Laodicean church is "Behold, I stand at the door, and knock: if any man hear my voice, and open the door, I will come in to him, and will sup with him, and he with me" (Rev. 3:20). At the last trump, He will call His church out of the world. That will be the last call. The one single trumpet, which is the voice of the Lord Jesus, will bring the believers together. This is what we call the Rapture of the church.

When ye blow an alarm, then the camps that lie on the east parts shall go forward.

When ye blow an alarm the second time, then the camps that lie on the south side shall take their journey: they shall blow an alarm for their journeys.

But when the congregation is to be gathered together, ye shall blow, but ye shall not sound an alarm [Num. 10:5–7].

The trumpets were used to bring this tremendous number of people into formation for the march through the wilderness.

And if ye go to war in your land against the enemy that oppresseth you, then ye shall blow an alarm with the trumpets; and ye shall be remembered before the Lord your God, and ye shall be saved from your enemies [Num. 10:9].

Another use of the trumpets was to blow the alarm for war.

Also in the day of your gladness, and in your solemn days, and in the beginnings of your months, ye shall blow with the trumpets over your burnt offerings, and over the sacrifices of your peace offerings; that they may be to you for a memorial before your God: I am the Lord your God [Num. 10:10].

The sounding of the trumpets also would denote certain segments of time and special occasions.

These trumpets, made of silver, which is the metal of redemption, sounded the call for a redeemed people. This was the way God moved them on the wilderness march. They were used as a way of signalling to the people how they should march through the wilderness.

ORDER OF MARCH

And it came to pass on the twentieth day of the second month, in the second year, that the cloud was taken up from off the tabernacle of the testimony.

And the children of Israel took their journeys out of the wilderness of Sinai; and the cloud rested in the wilderness of Paran [Num. 10:11–12].

They have been here at Sinai for about a year, getting the Law from God. The instructions for the silver trumpets have been given, and the trumpets have been made. Now they are blown and the children of Israel begin their wilderness march.

This becomes very detailed in its instructions here in this chapter. Let us go back for a moment to the plan of encampment which we had in chapter 2. You remember that the families of Levi were encamped around the tabernacle. Moses and Aaron were on the east side, Merari on the north, Gershon on the west, and Kohath on the south. Then the camps of the twelve tribes were out beyond that. Judah, Issachar, and Zebulun were on the east; Dan, Ashur, and Naphtali on the north; Ephraim, Manasseh, and Benjamin on the west; and Reuben, Simeon, and Gad on the south.

Early one morning the people of Israel strike camp because the pillar of cloud is lifted. Each family packs their things; the tabernacle is taken down. The time has come to move. What do they do first? Moses and Aaron give the signal and the silver trumpets are blown to sound an alarm. Who moves first? The family of Kohath which carries the ark moves out in front. The ark leads the wilderness march.

Also Christ leads His church through the wilderness of this world. The ark is a picture of Jesus Christ.

So the first trumpet puts Moses and Aaron and the ark out in front. The trumpet blows again and Judah moves out from the east side, with Issachar and Zebulun marching with Judah under his banner. After them come Gershon and Merari, bearing their part of the tabernacle—they had the heavier things, such as the boards and the bars and the coverings.

Then the trumpet blows and Reuben with Simeon and Gad move out, marching under the standard of Reuben. The trumpet blows again and the Kohathites follow them. They are carrying all the articles of furniture of the tabernacle except the ark, which has gone ahead to the front of the march. All these articles of furniture were equipped with poles and the Kohathites bore them on their shoulders. The trumpet sounds again and Ephraim moves out with Manasseh and Benjamin under his standard. Finally, Dan moves out with Asher and Naphtali, under the standard of Dan. Bringing up the rear is the mixed multitude, folk who were part Israelite and part Egyptian. They didn't know whether they should stay or go. Each one was mixed up. As a result, they were stragglers who came along on the wilderness march. The young man who blasphemed (whom we read about in Leviticus 24), who had an Egyptian father and an Israelite mother, had been part of this group.

Did you notice that the trumpet was blown seven times? In the Book of Revelation there is the blowing of the seven trumpets. Those seven trumpets are connected with the children of Israel. The blowing of those trumpets in the Great Tribulation period will move the children of Israel from all corners of the earth back into that land.

A great many people try to associate the last trump that is mentioned in 1 Corinthians 15:52 with the last trumpet in the Book of Revelation, and then they draw the conclusion that the church is going through the Great Tribulation period. However, that last trump which is mentioned in Corinthians is the voice of the Son of God, which is detailed in 1 Thessalonians 4:16, "For the Lord himself shall descend from heaven with a shout, with the voice of the archangel, and with the trump of God. . . ." His voice is like the voice of an archangel and like the sound of a trumpet. We know this because in Revelation 1:10–11 John writes, "I was in the Spirit on the Lord's day, and heard behind me a great voice, as of a trumpet, Saying, I am Alpha and Omega, the first and the last. . . ." Whom did John see when he turned to see who had spoken to him? He saw the glorified Christ, the Great High Priest. *His* voice is like a trumpet. His voice is going to raise the dead and change the mortal bodies of those who are living when He comes for His church. The trumpet sound for the church is the voice of the Son of God.

Trumpets are connected with the children of Israel. It is the trumpet that moved them on the wilderness march. It will be the trumpets that will bring them from the wilderness of this world back into the land.

And Moses said unto Hobab, the son of Raguel the Midianite, Moses' father in law, We are journeying unto the place of which the LORD said, I will give it you: come thou with us, and we will do thee good: for the LORD hath spoken good concerning Israel [Num. 10:29].

Here we have recorded an encounter with Moses' father-in-law and Moses' invitation to him. This could be applied to the church. We are strangers and pilgrims going through this world today. We are in a wilderness here, but we are on the way to the presence of the Lord Jesus Christ. Our invitation is the same invitation that Moses gave, "Come thou with us."

If you are not a child of God by faith in Jesus Christ, you may join the party. It is a great one, by the way, as we are marching to go into the presence of Jesus Christ. We are not a group that is marching because we are better than anyone else. We are sinners who have been saved by the grace of God. If you see yourself as a sinner and you need a Savior, turn to Him by simple faith and trust Him. Join the march! This is no protest march; it is a salvation march, a redemption march. It is the march that is going to Zion, not the earthly Zion but the heavenly one, the city of Jerusalem which will come down from God out of heaven, adorned like a bride for the bridegroom.

And he said unto him, I will not go; but I will depart to mine own land, and to my kindred [Num. 10:30].

Now Moses keeps on talking, and maybe he shouldn't have done that. Old Hobab, the father-in-law, didn't want to go along. He wanted to go home. So Moses answered him,

And he said, Leave us not, I pray thee; forasmuch as thou knowest how we are to encamp in the wilderness, and thou mayest be to us instead of eyes [Num. 10:31].

I want to say to you right here that I don't understand Moses. God has made it clear to Moses that the pillar of cloud by day and the pillar of fire by night would guide them and that the ark was leading them, both of which speak of Christ. He is the leader. Now Moses is suggesting to his own father-in-law that he needs him to lead them. The old man had been raised in the desert of Midian. He was a Midianite and he knew that area. He could have been a great help, I'm sure. But, you see, they were not to depend upon natural means. This old man didn't know the way God wanted them to go.

Unfortunately, the church is listening to the voice of the "experts," men without real spiritual discernment. As a result, the church is being led down the garden path in many instances. And the church is brought to a very sad place many times. What a responsibility rests upon the church leaders today, the ministers and the church officers! Are you sure Christ is the Head of your church? Are you sure that He is leading and guiding you, or are you today asking some man to come and be eyes for you?

Moses made a mistake here, friends. Moses could make mistakes, by the way. He was a sinner. The interesting thing is that he wrote this; so he recorded his own mistake. I'm afraid that if some of us had made these mistakes, we wouldn't have mentioned them.

And they departed from the mount of the LORD three days' journey: and the ark of the covenant of the LORD went before them in the three days' journey, to search out a resting place for them.

And the cloud of the LORD was upon them by day, when they went out of the camp [Num. 10:33–34].

Now they are on their way. God is leading them. God Himself is searching out the land. There was no need to have the father-in-law of Moses do the searching for them.

And it came to pass, when the ark set forward, that Moses said, Rise up, LORD, and let thine enemies be scattered; and let them that hate thee flee before thee.

And when it rested, he said, Return, O LORD, unto the many thousands of Israel [Num. 10:35–36].

Apparently Moses followed this little ritual of prayer each morning and every evening when they were on the wilderness march.

CHAPTER 11

THEME: *The complaint of the people; the complaint of Moses; God provides quail*

The children of Israel now have left Mount Sinai, and chapters 11 and 12 tell of the march from Sinai to Kadesh. We will find that when problems arose, the people fell to murmuring. This was a very serious thing, and it carries important lessons for us.

THE COMPLAINT OF THE PEOPLE

And when the people complained, it displeased the LORD: and the LORD heard it; and his anger was kindled; and the fire of the LORD burnt among them, and consumed them that were in the uttermost parts of the camp [Num. 11:1].

Every time the people complained, the glory of the Lord appeared. He was displeased with their groaning and their complaining.

We can be sure that the Lord is displeased with many of the criticizing, complaining saints today. They are everlastingly finding fault and nothing seems to please them. God doesn't want it that way for you, my friend. He wants you to be a happy, joyful Christian.

And the people cried unto Moses; and when Moses prayed unto the LORD, the fire was quenched.

And he called the name of the place Taberah: because the fire of the LORD burnt among them [Num. 11:2–3].

Now, what is behind all this complaining? Who were the troublemakers? We can locate them here, and we are just as able to locate them today.

And the mixed multitude that was among them fell a-lusting: and the children of Israel also wept again, and said, Who shall give us flesh to eat? [Num. 11:4].

Who is it that started this? It is the mixed multitude. You will remember that the mixed multitude were those who were not sure who they were. They could not go up and join one of the tribes. They couldn't declare their pedigree. They weren't sure whether they should go on the wilderness march or not. They were the products of mixed marriages. Each of them had one parent back in Egypt and one parent in the camp of Israel. They were Egyptian enough to like Egypt, and they were Israelite enough to want to go on the wilderness march.

We have our churches filled with people like that today. They want to mix with church people and go to church. They want to be moral and live upstanding lives; so they join a church. Then, during the week, they run with the world. They are a mixed multitude. They are not quite sure where they do belong. They are not sure if they are born again—they don't know their pedigree.

I have discovered through my years as a pastor that the real troublemakers in any church are the mixed multitude. They are fellow travelers with the world and with the church people. They like to have a church banquet, but they don't want the Bible study. They don't want to be forward in the march, close to the ark of God; they want to stay way in the back because they are not sure but what they may want to turn and go back some time. They are not quite clear about what they believe. They are never happy when others are having a real time of spiritual blessing. They're uncomfortable in the church, but they are also uncomfortable with the world. They just don't seem to fit in. They are a square peg in a round hole and they are the trouble-makers.

Now out here in the wilderness, what do you think they wanted? Listen to them.

We remember the fish, which we did eat in Egypt freely; the cucumbers, and the melons, and the leeks, and the onions, and the garlick:

But now our soul is dried away: there is nothing at all, beside this manna, before our eyes [Num. 11:5–6].

Notice what they missed. Everything they liked was a condiment, except the fish. They couldn't catch fish out in that wilderness—there weren't any lakes out there. They remembered the fish they had in Egypt. There they had all the fish they wanted. I'm of the opinion that in Egypt they were tired of the fish, but now that is what they remembered. They fell to lusting.

The children of Israel became infected with this complaining, and they began to weep along with the mixed multitude. This was like a spreading, contagious disease which swept through the camp. Before long, the whole crowd was weeping, remembering Egypt.

So they start to complain about the manna. They have the manna to eat, and it is miraculously provided by God every day, but they don't like it.

And the manna was as coriander seed, and the colour thereof as the colour of bdellium.

And the people went about, and gathered it, and ground it in mills, or beat it in a mortar, and baked it in pans, and made cakes of it: and the taste of it was as the taste of fresh oil.

And when the dew fell upon the camp in the night, the manna fell upon it [Num. 11:7–9].

The Spirit of God describes manna for us the second time. The thing they didn't like—how wonderful it was! It was not a monotonous food. The fact of the matter is, as we will see in Deuteronomy, when they went through the wilderness, their feet did not swell. They did not get beriberi from eating the manna. That manna had all the necessary vitamins in it. It was God's food. That manna gave them complete nourishment. Manna, of course, is a picture of the Lord Jesus Christ and of the Word of God which reveals Him.

There were many ways the manna could be prepared. It could be baked or fried; they could grind it to make a bread or a cake out of it. Mrs. Moses probably compiled a cookbook with one hundred and one recipes for manna. The Spirit of God is saying this was an adequate food, a marvelous food, and He is showing to us that it was this food which the children of Israel despised.

Let's not sit back and say how terrible the children of Israel were. How about you, my friend? That manna speaks of Christ. How do you feel about Him? Do you get tired of Him?

Many Christians get tired of manna. A lot of people get tired of Bible study. I think it is safe to say that the largest segment of the church today does not want Bible study. They just won't go for it. The predicament of the church today is due to the fact that folk have turned from the Word and are trying to feed somewhere else other than on the manna which God has provided.

THE COMPLAINT OF MOSES

After this, even Moses gets a little weary of this crowd. I must say that I have a certain sympathy for him.

Then Moses heard the people weep throughout their families, every man in the door of his tent: and the anger of the LORD was kindled greatly; Moses also was displeased.

And Moses said unto the LORD, Wherefore hast thou afflicted thy servant? and wherefore have I not found favour in thy sight, that thou layest the burden of all this people upon me?

Have I conceived all this people? have I begotten them, that thou shouldest say unto me, Carry them in thy bosom, as a nursing father beareth the sucking child, unto the land which thou swarest unto their fathers?

Whence should I have flesh to give unto all this people? for they weep unto me, saying, Give us flesh, that we may eat.

I am not able to bear all this people alone, because it is too heavy for me.

And if thou deal thus with me, kill me, I pray thee, out of hand, if I have found favour in thy sight; and let me not see my wretchedness [Num. 11:10–15].

Is Moses complaining? It sounds to me as though he is complaining here. Moses wasn't a perfect man, by any means. He was just a plain human being who was mightily used of God. Moses said he would rather be dead than go through what he was going through with that crowd!

I know pastors who have ulcers and nervous breakdowns. I know several men who have left the ministry. They did the same thing Moses did—complained to the Lord that the burden was too great. They got tired of hearing the criticisms and the complaints and the whining and the difficulties.

And the LORD said unto Moses, Gather unto me seventy men of the elders of Israel, whom thou knowest to be the elders of the people, and officers over them; and bring them unto the tabernacle of the congregation, that they may stand there with thee [Num. 11:16].

Moses made a mistake in complaining like this to God. Moses said that he was the one who was bearing all these people. Well, he wasn't.

God never asked him to. God was bearing them and also bearing Moses, but Moses was not fully casting himself upon God. Now God says, "Alright, Moses, I'll give you help if that is what you want." God very patiently, very graciously, provides some assistance for Moses. Seventy elders were appointed.

By the way, these seventy elders continued down through the history of Israel. In the time of our Lord they were called the Sanhedrin. One night they met and decided to put the Lord Jesus to death. I don't think they needed this organization.

We seem to think in the church today that if we will multiply committees and organizations and methods, we will solve our problems. Well, it has not solved our problems. We don't need more organizations; we don't need Sanhedrins.

And I will come down and talk with thee there: and I will take of the spirit which is upon thee, and will put it upon them; and they shall bear the burden of the people with thee, that thou bear it not thyself alone [Num. 11:17].

God had called Moses to lead the people, and God would provide the strength for Moses to do that. God always does. He never asks anyone to do more than he can do. If you feel that you are overworked or that you are doing too much, maybe you really are. Maybe you are doing more than God wants you to do. God will not overburden those who are His own.

And say thou unto the people, Sanctify yourselves against to-morrow, and ye shall eat flesh: for ye have wept in the ears of the LORD, saying, Who shall give us flesh to eat? for it was well with us in Egypt: therefore the LORD will give you flesh, and ye shall eat.

Ye shall not eat one day, nor two days, nor five days, neither ten days, nor twenty days;

But even a whole month, until it come out at your nostrils, and it be loathsome unto you: because that ye have despised the LORD which is among you, and have wept before him, saying, Why came we forth out of Egypt? [Num. 11:18–20].

It is interesting to read the comment that the Spirit of God makes concerning this incident. Psalm 106 is an historic psalm, and there we read in verse 15, "And he gave them their request; but sent leanness into their soul."

God answered their request, but He sent leanness into their soul. I imagine some of them ran around and said they got their answer to prayer, but notice the cost.

We are to make our requests known unto God with thanksgiving (Phil. 4:6), because we know that God is going to hear and answer our prayer. Most of the time God will say no to our prayer, which is the very best answer. Sometimes we pray for things that aren't the best for us. If we beg and complain, God may answer our prayer but give us leanness in our soul.

I remember a certain man who was an officer in a church I served years ago. He came to me and asked me to pray for him. His business was shaky, and he wanted me to pray that the Lord would bless his business. He said it offered him the opportunity of becoming wealthy if he could get it past this critical period. I was a young preacher then, and I went immediately and prayed that the man would make money and that God would establish his business. He prayed for it too. God heard our prayers and the man got rich, which was the worst thing that could have happened to him. He had a fine family until they got more money than they needed. He lost all of his children. God granted their request, but sent leanness to their souls.

God tells Moses that for a whole month they will eat flesh until it becomes loathsome to them. He will do this because they have despised Him and have wept before Him.

And Moses said, The people, among whom I am, are six hundred thousand footmen; and thou hast said, I will give them flesh, that they may eat a whole month.

Shall the flocks and the herds be slain for them, to suffice them? or shall all the fish of the sea be gathered together for them, to suffice them? [Num. 11:21–22].

Moses is asking God how He is going to do this.

And the LORD said unto Moses, Is the LORD's hand waxed short? thou shalt see now whether my word shall come to pass unto thee or not [Num. 11:23].

God answers him that He will do it. We never need to ask the Lord how He is going to do something after He says He will do it. He will do it, and He doesn't need your *how* and my *how*. He does it the way He wants to do it.

And Moses went out, and told the people the words of the LORD, and gathered the seventy men of the elders of the people, and set them round about the tabernacle.

And the LORD came down in a cloud, and spake unto him, and took of the spirit that was upon him, and gave it unto the seventy elders: and it came to pass, that, when the spirit rested upon them, they prophesied, and did not cease [Num. 11:24–25].

Notice that there was actually no more power than there had been before. There was a lot more machinery than there was before, but there was no more power because the same Spirit was divided among them.

But there remained two of the men in the camp, the name of the one was Eldad, and the name of the other Medad: and the spirit rested upon them; and they were of them that were written, but went not out unto the tabernacle: and they prophesied in the camp.

And there ran a young man, and told Moses, and said, Eldad and Medad do prophesy in the camp.

And Joshua the son of Nun, the servant of Moses, one of his young men, answered and said, My lord Moses, forbid them.

And Moses said unto him, Enviest thou for my sake? would God that all the LORD's people were prophets, and that the LORD would put his spirit upon them!

And Moses gat him into the camp, he and the elders of Israel [Num. 11:26–30].

Joshua was very loyal to Moses, and that was wonderful. But even more wonderful is the revelation that there wasn't a jealous bone in the body of Moses. He was not jealous because these others were able to prophesy. I believe there are three great sins in the ministry: laziness, jealousy, and boredom. Some of us are guilty of all three. We have seen that Moses was not lazy or bored; now we know he was not a jealous man either. Jealousy is an awful thing.

GOD PROVIDES QUAIL

And there went forth a wind from the LORD, and brought quails from the sea,

and let them fall by the camp, as it were a day's journey on this side, and as it were a day's journey on the other side, round about the camp, and as it were two cubits high upon the face of the earth [Num. 11:31].

The Lord gives them the meat He promised. He is providing quail on toast—they couldn't have it better than this! I can't even imagine quail in abundance like this. I've been quail hunting all day and found two or three quail.

And the people stood up all that day, and all that night, and all the next day, and they gathered the quails: he that gathered least gathered ten homers: and they spread them all abroad for themselves round about the camp [Num. 11:32].

That is about eighty-six gallons. They didn't have cold storage; so they had to cook all that. They demonstrated real gluttony.

And while the flesh was yet between their teeth, ere it was chewed, the wrath of the LORD was kindled against the people, and the LORD smote the people with a very great plague.

And he called the name of that place Kibrothhattaavah: because there they buried the people that lusted.

And the people journeyed from Kibrothhattaavah unto Hazeroth; and abode at Hazeroth [Num. 11:33–35].

God judges those things. He still does. Remember that Paul writes, "For if we would judge ourselves, we should not be judged. But when we are judged, we are chastened of the Lord, that we should not be condemned with the world" (1 Cor. 11:31–32).

CHAPTER 12

THEME: Jealousy of Miriam and Aaron; judgment of Miriam

The Bible tells us very little about the home life of Moses. But from what we do know, I can't believe it could have been very happy. The incident recorded in this chapter is a family matter which occurred during the march from Sinai to Kadesh-barnea. In this chapter we will find rebellion in high places, among the leaders of the children of Israel.

JEALOUSY OF MIRIAM AND AARON

And Miriam and Aaron spake against Moses because of the Ethiopian woman whom he had married: for he had married an Ethiopian woman [Num. 12:1].

I do not think this wife was Zipporah, the daughter of the priest of Midian—she would be a Midianite. The last we hear of Zipporah is when her father brought her to Moses at Mount Sinai (Exod. 18:2). Did she return home with her father? Was she dead? Who is this Ethiopian or Cushite wife? Scripture is silent. All we can say is that this appears to be a second wife. The point here is that Miriam used this marriage as a pretext to protest the authority of Moses.

And they said, Hath the LORD indeed spoken only by Moses? hath he not spoken also by us? And the LORD heard it [Num. 12:2].

This is big sister talking. Miriam could say, "Who does this boy Moses think he is? Why, I can remember when he was a little baby in an ark and I watched over him. If I hadn't watched over him, where would he be today?" And Aaron, the high priest, Moses' big brother, joins in.

(Now the man Moses was very meek, above all the men which were upon the face of the earth) [Num. 12:3].

It is stated of Moses and of our Lord Jesus that they were meek. Remember that meekness is not weakness. Meekness is being obedient to God and doing His will.

And the LORD spake suddenly unto Moses, and unto Aaron, and unto Miriam. Come out ye three unto the tabernacle of the congregation. And they three came out [Num. 12:4].

This is a family affair, you see.

And he said, Hear now my words: If there be a prophet among you, I the LORD will make myself known unto him in a vision, and will speak unto him in a dream.

My servant Moses is not so, who is faithful in all mine house.

With him will I speak mouth to mouth, even apparently, and not in dark speeches; and the similitude of the LORD shall he behold: wherefore then were ye not afraid to speak against my servant Moses?

And the anger of the LORD was kindled against them; and he departed [Num. 12:6–9].

God is saying that *He* chooses the prophets. Also He says that Moses is greater than the others—he is faithful in all My house. God says that He deals differently with him than with any other prophet: He speaks with Moses directly.

I think we find this to be true as we study the Old Testament. I cannot find that He dealt with any other prophet as He dealt with Moses. God appeared in dreams to Abraham. He appeared in dreams to Joseph. But God dealt with Moses face to face. Moses is different from all the others. Later on we will see that God says, "I will raise them up a Prophet from among their brethren, like unto thee, and will put my words in his mouth; and he shall speak unto them all that I shall command him" (Deut. 18:18). That Prophet who would be like unto Moses is the Lord Jesus Christ.

JUDGMENT OF MIRIAM

And the cloud departed from off the tabernacle; and, behold, Miriam be-
came leprous, white as snow: and Aaron looked upon Miriam, and, behold, she was leprous [Num. 12:10].

They had been very foolish in what they had said. Miriam became leprous which was God's severe judgment on her. Moses prayed to the Lord for her—how forgiving and gracious Moses was! Although God healed her, she had to be shut out from the camp for seven days, and the people could not journey while she was shut out of the camp. She held up the march for a whole week.

And Miriam was shut out from the camp seven days: and the people journeyed not till Miriam was brought in again.

And afterward the people removed from Hazeroth, and pitched in the wilderness of Paran [Num. 12:15–16].

Why wasn't Aaron struck with the leprosy? Because Aaron was God's high priest. If he were a leper he could not serve in that capacity; Israel would have had no intercessor to stand between them and God. So God didn't use this family affair to judge Aaron at this time. It was Aaron who pleaded with Moses, ". . . Alas, my lord, I beseech thee, lay not the sin upon us, wherein we have done foolishly, and wherein we have sinned" (Num. 12:11). The judgment was caused by the jealousy in both of them, but Miriam was the leader in it. Her name is mentioned first, and the verb *spake* in verse 1 is in the feminine—"she spoke." Aaron was not a leader; he was a follower. He was weak and pliable, a characteristic we see in Exodus 32 regarding the making of the golden calf. The sins of jealousy and envy were nurtured in Miriam's heart, and God rightly judged her.

CHAPTER 13

THEME: Sending spies; misinterpretation of facts; right interpretation of facts

Israel has reached Kadesh-barnea, which borders the Promised Land. It is sad to see that Kadesh becomes their Waterloo because of their unbelief.

This chapter includes the cause of their sending spies, the choice of the spies, the commission of the spies, the conduct of the spies, the spies' confirmation of the facts, and the two interpretations of those facts—a majority and a minority report.

SENDING SPIES

And the LORD spake unto Moses, saying,

Send thou men, that they may search the land of Canaan, which I give unto the children of Israel: of every tribe of their fathers shall ye send a man, every one a ruler among them.

And Moses by the commandment of the LORD sent them from the wilderness of Paran: all those men were heads of the children of Israel [Num. 13:1–3].

Whose idea was it to send in the spies? Was it the idea of God? Was it His thought to spy out the land? No. We always need to get a composite picture from the Word of God, because many times one facet will be given in one place and another facet given in another place. As an example, we need all four of the Gospel records to have a total spectrum of the Lord Jesus Christ. Although we get the impression here that this is God's idea, we find that He was responding to their request. Listen to the account in Deuteronomy. "And I said unto you, Ye are come unto the mountain of the Amorites, which the LORD our God doth give unto us. Behold, the LORD thy God hath set the land before thee: go up and possess it, as the LORD God of thy fathers hath said unto thee; fear not, neither be discouraged. And ye came near unto me every one of you, and said, We will send men before us, and they shall search us out the land, and bring us word again by what way we must go up, and into what cities we shall come" (Deut. 1:20–22). It was not God's idea to send spies into the land. The sending in of the spies denoted a weakness and a fear on the part of the people. There was a fear that maybe they wouldn't be able to take the land. It was so easy for them to rationalize and decide on spies as a matter of wisdom.

However, God is leading Israel to the land He has promised them. Their request for spies reveals a lack of faith on their part. They are not trusting Him. God had already been in and spied out the land. He knew all about it. He would not have sent them into the land unless He knew they could take it. When they finally did enter the land, the giants were still there; all the difficulties and problems were still there, yet they took the land.

What an important message this is for us today! Are we really walking by faith? Of course we need to take precautions, but there is a time when we do need to commit our way unto the Lord. "Commit thy way unto the LORD; trust also in him; and he shall bring it to pass" (Ps. 37:5). You and I need to come to the place in our lives when we commit our way to Him and trust Him completely.

These folk have come to that place but they're not trusting God. They decide to send out spies to find out what lay ahead of them. We find this to be another instance where God yields to the desires of His people. He *permits* them to do this thing. Before it was said of them, ". . . he gave them their request; but sent leanness into their soul" (Ps. 106:15). This time it will be worse than leanness.

After they demonstrate their lack of faith and lack of trust in God, He orders the spy mission, in response to their request, and commands that it should be done in a fair and orderly way, and that a ruler from each tribe go as a spy.

CHOICE OF SPIES

The list of the spies is given here. We are especially interested in two of them.

Of the tribe of Judah, Caleb the son of Jephunneh.

Of the tribe of Ephraim, Oshea the son of Nun [Num. 13:6,8].

Oshea or Hoshea is Joshua. We will hear more of these two remarkable men who brought in the minority report.

COMMISSION OF SPIES

And Moses sent them to spy out the land of Canaan, and said unto them,

Get you up this way southward, and go up into the mountain:

And see the land, what it is; and the people that dwelleth therein, whether they be strong or weak, few or many;

And what the land is that they dwell in, whether it be good or bad; and what cities they be that they dwell in, whether in tents, or in strong holds;

And what the land is, whether it be fat or lean, whether there be wood therein, or not. And be ye of good courage, and bring of the fruit of the land. Now the time was the time of the firstripe grapes [Num. 13:17–20].

Now the spies are to go in. They have been given their commission and they know what they are to do.

CONDUCT OF SPIES

So they went up, and searched the land from the wilderness of Zin unto Rehob, as men come to Hamath [Num. 13:21].

Hamath is way up in the extreme north of the land. The spies did a thorough job. The fact of the matter is that they could have written a book entitled *Inside the Promised Land*. They knew a great deal about it. We are told the places they went and that they saw the children of Anak. These were giants.

And they ascended by the south, and came unto Hebron; where Ahiman, Sheshai, and Talmai, the children of Anak, were. (Now Hebron was built seven years before Zoan in Egypt.)

And they came unto the brook of Eshcol, and cut down from thence a branch with one cluster of grapes, and they bare it between two upon a staff; and they brought of the pomegranates, and of the figs.

The place was called the brook Eshcol, because of the cluster of grapes which the children of Israel cut down from thence.

And they returned from searching of the land after forty days [Num. 13:22–25].

Our translation gives the impression that it took two men to carry one bunch of grapes. At least they cut down enough grapes (and they were lush grapes) for two men to carry and it was put on a pole between them. They brought back samples of the fruit to show what a wonderful land it was.

CONFIRMATION OF FACTS

And they went and came to Moses, and to Aaron, and to all the congregation of the children of Israel, unto the wilderness of Paran, to Kadesh; and brought back word unto them, and unto all the congregation, and shewed them the fruit of the land.

And they told him, and said, We came unto the land whither thou sentest us, and surely it floweth with milk and honey; and this is the fruit of it [Num. 13:26–27].

Their report confirmed that God was accurate when He said it was a land flowing with milk and honey.

MISINTERPRETATION OF FACTS

Nevertheless the people be strong that dwell in the land, and the cities are walled, and very great: and moreover we saw the children of Anak there.

The Amalekites dwell in the land of the south: and the Hittites, and the Jebusites, and the Amorites, dwell in the mountains: and the Canaanites dwell by the sea, and by the coast of Jordan [Num. 13:28–29].

This all was true. There were giants in the land. The cities were walled and very great. They were right in their facts, but they misinterpreted the facts. That is where they went awry.

But the men that went up with him said, We be not able to go up against the people; for they are stronger than we.

And they brought up an evil report of the land which they had searched unto the children of Israel, saying, The land, through which we have gone to search it, is a land that eateth up the inhabitants thereof; and all the people that we saw in it are men of a great stature.

And there we saw the giants, the sons of Anak, which come of the giants: and we were in our own sight as grasshoppers, and so we were in their sight [Num. 13:31–33].

When you are afraid and you have lost your faith, difficulties and problems are magnified. They become greater than they really are. There were giants, but the men thought they were bigger than they actually were. They looked bigger because these men were afraid. What an interesting contrast they give us here. Giants and grasshoppers! Do you know what they left out? They forgot to include God! They compared themselves to the giants as grasshoppers. That is the way they saw themselves. They left God out of the picture. If only they had put Him in, what a different story it would have been.

RIGHT INTERPRETATION OF FACTS

And Caleb stilled the people before Moses, and said, Let us go up at once, and possess it; for we are well able to overcome it [Num. 13:30].

Here is the minority report. Caleb spoke up with this report but the other men refuted him. Only Joshua agreed with Caleb.

So there we have the whole picture. The report was accurate as to the facts. But there were two different opinions in the interpretation of those facts. The minority report was "Let's go in and take the land. We are well able to do it." The majority report was, "We can't do it." The people believed the majority report. They didn't believe they could take the land because they lacked faith in God.

CHAPTER 14

THEME: Israel's refusal to enter the land; Moses pleads for Israel; God's judgment; Israel defeated by Amalekites and Canaanites

Israel has now come to the place of decision. They must decide whether they are going to enter the land or not. We find Israel refusing to enter. The reason is their unbelief. The Bible is its own best commentary, and it is the writer to the Hebrews who puts it just that way. "But with whom was he grieved forty years? was it not with them that had sinned, whose carcases fell in the wilderness? And to whom sware he that they should not enter into his rest, but to them that believed not? So we see that they could not enter in because of unbelief" (Heb. 3:17–19). It was unbelief that kept them from going into the land!

ISRAEL'S REFUSAL
TO ENTER THE LAND

And all the congregation lifted up their voice, and cried; and the people wept that night.

And all the children of Israel murmured against Moses and against Aaron: and the whole congregation said unto them, Would God that we had died in the land of Egypt! or would God we had died in this wilderness! [Num. 14: 1–2].

I am of the opinion that poor Moses and Aaron at this time were wishing they *had* died in the wilderness so they would be rid of their continual complaining.

And wherefore hath the LORD brought us unto this land, to fall by the sword, that our wives and our children should be a prey? were it not better for us to return into Egypt? [Num. 14:3].

They are in such a bad frame of mind that they say, "Our wives and children will be a prey!" They are using their children as an excuse, pretending they are thinking of the safety of their children, but actually it is a reflection on God. They are saying that God did not care what happened to their children.

Do you know who it was that entered the land? It was these children—that next generation. The old folks sat there and cried and said they were thinking of the safety of the children. The fact of the matter is that God was thinking of the safety of the children, and He brought them into the land.

And they said one to another, Let us make a captain, and let us return into Egypt.

Then Moses and Aaron fell on their faces before all the assembly of the congregation of the children of Israel.

And Joshua the son of Nun, and Caleb the son of Jephunneh, which were of them that searched the land, rent their clothes:

And they spake unto all the company of the children of Israel, saying, The land, which we passed through to search it, is an exceeding good land.

If the LORD delight in us, then he will bring us into this land, and give it us; a land which floweth with milk and honey.

Only rebel not ye against the LORD, neither fear ye the people of the land; for they are bread for us: their defence is departed from them, and the LORD is with us: fear them not [Num. 14:4–9].

These two men, Caleb and Joshua, brought the same facts as the others. What is the difference in their report? The difference is in their interpretation of the facts because they included God. When you see yourself as a grasshopper in the presence of giants, that is when you need God. These people certainly needed God. Caleb and Joshua insisted that if God would delight in them, He would bring them into the land. But how can God delight in them unless they believe God? They must trust Him.

"They are bread for us" in our idiom would be like saying, "Those people in the land will be 'duck soup' for us!" How can they be so confident? They have faith in God!

But all the congregation bade stone them with stones. And the glory of the LORD appeared in the tabernacle of the congregation before all the children of Israel [Num. 14:10].

Have you noticed that every time there is a rebellion, or murmuring, or complaining, the glory of the Lord appears? God is highly displeased with this rebellion against Him.

And the LORD said unto Moses, How long will this people provoke me? and how long will it be ere they believe me, for all the signs which I have shewed among them?

I will smite them with the pestilence, and disinherit them, and will make of thee a greater nation and mightier than they [Num. 14:11–12].

God is saying, "I'll destroy them and make a nation from you to fulfill My promises."

MOSES PLEADS FOR ISRAEL

And Moses said unto the LORD, Then the Egyptians shall hear it, (for thou broughtest up this people in thy might from among them;)

And they will tell it to the inhabitants of this land: for they have heard that thou LORD art among this people, and thou LORD art seen face to face, and that thy cloud standeth over them, and that thou goest before them, by day time in a pillar of a cloud, and in a pillar of fire by night.

Now if thou shalt kill all this people as one man, then the nations which have heard the fame of thee will speak, saying,

Because the LORD was not able to bring this people into the land which he sware unto them, therefore he hath slain them in the wilderness.

And now, I beseech thee, let the power of my LORD be great, according as thou hast spoken, saying,

The LORD is longsuffering, and of great mercy, forgiving iniquity and transgression, and by no means clearing the guilty, visiting the iniquity of the fathers upon the children unto the third and fourth generation.

Pardon, I beseech thee, the iniquity of this people according unto the greatness of thy mercy, and as thou hast forgiven this people, from Egypt even until now [Num. 14:13–19].

Moses reminds God that the rumor will go around that although He was able to bring them out of Egypt, He was not able to put them into the land, to complete that which He had begun. God agrees to go ahead with them and put Israel into the land.

And the LORD said, I have pardoned according to thy word [Num. 14:20].

And then the Lord gives this prophecy:

But as truly as I live, all the earth shall be filled with the glory of the LORD [Num. 14:21].

As God brought these children of Israel out of the land of Egypt and did put them in the Promised Land, so God will complete the plan He had for you when He saved you. And He will complete the plan He is working on now for the entire earth, because the time is coming when the whole earth shall be filled with the glory of the Lord.

GOD'S JUDGMENT

Because all those men which have seen my glory, and my miracles, which I did in Egypt and in the wilderness, and have tempted me now these ten times, and have not hearkened to my voice;

Surely they shall not see the land which I sware unto their fathers, neither shall any of them that provoked me see it:

But my servant Caleb, because he had another spirit with him, and hath followed me fully, him will I bring into the land whereinto he went; and his seed shall possess it [Num. 14:22–24].

Judgment falls on the children of Israel. The generation that murmured will not enter the Promised Land. Joshua and Caleb are the only ones whom God singles out from the people. God promises that *they* shall enter the land, and God made good that promise.

Your carcases shall fall in this wilderness; and all that were numbered of you, according to your whole number, from twenty years old and upward, which have murmured against me,

Doubtless ye shall not come into the land, concerning which I sware to make you dwell therein, save Caleb the son of Jephunneh, and Joshua the son of Nun.

But your little ones, which ye said should be a prey, them will I bring in, and they shall know the land which ye have despised.

But as for you, your carcases, they shall fall in this wilderness [Num. 14:29–32].

Their children, that they implied God did not care about, would be brought safely into the land they had despised.

And your children shall wander in the wilderness forty years, and bear your whoredoms, until your carcases be wasted in the wilderness.

After the number of the days in which ye searched the land, even forty days, each day for a year, shall ye bear your iniquities, even forty years, and ye shall know my breach of promise.

I the LORD have said, I will surely do it unto all this evil congregation, that are gathered together against me: in this wilderness they shall be consumed, and there they shall die [Num. 14:33–35].

God tells them that they will wander in the wilderness for forty years—one year for each day the spies were in the land.

And the men, which Moses sent to search the land, who returned, and made all the congregation to murmur against him, by bringing up a slander upon the land,

Even those men that did bring up the evil report upon the land, died by the plague before the LORD [Num. 14:36–37].

The ten spies who brought the evil report and led in the rebellion died of a plague.

ISRAEL DEFEATED BY AMALEKITES AND CANAANITES

And Moses told these sayings unto all the children of Israel: and the people mourned greatly [Num. 14:39].

They had turned from the land, but as they face the wilderness, they are actually more afraid of the wilderness than they had been afraid of entering the land.

And they rose up early in the morning, and gat them up into the top of the mountain, saying, Lo, we be here, and will go up unto the place which the LORD hath promised: for we have sinned.

And Moses said, Wherefore now do ye transgress the commandment of the LORD? but it shall not prosper.

Go not up, for the LORD is not among you; that ye be not smitten before your enemies [Num. 14:40–42].

They had lost their opportunity. They would not go up into the land when God wanted them to go. Now they presume to go up. This is presumption. Faith is not presumption! They again want to go their way rather than God's way. There can be no victory when there is no submission to the will of God.

But they presumed to go up unto the hill top: nevertheless the ark of the covenant of the LORD, and Moses, departed not out of the camp.

Then the Amalekites came down, and the Canaanites which dwelt in that hill, and smote them, and discomfited them, even unto Hormah [Num. 14:44–45].

CHAPTER 15

THEME: God's purpose is not destroyed; death penalty for breaking the sabbath; the ribband of blue

We have seen that the children of Israel had come to a point of decision at Kadesh-barnea. As you know, decisions are the difficult things for all of us in this life. This is especially true for the Christian. Many times we come to the crossroad and we are not sure which way to go. But it was crystal clear to these people which way they should have gone. They faced the choice of entering the land by faith or turning back into the wilderness in unbelief. They made the wrong decision and turned in unbelief.

However, when they looked at the wilderness, they changed their mind and decided that the Promised Land with its walled cities and giants was not so bad as the wilderness; so they attempted to go into the land. This was not a decision of faith; it was a decision based on their experience of two years in the wilderness. They presumed to go into the land. Presumption is as dangerous as unbelief.

A businessman of my acquaintance had a responsible position, then was laid off from this position shortly after he had bought a new home and new furniture. His question to me was: "Why would God let this happen to me since He had led me to buy the house and furniture?" I told him, "I remember that while you were looking for the new house, you mentioned that you were not sure of the leading of God at that time and you specifically mentioned that you didn't like the area, yet you bought the house. Now you are blaming God for all of it. Could it be that you moved by presumption rather than by faith?" He said, "Well, I just thought God would bless me."

My friend, we need to be extremely careful whether we are moving by faith or by presumption. Somewhere between these two is the will of God. It is important to spend time waiting upon the Lord to find out what is His will.

Now we enter that division of the Book of Numbers from chapter 15 to 25, which I call "Faltering, Fumbling, and Fussing through the Wilderness." At Kadesh-barnea, God has turned them back into the wilderness. Walking is turned to wandering; marching is turned to murmuring; witnessing is turned to wailing; warring is turned to wobbling; singing is turned to sighing; and working is turned to wishing.

Unfortunately, I must say that a great many Christians go through life just like that!

Now, the interesting thing is that these are silent years. There is no record of them anywhere. We are given only a few incidents with no connected history. However, we are given indications of the general characteristics of those years. In chapter 33, which is about as uninteresting as any chapter could be, we will find the log of the journeys. We can fit the recorded incidents into this log, but it shows us that we are not given a detailed account of those years. The years are *wasted* years for the children of Israel.

When we get to Joshua, chapter 5, we will learn that they did not circumcise their children during this period. This shows that they were not fulfilling the will of God relative to the covenant which God had made to Abraham. We also know that they did not offer sacrifices to God. "Have ye offered unto me sacrifices and offerings in the wilderness forty years, O house of Israel?" (Amos 5:25). These sacrifices pointed to Christ and they were not offering them during the forty years. Not only that, but we also know they worshiped idols during this period. "But ye have borne the tabernacle of your Moloch and Chiun your images, the star of your god, which ye made to yourselves" (Amos 5:26). Stephen relates this again in Acts. "Then God turned, and gave them up to worship the host of heaven; as it is written in the book of the prophets, O ye house of Israel, have ye offered to me slain beasts and sacrifices by the space of forty years in the wilderness? Yea, ye took up the tabernacle of Moloch, and the star of your god Remphan, figures which ye made to worship them: and I will carry you away beyond Babylon" (Acts 7:42–43). So we see that the children of Israel were not faithful to God during this period.

These years of wandering have many lessons for us today. We are pilgrims and strangers in this world. In God's sight the world today is a wilderness. It may not look that way to us. Down here in Southern California, we have never felt this was a wilderness, but God sees it as a wilderness. You and I, believers, are just passing through this world. We are strangers and pilgrims.

Let me emphasize again: the whole theme of this chapter is that they can delay God's blessing but they cannot destroy God's purpose. Notice that although the children of Israel have turned back into the wilderness, God says they will enter the land, and as far as God is concerned, it is as good as done. That is the reason a great deal of prophecy is stated in what is known as the "prophetic tense" in the Old Testament. It is stated in the past tense although it speaks of a future event. You see, friends, as far as God is concerned, when He says something is going to come to pass, it has already come to pass in His program.

GOD'S PURPOSE IS NOT DESTROYED

And the Lord spake unto Moses, saying,

Speak unto the children of Israel, and say unto them, When ye be come into the land of your habitations, which I give unto you [Num. 15:1–2].

God is now telling them things which they are to do when they enter the land. Forty years later, Israel in a new generation entered the land and they did the things which their fathers neglected to do.

And will make an offering by fire unto the Lord, a burnt offering, or a sacrifice in performing a vow, or in a freewill offering, or in your solemn feasts, to make a sweet savour unto the Lord, of the herd, or of the flock:

Then shall he that offereth his offering unto the Lord bring a meat offering of a tenth deal of flour mingled with the fourth part of an hin of oil [Num. 15:3–4].

Now God goes on to talk to them about this offering. A hin of oil was to be put on it, which speaks of the Holy Spirit. Then there was to be the fourth part of a hin of wine for a drink

offering, and that speaks of joy. Notice how God says, "When thou preparest a bullock" (v. 8). God talks to them about what they will do in the land as definitely as if it were done. Although this generation in the wilderness will turn back to idolatry, the new generation that is coming into the land will offer these offerings which all speak of the person of the Lord Jesus Christ.

My friend, how is it with you today? Probably on Sunday you go to church and your thoughts center on the Bible and the Lord Jesus Christ. But what happens to you on Monday when you go out into the wilderness of the world? Do you join in the idolatry of the world? Do you serve the gods of this world? Do you live a sacred, religious life on Sunday and a secular life during the rest of the week? I tell you, the Lord Jesus wants to go into the market place with you. He wants to go on the streets of this world and into the trading places with you. He is as real there as He is in the church on Sunday.

Now he mentions something which we have previously seen in Leviticus, the offering for sins of ignorance.

Then it shall be, if aught be committed by ignorance without the knowledge of the congregation, that all the congregation shall offer one young bullock for a burnt offering, for a sweet savour unto the Lord, with his meat offering, and his drink offering, according to the manner, and one kid of the goats for a sin offering.

And the priest shall make an atonement for all the congregation of the children of Israel, and it shall be forgiven them; for it is ignorance: and they shall bring their offering, a sacrifice made by fire unto the Lord, and their sin offering before the Lord, for their ignorance.

And it shall be forgiven all the congregation of the children of Israel, and the stranger that sojourneth among them; seeing all the people were in ignorance [Num. 15:24–26].

Sins of ignorance remind us of a current issue. There is a great deal of debate about whether the heathen, who have never heard the Gospel, are lost. May I say to you, they are not lost because they are ignorant of the Gospel. They are lost because they are sinners. Sins of ignorance had to have an offering. So men are lost because they are sinners, whether or not they have heard the Gospel. I believe every man should have the opportunity to hear the Gospel and to make a decision, but men are lost long before they hear and reject the Gospel. Jesus Christ came to seek and to save that which was lost, and all men are lost. That is their natural state. Lost mankind is not sitting down in grief today because they have not heard the Gospel. If you have ever had the opportunity of taking the Gospel to those who have never heard it, you will recognize that they are not anxious to hear it.

DEATH PENALTY
FOR BREAKING SABBATH

One incident that happened during the wilderness wanderings is startling to read.

> And while the children of Israel were in the wilderness, they found a man that gathered sticks upon the sabbath day.

> And they that found him gathering sticks brought him unto Moses and Aaron, and unto all the congregation.

> And they put him in ward, because it was not declared what should be done to him.

> And the LORD said unto Moses, The man shall be surely put to death: all the congregation shall stone him with stones without the camp.

> And all the congregation brought him without the camp, and stoned him with stones, and he died; as the LORD commanded Moses [Num. 15:32–36].

This is very severe. This makes one thing very clear. The death penalty was the penalty for breaking any of the Ten Commandments. We need to see this to understand what it means that the Lord Jesus Christ died our death for us.

THE RIBBAND OF BLUE

And the LORD spake unto Moses, saying,

Speak unto the children of Israel, and bid them that they make them fringes in the borders of their garments throughout their generations, and that they put upon the fringe of the borders a ribband of blue:

And it shall be unto you for a fringe, that ye may look upon it, and remember all the commandments of the LORD, and do them; and that ye seek not after your own heart and your own eyes, after which ye use to go a-whoring:

That ye may remember, and do all my commandments, and be holy unto your God.

I am the LORD your God, which brought you out of the land of Egypt, to be your God: I am the LORD your God [Num. 15:37–41].

That border of blue, which is a heavenly color, was to remind them of the fact that they were God's people and they were to have a heavenly walk down here on this earth. There are many believers today who need to have that "border of blue" to remind them that as God's children they are set apart and are to live for the Lord Jesus Christ.

CHAPTER 16

THEME: Rebellion against divinely constituted authority; the sixth murmuring

Although we have no detailed account of the children of Israel during these wasted years in the wilderness, there are isolated incidents recorded. From chapter 16 through 19, we have four incidents which all concern the priesthood. Chapter 16 is the gainsaying of Korah. Chapter 17 is about Aaron's rod that budded. Chapter 18 is the confirmation of the priesthood, and chapter 19 concerns the offering of the red heifer.

REBELLION AGAINST DIVINELY CONSTITUTED AUTHORITY

This chapter opens with the murmuring of the children of Israel. This is the fifth murmuring, and before we get out of the chapter we will find the sixth murmuring. One can divide the wandering of the children of Israel according to their murmurings in the wilderness. This one is a murmuring among the priesthood. In fact, it is led by Korah, a very prominent Levite.

Now Korah, the son of Izhar, the son of Kohath, the son of Levi, and Dathan and Abiram, the sons of Eliab, and On, the son of Peleth, sons of Reuben, took men:

And they rose up before Moses, with certain of the children of Israel, two hundred and fifty princes of the assembly, famous in the congregation, men of renown:

And they gathered themselves together against Moses and against Aaron, and said unto them, Ye take too much upon you, seeing all the congregation are holy, every one of them, and the LORD is among them: wherefore then lift ye up yourselves above the congregation of the LORD? [Num. 16:1-3].

Korah was a Levite of great authority. Associated with him were 250 of the princes of the assembly who were also men of authority. A rebellion to be effective must have prominent men behind it. It takes brains and money. This rebellion was no small affair.

Maybe you thought that protest movements and marches were new. They are not new at all. Here is a protest movement against the establishment. These are men of ability and, as always, they appeal to the mob by making

charges—such as: "Your rights are being infringed upon. Your leaders are assuming too much authority. You are being deprived of something you should have."

Now, actually, the charges made in this rebellion were not true to the facts. They were absolutely unfounded. Moses was not taking too much upon himself. If we go back in his history, we find that when God called him, he refused. He didn't feel capable of leading these people. Even after God had trained him in the wilderness, he didn't want the job. He asked for a helper, and God gave him Aaron. Moses was the meekest man on earth. When Joshua wanted to silence the prophets, Moses said that he wished all of God's people might prophesy. He didn't have a jealous bone in his body. My friend, we have seen that Moses was not sinless, but he certainly was not guilty of taking too much upon himself.

What was really the root trouble here? It was the jealousy of Korah. This matter of jealousy is an awful thing. All authority is God-given. No man takes this honor upon himself. God had given the places in the camp, and He had given the Levites their specific jobs to do. Korah was a Kohathite, and their position and service were God-appointed. Moses had his position and duties. Frankly, a rebellion like this must be dealt with, and extreme measures are going to be used.

This is so important for us to see today. Churches everywhere are having problems. We are a problem-conscious people today because we do have problems. My experience is that a great deal of the problem in churches today and a great deal of rebellion among the people in the churches can be found rooted in one thing—jealousy! This is why the Bible enjoins us to walk in meekness and in lowliness of mind. We are to walk in humility. We are to recognize that all authority is God-given.

In 1 Corinthians 12, Paul pictures the church as a body, a human body. As the body has many members, so the church has many members. When God saves you, He puts you in the body by the baptism of the Holy Spirit. You are to function in a certain way in the body of believers. There are many gifts of the Spirit. If you are a Christian, you have been given a gift, and you are to use that gift as you function in the body of believers. The whole body is not a tongue. Therefore, everyone will not speak in tongues. Not all the body is an eye, nor is all the body an ear. Every individual has a gift and there are many gifts. One of those gifts is the gift of helps, and I can think of hundreds of ways in which you can help to get out the Word of God.

Every believer has a gift, and God wants us to function by exercising that gift. Your business is not to try to get someone else's office or job. We have too much insane vanity among Christians wanting to be chairman of a board or to do something publicly. My friend, most of the members of the body are not seen. We cover them or they are inside the body. Yet their function is essential to the body. It is just so in the church!

Jealousy motivates a great many people who are troublemakers in our churches. These people push themselves into a place of leadership. They attempt to usurp a gift which they do not have at all. They have no particular ability to do the thing that they are attempting. God never called them to do that. That is hurting the church today.

God is going to deal with this rebellion in a definite way. I tell you, the judgment of these men is going to be serious. Let us notice what God did.

And when Moses heard it, he fell upon his face:

And he spake unto Korah and unto all his company, saying, Even to-morrow the Lord will shew who are his, and who is holy; and will cause him to come near unto him: even him whom he hath chosen will he cause to come near unto him.

This do; Take you censers, Korah, and all his company;

And put fire therein, and put incense in them before the Lord to-morrow: and it shall be that the man whom the Lord doth choose, he shall be holy: ye take too much upon you, ye sons of Levi [Num. 16:4–7].

They had said to Moses and Aaron that they took too much upon themselves. Now Moses is telling them from God that they take too much on themselves.

And Moses said unto Korah, Hear, I pray you, ye sons of Levi:

Seemeth it but a small thing unto you, that the God of Israel hath separated you from the congregation of Israel, to bring you near to himself to do the service of the tabernacle of the Lord, and to stand before the congregation to minister unto them?

And he hath brought thee near to him, and all thy brethren the sons of Levi with thee: and seek ye the priesthood also?

For which cause both thou and all thy company are gathered together against the Lord: and what is Aaron, that ye murmur against him? [Num. 16:8–11].

Because the duties of Moses and Aaron were appointed by God, the murmuring is actually directed at God.

And Moses sent to call Dathan and Abiram, the sons of Eliab: which said, We will not come up:

Is it a small thing that thou hast brought us up out of a land that floweth with milk and honey, to kill us in the wilderness, except thou make thyself altogether a prince over us?

Moreover thou hast not brought us into a land that floweth with milk and honey, or given us inheritance of fields and vineyards: wilt thou put out the eyes of these men? we will not come up [Num. 16:12–14].

Their malicious charge against Moses ignores the fact that had they followed his leadership at Kadesh-barnea, by now they would be settled in the land of milk and honey.

And Moses was very wroth, and said unto the Lord, Respect not thou their offering: I have not taken one ass from them, neither have I hurt one of them.

And Moses said unto Korah, Be thou and all thy company before the Lord, thou, and they, and Aaron, to-morrow:

And take every man his censer, and put incense in them, and bring ye before the Lord every man his censer, two hundred and fifty censers; thou also, and Aaron, each of you his censer [Num. 16:15–17].

It is up to God to make known His will in this matter.

And they took every man his censer, and put fire in them, and laid incense thereon, and stood in the door of the

tabernacle of the congregation with Moses and Aaron.

And Korah gathered all the congregation against them unto the door of the tabernacle of the congregation: and the glory of the LORD appeared unto all the congregation.

And the LORD spake unto Moses and unto Aaron, saying,

Separate yourselves from among this congregation, that I may consume them in a moment [Num. 16:18–21].

Every man took his censer, put incense in it, and came to the tabernacle. We will see that the glory of the Lord appeared. We have noticed before that the glory of the Lord appeared at the time of the murmuring, and now it appears at this time of rebellion.

And they fell upon their faces, and said, O God, the God of the spirits of all flesh, shall one man sin, and wilt thou be wroth with all the congregation? [Num. 16:22].

Again Moses intercedes for his people.

And the LORD spake unto Moses, saying,

Speak unto the congregation, saying, Get you up from about the tabernacle of Korah, Dathan, and Abiram.

And Moses rose up and went unto Dathan and Abiram; and the elders of Israel followed him.

And he spake unto the congregation, saying, Depart, I pray you, from the tents of these wicked men, and touch nothing of theirs, lest ye be consumed in all their sins.

So they gat up from the tabernacle of Korah, Dathan, and Abiram, on every side: and Dathan and Abiram came out, and stood in the door of their tents, and their wives, and their sons, and their little children.

And Moses said, Hereby ye shall know that the LORD hath sent me to do all these works; for I have not done them of mine own mind.

If these men die the common death of all men, or if they be visited after the visitation of all men; then the LORD hath not sent me.

But if the LORD make a new thing, and the earth open her mouth, and swallow them up, with all that appertain unto them, and they go down quick into the pit; then ye shall understand that these men have provoked the LORD [Num. 16:23–30].

It is a terrible thing for a man or group of men to disobey God and His divinely appointed leaders. It is a terrible thing to set up a little system of worship and so divide the people of God. God must deal with this kind of rebellion, and He must judge it.

And it came to pass, as he had made an end of speaking all these words, that the ground clave asunder that was under them:

And the earth opened her mouth, and swallowed them up, and their houses, and all the men that appertained unto Korah, and all their goods.

They, and all that appertained to them, went down alive into the pit, and the earth closed upon them: and they perished from among the congregation [Num. 16:31–33].

It is awesome to see the way God judged them. Because they attempted to divide the people, God judges them in the same way in which they had sinned. He divides the people to separate them from Korah and his group, and then He divides the earth and it closes upon them. Galatians 6:7 says, "Be not deceived; God is not mocked: for whatsoever a man soweth, that shall he also reap." God judges the very same way in which the man sins. That was true of old Jacob; it was true of David; it was true of Paul, the apostle; and it will be true of you and me.

And all Israel that were round about them fled at the cry of them: for they said, Lest the earth swallow us up also.

And there came out a fire from the LORD, and consumed the two hundred and fifty men that offered incense [Num. 16:34–35].

These men had been leaders in Israel. They felt they should have had more prominence in their service. What a warning for us today! Too many people have a marvelous gift for serving God, but it would put them into some humble service, and they have the impression they should be running the church. Do you remember Dorcas who had the gift of sewing?

That gift was so important to the early church that God used Peter to raise her from the dead. I think that today we need fewer voices trying to do the speaking and more people who will do the tasks such as sewing. We need people to do the humble tasks around the church today. Each and every gift is important. Jealousy and rebellion will be judged by God.

And the Lord spake unto Moses, saying,

Speak unto Eleazar the son of Aaron the priest, that he take up the censers out of the burning, and scatter thou the fire yonder; for they are hallowed.

The censers of these sinners against their own souls, let them make them broad plates for a covering of the altar: for they offered them before the Lord, therefore they are hallowed: and they shall be a sign unto the children of Israel.

And Eleazar the priest took the brasen censers, wherewith they that were burnt had offered; and they were made broad plates for a covering of the altar:

To be a memorial unto the children of Israel, that no stranger, which is not of the seed of Aaron, come near to offer incense before the Lord; that he be not as Korah, and as his company: as the Lord said to him by the hand of Moses [Num. 16:36–40].

Now God told Moses that the censers of the rebels should be molded into broad plates for a covering of the altar. These were to be a memorial to the children of Israel that no one was to offer incense before the Lord unless he was in the line of Aaron, the priest.

THE SIXTH MURMURING

But on the morrow all the congregation of the children of Israel murmured against Moses and against Aaron, saying, Ye have killed the people of the Lord.

And it came to pass, when the congregation was gathered against Moses and against Aaron, that they looked to-ward the tabernacle of the congregation: and behold, the cloud covered it, and the glory of the Lord appeared [Num. 16:41–42].

The next day, after they had brooded over it all night, they charge Moses and Aaron with murdering the rebels! Moses and Aaron didn't do it, you see; God did it. Notice again that after their murmuring, the glory of the Lord appears.

Now God is ready to judge this murmuring people. The very man about whom they are complaining is the one who stands between the people and God in order to avert His judgment from them.

And the Lord spake unto Moses, saying,

Get you up from among this congregation, that I may consume them as in a moment. And they fell upon their faces.

And Moses said unto Aaron, Take a censer, and put fire therein from off the altar, and put on incense, and go quickly unto the congregation, and make an atonement for them: for there is wrath gone out from the Lord; the plague is begun.

And Aaron took as Moses commanded, and ran into the midst of the congregation; and, behold, the plague was begun among the people: and he put on incense, and made an atonement for the people.

And he stood between the dead and the living; and the plague was stayed.

Now they that died in the plague were fourteen thousand and seven hundred, beside them that died about the matter of Korah.

And Aaron returned unto Moses unto the door of the tabernacle of the congregation: and the plague was stayed [Num. 16:44–50].

The man they rebelled against is the very man who saved them. He stood between them and God. Likewise, the very One whom the human family crucified on the cross is the One who saves us. He stands between God and the sinner.

CHAPTER 17

THEME: *Office of Aaron is attested by resurrection*

Now God is going to confirm the priesthood of Aaron and establish the fact that he is the high priest. He will establish this by resurrection!

OFFICE OF AARON IS ATTESTED BY RESURRECTION

And the Lord spake unto Moses, saying,

Speak unto the children of Israel, and take of every one of them a rod according to the house of their fathers, of all their princes according to the house of their fathers twelve rods: write thou every man's name upon his rod.

And thou shalt write Aaron's name upon the rod of Levi: for one rod shall be for the head of the house of their fathers.

And thou shalt lay them up in the tabernacle of the congregation before the testimony, where I will meet with you.

And it shall come to pass, that the man's rod, whom I shall choose, shall blossom: and I will make to cease from me the murmurings of the children of Israel, whereby they murmur against you [Num. 17:1–5].

The children of Israel were murmuring against Aaron saying that he was not the only one who could represent them before God. It was a rebellion against him.

And Moses spake unto the children of Israel, and every one of their princes gave him a rod apiece, for each prince one, according to their fathers' houses, even twelve rods: and the rod of Aaron was among their rods.

And Moses laid up the rods before the Lord in the tabernacle of witness [Num. 17:6–7].

Now God confirms his priesthood in a most remarkable manner. God had the prince of each of the twelve tribes bring a rod. These rods were picked up out on the desert—probably whittled out and decorated by carvings—but they were dead wood. Then these rods were placed before the Lord in the tabernacle. Aaron's rod was there among the others, and his rod was as dead as all the others. But what happened?

And it came to pass, that on the morrow Moses went into the tabernacle of witness; and, behold, the rod of Aaron for the house of Levi was budded, and brought forth buds, and bloomed blossoms, and yielded almonds [Num. 17:8].

This is life out of death. Aaron's priesthood was confirmed by resurrection. Aaron's rod brought forth buds, and blossoms, and fruit! Life out of death. Resurrection. In the springtime the blooming of plants which have been dormant all winter does not illustrate life out of death. Neither does the egg. There is a germ of life in the egg. The perfect illustration of the resurrection of Christ is Aaron's rod that budded.

The priesthood of the Lord Jesus Christ rests upon the fact of His resurrection. We are told very frankly in the seventh chapter of Hebrews that if He were here on earth, He would not be a priest. He did not come from the priestly tribe of Levi. His *resurrection* made Him a priest. Then it tells us that not every man becomes a priest. "And no man taketh this honour unto himself, but he that is called of God, as was Aaron" (Heb. 5:4). Aaron was God's called priest. The evidence was the budded rod—the resurrection.

The Lord Jesus Christ was raised from the dead and He became our High Priest. He has an unchangeable priesthood and so ". . . he is able also to save them to the uttermost that come unto God by him, seeing he ever liveth to make intercession for them" (Heb. 7:25).

At this very moment, He is at God's right hand. He is there for you and for me today. One of the greatest privileges we have is being able to go to Him. He is our Great High Priest who makes intercession for us. "Seeing then that we have a great high priest, that is passed into the heavens, Jesus the Son of God, let us hold fast our profession. For we have not an high priest which cannot be touched with the feeling of our infirmities; but was in all points tempted like as we are, yet without sin. Let us therefore come boldly unto the throne of grace, that we may obtain mercy, and find grace to help in time of need" (Heb. 4:14–16).

Friend, do you need mercy? Do you need help today? Is life monotonous? Is it stale, flat, and unprofitable? Then go to the Lord Jesus. He is up there for you, your Great High Priest. Are you lonely? Go to Him. Is life a battle that you are losing? Are you defeated? Go to Him. Is life a struggle against temptation that you cannot overcome? Go to Him. Is life a horrible mistake and you need wisdom at the crossroads of decision? Go to Him. Is life shrouded with sorrow for you today? Go to Him. He is our Great High Priest by His resurrection from the dead. He is alive! He is up there for us today!

And Moses brought out all the rods from before the LORD unto all the children of Israel: and they looked, and took every man his rod.

And the LORD said unto Moses, Bring Aaron's rod again before the testimony,

to be kept for a token against the rebels; and thou shalt quite take away their murmurings from me, that they die not [Num. 17:9–10].

Aaron's rod that budded and blossomed and brought forth almonds is to be kept for a testimony and for a token. This rod was one of the three items which were kept in the ark of the covenant: ". . . the ark of the covenant overlaid round about with gold, wherein was the golden pot that had manna, and Aaron's rod that budded, and the tables of the covenant" (Heb. 9:4). The tables of stone on which were written the Ten Commandments, a pot of manna, and the rod that budded were preserved inside the ark of the covenant in the tabernacle. The rod forever settled the question as to the priesthood of Aaron.

CHAPTER 18

THEME: *Aaron and the Levites confirmed in their position and responsibilities*

We have seen the rebellion of Korah and the 250 princes of Israel against the constituted authority of Moses and Aaron. God judged him and his followers with a very severe judgment because his rebellion was actually against God. Then there were repercussions throughout the camp and a murmuring of the people. They felt the judgment had been too harsh. After all, these had been attractive men, leaders in Israel. Because these soft-hearted folk had no spiritual discernment, they found fault with Moses. Well, Moses was no more guilty of their death than Simon Peter was guilty of the death of Ananias and Sapphira. I'm of the opinion that Moses himself was quite surprised at what really took place.

Then a plague came upon the people because of their murmuring. Aaron stood between the living and the dead, and he became, actually, their intercessor at that time. Then God testified to the priesthood of Aaron by resurrection—He caused Aaron's rod to bud, blossom, and bear fruit. Now God finds it necessary to confirm the priesthood.

AARON AND THE LEVITES CONFIRMED

And the LORD said unto Aaron, Thou

and thy sons and thy father's house with thee shall bear the iniquity of the sanctuary: and thou and thy sons with thee shall bear the iniquity of your priesthood [Num. 18:1].

God is telling the Levites that they are responsible for what takes place. We need to remember that Korah was a Levite; the rebellion arose within the tribe of Levi. It was very serious. God is telling them they are responsible.

You and I are responsible today for our Christian testimony, for our families, and for our church. A great many people like to pull their skirts around them and assume a holier-than-thou attitude, shine up their halo, and then look down at the church today and talk about it going into apostasy. Now that is true; the church *is* going into apostasy. But it is also true that when there is sin in the church, you and I bear a certain amount of responsibility. We cannot escape the responsibility for sin in our lives, sin in our families, and sin in our church.

You see, this is the thing God is saying to Aaron. Aaron cannot look at all that is happening among the Levites and take a holier-than-thou attitude. Aaron cannot elevate himself by pointing out that he is God's elect, the one whom God has chosen as the high priest. God's man is to walk in humility. God's man bears responsibility!

And thy brethren also of the tribe of Levi, the tribe of thy father, bring thou with thee, that they may be joined unto thee, and minister unto thee: but thou and thy sons with thee shall minister before the tabernacle of witness.

And they shall keep thy charge, and the charge of all the tabernacle: only they shall not come nigh the vessels of the sanctuary and the altar, that neither they, nor ye also, die [Num. 18:2–3].

God outlines for them very specifically that they, that is Aaron and his sons, are in charge of the sanctuary, the vessels of the sanctuary, and the altar.

Then God goes into detail concerning the part of the offerings that belongs to the priesthood. They were to be sustained by their part of the offerings, and the entire "wave offering" was given to the priest. The wave offering was not offered as a burnt sacrifice, but was given to the priests.

All the heave offerings of the holy things, which the children of Israel offer unto the LORD, have I given thee, and thy sons and thy daughters with thee, by a statute for ever: it is a covenant of salt for ever before the LORD unto thee and to thy seed with thee [Num. 18:19].

That was the way a covenant was sealed in that day. Salt was regarded as a necessary ingredient of the daily food and was used in the sacrifices to the Lord. A covenant of salt became a covenant of permanent obligation.

And the LORD spake unto Aaron. Thou shalt have no inheritance in their land, neither shalt thou have any part among them: I am thy part and thine inheritance among the children of Israel [Num. 18:20].

Aaron and all the Levites would have no part in the land. They would not have farms to keep, or vineyards to tend, or olive groves to protect. God, Himself, was their inheritance.

May I put this in very plain terms for today? The people in the church are to pay their preacher. You are to pay the one who is bringing you spiritual food. The man who is spending his time doing that cannot be working on a farm or in a field or in an office. It is a tragic thing to see that many of God's finest workmen, both here and in the mission fields, must take a secular job in order to survive. The ministry suffers, and the church suffers. God provided support for the Levites, and He expects the church to support its pastor.

Now I recognize there are problems in looking to the Lord for His provision, but it is also a wonderful thing. I have been a minister for many, many years, and, although there have been difficult times which have tried our faith, it has been quite marvelous to be in this position. I want to testify how good God is. He has been mighty good to this poor preacher. That is what David said in the sixteenth Psalm: "The LORD is the portion of mine inheritance and of my cup: thou maintainest my lot" (Ps. 16:5). It is a wonderful thing to have God as your inheritance, and to have Him as your paymaster, and to look to Him for every need. It is really a glorious position to be in.

The Lord places the Levites in that position. They lived by faith.

And, behold, I have given the children of Levi all the tenth in Israel for an inheritance, for their service which they serve, even the service of the tabernacle of the congregation.

Neither must the children of Israel henceforth come nigh the tabernacle of the congregation, lest they bear sin, and die.

But the Levites shall do the service of the tabernacle of the congregation, and they shall bear their iniquity: it shall be a statute for ever throughout your generations, that among the children of Israel they have no inheritance [Num. 18:21–23].

They were to serve in the tabernacle of the congregation, and they were to be supported by the tenth in Israel. This meant that the Levites must walk by faith.

Now the question often arises whether preachers, missionaries, and church staff members should give to the church. I find that today a great many feel that they should not. I'd like to say a word in that connection. We are dealing here with rules and regulations in the Mosaic Law. Although you and I do not live under the Mosaic system, I believe it furnishes great principles by which we are to live. They are road maps for us to help us out in these questionable areas.

And the LORD spake unto Moses, saying.

Thus speak unto the Levites, and say unto them. When ye take of the children of Israel the tithes which I have given you from them for your inheritance, then ye shall offer up a heave offering of it for the LORD, even a tenth part of the tithe [Num. 18:25–26].

God told the Levites that they were to offer a tenth part of what they received. May I say to you, I think that the Christian worker, whoever he is, is to give to the Lord's work also. I think he ought to give to his church and through his church into his church's program. I have always given to missions and I have always encouraged my staff to give. I always had the offering plate passed on the pulpit platform so we might set an example for the congregation in this matter of giving.

We have had some thrilling experiences, by the way. It is our policy to send out books and tapes to missionaries and not to charge them a thing. But do you know that half of them pay for them? We had a missionary from one of the leading faith mission boards who was home on furlough. He was discouraged and felt he was losing his faith, but he started listening to our program. He never missed one, and then he came to our headquarters to get our tapes. We wanted to give him the tapes, but he insisted he was going to pay for them. May I say to you, he had the right principle.

Many of our missionaries simply cannot pay and we are glad to give them our tapes and materials. I have been impressed by the poverty of the missionaries out on the foreign fields I have visited. They have driven me in cars that were like the one-horse shay, ready to fall apart. Often the gas tank would be so nearly empty I would wonder whether we would make it to the airport. It is a shame and a disgrace that we do not pay our missionaries adequately, nor do we give them the proper instruments and tools to carry out their work.

This eighteenth chapter is a very practical chapter. It has a very definite message for us today.

CHAPTER 19

THEME: *The offering and ashes of the red heifer*

We come now to one of the most interesting offerings. It is called the offering of the red heifer, and it is most unusual.

THE OFFERING AND ASHES OF THE RED HEIFER

And the LORD spake unto Moses and unto Aaron, saying,

This is the ordinance of the law which the LORD hath commanded, saying, Speak unto the children of Israel, that they bring thee a red heifer without spot, wherein is no blemish, and upon which never came yoke [Num. 19:1–2].

This is the first time an offering is to be a female animal.

And ye shall give her unto Eleazar the priest, that he may bring her forth without the camp, and one shall slay her before his face:

And Eleazar the priest shall take of her blood with his finger, and sprinkle of her blood directly before the tabernacle of the congregation seven times:

And one shall burn the heifer in his sight; her skin, and her flesh, and her blood, with her dung, shall he burn:

And the priest shall take cedar wood, and hyssop, and scarlet, and cast it into the midst of the burning of the heifer.

Then the priest shall wash his clothes, and he shall bathe his flesh in water, and afterward he shall come into the camp, and the priest shall be unclean until the even.

And he that burneth her shall wash his clothes in water, and bathe his flesh in water, and shall be unclean until the even [Num. 19:3–8].

Now what is the purpose of this?

And a man that is clean shall gather up the ashes of the heifer, and lay them up without the camp in a clean place, and it

shall be kept for the congregation of the children of Israel for a water of separation: it is a purification for sin [Num. 19:9].

How was this to be used?

And for an unclean person they shall take of the ashes of the burnt heifer of purification for sin, and running water shall be put thereto in a vessel:

And a clean person shall take hyssop, and dip it in the water, and sprinkle it upon the tent, and upon all the vessels, and upon the persons that were there, and upon him that touched a bone, or one slain, or one dead, or a grave:

And the clean person shall sprinkle upon the unclean on the third day, and on the seventh day: and on the seventh day he shall purify himself, and wash his clothes, and bathe himself in water, and shall be clean at even [Num. 19:17–19].

This is an unusual ordinance, and it sounds very strange, but there is a good reason for it. When the children of Israel were on the march and a man sinned, they couldn't stop right there, put up the tabernacle, and go through the ritual of offering a trespass offering or a sin offering. So what were they to do when a man sinned on the way? They would take the ashes of this heifer, mix those ashes with running water, then with hyssop sprinkle the individual who had sinned. That sounds very strange, doesn't it? But that was the way God dealt with sin for those people.

Let me tell you another strange incident. When our Lord Jesus Christ went into the Upper Room with His disciples, the first thing he did was to get a basin of water and wash the disciples' feet. Now why did He do that? He tells Simon Peter the reason. ". . . If I wash thee not, thou hast no part with me" (John 13:8). If the Lord Jesus had not washed the feet of Peter, Peter could not have fellowship with Him. He had come from the Father and He was going back to the Father. "Jesus knowing that the Father had given all things into his hands, and that he was come from God, and went to God; He riseth from supper, and laid aside his garments; and took a towel, and girded himself" (John 13:3–4).

Jesus Christ has gone back to the Father now, and He is still girded with the towel of service. The basin of water is the Word of God,

the Holy Spirit is the One who applies it, and the hyssop speaks of faith.

When you and I sin today, Christ is not going to die all over again. We are told, "But if we walk in the light, as he is in the light, we have fellowship one with another, and the blood of Jesus Christ his Son cleanseth us from all sin" (1 John 1:7). That "light" is the Word of God. If we walk in the light, what do we see? We see that we are dirty and that we need cleaning. The Spirit of God convicts us. The Word tells us that the blood of Jesus Christ, God's Son, will keep on cleansing us from all these sins. But the water of the Word and the cleansing blood of Jesus Christ must be applied to us. "If we confess our sins, he is faithful and just to forgive us our sins, and to cleanse us from all unrighteousness" (1 John 1:9). He died down here to save us. He lives up yonder to keep us saved. When Jesus Christ died for our sins, He did not die only for those sins up to the time we came to Him. He died for our sins from the time we came to Him at the cross until He gives us a crown.

Don't tell me that you don't sin after you have been saved. Sin in our lives is a fact which so many Christians neglect. Christian people get cleaned up for church. They take their Saturday night bath to be clean for Sunday. Congregations smell better today than they used to smell because they use deodorants, perfumes and colognes, but to God they smell worse because they are dirty. How many have been looking at things they shouldn't look at? They come with dirty eyes. How many have been listening to gossip during the week? How many have been hearing filthy things they shouldn't hear? They come with dirty ears. Some have dirty hands because they have been doing things they shouldn't have done. Some have dirty feet because they have been walking where they shouldn't have walked. They think that coming to church makes everything all right. Well, it's not all right. That's the reason the Lord Jesus says, ". . . If I wash thee not, thou hast no part with me" (John 13:8). If the church service seems dead, and the sermon boring, perhaps it's because you need a bath, a spiritual bath. "If we say that we have fellowship with him, and walk in darkness, we lie, and do not the truth" (1 John 1:6). We don't want to lie. If we do, then we have to confess that to Him. It is so important to go to Him and to tell Him all our sins. And you might just as well tell Him because He already knows all about you anyway. But it makes fellowship so wonderful if we confess our sins to Him.

Why don't you go to Him for cleansing?

Someone may ask how often this should be done. Well, I don't know about you, but I try to take a shower every day. And I find that I must go to Him two or three times every day and tell Him that McGee has been wrong and that McGee shouldn't have seen this, or done this, or said that. May I say to you, we want to keep sweet with Him, and the only way we can do that is to confess our sins.

This offering of the red heifer is a marvelous offering. It kept the children of Israel sweet on the wilderness march. This was their deodorant for the wilderness march so that they might walk in fellowship with Him.

CHAPTER 20

THEME: At Kadesh again (after 37 years); the seventh murmuring; water from rock, disobedience of Moses; Edom refuses Israel passage through their land; death of Aaron

The chapter before us opens with the death of Miriam and it closes with the death of Aaron. The chapter is bounded by death. It also contains the sin of Moses and the sin of Edom. Yet this is an important chapter because it marks the end of wandering for the children of Israel and the beginning of marching.

This section, from chapters 14 to 20, is the only section which deals with the forty years of wandering in the wilderness—and that's not very much. We have only a few incidents that took place during these forty years, Israel is out of God's will, and there is little to tell. We can talk about Israel being God's chosen people, but they didn't amount to anything except when they were in God's will. And that is still true today.

It is also true of you and me that we don't amount to anything when we are out of the will of God. When you and I are not functioning in the body of believers, exercising the gift that He has given to us by the power of the Holy Spirit, we are as unnecessary as a fifth leg on a cow. Actually, we get in the way.

AT KADESH AGAIN
(AFTER 37 YEARS)

Then came the children of Israel, even the whole congregation, into the desert of Zin in the first month: and the people abode in Kadesh; and Miriam died there, and was buried there [Num. 20:1].

Here we have the death of Miriam and only one verse is given to it. There is no long funeral oration, no days of mourning, no effort to eulogize. Miriam died and was buried. That's all.

They are back at Kadesh. They had been here almost thirty-eight years before and now they are back again. Thirty-eight years of wandering, going nowhere. Although these years of wandering were not years of great blessing for the people, they provide great lessons to be learned because many of us today are not marching as pilgrims through the world; we are simply wandering pilgrims in this world down here.

THE SEVENTH MURMURING

And there was no water for the congregation: and they gathered themselves together against Moses and against Aaron.

And the people chode with Moses, and spake, saying, Would God that we had died when our brethren died before the LORD [Num. 20:2–3].

Of course they don't really mean that. None of us want to die. Death is unnatural for man. But they are complaining, whining again, and murmuring. This is the seventh murmuring, and it is over the lack of water.

And why have ye brought up the congregation of the LORD into this wilderness, that we and our cattle should die there?

And wherefore have ye made us to come up out of Egypt, to bring us in unto this evil place? it is no place of seed, or of figs, or of vines, or of pomegranates; neither is there any water to drink [Num. 20:4–5].

Here they are back at Kadesh where they had failed before, and again they are complaining instead of trusting. Well, the land of milk and honey is ahead of them, but it isn't here.

I don't care where you are today, or who you are—you as a child of God need to recognize that you are not here permanently. All of us are just pilgrims passing through this world; we won't be in any one place for long. So we ought not to spend so much time complaining.

And Moses and Aaron went from the presence of the assembly unto the door of the tabernacle of the congregation, and they fell upon their faces: and the glory of the Lord appeared unto them [Num. 20:6].

Again I call your attention to the fact that every time these people murmured or complained, the glory of the Lord appeared. God was displeased with their complaining. That should make us realize that if we are whining and complaining saints, we are not pleasing to God. That is true no matter who you are, or where you are, or what you are doing.

WATER FROM ROCK, DISOBEDIENCE OF MOSES

And the Lord spake unto Moses, saying,

Take the rod, and gather thou the assembly together, thou, and Aaron thy brother, and speak ye unto the rock before their eyes; and it shall give forth his water, and thou shalt bring forth to them water out of the rock: so thou shalt give the congregation and their beasts drink [Num. 20:7–8].

"Take the rod"—this rod was Aaron's, by the way. "Gather the assembly together and speak unto the rock." Why were they simply to speak to the rock this time? It is because many years before this (as recorded in the seventeenth chapter of Exodus) the rock was smitten and water came forth. The rock is to be smitten only once!

And Moses took the rod from before the Lord, as he commanded him.

And Moses and Aaron gathered the congregation together before the rock, and he said unto them. Hear now, ye rebels; must we fetch you water out of this rock? [Num. 20:9–10].

Not only are the children of Israel complaining, but Moses is complaining now, don't you think? I have great sympathy for him. He's been with them all of forty years in the wilderness, and frankly, he is getting pretty tired of them.

He is forgetting himself here when he says, ". . . must *we* fetch you water out of this rock?" (Num. 20:11). Moses is not going to fetch them water out of the rock at all. God is the One who will provide the water. They need to learn a great lesson here which is that the rock is a type of Christ. Now Moses became angry and he did something that he should not have done. This is going to keep him from entering the Promised Land.

And Moses lifted up his hand, and with his rod he smote the rock twice: and the water came out abundantly, and the congregation drank, and their beasts also [Num. 20:11].

Some men teach that his error was in smiting the rock twice. He should not have smitten it at all, friends. It had already been smitten. The rock is a type of Christ (1 Cor. 10:4). Christ suffered once for sins, never the second time. He died once. God was teaching this to them in a type, and Moses should have protected and guarded the type by obeying God. God told him very clearly that he was to *speak* to the rock. That was all he needed to do. But Moses failed to obey God. The importance of this act of disobedience was that the rock pictures Christ. "Moreover, brethren, I would not that ye should be ignorant, how that all our fathers were under the cloud, and all passed through the sea; And were all baptized unto Moses in the cloud and in the sea; And did all eat the same spiritual meat; And did all drink the same spiritual drink: for they drank of that spiritual Rock that followed them: and that Rock was Christ" (1 Cor. 10:1–4).

The water came out abundantly. The error of Moses did not keep the water from coming out. How gracious God is!

And the Lord spake unto Moses and Aaron, Because ye believed me not, to sanctify me in the eyes of the children of Israel, therefore ye shall not bring this congregation into the land which I have given them [Num. 20:12].

God is saying here that Moses and Aaron did not believe Him, neither did they sanctify Him in the eyes of Israel. That is, they took to themselves the credit for the miracle.

When we read the New Testament, we find that Moses did reach the Promised Land eventually; he apeared on the Mount of Transfiguration with Christ in that land.

Canaan is actually the picture of where you and I should live by faith. It is not a picture of heaven. We are in this world which is a wilderness, but you and I ought to be enjoying the blessings of Canaan. That comes, as we shall see in the book of Joshua, by the death and resurrection of Christ. We are to reckon upon that, believing God and yielding to Him in this matter. That is what Moses and Aaron failed to do.

This is the water of Meribah, because the children of Israel strove with the LORD, and he was sanctified in them [Num. 20:13].

Today, unbelief is our great sin also. My, what a reflection it is on God when we don't take Him at His Word and believe Him!

EDOM REFUSES ISRAEL PASSAGE THROUGH THEIR LAND

And Moses sent messengers from Kadesh unto the king of Edom, Thus saith thy brother Israel, Thou knowest all the travail that hath befallen us:

How our fathers went down into Egypt, and we have dwelt in Egypt a long time; and the Egyptians vexed us, and our fathers:

Let us pass, I pray thee, through thy country: we will not pass through the fields, or through the vineyards, neither will we drink of the water of the wells: we will go by the king's high way, we will not turn to the right hand nor to the left, until we have passed thy borders [Num. 20:14-15,17].

Moses gives them a little history of their nation, and then he asks for permission to cross their land. Now that was a request that was made in a very kind sort of way. Edom was their brother, and Moses reminds them of this. Edom sinned by not letting them pass through.

And Edom said unto him, Thou shalt not pass by me, lest I come out against thee with the sword [Num. 20:18].

The children of Israel again told Edom that they had their cattle and little ones and wanted to come through. Again they assured them that they would not take anything or damage the land.

And he said, Thou shalt not go through. And Edom came out against him with much people, and with a strong hand.

Thus Edom refused to give Israel passage through his border: wherefore Israel turned away from him.

And the children of Israel, even the whole congregation, journeyed from Kadesh, and came unto mount Hor [Num. 20:20-22].

Now they are making a circuitous route which would not have been necessary had they been given permission to go through Edom. However, I think that Moses made a mistake here. Moses should have been following the cloud. He didn't need to worry. God would be leading him and guiding him. Instead of asking Edom for permission to go through, he should have simply followed the cloud. I think that the pillar of cloud would have led him in a way so he would never have had to fight Edom at all. I believe this is a case of running ahead of the Lord. Unfortunately, many of us do that.

DEATH OF AARON

We come now to the death of Aaron and that brings us to the end of the chapter which ends on a sad note. But there are very precious lessons in this chapter for you and for me.

And the LORD spake unto Moses and Aaron in mount Hor, by the coast of the land of Edom, saying,

Aaron shall be gathered unto his people: for he shall not enter into the land which I have given unto the children of Israel, because ye rebelled against my word at the water of Meribah [Num. 20:23-24].

You know, there are many people today who are saved but even in this life they never enjoy the fruits of salvation and they do not have the peace of the Spirit in their own lives. They do not know what it is to walk in fellowship with the Lord Jesus. Yet I would never for one moment question their salvation. Aaron was typical of that kind of life. He knew forty years of rugged experience in the wilderness, but he never knew what it was to sit down and enjoy the fruits of the Promised Land. He did not know what it was to drink the milk and eat the honey in the land of milk and honey. Many of us rob ourselves of that because of our unbelief.

Take Aaron and Eleazar his son, and bring them up unto mount Hor:

And strip Aaron of his garments, and put them upon Eleazar his son: and Aaron shall be gathered unto his people, and shall die there.

And Moses did as the LORD commanded: and they went up into mount Hor in the sight of all the congregation.

And Moses stripped Aaron of his garments, and put them upon Eleazar his son; and Aaron died there in the top of the mount: and Moses and Eleazar came down from the mount.

And when all the congregation saw that Aaron was dead, they mourned for Aaron thirty days, even all the house of Israel [Num. 20:25–29].

There is a precious lesson here for us. This was a very sad thing in Israel, but it has in it for us today something that should cause us to thank God.

The children of Israel mourned for thirty days. I think there were many in that company who had been to Aaron, the high priest. They knew Aaron, and Aaron knew them. They would bring their sacrifice and they would ask Aaron, "Oh, do you think God will forgive me?" And I think that Aaron would comfort them and tell them that our God is a gracious, merciful God. Then he would offer their sacrifice for them. Now they saw Eleazar come down, clothed in the garments of Aaron. Aaron is dead and gone. And they would say, "I don't know Eleazar and he doesn't know me. It's a different priest now."

May I say to you today that we have a High Priest who *ever* lives to make intercession for us. Our Lord is not a Priest after the order of Aaron but after the order of Melchizedek. He has neither beginning of days, nor end of life; He abides a Priest continually! Our High Priest will not die. He died once for us down here; He lives forever for us up there. He will always be there for us. We can always depend on Him. He knows each of us individually and we can know Him. To know Him is life everlasting. Knowing Him will occupy us for all eternity and it will never be changed. That is something to be thankful for today.

Israel has finished the wilderness wandering now and will be getting ready to enter into the Promised Land. Also God has a "promised land" into which He wants to bring us today. Christ is the One who can bring us there right now.

CHAPTER 21

THEME: Victory of Israel; the eighth murmuring; the serpent of brass; first song; the march of Israel

As we have seen, chapter 20 brought us to the end of the wilderness wanderings in the sense that the wandering is over and they begin to march. In this chapter are their first victories in warfare. Also the experience of their eighth and last murmuring is recorded, which brought about the fiery serpents and the serpent of brass, used by the Lord Jesus to illustrate His own crucifixion.

VICTORY OF ISRAEL

And when king Arad the Canaanite, which dwelt in the south, heard tell that Israel came by the way of the spies; then he fought against Israel, and took some of them prisoners.

And Israel vowed a vow into the LORD, and said, If thou wilt indeed deliver this people into my hand, then I will utterly destroy their cities.

And the LORD hearkened to the voice of Israel, and delivered up the Canaanites; and they utterly destroyed them and their cities: and he called the name of the place Hormah.

And they journeyed from mount Hor by the way of the Red Sea, to compass the land of Edom: and the soul of the people was much discouraged because of the way [Num. 21:1–4].

This is the first victory (since their conflict with Amalek shortly after they left Egypt) on the wilderness march. God clearly gave them this victory. However they now have to go by Mount Hor by way of the Red Sea. Since they can't go through the land of Edom, they are attempting to make a circuitous route around that land. The way is hard and becomes very discouraging to the people. In their plight of discouragement, they begin to complain and whine and murmur. Unfortunately this is characteristic of many of us today. When life is hard we complain and murmur.

THE EIGHTH MURMURING

And the people spake against God, and against Moses. Wherefore have ye brought us up out of Egypt to die in the wilderness? for there is no bread, neither is there any water; and our soul loatheth this light bread [Num. 21:5].

This is the eighth and last murmuring of the children of Israel. They are murmuring again about the manna. You will recall that the mixed multitude were the ones who had led them in rejecting the manna earlier in the march. Manna was a wonderful food, by the way. God reminds them in the book of Deuteronomy that their feet did not swell. A missionary doctor in the Philippines told me that the foot will swell and beriberi results from a diet deficiency. So they were getting all the correct nutrition in the manna, and it was a very tasty sort of food. Yet they complained.

There are people who will complain about steak—they would want a hamburger for variety! It's amazing how easy it is for us to complain, and especially to complain about that which pertains to the things of God. When I was a pastor, people complained about the seats in the church. Yet I've seen folk go to a football game and sit on hard seats in a stadium (and there is no back on those seats) for hours and never complain! Now I will admit that when they listened to me preach they noticed the seats more. But isn't it interesting how we whine and complain to God? How many times do we thank Him and rejoice in His goodness to us?

I think, frankly, that the Lord is getting just a little tired of all their murmuring. They say that their soul hates this manna. They don't want it. They charge God with bringing them into this wilderness to die. The Lord is tired of all their complaining and He is going to judge them for it.

THE SERPENT OF BRASS

And the Lord sent fiery serpents among the people, and they bit the people; and much people of Israel died.

Therefore the people came to Moses, and said. We have sinned, for we have spoken against the Lord, and against thee; pray unto the Lord, that he take away the serpents from us. And Moses prayed for the people [Num. 21:6–7].

"We have sinned." They are now ready to admit that they have sinned against the Lord and against Moses.

Now, that is a problem with many folk today. They want to begin with God as a church member, as a nice little girl or boy. We all must begin with God as *sinners*. The only way that God will begin with us is as sinners. You see, Christ died for sinners, and He loves sinners. If you can't come in under that category, then Christ is not for you. He came for sinners.

These people are going to have to give evidence of faith because they have no good works. They can't come to God with the promise that from now on they will be good because they won't be good. But they can believe God, and God is going to let them come to Him by faith.

And the Lord said unto Moses, Make thee a fiery serpent, and set it upon a pole: and it shall come to pass, that every one that is bitten, when he looketh upon it, shall live.

And Moses made a serpent of brass, and put it upon a pole, and it came to pass, that if a serpent had bitten any man, when he beheld the serpent of brass, he lived [Num. 21:8–9].

There is a marvelous lesson here, you see. They are to look at the brazen serpent, and they are to look in faith. In fact, they would not look if it were not in faith. I can well imagine some of the folk saying that this was just nonsense. They would want something else, something more tangible than just turning around to look at a serpent of brass. But, of course, if a man would not turn to look at the serpent of brass, he would die.

Now, we don't have to guess at the meaning of this and the lesson for us. When our Lord was talking to Nicodemus on that dark night, He said, "And as Moses lifted up the serpent in the wilderness, even so must the Son of man be lifted up: That whosoever believeth in him should not perish, but have eternal life. For God so loved the world, that he gave his only begotten Son, that whosoever believeth in him should not perish, but have everlasting life" (John 3:14–16).

How was the Son of man lifted up? You say, on a cross. Yes, but He was dying on the cross of Barabbas, and Barabbas was a thief and a murderer. Barabbas was guilty and was worthy of death. Jesus was not. Our Lord was made sin for us. On that cross, He not only has taken the place of Barabbas but also your place and my place. God permitted this and did this because He loves us. But God cannot save us by His love. It doesn't say that God so loved the world that He saved the world. Not at all. God so loved the world that He *gave* His only begotten Son. Now what God asks you to do, my friend, is to look and live. Look to Christ! He is taking *your* place there. You are a sinner and it is you who deserves to die. Christ did not deserve to die. He died for you.

We read here that this serpent of brass was made, and those who looked to it lived. Those who did not look to it—died. It is just that simple today. Either you are looking to Christ as your Savior because you are a sinner, or you are not doing it. If you are not doing it, I don't care how many times you have been baptized, how many ceremonies you have been through, how many churches you have joined, or who your father and mother happened to be, you are a lost, hell-doomed sinner. You must look to the Lord Jesus Christ. It is just as simple as that. And by the way, it is just as complicated as that. What a problem people have today. They would rather look to themselves and to their own good works, trusting that somehow their own good works might save them. It is a problem for people to admit they are sinners and to look to Christ and trust Him.

Now the children of Israel move on. They come to the River Arnon which you can trace on your map.

From thence they removed, and pitched on the other side of Arnon, which is in the wilderness that cometh out of the coasts of the Amorites: for Arnon is the border of Moab, between Moab and the Amorites [Num. 21:13].

Then they go on.

And from thence they went to Beer: that is the well whereof the Lord spake unto Moses, Gather the people together, and I will give them water [Num. 21:16].

FIRST SONG

Now listen to this. How different this is. This is the first time they sing a song of praise and thanksgiving. They have been singing the desert blues and murmuring. Now it's the Hallelujah chorus.

Then Israel sang this song, Spring up, O well; sing ye unto it:

The princes digged the well, the nobles of the people digged it, by the direction of the lawgiver, with their staves. And from the wilderness they went to Mattanah:

And from Mattanah to Nahaliel: and from Nahaliel to Bamoth:

And from Bamoth in the valley that is in the country of Moab, to the top of Pisgah, which looketh toward Jeshimon [Num. 21:17–20].

They were thanking God for the provision that He had made for them in supplying water. The princes digged the well and the nobles of the people digged. Here you find capital and labor joining together in this.

THE MARCH OF ISRAEL

And Israel sent messengers unto Sihon king of the Amorites, saying [Num. 21:21].

Israel now asks Sihon, king of the Amorites, for permission to pass through his land. Sihon refuses and gathers an army against Israel.

And Israel smote him with the edge of the sword, and possessed his land from Arnon unto Jabbok, even unto the children of Ammon: for the border of the children of Ammon was strong [Num. 21:24].

God gave Israel the victory over Sihon.

And they turned and went up by the way of Bashan: and Og the king of Bashan went out against them, he, and all his people, to the battle of Edrei [Num. 21:33].

The Lord told Moses not to fear Og, the king of Bashan. They smote him and his sons and his people and they possessed the land of Bashan.

The children of Israel are marching now. They are singing praises to God and God is giving them victory. God will help them against Moab, too. They will then be getting ready to enter the Promised Land.

CHAPTER 22

THEME: *The way of Balaam*

Chapters 22 to 25 comprise a section of Numbers which goes into the story of Balaam, the prophet. He comes across the page of Scripture as one of those strange individuals whom I wish I could interpret for you. I wish I knew more so that I could correctly evaluate him.

There are literally thousands of people recorded in the Word of God. The Holy Spirit customarily gives us a cameo-sharp picture of them, a clear delineation of their character in just a few words. We've seen that.

Then there are the exceptions—these few walk in the shadows. Darkness hides their true natures. They are distorted, twisted individuals. I am not sure about Cain, or about Esau, Samson, or Saul, Absalom, or this man Balaam. I am not sure how to interpret them. Then in the New Testament we have questions about that rich, young ruler who came to Christ. Did he ever come back to Christ? Then there is Judas. Who can understand him? I'm sure that most of us feel that he was a lost individual, but he's a strange person who followed our Lord for three years. No one detected that he was a phony except the Lord Jesus Himself. Then there is Demas—Demas who seemed to be so faithful and yet who finally forsook the apostle Paul. And what about Ananias and Sapphira?

Balaam is one of those enigmatic and mysterious characters. One writer says that he is the strangest of all characters in the Scripture. Some authors consider him a genuine prophet of God. Others say he was a religious racketeer. Is Balaam sincerely seeking to serve God, or is he a fake, a phony? Well, I'll have to let you be the judge of that.

We might say that we should dismiss him as unworthy of any consideration, but I must tell you that the Word of God attaches some importance to him. Micah writes, "Oh my people, remember now what Balak king of Moab consulted, and what Balaam the son of Beor answered him from Shittim unto Gilgal; that ye may know the righteousness of the LORD" (Mic. 6:5). Micah is telling Israel that they had better not forget him. So we had better not push this character aside.

Did you know that there is more said in Scripture about Balaam than there is about Mary, the mother of Jesus? There is more said about Balaam than about any of the apostles. The New Testament mentions him three times, and each time it is in connection with apostasy. In 2 Peter we are told about the *way* of Balaam. In Jude we are told about the *error* of Balaam. In Revelation we are told about the *doctrine* of Balaam.

This Balaam was a Midianite. He was a prophet with a wide reputation. He got results. Was he genuine? Let's read his story before we evaluate him.

THE WAY OF BALAAM

And the children of Israel set forward, and pitched in the plains of Moab on this side Jordan by Jericho.

And Balak the son of Zippor saw all that Israel had done to the Amorites.

And Moab was sore afraid of the people, because they were many: and Moab was distressed because of the children of Israel [Num. 22:1–3].

You see that Israel is ready to enter the land. Balak, king of the Moabites, had witnessed what had happened to the Amorites and to Og, the king of Bashan. He was wondering what he should do to get Israel out of the land. Should he attack them? Very candidly, he didn't know what to do. So he decided to engage the services of this prophet.

He sent messengers therefore unto Balaam the son of Beor to Pethor, which is by the river of the land of the children of his people, to call him, saying, Behold, there is a people come out from Egypt: behold, they cover the face of the earth, and they abide over against me:

Come now therefore, I pray thee, curse me this people; for they are too mighty for me: peradventure I shall prevail, that we may smite them, and that I may drive them out of the land: for I wot that he whom thou blessest is blessed, and he whom thou cursest is cursed [Num. 22:5–6].

He sends for Balaam. Apparently this prophet was well known in that entire land. Balak wants to hire him to come and curse the children of Israel. These people had poured into the area there by the Jordan River and Balak wanted them out of that land.

And the elders of Moab and the elders of Midian departed with the rewards of divination in their hand; and they came unto Balaam, and spake unto him the words of Balak [Num. 22:7].

He sent messengers down to Balaam to make this overture to him. The man has quite a reputation, you see. The messengers bring their rewards, or the pay, for the diviner. Balaam is a fortune teller. Balak offers a very handsome price to this man through his messengers.

And he said unto them, Lodge here this night, and I will bring you word again, as the Lord shall speak unto me: and the princes of Moab abode with Balaam [Num. 22:8].

Now he seems honestly to be trying to ascertain here the mind of God. He apparently is in touch with God. Now notice:

And God came unto Balaam, and said, What men are these with thee?

And Balaam said unto God, Balak the son of Zippor, king of Moab, hath sent unto me, saying,

Behold, there is a people come out of Egypt, which covereth the face of the earth: come now, curse me them; peradventure I shall be able to overcome them, and drive them out [Num. 22:9–11].

It is a very interesting thing that God did communicate with him.

And God said unto Balaam, Thou shalt not go with them; thou shalt not curse the people: for they are blessed [Num. 22:12].

Now that was a categorical, matter-of-fact answer. There was no way to be evasive about that. Now watch Balaam.

And Balaam rose up in the morning, and said unto the princes of Balak, Get you into your land: for the Lord refuseth to give me leave to go with you [Num. 22:13].

Balaam seems to be a sincere and honest man of God. If this were the end of the story, then I would have to assume that about him, but Balak was a persistent fellow.

And Balak sent yet again princes, more, and more honourable than they.

And they came to Balaam, and said to him, Thus saith Balak the son of Zippor,

Let nothing, I pray thee, hinder thee from coming unto me:

For I will promote thee unto very great honour, and I will do whatsoever thou sayest unto me: come therefore, I pray thee, curse me this people [Num. 22:15–17].

Actually, you see, they are offering him a better price.

And Balaam answered and said unto the servants of Balak, If Balak would give me his house full of silver and gold, I cannot go beyond the word of the Lord my God, to do less or more [Num. 22:18].

Well, they had upped the price but that does not seem to affect this man Balaam. He turns it down. He sounds very pious here. I feel like saying Amen. Then I have a second thought. He's too good to be true. Just why did he speak of a house filled with silver and gold? He said it because that is what he is thinking about. He is covetous, and his mind is turned in that direction.

Now therefore, I pray you, tarry ye also here this night, that I may know what the Lord will say unto me more [Num. 22:19].

Oh, oh, what is happening here, friends? Well, it's quite obvious. He already has an answer from God. He has no need to wait another night for a further answer from God. God had already told him not to go, but you see, this man is hoping that the Lord will open a little crack in the door so he can put his foot into it; and if he can get his foot into it, then he is going to go. This is all very interesting.

Do we sometimes do this same thing? We who are preachers make a great deal about a call from God. I heard the story of a preacher who came home and told his wife one day, "Honey, I just had a call to the church over in the next town. Now you know it's a bigger town, richer town, bigger church, more members, and fine folk over there. I've been called to go over there as pastor and I'm going upstairs to pray about it and find out what the Lord's will is for us." She answered, "I'll go upstairs to pray with you." "Oh no," he said, "you stay down here and pack!" He had made up his mind, as you can see. Old Balaam had made up his mind also.

Now notice what happens. God does not do this for Balaam only; He does it for you and for me. It is not good, friends, but God *permits* us to do what we want to do.

And God came unto Balaam at night, and said unto him, If the men come to call thee, rise up, and go with them; but yet the word which I shall say unto thee, that shalt thou do [Num. 22:20].

In other words, God is saying, "All right, you want to go and before it is through you will go, but if you go, you are to say what I want you to say. Be careful of that." We have here what is known as the permissive will of God. He permits us many times to do something that we insist on doing when it is not in His direct will. You remember how we learned from the children of Israel that God granted their request but sent leanness to their souls. Sometimes He also grants our requests and sends leanness to our souls.

And Balaam rose up in the morning, and saddled his ass, and went with the princes of Moab.

And God's anger was kindled because he went: and the angel of the LORD stood in the way for an adversary against him. Now he was riding upon his ass, and his two servants were with him.

And the ass saw the angel of the LORD standing in the way, and his sword drawn in his hand: and the ass turned aside out of the way, and went into the field: and Balaam smote the ass, to turn her into the way [Num. 22:21–23].

He had God's direct answer, but he didn't like that. God permits him to go. Now God sends His angel, but this prophet doesn't have the mind of God at all. We can see that he has no spiritual discernment, not even the discernment of this dumb animal.

But the angel of the LORD stood in a path of the vineyards, a wall being on this side, and a wall on that side.

And when the ass saw the angel of the LORD, she thrust herself unto the wall, and crushed Balaam's foot against the wall: and he smote her again.

And the angel of the LORD went further, and stood in a narrow place, where was no way to turn either to the right hand or to the left [Num. 22:24–26].

Balaam was determined to go, you see. He was a covetous man.

And when the ass saw the angel of the LORD, she fell down under Balaam: and Balaam's anger was kindled, and he smote the ass with a staff.

And the LORD opened the mouth of the ass, and she said unto Balaam, What have I done unto thee, that thou hast smitten me these three times? [Num. 22:27–28].

This is a miracle, of course. God is using this method to get His message through.

A wag once said that it was a miracle in Balaam's day when an ass spoke, and it's a miracle in our day when one keeps quiet! That's probably true.

And Balaam said unto the ass, Because thou hast mocked me: I would there were a sword in mine hand, for now would I kill thee.

And the ass said unto Balaam, Am not I thine ass, upon which thou hast ridden ever since I was thine unto this day? was I ever wont to do so unto thee? And he said, Nay.

Then the LORD opened the eyes of Balaam, and he saw the angel of the LORD standing in the way, and his sword drawn in his hand: and he bowed down his head, and fell flat on his face [Num. 22:29–31].

The angel warned Balaam again that he was to speak only the word which the Lord would tell him. So Balaam went on to his meeting with the king, Balak.

And the angel of the LORD said unto him, Wherefore hast thou smitten thine ass these three times? behold, I went out to withstand thee, because thy way is perverse before me:

And the ass saw me, and turned from me these three times: unless she had turned from me, surely now also I had slain thee, and saved her alive.

And Balaam said unto the angel of the LORD, I have sinned; for I knew not that thou stoodest in the way against me: now therefore, if it displease thee, I will get me back again.

And the angel of the LORD said unto Balaam, Go with the men: but only the word that I shall speak unto thee, that thou shalt speak. So Balaam went with the princes of Balak [Num. 22:32–35].

This is what Scripture calls the *way* of Balaam. Speaking of false prophets, Peter wrote, "Which have forsaken the right way, and are gone astray, following the way of Balaam the son of Bosor, who loved the wages of unrighteousness; But was rebuked for his iniquity: the dumb ass speaking with man's voice forbad the madness of the prophet" (2 Pet. 2:15–16). The *way* of Balaam was covetousness.

Unfortunately, this is the way that a great many Christians and Christian organizations are measured today—by the dollar sign. May God keep you and me from the sin of covetousness!

Now notice the scene here. Balaam goes on his way and arrives at the location where Israel is encamped.

And when Balak heard that Balaam was come, he went out to meet him unto a city of Moab, which is in the border of Arnon, which is in the utmost coast.

And Balak said unto Balaam, Did I not earnestly send unto thee to call thee?

wherefore camest thou not unto me? am I not able indeed to promote thee to honour?

And Balaam said unto Balak, Lo, I am come unto thee: have I now any power at all to say any thing? the word that God putteth in my mouth, that shall I speak.

And Balaam went with Balak, and they came unto Kirjath-huzoth.

And Balak offered oxen and sheep, and sent to Balaam, and to the princes that were with him.

And it came to pass on the morrow, that Balak took Balaam, and brought him up into the high places of Baal, that thence he might see the utmost part of the people [Num. 22:36–41].

Balak, the king of Moab, takes him to the top of a mountain where he can see the camp of Israel below.

CHAPTER 23

THEME: The error of Balaam

Here we see "the error of Balaam"—ignorance of God's righteousness. This is an impressive scene. Balaam has now come to Balak, the king of Moab. Balak takes Balaam to the top of a mountain so that he can see the camp of Israel below. The fact of the matter is that Balak is not satisfied with any of the prophecies of Balaam; so he will take him to four different mountains on four different sides of the camp.

THE FIRST PROPHECY

Balak took Balaam up into the high places of Baal. There they offered burnt offerings, and there the Lord put a word into Balaam's mouth.

And he took up his parable, and said, Balak the king of Moab hath brought me from Aram, out of the mountains of the east, saying, Come, curse me Jacob, and come, defy Israel.

How shall I curse, whom God hath not cursed? or how shall I defy, whom the LORD hath not defied?

For from the top of the rocks I see him, and from the hills I behold him: lo, the people shall dwell alone, and shall not be reckoned among the nations.

Who can count the dust of Jacob, and the number of the fourth part of Israel? Let me die the death of the righteous, and let my last end be like his!

And Balak said unto Balaam, What hast thou done unto me? I took thee to curse mine enemies, and, behold, thou hast blessed them altogether.

And he answered and said, Must I not take heed to speak that which the LORD hath put in my mouth? [Num. 23:7–12].

Here is the first of the remarkable prophecies concerning the people of Israel. This wasn't at all what Balak wanted him to say. He wasn't satisfied with this prophecy; so he took Balaam over to another mountain to give him another look at the children of Israel as they were camped in the valley.

THE SECOND PROPHECY

Balak took Balaam to the top of Pisgah and there they offered burnt offerings. They could see Israel down in the camp, and again the Lord met Balaam and put a word in his mouth.

And he took up his parable, and said, Rise up, Balak, and hear; hearken unto me, thou son of Zippor:

God is not a man, that he should lie; neither the son of man, that he should repent: hath he said, and shall he not do it? or hath he spoken, and shall he not make it good?

Behold, I have received commandment to bless: and he hath blessed; and I cannot reverse it.

He hath not beheld iniquity in Jacob, neither hath he seen perverseness in Israel: the LORD his God is with him, and the shout of a king is among them.

God brought them out of Egypt; he hath as it were the strength of an unicorn.

Surely there is no enchantment against Jacob, neither is there any divination against Israel: according to this time it shall be said of Jacob and of Israel, What hath God wrought!

Behold, the people shall rise up as a great lion, and lift up himself as a young lion: he shall not lie down until he eat of the prey, and drink the blood of the slain [Num. 23:18–24].

Instead of cursing Israel, he actually blesses them again. God makes it very clear that he is not to curse Israel.

THE ERROR OF BALAAM

Now we see what Balaam is doing. He uses his own reasoning and rationalizing, and concludes that God must condemn Israel. There was evil in the camp. Sin was in evidence. They failed miserably. We have just seen the incident of the brazen serpent, and the people there confessed that they had sinned. So Balaam came to this natural conclusion: God must judge Israel because of their sins.

The natural man always concludes that God must judge Israel because of their sin, and that God must judge the individual sinner. So many times I hear a question like this: "How could God call David a man after His own heart?" Well, there is a higher righteousness than human righteousness, and that is the righteousness of Christ. "What shall we then say to these things? If God be for us, who can be against us? He that spared not his own Son, but delivered him up for us all, how shall he not with him also freely give us all things? Who shall lay any thing to the charge of God's elect? It is God that justifieth. Who is he that condemneth? It is Christ that died, yea rather, that is risen again, who is even at the right hand of God, who also maketh intercession for us" (Rom. 8:31–34).

God does not judge the sinner because He has already judged him in Christ Jesus—when he came to God by faith in Christ. The world does not understand that. Old Balaam didn't understand that. He thought that God must condemn Israel. He figured that if God was going to judge Israel, he might as well get the benefit of the rewards from King Balak. He thought that God would condemn Israel and that he would be permitted to get a handsome reward as a result of it.

Balaam did not understand the righteousness of God. He did not understand that the believing sinner, just like the people of Israel, could not come under the judgment and condemnation of God. When the believer sins, he comes under the disciplining hand of God, not under the condemnation of God.

Again Balak is not satisfied. He takes Balaam to the top of Peor for another view of Israel.

CHAPTER 24

THEME: Balaam's third and fourth prophecies

The story of Balaam continues uninterruptedly from the previous chapter.

THE THIRD PROPHECY

And when Balaam saw that it pleased the LORD to bless Israel, he went not, as at other times, to seek for enchantments, but he set his face toward the wilderness.

And Balaam lifted up his eyes, and he saw Israel abiding in his tents according to their tribes; and the spirit of God came upon him [Num. 24:1–2].

Here is something which leaves us in amazement. The Spirit of God came upon this man. Listen to his prophecy.

And he took up his parable, and said, Balaam the son of Beor hath said, and the man whose eyes are open hath said:

He hath said, which heard the words of God, which saw the vision of the Almighty, falling into a trance, but having his eyes open:

How goodly are thy tents, O Jacob, and thy tabernacles, O Israel!

As the valleys are they spread forth, as gardens by the river's side, as the trees of lign aloes which the LORD hath planted, and as cedar trees beside the waters.

He shall pour the water out of his buckets, and his seed shall be in many waters, and his king shall be higher than Agag, and his kingdom shall be exalted.

God brought him forth out of Egypt; he hath as it were the strength of an unicorn: he shall eat up the nations his enemies, and shall break their bones, and pierce them through with his arrows.

He couched, he lay down as a lion, and as a great lion: who shall stir him up? Blessed is he that blesseth thee, and cursed is he that curseth thee [Num. 24:3–9].

There was sin in the camp of Israel, but God had dealt with that. He had set up the brazen serpent. The sins had been forgiven. God is not going to permit anyone on the outside to bring a charge against them. All that Balaam can do is to bless them and to praise them.

Just so, Satan cannot bring a charge against God's elect. "Who shall lay any thing to the charge of God's elect? It is God that justifieth. Who is he that condemneth? It is Christ that died, yea rather, that is risen again, who is even at the right hand of God, who also maketh intercession for us" (Rom. 8:33–34). "What shall we then say to these things? If God be for us, who can be against us?" (Rom. 8:31). I haven't anything to say but hallelujah! Who can make a charge against God's elect? No one. God has already declared them righteous.

And Balak's anger was kindled against Balaam, and he smote his hands together: and Balak said unto Balaam, I called thee to curse mine enemies, and, behold, thou hast altogether blessed them these three times.

Therefore now flee thou to thy place: I thought to promote thee unto great honour: but, lo, the LORD hath kept thee back from honour.

And Balaam said unto Balak, Spake I not also to thy messengers which thou sentest unto me, saying,

If Balak would give me his house full of silver and gold, I cannot go beyond the commandment of the LORD, to do either good or bad of mine own mind; but what the LORD saith, that will I speak?

And now, behold, I go unto my people: come therefore, and I will advertise thee what this people shall do to thy people in the latter days [Num. 24:10–14].

Of course Balak is angry, but Balaam reminds him that he cannot prophesy anything beyond the commandment of the Lord.

THE FOURTH PROPHECY

And he took up his parable, and said, Balaam the son of Beor hath said, and the man whose eyes are open hath said:

He hath said, which heard the words of God, and knew the knowledge of the most High, which saw the vision of the Almighty, falling into a trance, but having his eyes open [Num. 24:15–16].

Notice this carefully. It is a most remarkable prophecy, and this is the one we hear at Christmas time.

I shall see him, but not now: I shall behold him, but not nigh: there shall come a Star out of Jacob, and a Sceptre shall rise out of Israel, and shall smite the corners of Moab, and destroy all the children of Sheth.

And Edom shall be a possession, Seir also shall be a possession for his enemies; and Israel shall do valiantly.

Out of Jacob shall come he that shall have dominion, and shall destroy him that remaineth of the city [Num. 24:17–19].

Have you ever stopped to wonder where the wise men learned to look for a star? How did they associate a star with a king born over in Israel? Why would they make such a long trek?

About 1500 years after this prophecy was given, we find coming out of the east, the land of Balaam, a whole company of wise men. Apparently this prophecy of Balaam was retained, since Balaam was considered an outstanding prophet in the east, and the wise men knew his prophecy. When they saw the remarkable star, they remembered that Balaam had said, ". . . There shall come a Star out of Jacob, and a Sceptre shall rise out of Israel . . ." (Num. 25:17). When the wise men came to Jerusalem, their question was, "Where is he that is born King of the Jews? for we have seen his star in the east, and are come to worship him" (Matt. 2:2). When we add to these Scriptures the prophecy of Daniel (and Daniel likewise had prophesied in the east) which gives the approximate time that the Messiah would come, we see that the coming of the wise men to Jerusalem is very understandable.

The thing that makes it very remarkable is that Israel, the people who had the Old Testament with all the prophecies of Christ's coming, was not looking for Him—with the exception of a very small minority, such as Anna and Simeon. When this company of wise men (there were probably nearer three hundred than three!) converged on Jerusalem, the entire city, including Herod the king, was stirred. Their coming adds a thrilling dimension to the Christmas story. And it is quite interesting to trace it to this old rascal, Balaam.

Now Balaam prophesied concerning the nations around Israel.

And when he looked on Amalek, he took up his parable, and said, Amalek was the first of the nations; but this latter end shall be that he perish for ever.

And he looked on the Kenites, and took up his parable, and said, Strong is thy dwelling place, and thou puttest thy nest in a rock.

Nevertheless the Kenite shall be wasted, until Asshur shall carry thee away captive.

And he took up his parable, and said, Alas, who shall live when God doeth this!

And ships shall come from the coast of Chittim, and shall afflict Asshur, and shall afflict Eber, and he also shall perish for ever [Num. 24:20–24].

He certainly didn't satisfy king Balak with his prophecies.

And Balaam rose up, and went and returned to his place: and Balak also went his way [Num. 24:25].

That is a very strange statement concerning Balaam. He rose up and went and returned to his place. There is only one other man in Scripture who is said to have gone to his place and that man is Judas (Acts 1:25). The Scriptures are pretty silent about that.

We learn in Numbers 31:8 that Balaam was killed in battle along with the kings of Midian. ". . . Balaam also the son of Beor they slew with the sword." Balaam was slain and, like Judas, he went to his place.

CHAPTER 25

THEME: *The doctrine of Balaam—fornication with the Moabites and embracing their idolatry*

In this chapter we shall see the most subtle and satanic thing which this man Balaam really did. We have discovered the *way* of Balaam (2 Pet. 2:15) which is the way of covetousness. He was after the almighty dollar, and he was willing to sacrifice his principles for that. Then, in Jude 11, we read of the *error* of Balaam. His error was that he was not aware of the fact that God could declare righteous those sinners who trust in Him. Now we see in Revelation the doctrine of Balaam, the damnable thing which this man taught. "But I have a few things against thee, because thou hast there them that hold the doctrine of Balaam, who taught Balac to cast a stumbling block before the children of Israel, to eat things sacrificed unto idols, and to commit fornication" (Rev. 2:14). When Balaam saw that he could not curse Israel, he taught Balak how he might corrupt these people. We hear this same idea today. "If you can't lick 'em, join 'em." Because Balak couldn't fight these people, Balaam taught him to join them and corrupt them from within.

THE DOCTRINE OF BALAAM

And Israel abode in Shittim, and the people began to commit whoredom with the daughters of Moab.

And they called the people unto the sacrifices of their gods: and the people did eat, and bowed down to their gods.

And Israel joined himself unto Baal-peor: and the anger of the LORD was kindled against Israel [Num. 25:1–3].

Do you see what happened? Balaam couldn't curse Israel, but he could tell Balak what to do. They should infiltrate Israel, integrate with them, intermarry with them, and introduce idolatry to them to turn them away from their God.

I'm sure they told Israel not to be a bunch of squares, not to be so narrow-minded. They insisted they were broad-minded and invited Israel to come over and worship with them. But they never went to worship with the children of Israel.

It has always interested me that a liberal in the church wants me, a fundamentalist, to come over on his side and agree with him. But I have never been able to get him to come over to my side and agree with me—yet he claims to be the broad-minded fellow and I am the narrow-minded fellow. It is very interesting that the tendency of the human heart is always downward and away from God. This is the reason religious rackets prosper—radio religious rackets, church religious rackets, and educational religious rackets. Look how the people support such things. They appeal to the natural man. This is the reason some of those people think I am pretty foolish to teach the Bible. If I introduced something other than the Word of God, the program would prosper. I am very sorry to have to tell you that that is the way it is. Old Balaam knew that Balak could corrupt the people by getting a religious racket going. He could appeal to them and get the children of Israel to turn to the worship of Baal. And that is exactly what happened.

And the LORD said unto Moses, Take all the heads of the people, and hang them up before the LORD against the sun, that the fierce anger of the LORD may be turned away from Israel.

And Moses said unto the judges of Israel, Slay ye every one his men that were joined unto Baal-peor [Num. 25:4–5].

You say that is extreme surgery. It certainly is. And do you know why? Because the disease is fatal! This would turn a man away from God and send him to hell; therefore, God is performing an act of mercy to save the nation Israel.

And, behold, one of the children of Israel came and brought unto his brethren a Midianitish woman in the sight of Moses, and in the sight of all the congregation of the children of Israel, who were weeping before the door of the tabernacle of the congregation.

And when Phinehas, the son of Eleazar, the son of Aaron the priest, saw it, he rose up from among the congregation, and took a javelin in his hand;

And he went after the man of Israel into the tent, and thrust both of them through, the man of Israel, and the woman through her belly. So the

plague was stayed from the children of Israel.

And those that died in the plague were twenty and four thousand [Num. 25:6–9].

You see, this was the way that Balaam was able to curse Israel. This is the doctrine of Balaam.

Our Lord tells us in Revelation that that same doctrine gets into the church, and is in the church today. My viewpoint is that the enemy can't hurt God's people or God's work or God's church from the outside. The church has never been hurt from the outside. To the church at Pergamos our Lord said, "But I have a few things against thee, because thou hast there them that hold the doctrine of Balaam, who taught Balac to cast a stumbling block before the children of Israel, to eat things sacrificed unto idols, and to commit fornication" (Rev. 2:14). This is the doctrine of Balaam. In the history of the early church, Pergamos marked the union of the world and the church. The world came in like a flood, and the devil joined the church at Pergamos. It was not persecution from the outside, but the doctrine of Balaam on the inside that hurt the church.

This great principle is applicable in all relationships of life.

After World War II, we stationed missiles everywhere. We did everything to keep the enemy outside. What happened? We began to fall from the inside. There began a moral decay such as we had never before seen in our country. Today we find the revolutionaries are on the inside of our nation. We are being destroyed from within. Rome didn't fall from the outside. No enemy from the outside destroyed Rome, but Rome fell from within.

Have you ever noticed that the Lord Jesus was betrayed from the inside? It wasn't a Roman soldier who betrayed Him. It was one of His own apostles who betrayed Him. It was His own nation that turned Him over to Rome to be crucified. Jesus is always betrayed from the inside. That is still true today. That is the doctrine of Balaam and it is a damnable doctrine.

Now the covenant of the priesthood is given to Phinehas, the son of Eleazar, the son of Aaron the priest. And the Lord tells Moses to vex the Midianites and smite them. And that closes this chapter.

And the LORD spake unto Moses, saying,

Phinehas, the son of Eleazar, the son of Aaron the priest, hath turned my wrath away from the children of Israel, while he was zealous for my sake among them, that I consumed not the children of Israel in my jealousy.

Wherefore say, Behold, I give unto him my covenant of peace:

And he shall have it, and his seed after him, even the covenant of an everlasting priesthood; because he was zealous for his God, and made an atonement for the children of Israel.

Now the name of the Israelite that was slain, even that was slain with the Midianitish woman, was Zimri, the son of Salu, a prince of a chief house among the Simeonites.

And the name of the Midianitish woman that was slain was Cozbi, the daughter of Zur; he was head over a people, and of a chief house in Midian.

And the LORD spake unto Moses, saying,

Vex the Midianites, and smite them:

For they vex you with their wiles, wherewith they have beguiled you in the matter of Peor, and in the matter of Cozbi, the daughter of a prince of Midian, their sister, which was slain in the day of the plague for Peor's sake [Num. 25:10–18].

CHAPTER 26

THEME: Census of the new generation

This is the beginning of a new section of the Book of Numbers. The new generation is preparing to enter the land. The remainder of the Book of Numbers is occupied with this preparation.

CENSUS OF THE NEW GENERATION

When we compare the census taken the second year of their wilderness march with the census taken the fortieth year of their march, we find a considerable difference. The following chart, prepared by Keil and Delitzsch in their *Commentary on the Old Testament* shows that while there was considerable increase in some of the tribes, there was a decided decrease in others. The total decrease for Israel was 1,820.

	First Numbering	Second Numbering
Reuben	46,500	43,730
Simeon	59,300	22,200
Gad	45,650	40,500
Judah	74,600	76,500
Issachar	54,400	64,300
Zebulon	57,400	60,500
Ephraim	40,500	32,500
Manasseh	32,200	52,700
Benjamin	35,400	45,600
Dan	62,700	64,400
Asher	41,500	53,400
Naphtali	53,400	45,400
Total	603,550	601,730

For example, the tribe of Reuben became smaller by 2,770 persons.

These are the families of the Reubenites: and they that were numbered of them were forty and three thousand and seven hundred and thirty [Num. 26:7].

If you turn back to the census in the first chapter, you will find, "Those that were numbered of them, even of the tribe of Reuben, were forty and six thousand and five hundred" (Num. 1:21). That was forty years earlier when they started out in the wilderness.

In contrast to Reuben, the tribe of Dan showed a marked increase.

These are the sons of Dan after their families: of Shuham, the family of the Shuhamites. These are the families of Dan after their families.

All the families of the Shuhamites, according to those that were numbered of them, were threescore and four thousand and four hundred [Num. 26:42–43].

At the first census it was said of Dan, "Those that were numbered of them, even of the tribe of Dan, were threescore and two thousand and seven hundred" (Num. 1:39). In other words, Dan increased by 1,700 persons.

However, the second census revealed that Israel was smaller by 1,820 persons. The old generation died in the wilderness, just as God had told them. "Your carcases shall fall in this wilderness; and all that were numbered of you, according to your whole number, from twenty years old and upward, which have murmured against me" (Num. 14:29).

But among these there was not a man of them whom Moses and Aaron the priest numbered, when they numbered the children of Israel in the wilderness of Sinai.

For the LORD had said of them, They shall surely die in the wilderness. And there was not left a man of them, save Caleb the son of Jephunneh, and Joshua the son of Nun [Num. 26:64–65].

This is now the new generation. All the old generation, except Caleb and Joshua, have died. God did not hold those who were under twenty responsible for the failure and rebellion at Kadesh-barnea. This may give us some indication as to the age of accountability. I do not know when it is, and I do not mean to suggest that it is twenty, but I think it is older than many of us suspect.

This is a new generation with the exception of two men. We are going to get better acquainted with these two interesting men when we come to the book of Joshua.

CHAPTER 27

THEME: The women's problem; God grants their request; Moses is to prepare for death

We are in the section of the Book of Numbers which we have labeled "A New Generation." We saw last time that when the census was made, Joshua and Caleb were the only persons living who were enlisted in the census the first time. In other words, every one twenty years and over had died in that forty-year period. Those were rigorous years out on that desert, and they had perished. Now Israel is comprised of a new generation, and this new generation will have new problems.

It has always been a problem for one generation to understand another generation because each generation faces its own particular problem. It is quite interesting that someone has divided it this way. When you are young, you criticize the old generation, and when you are old, you criticize the young generation. That seems to be human nature.

As we come to this twenty-seventh chapter of the Book of Numbers we see that the new generation is presented here with a new problem. Actually, Moses didn't know what to do. He had to appeal to the Lord, because according to the laws of other nations the women just didn't count. In fact, they were treated as chattel.

THE WOMEN'S PROBLEM

Then came the daughters of Zelophehad, the son of Hepher, the son of Gilead, the son of Machir, the son of Manasseh, of the families of Manasseh the son of Joseph: and these are the names of his daughters; Mahlah, Noah, and Hoglah, and Milcah, and Tirzah [Num. 27:1].

If you have a lot of daughters in your family, friends, and you run out of names, and you don't like ordinary names, here is a list I'd like to suggest to you: Mahlah, Noah, Hoglah, Milcah, and Tirzah! I have never heard of a woman named any of these names, and I think I know why! But these were the daughters of Zelophehad.

And they stood before Moses, and before Eleazar the priest, and before the princes and all the congregation, by the door of the tabernacle of the congregation, saying,

Our father died in the wilderness, and he was not in the company of them that gathered themselves together against the LORD in the company of Korah; but died in his own sin, and had no sons.

Why should the name of our father be done away from among his family, because he hath no son? Give unto us therefore a possession among the brethren of our father.

And Moses brought their cause before the LORD [Num. 27:2–5].

You can see the problem. This man Zelophehad died in the wilderness. He had five daughters and no sons. According to the Mosaic Law, it looked as if a son were the one who inherited the property, and the women were just left out. Certainly the laws of the other nations did leave them out. They did not count at all. Now what are they to do?

These daughters of Zelophehad are very aggressive. We are hearing a great deal today about women's rights. Well, they certainly got their rights in the Bible. There are those who said years ago that the Bible was a man's book. However the more I read the Bible, the more I see that the Word of God gives women their rights. And I believe that they should have their rights, by the way.

Moses didn't really know what to do. I suppose he said to them, "Well, girls, I don't know what to say to you. I can see that you have a just cause, but according to the laws and customs of the day you certainly would not get anything." So Moses brought their case before the Lord.

GOD GRANTS THEIR REQUEST

And the LORD spake unto Moses, saying.

The daughters of Zelophehad speak right: thou shalt surely give them a possession of an inheritance among their father's brethren; and thou shalt cause the inheritance of their father to pass unto them [Num. 27:6–7].

The Lord is on the side of women's rights, you see. This is one of the most remarkable laws that is imaginable. We live in a day when a ruling such as this is commonplace. It is difficult for us to put ourselves back in that day when women were treated like chattel. Missionaries who work among the tribes on the Orinoco River were telling me recently that in Venezuela a little girl in the family is sold to a man even before she reaches the age of ten years. Girls are traded just as one would trade an animal. This custom still exists among primitive people. Every woman today ought to be thankful for the Word of God because it is the Bible that first gave women their rights. I think this is a marvelous thing. "The daughters of Zelophehad speak right: thou shalt surely give them a possession of an inheritance." Now, on the basis of that, God puts down a principle and a law for them.

And thou shalt speak unto the children of Israel, saying, If a man die, and have no son, then ye shall cause his inheritance to pass unto his daughter.

And if he have no daughter, then ye shall give his inheritance unto his brethren.

And if he have no brethren, then ye shall give his inheritance unto his father's brethren.

And if his father have no brethren, then ye shall give his inheritance unto his kinsman that is next to him of his family, and he shall possess it: and it shall be unto the children of Israel a statute of judgment, as the LORD commanded Moses [Num. 27:8–11].

This is a marvelous step forward, and it was made about 1500 years before Christ came into the world. I marvel at the aggressiveness and the forwardness of these women. I marvel at the faith of these women. "But without faith it is impossible to please him: for he that cometh to God must believe that he is, and that he is a rewarder of them that diligently seek him" (Heb. 11:6). The five girls wanted to possess their father's inheritance. It was not the custom of the day nor a written law that they could have it. Therefore, they asked by faith, and by faith God gave the inheritance to them.

There is a marvelous lesson in this for us today. We are told that we are blessed with all spiritual blessings in heavenly places in Christ (Eph. 1:3). I believe that God hears and answers us, not only in the spiritual blessings but also in the material things. I'm of the opinion that most of us are more or less paupers because we do not come to God as his children

and ask Him for things. God wants to be good to us.

In my Christian life I have always hesitated to ask God for any material thing. When I was attending seminary, I worked for a Memphis newspaper, taking in ads at night. When there was an ad to sell a car, I'd go out and look at the car. If it was a bargain, I would buy it. I would drive it a year or so, then sell it for what I had paid for it. When I graduated from seminary, I asked the Lord to give me a *good* second-hand car. Do you know what the Lord did? He gave me a new car. Now, why didn't I ask Him for a new car? Perhaps we are poor because we just don't know what to ask for.

More than this, we have possessions— wonderful spiritual possessions in Christ Jesus. He would like for us to claim these in faith. The daughters of Zelophehad came and asked for the possession that was their father's. Today we have spiritual possessions which we should ask for. Let's tell our Father that we want our inheritance and that we want these spiritual blessings. He wants to bless us! How wonderful He is!

MOSES IS TO PREPARE FOR DEATH

We come to a sad note here. We've been following Moses for a long time. Actually, because he is the writer of Genesis, we have been with him from Genesis until now. At this point he is to prepare to pass from this earthly scene.

And the LORD said unto Moses, Get thee up into this mount Abarim, and see the land which I have given unto the children of Israel.

And when thou hast seen it, thou also shalt be gathered unto thy people, as Aaron thy brother was gathered.

For ye rebelled against my commandment in the desert of Zin, in the strife of the congregation, to sanctify me at the water before their eyes: that is the water of Meribah in Kadesh in the wilderness of Zin [Num. 27:12–14].

God is referring to the time Moses smote that rock twice after God had told him to speak to it. God says here that it was rebellion against His commandment. Because Moses did this, he is only permitted to take a look into the land; he is not permitted to enter the land.

I used to ask my classes a trick question. Did Moses ever enter the Promised Land? Most of the students would say that he did not. Every now and then a sharp student would say, "Yes, he did." And, of course, he did. He was there on the Mount of Transfiguration with the Lord Jesus. That was after his death.

Here he only got a view of the Promised Land. God will not permit him to enter into the land. You see, disobedience keeps many of us from entering into our spiritual possessions. Disbelief will always lead to disobedience. That is exactly what happened to Moses.

And Moses spake unto the Lord, saying,

Let the Lord, the God of the spirits of all flesh, set a man over the congregation.

Which may go out before them, and which may go in before them, and which may lead them out, and which may bring them in; that the congregation of the Lord be not as sheep which have no shepherd.

And the Lord said unto Moses, Take thee Joshua the son of Nun, a man in whom is the spirit, and lay thine hand upon him;

And set him before Eleazar the priest, and before all the congregation; and give him a charge in their sight [Num. 27:15–19].

There is to be a successor appointed to take the place of Moses. He must be a Spirit-filled man. Now I want to make it clear that the laying on of hands did not make him Spirit-filled, nor did it give him any power. The only thing that can be communicated by the laying on of hands is disease germs. What this does indicate is succession or partnership in an enterprise. You will remember that the church put their hands on Paul and Barnabas and sent them out from Antioch. Did that give them power? Not at all. The power came through the Holy Spirit of God. It was to show that the church was acknowledging their association with these two men in the missionary enterprise. That is the meaning of the laying on of hands.

Joshua is to be the successor of Moses. After Moses lays down the work, Joshua will pick it up. We will learn a great deal about this man when we get to the Book of Joshua. I want to say here that I think Joshua was the most surprised man in the camp when he was chosen to succeed Moses. In one sense he was the most unlikely one to succeed Moses. Do you know why? He was an average man. No one went around saying that Joshua had great potential, great leadership ability, and all that sort of thing you hear today. Apparently Joshua didn't have that. He was an ordinary individual. Joshua reveals what God can do with an ordinary man.

I must tell you that the Books of Joshua and Judges have always been a great encouragement to me. I love those two books because they reveal what God can do with ordinary men. If a person will be yielded to Him, God can take him and use him. That means He can use me, because He can use the ordinary. It means He can use you.

So Joshua is the chosen one. He is appointed to take the place of Moses. We will see that in due time, after the death of Moses at the end of the book of Deuteronomy, Joshua takes over.

And Moses did as the Lord commanded him: and he took Joshua, and set him before Eleazar the priest, and before all the congregation:

And he laid his hands upon him, and gave him a charge, as the Lord commanded by the hand of Moses [Num. 27:22–23].

CHAPTERS 28 AND 29

THEME: *Law of the offerings*

Now that Israel is prepared to enter the Promised Land by a new census which mustered the able-bodied men for warfare, and by the appointment of Joshua as commander, its spiritual life is dealt with. The offerings have already been instituted, but here, for the sake of completeness, all the national sacrifices which were to be offered during the whole year are reviewed.

Because in Leviticus we looked at these offerings in detail, we will only touch on certain points here that are particularly interesting and meaningful.

Why did God spend so much time with the details of these offerings? Very candidly, it is rather tedious. This is especially true in our day when we do not offer bloody sacrifices. And it must have been tedious for them also. I marvel at how meticulous things had to be for the offering unto God. Why is there such detail? The reason is so wonderful that I wouldn't want you to miss it for anything in the world. It is actually the preciousness of Christ that is brought to our attention here—in fact, the abiding preciousness of Christ.

LAW OF THE OFFERINGS

And the Lord spake unto Moses, saying,

Command the children of Israel, and say unto them, My offering, and my bread for my sacrifices made by fire, for a sweet savour unto me, shall ye observe to offer unto me in their due season [Num. 28:1–2].

Notice the emphasis—"*My* offering . . . *my* bread . . . *my* sacrifice . . . unto *me.*" You recall from the Book of Leviticus that there were two kinds of offerings. Of the five offerings, three of them were sweet savor offerings; two of them were non-sweet savor offerings. The sweet savor offerings represent the *person* of Christ; the non-sweet offerings speak of the *work* of Christ in redemption for you and me. Now here God is talking about sweet savor offerings, and He calls them *My* offerings. These offerings represent not what Christ has done for us, or our thoughts of Him, but they speak of what *God* thinks of Him.

Now what does this mean to you and me? We hear a lot today about worship and worship services. But how much is true worship in our services? How much is just aimless activity? Real worship is when we think God's thoughts after Him. This sweet savor offering which God speaks of as *My* offering, *My* bread, *My* sacrifice, represents what God thinks of Christ. God is satisfied with what Christ did for you and me on the cross. What about you? Are you satisfied with what Christ did for you on the cross? Are you resting in that today? His invitation is "Come unto me, all ye that labour and are heavy laden, and I will give you rest" (Matt. 11:28). Have you brought your burden of sin to Him and received Him as your Savior? Are you satisfied with whom He is? If He is not the Son of God, then what He did is absolutely meaningless. True worship is a recognition of who He is and an adoration of His Person. In other words, it is thinking God's thoughts after Him.

And thou shalt say unto them, This is the offering made by fire which ye shall offer unto the Lord: two lambs of the first year without spot day by day, for a continual burnt offering [Num. 28:3].

That burnt offering, speaking of the Person of Christ, all went up in smoke; it all ascended to God. And this is the aspect of this sacrifice that is all important.

When we come to chapter 29, we find it is a continuation of the laws of the offerings.

God wanted His people to come to Him with joy on these wonderful, high, holy days, the feast days. The exception was the Day of Atonement.

And ye shall have on the tenth day of this seventh month an holy convocation; and ye shall afflict your souls: ye shall not do any work therein [Num. 29:7].

This was a repetition of the law as given in Leviticus. "Also on the tenth day of this seventh month there shall be a day of atonement: it shall be an holy convocation unto you; and ye shall afflict your souls, and offer an offering made by fire unto the Lord" (Lev. 23:27).

The chapter concludes with the law of offerings for the Feast of Tabernacles. Offerings for their sins and trespasses are mentioned, but always this is given in addition to the burnt offerings.

There are marvelous lessons for us in these two chapters. Friend, you and I are sinners. Even if you didn't know it, you are a sinner. If you and I pay close attention to the Word of God, we will find that we are sinners and need a Savior. We need Christ! We need a Savior who died for us and paid the penalty for our sins.

Sin is what has brought sorrow into this world. Sin has brought the tears and the broken heart. God hates sin. I'm glad He hates sin. God is moving forward today—undeviatingly, unhesitatingly, uncompromisingly—against sin. He intends to drive it out of His universe. God will not compromise with it at all. He will not accept the white flag of truce. He intends to eliminate it, and I'm thankful for that.

Because it is sin that has robbed you and me of our fellowship with Him, sin is an occasion for mourning. When was the last time you wept over your sins? Have you been before God, my friend, and wept over your sin, over the failure of your life, over your coldness and indifference? My, how we need to confess that to Him today. It is not because God is high and we are low, or because He is great and we are small, nor because He is infinite and we are finite that we are separated from Him. He says it is our sins that have separated us from Him. That is the occasion for weeping.

Let me be very frank with you. I was ordained into the ministry in 1933, and was an active pastor for thirty-seven years. I have had successful pastorates, as man judges those things. There has always been an increase in attendance, and a new interest in Bible study, thriving and growing young people's work, and people being saved. You may ask, "Isn't that a cause for rejoicing?" I confess to you that I don't rejoice. I look back and I see my failure, and I see it in a very glaring way. Don't misunderstand—I'm not guilty of shooting anybody or of committing adultery, but I failed my Savior in so many ways, so many times, and I confess that to Him. I let things come in to separate me in times when I needed His fellowship and wanted His fellowship. But I'd let these things come in the way. That is occasion for mourning, even for weeping to this day.

But God did not want His people to spend a life of mourning. There was only one day of mourning. All the others were feasts of joy. There were the sin offerings and the trespass offerings. Christ has atoned for our sins on the cross. How we needed that! But the emphasis is on the burnt offerings, the burnt offering continually every day and the burnt offerings of the feast days. God is delighted in His Son.

All of the details speak of our Savior and how wonderful He is. He is a sweet savor offering; that is who He is. He is the non-sweet savor offering; that is what He did. He was made sin for us, He who knew no sin. I am the sinner, but He died in my stead so that I might be made the righteousness of God in Him. He took my place down here and He has given me His place up there. If you are saved today, you have as much right in heaven as Christ has. Did you know that? You have *His* right to be there, and if you don't have His right, then you have no business there—in fact, you *won't* be there. We are accepted in the Beloved. That is the basis on which God receives us. If you are in Him, you just can't improve on that at all. How wonderful this is.

CHAPTER 30

THEME: A vow is inviolate; a woman's vow depends upon her father or husband; the vow of a widow or divorced woman must stand

After the law of the offerings, we have the law of the vows. The law of the vows in this chapter has special reference to women. We have seen that women have been given the right to claim their inheritance. Now we learn that women also have responsibility.

A VOW IS INVIOLATE

We had a whole chapter on vows in Leviticus and there we called attention to the importance which God attaches to vows. He warns His children that they should be careful if they are making a vow to God. God will hold a person to his vow; so the warning is not to make a vow foolishly.

I think there is a grave danger today for people to promise the Lord too much. As I neared the end of my ministry, I became very reluctant to ask people to take any kind of a vow before God, except to accept Christ Jesus as Savior. Why? Because I've seen multitudes come to an altar to dedicate their lives and then I've seen those people break their vows. God doesn't ask us to make vows—they are voluntary—but if we make a vow, God means business with us, and He will hold us to our vow.

And Moses spake unto the heads of the tribes concerning the children of Israel, saying, This is the thing which the LORD hath commanded.

If a man vow a vow unto the LORD, or swear an oath to bind his soul with a bond; he shall not break his word, he shall do according to all that proceedeth out of his mouth [Num. 30:1–2].

This is very important for Christians today. Paul has this in mind when he says, ". . . if thou shalt confess with thy mouth the Lord Jesus, and shalt believe in thine heart that God hath raised him from the dead, thou shalt be saved. For with the heart man believeth unto righteousness; and with the mouth confession is made unto salvation" (Rom. 10:9–10). How do you believe on the Lord Jesus Christ? With your heart. And then what happens? Confession is made by your mouth. Confessing with your mouth is your vow, that is your statement of faith. The point of it is not just what the mouth says, but that the heart must believe what the mouth is saying. These

two must be in agreement. "For with the heart man believeth unto righteousness." You don't believe with your mouth; you *say* it with the mouth. "And with the mouth confession is made unto salvation." The heart and the mouth must be singing the same tune, in a duet together. That is exactly what is meant in this matter of vows.

A WOMAN'S VOW DEPENDS UPON HER FATHER OR HUSBAND

If a woman also vow a vow unto the LORD, and bind herself by a bond, being in her father's house in her youth;

And her father hear her vow, and her bond wherewith she hath bound her soul, and her father shall hold his peace at her: then all her vows shall stand, and every bond wherewith she hath bound her soul shall stand [Num. 30:3–4].

In other words, if a woman makes a vow while she is still single and in her father's home, the father can be held responsible for her. If the father keeps quiet when he hears her make the vow, then that vow which she made will stand. However, if the father speaks up and says, "Wait just a minute. She has bought this dress, and I don't intend to pay for it," then he is protected in the matter. That vow is not binding.

But if her father disallow her in the day that he heareth; not any of her vows, or of her bonds wherewith she hath bound her soul, shall stand: and the LORD shall forgive her, because her father disallowed her [Num. 30:5].

Now what happens if the woman is married?

And if she had at all an husband, when she vowed, or uttered aught out of her lips, wherewith she bound her soul;

And her husband heard it, and held his peace at her in the day that he heard it: then her vows shall stand, and her bonds wherewith she bound her soul shall stand.

But if her husband disallowed her on the day that he heard it; then he shall make her vow which she vowed, and

that which she uttered with her lips, wherewith she bound her soul, of none effect: and the LORD shall forgive her [Num. 30:6–8].

If the married woman goes out and makes expensive purchases and obligates herself, the husband can say that he disallows it and will not be responsible to pay for it. The vow will not stand and he is not obligated. So you see that either a father or a husband could be held responsible for the vow a woman made, unless they had disallowed it.

Sometimes we see this principle bypassed today. There are women who are gold-diggers. They marry a man for his money. One sees this at times when a younger woman marries an older man. After she has his name, she can go to court and get practically everything that he owns. I've seen that happen several times. I knew a Christian man who was lonely after the death of his wife, and who then married a younger woman who was really after the money. This man had willed his money to mission boards and Christian organizations, but the young widow was able to break the will and get the money for herself so that the Christian organizations got none of it. Also I have had men tell me about marrying women who have taken them for everything they had. Well, that's the foolishness of mankind. God says a man does not need to permit this sort of thing.

THE VOW OF A WIDOW OR DIVORCED WOMAN MUST STAND

But every vow of a widow, and of her that is divorced, wherewith they have bound their souls, shall stand against her [Num. 30:9].

A widow must stand on her own two feet. The vow that she makes stands. You notice how important these details are to God. He wants His people always to be as good as their word.

God keeps His vows, and He expects His children to keep theirs. He made a vow to Abraham. He made a promise to David. God will stand behind His vows. He has kept His promises in the past and will keep His promises in the future. "For God so loved the world, that he gave his only begotten Son, that whosoever believeth in him should not perish, but have everlasting life" (John 3:16). That is the Word of God, God's promise to you and me. And the Word of God stands. He has vowed that He will save you if you trust in Christ, and that vow stands. A dear, little Scottish woman had an unbelieving son, who returned home from college with some new ideas and told her, "Your soul doesn't amount to anything in this vast universe." She thought it over and replied, "I agree my soul isn't worth very much, but if my soul is lost, God would lose more than I would lose. God would lose His reputation because He said that He would save me if I trusted Him." Friends, God will stand by His Word. He doesn't have to take an oath; all He needs to do is to say it, and it is truth. He wants those who represent Him down here to be that kind of a people. If they make a vow, they should stand by that vow. This kind of responsibility should be representative of the Christians in this world today.

CHAPTER 31

THEME: *Judgment of Midian*

Remember that we are dealing with things that pertain to the new generation which has come through the wilderness. Many of them were just little fellows when they started out. Some were grade schoolers, some were high schoolers and some had not even been born when they started the wilderness march. God is preparing this new generation for their entrance into the Promised Land.

The Midianites, you recall, joined the Moabites in hiring Balaam to curse Israel and afterwards seduced the people to idolatry and licentiousness. The only woman named in this seduction was Cozbi, a Midianite (Num. 25:6–15). After this episode God commanded His people, "Vex the Midianites, and smite them: For they vex you with their wiles, wherewith they have beguiled you in the matter of Peor, and in the matter of Cozbi, the daughter of a prince of Midian, their sister, which was slain in the day of the plague for Peor's sake" (Num. 25:17–18).

Midian in the wilderness is a type of the world. For the child of God there is to be a spiritual separation from the world today.

JUDGMENT OF MIDIAN

We are now going into the last official acts of Moses. When we get to Deuteronomy, we will have the last private acts of Moses. One of his last official acts is this war against the Midianites.

And the LORD spake unto Moses, saying,

Avenge the children of Israel of the Midianites: afterward shalt thou be gathered unto thy people.

And Moses spake unto the people, saying, Arm some of yourselves unto the war, and let them go against the Midianites, and avenge the LORD of Midian [Num. 31:1–3].

Now God commands Moses to make war against them. He is going to avenge Israel. They are to deal very harshly with them.

And Moses sent them to the war, a thousand of every tribe, them and Phinehas the son of Eleazar the priest, to the war, with the holy instruments, and the trumpets to blow in his hand [Num. 31:6].

Moses sent out twelve thousand men to go to war—one thousand from each tribe. The holy instruments, the articles of furniture in the tabernacle, were to go along, indicating that this was a spiritual warfare.

And they warred against the Midianites, as the LORD commanded Moses; and they slew all the males.

And they slew the kings of Midian, beside the rest of them that were slain; namely, Evi, and Rekem, and Zur, and Hur, and Reba, five kings of Midian: Balaam also the son of Beor they slew with the sword [Num. 31:7–8].

The kings of Midian were slain, and we note here the death of Balaam, the prophet. God is giving them a victory over the Midianites. There is a judgment on the Gentiles here, prior to the entering into the Promised Land. This is the same thing that will consummate the age before Christ comes. For in the Millennium, Israel, which is having such great problems today, will be put in the land and they will have peace.

But now there is a problem.

And the children of Israel took all the women of Midian captives, and their little ones, and took the spoil of all their cattle, and all their flocks, and all their goods [Num. 31:9].

God gave them a tremendous victory—they did not even lose one man (v. 49).

And Moses was wroth with the officers of the host, with the captains over thousands, and captains over hundreds, which came from the battle.

And Moses said unto them, Have ye saved all the women alive?

Behold, these caused the children of Israel, through the counsel of Balaam, to commit trespass against the LORD in the matter of Peor, and there was a plague among the congregation of the LORD [Num. 31:14–16].

There was a great problem with the children of Israel. God had taken them out of Egypt in one night. But it took God forty years to get Egypt out of them. And even now, after they had been tricked into idolatry through the advice of Balaam to the Midianites, they still bring the Midianite women into their camp. That is the problem with worldliness. It is not wrong for us to be in the world—that is where God has placed us—the great issue is whether the world is in us, in our hearts and lives.

The important lesson of this chapter is that it calls for spiritual separation from the world. Where are you walking? Do you walk in the light? Are you in the Word of God? Are you in fellowship with Christ? That is the important thing for the child of God.

CHAPTER 32

THEME: Reuben and Gad ask for land on the wrong side of Jordan

This chapter tells us about the half-hearted tribes. Reuben, Gad, and the half tribe of Manasseh ask for land on the wrong side of the Jordan River.

This incident has a tremendous spiritual application for us, as we consider the Jordan River as a type of the death and resurrection of Christ.

REUBEN AND GAD ASK FOR LAND ON THE WRONG SIDE OF JORDAN

Now the children of Reuben and the children of Gad had a very great multitude of cattle: and when they saw the land of Jazer, and the land of Gilead, that, behold, the place was a place for cattle;

The children of Gad and the children of Reuben came and spake unto Moses, and to Eleazar the priest, and unto the princes of the congregation, saying,

Ataroth, and Dibon, and Jazer, and Nimrah, and Heshbon, and Elealeh, and Shebam, and Nebo, and Beon,

Even the country which the LORD smote before the congregation of Israel, is a land for cattle, and thy servants have cattle:

Wherefore, said they, if we have found grace in thy sight, let this land be given unto thy servants for a possession, and bring us not over Jordan [Num. 32:1–5].

Moses is very disturbed at their request.

And Moses said unto the children of Gad and to the children of Reuben, Shall your brethren go to war, and shall ye sit here?

And wherefore discourage ye the heart of the children of Israel from going over into the land which the LORD hath given them? [Num. 32:6–7].

He remembers all too vividly the utter discouragement of the people when they heard the report of the men who had spied out the land almost forty years earlier.

Thus did your fathers, when I sent them from Kadesh-barnea to see the land.

For when they went up unto the valley of Eshcol, and saw the land, they discouraged the heart of the children of Israel, that they should not go into the land which the LORD had given them [Num. 32:8–9].

Remember this is a new generation that Moses is talking to. They were too young to remember that tragic experience, and Moses is reviewing it for them.

And the LORD's anger was kindled the same time, and he sware, saying,

Surely none of the men that came up out of Egypt, from twenty years old and upward, shall see the land which I sware unto Abraham, unto Isaac, and unto Jacob; because they have not wholly followed me:

Save Caleb the son of Jephunneh the Kenezite, and Joshua the son of Nun: for they have wholly followed the LORD.

And the LORD's anger was kindled against Israel, and he made them wander in the wilderness forty years, until all the generation, that had done evil in the sight of the LORD, was consumed [Num. 32:10–13].

Moses fears this young generation will repeat the failure of their fathers.

And, behold, ye are risen up in your fathers' stead, an increase of sinful men, to augment yet the fierce anger of the LORD toward Israel.

For if ye turn away from after him, he will yet again leave them in the wilderness; and ye shall destroy all this people [Num. 32:14–15].

You can well understand Moses' fears here. After enduring the hardships and discouragements of forty years in that terrible wilderness, the thought of again failing to enter the Promised Land seemed too much to risk.

And they came near unto him, and said,

We will build sheepfolds here for our cattle, and cities for our little ones:

But we ourselves will go ready armed before the children of Israel, until we have brought them unto their place: and our little ones shall dwell in the fenced cities because of the inhabitants of the land.

We will not return unto our houses, until the children of Israel have inherited every man his inheritance.

For we will not inherit with them on yonder side Jordan, or forward; because our inheritance is fallen to us on this side Jordan eastward [Num. 32:16–19].

They offered to send their men of war to help the other nine and one half tribes to take the Promised Land. On this basis, Moses agreed to let them settle on the east side of Jordan. They not only agreed to do it, but we find in Joshua 12–16 that they made good their promise.

Moses warned them:

But if ye will not do so, behold, ye have sinned against the LORD: and be sure your sin will find you out [Num. 32:23].

The way this is usually interpreted is, "Your sin will be found out." In other words, if you sin, you won't get by with it. You will be found out. That is not what it says at all. There are a great many sinners who get by with their sins and are never found out by anyone else.

This verse says that your sin will find *you* out. There will come that time when the chickens come home to roost. "Be not deceived; God is not mocked: for whatsoever a man soweth, that shall he also reap" (Gal. 6:7). I don't care who you are, or where you are, how you are, or when you are, your sins will find *you* out. In the way that you sin, that is the way it is going to come home to you sometime. That is the meaning of this statement, "Be sure your sin will find you out."

And Moses gave unto them, even to the children of Gad, and to the children of Reuben, and unto half the tribe of Ma-

nasseh the son of Joseph, the kingdom of Sihon king of the Amorites, and the kingdom of Og king of Bashan, the land, with the cities thereof in the coasts, even the cities of the country round about [Num. 32:33].

These tribes that chose the wrong side of Jordan did not have the opportunity of crossing over the river Jordan.

We need to realize, friends, that the river Jordan does not symbolize our death. When we get to the Book of Joshua, we'll see that it teaches how we pass over into Canaan. In other words, there are two places for the child of God to live today. You can live in the wilderness of this world and be a spiritual pauper, or you can enter into the place of spiritual blessings, represented by Canaan. Now how can we pass over the Jordan into the place of spiritual blessing? When we see the children of Israel crossing over Jordan, we find two great lessons there. The stones that were put in Jordan speak of the death of Christ. The stones that were taken out of Jordan speak of the resurrection of Christ. You and I get our spiritual blessings by the death and resurrection of Christ. We today are to know that we've been buried with Him and raised with Him. We are to reckon on the fact that we are joined to Him. We are to yield to Him on that kind of basis so that you and I can appropriate the spiritual blessings that are ours.

The two and one half tribes did not cross the Jordan. Did this work out to their disadvantage? Yes. Our Lord said that by their fruits ye shall know them. When He was here on earth, one time He was trying to get away from the crowd, "And they came over unto the other side of the sea, into the country of the Gadarenes" (Mark 5:1). Now who are the Gadarenes? They are the tribe of Gad, living on the wrong side of the Jordan River. And when Jesus came to them, He found them in the pig business, you remember. And when He healed the demon-possessed man, the Gadarenes asked the Lord Jesus to leave their country! They had gotten into a sad condition. This always happens to the child of God who fails to cross Jordan and get into the Land of Promise.

CHAPTER 33

THEME: *The log of the journeys; the law of the possession of the land*

Here we have a log of their journeys. We said before that we do not have a record of the happenings during their forty years of wandering, only a few isolated incidents, but here is the log of the journey, a record of the places they camped.

THE LOG OF THE JOURNEYS

These are the journeys of the children of Israel, which went forth out of the land of Egypt with their armies under the hand of Moses and Aaron [Num. 33:1].

Here are a couple of verses to show you that this is not very exciting reading.

And they removed from Haradah, and pitched in Makheloth.

And they removed from Makheloth, and encamped at Tahath.

And they departed from Tahath, and pitched at Tarah.

And they removed from Tarah, and pitched in Mithcah [Num. 33:25–28].

I'd call it pretty monotonous. We would like to know what happened there, but nothing is said about what took place.

If you went to visit a friend who had just returned from Europe, you would ask him to tell you about his trip. Suppose he said that they went to Rome, then they went to Milan, then they went to Florence, then they went into Switzerland to Lucerne, then to Zurich and to Geneva, and then into Germany into Frankfurt, and so on and on. You would want to ask him what they saw and what they did. You'd find a recital of all the places they had been a pretty boring account of their trip. That is my opinion of this chapter; it's not very interesting reading.

And yet, just as each portion of Scripture has a great spiritual lesson, so this chapter has a great spiritual lesson for us. Although this chapter is like a road map, and not interesting to read, it reveals that God noted and recorded every step that these people took. In fact, He was with them every step of the way through the wilderness march.

We sing a song today which is entitled "I'll go with Him all the way." Very candidly, I don't like it, and I think it expresses exactly the opposite viewpoint from what it should say. When I was a pastor, I used to look out on the congregation singing, "I'll go with Him all the way," and then I wouldn't see many of those people on Sunday night, or at any Bible study, or when there was any work to be done for God. I wonder how far would they really be willing to go with Him? I must confess that I have failed Him. I can't promise that I will go with Him all the way. I think we should turn that song around. *He* will go with *me* all the way, for He has said, ". . . I will never leave thee, nor forsake thee" (Heb. 13:5).

So here we have the log of their journey. Everywhere they went, every time they camped, He was with them. Frankly, they weren't going with Him. That is, their hearts were in rebellion against Him a great deal of the time. But He never left them. He never did forsake them.

This is one of the great truths of the Word of God. "I will never leave thee, nor forsake thee." Jesus said the same thing in His upper room discourse, "I will not leave you comfortless" (which is, literally, I will not leave you orphans): "I will come to you" (John 14:18). How? By sending the Holy Spirit. The Holy Spirit indwells every believer. If you are a child of God, you couldn't possibly get away from Him. He wouldn't let you go. He will go with you all the way. We may stumble, falter, and fail. We don't follow Him as we ought. But, thank God, He goes with us all the way!

THE LAW
OF THE POSSESSION OF THE LAND

The chapter closes with an order the Lord gives to Moses as Israel is preparing to enter the land.

Speak unto the children of Israel, and say unto them, When ye are passed over Jordan into the land of Canaan;

Then ye shall drive out all the inhabitants of the land from before you, and destroy all their pictures, and destroy all their molten images, and quite pluck down all their high places:

And ye shall dispossess the inhabitants of the land, and dwell therein: for I have given you the land to possess it.

And ye shall divide the land by lot for an inheritance among your families:

and to the more ye shall give the more inheritance, and to the fewer ye shall give the less inheritance: every man's inheritance shall be in the place where his lot falleth; according to the tribes of your fathers ye shall inherit.

But if ye will not drive out the inhabitants of the land from before you; then it shall come to pass, that those which ye let remain of them shall be pricks in your eyes, and thorns in your sides, and shall vex you in the land wherein ye dwell.

Moreover it shall come to pass, that I shall do unto you, as I thought to do unto them [Num. 33:51–56].

Here is something many folks, especially the skeptics, raise questions about. People say they think it is very cruel and unfair for the Lord to tell Israel to wipe out the inhabitants of the land, when Israel also had been disobedient. They contend that because the people in the land were such lovely folk that the Lord's wanting to put them out is indefensible. That is the way the liberal and the skeptic have been talking for years. The chances are that every liberal today is living on a piece of ground that once belonged to the Indians, and I don't see them giving back their property to the Indians!

Look at this with me for just a moment. "The earth is the LORD's, and the fulness thereof; the world, and they that dwell therein" (Ps. 24:1). This is His earth. He commands what is to be done. He told Israel to go into the land and to destroy their pictures; that is, their idols. The archaeologists are digging them up today. And they were to destroy their melted images. They were to demolish their high places. These were places of pagan and heathen worship where the vilest practices took place. The Canaanites were in a very low spiritual state. Not only were they idolators, far from the living and the true God, but promiscuity and sexual sins were a way of life and a part of their worship. As a result, the Canaanites were eaten up with venereal disease.

Our promiscuous society tries to minimize the terribleness of sexual sins. We have an epidemic of venereal disease today, a plague, and it is a grave danger. It does great injury to the human race. These disease-ridden Canaanites lived at the crossroads of the world. That land is one of the most sensitive spots that there is on earth. It is that yet today; it always has been; I think it always will be. It is a strategic land and the armies of the world have marched through that land. Trade routes of the world go through that land. The Canaanites had contact with a great number of people, and they were disseminating their loathsome diseases everywhere. So God is going to put a new tenant in the land. The Canaanites were destroying His property, and they were hurting the rest of mankind; so God is going to put them out.

Don't come to me, my friend, and say that God did not have the right to do that. It was actually an act of mercy. God destroyed the Canaanites for the sake of the oncoming generations. That is the same reason that God sent the Flood—God was preserving the future generations.

My friend, do not criticize God. Do not sit in judgment on God. We cannot realize all that is involved in any situation. One thing we do know—we will not experience peace on this earth until the rule of the Prince of Peace. Until that time, God will use nations in judgment upon other nations.

CHAPTERS 34, 35, AND 36

THEME: Borders of the Promised Land; cities given to the Levites; law regarding the inheritance of the land

BORDERS OF THE PROMISED LAND

This is an important chapter because it defines in unmistakable terms the extent of the land that God gave to Israel. Also it underscores the fact that God gave the land to Israel for an eternal possession. Regardless of who claims it today, that land belongs to Israel.

And the LORD spake unto Moses, saying,

Command the children of Israel, and say unto them, When ye come into the land of Canaan; (this is the land that shall fall unto you for an inheritance, even the land of Canaan with the coasts thereof:) [Num. 34:1–2].

He gives the south border:

Then your south quarter shall be from the wilderness of Zin along by the coast of Edom, and your south border shall be the outmost coast of the salt sea eastward [Num. 34:3].

Then He points out the west border:

And as for the western border, ye shall even have the great sea for a border: this shall be your west border [Num. 34:6].

And He establishes the north border:

And this shall be your north border: from the great sea ye shall point out for you mount Hor:

From mount Hor ye shall point out your border unto the entrance of Hamath; and the goings forth of the border shall be to Zedad:

And the border shall go on to Ziphron, and the goings out of it shall be at Hazar-enan: this shall be your north border [Num. 34:7–9].

Then He defines the east border:

And ye shall point out your east border from Hazar-enan to Shepham:

And the coast shall go down from Shepham to Riblah, on the east side of Ain; and the border shall descend, and shall reach unto the side of the sea of Chinnereth eastward:

And the border shall go down to Jordan, and the goings out of it shall be at the salt sea: this shall be your land with the coasts thereof round about [Num. 34:10–12].

The Lord then specifies who is to be responsible for the division of the land among the tribes.

And the LORD spake unto Moses, saying,

These are the names of the men which shall divide the land unto you: Eleazar the priest, and Joshua the son of Nun.

And ye shall take one prince of every tribe, to divide the land by inheritance [Num. 34:16–18].

He even lists by name each prince that is to have this responsibility. I won't quote these verses, because it is a little monotonous to us today. But it was very important to Israel in that day. The chapter concludes by saying,

These are they whom the LORD commanded to divide the inheritance unto the children of Israel in the land of Canaan [Num. 34:29].

CITIES GIVEN TO THE LEVITES

As we have learned, the Levites were taken from among the children of Israel instead of all the firstborn. The Levites belonged to the Lord. They were not given a section of the land of Israel, but they were given cities to live in.

And the LORD spake unto Moses in the plains of Moab by Jordan near Jericho, saying,

Command the children of Israel, that they give unto the Levites of the inheritance of their possession cities to dwell in; and ye shall give also unto the Levites suburbs for the cities round about them.

And the cities shall they have to dwell in; and the suburbs of them shall be for their cattle, and for their goods, and for all their beasts [Num. 35:1–3].

The suburbs are the pasture lands which were also reserved for the Levites.

And the suburbs of the cities, which ye shall give unto the Levites, shall reach from the wall of the city and outward a thousand cubits round about [Num. 35:4].

Of the forty-eight cities which were assigned to the Levites, six of them were designated as cities of refuge.

And the LORD spake unto Moses, saying,

Speak unto the children of Israel, and say unto them, When ye be come over Jordan into the land of Canaan;

Then ye shall appoint you cities to be cities of refuge for you; that the slayer may flee thither, which killeth any person at unawares.

And they shall be unto you cities for refuge from the avenger; that the manslayer die not, until he stand before the congregation in judgment.

And of these cities which ye shall give six cities shall ye have for refuge [Num. 35:9–13].

The Levites were to set up three such cities on the east side of Jordan and three on the west side of Jordan. A man who had unwittingly killed a person could flee to the city of refuge. This would save him from mob action or from the action of some zealous person or relative who might be emotionally wrought up at the time. This gave time for a fair trial later.

Then the congregation shall judge between the slayer and the revenger of blood according to these judgments:

And the congregation shall deliver the slayer out of the hand of the revenger of blood, and the congregation shall restore him to the city of his refuge, whither he was fled: and he shall abide in it unto the death of the high priest, which was anointed with the holy oil [Num. 35:24–25].

Notice, however, that the protection of the cities of refuge did not apply for the willful murderer.

Whoso killeth any person, the murderer shall be put to death by the mouth of witnesses: but one witness shall not testify against any person to cause him to die [Num. 35:30].

Now the Lord gives the reason for these commandments.

So ye shall not pollute the land wherein ye are: for blood it defileth the land: and the land cannot be cleansed of the blood that is shed therein, but by the blood of him that shed it.

Defile not therefore the land which ye shall inhabit, wherein I dwell: for I the LORD dwell among the children of Israel [Num. 35:33–34].

LAW REGARDING THE INHERITANCE OF THE LAND

The chiefs of the families of the sons of Joseph presented a problem to Moses. If the daughters of Zelophehad should marry men outside their own tribe, then their land would pass into another tribe. So Moses tells them the Word of the Lord concerning this.

This is the thing which the LORD doth command concerning the daughters of Zelophehad, saying, Let them marry to whom they think best; only to the family of the tribe of their father shall they marry.

So shall not the inheritance of the children of Israel remove from tribe to tribe: for every one of the children of Israel shall keep himself to the inheritance of the tribe of his fathers.

And every daughter, that possesseth an inheritance in any tribe of the children of Israel, shall be wife unto one of the family of the tribe of her father, that the children of Israel may enjoy every man the inheritance of his fathers. Neither shall the inheritance remove from one tribe to another tribe; but every one of the tribes of the children of Israel shall keep himself to his own inheritance [Num. 36:6–9].

The land was to stay in the tribe. No man could lose his property permanently. At the year of jubilee, all property which had been mortgaged reverted to the original family again. This was a marvelous arrangement which God made for His people. It was the way He protected them.

These are the commandments and the judgments, which the LORD commanded by the hand of Moses unto the

children of Israel in the plains of Moab by Jordan near Jericho [Num. 36:13].

This concludes the Book of Numbers. Also it concludes the public ministry of Moses— Deuteronomy will continue with the private ministry of Moses. It has given us only a glimpse into the lives of God's people during the wilderness experience. Marked by failure, rebellion, complaining, and tears, it provides valuable lessons for our own lives as we move through the wilderness of this world.

BIBLIOGRAPHY

Epp, Theodore H. *Moses*, Lincoln, Nebraska: Back to the Bible Broadcast, 1975.

Gaebelein, Arno C. *Annotated Bible*, vol. 1. Neptune, New Jersey: Loizeaux Brothers, n.d.

Grant, F. W. *Numerical Bible*. Neptune, New Jersey: Loizeaux Brothers, 1891.

Gray, James M. *Synthetic Bible Studies*. Westwood, New Jersey: Fleming H. Revell Co., 1906.

Jensen, Irving L. *Numbers: Journey to God's Rest—Land*. Chicago, Illinois: Moody Press, 1967.

Jensen, Irving L. *Numbers & Deuteronomy— Self Study Guide*. Chicago, Illinois: Moody Press.

Kelly, William. *Lectures Introductory to the Pentateuch*. Oak Park, Illinois: Bible Truth Publishers, 1870.

Mackintosh, C. H. (C.H.M.). *Notes on the Pentateuch*. Neptune, New Jersey: Loizeaux Brothers, 1880. (Excellent devotional study.)

Meyer, F. B. *Moses: The Servant of God*. Fort Washington, Pennsylvania: Christian Literature Crusade, n.d.

Thomas, W. H. Griffith. *Through the Pentateuch Chapter by Chapter*. Grand Rapids, Michigan: Wm. B. Eerdmans Publishing Co., 1957.
(Excellent summary.)

Unger, Merrill F. *Unger's Bible Handbook*. Chicago, Illinois: Moody Press, 1966.

The Book of
DEUTERONOMY

INTRODUCTION

As we come to the Book of Deuteronomy, I should remind you that this is the last book of the Pentateuch. The first five books in the Bible were written by Moses and they are called the Pentateuch. These books are Genesis, Exodus, Leviticus, Numbers, and Deuteronomy.

The Greek word *deutero* means "two" or "second," and *nomion* is "law." So the title *Deuteronomy* means "the second law." We are not to infer that this is merely a repetition of the Law as it was given to Moses on Mount Sinai. This is more than a recapitulation. It is another illustration of the law of recurrence, as we have already seen in Scripture. The Spirit of God has a way of saying something in an outline form, then coming back and putting an emphasis upon a particular portion of it.

There are four Hebrew titles of Deuteronomy: (1) *Debarim*, meaning "The Words" or "These be the Words," is derived from the opening expression, "These are the words which Moses spake." (2) The *Kith*, or the Fifth of the Law. (3) The Book of Reproofs. (4) The Iteration of the Law.

The theme of Deuteronomy may surprise you. The great theme is *Love and Obey*. You may not have realized that the love of God was mentioned that far back in the Bible, but the word *love* occurs twenty-two times. The Lord Jesus was not attempting to give something that was brand new when He said, "If you love me, keep my commandments." Deuteronomy teaches that obedience is man's response to God's love. This is not the gospel, but the great principle of it is here. And let's understand one thing: the Law is good. Although I emphasize and overemphasize the fact that God cannot save us by Law, that does not imply that the Law is not good. Of course the Law is good. Do you know where the trouble lies? The trouble is with you and me. Therefore God must save us only by His grace.

Moses wrote Deuteronomy. Moses was a man who knew God; he talked with God face to face. The Psalmist says, "He made known his ways unto Moses, his acts unto the children of Israel" (Ps. 103:7). The children of Israel saw the acts of God, but did not know Him. Moses knew His ways. Deuteronomy is the result of this intimate knowledge, plus the experience of forty years in the wilderness.

The section dealing with the death of Moses (Deut. 34:5-12) was probably written by Joshua and belongs to the Book of Joshua. When the Book of Joshua was written, it was placed on the scroll of the Pentateuch, making a Hexateuch.

The authorship of Deuteronomy has been challenged by the critics. The original criticism was that Moses could not have written it because no writing existed in Moses' day. That theory has been soundly refuted, as we now know that writing existed long before Moses' time. Also the critics stated that the purpose of the book was to glorify the priesthood at Jerusalem, yet neither the priesthood nor Jerusalem is even mentioned in the Book of Deuteronomy. It is amazing to see that this Graf-Wellhausen hypothesis, as it is known, which came out of the German universities years ago, is still being taught in many of our seminaries in the United States.

The Book of Deuteronomy was given to the new generation that was unfamiliar with the experiences at Mount Sinai. The new generation had arrived on the east bank of the Jordan River, and it was one month before they would enter the Promised Land. The adults of the generation which had left Egypt were dead, and their bones were bleaching beneath the desert skies because of their unbelief and disobedience. They had broken God's Law—those were sins of commission. They had failed to believe God—those were sins of omission. You see, unbelief is sin. The Law was weak through the flesh. It was the flesh that was wrong, as wrong as it is today. This is the reason God has an altogether different basis on which He saves us.

The new generation, now grown to adulthood, needed to have the Law interpreted for them in the light of thirty-eight years' experience in the wilderness. New problems had arisen which were not covered by the Law specifically. Also God tells His people that they are to teach the Law constantly to their children. By the way, I wonder if this isn't the great neglect in the modern home. We talk about the failure of the school and the failure of the church today, and I agree that both have miserably failed in teaching boys and girls, but the real problem is in the home where instruction should have originated.

Moses gives to this new generation his final instructions from the Lord before he relinquishes his leadership of the nation through death. He reviews the desert experiences, he reemphasizes certain features of the Law, and he reveals their future course in the light of the Palestinian covenant that God had made with him relative to the land of promise. We will see in this book that the Mosaic Law was not only given to a people, it was given to a land also.

Finally, Moses teaches them a new song; he blesses the twelve tribes; and then he prepares to die. A requiem to Moses concludes the Book of Deuteronomy.

One Hebrew division of Deuteronomy is very good and follows the generally accepted pattern:

EIGHT ORATIONS

First Oration—1:6–4:40
Second Oration—4:44–26:19
Third Oration—27–28
Fourth Oration—29–30
Fifth Oration—31:1-13
Sixth Oration—32 (Song of Moses)
Seventh Oration—33
Eighth Oration—34

OUTLINE

CHAPTER 1

THEME: Israel's failure at Kadesh-Barnea

Moses is reviewing the journeys of the children of Israel and interpreting a great deal of what had taken place. All of that generation is now dead, with the exception of Caleb and Joshua. He is preparing the new generation to enter the land, and rehearsing the experiences of their fathers so that they might profit from them rather than repeat the failures.

These be the words which Moses spake unto all Israel on this side Jordan in the wilderness, in the plain over against the Red sea, between Paran, and Tophel, and Laban, and Hazeroth, and Dizahab [Deut. 1:1].

In that same area I stood on Mount Nebo—I have pictures which I made there—and I actually could see the city of Jerusalem from that elevation. What I saw did not look like a promised land at all. It looked like a total waste, and this reveals what has happened to that land down through the centuries. When Moses looked at it, I think he was seeing a green and a good land. Today it is a desert. It looks like the desert area of California and Arizona.

(There are eleven days' journey from Horeb by the way of mount Seir unto Kadesh-barnea.) [Deut. 1:2].

Mount Sinai is in Horeb. It was a journey of eleven days from Horeb to Kadesh-Barnea, which was the entrance point into the land of promise. Israel spent thirty-eight years wandering when it should have taken them only eleven days to get into the land. Why? Because of their unbelief. Their marching was turned to wandering, and they became just strangers and pilgrims in that desert. Because they were slow to learn, they wandered for thirty-eight years in that great and terrible wilderness.

We also are slow to learn, friends. I think we would characterize ourselves by saying we have low spiritual I.Q.'s. It seems as if the Lord must burn down the school in order to get some of us out of it!

And it came to pass in the fortieth year, in the eleventh month, on the first day of the month, that Moses spake unto the children of Israel, according unto all that the Lord had given him in commandment unto them [Deut. 1:3].

At the close of their time of wandering, Moses delivers his first oration to them. Obviously his words were first given orally and then were written down later. The critics formerly found fault with this, claiming there was no writing at the time of Moses. Of course, now it has been shown that writing was in existence long before Moses. Moses was the spokesman who gave the oration, yet he makes it clear that this was given him by the Lord.

In reviewing their history and in going over their journeys in detail, Moses mentions his great mistake.

And I spake unto you at that time, saying, I am not able to bear you myself alone:

How can I myself alone bear your cumbrance, and your burden, and your strife?

Take you wise men, and understanding, and known among your tribes, and I will make them rulers over you [Deut. 1:9, 12–13].

We find the account of this back in Exodus 18. Moses became provoked, burdened, and frustrated. He thought he alone carried the burden of Israel. The Lord permitted him to appoint elders; so a committee of seventy was appointed. This later became the Sanhedrin, the organization which committed Christ to death many years later.

Moses, in his frustration, lost sight of the fact that *God* was bearing Israel. Moses was God's appointed leader; he didn't need a board or a committee. Moses made a real mistake and he mentions it here. Very few people will mention their mistakes, but Moses does. He says it sounded so good, but it didn't work and it caused a great deal of difficulty.

This same thing can happen in a church. I think one of the worst things that can happen to a church is a board that will not follow the pastor. In that kind of conflict, either the board should go or the pastor should go. If the pastor is standing for the Word of God and is preaching it, then it is the duty of the board to support him. If they don't like the way the pastor parts his hair, they should get out. Unfortunately, usually they stay on, split the church, and try to crucify the preacher.

Do you want to know Moses' estimation of the wilderness they went through?

And when we departed from Horeb, we went through all that great and terrible wilderness, which ye saw by the way of the mountain of the Amorites, as the LORD our God commanded us; and we came to Kadesh-barnea [Deut. 1:19].

I'll take his word for it, because he was there. It was both great and terrible. The wilderness march was no nice daisy trail which they were following.

The second mistake which Moses records was the decision at Kadesh-Barnea. This was a mistake of the people. Again, it was the problem of having a board or committee.

And I said unto you, Ye are come unto the mountain of the Amorites, which the LORD our God doth give unto us.

Behold, the LORD thy God hath set the land before thee: go up and possess it, as the LORD God of thy fathers hath said unto thee; fear not, neither be discouraged.

And ye came near unto me every one of you, and said, We will send men before us, and they shall search us out the land, and bring us word again by what way we must go up, and into what cities we shall come.

And the saying pleased me well: and I took twelve men of you, one of a tribe [Deut. 1:20–23].

Here we go again! We must have a board or a committee to go in and search out the land. God had already searched it out! God had said it was a land of milk and honey. Sure, there were giants in the land, but God had said that He would take care of them. The people wanted a board; Moses wanted a board. Look what happened. This was the reason they were turned back into that awful wilderness.

The basic problem is unbelief. God had said it was a good land. The spies looked it over and agreed that it was a good land. But they said there were giants in the land. God had said that He would take care of the giants because He would enable Israel. They did not believe God.

Many times the Christian today finds himself confronted by giants in this life. I'm sure that as a child of God you have found yourself in giant country. Believe me, it is difficult to know how to handle a giant when you are just a pygmy yourself. God has given us the same promise that *He* is able to handle the giants for us. It is wonderful to know that. It is not our circumstances on the outside which are our real problem. It is the circumstance on the inside of us, the unbelief in our hearts, which is the cause of our problems.

Now God makes it clear to them that the whole generation which came up to Kadesh-Barnea and turned back in unbelief will die. Only two men of the old generation will be permitted to enter the land. They are Joshua and Caleb.

And the LORD heard the voice of your words, and was wroth, and sware, saying,

Surely there shall not one of these men of this evil generation see that good land, which I sware to give unto your fathers.

Save Caleb the son of Jephunneh; he shall see it, and to him will I give the land that he hath trodden upon, and to his children, because he hath wholly followed the LORD.

Also the LORD was was angry with me for your sakes, saying, Thou also shalt not go in thither.

But Joshua the son of Nun, which standeth before thee, he shall go in thither: encourage him: for he shall cause Israel to inherit it [Deut. 1:34–38].

Caleb and Joshua were different from the others. They were spies who believed God and had brought back an accurate report, a good report. The fact of the matter is that Caleb will lay hold of the land that he wanted. We will find later, in the Book of Joshua, that he was a remarkable man. He walked up and down the land, and he claimed the mountain where the giants lived! "This is what I want," he said, and God gave it to him for an inheritance.

By the way, what do you want of God, friends? Are you a parent? Are you a young person starting out in life? What do you want of God? Let me say this: If you think you can sit on the sidelines and get it, you are wrong. There are a great many folks who think they should just sit and pray and pray and pray. I certainly agree that we must pray and live in fellowship with Him, but, my friend, you are going to have to go out there and take it. Did you know that? God said He would give to Caleb the land that he had *trodden* upon. A great many of us today are not being blessed because we are spending too much time sitting down. That is the wrong place to be if we want the blessing of God. We are to walk. There is a great deal said in the Scriptures about the Christian's walk and very little said about the Christian's sitting down. We need to lay hold of God's promises.

Joshua is the man who is to become the leader to succeed Moses. Why was he chosen? Well, he is a man of experience, and he is a man who wholly followed God. He and Caleb brought back the good report because they believed God. Faith was the essential thing. They believed God and they were willing to step out in faith. Friend, you don't believe God by just sitting down and claiming great blessings. You have to step out in faith for Him.

Moreover your little ones, which ye said should be a prey, and your children, which in that day had no knowledge between good and evil, they shall go in thither, and unto them will I give it, and they shall possess it [Deut. 1:39].

There are some very important things here that we don't want to miss. First, the age of responsibility is older than we may think it is. Some of these folk who entered the land were teenagers at Kadesh-Barnea. We know from Numbers 14:29 that God set the age at 20, and all from twenty years old and upward died in the wilderness.

Something else to note here is that children who die in infancy are saved. How do I know? God did not hold responsible those young folk who had not reached the age of accountability when their elders refused to enter the land. He permitted them to enter the land. You see, the older generation had said they did not want to enter the land because they feared for their children's safety—they were thinking of their children. God made it very clear to them that this was not their real reason. They were insulting God; they were really saying that *God* didn't care for their children. In effect God says to them, "I do care for your children, and those little ones whom you thought would be in such danger are the very ones who are going to enter the land." Now it is that generation of young folk who have come to the border of the land and are ready to enter the Promised Land. It is to them that Moses is speaking.

But as for you, turn you, and take your journey into the wilderness by the way of the Red sea.

Then ye answered and said unto me, We have sinned against the LORD, we will go up and fight, according to all that the LORD our God commanded us. And when ye had girded on every man his weapons

of war, ye were ready to go up into the hill [Deut. 1:40–41].

After the children of Israel refuse to go into the land at Kadesh-Barnea, they face a terrible dilemma. They face the wilderness if they turn back—remember that Moses called it "that great and terrible wilderness." Realizing they have sinned, and realizing they face the wilderness if they turn back, they decide to go into the Promised Land after all.

And the LORD said unto me, Say unto them, Go not up, neither fight; for I am not among you; lest ye be smitten before your enemies [Deut. 1:42].

May I say to you that such a type of fighting is no good. Do you know why? Because they were out of the will of God. The reason they were willing to fight at this time was not because they believed God but because they were afraid. Their motivation was fear, not faith! They were motivated by fear, not by faith in God.

So I spake unto you; and ye would not hear, but rebelled against the commandment of the LORD, and went presumptuously up into the hill [Deut. 1:43].

This was not faith, you see. If they had gone up at the beginning because they believed God, that would have been one thing. This now is acting presumptuously and is altogether different.

I think there is a very fine distinction between faith and presumption. In the course of my ministry, I have counseled with many people. One man told me, "You know, Brother McGee, I believed God and I thought He would bless my business. I went into business believing He would bless me, but He didn't. In fact, I went bankrupt." Well, friend, was it faith in God or was it presumption? When we got down to the nitty-gritty, I learned that this man had heard another business man speak at a banquet. His message had been that he had taken as his motto, "God is my partner," and he had been very successful in business. He told about how he had taken God into partnership with him, and God had blessed and prospered him. Obviously, God led that man; I'm confident of that. However, I believe that my friend went home and presumptuously said, "Well, if God will make me prosperous, I'll take Him as my partner in business." God didn't lead him, you see. Believe me, friends, there is a difference between faith and presumption.

And the Amorites, which dwelt in that mountain, came out against you, and chased you, as bees do, and destroyed you in Seir, even unto Hormah.

And ye returned and wept before the Lord; but the Lord would not hearken to your voice, nor give ear unto you.

So ye abode in Kadesh many days, according unto the days that ye abode there [Deut. 1:44–46].

Notice this. They came before the Lord and they shed crocodile tears. They wept, and they repented. Yes, but what kind of a repentance was this? Listen to Paul in 2 Corinthians 7:10:

"For godly sorrow worketh repentance to salvation not to be repented of: but the sorrow of the world worketh death."

Did they weep because they disobeyed God? No. They wept because the Amorites had chased them. Their defeat was the reason for their weeping. You know of incidents when a thief is caught, and he begins to shed tears and repent. But wait a minute. What kind of tears are they? Does he weep because he is a thief? No, he weeps because he has been caught. There is a world of difference in that. This is exactly the case with these people.

As a result of all this, they apparently spent a lot of time at Kadesh.

CHAPTER 2

THEME: *Moses reviews Israel's wanderings*

This discourse of Moses gives a continuation of his review of their journeys. After they turned back from Kadesh-Barnea, the children of Israel went to Mount Seir.

Then we turned, and took our journey into the wilderness by the way of the Red sea, as the Lord spake unto me: and we compassed mount Seir many days [Deut. 2:1].

I have always thought that the Lord has a sense of humor, and I think we can see it here.

And the Lord spake unto me, saying,

Ye have compassed this mountain long enough: turn you northward [Deut. 2:2–3].

You see, they didn't know where to go. All they have been doing is just going around and around Mount Seir. It was sort of a ring-around-the-rosy; round and round they go. Finally God says that He is getting tired of that. He probably said, "Let's quit this round and round business."

I'm afraid many Christians are doing that very same thing. Because they fail to take God at His Word, they are just marking time, and are on a merry-go-round of activity.

GOD'S CARE FOR ESAU

And command thou the people, saying, Ye are to pass through the coast of your brethren the children of Esau, which dwell in Seir; and they shall be afraid of you: take ye good heed unto yourselves therefore:

Meddle not with them; for I will not give you of their land, no, not so much as a footbreadth; because I have given mount Seir unto Esau for a possession [Deut. 2:4–5].

Here is something else which is important for us to learn. Back in Genesis 36 we learned that Esau lived in Seir and that Esau is Edom. Jacob had received the birthright and God gave to him and his descendants the Promised Land. Esau went to Seir, and it is now clear that God has given that to the people of Esau as their possession. This is in the country where the rock-hewn city of Petra stands to this day. God clearly tells Israel that they cannot touch the possession of Esau.

There is a lesson here for the nations today. God has set the bounds of the nations (Acts 17:26). Most wars are fought because the boundaries of nations are not respected.

Another lesson to learn is that God always keeps His promises. Even to a people such as the people of Esau, God remains true to His promise.

For the Lord thy God hath blessed thee in all the works of thy hand: he knoweth thy walking through this great wilderness: these forty years the LORD thy God hath been with thee; thou hast lacked nothing [Deut. 2:7].

Here is the overall view of their forty years. God knew all their trials and troubles because God had walked with them all those years. Moses could honestly say, "Thou hast lacked nothing." How wonderful! It is the same as when David looked back over his life and said, "The LORD is my shepherd; I shall not want" (Ps. 23:1). How could he say that? Because he had never wanted! God does not give us the promise of the luxuries of life, but God provides the necessities of life. He will do that for you and for me, also.

GOD'S CARE FOR OTHER NATIONS

We have seen how God protected the boundaries of Esau. We find that He does the same for other nations.

And the LORD said unto me, Distress not the Moabites, neither contend with them in battle: for I will not give thee of their land for a possession; because I have given Ar unto the children of Lot for a possession.

And when thou comest nigh over against the children of Ammon, distress them not, nor meddle with them: for I will not give thee of the land of the children of Ammon any possession; because I have given it unto the children of Lot for a possession [Deut. 2:9, 19].

Israel will face giants in the land, but God encourages them by showing them that for Esau to conquer his land, he had to destroy the giants called Horims (v. 22). For the children of Ammon to possess their land, they had to conquer the giants which were called the Zamzummims (v. 20). We still have giants today. Every now and again we produce people who are 7 and 8 feet tall.

CONQUEST OF TRANS-JORDAN

Rise ye up, take your journey, and pass over the river Arnon: behold, I have given into thine hand Sihon the Amorite, king of Heshbon, and his land: begin to possess it, and contend with him in battle [Deut. 2:24].

Israel passed around Moab and Ammon and did not possess their land. These nations sold them food and water. Now Moses tells of the overtures he made to Sihon, the king of Heshbon.

And I sent messengers out of the wilderness of Kedemoth unto Sihon king of Heshbon with words of peace, saying,

Let me pass through thy land: I will go along by the high way, I will neither turn unto the right hand nor to the left.

Thou shalt sell me meat for money, that I may eat; and give me water for money, that I may drink: only I will pass through on my feet;

(As the children of Esau which dwell in Seir, and the Moabites which dwell in Ar, did unto me;) until I shall pass over Jordan into the land which the LORD our God giveth us [Deut. 2:26–29].

Instead of allowing Israel to pass through his land, King Sihon came out against them with his armed forces.

But Sihon king of Heshbon would not let us pass by him: for the LORD thy God hardened his spirit, and made his heart obstinate, that he might deliver him into thy hand, as appeareth this day.

And the LORD said unto me, Behold, I have begun to give Sihon and his land before thee: begin to possess, that thou mayest inherit his land.

Then Sihon came out against us, he and all his people, to fight at Jahaz (Deut. 2:30–32).

God preserved His people from destruction.

And the LORD our God delivered him before us; and we smote him, and his sons, and all his people [Deut. 2:33].

This land that God allowed Israel to conquer and possess had formerly belonged to the Moabites. The Amorites under King Sihon's leadership had driven out the Moabites from this section of land and had taken over this territory. God permitted him to dispossess the Moabites, but when he led the attack against Israel, he was killed and his forces scattered. His capital was taken and the territory given to Israel. This episode is often referred to as a reminder to Israel of what God had done for them and became a source of encouragement to them. God is showing them that He is with them and will keep His promises to them.

As you know, the Lord does that for many of us today. He permits us to have a difficult experience, maybe a sad one, to prepare us for life—or to prepare us to be helpful to others.

CHAPTER 3

THEME: Moses reviews Israel's conquest of Bashan

Continuing the rehearsal of Israel's experience in the wilderness, Moses tells of the resistance of another Amorite king and the victory God gave to Israel.

Then we turned, and went up the way to Bashan: and Og the king of Bashan came out against us, he and all his people, to battle at Edrei.

And the LORD said unto me, Fear him not: for I will deliver him, and all his people, and his land, into thy hand; and thou shalt do unto him as thou didst unto Sihon king of the Amorites, which dwelt at Heshbon [Deut. 3:1–2].

Notice how the Lord stills their fears.

So the LORD our God delivered into our hands Og also, the king of Bashan, and all his people: and we smote him until none was left to him remaining [Deut. 3:3].

Og was an Amorite king, a man of gigantic stature, whose kingdom seemed invincible.

And we took all his cities at that time, there was not a city which we took not from them, threescore cities, all the region of Argob, the kingdom of Og in Bashan [Deut. 3:4].

Og held sway over sixty separate communities.

All these cities were fenced with high walls, gates, and bars; beside unwalled towns a great many [Deut. 3:5].

The fact that Israel was able to conquer this great, well-fortified kingdom was evidence that God fought for Israel. This was a great encouragement to them as they faced giants and the cities "walled up to heaven" in the Promised Land.

Now let me call your attention to the size of this man Og.

For only Og king of Bashan remained of the remnant of giants; behold, his bedstead was a bedstead of iron; is it not in Rabbath of the children of Ammon? nine cubits was the length thereof, and four cubits the breadth of it, after the cubit of a man [Deut. 3:11].

If a cubit is 18 inches, this bed is 13½ feet long! We think today that the king-size bed is something new. Well, it is not. Here is really a king-sized bed, friends. Apparently it was preserved as a museum piece at Rabbath among the Amorites.

POSSESSION OF THE LAND

And this land, which we possessed at that time, from Aroer, which is by the river Arnon, and half mount Gilead, and the cities thereof, gave I unto the Reubenites and to the Gadites.

And the rest of Gilead, and all Bashan, being the kingdom of Og, gave I unto the half tribe of Manasseh; all the region of Argob, with all Bashan, which was called the land of giants [Deut. 3:12–13].

The conquered kingdom of Og was given to the tribes of Reuben, Gad, and the half-tribe of Manasseh which chose to stay on the east side of the Jordan River.

And I commanded you at that time, saying, The LORD your God hath given you this land to possess it: ye shall pass over armed before your brethren the children of Israel, all that are meet for the war [Deut. 3:18].

Moses is reminding them that their being comfortably settled in their new homes does not free them from the responsibility of helping the other tribes in their conquest of the land on the west side of the Jordan River.

But your wives, and your little ones, and your cattle, (for I know that ye have much cattle,) shall abide in your cities which I have given you:

Until the LORD have given rest unto your brethren, as well as unto you, and until they also possess the land which the LORD your God hath given them beyond Jordan: and then shall ye return every man unto his possession, which I have given you [Deut. 3:19–20].

PRAYER OF MOSES

Now Moses recounts his personal experience with the Lord and the reason he will not be permitted to go into the Promised Land with them.

And I besought the LORD at that time, saying,

O Lord God, thou hast begun to shew thy servant thy greatness, and thy mighty hand: for what God is there in heaven or in earth, that can do according to thy works, and according to thy might?

I pray thee, let me go over, and see the good land that is beyond Jordan, that goodly mountain, and Lebanon.

But the Lord was wroth with me for your sakes, and would not hear me: and the Lord said unto me, Let it suffice thee; speak no more unto me of this matter [Deut. 3:23–26].

Like a good parent, God is true to His Word. In essence He says, "That's enough, Moses. I don't want to hear anymore about it."

Get thee up into the top of Pisgah, and lift up thine eyes westward, and north-ward, and southward, and eastward, and behold it with thine eyes: for thou shalt not go over this Jordan [Deut. 3:27].

Our hearts go out to this man Moses as he begs the Lord to let him enter the land which has been his goal for forty years. What a lesson this is for us, friends. Though we repent of our sin, we will have to take the consequences of it in this life whether we like it or not.

But charge Joshua, and encourage him, and strengthen him: for he shall go over before this people, and he shall cause them to inherit the land which thou shalt see [Deut. 3:28].

Moses is making it clear to this new generation that stands ready to enter the Promised Land that Joshua is the man the Lord has chosen to be their leader.

CHAPTER 4

THEME: *Moses admonishes Israel's new generation*

This chapter concludes Moses' review of Israel's wilderness journey. They have come up the east bank of the Jordan River and are near Mount Nebo as Moses gives his final instructions to the people. Only two of the people who made the entire journey stand there—Joshua and Caleb. Most of the people are buried out there in the wilderness, or their bones are bleaching under the desert sun. The new generation is ready now to go into the Promised Land, but before they enter, Moses reviews the wilderness experiences and pleads with them to obey God who loves them.

MOSES PLEADS WITH THEM TO OBEY GOD

Now therefore hearken, O Israel, unto the statutes and unto the judgments, which I teach you, for to do them, that ye may live, and go in and possess the land which the Lord God of your fathers giveth you.

Ye shall not add unto the word which I command you, neither shall ye diminish aught from it, that ye may keep the commandments of the Lord your God which I command you [Deut. 4:1–2].

They are to *do* the Word of God—not only to hear it, but do it. Notice that they were not to add to the Law, neither were they to take away from the Law. They were to obey it as God gave it.

If Israel had kept the Law, what a blessing it would have been. But we find here a demonstration in history of a people who were given the Law under favorable circumstances but who could not keep it. No flesh will be justified before God by the Law. Why not? Is it because God is arbitrary? No, it is because the flesh is radically wrong. That is the problem.

As I have already indicated, this book emphasizes two great themes: love and obedience. Maybe you never realized that love is a great theme of the Old Testament, but it is. Here, in this fourth chapter, Moses is pleading with this new generation, and he is giving to them reasons why they are to obey God.

1. God wants to preserve and prosper Israel.

This first verse tells us that they are to obey the Lord and hearken to His statutes and judgments "that ye may live, and go in and possess the land." Obedience to God is the only basis on which He can bless them. He desires their obedience because it is His desire to bless them.

2. Israel's obedience would show their gratitude to God.

Behold, I have taught you statutes and judgments. . . .

Keep therefore and do them. . . .

For what nation is there so great, who hath God so nigh unto them, as the Lord our God is in all things that we call upon him for?

And what nation is there so great, that hath statutes and judgments so righteous as all this law, which I set before you this day? [Deut. 4:5–8].

God had so marvelously blessed them that they are to show their gratitude through obedience.

3. God's love should prompt their obedience.

And because he loved thy fathers, therefore he chose their seed after them, and brought thee out in his sight with his mighty power out of Egypt [Deut. 4:37].

This is the first time in the Bible that God tells anybody that He loves them. God has *demonstrated* that He loves man from the very first of Genesis, but, up to this point, He hasn't said anything about it. This is the first time He mentions it. He gives this as His motive for what He has done. He has already delivered them out of the land of Egypt, and He is going to do greater and mightier things for them. The basis of it all, the motive for it all, is that God loves them.

This is something which every person today needs to recognize. I don't care who you are, God loves you! You may not always *experience* the love of God. Ours sins put up an umbrella between God and us. In spite of our sin, God loves you and He loves me. He has demonstrated that love at the cross of Christ. When we receive Christ as Savior, we can experience the love of God.

4. They are to obey God because they belong to God.

"Ye are the children of the Lord your God: ye shall not cut yourselves, nor make any baldness between your eyes for the dead" (Deut. 14:1).

Obedience to God is the first law of life, friends. Man has a natural, innate hatred of God. Man doesn't want to obey God; in fact, he is very much opposed to God. All the way through the Word of God we find that there is a resistance on the part of man against God. We find that in man even today.

I am rejoicing in something I heard recently. After I preached in a little church, a lady came up to me and said, "I was saved listening to your program, but I have never been able to get my husband into a church. I have never been able to get him interested, and he has always resisted. Now he is beginning to listen to your program, and it is the only thing he will listen to." If the Word of God won't break down the resistance of a man, nothing else will do it.

If Israel had only kept God's Law! What a blessing would have come to them!

RESULTS OF OBEDIENCE AND OF DISOBEDIENCE

Your eyes have seen what the Lord did because of Baal-peor: for all the men that followed Baal-peor, the Lord thy God hath destroyed them from among you.

But ye that did cleave unto the Lord your God are alive every one of you this day [Deut. 4:3–4].

He is referring to the time when Balaam was called upon to curse Israel, and he could not do it. The fact of the matter is he could pronounce only blessings. But he did make a suggestion to the king of Moab that since he could not curse Israel, the king should let his people go down and intermingle and intermarry with the children of Israel. This would introduce false worship among them which would bring God's judgment down on them. This is exactly what happened, as we saw in chapter 25 of Numbers.

This was to be an example to this new generation. It is to be an example to us also.

There is a reward for obedience. Those who did cleave to the Lord were kept alive and would enter the land. God reminds them again that obedience brings with it a blessing.

Behold, I have taught you statutes and judgments, even as the Lord my God commanded me, that ye should do so in the land whither ye go to possess it [Deut. 4:5].

Obedience would bring the blessing of God. They would go into the land to possess it. And their obedience was to serve yet another purpose:

Keep therefore and do them; for this is your wisdom and your understanding in the sight of the nations, which shall

hear all these statutes, and say, Surely this great nation is a wise and understanding people [Deut. 4:6].

Israel was to be a witness to all the world. Israel was to witness to the world in the opposite way from the way the Church is to witness to the world. We are told "Go ye into all the world, and preach the gospel . . ." (Mark 16:15). That command is given to every believer. Every believer in Christ should have some part in getting the Word of God out to the ends of the earth. Now, very frankly, the nation Israel was never asked to go as missionaries. They were to invite, "Come, let us go up to the house of the Lord." Their obedience, their faithfulness to God, would cause the other nations to hear these statutes and to notice that God's blessing made Israel a great nation. Then what would they do? What did the Queen of Sheba do? She came from the ends of the earth. There were no jet planes at that time. She made a long, arduous, hard trip. If a woman would come that distance under such circumstances, don't you think some men would come to see? And they did. That was the way Israel witnessed to the world. If they would obey, God would bless them, and they would be a witness to all nations. If they would not obey, and if they would turn from the Lord, then God would bring judgment upon them.

Only take heed to thyself, and keep thy soul diligently, lest thou forget the things which thine eyes have seen, and lest they depart from thy heart all the days of thy life: but teach them thy sons, and thy sons' sons [Deut. 4:9].

God gave to the nation Israel the great burden of a teaching ministry. They were to obey God, and they were to teach these things to their children and to their grandchildren.

The greatest undertaking of any nation is the education of the young. Probably the greatest failure of any nation is the failure in education. Look at America today and see the dismal failure we are making in this matter of education. Now I am not blaming the colleges and the schools. Do you know where the problem lies? It is right in the home. God tells these people, "I want *you* to teach your children and your grandchildren." The failure to teach is the failure of mom and dad in the home. This was the great responsibility which God placed upon every father and mother in Israel. Friend, if you are going to bring a child into this world, you are responsible for that child. Our problem today is not foreign affairs or national economy; our problem is the home. God will hold

divorced and preoccupied parents responsible for the vagrants of the world today who never knew the instruction and the love and the concern and the communication from parents. What a responsibility parenthood is! God makes this very clear to Israel. When that nation failed, it failed in the home, and God judged it.

And the Lord spake unto you out of the midst of the fire: ye heard the voice of the words, but saw no similitude: only ye heard a voice [Deut. 4:12].

The Lord Jesus stated it very clearly: "God is a Spirit: and they that worship him must worship him in spirit and in truth" (John 4:24). People were never to have any likeness of God whatsoever. The Lord Jesus became a man, but the Bible does not give us any physical description of Him. Now you will probably think I am picayunish, if you haven't already come to that conclusion, but I do not believe in pictures of Jesus. I know that many lovely people feel that a picture of Jesus helps them to worship Him. Let me tell you what was said by an old Scottish commentator: "Men never paint a picture of Jesus until they have lost the presence of Him in their hearts." We need Him in our hearts today, not in color on a canvas. These are tremendous and eternal truths which God is giving us in this chapter. The instructions which were given to Israel in that day are great principles for us to carry over for ourselves today, because truth is eternal.

For the Lord thy God is a consuming fire, even a jealous God.

When thou shalt beget children, and children's children, and ye shall have remained long in the land, and shall corrupt yourselves, and make a graven image, or the likeness of any thing, and shall do evil in the sight of the Lord thy God, to provoke him to anger:

I call heaven and earth to witness against you this day, that ye shall soon utterly perish from off the land whereunto ye go over Jordan to possess it; ye shall not prolong your days upon it, but shall utterly be destroyed.

And the Lord shall scatter you among the nations, and ye shall be left few in number among the heathen, whither the Lord shall lead you [Deut. 4:24–27].

That nation is still a witness to the world today, a witness in their disobedience. They are scattered over the world today. Why? Because they did the thing God forbade them to do. I know someone will point out that they are back in the land and they are a nation now. Yes, but they are in trouble, aren't they? When God brings them back into that land as He predicted, they won't be having the trouble they are having today. The nation of Israel is still under the judgment of God today because it has turned its back upon God. Judgment will come upon any nation which rejects Him. This is a tremendous lesson for us today.

When thou art in tribulation, and all these things are come upon thee, even in the latter days, if thou turn to the Lord thy God, and shalt be obedient unto his voice [Deut. 4:30].

This is the first mention of the Great Tribulation which is ultimately coming. "In the latter days" is a technical term in the Old Testament which refers to the Great Tribulation period. God sets up a condition: "If thou turn to the Lord thy God, and shalt be obedient unto His voice."

(For the Lord thy God is a merciful God;) he will not forsake thee, neither destroy thee, nor forget the covenant of thy fathers which he sware unto them [Deut. 4:31].

Will the Lord scatter them because He is a big bully or because He is being harsh? No, listen. God is merciful. "He will not forsake thee, neither destroy thee." The reason Israel has not been consumed is because God is merciful.

That is the same reason you and I have not been consumed. If you are saved, it is not because you are nice and sweet; it is because of the mercy of God. He is merciful to us as well as to Israel.

Moses goes on to show them the evidence of God's great mercy to them.

Did ever people hear the voice of God speaking out of the midst of the fire, as thou hast heard, and live?

Or hath God assayed to go and take him a nation from the midst of another nation, by temptations, by signs, and by wonders, and by war, and by a mighty hand, and by a stretched out arm, and by great terrors, according to all that the Lord your God did for you in Egypt before your eyes? [Deut. 4:33–34].

God did all these things before the very eyes of their fathers. God does not want them to forget that. God has been gracious to them, and He wants them to remember it.

And because he loved thy fathers, therefore he chose their seed after them, and brought thee out in his sight with his mighty power out of Egypt [Deut. 4:37].

God did it because He loved them. That is the explanation. There was no good in them, but there was good in God.

God loves us today. But He does not save us by love; He saves us by grace. He couldn't just open the back door of heaven and slip us in. He couldn't be righteous and do that. A sacrifice for our sins had to be made. His love sent Christ to die for us, and Christ loved us enough to die so that you and I might have a pardon. The Bible does not say, "God so loved the world, that he saved the world." It says, ". . . God so loved the world, that he *gave* His only begotten Son . . ." (John 3:16). He did this that whoever—it makes no difference who it is— "believeth in Him should not perish, but have everlasting life."

And this is the law which Moses set before the children of Israel:

These are the testimonies, and the statutes, and the judgments, which Moses spake unto the children of Israel, after they came forth out of Egypt [Deut. 4:44–45].

CHAPTER 5

THEME: Moses restates and interprets the Law

This is now the second oration of Moses. It is a restating of the Law, and the emphasis is still on love and obedience. In chapters 5–7 we will find a repetition and interpretation of the Ten Commandments. The generation that had originally heard the Law at Mount Sinai is now dead—their bones are bleaching out there on the desert. This new generation, the Israel that is going into the land, needs to have the Law restated and also interpreted for them. Moses will interpret this in the light of the forty years of experience in the wilderness.

Some of you will say that this is a duplicate of chapter 20 of Exodus. Well, it is almost a duplicate. This shows that the Ten Commandments are important enough to repeat. They are basic, moral laws.

And Moses called all Israel, and said unto them, Hear, O Israel, the statutes and judgments which I speak in your ears this day, that ye may learn them, and keep, and do them [Deut. 5:1].

Here are the four important steps we are to take in relation to the Word of God. The first is to *hear* it. The second is to *learn* it, to become acquainted with what God is saying. The third is to *keep* it. That means to have the Word of God down in your heart. Remember how David spoke of this fact: "Thy word have I hid in mine heart, that I might not sin against thee" (Ps. 119:11). The fourth is to *do* it. Not only should the Word of God be in your head and in your heart, but it should get down there where your feet and hands are.

You hear, as I do, a great many people say that they live by the Ten Commandments, and that's their religion. If you quiz such people, as I have done several times, you will find that what they really mean is they have voted for them—that is, they have heard them and they think they are good. But they certainly are not keeping them and are not obeying them.

The Law actually is like a plumb line to determine the verticality of a crooked wall. The Law is a mirror that is held up to the heart. It is a headlight on a car to show the way into the darkness and to reveal the curves ahead.

God makes it very clear that He is not saving men through the keeping of a moral code. There is nothing wrong with the moral code, the Law, but there is something radically wrong with us. Paul states this in Galatians 2:16: "Knowing that a man is not justified by the works of the law, but by the faith of Jesus Christ, even we have believed in Jesus Christ, that we might be justified by the faith of Christ, and not by the works of the law: for by the works of the law shall no flesh be justified." No one is justified by the Law. Why not? Because no one can do the works of the Law.

"Wherefore then serveth the law? It was added because of transgressions, till the seed should come to whom the promise was made; and it was ordained by angels in the hand of a mediator" (Gal. 3:19). It is logical to ask what the purpose of the Law is. The answer is that it was added because of (or for the sake of) transgressions, until the time when the Seed should come. That is, it was temporary until the Seed should come, and that Seed is Christ. "Wherefore the law was our schoolmaster to bring us unto Christ, that we might be justified by faith. But after that faith is come, we are no longer under a schoolmaster" (Gal. 3:24–25). The Law served as a schoolmaster, a servant to take us by the hand and bring us to the cross, just as the schoolmaster brought the child to school. The Law brings us to the cross and says, "Little fellow, you are a sinner and you need a Savior." The purpose of the Law is to show us our need for a Savior. The Law is good, friends; there is no doubt about that. The Law reveals the mind of God. The Law reveals how far short you and I come of the glory of God. The Law reveals that "all have sinned . . . , and come short of the glory of God" (Rom. 3:23). Put this Law down on your life and let it bring you to Christ.

The LORD our God made a covenant with us in Horeb.

The LORD made not this covenant with our fathers, but with us, even us, who are all of us here alive this day [Deut. 5:2–3].

God did not give the Law to them down in Egypt. The Law was not given until they were out in the wilderness at Horeb, which is Mount Sinai. The Law was given to the nation Israel.

The LORD talked with you face to face in the mount out of the midst of the fire,

(I stood between the LORD and you at that time, to shew you the word of the LORD: for ye were afraid by reason of the fire, and went not up into the mount;) saying,

I am the LORD thy God, which brought thee out of the land of Egypt, from the house of bondage [Deut. 5:4–6].

You see, Israel was in a land of idolatry when they lived in Egypt, and Israel lived in an age of idolatry.

Thou shalt have none other gods before me [Deut. 5:7].

Man's first sin was not to become an atheist; his sin was to become a polytheist. He worshiped many gods. For example, at the tower of Babel, men built a ziggurat, a tower. On the top of this they offered sacrifices, apparently to the sun. The sun and the planets were some of the first objects men worshiped when they turned away from God. After the Flood, they certainly were not worshiping thunder and lightning, because they feared them. They worshiped the sun, the creation rather than the Creator. It was for the polytheist that God said, "Thou shalt have none other gods before me." It was not until the time of David that atheism came in. Earlier than that, men were too close to the mooring mast of revelation to be atheists. The revelation of God was still in their memory, and no one was denying the existence of God. In David's day it was the fool who ". . . said in his heart, There is no God" (Ps. 14:1). That word *fool* means "insane." A man who says there is no God is insane or else he is not sincere. This first commandment does not even mention a disbelief in the existence of God, it prohibits the worship of many gods.

Thou shalt not make thee any graven image, or any likeness of any thing that is in heaven above, or that is in the earth beneath, or that is in the waters beneath the earth:

Thou shalt not bow down thyself unto them, nor serve them: for I the LORD thy God am a jealous God, visiting the iniquity of the fathers upon the children unto the third and fourth generation of them that hate me,

And shewing mercy unto thousands of them that love me and keep my commandments [Deut. 5:8–10].

There are only two kinds of people in the world: those who hate God and those who love Him. He goes into detail when He forbids the making of any likeness of anything that could be worshiped. Later on God will say, "Thou shalt love the LORD thy God with all thine heart, and with all thy soul, and with all thy might" [Deut. 6:5]. The Lord Jesus says that this is the greatest commandment. Over against that is the great company of those who hate God even today.

Today many people maintain that they do not worship an idol at all. Yet Paul tells us in Ephesians 5:5 that covetousness is idolatry. Anything that you give yourself to, anything that stands between you and God, becomes your god. You say you have no idol? To some people, their bankbook is their god. Other people worship the golf club. Others may let a child or a grandchild become their idol. The television screen can become your idol. Anything that takes first place in your heart is your idol.

Thou shalt not take the name of the LORD thy God in vain: for the LORD will not hold him guiltless that taketh his name in vain [Deut. 5:11].

Remember that when Paul shows that all mankind is sinful, he writes, "whose mouth is full of cursing and bitterness" (Rom. 3:14). All you have to do is walk down the street today or be in any public place and you will hear the people with foul mouths. I wonder if there ever have been so many foul-mouthed, dirty-minded folk as there are at the present time. God hates it. God says He will not hold guiltless those who take His name in vain.

A friend of mine challenged me one day and said it wasn't fair to say that man's mouth is full of cursing. I asked him to do a little experiment with me. I suggested we stand on the street corner and hit the first man who came along— hit him in the mouth to see what would come out. My friend, you know what would come out!

The first three commandments are negative; now we come to a positive commandment.

Keep the sabbath day to sanctify it, as the LORD thy God hath commanded thee.

Six days thou shalt labour, and do all thy work:

But the seventh day is the sabbath of the LORD thy God: in it thou shalt not do any work, thou, nor thy son, nor thy daughter, nor thy manservant, nor thy maidservant, nor thine ox, nor thine ass, nor any of thy cattle, nor thy stranger that is within thy gates; that thy manservant and thy maidservant may rest as well as thou.

And remember that thou wast a servant in the land of Egypt, and that the Lord thy God brought thee out thence through a mighty hand and by a stretched out arm: therefore the Lord thy God commanded thee to keep the sabbath day [Deut. 5:12–15].

The very interesting thing is that all of the commandments are repeated in the New Testament with the exception of the commandment about the Sabbath day. Why? Because the Sabbath was not given to the church. The church has always met on the first day of the week, the day on which Christ rose from the dead. The Sabbath day has a peculiar relation to the nation Israel. Back in the Book of Exodus, God said, "Speak thou also unto the children of Israel, saying, Verily my sabbaths ye shall keep: for it is a sign between me and you throughout your generations; that ye may know that I am the Lord that doth sanctify you" (Exod. 31:13). The Sabbath was given to Israel.

It is of interest to notice that in Exodus 20 the children of Israel were told to observe the Sabbath because in six days God had created the heavens and the earth. Here in Deuteronomy the Sabbath is to show the peculiar relationship between God and the children of Israel. Why was the Israelite to keep the Sabbath day? Because he had been a slave in Egypt, and God had brought him out by His great power.

These commandments have been concerned with duty toward God. Now we come to the section concerning duty toward man.

Honour thy father and thy mother, as the Lord thy God hath commanded thee; that thy days may be prolonged, and that it may go well with thee, in the land which the Lord thy God giveth thee [Deut. 5:16].

I believe this commandment is related to duty toward God and man. The father and mother stand in the place of God to the little one who is growing up. The little one looks up to the father and the mother, and that is the way it should be. "My son, hear the instruction of thy father, and forsake not the law of thy mother" (Prov. 1:8). Father and mother are to stand in the place of God while their children are small.

Now as these people are going into the land promised to them, they are to honor their father and their mother. A nation that does not observe this commandment will not be blessed. This very thing is a great problem in America right now, although I realize full well

that not all fathers and mothers are worthy of this respect. God has something to say to parents also: "And, ye fathers, provoke not your children to wrath: but bring them up in the nurture and admonition of the Lord" (Eph. 6:4). Both commandments go together.

Thou shalt not kill [Deut. 5:17].

The word for "kill" here is a very technical word, the Hebrew *ratsach*, and it means to murder. Thou shalt not murder. This is personal. This word has it in the thought of premeditated killing, of anger and of personal grievance. This has nothing to do with war—we will read a little later on that God tells these people to destroy their enemy in the land. This commandment does not apply to a soldier under the orders of war. A young man told me a few years ago that he did not want to go to Vietnam. He said, "I'm not angry at anyone over there. I don't want to go over there to kill." I answered that it was a good thing he was not angry with someone over there. If that were the case, and he went to seek that person out in order to kill him, he would be guilty of murder. We will speak more of this when we talk about our duty to government. The ninth commandment was not intended for a serviceman in combat.

Neither shalt thou commit adultery [Deut. 5:18].

We live in a sex-mad age. Every conceivable product is advertised by sex. It is around us on every hand. God's commandment still stands today. Thou shalt not commit adultery. This is one of the great sins that is pulling our nation down today.

Neither shalt thou steal [Deut. 5:19].

It is true there are many people who can say that they never held up a supermarket or a bank, yet there can be the desire to steal in the heart. Our Lord taught that the very thoughts of our heart are sinful. Hatred in the heart makes one guilty of murder. Lust in the heart makes one guilty of adultery.

Neither shalt thou bear false witness against thy neighbour.

Neither shalt thou desire thy neighbour's wife, neither shalt thou covet thy neighbour's house, his field, or his manservant, or his maidservant, his ox, or his ass, or any thing that is thy neighbour's [Deut. 5:20–21].

The command against covetousness shows that it is a sin just to feel an excessive desire for what belongs to another.

Moses rehearses for this younger generation the tremendous experience of receiving the Law directly from God.

And it came to pass, when ye heard the voice out of the midst of the darkness, (for the mountain did burn with fire,) that ye came near unto me, even all the heads of your tribes, and your elders;

And ye said, Behold, the LORD our God hath shewed us his glory and his greatness, and we have heard his voice out of the midst of the fire: we have seen this day that God doth talk with man, and he liveth.

Now therefore why should we die? for this great fire will consume us: if we hear the voice of the LORD our God any more, then we shall die.

For who is there of all flesh, that hath heard the voice of the living God speaking out of the midst of the fire, as we have, and lived? [Deut. 5:23-26].

It was such a terrifying experience that they wanted Moses to get the message from the Lord and relay it to them:

Go thou near, and hear all that the LORD our God shall say: and speak thou unto us all that the LORD our God shall speak unto thee; and we will hear it, and do it [Deut. 5:27].

The children of Israel promised to keep the Law, but they did not do it.

Listen now to God's heart-cry for His people:

O that there were such an heart in them, that they would fear me, and keep all my commandments always, that it might be well with them, and with their children fore ever! [Deut. 5:29].

The problem was that the nation failed to keep the Law. These people were under favorable conditions, living in the land promised to them—the Law was given for that land as well as that people—but they were unable to keep the Law. That should be a lesson to us. Just as they were unable to keep it so you and I are unable to keep it.

The Law is a mirror held up to us. We are to look in it, and it will reveal to each of us that we are sinners. The mirror in the bathroom will show the smudge spot on the face, but the mirror won't wash off that spot. The Law can show us our sin, but it cannot save us. In no way can the mirror remove the smudge spot. We must come to the basin and wash it away. The Law is the mirror that tells us to start washing. It tells us to come to Christ. It is the blood of Jesus Christ, God's Son, that will wash us and keep on cleansing us from all sin. William Cowper wrote, "There is a fountain filled with blood, drawn from Emmanuel's veins; And sinners plunged beneath that flood lose all their guilty stains."

The important thing is not whether you approve the Ten Commandments or what you think of them; the important question, my friend is: Have you kept them? If you are honest, you know that you haven't measured up. That means you need a Savior. "Come now, and let us reason together, saith the LORD: though your sins be as scarlet, they shall be as white as snow; though they be red like crimson, they shall be as wool" (Isa. 1:18). When you come to Christ, He forgives you and cleanses you from all unrighteousness. Then you stand spotless before Him.

CHAPTER 6

THEME: Love and obey

As we have noted before, in the Book of Deuteronomy there has been an emphasis on two words: love and obedience—not *law* and obedience, as we may have supposed.

God's love is actually expressed in law. The great principle of law is love. Therefore the principle of the Gospel itself is expressed in Deuteronomy. ". . . God so loved the world, that he gave his only begotten Son . . ." (John 3:16).

You and I express our love for God in our obedience. The Lord Jesus put it like this: "If ye love me, keep my commandments" (John 14:15). This is still the acid test today. If we love Him, we will keep His commandments. Salvation is a love affair. "We love him, because he first loved us" (1 John 4:19). The Lord Jesus cited this as the greatest commandment of all: "And thou shalt love the LORD thy God with all thine heart, and with all thy soul, and with all thy might" (Deut. 6:5). Our obedience is the manifestation of our love.

Obedience is the important thing all the way through—it is "*if* they keep these commandments."

Now you may wonder what is new about love in the New Testament if love is in the Old Testament. The difference is that in the New Testament the love of God has been translated into history by the incarnation and death of Christ. "But God commendeth his love toward us, in that, while we were yet sinners, Christ died for us" (Rom. 5:8). He died for us! You see, it is one thing to express love by bringing Israel out of Egypt; it is another thing to die for them. It is one thing to say something from the top of Mount Sinai; it is another thing to come down and take our frail humanity upon Himself, to be made in the likeness of Man, and to die on a cross for our sins. I repeat, salvation is a love affair. "Herein is love, not that we loved God, but that he loved us, and sent his Son to be the propitiation for our sins" (1 John 4:10).

We are still in the second oration of Moses. In chapters 5 to 7, he is giving a repetition and interpretation of the Ten Commandments.

THE GREAT COMMANDMENT

Now these are the commandments, the statutes, and the judgments, which the LORD your God commanded to teach you, that ye might do them in the land whither ye go to possess it:

That thou mightest fear the LORD thy God, to keep all his statutes and his commandments, which I command thee, thou, and thy son, and thy son's son, all the days of thy life; and that thy days may be prolonged [Deut. 6:1–2].

The emphasis is on obedience. There are actually only two classes of people in the world: those who love God and those who hate God. The heart attitude of people is evidenced by their obedience or disobedience. Listen to Deuteronomy 5:29: "O that there were such an heart in them, that they would fear me, and keep all my commandments always, that it might be well with them, and with their children for ever!" Through the prophet Isaiah, God had this to say: "Wherefore the Lord said, Forasmuch as this people draw near me with their mouth, and with their lips do honour me, but have removed their heart far from me, and their fear toward me is taught by the precept of men" (Isa. 29:13). Do you remember how the prophet Samuel rebuked King Saul? "And Samuel said, Hath the LORD as great delight in burnt offerings and sacrifices, as in obeying the voice of the LORD? Behold, to obey is better than sacrifice, and to hearken than the fat of rams" (1 Sam. 15:22). When the Lord Jesus gave His commission to Simon Peter, He asked only one question, "Simon, son of Jonas, lovest thou me?" (John 21:16).

The most wonderful thing in heaven will be to see the Lord Jesus and realize fully that He loves me and that He gave Himself for me. But the next best thing in heaven is going to be that I will love everybody, and everybody is going to love me. Now that, my friend, is going to make heaven a very wonderful place!

Hear therefore, O Israel, and observe to do it; that it may be well with thee, and that ye may increase mightily, as the LORD God of thy fathers hath promised thee, in the land that floweth with milk and honey [Deut. 6:3].

They had promised to keep all the commandments of the Lord, and yet they fell so short—as we still do today.

Now we come to a statement which is considered by many theologians to be the greatest doctrinal statement in the entire Scripture.

Hear, O Israel: The LORD our God is one LORD [Deut. 6:4].

That is a tremendous statement. "The LORD" is the Hebrew tetragram transliterated

YHWH or JHVH, translated in English as Jehovah. "God" is the translation for *Elohim. Elohim* is a plural word. Since there is no number given with it, one can assume the number is three. In the Hebrew language a noun is singular, dual, or plural. When it is plural, but no number is given, one can assume it to be three. This is, therefore, a reference to the Trinity. It could be translated, "Hear, O Israel: Jehovah, our Trinity is one Jehovah."

Israel lived in a world of idolatry. The nations were polytheists who worshiped many gods. The message that the nation Israel was to give to the world was the message of the unity of the Godhead, the oneness of the Godhead. Jehovah, our Elohim, is one Jehovah. That is the message for a world given over to idolatry.

Today we live in a world, not so much of idolatry and polytheism, but of atheism. In our age we also are to give the message of the Trinity. God is Father, Son, and Holy Spirit. We are talking about the same Jehovah. He is our Elohim, our Trinity. But He is one Jehovah.

And thou shalt love the LORD thy God with all thine heart, and with all thy soul, and with all thy might [Deut. 6:5].

Our Lord Jesus quotes this as being the greatest commandment of all. "And one of the scribes came, and having heard them reasoning together, and perceiving that he had answered them well, asked him, Which is the first commandment of all? And Jesus answered him, The first of all the commandments is, Hear, O Israel; The Lord our God is one Lord: And thou shalt love the Lord thy God with all thy heart, and with all thy soul, and with all thy mind, and with all thy strength: this is the first commandment. And the second is like, namely this, Thou shalt love thy neighbour as thyself. There is none other commandment greater than these" (Mark 12:28–31).

How do you measure up to this? Many of us would have to confess that we do not measure up to this. We do not love Him with all our mind and heart and soul. I must confess that I do not measure up to this; I wish I could, but I must say with Paul, "Brethren, I count not myself to have apprehended: but this one thing I do, forgetting those things which are behind, and reaching forth unto those things which are before, I press toward the mark for the prize of the high calling of God in Christ Jesus" (Phil. 3:13–14). I do want to say that I love Him. I wish I loved Him more than I do, but He is the object of my affection today. I can truly say

that I love Him. That is what He asked Simon Peter. "Do you love Me?" I think He would ask you and me that same question today. To learn to love Him, we must sit at His feet and come to know Him. He is the chiefest among ten thousand. He is the One altogether lovely. He is our God. Peter said, "Lord, to whom shall we go? thou hast the words of eternal life. And we believe and are sure that thou art that Christ, the Son of the living God" (John 6:68–69). He is our Savior. He is our Lord. He is our God. I worship Him. I want to know Him better. What does He mean to you?

"Thou shalt love the Lord thy God with all thine heart, and with all thy soul, and with all thy might." Then the Lord Jesus reached into Leviticus 19:18, and lifted out, "Thou shalt love thy neighbour as thyself." He said the second is like unto the first. Friend, there is no such thing as loving God and hating His people. Remember that when Saul was persecuting the Christians, the Lord Jesus asked him, "Saul, Saul, why persecutest thou me?" (Acts 9:4).

He may be saying the same thing to some Christians today. Although they profess to know and to love the Lord, He asks, "Why are you persecuting Me?" They would protest, "I'm not persecuting You, Lord; I love You!" Then the Lord would answer, "Then why do you criticize Mr. So-and-So so severely? Why are you so opposed to those who are giving out the Word of God today? Why is it that you have become a hindrance instead of a helper?" May I say to you, we must be careful about saying we love Him and then showing our hatred to other believers. It is impossible to talk about loving the Lord while you spend your time trying to destroy the ministry of someone else. That is just blatant, bald, bold hypocrisy.

And these words, which I command thee this day, shall be in thine heart [Deut. 6:6].

You remember that David said, "Thy word have I hid in mine heart, that I might not sin against thee" (Ps. 119:11). That is the place where you and I should have the Word of God today, my friend. It should be in our hearts.

And thou shalt teach them diligently unto thy children, and shalt talk of them when thou sittest in thine house, and when thou walkest by the way, and when thou liest down, and when thou risest up.

And thou shalt bind them for a sign upon thine hand, and they shall be as frontlets between thine eyes.

And thou shalt write them upon the posts of thy house, and on thy gates [Deut. 6:7–9].

Paul says the same thing in Ephesians 6:4: "And, ye fathers, provoke not your children to wrath: but bring them up in the nurture and admonition of the Lord." God holds parents responsible to bring up their children in the discipline and instruction of the Lord. All through the Scriptures there is a great deal said concerning the responsibility of parents. "Train up a child in the way he should go: and when he is old, he will not depart from it" (Prov. 22:6). That does not mean to train him the way *you* want him to go. It means that God has a way for him to go, and you are to cooperate with God. That means, parent, that you need to stay close to Him!

These words were to be kept before them at all times. We see advertising on billboards and in signs and in neon lights. It is no wonder that America today is turning to liquor and to cigarettes and to drugs. This is what is held before our eyes. It is on the television screen, on the radio, in all the advertising. Young people turn to these things because this is what greets them on every hand. God wants His Word to be taught to His people just like that. It should greet them at every turn. Why? Because the human heart is prone to forget God and His ways.

Then God warns His people that they should not forget Him after they get into the land and experience His blessings. It is a strange thing that when people are blessed, they tend to forget the One who blesses them.

Thou shalt fear the LORD thy God, and serve him, and shalt swear by his name [Deut. 6:13].

Our Lord Jesus used this verse when He was tempted by Satan, as recorded in Matthew 4:10 and in Luke 4:8.

Ye shall not tempt the LORD your God, as ye tempted him in Massah [Deut. 6:16].

This is another verse which our Lord used when He withstood the temptation of Satan, which is quoted in Matthew 4:7 and in Luke 4:12. No wonder that Satan hates the book of Deuteronomy and levels his attacks against it!

Again God admonishes His people to diligently do His commandments that they might keep the land He is giving to them, and to explain this to their children, also.

And he brought us out from thence, that he might bring us in, to give us the land which he sware unto our fathers.

And the LORD commanded us to do all these statutes, to fear the LORD our God, for our good always, that he might preserve us alive, as it is at this day.

And it shall be our righteousness, if we observe to do all these commandments before the LORD our God, as he hath commanded us [Deut. 6:23–25].

God had brought them *out* of the land of Egypt. His purpose is to bring them *into* the Promised Land. It is just so with our salvation. God has saved us out of death and sin and judgment. He brings us into the body of Christ, into the place of blessing, into fellowship with Himself, and finally, into heaven itself. However, our salvation is still not complete. He was "delivered for our offenses and was raised again for our justification" (Rom. 4:25). He is our righteousness so that we might stand complete before Him. He has brought us out; He intends to bring us in. Because of this we can say today:

I have been saved. We already have eternal life. We already stand before God in all the righteousness and merit of our Savior. "And this is the record, that God hath given to us eternal life, and this life is in his Son. He that hath the Son hath life; and he that hath not the Son of God hath not life" (1 John 5:11–12).

I am being saved. God is working in my life, shaping, guiding, molding me to conform me more and more to His own dear Son. ". . . Work out your own salvation with fear and trembling. For it is God which worketh in you both to will and to do of his good pleasure" (Phil. 2:12–13). This is not working *for* salvation, but the working *out* of salvation in our lives.

I shall be saved. Don't be discouraged with me, because God is not through with me yet. And I won't be discouraged with you, because God is not through with you either. "Beloved, now are we the sons of God, and it doth not yet appear what we shall be: but we know that, when he shall appear, we shall be like him; for we shall see him as he is" (1 John 3:2).

A dear little lady got up in a testimony meeting and said that every Christian should have printed on his back a sign that reads: "This is not the best that the grace of God can do." How true that is! God is not through with any one of us. But "when he shall appear, we shall be *like him.*"

CHAPTER 7

THEME: Israel to be separate from other nations

When the Lord thy God shall bring thee into the land whither thou goest to possess it, and hath cast out many nations before thee, the Hittites, and the Girgashites, and the Amorites, and the Canaanites, and the Perizzites, and the Hivites, and the Jebusites, seven nations greater and mightier than thou;

And when the Lord thy God shall deliver them before thee; thou shalt smite them, and utterly destroy them; thou shalt make no convenant with them, nor shew mercy unto them [Deut. 7:1–2].

This is very strong language. Remember that God had said, "Thou shalt not kill." That is a command against personal animosity, personal hatred which leads to murder. The Hebrew word is *ratsach*. Here they are directly commanded to *destroy* these people who were living in the land. It is an altogether different Hebrew word—*charam*, meaning to devote (to God or destruction). You may think that is terrible. The liberal today hates the God of the Old Testament. I heard one call God a bully. They don't like the idea that God would actually destroy whole nations. God also says this:

Neither shalt thou make marriages with them; thy daughter thou shalt not give unto his son, nor his daughter shalt thou take unto thy son.

For they will turn away thy son from following me, that they may serve other gods: so will the anger of the Lord be kindled against you, and destroy thee suddenly [Deut. 7:3–4].

Here we have the reason for God's command. These people were eaten up with venereal disease. Had Israel intermarried with them, they would have destroyed the race. Moses didn't understand much about disease germs, but God knows a great deal about them. These people were so polluted and corrupt that God put them out of the land. Not only that, these people were idolatrous, and they would have led Israel into idolatry. So God goes on to tell them that they are to utterly destroy their altars and break down their images. All this polluting influence is to be completely destroyed.

God gives Israel a solemn warning. If they do intermarry and turn to other gods, then God

will put them out of the land. And yet, God makes it very clear to Israel that He is the God of love. He gives these commands because He loves them.

For thou art an holy people unto the Lord thy God: the Lord thy God hath chosen thee to be a special people unto himself, above all people that are upon the face of the earth.

The Lord did not set his love upon you, nor choose you, because ye were more in number than any people; for ye were the fewest of all people [Deut. 7:6–7].

Never a great nation numerically, they would not compare to China or India or other great nations of the world.

But because the Lord loved you, and because he would keep the oath which he had sworn unto your fathers, hath the Lord brought you out with a mighty hand, and redeemed you out of the house of bondmen, from the hand of Pharaoh king of Egypt [Deut. 7:8].

You remember that God said in Exodus that He had heard their cry, that distress cry. He responded because He loved them. He delivered them from bondage for that reason. He keeps repeating this.

Know therefore that the Lord thy God, he is God, the faithful God, which keepeth covenant and mercy with them that love him and keep his commandments to a thousand generations [Deut. 7:9].

What is man's answer to the love of God? It is obedience.

And repayeth them that hate him to their face, to destroy them: he will not be slack to him that hateth him, he will repay him to his face.

Thou shalt therefore keep the commandments, and the statutes, and the judgments, which I command thee this day, to do them [Deut. 7:10–11].

God will bless any people who respond to His love by obedience.

Wherefore it shall come to pass, if ye hearken to these judgments, and keep, and do them, that the Lord thy God

shall keep unto thee the covenant and the mercy which he sware unto thy fathers:

And he will love thee, and bless thee, and multiply thee: he will also bless the fruit of thy womb, and the fruit of thy land, thy corn, and thy wine, and thine oil, the increase of thy kine, and the flocks of thy sheep, in the land which he sware unto thy fathers to give thee [Deut. 7:12–13].

How wonderful it would have been if Israel had believed God!

God encourages them, and He promises them victory—

Thou shalt not be afraid of them: but shalt well remember what the Lord thy God did unto Pharaoh, and unto all Egypt [Deut. 7:18].

The faithfulness of God in the past should be an encouragement for them in the future. Isn't it precisely the same with us?

Thou shalt not be affrighted at them: for the Lord thy God is among you, a mighty God and terrible.

And the Lord thy God will put out those nations before thee by little and little: thou mayest not consume them at once,

lest the beasts of the field increase upon thee [Deut. 7:21–22].

We see God's wisdom here. He is thinking of their safety, knowing that if the population were destroyed suddenly, the wild animals would take over the land.

But the Lord thy God shall deliver them unto thee, and shall destroy them with a mighty destruction, until they be destroyed [Deut. 7:23].

All these nations were to be put out of the land and utterly destroyed because of their abominations. Now don't say that God had not been patient with them. Way back in Genesis 15:16 God had told Abraham that his descendants would not come back into the land until the fourth generation "for the iniquity of the Amorites is not yet full." God gave these people 430 years to see whether they would turn to God and turn from their sins. Friends, how much more time do you want God to give them? Do you know any other landlord who will give his tenant that long a time to pay his rent? God gave them a time of mercy that lasted for 430 years. Then the cup of iniquity was full, and the judgment of God fell upon them. So let us not have a false kind of pity for these nations. Rather, let us learn from these events. God is a God of mercy and of love in the Old Testament as well as He is in the New Testament.

CHAPTER 8

THEME: *God's past dealings give assurance for the future*

In this section of the restating of the Law, we come now to the portion dealing with religious and national regulations, which will be continued through chapter 21.

All the commandments which I command thee this day shall ye observe to do, that ye may live, and multiply, and go in and possess the land which the Lord sware unto your fathers [Deut. 8:1].

Here is the new generation, standing on the east bank of the Jordan river. They are ready to cross over into the land with high anticipation and hope. As Moses is preparing them to enter the land, he encourages them to obey God.

And thou shalt remember all the way which the Lord thy God led thee these forty years in the wilderness, to humble thee, and to prove thee, to know what was in thine heart, whether thou wouldest keep his commandments, or no [Deut. 8:2].

God wants them to remember the past. They should see in the past that God has been dealing with them, that He has been testing and training them.

God wants us to remember our past, too. Paul put it like this for the believer: "Being confident of this very thing, that he which hath begun a good work in you will perform it until the day of Jesus Christ" (Phil. 1:6). We are to remember that God has led us and blessed us. Isn't this true for you? Can't you say that God has brought you up to this very moment? If He has done that in the past, He will continue to do so in the future. Remembering is for our encouragement. It is to give us assurance for the future.

Why did God test Israel in the wilderness? It was to humble them and to prove what was really in their hearts. That explains why God puts you and me through the mill. Sometimes He puts us in the furnace and heaps it on very hot. Why? To test us and to humble us. Little man is proud, he's cocky, he is self-confident, and, to be frank, he is an abomination! Listen to the boasting and bragging and the pride with which little man walks the earth. So God must take His own people and put them through the mill in order to humble them and to prove them.

You know, testing really proves the metal. Tests will reveal whether or not a person is really a child of God. Our churches today are filled with affluent people who have never been tested. I can't tell whether or not they are genuine. The man who has been tested is the man in whom you can have confidence.

And he humbled thee, and suffered thee to hunger, and fed thee with manna, which thou knewest not, neither did thy fathers know; that he might make thee know that man doth not live by bread only, but by every word that proceedeth out of the mouth of the LORD doth man live [Deut. 8:3].

Our Lord quoted this verse when He was tempted in the wilderness (Matt. 4:4 and Luke 4:4). If the Lord Jesus had not quoted this, we would probably pass by the great spiritual lesson that is here. God has been good to us. He has blessed us in many, many ways with material things. The important lesson is that God gives us those things in order that we might see that there is a spiritual wealth, the Word of God. It is the Word of God that is the real wealth for the child of God today.

Thy raiment waxed not old upon thee, neither did thy foot swell, these forty years [Deut. 8:4].

Here is a strange, marvelous, miraculous statement! Imagine having a suit of clothes that would not wear out. I know the ladies would not like this at all. Year after year the wife could tell her hubby that she needed a new dress, and year after year the husband could say that the one she was wearing looked brand new. I tell you, after that went on for forty years, the women would be pretty far behind in the styles. However in the wilderness the styles didn't change; so it really didn't make any difference. Seriously, this is marvelous; it is a miracle.

"Neither did thy foot swell, these forty years." A missionary doctor explained to me that out in the Orient where he served, the people had a sameness of diet. They did not get all the vitamins they needed; so they would show the manifestations of beriberi. One of the symptoms is a swelling of the feet. Now, you see, Israel got all their vitamins. They got all the nourishment that they needed. What did these folks eat for forty years? Why, it was manna. God fed them with manna, which was a miracle food. It provided everything they needed for the nourishment of their bodies.

Spiritual manna is the Word of God. It is a wonderful food. It will supply all your needs. I marvel at the letters I receive that attest to this. Someone will say that when I spoke on a certain chapter, that passage brought comfort to his heart. Someone else will write that he was in sin and had gotten away from God, had become cold and indifferent, and that passage from the Word of God brought him back. Someone else writes to say he listened and was saved. You see, friend, you won't get any swelling of the feet if you will read the Word of God. In other words, the Bible will meet your individual needs, whatever they may be. This is manna.

God promised temporal blessings to the nation Israel if they would serve Him.

Thou shalt also consider in thine heart, that, as a man chasteneth his son, so the LORD thy God chasteneth thee.

Therefore thou shalt keep the commandments of the LORD thy God, to walk in his ways, and to fear him.

For the LORD thy God bringeth thee into a good land, a land of brooks of water, of fountains and depths that spring out of valleys and hills;

A land of wheat, and barley, and vines, and fig trees, and pomegranates; a land of oil olive, and honey;

A land wherein thou shalt eat bread without scarceness, thou shalt not lack any thing in it; a land whose stones are iron, and out of whose hills thou mayest dig brass [Deut. 8:5–9].

God does not give this promise to Christians today. I would have you note this. There is a lopsided notion that if you are a faithful Christian, God will prosper you in temporal things. My friend, that is not true. God promised to prosper Israel in the land. He does not promise to prosper the Christian in the things of this world.

Now I know that there are Christians who are outstanding, successful business men. They say they took God into partnership, and God blessed them abundantly. He does do that, and we praise Him for it. But that is not what He has promised to do. This is the *promise* to the Christian: "Blessed be the God and Father of our Lord Jesus Christ, who hath blessed us with all spiritual blessings in heavenly places in Christ" (Eph. 1:3). He has promised us *spiritual* blessings. There is no verse in the New Testament which promises temporal blessing to the child of God today.

May I also add that although God does not *promise* temporal blessings, He sometimes does add them. God does this for some, but not for all. There are wonderful Christians whom the Lord has blessed financially. Some of them have been a great help to us in broadcasting the Word of God by radio. But I also want to say that some of the choicest children of God today have been blessed with spiritual blessings and not with the things of this world. They seem to be the happiest, and they seem actually to do more for God than anyone else. Certainly they have been a blessing to this poor preacher and a blessing to the cause of Christ in the world.

One of the major distinctions between the nation Israel in the Old Testament and the church in the New Testament is that God promised Israel temporal blessings and He promises us spiritual blessings. If you keep this straight it will prevent a great deal of heartache. Also, it will cause a great many children of God to rejoice rather than to lapse into a backslidden condition. My friend, if you are on a low economic level, cash in on some of your spiritual blessings so that you may enjoy the riches He has promised you.

When thou hast eaten and art full, then thou shalt bless the LORD thy God for the good land which he hath given thee.

Beware that thou forget not the LORD thy God, in not keeping his commandments, and his judgments, and his statutes, which I command thee this day [Deut. 8:10–11].

He continues his warning to Israel for the coming days of prosperity.

Then thine heart be lifted up, and thou forget the LORD thy God, which brought thee forth out of the land of Egypt, from the house of bondage;

Who led thee through that great and terrible wilderness, wherein were fiery serpents, and scorpions, and drought, where there was no water; who brought thee forth water out of the rock of flint;

Who fed thee in the wilderness with manna, which thy fathers knew not, that he might humble thee, and that he might prove thee, to do thee good at thy latter end [Deut. 8:14–16].

At the "latter end," in the future Millennium, God promises to make Israel the leading nation with earthly blessings. God has not promised that to the church, my friend; so don't appropriate that promise for yourself. The Lord Jesus said, ". . . I go to prepare a place for you. And if I go and prepare a place for you, I will come again, and receive you unto myself; that where I am, there ye may be also" (John 14:2–3). The hope of the child of God today is that Christ is coming to take us out of this world. The hope of Israel is *in* this world. That distinction is of utmost importance.

If you try to mix these promises, it will cause utter confusion. Too many so-called theologians use a blender. They put the whole Bible into a blender, and they really mix it up! If you let the Bible stand as it is, you will see that God is very specific when He makes promises.

And thou say in thine heart, My power and the might of mine hand hath gotten me this wealth.

But thou shalt remember the LORD thy God: for it is he that giveth thee power to get wealth, that he may establish his covenant which he sware unto thy fathers, as it is this day [Deut. 8:17–18].

When the nation of Israel is in the land and is being prospered, then you can know it is obeying God. When it is not prospering in that land, it is an indication that it is not obeying God. Look at Israel today and make your own decision.

And it shall be, if thou do at all forget the LORD thy God, and walk after other gods, and serve them, and worship them, I testify against you this day that ye shall surely perish.

As the nations which the LORD destroyeth before your face, so shall ye perish; because ye would not be obe-

dient unto the voice of the Lord your God [Deut. 8:19–20].

This is God's warning to them. He promises to bless them if they will be obedient to Him. If they are not obedient, He will treat them as He treated those nations that were in that land before them. The fact of the matter is that God treated them even worse than the nations that preceded them. Do you know why? Because Israel had been given more light. Light creates responsibility before God.

CHAPTER 9

THEME: God knew Israel's past failure

God is reviewing for this new generation the past of the nation Israel. Their past was not good. God did not save them because they were good. He didn't call them because they were an outstanding nation. They were not.

God has not saved us because we are outstanding, or superior, or even good. The only kind of people God is saving is bad people. I am reminded of an incident when I was walking behind some members of the church I was serving. As we were walking through a park, a bum begged them for some money. We had encouraged our members to send such people to the mission where they would be helped. But this fellow didn't want that—he wanted money to buy wine. When I came along, the beggar told me that the folk ahead, who had gone into the church, thought they were better than anybody else. I answered him, "It's quite interesting that you say they think they are better than anyone else. I happen to know them, and I remember the day they came to Christ. Do you know why they came?" He looked at me in amazement. "They came because they thought they were *worse* than anybody else. They thought they were sinners and needed a Savior. That is why they came to Christ." You see, he had the idea, which is commonly expressed, that the church is made up of people who think they are better than other folks. Now that may be true in some cases. If it is true, the church is certainly not a church in the New Testament sense. God saves us because we are bad, because we are sinners.

Hear, O Israel: Thou art to pass over Jordan this day, to go in to possess nations greater and mightier than thyself, cities great and fenced up to heaven [Deut. 9:1].

"This day" does not refer to a twenty-four-hour day, but to the time when they will enter the land.

A people great and tall, the children of the Anakims, whom thou knowest, and of whom thou hast heard say, Who can stand before the children of Anak! [Deut. 9:2].

God gives a report on the land which is worse than the report the spies had brought back. God knew the land and God knew who was in the land, yet God had told them to go in. They had refused to go in because they didn't believe God. God knew that the people there were giants. He knew all the difficulties. He had promised to go into the land with them.

It was Martin Luther who said, "One with God is a majority." My friend, if you are with God, you are with the majority. Actually, Christians belong to a minority group down here in this world. But I'll tell you something the world doesn't know: with God, we are a majority. One with God is a majority.

Understand therefore this day, that the Lord thy God is he which goeth over before thee; as a consuming fire he shall destroy them, and he shall bring them down before thy face: so shalt thou drive them out, and destroy them quickly, as the Lord hath said unto thee [Deut. 9:3].

God takes the responsibility of putting them out of the land. God is the Landlord. He is the Creator. He has a right to do this. When I hear a fellow who is liberal in his theology complain about this, I feel like saying, "You little pipsqueak, you keep quiet. You and I are just little creatures down here." God is the sovereign Creator; we are the creatures.

Speak not thou in thine heart, after that the Lord thy God hath cast them out

from before thee, saying, For my righteousness the LORD hath brought me in to possess this land: but for the wickedness of these nations the LORD doth drive them out from before thee [Deut. 9:4].

God is saying that He is driving the other nations out because they are wicked nations—not because the people He was putting in there were righteous. God makes that abundantly clear.

Not for thy righteousness, or for the uprightness of thine heart, dost thou go to possess their land: but for the wickedness of these nations the LORD thy God doth drive them out from before thee, and that he may perform the word which the LORD sware unto thy fathers, Abraham, Isaac, and Jacob [Deut. 9:5].

God did not come down to deliver Israel because they were a wonderful people. He knew all the time that they were a stiff-necked people, but He heard their cry in Egypt. And friend, if you recognize that you are a sinner and need a Savior, then you will need to cry to Him for salvation. He will hear you. Do you know why? Not because of who you are, but for Christ's sake. If you will turn to Christ in faith, He will save you.

Understand therefore, that the LORD thy God giveth thee not this good land to possess it for thy righteousness; for thou art a stiffnecked people [Deut. 9:6].

Do you know that God does not save you and me because we are good? We are sinners. He saves us for Christ's sake, not for our sake. Friend, if you think that somehow or other God will find something in you that merits salvation, forget it, because you will be disappointed. God knows you, and He says He can't find anything righteous in you at all. It is for Christ's sake that God saves us, and God finds everything we need in Him. How wonderful that is! You see that in this passage of Deuteronomy there is the seed for the gospel of the grace of God.

ISRAEL'S PAST FAILURE

Remember, and forget not, how thou provokedst the LORD thy God to wrath in the wilderness: from the day that thou didst depart out of the land of Egypt, until ye came unto this place, ye have been rebellious against the LORD [Deut. 9:7].

Moses directs them back over their past history and refers specifically to the time when they made the golden calf. If we turn back to Exodus 32:4 we read, "And he received them at their hand . . . ," referring to the golden earrings. The women, and the men, too, took off their golden earrings and gave them to Aaron. Those golden earrings were a sign of idolatry (generally they were worn in one ear only). These people had lapsed back into idolatry very quickly. Aaron took the golden earrings, and with a graving tool he fashioned a molten calf. And they said, "These be thy gods, O Israel, which brought thee up out of the land of Egypt." Now God calls them to remember this. God reminded them of that again in Psalm 106:19. "They made a calf in Horeb, and worshiped the molten image." God asked them to remember, but they forgot.

Also in Horeb ye provoked the LORD to wrath, so that the LORD was angry with you to have destroyed you [Deut. 9:8].

Moses goes on with his narrative:

And the LORD said unto me, Arise, get thee down quickly from hence; for thy people which thou hast brought forth out of Egypt have corrupted themselves; they are quickly turned aside out of the way which I commanded them; they have made them a molten image [Deut. 9:12].

At the very time they were making the molten calf, Moses was in the mount getting the commandments, and two of these commandments were against that very thing: "Thou shalt have no other gods. Thou shalt not make unto thee any graven image." Notice that God says to Moses, "They're your people. You brought them out of Egypt." Moses will answer that in just a moment.

Furthermore the LORD spake unto me, saying, I have seen this people, and behold, it is a stiffnecked people [Deut. 9:13].

The Lord repeats this again—He knew all the time that Israel was a stiffnecked people. He knows you and me also, and can probably say the same thing about us.

Let me alone, that I may destroy them, and blot out their name from under heaven: and I will make of thee a nation mightier and greater than they [Deut. 9:14].

This must have been a temptation for Moses, but he resisted it. His pleading for Israel is recorded in Exodus 33:12–17. Moses would not go up into the land without the presence of the Lord. He said, "If thy presence go not with me, carry us not up hence." Moses identified himself with the people.

When Moses came down from the mount, he saw what they had done.

And I looked, and, behold, ye had sinned against the Lord your God, and had made you a molten calf: ye had turned aside quickly out of the way which the Lord had commanded you [Deut. 9:16].

At the very moment when God was giving them the commandments, they were turning from Him—yet they were saying they would obey Him. People can be more phony in religion than in anything else. It seems to be something that is characteristic of the human nature. Even people who are really sincere are as phony as can be. We all need to pray the prayer of the psalmist, "Search me, O God, and know my heart: try me, and know my thoughts: And see if there be any wicked way in me, and lead me in the way everlasting" (Ps. 139:23–24). Every child of God needs to pray this. Paul has this admonition for the believers: "Examine yourselves, whether ye be in the faith; prove your own selves. Know ye not your own selves, how that Jesus Christ is in you, except ye be reprobates?" (2 Cor. 13:5). Check whether you are in the faith or not. I believe and I preach the security of the believer, my friend. I believe that the believer is secure. But I also believe and preach the insecurity of the make-believer. There are a lot of make-believers. We need to search our hearts, every one of us.

And I took the two tables, and cast them out of my two hands, and brake them before your eyes.

And I fell down before the Lord, as at the first, forty days and forty nights: I did neither eat bread, nor drink water, because of all your sins which ye sinned, in doing wickedly in the sight of the Lord, to provoke him to anger [Deut. 9:17–18].

I want you to notice that Moses knew God. The psalmist says, "He made known his ways unto Moses, his acts unto the children of Israel" (Ps. 103:7). The children of Israel saw the mountain smoke, they saw the judgment of God, they saw His glory, but they did not know Him. Moses knew Him! Moses knew His ways.

Moses understood two things about God which are revealed here. They are paradoxical, but they are not contradictory.

Moses knew that God hates sin. May I say to you that we today do not have the faintest conception of how God hates sin and how He intends to punish it. Moses went down on his face before God and fasted and cried out to God for forty days and forty nights! Why? Because Moses knew the ways of God. He knew how God hates sin.

The average Christian today does not seem to realize how God hates sin in his life. My friend, God never ignores a sin we commit. God will deal with sin in your life and in my life. I have been a pastor for a long time, and I have observed church people over the years. I want to say to you that I have watched people in the church play fast and loose with God. I have seen them cut corners and put up a front. The days melt into years, and then I have seen the hand of God move in judgment on their lives. Sometimes the judgment has been extremely severe. I can especially remember a man who came to me and actually dropped down on his knees and cried out that he just could not stand what God was putting him through. He had lost his children, lost his family. I can remember him as a young upstart, a young married man, who thought he could play fast and loose with God. God hates sin. God punishes sin.

Moses also knew the mercy of God. Moses comes to God because he trusts in His mercy. God will punish sin, but, my friend, we do not comprehend how wonderful He is. He is so gracious. He extends mercy to the sinner. He has extended His mercy to you, I am sure. I know He has to me. And the Lord extended mercy to Israel. Listen:

For I was afraid of the anger and hot displeasure, wherewith the Lord was wroth against you to destroy you. But the Lord hearkened unto me at that time also [Deut. 9:19].

God did not hear the prayer of Moses because of who he was. God heard his prayer because He is merciful. Paul makes this clear in Romans 9:15, "For he saith to Moses, I will have mercy on whom I will have mercy, and I will have compassion on whom I will have compassion." God is sovereign, and He sovereignly extends His mercy. How wonderful He is. You and I do not fully comprehend those two attributes of God: His hatred of sin and His mercy.

And the Lord was very angry with Aaron to have destroyed him: and I prayed for Aaron also the same time.

And I took your sin, the calf which ye had made, and burnt it with fire, and stamped it, and ground it very small, even until it was as small as dust: and I cast the dust thereof into the brook that descended out of the mount [Deut. 9:20–21].

If this incident weren't so tragic, it would be humorous. Moses makes the people drink their idol.

And at Taberah, and at Massah, and at Kibroth-hattaavah, ye provoked the LORD to wrath.

Likewise, when the LORD sent you from Kadesh-barnea, saying, Go up and possess the land which I have given you; then ye rebelled against the commandment of the LORD your God, and ye believed him not, nor hearkened to his voice.

Ye have been rebellious against the LORD from the day that I knew you [Deut. 9:22–24].

This is a summary. There never was a day when these people were really found faithful to God. What a picture! We tend to point to them in criticism, but what about the believer today? I am afraid there are many of us, even in conservative churches, who are not faithful to God for a single day. We boast that we are sound in the faith—sound all right—sound asleep!

Thus I fell down before the LORD forty days and forty nights, as I fell down at the first; because the LORD had said he would destroy you [Deut. 9:25].

This was after they refused to go into the land

at Kadesh-Barnea. Moses knew God. Moses knew that God judges sin.

I prayed therefore unto the LORD, and said, O Lord GOD, destroy not thy people and thine inheritance, which thou hast redeemed through thy greatness, which thou hast brought forth out of Egypt with a mighty hand.

Remember thy servants, Abraham, Isaac, and Jacob; look not unto the stubbornness of this people, nor to their wickedness, nor to their sin:

Lest the land whence thou broughtest us out say, Because the LORD was not able to bring them into the land which he promised them, and because he hated them, he hath brought them out to slay them in the wilderness.

Yet they are thy people and thine inheritance, which thou broughtest out by thy mighty power and by thy stretched out arm [Deut. 9:26–29].

Moses knew how to pray. I wish I knew how to pray like that! Remember that back in verse 12 God said, "For thy people which thou hast brought forth out of Egypt have corrupted themselves." Now imagine Moses saying to God that He has made a mistake! Moses says, "They are not my people; they are Yours. I didn't bring them out of Egypt; *You* did. They belong to You." Moses reminds God that the people in the land would think He was unable to bring Israel into the land—that He was able to bring Israel out of Egypt, but He was not able to bring them into the land. That kind of praying moves the hand of God. Here Israel stands, ready now to enter the land which reveals that Moses knew how to pray!

CHAPTER 10

THEME: *God sent Israel to Egypt; God brought them out of Egypt*

As Moses has said in his prayer, Israel belongs to God; they are His inheritance. He will not destroy them because of their sin but graciously give them again the Ten Commandments, written by Himself.

At that time the Lord said unto me, Hew thee two tables of stone like unto the first, and come up unto me into the mount, and make thee an ark of wood.

And I will write on the tables the words that were in the first tables which thou brakest, and thou shalt put them in the ark [Deut. 10:1–2].

Moses brought the tables of stone down and placed them in the ark. Then the children of Israel continued on their journey.

At that time the Lord separated the tribe of Levi, to bear the ark of the covenant of the Lord, to stand before the Lord to minister unto him, and to bless in his name, unto this day.

Wherefore Levi hath no part nor inheritance with his brethren; the Lord is his inheritance, according as the Lord thy God promised him [Deut. 10:8–9).

There are great spiritual lessons in this for us. As Levi was the priestly tribe, so today the church is a kingdom of priests. That is, every believer in Jesus Christ is a priest. I am not a Roman Catholic priest, but I am a "catholic" priest (as is every believer in Christ) in the sense that *catholic* means "general." The New Testament priest is to offer himself to God for worship, intercession, and service (Rom. 12:1–2). And he is to exercise a gift as a priest according to 1 Corinthians 12. And every believer, as a priest, has a gift to exercise in the church.

Notice that the tribe of Levi was to have no material inheritance. God was their inheritance. God had promised to give land, a certain amount of acreage, to the other tribes. And when He blessed them, it was temporal blessing. He did not promise that to Levi. This is also the position of the believer today. Like Levi, our inheritance is in God. We are blessed with all spiritual blessings in the heavenlies.

And now, Israel, what doth the Lord thy God require of thee, but to fear the Lord thy God, to walk in all his ways, and to love him, and to serve the Lord thy God with all thy heart and with all thy soul [Deut. 10:12].

Now do not make the mistake of thinking this is the gospel. It is not the gospel. You and I ought to thank God for that, because if it depended on this, you and I wouldn't be blessed very much.

To keep the commandments of the Lord, and his statutes, which I command thee this day for thy good? [Deut. 10:13].

If Israel had kept them, they would have been blessed. When they broke them, judgment came upon them. God, for fifteen hundred years, demonstrated through Israel to the world and to you and me that He cannot save people by Law. These people under favorable circumstances, in a land geared to the Law, were unable to keep it. And if *they* were unable to keep it, then you and I are unable to keep it. Thank God, He saves by grace today. In fact, grace has always been His method. In the Old Testament He never saved anyone by Law. They were saved by His mercy and grace to them, looking forward to the coming of Christ to die on the cross to take away their sins.

He doth execute the judgment of the fatherless and widow, and loveth the stranger, in giving him food and raiment [Deut. 10:18].

God loved the stranger. And He reminded these people that they had been strangers in the land of Egypt.

Love ye therefore the stranger: for ye were strangers in the land of Egypt.

Thou shalt fear the Lord thy God; him shalt thou serve, and to him shalt thou cleave, and swear by his name [Deut. 10:19–20].

The Lord Jesus quoted this to answer Satan, you remember. Our Lord certainly was familiar with the Book of Deuteronomy, as probably every Israelite was in that day.

Thy fathers went down into Egypt with threescore and ten persons; and now the Lord thy God hath made thee as the stars of heaven for multitude [Deut. 10:22].

The evident blessing of God was upon them. He sent them down into Egypt; He brought them out of Egypt. God was responsible, and He didn't mind taking that responsibility.

CHAPTER 11

THEME: *The Promised Land unlike Egypt; principle of occupancy of the land.*

God talks to them here about the land they are about to enter. The Promised Land will not be at all like Egypt. And God will give them the principles required for occupancy of the land.

A CALL TO COMMITMENT

Therefore thou shalt love the Lord thy God, and keep his charge, and his statutes, and his judgments, and his commandments, always [Deut. 11:1].

The response to the love of God is obedience.

Therefore shall ye keep all the commandments which I command you this day, that ye may be strong, and go in and possess the land, whither ye go to possess it;

And that ye may prolong your days in the land, which the Lord sware unto your fathers to give unto them and to their seed, a land that floweth with milk and honey [Deut. 11:8–9].

They were accustomed to irrigated fields down in Egypt.

For the land, wither thou goest in to possess it, is not as the land of Egypt, from whence ye came out, where thou sowedst thy seed, and wateredst it with thy foot, as a garden of herbs [Deut. 11:10].

When I was in Egypt I was told that the rainfall there is less than one inch a year. Now that is not much rainfall! I've been to a place in the Hawaiian Islands where the rainfall is over 100 inches a year. That is quite a difference. Obviously, Egypt was dependent upon irrigation.

PRINCIPLE OF OCCUPANCY
OF THE LAND

But the land, whither ye go to possess it, is a land of hills and valleys, and drinketh water of the rain of heaven:

A land which the Lord thy God careth for: the eyes of the Lord thy God are always upon it, from the beginning of the year even unto the end of the year.

And it shall come to pass, if ye shall hearken diligently unto my commandments which I command you this day, to love the Lord your God, and to serve him with all your heart and with all your soul.

That I will give you the rain of your land in his due season, the first rain and the latter rain, that thou mayest gather in thy corn, and thy wine, and thine oil.

And I will send grass in thy fields for thy cattle, that thou mayest eat and be full [Deut. 11:11–15].

The land these people were going to enter would be a little difficult to irrigate because it was hilly. Of course they didn't have the equipment for it in that day. The land would depend upon the rain from heaven. God did this purposely. He put them on a land that had to depend upon Him for rainfall. This would draw the people closer to God.

The reason that land is desolate today, as we shall see in Deuteronomy, is because the judgment of God is upon it. The minute water is put into that soil, the desert blossoms as a rose. It is water that it needs, and they are having trouble with water there even today. God told them that they would be dependent upon rain. If they would obey Him, He would bless them with the former and latter rains; that is, the fall and spring rainfall. By looking at that land you can see the spiritual condition of the people.

In an affluent society such as we live in today, where things come so easily, I am afraid that people assume God has nothing in the world to do with it. I do not understand why people think that if things come easily, they have done it; if things come with difficulty, then God must be in it. Well, God is the One who provides for all our physical needs. Whether things come to us easily or with difficulty, He still is the Provider.

> For if ye shall diligently keep all these commandments which I command you, to do them, to love the LORD your God, to walk in all his ways, and to cleave unto him [Deut. 11:22].

The great principle of their occupancy of the land is given here.

> Then will the LORD drive out all these nations from before you, and ye shall possess greater nations and mightier than yourselves.

> Every place whereon the soles of your feet shall tread shall be yours: from the wilderness and Lebanon, from the river, the river Euphrates, even unto the uttermost sea shall your coast be.

> There shall no man be able to stand before you: for the LORD your God shall lay the fear of you and the dread of you upon all the land that ye shall tread upon, as he hath said unto you [Deut. 11:23–25].

You will notice that the land is a gift from God. He has given to them a land which is much greater than anything they have ever occupied. It was from the river Euphrates to the Mediterranean Sea, and from Lebanon all the way south into the desert that they had come through. This was approximately 300,000 square miles. They have never occupied more than about 30,000 square miles of it, even at the time when the kingdom reached its zenith under David and Solomon.

"Every place whereon the soles of your feet shall tread shall be yours." It had been given to them by God and it was theirs, but they failed to walk upon it, claim it, and enjoy it. God told Joshua the same thing. He told him that the land was right there before them and that it belonged to Israel. But He told them they had to go in and walk up and down in the land. They had to possess it.

Why is there such a difference in believers today? Some Christians are sitting on the side lines and are poverty stricken spiritually. Others are fabulously rich spiritually. God makes it clear that He has blessed all believers with spiritual blessings in the heavenlies in Christ Jesus. Some believers claim those blessings; some do not. Some believers enjoy those blessings; some do not. It is a matter of appropriating that which we already possess.

> Behold, I set before you this day a blessing and a curse [Deut. 11:26].

Israel was commanded to obey. Obedience was the very nub of the matter.

> A blessing, if ye obey the commandments of the LORD your God, which I command you this day [Deut. 11:27].

Obedience is something which has been dropped into the background today. I believe in the grace of God. I preach the grace of God. We are saved by grace, we are kept by grace, we grow by the grace of God. We are going to get to heaven by the grace of God. When we've been there ten thousand years, it will still be by the grace of God. But, my friend, there are great spiritual blessings today which you are going to miss if you are not obedient to Him. Jesus told us, "If ye love me, keep my commandments" (John 14:15). Obedience offers a personal, wonderful, glorious relationship with God.

The opposite is also true. Disobedience brings with it a curse.

> And a curse, if ye will not obey the commandments of the LORD your God, but turn aside out of the way which I command you this day, to go after other gods, which ye have not known [Deut. 11:28].

You will notice that the great issue over which God is pleading with Israel is idolatry. There was always the danger that they would turn from Jehovah, their God, and lapse back into idolatry.

CHAPTER 12

Later in the history of Israel, God chose Jerusalem as the place where the temple was to be built. They were to go there to worship God. Why didn't God permit the worship in every other place? I think the reason is obvious. There was idolatry in the land, and they were commanded to destroy it. Because they did not destroy it, they were commanded to assemble in one place for worship. This unified their worship and brought them closer together as a nation. They were one when they went up to Jerusalem for the feasts.

Today we do not need to meet in one place to worship God. The Lord Jesus told the Samaritan woman the reason why this is true. "Jesus saith unto her, Woman, believe me, the hour cometh, when ye shall neither in this mountain, nor yet at Jerusalem, worship the Father. Ye worship ye know not what: we know what we worship: for salvation is of the Jews. But the hour cometh, and now is, when the true worshipers shall worship the Father in spirit and in truth; for the Father seeketh such to worship him. God is a Spirit: and they that worship him must worship him in spirit and in truth" (John 4:21–24).

Believers do not meet in one *place* to worship God today; we meet around One *Person* and that Person is the Lord Jesus Christ. That is the important thing to keep in mind today. The name of your church doesn't make the difference. The denomination or lack of denomination of your church doesn't make the difference. The all-important question is this: do you meet around the person of Jesus Christ? Now, friends, if you don't, that is idolatry, because then you are meeting around something that is replacing Christ. If you are meeting to socialize or be entertained, that is idolatry. The thing that is to draw us together into a oneness is the person of Jesus Christ. How important that is!

These are the statutes and judgments, which ye shall observe to do in the land, which the LORD God of thy fathers giveth thee to possess it, all the days that ye live upon the earth.

Ye shall utterly destroy all the places, wherein the nations which ye shall possess served their gods, upon the high mountains, and upon the hills, and under every green tree:

And ye shall overthrow their altars, and break their pillars, and burn their groves with fire; and ye shall hew down the graven images of their gods, and destroy the names of them out of that place.

Ye shall not do so unto the LORD your God [Deut. 12:1–4].

The reason the judgments of God came upon Israel, one after the other in the times of the judges, was because the people had lapsed into idolatry. Then that great prophet Elijah leveled his message against idolatry in the land. The reason Israel went into the Babylonian captivity was idolatry. The warning in the last book of the Old Testament is about the danger of idolatry.

We should not think we are immune to idolatry today. We tend to think we are such enlightened folks that we would not fall down and worship an idol. Can we be so sure about that, friends? Anything, *anything* that comes between our souls and God becomes an idol. I know a young man whom I saw grow up in the church and seemingly become a sweet Christian. Later he became a member of a large corporation. Because he had wonderful ability, he began to move up in the organization. The farther he moved up in the corporation, the farther he moved away from God. Today his job comes first. I was holding meetings in a distant city where he lives, and he invited Mrs. McGee and me for dinner, for old time's sake. He made it very clear to me that he would not be able to come to any of the meetings because of his business. Business, his position, his advancements—they had become his idol, his god. Talk about worship! He fell down before that idol seven days a week!

Anything that comes between your soul and your God is your idol.

But unto the place which the LORD your God shall choose out of all your tribes to put his name there, even unto his habitation shall ye seek, and thither thou shalt come [Deut. 12:5].

Eventually, the designated place was Jerusalem. But even before that, Israel was to worship in one place only. There was to be one place for their burnt offerings, sacrifices, tithes, and vows. The tithes of food which they brought before the Lord had to be eaten in this one place.

Notwithstanding thou mayest kill and eat flesh in all thy gates, whatsoever thy soul lusteth after, according to the blessing of the LORD thy God which he hath given thee: the unclean and the clean may eat thereof, as of the roebuck, and as of the hart.

Only ye shall not eat the blood; ye shall pour it upon the earth as water [Deut. 12:15–16].

There was also food which they ate at home. This was not a part of their worship, but this, too, was regulated by dietary laws. In Chapter 14 we will find an extensive list of clean and unclean animals. A person did not need to be ceremonially clean to be able to eat at home. Also, in addition to the animals which were sacrificial animals, he could eat wild game so long as it was a clean animal. The stipulation given was that the blood was not to be eaten. In contrast, anything that was an offering to the Lord had to be eaten before the Lord in the one place which God would designate.

If the place which the LORD thy God hath chosen to put his name there be too far from thee, then thou shalt kill of thy herd and of thy flock, which the LORD hath given thee, as I have commanded thee, and thou shalt eat in thy gates whatsoever thy soul lusteth after.

Even as the roebuck and the hart is eaten, so thou shalt eat them: the unclean and the clean shall eat of them alike.

Only be sure that thou eat not the blood: for the blood is the life; and thou mayest not eat the life with the flesh.

Thou shalt not eat it; thou shalt pour it upon the earth as water.

Thou shalt not eat it; that it may go well with thee, and with thy children after thee, when thou shalt do that which is right in the sight of the LORD [Deut. 12:21–25].

In Leviticus 17, while Israel was in the wilderness camp, they were told that every time an ox, or lamb, or goat was killed, it had to be brought to the door of the tabernacle and the priest would sprinkle the blood upon the altar and would offer the fat as a sweet savor to God. This was to prevent them from making any offering to devils. After they will settle in the land, it is obvious that many people will live too far away from Jerusalem to bring every animal there before they kill it for food. So the Lord tells them again that an animal may be killed for food, but they shall not eat the blood of the animal. The blood represents the life, which is the reason that Scripture puts such an emphasis on the blood of Jesus Christ.

When the LORD thy God shall cut off the nations from before thee, whither thou goest to possess them, and thou succeedest them, and dwellest in their land;

Take heed to thyself that thou be not snared by following them, after that they be destroyed from before thee; and that thou inquire not after their gods, saying, How did these nations serve their gods? even so will I do likewise.

Thou shalt not do so unto the LORD thy God: for every abomination to the LORD, which he hateth, have they done unto their gods; for even their sons and their daughters they have burnt in the fire to their gods [Deut. 12:29–31].

They are told over and over again that they are to destroy the nations which are in the land so that they do not become ensnared by them. These nations were idolatrous. In the worship of Baal, as in the worship of many pagan religions, they had that most cruel practice of offering their own children. They would heat an idol red hot and then drop their babies into the arms of this red hot idol. I can't think of anything more horrible than that. God says He hates such a practice. It is an abomination to Him. I find that God hates many things that I hate. I hope that I can learn more and more to hate what He hates and love what He loves.

What thing soever I command you, observe to do it: thou shalt not add thereto, nor diminish from it [Deut. 12:32].

They are to give heed to these commandments which the Lord gives them. If they disobey God, God will treat them as He treats the other nations. God doesn't watch the actions of some people and disregard others. I have never understood why some Christians think they can get by with certain things that other people do not get by with. Sin is sin. If Israel does not obey the Lord, she will not be spared. So the encouragement for them is to observe to do what the Lord commands them.

CHAPTER 13

THEME: Warning against and test of false prophets

This is a very important chapter because it deals with false prophets and false gods. When we get to chapter 18 of Deuteronomy, we will find the test which would identify a false prophet. Israel had no problem in detecting the false prophets because they had a biblical, God-given test that surely would ferret them out. However, the chapter before us deals with the action that was to be taken against anyone who attempted to lead God's people away from Him by introducing false religions.

> If there arise among you a prophet, or a dreamer of dreams, and giveth thee a sign or a wonder.
>
> And the sign or the wonder come to pass, whereof he spake unto thee, saying, Let us go after other gods, which thou hast not known, and let us serve them;
>
> Thou shalt not hearken unto the words of that prophet, or that dreamer of dreams: for the LORD your God proveth you, to know whether ye love the LORD your God with all your heart and with all your soul.
>
> Ye shall walk after the LORD your God, and fear him, and keep his commandments, and obey his voice, and ye shall serve him, and cleave unto him [Deut. 13:1–4].

This is pertinent for today. People ask me how I explain the fact that some of the false prophets today are accurate part of the time. Or they ask me to explain how some people seem to be healed in certain meetings. Well, I don't explain it. To begin with, I think there would probably be a natural explanation in many instances, but even if there is something supernatural, God has warned that this can be accomplished through false prophets. It is well for us to mark that. God says that when a false prophet comes along and performs signs which come to pass, we are not to believe him if he denies the great truths of the Christian faith. That is the great principle which is put down here, and that is very important.

> And that prophet, or that dreamer of dreams, shall be put to death; because he hath spoken to turn you away from the LORD your God, which brought you out of the land of Egypt, and redeemed you out of the house of bondage, to thrust thee out of the way which the LORD thy God commanded thee to walk in. So shalt thou put the evil away from the midst of thee [Deut. 13:5].

Notice that any false prophet who attempted to take the people into some false cult or false religion was to be stoned to death. Does that sound extreme? Does that sound severe? Such a false prophet is like a cancer, and a cancer must be cut out as soon as possible—I know that from personal experience. God here is the Great Physician and He says the cancer must be cut out from among His people.

This reveals the mind of God concerning false prophets who lead the people to false gods and false religion. I can remember when I was a boy that the reading of the Bible in the schoolroom was a normal procedure. I don't think it was particularly meaningful to me at that time, yet I understood it was the Word of God and that impressed me. Today we have let the unbeliever come in, the cults, and those who oppose Christianity and the Bible, and they have taken over so that Bible reading and prayer are no longer permitted in public schools.

God laid down these rules to prevent this from happening in Israel. If one appeared in Israel who was attempting to take God's people away from the worship of God, that person was to be put to death.

Some soft-hearted and soft-headed folk will say this is too extreme. God understood how terrible it would be if false prophets were permitted to multiply and to lead Israel into idolatry. History reveals that Israel did not obey God and they did permit this to happen. If you want to know how bad it was for God's people in that day, read the story of Ahab and Jezebel who plunged God's people into idolatry. This brought the judgment of God upon them so that eventually the northern kingdom was carried into captivity. That is how serious it is.

> If thy brother, the son of thy mother, or thy son, or thy daughter, or the wife of thy bosom, or thy friend, which is as thine own soul, entice thee secretly, saying, Let us go and serve other gods, which thou hast not known, thou, nor thy fathers;
>
> Namely, of the gods of the people which are round about you, nigh unto thee, or

far off from thee, from the one end of the earth even unto the other end of the earth;

Thou shalt not consent unto him, nor hearken unto him; neither shall thine eye pity him, neither shalt thou spare, neither shalt thou conceal him:

But thou shalt surely kill him; thine hand shall be first upon him to put him to death, and afterwards the hand of all the people [Deut. 13:6–9].

This is extreme. This is radical. This sounds like a foreign language to the soft and affluent society in which we live. It is a serious matter for a man to be the first one to throw a stone in the execution that would stone his own brother to death. That seems very severe, but ultimately it would save many lives. When the northern kingdom went into idolatry, what happened? Literally thousands of them were slain, and most of the survivors were taken as slaves to the brutal nation of Assyria. Wouldn't it have been better if they had stoned the false prophets who led them into idolatry instead of a whole multitude being slain?

We see the same kind of thing in our nation today. We have so many soft-hearted and soft-headed judges who have no Christian background whatsoever. They do not think of our laws in the Christian context in which they were originally formulated—that is, obedience to law and a penalty exacted for disobedience. Our judges turn criminals loose to again prey on society. Right here in my town, a known criminal attacked seven women in one night. Several were killed, one was raped, others were hospitalized with severe injuries. Now wouldn't it be wiser for the criminal to be given the utmost penalty than for many innocent people to be murdered? God's way is the way that will save lives and protect a host of people. I am afraid that we have become so short-sighted that capital punishment sounds extreme to us today.

And thou shalt stone him with stones, that he die; because he hath sought to thrust thee away from the LORD thy God, which brought thee out of the land of Egypt, from the house of bondage [Deut. 13:10].

God exacts the death penalty. Today we feel that the death penalty is uncivilized. I guess the crowd who feels that way would call God uncivilized. I would like to ask that crowd where they got the little civilization and the little culture which they do have. All of it came from the Word of God, friends. Now we are moving away from the Word of God and folk think that is being more civilized. It is more dangerous to walk on the streets of the cities in the United States than it is to walk on the jungle trails of Africa. Why? Because we think the death penalty is uncivilized and so we have abolished it. Some time ago as I was walking by night on a jungle trail in the mountain regions of Venezuela, I felt safer than I do in Los Angeles, although they said there might be a few boa constrictors around. And I noticed that nobody locked their doors. I wondered whether they should send missionaries to us instead of our sending missionaries to them.

And all Israel shall hear, and fear, and shall do no more any such wickedness as this is among you [Deut. 13:11].

They were not to depart from the living and true God. As long as they would obey Him, there would be blessing. However, they failed to obey Him, and the judgments did come upon them—that is their story.

If thou shalt hear say in one of thy cities, which the LORD thy God hath given thee to dwell there, saying,

Certain men, the children of Belial, are gone out from among you, and have withdrawn the inhabitants of their city, saying, Let us go and serve other gods, which ye have not known;

Then shalt thou inquire, and make search, and ask diligently; and, behold, if it be truth, and the thing certain, that such abomination is wrought among you [Deut. 13:12–14].

They were not to do anything rashly. A thorough investigation must be made and truth arrived at before any action was to be taken.

Thou shalt surely smite the inhabitants of that city with the edge of the sword, destroying it utterly, and all that is therein, and the cattle thereof, with the edge of the sword.

And thou shalt gather all the spoil of it into the midst of the street thereof, and shalt burn with fire the city, and all the spoil thereof every whit, for the LORD thy God: and it shall be an heap for ever; it shall not be built again [Deut. 13: 15–16].

Again, this is severe. A city, an entire city, would be destroyed. Suppose there was someone in that city who hadn't gone into idolatry. Had they protested? Had they just sat by and done nothing? If they had done nothing about it, they were to be judged along with the rest.

There are too many Christians today who think that it is Christian to be silent. There are so many Christians who do not take a stand on important issues even when truth is at stake. You hear the old cliché, "Silence is golden." Friends, sometimes it is yellow—not golden—

to remain silent and not to take a stand. The minority is to protest that which is wrong.

Everything in such a city was to be completely destroyed.

And there shall cleave nought of the cursed thing to thine hand: that the Lord may turn from the fierceness of his anger, and shew thee mercy, and have compassion upon thee, and multiply thee, as he hath sworn unto thy fathers [Deut. 13:17].

CHAPTER 14

THEME: *Diet for Israel*

Although Leviticus 11 and Deuteronomy 12 deal with the diet for God's people, we have in this chapter regulations that may be a little clearer than those in Leviticus. The reason for this is that the dietary law recorded in Leviticus has now been tested during the wilderness march for forty years.

PAGAN RITES FORBIDDEN

Ye are the children of the Lord your God: yet shall not cut yourselves, nor make any baldness between your eyes for the dead.

For thou art an holy people unto the Lord thy God, and the Lord hath chosen thee to be a peculiar people unto himself, above all the nations that are upon the earth [Deut. 14:1–2]

These were heathen, pagan practices in that day. We see the carry-over of this among certain tribes on the earth today who still disfigure their faces. It is a part of their worship, a part of their religion. God's people were never to do anything like that.

In my book, *Learning Through Leviticus*, I have gone into more detail regarding the clean and unclean animals. The diet which God gave to His people was more than just a religious ritual. There was actually a physical benefit from their observation of it. This has been tested down through the centuries.

When the plague broke out in Europe years ago, the Jewish population was hardly touched by the plague at all, while a large percentage of the Gentile population died. So the people be-

gan to blame the Jews for the plague. Of course, they had nothing in the world to do with it, but their dietary habits and living habits had protected them from the plague.

We are living in a day of diets of all sorts. Everyone seems to be interested in diet. God has not given specific dietary laws for you and me. It makes no difference whether we eat meat or don't eat meat as far as our relationship to God is concerned. However if you observe these laws, you may stay in this world a little longer, and if you don't, it may get you into His presence a little sooner!

Now He will make it clear what animals are included and which are excluded:

Thou shalt not eat any abominable thing.

These are the beasts which ye shall eat: the ox, the sheep, and the goat,

The hart, and the roebuck, and the fallow deer, and the wild goat, and the pygarg, and the wild ox, and the chamois.

And every beast that parteth the hoof, and cleaveth the cleft into two claws, and cheweth the cud among the beasts, that ye shall eat [Deut. 14:3–6].

These were the clean animals which they could eat. There were two marks that identified the clean animals. These marks also teach us spiritual lessons.

The hoof of the animal was to be divided or separated. That could symbolize the walk of the believer. The separated hoof speaks of a separated life. Now I know that there is a lot of legalism which is brought into Christian conduct today. There are a great many people who don't restrict themselves to the Ten Commandments, but they have added about twenty-five others, and they live by them. I do not believe that is what God is indicating by the separated hoof. The word "cleave" actually has two opposite meanings. Cleaving can mean to break apart or break asunder, or it can mean to be attached to something. This is true also of separation. One can be separated *from* something or separated *unto* something. The important thing is not to be separated from certain activities or habits but to be separated unto *Christ*. When you are separated unto Christ joined to Him, your "walk" will undergo a radical change.

The second mark of the clean animals was the chewing of the cud. The spiritual lesson here is that we should spend time in the Word of God. "But his delight is in the law of the LORD; and in his law doth he meditate day and night" (Ps. 1:2). The first verse starts out with "Blessed is the man." The blessed man delights in the law of the Lord and meditates on it. That word "meditate" has the idea of chewing the cud. It is illustrated by the cow which has a complex stomach. As she grazes on the grass in the morning, it goes into one chamber of her stomach. In the heat of the day she lies down under a tree or stands in the shade, and chews her cud, which transfers that grass from one chamber to the other. Chewing the cud is rechewing the grass, going over it again. That is what we are to do with the Word of God—we are to go over and over it, meditating on it.

The unclean animals fail to meet these two requirements. Some chew the cud but do not have the divided hoof. The pig has the divided hoof but does not chew the cud. Such animals were designated as unclean and were not to be eaten.

Also certain marine life was designated as unclean:

These ye shall eat of all that are in the waters: all that have fins and scales shall ye eat:

And whatsoever hath not fins and scales ye may not eat; it is unclean unto you [Deut. 14:9–10].

Water creatures must be characterized by two visible marks—fins and scales—to be edible.

There follows a list of clean and unclean birds. There are a great number of people who try to put themselves back under the Mosaic Law, and they know a great deal about not eating pork. So when one of them begins to chide me about eating pork, I remind them of verse 12.

Of all clean birds ye shall eat.

But these are they of which ye shall not eat: the eagle, and the ossifrage, and the osprey [Deut. 14:11–12].

A few years ago I had a doctor friend, who was a legalist, tell me repeatedly that I should not eat pork. One day while we were playing tennis, I asked him, "Did you ever eat an ossifrage or an osprey?" He looked at me with a puzzled expression and said that he didn't even know what they were. I said, "Well, you sure better find out. I might invite you over someday for dinner and have roast ossifrage. That would be as bad as eating pork!" He said, "I didn't know that!" So I told him he had better look it up, and I sent him to this verse and to Leviticus 11.

RULES CONCERNING THE TITHE

Thou shalt truly tithe all the increase of thy seed, that the field bringeth forth year by year.

And thou shalt eat before the LORD thy God, in the place which he shall choose to place his name there, the tithe of thy corn, of thy wine, and of thine oil, and the firstlings of thy herds and of thy flocks; that thou mayest learn to fear the LORD thy God always [Deut. 14:22–23].

God had promised to bless his people in a material way if they would serve Him. Out of that blessing, they were to tithe for the Lord from the produce of the land as well as from their flocks. This tithe was to be eaten before the Lord at the place of the sanctuary. This would be a special feasting before the Lord.

Then shalt thou turn it into money, and bind up the money in thine hand, and shalt go unto the place which the LORD thy God shall choose:

And thou shalt bestow that money for whatsoever thy soul lusteth after, for oxen, or for sheep, or for wine, or for strong drink, or for whatsoever thy soul desireth: and thou shalt eat there before the LORD thy God, and thou shalt rejoice, thou, and thine household [Deut. 14:25–26].

If they lived too far from the temple to bring their tithe of produce or livestock, they could turn it into money, then buy their offering to the Lord when they got there.

At the end of three years thou shalt bring forth all the tithe of thine increase the same year, and shalt lay it up within thy gates [Deut. 14:28].

If you will examine the Law carefully, you will find out that they actually paid three tithes. That is, 30% of what they made went to the Lord, not just 10%. It seems that the tenth went to the temple immediately, but also there was this tithe at the end of three years.

And the Levite, (because he hath no part nor inheritance with thee,) and the stranger, and the fatherless, and the widow, which are within thy gates, shall come, and shall eat and be satisfied; that the LORD thy God may bless thee in all the work of thine hand which thou doest [Deut. 14:29].

God wanted the Levites, who did the spiritual service for the nation, to be cared for. Also note that God had a concern for the poor.

CHAPTER 15

THEME: God's poverty program; the permanent slave; the perfect sacrifice is Christ

Today we hear a great deal about poverty programs. Man has devised many programs, but they do not work. God has a poverty program that works.

Then in this chapter there is a section about a permanent slave. And, finally, we find in this chapter a type of the perfect sacrifice which is Christ.

THE SABBATIC YEAR

At the end of every seven years thou shalt make a release [Deut. 15:1].

Every seventh year is a sabbatical year. In that year a release was to be made.

And this is the manner of the release: Every creditor that lendeth aught unto his neighbour shall release it; he shall not exact it of his neighbour, or of his brother; because it is called the LORD's release [Deut. 15:2].

God had already told them that the land was to lie fallow every seventh year. Now we learn about the release on the seventh year. The Israelite could not take a mortgage that went beyond seven years. There could be no foreclosure on a mortgage. When the seventh year came around, money that had been lent or mortgages that had been made were all to be canceled out. This was a great equalizer of the wealth. It gave every man an equal opportunity.

Socialism as it is advocated today does not take into account the fact that man is a sinful creature. If he can get something for nothing, he is not going to work for it; that's for sure. Democracy and capitalism as we have it today allows for extremes. We have the extremely poor who do not work, but we also have the extremely wealthy who do not work. God had a system for Israel which equalized the opportunity so that it was possible for the poor man who really wanted to work to get something for himself. God's system guarded against extreme wealth and extreme poverty.

Of a foreigner thou mayest exact it again: but that which is thine with thy brother thine hand shall release [Deut. 15:3].

This rule held for fellow Israelites. Every seventh year the debt of the poor would be canceled out and they would have an opportunity to start again.

If Israel would observe this carefully, notice what would happen:

Save when there shall be no poor among you; for the LORD shall greatly bless thee in the land which the LORD thy God giveth thee for an inheritance to possess it [Deut. 15:4].

Wherever one goes today, whatever nation one visits, one is impressed by the extremes of poverty and wealth. This is true in Europe,

Asia, South America, the United States, wherever one goes. On one side of town there is extreme poverty, and on the other side of town there is extreme wealth. This is the result of the sin of man. One can blame certain individuals, of course, but the basic cause is the sin of man. If man had obeyed God in this respect, there would have been no poor among them; there would have been a balance of wealth.

Until the heart of man is changed, socialism as it is practiced in the communist countries becomes the most frightful dictatorship that is imaginable. Capitalism is still so much better than socialism; but whether a nation has socialism or capitalism, the basic problem is the human heart. God called Israel to obedience. Had they obeyed Him, poverty would have been eliminated. We think that we can eliminate poverty by funding poverty programs. And what happens? We see the worst corruption we have ever seen in this nation. It has become a disgrace. Why? Because of the kind of men we are dealing with. It is not the system that is wrong; it is man that is wrong. There is no use running down one system and promoting another, because until you change man, no system will work. God is dealing with the nitty-gritty here, friends. The basic problem is with the heart of man. What would happen if the wealth of this nation were all divided equally? Well, in ten years the other fellow would have it and I'd be poor again. That is the way it would be because of what is in the heart of man. God makes it very clear that if His system had been used, the problem would have been solved.

For the Lord thy God blesseth thee, as he promised thee: and thou shalt lend unto many nations, but thou shalt not borrow; and thou shalt reign over many nations, but they shall not reign over thee [Deut. 15:6].

This is a remarkable statement concerning the nation Israel. It is true that many Jewish financiers have become the bankers of the world. The house of Rothschild has financed quite a few nations, by the way. "Thou shalt lend unto many nations" has certainly been fulfilled. "Thou shalt reign over many nations, but they shall not reign over thee" has not yet been fulfilled. Why? Because Israel has never obeyed God up to the present.

If there be among you a poor man of one of thy brethren within any of thy gates in thy land which the Lord thy God

giveth thee, thou shalt not harden thine heart, nor shut thine hand from thy poor brother:

But thou shalt open thine hand wide unto him, and shalt surely lend him sufficient for his need, in that which he wanteth [Deut. 15:7–8].

This is a remarkable passage of Scripture. The nation never fully obeyed it, and the Jewish people don't obey it fully today. But have you observed that the little nation of Israel receives gifts from Jewish people all over the world? That nation probably receives more gifts than any other nation ever received. One might think that Christians, certain denominations, certain churches, lead the list in charitable giving, but they do not. Jewish people today are giving millions of dollars to the little nation of Israel. You see, God taught them at the very beginning that they were to take care of their brother. This same principle was also given to the Christian believers—there are certain great, fundamental principles which are eternal truths and which God carries over from one dispensation to another. This is what believers should be doing today. But we are not even in the same league when it comes to helping our brothers. However, I don't think that even Jews come near to what God intended for them when He gave these instructions.

Beware that there be not a thought in thy wicked heart, saying, The seventh year, the year of release, is at hand; and thine eye be evil against thy poor brother, and thou givest him nought; and he cry unto the Lord against thee, and it be sin unto thee [Deut. 15:9].

God warns that they shouldn't rationalize away their responsibility. They could say that since on the seventh year the brother will be out of debt anyway, it will be unnecessary to help him for a year or two. God tells them to go in and help the poor brother right at that very moment.

Thou shalt surely give him, and thine heart shall not be grieved when thou givest unto him: because that for this thing the Lord thy God shall bless thee in all thy works, and in all that thou puttest thine hand unto.

For the poor shall never cease out of the land: therefore I command thee, saying, Thou shalt open thine hand wide unto thy brother, to thy poor, and to thy needy, in thy land [Deut. 15:10–11].

God had told them that if they would obey Him, there would be no poor in the land. But because God knows the human heart, He tells them that there will always be poor people in the land. You remember that the Lord Jesus said the same thing: "The poor always ye have with you" . . ." (John 12:8). There will always be poverty because of the heart of man. Candidly, many are lazy; many people are shiftless and have no initiative. On the other hand, those who are able will not normally help the poor. It is not natural for man to do that. It is supernatural for a man to share what he has with the less fortunate. Therefore, He commands His people, "Thou shalt open thine hand wide unto thy brother, to thy poor, and to thy needy, in thy hand."

Slaves were to be freed on the seventh year.

And when thou sendest him out free from thee, thou shalt not let him go away empty:

Thou shalt furnish him liberally out of thy flock, and out of thy floor, and out of thy winepress: of that wherewith the LORD thy God hath blessed thee thou shalt give unto him [Deut. 15:13–14].

When the slave was freed, he was not to be sent away empty-handed.

THE PERMANENT SLAVE

And it shall be, if he say unto thee, I will not go away from thee; because he loveth thee and thine house, because he is well with thee;

Then thou shalt take an awl, and thrust it through his ear unto the door, and he shall be thy servant for ever. And also unto thy maidservant thou shalt do likewise [Deut. 15:16–17].

We saw back in Exodus 21 that a man could sell himself as a slave. If his master had given him a wife—that is, a girl who was his master's slave—when the sabbatical year came, the man could go free. But, perhaps he would choose to stay with his wife and his children and become the permanent slave of his master. Then his ear was to be pierced to signify that he had become a permanent slave.

This is a beautiful picture of the Lord Jesus Christ. He "made himself of no reputation, and took upon him the form of a servant, and was made in the likeness of men: And being found in fashion as a man, he humbled himself, and became obedient unto death, even the death of the cross" (Phil. 2:7–8). Jesus could have gone out free. He owed no debt of sin; He was no sinner. He had no penalty to pay. But He loved us and He gave Himself for us. Just as the servant had his ear thrust through by the awl, so the Psalmist says, ". . . mine ears hast thou opened. . ." (Ps. 40:6). The Book of Hebrews takes the same passage from Psalm 40 and says, ". . . but a body hast thou prepared me . . ." (Heb. 10:5). The Lord Jesus took on Himself a human body so that He could be crucified for you and for me. It is one of those remarkable pictures which we find of the Lord Jesus Christ in the Old Testament.

CHAPTER 16

THEME: Three main feasts: Passover, Pentecost, Tabernacles

Israel was give three feasts which all the males were required to attend: Passover, Pentecost (or Weeks), the Tabernacles.

THE FEAST OF PASSOVER

The Feast of Passover was instituted as a memorial to Israel's deliverance from Egypt and their adoption as Jehovah's nation. The Passover is a festival that laid the foundation of the nation, Israel's birth into a new relationship with God.

Observe the month of Abib, and keep the passover unto the LORD thy God: for in the month of Abib the LORD thy God brought thee forth out of Egypt by night.

Thou shalt therefore sacrifice the passover unto the LORD thy God, of the flock and the herd, in the place which the LORD shall choose to place his name there [Deut. 16:1–2].

To get the background of the celebration of Passover, turn back to Exodus 12. The children of Israel were in slavery in Egypt. Moses had been chosen by God to lead His people out of Egypt and to the Promised Land. Pharaoh had stubbornly refused to release them, and God revealed His power to Pharaoh by bringing plague after plague upon Egypt. On the fateful night that the final plague was about to descend upon the people, the children of Israel were to express their faith by slaying a lamb, and placing its blood outside the door of the home. Upon seeing the blood, the death angel would pass over the house, which spared the firstborn from death. Because the firstborn died in every home where the blood was absent (including his own), Pharaoh released the children of Israel.

God wanted His people to remember this tremendous deliverance and so instituted the yearly Feast of Passover.

Thou mayest not sacrifice the passover within any of thy gates, which the LORD thy God giveth thee:

But at the place which the LORD thy God shall choose to place his name in, there thou shalt sacrifice the passover at even, at the going down of the sun, at the season that thou camest forth out of Egypt.

And thou shalt roast and eat it in the place which the LORD thy God shall choose: and thou shalt turn in the morning, and go unto thy tents.

Six days thou shalt eat unleavened bread: and on the seventh day shall be a solemn assembly to the LORD thy God: thou shalt do no work therein [Deut. 16:5–8].

That was the Feast of Passover. It was to be observed in one place, which was in Jerusalem. All the males of Israel were to go to Jerusalem at that time.

THE FEAST OF PENTECOST

Seven weeks shalt thou number unto thee: begin to number the seven weeks from such time as thou beginnest to put the sickle to the corn.

And thou shalt keep the feast of weeks unto the LORD thy God with a tribute of a freewill offering of thine hand, which thou shalt give unto the LORD thy God, according as the LORD thy God hath blessed thee:

And thou shalt rejoice before the LORD thy God, thou, and thy son, and thy daughter, and thy manservant, and thy maidservant, and the Levite that is within thy gates, and the stranger, and the fatherless, and the widow, that are among you, in the place which the LORD thy God hath chosen to place his name there [Deut. 16:9–11].

Notice that they were to number seven weeks after Passover, which would be forty-nine; then the next day would be the Sabbath, the fiftieth day. Because the Greek word for "fifty" is *pentecoste*, this Feast of Weeks is known as *Pentecost*. It is also called the Feast of Harvest or the Day of First Fruits. It celebrated the first or earliest fruits of the harvest.

THE FEAST OF TABERNACLES

Thou shalt observe the feast of tabernacles seven days, after that thou hast gathered in thy corn and thy wine [Deut. 16:13].

This was another feast of rejoicing. It lasted seven days and it, too, was to be kept in the place which the Lord should choose, which was Jerusalem.

Three times in a year shall all thy males appear before the LORD thy God in the place which he shall choose; in the feast of unleavened bread, and in the feast of weeks, and in the feast of tabernacles: and they shall not appear before the LORD empty:

Every man shall give as he is able, according to the blessing of the LORD thy God which he hath given thee [Deut. 16:16–17].

These are the three feasts which were to be celebrated in Jerusalem, which all males were required to attend. Three times a year they were to travel to Jerusalem to keep these feasts. It was to be a time of rejoicing. Notice they were to come before the Lord with *joy*.

JUDGES IN THE GATES

The chapter concludes with commandments regarding judges.

Judges and officers shalt thou make thee in all thy gates, which the LORD thy God giveth thee, throughout thy tribes: and they shall judge the people with just judgment [Deut. 16:18].

The courthouse in that day was not a building in the center of town or even in a courthouse square. Instead of being in the center of town, it was at the edge of town, at the gate in the wall around the city. The reason for that was that it was the place where all the citizens entered or left the city. It was the gathering place, just as the square is the gathering place in some of our little towns.

Knowing the human heart as God does, He warns against distorting justice, about respect of persons, and about accepting a bribe.

Thou shalt not plant thee a grove of any trees near unto the altar of the Lord thy God, which thou shalt make thee.

Neither shalt thou set thee up any image; which the Lord thy God hateth [Deut 16:21-22].

A grove was connected with idolatry and with sinful worship in that day. That was the reason they were not to make groves. It was in those groves that the altars and images and idols were made to heathen and pagan gods. You can see that this is very close to the worship of the Druids in Europe. Paganism goes in for that type of thing, and God is warning His people against it.

CHAPTER 17

THEME: Sundry laws

In chapters 17 and 18 we come to a section which deals with the regulations that would control a king, a priest, and a prophet. These were the three main offices in the nation Israel, in the theocracy which God had set up for these people. God laid down rules for each of these offices.

OFFERING MUST BE WITHOUT DEFECT

Thou shalt not sacrifice unto the Lord thy God any bullock, or sheep, wherein is blemish, or any evilfavouredness: for that is an abomination unto the Lord thy God [Deut. 17:1].

God had said that the firstborn of every creature belongs to Him. Also that every offering presented to Him was to be without spot or blemish. When you come to the last book of the Old Testament, you will find that Malachi lists the charges which God brought against His people—the sins that brought His judgment down upon them. The number one charge was that they were offering sick animals to God.

Suppose a farmer had a very fine bullock which he had decided to keep. One morning he goes out to his barn lot and finds that this animal is sick. He would say to his boys, "Hustle up, boys; we'll put this bullock in the cart and rush it over to the temple and we'll offer this prize bullock to the Lord." The neighbors would say, "My, my, look at Mr. So-and-so. Isn't he generous! He's giving God that prize bullock." But God, who knows the heart, says,

"I will not accept it. Such an offering is absolutely meaningless."

Do you realize that if we as believers were checked out on the way we do business with God, we would be arrested and put in the penitentiary? If we did business with the world or with other individuals in the same manner, we would be put in jail! Each of us should check up on ourselves. How honest are we with God in our financial matters? Don't misunderstand: God is not poor—He owns all the silver and the gold. The cattle on a thousand hills belongs to Him; He doesn't need our offering of an old sick cow. Actually, we can't give God anything. Then why does He ask for an offering? He permits us to offer to Him because it is a blessing to our own souls, and we are not blessed when we are beggarly and stingy with God. For instance, we ought to consider what we do for missions. A great many folk today give their castoffs and their secondhand clothes to the missions and to the missionaries. Friends, God does not want our leftovers. He wants our best.

DEATH PENALTY FOR IDOLATERS

If there be found among you, within any of thy gates which the Lord thy God giveth thee, man or woman, that hath wrought wickedness in the sight of the Lord thy God, in transgressing his covenant,

And hath gone and served other gods, and worshipped them, either the sun, or moon, or any of the host of heaven, which I have not commanded;

And it be told thee, and thou hast heard of it, and inquired diligently, and, behold, it be true, and the thing certain, that such abomination is wrought in Israel:

Then shalt thou bring forth that man or that woman, which have committed that wicked thing, unto thy gates, even that man or that woman, and shalt stone them with stones, till they die [Deut. 17:2–5].

This is an absolute law against idolatry. From this and other examples that are given to us, I judge that the penalty for breaking any one of the Ten Commandments was death. Today we are so "loving" and so "civilized" that we have gotten rid of the death penalty. But the interesting thing is that we have one of the most lawless societies that the world has ever seen. Doesn't it make you wonder if God wasn't right, after all? Stoning was the penalty for idolatry.

You will notice that he mentions idolatry, which was common in the cultures of that day. Greek mythology and the idolatry of the Orient have many gods and goddesses who were associated with the sun, moon, and stars. Apollo was the god of the sun and Diana the goddess of the moon in the Greek mythology. They worshiped the creature rather than the Creator.

Where did all this begin? I think it began at the tower of Babel. That tower of Babel was actually a rallying place for all those who were against God. Why? God had sent a Flood, and now they were going to worship the sun because the sun, according to their reasoning, never sent a flood. The very interesting thing is that they didn't know that the sun is responsible for drawing the water up. The clouds move across the sky and rain falls. The idolatry of that day wasn't very accurate; neither was their science. And maybe the science of our day doesn't have the final word either. A great many people today feel that man's wisdom and knowledge is accurate. Well, we know it has been inaccurate in the past. They worshiped the sun, the moon, and the stars because they thought the heavenly bodies were friendly to them. They worshiped these rather than the Creator who had made them.

At the mouth of two witnesses, or three witnesses, shall he that is worthy of death be put to death; but at the mouth of one witness he shall not be put to death [Deut. 17:6].

Notice how carefully God protects the innocent. A man couldn't rush to the authorities because he didn't like one of his neighbors and accuse his neighbor of worshiping the sun god or Ashtaroth, the Babylonian god, or Baal or Aphrodite or any of the false gods. There had to be two or more witnesses to condemn a man. In our society, one witness could send a man to the gas chamber or the electric chair. I personally think this should not be permitted. God always required two or more witnesses. God is very fair in His dealings.

OBEDIENCE TO AUTHORITY

In the theocracy, they were to refer their cases to the priest or to the judges whom God would put over them. In a theocracy they should never have had a king. We know that later on they asked for a king and God granted their request. Remember Psalm 106:15: "And he gave them their request; but sent leanness into their soul." This was said of their experience in the wilderness, but it is a truth for all time. If God would answer many of our prayers as we pray them, it would be the biggest mistake in he world. God is gracious and many times refuses our requests. He does that for me, and I'm sure He does that for you. However, God yielded to Israel's request for a king. In fact, way back here—before they were even in the land—He was laying down regulations for their king.

If there arise a matter too hard for thee in judgment, between blood and blood, between plea and plea, and between stroke and stroke, being matters of controversy within thy gates: then shalt thou arise, and get thee up into the place which the LORD thy God shall choose [Deut. 17:8].

If two men disagree on an important matter, how is it to be solved when evidence seems to be equally impressive on both sides?

And thou shalt come unto the priests the Levites, and unto the judge that shall be in those days, and inquire; and they shall shew thee the sentence of judgment:

And thou shalt do according to the sentence, which they of that place which the LORD shall choose shall shew thee; and thou shalt observe to do according to all they that inform thee:

According to the sentence of the law which they shall teach thee, and according to the judgment which they shall tell

thee, thou shalt do: thou shalt not decline from the sentence which they shall shew thee, to the right hand, nor to the left [Deut. 17:9–11].

Because the Law didn't cover every situation, disagreements were to be taken to the priest. Then the people were to abide by the decision given. Disobedience to the judgment of the priest was to be punished with the death penalty.

The only instance we have recorded of this being used is in Haggai 2:11. I'm sure there were many instances like this. If the Law specifically covered an issue and dogmatically gave a ruling about it, then, obviously, there was no need to take the matter to the priest. If, however, a matter had to be taken to the priest or the judge for a decision, that decision was final and was to be obeyed.

LAWS CONCERNING A KING

God knows that the time will come when they will demand a king like the other nations had. God says that their king must be an Israelite and not a foreigner.

But he shall not multiply horses to himself, nor cause the people to return to Egypt, to the end that he should multiply horses: forasmuch as the LORD hath said unto you, Ye shall henceforth return no more that way.

Neither shall he multiply wives to himself, that his heart turn not away: neither shall he greatly multiply to himself silver and gold [Deut. 17:16–17].

Here are the rules for the king. It is interesting to note that King Solomon transgressed these rules. First of all, he multiplied horses. When I was at Megiddo, the thing that impressed me there was not so much the battlefield of Armageddon as the ruins of the stables of Solomon. The stables of Solomon would have made any of the racetracks in this country look like a

tenant farmer's barn down in Georgia. And other stables have been excavated at several additional sites. This man, Solomon, went all out in that direction. God warned against this. The raising of horses would get one entangled with Egypt because that was the place where very find horses were bred.

Then, Solomon transgressed by multiplying wives to himself. God put up warning signs long before Israel ever had a king: "Don't go this way. Be careful." Yet Solomon had many, many wives. It was his wives who turned his heart away from God.

Third, God warned against trying to corner the silver and gold market of that day. Yet that is exactly what Solomon did. David had begun it—but David was collecting silver and gold to build the temple, but Solomon continued collecting silver and gold for himself. This was the undoing of Solomon, and the grievous taxation was the direct cause of the division of Israel as a nation into the northern and southern kingdoms after Solomon's death.

And it shall be, when he sitteth upon the throne of his kingdom, that he shall write him a copy of this law in a book out of that which is before the priests the Levites:

And it shall be with him, and he shall read therein all the days of his life: that he may learn to fear the LORD his God, to keep all the words of this law and these statutes, to do them:

That his heart be not lifted up above his brethren, and that he turn not aside from the commandment, to the right hand, or to the left: to the end that he may prolong his days in his kingdom, he, and his children, in the midst of Israel [Deut. 17:18–20].

The king was to be a man of the Word of God. He was to have a private copy of the Law of God, and he was to read in it every day of his life.

CHAPTER 18

THEME: *Priests and prophets; the test of a true prophet*

God gives rules regarding the maintenance of the priests. Then there is another warning against idolatrous practices which resort to the satanic powers. This is followed by one of the outstanding sections of the Book of Deuteronomy which deals with prophets, and there is a wonderful prophecy about the Lord Jesus, the Prophet who was to come. The section on prophets concludes with the very interesting and important test for determining true and false prophets.

THE CARE OF THE PRIESTS

The priests the Levites, and all the tribe of Levi, shall have no part nor inheritance with Israel: they shall eat the offerings of the Lord made by fire, and his inheritance.

Therefore shall they have no inheritance among their brethren: the Lord is their inheritance, as he hath said unto them [Deut. 18:1–2].

The priests came from the tribe of Levi. All the Levites were employed in the temple service. They had no land inheritance among the children of Israel, but the Lord was their inheritance. The Lord provided for them in this particular way. It is interesting that God did not mention how a king was to get his salary, but He did give instructions about how a priest was to get his. Yet the preacher's salary is the one thing that is always a touchy issue in the church. God just laid it on the line. He said, "This is what the priests are to receive."

And this shall be the priest's due from the people, from them that offer a sacrifice, whether it be ox or sheep; and they shall give unto the priest the shoulder, and the two cheeks, and the maw.

The firstfruit also of thy corn, of thy wine, and of thine oil, and the first of the fleece of thy sheep, shalt thou give him.

For the Lord thy God hath chosen him out of all thy tribes, to stand to minister in the name of the Lord, him and his sons for ever [Deut. 18:3–5].

This is a great principle that God is laying down here. This is still the method God uses to carry on His work in the world. He expects His people to support the people who are giving all of their time in getting out the Word of God to the world. If people started bringing shoulders of beef and of lamb we might have T-bone steaks and lamb chops—of course I do not think He means for us to do it in this same way, but the principle is still true.

When thou art come into the land which the Lord thy God giveth thee, thou shalt not learn to do after the abominations of those nations.

There shall not be found among you any one that maketh his son or his daughter to pass through the fire, or that useth divination, or an observer of times, or an enchanter, or a witch.

Or a charmer, or a consulter with familiar spirits, or a wizard, or a necromancer.

For all that do these things are an abomination unto the Lord: and because of these abominations the Lord thy God doth drive them out from before thee [Deut. 18:9–12].

When these people would go into the land, they were not to resort to the pagan, heathen practices of the people in the land. This warning is repeated in the New Testament. Paul warns ". . . that in the latter times some shall depart from the faith, giving heed to seducing spirits, and doctrines of devils" (1 Tim. 4:1). They will be resorting to the unseen satanic world.

Now let me venture my own judgment, and you can take it for what it is worth. I believe we have now come into that period. As I write, there is a great manifestation of Satan worship. Here, in Southern California, there are churches of Satan where he is actually worshiped. In Hawaii, I saw a group of young people falling down before a picture of Krishna, which is nothing in the world but satanic worship. Some people pass this off as a fad because it is a tendency of human nature to go after fads—especially in America. However, there is a great deal of reality in Satan worship. It is not a group of stupid people, nor is it only the uneducated who are indulging in this sort of thing. There must be reality in it and, since Satan is real, I believe there is a certain amount of reality in it. But God warns against this. He says it is an abomination unto Him.

I want to add this because someone needs to say it today. There is a danger in playing with astrology. Remember that in the previous chapter we read the condemnation of the worship of sun, moon, and stars. There are a great many people today who are placing more emphasis on astrology than they are on the Bible. Stores and magazine racks are loaded with material on astrology. The media is promoting it. We see it everywhere we turn. My friend, astrology is an abomination unto the Lord. Don't find fault with me for saying this. It is God who calls it an abomination. Why is it an abomination? It takes people away from the living and true God. It plunges them into darkness and demonism. There is reality in the world of demons. There are fallen angels and a spirit world. This thing is real, and today people are intrigued with it. They use drugs and every other means they can think of to try to make contact with this unseen world. And the satanic world is very glad to make contact with them. A child of God should let this thing alone. Any one who turns in that direction has a weak faith and is not really trusting Christ as Savior. He is turning away from the Holy Spirit and the Word of God. God has given warnings about this sort of thing. His warnings have happened to be very accurate in the past. His batting average, friends, is excellent—He hasn't missed yet. He hits a home run every time, and I am going to go along with Him.

Thou shalt be perfect with the Lord thy God.

For these nations, which thou shalt possess, hearkened unto observers of times, and unto diviners: but as for thee, the Lord thy God hath not suffered thee so to do [Deut. 18:13–14].

These nations in the land were judged and would be removed from the land because of this very thing. Israel has been called to be a witness to the true and living God.

PROMISE OF THE COMING MESSIAH

The Lord thy God will raise up unto thee a Prophet from the midst of thee, of thy brethren, like unto me; unto him ye shall hearken:

According to all that thou desiredst of the Lord thy God in Horeb in the day of the assembly, saying, Let me not hear again the voice of the Lord my God, neither let me see this great fire any more, that I die not.

And the Lord said unto me, They have well spoken that which they have spoken [Deut. 18:15–17].

The children of Israel were to listen to God's prophets. Why? Because they were telling them the truth. That was the basic reason. But the second reason was to prepare them to listen to the final messenger, the final Prophet, the Lord Jesus Christ.

Some people still ask why God does not reveal Himself today. Friend, in the person of the Lord Jesus Christ, God put the period at the end of the sentence. God wrote *finis* at the end of the book. He has nothing more to say to the world than He has said in Jesus Christ. We are to hear *Him*. We are to hearken unto *Him*. At the transfiguration, God the Father said, "This is my beloved Son, in whom I am well pleased; hear ye him" (Matt. 17:5). Listen to Him. He has the final Word. For believers today the Lord Jesus Christ is God's ultimate, God's full, God's final revelation to man. This is what Moses is saying way back here in Deuteronomy.

I will raise them up a Prophet from among their brethren, like unto thee, and will put my words in his mouth; and he shall speak unto them all that I shall command him.

And it shall come to pass, that whosoever will not hearken unto my words which he shall speak in my name, I will require it of him [Deut. 18:18–19].

You will recall that the Lord Jesus said again and again that the words He spoke were not His own but the Father's. For instance, in John 5:30, and several times in John 6, the Lord Jesus says that He came not to do His own will but to do the will of the Father. After the Lord's earthly ministry was finished, he prayed in that great high priestly prayer, where He is turning in His final report to the Father. ". . . I have finished the work which thou gavest me to do. . . . For I have given unto them the words which thou gavest me . . ." (John 17:4, 8). If God were to speak out of heaven at this very moment, He would not say anything that He had not already said. He would just repeat Himself, because all He intends to say to you and to me is in the person of Christ.

That is the reason we are to let astrology alone. It is the tendency of human nature to want to explore the unknown, to know about the future. There is an insatiable desire to probe the mysterious. There is some of the spirit of Columbus in all of us. Right now we are exploring space and the depths of the oceans. We like to reach out into new areas. Not only do we do this in space, but man also likes to reach out in time. He wants to know about that mysterious future. What is beyond tomorrow? What does the future hold? All would like to know that, would they not? People are anxious about the future. There is always the question: what about tomorrow? The future is a closed door. Memory can take you back into the past, but there is no vehicle to take you into the future. Written on the door of the future are the words, "Keep Out!" Today was tomorrow only yesterday. Man is limited as to time and also space.

To satisfy this insatiable longing, there arose among the heathen, spiritualists, necromancers, and diviners. God warned His people against it. This was connected with idolatry and was satanic in origin. Could they tell the future? Yes, there was a certain degree of accuracy. The Greeks used the oracle of Delphi and, apparently, got a certain amount of accurate information there—but it was satanic. They say that Hitler resorted to some type of fortune teller. I understand in Washington today, fortune tellers do a land-office business. The classified ads in any city will show you that there are many fortune tellers making a very fine living by speaking of the future.

Now the future is an area in which man has never been given dominion. God alone can predict the future, and it belongs to Him. A unique character of the Word of God is that it moves beyond the present. The greatest proof to me that the Bible is the Word of God is the fulfillment of prophecy. One fourth of the entire Bible was prophecy at the time it was written, and a large portion of that has already been fulfilled. God has recorded prophecies concerning cities and nations and great world empires. Under such circumstances, there would arise false prophets, as there are today. They wanted the status and the position that belonged to the true prophet of God. How could Israel protect themselves from the false prophets? God lays down a test by which they could be certain a man was either a true prophet of God or a phony.

TEST FOR DETERMINING TRUE AND FALSE PROPHETS

There were false prophets among the people; that's quite evident. Unfortunately, Israel would not apply God's rules by which they could identify them. We find this passage in Jeremiah 14:14: "Then the LORD said unto me, The prophets prophesy lies in my name: I sent them not, neither have I commanded them, neither spake unto them: they prophesy unto you a false vision and divination, and a thing of nought, and the deceit of their heart." It was easy enough for a false prophet to speak of the coming kingdom—centuries in the future. The prophet Jeremiah spoke of the future. How could one tell which was the true prophet? Today we can know because a great deal of Jeremiah's prophecy has been fulfilled, but how could people know at the time it was spoken? Well, God put down a very accurate test. Listen to Him:

But the prophet, which shall presume to speak a word in my name, which I have not commanded him to speak, or that shall speak in the name of other gods, even that prophet shall die.

And if thou say in thine heart, How shall we know the word which the LORD hath not spoken?

When a prophet speaketh in the name of the LORD, if the thing follow not, nor come to pass, that is the thing which the LORD hath not spoken, but the prophet hath spoken it presumptuously: thou shalt not be afraid of him [Deut. 18: 20–22].

Let us take time to look at this for a moment. Isaiah is a prophet of God, a true prophet of God. How do we know? He prophesied that a virgin would conceive and bring forth a son. He clearly marked out the coming of the Lord Jesus, His birth, His life, His death. Suppose someone had asked Isaiah when all this would take place. He would have answered that he was not quite sure but that it could be hundreds of years. (Actually, it was seven hundred years.) Well, that crowd would laugh and say they would never be around to know whether he was telling the truth or not. The test of the prophets was that they had to give a prediction about a local situation that would come to pass right away, and they had to be *completely accurate.* They couldn't miss in any point of their predictions. Any inaccuracy at all would immediately disqualify them as a true prophet of God.

Now let us look at Isaiah again. He prophesied the virgin birth, and we today can look back 1900 years to the fulfillment of that and know that he was accurate. But how could the people in his day know that? They could know because Isaiah went to the king, Hezekiah, with a prophecy concerning a local current event. There was a great Assyrian army of trigger-happy soldiers surrounding the city, but Isaiah said that not one arrow would enter the city. Those Assyrians had conquered other nations and they were there to conquer Jerusalem and to carry Israel into captivity. Isaiah told them what God had said about it:

"Therefore this saith the LORD concerning the king of Assyria, He shall not come into this city, nor shoot an arrow there, not come before it with shields, nor cast a bank against it. By the way that he came, by the same shall he return and shall not come into this city, saith the LORD" (Isa. 37:33–34).

All of those fellows in the Assyrian army had bows and arrows. You'd think that just one of them might let an arrow fly over the wall just to see if he could hit someone. Now if one arrow was shot into the city, Isaiah would lose his job as a true prophet of God. He would be out of business. That was one of the tests which Isaiah passed. There were others where Isaiah spoke to a local situation, and it came to pass just as he had said. The true prophet had to be correct 100 percent of the time.

Now what about today? This test would disqualify everyone on the contemporary scene who claims to be a prophet by predicting the future. I grant you that some of them sometimes hit the nail right on the head, but more often they miss the nail altogether. You don't hear of their misses; you only hear of their accurate guesses. I could give many instances of false prophecies. We have folk predicting the end of the world on a certain date, the Rapture of the church on a certain date, calamities that will come to a particular section of the country on a specific date, and a host of other things. If we applied God's test to these self-acclaimed prophets, they would be out of business in short order. A true prophet must be accurate in every detail every time.

But do you know that there are no warnings about false prophets for the church today? Why? Because there is no more prophecy to be revealed. Everything has been revealed in the Lord Jesus Christ and in His Word. Our warning today is not against false prophets; our warning is against false teachers. "But there were false prophets also among the people, even as there shall be false teachers among you . . ." (2 Pet. 2:1). The warning to us is to listen very carefully today, because there are many sweet, soothing voices that sound very pious, but are not teaching the Word of God. Oh, how important it is for us to beware of false teachers!

CHAPTER 19

THEME: *Cities of refuge; extent of the land and the extremity of the Law*

The provision of cities of refuge, the protection of property rights, and the severity of the Law reveal again God's concern for the innocent person.

CITIES OF REFUGE

In the Book of Numbers, chapter 35, we learn that the Levites were to set up three such cities on the east side of Jordan and three on the west side of Jordan.

Thou shalt separate three cities for thee in the midst of thy land, which the LORD thy God giveth thee to possess it.

Thou shalt prepare thee a way, and divide the coasts of thy land, which the LORD thy God giveth thee to inherit, into three parts, that every slayer may flee thither.

And this is the case of the slayer, which shall flee thither, that he may live: Whoso killeth his neighbour ignorantly, whom he hated not in time past [Deut. 19:2–4].

A man who had unwittingly killed a person could flee to a city of refuge. This would save him from mob action or from the action of some hotheaded relative who might be emotionally wrought up at the time. In a city of refuge he would be protected until a fair trial could be held.

God makes it perfectly clear that the cities of refuge were to be protection for the innocent man. He gives an example of what He means by an accidental killing.

As when a man goeth into the wood with his neighbour to hew wood, and his hand fetcheth a stroke with the axe to cut down the tree, and the head slippeth from the helve, and lighteth upon his neighbour, that he die; he shall flee unto one of those cities, and live:

Lest the avenger of the blood pursue the slayer, while his heart is hot, and overtake him, because the way is long, and slay him; whereas he was not worthy of death, inasmuch as he hated him not in time past [Deut. 19:5–6].

The Lord is specific that the cities of refuge are not to be protection for those guilty of murder.

But if any man hate his neighbour, and lie in wait for him, and rise up against him, and smite him mortally that he die, and fleeth into one of these cities:

Then the elders of his city shall send and fetch him thence, and deliver him into the hand of the avenger of blood, that he may die [Deut. 19:11–12].

PROTECTION OF PROPERTY

Thou shalt not remove thy neighbour's landmark, which they of old time have set in thine inheritance, which thou shalt inherit in the land that the LORD thy God giveth thee to possess it [Deut. 19:14].

Here is the fact that landmarks were sacred. This was a protection of human property and establishes the rights to property.

One witness shall not rise up against a man for any iniquity, or for any sin, in any sin that he sinneth: at the mouth of two witnesses, or at the mouth of three witnesses, shall the matter be established [Deut. 19:15].

This passage reveals to us the awesomeness of the Law. The demands of the Law were terrible, and under no circumstances was one witness sufficient. Anyone today who says that he wants to live under Law should really find out what it is.

If a false witness should arise, then the accused and the accuser were to stand before the Lord, represented by the priests and the judges. If the judges decided that the witness was false, then whatever he wanted to have done to the accused was the punishment which should be given to him. In that way, evil was to be removed from the nation (vv. 16–20).

And thine eye shall not pity; but life shall go for life, eye for eye, tooth for tooth, hand for hand, foot for foot [Deut. 19:21].

That is Law, friends. There is no mercy in Law. I thank God today that the Lord is not judging me on the basis of Law. He saves me by grace. If He were saving me by Law, I would be lost forever, because I could never, never measure up to the requirements of the Law. Law is *law*—we have developed such a careless attitude about it today—but God *enforces* His Law. It was eye for eye, tooth for tooth. How I thank God that Jesus Christ paid the penalty of the Law so that there is pardon for sinners. The throne of God has become a mercy seat because Christ died and His blood has been sprinkled there—and that's the blood of the covenant. God saves us by His grace. We have not kept the Law; we have broken it. We are all guilty before God. Christ paid the penalty; so the requirements of the Law have been fulfilled. Now God is free to save sinners by His marvelous, infinite, wonderful grace.

CHAPTER 20

THEME: *Laws regulating warfare*

This Book of Deuteronomy is a very practical book. It touches life where we live it today. Although these laws were given to Israel, there are certain basic principles here which would contribute to the happiness and the welfare of mankind if they were incorporated into the laws of modern nations. I'm convinced that the men who originally drew up our constitution were men who were Bible-oriented. The problem today is that we have a society made up of people who are entirely ignorant of the Bible, and lawmakers who are actually stupid as far as the Word of God is concerned. The blunders they make in their policies are enough to cause us to weep and howl—all because they are so far from God and not following Him at all. This Book of Deuteronomy covers problems which Washington has been trying to solve in its own way. Our lawmakers have been wrestling with these problems for years.

They have dealt with the problem of our young men for service in the armed forces. They are troubled to know what should be the conditions on which a man should serve or not serve. Israel had these same problems. God put down certain very basic rules that would prevent a man from going to war. Very candidly, I am of the opinion that if our government had paid attention to God's Law relative to this, we wouldn't be in the mess we are in today.

When thou goest out to battle against thine enemies and seest horses, and chariots, and a people more than thou, be not afraid of them: for the LORD thy God is with thee, which brought thee up out of the land of Egypt [Deut. 20:1].

Here was something that was important for Israel, and I believe it is important for us today. We see little mottos which read, "Make love, not war." That may sound good, but like so many little mottos, it is absolutely meaningless. Because we are living in a sinful world where the heart of man is desperately wicked, there are times to make war. There are times when we need to protect ourselves. There are wars in which God is on one side. Frankly, the important question any nation should consider—and certainly a so-called civilized and Christian nation—is whether this is a war that God is in. If He isn't in it, then we shouldn't be in it either.

And it shall be, when ye are come nigh unto the battle, that the priest shall approach and speak unto the people,

And shall say unto them, Hear, O Israel, ye approach this day unto battle against your enemies: let not your hearts faint, fear not, and do not tremble, neither be ye terrified because of them;

For the LORD your God is he that goeth with you, to fight for you against your enemies, to save you [Deut. 20:2–4].

This is something that is very important in warfare. Make sure that you are on God's side. God commanded them to war against these nations and promised that He would be with them.

Now God puts down four conditions, or four excuses, which would keep a man from going to battle.

And the officers shall speak unto the people, saying, What man is there that hath built a new house, and hath not dedicated it? let him go and return to his house, lest he die in the battle, and another man dedicate it [Deut. 20:5].

If a man has built a new home and has not had the opportunity to live in it, he was not to go into battle. Why not? Because his heart, naturally, would be in that new home. He had set his heart and his affection on it. He wanted to live in that new home, and he is to be given the opportunity to live in it.

And what man is he that hath planted a vineyard, and hath not yet eaten of it? let him also go and return unto his house, lest he die in the battle, and another man eat of it [Deut. 20:6].

These people were agrarian; they were farmers. Here is a man who has just gotten started in business; he had just planted a vineyard. Because he hasn't had the opportunity to eat a grape off it yet, he is not to go to battle. His heart is in his vineyard; his interest is there. He is to stay until he gets to eat of it, until he gets established. Otherwise he might be killed in battle, and another man would reap the fruit of his labors. This is quite interesting, is it not?

And what man is there that hath betrothed a wife, and hath not taken her?

let him go and return unto his house, lest he die in the battle, and another man take her [Deut. 20:7].

Here is a young man who is engaged to a girl and he gets drafted. He is not to be taken. He is in love with that girl; he wants to marry her. Let him stay home, and let him marry the girl. That is where his heart is, and he is not to go to battle.

Now here is the fourth excuse:

And the officers shall speak further unto the people, and they shall say, What man is there that is fearful and fainthearted? let him go and return unto his house, lest his brethren's heart faint as well as his heart [Deut. 20:8].

There might be a man who very frankly says, "I am a coward. I am afraid to fight, and I don't want to fight." So here are four good reasons for a man not to go to war. I could not have used the first three reasons, but that last one I could have used. If a man was afraid, fainthearted, fearful, he was not to go. I believe I would have turned and gone home.

This law was applied to Gideon's army. You may remember that Gideon started out with quite an army—32,000 men who rallied to him to free their nation from the oppression of the Midianites who had actually impoverished them. Then the Lord told him he had too many soldiers, and that whoever was fearful and afraid could go home! When that word went out, 22,000 men picked up their gear and went home! Then God told Gideon that he still had too many men. How were they separated? They came to a stream and some of the men got down on all fours to drink. There were others who lapped up the water like a dog and were all set to go. They were eager to get to the enemy and get the job done. They wanted to free and save their nation. So they were the ones who went to battle, and the others were sent home.

In America we have had problems with our young men dodging the draft and burning their draft cards. I have great sympathy with many of these young men, but I wish instead of trying to blame the government and blame everybody else, they would just come out and say they are afraid to go fight. That is a good reason. That would have kept me out of the battle, I can assure you of that. I don't mind admitting I'm a coward. For example, because I had to work my way through high school and

college, and support my mother, I could never have proven that I was a good enough football player to earn a scholarship. But I played a little and enjoyed it. I remember how I felt just before that kickoff. When the whistle was blown—I played the backfield—standing way back there, my knees would buckle. There were times when I'd actually go down on one knee, I was so scared. But the minute I got the ball and I was hit, from then on I was all right. But I would never have made it in combat on the battlefield, I can assure you!

God says here that He wants His people to know two things before they go to war. First of all, they must be on His side. They must be fighting for what is right and know that God is with them. Secondly, they must be enthusiastic about it. There is a time when one should fight for his country, and there is a place for the flag and for patriotism. The way things are carried out by our politicians actually encourages this motley mob who burn their draft cards. But the way God does it is very wise. He had a marvelous arrangement for His people, even in time of war.

When thou comest nigh unto a city to fight against it, then proclaim peace unto it.

And it shall be, if it make thee answer of peace, and open unto thee, then it shall be, that all the people that is found therein shall be tributaries unto thee, and they shall serve thee.

And if it will make no peace with thee, but will make war against thee, then thou shalt besiege it [Deut. 20:10–12].

Here is another great principle which is laid down. You may remember that General Douglas MacArthur did not believe in fighting a war which we did not intend to win. This kind of compromise is the curse of our nation today, and we do it with a phony piousness. This has pervaded our churches, and today it is in our government. We pretend to be the great big wonderful brother. MacArthur warned, in his day, not to fight a land war in Asia. But if we fight a war, we are to fight to win—that is the purpose of it. And that is exactly what God says. We have no business to fight a war unless we are fighting to win it.

God has put down some very good principles here, friends, but today we have departed far from them.

CHAPTER 21

THEME: *Laws regarding murder, marriage, and delinquent sons*

This chapter concludes the section concerning religious and national regulations which began with chapter 8. We find here interesting and remarkable laws regulating many different aspects of the life of Israel.

> If one be found slain in the land which the LORD thy God giveth thee to possess it, lying in the field, and it be not known who hath slain him:
>
> Then thy elders and thy judges shall come forth, and they shall measure unto the cities which are round about him that is slain:
>
> And it shall be, that the city which is next unto the slain man, even the elders of that city shall take an heifer, which hath not been wrought with, and which hath not drawn in the yoke:
>
> And the elders of that city shall bring down the heifer unto a rough valley, which is neither eared nor sown, and shall strike off the heifer's neck there in the valley [Deut. 21:1–4].

If a man has obviously been murdered and his body is found, the officials of the city are to measure to find the closest city. Then that city is held responsible for the murder. It may not be that he was slain in the city, but the city is still held responsible.

This is what they are to do:

> And the priests the sons of Levi shall come near; for them the LORD thy God hath chosen to minister unto him, and to bless in the name of the LORD; and by their word shall every controversy and every stroke be tried:
>
> And all the elders of that city, that are next unto the slain man, shall wash their hands over the heifer that is beheaded in the valley:
>
> And they shall answer and say, Our hands have not shed this blood, neither have our eyes seen it.
>
> Be merciful, O LORD, unto thy people Israel, whom thou hast redeemed, and lay not innocent blood unto thy people of Israel's charge. And the blood shall be forgiven them.

> So shalt thou put away the guilt of innocent blood from among you, when thou shalt do that which is right in the sight of the LORD [Deut. 21:5–9].

There is a basic truth taught in this procedure. When a crime takes place in a city, the inhabitants of that city have a certain responsibility. This is my reason for believing that ultimately there will have to be a demand made by concerned citizens that laws be *enforced* to get rid of the crimes that are taking place. God holds a community responsible. Even if the murder was not committed in the city, the city still is responsible. The elders of that city were to come and ask for forgiveness for the city, and forgiveness would be granted them.

In America I wonder if there ever is even a suggestion that we ask God for forgiveness for our many crimes and the many things happening in our land. It is one thing to say that things are terrible, things are awful. It is another thing to go to God and say, "Oh, God, forgive us as a nation. God, forgive us for our sins today."

Do you know that Christ was murdered outside a city? Yes, He was. But His death could save His murderers. I think the Roman centurion who had charge of His crucifixion is one of the men who was saved.

Verses 10–17 give the law regulating marriage with a woman who was captured in warfare. Also there is the legal protection of the rights of the firstborn in the case of dual marriage where one wife was loved and the one was hated. We have seen this illustrated in the life of Jacob.

> If a man have a stubborn and rebellious son, which will not obey the voice of his father, or the voice of his mother, and that, when they have chastened him, will not hearken unto them:
>
> Then shall his father and his mother lay hold on him, and bring him out unto the elders of his city, and unto the gate of his place;
>
> And they shall say unto the elders of his city, This our son is stubborn and rebellious, he will not obey our voice; he is a glutton, and a drunkard.
>
> And all the men of his city shall stone him with stones, and he die: so shalt

thou put evil away from among you; and all Israel shall hear, and fear [Deut. 21:18–21].

Here is the law concerning the "prodigal son." We can understand how our Lord shocked the crowd listening to Him when He told them the parable of the prodigal son. When that boy came home, the listening crowd would expect that he would be stoned. Imagine their surprise when our Lord said that the father went out with open arms to meet the boy. They had expected the boy to get what he justly deserved. He had been a disgrace. He deserved to die. But what does the father do? He puts his arms around the boy and kisses him. He says, ". . . let us eat, and be merry: For this my son was dead, and is alive again; he was lost, and is found" (Luke 15:23-24).

Friends, aren't you glad that we are not under Law today? When we come to God, and we confess our sins, "He is faithful and just to forgive us our sins, and to cleanse us from all unrighteousness" (1 John 1:9). Instead of judgment, there is mercy for us. How wonderful and how merciful God is to accept us and receive us when we come to Him!

Now we have the strange case of one being hanged on a tree.

And if a man have committed a sin worthy of death, and he be to be put to death, and thou hang him on a tree:

His body shall not remain all night upon the tree, but thou shalt in any wise bury him that day; (for he that is hanged is accursed of God;) that thy land be not defiled, which the LORD thy God giveth thee for an inheritance [Deut. 21:22–23].

A criminal who was executed by hanging was not to remain on the tree all night. This was because everyone who hangs on a tree is accursed. It seems strange to us that this law is mentioned here. The form of capital punishment which was used in Israel was stoning. Apparently Israel did not use hanging as a form of capital punishment. So what this really means is that a person who was put to death by stoning was then hung on a tree. This applied to criminals of the worst type, to let it be seen that he had died for his terrible crime. It would be a warning to others. The body was to be taken down from the tree by nightfall and buried. The reason was that the criminal was accursed of God.

Probably Moses did not realize, and certainly the children of Israel did not realize, the full significance of this law. In Galatians 3:13, Paul picks up this statement in the law and applies it to Christ. "Christ hath redeemed us from the curse of the law, being made a curse for us: for it is written, Cursed is every one that hangeth on a tree." In the time when our Lord Jesus lived on earth, He was delivered into the hands of the Romans for execution. Because Rome was in control of the land, the death penalty could only be executed by Rome. Our Lord was crucified on a Roman cross, sometimes called a tree. Now Paul picks that up and says that when Christ was hanging there on the tree, He was taking our sins and was accursed of God in that condition. Because of what He had done? No. He became a curse for us to redeem us from the curse of the Law. He redeemed us from the curse of sin. He redeemed us from the penalty of sin, and He has bought our pardon. Why? Because He was made a curse for us.

I get weary of people arguing about whether the Romans or the Jews were to blame for the death of the Lord Jesus. Actually you and I were responsible for His death. Christ was made a curse for us. This is the thing He did for us on the cross, which makes *us* responsible for His death.

CHAPTER 22

THEME: Miscellaneous laws concerning brother relationships, mixtures, and marriage

This chapter brings us to another division of the Book of Deuteronomy. We have seen the repetition and interpretation of the Ten Commandments in chapters 5–7. Then there are the religious and national regulations in chapters 8–21. Now we come to regulations for domestic and personal relations in chapters 22–26. God directed many of these laws to the nation; now He gets right down to the nitty-gritty where the people live with laws relative to their domestic and their personal relations.

BROTHER RELATIONSHIPS

Thou shalt not see thy brother's ox or his sheep go astray, and hide thyself from them: thou shalt in any case bring them again unto thy brother.

And if thy brother be not nigh unto thee, or if thou know him not, then thou shalt bring it unto thine own house, and it shall be with thee until thy brother seek after it, and thou shalt restore it to him again [Deut. 22:1–2].

In my day we have heard a great deal about a good neighbor policy, and we see that God had a good neighbor policy for His people in that day. I remember during Franklin Roosevelt's administration when he came out with the "good neighbor policy," all the pundits and reporters acclaimed it as something brand new. They hailed Roosevelt as a sort of Messiah and thought he had come up with something wonderful. May I say to you that the good neighbor policy is as old as Moses—actually much older than Moses. It goes back to the very throne of God in eternity. He is the One who says we are to adopt a good neighbor policy, and it is to be demonstrated in our everyday life.

Thou shalt not see thy brother's ass or his ox fall down by the way, and hide thyself from them: thou shalt surely help him to lift them up again [Deut. 22:4].

They were not to assume a nonchalant attitude toward the neighbor, nor were they to pass by as if the neighbor's problem was none of their business. They were to extend their help to the neighbor.

DRESS CODE

The woman shall not wear that which pertaineth unto a man, neither shall man put on a woman's garment: for all that do so are abomination unto the LORD thy God [Deut. 22:5].

Someone will say this does not apply to us today because we are not under the Law. That is true. However, all these laws which we are studying do lay down certain principles which we do well to notice. I may be out of step with the times, but I believe it is still true today that a woman looks better dressed as a woman, and a man looks better dressed as a man.

As my wife and I were driving in San Francisco, we were behind a little Volkswagen. I remarked that the wife was driving and the man was sitting next to her, and she was driving pretty fast. When they were going up a hill, they couldn't mantain their speed, so I passed them. Do you know that I was wrong? The man was driving and the woman was sitting beside him. That man looked like a woman, and the woman looked like a man. Frankly, I don't see the benefit of that.

God created us male and female. God is saying here that a man ought to look like a man, and a woman ought to look like a woman. We are having a great deal of trouble today because the sexes are trying to look alike and are trying to act alike. I personally feel that womanhood is paying an awful price for demanding equal rights. Men would like to treat women as women, and that means men would like to elevate them, and give them more than equal rights.

PROTECTION FOR BIRDS

If a bird's nest chance to be before thee in the way in any tree, or on the ground, whether they be young ones, or eggs, and the dam sitting upon the young, or upon the eggs, thou shalt not take the dam with the young:

But thou shalt in any wise let the dam go, and take the young to thee; that it may be well with thee, and that thou mayest prolong thy days [Deut. 22:6–7].

It is a wonderful thing to see that God is concerned for the birds. Remember the

Lord Jesus said that not even a single sparrow falls without the Father (Matt. 10:29). Actually, the language has the thought that a sparrow always falls into the lap of the Father. Just a bird—yet the Father is concerned about it! The Lord Jesus said, "Fear ye not therefore, ye are of more value than many sparrows" (Matt. 10:31). How wonderful that is. If the Father is concerned about a sparrow, He is also concerned and knows all about you.

BUILDING CODE

When thou buildest a new house, then thou shalt make a battlement for thy roof, that thou bring no blood upon thine house, if any man fall from thence [Deut. 22:8].

One must understand that the roof of the house in that day in Israel served as the front porch, the patio, the deck, whatever you wish to call it. It was the place where the family went to sit in the cool of the evening. Now God says that the area is to be protected. There was to be a railing around it so little children would not fall off and so that people would not step off the roof in the darkness.

Do you know that it is only in recent years that our nation has had building codes to protect people? God is not behind the times as a great many people seem to think He is. God has a concern about the way people build their homes. He is interested in that.

He wants your home to be dedicated to Him, and He wants that home to be a safe place. Do you have a railing around your home? Do you protect your children from the things of this world? Many parents let their children move from the home and do not even know where the children are. Many children have gone out to live on the street or in communes. The railing, the protection, is not there as it should be in the modern home.

MIXTURES

Thou shalt not sow thy vineyard with divers seeds: lest the fruit of thy seed which thou hast sown, and the fruit of thy vineyard, be defiled.

Thou shalt not plow with an ox and an ass together [Deut. 22:9-10].

This sounds to me like a humorous thing which the Lord is saying here. Actually I saw this done over in Israel. In fact, I have a slide that I took showing an Arab plowing with an ox and an ass yoked together. So they do this over there even today. God says that

Israel should not plow that way. Someone may ask, "What is wrong with that?" Well, an ox is an ox and an ass is an ass, and they do not go together. They don't walk together—their gait is different, and they do not pull together.

Have you noticed that the Lord does not like mixtures? The same thing is true in marriage. God does not want a mixture of the saved and the unsaved. Unfortunately, I have seen quite a few marriages that reminded me of an ox and an ass yoked together—a Christian girl marries an unsaved fellow, or vice versa.

Thou shalt not wear a garment of divers sorts, as of woollen and linen together [Deut. 22:11].

Do you know what happens with a mixture like that? When you wash it, the wool will shrink but the linen will not. Then you have a real problem.

Thou shalt make thee fringes upon the four quarters of thy vesture, wherewith thou coverest thyself [Deut. 22:12].

That fringe was most generally blue. We know it was blue on the garment of the high priest. The fringe was a reminder of their relationship to God. Later the fringes became distinct badges of Judaism.

God warns against mixtures. The child of God cannot mix with the world. I hear Christians say that they go the way of the world in order to reach the people of the world. I have news for you. That is not the way to reach them. If you ever hear of anybody being reached because a Christian went the way of the world, let me know. The seeds were not to be mixed. The ox and the ass were not to try to work together. The wool and the linen were not to be mixed. The Christian is not to mix with the world, my friend.

MARRIAGE

If any man take a wife, and go in unto her, and hate her,

And give occasions of speech against her, and bring up an evil name upon her, and say, I took this woman, and when I came to her, I found her not a maid:

Then shall the father of the damsel, and her mother, take and bring forth the tokens of the damsel's virginity unto the elders of the city in the gate [Deut. 22:13–15].

Here was a law to protect the innocent wife, and it was to keep a wife from being falsely charged. This protected a wife from a godless and hateful husband. It was a way we do not have today, but God had made an arrangement to protect a wife under such circumstances.

> **But if this thing be true, and the tokens of virginity be not found for the damsel:**

> **Then they shall bring out the damsel to the door of her father's house, and the men of her city shall stone her with stones that she die: because she hath wrought folly in Israel, to play the whore in her father's house: so shalt thou put evil away from among you [Deut. 22:20–21].**

Suppose the woman was guilty. Then she was to be stoned.

Today people talk about the "new" morality and consider sex apart from marriage a great step forward. God gave a standard of morality to His people, Israel. God-given morality has always been a blessing to any nation. Any nation that has broken over at this point has gone down. When I think of this, and when I think of the condition of my country, I weep. Under God's law to Israel, a person guilty of adultery was stoned to death, whether man or woman. If we did that here in Southern California, there would be so many rock piles it would be impossible to drive a car through this part of the country.

God honors marriage and God honors sexual purity. Adultery in Israel was to be punished by stoning. This tells us how God feels about adultery, friends. Remember that God's love for His people is expressed in His Law. This law regarding the protection of the sanctity of marriage is a very fine example of His love and concern for the human family.

CHAPTER 23

THEME: The world, the flesh, and the devil

Chapter 23 continues this very interesting section regarding regulations for domestic and personal relationships. The world, the flesh, and the devil are the three enemies a believer contends with daily, even hourly, and moment by moment.

We are living in a day when very plain language is being used—in fact, vulgar language. God in His Word also uses very plain language, but it is by no means vulgar. Where the Bible deals with very personal issues, that section is generally avoided. However, I do not think we should avoid it, as it holds very practical spiritual lessons for us.

> **He that is wounded in the stones, or hath his privy member cut off, shall not enter into the congregation of the LORD [Deut. 23:1].**

This is a most unusual law, is it not? What is God trying to teach us here? I believe that this would correspond to asceticism, and God condemns it.

During the Middle Ages, men saw the corruption in Europe and in Asia and in North Africa, and they turned from the things of the world to become ascetics. They retired to monasteries to get away from the world. Very candidly, one probably couldn't blame them for doing it at that time. But this is an extreme and God warns against it.

In Protestantism one can find that same type of legalism today. There are those who feel they are living the "separated life." Yet I have never found one of those folk to be a joyful person. As a matter of fact, I have found some of them to be dangerous people. They act very pious and seem very shocked when anything that is worldly is mentioned before them. I have found that those same people can be the meanest gossips, and that they are not always honorable in their business relations. I have had a very bitter experience in my own life with a little group of "separated Christians" who were totally, absolutely dishonest. I believe God is warning against asceticism. He does not accept that kind of thing.

> **A bastard shall not enter into the congregation of the LORD; even to his tenth generation shall he not enter into the congregation of the LORD [Deut. 23:2].**

God uses some pretty strong language here. An illegitimate child could not enter the congregation of the Lord. What does that mean for us today?

You must be born again to be a child of God. There are a lot of people today who say, "I am a child of the King," but they are not a child of the King. They are illegitimate. One can be religious and not be born again. Such a one is not a child of God at all. God makes that very clear. Nicodemus was a Pharisee, a very religious man, a spiritual ruler of the people, a man who wore his phylacteries. Yet that man was illegitimate, and our Lord said to him that he must be born again. Our Lord almost rudely interrupted him to make that clear to him (John 3:3).

As I hold many meetings all over this country, I meet many pastors. One Baptist pastor told me, "There are a lot of baptized pagans today. They are hell-doomed sinners, and they think because they have been baptized they are children of God." God says that an illegitimate son is not going to heaven—he shall not enter the congregation. God doesn't have illegitimate children. His children are all legitimate because they have been born again.

There is a good question for you to ask yourself today. Have you been born again? Do you know Christ as your Savior? "But as many as received him, to them gave he power to become the sons of God, even to them that believe on his name: Which were born, not of blood, nor of the will of the flesh, nor of the will of man, but of God" (John 1:12–13). Do you qualify as a legitimate child of God? I don't care how many ceremonies you have been through, or how many churches you have joined, or how religious you may be—unless you are a child of the King, you are illegitimate.

FALSE RELIGIONS

An Ammonite or Moabite shall not enter into the congregation of the Lord; even to their tenth generation shall they not enter into the congregation of the Lord for ever:

Because they met you not with bread and with water in the way, when ye came forth out of Egypt; and because they hired against thee Balaam the son of Beor of Pethor of Mesopotamia, to curse thee [Deut. 23:3–4].

Archaeologists have discovered that the Ammonites and the Moabites were pagan to the worst degree. They have found a great many of their little images to Baal. False religion is not to enter into the congregation of the Lord. And how can one recognize false reli-

gion? "By their fruits ye shall know them." The evidence was that they "met you not with bread and water" in that great and terrible wilderness, and they hired Balaam to curse Israel.

Nevertheless the Lord thy God would not hearken unto Balaam; but the Lord thy God turned the curse into a blessing unto thee, because the Lord thy God loved thee.

Thou shalt not seek their peace nor their prosperity all thy days for ever [Deut. 23:5–6].

This sounds harsh, but it is a warning against linking up with false religions. False religion is satanic in origin. The devil is not to enter into the congregation of the Lord. It is false religion that has damned this world more than anything else. It is possible for a beautiful church building with a high steeple and a lovely organ to be the very den of Satan. We are to beware of false religion. False religion has no place in the congregation of the Lord.

Thou shalt not abhor an Edomite; for he is thy brother: thou shalt not abhor an Egyptian; because thou wast a stranger in his land [Deut. 23:7].

We saw back in the Book of Genesis that Edom is Esau, and Esau and Jacob were twin brothers. Ammon and Moab were to be abhored. Why not Edom also? Because an Edomite was their brother.

For the believer, Esau represents our old nature, the flesh. We can hate the flesh, try to step on it, try to punish it, or multilate it but none of that will do any good. We are not to abhor the flesh, but we are not to yield to it. The old nature is not to control us. The flesh is in rebellion against God, but it is a part of us, and hating it will not get us anywhere.

They were not to abhor an Egyptian. Why? "Because thou wast a stranger in his land."

Egypt in Scripture represents the world. We are told "Love not the world, neither the things that are in the world. If any man love the world, the love of the Father is not in him" (1 John 2:15). Again let me say that this does not mean we are not to appreciate the beauties of nature or our homes, our cars, and other conveniences that are part of the world around us. The point is that we are not to fall in love with these things. Of course we are not to despise them, but we are not to love them. You and I are strangers and pilgrims down here in this world. Just as the children of Israel were never called upon to plant flowers in the wilderness, neither are we called upon to join movements that try to straighten out the world. We are to give out the Word of God—that is our business—but we are pilgrims and strangers here, just passing through.

CLEANLINESS

Now beginning with verse 9 is a section on cleanliness. Even when they were out in the field of battle, they were to maintain a clean camp.

Thou shalt have a place also without the camp, whither thou shalt go forth abroad:

And thou shalt have a paddle upon thy weapon; and it shall be, when thou wilt ease thyself abroad, thou shalt dig therewith, and shalt turn back and cover that which cometh from thee [Deut. 23:12–13].

God is interested in sanitation. Wherever Christianity has gone, there has been an improvement in sanitary conditions.

We hear so much about pollution today. Who polluted this universe? Certainly, it was not God who did it. He gave us clean streams, clean air, clean water. It is sin, sinful man, who pollutes this earth today. If men would follow the rules which God has given, this earth would be a sanitary place.

For the LORD thy God walketh in the midst of thy camp, to deliver thee, and to give up thine enemies before thee; therefore shall thy camp be holy: that he see no unclean thing in thee, and turn away from thee [Deut. 23:14].

God is interested in cleanliness. I think it was Webster who said that cleanliness is next to godliness. I think it is even closer than that—I would classify cleanliness as a part of godliness. God wants us clean in body, clean in environment, clean in thought, clean in action. We are to be a holy people in this world today. Say, this book is very practical, is it not?

There shall be no whore of the daughters of Israel, nor a sodomite of the sons of Israel.

Thou shalt not bring the hire of a whore, or the price of a dog, into the house of the LORD thy God for any vow: for even both these are abomination unto the LORD thy God [Deut. 23:17–18].

God said there were not to be harlots or sodomites among His people. God says that under no circumstance will He accept income from that which is illegal or from that which is immoral or wrong. He does not want any of it.

Now I am going to say something that I know is not popular to say. I do not believe that any Christian organization should receive money from any industry that is illegal or immoral. I thank God for the two schools that turned down a gift from a large brewery. Many questionable businesses try to gain respectability by giving to charity, as you know.

Thou shalt not lend upon usury to thy brother; usury of money, usury of victuals, usury of any thing that is lent upon usury:

Unto a stranger thou mayest lend upon usury: but unto thy brother thou shalt not lend upon usury: that the LORD thy God may bless thee in all that thou settest thine hand to in the land whither thou goest to possess it [Deut. 23:19–20].

Here again God is insisting that they take care of their brother. And if they lend him money, they are not to charge him usury, which is interest.

When thou shalt vow a vow unto the LORD thy God, thou shalt not slack to pay it: for the LORD thy God will surely require it of thee; and it would be sin in thee.

But if thou shalt forbear to vow, it shall be no sin in thee [Deut. 23:21–22].

A vow to the Lord was a voluntary act. No one was required to take a vow. However, once a person had made a vow to the Lord, that vow was absolutely binding, as we have mentioned before.

When thou comest into they neighbour's vineyard, then thou mayest eat grapes thy fill at thine own pleasure; but thou shalt not put any in thy vessel.

When thou comest into the standing corn of thy neighbour, then thou mayest pluck the ears with thine hand; but thou shalt not move a sickle unto thy neighbour's standing corn [Deut. 23:24–25].

We will find that the disciples of our Lord did this very thing. Because they were hungry, they began to pluck the grain and eat it as they passed through a field. As we see here in Deuteronomy, this was not illegal. God said that a farmer was to extend this courtesy.

CHAPTER 24

THEME: *Divorce*

This chapter begins with the Mosaic Law of divorce. The remainder of the chapter is devoted to people-to-people relationships in which mercy is to be shown. Friends, God is merciful, and He expects His people to exhibit mercy toward each other.

THE MOSAIC LAW OF DIVORCE

When a man hath taken a wife, and married her, and it come to pass that she find no favor in his eyes, because he hath found some uncleanness in her: then let him write her a bill of divorcement, and give it in her hand, and send her out of his house.

And when she is departed out of his house, she may go and be another man's wife.

And if the latter husband hate her, and write her a bill of divorcement, and giveth it in her hand, and sendeth her out of his house; or if the latter husband die, which took her to be his wife;

Her former husband, which sent her away, may not take her again to be his wife, after that she is defiled; for that is abomination before the LORD: and thou shalt not cause the land to sin, which the LORD thy God giveth thee for an inheritance [Deut. 24:1–4].

Now you may wonder why remarriage was put on that kind of basis. Well, because God doesn't agree to wife-swapping, which this would amount to. There is to be no trading back and forth.

This seems like a very easy form of divorce, does it not? It was very easy. Why did God permit it? Well, the Lord Jesus was approached with that question. "They say unto him, Why did Moses then command to give a writing of divorcement, and to put her away? He saith unto them, Moses because of the hardness of your hearts suffered you to put away your wives: but from the beginning it was not so. And I say unto you, Whosoever shall put away his wife, except it be for fornication, and shall marry another, committeth adultery: and whoso marrieth her which is put away doth commit adultery" (Matt. 19:7–9). Unfaithfulness to the marriage vow was the only grounds for divorce. (There is some speculation about 1 Corinthians 7 opening up another reason or basis for divorce.)

Jesus said that Moses was permitted to make this law because of the hardness of their hearts. There are a great many things which God permits in His permissive will. He permits it because of the hardness of our hearts. This is still true today in many cases of divorce. It is also true in many of our homes, and it is true in the personal lives of many individuals. God is merciful and gracious to us and permits things in our lives that are not in His direct will. It is His permissive will that manifests His grace to us. Knowing this, it would behoove some of the more spiritual brethren not to be so critical of other folk today.

When a man hath taken a new wife, he shall not go out to war, neither shall he be charged with any business: but he shall be free at home one year, and shall cheer up his wife which he hath taken [Deut. 24:5].

God protects the home even in the time of war. God regards the sacredness of the marriage vow.

VARIED REGULATIONS

If a man be found stealing any of his brethren of the children of Israel, and maketh merchandise of him, or selleth him; then that thief shall die; and thou shalt put evil away from among you [Deut. 24:7].

God condemns slavery. There is no question about that.

When thou beatest thine olive tree, thou shalt not go over the boughs again: it shall be for the stranger, for the fatherless, and for the widow.

When thou gatherest the grapes of thy vineyard, thou shalt not glean it afterward: it shall be for the stranger, for the fatherless, and for the widow.

And thou shalt remember that thou wast a bondman in the land of Egypt: therefore I command thee to do this thing [Deut. 24:20–22].

God was taking care of those who were helpless, those less fortunate ones. God had a good poverty program, and the interesting thing is that it worked. We will see this a little later on when we get to the Book of Ruth.

CHAPTER 25

THEME: Punishment of the guilty; law protecting widows; judgment of Amalek

This is a remarkable chapter that expresses God's concern for protecting the innocent by punishing the guilty and by perpetuating a brother's name in Israel. It concludes with the command to "blot out the remembrance of Amalek from under heaven."

FORTY STRIPES

There were certain crimes that arose through difficulties between individuals. I think that in our legal nomenclature today we would call them misdemeanors. These would not be serious crimes which would merit the death sentence. However, they would require punishment.

If there be a controversy between men, and they come unto judgment, that the judges may judge them; then they shall justify the righteous, and condemn the wicked.

And it shall be, if the wicked man be worthy to be beaten, that the judge shall cause him to lie down, and to be beaten before his face, according to his fault, by a certain number.

Forty stripes he may give him, and not exceed: lest, if he should exceed, and beat him above these with many stripes, then thy brother should seem vile unto thee [Deut. 25:1–3].

Forty stripes would be the limit. Otherwise there would be the danger of killing the man. The number of the stripes, one to forty, depended on the seriousness of the crime.

This method of punishment has gone entirely out of style. It was interesting to me to hear several outstanding attorneys discussing this. They agreed that it would break up a great deal of this lawlessness if there were public floggings. That is, when a person commits a minor crime, instead of putting him in an air-conditioned jail to loaf for a few days, he should be taken out and publicly flogged. Apparently God thought that is the way it should be handled, and the answer as to whether or not it was effective is found in the fact that Israel had a very low crime level.

THE OX NOT TO BE MUZZLED

Thou shalt not muzzle the ox when he treadeth out the corn [Deut. 25:4].

Here is a lovely thing. God is protecting the ox. When I was in Israel, I took pictures of this very thing because they still do this over there. For a long time I watched an Arab who had his ox going round and round, treading out the corn, and, do you know, he had his ox muzzled. God had said, "Don't do that. The ox is working for you; he is treading out your corn—let him eat." God's concern is a very wonderful thing.

It is interesting that Paul reaches into the Book of Deuteronomy and uses this verse in his letter to the Corinthian Christians. "For it is written in the law of Moses, Thou shalt not muzzle the mouth of the ox that treadeth out the corn. Doth God take care for oxen? Or saith he it altogether for our sakes? For our sakes, no doubt, this is written: that he that ploweth should plow in hope; and that he that thresheth in hope should be partaker of his hope. If we have sown unto you spiritual things, is it a great thing if we shall reap your carnal things?" (1 Cor. 9:9–11). Do you see how Paul is applying this? He is saying, "Pay your preacher." "Even so hath the Lord ordained that they which preach the gospel should live of the gospel" (1 Cor. 9:14). The man who is ministering to you in spiritual things is feeding you spiritual food. You, in turn, are to feed him with material things. That is how Paul is making the application of this verse.

While I sit and talk into a microphone, making a record on tape for broadcasting on radio, I see the tape going round and round, and I feel like an ox treading out the corn. And you know, that is what I am trying to do—tread out the corn. God says not to muzzle the ox that treads out the corn. I'll let you make your own application of that!

LAW PROTECTING WIDOWS

Now we move on to another point. You can't make me believe that God does not have a sense of humor. God has a law here to take care of widows. It worked effectively, as we shall see in the Book of Ruth. But to me it is very humorous.

If brethren dwell together, and one of them die, and have no child, the wife of the dead shall not marry without unto a stranger: her husband's brother shall go in unto her, and take her to him to wife,

and perform the duty of an husband's brother unto her.

And it shall be, that the firstborn which she beareth shall succeed in the name of his brother which is dead, that his name be not put out of Israel [Deut. 25:5–6].

God was protecting womanhood. We hear a great deal about women's rights, and it is interesting that God guarded their rights. We need to remember that in Israel most of the people were farmers. The land was divided among the people and each had his own piece of land. When a man died, he would leave a farm with all his wheat and corn and also his livestock of sheep and oxen. The widow was left with this farm to care for. Suppose some man from the outside, a foreigner, or a man from another tribe wanted to marry her and thus come into possession of the land. This was forbidden. She was not permitted to marry outside. Here is a case where the widow does the proposing. What she was to do was to go and claim one of her husband's brothers, a cousin, or the nearest relative and ask him to marry her.

And if the man like not to take his brother's wife, then let his brother's wife go up to the gate unto the elders, and say, My husband's brother refuseth to raise up unto his brother a name in Israel, he will not perform the duty of my husband's brother [Deut. 25:7].

If the brother, or relative, doesn't want to marry her, she can take him to court, you see.

Then the elders of his city shall call him, and speak unto him: and if he stand to it, and say, I like not to take her;

Then shall his brother's wife come unto him in the presence of the elders, and loose his shoe from off his foot, and spit in his face, and shall answer and say, So shall it be done unto that man that will not build up his brother's house.

And his name shall be called in Israel, The house of him that hath his shoe loosed [Deut. 25:8–10].

If the man refused to marry her, the woman could take him to court—the city gate was where court was held in those days. She would tell the elders how it was. If he still refuses to marry the widow, there is a penalty. He is disgraced for not performing that which he should do according to the Law. It reveals the fact that he is not being true to his brother, or

to his family, or to his tribe, or to his nation, or to his God. The man is disgraced.

Here is a marvelous example of how God protected the widow. We will see this law in operation when we get to the Book of Ruth. It was used effectively in that book.

Can you imagine how this would affect a family in Israel? Suppose there was a family of four sons living on a farm in Ephraim country. Suppose that night after night one of the boys went off with the lantern and when he came back to go to bed, he would be whistling. Pretty soon the family would get into a huddle and the brothers would ask him, "Where are you going every evening?" They'd do a little investigating of their own and find there was a daughter in the family that lived down the road. So the brother would admit, "I believe in the good-neighbor policy, and I have been going down there to visit that family that just moved in." And he would admit that he was thinking of marrying the girl. Now, if those brothers didn't care too much for that girl, can you imagine what would happen? They'd say, "Listen—before you get any notions, you go to the doctor and have a physical check-up. We want to be sure you are in good health before you marry her, because none of us want to get stuck with her." Believe me, they got down to business. Getting married was a family affair. This was God's way of drawing families very close together, of protecting the widows, and also of protecting the land. You see, this was the way the land would always stay in the same family. It was a very good law for them.

The next verses give a severe punishment for involvement when men strive together. Also God commands His people to be accurate in their measurements and in their weights. They are to be absolutely honest in their business dealings.

JUDGMENT OF AMALEK

In Exodus 17 we have the record of Amalek's attack upon the children of Israel when they came out of Egypt. The Amalekites were marauding nomads out on that desert.

Remember what Amalek did unto thee by the way, when ye were come forth out of Egypt;

How he met thee by the way, and smote the hindmost of thee, even all that were feeble behind thee, when thou wast faint and weary; and he feared not God.

Therefore it shall be, when the LORD thy God hath given thee rest from all thine

enemies round about, in the land which the Lord thy God giveth thee for an inheritance to possess it, that thou shalt blot out the remembrance of Amalek from under heaven; thou shalt not forget it [Deut. 25:17–19].

Israel had suffered an unprovoked attack by Amalek at Rephidim. That was the battle when Moses was on the top of the mountain and Aaron and Hur held up his arms in prayer to God. When his hands were up, Joshua and the army of Israel won; when his hands were down, they lost. They finally won a victory over Amalek. At that time the Lord said a very interesting thing, ". . . thou shalt blot out the remembrance of Amalek from under heaven."

As I have mentioned before, Amalek represents the flesh; that is, the fallen nature we inherited from Adam. God intends eventually to get rid of that old nature—it would be impossible to go to heaven with it. You and I have an old nature that can never be obedient unto God. We will deal with this subject quite thoroughly when we get to the Epistle to the Romans. Amalek is an illustration of the flesh. As long as we are in this life, we shall never get rid of the flesh—"Because the Lord hath sworn that the Lord will have war with Amalek from generation to generation" (Exod. 17:16). We saw in chapter 23 that the flesh is not for us to despise. We cannot overcome the flesh by becoming ascetic or by trying to beat it down or by becoming super pious. That won't accomplish anything. But we do need to recognize that there is a war going on in each one of us. It is a war between the spirit and the flesh.

"For the flesh lusteth against the Spirit, and the Spirit against the flesh: and these are contrary the one to the other: so that ye cannot do the things that ye would" (Gal. 5:17). We cannot overcome the flesh by fighting. The only way we can overcome the flesh is by yielding to the Spirit of God. Only the Spirit of God can produce the fruits of the Spirit in our lives. The Lord says that He is going to blot out the remembrances of Amalek from under heaven. I thank God that He intends to get rid of the flesh someday!

CHAPTER 26

THEME: *First fruits—thanksgiving*

The chapter before us presents the beautiful ceremony in connection with the offering of firstfruits. Acknowledging that all the produce of the land came from God, and as an expression of thankfulness for His goodness, the Israelites brought as an offering to Him a portion of the fruit that ripened first.

And it shall be, when thou art come in unto the land which the Lord thy God giveth thee for an inheritance, and possessest it, and dwellest therein;

That thou shalt take of the first of all the fruit of the earth, which thou shalt bring of thy land that the Lord thy God giveth thee, and shalt put it in a basket, and shalt go unto the place which the Lord thy God shall choose to place his name there.

And thou shalt go unto the priest that shall be in those days, and say unto him, I profess this day unto the Lord thy God, that I am come unto the country which the Lord sware unto our fathers for to give us.

And the priest shall take the basket out of thine hand, and set it down before the altar of the Lord thy God [Deut. 26:1–4].

As he presented his offering of firstfruits to the Lord, he was to review God's gracious dealings with his people in delivering them from oppression in Egypt and in bringing them to the bountiful land He had promised them.

And thou shalt speak and say before the Lord thy God, A Syrian ready to perish was my father, and he went down into Egypt, and sojourned there with a few, and became there a nation, great, mighty, and populous [Deut. 26:5].

There is something here I would like to have you note. He comes to God first with confession. The Israelite would confess, "A Syrian ready to perish was my father." Was Abraham an Israelite? No, he actually was not. What about Isaac? Well, he was not either. What about Jacob? Technically, Jacob was not an Israelite. The crowd that went down to Egypt were Syrians. Abraham was no more an Israelite than he was an Ishmaelite—since both peoples descended from him. Abraham was a Syrian as to nationality.

And the Egyptians evil entreated us, and afflicted us, and laid upon us hard bondage:

And when we cried unto the LORD God of our fathers, the LORD heard our voice, and looked on our affliction, and our labour, and our oppression:

And the LORD brought us forth out of Egypt with a mighty hand, and with an outstretched arm, and with great terribleness, and with signs, and with wonders:

And he hath brought us into this place, and hath given us this land, even a land that floweth with milk and honey.

And now, behold, I have brought the first fruits of the land, which thou, O LORD, hast given me. And thou shalt set it before the LORD thy God, and worship before the LORD thy God [Deut. 26:6–10].

To the Israelite it was to be a time of true thanksgiving. Thanksgiving for us is a day when we bring a sacrifice of praise and thanksgiving unto God—and that's good. Most of us,

and I confess I am in the category, eat a big turkey dinner. Usually friends invite us out to dinner. This past Thanksgiving was a glorious time. But how many of us really made an offering to God on Thanksgiving Day? Israel did—this was the beginning of Thanksgiving. If we go back and check the Pilgrims and the Puritans, we will find that they, out of their meager resources, made an offering unto God on that day. Wonderful as it is to make an offering of thanksgiving and praise with out lips, we ought to back it up with our purse. Praise and purse go together in God's Word.

The second part of this chapter deals with the Israelites' declaration of obedience to God.

When thou hast made an end of tithing all the tithes of thine increase the third year, which is the year of tithing, and hast given it unto the Levite, the stranger, the fatherless, and the widow, that they may eat within thy gates, and be filled;

Then thou shalt say before the LORD thy God, I have brought away the hallowed things out of mine house, and also have given them unto the Levite, and unto the stranger, to the fatherless, and to the widow, according to all thy commandments which thou hast commanded me: I have not transgressed thy commandments, neither have I forgotten them [Deut. 26:12–13].

If Israel would keep His commandments, He promises to make them His peculiar people and to place them above all nations of the earth.

CHAPTER 27

THEME: *The future of the land: curses for disobedience*

We come now to one of the most vital sections of the Book of Deuteronomy. This is now Moses' third oration. It belongs to the next major section of the book which is regarding the future in the land. This is the third main section of the book and extends from chapter 27–30. In it we find the so-called Palestinian covenant which God made with the nation Israel.

I have called Deuteronomy 28–30 the prewritten history of Israel in the land before they

enter the land. The section from Deuteronomy 29–30:10 is the Palestinian covenant.

As we begin this new section, I think we ought to say something about a covenant. That word has occurred several times already. There are different kinds of covenants. We find that individuals make covenants with each other. There are covenants of this kind mentioned in the Bible. Then there are nations that make covenants, and some of them are mentioned in the Bible. Then there are the covenants which God made with His people and with all humanity in the Old Testament. We have already studied the Adamic covenant, the Noahic covenant, the Abrahamic covenant, and the Mosaic covenant. Now we have come to the Palestinian covenant.

The covenants which God makes are divided into two different classifications: conditional and unconditional. We could call them eternal covenants and temporary covenants. The eternal covenant is a permanent covenant and it is unconditional. The temporary covenant is a conditional covenant. It is important to distinguish between the two.

The covenant which God made with Abraham was an unconditional covenant. The covenant God made with Moses, the Ten Commandments, was a conditional covenant—"Now therefore, *if* ye will obey my voice indeed, and keep my covenant, then . . ." (Exod. 19:5). The Palestinian covenant which God made in the chapters we are about to study is an unconditional covenant.

This covenant has to do with Israel's future. We understand that these people are now standing on the east bank of the Jordan River. They are preparing to enter the land. This is the new generation; the old generation has died in the wilderness. Moses himself will not enter into the land. We shall see that this book closes with a requiem to Moses. He dies, but the people enter the land under a new leader. Now this particular section is prophetic and has to do with their future in the land which they are about to enter. We find here some of the most remarkable prophecies in the entire Word of God.

And Moses with the elders of Israel commanded the people, saying, Keep all the commandments which I command you this day.

And it shall be on the day when ye shall pass over Jordan unto the land which the Lord thy God giveth thee, that thou shalt set thee up great stones, and plaster them with plaster:

And thou shalt write upon them all the words of this law, when thou art passed over, that thou mayest go in unto the land which the Lord thy God giveth thee, a land that floweth with milk and honey; as the Lord God of thy fathers hath promised thee [Deut. 27:1–3].

They were told that when they crossed over into the land, the Ten Commandments were to be written in stone and displayed. Their tenure in the land, their dwelling there, would be determined by their obedience to God. That was a conditional arrangement. But the *land* was given to them with no conditions attached whatsoever. God has given that land to Israel, and that is an unconditional covenant. God will bring Israel back into that land because it belongs to them. That is something very important for us to realize at the present time.

Therefore it shall be when ye be gone over Jordan, that ye shall set up these stones, which I command you this day, in mount Ebal, and thou shalt plaster them with plaster.

And there shalt thou build an altar unto the Lord thy God, an altar of stones: thou shalt not lift up any iron tool upon them.

Thou shalt build the altar of the Lord thy God of whole stones: and thou shalt offer burnt offerings thereon unto the Lord thy God:

And thou shalt offer peace offerings, and shalt eat there, and rejoice before the Lord thy God.

And thou shalt write upon the stones all the words of this law very plainly [Deut. 27:4–8].

God's law was to be prominently displayed. In fact, it was to be put in front of them wherever they went—even on the doorposts of their homes.

And Moses and the priests the Levites spake unto all Israel, saying, Take heed, and hearken, O Israel; this day thou art become the people of the Lord thy God.

Thou shalt therefore obey the voice of the Lord thy God, and do his commandments and his statutes, which I command thee this day.

And Moses charged the people the same day, saying,

These shall stand upon mount Gerizim to bless the people, when ye are come over Jordan; Simeon, and Levi, and Judah, and Issachar, and Joseph, and Benjamin [Deut. 27:9–12].

When they get into the Promised Land, the blessing of the people is to be declared from Mount Gerizim. He mentions the tribes who will do the blessing.

And these shall stand upon mount Ebal to curse; Reuben, Gad, and Asher, and Zebulun, Dan, and Naphtali [Deut. 27:13].

The tribes who are to declare the curses are to go over to Mount Ebal. These mountains are in the area where the Samaritan woman was at the well. That well is still there today. The blessings were from Mount Gerizim and the curses from Mount Ebal.

Now a list of the curses are given. After they are in the land, their tenure there is on a condition. We might say that each generation are tenants and they are to pay rent. God is the land owner, and that rent is *obedience* to God. Actually, the nation is more than a tenant because God has given Israel that land as an eternal possession. However, when a generation will not obey God, that generation would be put out of the land, even though the land remained theirs as an eternal inheritance. This is the reason that that piece of real estate is the most sensitive spot on the topside of this globe. It is the belief of a great many people that right now a world war could be triggered by what takes place in that land, and certainly this is true.

There are twelve curses given here, and I am not going into detail about them as they are self-explanatory.

Cursed be the man that maketh any graven or molten image, an abomination unto the LORD, the work of the hands of the craftsman, and putteth it in a secret place. And all the people shall answer and say, Amen [Deut. 27:15].

This has to do with the first two of the Ten Commandments.

Cursed be he that setteth light by his father or his mother. And all the people shall say, Amen [Deut. 27:16].

This deals with the fifth of the Ten Commandments.

Cursed be he that confirmeth not all the words of this law to do them. And all the people shall say, Amen [Deut. 27:26].

As you read all the verses in this chapter, you will see that they all deal with the breaking of the Ten Commandments.

CHAPTER 28

THEME: Israel's pre-written history

This chapter continues the section regarding the future of Israel. Moses pronounces the conditional part of the covenant. The people of Israel would be blessed only as they obeyed God. Their disobedience would bring curses, which are spelled out for them here.

Then we have one of the most remarkable passages of Scripture which gives their pre-written history in the land before they had even set foot on it. There are three prophecies of their dispossession—all have been fulfilled. There are three prophecies of their restoration—two have been fulfilled. Israel's third return to the land is yet future.

And it shall come to pass, if thou shalt hearken diligently unto the voice of the LORD thy God, to observe and to do all his commandments which I command thee this day, that the LORD thy God will set thee on high above all nations of the earth:

And all these blessings shall come on thee, and overtake thee, if thou shalt hearken unto the voice of the LORD thy God [Deut. 28:1–2].

"*If* thou shalt hearken diligently"—notice the great big "if." This is a conditional part of the covenant. They are going to be blessed only as they obey God.

Blessed shalt thou be in the city, and blessed shalt thou be in the field.

Blessed shall be the fruit of thy body, and the fruit of thy ground, and the fruit of thy cattle, the increase of thy kine, and the flocks of thy sheep.

Blessed shall be thy basket and thy store.

Blessed shalt thou be when thou comest in, and blessed shalt thou be when thou goest out [Deut. 28:3–6].

As you read this, perhaps you are struck by the fact that there are twelve curses pronounced but that there are only six blessings. If you want to know why this is so, I'll tell you where we pick up the rest of the blessings. Our Lord stood on the mount and delivered what is called the Sermon on the Mount. How did He begin it? *"Blessed* are the poor in spirit: for theirs is the kingdom of heaven"* (Matt. 5:3)—then the other beatitudes follow. Beginning His message like this would make the instructed Israelite listen. He was hearing of the blessings which would come to them even after their long, checkered history. At that time they had already experienced captivity twice, and they were yet to go into another captivity that would scatter them throughout the entire earth.

There is the promise of an abundance of blessing if they will obey.

And the LORD shall make thee the head, and not the tail; and thou shalt be above only, and thou shalt not be beneath; if that thou hearken unto the commandments of the LORD thy God, which I command thee this day, to observe and to do them:

And thou shalt not go aside from any of the words which I command thee this day, to the right hand, or to the left, to go after other gods to serve them [Deut. 28:13–14].

Now he returns to the curses and mentions that they all rest upon this matter of an "if."

But it shall come to pass, if thou wilt not hearken unto the voice of the LORD thy God, to observe to do all his commandments and his statutes which I command thee this day; that all these curses shall come upon thee, and overtake thee [Deut. 28:15].

Again we see that this is conditional.

Now we come to one of the most remarkable passages of Scripture. It is the history of Israel in the land, pre-written. Scripture prophesied concerning Israel's being dispossessed out of the land three times and regathered into the land three times. There are to be three dispossessions and three regatherings of Israel.

The first of these was prophesied by God to Abraham. "Know of a surety that thy seed shall be a stranger in a land that is not theirs and shall serve them; and they shall afflict them four hundred years. . . . But in the fourth generation they shall come hither again

. . . (Gen. 15:13, 16). They went down into Egypt for 430 years; then God brought them out of Egypt. That is what we are following now in Deuteronomy. They are on the east bank of the Jordan River, and God is bringing them back to the land for the first regathering. In the Book of Joshua, we will find them entering into the land, and in the Book of Judges we will find them settled in the land, which is a complete and literal fulfillment.

Now, before they have even entered the land, the second time they are to be put out of the land is mentioned here. This is a very remarkable chapter.

Thy sons and thy daughters shall be given unto another people, and thine eyes shall look, and fail with longing for them all the day long: and there shall be no might in thine hand.

The fruit of thy land, and all thy labours, shall a nation which thou knowest not eat up; and thou shalt be only oppressed and crushed alway:

So that thou shalt be mad for the sight of thine eyes which thou shalt see [Deut. 28:32–34].

This verse was accurately fulfilled in Judah's last king, Zedekiah, whose sons were slain before him; then his eyes were put out. Blind and helpless, he was carried away into Babylonian captivity.

The LORD shall smite thee in the knees, and in the legs, with a sore botch that cannot be healed, from the sole of thy foot unto the top of thy head.

The LORD shall bring thee, and thy king which thou shalt set over thee, unto a nation which neither thou nor thy fathers have known; and there shalt thou serve other gods, wood and stone.

And thou shalt become an astonishment, a proverb, and a byword, among all nations whither the LORD shall lead thee [Deut. 28:35–37].

This was to be the Babylonian Captivity which is now a matter of history. We have the record. We will learn of it later in our study of the Bible where we will read more prophecies about it and then will actually see it come to pass in both Kings and Chronicles.

Why did all this happen to them? It was because of their disobedience. God had given them the "if"s. God said, "If you obey, you will be blessed. If you disobey, you will be put out of the land."

Israel was regathered from the Babylonian Captivity. Their return to the land is recorded in Ezra and Nehemiah. The prophets, Haggai, Zechariah, and Malachi, tell of their return to the land. So then, this is the second prophecy concerning their return to the land. This has been literally fulfilled.

The third scattering of Israel was the result of being conquered by Rome. This is described prophetically.

Therefore shalt thou serve thine enemies which the LORD shall send against thee, in hunger, and in thirst, and in nakedness, and in want of all things: and he shall put a yoke of iron upon thy neck, until he have destroyed thee [Deut. 28:48].

Here in my study I have two volumes of Flavius Josephus' history in which he tells about the coming of the Romans under Titus. Rome, known as the iron kingdom, fulfilled the prediction, "He shall put a yoke of iron upon thy neck."

The LORD shall bring a nation against thee from far, from the end of the earth, as swift as the eagle flieth; a nation whose tongue thou shalt not understand [Deut. 28:49].

Rome, coming all the way from the West, spoke a language that was entirely different from Hebrew. Our English is based on Latin and the European languages, but Hebrew is a language that is related to the Asian and African and Oriental languages. It is altogether different. God says the conquerors would be "whose tongue thou shalt not understand."

It is interesting that Rome carried standards bearing the emblem of the eagle. I am of the opinion that many an instructed Israelite, when he looked over the battlements of the wall and saw the standards of Titus with an eagle on them, said, "This is *it!*"

A nation of fierce countenance, which shall not regard the person of the old, nor shew favour to the young:

And he shall eat the fruit of thy cattle, and the fruit of thy land, until thou be destroyed: which also shall not leave thee either corn, wine, or oil, or the increase of thy kine, or flocks of thy sheep, until he have destroyed thee.

And he shall besiege thee in all thy gates, until thy high and fenced walls come down, wherein thou trustedst,

throughout all thy land: and he shall besiege thee in all thy gates throughout all thy land, which the LORD thy God hath given thee.

And thou shalt eat the fruit of thine own body, the flesh of thy sons and of thy daughters, which the LORD thy God hath given thee, in the siege, and in the straitness, wherewith thine enemies shall distress thee [Deut. 28:50–53].

Josephus tells in his history how mothers were forced to give up their babies, and the flesh of the babies was eaten. The people died, and their corpses collected inside the city. They had to throw them over the wall. May I say to you that this prophecy was literally fulfilled.

And now the Jewish people are scattered throughout the world.

And the LORD shall scatter thee among all people, from the one end of the earth even unto the other; and there thou shalt serve other gods, which neither thou nor thy fathers have known, even wood and stone [Deut 28:64].

They have never returned from that dispersion. That has yet to be fulfilled. There are three prophecies of dispossessions. There are three prophecies that they will return. They have returned twice. They have not returned the third time.

So we have six prophecies. Five of them have been literally fulfilled. What do you think about the sixth one? I can tell you what I think about it. I think it will be literally fulfilled. It is yet to come in the future.

And among these nations shalt thou find no ease, neither shall the sole of thy foot have rest: but the LORD shall give thee there a trembling heart, and failing of eyes, and sorrow of mind:

And thy life shall hang in doubt before thee; and thou shalt fear day and night, and shalt have none assurance of thy life:

In the morning thou shalt say, Would God it were even! and at even thou shalt say, Would God it were morning! for the fear of thine heart wherewith thou shalt fear, and for the sight of thine eyes which thou shalt see [Deut. 28:65–67].

How literally all this has been fulfilled in the persecutions of the Jews down through the centuries! This is all the consequence of their continued disobedience. They have no rest, and they have a trembling heart. In the morning they wish for evening, and in the evening they wish for morning. How sad. God is true to His Word, friends. What a lesson there is in that for us.

This should move us to tell the gospel to these people who are dispossessed from the land. The gospel of the Lord Jesus Christ is for Jew and Gentile alike, and it is for the "obedience to the faith among all nations" (Rom. 1:5).

CHAPTER 29

THEME: Palestinian Covenant (introduction)

Chapters 29 and 30 are considered the Palestinian covenant. Dr. Lewis Sperry Chafer considered chapters 28–30 to be the covenant. The Scofield Reference Bible considers it to be 29–30:10 with chapter 29 as the introduction. In my notes I take chapter 29 through the first ten verses of chapter 30 as being the covenant, although the covenant proper is in the first ten verses of chapter 30. This chapter 29 is a preliminary.

RESUMÉ OF GOD'S CARE

This is now the fourth oration of Moses.

These are the words of the covenant, which the Lord commanded Moses to make with the children of Israel in the land of Moab, beside the covenant which he made with them in Horeb [Deut. 29:1].

The covenant made in Horeb was the Ten Commandments or what we know as the Mosaic Law. The covenant which God is going to make with them here relates to the land, and it is called the Palestinian covenant. God makes this covenant with them just before they enter the land.

And Moses called unto all Israel, and said unto them, Ye have seen all that the Lord did before your eyes in the land of Egypt unto Pharaoh, and unto all his servants, and unto all his land [Deut. 29:2].

These people would have been children and teenagers when they witnessed these things. The oldest people in the nations would have been about sixty years old after wandering through the wilderness since the failure at Kadesh-Barnea. Only Joshua and Caleb remained of the old generation.

The great temptations which thine eyes have seen, the signs, and those great miracles:

Yet the Lord hath not given you an heart to perceive, and eyes to see, and ears to hear, unto this day [Deut. 29: 3–4].

In spite of seeing all the signs, they still did not perceive. Isaiah has a great deal to say about that. Paul in Romans deals with the blindness of Israel. "(According as it is written, God hath given them the spirit of slumber, eyes that they should not see, and ears that they should not hear;) unto this day" (Rom. 11:8). Does this mean that God will not permit them to comprehend, that God turns them off? No, it means they are already off. God has to turn us on! That is something which we need to recognize today. Until God opens the eyes and the ears of men and women, they cannot hear the gospel. Now do not misunderstand me—they can hear the words, but they cannot hear the gospel with understanding.

A writer of a magazine article classified our program of going through the Bible in five years with religious racketeers. He seems to think that if you attempt to teach the Bible you are running a religious racket! I wish the man would listen to the program to see what we are trying to do. And yet I still feel frustrated because if he did listen, he wouldn't understand. He wouldn't be able to comprehend. He would still feel that we are teaching the Bible on the radio for some ulterior motive. He would feel that the Bible is just being used as propaganda. Why? Because it would take the Spirit of God to work through the Word of God to open his eyes and his heart. Then he would see that the Word of God is effective in the lives of many people.

Now God says that he just left these people as they were. They had no intention to turn to

Him. They had broken communication with the living and true God. Therefore, God would just leave them in their state of unbelief.

And I have led you forty years in the wilderness: your clothes are not waxen old upon you, and thy shoe is not waxen old upon thy foot [Deut. 29:5].

Imagine walking for forty years in the same pair of shoes, and their not getting old! Now Moses goes on to describe their journey through the wilderness and how this should have opened their eyes.

A great many people today say that if God would only perform a miracle before their eyes, they would believe. Well, these children of Israel saw miracles for forty years, and yet they did not believe. It is not for want of evidence that men are unbelievers. They are unbelievers not because of what they read in the Bible nor because of what they see around them. The problem is on the inside. They are unbelievers because they are innately enemies of God. They have no capacity for the things of God. What a picture God presents of the human heart! He says that it is desperately wicked and that none of us can actually conceive how terrible it really is. "Because the carnal mind is enmity against God: for it is not subject to the law of God, neither indeed can be. So then they that are in the flesh cannot please God" (Rom. 8:7–8). Paul wrote this after God had tested Israel for about 1500 years under the Law. What a picture of humanity this is! Those who are in the flesh cannot please God.

Moses gives them a resumé of their history, reminding them of God's wonderful provision and care for them. This is the preliminary to the covenant.

Remember that the Palestinian covenant is unconditional, but that their tenure in the land will depend on their obedience.

Ye stand this day all of you before the Lord your God; your captains of your tribes, your elders, and your officers, with all the men of Israel,

Your little ones, your wives, and thy stranger that is in thy camp, from the hewer of thy wood unto the drawer of thy water:

That thou shouldest enter into covenant with the Lord thy God, and into his oath, which the Lord thy God maketh with thee this day:

That he may establish thee to-day for a people unto himself, and that he may be unto thee a God, as he hath said unto thee, and as he hath sworn unto thy fathers, to Abraham, to Isaac, and to Jacob [Deut. 29:10–13].

As we read Moses' warning that disobedience to the covenant will affect both the people and the land, it sounds to us like a prediction, because Israel did forsake the covenant.

So that the generation to come of your children that shall rise up after you, and the stranger that shall come from a far land, shall say, when they see the plagues of that land, and the sicknesses which the Lord hath laid upon it;

And that the whole land thereof is brimstone, and salt, and burning, that it is not sown, nor beareth, nor any grass groweth therein, like the overthrow of Sodom, and Gomorrah, Admah, and Zeboim, which the Lord overthrew in his anger, and in his wrath:

Even all nations shall say, Wherefore hath the Lord done thus unto this land? what meaneth the heat of this great anger?

Then men shall say, Because they have forsaken the covenant of the Lord God of their fathers, which he made with them when he brought them forth out of the land of Egypt:

For they went and served other gods, and worshiped them, gods whom they knew not, and whom he had not given unto them:

And the anger of the Lord was kindled against this land, to bring upon it all the curses that are written in this book [Deut. 29:22–27].

Years ago I heard the late Dr. George Gill tell about a trip he made by train, going down through Asia Minor and into Palestine. Late in the afternoon they were leaving Jerusalem and dropping down into the Dead Sea area. As they did, he was standing out on the back vestibule of the train with a very wealthy American. The American said, "I always heard this was the land of milk and honey. Why, I've never seen a land that is as bad as this. I've never seen anything like it." Dr. Gill said, "It is interesting that you said that." Then he opened his Bible and showed the American in verse 24 that strangers shall come from a far land and ask that very question, "Wherefore hath the

LORD done thus unto this land? what meaneth the heat of this great anger?" And Dr. Gill told him the exact reason which Moses had given 3500 years ago. "Because they have forsaken the covenant of the LORD God of their fathers."

The land and the people go together. Actually, the whole Mosaic system is geared for that land. It is not only for the people but also for that land. That is important to see. In our Lord's day, the Mount of Olives was covered with trees. It was a real wooded area. The enemies who came to conquer cut out all the timber and left the land desolate. God's judgment does not fall only on the people. It also has fallen on the land.

And the LORD rooted them out of their land in anger, and in wrath, and in great indignation, and cast them into another land, as it is this day.

The secret things belong unto the LORD our God: but those things which are revealed belong unto us and to our children for ever, that we may do all the words of this law [Deut. 29:28–29].

But even before the covenant is given, they are told what will ultimately happen.

Now friends, God hasn't told us a lot of things, but there are certain things He has told us, and He surely has told us about that land. It lies over their right now, desolate, and they are trying to get water on it. Agricultural authorities have said that if the land could be revived by getting water to it, it should be able to support fifteen to twenty-five million people.

I have traveled in that land from Jericho to Jerusalem, back and forth several times. Anyone who travels there is bound to ask, "What meaneth all the judgment on the land of milk and honey?" Israel was put out of the land because God said, "You go into it and live in it *on condition.*" They did not meet His condition; they did not obey Him.

Does this mean that since Israel failed to keep the covenant, they will not go back to the land? No, God made the Palestinian covenant with these people *unconditionally.* We shall see that in the next chapter.

CHAPTER 30

THEME: *The Palestinian covenant*

We come now to the Palestinian covenant which God made with Israel. Read it carefully. You will notice there are no "if's" in this covenant. It is an unconditional promise of future blessing.

And it shall come to pass, when all these things are come upon thee, the blessing and the curse, which I have set before thee, and thou shalt call them to mind among all the nations, whither the LORD thy God hath driven thee,

And shalt return unto the LORD thy God, and shalt obey his voice according to all that I command thee this day, thou and thy children, with all thine heart, and with all thy soul [Deut. 30:1–2].

There are seven great promises which God makes here. He makes these statements which are unconditional. Verse 1 tells that they will be dispersed among all the nations. The nation would be plucked off the land for its unfaithfulness. That has taken place.

Verse 2 tells that there will be a future repentance of Israel in the dispersion. They are going to come back to God. Someone may ask whether their return will be on the basis of their obedience. It seems logical that if they were dispersed because of disobedience, they will return because of their obedience. No, friend, this is the order of grace, not law. They will not be returned because of their obedience, but they will be obedient because of their return. God will bring them back to the land. The regathering of Israel into her own land is the theme of at least twelve major prophecies in the Old Testament. We will call your attention to them when we come to them.

That then the LORD thy God will turn thy captivity, and have compassion upon thee, and will return and gather thee from all the nations, whither the LORD thy God hath scattered thee [Deut. 30:3].

This verse tells that their Messiah will return. Notice that, for it is very important. This is the first mention of the return of Christ to the earth that is recorded in Scripture. (When we get to the Book of Jude, we will find that Enoch mentioned the fact that He is coming back, but that was not recorded in the Old Testament.) This is a remarkable prophecy, and it has not yet been fulfilled. Not until its fulfillment will the land be blessed and be at peace.

If any of thine be driven out unto the outmost parts of heaven, from thence will the LORD thy God gather thee, and from thence will he fetch thee:

And the LORD thy God will bring thee into the land which thy fathers possessed, and thou shalt possess it; and he will do thee good, and multiply thee above thy fathers [Deut. 30:4–5].

Here is the fourth great promise of God. Israel is to be restored to the land. This is an unconditional promise. No amount of scattering can change the fact that in the future God will bring them into the land, as verse 4 makes clear.

The fifth promise is that there will be a national conversion.

And the LORD thy God will circumcise thine heart, and the heart of thy seed, to love the LORD thy God with all thine heart, and with all thy soul, that thou mayest live [Deut. 30:6].

We find this same promise reaffirmed in Jeremiah and Hosea and stated by Paul in the Book of Romans.

The sixth thing mentioned here is that Israel's enemies will be judged. Israel will return and then obey the voice of the Lord. That is the order of grace. And then their enemies will be judged.

And the LORD thy God will put all these curses upon thine enemies, and on them that hate thee, which persecuted thee.

And thou shalt return and obey the voice of the LORD, and do all his commandments which I command thee this day [Deut. 30:7–8].

Finally, the seventh wonderful thing is that Israel will then receive her full blessing.

And the LORD thy God will make thee plenteous in every work of thine hand, in the fruit of thy body, and in the fruit of thy cattle, and in the fruit of thy land, for good: for the LORD will again rejoice over thee for good, as he rejoiced over thy fathers:

If thou shalt hearken unto the voice of the LORD thy God, to keep his commandments and his statutes which are written in this book of the law, and if thou turn unto the LORD thy God with all thine heart, and with all thy soul [Deut. 30:9–10].

When will the day of return be? Is it actually happening now? We cannot be dogmatic about what we do not know. It clearly states that when they return to the land, it will be in obedience to God. There will be no blessing for them in the land until the time when they return in obedience with the new heart which God will give them. This will be at the time when God returns them to the land. The present return to Israel is not in obedience to God. I believe that the return of Israel under the covenant promise is yet in the future. It is unconditional because it is God who will return them to the land.

For this commandment which I command thee this day, it is not hidden from thee, neither is it far off.

It is not in heaven, that thou shouldest say, Who shall go up for us to heaven, and bring it unto us, that we may hear it, and do it?

Neither is it beyond the sea, that thou shouldest say, Who shall go over the sea for us, and bring it unto us, that we may hear it, and do it?

But the word is very nigh unto thee, in thy mouth, and in thy heart, that thou mayest do it [Deut. 30:11–14].

Israel can plead no excuse that they do not know the commandment of God. God has brought it right to them, and they know it.

We also have a responsibility—we who live in the land where we can hear the gospel. My friend, you don't have to go to heaven to get salvation. You don't need to cross the ocean to get it. May I say to you, it's right near you. It is as near as your radio; it is as near to you as a preacher or another Christian who will give you the Word of God. And *you* are responsible to act upon what you have heard. That is where your free will comes in. It is my business to get out the Word of God—I try to get it right up to your eardrums by radio, and right before your eyes by the printed page. That is as far as I can go. From then on, it is up to you.

Now notice that verses 12 and 13 are quoted by the apostle Paul in Romans. "But the righteousness which is of faith speaketh on this wise, Say not in thine heart, Who shall ascend into heaven? (that is, to bring Christ down from above:) Or, Who shall descend into the deep? (that is, to bring up Christ again from the dead.) But what saith it? The word is nigh thee, even in thy mouth, and in thy heart: that is, the word of faith, which we preach; That if thou shalt confess with thy mouth the Lord Jesus, and shalt believe in thine heart that God hath raised him from the dead, thou shalt be saved. For with the heart man believeth unto righteousness; and with the mouth confession is made unto salvation" (Rom. 10:6–10).

Paul does not say that Moses said this, but rather the "of-faith-righteousness" is the speaker. Paul is not making a substitution of faith here for the Law. The passage in Deuteronomy is prophetic and speaks of a day when Israel will turn to God with all their heart and soul. (See Deut. 33:10). It looks forward to the new covenant which God will make with Israel.

"And I will give them an heart to know me, that I am the LORD: and they shall be my people, and I will be their God: for they shall return unto me with their whole heart" (Jer. 24:7).

"Behold, the days come, saith the LORD, that I will make a new covenant with the house of Israel, and with the house of Judah: Not according to the covenant that I made with their fathers in the day that I took them by the hand to bring them out of the land of Egypt; which my covenant they brake, although I was an husband unto them, saith the LORD: But this shall be the covenant that I will make with the house of Israel; After those days, saith the LORD, I will put my law in their inward parts, and write it in their hearts; and will be their God, and they shall be my people" (Jer. 31:31–33).

"For finding fault with them, he saith, Behold, the days come, saith the Lord, when I will make a new covenant with the house of Israel and with the house of Judah" (Heb. 8:8).

Christ is the One to institute this new covenant which is yet future. Righteousness by faith is indeed witnessed to by the Law and prophets. In the meantime, it is not necessary to ascend to heaven to bring Christ down. He has already come the first time and died. It is not necessary to raise Him from the dead. He has been already raised from the dead.

They had the Law for 1500 years and they knew it as a matter of rote and ritual, but it had not brought righteousness. Christ had *come* to them just as the Law had come. It was not something that was far off, and Christ had come among them. He died and rose again in

their midst. The "of-faith-righteousness" was available to them as it is to us because it has been preached down through the ages. The Law bore witness to both the righteousness by law and righteousness by faith. It is not "the commandments" in Deuteronomy 30, but "commandment." The "of-law-righteousness" had not brought salvation, but the "of-faith-righteousness" does bring salvation.

A careful examination of the passage in Deuteronomy 30 will reveal that Paul is not giving an exact quotation, but that he is making an application of the passage. The statement of Beet is pertinent, "This appeal to Moses is a remarkable example of skillful and correct exegesis."

See, I have set before thee this day life and good, and death and evil;

In that I command thee this day to love the LORD thy God, to walk in his ways, and to keep his commandments and his statutes and his judgments, that thou mayest live and multiply: and the LORD thy God shall bless thee in the land whither thou goest to possess it [Deut. 30:15–16].

Their stay in the land will be determined by their obedience. He outlines their history and says they will go out of that land when they disobey. But God promises to bring them back. Finally, He will return them and they shall never, never go out again. Why? Because they will obey Him? No. Because God makes good His covenant. He will bring them back, and then they will obey Him.

It is exactly the same with us. God asks us to trust the Lord Jesus Christ as our Savior. After that He talks to us about obedience—"If ye love me, keep my commandments" (John 14:15).

That thou mayest love the LORD thy God, and that thou mayest obey his voice, and that thou mayest cleave unto him: for he is thy life, and the length of thy days: that thou mayest dwell in the land which the LORD sware unto thy fathers, to Abraham, to Isaac, and to Jacob, to give them [Deut. 30:20].

I repeat it again: Love and obedience is the great theme of Deuteronomy. If this was so important for the children of Israel, how important it is for you and me in this day of grace when we have been given so much more light. Since we have been given more, our responsibility is greater. One of the things I pray for more devoutly than anything else is that I may be kept close to Him today. Oh, friends, we need to be kept close to the Lord Jesus Christ. How important it is!

CHAPTER 31

THEME: *Moses' last counsels*

We have come now to the last section of the Book of Deuteronomy. It is a requiem to Moses and extends from chapter 31 through 34. It begins with the fifth oration which Moses gave to the children of Israel and which is recorded in this book.

We are coming to the end of the life of Moses. The entire Bible up to this point has been written by Moses. A great deal of it has been about Moses. He has been a key person ever since the time they came out of the land of Egypt. He has been concerned with Israel for forty years, and he has left us a record of the 120 years of his life. Now he is getting ready to die.

And Moses went and spake these words unto all Israel.

And he said unto them, I am an hundred and twenty years old this day; I can no more go out and come in: also the LORD hath said unto me, Thou shalt not go over this Jordan [Deut. 31:1–2].

Note the two statements about himself. He is getting old. We all get old, and most of us will not make it to 120. When we move toward that area, we are no longer vital as far as God's program is concerned. Moses is not the essential one to bring Israel into the Promised Land. God has made it very clear to him that a new leader will take the people over the Jordan River and into the land. Moses will not be the leader much longer.

The LORD thy God, he will go over before thee, and he will destroy these nations from before thee, and thou shalt possess them: and Joshua, he shall go over before thee, as the LORD hath said [Deut. 31:3].

Moses did not choose Joshua; *God* selected him to be the leader to succeed Moses. I doubt whether Moses would have chosen Joshua if the choice had been left to him. Actually, Caleb seems more impressive than Joshua, and it would seem more natural for him to be the new leader. Or, (after all, Moses is human) wouldn't he have been apt to choose one of his own sons to succeed him? That was the way the Pharaohs did down in Egypt, and it would be natural for Moses to do the same thing. So God chose Joshua to lead them over the Jordan. Moses is no longer essential.

That has a great lesson for us. It teaches us that none of us are essential to God's program. God uses each man in his own time, but when the time of work for the man is finished, God's work still goes on.

I can remember a pastor who was up in years telling me, "I just can't retire because I am so essential to this work." Since then he died in the harness, but the interesting thing is that the work prospered more after he died than it had before. We may think we are essential, but we are not. When the time comes for us to step aside, God will raise up someone else. That is what is happening to Moses here.

Be strong and of a good courage, fear not, nor be afraid of them: for the LORD thy God, he it is that doth go with thee; he will not fail thee, nor forsake thee [Deut. 31:6].

Moses is encouraging these people not to fear the enemy tribes that are in the land. You will notice that he encourages this generation over and over, telling them to cross over into the land. He had lived through the experience of Kadesh-Barnea. He had seen the older generation turn yellow and run back into the wilderness. So Moses over and over again encourages this new generation to go on in, assuring them that God will lead them into the land.

And Moses called unto Joshua, and said unto him in the sight of all Israel, Be strong and of a good courage: for thou must go with this people unto the land which the LORD hath sworn unto their fathers to give them: and thou shalt cause them to inherit it [Deut. 31:7].

This was good; this is as it should be. He encourages Joshua before all the people. By encouraging Joshua, he is also encouraging the people.

> **And the LORD, he it is that doth go before thee; he will be with thee, he will not fail thee, neither forsake thee: fear not, neither be dismayed [Deut. 31:8].**

This was the same lesson that Isaiah had to learn. Remember that the sixth chapter of Isaiah starts, "In the year that king Uzziah died I saw also the Lord sitting upon a throne . . . ." Poor Isaiah! Uzziah had been a good king, and now that he was dead, Isaiah thought things were really going to be bad. Another king would be raised up and the nation would just go to the dogs, so to speak. But what did he find when he went into the temple? He found that God was still on the throne, that the real King of Israel and of Judah was still on the throne. He wasn't dead. He wasn't even sick. Isaiah learned that although Uzziah had died, God was still very much alive.

> **And Moses wrote this law, and delivered it unto the priests the sons of Levi, which bare the ark of the covenant of the LORD, and unto all the elders of Israel [Deut. 31:9].**

Remember that Deuteronomy began, "These are the words which Moses spoke." There are about eight orations of Moses in the book—given orally, then written down. Moses wrote this Law. As you may know, the Graf-Wellhausen theory rejects the Mosaic authorship, considering the Pentateuch as historical documents compiled shortly before 400 B.C. The original argument for this theory was that writing was not in existence at the time of Moses. Of course archaeologists have found that writing was in existence long before Moses' day, but the Graf-Wellhausen theory is still held by the liberal wing of the church for the obvious reason that the prediction of Israel's declension after entering the land is so accurate that the unbeliever would like to think it was written as history rather than prophecy.

Now even at this time, when the children of Israel are ready to enter the land, you would think that God wouldn't take them in if there was a chance of their failing. Yet He tells Moses here this is exactly what will happen. God knows human nature. He knows your being and my being. My friends, you and I would walk away from God in the next ten minutes if He didn't keep us close to Himself.

Now notice what the Lord says to Moses:

> **And the LORD said unto Moses, Behold, thy days approach that thou must die: call Joshua, and present yourselves in the tabernacle of the congregation, that I may give him a charge. And Moses and Joshua went, and presented themselves in the tabernacle of the congregation.**

> **And the LORD appeared in the tabernacle in a pillar of a cloud: and the pillar of the cloud stood over the door of the tabernacle.**

> **And the LORD said unto Moses, Behold, thou shalt sleep with thy fathers; and this people will rise up, and go a-whoring after the gods of the strangers of the land, whither they go to be among them, and will forsake me, and break my covenant which I have made with them.**

> **Then my anger shall be kindled against them in that day, and I will forsake them, and I will hide my face from them, and they shall be devoured, and many evils and troubles shall befall them; so that they will say in that day, Are not these evils come upon us, because our God is not among us? [Deut. 31:14–17].**

Now I know that there are people who say today, "We are different today. We'll not turn away from God." But do you know that the Lord Jesus said the same thing about the church? In Luke 18:8 He said, "Nevertheless when the Son of man cometh, shall he find faith on the earth?" "Faith" is *the* faith, the whole body of revealed truth. The answer to that is no, He won't. In fact, the way the question is couched in the Greek demands a negative answer. In the New Testament there is predicted the apostasy of the church, just as it was predicted of Israel, and you and I are living in it today. I have seen in my day that which curdles my blood. I have watched church after church, which at one time was conservative, take the emphasis off the Word of God and finally depart from the faith. And I have seen man after man, who at one time professed to be sound in the faith, turn away from the things of God. Now don't say that *you* can't do it or that *I* can't do it. In these days I pray more than anything else, "Oh, God, keep me close to Thee."

> **Now therefore write ye this song for you, and teach it the children of Israel: put it in their mouths, that this song**

may be witness for me against the children of Israel.

For when I shall have brought them into the land which I sware unto their fathers, that floweth with milk and honey; and they shall have eaten and filled themselves, and waxen fat; then will they turn unto other gods, and serve them, and provoke me, and break my covenant.

And it shall come to pass, when many evils and troubles are befallen them, that this song shall testify against them as a witness; for it shall not be forgotten out of the mouths of their seed: for I know their imagination which they go about, even now, before I have brought them into the land which I sware [Deut. 31:19–21].

Music is a very important factor. We are all greatly influenced by music. Right now some of the music that is getting into our churches is a disgrace, according to this poor preacher's opinion. Someone needs to speak out against it. The music must say something, must have a message that will draw people closer to the Lord Jesus. Too much of our music attempts to reach the modern generation all right, but fails to meet them with the gospel of Jesus Christ.

In the next chapter we will read the song. The interesting thing about the song is that it is rock music. Do I really mean that? Yes, it is all about the Rock, who is Christ. That is the kind of rock music that Moses taught to Israel, and that is the kind of rock music we need today.

And it came to pass, when Moses had made an end of writing the words of this law in a book, until they were finished,

That Moses commanded the Levites, which bare the ark of the covenant of the Lord, saying,

Take this book of the law, and put it in the side of the ark of the covenant of the Lord your God, that it may be there for a witness against thee [Deut. 31:24–26].

This "book," you understand, was not a book such as we have today. It was a scroll or it may even have been a clay tablet. However, in Moses' day they had scrolls and this law was probably written on a scroll.

Remember that we are in the section which we have labeled the requiem of Moses. He is getting into his final report to the nation. He calls the tribes around him just as old Jacob had called the twelve sons around him. The twelve sons have now become the twelve tribes, and they are a great nation. Moses calls them to him.

For I know thy rebellion, and thy stiff neck: behold, while I am yet alive with you this day, ye have been rebellious against the Lord; and how much more after my death?

Gather unto me all the elders of your tribes, and your officers, that I may speak these words in their ears, and call heaven and earth to record against them.

For I know that after my death ye will utterly corrupt yourselves, and turn aside from the way which I have commanded you; and evil will befall you in the latter days; because ye will do evil in the sight of the Lord, to provoke him to anger through the work of your hands.

And Moses spake in the ears of all the congregation of Israel the words of this song, until they were ended [Deut. 31:27–30].

May I say that this statement which Moses made about 3500 years ago is still accurate, still true. It has been fulfilled quite literally. It is also true of the entire human family, for God has said that mankind apart from God will utterly corrupt itself. All we need to do is look around us today and we can see that this is true.

CHAPTER 32

THEME: *Moses' final song*

The Song of Moses is a great song, in fact, a magnificent song in many ways. The nation of Israel was to learn it. It was to be somewhat like their national anthem. It was a song given to them by God; every Israelite was to learn it and teach it to their children.

As I indicated before, music is a very important factor in the life of a nation. Someone has said, "Let me write the music of a nation, and I do not care who writes the laws." In other words, the songs have more influence than do the laws! If this is true, we today are in a sad predicament. Modern music has sunk to a level that is absolutely frightening.

The first four verses of the Song of Moses are the introduction.

Give ear, O ye heavens, and I will speak; and hear, O earth, the words of my mouth [Deut. 32:1].

God calls heaven and earth to witness that these are the conditions under which He is putting Israel into the land. When He is ready to put Israel out of the land in judgment, Isaiah records this same call. In fact, that is the way the Book of Isaiah opens: "The vision of Isaiah the son of Amoz, which he saw concerning Judah and Jerusalem in the days of Uzziah, Jotham, Ahaz, and Hezekiah, kings of Judah. Hear, O heavens, and give ear, O earth: for the LORD hath spoken, I have nourished and brought up children, and they have rebelled against me" (Isa. 1:1–2). When God put Israel into the land, He called heaven and earth to witness. When God is ready to put them out of the land, about seven hundred years later, He again calls heaven and earth to witness. God is not doing this in a corner; this is not something which He does under cover. He is justified in putting them out of the land.

My doctrine shall drop as the rain, my speech shall distil as the dew, as the small rain upon the tender herb, and as the showers upon the grass [Deut. 32:2].

That is the way the Word of God is. The Psalmist says, "He shall come down like rain upon the mown grass: as showers that water the earth" (Ps. 72:6). I love that statement. A dear saint in Dallas, Texas, lost her husband whom she loved dearly. She told her pastor that now she understood the meaning of that verse in the Psalms. She was the mown grass, but God came to her through His Word like the gentle rain. That is the way the Word of God should come down in our lives. Here in Southern California, we go through an entire summer without rain. Normally, in the fall we have quite a rain that begins the autumn season. The earth just opens up to receive it. It washes the leaves on the trees, and everything becomes clean and sharply clear. God desires that the Word of God should come down into our hearts and lives like this.

Because I will publish the name of the LORD: ascribe ye greatness unto our God [Deut. 32:3].

How little of our literature today promotes God or has anything good to say about Him! Usually His name is taken in vain if it is used at all.

He is the Rock, his work is perfect: for all his ways are judgment: a God of truth and without iniquity, just and right is he [Deut. 32:4].

This is the song about the Rock, you see. The word "Rock" is used about seven times in the song. The Lord Jesus Christ is called the Rock. Christ is the chief Cornerstone of 1 Peter 2:6. His work is perfect. Oh, how this song exalts God, and He needs to be exalted by us today.

They have corrupted themselves, their spot is not the spot of his children: they are a perverse and crooked generation.

Do ye thus requite the LORD, O foolish people and unwise? is not he thy father that hath bought thee? hath he not made thee, and established thee? [Deut. 32:5–6].

God is the Father of Israel because of creation—He doesn't mention redemption here. In one sense God is the Father of all mankind because He created all mankind. When God created Adam he was called a son of God, but Adam sinned. After that, none of the offspring of Adam are called the sons of God unless they have become sons of God by faith in Jesus Christ. The whole human family may be pictured as a crooked generation, a foolish people.

Now we have a wonderful stanza on the goodness of God—verses 7–14.

Remember the days of old, consider the years of many generations: ask thy father, and he will shew thee; thy elders, and they will tell thee.

When the Most High divided to the nations their inheritance, when he separated the sons of Adam, he set the bounds of the people according to the number of the children of Israel.

For the LORD's portion is his people; Jacob is the lot of his inheritance [Deut. 32:7–9].

Verse 8 is most unusual. I have never yet heard a satisfactory explanation of it. The nations of the earth are measured according to the number of the children of Israel. In other words, the bounds that the nations have are arranged according to the number of Israelites. This is something that needs a great deal of study today. It explains why the Jew and his land are the most sensitive areas on the earth.

He found him in a desert land, and in the waste howling wilderness; he led him about, he instructed him, he kept him as the apple of his eye [Deut. 32:10].

For forty years in that howling wilderness, that great and terrible wilderness, God led His people and kept them. Why? They were the apple of His eye—a lovely expression.

Now we have one of the great statements in Scripture:

As an eagle stirreth up her nest, fluttereth over her young, spreadeth abroad her wings, taketh them, beareth them on her wings:

So the LORD alone did lead him, and there was no strange god with him [Deut. 32:11–12].

At the time when the little eaglets ought to be out spreading their wings, they are perfectly willing to stay in the nest and let mamma and papa bring them food all day long, then take care of them at night. The day comes when the mother eagle pushes those little ones off the cliff, and they have to stretch those wings. But suppose a little eaglet does not do very well. That mother, with those tremendous wings of hers, comes right up under the little eaglet, catches him on her wings, them lifts him back up to the rock and gives him a few more worms to eat for the next few days. Then she tries him out again. This is the way God watches over those who are His own. God pushes *us* out of the nest sometimes, not because He doesn't love us but because He wants us to learn to fly—He wants us to learn to live for Him.

This is a wonderful description of the goodness of Jehovah.

But Jeshurun waxed fat, and kicked: thou art waxen fat, thou art grown thick, thou art covered with fatness; then he forsook God which made him, and lightly esteemed the Rock of his salvation [Deut. 32:15].

"Jeshurun" is another name for Israel. Israel waxed fat, and kicked! What a picture this is of the affluent society we have in America today. And what a bunch of complainers there are— and the Christians join with them. "Thou art waxed fat, thou art grown thick" means these folk were getting fat. In their prosperity, they didn't think their Rock was important anymore.

They provoked him to jealousy with strange gods, with abominations provoked they him to anger.

They sacrificed unto devils, not to God; to gods whom they knew not, to new gods that came newly up, whom your fathers feared not.

Of the Rock that begat thee thou art unmindful, and hast forgotten God that formed thee [Deut. 32:16–18].

In this next section (vv. 19–25) we see the judgment of God upon His people.

And when the LORD saw it, he abhorred them, because of the provoking of his sons, and of his daughters.

And he said, I will hide my face from them, I will see what their end shall be: for they are a very froward generation, children in whom is no faith [Deut. 32:19–20).

God says that He will hide Himself from them. He will not manifest Himself to them.

The next section, verses 26–42, expresses God's longing for His people.

I said, I would scatter them into corners, I would make the remembrance of them to cease from among men:

Were it not that I feared the wrath of the enemy, lest their adversaries should behave themselves strangely, and lest they should say, Our hand is high, and the LORD hath not done all this [Deut. 32:26–27].

God says He would scatter Israel into corners, were it not that He feared for them the wrath of the enemy. He says, "I don't want them to hurt My people or destroy them, 'Lest their adversaries should behave themselves strangely, and lest they should say, Our hand is high, and the LORD hath not done all this.' "

For they are a nation void of counsel, neither is there any understanding in them.

O that they were wise, that they understood this, that they would consider their latter end!

How should one chase a thousand, and two put ten thousand to flight, except their Rock had sold them, and the LORD had shut them up?

For their rock is not as our Rock, even our enemies themselves being judges [Deut. 32:28–31].

What a picture we have here! God has a longing for His people. He wants to redeem them. He wants to save them.

Now we come to the final stanza of the song: the nations of the world will be blessed with Israel.

Rejoice, O ye nations, with his people: for he will avenge the blood of his servants, and will render vengeance to his adversaries, and will be merciful unto his land, and to his people [Deut. 32:43].

This concludes this magnificent Song of Moses.

And Moses came and spake all the words of this song in the ears of the people, he, and Hoshea the son of Nun [Deut. 32:44].

"Hoshea" is Joshua, by the way.

And Moses made an end of speaking all these words to all Israel [Deut. 32:45].

THE FINAL EXHORTATION

And he said unto them, Set your hearts unto all the words which I testify among you this day, which ye shall command your children to observe to do, all the words of this law.

For it is not a vain thing for you; because it is your life: and through this thing ye shall prolong your days in the land, whither ye go over Jordan to possess it [Deut. 32:46–47].

Again, their tenure in the land would depend on their obedience.

And the LORD spake unto Moses that selfsame day, saying,

Get thee up into this mountain Abarim, unto mount Nebo, which is the land of Moab, that is over against Jericho; and behold the land of Canaan, which I give unto the children of Israel for a possession:

And die in the mount whither thou goest up, and be gathered unto thy people; as Aaron thy brother died in mount Hor, and was gathered unto his people:

Because ye trespassed against me among the children of Israel at the waters of Meribah-Kadesh, in the wilderness of Zin; because ye sanctified me not in the midst of the children of Israel.

Yet thou shalt see the land before thee; but thou shalt not go thither unto the land which I give the children of Israel [Deut. 32:48–52].

Moses, the representative of the Law, the lawgiver, cannot enter into the land. Legalism is actually a hindrance. The Law is a *revealer*, not a *remover* of sin. The Law cannot save. The Law could not bring Moses into the land. Neither can the Law bring us into the place of blessing.

CHAPTER 33

THEME: Moses' final blessing of the tribes

The last public act of Moses before his death is to gather his people about him by tribes and give a blessing to each one.

And this is the blessing, wherewith Moses the man of God blessed the children of Israel before his death [Deut. 33:1].

He begins with Reuben.

Let Reuben live, and not die; and let not his men be few [Deut. 33:6].

Moses prays that Reuben will never become extinct as a tribe in Israel.

And this is the blessing of Judah: and he said, Hear LORD, the voice of Judah, and bring him unto his people: let his hands be sufficient for him; and be thou an help to him from his enemies [Deut. 33:7].

Judah is the royal tribe from which the Messiah is to come.

And of Levi he said, Let thy Thummim and thy Urim be with thy holy one, whom thou didst prove at Massah, and with whom thou didst strive at the waters of Meribah;

They shall teach Jacob thy judgments, and Israel thy law: they shall put incense before thee, and whole burnt sacrifice upon thine altar.

Bless, LORD, his substance, and accept the work of his hands: smite through the loins of them that rise against him, and of them that hate him, that they rise not again [Deut. 33:8, 10–11].

This tribe was honored by the priesthood in the family of Aaron. They had the privilege of teaching the Law. The nation will be blessed through Levi.

Blessing is to come to Israel through the tribes of Joseph which are Ephraim and Manasseh.

An interesting blessing is in verse 24.

And of Asher he said, Let Asher be blessed with children; let him be acceptable to his brethren, and let him dip his foot in oil [Deut. 33:24].

It is interesting that years ago a pipeline of oil came into the northern part of the kingdom through the land of Asher. It may be that that pipeline will be opened.

There is none like unto the God of Jeshurun, who rideth upon the heaven in thy help, and in his excellency on the sky.

The eternal God is thy refuge, and underneath are the everlasting arms: and he shall thrust out the enemy from before thee; and shall say, Destroy them.

Israel then shall dwell in safety alone: the fountain of Jacob shall be upon a land of corn and wine; also his heavens shall drop down dew.

Happy art thou, O Israel: who is like unto thee, O people saved by the LORD, the shield of thy help, and who is the sword of thy excellency! and thine enemies shall be found liars unto thee; and thou shalt tread upon their high places [Deut. 33:26–29].

Oh, if only Israel had obeyed God!

CHAPTER 34

THEME: The death of Moses

The question arises whether Moses wrote of his own death. He could have. The Lord had told him he would die. I have had funeral services for individuals who wrote out the details of the entire service before they died. However, a great many believe that this is part of the Book of Joshua. This certainly may be, since originally there were not the book divisions that he have today. The Old Testament was written on scrolls with one book following another. Therefore, this may actually be the beginning of the Book of Joshua.

And Moses went up from the plains of Moab unto the mountain of Nebo, to the top of Pisgah, that is over against Jericho. And the Lord shewed him all the land of Gilead, unto Dan,

And all Naphtali, and the land of Ephraim, and Manasseh, and all the land of Judah, unto the utmost sea,

And the south, and the plain of the valley of Jericho, the city of palm trees, unto Zoar.

And the Lord said unto him, This is the land which I sware unto Abraham, unto Isaac, and unto Jacob, saying, I will give it unto thy seed: I have caused thee to see it with thine eyes, but thou shalt not go over thither.

So Moses the servant of the Lord died there in the land of Moab, according to the word of the Lord.

And he buried him in a valley in the land of Moab, over against Beth-peor: but no man knoweth of his sepulchre unto this day [Deut. 34:1–6].

Why was his sepulchre unknown? Because of the fact that Moses was to be raised from the dead and brought into the Promised Land. You will remember that when the Lord Jesus was transfigured on the mount, both Moses and Elijah appeared with Him and spoke about His approaching death. So, you see, Moses did get to the Promised Land eventually. The Law could not bring Moses into the land, but the Lord Jesus Christ brought him in.

And Moses was an hundred and twenty years old when he died: his eye was not dim, nor his natural force abated.

And the children of Israel wept for Moses in the plains of Moab thirty days: so the days of weeping and mourning for Moses were ended [Deut. 34:7–8].

By Nebo's lonely mountain,
  On this side Jordan's wave,
In a vale in the land of Moab,
  There lies a lonely grave.

And no man knows that sepulchre,
  And no man saw it e'er,
For the angels of God upturned the sod,
  And laid the dead man there.

Cecil Frances Alexander,
"The Burial of Moses"

Again, why was his grave kept secret? Well, after all, Satan would not want Moses to appear on the Mount of Transfiguration. God took care of this performing the burial of Moses Himself.

Although to us it may seem like a lonely death, one translation has it, "He died by the kiss of God." It is a lovely thought that God just kissed Moses and put him to sleep. What a picture we have here!

It is with a note of sadness that we close the book of Deuteronomy, but we will be going with the children of Israel into the land of promise in the book of Joshua.

BIBLIOGRAPHY

Epp, Theodore H. *Moses*. Lincoln, Nebraska: Back to the Bible Broadcast, 1975.

Gaebelein, Arno C. *Annotated Bible*. Vol. 1. Neptune, New Jersey: Loizeaux Brothers, n.d.

Grant, F. W. *Numerical Bible*. Neptune, New Jersey: Loizeaux Brothers, 1891.

Gray, James M. *Synthetic Bible Studies*. Westwood, New Jersey: Fleming H. Revell Co., 1906.

Jensen, Irving L. *Numbers & Deuteronomy—Self Study Guide*. Chicago, Illinois: Moody Press, 1967.

Kelly, William. *Lectures Introductory to the Pentateuch*. Oak Park, Illinois: Bible Truth Publishers, 1870.

Mackintosh, C. H. (C.H.M.). *Notes on the Pentateuch*. Neptune, New Jersey: Loizeaux Brothers, 1880.

Meyer, F. B. *Moses: The Servant of God*. Fort Washington, Pennsylvania: Christian Literature Crusade, n.d.

Schultz, Samuel J. *Deuteronomy: The Gospel of Love*. Chicago, Illinois: Moody Press, 1971.

Thomas, W. H. Griffith. *Through the Pentateuch Chapter by Chapter*. Grand Rapids, Michigan: William B. Eerdmans Publishing Co., 1957.

Unger, Merrill F. *Unger's Bible Handbook*. Chicago, Illinois: Moody Press, 1966.